Africa
Continent of Economic Opportunities

DAVID FICK

First published in 2006 by
STE Publishers
4th Floor Sunnyside Ridge,
Sunnyside Office Park,
32 Princess of Wales Terrace,
Parktown 2143
Johannesburg, South Africa

© David Fick 2006

ISBN 1-919855-44-0

Cover artwork: "African Connection" (Batik cloth) by Nuwa Nnyanzi, Uganda

Publishing Manager:	Kevin Humphrey
Editor:	Monica Seeber
Marketing & Publicity:	Angela McClelland
Design:	Adam Rumball, Mad Cow Studio
Printing:	Jakaranda Printers

The opinions expressed in this book remain that of the entrepreneurs profiled in these pages and those of the author. Whilst every effort has been made to ensure the factual accuracy of information contained in quotes and excerpts from the numerous sources, the publishers cannot be held responsible for any incorrect information. Where information has been incorrectly attributed, we welcome your input in this regard. Every effort has also been made to acknowledge all sources. In the event that there has been an omission, we will include the source in subsequent reprints.

All rights reserved. Without limiting the rights under copyright reserved above, no part of this publication may be reproduced, stored in or introduced into a retrieval system, or transmitted, in any form or by any means (electronic, mechanical, photocopying, recording or otherwise) without prior written permission of both the copyright holder and the publishers of the book.

This book is sold subject to the condition that it shall not, by way of trade or otherwise, be lent, re-sold, hired out or otherwise circulated without the publisher's prior consent in any form of binding or cover other than that in which it is published and without a similar condition being imposed on the subsequent purchaser.

Publishers Note

During the second half of 2004, STE received an email from David S Fick, author of the popular book, *Entrepreneurship in Africa: A Study of Successes*, published in 2002 by Quorum Books in the USA. Whilst researching companies in Africa for his second book, David came across STE Publishers. As always, appreciative of the efforts of African business, David entrusted us with this, his latest manuscript – *Africa: Continent of Economic Opportunities*.

During the time taken to ready the book for printing, we have been delighted to note that there is keen interest from people all over the world – from Mogadishu and Somalia to the US, UK and Australia.

Working with David has been quite an experience; he must be one of the world's most prolific e-mailers and has certainly brought us many valuable contacts.

In publishing *Africa: Continent of Economic Opportunities*, we have experienced first hand David's aim of "encouraging a dialogue so that knowledge and ideas may be presented and exchanged for the benefit of Africans and their trading and business partners all over the world". The book also actively advocates that African countries do more business with each other by means of regional groupings and provides examples of how this has worked and can continue to improve.

This book has created opportunities for us to partner with booksellers and businesses throughout the African continent, thus ensuring that the publishing process is in keeping with the goals of the book.

Assisting David to share his considerable knowledge and vision whilst promoting a culture of reading and entrepreneurship in Africa is truly a privilege.

DAVID S FICK is a graduate of the Wharton School, University of Pennsylvania, and has spent his entire business career as an entrepreneur in Kansas.

His interest in African entrepreneurs began whilst travelling through Africa in 2000. This visit ignited a passionate interest in the opportunities for entrepreneurs in Africa as he found success stories everywhere, in spite of the numerous obstacles.

For the past six years he has dedicated himself to searching for projects and business opportunities that are beneficial to the people of Africa and the wider entrepreneurial environment.

Contents

Introduction		6
PART 1	AFRICAN CONTINENT	9
Chapter 1	Economic and Political Policies	11
Chapter 2	Challenges and Opportunities	24
PART 2	WEST AFRICA	39
Chapter 3	Ghana	41
Chapter 4	Nigeria	61
Chapter 5	The Gambia, Sierra Leone, Liberia, Guinea, Senegal, Côte d'Ivoire, Togo, Benin, Burkina Faso, Mali, Niger, Guinea-Bissau and Cape Verde.	82
PART 3	SOUTHERN AFRICA	111
Chapter 6	Namibia, Botswana, Lesotho and Swaziland	113
Chapter 7	Madagascar, Mauritius, Seychelles, Comoros, Mozambique and Zimbabwe	142
Chapter 8	South Africa: Mining, Agriculture, Construction, Transport and Tourism	166
Chapter 9	South Africa: Business, Manufacturing, African Arts & Crafts, Health, Education and Media	199
Chapter 10	South Africa: Investors, Bankers and Exchanges	235

PART 4	EAST AFRICA	261
Chapter 11	Horn of Africa: Ethiopia, Eritrea, Djibouti and Somalia	263
Chapter 12	Kenya	292
Chapter 13	Tanzania	322
Chapter 14	Uganda	340

PART 5	CENTRAL AFRICA	369
Chapter 15	Republic of Congo, Gabon, Central African Republic, Cameroon, Chad, Equatorial Guinea and São Tomé and Príncipe	371
Chapter 16	Democratic Republic of Congo, Rwanda and Burundi	387
Chapter 17	Angola, Zambia and Malawi	417

PART 6	NORTH AFRICA	441
Chapter 18	Egypt and Sudan	443
Chapter 19	Arab Maghreb Union: Mauritania, Morocco, Algeria, Tunisia and Libya	471

PART 7	AFRICA'S FUTURE	493
Chapter 20	Commentary and Conclusions	495

AFRICA: CONTINENT OF ECONOMIC OPPORTUNITIES

Introduction

My wife and I were guests of the people of Kenya, Tanzania and Ethiopia in 2000. We found ourselves impressed by the beauty of Africa and the hospitality of its people. The Ethiopia of 2000 reminded me of South Korea as it was in 1962 and 1963, when I had the pleasure of serving in Korea as a lieutenant with the United States Army's Transportation Corps. Our suppliers were from the private sector in South Korea, and it was the local Korean entrepreneurs who became the engines of growth for the future development of the country.

Having graduated from the Wharton School at the University of Pennsylvania in Philadelphia in 1961, having spent my business career in the United States, and having travelled to 33 countries in six continents, I found myself becoming interested in the opportunities for entrepreneurs in Africa. Upon returning to the US, I began researching successful entrepreneurs in Africa. During my search, I became aware of the opportunities and roadblocks that the cultural, economic, social, political and physical environments provide in Africa. This new-found awareness led me to also search for actual or proposed projects and policy changes that are, or could be, of great benefit for the people of Africa and the entrepreneurial environment.

In March 2002, Quorum Books, an imprint of the Greenwood Publications Group, published my first book, *Entrepreneurship in Africa: A Study of Successes*, which is now one of the best-selling books on the Amazon.com website concerning microeconomics and entrepreneurship in Africa. My second book, *Africa: Continent of Economic Opportunities*, which you are now reading, is based on correspondence with people in Africa and around the world who are interested in the sustainable development of Africa. These correspondents included professors of economics interested in the future of Africa, entrepreneurs doing business in Africa, non-governmental agencies involved with the economic development of Africa, journalists and people in general who are interested in Africa's development.

There is a growing interest concerning the continent's being developed to fulfil its immense potential. *Africa: Continent of Economic Opportunities* shows the business opportunities that can be found in Africa, and also the problems people encounter in realising them. Most books deal with macroeconomics when actually it is the small and medium enterprises of the world that create the majority of new jobs. By presenting interesting case studies of individual small, medium and large enterprises, and community projects creating jobs in Africa, this book is a guide to the way business should be conducted in Africa.

Africa: Continent of Economic Opportunities is meant to tell the story of people and their communities that are successful in developing Africa. It is meant to get across the idea that all ethnic groups (native Africans, Europeans, Arabs, Asians and Americans) can be successful in Africa, which can, like the Americas, welcome immigrants and prosper through their efforts. All citizens of Africa will benefit and all can become successful in Africa if they have the imagination, education and persistence. It also will tell how these people give back to the communities that they live in. It will advocate that African countries do more business with each other by means of regional groupings.

Africa: Continent of Economic Opportunities is meant to encourage a dialogue so that knowledge and ideas may be presented and exchanged with the goal of improving Africa and the world. In all the cases and commentary presented in this study, I have tried to retain the sense and substance of the information I have obtained. Whether from websites, press releases, books, newspapers and periodicals, or from personal meetings, letters, e-mail correspondence and phone calls with interested parties in Africa and around the world, I have tried not to colour someone else's inspirations, ideas or plans with my views of how the world should be. Wherever possible, I have endeavoured to use the exact words of my sources in presenting or summarising their ideas. When I mention a source, it is their ideas and words that I present. I do not claim credit for their ideas, only the blame if I have not adequately presented them.

I should like to thank everyone who helped with editing their stories. Frequently, I learned about their entrepreneurial efforts to create jobs in Africa from news articles, magazine articles, press releases and

INTRODUCTION

websites. Through personal e-mail correspondence, everyone was very helpful in creating a book of interesting profiles of successful entrepreneurs in Africa. I should also like to thank the owners of websites, the authors of the articles and the editors of the publications that I have cited as references in this book. I would especially like to thank all the entrepreneurs who so kindly gave permission for the reproduction of their stories.

By sounding out African entrepreneurs about the visions they harbour of their continent, I have tried to present the successes and the philosophies of these entrepreneurs, and also the philosophies of the economists, educators and political leaders who are interested in developing Africa to its full potential for the benefit of Africans and the world. The selection and editing of the views presented in this book naturally reflect my thinking and stance on the issues involved in developing a new Africa and making it a continent of opportunity. I believe that Africans need to think about and determine their own destiny, keeping in mind the welfare, happiness, rights and opportunities of all ethnic groups.

For the latest updates on the entrepreneurs presented in this book, please do both a 'Google search' at www.google.com, and an information search with AllAfrica Global Media, a multi-media content service provider, a systems technology developer, and the largest electronic distributor of African news and information worldwide. Registered in Mauritius, with offices in Johannesburg, Dakar, Abuja and Washington, AllAfrica is one of a family of companies that aggregate, produce and distribute news from across Africa to tens of millions of end users. Their website, www.allAfrica.com, is among the Internet's largest content sites, posting over 800 stories daily in English and French and offering a diversity of multilingual streaming programming and well over 600,000 articles in their searchable archive (which includes the archive of Africa News Service dating from 1997).

In recognition of everyone's support, author's royalties due to me from the sales of this book are going to Médecins Sans Frontières/Doctors Without Borders (MSF) to support their medical relief projects in Africa. MSF is an international humanitarian aid organisation that provides emergency medical assistance to populations in danger in nearly 70 countries. In countries where health structures are insufficient or even non-existent, MSF collaborates with authorities such as ministries of health to provide assistance. MSF works in the rehabilitation of hospitals and dispensaries, vaccination programmes and water and sanitation projects. MSF also works in remote health-care centres and slum areas, and provides training of local personnel. All this is done with the objective of rebuilding health structures to acceptable levels. In carrying out humanitarian assistance, MSF seeks also to raise awareness of crisis situations; MSF acts as a witness and will speak out, either in private or in public, about the plight of populations in danger for whom it works. In doing so, MSF sets out to alleviate human suffering, to protect life and health and to restore and ensure respect for human beings. (Source: www.doctorswithoutborders.org)

I am presently making contact with all the people interested in Africa's future development in the 21st century for a possible third book entitled *African Entrepreneurs in the 21st Century*. I am looking forward to feedback from readers of my first book, *Entrepreneurship in Africa: A Study of Successes* (2002), and readers of this book, *Africa: Continent of Economic Opportunities* (2006), concerning their information on successful entrepreneurs in Africa that I might profile in my third book.

Generally, I look for entrepreneurs who strive for excellence in order to be competitive in regional, national and international markets. Their enterprises are well established, in good financial shape and enjoy a reputation for quality, integrity and service. They act in a socially responsible way, support community development efforts and create a work environment in which their employees can learn and grow.

To be more precise, I try to illustrate the following factors:
- What the enterprise does (establishment, key dates, past, current and future projects);
- growth of the business, how it has grown (turnover, profits, the number of employees, or anything that illustrates that the enterprise has grown);
- marketing strategy (ways used to grow the business such as marketing and expansion strategies);
- hardships or difficulties that might have been experienced, and how they were overcome;
- team management structure of the business;

- quality certification and awards received;
- training done within the enterprise; and
- social involvement – how the enterprise contributes towards job creation and social upliftment.

I try, however, to keep it interesting, and not too factual, and so I find that I sometimes skip over some of the factors I am considering in order to keep the stories interesting. It is most important to also include the secrets of success from successful entrepreneurs that will motivate and help others to start new businesses. I am looking at best practices within Africa so that we can replicate those success stories in other parts of the continent. For uniformity, most stories are told in the third person.

I am also looking for commentary for inclusion in the third book concerning how best to create economic environments and opportunities for skilled, innovative and passionate entrepreneurs in Africa to successfully implement their ideas, achieve their dreams and bring benefits to their communities.

African Entrepreneurs in the 21st Century will feature examples of African entrepreneurs who have demonstrated visionary and strategic entrepreneurial leadership across the continent. These individuals are an inspiration to others with their ability to spot market opportunities, and arrange resources to create viable businesses in spite of significant challenges. Through their personal stories, readers of *African Entrepreneurs in the 21st Century* will gain invaluable insights on how to recognise gaps in the marketplace and lead or partner with others to establish profitable ventures.

As with my first and second books, in recognition of everyone's support, author's royalties due to me from sales of the third book will also go to Médecins Sans Frontières/Doctors Without Borders (MSF) to support their medical relief projects in Africa.

David S Fick
Email: AfricanEntrepreneurs@gmail.com

Part 1

The African continent

AFRICA: CONTINENT OF ECONOMIC OPPORTUNITIES

The continent of Africa is the world's second largest after Asia, with a total surface area, including several surrounding islands, of 30,313,000 square kilometres. It stretches from 40° in the north to 34 35° south and encompasses 54 independent countries — 48 mainland and six island states — with an estimated total population of around 800 million.

While many write off Africa as the continent of despair, other enterprising individuals and organisations have recognised the huge, untapped potential of Africa and are actively pursuing business ventures across the continent. Africa's opportunities include:

- oil and gas (OPEC members Nigeria, Algeria and Libya are key African producers which can potentially reduce dependence on Persian Gulf oil. Angola, Cameroon, Chad, Congo, Gabon and Côte d'Ivoire are non-OPEC African producers who can be expected to reap the benefits of substantial exploration activity);
- mining (West and Central Africa);
- privatisations (South Africa and Nigeria);
- international trade (oil producers and SADC);
- infrastructure (pipelines, roads, telecommunications);
- stock exchanges that are mushrooming in many countries;
- using educated English and French-speaking African nationals;
- leisure (big game, beaches, golf, climate); and
- a huge telecommunicating opportunity (satellite, Internet, cellphones, low cost structure).

Perhaps Africa's greatest opportunity, however, lies in its biodiversity, which ranges from Saharan desert to tropical jungle, from snow-capped volcanic Mount Kilamanjaro to the beaches of East and West Africa. Then there is the excitement of stalking big game in the African bush, the thrill of whitewater rafting through the gorges below the Victoria Falls or the awe of seeing the Egyptian pyramids at sunrise. While Africans have a vision of Africa one day becoming the telecommunications centre of the world, in the short- to medium-term, ecotourism provides the opportunity to develop leisure complexes which can take advantage of game parks, golf courses, beaches and beautiful scenery.

The biggest challenges to doing business in Africa are:

- the lack of quality information about the continent;
- fluctuating currencies;
- bureaucratic red tape (which is slowly getting easier to wade through);
- graft and corruption, as much a fault of the non-Africans who pass the brown paper bags as the poor and often unpaid civil servant who accepts the bag;
- nepotism;
- wars and unrest, though the changes in South Africa are starting to create a ripple of peace and democracy throughout the region;
- lack of local capital;
- monopolies such as marketing boards, state trading firms, foreign exchange restrictions, trade taxes and quotas and concentration on limited commodities all place a disincentive on exports, thus delinking Africa from the world economy; and
- lack of infrastructure, though in areas such as telecommunications and energy, Africa is able to use new technologies to leapfrog more advanced economies.

None of these challenges, however, is insurmountable.

(Source: www.mbendi.co.za)

Chapter 1: Economic and Political Policies

'Old' Africa is well known for its many challenges. In a 'new' Africa, the continent's challenges will be addressed and overcome with new strategies, new approaches and new ways of doing things, in order for Africa's vast opportunities to be exploited for the benefit of its entire people.

Africa: Continent of Economic Opportunities focuses on identifying business opportunities within Africa, on factors critical to building a successful company, on variables influencing future growth, and on exploring the collaboration that needs to exist between government, businesses and citizens. In the 21st century, there must be increased private sector participation in the development, rehabilitation and maintenance of Africa's roads, ports, rail, water, telecommunications and energy industries. Funding from the government and donors will diminish in the face of heightened social demands for education and health. African countries must successfully involve private investors in the development of its infrastructure.

In 2004, at the Developing Business and Infrastructure in Africa conference in Nairobi held by the International Finance Corporation in conjunction with the *Financial Times* of London, the president of Madagascar, Marc Ravalomanana, said, 'It's morning in Africa, and we are waking up. We are ready to move to improve our lives, our future and that of our children. We must show the world Africa's new face. The new Africa is a dynamic and competitive continent where the public and private sectors work in partnership to achieve growth and eradicate poverty. We should be proud and self-confident, ready to shape our future and take destiny in our own hands. It is up to us to lead our country to prosperity. Africa should stand up and meet that challenge.'

In the 2001 publication *The Elusive Quest for Growth*, Professor William Easterly points out that, in the past, African countries have borrowed heavily because they were willing to mortgage the welfare of future generations to finance their current standards of living. In addition to incurring high debt, irresponsible governments sold off national assets such as oil, diamonds, gold and lumber in order to live well while their people remained mired in poverty. African governments have often chosen destructive policies because they act in the interest of a particular class or ethnic group and not in the interest of the nation. Easterly demonstrates that neither aid nor investment nor debt forgiveness has proved to be the answer to developing African countries that have bad governments. He emphasises that only African governments displaying a fundamental shift in behaviour should receive aid, or be eligible for debt relief.

Easterly believes that a favourable climate for new generations of business people and entrepreneurs, which encourages them to invest in knowledge, machinery, technology and skills, is essential for Africa's future growth and development. High inflation, black markets, corruption, high interest rates, high budget deficits, restrictions on free trade and poor public services all create poor incentives for growth. He proposes that a just rule of law, democracy, independent central banks, independent finance ministers, and other good quality institutions are needed to stop the endless cycle of bad policies that perpetuate poor growth in Africa.

Easterly would agree that for Africa to have a bright future it must be a democratic continent with institutions that protect the rights and interests of minority groups, and that protect the right of private property and of individual economic freedom. Governments must be faced with the proper incentives in order to create private sector growth. Easterly imagines an Africa in which governments do not devote themselves to theft, but instead provide a national infrastructure — health clinics, primary schools and well-maintained roads — and assistance to the poor. He encourages the World Bank, the International Monetary Fund and other donors to support aid only to African governments able to present credible intentions to build a national infrastructure, and to give aid where it will help the poor most. Perhaps, then, the pursuit of growth in Africa will be more successful than in the last 50 years.

Easterly suggests that poor countries can leap to the technological frontier by imitating technologies from industrialised nations, and recommends that African governments and world organisations encourage this transfer of technologies from industrial nations to developing nations. He points out that electric power, a phone line and a computer translate into a vast store of knowledge on the internet. He believes that the decentralised nature of the electronics revolution could be very good for Africa.[1]

Professor Daron Acemoglu is an economist at the Massachusetts Institute of Technology. He believes the key to Africa's economic future is the good social institutions — such as political parties and courts — which it builds, and thinks that one model for Africa might be Botswana. Many African countries are rich in natural resources. Botswana is rich in diamonds. And, like most African countries, Botswana went through a transition in 1966 when it achieved independence from the United Kingdom. Since then, Botswana's economy has grown at a blistering average annual rate of 7.5 per cent. Acemoglu believes it happened because of political institutions that helped limit the powers of politicians and business leaders, and effected the right policies. Seeds of democracy existed in long-standing tribal institutions that encouraged broad-based participation and placed constraints on the political elite. Using this as a base, Botswana distributed power evenly. A broad cross-section of Botswana society has effective property rights and economic opportunities for investment and development. Sub-soil mineral rights are vested in the national government, which receives a 50 per cent share of diamond profits. Income from diamond mining has been reinvested in health, education and infrastructure, rather than being hoarded by rulers.[2]

The Common Market for Eastern and Southern Africa (COMESA) is a regional trade and economic integration grouping of 20 African nations: Angola, Burundi, Comoros, Democratic Republic of Congo, Djibouti, Egypt, Eritrea, Ethiopia, Kenya, Madagascar, Malawi, Mauritius, Namibia, Rwanda, Seychelles, Sudan, Swaziland, Uganda, Zambia and Zimbabwe. Intra-COMESA trade in goods reached US$5.3 billion in 2003 and was expected to grow by 20 per cent in 2004. In October 2002, in an interview with Charles Cobb, a correspondent for allAfrica.com (the website of AllAfrica Global Media), Erastus Mwencha, the secretary general of COMESA, spoke out on United States and European Union trade barriers that African nations continue to face, and on the need for greater regional integration in Africa. He pointed out that Africans have come forward with the New Partnership for Africa's Development (NEPAD). He has seen statements which say NEPAD is a good basis for sustainable African growth. 'Now,' he says, 'let's get down to business!' Africa has seen good trade movement with the United States African Growth and Opportunity Act (AGOA). Trade has increased; for instance, the value of African garment exports to the US rose from about US$600 million in 1999 to US$1.5 billion in 2003.

Mwencha points out, however, that such improvement does not necessarily apply in the case of other products where Africa ought to have a comparative advantage. For example, Africa still has problems of access to the US market, in the form of non-tariff barriers, when it comes to agricultural products. He encourages reducing these barriers of entry to assist Africa in tackling the problem of development. Mwencha talks of market access and of subsidies to agriculture in the developed world that are affecting both the marketplace and production and making an impact on the local producer and consumer. He says that all should agree that a subsidy is a subsidy, and should try to find a long-term solution to their elimination. Since 2000, Mwencha has been citing the Organisation for Economic Cooperation and Development (OECD) for spending over US$300 billion a year on subsidies and he would like to see some significant advancement in cutting subsidies so that African agricultural products can compete.

AGOA gives market access that allows African garments to come into the US quota- and duty-free. In 2004, these tariff- and quota-free trade benefits were extended until 2008, and AGOA was extended until 2015. Now is the time that Mwencha would like to see technology transfers, investment and a two-way trade flow. He wants to encourage yarn-making, fabric-making and, only then, garment-making — whereas at the moment Africans have only the capacity for garment making, with 'upstream' industries yet to be developed. This is the potential Mwencha wants to look at. AGOA has been running since 2001; from the perspective of the trade flow, the trend is promising, shows opportunities, and holds a lot of potential, but Africans need to act if they are going to have sustainable development in this area. They need long-term stability so that the garment trade doesn't crash in 2008 when the multi-fibre AGOA agreement ends.

Mwencha is trying to create a viable marketplace under COMESA. In 2000, COMESA created Africa's largest and most dynamic free trade area. In 2002, the COMESA nations, with a population of 380 million, constituted a free trade area for nine countries (Djibouti, Egypt, Kenya, Madagascar, Malawi, Mauritius, Sudan, Zambia and Zimbabwe) with 200 million people; within this free trade area, the members are able to trade free of duty, thus creating a huge market. COMESA is the first African grouping to be a free trade area and the third in the world after the European Union and the North America Free Trade Agreement (NAFTA). Burundi and Rwanda joined the FTA on 1 January 2004, and there are four other countries (Uganda, Swaziland, Comoros and Eritrea) that have made significant moves toward being part of the free trade area.

But removing barriers to trade is not enough. Member nations need to start tackling investment in the region. Mwencha puts forward three ideas:
- One is the fiscal infrastructure and an environment which makes it very difficult to do business in the region because of high transaction costs.
- The second is the ability to attract foreign direct investment into the region and create an environment conducive to investment.
- The third involves looking at the macroeconomic environments and the political scenarios of the region so that COMESA countries offer an attractive investment destination.

Mwencha has established a COMESA AGOA desk in Washington, to match business communities in the two continents so that Africa can get investment. Even under AGOA, he has seen in COMESA, and encouraged, cross-border investments of cumulative value where one country may have yarn but no garment-making facilities; for example, yarn is moving from Zambia to Mauritius to Madagascar to produce garments for the US.

NEPAD has a coordination mechanism based in Johannesburg. It is not intended to be a bureaucratic arrangement. NEPAD is a concept. It's also a programme of action, which will be implemented by regional organisations such as COMESA. If one looks at the agenda of NEPAD and the agenda of COMESA — whether one is talking of ICT, of infrastructure, or of agriculture — one sees that exactly the same programme is being pursued. So NEPAD is the concept while the vehicle is COMESA. The African Union is the finality of what is seen as regional integration groupings, for regional integration groupings are the building blocks which will eventually become the African Union. COMESA's achievement of a customs union is also, partially, an achievement of the AU. And what Africa now needs, and what Africans are working on, is for each of the two blocks to slot into each other.

Mwencha points out that investment in Africa holds a number of challenges. One is the high debt factor combined with low savings. Africa needs substantial resources for growth. Africans have agreed on the Millennium Development Goals but the continent must reach at least a 7 per cent growth rate to achieve them by 2015. And for this Africa needs huge investments. Foreign direct investment going to Africa in 2002 was only 4.8 per cent of world foreign direct investment flows, and this is totally inadequate. Africa should be looking at 15 per cent or more.

Why isn't it coming to Africa? Mwencha thinks, first of all, that there is unwarranted bad publicity about Africa. In many African countries it is the negative events which catch the headlines. He believes that culpability for the problem of continued negative publicity lies both with Africans and with those he calls partners for, as he points out, all nations are now in an indivisible world where interdependence is undeniable. As he says, 'we all need to confront this problem so that we can turn the tide and see Africa grow.'[3]

Leon Louw, Executive Director of the Free Market Foundation of South Africa, believes that prosperity is the natural outcome of relative economic freedom. African governments have succeeded in preventing prosperity although Africa is a continent of manifestly energetic, resourceful and enterprising people who, if left alone, would prosper. Louw, however, asserts that eco-imperialism, imposed by many first world governments, academics and scientists, NGOs and passionate activists, threatens to hamper the progress of developing African countries. Louw maintains that new eco-imperialists do not want poor African countries to follow the development paths that made possible the prosperity of developed countries which mined minerals, harvested timber, converted jungles, rain forests, swamps and wetlands into cities and farms, domesticated and commercialised their wild life, and laboured under harsh conditions by choice. These enemies of globalisation seek to extend policies which, Louw says, are known to perpetuate and exacerbate poverty.[4]

Callisto Madavo, the World Bank former vice president for the Africa Region, has written that Africans need jobs, millions of them, in cities, on farms, in small enterprises, in multinational corporations, in export industries, and in services. Jobs would raise incomes, lower poverty, and create the tax base necessary to finance critical work in combating HIV/AIDS, malaria and tuberculosis. Madavo understands that African leaders are prepared to take specific actions to help deliver more and better-paying jobs.

There are three steps that, he believes, would make a difference.

First, Africa must invest in infrastructure. Access to roads and electricity pays off in multiple ways. Improved rural infrastructure helps both farmers and other workers. Madavo points out that this is evident in community-driven development programmes that have empowered villages to improve their wellbeing by improving roads and water supply. Enterprises stand to benefit enormously from improved provision of energy and electrical power.

Second, African leaders can improve the business climate in their countries.

Third, the time has come to accelerate regional integration. Africa's small, narrowly-based economies can benefit from being knit together, with lower tariffs, shared infrastructural projects and harmonised regulations.

Madavo recommends that each country look closely at its own opportunities and constraints. Success depends upon working in an integrated fashion and involving the private sector in working with government to tackle problems. Strategies must be multifaceted. It doesn't make sense to free up farm prices, but allow the deterioration of the roads which farmers use to get their goods to the marketplace. It's not enough to provide workers with new skills to compete if the regulatory environment drives investors to other countries.

Finally, both African decision-makers and their international partners must stick to their pledge to keep jobs very much at the centre: jobs for the 35 million Africans who are unemployed and better-paying work for the 140 million Africans who earn less than US$1 a day.[5]

David Dichter, founder of the company Technology for the People, has tried for many years to convince the development community in general, and development banks in particular, about the advantages which African businesspeople could derive from south-to-south transfers of production technology. This involved his taking many, many trips to the region and much proposal writing — but it was to no avail. Dichter asserts that the movers and shakers in the World Bank simply couldn't be bothered to listen because they were so busy trying to drum up business for their own financial outlets and to push their own pet theories. They felt that to go out of their own orbits and bypass the special interest groups was somehow too unorthodox and too untrustworthy, and they also took the position that any ideas, strategies, or programmes which didn't originate with them in the first place were not worth doing! Also, they were so intent on trying to make sure that African entrepreneurs didn't take advantage of them that any loan programmes they did devise were so over-regulated and top-heavy that they were doomed from the outset. David Dichter felt that it was impossible to cure with a bandage what required a major operation. And he was afraid that the powers-to-be in the World Bank, the African Development Bank, and national development programmes like USAID are so set in their ways, and have such entrenched positions, favouring their own sacred cows, that he simply gave up in disgust.

In sharing some further thoughts on entrepreneurship in sub-Saharan Africa, David Dichter feels that the World Bank, various regional banks and national banks make a point of telling everyone that they are guided in all of their decisions, as far as small and medium enterprises (SMEs) are concerned, by several main considerations. These are conveniently expressed as economies of size and due diligence. And, also as bankers, they are also committed to justifying their own positions by trying to delegate their responsibilities to other banks down the line. Dichter maintains that these considerations have one thing in common: that the individuals involved are essentially seeking to protect themselves every step of the way. This leaves very little room, of course, for innovation — and certainly for any sort of real trust and understanding where the needs and requirements of SMEs are concerned. As part of the game that is being played out, Dichter says these banks pay outrageous fees to professional consultants, fees established by the banks themselves. These fees are for 'checking on things' even though the megabucks firms have little or no competency in such matters, or haven't a clue what works — or doesn't work — in the country concerned.

Dichter suggested to the bankers that as far as due diligence was concerned carefully selected in-country NGOs could effectively do the job at a fraction of the cost. He pointed out that at the same time they could do a very creditable job in monitoring the activities of SMEs which might receive modest loans from a local World Bank or ADB affiliate bank. You might have thought that he was trying to undermine their very existence — the banks and national aid programmes do everything possible to convince themselves, as well as the people and governments who keep them in business, that they are totally supportive of everything connected with SMEs and the free enterprise spirit. Dichter's sense is that they are in fact very suspicious of SMEs and their intentions. They seem to feel that they must not only be constantly on guard against being ripped off by SMEs, with whom many bankers feel decidedly uncomfortable in spite of all the rhetoric to the contrary. They seem to prefer to use their economies of size argument, which effectively means that giving loans to SMEs is more wasteful, and then they follow up by saying that administering such loans simply isn't very cost-effective.

Over the years Dichter has observed that the World Bank has tried to shift attention away from SMEs by passing responsibility to other affiliate agencies, including the United Nations Development Programme and Technical Cooperation Amongst Developing Countries. Their results have been equally disastrous. In addition, the World Bank and African Development Bank have tried over the years (with very little success) to make selected local and regional banks more responsive to the needs of SMEs — for instance serving as conduits for such loan funds. These efforts, however, have also lacked any real conviction or follow-through. When mistakes were made or funds squandered by these local banks, little or no due diligence was exercised for fear that local or national politicians would somehow be offended and that the World Bank would be criticised for interfering in their national affairs. Thus, time and time again it is the little guys who have suffered. No-one trusts them, but on the other hand no-one has ever bothered to trust them.

Graham Bannock is a British consultant whose 2002 study identified domestic private sector development as a key aspect of economic growth. The study found that economic policies to regulate the institutional environment in the private sector are essential. Bannock maintains that in the early stages of development, small firms help to develop markets through trading activities and, in the process, accumulate capital. They help to develop a widespread commercial culture with the necessary skills, disciplines and organisation upon which further progress can be built. In later stages these functions continue, but as larger organisations emerge SMEs can increasingly be sub-contracted to carry out activities which cannot be carried out optimally on a large scale — and therefore complement large firms. People also move from large firms to small and vice versa. This explains why tiny firms have played such a large role at the start of the recent information technology boom in the West and where the flexibility, speed of reaction and openness of small firms has been so important. As development proceeds, large firms become increasingly capital-intensive, creating added value which can increase wealth at a rapid rate. This allows new, more labour-intensive small firms to serve the new markets which greater wealth creates. As new activities mature to a point where large-scale activity is viable, these activities are taken over by large firms. In all these ways, large and small firms complement one another.

Bannock reports that effective policies for promoting private sector development cannot be developed or implemented without the full participation of private business at national, regional and local levels. Tanzania has set up an official National Business Council. In Uganda, an umbrella organisation, the Private Sector Foundation, was created in 1995 to improve dialogue between business representatives and government. In Kenya, an umbrella organisation, the Private Sector Forum, was set up in 2000. In most countries, the private sector policy framework was created essentially for the large-scale enterprise sector, which subsequently forced SMEs to operate in a less favourable business environment than larger firms.

Bannock acknowledges that in Africa lack of finance, and bank finance in particular, is universally regarded as the major impediment to the development of SMEs. Behind the financing problems of SMEs are a series of institutional and regulatory barriers which prevent capital markets from working properly. The most important of these obstacles is a lack of property rights and other institutional mechanisms which would allow people in the informal sector to pledge their assets against borrowings and participate in the capital markets for business assets. Informal sector entrepreneurs have erected buildings, for example, which represent considerable collateral value, but they cannot pledge these assets because the buildings are on land (such as government land or common land) to which they do not have clear title. Although they may have reasonable security of occupation by usage or custom, and they may have purchased the property on that basis, this does not count as a legal title. Not only do banks find it difficult to obtain sound collateral, but even where they have it there are often difficulties in realising it in cases of default. Hernando de Soto has calculated that the world's poor have in fact accumulated property many times greater than all the foreign aid and investment received since 1945 but that these properties cannot be utilised in the capital markets of the formal sector because of a lack of property rights.[6] Bannock concludes that these problems need to be overcome in the present developing economies before they are able to embark on rapid industrial expansion.

Bannock maintains that market economies cannot function effectively unless contracts can be established and enforced. The problem is not that laws are outdated or not administered with impartiality; rather it is that these formal legal systems are not accessible to the vast majority of business people. Those in the informal sector are excluded by cost.

Greatly expanding private sector economic activity and increasing its productivity, Bannock believes, is the only route by which developing countries can reduce aid dependency and alleviate poverty by their own efforts. Lower regulatory costs, smaller informal economies, less corruption, and more effective public revenue-raising, as well as the alleviation of poverty, are all associated with higher economic development. Inappropriate regulation deters inward investment, raises business costs and erects a barrier to entry into modern economic activity — in short, it prevents markets from working to channel human and physical resources into productive use. Moreover the regulatory framework fosters corruption, which deprives governments of the revenues needed to create conditions which could favour development.

Bannock states that not only is regulation too complex, and therefore costly, but it is, in general, inefficiently administered and many of the techniques recently adopted for lightening and controlling the burden in advanced countries have yet to be imported into the developing world. Procedures for business registration and licensing, employment, foreign trade, taxation and other matters are unnecessarily protracted and costly. Regulation or, in a few cases, the lack of it, has obstructed the emergence of capital markets that could channel savings into productive use. African countries do not, in general, have fully integrated and articulated policy statements for promoting private sector development, nor do they have adequate machinery for formulating policy or implementing it.

Whilst donors are increasingly devoting attention to providing means and opportunities for environmental issues to assume importance, Bannock points out that the political will to effect change in Africa, in particular, remains muted for a variety of reasons which include the power of vested interests, a lingering hostility to private sector activity and motivations, and a lack of understanding, perhaps, of the ways in which development took place in advanced countries and continues to progress there, in Asia and elsewhere. There are, however, clear signs in most countries of a growing appreciation that interventionist strategies for promoting private domestic activity — support systems, subsidies, state ownership and controls — must give way to creating the conditions in which the indigenous population can help itself.

The processes of private economic development in market economies are essentially similar everywhere, and in all epochs, including those which saw the early industrialisation of the advanced countries of today. Bannock says that it is wrong to assert that countries cannot develop without large inflows of foreign capital, or transport infrastructure, or large enterprises, or massive programmes for education. These may be all good things, but in the developed countries these things followed development rather than preceding it. The argument that things are different now might have some force were it not that some emerging countries in

Asia have broken out of the cycle of underdevelopment to achieve living standards comparable to those of some OECD countries. Bannock agrees that export-led growth, which took advantage of low labour costs in Asia — an advantage certainly shared by African countries — played a major part in Asia.

Bannock concedes that the enabling environment was, and is, less favourable in Africa than in Asia. He points out that virtually all studies of the 'Asian Miracle' seem to be focused on macroeconomic and cultural issues. He stresses that political stability and sound macroeconomic polices are requisites for sustained development, and that some regulation is necessary for markets to function effectively and for reasons of social cohesion. The strong influence of local, cultural and other conditions must be recognised; for example, some cultures limit the role of women. Bannock reminds us that what has worked in one place may not work in others without adaptation to indigenous factors. Nonetheless, he emphasises that inappropriate regulatory policies are a major impediment to private sector growth and, moreover, that despite the formidable political obstacles, if the will exists, these impediments can be reduced and it is a priority that they should be reduced.[7]

Firms and entrepreneurs of all types, from micro enterprises to multinationals, play a central role in growth and poverty-reduction. Their investment decisions drive job creation, the availability and affordability of goods and services for consumers, and the tax revenues governments can draw on to fund health, education and other services. Their contribution depends largely on the way governments shape the investment climate in each location, through the protection of property rights, regulation and taxation, strategies for providing infrastructure, interventions in finance and labour markets, and broader governance features such as cracking down on corruption. Botswana and South Africa developed the strongest investment climates in Sub-Saharan Africa between 2003 and 2004, but too few other African nations were following suit and most continued to rank among the world's least friendly for business, according to the September 2004 report *Doing Business in 2005: Removing Obstacles to Growth*, co-sponsored by the World Bank and the International Finance Corporation, the private sector investment arm of the World Bank Group. The report found that investment climate reforms, while often simple, can help create job opportunities for women and young people, encourage businesses to move into the formal economy, and promote growth. The report found that sub-Saharan African countries reformed less than any other region in 2004 and retained the most regulatory obstacles to doing business. Sixteen of the 20 countries with the most cumbersome business regulations and weakest protection of property rights were in Africa.

The report found that poor countries, which desperately need new enterprises and jobs, risk falling even further behind rich ones which are simplifying regulations and making their investment climates more business-friendly. Businesses in poor countries face larger regulatory burdens than those in rich countries. Poor countries impose higher costs on businesses to fire a worker, enforce contracts or file for registration; they impose more delays in going through insolvency procedures, registering property, and starting a business; and they afford fewer protections in terms of legal rights for borrowers and lenders, contract enforcement, and disclosure requirements. In administrative costs alone, the report found a threefold difference between poor and rich nations. The number of administrative procedures and the delays associated with them were twice as high in poor countries. The payoffs from reform appeared to be substantial.

The report concluded that the payoff comes because businesses waste less time and money on unnecessary regulation and devote more resources to producing and marketing their goods, and because governments spend less on ineffective regulation and more on social services. Heavy regulation and weak property rights exclude the poor — especially women and younger people — from doing business and from joining the formal economy. Heavy regulation has thus not only failed to protect those it was intended to serve, but has often harmed them. Countries with simpler regulations can provide better social protection and a better economic climate for business people, investors, and the general public. The report built on noted economist Hernando de Soto's work, showing that while it is critical to encourage registration of assets, it is as important, and harder, to stop them from slipping back into the informal sector.[8]

The high level of informality among micro firms in African countries and other LDCs has been extensively documented. The common view is that the informal sector arises mainly from disequilibrium in labour or product markets. In their 1997 paper 'An evolutionary approach to the informal sector in Africa', Nottingham Business School lecturers Gamal Ibrahim (Sudan) and Francis Neshamba (Zimbabwe) offer an alternative approach based on evolutionary economics. They argue that the informal sector has it own dynamics, embedded in a specific socio-cultural context. They point out that informality is a survival mechanism by business owners, who are constrained by socio-economic factors. Therefore, the transition to formality is an evolutionary process building on the networks, habits and relationships active in the second market. They believe this indicates that such transition from informality to formality does not always result from excessive government regulations and market failure but, rather, from an entrepreneurial capability to participate successfully in societal institutions. Ibrahim and Neshamba assert that this has direct implications for government policies towards small firms in Africa. They conclude that, given time and appropriate policies by formal institutions in terms of providing benefits and imposing fiscal costs, organisations operating in the second markets will adapt their behaviour and see the benefits of becoming legitimate.

I believe the following political and economic policies would support free enterprise and free markets in assisting in the just and sustainable development of Africa:

- The cure for Africa's ills is to return to African roots, to build upon the African indigenous institutions of free village markets, free enterprise and free trade, and to empower the individual — politically, socially, and economically. In traditional African society, chiefs are answerable to their subjects though not necessarily in forms recognised in the West. There is hardly any African country today that cannot manage itself if its resources are put to proper use (Ayittey 2005).
- Economic programmes that are geared to help the group or the family have their best chance of success in alleviating poverty when they assist and allow individuals to become successful through their own excellence and hard work.
- Priority should be given to the agricultural sector's adequately feeding all the people within its society before exporting commodities such as tea, coffee, cocoa, cotton and other cash crops.
- Farmers should be given greater access to land, credit, technology, and the knowledge that would help them grow more resistant crops as well as ensuring plant and animal safety.
- Farmers should be provided with reasonable private financing for land, equipment, and supplies of fertilizer, seeds and pesticides, in addition to an efficient and competitive market for their surplus, and extension services from experts.
- Efficient organic farming methods should be considered wherever they will produce the same competitive surplus for market while preserving the environment.
- Genetic research that answers the safety questions posed by Europeans should be completed. Furthermore, some people think that GM crops should not be introduced into Africa, because they make poor farmers dependent on greedy large seed-producing companies.
- Governments should create a healthy and positive enabling environment that will encourage investment and growth in the indigenous private sector. Without a strong local private sector offering opportunities for jobs and income, a country's growth targets will not be met (Bannock 2002).
- Government policies related to inflation and pricing, competition and monopoly, property rights, and contract enforcement provide the enabling framework for all businesses, including SMEs, in the economy. If these general policies, taken as a whole, work to minimise the cost of transacting business, they make the whole economy more efficient, and allow indigenous enterprises to focus their attention on the production of goods and services for the marketplace (Bannock 2002).
- Local producers should have ready access to markets, should be able to know the status of the markets in advance, and should have access to adequate credit.
- Government policies should help the struggling farm families and the entrepreneurs in Africa and reflect solutions developed out of African genius on African soil and in tune with the African spirit and family values.
- What is needed is governmental regulation to support a healthy, growing economy where personal

freedoms can exist and economic benefits are realised, without the abuses that unregulated capitalism can bring. A healthy economy is the result of a careful balance of personal freedoms, the productive application of capital (entrepreneurial capitalism), and appropriate governmental regulation.
- There are proper areas of responsibility for government. Government should collect revenue and user fees to provide services and infrastructure such as decent schools and medical facilities, safe drinking water, good roads and railways, electricity, and access to the internet. Africa's great natural wealth in oil, diamonds and lumber should be invested in its citizens, not used to fuel endless conflict.
- Governments should not try to own and manage businesses directly or through their cronies.
- Governments should provide security and police forces to provide protection for all citizens and a rule of law that includes property rights and protection of minorities and all ethnic groups.
- Tribalism is a serious cause of conflict in Africa. Within each African country a council of traditional tribal chiefs could be consulted by government leaders concerning tribal issues, and with this council in place there might be fewer issues between the tribes.
- Competent, efficient and adequately compensated government bureaucracies and independent judiciaries should work towards eliminating graft and corruption by just laws, good governance and accountability.
- Respected government bureaucracies should gather information on external markets, enforce standards among local producers, and provide advice and incentives that help these local firms better to thread their way through the labyrinth of rapidly changing world markets and to find their own niches in which to succeed.
- Developed countries should provide access to their markets without unfair subsidies and regulations that discriminate against Africa and other developing areas.
- Regional neighbours in Africa should work together to provide larger markets for member countries. It is hoped that initiatives like NEPAD will facilitate and speed up the desired changes.
- In order to allow trade to flow regionally, regional neighbours should work together to provide an efficient physical infrastructure of roads, railways, pipelines, power lines, air services and telecommunications within Africa.
- An adequate banking and investment system should be constructed that will provide capital, enabling entrepreneurs to achieve their visions while creating jobs for all Africans looking for work.
- Protection of the environment should be accomplished in a way that provides for the wellbeing of present and future generations.
- The export of natural resources like gold, diamonds and petroleum must adequately benefit all Africans by building infrastructure, creating jobs, and providing good health and education within Africa.
- Actions should be taken to increase competition and lower costs on maritime and air transport routes to and from Africa and road and rail transport within Africa.
- Wherever possible the export of finished products instead of raw materials must be encouraged.
- The competitive regional production of finished products such as automotive vehicles, steel, and clothing should be encouraged. This is preferable to importation from abroad since local production within Africa provides jobs and accumulates investment capital for use within Africa.
- Entrepreneurs and business leaders who are successful in Africa should strive to give back to their communities.
- Africans, wherever they are, should get back home with their diversified experience and expertise to help out their motherlands.

Africa is composed of 54 countries and there are success stories in some African countries that the other African countries should learn from:
- African countries should learn the secrets of capital, its creation, preservation and expansion. In creating, preserving and expanding capital, certain institutional and infrastructural frameworks have to be developed concurrently: rule of law, financial transparency, and a culture of saving and investment.
- The economic impact of the HIV/AIDS pandemic in Africa, the cultural impact, the family impact, the

impact on children, on all the coping mechanisms of a family or a country, and on the bureaucracy with its loss or depletion of human resources, is enormous. There are leadership issues and there are resources issues. Africa and the world need to be as thoughtful about this set of issues as about anything on their agenda in the 21st century.

Bad government and cultural differences have been fundamental problems in Africa. Therefore, good government and enabling cultures are prerequisites for putting these suggested policies into action. The Nigerian Amy Jadesimi asserts that Africa cannot feed itself largely because of a lack of long-term investment from governments and the private markets. A significant amount of the latter has been due to trade barriers, political interference and colonial legacies. She believes that Africans should focus on fixing Africa's problems and should hold themselves accountable and maintains that, rather than repeating the mistakes of the West, environmental or otherwise, Africans should aim to create a society built without many of the West's mistakes. That Africa as a developing continent does not absolve its leaders of their responsibility to safeguard their children's futures — which, after all, is where the salvation of Africa lies.

For David Mpanga of Uganda, the solution lies in good governance: the building of institutions (which of necessity have no family and belong to no tribe) instead of personalities; instilling a sense of personal responsibility instead of lamenting a colonial past that cannot be changed; building a deep sense of fiscal responsibility in leaders and making them more accountable to their own people, and concentrating on building the nation instead of lining leaders' pockets. Mpanga believes good governance will make Africa a more attractive investment destination. With increased investment, a reduction in red tape and senseless regulations will follow. The economic cake will grow bigger and national resources will go where they are supposed to go, thus leading to a reduction in corruption and poverty.

Alhaji Bamanga Tukur, executive president of the African Business Round Table, explains that capital flight exists in Africa because of fear on the part of foreign investors. Tukur maintains that for Africa to allay the fears of foreign investors and to be able to stop massive capital flight, it should smooth the environment and investment terrain for investors. Governments in Africa should address the lack of infrastructure and initiate legislation which would promote investments as well as partnerships. 'We need to look at our environment and see what is wrong. We talk glibly. If the Nigerian government, for instance, wants investments to come in, it should fix power, energy and open up roads, as well as strengthen transportation,' he advises. He states that investment is prepared to go anywhere there are benefits and that is why governments should strive to create the enabling environment. 'If the business and investment environment is good, we don't need to call anyone to come and invest because entrepreneurs will come by themselves,' he explains.[9]

Patterson Timba of Zimbabwe points out that both economic and political arguments suggest that increased intra-African trade can foster a regional take-off. Infrastructure (especially telecommunications networks and transport communications), and economic policy conduct (relating to sound economic policies and good exchange rate management), are conducive to intra-African trade. Insofar as regional intra-trade arrangements contribute to increased bargaining power, more policy credibility and extra regional security, its welfare effect, he believes, is indisputably positive.

Timba says that regionalism, coupled with sound macroeconomic management, lower political tensions and better physical infrastructure, can produce welfare gains. Even if pure economic arguments do not alone constitute a sufficient rationale for regional intra-trade arrangements, their interplay with politics and policies may nonetheless turn integration into an efficient solution. A market enlargement can attract foreign direct investment to a region. Economies of scale favour limiting the number of locations. If intra-African trade is tax-exempt, market size and access considerations reinforce cost considerations in convincing investors to locate to Africa.

Without the dynamic advantages accruing from foreign direct investment, in terms of technology transfer, organisational know-how and market intelligence, Timba believes that Africa risks being further marginalised. Economic integration could generate the threshold scales necessary to trigger the much needed strategic complement and to attract the adequate levels of investment (especially foreign direct investment) necessary for the development of modern manufacturing cores and the transfer of technology within the region. Apart from fostering regional peace, if increased intra-African trade succeeded in fostering regional economic take-off and initiating an 'African virtuous circle', it could contribute to reducing political tensions.

Africa has always had a lot of well-intentioned plans, but few implementers of good political and economic policies to support free enterprise and free markets in assisting in its just and sustainable development. Julian Morris is the editor of a thought-provoking book that brings together the experience and thoughts of 17 experts from five continents.[10] He says true sustainable development requires a shift in focus away from false perceptions and supposedly desirable outcomes — and toward an institutional framework that allows and encourages people to better their lives, make the best use of available resources, and improve the environment. This framework must include decentralised ownership and control of property and natural resources, enforceable property and contract rights, free markets, limited regulation, and the empowerment of individuals and communities to take charge of their own lives. Morris observes that the needs, views and concerns of poor people in poor countries must be accounted for. People need to focus more on the real, immediate, life-and-death needs of present generations by fostering economic development, not restricting development in the name of protecting the environment. It is their duty to ensure that the institutions they pass on to their children, and their children's children, enable them to progress. And they must strive to ensure that institutions which enable progress are adopted widely, so that people alive today are able to improve their lot; to live rather than subsist; to create rather than copy; to be free rather than oppressed (Morris 2002).

Is economic development under authoritarianism feasible? Can it be argued that if only a country could get its economy right the people would prosper and, as they become wealthier, demand greater political rights? George Ayittey, Distinguished Economist in Residence at the American University in Washington, asserts that economic reform (to establish more economic freedom) without concomitant political reform or freedom (democratisation) is an exercise in futility, because a liberalising and prospering economy would eventually hit the 'political ceiling'. If the leadership is enlightened and opens up the political space, the country will be saved and the prosperity will continue, but if the leadership refuses to open up the political space, economic progress and achievements will unravel.

Ayittey has stated[11] that the following African countries would implode if the political space was not opened up to permit democratisation: Cameroon, Chad, Eritrea, Ethiopia, Equatorial Guinea, Gabon, Guinea, Togo and Zimbabwe. He believes that three types of reform or freedom are needed to move a state-controlled society to a free one:

- Intellectual reform/transparency or freedom. By this is meant freedom of expression, free media, tolerance of dissent and the freedom to criticise government policies. According to Freedom House's Freedom in the World 2005 report, in 2004 only eight of Africa's 54 countries had free media and tolerated criticism of unwise government policies and exposure of corruption.
- Political reform. This essentially means democratisation and giving the people the political freedom to choose their leaders. In 2004, only 16 African countries were judged by Freedom House in their Freedom in the World 2005 report to be granting their people such freedom.
- Economic liberalisation. This rolls back the pervasive influence of the state from the economy, and grants the people the economic freedom to go about their activities. It requires removal of price and state controls on the economy and privatisation of inefficient state enterprises. According to the Heritage Foundation 2005 Heritage Foundation/*Wall Street Journal* Index of Economic Freedom, in 2005 only seven African countries were classified as largely economically free, while none received a totally free rating.

Ayittey maintains that the ideal sequence of reform starts with intellectual reform. If Africans are to craft their own solutions to their problems, then they need the intellectual freedom to expose problems and permit an open and free debate of possible solutions. Next comes political freedom, opening up of the political space so that the people can throw out of office corrupt leaders who have failed them. Ayittey has written extensively about this sequence of reform.[12] He asserts that the sequence should run: Intellectual-Political-Economic.

In the two decades before 1989, western governments and multilateral development agencies such as the World Bank focused only on economic reform. Taking a page from the West's own economic history, they argued that the ensuing prosperity would lead people to demand economic freedom. However, when the former Soviet Union collapsed in 1989, a 'political conditionality' (multi-party democracy) was added by the West as a condition for its aid. In 1991, the World Bank suspended loans to Malawi and Kenya until those countries implemented multiparty democracy. There was no mention of intellectual reform. But shrewd African despots resorted to chicanery and acrobatics, holding cosmetic and 'coconut' elections in order to continue receiving western aid. Africans dismissed the charade as the 'Babangida boogie' — one step forward, three steps back, a flip and a sidekick to land on a fat Swiss bank account. The sequence demanded by western donors (Economic-Political-Intellectual) is simply a reversal of the ideal proposed by Ayittey. This, he believes, is why Africa has not progressed, after decades of 'reform' — because they are doing it backwards.

Ayittey takes a fresh look at Africa's future and makes a number of daring suggestions.[13] First, he says that economic development requires investment, both foreign and domestic. Investment, however, does not take place in a swamp or vacuum but in an enabling environment, which must incorporate, inter alia, security of persons and property, rule of law and a basic functioning infrastructure. This environment does not exist in many parts of Africa because of the absence of a few key critical institutions such as an independent media, an independent central bank and an independent judiciary. These institutions are established by civil society or parliament and not by corrupt leaders, since they are fundamentally opposed to the establishment of institutions that will check their arbitrary use of power.

Second, an African economy is composed of three sectors: the modern, the informal and the traditional. The vast majority of African people live in the informal and traditional sectors. Africa cannot be developed by ignoring the informal and traditional sectors, but that was precisely what African elites did after independence; for instance over 80 per cent of Côte d'Ivoire's development was concentrated in Abidjan, the capital (or the modern sector). But the modern sectors in many African countries have become dysfunctional and non-reformable. The World Bank and western donors have spent billions of dollars trying to persuade and cajole the elites to reform the modern sector but they refuse because they benefit from the status quo. At some point, the World Bank and western donors would come face to face with the law of diminishing returns.

Rather than waste more money on modern sector reform, Ayittey argues that greater results can be achieved by focusing on the informal and traditional sectors, where the majority of the African people live. That is, these sectors should de-coupled or unchained from the parasitic modern sector for Africa to grow economically by modernising, building and improving upon its indigenous institutions. These institutions have often been castigated by African elites but they are the same institutions of free trade, free enterprise and free markets which Africans used to engineer what historians regard as the 'Golden Era of African Peasant Prosperity' from 1890 to 1950. Asking why the poorest Africans haven't been able to prosper in the 21st century, Ayittey answers that their economic freedom was snatched from them. War and conflict replaced peace, and the infrastructure crumbled. In a book that will be pondered over and argued about as much as were his previous volumes, Ayittey looks at the possibilities for indigenous structures to revive a troubled continent (Ayittey 2005).

Reuel Khoza, chairman of Eskom, and representative of the South African NEPAD Business Group, as well as the black empowerment private equity and investment group Aka Capital, says idealism has an important role to play in shaping Africa, but it must be an idealism tempered by pragmatism. Known for his robust views, Khoza maintains that the continent has enormous potential for growth if it is given the right kind of leadership. 'We have to develop African leaders anchored in African tradition for an African environment to meet African challenges, and equip them with requisite skills and competencies to handle the paradoxes and challenges of their times,' says Khoza. 'It is a leadership that does not consume seed capital but invests for the generations to come. A leadership that bridges the schisms and cleavages wrought by religious, tribal, social, ideological, economic and political diversity that characterises much of Africa's politics.'

The African concept of ideal leadership is characterised by probity, humility, integrity, compassion and humanity, says Khoza. This value-centred leadership is based on the philosophy of *ubuntu*, or African humanism. 'We believe in the ability of Africans to rebuild a vibrant, productive African leadership spirit, and produce leaders who are role models in many spheres of human endeavour,' he says. For Khoza, the idealism inherent in restoring Africa to itself is a necessary part of economic revival. In an Africa whose intellectuals are nurtured by native founding principles, innovation and industry will forge ahead, based on native technology and skills, combined with the best universal practices.[14]

Now is the time for action, and not merely words, to make Africa a continent of new opportunity for all Africans: where the basic needs of all Africans will be met; where all Africans will be extended the opportunity to fulfil their aspirations for a better life; and where each generation will create a better-ordered society, thereby building a better Africa for the next generation.

1 William Easterly. *The Elusive Quest for Growth*, Cambridge: The MIT Press, 2001.
2 Daron Acemoglu, Simon Johnson and James Robinson. *'An African success story: Botswana'*, in *In Search of Prosperity: Analytic Narratives on Economic Growth*, ed. D Rodrik, Princeton: Princeton University Press, 2003.
3 Charles Cobb Jr. *'Common Market Leader Seeks Level Global Field'*, allAfrica.com, 10 October 2002, allafrica.com/stories/200210110004.html
4 Leon Louw. *'The miracle of poverty'*, *Wall Street Journal*, 29 August 2002.
5 Callisto Madavo. *'Les Africains doivent trouver des employs'*, *Africa International Magazine*, No 381, November 2004.
6 Hernando De Soto. *Mystery of Capital*, New York: Basic Books, 2002.
7 Graham Bannock. *Improving the Enabling Environment for Indigenous Enterprise Development: A 10-Country Study*, Bannock Consulting, 2002.
8 World Bank. *Doing Business in 2005: Removing Obstacles to Growth*. Oxford: Oxford University Press, 2004.
9 Emmanuel Yashim. *'Bamanga lists ways to stop capital flight'*, Abuja: *Daily Trust*, 5 December 2003.
10 Julian Morris (ed.). *Sustainable Development: Promoting Progress or Perpetuating Poverty?* London: Profile Books, 2002.
11 Correspondence with the author, January 2004.
12 George Ayittey. *Africa Betrayed*. London: St Martin's Press, 1993 and *Africa in Chaos*, London: St Martin's Press, 1998.
13 George Ayittey. *Africa Unchained: The Blueprint for Africa's Future*. Basingstoke: Palgrave Macmillan, 2005.
14 *'African leaders needed for African challenges'*. Johannesburg: *Sunday Times*, 4 October 2004.

Chapter 2: Challenges and Opportunities

Ugandan President Yoweri Museveni says that there are challenges and opportunities for leadership in the era of globalisation in Africa. He asserts that leaders across Africa, and the people of Africa, must be committed to deepening and broadening regional economic integration, for this will create economies of scale, harmonise policies, pool resources, consolidate private investment and promote intra-regional and international trade. The rich countries of the world need to encourage these positive trends in Africa by opening up their markets on a quota-free, tariff-free basis, and this will encourage the multinational investors to come to Africa. Investment creates jobs for Africans and earns foreign exchange. Through a new pact for development between rich and poor countries, equitable world development is possible and desirable for everybody.

Museveni believes that there is a new dynamic evolving between Africa and the wealthier countries of the world. Africans are no longer looking for handouts. Rather, they are asking for the opportunity to compete, to sell their goods in western markets, to be considered for private investment funds, and to participate more fully in the global trading system. In short, they want to trade their way out of poverty and ask that the US and other developed countries support them in this effort. The call should go out for solidarity, hope and progress in the promotion of prosperity, peace and health for all humanity in the 21st century.[1]

A voice from South Africa suggests that history is the past; we can learn from it, but revisiting slavery and colonialism will not solve Africa's problems. In order to make Africa a better place, poverty and conflict should be eradicated by promoting trade, education and respect for existing cultures. Greed and despotism work against real development. Africa needs enlightened intelligent leaders, not opportunists elected because of stupid promises. Leadership is important. Educate the African people. Empower them through education and real opportunities to trade. Fighting poverty and oppression is the only way to make sure that terrorism disappears from the face of the world.[2]

Tony Colman has been an elected member of the British Parliament for Putney since 1997. From 1964-69, he worked for the then Unilever in East and West Africa and then moved to the Burton Group where he was a member of the Board from 1969-90. His parliamentary interests include trade and industry, the environment, pensions and finance. He points out that one of the great successes of Unilever in Africa in the 1960s and 1970s was the movement to local personnel, so that people were not being flown in from the north, from Europe, with cultural standards and interests that did not reflect local concerns. He also believes that it is very important for European countries to support fledgling industries in the developing countries of Africa.

He has proclaimed that development would not come to Africa through policies dreamed up in western think tanks and universities. It had to come from within and it had to be designed and supported by African people themselves. It had to be development for the people and by the people. Colman believes that the creation of the African Union (AU) and the New Partnership for Africa's Development (NEPAD) is cause for optimism. The key to development is fair trade, and with only a 2 per cent share, Africa has been on the periphery of global trading for too long. South-south trading, or, more specifically, intra-African trade, has the potential to spur on economic development. In this way, the African Union has the potential to bring economic integration, and eventually prosperity, to its member states.

The African Union offers the continent a chance to develop its existing trade blocks: the Southern African Development Community (SADC), the Economic Community of West African States (ECOWAS), the East African Community (EAC), the Common Market for Eastern and Southern Africa (COMESA), and the Economic Community of Central African States (ECCAS). Intra-continental trade relations must be energetically reshaped. ECOWAS's initial attempts at regional trade liberalisation have begun to bear the fruits of success, and increasing trade within the African Union should be a top priority for the new organisation. The AU will be looking towards a single currency as a stabilising and trade-facilitating economic measure, and although this may be some way off it is an important objective. The question of feasibility can be addressed by learning from the experience of Francophone African countries which have spent years with a fixed exchange rate between the French franc and the franc CFA, a currency used by 13 African countries, and which now have links to the euro.

NEPAD is more than a symbol. It is a realisation of the political will now present in Africa to take the developmental bull by the horns, and to do so with a home-grown and integrated strategy. The ideas that make up NEPAD are not revolutionary; on the contrary, the plan is an amalgamation of existing best practices. NEPAD needs to be developed with input from African civil society organisations and research institutions. In essence, NEPAD is a pan-African pact, an integrated development strategy. African governments are making serious commitments to good governance, which is in effect a precondition for economic growth. They are committed to placing their countries, both individually and collectively, on a path to sustainable growth and development and to active participation in the world economy. As a mirror undertaking, the international community is asked to ensure fairer terms of trade and market access for Africa's exports, continued support for debt relief, and the streamlining of aid flows to minimise transaction costs and increase efficiency.

In November 2002, during a meeting of the NEPAD implementation committee in Abuja, Nigeria, 12 African nations agreed to create an all-Africa peer review system for monitoring their governments' conduct: an attempt to help attract trade and aid from western governments tired of wars and human rights abuses on the African continent. The decision marked the first time that African nations had agreed to monitor each other's progress towards good governance and sound fiscal management. Stressing that wars and civil unrest are hindering development on the continent, Nigerian President Olusegun Obasanjo said that peer review was essential and that African governments should work to enthrone genuine democracy, the rule of law and good governance in all its ramifications. NEPAD is a programme of the African Union, and so the peer review mechanism would be a part of the African Union. It is obvious that any African country that does not agree to peer review is unlikely to obtain any of the extra aid and investment that NEPAD is trying to attract to the continent.

Tony Colman asserts that peace and security is a pre-condition to development. Investors want stability; legitimate trade requires stability; the development of national systems of taxation requires stability; the people of Africa need peace — and the international community has a responsibility to assist in these matters. western countries need to start practising what they preach in terms of open and fair trade relations and the renegotiating of international terms of trade, in order to halt Africa's increasing marginalisation. Strong leadership will integrate Africa into the world trading system and strong African leaders must unite to bring their people back into global trade and out of the sidelines of stagnation. Tony Colman concludes that there is a need for an African Union built on the same principles of cooperation as the European Union. It is this unity that will reinforce the sense of possibilities now being talked about; it is integration that will bring stability to the continent; and it is engagement that will bring opportunities to African entrepreneurs. It is African ownership of the development process that will bring economic, social and institutional development to the 600 million people of sub-Saharan Africa.[3]

In September 2002, Britain's former Secretary of State for International Development, Clare Short, advocated the reform of international trade rules. This had been UK government policy for many years and was well articulated in the 2000 White Paper 'Eliminating world poverty: making globalisation work for the poor'. Short maintained that for too long the rich countries of the world have lectured the developing world about trade liberalisation while creating barriers to developing country access to their markets. She feels that the world community needs to make trade rules fairer and to reform perverse subsidies. The European Union needs to show leadership on this; the Common Agricultural Policy must be reformed and the EU needs a policy that ceases to subsidise European farmers to dump surpluses on world markets, undercutting poor farmers. The developing countries are beginning to recognise the importance, both political and economic, of good governance. The members of the Organisation for Economic Cooperation and Development (OECD) are becoming committed to providing more and better aid, a sustainable exit from debt relief, better trade access, and a stronger voice for developing countries in international decision-making. The environment and development movements have also come together in a common endeavour to both reduce poverty and pursue sustainable development. The world community now needs a period of intensive implementation.

Short points out that this requires political will and action in all countries, developed and developing alike. It is essential for the effectiveness of aid to be improved. She says this means moving away from funding a proliferation of projects to backing poverty-reduction strategies drawn up by developing countries themselves. She believes that this is the true meaning of partnership: developing countries in the lead in developing their own poverty-reduction strategies; development assistance supporting these strategies, building national capacity rather than undermining it. It represents a new approach to development assistance — from seeing aid as a drop of charity in an ocean of poverty, to being part of the process of building modern, effective states and strengthening local communities in order to deliver long-term improvements in the lives of the poor. The opportunity to eliminate poverty and leave a sustainable planet to future generations is within reach. If the world community can grasp this, it can help build a world in which mass poverty exists only as a memory, and a world that is more sustainable and secure for our grandchildren. Short feels that it is time for the world community to deliver on its promises to reduce poverty in the world.[4]

Senegalese President Abdoulaye Wade says that the struggle to harness the benefits of new technologies is well under way in Africa, and that signs are pointing in the direction of a digital revolution for the continent. One example of recent advances is the use of underwater fibre optic networks that now link millions of Africans with their neighbours and with people living in other regions — technology that aims to connect the African economy with the global network at a lower cost. President Wade dreams of the construction of a tunnel linking Africa to Europe under the Mediterranean, from the northern tip of Morocco to Gibraltar. The tunnel would strengthen trading potential between the two continents. Other dreams include the construction of a highway linking the Moroccan coastal city of Tangiers to Mali further south, and an inter-Africa road network linking Dakar to Indian Ocean seaports, airports, and railway lines on the eastern side of the continent.

Convening every two years, the Corporate Council on Africa is the premier gathering in the United States of business and government leaders who are united by their shared commitment to promoting trade and investment between the US and Africa. 'Assistance doesn't mean charity,' said participants from Africa who attended the CCA's US-Africa Business Summit in November 2001 in Philadelphia, 'It means investment.' Six hundred of the approximately 1,500 people who attended the summit were African businesspeople. The director general of Madagascar's Hotel Le Glacier Group, which is expanding into eco-tourism, said that he wanted joint ventures with American business and had come to network and, if possible, nail down some deals. That a meeting like this was being held in the United States was in itself an encouragement. The summit, the largest gathering of African leaders (outside the United Nations) ever to convene on American soil, was organised by the Corporate Council on Africa (CCA), a private sector organisation established in 1992 that seeks strengthened trade and investment ties between the US and Africa. Nearly 200 American companies make up the CCA, representing approximately 85 per cent of the total US private sector investments in Africa.

This was the third CCA summit. CCA president Stephen Hayes says Africa is going to require hard and intense work because it is still, somewhat unfairly, seen as a high-risk venture by most businesses in the United States. Hayes says that small- and medium-sized businesses are especially crucial and that the African businesspeople came to do business and create partnerships. He believes American businesspeople need reliable, trustworthy partners in Africa and particularly small- and medium-sized businesses, for the future of African development depends more on small- and medium-sized businesses than on the large corporate presence. About a third of the summit agenda focused on ways and means for small businesses in Africa and the United States to take advantage of trade opportunities. Hayes says that many small- and medium-sized businesses don't need as much as a million dollars, but, ironically, it's harder to get smaller than larger grants.

The African Growth and Opportunity Act (AGOA) also formed a large part of the discussion in

Philadelphia. AGOA was enthusiastically embraced there as important in opening the door of US-Africa partnership a little wider. Another key concern at the Summit was regional integration. The fact of a global economy requires a regional approach, most participants believed.[5]

An international business committee, the NEPAD Business Group, works with NEPAD coordinating business policy. The CCA is the US representative on their executive committee, which also comprises the International Chamber of Commerce (ICC), the world business organisation; the Commonwealth Business Council in London; the Conseil Français des Investisseurs en Afrique (CIAN) in Paris; and the African Business Round Table in Johannesburg.

What is the NEPAD Business Group? It comprises leading business organisations which have a broad constituency both inside and outside Africa and are committed to helping the continent realise its full economic potential. The group acts as the medium between NEPAD and private companies which support its aims. It shares information on trade and investment opportunities in Africa and encourages private sector involvement in sustainable development projects.

James Harmon, 2002 chairman of the CCA, calls for the private sector to lead efforts to address the needs of the developing world. He states that the private sector is an essential part of the solution. He lauds the potential of private sector-led trade and investment to lift the economies of developing countries, and adds that the private sector's ability to manage, to move quickly, to bring to bear immense resources, to be imaginative and entrepreneurial far outpaces even the finest government and multilateral institutions. For example, South African-produced cars are now exported to the United States (the largest South African export item by value in 2004) and manufacturers like BMW have increased their investment in South Africa.

The fourth US-Africa Business Summit was held from 24 to 27 June 2003 in Washington. The summit's theme was 'Building Partnerships', and its mission was facilitating export/import trading; identifying agents, representatives and distributors; exploring joint venture partnerships and strategic alliances; and promoting foreign direct investment in Africa.

As in past years, the format of the event provided the opportunity for participants to interact with the African private sector, the American private sector, and African and US government leaders. The summit attracted a number of African heads of state and prime ministers as well as senior-level US government officials, and it helped advance, in tangible terms, their common ambition of strengthening trade and investment ties between the United States and Africa.

In November 2002, at the Africa Business Forum organised by the Wharton African Students Association, James Harmon identified the Millennium Challenge programme announced in March 2002 by the Bush Administration as being a watershed event in US foreign assistance. Under this programme, US foreign aid was increased from US$10 billion to US$15 billion a year with grants targeted to poor countries pursuing economic reforms. Harmon says African nations may receive anywhere from a third to half of those grants. According to Harmon, African nations have to look to foreign capital because it will be many years before the rate of internal savings can grow the economy. He notes, however, that African nations have to solve some problems on their own to cause that capital to flow. He realises that no amount of international goodwill will matter until African countries adopt policies of transparency, reduce corruption, and accept the rule of law and other reforms. Graft tops the list of reasons why some investors will not invest in Africa, followed by red tape, low supply of skilled labour, poor access to finance and undeveloped infrastructure.

At the forum, Roger Jantio, managing director and CEO of Sterling Merchant Finance, said his firm benefits from the paucity of venture capital in Africa. Sterling loves it and is buying a bank that has been privatised in Togo. No one else negotiated to take over a company that has promise and so Sterling is getting some very good deals. Jantio notes that his firm's first African fund, set up 10 years ago, didn't do well. Sterling was focused on smaller businesses with a high learning curve. Fish farming projects were exciting but at the end of the day, they didn't do Sterling any good. A reconstituted fund now specialises in banking, insurance and hotels and goes after only the largest operators, taking majority control and hiring the managers. Sterling's maximum investment is US$1 million per company, but in Africa, he says, a million is a lot of money.

According to Tunde Onitiri, assistant director of Emerging Markets Partnership, who also attended the Wharton forum, what makes Africa a good place to invest in is 'great demand'. The demand for wireless service has been beyond Emerging Markets Partnership's dreams. In Nigeria, there are close to a million new subscribers a year, which is favourable to private equity investors. Onitiri's firm, founded in 1992, became active in Africa in 2000 and, as of November 2002, has invested about US$200 million in six countries. His firm's strategy is to invest only in large, primarily regional, companies, such as a telecom or an airline, with investments ranging from US$10 million to US$40 million. His firm looks for companies strong enough to attract international sponsors and with strong local management, and takes a significant minority stake which can be anywhere from 10 per cent to 49 per cent of the company. His firm insists on at least one seat on the board of directors with the right to veto appointments of senior management people. The firm's goal is to achieve its return on investment by selling the company through a stock sale in three to five years.

At the forum, Mitchell Fenster, an investment officer for Modern Africa Fund Managers, said his firm concentrates its interest in a geographic region, central Africa, rather than in specific business sectors. The fund, in 2002 and in the fifth year of a 10-year plan, has invested US$105 million in amounts ranging from US$2 million to US$15 million in companies ranging from a US$100 million firm to start-ups. His firm doesn't play an active role in management but merely provides capital and financial expertise. However, every deal is preceded by exhaustive research and it takes at least a year to close a deal. In addition, the principals of the business are people they already know. In Ghana, for example, the business community is small and the people in it are well-known.

Samer Khalidi, who attended the Wharton forum, is not involved with a venture capital fund per se. His role is to advise wealthy individuals and families. Based in the Middle East, Khalidi says the single greatest challenge in entrusting funds is finding the right managers. He spends a lot of time with the people with whom he is investing, to determine if they can learn. He taps executives of other companies in his portfolio to offer advice. Khaldi's goal is to build up businesses to the point that multinational companies will want to buy them.

Stephen Sammut, chair and CEO of Buttonwood Ventures, believes that successful small private enterprises can provide social good through housing and jobs, a case of doing good by doing well. Onitiri says his group makes sure the businesses in which they invest meet environmental standards with which they are comfortable, and they hire local staff. They rely on the trickle down effect.[6]

Kevin Watkins, senior policy adviser at Oxfam, proposes that the international trading system offers real opportunities for sub-Saharan Africa and developing countries and has the potential to reduce poverty. But in order to take advantage of the opportunities provided by international trade, Watkins believes developing countries need better access to northern economies and they need to better regulate their own economies — and that includes foreign investment and imports into their economy in a manner that is in the best interest of poverty-reduction. Watkins declares that developing countries are not in the same position as industrialised countries when it comes to adjusting to international trade pressures, and rich countries should take into account the special circumstances of developing countries.[7]

Trade can realise its full potential only if rich and poor countries alike take action to redistribute opportunities in favour of the poor. This requires action at the national level, new forms of international cooperation, and a new architecture of global governance at the World Trade Organisation, says the Oxfam report 'Rigged rules and double standards' released in April 2002. National policies, the report notes, include tackling inequalities in health and education services, ownership of assets and access to land, financial resources and marketing infrastructure. At the international level, unsustainable debt burdens and the lack of effective representation of developing countries at the WTO has meant further marginalisation. The Oxfam report concludes that there is need for a new world trade order, grounded in new approaches to rights and responsibilities, and in a commitment to make globalisation work for the poor.

In May 2002, trade and development issues were at the heart of US Treasury Secretary Paul H O'Neill's agenda as he departed for Africa. He went with Irish rock star Bono for a 10-day visit to Ghana, South Africa, Uganda and Ethiopia to find out which policies did and didn't work. Part of Bono's intention was to use his fame to draw greater attention to his African concerns, especially in media that do not often pay much attention to the continent — which seemed to work since CNN, *Rolling Stone* magazine and MTV were among the media organisations on the trip. O'Neill went to learn, to hear from entrepreneurs, investors, farmers, artisans and vendors in the market. He wanted to hear about their hopes and dreams and he hoped they would share with him their insights into how best to eliminate the obstacles to Africa's prosperity. He went to Africa with an open mind, convinced of only one thing: human beings everywhere have the potential to succeed.

O'Neill says that the world's policy-makers need to move towards creating a global economy free of trade and tariff barriers so that the world would be better for its inhabitants in the sense that economic productivity would improve and economic life would be better. The real challenge is to figure out a way towards the idea of no trade and tariff barriers.

African nations are told to show that they are opening their markets, reducing subsidies and privatising industries through a variety of mechanisms such as International Monetary Fund/World Bank loan conditions, regional and bilateral trade agreements, and general policy advice. The paradox, however, is that the US and the European Union are not implementing at home the policies they insist African countries must take. This was starkly seen in April 2002 when the US announced its new Farm Bill, which increased US farm subsidies by US$35 billion, or more than US$20,000 to each farmer. European subsidies are only slightly lower, but the effect is that rich countries can continue to flood African markets with artificially cheap food and products and that African producers find it ever harder to export.

In Ghana, Finance Minister Yaw Osafo-Maafo objected to European tariffs on processed cocoa, because they wall out Ghanaian exports that would help development. It was also noted that the US-backed International Monetary Fund has pressured Ghana to drop its farm subsidies, while America dumps its own subsidised rice on Ghana resulting in the collapse of the Ghanaian rice industry in recent years, as heavily subsidised US and Thai imports have flooded in. From being an exporter, Ghana now imports US$100 million of rice a year. O'Neill says people should not be expected to live without clean water, as do about half the population of Ghana. He thinks we should do something about it, and we should do it now. He sees three types of investments in people vital to realising Africa's potential: clean water, higher primary education enrolment, and health care.

In South Africa it is noted that the whole issue turns around empowerment. As has been said, if you want to empower people, don't give them fish, rather teach them how to fish. In the early 1990s, the United States and European countries put a lot of pressure on South Africa to sign the GATT agreement. The purpose was said to be to create more opportunities for world trade. Conditions to this agreement were that signatories stop giving incentives, restitution and other financial help to producers and exporters. Subsequently the South African government stopped financial incentives to farmers and exporters. But for the past 10 years South Africa has been unable to sell many of its products to West Africa because prices from European countries were always cheaper. South Africans subsequently discovered that European countries continued giving subsidies to their producers and exporters of meat, dairy products and cereals. South African barley malt for a West African brewery could not compete against subsidised European barley malt.[8]

South Africans ask the same questions many other African traders and manufacturers have asked: why were Europe and the US so keen and so adamant to push for GATT to be signed and for South Africa to stop giving support for subsidies when both Europe and the US have continued giving billions of dollars of incentives to their producers and exporters? Does this mean that there is a rule for powerful nations (the rule of the strongest) and a rule for the rest of the world? Do the American people and the European people think that world poverty and resentment will disappear with such policies? South Africans ask for explanations, and Africans know very well that no support obliges the free market to take over and the more efficient producers to win. It should also enable locals to produce and earn a living. Africa used to produce large quantities of food and has very fertile lands for agriculture. Africans therefore ask only for level playing fields upon which to compete with their international rivals.[9]

When O'Neill and Bono visited Uganda, Museveni stressed to them that rich western nations should open their markets to developing countries and give them grants instead of loans. Museveni believes that debt relief is a short-term measure to allow the body to recover, but that the body must also get up and start being active. That is why the developed countries should link debt cancellation, grants, trade access, and market access — and then Africans will emerge from the quagmire. Museveni maintains that African mismanagement and the bad policies adopted by postcolonial leaders are responsible for the perilous state of economies in Africa. He points out that in 1965 Uganda was at the same level of development as South Korea while now South Korea is an industrialised country and yet Uganda is struggling.

O'Neill says President George W Bush has proposed that western nations should stop lending money to countries that can't afford to pay it back and should instead give grants to those showing good leadership. One way to get Africa out of the debt business is to stop making loans to people who should get grants for water assistance and primary education. Uganda was the first country to benefit from the World Bank's relief plan for heavily indebted poor countries and has been spending the money it didn't have to service the debt on primary education and expanding basic health services and treatment for victims of HIV/AIDS.

The Ethiopian Prime Minister, Meles Zenawi, has lambasted the United States and other developed nations for coddling their own farmers with agricultural subsidies while exhorting Africans to rely on trade, not development aid. Meles called this blatantly hypocritical. African Development Bank President Omar Kabbaj said subsidies prevented the creation of a level playing field for African exporters and called on developed nations to reconsider their policies. O'Neill turned the issue back to Africa and criticised many countries for imposing trade and tariff barriers that impede regional integration and development. He says that one of the things true of the countries of Africa is that the trade and the tariff barriers between them are high, and represent significant barriers to internal development.

O'Neill says that while the problems and challenges facing Africa are substantial, the trip showed him that the resolve of the people will not bend. Africans are brimming with hope, confidence and dreams, but Africa can't do it alone. The US shouldn't adopt an offhand attitude, saying that as long as Africans are just like Americans all will be well. American leaders can offer an opinion or advice, can remind everyone of their belief that the best route to economic growth is private enterprise, free markets and the rule of law, but O'Neill thinks it's a mistake for America to impose its values on the rest of the world.

Bono believes the 21st century is Africa's century. He is looking for big change, and big change is the relationship between the north and the south. Bono praises South African President Mbeki's NEPAD initiative, and expresses the hope that the north will rise to the challenge. The idea of creating partnerships is central to success; it is about reciprocal commitments, about what Africans do and what help they receive from the northern developed countries. Among Bono's reasons for being in Africa was to ensure that a comprehensive approach to the problems of the continent is started there and matched in Europe and America.

The trip to Africa gave O'Neill an opportunity to highlight the effectiveness of US trade policy. He met the people on the frontline working with, and benefiting from, this policy. He listened and learned, and he had the opportunity to talk to his counterparts about the millennium challenge account that provides increased US development assistance to nations working to eliminate corruption and to reform their economic systems, nations that exhibit stronger governance and that implement policies to promote greater productivity. This policy, initiated by US President Bush, significantly increased US development assistance to Africa, including assistance to build trade capacity. It increased US foreign aid by US$10 billion over three years for projects in nations that govern justly, invest in their people and encourage economic freedom.

In 2002, the US was working with African countries and others in the WTO to address subsidies and other issues related to market access. George Melloan, deputy editor international for the *Wall Street Journal*, reported that the Bush administration was proposing a sweeping reform in world trade in agricultural products. It had called on the rich industrial nations to reduce farm subsidies and allow poor regions greater access to lucrative markets. Interestingly, few complaints came from the US farm states of the Midwest, Great Plains and south, where farmers tend to understand the advantages of freer trade in agricultural products, so that there is enough food for third world urbanites who no longer have access to subsistence farming. The proposal came at a time when both European and Japanese politicians had urgent reasons to address farm subsidies. Japan's huge national debt, piled up in part by government generosity to marginal farmers, had become a drag on economic growth. European lawmakers knew that they had to do something about the monstrous common agricultural policy. It was squandering more than US$40 billion a year on farm support programmes.

Melloan pointed out that the Bush administration's farm proposal targeted trade-distorting industrial nation farm subsidies and hinted at a willingness to put the much criticised 2002-2012 US$190 billion US farm programme on the table. The EU would of course have to throw its own programme, which was about three times as expensive, into the pot. The US goal was to knock total global subsidies down by US$100 billion, capping individual programmes at no more than five per cent of total production. The US also wanted the elimination of export subsidies, claiming that EU farm export aid, at US$2 billion, dwarfed the US$20 million the US was spending. Tariffs on farm products were another target, with the US proposing a 15 per cent global average, compared to 62 per cent in 2002. The average US agricultural tariff was 12 per cent compared with 30 per cent for the EU and over 50 per cent for Japan. This would have to be addressed multilaterally. Most of Africa's agricultural products were covered by AGOA. So under AGOA, the Generalised System of Preferences Programme, as well as the Most Favoured Nation initiative, most African agricultural products were coming into the US duty-free.

Melloan concluded that the farm products initiative was an interesting exercise in global politics. He believed economists would find it hard to come up with a moral argument against giving the agricultural products of poor nations better access to the markets of rich nations. As for the Europeans and Asians, their initial reaction to the Bush farm proposal was negative — which was as predictable as the support it received in the US farm belt. American farmers may be dependent on the dole, but they are on the whole highly efficient compared to other growers in the world. The Europeans know this and were not very interested in opening themselves up to more American competition. Yet the stage was set for some wheeling and dealing, with the possibility that there just might be some benefits for all concerned.[10]

One effort that was working, thought former assistant United States trade representative for Africa, Rosa M Whitaker, in a May 2002 interview with Charles Cobb of allAfrica.com, is the African Growth and Opportunity Act (AGOA) signed into law by former President Bill Clinton in 2000. Whitaker says that AGOA provides substantial opportunities for Africa to expand its exports if the capacity required to compete in international markets can be developed and so long as the restrictions that hamper African trade can be reduced within the framework of the World Trade Organisation.

The process of bringing Africans from the margins to the mainstream of the global economy includes various elements. The United States has taken some of the most important steps in that process by opening up the largest market in the world — duty-free and quota-free for essentially all African products. Whitaker says trade capacity building is very important, because unless African countries build the capacity to take advantage of this opportunity, they are not going to see much progress. The US has coupled their market access with trade capacity building. By May 2002, the US had devoted US$192million to building trade capacity in Africa.

Trade capacity-building means helping African countries to develop commercial laws, intellectual property protection and harmonised tariff schedules; to understand how to market and how to develop a business; and to help develop the kind of economic reforms that are necessary in order to track trade and investment. It means helping African countries to improve their customs and trade facilitation organisations, to build expertise in the trade ministries, and to assist with WTO issues. This is all part of broad trade capacity building.

Whitaker reported that in the whole of Africa there is a need to build this kind of trade capacity, really a direct result of African countries not being fully integrated into the trading system. She said that when you have a region of the world that has been isolated from the system for so long, you can't expect it to have capacity, and she wanted to help African countries build the fundamental building blocks of running a trade regime.

Priorities are constructed in consultation with African countries, and those priorities are based on the needs of the country and where significant opportunities are seen to exist. For example, AGOA provides a significant opportunity, but in order to take advantage of that opportunity African countries have to have a functioning customs system — and so developing the customs procedure becomes an important priority. When a company might not want to come into a country with a weak intellectual property regime, intellectual property rights could become an important priority.

Whitaker targeted institutional capacity, saying that intellectual capacity and entrepreneurial spirit already exist in Africa and pointed out that African people come from a long tradition of trading. What she was primarily trying to do, therefore, was to strengthen institutional capacity and help those on the front lines of the government ministries and the private sector to play a more meaningful role. An example was an American project in Nigeria. US industry wanted gum arabic, which it uses a lot in food and in pharmaceuticals. Nigeria had the gum arabic growing wild but wasn't exporting in bulk to the US, so this was a significant opportunity. American industries wanted to come in but were unable to because in the first place the farmers had to be trained to harvest the trees. So trainers were brought in; a laboratory that would take the product and prepare it for export; training to the farmers in how to get the product from the village to the market. As a result, American industry made bulk purchases. If the US had merely given the Nigerians the market opportunity, it would not have been enough, without the laboratory, without the training, without knowing how to harvest the trees.

In Nigeria, and in other countries, the US is training officials to negotiate and better understand the intricacies of the World Trade Organisation and how to prepare the notification and the documentation. There has been a series of WTO workshops and of AGOA trade capacity-building workshops in Nigeria and there have also been workshops in Cameroon and Uganda. regional officials have been trained in AGOA: what it is, how to take advantage of it and how to comply with the various provisions.

Whitaker thinks there are many people speaking for the poor now, and since Africa is the poorest region of the world, she believes they should talk to African countries and find out how they feel about trade. What she hears when she is in Africa is that Africans are asking for more trade, not less. The US is helping the expansion of trade. People who have an issue with this should go, she suggests, to some of these countries — for instance to Lesotho where, because of AGOA, employment in the manufacturing sector outpaces employment in the public sector for the first time. They should talk to women who have been working and supporting whole villages on their salaries and providing new opportunities such as the education of girls as well as boys. When there is talk about what is good for the poor, Whitaker thinks, the poor know best, and we should have more dialogue with them.

Rosa Whitaker thinks that AGOA is showing fundamental results because it was a historic step towards eliminating some of the barriers to African products in the US market. Referring to her office's 2002 Comprehensive Report on US Trade and Investment Policy toward Sub-Saharan Africa and Implementation of AGOA, we learn that, since its enactment in 2000, AGOA has helped to transform the economic landscape of Sub-Saharan Africa. It has stimulated new trading opportunities for African businesses and entrepreneurs, creating new jobs and bringing hundreds of millions of dollars in much needed investment to the region. US imports from sub-Saharan Africa increased 61.5 per cent from 1999 to 2001. Most products from sub-Saharan Africa are now eligible to enter the US duty-free under AGOA. The US imported US$8.2 billion of duty-free goods in 2001 under AGOA, including the Act's generalised system of preferences (GSP) provisions, representing almost 40 per cent of all US imports from sub-Saharan Africa, and the US is sub-Saharan Africa's largest single market, purchasing 27 per cent of the region's exports in 2000. In addition, US exports to sub-Saharan Africa reached record levels in 2001, growing to nearly US$7 billion, a 17.5 per cent increase from 2000. Between 2002 and 2003, imports from sub-Saharan Africa grew by 55 per cent, and totalled US$14.1 billion in 2003. Even the non-oil imports grew by 30 per cent over the 2002 figure in 2003. It has meant that sub-Saharan Africa has received probably over US$300 million in investment, and that tens of thousands of jobs have been created, most in the textiles and apparel sector, although there has been growth in other areas as well.

Farm subsidies are a frequent flash point in trade relations between wealthy and poor nations, for which agriculture is one of the few potential economic engines. While the US and Europe push the developing world to open borders to imported goods and services, the industrialised countries often protect their own farmers from foreign competition. The US position in the WTO is that if others do so, the US will lower or eliminate their agricultural subsidies, which are much lower than Europe's and Japan's (EU agricultural export subsidies were 26 times higher than those of the United States in 2002).

Rosa Whitaker believes that Africa, the poorest region in the world, is the only area where the number of people living on less than one dollar a day is actually growing. In 2002, that number was at 290 million, more than the entire population of the United States. She points out that if the US wants to expand its exports (and 25 per cent of US GDP is dependent on exports) it needs healthy Africans, capable of buying. Since sub-Saharan Africa represents, to the US, a very important potential market of over 600 million people, the US stands to gain through expanded trade with Africa. The importance of trade as a vehicle for economic growth and development in Africa and elsewhere is broadly recognised. Some of the challenging issues are being addressed in the WTO but Whitaker believes that the sense of pessimism one might find in Africa has to do with the burden of the challenges there — and as one challenge is addressed, new ones emerge. Whitaker points out that the US has, through two administrations, been a very powerful ally of African countries, and would continue to support African effort. She concludes that these are challenges that no region of the world should face alone. [11]

In December 2002, Whitaker left her position as the US trade representative for Africa. She planned, however, to continue working in the same field and has created her own institution, The Whitaker Group (TWG), which is devoted to promoting trade and investment in Africa. She wants to bridge what she says is still a huge gap between US investors and Africa and points out that sub-Saharan Africa is the only region of the world not represented in the United States by a strong private sector association — which is usually where the bulk of trade takes place. She asked a number of questions. Who is going to actually work with the investors? Who has their confidence? Who has been working with the private sector? Who's been working with the countries to build bridges and provide for more US investment, more dialogue, more contact and more investment capital flowing into the region? She had tried to do this from a government position but realised she needed to be freer to perform more effectively. African countries do not know how to create access and have not been able to build sufficiently strong links with the American private sector to bring in its investment. This was the void she intended to fill with TWG.[12]

Since its launch in early 2003, TWG has generated trade and investment for its African clients, valued in July 2004 at over US$50 million. TWG consultancy works in practical, innovative ways to help knit Africa into the mainstream of the global economy for the benefit of government and private sector clients both in and out of the continent. The core of TWG's business is making sure AGOA delivers real, bottom-line results to help grow African economies and markets. TWG is about matching entrepreneurs, investors and traders with African opportunities — opportunities that it works to identify, create and promote. Since its primary benchmark is the value of the deals it facilitates, it fosters conditions conducive to getting deals done. That is why TWG works to ensure American policy makers and regulators, as well as the business and investment community, are fully supportive and share its enthusiasm for the opportunities Africa presents, and why it spearheaded the successful campaign to expand and improve AGOA.

Importers and retailers would do well to keep Africa in their sourcing plans after the elimination of quotas on China and other major suppliers in 2005, Rosa Whitaker told the US fashion industry on 1 September 2004, at the annual MAGIC show in Las Vegas, which attracts key buyers and sellers of apparel from all over the world. Whitaker said that thanks to the recently expanded AGOA, 'Africa can and will be competitive after 2005'. 'I would encourage you to build partnerships with Africa,' she told the industry, noting that there was a strong national consensus on the need to bring Africa into the mainstream of the global economy by opening US markets to its products. 'It makes sense on every level. It will be good for your business. The future is exciting, especially if textile production can be ramped to take advantage of the

US market access now locked in until 2015. And the constituency for African trade is such that you won't have to worry about the kind of safeguard actions now being proposed for China.'

(Source: www.thewhitakergroup.us).

Africa's time has come and this will be Africa's century for economic growth and development, she confidently predicted on 17 September 2004. Speaking to hundreds of students attending the Teach Africa Youth Forum at the US State Department, Whitaker pointed to the many countries in Asia that were once 'so incredibly poor' but now are 'experiencing a kind of prosperity that we in America take for granted'. They had gone from desperate poverty to prosperous members of the international trade community in just a few decades, and in her estimation the 21st century would see African countries transform their economies from poor to prosperous by strengthening their trade links with the international economy — just as South Korea and Taiwan had done not so long ago. 'When I was a child,' she told the students and Africanists in attendance, 'these countries [South Korea, Taiwan and Singapore] were just very, very poor. In fact, some of them were poorer than [some countries now are in] Africa.'

Although analysts are still debating the variables that contributed to the dramatic economic take-offs of these Asian nations, she said, most agree that trade was a major factor contributing greatly to their overall economic growth and development and making them vibrant and contributing members of the world economy. Citing South Korea to illustrate her point, Whitaker said that the key ingredients to that country's success had been the production of new products, the exportation of these products abroad at a competitive price, and the subsequent lure of foreign capital to invest in South Korean markets.

Whitaker explained that the 2004 reauthorisation and extension of AGOA has given Africa the advantages needed to build up its economies and emulate the success stories of its Asian counterparts, which were known as the 'Asian Tigers' — Hong Kong, Korea, Indonesia, Malaysia, the Philippines, Singapore, Taiwan and Thailand.

'We decided that if Africa was to have a real shot at what Malaysia and all the Asian countries developed, we were going to have to give Africa some preferential advantages and treatment. And that is what we did in the African Growth and Opportunity Act,' she said.

South Africa, Whitaker told her audience, has already begun to follow the examples of its Asian counterparts by taking advantage of the tariff-free entry of its products into the US market and exporting BMW and Mercedes Benz automobiles to the United States at a very competitive price. Africa's trade advantages under AGOA, Whitaker said, are bringing clothing retailers like GAP and The Limited to the continent to start producing their shirts in Africa instead of China. Whitaker held up two Ann Taylor brand shirts produced in Lesotho to demonstrate how AGOA was changing the face of trade in and with Africa. Before clothing companies like Ann Taylor began investing there, Lesotho was considered one of the poorest countries in the world; gold mining was its only major industry and companies employed mostly men, leaving women to scrounge for a living off the land. 'Now,' Whitaker explained, 'there are hundreds of factories in Lesotho producing these tops for the US market,' with a high percentage of women now employed in the industry.

The Overseas Private Investment Corporation's political risk insurance and loans help US businesses of all sizes to invest and compete in more than 140 emerging markets and developing nations worldwide. OPIC is a US government agency that assists American private investment overseas because it is in the country's economic and strategic interest. By charging user fees, OPIC operates at no net cost to US taxpayers, and its reserves in 2003 exceeded US$4 billion. OPIC has pushed an aggressive agenda in sub-Saharan Africa. A Botswana company which benefited from investment projects is the Game Trackers eco-tourism project; OPIC's US$4 million commitment helped expand and upgrade the northern Botswana attraction, develop the country's tourism sector, and provide local employment and training. In addition, Lobatse Clay Works was formed following an OPIC mission to Botswana. The number of OPIC projects in Africa has increased dramatically. The majority are with small businesses.

In Angola, OPIC has enabled the Seaboard Corporation from Kansas to rehabilitate a flourmill, more than tripling its production capacity and thereby helping that country address a scarcity of domestically produced food. In 2003, OPIC provided US$6 million in insurance to Seaboard for the rehabilitation and operation of a flour mill formerly known as Moagem Herois De Kangamba, located in Viana, nine miles east of the capital of Luanda. The mill produces and markets wheat flour and wheat bran for animal feed at a rate of 200 metric tons per day (MTD), compared to its 1999 capacity of 70 MTD. The project helped to alleviate scarcity in the Angolan domestic wheat flour market, making bread in particular more affordable to Angolans. By providing a staple food item at a reduced cost, as well as jobs for local residents, the project directly benefited the Angolan population and economy.

Michael Durney has been doing business in Angola for decades despite the civil war that ravaged the country. Durney turned to OPIC when business growth and the need to meet improving health and safety standards made it time to expand Mampeza International, his family's California-headquartered tuna canning and processing business. A US$1.8 million OPIC loan helped Mampeza's tuna canning facility in Angola improve its operating standards, diversify its product base and reach new customers in Europe. Mampeza employs fishermen and factory workers in Angola, and was already the local province's largest employer. An expanded Mampeza has created new jobs and training programmes and has generated new opportunities for local suppliers and contractors.

A US$1.68 million OPIC loan assisted Camas International from Idaho to support the organisation, deployment and operation of two mobile agricultural processing units to clean and separate cocoa beans in Ghana. By facilitating the cleaning of cocoa beans, Ghana's main source of export earnings, these new machines have increased Ghanaian cocoa bean export prices. The processing units are manufactured by Camas International using Camas's patented technology. In all, the project has generated 25 US jobs, supported 45 local jobs and provided a strong source of foreign exchange earnings for Ghana. And in Kenya, to help manage the water hyacinth infestation choking Lake Victoria, D& D Products of Wisconsin used American-made machinery. US$1.4 million in OPIC political risk insurance allowed D&D to convince its local bank to finance the project.

OPIC believes that its success in sub-Saharan Africa suggests a change in the international marketplace — an appreciation of the great opportunities on the African continent and the increasingly attractive investment environment in many African countries. OPIC's mission is to mobilise and facilitate the participation of US private capital and skills in the economic and social development of developing countries, thereby complementing the development assistance objectives of the United States.

In 1999, OPIC's first micro-credit initiative in Africa, the People's Investment Fund for Africa, which generates grassroots loans for local entrepreneurs, was launched with the help of the Reverend Leon Sullivan and his International Foundation for Self-Help. In 2001, OPIC established the Africa Millennium Fund as mandated by the AGOA legislation. This $350 million fund invests in telecommunications, transportation, electricity, water and sanitation projects. OPIC has also committed US$1 million to support micro-finance in Africa. This fund joins OPIC's Modern Africa Fund and its US$350 million Infrastructural Development Fund for sub-Saharan Africa (both of which invest in west and East Africa), and its New Africa Opportunity Fund which is active in southern Africa. In the 41 sub-Saharan African nations where OPIC financing, insurance and equity funds are available, OPIC-assisted investment projects will create jobs and economic growth in Africa and the US.

In December 2002, *Wall Street Journal* correspondent Roger Thurow reported a heated exchange between the US and Europe over the future of genetically modified foods. The American government and the biotech industry are pushing to bring genetically modified (GM) seeds to Africa. The European Union, where consumers are deeply suspicious of the safety of laboratory-altered food, is trying to convince Africans to adopt their own go-slow approach to biotech. The US industry hopes to polish its image with examples of biotechnology helping African farmers overcome pests, poor soil and drought whereas European countries have hinted that imports from their former colonies could be jeopardised if they switched to bio-engineered crops — which would dent the already bruised economies of Africa, whose biggest export customer is Europe. Africa, which desperately needs to find a way out of its chronic food crises, is the proxy battleground in the biotech struggle. Thurow says it brings to life the popular African proverb that says when two elephants fight it is the ants that get trampled.

Thurow points out that in 1999 the Ugandan government was moving aggressively toward embracing biotech crops. Then the contretemps over the safety of bio-engineered food between the US and the EU erupted in Uganda, and the fast-track progress hit the brakes. Economic risks also clouded African biotech efforts. When Ugandan scientists considered an application by US crop biotechnology giant Monsanto to test genetically modified cotton in Uganda, the country's cotton industry lodged an urgent protest. The United Kingdom and other European countries, it said, were threatening to stop imports of Ugandan cotton, worth US$19 million a year, if its character was genetically altered.

Thurow says that how the fight between the US and Europe plays out could well determine to what extent Africa uses biotechnology to tackle its most intractable problems. Millions of tons of sweet potato, maize, bananas and cassava, crops upon which Africa's poorest depend, are lost each year to pests, disease and drought. Projects underway to give these plants the genetic blueprints to resist assault from the elements could mean the difference between life and death for many Africans. Other scientists are exploring using biotech crops to deliver vaccines and vitamins that can ward off human disease where medical care is scarce. Patrick Rubaihayo, professor of plant breeding and genetics at Uganda's Makerere University, who is overseeing students working on the banana biotech project, says that Africans missed the green revolution and don't want to miss the GM revolution. He says the Ugandan government is asking who's telling the truth about GM. European organisations say it's not safe while the US says it is. His government wants to know which way Uganda should go.

Thurow points out that the 2002 food crisis in southern Africa brought the biotech battle to a fevered pitch. The government of Zambia turned away about 20,000 metric tons of US food aid in October 2002, saying that the shipments contained genetically modified corn that was unsafe, capable of polluting the country's seed stock and jeopardising its export markets, particularly to Europe. The US government, for its part, is spending about $12 million annually on African biotechnology. It has funded scientists in America and Africa to genetically engineer potatoes and sweet potatoes to resist attack by disease and pest. Alarmed by the American push, the development aid arms of various EU governments are countering with their own bio-safety and regulatory funding in Uganda and the East African region. Thurow reflects that the world's leading scientists say there is no evidence whatsoever that biotech crops are harmful to humans; if anything, they are probably safer to eat than conventional food because of the additional regulation to which they're subjected. Priver Namanya, one of the Ugandan scientists, tells Ugandan villagers that biotech bananas would boost production and incomes. Farmer Yusufu Konyogo says that he would like that, as long as the bananas will taste the same. Thurow concludes that the debate over genetically modified food is difficult because it turns on fears of long-term consequences.[13]

Daniel Steinmann, editor of the Namibia Economist, writes that 'GMO cereals have the capacity to provide harvest yields substantially above what we are used to so we need less land to feed more people. They can also be modified in such ways that they resist pests so we need less pesticide; that they grow on poor soils so we need less fertiliser; that they can be irrigated with salty water so we need less fresh water; that they modify soil for the better so we can plant the same crop on the same soil longer; and that they cannot proliferate in the wild so that we need not fear our wheat and maize will develop intentions of ruling the world. I think in short it comes down to the fact that GMO is a fait accompli and that the debate on the ethics has been overtaken by events. We shall need to decide very soon where we stand on this issue and what laws we need to regulate GMO in Namibia.'[14]

1 Museveni, Yoweri. Speech delivered at the Woodrow Wilson International Centre, Washington, 14 May 2002.
2 Georges Jaumain. Correspondence with the author, 2002.
3 Tony Colman. *African success through African ownership*, allAfrica.com, 12 February 2002.
4 Clare Short. Article published in West Africa Magazine, 7-13 October 2002.

5 Charles Cobb. *'Investment needed, not welfare, Africans tell Business Summit'*, allAfrica.com, 1 November 2001.
6 *'Global investment comes slowly to Africa'*, http://knowledge.wharton.upenn.edu/, 2002.
7 Akwe Amosu. *'The AGOA bargain is unequal - Oxfam'*, allAfrica.com, 21 May 2002.
8 Georges Jaumain. Correspondence with the author, 2002.
9 Ibid.
10 George Melloan. *'Those amber waves of grain are again a trade issue'*, Wall Street Journal, 6 August 2002.
11 Charles Cobb. *'Expanding African trade is the key to the future'*, interview with Rosa Whitaker. allAfrica.com, 20 May 2002.
12 Charles Cobb. *'US trade rep for Africa confirms move to private sector'*, allAfrica.com, 17 November 2002.
13 Roger Thurow, Brandon Mitchener and Scott Kilman. *'Amid a heated US-EU clash on biotech, Africa goes hungry'*, Wall Street Journal, 26 December 2002.
14 Daniel Steinmann. *'Give us this day our daily blend'*, Namibia Economist, 20 February 2004. www.economist.com.na

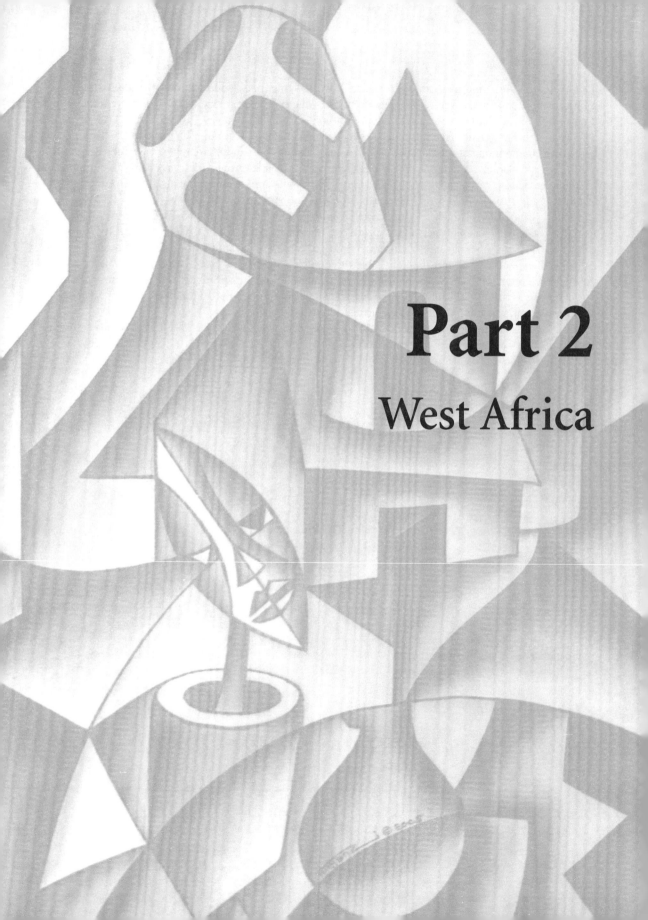

Part 2
West Africa

AFRICA: CONTINENT OF ECONOMIC OPPORTUNITIES

The West African region consists of 15 countries with a total population estimated at approximately 240 million people, spanning over 2,500 miles from the Atlantic Ocean to the interior of the continent. The desert lands of the southern Sahara, the lush rainforest of the coastal areas, the rich natural resources and, of course, the slave trade have influenced the development of this region. The spread of Islam and the aggressive competition between France and Britain to exploit the region have left a powerful legacy.

English is the official language in the coastal countries of Ghana (principal exports being gold, timber and cocoa); Nigeria (oil, cocoa and rubber); The Gambia (peanuts and peanut products and fish); Sierra Leone (diamonds and rutile) and Liberia (diamonds, iron ore, rubber, timber and coffee).

French is the official language in the coastal countries of Guinea (alumina, diamonds, gold, coffee and fish); Senegal (fish, peanuts, petroleum products, phosphates and cotton); Côte d'Ivoire (cocoa, coffee, tropical woods and other agricultural products); Togo (cocoa, coffee and cotton); Benin (cotton, crude oil, palm products and cocoa) and the sub-Saharan countries of Burkina Faso (cotton, animal products and gold); Mali (cotton, gold and livestock) and Niger (uranium, livestock products and agricultural products).

Portuguese is the official language in the coastal country of Guinea-Bissau (cashews, fish and seafood) and the island country of Cape Verde (shoes, garments, fish and bananas).

There are also hundreds of indigenous African languages such as Hausa, Wolof and Yoruba commonly spoken in this region. The Economic Community of West African States (ECOWAS) forms a solid geographical bloc of these 15 countries, from Senegal in the west to Nigeria in the east.

Chapter 3: Ghana

In the 1960s, the people of Africa emerged from colonial rule with optimism and determination to transform their society and bring prosperity to the continent, but in 1991 there was neither economic nor political freedom. Kofi Apraku believes that in order to seize control of its destiny, Africa must mobilise all of its resources and recognise the contributions that emigrants in the United States can make toward its development. In his book, African Émigrés in the United States: *A Missing Link in Africa's Social and Economic Development*,[1] Apraku offered a comprehensive look at these African emigrants and the role they may play in contributing to Africa's development. He demonstrated that Africa has well-trained, experienced and productive personnel in the United States, and that they are willing to return to their native lands only if African leaders are willing to undertake the necessary political and economic reforms.

Apraku's study addressed four main questions: Who are the skilled emigrants employed in the United States? Why did they come to America? What potential role can they play in Africa's development? What types of reforms are needed to allow them to contribute to Africa's development? In addition, the book discussed contemporary African issues, including agriculture and food production, population growth, economic integration, economic aid, diversification of African economies, privatisation, democratisation of political systems, and industrial policy for the 1990s. A review of failed economic policies was presented, together with suggestions for new approaches and a new emphasis on sustained economic growth and political stability. During the 1990s, Apraku's work became an important reference source for students of African studies and international development, as well as for international policymakers and professionals in development agencies.

Apraku has said that a competitive modernisation of Ghana's ports of entry is a logical step in achieving the so-called Gateway objective. Under the Gateway programme, the Ghanaian government is determined to make Ghana the hub of business activity in the sub-region. For that reason, it is planned that the private sector be more involved in the operations of the ports to shape the economic destiny of the nation. In a keynote address to commission the 60,000 square metre Tema Container Terminal (TCT) based in Tema, Apraku emphasised that the government cherished the desire for a genuine, functional relationship with the private sector as partners in development. TCT is a privately operated container terminal resulting from a joint venture between Antrak Ghana Ltd and SDV Ghana Ltd and aims to significantly increase Ghana's cargo reception, storage, bonded warehousing and clearance capabilities, providing consumers with a broader commercial choice.

The site started life as a dedicated timber terminal, but when timber exports via Tema port were re-directed to Takoradi in the early 1990s in order to boost the economy of the western region, it was decided to upgrade and convert the site into a container terminal. The US$10 million terminal, opened in March 2002, employs over one hundred staff and will be seen as an important long-term investment in the infrastructural needs of Ghana. No other private organisation has invested so heavily in Ghana's transport system and this project is the first of its kind in Ghana.

The Ghana Gateway project opened the door to private investors and encouraged new ideas of this kind, envisaging the harnessing of Ghana's potential as an export processing zone and regional trading, transhipment and relay hub. The terminal compliments Ghana's growing use of containers and its prospects as a cargo hub and transit route to land-locked Africa, attracting more external business through Ghanaian ports and borders.

The founder and executive chairman of both the OT Africa Line (OTAL) and the Antrak Group Ghana, Alhaji Asoma Banda, says that his desire has been to develop a competitive facility to serve the needs of shipping and trading communities and also to attract cargo moving to and from Burkina Faso, Mali, Niger and elsewhere along the coast. He says the terminal will greatly help the Gateway process whilst significantly increasing capabilities and improving facilities to provide a range of cargo services that will enhance the economic prospects of the nation.

(Source: Fred Oppong-Botwe. *'Trade Minister on modernisation of port', Ghanaian Chronicle*, 4 April 2001)

In 2001, Banda was elected chair of the Shipowners and Agents Association of Ghana (SOAAG), an appointment that reflected his outstanding contribution to the maritime industry in Ghana and west Africa. At the time of his appointment he looked forward to improving and assisting Ghana's overall prospects as a maritime hub and transport gateway to other parts of the sub-region, prospects including the improvement of Tema's deepwater capacity through a major capital dredging project; the development and of off-port cargo facilities; the encouragement of global shipping lines requiring ever greater economies and efficiencies; and the 'hubbing' concept taking deeper root in West Africa; and starting to bring down sub-regional market protectionism and customs barriers.

The Antrak Group specialises in ships agency, land side transport and project transportation in countries throughout west Africa and it has the largest trucking fleet in Ghana. Antrak is well established as the leading specialist project transporter for the construction, mining, power, oil and gas sectors, handling awkward loads, heavy lifts, large volumes and project documentary processing, route-surveying, logistics-planning, shipping, airfreight, trucking and other associated services. Through its Perth, London and Accra offices, Antrak managed the movement of an 11-ton engine from the manufacturer's premises in Korea direct to a mine site 200 kilometres into the heart of Ghana. Antrak coordinated and physically moved this fragile piece, covering all documentation, PSI, customs clearance, onward carriage, air clearance and port clearance. It has also transported the largest grinding mills ever imported into Ghana. The consignment, consisting of two 70-ton mill shells, was moved from southern Germany to a green field site more than 200 kilometres into the African interior. A 24-hour armed guard was provided and 600 power cables were removed and reconnected. An engineering study resulted in the strengthening of several bridges by means of three escort vehicles carrying 120 tons of road aggregate, which was used to fill in the potholes. The consignment was delivered safely, securely and ahead of schedule.

In June 2005, Antrak Air started flying passengers from Accra, Kumasi and Tamale to 12 cities in the west African sub-region: Abidjan, Abuja, Bamako, Banjul, Cotonou, Dakar, Freetown, Lagos, Lome, Monrovia, Niamey and Ouagadougou. This followed the purchase of two DC9 aircraft, each with a seating capacity of 1ten, by from Boeing International Corporation. Antrak Air chair Alhaji Banda recalls that his outfit started operating the domestic routes of Accra, Kumasi and Tamale in 2003 with a leased ATR 42 aircraft. The purchase of the two aircraft resulted from the hard work and vision of the board members, management and entire staff of Antrak Air. The decision for Antrak Air to operate in the sub-region was in line with the vision of the company to offer 'excellent service' to the public at moderate rates. Banda notes that there was competition along the west coast which, he says, was healthy for business since the beneficiary was the customer. He urges entrepreneurs to emulate the achievements of Antrak Air and realise that Ghana's 'destiny lies in our own hands,' and stresses that 'we should not always think that the salvation of this nation lies in the hands of foreigners.'

Antrak Air should continue to be a major force in the west African transportation sector. The purchase of DC9s is an excellent choice for regional routes as it was designed to operate from short runways and on short- to medium-range routes so that the speed, comfort and reliability could be extended to many communities. Planned operations of Antrak Air in the west African sub-region are in line with Ghana's aim of creating a hub in the sub-region.

(Source: www.antrak-gh.net)

One of Africa's premier shipping services is the OTAL shipping line and intermodal transport organisation carrying world-wide cargo to, from and within west Africa. OTAL operates a vast range of transport services complementing its regular liner and logistic operations. The company handles cargo throughout west Africa — from Morocco down to Angola — including destinations in the region's land-locked countries Burkina Faso, Chad, Central African Republic, Mali and Niger.

As a liner operator, OTAL transports cargo from northern Europe to west Africa using a fleet of no fewer than four 920 TEU container vessels, seven 1500 TEU container vessels, and six 660 TEU roll-on/roll-off (ro-ro) vessels. These vessels sail from Europe roughly every seven to ten days and perform 41-day round trips to Africa and back. Three new feeder services adding new port calls to OTAL's service play an integral part in these operations. A north African feeder service served by two 400 TEU vessels provides a weekly service to and from Dakar calling at Banjul (Gambia), Nouakchott (Mauritania) and Casablanca (Morocco). A west African feeder container service operates one 230 TEU vessel providing a weekly service to and from Dakar calling at Conakry (Guinea), Freetown (Sierra Leone) and Monrovia (Liberia). A southern African weekly feeder service operates one 270 TEU vessel connecting Pointe Noire (Congo), Soyo (Angola) and Matadi (DRC). OTAL's cross trading department, otherwise known as OTAL Crosstrades, oversees the transportation of container cargoes from outside the liner service's immediate sphere of operations in Europe and west Africa. This means it manages Connecting Carrier Agreements (CCAs) with other reputable carriers and tranships cargo over its European ports, using its own ships to Africa.

OTAL's mission is to be the first-choice carrier to, from and within Africa and it aims to achieve this by establishing close long-term relationships with its customers, enabling it to anticipate and cater for their needs. In the past few years, OTAL has extended its global agency network to cover close to 140 offices in 62 countries. This brings together the worldwide representation and expertise needed to give OTAL coverage in every major market trading with west Africa, particularly amongst the region's newly emerging or expanding trading partners in the Far East and the Indian sub-Continent.

In 2002, in response to the rising demand for specialist containers on the steadily maturing west African trade, OTAL introduced a range of refrigerated containers (reefers). These containers are a new addition to the OTAL fleet, which comprises of 20ft reefers, ventilated containers, dry vans, flat racks, collapsible flat racks and open tops, and 40ft high cubes, dry vans, flat racks, collapsible flat racks, and open tops. The new reefers are used to transport the growing number of perishable products imported and exported by west Africa every day. Movements of perishable cargo such as meat, dairy products, fresh fish and fruit require special care and attention. Reefers are ideal for the transportation of such goods as they are specially insulated and have built-in refrigeration units. While a reefer unit is in operation, a constant flow of air (set to a specific temperature) is circulated around the cargo by the container's evaporator fans (located at the base of the unit) before it is extracted. The most advanced reefer containers, such as those used by OTAL, are computerised, enabling an exact temperature setting to be programmed and maintained. This type of precision control has made the transportation of perishable goods easier, something especially important when shipping goods to and from west Africa where temperatures and humidity are often very high.

Using reefers to move perishable goods has proved to be a very effective way of transporting cargo with the confidence that the goods will arrive at their destination as fresh as when they were packed. It also means that shippers have the option of shipping goods by sea, a much cheaper alternative than air freight. OTAL has a comprehensive fleet of containers, making the line even more flexible. Shipping goods to and from west and central Africa can be a fairly tricky process and it is important for those with business dealings in the region to know what they're doing. For many, being able to use an agent who knows the region well, and who is willing to take responsibility for every step of the journey including the customs formalities at the ports, is a welcome relief. As an experienced operator in this complex shipping environment, OTAL is ideally placed to ship, truck and manage all the documentary formalities of delivering goods to some of the most demanding markets in the world.

(Source: www.otal.com)

Kwesi Nduom was a partner of Deloitte & Touche, USA, between 1986 and 2001, consulting with clients in Wisconsin, with Nestlé and the Ashanti Goldfields Company in Ghana, with Fan Milk in Nigeria and with the social security authority in Zimbabwe — and many other enterprises across the world. He started Gold Coast Securities, an investment banking firm with a broad distribution network in Ghana. Gold Coast has offices in Accra, Kumasi, Tamale, Takoradi, Ho and Hohoe and has become very successful. It is the local correspondent for Standard and Poors, and for Bloomberg. It has developed a number of innovative collective schemes in Ghana. In 2004, the Ghana Gold fund was launched in Accra by Gold Coast Securities and is being aggressively marketed to Ghanaians (and, indeed all Africans) with an interest in contributing funds to Ghana's local economy.

Nduom has also built a very successful hotel group, Coconut Grove Hotels, one of the significant investments made by the Nduom family over the past ten years. Coconut Grove Hotels is one of the few private multiple location hotel establishments owned and managed by Ghanaians. The hotel chain has four properties in Elmina, Obuasi and Accra, employs 160 people and has become a recognisable brand name in west Africa. Coconut Grove has won hotel of the year awards over the past four years from the Ghana Tourist Board. Ndoum also developed TSS Ltd, an innovative information technology company that has successfully developed and implemented software products for the insurance, mining and hotel industries. Its clients can be found in Zimbabwe, Guinea, Nigeria and Ghana.

As Ghanaian Minister of Economic Planning, Regional Cooperation and Integration from 2001 to 2003, Ndoum institutionalised a west Africa public-private sector round-table to assist the private sector to attract investments, increase exports and diversify the economy. The forum helped to formulate and implement policies and programmes in line with the country's aim of expanding trade and industrial relations with its sub-regional neighbours. Convinced that regional trade expansion provided a strong basis for the effective participation of Ghana and ECOWAS countries in the evolving linkages and interdependence of production units, his ministry promoted sub-regional economic cooperation and integration by focusing on expanding trade through the creation of a single free trade area and borderless zone. Access to this type of market enhances Ghanaian enterprise ability to gain access to global funds. The ECOWAS Trade Liberalisation Scheme seeks to promote intra-community trade and the free flow of unprocessed goods and traditional handicrafts duty-free between member countries.

As Minister of Energy from 2003 to 2004, Nduom's main contribution to the energy sector was to give it a firm vision and to ensure that a road map was put into place for his vision's implementation. It is only abundant and relatively cheap energy that will provide the fuel to power the private sector engine. The point is that the public and private sectors in Ghana must pay particular attention to the energy sector if the Ghanaian economy is to grow to the extent that will allow the average Ghanaian to achieve an appreciable level of micro-level prosperity. Mechanised agriculture requires fuel. ICT and any kind of advanced technology depend on sustained and reliable electricity and other energy resources. Industry needs appropriately cost-effective fuel and power in order to be profitable. The Internet revolution was developed on the back of abundant, cost-effective, reliable energy. The media cannot disseminate information effectively without power. Nduom has led the Ministry of Energy to carefully craft the vision to overcome challenges, supply the domestic demand and lead Ghana to become a net exporter of power and fuel by 2009.

(Source: www.nduom.com)

A few firms have begun tapping the African market. For instance, there's a good chance that many Americans who have recently filed a health insurance claim have had it processed by a clerical worker in Ghana. Affiliated Computer Services of Dallas sends digital images of the information from Lexington, Kentucky, to Accra through a high-speed satellite link. The arrangement allows ACS to tap Ghana's ample supply of low-wage workers. In June 2001, President Kufuor and Ndoum paid a visit to ACS's data transmitting business office operating in Ghana's free zone area. President Kufour was visibly impressed by what he saw and in brief remarks told his hosts that he would like them to be partners with government in job creation to fall in line with his policy of a 'Golden Age of Business in Ghana'.

President Kufuor has said that the government was determined to make Ghana the hub of information technology facilities in the west African sub-region. Commending the capabilities, competence and dynamism of the people of Ghana, he considered the major challenge facing the government to be how to move the economy forward and expand it to create more opportunities for jobs, building happiness and security, for if the economy is not well managed there may be all sorts of brilliant ideas but their implementation will be a problem.

ACS Ghana's first office in Africa was established in 2000. ACS employs about 1,000 people in Ghana and will possibly increase employment in the future on account of the high calibre of Ghanaian technicians, comparable to technicians at other ACS offshore offices. ACS, one of the world's largest information technology outsourcing companies, offering a broad range of technology and business solutions, chose Ghana as a location because it wanted a country with a stable and willing government to support their operations. ACS also needed a country that had the right technology and skills.

ACS management is very pleased that the quality of work has been excellent. Ghana plans to build on the positive image it has attained and translate it into economic growth. As Ghana garners a reputation as a bastion of peace and stability in west Africa, American business will grow increasingly aware of the economic opportunities there and dedication to democracy, peaceful transitions of power and the rule of law will increasingly cause American business to look at what Ghana has to offer. As American and British businesses look at Ghana, many will be encouraged by the importance government places on a business climate that promotes growth of the private sector and by the avowed objective of zero tolerance for corruption. The ACS Ghana venture demonstrates the possibilities of the global workplace in the information age — the opportunities for mutually beneficial private sector investment and economic dividends that can be reaped when a nation demonstrates devotion to peace and stability.

(Source: www.acs-inc.com)

Ghana's government has a vision of accelerated and sustained economic growth that provides equal opportunities for all. Ghanaian voters increasingly believe that a free enterprise economy is the surest guarantee of economic growth and prosperity and that only a positive partnership between the government and the private sector can deliver prosperity. The Ghanaian government is aware of the challenges that globalisation and liberalisation present and realises that it is imperative for Ghana to introduce even more dynamic programmes, to prepare the country to withstand the intensity of increasing worldwide competition.

Ash-Geo Handmade Textile Training Centre is a medium-scale textile weaving enterprise located in Keta, a coastal district capital in the Keta District of the Volta region of Ghana. The company started in 1987. Its main product is Kente cloth produced on both local and broad looms. Ghanaian batiks, tie-and-dyes and apparels are also produced using the centre's own original designs and motifs. George Ashiagbor, the proprietor and managing director of Ash-Geo is a young dynamic entrepreneur with vision, initiative and drive. He is an accomplished designer and produces the original kente patterns before they are transferred onto looms for actual production. The centre, which is managed with the support of an administrator, has employed 32 artisans comprising weavers, designers and tailors and has become the primary training centre for the Keta District Weavers Association, a cooperative organisation of 15 handloom textile weaving enterprises, and of which Ashiagbor is the current chairman. Each of the enterprises has an average of 12 workers most of whom had previous training at his centre. The formation of the association has set a firm production base for meeting any large orders that cannot be met by an individual producer. Ash-Geo takes the lead in the coordination and delivery of these large orders which are exported to neighbouring Benin, Burkina Faso, Côte d'Ivoire, Mali and Nigeria. On behalf of the centre, Ashiagbor has participated in some international textile conferences and fairs including the Trade Fair in Florence, Italy, in 1999, as well as the

Corporate Council on Africa Conference in Atlantic City, USA, in 2002, and has supplied a variety of designers and academic institutions with his kente designs. Ash-Geo was a finalist in the 2004 Africa SMME Awards. The company is interested in establishing business and marketing partnerships with companies abroad; in 2004, it expanded the market of its unique product line of kente designs and batik tie-dye textiles into North America, shipping from Tema Port near Accra, or by air from Accra.

Printex (Ghana) Ltd, a textile manufacturing company in Accra, was established in the 1950s as the Millet Textile Company, to manufacture towels. It operated under the name Spintex Ltd in the 1980s with spinning, weaving and finished departments, producing furnishing, suiting and shirting materials, traditional clothes, school uniforms, and uniforms for factory workers, the security services and commercial banks. In 1998, the company changed its name to Printex when it started making African prints. To adjust production of uniform materials in Ghana into fashionable fabrics was a challenging task. Printex aspired to operate in the competitive market of other high quality products from Africa and beyond.

Milad F Millet, managing director of the family-owned company has described the varied fabric designs as a blend of the exotic colours of the African forest, the flame of the rays of the sunset and the mystical mountainous areas of the African highlands. The Ghanaian market has been favourable to Printex's products owing to their high quality, and each new range of fabrics attracts increased patronage. Millet believes that the patronage of Printex's high quality fabrics is a beacon of hope for 'made in Ghana' products and challenges Ghanaian manufacturers to produce superior quality goods. He asserts that Ghanaians must learn to patronise goods made in Ghana in order to develop the technology and expertise of Ghanaian entrepreneurs to produce goods needed for development.

Printex employs 400 and turns over approximately US$20 million in annual sales. It supplies printed cloth to wholesalers, which then distribute it to market women, the traditional textile dealers. A team of designers produces more than 500 copyrighted patterns a year. Printex maintains strict secrecy until the point of production, keeping huge bolts of cloth printed with copyrighted designs under lock and key; they are often pirated by companies in other developing countries since once the new Ghanaian designs are released it is only a matter of time before knockoffs appear. Fakes tend to be made of fabric flimsier and less regular than cotton, and the colours do not always line up. Millet believes that piracy and smuggling cost the four local textile producers about two-thirds of the US$150 million annual local market.

(Source: Michael Phillips. *Ghana's fabric makers combat textile pirates, cheap knockoffs*, The Wall Street Journal, July 12 2002)

But while copyright infringement is an issue, smuggling is by far a greater problem for the local industries — one that could easily be reduced, according to Millet, if customs carried out checks at points of sale (retailers) and seized goods without adequate documentation to show evidence of correct duty payment. Millet also stresses the need for custom, excise and preventive officials along the borders to endeavour to put an end to the smuggling of fakes and the evasion of taxes by importers, adding that if the appropriate taxes were paid local companies would become competitive. After several years of meeting and pointing out the issue of smuggling as the biggest single factor hampering the growth of local textile manufacturers, the government seems unable or unwilling to tackle this, so whilst Printex continues to innovate, growth is being stifled.

Millet pledges to keep standards high. He hints at prospects for export but stresses that the immediate priority of Printex is the local market. He will keep increasing local market share by introducing and developing more varieties and by also increasing exports into neighbouring countries and possibly Europe or the US. In a very short period of time, and in a traditional market, Printex has become a household name, synonymous with quality and innovation. The introduction of pioneering innovations such as seersucker, diamond, and oheneba, openyin, and adinkra (showing the richness of the African culture), into the local market will no doubt be copied by smugglers soon, unless government acts quickly to curb such practices.

Printex, the newest made-in-Ghana fabric, is now firmly established both on the Ghanaian market and globally. In May 2002, Printex held a colourful fabric and design show at the Banquet Hall of the State House in Accra, a fashion extravaganza dubbed Ya tinase ('we are seated and here to stay'), to display the quality and beauty of Printex fabrics. The purpose of the show was to expose the public to Printex varieties, and increase patronage so that it would continue flourishing. Millet says he is happy that the fabric has been able to meet the competition on the Ghanaian market and has also been accepted globally. He believes it will 'climb high depending on Ghanaians' patronage to promote it'.

(Source: Isaac Essel and Kent Mensah. *'Printex is here to stay'*, Accra Mail, 3 May 2002)

In 2003, Ghana's Minister of Trade, Industry and Presidential Special Initiatives, Alan Kyerematen, announced that the President's Special Initiative (PSI) on garments was expected to generate US$3.4 billion, 70,000 jobs directly and 20,000 indirect jobs within four years. To make this a reality, a 178-acre piece of land was acquired at the Tema Export Processing Zone to develop a modern garment city with factory units that would be rented out to companies. The city was to consist of 92 medium-scale, ten large-scale and ten extra large-scale factories. The first batch of factory shells was finished in December 2003.

As of September 2003, a hundred entrepreneurs had been selected and were being assisted to develop into medium-sized garment manufacturers through a well-structured technical assistance programme. A modern clothing technology and training centre was established in Accra to train the youth in industrial sewing machine utilisation and mass production techniques, providing 400 mechanists with employable skills every month. By August 2003, about 1,800 operators had been trained. Similar training centres started operations in Kumasi and Takoradi in September and December 2003 respectively and a model commercial production unit was set up to give the entrepreneurs a true impression of a medium-sized factory. Supervisory and managerial personnel are trained within this unit, which is equipped to produce garments for export, and is to be replicated by the entrepreneurs.

By August 2003, cultivation of cotton to feed the President's Special Initiative on textiles and garments was in the pipeline, but in the meantime Ghana was importing cotton from Togo, Burkina Faso and Benin, to strengthen ECOWAS and enhance NEPAD in terms of regional trade. Kyerematen noted that his ministry was promoting the consumption of made-in-Ghana goods, especially locally-manufactured garments, and that the convention of wearing locally-sewed attire to work had been revitalised.

Problems facing another President's Special Initiative on salt are being systematically addressed to transform the industry into an internationally competitive one. By August 2003, six production sites had been identified, 15 production units registered, ten new companies licensed and four local industry experts engaged to boost the industry. Furthermore, 100,000 hectares of new oil palm plantation is under cultivation for the next five years under the oil palm President's Special Initiative to meet local demand, to be expanded to 300,000 hectares eventually. The Oil Palm Research Institute has been commissioned to produce two million pre-germinated seedlings for distribution to nursery operators.

Kyerematen estimates that Ghana needs to establish five factories to meet foreign demand for cassava starch. It is because of this that Sika Starch and Eastern Starch, in the Ashanti and Eastern Regions respectively, were incorporated in November 2003, and commenced operations in 2004. As of 2003, the Ghanaian government had spent US$1 million on infrastructural development and the formation of cassava grower associations to support the Ayensu Starch Company (ASCo) factory at Bawjiase in the Central Region, which began full production in July 2003.

The US$7 million ASCo project was financed initially by the Agricultural Development Bank (ADB), the National Investment Bank (NIB), the Ghana Commercial Bank (GCB), the Export Development and Investment Fund (EDIF) and Oerko, a Dutch credit financial institution. The project will be replicated in 50 districts in all the ten regions of the country.

Kyerematen points out that a lot of hard work went into the project, the aim of which is to bring rural communities into the mainstream of economic activities. The unique features of the project include that the conceptual framework, including construction, engineering and supervision, was designed by Ghanaians. This gives a sense of hope and serves as an example that Ghanaians can do better in the area of technology for the golden age of business by starting with the rural communities.

The ASCo project is primarily owned by Ghanaian farmers and the PSI Secretariat is working to separate ownership from management. The ADB and the NIB have agreed to convert part of their loans into equity for farmers. PSI is establishing additional cassava starch projects in the Eastern and Ashanti regions and it also inaugurated two more cassava plants in the last quarter of 2004. Serious discussions are ongoing to secure funding for three additional cassava starch projects in other parts of the country because the number of farmers who expressed interest in the project rose from 1,000 in September 2001 to 5,000 in 2002, and to the 10,000 mark in 2003.

Ceramica Tamakloe, a small company in Accra, won the Crown Agents Foundation Award for Small Business in the annual Worldaware Business Awards 2000. The company produces decorative pottery for export to Europe and America, and ceramic roofing tiles for the local market. It makes products of the right quality, design and price to win overseas orders and has the right business skills to fulfil them. It is now the largest single exporter of ceramic products from Ghana. The company was one of five winners from a high quality crop of entries for the Worldaware Business Awards scheme that began in 1989. The Award for Small Businesses is given to a company with not more than 100 employees, for commercial activity contributing to viable economic development, employment creation and community development in developing countries.

Founder Peter Tamakloe tells how the gift of a tie-pin and the closure of Ghana's universities in 1983 set him on the way to creating a business making decorative and garden pottery for the United States and tiles for the roofs of Accra. The closure of the University of Science and Technology in Kumasi, where he was studying ceramics at the College of Art, led him to visit potteries in Britain including that set up by Michael Cardew who had introduced contemporary pottery to Ghana 40 years before. A college instructor who knew Cardew gave him the tie-pin as a gift for another friend, the publisher Peter Kindersley. Hearing that Tamakloe wanted to start his own pottery in Ghana, Peter and Juliet Kindersley raised the money to buy him an electric kiln.

Tamakloe had not wanted to risk trying to build a kiln himself, but he returned to Ghana with a book of instructions, and the following year he built a gas-fired kiln based on the book. Unfortunately, the kiln was still cold at the bottom when it was hot at the top, but later models improved, and he went on to build electric kilns, lining them with used refractory bricks from the Tema Aluminium works. Other potters copied his work. He and a relative used the kilns to make very cheap crockery for Ghana's tables, selling it as fast as they made it. However, they could not agree over ownership of the firm and broke up, which left Peter to start again without capital. He kept going by borrowing small sums from relatives and got help from an old college friend.

A key difficulty for Tamakloe and other potters was that imported glazes were expensive. In 1993, he was by chance asked to undertake for Pier One in the United States an order worth US$15,000 which another firm had rejected because the price was low. This order, the work of an international designer, was for unglazed pots with cane handles. The Tamakloe pottery delivered them on time and without making a loss, and received a better-paying US$25,000 order the following year. Peter took a ten-day course with the Empretec business development agency to learn more about running an enterprise. In 1995 he was asked to build a gas kiln in Honduras and called at the New York International Fair on the way. He realised there was a huge market for unglazed fruit bowls, candleholders, vases, incense burners and planters and decorated them with Adinkra motifs expressing Ghanaian folklore which, he says, appeals to African Americans who like to identify with their roots.

In 2002, Tamakloe gave up making glazed crockery in favour of clay tiles, the preferred roofing material in Accra. Ceramica's expansion into the production of ceramic roof tiles is not only a good business opportunity but also moves away from the use of asbestos in this industry. Most of them have been concrete, made with cement. Peter Tamakloe says that Ceramica believes the locally-abundant clay should be used to reduce the need to import costly clinker for cement making and to continue the replacement of asbestos. The switch to tiles hit Ceramica's turnover because making them was difficult, while the pottery export orders were not big enough to compensate for giving up crockery. An adviser from British Executive Service Overseas helped to get tile production up to 500 an hour but a plan to buy a brick works fell through. The bank which was to lend the money feared it would not get its money back.

Peter Tamakloe, however, believed that, firing with sawdust from local sawmills, he could make tiles at only a fifth of the fuel cost of a government-owned brick works. The first sawdust-blower he tried was too powerful, causing damage to the refractory bricks insulating the kiln. A smaller one proved adequate. In 1999, he decided to use the profit from a US$178,000 pottery order from Pier One to buy a five-acre clay-bearing site at Mobole outside Accra. In 2001, Ceramica Tamakloe was making bricks, tiles and pottery at this site. It has saved money by buying equipment second hand. In the first eight months of 2000, Ceramica Tamakloe exported 20 containers of pots, worth US$233,000 in all, to the United States and Europe. The pots come in a wide range of shapes and sizes, artistically decorated with metal, straw, cane, beads or shells. Peter Tamakloe is chief designer but he has worked with other designers as well. He is also on a committee seeking to set up a Ghanaian design centre.

Ceramica Tamakloe has participated in various exhibitions, both local and foreign: the New York Gift Fair; the Spring Fair in Birmingham, UK; the Ambiante and Tendence Fairs in Frankfurt, Germany — and local exhibitions of the Handicraft Exporters Association of Ghana. Ceramica Tamakloe has 38 full-time employees who receive at least twice the minimum wage and have benefited from an apprenticeship scheme. It has sub-contracted work to four other potters, two of them former employees. The firm uses two acres to grow corn, cassava and cow peas for workers' meals and it allows local people to use water from its clay pits. Its power transformer supplies electricity for grinding corn. Tamakloe has also promised to build a health clinic, and he is keen to help with village planning to prevent what he calls the usual mess of scattered buildings.

Demand for Ceramica Tamakloe roof and floor tiles continued to increase in 2002 but Ceramica was not producing as efficiently as it should because of obsolete machinery. It decided to acquire and install a complete plant for producing floor tiles for the Ghanaian and West African sub-region. In 2002, a team comprising technicians and a manager visited Italy to learn about the equipment before the plant and machines were shipped down in ten 40-foot containers with about 95 per cent of the installation being completed by the local Ghanaian team. The Italian technician failed to come and complete the final installation and test running of the plant so Ceramica had to look at other ways of getting the machines working. When finally Ceramica found a good local engineer to help complete the installation, it was realised that parts of the used equipment still had to be imported from Italy. During 2003 Ceramica went back and forth trying to put necessary pieces together to start the production of floor and wall tiles. It waited for the arrival of moulds from Italy to begin production of floor and wall tiles and it kept in close contact with local engineers who manufactured the hammer mills, silos, conveyors and sieves for the dry body preparation unit. Trial production finally started in December 2003. The pottery department continued to support this expansion even though orders had dwindled since 9/11. It is very much Ceramica's desire to continue research into making tiles efficiently to compete with the imported tiles from Europe but Tamakloe advises any third world company buying or importing advanced equipment to tie into the contract, the installation and commissioning of the equipment before final payment is made.

In 1995, when Peter Tamakloe visited Honduras to build a kiln for a friend, he met Ron Rivera, a ceramist, and they briefly discussed the possibility of producing inexpensive water filters to provide potable water to rural areas. Over the years the discussions went on as Ron's NGO, Potters for Peace, researched and developed the water filters. In 2003, with funding from the Dutch Practica Foundation, the Potters for Peace team arrived in Ghana. Development and production began, together with Ceramica Tamakloe, of inexpensive colloidal silver water filters using local clays and sawdust to form the clay pot, and later treating it with colloidal silver after firing. Ceramica hoped to produce about 100,000 water filters for as many households in 2004.

(Source: www.ceramicatamakloe.com and www.worldaware.org.uk)

Ghana is one of the main attractions for people of African descent moving back from the West. Jamaican music producer Stewart Brown has repatriated there with his famous sound system, African Star, and now lives in an Accra suburb. Singer and actor Isaac Hayes, known in Ghana as Nene Katey Ocansey I, the King for Development of Ada, plans to have a home soon on a nearby island of his own, close to where he has been working on the development of information technology. Isaac Hayes believes it is his duty to unlock the heavy chains of illiteracy which still continue to keep the minds of his people in abject poverty in the midst of plenty. He is deeply humbled to have the opportunity of seeing the fulfilment of this duty in his lifetime through the Nene Katey Ocansey I Learning and Tech Centre (Neko). He knows that health and technology are the two anchors that will help improve the plight of Africa in the 21st century.

Neko Tech is a non-profit non-governmental organisation located in the rural village of Ada, co-founded in August 1998 by Isaac Hayes and Naa Asie Ocansey. Ada is designated as a deprived area in rural Ghana, with very little development — electricity for instance was not installed until 1996. With the assistance of the Isaac Hayes Foundation, the 8,000 square feet (approximately 750 square metre) world-class ultra-modern teaching and learning Neko Tech Centre building project in Ada was completed in July 2000.

Neko's mission is to facilitate the quality of life of under-served populations, particularly in rural Africa, through education in technology, healthcare, entertainment and spiritual and economic development. Its vision is to become a sustainable world class institution and research facility that re-educates rural Africans to enable them fully to participate in the new networked economy. Meanwhile Neko will also be sensitising the international community, students, stakeholders and donors to rural development issues by the collaborative development of scaleable pilot projects that will effectively eradicate illiteracy, alleviate poverty and improve health and life in general and especially for the poor. Neko Tech is used as a case study for rural development in a programme called eDevelopment, conducted jointly by Harvard University and the Massachusetts Institute of Technology.

(Source: www.nekotech.org.gh)

The Save a Million Lives project, an HIV/AIDS education, prevention and support project, is a partnership between African-American medical associations the National Medical Association, the Student National Medical Association, the Neko Tech Centre/Isaac Hayes Foundation and the Ghana Ministry of Health. This is an important pilot project whose results will help fight HIV/AIDS virus all over the continent of Africa. In 2002, it was presented at the White House, and its documentary Save a Million Lives won the best documentary of the year from the Ghana Film Awards.

Skyy Power Fm, a Takoradi-based radio station, supports the economic growth of the western region of Ghana. Wilson Arthur, Chief Executive Officer of Skyy Power Fm and Skyy TV, says the western region is arguably one of the most naturally endowed regions in Ghana, and contributes 52 per cent of the natural wealth of the nation, yet it has the least infrastructure for development. As a result of this apparent neglect, Arthur believes that it is about time the region took steps to state its own case.

Arthur has contacted experts in the various fields of human endeavour, and opinion leaders, for ideas on what could move the region forward. A 40-page document, The Western Region Development Agenda, came out of this effort. Besides the radio station and a local monthly development newspaper, *Skyy Focus*, Arthur's holding company, Wilsad Support Ltd, has established a four-channel television service, Skyy TV to help expose the western region to the outside world.

Arthur adds that through the media support of Skyy TV and Skyy Power Fm, the former white elephant, the Apremdo Market built in 1996, is finally serving the purpose for which it was built. The metropolitan authorities had been struggling for nine years to get the market women and other sellers to move from the congested Market Circle to the over ten billion-cedi Apremdo Market with no success.

The Apremdo Market used to be empty while traders were willing to sell close to refuse dumps, open drains and places of convenience. The Apremdo Market initially lacked toilet facilities, water, lighting, security and a day care centre. The metropolitan chief executive, Philip Kwesi Nkrumah, says the Apremdo Market was finally provided with water, electricity, security and warehouse facilities to make trading activities safe, conducive and disease free but the traders and shop owners still persistently refused to use it. Madam Adwoa

Moncar, a trader, said the discharging of goods at the Apremdo market by large trucks would ease congestion and facilitate vehicular flow. She also had called for the provision of a day care centre at the market.

(Source: *'SAEMA evicts illegal traders from Takoradi Market Circle'*, *Ghana News Agency*, 7 February 2005, www.ghananewsagency.com)

With the blessing of Nkrumah, Skyy developed a media campaign to support the effort of the assembly to get the market women and other sellers to move from the congested Market Circle. In a matter of six weeks, the Apremdo Market came alive. The three-month (March to May 2005) campaign was valued at 60 million cedi (the value of the billboard advertising space within the metropolis provided to Skyy as payment), which illustrates the impact Skyy is making on the development of the western region.

Arthur became the Personality of the Year for the western region's annual awards ceremony on 19 March 2005 and was honoured for his contributions in the area of event organisation, promoting the development agenda of the region and bringing radio and TV to the region. Arthur is chairman of the 12-member Western Region Education Trust Fund Board of Trustees, other distinguished members of which include Professor Addae Mensah, former vice-chancellor of the University of Ghana and Nana Kobbinah Nketsia V, paramount chief of Essikado. In 2005, Wilsad Support, Wilson Arthur's holding company for Skyy Power Fm and Skyy TV, was a winner in the open category for an Africa SMME Award.

Sam Mensah is the chief executive officer of SEM Financial Group Ltd, a diversified financial services firm in Accra with operating subsidiaries engaged in management consulting, training, investment management and advisory services. Mensah was born in Ghana in 1949, immigrated to Canada in 1972 after completing a BA in political science at the University of Ghana and studied for many years in Canada where he obtained postgraduate degrees in political science and economics and a doctorate in finance from the University of Toronto. He came back in 1996, after resigning from the University of Michigan, in order to make himself useful to Africa. He started his re-entry into Africa by organising the first African Capital Markets Conference in Nairobi, Kenya, in 1993, a movement which eventually culminated in the formation of the African Capital Markets Forum of which he is now executive secretary. The African Capital Markets Forum is a regional organisation of regulatory and policy agencies, capital market operators, stock exchanges and donor agencies. Mensah has consulted extensively for Ghanaian firms and international clients including the Ghana Stock Exchange (GSE), USAID, the Commonwealth Secretariat, the World Bank and the Canadian International Development Agency (CIDA).

In May 2002, Mensah was the project leader for the Ghana Central Securities Depository Project. He led a team of consultants in preparing a feasibility analysis, business plan, and legal analysis for the establishment of a central securities depository and automated clearing and settlement system for the securities market and he advised the government on implementation. Mensah strongly recommended that the GSE should take a hard look at its activities and operations and be made to run strictly as a profitable business to enable it to perform its role on the financial market. The GSE was set up in 1989 to serve as a vehicle for long-term funds mobilisation for the national economy. Despite the fact that many activities and events have taken place since 1990 on the local and international financial markets, the listing and membership rules had remained the same. Mensah suggested that there was a need to take a hard look at the various laws governing the operations of the exchange once declared a star performer on the African continent. He insisted that existing laws and regulations that impinge on the growth of the market should be changed to enable the exchange to serve the purpose for which it was established. Mensah thought the structure of the exchange board should consist of core participants or players in the market and declared that Africa is entering an era in which stock exchanges should have to reform themselves to survive as institutions. He believed that regionalisation is a step in the right direction since it helps provide the expertise and economies of scale African countries need to integrate into the global economy.

(Source: www.semfinancial.com)

Judith Aidoo is a Ghanaian financier and private hedge fund manager specialising in media and entertainment, financial services, and real estate and serves as the chief executive of two Wall Street-based merchant banks: the Aidoo Group Ltd and its African regional affiliate, Capital Alliance Company Ltd (a registered broker-dealer, investment advisor, and a member of the Ghana Stock Exchange); and the US-focused firm, Caswell Capital Partners, which invests in and raises capital for media and real estate ventures.

Born in the US, Aidoo is the daughter of a physician from Ghana and an American mother. She contends that her entrepreneurial spirit was nurtured in her earliest years, surrounded by strong, savvy Ghanaian women who ran everybody's lives and businesses. She attended Rutgers University, graduating Phi Beta Kappa and magna cum laude with degrees in business administration and French, and then entered Harvard and received a Juris Doctor degree from the Harvard Law School. She joined Goldman Sachs & Co in 1987 in fixed income sales and trading and stayed until 1991, when the lure of her own ideas proved too difficult to resist.

In 1991, Aidoo started The Aidoo Group Ltd, an investment bank boutique specialising in providing financial advice to emerging market companies and international investors. The Aidoo Group's mission is to make Africa understandable to international investors and corporations, so that they can make effective business decisions. During her years as an investment banker, first at Goldman, Sachs & Co and then in her own firms, Aidoo has advised on transactions in wireless and satellite telecommunications, Internet, broadcasting and entertainment, real estate and financial services. Her clients include governments, multilateral institutions, global corporations, and large institutional investors. Specifically, she has connected African companies to international financing, advised African governments on privatisation and capital markets development and structured and managed a US$500 million asset securitisation of African trade receivables for the PTA Bank. This final programme refinanced dollar-denominated trade loans of large African exporters in 22 eastern and southern African countries. The deal marked the first time in history that a purely African related financing received the highest possible US short-term credit rating from Standard & Poor's (A1+) and Fitch Investor Service (F1+).

In the continent of Africa, Aidoo sees a huge, wealthy, and undervalued region, full of natural resources and talent, and notes that what Africans need most is more business know-how and capital, in addition to aid. One area of potential interest for investors is in financial services. Africa is seriously under-banked in most regions. She adds that there is also ample room for insurance companies and mutual funds to put down roots in Africa. Another sector presenting massive potential across the African continent is telecommunications and media.

In the telecommunications sector, Judith has advised Northern Telecom; Titan Wireless, a subsidiary of Titan Corporation; Telecel International (Pty) Ltd; and the Regional African Satellite Communications Organisation. In 1999-2000, she was CEO of Titan Wireless Africa, which was bringing advanced telecommunications, including cell phones, to West Africa. Rapid government deregulation and unmet consumer demand for telecommunications services in Africa opened vast new markets for companies able to provide value-priced, high quality, voice, data and Internet connections.

The challenge for Aidoo is not finding business opportunities in the sub-region but, rather, continuing to make measured and timely investments in Africa. Aidoo comments that many Africans see technology as the great equaliser, with a focus on the individual versus institutional investments. She says that a new generation of African entrepreneurs is capable of competing on a global level.

Aidoo suggests that the biggest job is getting the word out on Africa, which she sees as the last frontier. She insists that anyone taking the time to understand the African landscape will see that there is plenty of business to be done, not much competition in most areas, and a lot of opportunity for pioneering spirits.

(Source: Lorna Cox. *'Into Africa: One woman's attempt to throw light on the Dark Continent'*, Global Custodian, June 1992; and Anita Spring. *'Gender and the range of entrepreneurial strategies: The 'typical' and the 'new' women entrepreneurs'*. In Alusine Jalloah and Toyin Falola (Eds.). *Black Business and Economic Power*, Rochester: Rochester University Press, 2000)

Edward Effah is the founder and chief executive officer of Fidelity Group, a Ghanaian financial services group whose activities includes a discount house operation, investment management, venture capital funds management and corporate finance advisory services. Fidelity Discount House Ltd was incorporated in 1997 as a discount house and commenced business in 1998.

The Fidelity Group is owned by strategically selected shareholders comprising well-known and respected Ghanaian commercial banks, foreign investors and local private shareholders, each of whom brings to the Group financial strength, expertise in the money and capital markets and a unique network of local and international contacts. The shareholding structure also offers the Group diversified international and local experience at the Board level to assist management in achieving its goals.

The Group's primary motivation is to contribute towards the development of the money and capital markets in Ghana by offering clients a broad spectrum of specialist investment services. In particular, Fidelity plans to work closely with the domestic financial authorities to improve the domestic money market and monetary policy implementation. Fidelity Investment Advisors Ltd (a 100 per cent subsidiary of Fidelity Discount House Ltd) works with growing Ghanaian corporations and assists with promoting exports, increasing the access of the Ghanaian business sector to the international capital markets, and offers advisory services to small and medium scale enterprises. Fidelity Equity Funds Holding Ltd is a US$ 30 million venture capital fund, a 50:50 joint venture between Fidelity Investment Advisors Ltd and the Netherlands Development Finance Company. It was set up to raise long-term equity funds to acquire, hold and dispose of a portfolio of investments in Ghana, and is managed by Fidelity Investment Advisors.

Effah leads the executive management team and brings to the Fidelity Group over ten years of experience in senior executive positions in finance and treasury management. His previous positions include: resident director of Global Emerging Markets Ghana Ltd (1995-1998), chief finance officer of Inter-Afrique Group (1994-1997) and risk manager (1990-1994) of Rudolf Wolff, the City of London based derivatives and foreign exchange traders. Effah is a chartered accountant by profession and is a member of the Institute of Chartered Accountants in England and Wales. He spent four years (1987-1990) of his professional career with Coopers & Lybrand, London, as an auditor and management consultant.

Effah is always in aggressive pursuit of partnerships in the financial sector with reputable south-south partners. He has learned that there are good investment opportunities in Ghana, which can yield 25 per cent and above in US dollar returns over the life of the investment. There are, however, many pitfalls, depending on the industry, the macro-environment, the sponsor and the type of investment. Foreign investors must be aware of the quality of their fund manager versus cost (limited local expertise). One should hedge against foreign exchange risk/cedi depreciation. Exiting profitability needs to be thought through at the point of entry. Cultural attitudes are real and can be a problem. There is a need to look out for opportunities to make money out of investment other than through the dividend stream. A fund manager often has to be a sponsor to improve deal flow. There must be an understanding of the relationship with the venture capital fund. Some entrepreneurs are unwilling to share; they are suspicious and more used to debt. They have a 'free' equity attitude. Then there are the big fund versus small fund advantages and disadvantages.

Effah's factors of success are:
- management (an experienced, hungry team with all-round skills);
- established companies with track records (start-ups have to be exceptional);
- sponsors must be committed, focused and driven, with good relationships and shared visions; and
- there must be a close relationship plus monitoring by the venture capital fund's management.

On the other hand, his checklist of issues to be concerned about ('red flags') encompasses:
- the quality of diligence by the local sponsor;
- the quality of diligence by the technical partner;
- management with no industry experience;
- a technical partner who is the supplier of equipment;
- technical fees not related to performance;

- limited or no equity participation by technical partner;
- new industry to the local sponsor;
- in-kind contribution by the local sponsor;
- high business promotion costs;
- new product/time to educate market;
- lack of commitment on the part of sponsor (involved in too many other things);
- high start-up cost due to generous use of expatriates;
- government licensing requirement;
- family business/management team with majority voting rights;
- weak unassertive Board versus dominant entrepreneur;
- high cost/lifestyle of maintaining senior management team such as cooks, watchmen and drivers; and
- controls and financial discipline.

Effah proclaims that the macro-fundamentals for private equity are in place in Ghana.

He observes that the Ghanaian economy is expanding, with access to international markets. He points out that useful lessons have been learned concerning the future opportunities for private equity and concerning the many pitfalls. He asserts that knowledge of the local environment is essential and that there is an increasing role for private equity, which provides 'more than money'.

(Source: www.fidelitysite.com and www.fidelitycapitalpartners.com)

Dzifa Amegashie was selected in December 2002 to be one of the World Economic Forum's Global Leaders for Tomorrow 2003. She is currently a partner at BDC Consulting, a management consulting firm. Edward Effah is a member of its board of directors and his Fidelity Group is a client. Primarily, BDC assists its clients to structure their businesses in a way that ensures the maximisation of stakeholder value. By clearly identifying the right corporate strategic direction, as well as defining and measuring the key drivers of corporate performance, BDC assists executive management to implement sustainable business improvement programmes. From complete corporate transformations to stand-alone projects, BDC employs effective technologies and methodologies to ensure that it exceeds the expectations of its clients and their stakeholders.

The professionals who work in BDC bring years of varied experience in many different disciplines and types of businesses to bear on their assignments. Within the firm, creativity, quality, innovation and technical excellence are encouraged. Above all, each individual shares in BDC's core value of delivering tangible results to each client by always exceeding client expectations. Ms Amegashie's work experience covers corporate and project finance, principally involving structuring and raising medium term finance from local and foreign institutions for SME projects in Ghana and The Gambia. Before joining BDC, she served as an investment officer with the International Finance Corporation (World Bank Group), Ghana. She has also worked at CAL Merchant Bank, Ghana, and Ashanti Goldfields Corporation. Ms Amegashie obtained a BSc in economics at the London School of Economics, and an MBA at Imperial College, University of London.

Nicholas Manu is the founder and director of 5M Ghana Ltd a company dedicated to providing computer training and developing software for small- and medium-sized companies. 5M Ghana has a software developing alliance with System Solutions in Bangalore, India, and maintains server farms in Atlanta, USA. The products, applications and tools developed at 5M Ghana are simple to use and effective when used in the web environment. Particularly significant software developed are the educative software, the e-learning and Digital Café Ver, which are suitable for distance and self-tuition learning. Student Welfare System Software was also developed to bring students, parents and institutions of higher learning closer online. 5M Ghana has a team of professionals who can develop visually stimulating yet content-rich websites. Manu was trained in Germany, graduating with a diploma in international logistics from the Hamburg College of

Professional Studies. He has also worked in Germany, Canada, Russia, Cameroon, Nigeria and the Scandinavian countries.

(Source: (www.5mghana.com)

Cordelia Salter-Nour has worked in IT in aid and development work in Africa since 1979, and during that time has lived in Egypt, Sudan, Sierra Leone, Ethiopia and Ghana. In 1998, she started a web design business, cordelia.net, which aims to bring more African business online and to raise Africa's profile on the Internet. The company's work is carried out in partnership with local IT professionals. In 1999, Cordelia founded eShopAfrica.com, an e-commerce website based in Ghana that supplies African arts and crafts direct from the artisan. The artisans that supply eShopAfrica are looking for new markets, as local economies are depressed. A wide range of products from many African countries is already represented on the site. eShopAfrica's aim is to carry arts and crafts from as many African countries as possible. Following two citations in The Wall Street Journal during 2002, eShopAfrica has seen a steady growth of orders. In 2003, it launched a major initiative to publicise fair trade and the use of African products within the European fashion industry.

(Source:www.eshopafrica.com)

Kwabena Darko heads one of Ghana's most successful private enterprises, Darko Farms & Co Ltd. He is the principal shareholder of the family enterprise, which produces more than 50 per cent of Ghana's day-old chicks, and a large proportion of its table eggs and dressed chicken. Darko has advanced poultry science in Ghana, receiving numerous awards of recognition for his contribution to the field. Darko Farms actually consists of a group of farms, plants and office complexes scattered across Ghana, with headquarters in Kumasi, in the culture-rich Ashanti region.

The company consists of:
- a hatchery, which produces about 5 million day-old chicks a year (about 50 per cent of the nation's requirements);
- a layer parent farm with a bird population of about 40,000;
- two commercial layer farms with a bird population of 110,000;
- a broiler commercial farm with a bird population of about 110,000;
- a pullet-rearing farm with a capacity for 70,000 pullets;
- a feed mill with an installed capacity of 40 tons of feed per day;
- a processing plant with an installed capacity of 7,500 birds per day; and
- branch offices and sales outlets across the country.

Darko and his wife Christiana have six children, including Samuel, Jonathan and Maxine, who have all followed their father, having been groomed under his mentorship to assume top management positions in the company. Samuel, with a degree in poultry science from Kansas State University, currently heads the day-to-day administration of the company as executive director. Jonathan, a graduate of the University of Houston, serves as the chief financial officer. And Maxine, with a degree in biology from the University of Texas, oversees the day-to-day operations of the Accra regional office as regional director.

For Darko all this did not come easily. Born to working class parents in a small town in Ghana's Ashanti region, Darko lost his father at an early age. With the loss of the family breadwinner, young Darko had to combine petty trading with his schooling in order to supplement the family income. Times were hard, resources were scarce, and there were many mouths to feed. In fact, on many occasions the family did not know where the next meal was coming from but Darko did not lose hope. Eventually, he had to continue his education on a part-time basis in order to devote more time to his petty trading activities.

In the course of time, his mother remarried. His new father had a small chicken farm, and the enterprising young Darko set out about helping his stepfather on the farm. In typical fashion, Darko applied himself to the work, and soon proved he was capable of managing the farm in the absence of his stepfather. With the help of his stepfather, he was able to gain a scholarship for further training at the Ruppin Institute in Israel, where he studied agriculture in general but majored in poultry science. On his return to Ghana, he worked at the Ghana State Farms Corporation, which had established a new poultry project in Africa. Six months later, he resigned and joined his stepfather, who had by then embarked on commercial poultry farming. In those days, selling table eggs was regarded as the most viable commercial activity in the poultry industry, but it involved a lot of hard work, and Darko was not one to shy away from hard work. As a result, his stepfather's business prospered under his hand, growing from 5,000 layer birds to 100,000 layer birds within five years. That was the beginning of great things to come.

Darko's long-term objective was to build a giant complex; similar to those he had seen in Israel. He was convinced in his spirit that he could succeed on his own. All he had was savings of US$1,000, his faith and a dream many thought was impossible. He bought 900 chickens and a three-acre piece of land for US$50, and in April 1966 Darko Farms & Company was founded.

Since then, the company has grown from strength to strength, fuelled by the tireless energy of a man who sees himself as merely a steward of God's business. In fact, Darko refuses to be called a self-made man, and insists that he is 'God-made'. From the very beginning, his vision has been to build a vast business empire, which would support missions, orphanages and ministry work in general, and he has stuck to this commission with fervour. Often, other industrialists question his wisdom in 'throwing all that money away', but Darko calmly replies, 'Any decision which helps me to obey the Lord is a good business decision. True success is to know the Lord and to obey him.'

(Source:www.darkofarms.com)

Leticia Osafo-Addo is the managing director and founder of Processed Foods and Spices Ltd in Tema. Processed Foods was the first company to package Shitto, a traditional Ghana pepper sauce. Shitto (pronounced SHEE-toe) — from the word for pepper in the Ga language — is a spicy hot chilli pepper condiment that, like ketchup in the United States and salsa in Mexico, is served with anything and everything in Ghana, and is sometimes used as an ingredient in Ghanaian recipes. Shitto has been picked-up nationally and internationally by the student population in boarding institutions and is usually referred to as the student companion because it can be preserved for a long time. Today, through the awareness created by Processed Foods and Spices Ltd, the product is being produced by many people and is used as an instant sauce in most homes and especially during parties and funeral gatherings. Shitto has become indispensable in Ghana. If production is well harnessed and supported, it could become a premium Ghanaian export.

Since 1991, Processed Foods has grown from a one-woman business to a staff of 18 in 2004. Starting with one product, Shitto pepper sauce, the company has added on other products such as peanut butter, jams, marmalade, fruit juice, spices and snack peanuts. Osafo-Addo supplies all her products to most parts of Ghana, exports to the USA, and has supplied the Ghana Armed Forces during peacekeeping operations in Cambodia, Liberia, Sierra Leone, Rwanda and the Democratic Republic of Congo. Her future projects will include the increased production of her core products and the fortification of most staple foods in Ghana with micronutrients, vitamins and mineral substances in order to address the micronutrient deficiency syndrome in Ghana and the west African sub-region. Osafo-Addo's ultimate objective is to establish a modern food processing emporium with an academy to train people in food processing and entrepreneurial development.

Osafo-Addo is a German trained nurse anaesthetist and intensive care therapist. In 1995, she won an award from the Swedish Academy of Directors to undergo training in directorship in Stockholm. In 1997, she received a fellowship to study quality assurance and marketing in the food processing industry at the Wageningen Agricultural University in the Netherlands. At the same university she received an MBA in management technology and innovation. She won the Ghana Chartered Institute of Marketing's Marketing Woman of the Year 2000 award for introducing packaged Shitto in commercial quantity for the Ghana market. In 2002, she was elected to be one of the Association of Ghana Industries' seven National Council members, and in 2004 she was appointed first vice president.

AGI helps local industries to grow by providing tailored business solutions to industrial companies. Since AGI is the voice of Ghana's manufacturing and service industries, Osafo-Addo appeals to the Ghana government to address the unfortunate economic situation of high taxes and tariffs, irregular utility services, lack of long-term and low interest rate capital for investment, lack of access to foreign markets, and the influx of inferior imports into Ghana. She says the AGI is actively involved in finding ways of assisting women industrialists through workshops, seminars and conferences. She asks that women industrialists take advantage of the present enabling environment towards women's empowerment and growth, and aspire to leadership positions.

West African women are supplying Americans with their newest beauty fix. Vitamin-rich shea butter, a natural moisturiser extracted from African shea tree nuts, is fast becoming an essential ingredient for the American cosmetics industry, and the United States annually imports more than 500 tons of it from Africa. Shea butter is found in lip balms, shampoos, anti-wrinkle creams and other products carried by trendy retailers such as Origins, Bath & Body Works and l'Occitane. The product is known as 'women's gold' in Africa, where women are the primary producers. Recognising the potential of shea butter, Eugenia Akuete, a Maryland businesswoman, opened a shea butter processing plant in Ghana in June 2003.

Akuete was born in Ghana to parents regarded as pioneering business leaders in their respective fields. It is no wonder that she found her way back into business after six years in banking and 20 in accounting. Her father, the late Felix Brenya, was a pioneer in the field of commercial poultry farming and animal feed production from the 1950s to the 1970s. Under his leadership Muus poultry feed became a household name. Her mother was one of the first crop of midwives who the British colonial government trained at Korlebu Hospital in the 1940s and she went on to become a very successful private practising midwife with her own 12-bed clinic until she retired in the 1970s.

After Akuete left sixth form she went to college in London and in four years obtained both the Institute of Bankers (UK) diploma and the Chartered Institute of Administrators diploma. In 1975 she joined the Ghana Commercial Bank as an accountant. After a year in their London office she was transferred to Accra, and worked in the foreign branch, in charge of letters of credit. By the time she left in 1981 she was an assistant manager. In 1981, she had requested a leave of absence for a year to travel with her husband and two sons aged four and two to the US. One year turned into 23 years, and in the process, she became an American citizen.

Akuete was familiar with shea butter and sold it to friends in the Washington area. Wanting to become more involved in the shea butter trade, she attended the West Africa International Business Linkages programme's shea butter conference series in Washington and Bamako, Mali, in early 2003. After learning more about the industry, examining issues with quality standards and seeing shea butter made in Malian villages, Eugenia decided to open her own shea butter processing factory in Ghana. Her factory, named Naasakle, has been operating since June 2003, and by November 2003 the plant had already recovered its initial investment by selling more than 12 000 pounds of the cherished butter. Akuete says she decided to go into production of shea butter better to control the quality and also to help the women and their communities.

Naasakle employs sixteen workers, three of whom are women recruited from northern villages in Ghana, to monitor production. In addition to a competitive salary, employees receive lodging and paid medical for the immediate family as part of their benefit package. Naasakle maintains high quality standards, and each employee is trained in all steps of the processing. Shea nuts are purchased in bulk from women's co-operatives before being inspected by hand for processing. Due to an increase in demand, Naasakle has purchased more grinders and a kneading machine to increase capacity and efficiency.

(Source: *A new quantity of shea butter*, West Africa International Business Linkages Programme, www.ccawaibl.com/article.php?did=112e&scid=2)

Naasakle's machines are locally-made in Ghana to help increase efficiency and reduce worker fatigue and reducing cost. Naasakle exports the finished shea butter mainly to the US for small cosmetic companies that produce soap, body and bath/beauty products.

In 2004, Naasakle trained the women to make soap and bath products from shea butter and citronella essential oil in order to diversify its own local product line. These products, they hope, will help ward off mosquitoes because citronella is a natural insect repellent. Their hope is that users can have the benefits of the healing and moisturising properties inherent in shea butter; thus beautifying the skin at an affordable price for the average Ghanaian while avoiding mosquito bites. Virgin shea butter has only a very low sun protection factor (SPF), so its SPF would have to be chemically increased in order to label it a sunscreen; however, its high ultraviolet A spectrum makes it an effective anti-wrinkle cream. Akuete's medium-term five-year plan is to build an ultra-modern factory with a laboratory and research and development departments to meet the ever growing demand by end users for quality shea. Her short-term 2004-2005 goals were to attend a number of trade shows to get more exposure for her products. As natural products gain popularity, many US companies have followed Akuete's lead by directly sourcing their shea butter from west Africa. This defies traditional trade patterns that often passed through Europe. By selling directly to the US, west African women capture for themselves more of the butter's value.

(Source: www.bestsheabutter.com)

Esther Afua Ocloo, who died in 2002, exemplified the true African entrepreneurial dream. She was a highly successful entrepreneur, industrialist, philanthropist, international leader and, in 1990, the first woman to receive the Africa Prize for Leadership. She was a model to women and men in Africa and worldwide, producing creative solutions to the problems of poverty, hunger and the distribution of wealth. Ocloo believed that the problem in Ghana was that the people had turned their backs on agriculture. She said that Ghana was producing young people with degrees, and who didn't want to work in the fields or have anything to do with agriculture. She pointed out that Ghana was made to be an agricultural nation, that Ghana used to be the world's leading producer of cocoa, and that Ghana used to export surplus agriculture. She lamented that now Ghana was hungry and had to import food.

Ocloo's own business focused on feeding Africa. In 1942, with ten shillings given to her by her aunt, she bought oranges and made 12 jars of marmalade. Her teachers invited her to supply her school with her marmalade twice a week. They were so impressed with how successful her business was that they began reserving a percentage of her profits to save money for her to go to England for further training. After six years, enough money had been saved. Ocloo was sent to England, where she studied food technology, preservation, nutrition and agriculture. She brought back all that she had learned to her homeland and sought to help the underprivileged and marginalised in her society. From these humble beginnings in 1942 grew Nkulenu Industries, of which Ocloo was the founder and managing director. Today it packages foods using Ghanaian produce ranging from fruit juices to soup.

Ocloo was a pioneering leader from the time of Ghana's independence. In 1958, she was the founder and first national president of the Association of Ghana Industries. She served as a consultant and held senior positions on various international committees. In 1964, she became the first female executive chairman of the Ghana National Food and Nutrition Board and in 1978, she founded the Ghanaian chapter of the International Federation of Business and Professional Women. Ocloo was committed to providing two essential opportunities to African women — appropriate training and access to credit, so that they could start their own enterprises. She accepted the request of the African Training and Research Centre for Women of the UN Economic Commission for Africa to assist in the training of women from many countries in processing and preserving food.

At a workshop in Mexico City preceding the International Women's Year conference in 1975, she put forth the idea of an international bank directed specifically to women. The result, Women's World Banking, plays a vital role for the empowerment of women. Historically, women have lacked access to credit because they did not own, and often were not permitted to own, assets that would stand as collateral. Women's World Banking provides guarantees for women who cannot provide collateral, so that they are eligible for bank loans. Ocloo became the first chairperson of its board, serving in that capacity from 1980 to 1985.

In 1990, Ocloo felt rather overwhelmed, as she stood before an august gathering to receive the African Leadership Award for the Sustainable End of Hunger. This was indeed an unexpected honour and privilege, which she received with humility, appreciation and gratitude. In her acceptance speech she announced that African women farmers had remained small entrepreneurs for far too long. They were anxious to increase the acreage of their farms and to provide themselves with appropriate and affordable equipment, machinery and technology. They would have liked special courses organised for them to teach them these skills in their own local languages. Ocloo said that they would like their governments to recognise their work in mainline national planning and make adequate provisions for them. With such help, food production would be increased.

Ocloo believed that food wastage and spoilage in the absence of good storage, processing and marketing is of great concern. It is estimated that about a third of the post-harvest losses are due to lack of motorable roads and good storage. Although African women carry out some food preservation using indigenous methods, much still goes bad. Between 1980 and 1990, efforts were made to teach the women skills to upgrade the traditional methods of food preservation and also to introduce to them new and scientific methods of work. Ocloo concluded that technology was available within the continent to carry this out, but that the main constraint had been the lack of funds to purchase suitable materials for the construction of solar dryers, inexpensive small silos, preserving jars, packaging materials and preservatives.

At the launch of the African Entrepreneurship Awards in Nairobi, Kenya, in October 2001, Ocloo received a five-minute standing ovation as she accepted one of the six awards honouring African women entrepreneurs. Initiated by the *EnterpriseAfrica* magazine, the continent's premier journal on investment and entrepreneurship, the awards are EnterpriseAfrica's initiative to annually recognise, celebrate and reward African entrepreneurial excellence. The award ceremony was the culmination of EnterpriseAfrica's second annual entrepreneurship round table featuring two days of discussions on how Africa's emerging enterprises can improve their competitiveness through improved access to finance and the use of new technologies. Over a hundred financial experts, entrepreneurs, and policy-makers from across Africa attended.

In February 2002, Ghana mourned the death of Esther Afua Ocloo. Ghana's President Kufuor said that Ocloo, who died at the age of 83, was in all respects a trail blazer and role model, and personified the Ghanaian dream. He praised her commitment and contribution to the private sector, especially the development of the indigenous entrepreneurial base of the country, and said she was undoubtedly one of the most decorated Ghanaians in the country's history. She would forever be remembered for her selfless and genuine advocacy and her devotion to the cause of advancement and empowerment, especially of women, both nationally and internationally.

(Source: www.thp.org and www.enterpriseafrica.com)

Lucia Quachey, president of the Ghana Association of Women Entrepreneurs (GAWE), is very interested in the Build, Operate and Transfer (BOT) programme. GAWE has an interest in establishing a big factory with, to begin with, 1,000 industrial machines to weave, knit, sew and package ready to wear clothes. This would help GAWE and its members benefit from AGOA and EU/ACP programmes. GAWE wants to use BOT for a US$20 million project in agriculture and its related activities in Ghana and, in 2002, it proposed a project for commercialising the subsistence farming and off-farm activities of women and youth. This would involve integrated entrepreneurial and technical skills training for women and youths for poverty reduction in the East Mamprusi area, in northern Ghana and ten other districts in ten regions of Ghana. The project would reduce poverty and urban drift by establishing holistic entrepreneurial skills in rural women and youth to enhance their earning capacities and their income earning opportunities and living standards, through expansion of agricultural activities, reduction of post-harvest losses and introduction of affordable non-farming income generating activities.

The project would eventually train 70 groups of women and youth, involving 3,500 individuals in functional literacy in each of the pilot districts as the basis for improving and commercialising their subsistence activities in all the ten regions in Ghana. It would:
- raise the collective literacy rate in business management;
- build the self-confidence of people to create new jobs and expand existing jobs;
- improve the entrepreneurial capacity of women and youths;
- initiate activities to establish micro credit facility;
- increase earning from farm activities, diversify rural livelihoods and income sources; and
- enhance the ability and confidence of rural people to transact business in the formal sector of society.

Women and youth would be trained within their own surroundings to create jobs and reduce unemployment and the drift of youth from rural to urban areas. The group ownership of business would be encouraged by the project in order to enhance rural women's and youths' opportunities to access credit. In addition to extending the economic value of farm products through post-harvest technologies, the project would enhance the ability of rural communities to utilise resources available to their nutritional and economic advantage. For example, integration of farming activities would be a conscious effort and existing rural industries, such as the processing of shea butter and groundnut oil would be made more efficient and commercial. There would be an expansion of appropriate and wise use of resources available to communities. For example, the use of plant products in the tie-and-dye industry, snail farming and bee keeping would be encouraged, thus increasing earning opportunities and upgrading living conditions.

The primary beneficiaries of the project outputs would be the women, youth and general communities of Naleregu, Gambaga, Langbensi and Nankpanduri, all in the East Mamprusi area in northern Ghana where the pilot projects are to be established. The project would be replicated in adjacent communities and in each district in all the ten regions of Ghana within five years. Eventually, the creation of employment opportunities by the project to reduce urban drift would benefit Ghanaian society at large by a reduction of vulnerable groups in urban areas. Mrs Lucia Quachey promises to continue searching for working capital for subsistence farmers to enable them to employ themselves and escape the cycle of poverty.

1 Kofi Apraku. African Émigrés in the United States: *A Missing Link in Africa's Social and Economic Development*, Westport: Praeger Publishers, 1991.

Chapter 4: Nigeria

Nigerian entrepreneurs have been urged to invest in water transportation to boost the transport and tourism sectors of the nation's economy. The chairman of Nigeria's leading marine transport firm, Arco Marine and Oil Services Ltd, Alfred Okoigun, says such investment is imperative considering the inadequacy of Nigeria's transport sector, adding that investment in marine transportation is vital and strategic to boosting the neglected tourism sector. Okoigun wants to draw attention to the state of water transportation in Nigeria and the need to utilise Nigeria's waterways effectively, noting that water transportation (Nigeria has 8,575 kilometres of waterways) is one of the least developed areas of the transport sector of the Nigerian economy. There is so much preference for road, air and rail transportation that Nigerians have not fully exploited the potentials of water transportation.

Arco as a group started business in 1980. It has remained a family business but now, in line with the vision of its founders, it will open business to other potential investors, as it has started to create subsidiaries and restructure the business to make it investor-friendly. Arco Marine is number one on the list of ten such subsidiaries created and made viable for potential investors by 2010, when Arco will clock up 30 years in business. Arco places a premium on strategies leading to sustainable investments that will make the company grow and outlive the founders. According to Okoigun, the crop of committed and creative young Nigerians in the company's employ gives Arco confidence that all goals are realisable.

Nigerians can now cruise on the ultra-modern Arco River Runner 150-seater boats by which Arco provides safe, comfortable modern boat services. Bothered by many Nigerians' apprehension of water transportation, Arco demonstrated that safer, faster and more comfortable ferry services could be provided. The Arco River Runners were the first of their kind in West Africa. A lot of people were afraid of water transportation for various reasons, among them stories of accidents, and the dilapidated condition of most water vessels — which are in addition slow — so Arco marine set out to reverse the trend by providing a world-class ferry service which offers a safe and fast transportation system in offshore operations. In addition, two luxury boats help ease transport congestion between Victoria/Lagos Island and Mile 2/Apapa. Each of the two state-of-the-art boats is fully air conditioned, with audio-visual entertainment and refreshment on board, and is capable of seating between 150 and 200 passengers comfortably. This is an added advantage over the hovercraft and helicopter used by some oil companies, which must make many trips to be able to convey a large number of people. Each of the Arco River Runner boats has life rafts for quick evacuation of passengers in the unlikely event of an emergency, and in addition there are life buoys and jackets for the safety of passengers.

Arco Marine intends to change the phobia about water transportation, and has decided to make it a thing of pleasure rather than fear; the next generation of transportation, with all the features of an aircraft as far as comfort is concerned. The company's foray into ferry services will not only boost tourism development in Lagos State and the Niger Delta, but will also help to alleviate the severe hardship visited on Lagos commuters by the existing public transportation system. In its fleet the company also has houseboats, speedboats and barges, and its operations include marine emergency rescue services, offshore surveillance facilities and general marine works. Visits to the historic Bonny Kingdom will help to rekindle interest in tourism through the effective utilisation of Nigeria's waterways, which Arco Marine has been pioneering since 2001. The latest boats brought the number in Arco Marine's fleet to 13. Okoigun reveals that his ultimate aim is to make even more high-quality boats and have them available for use by the general public.

Okoigun looks for support to the people of the Niger Delta, the host communities of Arco Marine's two new ferries launched in 2003. He asserts that oil companies in the area need to do more to assuage people's concerns, and if they were to provide jetties and boats such as these to transport people living in villages, in comfort, they would sing the oil companies' praises. Nigerians are entitled to the good things in life. Oil companies should better the condition of those suffering from neglect. Okoigun has demonstrated his love for Nigeria by bringing to Nigeria good things he has seen in foreign lands.

(Source: Emeka Ugwuanyi. *'Entrepreneurs should invest in marine transport'*, Lagos: *Vanguard*, 21 November 2003)

The Totalsupport Group, founded in 1990, provides engineering and logistical support to blue-chip oil, oil service and engineering companies in West Africa. Composed predominately of engineers and technicians, the highly expert staff offers expertise and technical support in oilfield and energy-related operations, base power and standby power generation, process plant design and fabrication, and energy logistics and support services. In pursuit of performance excellence, the company is committed to achieving zero downtime in a safe, smart, and cost-effective manner. Taking a 'mission-critical, never go down' approach, Totalsupport believes leading technology is an investment in superior engineering and technique, with ultimate savings to its clients. The Totalsupport Group consists of Group Operations & Logistics Ltd, Measurement & Control Ltd, Personnel Managers Ltd, Distributed Power Systems Ltd, Heavy-lift Ltd, Totalsupport Ltd, and Totalsupport Refineries. Each company brings its specialty to bear on the overall Group performance. In 2004, it employed 386 persons, mainly engineers and technicians working at client sites.

(Source: www.Totalsupportltd.com).

In 2004, a consortium of six banks, led by First Bank Nigeria, put together a financing package for the construction of a private oil refinery expected to cost $100 million (N13.3 billion). The consortium was charged with the task of raising loans for funding the project as well as packaging the equity financing for the construction of the refinery owned by Totalsupport Refineries and sited to the immediate right of Calabar Port in the Calabar Free Trade Zone, Cross River State. The Totalsupport refinery signalled the take-off of a private refinery in Nigeria, more than two years after the federal government first granted preliminary licences to 18 companies. The president of the Totalsupport Group, Ubani Nkaginieme, says crude oil feed stock for the refinery can be sourced from ExxonMobil's Qua Iboe Crude Oil Terminal, Shell's Bonny terminal, or from indigenous oil producer MoniPulo. These oil producing firms have their operations a few kilometres away from the refinery. He says the refinery, expected to be on stream in early 2007, will initially take crude oil supply through the use of two self-propelled barges with installed capacity for 24,000 barrels each.

Nkaginieme says that, unlike other refineries, theirs will utilise all the flue gas (off-gas) for clean power generation, thereby achieving up to 80 per cent energy conversion efficiencies as opposed to the approximately 30 per cent of current refineries. The company president says emissions will be less than three per cent of most current refineries and adds that the refinery is designed to be the one of the most environmentally friendly in the world. He also says that the refinery was planned to be an export refinery, but that since Nigeria imports about 70 per cent of its fuel supply needs, it would be expected to produce for the local market. The 12 000-barrel per day refinery will produce unleaded gasoline (petrol), diesel, kerosene and fuel oil for local market. It will operate on hydro reformer technology. The modular design eliminates process bottlenecks, making maintenance and expansion easy and very fast. Being a small refinery, it would not use the cracking technology since only large refineries can have expensive catalytic crackers.

(Source: Mike Oduniyi. *'First Bank, 5 others to finance $100m refinery'*, Lagos: *ThisDay*, 15 September 2004)

Nkaginieme has an electrical engineering degree from the University of Nigeria in Nsukka. He is a leading member of the Gershom Lehrman Group/Council of Energy Advisors, an association of leading electrical engineers, petroleum geologists, consultants and energy professionals who collaborate part-time with investment professionals to promote business innovation and investor education. He is the recipient of the Rotary/Jaycees National Merit Best Young Company CEO Award for 1999; the Society of Petroleum Engineers Corporate Gold Award for 2001; Distinguished Alumnus Award of the University of Nigeria, Nsukka for 2001; and the National Association of Chambers of Commerce Gold Award for Excellence for 2002. In 2005 Ubani Nkaginieme received the West Africa Business Integrity Award.

Nkaginieme is interested in viable mid- to long-term projects in the oil/energy sector that benefit his business, the community, his clients, the government and the environment. He reports that these are indeed interesting times in Africa, especially in Nigeria. Since 1999, Totalsupport has focused on clean energy and its distribution because it is convinced that distributed energy is the preferred way to quickly deploy desperately needed energy, especially to rural communities where most of their people live and work. Progress with the refinery project, twelve Capstone micro-turbine units deployed to Mobile Telephone Networks (MTN) and Shell Petroleum Development Company, SPDC sites as of September 2004, and an ongoing commitment to small Liquefied Natural Gas plants with Shell Nigeria Gas and MTN, are pointers to where they are heading.

Ocean & Oil Holdings is a private company managing diversified interests in various sectors including energy, real estate, information technology and communications and financial advisory. Wale Tinubu, Mofe Boyo and Jite Okoloko are friends in their mid-thirties, and joint owners. Tinubu is a law graduate from the University of Liverpool, from where he proceeded to the London School of Economics for an LL M. Boyo studied law at the University of London. Okoloko is a graduate in economics from the University of Benin. From their varied backgrounds they found a common purpose in a partnership to build a new and flourishing business empire.

By 2004, Oando, a subsidiary of Ocean & Oil, had grown from 300 filling stations to 598. It has two lubricant plants, one of which is the largest lubricant blending plant in Nigeria. Oando's subsidiary, Gaslink, is the first Nigerian gas distribution company. Oando's sales for 2003 were in excess of N63 billion and the target for 2004 was well over N100 billion. The company is investing aggressively in infrastructure and has half-million ton storage facilities in Lagos, Port Harcourt, Kano and Kaduna. It is building a 45-million litre storage facility at the export-free zone in Onne, Rivers State, and depots in other places. It has operations in Ghana, Sierra Leone, Benin, Togo and even Liberia. As Tinubu says, it is heading for the number one spot.

(Source: www.oandoholdings.com; and Simon Kolawole. *'Why I abandoned my law practice'*, This Day, 24 May 2004)

Femi Otedola is the undisputed king of diesel within Nigeria's oil industry. This is because he controls the entire diesel market, via his company Zenon Petroleum and Gas. Otedola enjoys intimidating those who consider themselves his competitors. He has two oil vessels and close to 1,000 DAF trucks. In 2004, he launched another set of 100 DAF oil tankers at close to N5 billion, further scaring away his competitors. One thing Otedola has going for him is that he is focused — he also has access to cash that he can use to back up his business.

He also dominates the dry cleaning business with Garment Care and once told friends that what he is out to achieve by delving into the capital-intensive world of business is to invest in human development and create employment. He has let it be known that profits would not be taken out of Nigeria but would be ploughed back into the economy to help create jobs for young Nigerian graduates. He says it is not all just about making money. Nigerians need to build a better country so that the youth can have a decent society to live in.

(Source: Mike Oduniyi and Shaka Momodu. *'Zenon's N15b investment: Celebrating deregulation'*, ThisDay, 24 May 2004)

Oba Otudeko is the chair of the Honeywell Group, one of the leading indigenous conglomerates in Nigeria. He is a frontline businessman whose entrepreneurial pursuits span the key sectors of the Nigerian economy — and beyond. A man of impeccable credentials, he relentlessly pursues a vision of being the best at all he does. Born in 1943 in Ibadan into the royal Otudeko and Omo Oba Adejonwo lineage of Odogbolu and Ijebu Igbo, Oba distinguished himself as a staff of Cooperative Bank Ltd, Ibadan, and proceeded on a scholarship to study accountancy at the Leeds College of Commerce, England, finishing in 1968. He worked with the Cooperative Bank, Ibadan for 23 years, an experience that culminated in his acting as Chief Executive Officer of the bank. In the early 1980s, he devoted his time to the Honeywell Group, which has since grown to become one of the most formidable conglomerates in Nigeria, with interests in oil and gas, engineering, foods, deep-sea trawling, marine services, hospitality and real estate. Otudeko currently chairs the boards of all Honeywell Companies.

Oba Otudeko's father came originally from Ijebuland and settled in Ibadan in 1909. He worked with Nigerian Railways before going into produce dealing in cocoa and palm kernels, and gold mining at Ilesha. This led to an investment in EO Waters, a mineral water and soft drink bottling plant in Ibadan. Otudeko's mother was a very energetic trader and traveller. She settled in Sokoto, where she pioneered the introduction of grinding machines in the early 1950s. Her trading network in foodstuffs extended to the Nigerian towns of Gusau, Minna, Zaria and Kaduna and she traded across the border to Niger, Ghana and Côte d'Ivoire.

Honeywell gradually evolved out of the transformation and redirection of his mother's business in foodstuffs, through the introduction of modern management techniques. Capital from that source was used to develop the importation of sugar, milk and baking yeast. The group was initially active mainly in the Lagos and Ibadan markets but has grown rapidly and is now being managed by seasoned and well-trained managers. Currently, the group employs over 4,000 persons spread across eight unit companies: Honeywell Flour Mills Ltd (a wheat milling company); Pivot Engineering Company Ltd (an electrical and mechanical contracting firm); Honeywell Fisheries Ltd (a deep-sea trawling company); Honeywell Oil and Gas Ltd (an operator in the downstream sector of the oil industry); Hudson Petroleum Ltd (representing the upstream oil activities of the Honeywell Group); Skyview Estates Ltd (a property development company); Broadview Engineering Ltd (an EPC contracting company in oil and gas); and Metropolitan Trust Ltd (an investment outfit).

By global standards, Oba Otudeko stands out as an entrepreneurial model with demonstrable core attributes. An integral part of his legacy-building is turning his businesses into enduring institutions able to compete and deliver on a universal basis. In particular, this uncommon foresight translates into the creation of employment opportunities for over 4,000 Nigerians and expatriates, contributing to Nigeria's gross national product and oiling the wheels of commerce. His indirect contributions towards employment creation in companies where he is an investor or non-executive director are also worthy of note.

Oba Otudeko's passion for entrepreneurial studies is deep-rooted. He made a substantial financial donation to the Lagos Business School (now Pan-African University) for the development of an Entrepreneurship Centre. His conglomerate, the Honeywell Group, has taken up the challenge of bequeathing a worthy legacy to generations of Nigeria's greatest assets - its human capital. He declares that the time has come for Nigeria to progress from the status of a less developed country to a developed nation and states that this can only be achieved through the consistent commitment of local businesspeople and companies, as well as ordinary citizens, to this aspiration. He concludes that Nigeria needs to build a virile, knowledge-based economy driven by proven technologies to create value-added products and services that progressively make the world in general, and Nigeria in particular, a better place. This will all be possible if Nigeria has a system of developing upcoming generations into entrepreneurs and visionary business leaders.

(Source: www.honeywellgroup.com)

Mike Adenuga, chairman of Globacom Ltd, is another of Nigeria's most successful business moguls. His resounding success in business was achieved through hard work, resourcefulness and sheer determination. Adenuga attributes his success to hard work, God's blessing and luck. His business philosophy is to add value to the lives of Nigerians. From a humble beginning, Adenuga shot into the limelight as an extraordinary entrepreneur. He started early in life to imbibe the entrepreneurial spirit. His interest in business developed when he returned from the United States where he had acquired higher education. His parents, who had a sawmill factory in Ijebu-Ode, Ogun State, handed over the management of the enterprise to him.

Bubbling with the zeal to excel, he transformed the sawmill factory through the importation of equipment. Determined to expand his business horizons, Adenuga started importing beer and laces, for according to him any businessman who desired success must of necessity be a 'Jack of all trades'. The modest sawmill business Adenuga took over from his parents has today produced a large business conglomerate. He has diversified into oil prospecting, banking and telecommunications (he is said to be one of the first Nigerians to find oil and produce it in commercial quantities). He is the chairman of Consolidated Oil which is involved in upstream and downstream oil prospecting and marketing. In the banking sector, which he sees as a catalyst for economic growth, Adenuga is the chairman of Devcom Merchant Bank and Equitorial Trust Bank.

Following the deregulation of the telecommunications industry, Adenuga set up Globacom Ltd when the opportunity to bid for the second national carrier licence opened up. Luck smiled on him. Globacom secured the all-encompassing licence, a 'basket of licences', which includes fixed line phone, mobile and international gateway services. In August 2003, he recorded a landmark in the telecommunications sector with the smooth roll-out of the Globacom GSM network. Adenuga has described Globacom as the fastest growing GSM network in Africa. Its mobile arm, Glo Mobile, spread coverage and area expansion to 60 towns in eight months; the feat put Globacom on a fast track towards realising its dream of becoming Nigeria's biggest and most successful GSM network.

Apart from its vastly expanding coverage areas, which span 11 states of the federation and Abuja, Glo Mobile has also emphasised its commitment to the provision of world class telecommunications services in Nigeria. The commitment was the driving force behind the network's deployment of the only 2.5G network in Nigeria. Glo Mobile next launched its service in Enugu with 37 base stations, making it the network with the highest number of base stations in the coal city which is also regarded as the political capital of the south east. The list of Glo Mobile's coverage areas is growing bigger as it intensifies efforts to launch its services in the core north and other parts of the country. No fewer than 20 northern cities will be covered in this phase. Two world class GSM vendors, Alcatel and Siemens, are handling the deployment of Globacom infrastructure around the country.

In May 2004, Glo Mobile's subscriber base was about 850,000. Globacom's quick penetration of the market can be attributed to innovative service and friendly pricing policy. Adenuga's motivation in business is not to become the richest man in Nigeria, but to add value to the life of Nigerians. His rise to prominence was largely propelled by his solid educational background and creative mind. He attended Ibadan Grammar School; North Western State University, Alva, Oklahoma; and Pace University, New York, USA. Adenuga is also the president of the Nigerian Association of Oil Explorationists. In recognition of his immense contribution to societal growth, he was conferred with national honours as Member, Order of Niger, by the Federal government. In February 2006, Mike Adenuga received the 11th Annual *ThisDay* Award for Brand of the Year — Glomobile; and Company of the Year — Globacom.

(Source: www.gloworld.com; Ajaero, Chris. *'Profile: Adenuga, The gold digger'*, *Newswatch*, 1 September 2003; and Osuagwu, Prince. *'Globcom mobile spreads to 60 towns in 8 months'*, *Vanguard* 3 May 2004)

Austin Okere is a big player in the information technology sector of the Nigerian economy. He is managing director of the Computer Warehouse Ltd, Lagos, which he founded in September 1992. A 1986 graduate in computer science from the University of Lagos, Okere is a young man with eagle eyes for business. He saw beyond the fog of Nigeria's economic and political impasse when he resigned his sales and marketing job with Inlaks Computers to found Computer Warehouse, which supplies and maintains computer hardware and ancillary equipment (it was particularly helpful that Okere left Inlaks on a friendly note, as he soon became their dealer).

Okere's business philosophy is to keep the customer happy. 'Let them speak well of you,' he says. That was how he acquired many references, from one corporate customer to another. In 1997, Dell Corporation,

UK, invited him to accept the Dell Distribution Award for the fastest growing business in Africa and the Computer Warehouse is Dell's sole service centre in Nigeria. Through Okere's effective salesmanship, Dell computers have outsold many of the older, more entrenched computer names in Nigeria.

Okere is a motivating self-starter whose greatest joy is motivating young people and inspiring them to a fuller life. His successes derive from clear-headed, far-sighted business strategies.

The growth in the Computer Warehouse Group saw the birth of Digital Computer Communications Ltd (DCC), which specialises in wide area network, local area network and systems integration. Expert Edge Software and Systems Ltd is another company incorporated as a result of the tremendous growth of the parent company, Computer Warehouse. Expert Edge is involved in software development, systems analysis, design and implementation, smart card application and packaged training on software. The company's growth is impressive; it controlled 20 per cent of the market in 2004. DCC stands on the first rung among computer communications companies. Expert Edge has tied up strategic alliances with some of the world's software development giants to deliver some of the most sought-after products.

Okere is a member of the Nigeria Economic Summit Group, where he serves on the infrastructure development committee. He attended the University of Ghana, Legon, for a year before transferring to the University of Lagos where he graduated with a B Sc (Hons) in Computer Science. Okere also has an MBA from the prestigious Lagos Business School. The author of several publications, Okere is a member of several professional bodies including the Nigerian Economic Summit Group, the Computer Association of Nigeria, the Institute of Directors and the Executive Committee of the Nigerian-South African Chamber of Commerce.

Over the years, Okere has received many international and local awards. In 1997, Corporate Press Services honoured him with the Men of Achievement Award. In 1997, *The Guardian* newspapers honoured him an Outstanding Personality of the year, and Diet Communications Ltd named him among ten Dynamic Leaders in Corporate Nigeria. In 1999, *This Day* newspaper and *The Week* magazine took turns to honour him. *This Day* named Okere among 50 Most Dynamic CEOs while *The Week* named him among ten Distinguished Men of Excellence in Nigeria

(Source: www.cwlgroup.com; www.onlinenigeria.com and e-mail correspondence with Austin Okere)

Florence Seriki, chemical engineer and graduate of the University of Ife (now Obafemi Awolowo University), is the chief executive officer of the small but energetic Lagos company Omatek Computers. Seriki started as a computer instructor to CEOs of financial institutions, then went into computer sales and, with her Omatek Ventures Ltd, became a vendor for some of the world's top class brands. She soon developed a passion for local assembly of PCs, and in 1993 Omatek Computers was launched.

From her Ojota factory, Seriki has been able to penetrate the public and private sectors with her Omatek brand. Omatek produces 42-inch plasma screen televisions, office computers and the latest generation PCs. The technology is imported, but the production is 100 per cent Nigerian. Omatek's production lines, where some 250 people work, can produce up to 60,000 computers a year. The range of Omatek products, besides TVs and computers (where the only imported elements are the motherboards and processors) includes hi-fi and home theatre systems, as well as monitors for presentations.

The company, whose main stakeholders are two of Nigeria's main banks, wants to support the technological growth of Africa's most populous nation. In 2005, Seriki approved an e-youth initiative, to provide families and schools, at competitive prices and instalment payments, with PCs installed with educational software and wide-band access to the Internet. In recognition of Seriki's success, Omatek Computers won 'The System Builder Partner' 2005 award for the west, east and central Africa region conferred on it by software giant Microsoft.

In 1990, Fola Adeola and Tayo Aderinokun co-founded the Guaranty Trust Bank Plc (GTB). Adeola served the bank as its pioneer managing director and chief executive officer for 12 years, while Aderinokun served as deputy managing director before taking over in his current position as managing director/chief executive officer in August 2002. Aderinokun is responsible for strategic policy direction as well as day-to-day administration of the bank. By 2000, GTB had grown to become one of Nigeria's biggest and most profitable companies.

The focus of GTB is specialised banking services to the top end of the business community, which includes working with local and multinational oil conglomerates. GTB has been quoted at the Nigerian stock exchange since 1996 when it won the prestigious President's Merit Award for best company performance. It remains the philosophy of GTB to constantly support social projects. To this end, the bank reserves 2.5 per cent of its profit before tax for such social projects.

The bank's success has turned it into a Harvard Business School case study for growth in adverse market conditions. Part of GTB's secret has been the singular vision of its two founders, Adeola and Aderinokun. From the start, they did not want to be the typical Nigerian bank. GTB revolutionised the concept of banking by introducing technology at a time when competitors sat around waiting for business. In February 2005, GTB clinched the *ThisDay* 'Bank of the Year' award for excellent corporate and operational performance during 2004.

(Source: www.gtbplc.com)

Fola Adeola and Chima Onyekwere are co-founders of Linkserve Ltd, the first Internet service provider in Nigeria. As a wholly-owned Nigerian company incorporated in 1996, Linkserve commenced business operations in 1997 with an IP connection to the Internet offering full Internet services to the public in real time. Its client base cuts across financial institutions, foreign missions, NGOs, the oil sector, government, the manufacturing sector and trading concerns. Linkserve is globally recognised as the premier Internet service provider (ISP) in Nigeria and is the industry leader. Linkserve is strategically located in Lagos, the most populous and industrious state in Nigeria, and at present, the head office is located on Victoria Island (a perfect choice owing to its proximity to the necessary digital telephone lines for dial-up access).

A fast-growing client base led the company to consider setting up offices in different parts of the country, in order to be in a better position to cater for customers outside Lagos. Linkserve also considered the problems associated with making long distance calls by subscribers outside Lagos. Based on these facts, Linkserve concluded arrangements to situate satellite offices in strategic parts of the country and to offer access to the Internet to a wider range of people. Linkserve now has coverage in the 36 states of the federation, with offices in Lagos, Abuja, and Port Harcourt. The company's coverage also includes some West African countries such as Cameroon, Ghana and Liberia, with an office in Accra. Chairman Chima Onyekwere says that Linkserve remains committed to providing quality service as a way of driving the information economy forward. He says this was what impelled the company's acquisition of its own satellite hub in the United States.

(Source: www.linkserve.com.ng)

In December 2005, the board of directors of Transnational Corporation of Nigeria Plc (TransCorp) announced the appointment of Fola Adeola, as the group managing director/chief executive officer for this mega corporation. TransCorp was incorporated in November 2004 in response to the need to establish a mega corporation, created in Nigeria, and owned by all Nigerians, which would respond to market opportunities that require heavy capital investment not just at home but in sub-Saharan Africa and around the world. TransCorp is to be the vehicle to reposition Nigeria in Africa and the world, as a nation ready to compete in global markets. TransCorp is made up of Nigeria's most influential businesspeople and most successful businesses. Household names and the nation's premier brands are all part of TransCorp.

(Source: www.transcorpnigeria.com)

In 2000, Adeola founded the FATE Foundation, a non-governmental organisation committed to fostering wealth creation by promoting business and entrepreneurial development among Nigerian youth. FATE was created to fill a gap in Nigeria, by offering an innovative approach to wealth creation among Nigerian youth. It is a private sector-led initiative, created and funded by Nigerians concerned about the poor state of the country. FATE established over 1,800 new businesses by 2005 and its vision is to foster the establishment of an additional 4,200 new businesses by 2015. These business start-ups will lead to the creation of employment for at least 60,000 Nigerians by 2015. FATE relies on the voluntary services of professionals and entrepreneurs from the private sector, and provides a one-stop shop for aspiring and emerging entrepreneurs. Its philosophy is if Nigeria's enterprising youth are equipped with skills, tools, networks and financing they can create successful businesses that will in turn offer gainful employment to the teeming masses in the nation. FATE offers three main programmes, the Programme for Aspiring Entrepreneurs, the Programme for Emerging Entrepreneurs and the Enterprise Promotion Service. Participants enrolled in FATE's Programme for Aspiring Entrepreneurs benefit from the five-month School of Entrepreneurship, mentoring programme, business library, computer centre, consulting service, internship programme, business plan competition and investors' forum. Graduates of this programme can also take advantage of the organisation's broad array of alumni services, which include its loan support scheme and business incubator.

Adeola is convinced that it is possible for young people to break through the poverty barrier through hard work and entrepreneurship. As chairman of FATE, Adeola strongly believes that tactics promoting wealth creation, as opposed to poverty alleviation, will significantly reduce the intense suffering in Nigeria. Given the large numbers of innovative and driven Nigerian youth, Adeola believes that he can foster wealth creation by training individuals, providing mentoring and offering some financing. FATE currently has a 17-member board, composed of business and public sector leaders from different parts of Nigeria. It also has 15 full-time employees and over 300 volunteers. Since its inception, FATE has graduated over 260 aspiring and emerging entrepreneurs from its programmes. In addition, over 4,000 young people have benefited from its monthly workshops. FATE was recognised as a winner of the 2002 World Bank Development Marketplace Competition and received funds from the IFC to expand its operations to Port Harcourt.

Nike volunteers for FATE as a facilitator and a mentor, giving of her time and energy to teach and counsel participants of the FATE School of Entrepreneurship. She runs a textile business in Lagos, employing 60 people in her factory, and even offers housing loans to its staff. She makes children's wear under her own label, Ruff 'n Tumble, filling a niche market for American-style kids' clothes for middle-class Nigerians. In recognition of her remarkable achievements as an entrepreneur, she was honoured with the prestigious FATE Model Entrepreneur Award for 2005. (Source: www.fatefoundation.org)

In 2005, Nike was one of ten African entrepreneurs who were featured in a new one-hour documentary, *Africa Open for Business*, by Carol Pineau, writer, director and producer. Pineau's documentary seeks to dispel the myths about business in Africa by showcasing ten entrepreneurs on the continent who tell in their own words their path to success.

In Pineau's documentary, Nike says she started in the business by accident. Her kids ran out of pyjamas, and she used to make clothing for women so she decided that she'd just make some pyjamas for her kids. From there, Nike made children's clothing for a friend and took to selling children's clothes in bazaars. An inspired idea to use her own children — dressed in her label — for an advertising promotion led to immediate success.

'It was the first time that anybody had ever marketed children's clothes — not a clip out of a foreign magazine, but actually using Nigerian children. The response was incredible. People actually wanted the 'made in Nigeria' garments.' She smiles when she says she is not interested in exporting to the United States or England. Nike has her eye firmly on West Africa. If 40 per cent of the 120 million Nigerians are children, she has the potential of a huge market in Nigeria.

(Source: www.africaopenforbusiness.com)

Gbonju Awojuyigbe is the managing director of Wandy Foods, a fast growing food stuffs enterprise located in the technology business centre in Agege, Lagos, where she produces Wandy Honey, Wandy chilli pepper, Wandy ground rice, Wandy plantain flour, Wandy beans, Wandy confections (cookies and shortbread), and other items with the label of Wandy Foods. All products are certified by the National Agency for Food and Drug Administration and Control. From there, these products find their way into supermarkets and other sales outlets. Gbonju, an avid reader of books on marketing, leadership and business, says her philosophy of life is that nothing is impossible. She believes that if you can dream it, if you can see it, you can work hard to achieve it. She read law, and did substantial research before she started her business. She doesn't believe anything is impossible or too difficult.

Gbonju, a member of the National Association of Small Scale Industrialists, urges the government to stop paying lip service to the sub-sector and to assist the sector with funds. She laments that many of her colleagues in the association have gone back to paid employment because of lack of financial assistance and the unfavourable economic climate. However, she advises Nigerians who are unemployed to take advantage of many untapped business opportunities in the country. She sees business opportunities every day and says that you do not need a lot of money before you take advantage of them. She encourages women to sit down and think about what they can do best — and start doing it. She asks Nigeria's educated young people to stop making excuses concerning the government and finance, and look for how they can create employment. Gbonju was awarded the FATE Alumni Model Entrepreneur Award for 2005

(Source: www.fatefoundation.org)

Husband and wife team Folu and Bose Ayeni, originators of Tantalizers, were the winners of the 2004 edition of the FATE Model Entrepreneur Award organised by the FATE Foundation. They beat over 50 other business leaders nominated for the award to emerge winners after the final selection by the FATE Foundation Board of Directors.

Folu and Bose won the award for the touch they brought to bear on the burgeoning fast food industry in Nigeria occasioned by a phenomenal growth that has continued to amaze analysts. This growth has been achieved in a very short time without compromising standards. Expressing his delight at the award, Tantalizers chairman and owner, Folu Ayeni, said the award would go a long way in strengthening their confidence and resolve to support the development of entrepreneurship in Nigeria, stressing that there was no alternative to unleashing the Nigerian entrepreneurial spirit.

From the single Lagos outlet where it commenced operations in 1997, Tantalizers has rapidly expanded and, by December 2005, boasted 30 outlets in its chain of eateries located in Lagos, Ibadan, Abuja and Port Harcourt, with plans for further growth to include ten new outlets in 2006. The brand advertising campaign, 'Have you tantalised her lately?' and its follow-up 'She has been tantalised lately' have been adjudged one of the most effective ad campaigns in Nigeria targeted at young dates. Tantalizers are recognised as a leader in the fast food industry and have pioneered a range of innovations including the introduction of Nigerian cuisine onto the fast food scene.

Prior to establishing Tantalizers, Folu served as a brand manager and product group manager for Lever Brothers Nigeria. He also worked with Xerox HS (Nigeria) in a number of roles, culminating in deputy manager director. Folu graduated with a degree in psychology from the University of Nigeria in Nsukka, and obtained his MBA from McGill University in Montreal, Canada. A FATE mentor, Folu is widely recognised for his commitment to service and dedication to supporting entrepreneurs and youth in Nigeria. He serves on a range of boards and has received numerous honours.

(Source: www.tantalizersnig.com and www.fatefoundation.org)

Some people, unknown to them, have their paths cut out for them in life. Until they discover this they search for alternative means of livelihood and the bright light of success and fulfilment continues to elude them until they chance upon their true vocation. This is the story of Toyin Olaleye. When Toyin left the University of Lagos with an upper second class in sociology, she envisaged a corporate career for herself. In her mind she had her life well structured as a top-shot in a corporate boardroom. She plotted a career path for herself in the banking, oil or service sectors of the economy. Was she wrong? Today, she has made an about-turn as fate has pushed her away from that initial desire for a corporate career. Rather, as the managing director and culinary specialist of Teeto Ltd, Toyin leads a team of young men and women in making a living from kneading dough.

The development of her culinary and entrepreneurial skills started during her teens under the tutelage of her mother. She then studied at the Wavecrest Training Centre, Surulere, Lagos. Her involuntary separation from paid employment during a reorganisation exercise saw her embarking on a journey into full-time entrepreneurship. In a bid to ensure the success of her entrepreneurial adventure, Toyin decided to enrol in the aspiring entrepreneurs programme at the FATE Foundation.

Taking a cue from the expression 'Don't compete if you do not have competitive advantage', Toyin took time to study the pastry and baked food market in order to identify any gap she could successfully fill. She started by producing home baked quality cakes to be sold in offices on Fridays by existing retailers in schools and public places. Not satisfied with modest progress, she embarked on creating a new product that would position her as the leader, ahead of the pack, and developed a specialty bread recipe which is being used to produce the 'Teeto Bread' brand that is gaining wide acceptance in many parts of Lagos.

Many mobile phone messages, phone calls and e-mails are received confirming customer satisfaction with Teeto products. Retailers also attest to the quick turnover of the products supplied to their outlets. At times, the company gets requests from people who, having tried Teeto Cookies on visits to Lagos; call to make enquiries about the possibility of extending the products to other cities — Ibadan, Warri, Jos and Kaduna.

The choice of Toyin as the FATE Alumni Model Entrepreneur of the year 2004 is therefore an open recognition of the industry, enterprise and determination that have gone into making Teeto such a huge success. Toyin plans to offer training programmes for candidates interested in developing culinary skills, either to enhance their professional or vocational skills or simply to acquire such basic knowledge and skills as a hobby or alternate source of income.

(Source: www.fatefoundation.org)

Kayode Odukoya, CEO of Bellview Airlines, one of the leading carriers in Nigeria, was recognized as FATE's Model entrepreneur for the year 2003. An economist, with a degree in public administration, and a seasoned aviation administrator, Kayode Odukoya had, within the space of ten years, rapidly grown Bellview into a strong regional carrier with a high rate of return on capital. Bellview started out as a travel agency in Lagos in 1989. Three years later saw it leasing a Russian aircraft, a Yak 40 with a capacity of 30 passengers, with which it commenced executive charter operations for Chevron-Texaco in October 1992. By the very next year, Bellview Airlines commenced scheduled passenger services into the three major Nigerian cities — Lagos, Abuja and Port Harcourt. It did so by using two McDonnell Douglas DC-9-32 Series passenger jets. In three years, it went from obscure to obvious and became a regional airline providing services into the cities of Banjul and Freetown.

In November 2004, Bellview Airlines bagged the African Regional Airline of the Year award. Organisers of the awards, the London-based *African Aviation* magazine, in collaboration with African Airlines Association, said the airline worked very hard to fulfil its ambitious mission statement, which is to be the undisputed leader in the aviation industry in Nigeria and the West African sub-region by providing the highest level of customer service. In 2005, Bellview was operating in eight African countries: Nigeria, Ghana, Côte d'Ivoire, Sierra Leone, Senegal, Guinea, The Gambia and Liberia, using five Boeing 737-300 series. With 23 daily flights into 11 cities in eight West African countries, Bellview has the largest route network in Nigeria and the largest jet aircraft fleet in the entire West African region.

The immense success of this airline has been traced to what Kayode Odukoya refers to as its three S principles: safety (an avowed commitment to universally accepted procedure); schedule (a sound commitment to on time departure of flights); and service (a total commitment to improved in- and post-flight services). These factors have, understandably, earned Bellview well deserved accolades: the loyal patronage of its customers; a popular endorsement as the 'the preferred airline'; and the award of the best domestic carrier for four consecutive years — 1995, 1996, 1997 and 1998. In addition to this, Bellview Airlines was the first domestic and privately owned airline established with automated operations.

In terms of impact on the economic well-being of Nigerians, this airline company has created several employment opportunities — from 12 employees in 1992 to 530 in 2003. It employs new graduates on a regular basis and provides them with training to keep them and the company abreast with, and ahead of, industry standards. Bellview also extends its employment opportunities to the handicapped, giving testimony to the fact that there is 'ability in disability'. Bellview Airlines also extends the hand of charity, as in its active participation in the collection of funds on behalf of the Sickle Cell Foundation for the completion of the National Sickle Cell Centre.

(Source: www.fatefoundation.org)

Abolaji Osime, FATE Alumni Model Entrepreneur 2003 Award recipient, is the group managing director of World of Fun. With its focus on children and the various ways to engage them in healthy, lively and creative recreational activities, this unique organisation is already a force to be reckoned with in Nigeria. World of Fun was established in 1999. The company aims to expand its current location to accommodate more clients, establish an amusement park for leisure and entertainment for children and, through the Global International College, make an impact on the Nigerian educational system. The organisation currently has a turnover of N250 million and employs 120 full-time staff and 10 on a contract basis. Osime is the chairman of several successful Nigerian companies including Party Planners Ltd, World Of Fun Inc and Multi-properties Ltd.

Mrs Osime is an accomplished entrepreneur and a legal consultant. She has brought her enormous wealth of knowledge of the Nigerian and international business terrains, borne out of over 17 years of hands-on experience in legal, corporate and management positions in various organisations, to bear on her invaluable contribution as the chief executive of Integral Consultants Ltd. She is also the Principal Partner in Andu & Andu Solicitors and has a Masters in corporate law from the London School of Economics. She is the director of admission at Global International College and Global Counselling Ltd, a company that places students in various universities in the UK and all over the world.

As an educationist, Mrs Osime says that secondary school students in Nigeria take too many subjects. The negative effect of this is that in an attempt to pass examinations, students memorise without actually comprehending what they are taught. She makes a comparison with the British curriculum, which places more emphasis on comprehension and application and concludes that there is a need to overhaul the curriculum in Nigeria to emphasise thinking skills, using your brain and applying the information you have.

(Source: www.fatefoundation.org and http://nigerianewsnow.com)

FATE presented the FATE Model Entrepreneur Award for 2001 to Frank Nneji, the managing director and chief executive officer of the ABC Transport and Rapido Group. Nneji established Rapido at the early age of 23 with his National Youth Service Corps allowance of N720. Between 1984 and 1992, Rapido emerged as the major supplier of educational materials in Nigeria and, indeed, across West Africa. In addition, Nneji has radically transformed the luxury bus industry in Nigeria through the introduction of ABC, an upscale bus company, which directly meets the needs of discerning customers because of its high level of customer service, consistency and brand image. He employs over 800 and invests in training and developing his staff. Nneji has contributed immensely to his local community as well as to improving the lives of individuals and organisations across the nation.

Frank is a graduate in biological science of the University of Nigeria, Nsukka. He is responsible for the day to day running of the transport company. Frank has won many awards for his innovative and successful business initiatives, including the FATE Model Entrepreneur Award from FATE Foundation for creativity, excellence and ethics in business.

Associated Bus Company Ltd, operators of ABC Transport, commenced operation in road passenger transportation in 1993 as an off-shoot of Rapido Ventures with a view to running a modern road transportation system in Nigeria. ABC Transport operates luxury bus services according to accepted international standards of road transportation. Its services are specially designed for travellers who would otherwise fly. The operations within Nigeria use ultra modern terminals, with comfortable lounges in cities like Lagos (Jibowu and Festac), Aba, Owerri, Port Harcourt, Abuja, Enugu, Okene, Onitsha and Umuahia. ABC buses bear the company's trademark, the reindeer, the choice of which was made after a careful study of the animal — which is strong, fast and moves in herds.

In July 2004, ABC Transport inaugurated the Accra route, Coach West Africa. Besides transportation to Ghana and other neighbouring countries, there is also West Link Tours, a holiday/tour guide package. The latter offers a three- or six-day vacation/guided tour in Ghana. With this, the company operates internationally. For its remarkable achievements in transportation, ABC Transport was adjudged the Best Transporter in Nigeria by the Chartered Institute of Transport, Nigeria and has since then consistently won the National Bus Operator of the Year Award along with other accolades.

Frank says that ABC Transport first brought educated, decent, young men into the profession of driving buses, and attendants with secondary education. Other novel introductions were on-board video entertainment and meals, as well as mail delivery and cargo haulage. Frank also says his company was the first in the industry to be hosted on the Internet. It has created a unique brand name, employs hundreds of young people and sustains tens of thousands of others.

(Source: www.abctransport.com, www.fatefoundation.org, and www.thisdayonline.com 16 November 2004).

As a result of the challenges experienced by upcoming Nigerian entrepreneurs, Olakunle Kasumu and Adeniyi Adekunle, the founders of Awake Africa (an organisation which researches, educates, advocates and promotes entrepreneurship) wrote the book *Even Here, Even Now* (published in Lagos in 2005). The authors had noticed the need for entrepreneurial education, inspiration, and 'real life' credible examples for Nigerian entrepreneurs and budding entrepreneurs. They had also seen that because of the enormous socio-political and economic challenges in Nigeria, many budding entrepreneurs were fast losing faith in their ability to venture out to build businesses and organisations. Finally, they had observed that a number of so-called successful Nigerian entrepreneurs lacked credibility and 'traceable' histories.

Kasumu and Adekunle were inspired to put a book together for entrepreneurs and budding entrepreneurs, chronicling the way to success of 12 Nigerian entrepreneurs. They decided to seek out Nigerians who could serve as positive role models and examples for would-be entrepreneurs, role models the man on the street could identify with.

Like many upcoming Nigerian entrepreneurs, Adekunle and Kasumu did not have the opportunity of acquiring formal entrepreneurial training, so they decided to research credible businesses that were adding value to society. Their intention was to find inspiration. What they learned from these 12 entrepreneurs was very educative and has been put in their book to encourage upcoming entrepreneurs. The book includes the stories of FATE award winners Frank Nneji of ABC Transport, Abolaji Osime of World of Fun, and Adenike Ogunlesi of Ruff'n' Tumble.

The book is doing well. The authors are getting feedback from all over Nigeria and beyond that people like the book and find it useful. The authors plan to research more entrepreneurs successful in Nigeria, put their stories together, get more books published and into schools, libraries, companies, higher institutions and the hands of both budding and established entrepreneurs, as well as Nigerians who desire to start their own businesses but lack the courage to step out. In the future, the authors will look at the possibility of compiling the stories of Nigerians in the diaspora who are successful creating jobs and improving the quality of life in their adopted communities.

(Source: Omodele Adigun. 'Studying successful people is shortest way to success', *Daily Sun*, www.sunnewsonline.com, 1 December 2005)

Ndidi Nwuneli was the pioneer executive director of the FATE Foundation. Prior to assuming this position, Ndidi worked as a management consultant with McKinsey and Company, a leading international management consulting firm. Even though she had worked for top blue-chip companies outside Nigeria, her soul was in her country. Based on the conviction that Nigerians were not fulfilling their potential, she decided to return to assist the country. She notes that 40 years ago Nigerians were richer than Malaysians and Indonesians but today the story is different.

Ndidi holds an MBA from the Harvard Business School. She received her undergraduate degree with honours in multinational management and strategic management from the Wharton School at the University of Pennsylvania. Ndidi points out that, historically, Nigerian initiatives have focused on micro entrepreneurs in the rural areas, or on established entrepreneurs in the urban areas. While these are all laudable initiatives, with noble goals, Ndidi says that they have not attempted to address the unique needs of urban youth. As a result, these youths remain a vulnerable and neglected segment of society.

In December 2002, Ndidi was chosen as one of the World Economic Forum's Global Leaders for Tomorrow. Ndidi is the founder and managing partner of a new organisation, LEAP Africa (Leadership, Effectiveness, Accountability and Professionalism) which is focused on building management capacity in Africa. She still serves on the board of FATE Nigeria and FATE USA. In February 2006, Ndidi received 11th Annual *ThisDay* Award as Young Manager of the Year.

Godwin Ehigiamusoe is the founder, initiator and coordinator of the Lift Above Poverty Organisation (LAPO), one of the leading micro-credit organisations in Nigeria. LAPO is a poverty-focused development membership organisation, with the broad aim of assisting its members, poor women, to improve their well-being. LAPO's activities are directed by the operating assumptions that poor women are too disadvantaged to benefit from the services of formal financial institutions and that the poor are not necessarily lazy. LAPO believes that the socio-economic situation of the poor would improve if credit was added to support their labour and skills, and that poverty is reinforced by factors such as too large a family, malnutrition, ignorance, disease and social injustice. LAPO has learned that small groups have a tremendous influence on getting each individual in the group to cooperate, and that poor women and children have previously been the most neglected by society.

In 2001, in a paper entitled 'Micro-credit as a tool for poverty alleviation of Nigerian women — our experience', Ehigiamusoe states that the condition of women remains critical, especially in the areas of poverty and their exclusion from participation in the public sphere. Improvement in their condition is paramount. LAPO's focus on the poor, especially poor women, is not negotiable. It believes that the world has the resources and technological capability to eradicate the worst manifestations of poverty — if the will is there. LAPO conceives of poverty as a monster with many faces. Gone are the days when simplistic interpretations and explanations of poverty gave prominence to 'laziness' or 'destiny'. People, especially women, are poor because they are largely illiterate so do not participate in the decision-making process of the country. They lack access to assets and have limited access to health and other welfare services. LAPO believes that poverty leads to material deprivation, loss of self-esteem, powerlessness and poor health. The success of a unilineal attack on poverty is therefore doubtful.

LAPO is known for its delivery of micro-financial services operating a credit and savings scheme which targets poor women. Intended beneficiaries are expected to organise themselves into groups, and members of a group of five members guarantee one another. No collateral is required. Banks deal with faceless clients, but LAPO knows its loan beneficiaries as members because they are involved in decision-making through the basic phases of loan cycle and in the institution. The micro-credit scheme has therefore provided an avenue for women to have access to an array of responsive financial products for their micro enterprises. Loan products include regular loans for working capital requirements, Christmas business loans, asset loans, and joint project loans. An innovation credit-for-shares product provides fund to poor women to purchase shares in profitable companies. Savings products include regular savings, Christmas savings and business savings. As they have access to these products, women are able to enhance their income earning capacity and build up assets, which eventually propel them to break out of the vicious cycle of poverty to the virtuous cycle of prosperity. A 100 per cent to 250 per cent increase in the level of women's income, within 12 months of access to LAPO's loans, is the norm.

Besides credit and savings opportunities, LAPO has introduced a micro insurance scheme for women to reduce their vulnerability. The project, which covers over 4,000 women, was implemented in conjunction with the American International Insurance Company. It is envisaged that the creative risk management arrangement will be extended to all members and to cover additional risks. Economic empowerment and risk management is central to playing a dominant role in decision-making in the family. When women have their own resources, they are able to make decisions about the utilisation of such resources without having to seek approval from the male head of the household. With adequate resources, women no longer suffer or watch their children die from conditions that can be helped with a little money.

LAPO realises that poverty goes beyond the possession of financial resources. Certain factors beyond money have been identified as major causes of poverty or reinforcement where it already exists: ill health, ignorance and exclusion from decision-making opportunities. Beyond the provision of access to financial resources to engage in income-generating activities, LAPO realises the need to equip its members with tools to enable them to challenge and break down structures that sustain poverty. Without doing this, it would be a question of helping them cope today without facing the challenges of life tomorrow. Women, whether urban or rural, do have political interests to pursue. They are confronted with power relations, which constrain the opportunities open to them in both private and public spheres. Women's demands to meet basic needs like food, shelter, education and health care, for themselves and members of their family, have direct political implications.

In 1996, the knowledge that the allocation of resources within a society can be influenced by a politically active population prompted the creation of the LAPO Development Centre. The centre has the primary responsibility for the promotion of social development for the maximum impact of the economic empowerment programme. The strategy consists of creative sensitisation packages such as GELT (Gender Environment and Leadership Training), a two-day participatory training programme. With essential codes such as drama, storytelling, songs and sharing, poor women are sensitised to the role of cultural norms and practices in the process of poverty. They are also encouraged to challenge, and indeed seek to destroy, such gender-hostile practices. LAPO women called the GELT package an eye opener. Development Education and Leadership Training is a four-week training programme segmented into four phases and designed to sensitise LAPO women on issues such as self-esteem, group dynamics, the process of poverty, social injustice and inequity, political participation and household power relations. According to Ehigiamusoe the number of women trained by the LAPO Social Envelopment Unit was 10 520 as of 31 October 2005. LAPO's television programme, Bridging the Gap, is also aimed at social and political sensitisation. Health awareness activities have been a part of LAPO since its inception in the late 1980s. Key strategies are community health discussion sessions, publication and distribution of graphic-dominated health awareness journals, the radio health talk '15 minutes with LAPO', the production and distribution of posters, and the training of rural health sensitisation agents.

LAPO's focus is on rural women, and the organisation has been structured to deliver these services effectively. Within the LAPO system are semi-autonomous units, which implement the various components. LAPO Fund delivers financial services through 14 branches and a community bank in Edo state, 12 branches in Delta state, one branch in Kogi state, six branches in Lagos and four branches in Federal Capital Territory. The LAPO Development Centre (LADEC) is the think tank of the LAPO system and implements social development programmes in addition to conducting surveys and researches. LAPO Health implements health awareness programmes. The Micro Investment Unit supports enterprising women and groups in setting up micro enterprises.

LAPO insists on serving only poor women, and eligibility criteria are set and vigorously applied. LAPO de-emphasises charity and involves beneficiaries from the community-based groups in the governing board. There is intensive interaction between beneficiaries and programme staff, with emphasis on programme monitoring, responsive products and services, commitment of programme staff and support from donor agencies. All these factors have contributed to LAPO's success.

Godwin Ehigiamusoe estimates that more than a million Nigerians are in some micro credit programme. And that, he says, doesn't begin to approach the need. He says, 'If we are going to make a meaningful impact on poverty in Nigeria, we need to reach a higher number of people.' Ehigiamusoe thinks he sees a way. He is lobbying the government to create a national fund for micro credit finance. The way he sees it, if the government and private sector are serious about developing the economy, there is no way they can get around micro credit finance. 'If we are able to provide capital on an affordable condition — because that is important to a very large number of people, and this large number of people is able to use that resource to increase their productivity, their capacity, their income capacity — that means that first of all the income of the household, of a large number of households, will be enhanced.' Ehigiamusoe is also finding more interest among Nigerian banks interested in micro finance. He tells the banks, 'Don't be afraid. Your money will come back. Don't be so concerned. This business is very profitable.' If the lure of profits is not enough, a growing number of governments in the developing world, like that of Nigeria, are beginning to require that banks provide some funding for micro-enterprises and small to medium businesses.

(Source: Kenneth Walker. 'Nigeria: Building its future: Part 4 - Making the micro credit Connection', www.nbr.com, 16 June 2005)

Nigeria hopes to generate US$5 billion in revenue annually from the export of cassava and related products according to Nigeria's Minister for Agriculture, Chief Bamidele Dada. Nigeria is the world's largest producer of cassava tubers. In 2003, the country was producing between 35 and 40 million metric tons of cassava annually and by 2007 production could be increased to 150 million metric tons. Bamidele says cassava has become an important product worldwide, especially in developed countries, where it is used for poultry feeds. Bamidele states that if Nigerians are able to access the export market to produce cassava pellets and cassava chips of world market quality, they can start to earn part of this projected amount. He reveals that there is tremendous potential for the use of cassava for industrial starch, as livestock feed and in the production of ethanol and some derivatives for pharmaceuticals. What Nigerians need to do is to establish appropriate agro-industries to make use of raw cassava tubers so that they can export these products as import substitutes and meet the needs of other African countries as well as European and other developed countries. A number of equipment producers are interested in partnering Nigerian entrepreneurs to explore business opportunities in the agricultural sector, especially in the processing of cassava.

Nigeria's blueprint for agricultural development is intended to boost food production and alleviate poverty. The launching of the National Agricultural Development Fund in 2003, with an initial take-off fund of N10 billion, was one of the measures put in place to increase food production. Nigeria also entered into an agreement with China to provide 500 technicians to help the country's farmers. Agriculture remains a potent tool with which the twin goals of poverty reduction and food security can be achieved in the short term. The sector has therefore been incorporated as a major sector in fulfilling the requirements of the ongoing NEPAD initiative. Speaking on the theme 'Competitive agriculture: the pathway to economic transformation', the chairman of the 10th Nigeria Economic Summit (2003), Mohammed Hayatu-Deen, said it was no longer a matter of debate that agriculture and food security were basic factors for the economic transformation of the country. 'We already know from our own history and those of developed economies that the strength, capacity and sustainability of any economy are dependent on the extent of agriculture and food security,' the chairman stated. He added that in the past the cycle of economic instability in Nigeria was directly related to what he called the continuous neglect of agriculture.

(Source: Cletus Akwaya. 'N5 billion targeted from cassava export', Lagos: *ThisDay*, 21 November 2003).

    Mohammed Hayatu-Deen is also chairman and CEO of FSB International Bank Plc. In 1992, he assumed office with the special task of transforming the moribund Federal Savings Bank into a viable and profitable commercial bank. He had earlier worked in the Northern Nigerian Development Company from which he retired as managing director. He then set up and managed a private consulting firm. Today FSB International has become one of the high-flying banks in Nigeria, measured by any indicator. By investing heavily in leading edge technology, the bank has been an efficient provider of banking services locally, offering premium services to its clients such as electronic banking that grants customers easy access to their accounts from their offices. It also offers real time on-line services, which enable their customers to transact their business from any of its branches. FSB has 25 branches and is a leading provider of specialised services, particularly project financing and cross-border credit from the bank's strategic partners. 'As the middle class grows more people will require banking services. That's where the private banking arm of FSB will be really important,' says Hayatu-Deen.

    FSB under Hayatu-Deen is quoted on the Nigerian stock exchange and its performance is quite commendable. The bank, in league with 18 other banks, has invested in the smart card consortium Smart Card Nigeria Plc, which provides a safer and less burdensome alternative payment system. Similarly, FSB is invested in Pioneer Currency Sorting Company Ltd, which operates from eight centres to service the Nigerian banking industry. FSB also has investments in First Security Discount House Ltd, the first and leading discount house in the country. FSB is not merely interested in investing in computers; the bank has launched its own website on the Internet and introduced electronic mail technology both within and outside the bank in order to enhance communication and transform it into a paperless institution. Hayatu-Deen is one of the moving spirits behind the Nigerian Economic Summit that has set the agenda for restructuring the Nigerian economy and putting it on a firm foundation. The Nigerian Economic Summit served as a precursor to Vision 2010 in which Hayatu-Deen also played a prominent role.

(Source: www.fsbint.com)

    Talon (Nigeria) Ltd is an Apapa-based company in agriculture and agro-allied products. For export, it undertakes product coordination, provides suitable advisory services for a number of commodities and guides its customers in those areas — oil seeds, spices, aquatic products, fish, shellfish, and so on. Dr Samuel Olanrewaju Talabi, executive chairman, says that in the future they will be going into some more technological areas such as biotechnology products. Talon was established in 1984 as an agro-based research and development company principally involved in bringing cost-effective, sustainable and appropriate technology and management know-how to bear upon food, agriculture, fisheries and the environment in Nigeria. Since its establishment, Talon has undertaken various agro-based nationwide projects through which it has steadily built up and consolidated its technical expertise in the agro-based sector, resulting in major contributions in food, agriculture, fisheries and the environment.

    Talon has about 20 permanent staff and 40 regular consultants and associates, most of whom are members of one or more professional institutions. The cultural diversity of its permanent staff and associates provides a rich pool of language capability for its consultants: English, Yoruba, Hausa and Igbo, Spanish, French, German and Dutch. Talon also provides services such as project coordination, mass data processing, specialist information and technology procurement. The company has access to several well-equipped laboratories (local and abroad) to provide a wide range of analytical services on water, food and soil. Talon's multi-disciplinary approach to projects and its 50-hectare research and development farm at Omilende in Ogun State enable it to provide appropriate solutions to problems in agriculture, fisheries and the environment. In the various stages of sustainable agricultural development, Talon uses the most advanced techniques such as tested processing from its research and development farm, remote sensing, geographic information systems, and computer simulations. Transfer of knowledge about the applications of these techniques to counterpart staff forms an important aspect of the assistance provided to the client in order to ensure project sustainability.

Export marketing companies, according to Talabi, are critical to the export business in Nigeria. Small and medium enterprises producing exportable products on a small scale must work with export marketing companies, and export marketing companies should continuously train small-scale entrepreneurs in quality aspects and pay them appropriately for their products. He believes it is the medium and large export marketing companies that will tap into the export market and monitor the market environment and trends that will have to do with exports. Back in Nigeria, the export marketing companies should engage in training the SMEs and put them in the network correctly so that they can benefit. He does not think that small-scale entrepreneurs should themselves look forward to exporting. Rather, they should produce, forming the basis for exports, and let export marketing companies take their products in exchange for appropriate prices.

Talabi recommends that the various tiers of government should identify and use people with experience in exports, who should be paid for providing SMEs with necessary information. He adds that the government should also be prepared to provide export infrastructure at ports and airports. Government should provide offices and warehouses in big centres like London, Amsterdam and Rotterdam for the Nigerian produce. Nigerian embassy staff should be linked with these offices, in order to advise Nigerian exporters, and protect them from dealing with criminal elements.

Talabi suggests that Nigerian research institutes should have export programmes and look at the research components of exports which invariably should involve a lot of technology and research in trade matters such as the WTO, sanitary regulations and services. The three tiers of government have a responsibility to promote export trade. He urges local government councils to promote export development in their areas of jurisdiction since they can promote the production of exportable goods to a very high standard. They can advise on quality; provide training for operators aspiring to export; and provide a clean environment for minimising the cross-contamination of exportable products with extraneous substances, materials and organisms. They can also reclaim some areas and set up small industrial estates purely for exports; work with the port authorities to provide support services; and develop new areas and designate them as industrial estates for small businesses that would principally support export.

On what Nigeria should do to develop the potential to export non-oil products to bring in much-desired foreign exchange, Talabi maintains that Nigeria is already doing a lot in cocoa, spices (especially ginger) and traditional vegetables, but that more needs to be done in other areas like herbs and fruits, especially mangoes, pineapples, oranges and pawpaw. He points out that there are still a lot of areas to be developed and it is the way they are developed that will determine the sustainability of Nigeria's export drive. However, the country can still expand and improve, especially where quality is concerned. There are new areas like furniture and forest products, non-tree forest products and aqua-culture products, especially shrimp.

(Source: Daniel Gumm. 'Marketing companies are critical to export business - Talon Boss', Lagos: *Vanguard*, 23 July 2004)

Spectra Nigeria Ltd is a member of the Nigeria Association of Small Scale Industrialists (NASSI) and employs 80 people. Its major operation is food processing. The company has been involved in small-scale processing of Suco cocoa drink powder, instant soya powder, pineapple juice and sesame seed oil. All these products have been fully developed and marketed. Spectra's Frute pineapple juice and Frute pineapple/ginger are natural: fresh pineapples and ginger are processed with no chemical additives, flavouring or colouring. The juice is bottled in brown bottles which, says Spectra's founder and managing director, Duro Kuteyi, shields the contents from the sun and prevents deterioration.

Spectra was incorporated and started operations in Lagos in August 1992 producing the Suco cocoa drink powder and instant soya powder with a staff of six including the managing director, production supervisor, driver and saleswoman. In the quest to modernise the production process and also to make contact with other food processing companies, the company moved to the Lagos Technology Business Incubation in 1994, where it was recognised as the best business of the year for five years. In 1998, the company moved to its present location. For economy of scale, it was important that production lines should be expanded. In recognition of the company's performance over the years and its potential, the government approved and leased this bigger manufacturing space to the company. The support, constructive ideas and assistance of other Spectra directors should also be recognised. Today, the company has a standard factory comprising the production section, the administrative and quality control sections, and has been able to maintain and expand its market position despite stiff competition from multinationals.

Kuteyi attended the University of Ife (now Obafemi Awolowo University), Ile-Ife, between 1972 and 1977, where he obtained a Bachelor of Food Science and Technology. As Spectra's chief operating officer, Kuteyi is demonstrating in practical terms what it is to be a manufacturer. With a wide product range and many more new products being developed, he is in the thick of entrepreneurial developments. His indigenous efforts in this regard are highly regarded by his fellow industrialists and the Nigerians who are profiting from his investments either as employees, consumers or government agencies who regularly collect taxes from his productive engagements. As the national vice president of NASSI in 2004, he continued to play prominent roles in opening up the industrial space of the nation. At the international level, Kuteyi is no less active and vibrant in articulating the interests of Nigeria and he has at various times been commended for assisting in attracting foreign investors to Nigeria and for his efforts to promote Nigeria's agricultural development and food processing. In Kebbi, he was involved in developing processing methods for onions within the state.

Kuteyi is an executive council member of Technonet Africa, an intra-regional African SME network that assists in the development of small and medium enterprises in Africa. At various times, he has attended workshops in Europe, America, Asia and many countries in Africa, and in all of these meetings and workshops he has never shied away from articulating the interests of Nigeria in the area of investment, development of small- and medium-scale industries, and the economic empowerment of Nigerians. Kuteyi lobbied the president, Chief Olusegun Obasanjo, for the inclusion of micro-credit financing into the Small and Medium Industry Equity Investment Scheme, an initiative of the bankers' committee in 2002. He was a member of the Inter-Agency Technical Committee of Relevant SME Agencies and Organisations that prepared the Implementation Blueprint for the Establishment of National Credit Guarantee Scheme for Small and Medium Enterprises in Nigeria in 2003. In August 2004, Kuteyi received the prestigious Manufacturer of the Year Award from the Nigerian Leadership Foundation and *CELEBRITY* magazine in Lagos.

Leonard Okafor is the Nigerian UN volunteer specialist in business-community relations based at the Lagos UNDP office. He graduated in 1989 with a B Sc degree honours in economics and statistics from the University of Nigeria, Nsukka and has experience spanning banking, business and international civil service. One of his particular interests is development work, addressing poverty and finding ways to build capacity in civil society for self-reliance. Leonard enjoyed the opportunity to work in the Brazil-Argentina Commercial Centre, where he had the task of identifying and integrating similarities between Brazil and Nigeria with a view to adapting its cottage industrial experience to Nigeria's traumatised economy. Leonard has conducted the only known research into corporate responsibility/business-community relations in Nigeria, producing a national report and 10 case studies. He has worked extensively to understand and promote better relations between the oil multinational corporations and communities in the Niger Delta especially Elf Petroleum (TOTAL), ChevronTexaco and Schlumberger, providing involved stakeholders with options and strategies for their developmental goals within these relationships. Through extensive stakeholder consultations, national and several corporate-community workshops, he has developed a groundbreaking dialogue towards partnership for development between Elf Petroleum (TOTAL) and its host communities in Rivers state. The envisaged partnership aims to deliver peace and security to the company and its operations, and social services to the communities, including healthcare, education, skills acquisition and enterprise development, sustainable agriculture and environmental protection. It will employ delivery mechanisms that utilise baseline studies, programme planning and implementation. Also in 2004, he completed a research work, ready for publication, on the theme of 'Corporate citizenship in Africa: Retrospection and introspection – progress looking back; prospects looking forward'. He has established an African regional consultancy for companies involved with host communities, to deliver the following services: research and baseline surveys to support corporate sustainability programmes; impact assessments for corporate sustainability programmes (social and environmental impact assessments); social reports; corporate indexing; development of corporate sustainability programmes, and monitoring and evaluation.

The Fair Trade Network of Nigeria (FTNN) was founded as the Alternative Trade Network of Nigeria in 1994 in the city of Jos, as a membership, non-profit, non-governmental development organisation working with the disadvantaged grassroots communities and producers under the guiding principles and practices of the international fair trade movement. Its formation was facilitated by a research work conducted by Carol Bergin of the Irish Fair Trade Network (IFTN), who sought to evaluate the business development and export potentials of Nigerian handicraft to northern Alternative Trade Organisations (ATOs). The research results established immense potentials for Nigerian handicrafts and indigenous products albeit requiring more effort at product quality enhancement, product costing, packaging and marketing — all prerequisites for export market penetration. In response, the FTNN was established with an initial membership of 25 cooperatives drawn from various parts of Nigeria. The network is a registered affiliate member of the International Federation for Alternative Trade (now re-named the International Fair Trade Association, or IFAT, and still remains the only fair trade producer development organisation operating in Nigeria.

Semshak Gompil, FTNN's executive director, is the founding national executive coordinator. He studied tourism and worked for many years with the Plateau State Ministry of Tourism Corporation in Jos, Nigeria. Through his international fair trade involvement, he was elected to become the African regional representative on the board of the International Fair Trade Association, with its headquarters in the Netherlands), where he has been responsible for the establishment of an Africa regional secretariat of IFAT called the Cooperation for Fair Trade in Africa (COFTA) with membership (50 members from 22 African countries) drawn from all fair trade organisations and practitioners in Africa, and with headquarters in Nairobi. It was inaugurated in May 2004 in Mombasa, Kenya, with fair trade advocacy, market access and capacity-building as its key programme missions.

Mr Gompil met Carol Bergin during one of her tourism exchange programmes in Nigeria and started organising guided tours for her entourage with a view to ensuring and increasing economic opportunity and value for tourists' trips, purchases and the promotion of cultural exchange. In the course of these tours, he discovered the immense potential of the communities to generate wealth from arts and food production, but quickly realised how artisans and farmers were short changed and exploited through their business limitations and their involvement with middlemen who would buy products at very low rates to sell on to retail shops, hotels, airports, and township markets at highly inflated rates. This situation provided Gompil with the vision and idea to set up the FTNN programme. He expressed great optimism about the efforts of the Network to provide the technical means and support to effectively mobilise rural producer participation and sustainable development of small scale enterprises that, through growth and expansion, would assist producer development and reduce poverty. However, he worried about the lack of in-country support from government and non-government development organisations, and was and also concerned about the network's restrictive facilities, internal capacity and manpower — constraints which reduce the potential operational impacts and service output of the network and therefore threaten continuity, growth and sustainability. He hoped and expected that once support from government or funding organisations could be secured he could develop the network programme facilities, structure and capacities to make the programme a sustainable independent entity.

The development and marketing of traditional arts and crafts are FTNN's major focus, not merely for the promotion of fair trade, but also to encourage the development of responsible tourism and the eventual expansion of an African fair trade brand of 'world shops'. Part of its programme marketing strategy includes the promotion of member producers' arts and crafts at local and international levels, through coordinating and participating in regional and international trade fairs, developing channels for e-commerce, CD-ROM catalogues for export and also direct local retailing from its shop in Jos which is solely dedicated to the exhibition and marketing of member producers' goods. This is a pilot shop model for fair trade domestic marketing which is allied to periodic trade exhibitions and events in some key cities in Nigeria. A wide range of FTNN's craft products are also exported internationally, through partnerships with FTOs in Italy, Spain, the UK, Canada, Australia and the US.

While working mostly with its producer members, rural artisan craftsmen, FTNN also focuses on the physically challenged, widows, orphans and HIV/AIDS victims. FTNN believes that the greatest challenge facing Nigeria now is raising awareness about the negative economic impacts and dimensions of HIV/AIDS. Victims need money for drugs, to buy and eat good food, and to pay hospital bills. The physically challenged and HIV/AIDS victims in Nigerian society have had to put up with discrimination and social deprivation arising from stigma and some mythologies surrounding their dispositions. This has placed a huge burden on these groups, condemning them to poverty even when they have the potential skills and the determination to survive. Also, in most traditional Nigerian societies widows are often the most deprived and vulnerable. This is because women in the traditional society are usually dependent on their husbands. If a man dies, the woman usually finds herself and her family suddenly marginalised — exposed to further economic hardship and challenges, with little means, skills or opportunities to support herself.

This programme is therefore targeted at supporting disadvantaged groups in their most difficult and trying moments — providing beneficiaries with new skills and business opportunities and a new lease on life. FTNN believes that direct involvement with these groups can empower them with the skills to lift them from their social deprivation and consequent poverty, giving them a sense of self worth through capacity-building and other empowerment initiatives such as working capital or order pre-financing. A key aspect of FTNN's service is to provoke creativity and skills exchange between members through mutual skills development, training, workshops, and exchange programmes. For example, batik producers from the city of Ibadan are often engaged to train widows' groups on batik production as a means of empowerment.

FTNN has classified Nigerian crafts under three broad categories: organic crafts, which are ethnic and come from the tradition of forefathers in the communities (masks, carved works, beads, necklaces, and ornaments); inorganic or contemporary crafts, which involve modification of crafts with inorganic materials (beads, decorations, and other artwork made of such inorganic materials as plastic); and mechanical crafts, which are produced through mechanical processes and typified by the Asian mass-produced crafts of today. Examples are batik dresses or tie-and-dye, and other traditional attires.

Jai' Mariali Adba, an artist who produces souvenirs, cards and paintings, testifies that through his membership with FTNN his output and quality have improved through the workshops and training, which have enabled him to gain and effectively meet up with new export orders from Ten Thousand Villages, a United States fair trade organisation. This contract was secured for him through the FTNN export programme. He invested the income proceeds in new tools and the upgrading of his art studio. He also indicates how the Network-organised trade fairs have improved his local income, but he is concerned about member producers' inability to access micro-credit and believes that the FTNN should find the means to incorporate an internal micro-credit/loan facility into their programme structure to assist in this regard.

Ms Mercy Edeke, a fabric designer representing Resource Women on Mission Cooperative Society has said that FTNN is helping to open up opportunities for community arts and crafts cooperatives and individual producers and improving their businesses by challenging their creativity and business development through fair competition. She expects FTNN to develop an effective professional operational framework for better interaction and exchange between the network and producer members and to boost accountability and transparency as both stakeholders and beneficiaries are still learning to develop that aspect of their relationship. Further, she thinks that FTNN will be better appreciated if producers see it coming to help them with micro-credit.

Innocent Azuh, a professional painter and member producer, says that his business has grown in size from that of a sole worker to a workshop of four paid staff with periodic apprentices, since his involvement and collaboration with FTNN. He also reports that through the Network's recommendations he has now been able to secure a gift shop at the Wild Life Park in the Plateau State of Nigeria, a Tourism Corporation initiative, which provides him with a good retail outlet for his products.

Josephine Onwuka is a physically challenged producer member and also a shop assistant at the Network. She is happy with FTNN and sees the added value in its training support programmes, which have improved her skills, output and income, enabling her to gain new orders annually for her fabric dolls and products, from the United States, Australia, Italy and Canada — all secured through the Network's trading activities. For each order, 50 per cent mobilisation capital was advanced in accordance with fair trade principles and her customers expressed their appreciation for her product quality, price and timely delivery.

Esther Dokyoung is an industrial designer and FTNN producer representing Endless Options African Creativity, a training, capacity building and skills acquisition centre for youths and women, which focuses on dropouts and the unemployed. She believes that her group's involvement with the Network has improved their own public relations skills and ability to work with diverse groups, but she is concerned about the network's lack of internal capacity for producers' enlightenment — especially the lack of a technical resource library and information facilities, limited staff capacity in the Network, issues of accountability and poor financial support from development agencies. She campaigns for greater FTNN commitment from producer members, stating that producers can do a lot but are incapacitated by lack of money, and would appreciate micro-credits, for greater productivity and enhanced income, from FTNN.

(Source: Leonard Okafor. 'Enhancing business-community relations, alternative trade network of Nigeria case study', Bonn: United Nations Volunteers, and Bath: New Academy of Business, www.new-academy.ac.uk/research/businesscommunity/unvpages, November 2003)

In 2005, FTNN had a membership of over 87 producer cooperatives, with more than 2,200 individuals producing diverse handicrafts that capture and reflect the rich cultural and traditional heritage of Nigeria. Beyond this, their activities are silently but surely creating a social and economic revolution in the lives of people who ordinarily would have no chance of living life to its full potential. The next major project was the expansion of its fair trade shop in Jos into an African World Shop, and the establishment of a pilot collaborative cottage factory in Biu, Adamawa State, for the production of hand-woven straw baskets. The present retail outlet would also be enlarged to accommodate more artisans, thereby creating greater market access for producers. This informed Gompil's vision to set up the FTNN. He believes the network has the necessary potential to mobilise rural participation and sustainable development of small scale enterprises that will greatly assist in poverty reduction. However, he is worried about the lack of support from government and development organisations, and concerned about limited internal capacity and inadequate manpower, which have threatened sustainability. He expects that support from government or funding organisations would at least ensure the retention of a core group of staff that would continue to promote the Network's initiatives and further improve the capacities of producer groups for the export market.

Chapter 5: The Gambia, Sierra Leone, Liberia, Guinea, Senegal, Côte d'Ivoire, Togo, Benin, Burkina Faso, Mali, Niger, Guinea-Bissau and Cape Verde.

The Gambia

A special entrepreneur contributing to the development of both residential and commercial properties in Africa is Mustapha Njie, commonly known as Taf. With a solid reputation for hard work and efficiency behind him, built over the years by working in senior positions of reputable international firms, Taf embarked on a personal development programme by pursuing a diploma course in site management, and was admitted as a licentiate member of the British Chartered Institute of Building in 1987. Given Taf's business acumen and his rating at the time within the private sector, particularly the construction industry, he decided to take the bull by the horns by setting up his own construction outfit, Taf Construction Ltd. Taf is considered one of the most dynamic young Gambian entrepreneurs, and a shining example of the breed of private sector entrepreneurs to lead his country into the 21st century.

Over time, Taf established a conglomerate of businesses with a high degree of synergy: Taf Construction Ltd (TCL), Taf Building Materials Supplies, Taf Estate Developers (TED), and Tafbel Maisonettes. Taf Estate Developers (TED), while younger, is involved in the construction and management of modern housing estates. In 2000, Taf launched a housing project, 'Operation House the Nation'. The project, comprising more than 200 two-and three-bedroomed houses, was sold mainly to Gambians in the diaspora, through the Internet. After the successful completion of this project, another site four times the size of the former was allocated to Taf. This site is now being developed and it is envisaged that, when complete, will contain at least 500 houses. The project is being co-financed by Shelter Afrique, a pan-African housing finance institution based in Nairobi.

Taf Holding is the first and only private large-scale housing developer in The Gambia. Over the years Taf has expanded his business to neighbouring Senegal, and also has plans to launch low-cost housing projects in Mali and Guinea Bissau.

Taf's companies employ over 500 Gambians and contribute to civil society by donating to philanthropic organisations and giving scholarships to the poor and deserving students and to sports. Taf is an active member of the West African Enterprise Network (WAEN) and a founder member of the Gambia chapter (WAEN is a networking platform supported by USAID and Club du Sahel for West African entrepreneurs). In the course of his business career, he has received several awards and distinctions such as the European Commission Global Business Award for Excellence and Quality (1998) and The Gambia Chamber of Commerce Businessman of The Year (1992/93) and 2004. Taf is an example of what sheer determination, self-motivation, goodwill, and self-confidence can create and a role model for many young Gambians with ambition and aspirations. Taf is highly respected for his honesty, sincerity and hard work. He is an example for the next generation of Gambian and African entrepreneurs.

When the winners of the Africa 2004 SMME Awards were announced in October 2004, enterprises from all over the continent made their mark. Taf Holding Company was the winner of the award for the construction sector. In October 2004, Taf was also awarded an honorary doctorate in Global Enterprise Management by the Irish University Business School. Delivering a powerful address on entrepreneurship in Africa, he said:

'Starting up any business in Africa is always a major challenge. Entrepreneurs in Africa have to put in significant extra efforts in order to succeed, given the many hurdles they face, which may not be the same in the developed world ... despite all these challenges, there are great opportunities which exist in the continent and which may bring relatively high returns.'

Describing his own challenges, he said that when he decided to start his own company he had to convince relatives and friends who wanted him to stay employed and not to take the risk of having to compete with established enterprises. 'But as a potential entrepreneur, I was deeply convinced and determined to take the risk of venturing into my own business.' He had to overcome a negative image since, 'at 33 I was considered too young to have the ability and know-how to manage any enterprise.' Deciding that initial efforts should be dedicated to publicity, he had flyers and other materials developed by professional communications companies. He wrote letters of introduction and sent them, accompanied by flyers, to potential clients. Though well received in some institutions, they were viewed with scepticism in others.

A few clients asked him to build personal residences for them. This was an opportunity. Taf's guiding principle was to deliver to customers in a timely manner and to ensure that prices were competitive but that the end product was always of the best possible quality. He continued: 'Dealing with the negative image is not only a problem for Gambian entrepreneurs, but is indeed a huge challenge for most indigenous businesses in sub-Saharan Africa. Because of the existence of reputable international firms which have a solid foundation and good contacts at national level, it can sometimes be very difficult to get a foot in the door of this market. There is a need to persevere and to demonstrate to clients that the work done by the indigenous firms can be of the same quality as the international ones, that they will get their value for money, and that the added advantage of the indigenous firms is that they will likely always be around in the event that maintenance is needed.'

Taf advocated networking in the local private sector as another way of overcoming challenges. 'It is also advisable to develop professional associations who can lobby both international and national policy makers to facilitate the participation of indigenous enterprises in national development. At times it may be necessary to give additional incentives to local enterprises. This will not only ensure that they become involved in their development processes, but will also ensure that local capacity is developed. Capacity development is key to addressing the negative image problem, whilst, at the same time, it plays a critical role in sustaining the inputs into the development process from the private sector. If private sector-led growth is to be a reality in Africa, this will need to be given serious consideration.'

He continued that the lack of finance or start-up capital was always a major challenge to new and young enterprises in sub-Saharan Africa. There are few financial institutions involved in long-term development lending, especially for the start-up of small- and medium-size enterprises. The majority of financial institutions are involved in the financing of trade, with high interest rates, and mainly offer short term loans, so most African entrepreneurs are inclined to less risky ventures, mostly trade related, giving high returns on short-term investments. 'In order to overcome this major challenge, African governments, working in partnership with the international institutions, must encourage the setting-up of financial institutions that are involved in the management of low interest, long-term financing of indigenous enterprises. This will help encourage the development of the African private sector and also facilitate their effective participation in their respective national development processes. While this is an ideal solution, care must be taken and lessons learnt applied, so that the funds are not mismanaged and, further, are administered in a transparent and equitable manner. Experience has shown that in the past, where this has been done, the results have not been as expected, mainly because of political interference and the mismanagement of the funds through favouritism, the lack of clear criteria for eligibility and a general lack of transparency.'

On the subject of competitiveness, he commented that in The Gambia most businesses are owned by non-Gambians and it was only recently that Gambians had started venturing into both the formal and informal private sectors. 'Trading is one of the main activities also for local entrepreneurs. However, more and more locally manufactured goods are becoming less and less competitive because of the cheaper goods that can be obtained, particularly from South East Asia. It is not also certain that the requisite taxes and duties are paid on these imported goods, as such they can be sold at a cheaper price. In order to make locally manufactured goods more competitive for both the local and international markets, indigenous entrepreneurs should be encouraged by giving them incentives.'

On the subject of taxes he considered it important for African governments and policy makers to recognise that a vibrant private sector is critical to economic development, and that for any private sector to be vibrant and play an effective role, taxes and duties must be collected judiciously and should not to be an impediment to growth. He admitted that the poor state of the infrastructure in sub-Saharan Africa is one of the major challenges for entrepreneurs. 'The roads are in a deplorable state and sometimes certain areas are almost inaccessible ... good roads and access to potential construction sites are an imperative if enterprises are to succeed.'

'The state and cost of electricity supplies in Africa is another deterrent for the growth and prosperity of business enterprises. The cost of electricity in some African countries is amongst the most expensive in the world. Electricity supplies are also unreliable and in some areas non-existent. This makes the cost of doing business very expensive ... a possible solution ... is to encourage governments to forge partnerships between the public and private sectors in the supply and management of electricity in Africa. Cross border supplies of excess electricity should also be encouraged, since some countries have excess energy that can be exported to neighbouring countries.'

Taf praised the rapid development of telecommunications, noting that the advent of cellular phones in Africa has had a positive impact and in some instances has directly and indirectly reduced the transaction costs of doing business. He went on to say that Africa has diverse sets of norms, traditions and practices which can have an impact on businesses. These socio-cultural issues need to be understood and respected, 'though they may not be that apparent as they are usually not documented, nor are they formalised. Notwithstanding, they can have an important role to play in the success or otherwise of any business. These issues are mostly of a religious, ethnic, or cultural nature.' In most African countries, Taf said, religion plays a vital role in all aspects of life, and doing business is not an exception. 'With multiple religions and sects, one must understand the dos and don'ts of all these religions if one is to operate and succeed in business in Africa. Likewise different norms, values and beliefs exist for different ethnic groups ...culture is an important issue in all works of life. People's culture can influence the success or failure of any business enterprise in Africa. One must understand the best practices in any culture and put them positively into practice for the success of any business enterprise.'

The lack of a well trained and efficient human resources base in Africa remained a major challenge according to Taf. This was due to several contributing factors including the brain drain, the colonial histories, and the education and vocational policies being pursued. 'Currently some entrepreneurs don't invest in the training and development of their work force and this can have a negative impact on their output. For any enterprise to excel and succeed in its endeavours, it is important to engage in good, sustainable training and apprenticeship programmes.'

Taf pointed to a number of opportunities that exist and that have been made possible by advances in technology, the creation of an enabling environment at the regional level by NEPAD and the AU, and the improved governance regime in a number of countries. He believed that these regimes would improve with the establishment of the African peer review mechanism, and that this would further encourage private investment. Among the new opportunities, Taf mentioned improvements in telecommunications: Africa has recorded to date a total of over 35 million mobile phone users across the continent according to Yoshio Utsumi, secretary general of the International Telecommunications Union. Mobile phone users worldwide are expected to outnumber those with traditional phones by the year 2010 whereas in 2001, Africa became the first region where mobile phones outnumbered fixed-line phones. Entrepreneurs have achieved significant financial returns in their investments. The airline industry has also seen a significant number of private and national operators seizing and venturing into opportunities that not only were untapped but at times were operated as monopolies. The housing industry continued to attract opportunities. Most African countries were changing the traditional ways of housing delivery, moving from the conventional way of private individuals building their own homes to buying houses from developers whether public or private. Taf rated this an industry with major opportunities and profitable returns since governments were putting in place a conducive policy environment through attractive concessions to developers: issuance of land, tax holidays, non payment of custom duties on some materials and machinery. There existed regional, and national housing finance institutions offering medium- and long-term lending with low interest rates to both public and private developers.

Taf continued: 'An emerging profitable market which exists today in Africa, that not only affects housing but all other services, is the need to service the needs of Africans in the diaspora, who are remitting significant sums of money back to their countries of origin. As a private housing developer in The Gambia, we saw the need to service Gambians in the diaspora by marketing our houses to them. This we did by setting up a website with detailed descriptions of our projects. Interested applicants could apply by filling application and submitting them online. Financial transactions can also be carried out online. The Internet also offers them the opportunity to view the progress that is being made.'

He concluded: 'The definition of entrepreneurship varies and there are different interpretations. One school of thought is that entrepreneurs are born whilst another is that they are made. In my opinion, irrespective of the school of thought, there are certain characteristics that an entrepreneur needs to have. These include the ability to take risks on business opportunities at well-calculated moments; to be persistent in order to achieve the results that one is seeking; to be patient with any business pursuit; to be self-confident, as this is also important for image and the clientele; to be a visionary and to strive to be innovative and think ahead; to be passionate as this will nurture the love for one's business ideals.

As a continent, Africa is mostly portrayed in a negative light, full of problems and never-ending conflict. However, there is another side which is not seen much and which is reflected in a younger generation determined to succeed and to be agents of change in their communities. The numbers of these people is continuing to grow, irrespective of where they sit, be it in government or the private sector. There is a need to spread more of this positive message and to continue to explore how these islands of change can be nurtured, and the message spread, so that a conducive environment for investments that will improve the quality of life of the people, can be created and maintained.'

(Source: E-mail correspondence from Mustapha Njie, October 2004, and www.tafgambia.com)

The businessman Amadou Samba decided to bring clean quality water to The Gambia. Driven by market demand and since he owned land with natural springs, Samba established a natural mineral water bottling company, Gamwater. Prior to his company start-up, all bottled water was imported into the country. In order to get started, Samba needed high-end water purifying and testing equipment as well as financing. West African International Business Linkages (WAIBL) introduced him to various suppliers in the United States as well as an American private lender experienced in trade and structured finance, and he was able to secure a loan at competitive commercial rates and payment terms, which allowed Gamwater to move forward. As a result, Gamwater imported over half a million dollars of purifying and bottling equipment from the US that was supported by the US Export-Import Bank with a loan guarantee. At that time Gamwater was the only locally bottled natural mineral water available in The Gambia. Its state-of-the-art plant meets World Health Organisation (WHO) hygiene guidelines. Gamwater is available in restaurants, supermarkets, and hotels and because of its success the company is looking to export its water to the West African sub-region.

Amadou Samba is an alumnus of the University of Nigeria, where he obtained his law degree in 1980. He also attended the Nigerian Law School between 1980 and 1981. He holds a postgraduate diploma in international law from the Jawahal Nehru University, India and the Indian Academy of International and Diplomacy. He held various legal positions in The Gambia, including senior state counsel at the Ministry of Justice, before he set up a private legal practice in 1986. He is an industrialist and director/shareholder in several companies in The Gambia: the *Daily Observer* newspaper, Gamsen Construction, and Guaranty Trust Bank (Gambia).

Guaranty Trust Bank (Gambia) focuses on supporting the manufacturing, agriculture, tourism, and trade sectors of the economy. GTB is well connected and is collaborating with international financial organisations to arrange large foreign currency denominated credit facilities on a medium- to long-term basis. The bank has created a niche in international finance and payment systems supported by real time online technology links with its correspondent banks ANZ and Citibank. A happy customer of GTB says the bank continues to amaze him with the level of services he receives — a card on his birthday and even fruit for Ramadan; he never knew banking could be so rewarding. Other banks can longer take customer service for granted. According to Salieu Taal, GTB's head of corporate and legal affairs, GTB is not worried about other banks copying or trying to emulate their unique style of banking since competition brings out the best in everyone and ensures that customers will be spoilt for choices. On GTB's future plans, Taal says the bank will continue to introduce value added products that will make banking easier, simpler and more convenient, for example, a branch in Banjul was opened in 2004.

(Source: www.gambia.gtbplc.com, and Francis Pabai, 'Guaranty Trust Bank - Gambia's Service Bank', *Daily Observer*, 2 January 2003)

Adama Bah was judged the person who has contributed most significantly to responsible tourism, receiving a Responsible Tourism Award for 2004. Adama Bah became a founder member of Gambia Tourism Concern in 1994, and was instrumental in the formation of the Association of Small Scale Enterprises in Tourism (ASSET) which has since grown to a membership of around 50 organisations carrying an individual membership in excess of 500.

ASSETT has recently been the focal point of the Responsible Tourism Partnership (RTP) in The Gambia, with Adama as its destination office manager. The RTP has come a long way in a short time and is a leading destination organisation world wide. Much of the credit for this goes to Adama. He is always involved with raising awareness and quality through ongoing training programmes, workshops and constant interaction. This obviously raises income levels where needed most.

Adama also has international connections, having delivered papers on RTP and eco-tourism in Africa and Europe. He is the type of person the world needs to fight some of the problems facing the developing world. RTP is an obvious vehicle for this journey and Adama as good a captain as will be found anywhere along the road.

(Source: www.responsibletravel.com)

The 2005 Responsible Tourism Award for Poverty Reduction went to the ASSET, which has increased the income of impoverished Gambians by developing tourism employment opportunities. ASSET was established in April 2000 in order to bring together, advocate for, and promote a large number of small enterprises that were active in the tourism industry in The Gambia. These businesses include craft market vendors, tourist taxi drivers, official tourist guides, juice pressers and fruit sellers as well as a number of small hotels, guest houses and tour operators. ASSET's future goals include the training of large numbers of personnel working in tourism, the development and implementation of industry wide standards and the marketing of the diverse and excellent services that are provided by ASSET members.

(Source: www.asset-gambia.com)

Sierra Leone

Andrew Kromah, the founder, owner and operator of three private radio stations in Sierra Leone, was one of two international journalists honoured with the 2002 Knight International Fellowship Award. The Washington-based International Center for Journalists cited Andrew Kromah's 'extraordinary devotion' to his craft in the midst of conflict, and his efforts to improve the state of journalism in Sierra Leone. Kromah explains that he hadn't set out to pursue a career in journalism. After receiving master's degrees in development economics and agricultural economics from the University of Texas at Prairie View, he returned to Sierra Leone in 1989 to set up a development organisation aimed at helping local farmers and miners realise the value of their land. His efforts were disrupted in 1992 by the outbreak of his country's civil war. Kromah says he realised the need for citizen participation in resolving the conflict.

Kromah took his savings and in 1993 he launched the independent radio station KISS 104 FM in Bo with a staff of eight, five journalists and three support staff. The studio and transmitter are located on Candy Mountain overlooking Bo. Its signal is received throughout the entire township of Bo, and during the dry season KISS can be heard as far away as Calaba Town, in the East End of Freetown. Its programmes, which are aired in Krio and Mende, appealing to the broadest range of citizens, include topics such as health, farming, education, and Voice of America pre-recorded programming. KISS is also the only outlet in the area for government announcements. KISS is committed to the distribution of useful, unbiased information to citizens of the country. One of its programmes trains community singers and cultural groups to serve as 'community animators' to develop radio programmes on peace, reconciliation, and the democratic process. Radio Bo supplements these programmes with music and drama.

In 1996, Kromah launched Freetown-based SKYY 106 FM with a staff of 16, nine journalists and seven support staff. The station's transmitter is located at Leister Peak, behind Fourah Bay College, and its signal can be heard as far as Waterloo, 32 kilometres east of Freetown, and throughout the peninsular western area of the city. As the only private radio station on the air, SKYY is overwhelmingly received by the populace.

Kromah invested money into radio because there was a need for information, and he believed very much that a vigorous media institution would be able to pass information about the war. While promoting respect for human rights and a civil society in one of the world's most hostile press environments, Kromah nonetheless ensured that each side in the civil war — rebels, government forces or civilians — had its voice heard. He also developed a system of reporting corruption under the pseudonym 'Mr Owl', which led to increased transparency among commercial and governmental institutions. All was not smooth sailing but despite several attempts on his life, Kromah continued, undaunted. The stations were frequently plagued by shortages of funds due to the lack of wartime economic activity in the Bo area, and Sierra Leone's independent media received scant encouragement from the government. He persevered, and during the May 2000 election he was chosen to coordinate the *ad hoc* Independent Radio Network, which sent reporters equipped with mobile and satellite telephones around the country to report the election results as the votes were counted. The project was a success. It was a first step towards Kromah's dream of a permanent independent public radio network for Sierra Leone.

Kromah is working to institutionalise his radio stations and to ensure opportunities for the next generation of Sierra Leonean journalists. He has established the Media Foundation for Peace and Democracy to take over as an independent national public radio that will provide jobs for journalists and for the students who are graduating from the mass communications and journalism department at Fourah Bay College. There are plans to expand its radio broadcast coverage and services, and host more programmes on science and technology as well as agricultural development. In 2004, Kromah received the Elizabeth R Award for an Exceptional Contribution to Public Service Broadcasting from the Commonwealth Broadcasting Association.

Solar and Communications Equipment Limited (SolarCom) was established by Andrew Kromah in September 1992, initially to supply and install wireless two-way land mobile communication and solar-energy equipment to businesses, government and non-governmental organisations operating in remote areas and areas without dependable electricity. The company aims at manufacturing solar panels and batteries.

When the winners of the Africa 2004 SMME Awards were announced in October 2004, enterprises from all over the continent made their mark. SolarCom was the winner of the regional award for western Africa. The Africa SMME Awards are an initiative of the Africa Centre for Investment Analysis (ACIA) at South Africa's University of Stellenbosch Business School. The whole aim of the awards is to inspire the entrepreneurial spirit of Africa.

(Source: International Centre for Journalists, Press Release October 2002; and http://www.sierra-leone.org/slnews1002.html)

AFRICA: CONTINENT OF ECONOMIC OPPORTUNITIES

Since 1979, Trickle Up has helped launch or expand 46,417 businesses in Africa and in 2004 it launched 3,823 businesses through 42 coordinating partner agencies in Benin, Burkina Faso, Ethiopia, Kenya, Mali, Niger, Sierra Leone, South Africa and Uganda. In Sierra Leone, one Trickle Up entrepreneur is Sampa Turay, a married woman with seven children. Several years ago, rebels attacked her village of Rokupr, in northern Sierra Leone, forcing Sampa and her family to take refuge in Barbara. When they returned home to begin life again in Rokupr, Sampa found it difficult to provide for her family. She was selected for a Trickle Up grant by Community Action for Progress, which she used to start a business buying and selling fish. However, Sampa found it tiring to walk around the market and decided to open a small restaurant instead. She used the rest of her grant to buy raw materials and benches for her clients. Since then, her weekly profit has quadrupled. She can now buy food and clothes, pay her medical expenses, and send four children to school, instead of two. As a result of her business training, Sampa has also improved her management and marketing skills — for example, she has helped to start an association with other cooking businesses operating in the Luma market. By agreeing to competitive prices, the association has increased its market share and has also created an 'ususu' (savings group), to which the ten members contribute Leones 5,000 (US$2.50) a week. Sampa plans to increase her profits by expanding her business into more rural areas, where she will grow her customer base and buy cheaper vegetables and rice.

(Source: www.trickleup.org)

In 2004, the Sierra Leone Brewery officially commissioned an ultra-modern bottling line at the factory's industrial estate in Wellington, Freetown. The bottling line is estimated to cost some 6 million euros, the equivalent of 19 billion Leones. The managing director of the Sierra Leone Brewery, Ivan Carroll, has paid tribute to their overseas shareholders — Heineken International, Guinness Overseas Ltd and Peterson Zochonis Plc — for making the new bottling line available to the company, saying that the new bottling line would improve the yearly production capacity from 120,000 hectolitres to 250,000 hectolitres. The new bottling facility also has the capacity to produce 25,000 bottles — equivalent to 1,040 cartons an hour.

Thomas De Man of Heineken International said he was very impressed with the positive development and economic activity in the country, and pointed out that in addition to the 6 million euro investment in the new bottling line, his company would be developing the Sierra Leone Brewery's human resource base. 'We are committed to train, develop and expose the people to the best and introduce tools and processes that would afford them the opportunity to deliver the organisation's goals, aspirations and ambition, and also revamp the distribution network to ensure products are available, accessible, acceptable and affordable,' the Heineken International representative disclosed. In response to a suggestion put forward by Sierra Leone President Kabbah, De Man said Heineken International had decided to develop a programme for the growing of some of their required raw materials in the country, as a means of boosting the agriculture sector. He assured the president that he was committed to not only produce and market high quality products but also to contribute toward the development of the economy and the well-being of Sierra Leoneans. The possibility of exporting products to the surrounding countries would also be investigated.

The Minister of Trade and Industry, Kadie Sesay, said the Sierra Leone Brewery had shown its commitment to his country by risking capital of about six million euros by investing in this new bottling line and had demonstrated its optimism about the future prospects of Sierra Leone. With improved peace and stability in the country and the positive economic growth projections, the minister said, there had never been a better time for the private sector to invest in the future of the country. Sesay pointed out that the promotion and development of the private sector was the engine of growth and he thus looked forward to more investments of this nature. She said the Sierra Leone Brewery, according to data provided, contributed seven billion Leones to government revenue in 2003, in the form of duties and other taxes (and by the end 2004 the company hoped to make it 12 billion Leones), and pointed out that these were significant contributions which demonstrated the ability of the private sector to generate resources that the Government could use for socio-economic spending. She added that the aim of government was to have another hundred companies like Sierra Leone Brewery contributing similar revenues to the government treasury, and congratulated the board and management of the company for their stewardship and wonderful achievement.

President Kabbah recalled that over 40 years previously, when planners identified and mapped out suitable areas in the Wellington vicinity for industrial development, the Sierra Leone Brewery was one of the earliest industries to be established in the area. 'That was the birth of a testimony of success after success in the brewing and marketing of alcoholic and non-alcoholic beverages in this country,' the President recounted. At the time, with the formation of the West African Free Trade Area, which is today the Mano River Union, a deliberate decision was taken to locate industries in the respective member countries that would serve the rest of the union. This kind of synergistic pooling of resources was aimed at accelerating development within the sub-region. For instance, a brewery in Freetown, an iron ore treatment facility in Monrovia and a bauxite plant in Conakry, with one country producing for the three, was one of the visions of the free-trade concept. However, the President said that this brilliant idea and others like it had never materialised, largely because of conflict and instability in the sub-region. But in light of the present moves to reactivate the Mano River Union, the president suggested, to those responsible for planning the development of this particular industry, the possibility of future expansion of this brewery to meet the original dreams of producing for an expanding market.

(Source: Fatmatta Kamara, 'President Kabbah commissions ultra-modern brewery', 9 June 2004: www.statehouse-sl.org; and June 2005 e-mail correspondence with Thomas De Man).

In the Sierra Leone fishing sector, 60 per cent of the country's needs are provided by artesian fishermen whereas industrial fishing companies such as Sierra Fishing provide the remaining 40 per cent. The Sierra Fishing Company is owned by JS Mohamed & Sons.

All the existing cold rooms have been refurbished, ice plants have been installed and a major fresh fish business has been started. With depots country wide in Bo, Kenema, Kono, Makeni, Kambia, and Moyamba, and cold rooms for the distribution of fish continuing to open in other districts, the company is expanding. In 2005, it also opened a brand new processing plant built to EU Standards and, at a cost of US$900,000, a big investment.

At first the company sold 100 to 150 tons of fish a month, but in 2004, they reached the 1,000 ton mark. In 2003, the company's turnover was US$3.6 million, and around US$5.2 million was envisaged for 2004; in April 2004, they started opening export markets and there were strong indications that they would reach their US$5.2 million goal. Although the export markets are the main turnover generators for the company this doesn't mean the local markets will be neglected. However, although the local market is still very lucrative it has certain limits. It has helped Sierra Fishing to develop to this stage, but now it is time to look beyond national boundaries and to target the international markets.

Sierra Fishing's on shore landing is 100 per cent, which affects the economy directly by generating a lot of jobs. The Ministry of Fisheries and Marine Resources often complains to foreign companies because by carrying out most of their operations offshore they don't create jobs or involve local people. Sierra Fishing is changing that by bringing the industry back on shore. In 1999 they started with 30 employees and now have around 300 employees including casuals (178 are permanent workers while the rest work on contract).

Bassem Mohamed's father started the business. Originally in the diamond business, he was pulled into this investment through his contacts and at the beginning he did not believe in it. But later it turned out to be his major investment. Bassem also has a personal interest, since he likes fishing and diving. He took over the position of managing director in March 2003 and had to start from scratch as the company was heavily in debt; it is only through hard work and dedication that they have managed to reach the level where they are today. Internationally, there is still a lot to be done.

Sierra Fishing has had an important socio-economic impact on the development of the country, not only by providing jobs but also by providing the people with fish — and of course it is also a very good business. People don't invest their money in a charity but in order to make a profit. The country has a strong legal system to protect investors, and huge untapped fish and shrimp stocks. Sierra Fishing is looking forward to European companies with their advanced technology, coming to fish there, and bringing benefits. Bassem would like to see new European companies coming with their trawlers or fishing fleets because there is plenty of room for them.

(Source: 'Sierra Leone: on the path to recovery ', *World INvestment News*, 20 May 2004)

Liberia

In January 2006, Ellen Johnson-Sirleaf was sworn in as President of Liberia, Africa's oldest republic, making her Africa's first elected female leader. The ceremony was attended by Presidents Thabo Mbeki of South Africa, Nigeria's Olusegun Obasanjo, US First Lady Laura Bush, and Secretary of State Condoleezza Rice, among others. President Johnson-Sirleaf said her top challenge was to maintain peace, law, and order after 14 years of civil war in a country founded in 1847 by freed American slaves. She admitted knowledge of the fact that Liberians wanted change, peace, and security. She offered reassurance that she had heard them loudly. She vowed to wage a war on Liberia's 'major public enemy', corruption. This would start by leading civil servants and ministers declaring their assets. The President said her victory marked a new beginning for her country and for African women, and promised to lead by example. Saying that women have shattered the glass ceiling, she hoped they would seize the moment to become active in civil and political affairs at home and abroad.

The challenges which lay ahead as Johnson-Sirleaf began her six-year term were great. After a quarter of a century of war and misrule, Liberia's road network was in ruins; there was no national telephone network, national electricity grid or piped water. Unemployment ran at 80 per cent. Many of Liberia's three million people were illiterate. Hundreds of thousands were living in relief camps and many of the most educated were living overseas. A further challenge was to reintegrate the 100,000 ex-combatants, including many former child soldiers, into civilian life. She noted that it had been a long, hard journey to this happy ending. 2006 marked the beginning of a new era, the dawn of a new day for Liberia after so many years of turmoil and instability.

In her blueprint for improving the sagging Liberian economy, 'Liberia: A framework for change and renewal', presented at the Conference on the Liberian Economy on 4 November 1999, Harvard-educated economist Johnson-Sirleaf listed ten points of action to resuscitate Liberia. They included: (1) the need to formulate an economic vision — the determination of economic goals, consistent with national endowment, regional and global dynamics; (2) revisiting the system of land tenure so as to ensure that this fundamental resource is used in a manner that fosters the achievement of sustainable development goals; (3) revisiting the privileges and benefits of concession activities; (4) prioritising of agriculture; (5) restructuring and reform of the civil service; (6) revamping education and health; (7) improving economic infrastructure relating to roads, telecommunications, sea, airports and energy; (8) a secure environment; (9) regional cooperation and integration; and (10) gender empowerment.

The blueprint called for an environment of freedom, civil rights protection and the exercise of choice without penalty or repression, and hailed a political agenda that rebalances power between the presidency and the people. An imperial presidency which has the power of life or death, wealth or poverty, success or failure for everyone, and everyone in its hands, she observed, is an obstruction to progress. She decried monopolisation of power and privilege by any individual or ethnic group, and proposed a rotational system, which provides opportunity for all political subdivisions to have a chance at top leadership of the country.

Johnson-Sirleaf advised the opposition to be ready to play the role of what is called the loyal opposition, one which stresses loyalty to the nation, its people, laws, and prosperity, while strongly rejecting any course or action, particularly associated with violence that undermines the constitution, peace, and stability of the nation. Civil society, she noted, also has a role to play in ensuring that economic, social, and political systems provide the basis for growth and development. 'The real wealth of a nation is its people; and the purpose of development is to create an enabling environment for people to enjoy long, healthy, and creative lives,' she noted.

(Source: Josephat Juma, 'Mother Africa is born!', *The African Executive*, www.africanexecutive.com, Issue 39 (18-25 January 2006)

An entrepreneur in the Chicago area, Jackson Fiah Doe Jr, is very interested in helping equip Liberian entrepreneurs with skills and expertise requisite to becoming competitive and profitable, not only nationally but also internationally. In light of this, beginning in December 2006, he plans to conduct seminars and training on entrepreneurship at least twice a year in Liberia. Doe has a wealth of professional experience. He believes three excellent examples of successful Liberian-owned businesses that have succeeded are: Jungle Water Group of Investments (JWGI), The Liberian Observer Corporation, and Bonjal Fast Food Restaurant.

(Source: Jackson Fiah Doe Jr. 'Why many Liberian-owned businesses fail: A first person account', *The Perspective*, www.theperspective.org, 9 January 2006)

Founded by Tomah-Sehe Floyd, who is of Liberian and Lebanese lineage, Jungle Water Group of Investments (JWGI) is a conglomerate whose lines of business include stores and rental properties; buying and selling diamonds, gold, and cash crops; and providing electricity and DSTV services. Floyd's company saw its genesis during the Liberian civil war. At a time when businesses were fleeing Sanniquellie in droves because of security concerns, Floyd moved to the city. He saw an opportunity when no one else did. Undaunted by the political instability, he opened a store there. The store's value proposition was simple: offer customers all the basic essentials, everything from toiletries to food. As the only store in Sanniquellie, it quickly gained a critical mass of customers in the city and its environs, and he also won the loyalty of his customers. The store became so successful that Floyd broadened the scope of his business interests to include buying and selling diamonds, gold and cash crops. He purchased rental properties. Because of its numerous business ventures, Jungle Water Group of Investments has emerged as one of the most successful companies in Liberia, making Floyd one of Liberia's richest businessmen. Floyd calls on the government of President Sirleaf to create more conditions that would improve Liberia's business climate.

(Source: 'Take Liberia out of Monrovia', *Liberian Observer*: www.liberianobserver.com, 20 December 2005)

The Liberian Observer Corporation, which publishes the *Daily Observer*, saw its origins in 1981, when Kenneth Best founded it. Shortly thereafter, it emerged as the most trusted newspaper in the country. It was shut down numerous times by the Liberian government in the 1980s (it was critical of the Doe administration), and its publisher, Kenneth Best, was imprisoned. Despite these challenges, the newspaper did not go under. It kept operating. With the onset of the Liberian civil war, the Liberian *Observer* closed its doors, but it was revived in 2005. It also launched a very successful online site, which is frequented by thousands every day. The Liberian *Observer's* keys to success are its unwavering commitment to providing Liberians with quality news. The company should have crumbled during the Doe era but because of Best's tenacity the newspaper managed to survive amid difficulties and frustrations brought upon it by the government.

Another reason for the newspaper's success is its access to capital. Had it been undercapitalised, it wouldn't have survived. Additionally, Best made a great move by getting the next generation involved in the business. In 2005, he brought on board his daughter, Boto Bradford, as online editor. His son Bai is marketing manager of the company. Best has done a marvellous job of putting in place a succession plan, should he not be available to run the newspaper. This guarantees that the company will thrive well into the 21st century.

(Source: www.liberianobserver.com)

Founded by Samuel J Doe and his wife Annie, Bonjal Fast Food began in 1986 as a provision shop named Curve, which offered African dishes for lunch, and drinks from afternoon till late evening. Curve was renamed Bonjal in 1987, and its core business subsequently shifted to quality ice cream and fast food. In the late 1980, located just outside Monrovia on the Schiefflin-Robertsfield highway, which leads to Liberia's only international airport, Bonjal was a hot spot for college students. It was clean and comfortable, the quality of service was first class, the employees were helpful, the waiting time for orders was very short and the ice cream was delicious. It was always jam-packed, with standing room only. When the civil war started in 1989, the restaurant was forced to shut its doors but it re-opened in 1993 at a cost of about US$300,000 for renovations and equipment purchases. When the civil war flared up again in 1996, the owners again found themselves shutting the restaurant's doors. Now the restaurant is back. It re-opened, for the third time, before Christmas 2005, after Doe and his family invested an additional US$199,000.

More determined than ever to succeed, the company has plans to expand to the 16 counties. One of the reasons the restaurant has withstood the test of time has been its access to capital. If this was not so, it would not have re-opened for the third time. The restaurant has a very good relationship with its creditors, and the owners saved money, which they used to re-start the business. Its unwavering commitment to excellence has enabled Bonjal to enjoy success. Its entertainment environment is second to none in the country. Bonjal's employees are adequately trained. And of course the ice cream and fast food are of superior quality.

(Source: Kpeh-Kpeh Hindeh. 'Determined to rebuild and serve, Bonjal is back!'; www.liberianobserver.com, 12 December 2005)

The Haddad group of Companies is a multi-conglomerate of thriving business establishments headquartered in and around Monrovia, managed by the Haddad family and professional Liberians. The Haddad group is one of the largest corporate holdings in Liberia and includes the following listed companies:
- Bridgeway Corporation (BWC), importers of 110 lines of commodities and the mother company;
- The Alliance Motor Corporation (AMC), a vehicle company involved in the dealership/distributorship of Mercedes Benz, Volkswagen and Audi vehicles;
- The Liberia Group of Industries (LGI) is the only manufacturer of packaged fruit drink in the country. LGI is the producer of the famous Sun Top and Disco Drinks, managed by Ahed Haddad;
- Prestige Motor Corporation (PMC) involved in the dealership/distributorship of Land Rovers, BMW and Mitsubishi vehicles, managed by Elie Haddad; and
- Worldwide Impex (WWI), established in 1995 is involved in the purchasing, processing and exporting of cocoa and coffee.

The Haddad Group has carved for itself a very enviable record but, not content to rest on its laurels, is tirelessly working to sustain its position among the top businesses in the Liberian economy. George E Haddad, managing director, sums up the success of the Haddad group as resting on its firm reliance on professionalism.

The Group is pumping more lifeblood into the Liberian economy by diversification and has branched off into rice farming. The success story of the Haddad Group hopefully will stimulate more investors to venture into Liberia. The Haddad formula serves as an investment bible to lure entrepreneurs into Liberia. Haddad advises investors to come to Liberia and do some studies for themselves.

(Source: 'Too many opportunities, too few tappers ', 21 June 2001; www.winne.com)

Guinea

According to Madame Djéinabou Kanté, the growth and continued success of 'Raky Teinture', her cloth-dying business in Taouyah, Conakry, is due to the USAID-sponsored business training that she received in

1990. A schoolteacher by profession, Madame Kanté had long been supplementing her teaching income to support her family by dying cloth after her classes, an art that women in her family had been doing for generations. 'Still,' she says, 'I am a teacher by profession and I didn't know how to manage a business. I needed to learn business management to succeed.'

That changed, says Madame Kanté, after being sent on a three-week business training course at the University of Abidjan in Côte d'Ivoire, sponsored by USAID, where she learned a lot about money management. 'Before, I simply dyed cloth and sold it. I used the money from the sales for my personal needs, to buy shoes or something for the kids, and then I didn't always have enough money to invest back into my business. I learned that I needed to separate the funds, and that even though I run the business, I myself need to have a fixed salary, and that I shouldn't use the money set aside for the business to buy a dress for myself, for example. Before, I thought, 'Money is money, I'll spend it as I like,' but I learned that you can't run a business that way. I learned these basic management skills through the training.'

In 1991, Madame Kanté was again chosen among a group of six businesswomen to go on a USAID-sponsored training group in the US. As part of the training, the women visited a number of successful small businesses, many of which were run by African-American women. Through training, Madame Kanté learned about marketing, and the importance of knowing, and showing, what set her products off from others. 'We've always had a high-quality product, and still do, and that's why people come here, so that's what we advertise.'

Raky Teinture is now one of the best known names in Conakry for high-quality hand-dyed products. Her biggest sales come from batik tablecloths, though she also sells ready-made clothes, travel and handbags, backpacks, placemats, sheets and other items made with her characteristic African designs. Since her first training course in 2000, Madame Kanté has expanded her business, selling a higher volume of products and taking on more employees to help with the ever-increasing workload.

One of the biggest advantages of running a successful business, according to Madame Kanté, has been her ability to finance her children's education. 'The extra income helped me a lot, particularly with keeping my kids in school. They all did well and completed their high school degrees, which is not too bad for here in Guinea.'

Madame Kanté used to export her wares to France. In 2000, she found a reliable business contact in the US who is able to stay in touch by fax or phone, so she has started exporting some of her merchandise to Washington. Her client sends patterns of clothes that she thinks will suit the tastes of her American business clientele, and Madame Kanté's tailors then make the clothes out of her signature cloth for sale in the US. The extra business helped finance her three sons' college education in the US.

Madame Kanté says, 'With our work, you have to have a lot of initiative. You want to always have something new that your customers can discover when they come in. That's what sets Raky Teinture apart.'

(Source: Laura Lartigue. 'Madame Kanté: Making good on USAID-sponsored training'. www.usaid.gov, updated: February 2006).

Where can African businesswomen go to market their wares, promote new product lines, find competitive suppliers, or strike up new ventures? Hadja Mariama Bah, owner of a women's clothing enterprise in Guinea, has gone online. Hadja had always conducted business in person or through the mail, frequently relying on word of mouth to establish, maintain and expand her network of clients and partners. In 2005, through a USAID-supported programme, Hadja learned to use the Internet as a business tool for operational savings and also for access to a wider market and, therefore, increased revenues. USAID cooperated with the African Businesswomen's Information Service (ABIS) to bring Guinean women entrepreneurs, like Hadja and daughter Kadiatou Diallo, into a cyber cafe to learn the basics of computer use and how to access the Internet to enhance their businesses.

(Source: USAID Success Stories, 'Cyber skills bring business success'. www.usaid.gov)

A distinguished African businesswoman, Hadja M'Mah Sampil, was born in Kankan, attended primary school in Dakar and Conakry and secondary school in Conakry, and later earned the baccalaureate degree. Subsequently, she attended midwife school in Dakar and Algeria, earning a midwife degree in 1971. For the next 10 years she worked as a midwife, until 1981, when she started her first business. Since that time, with a tender touch, she has distinguished herself in the tough business world. She opened a sewing workroom in 1982. In 1984, she created a fire security company. In 1985, she started a duty free shop at the new airport in Conakry. And, in 1988, she created a printing house. With each of these businesses, she has forged new ground, blazed forbidden pathways and maintained a stature, as a woman, unmatched by most. While visiting the United States in 1993 as part of a Guinea delegation, she established herself as an effective ambassador of goodwill on behalf of her country.

Senegal

Manobi Sénégal was the overall winner in the organisational category of the African ICT Achievers Awards in November 2004, and was also named Africa's most innovative company. The four-year-old company has developed a multi-channel service platform (MCSP), which is able to provide value-added services through any telecommunications infrastructure. It seeks to provide cost-effective African-designed solutions that target rural areas in developing countries. The MCSP supplies sectors including commerce, agriculture and fisheries with a range of innovative services, such as business assistance, supply chain management and safety services. Information can be delivered through voice, WAP (Wireless Application Protocol), SMS (Short Messaging Service), MMS (Multimedia Messaging Service) and the Internet.

Founder and general manager Daniel Annerose says Manobi Sénégal aims at fighting poverty through modern technology. The Dakar-born Annerose has partners in different parts of Africa and abroad. He also has strategic partners in South Africa. He obtained a Ph D in vegetal biology from the University of Paris VII, has a degree in computer science from the University of Paris XI, and describes himself as permanently hooked into the field of ICTs. He has 20 years of experience as a scientist and developer in the field of rural agriculture and agro-industry in tropical countries. In his experience the impact of liberalisation and globalisation on small African farmers is enormous. They cannot compete in that market if they do not have access to certain information or to the data that their competitors have. He says Manobi wants to provide low-cost innovative services within the mobile sector of telecommunications and the Internet. By doing so, they want to contribute to the social and economical development of people. The company has developed what it calls a multi-channel service platform, which comprises software and hardware containing all the elements needed to access different services, such as Internet, SMS, WAP, MMS, EMS (Enhanced Messaging Service), iMode (packet-based means of wireless data transfer), and USSD (Unstructured Supplementary Services Data) from a single voice mobile network.

Manobi's innovative Internet and wireless e-services for the strengthening of Senegalese fisherman artisans is a project started in early 2003. This project uses WAP and SMS technology via cell phones to provide fishermen with up-to-date weather reports and market price information. In addition the fishermen are able to use the interactiveness of the technology to input fish stock information for marketing purposes, and to log their departures and estimated times of return, so that local fishing unions can be alerted if fishing boats fail to return on time. Manobi has also developed a rescue system for fishermen, using GSM and satellite tracking, which can cover areas up to 70 kilometres out to sea. One of the fishing unions reported how the service enabled them to detect and rescue one of their members and their eight-man crew that had not returned on time. The service also potentially enables fishermen to improve the quality of their products — by alerting all potential buyers (middlemen) as soon as they have landed their catch, the fish can be sold while still very fresh. Typically up to 30 per cent of the catch of artisan fishermen may be wasted while the fishermen wait to find a buyer.

An African farmer in Senegal can use his cell phone to check the market price for his crops and thus be in a good negotiating position when it comes to selling these crops. Manobi uses teams to gather information about the prices of foods and goods being sold in the markets in and around Dakar. Ordinarily, farmers have no way of finding out the prices before they travel to the market, or even if their crop is in short supply at a particular place. According to Annerose, middlemen often take advantage of this ignorance and offer to buy crops at prices far lower than they would get if they travelled to market themselves. The differences in prices can be significant. One farmer using Manobi's service found that he could get more than twice as much for grapefruit than he was offered by the middle men. Manobi independently collects prices and uploads them to its central database using mobile phones that dial in to the server via WAP. The price collectors note the price of every item they come across, be it garlic, peanuts, aubergines or any other food. Farmers in the field can use their mobile phones to check prices before they set off and find out where they will get the best offer for their produce. They can even check what European or American importers would pay.

Through this system, Manobi is creating a platform where all parties concerned with business transactions can find each other and interact — and not only on information concerning price of stock. It is also a platform where business relationships can be built and ideas exist. The secret of Manobi is that they try to keep the costs to a minimum for their customers. Prices are kept low and farmers pay for the service as part of a deal between Manobi and the national telephone company. It's well adapted to a cash economy. Farmers don't want to have a bill every month. As an open source company they developed cost-effective technology and services and in addition, a large group of small farmers and fishermen uses these services, at low costs. Finally, some clients are big companies that will pay a lot more because they use the services much more.

Manobi is a game the children play in Senegal. If one child says he will jump over that fountain, then the other children have to do the same. It is a game of challenges and therefore Annerose chose it for his company. The biggest challenge for Annerose in 2004 was expanding Manobi into a pan-African company, but winning an African ICT Achievers Award in 2004 will help him achieve that goal since the award will help him find partners and investors. With offices in Senegal and France, Annerose is in the process of setting up a South African office. Manobi wants to bring to South Africa its technology, its experience and its understanding of their customers and their needs.

Annerose says that although several European countries have already expressed an interest in the company's technology, Africa remains its focus. Its biggest market is still in Africa, as the company has a deep understanding of the market and has developed technology specifically for it. Nonetheless, they would be very proud if they were able to spin a strong European service out of their African market, and perhaps by taking an African service into the developed world, they may just help to change its image of the developing world.

(Source: www.manobi.net; Rodney Weidemann. 'African operator targets SA, Europe', *IT Web* www.itweb.co.za, 12 October 2004; and Ellen Hollemans, 'Roll out the red carpet for ICT', Johannesburg: *Mail & Guardian Online* www.mg.co.za, 5 November 2004)

The founders of a Senegalese cartoon studio described some of the challenges they overcame to put Africa on the animation map in the September-October 2005 edition of *WIPO Magazine*. 'Unless we know how to sell our culture, others will sell it for us, 'says Pierre Sauvalle, founder and co-director of Pictoon. 'The art industry is really important to Africa because it creates an image of us,' says Pictoon co-director, Aïda Ndiaye.

Sylvie Castonguay of the World Intellectual Property Organisation (WIPO) in Geneva tells us that Africa's traditional heritage is rich in storytelling, so it seems altogether fitting that the first animated film series to come out of the continent is about Kabongo the griot, a West African storyteller. Kabango strides through the countries of the world, his singing monkey Golo at his side, searching for a worthy pupil to whom he can pass on his art and skills. In each country he encounters misfortune and adventure and, through his storytelling, reveals the magic in the myths and legends of the country's past.

The 13-part cartoon series, the first to be entirely made in Africa, is the work of a small animation studio, Pictoon, based in Senegal's capital Dakar. Broadcast on the Canal France International (CFI) satellite service in December, 2003, Kabongo was an instant hit. 'It's a magnificent series, very ambitious, and very African,' CFI's programming director, Pierre Block de Freiberg, told *TIME Europe* Magazine in August 2004.

Kabongo was the brainchild of Pierre Sauvalle, who set up Pictoon in 1998 together with his co-director, Senegalese businesswoman Aïda Ndiaye. Sauvalle had worked for eight years in French production companies after graduating from the renowned animation school, Les Gobelins, in Paris. But he had always nursed the desire to return to Africa in order to start creating genuinely African productions. He engaged both African and French writers to work on the screenplay for Kabongo, but the storyboards, the animation, the colorization and the editing were all done by Pictoon in Dakar. Only post-production work (i.e. sound) was done in France.

With Kabongo, Pictoon has put Africa on the map of the animation industry and proved that Africa can produce seamless, high-quality cartoons. But that is just the start of Pictoon's ambitions. While the company could earn more than enough by producing local television commercials to keep it in business, its real aim is to attract some of the US$75 billion global animation industry its way.

Sauvalle and Ndiaye are unfazed by the challenge. So far they have found solutions to every difficulty they have encountered, be it a shortage of qualified artists, the power outages, or the problems of obtaining computer equipment and software appropriate for their use and sturdy enough for their environment. Unable to find trained cartoon artists, Sauvalle began training them himself. He set up a two-year drawing and computer-animation apprenticeship for promising young artists whom he talent scouted locally. As the apprentices gain experience and master the necessary skills, they in turn teach new arrivals. During busy periods, Pictoon now employs up to 120 people, all of them trained on site.

Other problems that Pictoon could not resolve, they worked around. 'You can put in all the surge protectors you like, but it doesn't change a thing,' says Ndiaye, the company's managing director. 'Every year we have to replace the entire computer system. '

The wages paid to the art apprentices in Senegal, which is classified as one of the world's least developed countries, allow Pictoon to compete on cost grounds with Asian countries, such as South Korea, to whom European and U.S. animation production firms currently outsource much of their artwork. Combining low costs with high quality — which Sauvalle notes has impressed animation professionals around the world — Pictoon is shaping up to be a serious competitor in the global marketplace.

But Pictoon does not want business at any cost. Its founders are determined to continue producing their own films in order to remain true to their cultural heritage. They plan to create more African cartoons, inspired from legends and stories that have been passed from father to son for generations. Such stories, they believe, hold a universal appeal. Following the success of Kabongo in France and across francophone Africa, Sauvalle is confident that the soon-to-be released English version will capture the world market.

Pictoon understands the value of its intellectual property and has registered Kabongo with the French collective management society, the Society of Authors and Composers of Dramatic Works. But Sauvalle is deeply concerned that the costs involved in protecting intellectual property are proportionally so much greater for developing countries. 'The cost of registering creations and applying for patents is often simply beyond the means of creators from African countries,' he observes. He would like to see fees waived for the poorest countries like Senegal, so that creators could register their works for free, 'just as a father registering the birth of his new child.'

(Source: 'Putting Africa on the animation map - the story of Pictoon, Senegal', *WIPO Magazine*, Geneva, September-October 2005)[1]

In 2001, Mamadou Cissokho, a Senegalese peasant farmer, was awarded the Rene Dumont French prize to honour 'his work in the service of the land and those who live on it'. Cissokho was particularly hailed for his involvement since 1977 in creating a village development committee in the Bamba-Thialene zone of Senegal. The association has since expanded to involve rural farmers from ten other countries of the West Africa region in rural development activities; part of these activities include the exchange of information and networking among rural farmers in the area of improved credit management as well as better natural resource management. Cissokho says that the prize was recognition of the struggle that peasant farmers in Africa have engaged in for the development of their countries. He is concerned that Africa is unable to be self-sufficient in food and yet the continent is rich in land and human resources and has a relatively good climate. He believes that the major handicap preventing the sector from playing a leading role in the continent's overall development is poor agricultural policies. 'Food production today cannot be attained unless we in Africa are better organised, and that is what we as rural farmers have begun to do through networking and the exchanging of ideas,' he states. He says African governments must respect peasant farmers and listen to their views before taking any decisions involving the sector if agriculture on the continent is to be boosted. For Cissokho, such close collaboration with farmers could begin by African governments refusing to imitate models that are not suitable for the continent. He says Africa must come up with its own agricultural models that best respond to the continent's needs.

Cissokho condemns what he terms subsidised agricultural exports from the North, which hurt poor farmers in Africa through the low prices they receive for their sweat. On the impact of genetically modified crops on the continent's agricultural sector, Cissokho says Africa should not embrace everything that is flouted as the panacea to its problems without weighing the long-term impact. Solutions must come from within and be rooted in models that are in the best interests of the continent. 'Africa should not take genetically modified food to be a priority or to be the only solution to its agricultural problems,' says Cissokho, the President of the Conseil National de Concertation des Ruraux (CNCR).

(Source: www.cncr.org, and 'Senegalese scoops French agriculture award', *Africa News Service*, 26 February 2001)

The development of both residential and commercial properties and infrastructure is critical for the economic growth of African countries and many individuals and companies have achieved great successes by establishing businesses in this sector. One such individual is Pierre Atepa Goudiaby, who is responsible for the design of some of Africa's most stunning buildings. Born in 1953, Goudiaby comes from the far-flung village of Baila, in Senegal's southern Casamance region, and was raised in the Medina, Dakar's tough inner-city slum. He now lives in the city's Fann suburb with his family. He has become not only one of Africa's top architects but a power-broker in the region and friend and advisor to African leaders. The architect's first love was acting, and as a boy he led a theatre troupe, but his parents said it was not a proper profession and then he realised that with architecture he could turn his dreams into reality. Guodiaby's first major buildings were banks. He wanted customers to see a vision of Africa in his buildings that would make them feel that this was where they wanted to put their money. His 25-storey West Africa Central Bank in Dakar is modelled on the sacred baobab tree, where village elders traditionally go to discuss important matters.

Recently, Goudiaby has been focused on The Gambia, a country that until recently didn't have a structure taller than four floors. Now, his new 250-bed hospital in the bush town of Farafenni might be mistaken for Africa's first space station, while the international airport, which opened in August 2002, looks like it could fly itself. Goudiaby's futuristic palace, monuments and grand public buildings can be seen in towns and cities all over West and Central Africa. From his Dakar headquarters, a giant pyramid, Pierre Goudiaby's Africa of tomorrow is planned using the latest technologies from all over the world, from which he makes his creations look and feel African.

(Source: www.atepa.com)

Côte d'Ivoire

The Aga Khan Fund for Economic Development (AKFED) is an international development agency which promotes entrepreneurship in the private sector in specific regions of the developing world. A for-profit institution, the fund helps to build economically viable enterprises through strong equity participation combined with management and technical expertise and support. AKFED companies promote sustainable economic development in south and central Asia and sub-Saharan Africa with projects in industry, tourism and financial services. The developing world needs more electricity, telephones, clean water and transport, and governments are encouraging the private sector to take a role in providing these basic services. AKFED is responding to the challenge and is looking at infrastructure projects in telecommunications, water and sewerage, and power generation. The Azito project is AKFED's first investment in the power sector and will shortly be followed by two other energy projects in East and West Africa. The Azito power facility is the largest private sector power plant in sub-Saharan Africa, developed and operated by the Swiss/Swedish ABB Energy Ventures, the French Electricité de France, and AKFED's venture capital arm in West Africa, Industrial Promotion Services. With the second phase of development completed, Azito is the largest gas-fired power station in West Africa.

The 288 megawatt project, developed on a build-own-transfer basis, commenced electricity production in March 1999, makes use of Côte d'Ivoire's offshore natural gas as fuel and is one of the lowest cost generators in Africa. Ocean Energy, Inc is an independent energy company engaged in the exploration, development, production and acquisition of crude oil and natural gas. Ocean holds a leading position among US independents in West Africa with oil and gas activities in Equatorial Guinea, Angola and Cote d'Ivoire. Ocean's offshore fields produce natural gas pumped through a pipeline to the Azito thermal power plants onshore. At full production, Azito produces 30 per cent of Côte d'Ivoire's electricity requirements and exports surplus electricity to neighbouring countries. The Azito project is a good example of the relevance of private sector support in economic development, responding to the growing demand in the developing world for improved and reliable infrastructure services.

(Source: www.akdn.org)

Mme Botti Rosalie is the president of Cocovico (Coopérative des commerçantes des produits vivriers de la commune de Cocody), an all-women's cooperative established in 1997. Cocovico is involved in the marketing of farm produce, normally supplied from almost all the major producing areas of Côte d'Ivoire, and also from Burkina Faso and Niger for fresh tomatoes and onions. Cocovico is based in the Marché d'Angré, a commune de Cocody market located in northern Angré in Abidjan. The market is built on a surface of 5,200 m^2 including 1,200 m^2 not yet exploited. This market currently has 59 storage areas and more than 1,000 displays, covered to avoid the bad weather, as well as toilets. To have a display, it is necessary to pay to be a member of Cocovico, and for the acquisition of a table. Mme Rosalie was the initiator of the project, which included the electrification and the asphalting of the market.

Togo

Shea butter has been used for centuries on the African continent and is enmeshed within the history and culture of the West African wooded savannah. Shea butter is mentioned in almost all African historical documents, including a reference as early as Cleopatra's Egypt, which mentions caravans bearing clay jars of shea butter for cosmetic use. Funeral beds of kings were carved in wood of old shea trees, and shea butter has always been a staple of African pharmacology.

Shea butter is the oil from the nuts that are gathered from wild trees scattered throughout the fields and forests of the wooded savannah. It has many useful properties and has been used as a decongestant, as an anti-inflammatory for sprains and arthritis, as a healing salve for babies' umbilical cords and after circumcision, as a lotion for hair and skin care, as a cooking oil, and as a lamp fuel — but its protective and emollient properties are most valued for skin care. Shea butter is a main ingredient in local soap production, and is applied to the skin and hair directly to protect them from drying out in the harsh African environment. It is an important natural resource for the savannah nations.

Until recently, Europeans have controlled all shea butter for export by purchasing the shea kernels and chemically extracting the oil using hexane. Chemically extracted shea butter, however, does not retain all the healing and moisturising properties of the traditionally-made product.

(Source: Michel Pobeda. 'Shea butter: the revival of an African wonder', Global Cosmetic Industry, April 1999)

Shea butter is a major part of the lives of many people in central and northern Togo. Since the 1960s, the Tchala and Agbanga families have been involved in gathering, making, and selling traditional shea butter in regional markets. In early 2003, Olowo-n'djo Tchala took the family business to another level by creating the Agbanga Karité Group, a multi-ethnic, member-controlled, and decentralised organization that produces, exports, and wholesales high quality, traditional unrefined shea butter, African black soap, and other indigenous products. Agbanga Karité's shea butter is produced using traditional techniques that preserve the healing and moisturising properties.

The goal of this organisation is to help empower the women of Togo by providing them with a means of bringing the products of their indigenous knowledge and wisdom to the rest of the world while receiving a fair, living wage for their efforts. Olowo-n'djo named this organisation Agbanga Karité to honour his mother's name and the years of struggle she endured to raise her family. The Agbanga Karité Group strives to be an example for other African organisations to follow by adhering to fair trade and organic production guidelines and giving back a percentage of earnings to its communities.

Agbanga has a main shea butter processing centre at Sokodé, Togo, with 60 permanent employees and a production capacity of 100 metric tons per year. A customer relations office in Olympia, Washington, facilitates sales and follow up with customers in the United States. Agbanga also runs a training centre and brings in local experts from different ethnic groups to exchange ideas about, and methods of, traditional shea butter production. Agbanga is also working with local ethnic groups to find ways to preserve the shea trees.

(Source: www.agbangakarite.com, and August 2005 e-mail correspondence with Olowo-n'djo Tchala)

Benin

Journalist John Matshikiza writes that Godfrey Nzamujo is a humble Catholic priest (in fact a monk) with a farm project in Benin. The Songhai Centre, Nzamujo's brainchild, was born in 1985. In that year Father Godfrey stepped into the small West African republic of Benin, neighbour to his native Nigeria, and asked the government of President Mathieu Kerekou for a piece of land to try out an experiment in small-scale sustainable development. Kerekou granted him a few acres just outside Benin's second city Porto Novo. Nzamujo took possession of the unpromising piece of swampland that he had been granted and he created something remarkable. His guiding principle was: 'The only way to fight poverty is to transform the poor person into an active producer.' His way of doing this was to create a living and teaching environment where ordinary Africans could learn the skills of self-advancement.

Applying all he had learned over the years about mechanical and electronic engineering, farming, economics, business, and husbandry in general (spiritual and temporal) he set about turning his vast, abstract knowledge into something practical. In less than 20 years, Nzamujo has developed an environment where the small portion of land produces pawpaw, bananas, giant mushrooms, pigs, a furry and nutritious rodent known as 'bush meat', cabbages, fish, chickens, ducks, turkeys, manioc, sheep, cattle, rabbits, giant snails, various varieties of beans, maize, cashew nuts, mangoes, rice, and sunflowers. These are harvested and transformed into consumable and saleable goods at the centre's bakery, cannery, bottling facility, restaurant and countless other mini-industries in this mini-economic environment. There are also mechanical workshops where young men and women make machinery to speedily husk maize and perform other vital agricultural tasks for small-scale farming, and the IT centre where communication skills are transferred to the young people of the community.

Nzamujo's masterpiece is the creation of a utopian African village in microcosm. The village is simply a living diagram of a sustainable model of production and survival. The centrepiece is the lavatory block; since human beings consume so much of what they themselves produce, recycling their own waste is the key to creating a self-sustaining environment. At Songhai, septic tanks are anathema. What you eat and drink goes straight into collection channels beneath the lavatory block, and is processed through a series of canals into a pool, where it is all cleansed through the natural agent of water hyacinths ('God put everything on earth for a reason,' says Nzamujo, putting an interesting new spin on battles that have been fought against this foreign-imported river plant from the Nile to the Niger) and then recycled back into the bio-system that has produced all the consumables. This recycling system not only produces fertilisers for the farm and makes it possible for used water to be recycled: it is capable of producing a power supply for the whole village. For example, the key communal functions of cooking, eating, and bonding take place around gas fires rather than the traditional wood-burning hearth; and the gas fires even provide sources of light, which have always been regarded as the remote and prohibitively expensive province of government.

Nzamujo has expanded his Songhai experiment well beyond the original smallholding near Porto Novo to include five others in Benin and another two sites in neighbouring Nigeria and the Songhai programme will soon start in Gabon and Congo Brazzaville. All are thriving examples of how African ingenuity can be made to work for Africa, rather than having to be exported to survive, and leaving its major work behind. Nzamujo's visions should be a central part of the much heralded New Partnership for Africa's Development and his models for economic development should be exported to other needy parts of Africa, to become part of a true attack on poverty and starvation.

Authorities in Liberia invited Father Nzamujo to see how the Songhai concept could help in rebuilding their war ravished country. He went around the country in August 2005, and he was overwhelmed by what needs to be done to get the country back on its feet. He paid a visit to Ellen Johnson-Sirleaf during this visit, and she demonstrated a strong determination to do every thing in her power to restore hope in Liberia. Nzamujo assured her of his prayers and willingness to work with her, and believes her presidential platform is a strong base for the reconstruction of Liberia. Liberia needs help and Nzamujo will be very delighted to be of help. He believes Africans should not miss this opportunity in Liberia, an opportunity for courage and unbending determination to change things in Africa, despite all the problems.

(Source: John Matshikiza. 'Africa's arsenal: the sustainable village', 24 June 2003, from online magazine www.opendemocracy.net; and January 2006 e-mail correspondence from Godfrey Nzamujo, website www.songhai.org)

Samuel Dossou-Aworet heads the Petrolin Group, an African owned upstream and downstream oil group, with significant African business interests. Since 1996, besides its involvement in the oil industry in Africa and the Middle East, the Petrolin Group has been developing, whenever possible, humanitarian and social activity through its subsidiary Fondation Espace Afrique (FEA). By providing free education and medical care and promoting culture and artistic talents, the Petrolin Group contributes to the improvement of the social conditions of disadvantaged rural populations in several African countries.

In Glo-djigbé in Benin, FEA is entirely financing the International Center for Experimentation and Enhancement of African Resources (ICEEAR). This project adopts an integrated approach to Africa development. It relies on local and traditional African resources to help the population become self-sufficient and capable of fulfilling their social and economic needs.

The ICEEAR started its activities in early 2004 and concentrates on two programmes. The objective of the Programme of Experimentation and Research on Pharmacopoeia and Health through Plants is to mobilise African human resources and knowledge of traditional pharmacopoeia to promote treatments made of African natural products. ICCEEAR's botanical garden is used as an educational tool in this programme, to teach the curative and nutritive properties of African plants. The goal of the Programme of Professional

Training and Support to the Creation of Micro-Projects is to strengthen African entrepreneurs' capacity to create and manage their own projects, and to facilitate their access to micro-credit. The main areas of activity are agriculture, carpentry, sewing, mechanical engineering and computer science.

This project comprises a conference room of 500 seats, more than 30 rooms equipped for training workshops, conferences, computer science, research and documentation, as well as a hotel, a medical centre and a campus with the capacity to accommodate more than 300 students.

(Source: E-mail correspondence; www.petrolin.com/humanitaire.htm; and www.f-spaceafrique.com)

Burkina Faso

Bernard Lédéa Ouedraogo, a teacher turned agriculturist, is the founder and leader of Africa's largest and most successful movement for self-reliance. He is a bold, visionary leader who has inspired hundreds of thousands of small-scale farmers. Having realised early in his career that government-organized cooperatives were not accepted by the people, Ouedraogo searched for a better way to stimulate the participation of farmers in the improvement of their own circumstances. In his own Mossi society, there existed a traditional structure called *Kombi-Naam*, in the local Mooré tongue, which gathered all the young men and women in a village for various agricultural, cultural and social activities. They were traditional youth associations, composed of girls aged 15 to 21 and young men of 20 to 35, with the purpose of both developing moral qualities such as solidarity, cooperation, friendship and loyalty in the young, and at the same time accomplishing socially useful tasks for the village. Positions within the *Naam* were not at all based on caste or social status, but rather on ability. The *Kombi-Naam* traditionally provided moral, civic and technical training for the village youth.

Since 1967, as a result of Ouedraogo's tireless work and leadership, in the closest collaboration with the villagers, the traditional *Kombi-Naam* mechanism has been transformed into pioneering, modern, self-help groups, open to all. The *Naam* became a form of development adapted to local needs, created by the people themselves, which instead of destroying traditional structures from the outside, slowly, like leaven, transforms them from the inside. It starts from where people are (based on a true appreciation of their African identity), what they know (respect for traditional knowledge and values), their know-how (rediscovery of traditional techniques, some of which, for example in the field of water and soil conservation, have proven invaluable) and what they wish to achieve (which implies meaningful grassroots participation in defining the very objectives of the development process).

The transition from the traditional to the modern *Naam* was gentle, enabling village groups to adapt little by little to their new roles. One important change was the opening up of the *Naam* to people of all ages, thereby involving the whole village rather than just one age group. The modern *Naams* also nominate counsellors from among the village elders, an innovation in line with the African tradition of respect for the wisdom of the elders. The *Naams* are primarily involved in village agricultural development, but they also work in income-generating activities.

Ouedraogo had built a community development institution to deal with migration and the erosion of village institutions. The *Kombi-Naam* was transformed from a temporary association into an institution that retained its membership over a period of years. As the lifespan of the institution was extended, it assumed responsibility for more ambitious projects such as land reclamation, the building of dams and reservoirs, revolving credit funds, and the operation of grain banks. In the late 1980s there were over 4,000 Naam and affiliated groups in the Yatenga area of Burkina Faso, with well over 200,000 members — unquestionably one of the largest, most powerful peasant organisations in Africa, and a formidable force for development. The *Naams* represent the triumph of the idea of developing without harming. In November 1988, the *Naam* movement declared its goal of ending chronic, persistent hunger in their villages. As of the early 1990s, the *Naam* institution had diffused broadly in northern Burkina Faso, Mali, and Senegal. The 'renovation' of traditional community groups can be an effective strategy for participatory development.

Ouedraogo is also co-founder of the 'Six-S' association, which embraces 3,600 village development groups in nine West African countries: Burkina Faso, Chad, The Gambia, Guinea-Bissau, Mali, Mauritania, Niger, Senegal and Togo. Six-S is almost unique in that it provides un-tied aid. Trusting the African people to find the best routes to economic and social advancement, funds entrusted to Six-S by donor countries are given to responsible local organisations as development loans with no strings attached. Six-S currently involves hundreds of thousands of individuals and benefits millions more. Ouedraogo's leadership and dedication to the people of Africa have brought him worldwide recognition. In 1987 he was awarded the UN World Environment Prize and the Unicef Prize for Peace. The Hunger Project acknowledged Ouedraogo's extraordinary contribution to humanity by awarding him the 1989 Africa Prize for Leadership for the Sustainable End of Hunger.

(Source: Address by Dr Bernard Lédéa Ouedraogo on the occasion of receiving the 1989 Africa Prize for Leadership, 14 September 1989, www.thp.org; Paul Harrison. 1987. *The Greening of Africa: Breaking Through in the Battle for Land and Food*. London: Paladin Grafton Books, 1987 (pp. 279-84); and Takehiko Uemura, Takehiko, 'Sustainable rural development in western Africa: The Naam Movement and the Six S', FAO Rural Development Division, www.fao.org)

Salif Yameogo is president and CEO of Groupe Soyaf, chairman of Telecel Faso since its creation, and president of the Burkina Faso Hoteliers and Restaurateurs Association. Born in 1949, Salif is a self-made man and a very successful entrepreneur. Equipped with experience in all the economic sectors of the Burkina Faso economy, Salif has directed the group since its creation in 1982. Groupe Soyaf is a company of international standard. Initially centred on a chain of three star hotels located in the two principal cities of Burkina Faso, the activities of the group quickly extended into various economic sectors such as real estate, mobile telecommunication, distribution of food stuffs, and the management of a casino and night club. In 2002, Groupe Soyaf opened a new four-star hotel in Bobo Dioulasso, the second city of Burkina Faso. The group now has three hotels in Burkina Faso that employ more than 225 people, and wants to be the ideal partner for multinationals in their development of the Burkina Faso market.

Salif's first chief managing deputy is his son, Cheick Kader Yameogo. Born in December 1975, Cheick Kader received his bachelor degree in economics at the University of Montreal and his MBA at Pepperdine University in California. After a passage at Ernst & Young in Paris and Los Angeles, he joined the group in 2000.

Since May 2002, Groupe Soyaf has been involved in the mineral water business. It established a new mineral water plant that produces and sells a mineral water called JIRMA. The new activity is managed directly by Cheick Kader and the unit has created about 45 new jobs and a total investment of US$2.7 million.

After its first six months, Soyaf Soft Drinks had a 58 per cent share of the market. From that point their strategy has been to diversify their activities in order to reach all the different social classes of the country. In January 2003, Soyaf started to produce mineral water in sachets and, in one week, sold all the production planned for four months. In December 2003, they began offering five gallon bottles and the dispensers for big corporations. That also was a big success, and now they are number one in the mineral water sector in Burkina Faso, and export the product to Niger — where they are also number one. The technical staff in the plant has accumulated extensive know-how regarding all the machines needed to produce mineral water.

Since July 2003, Cheick Kader has been in partnership with Edouard Napiontek, the owner of SEDI (the French company that has manufactured and sold to Soyaf Soft Drinks the entire equipment for the mineral water plant) in order to represent the brand SEDI in Africa. Soyaf has been involved since July 2003 in the selling of bottling equipment and production line in partnership with SEDI and Cheick Kader is the Associé-Directeur Régional of SEDI that makes 985 of its sales in Africa. Soyaf has already sold equipment in Niger, Algeria, Tunis, Côte d'Ivoire and Mali. Cheick Kader's job is to promote SEDI equipment in Africa and his team guarantees the after-sales service and maintenance of the SEDI equipment. In the future they aim to consolidate their position by continuing to give a very high quality product to their customers. Since they have the distribution network, they are planning to install another plant that will produce natural juice and take advantage of the network.

(Source: www.groupe-soyaf.com)

Mali

Mossadeck Bally, well-known Malian businessman, is chairperson of the Grand Hotel de Bamako, one of the main establishments in the capital of Mali. This medium-size hotel in the heart of the capital city was built by private investors in 1952, nationalised by a Marxist-oriented military regime after independence in the 1960s, and reverted to private management following the return to democracy and free markets in the 1990s. The 74-room, three-storey hotel is a prestigious building that combines both traditional and modern architectural designs. It is located in the administrative area of Bamako, close to the main official buildings and the railway station. Since the 1960s, the hotel had been owned by the Societe des hotelleries du Mali (SHM), a public company. Various attempts were made in the 1980s to renovate the state-run hotel and privatise its management. Over more than a decade, leasing contracts were signed for this purpose. In spite of the multiple changes in status and management, the SHM was unable to transform it into a successful and profitable venture.

In 1993, the government decided to fully privatize the hotel. Several offers were received and the sale was awarded to a group headed by Mossadeck Bally. The group had the support of the Africa Enterprise Fund/International Finance Corporation (AEF/IFC). The project consisted of buying and renovating the Grand Hotel. It took about a year to complete the renovation of the hotel, set up a management team and train the staff. The new hotel opened in March 1995. Privatisation is paying off. Results obtained so far show that a real turnaround has taken place. Clients generally agree that service is excellent by international standards and management has received high marks for efficiency. Since then, the IFC has supported Bally in the building of the Hotel Salam in Bamako, and in November 2005, they approved supporting Bally in the renovation and expansion of the Hotel Independence into a three-star international business hotel with 180 rooms, located in Ouagadougou, Burkina Faso.

(Source: www.ifc.org)

Mossadeck Bally is a member of the West African Enterprise Network, which was launched in 1993 in West Africa and expanded to East and Southern Africa in 1998. Today, the Enterprise Network initiative involves over 500 businesspeople who belong to one of 30 national units which, in turn, make up three regional enterprise networks: the West African Enterprise Network (WAEN), the East African Enterprise Network (EAEN) and the Southern African Enterprise Network (SAEN). The dual mission of each of the regional enterprise networks is to improve the business climate in member countries and to promote cross-border trade and investment in its geographic region. To achieve this mission, Enterprise Network members pursue four common objectives: enhance the competitiveness of individual member firms, facilitate access to financing, improve business information flows and promote opportunities for regional economic integration.

Laurent Coche is the United Nations Development Programme administrator responsible for the multifunctional platform programme, a programme to install multi-purpose power platforms in 500 Malian villages, and to put local women in charge of them. Laurent says they are empowering women in work that traditionally has been theirs. This does not require fancy new technology. The strategy is simple, elegant and effective: help an organisation of village women finance the purchase of a multifunctional platform built around a sturdy and simple one-cylinder diesel motor that has a long record of versatile service.

The multifunctional platform produces mechanical power to relieve women of back breaking, time consuming hand labour such as grinding meal and pumping water. It can power various tools, such as a cereal mill, husker, alternator, battery charger, pump, welding and carpentry equipment. It can also generate electricity and be used to distribute water. The platform reduces many of the women's burdensome and exhausting tasks such as fetching water and grinding cereals. It offers them income-generating opportunities, management experience and, as they become more economically independent, increases their social status.

The platform also stimulates the creation, development and modernisation of other artisan activities in the villages such as blacksmiths, mechanics, and carpenters. It is manufactured, installed and maintained by private mechanics. The seeds of the pourghere plant, which grows in Mali, can be crushed by an attachment to the platform. The motor uses a litre of pourghere oil while crushing enough seeds to produce 21 additional litres of the lubricating oil.

Not only does the work life of a village change when the platform arrives — the social structure changes, too. In 2002, 300 villages in Mali bore testimony to support Coche's assessment that the social structure changes. Since the machine has come to these villages, many girls who were kept home to help with the domestic work from dawn to dusk are now going to school. The women of the villages also have an incentive to become literate, and to learn arithmetic, in order to operate the machine and manage its use. Mothers and grandmothers who would have spent a lifetime pounding and grinding now have the free time to take literacy courses and start up small businesses, or to expand family farming plots and nurture a cash crop such as rice. When life in the villages improves, and with the addition of water systems and power supplies, there is less reason for young people to drift into the cities, where life often is more difficult for the poor.

The Mali government, one of the poorest in the world, would like to see one machine in every village, and it is funnelling some of its savings from international debt relief into the project. Nobody is giving the villagers a better life. They are investing in themselves, and working to protect that investment. For example, in the spring of 2002, in the village of Mountougoula, just outside Bamako, the village women raised additional money to connect a generator to their machine and rigged up a lighting network. For the first time ever, the village of 1,580 had lights, with 280 bulbs burning brightly from dusk to midnight. The dark is gone. Gradually the support system provided by the platform project will fade away. There is nothing in the project which cannot take on an economic life of its own in the villages of Mali and other countries of Africa.

(Source: www.ptfm.net, and Roger Thurow, 'Mali's makeshift 'Cuisinarts'create peanut butter and new possibilities', *The Wall Street Journal*, 26 July 2000)

American Elaine Bellezza has lived in West Africa since 1991, first as a crafts sector/small business development specialist in the non-profit sector. After ten years of helping and training artisans in various African settings, she decided to make the commitment and take the risk to open her own business, working with African craftspeople. Since 2002, Mia Mali has grown from a small retail business in her home, to a major retail and wholesale outlet in Bamako. Mia Mali has a large shop and a production workshop, and exports by container and airfreight regularly to Europe and the US. Mia Mali also facilitates design projects for international buyers and generates lines for wholesale clients.

The Mia Mali team see themselves as the pivotal point between producers and buyers, helping producers raise their level to meet the stringent demands of the international buyer. In addition, they help reduce the risk to the international buyer by assuring product quality, respecting deadlines and offering excellent product at decent prices. Their method is to work side by side with artisans in the artisans' workshops or in Mia Mali's workshops while developing new products. This could take days or weeks. Once the product is perfected the producers works on their own, while Mia Mali generates small-scale orders for the local market, building production capacity. Mia Mali then introduces these products to the international market in sample quantities. This way, by the time buyers are ready to order, artisans are ready to produce.

Through this methodology, Mia Mali has built a network of over 160 highly skilled and dedicated artisans. Through Mia Mali's efforts, workshops have been transformed from a few family members producing a few items a week for the tourist market into businesses with 15 employees producing thousands of highly developed products in a year.

(Source: www.miamali.com and July 2005 e-mail correspondence with Elaine Bellezza)

Niger

The Sudano Sahel is a region about 600 kilometres wide stretching from Mauritania on the Atlantic Ocean to Eritrea and Somalia on the Indian Ocean. Its borders are defined by the 300-800 mm rain isohyets. This region is home to the poorest people of the world. The subsistence rain-fed agricultural system is destructive to the environment and a major perpetuator of poverty. Through its biggest asset, its powerful partnerships, International Crops Research Institute for the Semi-Arid Tropics (ICRISAT) avidly pursues remarkable new science-driven opportunities for the long-suffering peoples of the Sahel. The New Sahel is a programme devised by ICRISAT to transform the current subsistence agricultural system into a productive, sustainable and market oriented system, thus helping the Sahelian population to exit from the current vicious cycle of poverty and land degradation. The programme is based on the development of both new rain-fed and of irrigated systems and on the introduction of a wide range of income-generating export-oriented crops. This vigorous new market-oriented agriculture is bound to transform lives and lands along this northern perimeter of sub-Saharan Africa.

The African Market Garden (AMG) is a cost-effective, integrated low-pressure drip irrigated system that should serve as a platform for a highly profitable, export oriented horticulture industry. The AMG comes with a package of proper management practices, quality vegetable varieties adapted to the region and new fruit tree species and varieties. The hardware components of the AMG system are a concrete reservoir, the plastic drip irrigation kit (a basic unit covers an area of $500m^2$, and can be extended to $1500m^2$ using the same reservoir), and a water pump. Manifold boosts in income are possible from cultivating date palm, papaya, table grapes, figs, citrus, pomegranates and vegetables for both domestic and international markets. The benefits of the AMG system include higher yields of improved quality vegetables and fruits, the ability to produce crops year round, an efficient utilization of water resources, decreased labour requirements for irrigation and weeding, and greater likelihood of maintaining the productive capacity of the soil. In 2005, the AMG was at the stage of mass dissemination in the region with some 2,000 AMG units successfully operating in eight Sahelian countries and in South Africa.

(Source: Dov Pasternak, 'The New Sahel: Transforming Sahelian agriculture through the intensification of rain-fed and irrigated systems', presentation at the Science and Technology Conference in Burkina Faso, 21-23 June 2004)

Dov Pasternak, an Israeli professor from Ben-Gurion University of the Negev, has formed a unique partnership and a special personal relationship with El Hadj Issaka Dandakoye, an African vegetable farmer from Niamey, Niger. Since 2001, Pasternak has been working since 2001 for ICRISAT in Niger, developing the AMG horticultural production system for farmers with small parcels of land and other rain-fed sustainable production systems. Known throughout the land affectionately as Professor Dov, the former head of Ben-Gurion University's Institute for Agriculture and Applied Biology developed AMG in Israel over a three-year period, before Pasternak moved to Africa. The major supporter of his research and development activities in Africa is a programme called the International Program for Arid Land Crops (IPALAC) that is financed by the governments of Finland and Israel. Pasternak is the director of IPALAC. IPALAC and ICRISAT began their cooperative activities in 1997.

When Professor Dov was looking for farmers to experiment with the AMG, he approached El Hadj Issaka Dandakoye, a fourth generation vegetable farmer in the area, a big person with a very good nature. He is a devoted Moslem approaching 60 and is the chief of a village touching Niamey called Gamkaley. Dandakoye volunteered to set up a 500m² AMG unit in one of his fields, and was duly impressed with the results. As a result of that experiment, at the end of April 2004, Pasternak and Dandakoye inaugurated a four-acre AMG vegetable farm featuring the first farmer-operated pressurised drip irrigation system in Niger. Since the inauguration of Dandakoye's field, Pasternak is receiving continuous requests for the pressurised AMG from farmers who visited Dandakoye's field. The city vegetable traders line up at Dandakoye's field to purchase the quality tomatoes. They sleep there at night to be the first to receive the produce that Dandakoye sells for double the price of the local produce.

The inauguration provided dramatic proof of the success of a three-year campaign to demonstrate the AMG concept in one of the poorest countries in the beleaguered continent, faced with grinding poverty and lack of food security. Pasternak sees the AMG as a way of optimising the use of scarce arable land through the production of high-valued crops such as vegetables and fruit, with high efficiency, thereby providing the farmer and his family with a steady source of income.

(Source: Nahum Finkelstein, 'Sub-Saharan Africa blooms with Israel's cooperation', www.israel21c.org, 20 June 2004)

Pasternak says that the AMG will not solve all the problems of rural Sahel, where agriculture relies solely on rain-fed systems, and he is working towards a solution that he calls the Sahelian Eco-Farm (SEF) system which incorporates high value multi-purpose plants with soil and water conservation structures, and promises to bring benefits to farmers in the form of fuel wood, forage, cash, plant nutrients, biomass for mulch, and protection from wind erosion.

Ingeniously planned, the SEF system features strategic choices in the placement of trees, hedges and annual crops. Livestock has a key role to play in increasing incomes in dry areas, but will have to be combined with, and preceded by, a higher productivity crop system to make possible better feeding. A unique aspect of the SEF system is that all the elements would generate cash income. To facilitate and ensure farmer adoption and continuing viability over time, each one of the system components is a separate income-generating centre. Tree products (fruit, firewood, animal feed) can add to farmer income and mitigate the effect of droughts because trees are much less affected by rain distribution or droughts than the annuals. Main advantages of the SEF system are: arrest of land degradation and restoration of degraded lands; requires little capital investment and is within the reach of every farmer; marked increase in farmers' incomes; marked increase in animal feed production; diminish tree cutting for firewood and higher carbon sequestration; improved socio-economical status of women by reducing firewood collection and through the supply of fruit and other products that can be sold in markets.

The SEF system and the multitude of new crops that are produced in it are still under development. It is estimated that the SEF system with its tree-shrub-crop components will increase profits per hectare by a factor of ten as compared with the present millet and sorghum based system — and is far more environmentally sustainable. The SEF system has the potential to change the life of rural Sahelians even more then the AMG system. The SEF system, with the judicious application of fertilisers, allows the available arable land to support more people. The technology will also alleviate another of Africa's growing problems, the exodus of rural people to the cities. By revitalising the rural areas it will lessen the need to seek work elsewhere.

(Source: Dov Pasternak, 'The Sahelian eco-farms: An integrated approach for combating poverty and land degradation in dry Africa', 2004, ICRISAT; and January 2006 e-mail correspondence from Professor Dov Pasternak)

Women working together in West Africa are making a difference. Throughout West Africa they have come together in formal and informal organisations to solve problems and explore new opportunities. They build a spirit of solidarity and purpose, learning from and supporting one another. Together they can do more in solving community problems, opening up business prospects, creating access to credit, and ensuring that families get better education and health care. Amina Hassane Wangari is the president of the Réseau de l'Entreprenariat Féminin en Afrique de l'Ouest (REFAO), also known as the West African Businesswomen's Network (WABNET), a regional organisation with national chapters in Benin, Burkina Faso, Côte d'Ivoire, Gambia, Ghana, Guinea, Mali, Niger, Nigeria, Senegal, Sierra Leone and Togo. Wangari is the president of the Réseau des Femmes Chefs d'Entreprises du Niger (REFCEN), the Niger Network of Women Business Owners, and also the president of the Union des Mutuelles d'epargne et de Credit (UMEC NIGER), which has 42 micro-finance institutions, about 30,000 members, and important training abilities.

The Internet is a formidable way to empower women in business. West Africans are getting online and going wireless by the millions. 'It's truly a revolution,' says Wangari. She founded Complexe Technique Wangari, a technological and management training centre, with a college of general education, a technical school, an institute of management and technology, and the largest cybercafe in Niamey. There are 35 permanent professors and 78 freelance. In July 2002, Amina Hassane Wangari opened her cybercafe using a 64kbit satellite connection and equipment imported from the US. In a country with one of the world's lowest rates of Internet connectivity, Wangari offers students of all ages access to the Internet at reduced rates and hosts training for businesswomen. In order to expand the success of this cybercafe and to offer more affordable Internet services, Wangari decided to acquire her own satellite or VSAT (very small aperture terminal). She is also the chairman of establishment CIMINTI, an import/export trading company. In 2003, Wangari's import/export trading establishment Ciminti purchased IT equipment from an American. Wangari's Ciminti is also seeking to represent foreign suppliers of construction materials and equipment in Niger.

The Corporate Council on Africa's West Africa International Business Linkages programme (WAIBL) sponsored Wangari to attend the CCA's 2001 US-Africa Business Summit in Philadelphia, and she also attended WAIBL's ICT conference in New Jersey in March 2004. More than a hundred ICT business leaders from Benin, Cape Verde, Gabon, Ghana, Guinea, Senegal, Niger, Nigeria, Togo and the US explored business opportunities at the 2004 conference. The WAIBL programme is a catalyst for trade and investment (import/export, joint ventures, and equity partnerships) between West African and US businesses. As of May 2004, WAIBL had generated more than US$130 million in business transactions. WAIBL is funded by the US Agency for International Development through the West Africa Regional Programme (WARP).

(Source: May 2004 e-mail correspondence with Amina Hassane Wangari)

Guinea-Bissau

Isabel Maria Garcia de Almeida is the first nutritionist in Guinea-Bissau. Her goal is to establish a nutrition 'museum' to address malnutrition and related health problems, matters of widespread concern in her country. Isabel's ambition is to develop a creative space to research food and nutrition issues, to develop imaginative ways of informing and educating the Bissau-Guinean people on the essential elements of nutrition and healthy eating habits. Malnutrition is one of the principal causes of morbidity, mortality and poverty in Guinea-Bissau.

This museum would be a new type of research centre, through which information on a variety of food-related issues, from the history and anthropology of nutrition to food groups and nutrients readily available in Guinea-Bissau, could be widely and attractively disseminated. The centre would also undertake basic analysis of national food policy and agrarian issues, principal factors in the country's socio-economic development. This nutrition centre is to be named Bemba, a local word meaning granary, and will be a place to gather useful information and ideas.

Isabel's strategy is well developed and multi-faceted. Her immediate priority is to establish a structure to house the library and exhibition space. The site she has chosen is in a rural location; the setting is also key to attracting travellers, as it will be situated on a busy crossroads linking the capital to major arteries which lead to the north, east, and south of the country.

An essential element of Isabel's strategy is to enliven the normally static approach to learning practiced by more conventional museums. Part of her aim is to create local employment and to make the site more productive through horticulture and animal-raising schemes. In the long-term, Isabel hopes to add other attractions to her centre, including a hostel which will provide lodging for workshop participants, and refreshment stands to attract visitors and passers-by. The overall intent is to contribute to a healthy, restful and attractive environment conducive to learning and reflection, and in doing so to help overcome the health and nutrition problems of her society.

In 1991, Isabel was one of six founding members of the Association for Research and Alternatives (Alternag), one of the first legally registered non-governmental organisations in the country. Alternag's objectives are to help develop, through participatory research techniques, alternative solutions to social and economic problems, and to help bring about an informed citizenry capable of participating in the decisions now facing the country.

During a trip to Switzerland a few years ago, Isabel was greatly stimulated by a visit she made to the Nestlé food museum, which provides public relations and educational displays along with Nestlé food products. Seeing in this museum the kernel of an idea worth building on, Isabel has imagined how effectively similar techniques could be improved and adapted to fit the context and needs of her own country. She has a dynamic approach to her work, and is ready and committed to putting her imaginative ideas into action. Isabel De Almeida was awarded the Ashoka Fellowship in 1994.

(Source: www.ashoka.org, and June 2004 e-mail correspondence from Isabel Maria Garcia de Almeida)

Cape Verde

Frescomar, a fish processing company based in Sao Vicente, Cape Verde, is an exporter of canned tuna and mackerel. In 2001, Frescomar was among the first companies in Cape Verde to export under AGOA, regularly shipping one container of canned fish every 45 days to distributors in New England. In December 2001, Frescomar became the first Cape Verdean company to be certified by the US Food and Drug Administration. Frescomar's products, targeted at a high-end niche market, are cut and trimmed by hand using high quality fresh fish. Manager Miguel Pinto says that Frescomar adheres to strict sanitary controls and its products are certified dolphin friendly. Established in 2000, Frescomar employs 150 people and processes over 16 tons of fish per day (or 30,000 cans).

Confeccoes Proto Grande (CPG), one of Cape Verde's leading apparel manufacturers, specialises in men's cotton shirts such as flannel shirts, sports shirts and outdoors shirts. Manager Adriano Pires says that in a 5,000 square metre factory with 155 workers, CPG has a daily production capacity of 1,600 shirts. CPG uses modern machinery primarily from Japan and Germany and its factory is less than one kilometre from the port. CPG exports to the US and Europe regularly and has been producing for brands such as Pierre Cardin, Cabela's and LLBean.

The Cape Verde Clothing Company manufactures women's and men's non-washed woven apparel such as blouses, shirts, jackets, pants, shorts, suits and skirts. With an annual turnover of over US$1 million it produces and exports between 500,000 and 1,000,000 pieces a year to an American customer who supplies Wal-Mart and other department stores. Manager Asanga Vithrana is proud that Cape Verde Clothing Company's factory has been certified by Wal-Mart. Total annual capacity is 1.5 million pieces. Currently Cape Verde Clothing Company imports fabrics from Asia. Vithrana is seeking additional American customers and is expanding to produce apparel using US fabric.

The African Development Foundation (ADF) promotes community-based, participatory development and finances small projects, focused on trade. In October 2004, ADF announced support for education in Cape Verde, mining in Uganda, inland fishing in Mali, and roads in Burkina Faso and Benin. ADF has been active in Cape Verde since 1993. Former local ADF liaison officer Julio Fortes says that one cannot overestimate the positive impact that ADF micro-enterprise programmes have had on the lives of his fellow citizens. 'Cape Verde is a small country, so any small project has a big, big impact. Some of our local projects even have impact at the national level.'

To illustrate his point, Fortes recalls how a micro-credit grant from ADF helped a sewing business flourish. The Cooperativa de Costura Simplicidade (CCS) is a woman's sewing cooperative created in 1991 in San Vicente when 12 employees of a publicly and formerly government-owned sewing plant that was privatised got together. As former employees, they had the knowledge and the skills to operate the business. ADF gave them the financial resources to purchase needed equipment, training, technical assistance, management, and working capital. The cooperative has grown and has become so large that it is no longer a micro-enterprise project but one of the country's largest clothing manufacturers, employing about 65 women, and grossing US$500,000 in annual sales.

The cooperative has gained a monopoly on sewing uniforms for schools, hotels, restaurants, factories, Cape Verde's national airline, and others. It has also negotiated a contract with a clothing company in Portugal. They export finished products to other European countries and sell T-shirts in Hawaii. People who were once jobless are now successful. The company's employees now operate their own credit union and social benefit programme. Institutions such as ADF deal directly with the people and work at the grassroots level. Fortes says that seeing people bettering their lives makes his job and ADF's mission worthwhile.

CCS has developed a new marketing strategy to enable it to export finished products to the US, taking into account the possibilities offered by the African Growth and Opportunity Act (AGOA). CCS undertook a market survey. Members of the cooperative visited textile manufacturing factories, negotiated with suppliers and collected market information for the development of its new strategy.

(Source: www.adf.gov/capeverde.html)

[1] Document originally provided by the World Intellectual Property Organization (WIPO), the owner of the copyright. The Secretariat of WIPO assumes no liability or responsibility with regard to the transformation or translation of this data.

Part 3
Southern Africa

The economic powerhouse of Africa south of the Sahara desert is South Africa, Africa's biggest exporter by far. The next biggest exporters are Algeria, Libya, Morocco, Tunisia and Egypt in North Africa, Nigeria in west Africa and Angola in central Africa. Through its well-developed infrastructure and deepwater ports, South Africa handles much of the trade for the whole southern African region. In 1970 its immediate neighbours, Botswana, Swaziland and Lesotho, and latterly Namibia, signed the Southern African Customs Union (SACU) enabling them to share in the customs revenue from their trade passing through South African ports.

In 1980, in order to counter the threat of economic dominance of then apartheid South Africa in the southern African region, the countries to the north of it organised themselves into the Southern African Development Community (SADC). Thirteen member states today include those of the SACU as well as Zimbabwe; Mozambique on the southeast coast; the island republic Mauritius; the Democratic Republic of Congo; Angola, Zambia, and Malawi in south central Africa; Tanzania in eastern Africa and South Africa itself. SADC's headquarters are in Gaborone, Botswana. The SADC enjoys the highest percentage of intra-regional trade on the African continent. Compared to other regional blocks such as ECOWAS and COMESA, SADC's trade figures in 2004 were the highest in Africa and constituted 24 per cent of total trade by the SADC countries.

In 2004, SADC deputy executive secretary, Albert Muchanga, was upbeat about the fact that the region was geared for the Free Trade Area by 2008 and the SADC Customs Union by 2012. He declared that they were happy to be the leading regional block in terms of intra-regional trade in Africa.

There are six independent island states associated with the continent of Africa. Off the southeast coast are the island republics of the Comoros and Madagascar (the world's third largest island with an area of 587,041 square kilometres). Further east in the Indian Ocean are the island republics of Mauritius and the Seychelles. Lying close to Mauritius is the island of Réunion, a dependency of France although its economy is closely linked to that of the southeast African coast and Indian Ocean islands.

Chapter 6: Namibia, Botswana, Lesotho and Swaziland.

Namibia

Namibia is blessed with a modern infrastructure and is the biggest anomaly on earth: a large, very dry country with relatively few people, yet modern, well developed, with well above average incomes. This is one of the main reasons why it is classified by the United Nations as a medium developed country.

Whenever one makes an assessment of Namibia, there are a number of fundamentals one must never lose sight of. Internationally, Namibia is minute, constituting about 4.2 per cent of the South African economy. So compared to first world economies, they are really small. But the country, in turn, is vast, slightly bigger than Texas, with only 1.7 million people. So one can imagine there are vast stretches of land hardly with a soul on it. Namibia is a very arid country. The western third is the Namib Desert, the middle third is the Karoo (bush shrub) and the eastern third is the Kalahari (savannah with large trees but also a desert of some sorts). One must also be aware of the operating background when forming an opinion of any local business, including the country's local business newspaper, *The Namibia Economist*.

Daniel Steinmann, editor of *The Namibia Economist*, has written the following:

'Trade is fast becoming the most important and most powerful political tool in the interaction between nations. By this I do not mean that trade has not been important historically, rather that it has not featured so prominently as the main motivator in international relationships and diplomacy. Trade has always played an important role in the history of nations but it was restricted in many ways and the conventional way to deal with unwanted goods was simply to bar them by saying no. Nowadays, and this has been happening concurrently with progress in technology and in particular information technology and data systems, trade has been refined to a fine tool, or perhaps, system. And as the global village has grown and the world has shrunk, trade has assumed the number one position as the determining factor between nations. The one that trades the best will in time become the leader and the other, to a large extent, will have to play by the rules set by the dominant player. We see this happening as the Southern African Customs Union (SACU) negotiating team engage their American counterparts to thrash out a deal that would supposedly give us and our neighbours preferential access to the lucrative US market, while at the same time, through quid pro quo principles, allow the Americans free access to our hopefully-growing consumer markets. But the road is fraught with dangers and many of these surfaced this week at a seminar organised by the Agricultural Trade Forum which describes itself as the voice of the agricultural private sector.

'One fact that we need to be aware of is that the USA is currently negotiating free trade agreements with 34 other nations. Thus, rules of origin become extremely important, and more important is that the two negotiating teams should agree on those rules. It is quite possible that an American importer can import mutton from Australia at less than a third our production price and then dump his entire shipload in Walvis Bay to enter the SACU market. The same could happen with cargoes from Argentina, Brazil or even Madagascar. This example is not far-fetched. It has actually happened twice in the last years, that I am aware of and this was before trade liberalisation became such a buzz word. What we must also not forget is that South Africa has just concluded a free trade agreement with the European Union and is in the process of talking to Mercosur as well, so again, instead of preferential access with original goods, it may turn out to be a case of preferential shunting, in the process killing local producers and local industry. Of course this holds true for both us and South Africa, but a quick trip around the country shows immediately there are economies of scale in SA and not in Namibia. So we are far more vulnerable when it comes to indiscriminately allowing so-called free-flow of goods. It could turn out to be a free-flow of local bankruptcies. Then again, rules of origin must not be so strict that they prevent, for instance, Ramatex to import raw materials and export apparel as currently allowed under the African Growth and Opportunities Act (AGOA).

'Of course, there are all sorts of ways to regulate trade and, in particular, to prevent certain types of trade but these, in principle, go against the basic tenets of a 'free trade' agreement. Still it was pointed out, in no uncertain terms, that for a free trade agreement with a behemoth, such as the US, the ultimate agreement will have to be asymmetrical. The SACU market is not insignificant with between 50 and 60 million consumers of which a substantial proportion generate a steady income: spending power! But it is still not a very large market and it is not homogenous by any standard. For a power like the US to flood us with certain items they don't need so much, will be very easy. The local producer has to be protected against this. Regarding subsidies, I presume it will take a very long time before the South and the West see eye to eye on this one, so in the meantime, a long list of subsidised items, mostly agricultural, will have to be excluded from free trade. Meanwhile, back home we shall have to figure out ways of complementing the fiscus as any free trade agreement reduces the revenue derived from customs duties. Fortunately, since the South Africans negotiated with the European Union, two things have happened. They have realised SACU consists of partners, so for the SACU USA FTA Namibia is actually part of the negotiating team, and secondly, FTAs must be implemented gradually (12 years with the TDCA), to enable countries to make up the revenue shortfall through other means.'

(Daniel Steinmann, 'We'll send you some and then think about yours', (c)*The Namibia Economist*, 27 February 2001, www.economist.com.na)

The Namibia Economist is Namibia's independent weekly business newspaper, published in Windhoek since 1988. It is one of the leading publications in Namibia, and certainly the leading economic and business publication. Daniel Steinmann started *The Namibia Economist* in February 1991 but its roots go back further; in December 1988, a group of businessmen started what they called the *SWA Ekonoom*, Afrikaans for the South West African Economist (this was before independence and Namibia was South West Africa — for all practical purposes a fifth province of South Africa).

The *SWA Ekonoom* had an up and down existence through 1989 and 1990, appearing erratically, and finally went bust in about October 1990. Steinmann then started negotiating with the previous owners to buy what was left. This proved to be a major mistake on his side. There was nothing left but, philosophically, he attributes this to experience. He basically started from scratch in February 1991 — actually he started from below zero because by that time there were so many negative perceptions in the market regarding the *SWA Ekonoom* that he spent his first six months persuading hundreds of people that *The Namibia Economist* was a drastic departure from its predecessor.

Things were extremely shaky in the beginning. It really was a one-man show in the truest sense of the word. Steinmann was everything: from receptionist, to marketer, to journalist, to delivery boy, to driver, to accountant. Only after four months could the newspaper afford a half-day receptionist. Thinking back today, he is not sure that he would have had the guts to tackle this venture had he known what was in store for him. He changed the name to *The Namibia Economist* from the start. At that stage the newspaper was a monthly knock-and-drop (local jargon for a publication distributed free of charge) and his first task was to get the paper at a level where it could at least pay its accounts. Break-even was nowhere in sight yet. Every cent was borrowed money and cash flow was almost non-existent.

Just before its second anniversary, The Namibia Economist had a receptionist, one (very junior) journalist, an advertising representative and a person responsible for distribution. Slowly things started turning for the better but Steinmann realised he needed help.

In the third year he struck a deal with Desere Lundon-Muller who was keen on doing the marketing. She joined *The Namibia Economist* as a shareholder assuming the position of marketing manager. This was in 1994. From then on they started growing very quickly. Steinmann could then devote all his attention to editorial content and to being in touch with the market, while Lundon-Muller made sure the market knew *The Namibia Economist* was the best analytical publication in the country. A year and a bit later the two partners decided to go weekly and to become a conventional retail newspaper. This was a wise decision. They have never looked back, only worked and worked and worked. In the business community, the 'Economist' (as it is fondly known) is certainly the most influential.

Being a newspaper, the Economist found it hard in its initial years to find a suitable marketing channel. The owners did not want to use other newspapers to create awareness for the Economist and listeners of the government controlled radio stations did not fit the targeted readers' profile. Hence, as marketing manager, Lundon-Muller was tasked to start projects, which would serve two purposes: first to act as an advertising medium for the newspaper itself, and secondly, to make a meaningful contribution to the economic and social development of Namibia.

Today, the Economist hosts the Economist Business Forum, the Namibian Businesswoman of the Year, the Economist Businesswoman Club and the Economist Businesswoman Conference in the North. The Namibian Businesswoman of the Year award has established a very proud tradition of awarding the spirit of the entrepreneur amongst women every odd year. The award is differentiated into two categories: entrepreneur and corporate-professional. The award is made every year, but the two categories are alternated. The award is sponsored by First National Bank and Castle Brewing Namibia as main sponsors.

Sara Elago was Namibian Businesswoman of the Year for 1999. She was the first black woman to receive this honour. Highly regarded in business circles, Sara Elago has become the darling of the business community, and also a role model for young people aspiring to go into their own businesses. Her history is now widely known: how as a young girl she trained to become a nurse, and then started selling groceries through her bedroom window until she could open her first little shop. This eventually grew into a family business and Elago Supermarket became a household name in Katutura, Windhoek's black township. She now has an extended business empire including several shops and SE Duty Free Trading with a warehouse in Windhoek and a duty-free shop at Hosea Kutako International Airport outside Windhoek. She is involved in import and export; she runs an investment company, Real Africa Investments and, in collaboration with her husband, has extensive interests in agriculture. She also has international business interests. Her companies today employ around 60 people.

As former Namibian Businesswoman of the Year, Elago was president of the Economist Businesswoman Club for the year 2000, whose members are all either entrepreneurs or career women. In 2001, she was the patron of the annual Businesswoman Conference in Ongwediva. She refers to women as key shapers of Namibian leadership. She says that as women address issues of leadership they should not think as women, but as leaders. Their concern should be how to empower themselves so as to better build their society and secure its future in the world.

(Source: 'Judges' convenor - Sara Elago', Windhoek: *The Namibia Economist*, 7 September 2001; www.economist.com.na)

On her farm in Brakwater, Elago has entered the agriculture sector, describing farming as one of the best business opportunities in Namibia. While, she says, it is a leap from retailing, she feels confident that vegetable farming will one day become a big industry, and she has dedicated twelve hectares of the 125 hectares she owns to tomatoes, onions and pumpkins. At the same time she is experimenting with other produce. She employs 12 people at the farm, and the produce is sold in her shops. The vegetables are seasonal, but she is working on plans to have a constant supply of vegetables and become a supplier rather than merely a grower-retailer. One of the problems in farming, she has realised, is that not many people have the money to buy land, so she is also encouraging those with land to use it effectively and reduce the import of vegetables from South Africa.

(Source: Desie Heita, 'Sara Elago leaves retailing for full-time farming', *The Namibia Economist*, 23 May 2003; www.economist.com.na)

Quality people make for a quality award. Five women were the finalists for the Namibian Businesswoman of the Year for 2001 award: Riana Jacobs, Zanthia Berkelmann, Adree Mudge, Marita Ernsting and Anita Devenish. Riana Jacobs is the owner of a guest house, Bird's Nest, and a hotel, Bird's Mansion, in

Keetmanshoop. Her hotel has brought new life to the central part of Keetmanshoop, a dusty desert town in the country's south. Zanthia Berkelmann is a co-owner of Corporate Gifts and Promotions, a company specialising in providing other businesses with promotional items for marketing purposes. Adree Mudge is a co-owner of Kleines Heim Hotel in Windhoek, a landmark establishment close to the city's central business district. Kleines Heim is also popular in the corporate sector as a conference venue. Marita Ernsting is the owner of PhotoBox and ProFoto Centre. Her shops provide film and film processing for amateur and professional photographers, as well as all the paraphernalia associated with photography.

Anita Devenish, the owner of Santorini Inn, a hotel in Oshakati, northern Namibia, as well as the owner of transport, agricultural and electrical contracting interests in Oshakati and Ruacana, was the fifth finalist and was chosen Namibian Businesswoman of the Year for 2001. Santorini Inn was established in December 1992. During the course of 1993, a restaurant, a storeroom, kitchen and seven more rooms were added. An a la carte menu was later completed and more staff employed. Today the hotel has 29 rooms. Devenish's hands-on management style is reflected in her willingness to fill in for any staff member when the need arises. She sometimes helps out at reception or in the dining hall, or she may show guests to their rooms. Although she also runs seven other businesses and now employs a total of 92 people, Devenish is in daily contact with her staff members and always has time for a kind word or a bit of advice.

In 1997, she and her husband bought a farm in the south to supply Santorini Inn with meat. In 1998, her husband died at a construction site in Angola in a freak accident. At that time, he was building a guesthouse similar to Santorini Inn for the Angolan government. With two small children to look after, Devenish decided to carry on with the hotel. She said she gave herself three years to survive in what she termed a man's world.

In October 1998, she had the guesthouse in Ondjiva completed and handed the keys to the governor. During the course of 1999, she bought five vehicles and formed Santorini Car Hire. In 1999, she also bought a lodge in Ruacana. In this deal she obtained the BP service station, as well as the Kunene Mini Market and filling station. In 2000, she added another house in Ruacana to her rapidly expanding business interests. This she turned into self-catering lodgings. She also has a private pilot's license. Her late husband would have been proud of her.

(Source: 'Namibian Businesswoman of the Year 2001', *The Namibia Economist*, 28 September 2001; www.economist.com.na)

By June 2003, Devenish's business operations had overtaken others, and she had ventured into new directions. She has expanded her electrical business across the border into Angola, where the results have been so impressive that she is thinking of opening a permanent branch there. Santorini Inn is also well poised to attract business from north of the border. Devenish is also promoting her lodge and guest house in Ruacana because she thinks businesspeople and communities need to come up with something that attracts tourists to the area. They need to promote their region and one way is through community based tourism. In Kaokoland, where she has a mini market, sales were not impressive until she realised the possible cause of the problem. She immediately talked to one of the banking institutions and a new automatic teller machine was installed; now, not only is the community happy about the shopping convenience — it regards the ATM as part of the development in that area.

(Source: www.santorini-inn.com, and 'Businesswoman of the Year regroups, crosses the border north', *The Namibia Economist* 20 June 2003; www.economist.com.na)

Barbara Rogl, the owner of Otjiruze Hunting and Guest Farm near Okahandja, was one of five finalists for the tenth Namibian Businesswoman of the Year award in 2003. Barbara's guests can feel the vibes of the African bush on a real Namibian cattle ranch on some 6,000 hectares of vast and beautiful acacia savannah. The hosts are Barbara, her sons Werner, Markus and Alexander, and her team. At Otjiruze, guests come and relax as part of the Rogl family and enjoy exclusive and personal attention on a typical Namibian cattle ranch.

Otjiruze offers eight double rooms and two more for tour guides all with facilities en-suite. Two of these are adapted for the handicapped in wheelchairs. Guests enjoy Otjiruze's relaxed atmosphere and tranquillity.

The Rogl family takes care of their guests, making them feel at ease and at home as they soak up the sun at the swimming pool or play tennis. Also on offer are nature drives, while those wanting to explore the African bush on foot have a choice of walks ranging from one to five kilometres. Guests can enjoy sitting at one of the waterholes for a few hours, watching the game quench their thirst, or do some serious birding at one of the many dams on the ranch. They can look forward to typical Namibian cuisine mixed with some German home-cooking. And, in season, guests can savour truly Namibian delicacies such as the Omajova mushroom growing on termite mounds during the January-February rainy season and, a few months later, Ovitjotjos, the Kalahari truffles.

Otjiruze still is an active cattle ranch. Grazing on the nutritious rangelands of Otjiruze are two well-known cattle breeds, Brahman and Simmentaler. Thus guests have the opportunity to gain a first-hand insight into the joys and set-backs of a ranch family on a producing ranch in Namibia. Right next to the Otjiruze River and just a few kilometres away from the ranch house is the Otjiruze River Camp; set among a cluster of camel-thorn and sweet-thorn trees, the camp gives the real 'out in the bush' feeling. Sitting around the campfire at night, listening to the yelping call of a jackal, or the hoot of an owl, gives visitors the feeling of being out in the wilds, and the morning wake-up call is a raucous choral performance by grey louries, hornbills, starlings, and francolins. The campsite offers ablution facilities with hot and cold water, a kitchen and two large braai (barbeque) areas together with a 'bush bar'. The only thing guests have to bring along is their camping equipment and their food supplies.

Otjiruze is also a hunting ranch, hosting trophy hunters, some of whom have returned every year for the last 15 years. It boasts kudu, gemsbok (oryx), red hartebeest and warthog. Barbara will make arrangements for other species to be hunted on other, nearby, ranches. The ranch is bow-hunting registered and her sons will assist anyone who would like to venture into this new technique of hunting. The Rogl family's 'new baby', born in 1999, is the Swakoptal Conservancy, where all surrounding farmers are members and take part. Barbara has been the chairlady of this organisation since 2003. Managing conservancies overall is the Conservancies Association of Namibia, where Barbara serves on the executive committee.

(Source: www.otjiruze.com, and www.swakoptal.com)

With over twenty years of experience in the tourism industry, Wilderness Safaris hosts guests in over 50 safari lodges in seven different southern African countries. The company is privileged to control, manage or lease over two and a half million hectares of prime wildlife and wilderness land and has approximately 1,700 employees drawn primarily from rural communities in the vicinity of the lodges.

Wilderness Safaris' Damaraland Camp was named by the World Travel and Tourism Council as the overall winner of the Tourism for Tomorrow Conservation Award 2005 at an awards ceremony held on 8 April 2005, in New Delhi, India. This award is one of the top two global travel environmental awards, and is adjudicated by independent judges who conduct on-site inspections of all the finalists.

In 1995, the area around Damaraland Camp was in decline; there was no formal conservation protection, wildlife numbers were rapidly diminishing and unemployment within the local community was close to 100 per cent. In 2005, due to the successful partnership between the Damaraland Community and Wilderness Safaris, and the implementation of a viable eco-tourism model, around 350,000 hectares of land are under conservancy protection, wildlife numbers are thriving and the local community has money in the bank and employment. Encouraged by this example, the neighbouring Doro Nawas Community has in turn created its own 400,000-hectare conservancy, and has entered into a similar partnership with Wilderness Safaris that includes significant equity shareholding.

The Tourism for Tomorrow Conservation Award 2005 was an accolade that bears testimony to the concerted efforts of all those involved in Damaraland Camp and, in particular, the members of the community who have had the foresight to invest in their future by protecting their wildlife and natural surroundings. Wilderness Safaris was extremely honoured to have received this acknowledgment of the Damaraland Camp success story, which has enabled and enriched the local community who are committed to preserving their environment and wildlife for future generations. This is a fulfilment of Wilderness Safaris' promise 'to protect and conserve our most precious natural treasures: our planet and our people'.

Situated on the northern face of the Huab River Valley and looking south toward the imposing Brandberg Mountains, Damaraland Camp offers its guests endless vistas. Early morning mists generated by the clash between the icy Atlantic Ocean and the warm desert air of the Skeleton Coast, drift inland along the river sand canyon, providing sustenance to the flora and fauna of the region. This comfortable and friendly camp offers walks and drives in one of the best wilderness areas in Namibia. Although wildlife is not concentrated, Damaraland Camp is situated where the rare desert elephant roams, alongside gemsbok (oryx), springbok, ostrich and other hardy desert animals. Rare succulent plants somehow manage to eke out an existence in this harsh countryside.

Damaraland Camp has 10 tented rooms, each with an en-suite bathroom including flush toilet and shower with hot and cold running water. The dining room and pub are combined under canvas, and an open fire is enjoyed on calm evenings. A feature of the camp is the unique rock pool. Activities throughout the area are in 4x4 vehicles and on foot. Mountain bikes are also available for guest use.

The Camp lies within the Torra Conservancy, 90 kilometres inland from Namibia's Skeleton Coast. It is an area that has been plagued in the past by poaching and destruction of the natural habitat. Committed to empowering the local community and giving them a sense of ownership, Wilderness Safaris set up a partnership whereby the local community's Trust earned significant cash revenues as well as jobs, mentoring and training. One of the poorest communities anywhere is now thriving and poverty alleviation has been achieved directly through conservation and tourism. This attitude has instilled a sense of pride and belonging in the community who now see their environment as being integrally linked to their future successes.

Poverty reduction, conservation and empowerment were placed together on the same agenda. Financial initiatives that earn the community a significant percentage of the camp's bed night accommodation revenue, coupled with conservation initiatives on the ground, are increasing the value of wildlife to the community and to the country. The result is that rare desert-adapted animals like the desert elephant and black rhino are increasing in numbers throughout the region. It is a win-win situation for all: The community prospers, the country wins and the surrounding environment is sustained and balanced — and Wilderness Safaris' guests can enjoy a wonderful experience.

(Source: www.wilderness-safaris.com)

Children in the Wilderness Camps were inspired by the concept of the Hole in the Walls Camps, the first of which was founded in 1988 by Paul Newman. Since then, the Association of Hole in the Wall Camps has grown to include five camps in the United States, camps in Ireland and France, and one scheduled to open in Israel in 2007. The camps are staffed by trained personnel and provide recreational and therapeutic activities for children with serious illness and life threatening conditions.

In August 2001, Paul Newman and his family travelled to Botswana and Namibia on a two-week safari with Wilderness Safaris. During this trip, it was suggested that the respective visions of the Hole in the Wall Camps and Wilderness Safaris could be combined and blended to create a sustainable and effective African programme. Within weeks of Paul Newman's return to the USA the wheels for the Africa version were set in motion and the project began to gain momentum. Educators were appointed from the USA and also from Wilderness Safaris' local staff, and some of Wilderness Safaris camps were closed to guests and opened to the children for a week-long educational and inspirational programme. Over the course of five weeks, 150 children were hosted for over 1,000 'safari-days' in that first year. The programmes successfully combined the missions and expertise of both Wilderness Safaris and The Association of Hole in the Wall Camps, while facilitating a wonderful and inspiring camp experience for the children.

The Children in the Wilderness programme was four years old in 2005, and had successfully hosted nearly 7,000 children in Wilderness Safaris lodges in Botswana, Malawi, Namibia, and South Africa. With the dedicated support of private, corporate and community sponsors, the programme has the potential to continue to grow and make a huge contribution to the sustainability of Africa's people and wildlife areas.

(Source: www.childreninthewilderness.com)

Namib Mills (Pty) Ltd plays an important role in Namibia's milling industry. Since 1982, the company has helped develop the industry through reinvestment in infrastructure and associated value adding activities. Today, Namib Mills is Namibia's leading miller and a major grain-derived foodstuff manufacturer. Its products include traditional flour and maize products, various types of pasta, milled indigenous millet, rice, sugar and animal feeds. An ambitious expansion program was initiated in 1986/87 when the construction of Namibia's first wheat mill enabled Namib Mills better to service its markets and increase its production capacity. The company's market share grew proportionately. In 1995, the company made another commitment to Namibia and erected one of the most advanced Buhler wheat mills in southern Africa.

In October 2001, Namib Mills opened a state-of-the-art pasta factory which produces a great variety of pastas from two huge, shiny machines. Peter Göttert, head of Pasta Polana, fondly calls them the 'long goods line' and the 'short goods line'. The long line machine produces spaghetti and tagliatelli, and the short line machine produces macaroni, elbows, shells, gnocchi, pasta rice and fusilli.

It is quite fascinating to see the ingredients being put together. 'Simply water and wheat flour,' says Göttert. 'The flour should be perfectly white for Pasta Polana,' he points out. He notes, however, that since no eggs are added, a bit of egg yellow colorant is added to the water in order to obtain a final product of a colour that matches consumer needs as expressed during research. Next, the flour is moved from the mill via a blow-line and blown into bins in the factory from a large bin at the mill. The smaller bins blow the flour to the two machines. The system is fully computerised; while they are mixing the dough the two high-tech machines are able to detect when they need more flour or water. The temperature is monitored and remains constant. According to Göttert any change in the temperature will affect the pasta — if it drops slightly, the pasta will crack before being packaged.

The factory floor is circled by big pipes carrying boiling water. The machines do almost everything except monitor themselves. There are 25 workers monitoring and servicing the machines. Control is handled from a separate room, where two computer monitors display all activities on the factory floor. All 25 employees are Namibian. They received their training before the plant opened, from the Italian machine manufacturers. Workers rotate eight-hour shifts. It takes six hours for the machinery to produce the first pasta to reach the final, packaging stage. In one hour the long-line machine can produce up to 400 kilograms of spaghetti, while the short-line spits out 700 kilograms of macaroni, shells or pasta rice.

(Source: Desie Heita. 'Macaroni does not grow on trees', *The Namibia Economist*, 28 February 2003; www.economist.com.na)

In 2005, Namib Mills had three milling facilities strategically located across the country. The Feedmaster processing plant ensures that by-products do not go to waste and that the country is self sufficient with regard to animal feed. Ten depots, positioned throughout Namibia, allow products to be delivered anywhere in the country within 24 hours. Namib Mills is also ideally positioned to export products to Angola, Botswana, Zambia and the markets of West Africa. Development of the milling industry has led to growth of other Namibian economic sectors. Wheat and maize farmers have a guaranteed market for their crops. Consistent supply to the baking industry has been the catalysis for growth in the baking industry. Transport contracts have stimulated the transport sector.

Namib Mills is focused on quality. Leading production technology and efficient quality assurance measures are the means to this end. The result of this focus on quality has been twofold. The company received ISO 9002 certification in 1999, and enjoys a high degree of trust in the retail and industrial sectors.

The company also received ISO 9001 certification in October 2003. It is marketing-driven and takes pride in its ability to launch new products to satisfy consumer demand. Underpinning this is the company's commitment to market research, consumer-based brand plans and local advertising campaigns. Namib Mills' leading brands are Top Score maize meal and Bakpro wheat flour. Recent additions to the stable have been Really Rice, Sugar First and highly successful pasta ranges.

Namib Mills has also taken the initiative in commercialising Namibia's traditional millet crop, mahangu, a subsistence crop grown and consumed primarily in the northern regions of Namibia. Meme Mahangu is Namibia's 'own brand' and a unique opportunity for northern communal farmers to generate additional income. Facilities for raw material intake have been established in Ondangwa, Rundu and Katima Mulilo. Pasta is rapidly becoming one of Namib Mills' most popular retail brands. In addition to the popular Polana Pasta range the company is in the process of launching new additions to the Pasta la Vita range, which is expected to capture the high end of the market.

Namib Mills is committed to the growth of the Namibian economy. In addition to substantial investment and growing foreign exchange earnings, the company provides approximately 500 employment opportunities. As a part of its commitment to the social well-being of Namibians, it is an active partner in many programmes to fight hunger. The company also supports various welfare organisations. A second facet to social commitment is the company's ability to store six months' grain, guaranteeing Namibia's food security. The company values its employees, customers, suppliers and all other stakeholders. It recognises that its future is intertwined with that of Namibia, and so works towards a better future for all.

Uri Offroad Vehicles began on a farm in the Kalahari. The Uri (Nama for jump) was developed by Ewert Smith, an Angora goat farmer from Namibia's Koes district. Smith ran a 4x4 touring business as a sideline. Because of the cost of vehicles and spares he began exploring alternatives. He wanted something light, rugged, reliable and affordable, so he decided to build his own off-road utility vehicle in his backyard workshop. When his invention hit the road, it attracted enough attention to warrant special orders from friends and acquaintances. Later, demand overtook production and the rest is history. To meet the demand the workshop was moved from the farm to a factory in Witvlei in October 1999. Later, a plant was also established in Pretoria, in conjunction with South African partners. Uri Offroad Vehicles managing director, Joachim Cranz, says vehicle production in South Africa commenced in March 2003 and is running smoothly as planned. The company ventured into South Africa to service the potential growth in that market and there had been much interest from the South African market, especially from the South African police and the mining industry.

Uri Offroad Vehicles are built from thick walled steel tubing and clad with sheet metal. Unlike conventional cars where the chassis structure is separate from the actual body shell, the body and the chassis is an integrated structure rather like a pipe cage clad with metal sheeting, creating a strong durable rigid body shell. Because of its unique features, the vehicle has attracted attention from as far as Iran. South African and Namibian police make use of Uri vehicles. The mining industry has also started using them, and approximately 80 are in use in mines in Namibia, Botswana and South Africa. Debswana (De Beers in Botswana) use their Uri to transport workers in the mine. Rosh Pinah and Ongopolo use theirs underground.

Cranz says the car has a longer life span than conventional cars, and lower maintenance costs. The vehicle has South African Bureau of Standard (SABS) approval and can be built to client specification. Several government agencies have shown strong interest and the Namibian police placed their first order in June 2004. A Windhoek-based security firm, ProForce, is using six of the vehicles for its security operations. According to Corinus Kotze, customer care and public relations manager for Proforce, they needed something strong, with the ability to run over pavements and through river beds during emergencies. The Uri can do all that and more. The car runs with Toyota engines. The smallest engine is the 2.2 litre petrol while the biggest is the 3.0 litre diesel.

In July 2004, the Namibian company relocated its plant in Windhoek to Pretoria and consolidated its facilities with Uri Vehicle Manufacturing (Pty) Ltd, the sister company in South Africa, in an effort to rationalise and cut costs. Uri Offroad Vehicles (Namibia) continues with sales and marketing, as well as after sales service in Namibia, while manufacturing has been centralised in South Africa. Uri Vehicle Holdings (Pty) Ltd, incorporated in Namibia, owns 100 per cent of Uri Offroad Vehicles in Namibia and 51 per cent of the South African business, of which Adriaan Booyse is the managing director and 49 per cent shareholder. Cranz is a shareholder in the holding and managing director of Uri Offroad Vehicles (Pty) Ltd. in Namibia. He says that much has improved since 2002. Apart from design improvements on the standard Uri, developments for heavy duty mining vehicles fitted with brand new Cummins engines were carried out. The company is negotiating with potential investment partners to increase capacity.

(Source: Desie Heita, 'Uri offroader needs government support to satisfy sudden demand', *The Namibia Economist*, 19 March 2004; www.economist.com.na; and 'Uri vehicles matures into a reputable company'. *The Namibia Economist*, 12 March 2004; www.economist.com.na)

In October 2003, Namibia's first-ever award was given to Novanam, a Lüderitz-based fishing company. Novanam won the overall award as well as the award in the category of fisheries. Exotic International Namibia, the grape company based in Aussenkehr, won the award in the agricultural category. The company exports world-class table grapes to Europe, and owns the biggest pack house and cooling rooms in Africa. At full production, this facility staffs 1,000 workers and generates some N$35 million in foreign exchange annually. At the time of winning, Exotic was only in its third year of production and had planted 102 hectares of vineyards. In the manufacturing category the award went to the Ohlthaver & List (O&L) Group of Companies, which has interests in food processing, beverages, fisheries, farming, retail trade, information technology, property, leisure and hospitality, marine engineering and the services sector.

In the mining category the award went to Ongopolo Mining and Processing Ltd, a Namibian-controlled company based in Tsumeb, which mines and processes base metals, mainly copper, but also associated precious metals such as gold and silver. It also produces by-products including arsenic trioxide. The national power utility NamPower won the award in the service category. NamPower has realised its main objectives of making power available, affordable, and accessible to as many Namibians as possible. This has included involvement in the government's massive rural electrification project, and overall expansion of Namibia's transmission system. NamPower has contributed significantly to national efforts to extend and strengthen vital infrastructure to service industry and enhance the quality of life. It has proposed the development of a 20MW hydro power station on the Okavango River, near Divundu, to meet the growing demand for power in Namibia and ensure reliability of power supply to the northern regions. Nature Investments Pty Ltd won in the category of tourism.

Fantastic, unbelievable, and phenomenal are the words heard over and over again from tourists standing at the eroding bank of the Fish River Canyon in southern Namibia. The canyon is one of Namibia's three biggest attractions and is included in the itinerary of almost every holidaymaker visiting the south. But the masterpiece of geology is not the only attraction. Just a few kilometres east of the canyon, businessmen and farm owners with a love for Namibia's south have set up a foundation, Namibia Natural Heritage Trust, which in turn formed a huge private conservation area called Gondwana Cañon Park, named after the ancient southern continent which broke apart millions of years ago and thereby contributed to the formation of the canyon. Nature conservation is costly. Gondwana Cañon Park is financed with the profits from its hospitality business. Since 1996, the non-profit company Nature Investments Pty Ltd has initiated and developed the largest single tourism investment in southern Namibia. The company has thus contributed to the restoration of economic and social vibrancy in southern Namibia.

Nature Investments runs several accommodation establishments in one part of the large park: the Cañon Lodge, the Cañon Roadhouse, the Cañon Mountain Camp, the Cañon Village and the Cañon Self Sufficiency Centre. The Centre is as much part of the concept guiding Gondwana Cañon Park as are the four lodgings. It is a farming business with poultry, pigs and cattle, a butchery, smoking-chamber and dairy. The Centre supplies fresh vegetables and fruit, meat, cold cuts and cheese to the Roadhouse, the Lodge and the Village. Whereas previously all fresh produce had to be shipped from South Africa, about 70 per cent of the requirements can now be met with home-made produce. Visitors to Gondwana Cañon Park are more than just holiday-makers enjoying the comfort, atmosphere, excellent cuisine, sightseeing or hiking trips. They are at the same time actively contributing to nature conservation, financing steps to protect nature or to resettle animals which used to inhabit the area long ago, and are also providing local people with jobs and hope for the future.

Cañon Village's new Cape Dutch cottage style lodgings are sited in mountainous surroundings to take best advantage of the beautiful view offered by the Gondwana Cañon Park. Cañon Village affords close access to the Fish River Canyon (the second largest canyon in the world), and offers privacy and exclusivity. Cañon Village is the result of harmoniously combining nature and comfort. The main building houses a restaurant, a separate bar, a room for a group, a souvenir shop and a partly covered beer-garden. The style of the 24 chalets (with a total of 60 beds) is similar: the bathroom with shower and toilet is the thatched little 'house within the house.' A stoep (veranda) with wooden railings, in front of the rooms, and the Cape Dutch style, impart a village quality. Indeed, the main building and the chalets look like a quaint village nestling in the valley between granite tops and table-mountains. More than 150 murals in the main building and the chalets depict the history and culture of the Bondelswart-Nama who have lived in the area for centuries. They bring personalities to life, depicting heroes of colonial resistance such as Captain Hendrick Witbooi and Jakob Marengo. The murals are the work of local Namibian artists whose paintings are also on sale in the souvenir shop.

(Source: www.gondwanapark.com)

Pescanova, the Spanish fishing giant, through Novanam, brought capital and technical expertise to one of the world's best fishing grounds to spark off an economic renaissance in the almost forgotten settlement of Lüderitz on the remote and formerly neglected shoreline. In pursuit of its pioneering tradition, Pescanova committed its resources to the new Namibia in order to develop a locally-based fishing industry. The port of Lüderitz was chosen as it was the most suitable Namibian harbour at the time of independence in 1990. This investment, the largest foreign investment in Namibia since its independence, led to the construction of a highly advanced factory complex. Novanam's huge Lüderitz waterfront plant employs 2,600 staff and is capable of processing more than 150 tons of fish a day, serviced by 19 owned fishing vessels and a further eight of its associates. Novanam packs more than 200 different retail products at its white fish factory in Lüderitz.

CEO and chairman of the Novanam Group of Companies, Angel Tordesillas, says 65 per cent of Novanam's on-shore production is now processed and packed for the retail market. Apart from the higher earnings in foreign revenue, retail products also help to enhance Namibia's image in foreign markets. Pescanova sends Namibian fish products mainly to four southern countries in Europe as well as to the equally lucrative American and Australian markets where, according to Tordesillas, Namibia is seen as a reliable fish exporting country. Every container of retail packs leaving the Novanam factory turns into an army of small ambassadors for the local industry. Wherever it is sold on supermarket shelves across the world, it clearly says 'Product of Lüderitz, Namibia'.

In 1996, the company tackled the process of Namibianisation that led to the formation of Novanam Ltd with 51 per cent of its voting equity in the hands of Namibian financial institutions and company staff. Tordesillas notes that there are other rich fishing grounds in the world, but that Namibia enjoys one of the world's best resources management. He adds that the Namibia government introduced a scientific and political framework that was a pragmatic, sensible model. Novanam was the first new investment to come back and its confidence has been vindicated 150 per cent — they're continuing to invest and expand, and are committed to the control and good management of the Namibian marine resource since Novanam's adherence to careful management, research and control ensure that these resources are protected for the future. The leadership status of the Pescanova brand is paramount in the company's endeavours to provide high quality premium products to the tables of the world.

(Source: www.novanam.com.na; www.pescanova.co.za; and 'Value-adding in the fishing industry starting to pay off', *The Namibia Economist*, 6 December 2002; www.economist.com.na)

Franz Schmidt, the 'father' of brewing in Namibia, built the first brewery in the country in Klein Windhoek, at the beginning of the 20th century. He was involved in the brewing industry from childhood, since his parents owned a brewery in Germany. In the early 1900s, three other small local breweries emerged, producing light, thirst-quenching beer. In 1920, Carl List and Hermann Ohlthaver acquired these four breweries and amalgamated them to form South West Breweries Ltd (SWB) — the nucleus of what was to become one of Namibia's largest industrial concerns. In 1923, Hermann Ohlthaver and Carl List founded the Ohlthaver & List Company. Carl List's son Werner took over O&L's chairmanship in 1964. In 1967, SWB bought a majority shareholding in Hansa Brauerei in Swakopmund.

A milestone in the history of the brewery was its relocation from the old Garten Street premises in the centre of town to the new premises in Windhoek's northern industrial area. The new brewery was officially opened in 1986. When Namibia gained its independence on March 21, 1990, the SWB changed its name to Namibia Breweries Ltd. In May 1996, the company obtained its listing on the Namibia Stock Exchange and became a public company. In 2002, the grandson of the late entrepreneur Werner List, Sven Thieme, was appointed the new chairman and chief executive officer of the O&L Group, and chairman of the board of Namibia Breweries.

Namibia Breweries currently operates a brewery in Windhoek with a capacity of 1.5 million hectolitres. In 2002, the company sold 1.1 million hectolitres of beer and 300,000 hectolitres of soft drinks. Its main beer brands are Windhoek Lager, Windhoek Light and Tafel Lager. Other beer brands include Windhoek Draught, Hansa Pilsener, Windhoek Special, Urbock and a beer shandy called Club Shandy, while Heineken and Beck's are brewed under licence. Export is playing an important role with more than 50 per cent of production finding its way to 25 countries outside Namibia. All local brands are brewed in strict accordance with the Reinheitsgebot or Purity Law (German Purity Law, adopted in 1516 that states that the only ingredients used for the brewing of beer must be barley, hops and water). The quality of Namibia Breweries beers was acknowledged when four of its brands became the first in Africa to be awarded international gold and silver medals by the Deutsche Landwirtschafts-Gesellschaft. The highest honour was bestowed on Windhoek Light when it was voted the world's best light beer at the Brewing Industry International Awards in 2005.

In July 2004, Diageo, Heineken, and Namibia Breweries announced a new joint venture company in South Africa trading under the name Brandhouse. The new company combines the sales, marketing and distribution of some of the world's top premium brands in this fast growing sector in South Africa. The formation of Brandhouse follows the acquisition by Diageo and Heineken of an effective 28.9 per cent stake in Namibia Breweries, which was finalised in April 2004 following unconditional approval by the South African Competition Commission. The new company has sales of around R3 billion annually. Brandhouse's managing director, Simon Litherland, says the emergence of an influential consumer group in South Africa who are trading up into premium brands has provided a great opportunity to create a new premium liquor business. Brandhouse draws together some of the most talented people in the industry and over 40 of the world's strongest brands into a new, re-engineered business structured for growth.

Namibia Breweries is an independent subsidiary of the O&L Group, as are the other subsidiaries such as Namib Sun Hotels and Namib Sun Hunting Safaris. The O&L Group employs a total workforce of over 4,000 employees. O&L has manifested its genuine commitment to economic empowerment by ceding a 49 per cent shareholding to EPIA, an empowerment group especially established to involve, as beneficiaries, local communities throughout Namibia.

(Source: www.ohlthaverlist.com)

Namib Sun Hotels consists of a hotel and lodge portfolio throughout Namibia, ranging from luxurious four-star establishments to business hotels and consisting of Mokuti Lodge, Strand Hotel, Midgard Lodge, Ghaub Guest Farm, King's Den, Zambezi Lodge and the recently upgraded Hotel Thuringer Hof for business travellers conveniently situated in the CBD of Windhoek. Mokuti Lodge has been awarded four stars in 1995, and the Namibia Best Hotel award four years running. Mokuti Lodge boasts unique African charm, combined with international standards of luxury, and is situated at Anderson Gate, on the eastern edge of Etosha National Park. The park is renowned as one of the most spectacular game viewing areas in Africa. In early 2003, Zambezi Lodge and King's Den joined Namib Sun Hotels.

In 2004, Henry Feris became the group general manager of Namib Sun Hotels. Feris draws his experience from the banking, mining, and consumer product manufacturing sectors. His business degree, well-developed leadership skills and commercial and general business acumen provide outstanding leadership for the Namib Sun properties. He points out that if visitors wish to see and experience Namibia's incredible diversity of ecosystems and wildlife, and to meet and interact with Namibia's many cultures, or to establish a foothold in a stable and peaceful business environment, they should stay at a Namib Sun Hotels property, which lie in or near most major Namibian tourist attractions and business centres.

(Source: www.namibsunhotels.com.na).

Namib Sun Hunting Safaris consists of Katemba Hunting Ranch and Otjiwa Hunting Ranch, which has been completely rebuilt to meet international standards in accommodation and hunting experience. Both lodges provide a hunting area of approximately 28,000 hectares. Different exciting environments and sceneries, from sandy bush plains to rock savannah, make Namib Sun Hunting Safaris a paradise for rifle or bow hunting safaris. Besides professionally executed hunting trips, they also offer game viewing, or simply a great place to relax. A leisurely walk through the savannah landscape will reward visitors with sights not only of rhino and giraffe, but also impala, springbok, blesbok and oryx, grazing on the open plains. Other wildlife includes zebra, wildebeest, the majestic kudu, and the largest of the antelope, the eland.

(Source: www.namibsunhunting.com)

Ongopolo Mining and Processing is working with Zambia and the Democratic Republic of the Congo (DRC) on joint ventures that include the setting up of a copper refinery plant located at Tschudi Mine on the outskirts of Tsumeb, and a foundry and copper rod and wire manufacturing plant in Walvis Bay. Ongopolo's managing director, Andre Neethling, says he is promoting the smelting of copper at Tsumeb from Zambia and DRC as part of a southern African regional initiative that promotes the use of the Trans Caprivi Highway, a road network that links Namibia's landlocked neighbours to the Atlantic Ocean via the port of Walvis Bay. According to Neethling, Tsumeb offers excellent infrastructure, is only 60 kilometres west of Grootfontein on the Trans-Caprivi highway, and is located along the railway line linking Grootfontein with Walvis Bay, which is also part of the system of routes that forms the Walvis Bay Corridor. Neethling believes that opportunities on the international markets and competitive advantages in Namibia, Zambia and the DRC can help forge economic cooperation among the three countries.

Namibia is endowed with copper resources that have been mined since the 1800s. Zambia and the DRC are home to world-class copper deposits. The investments are greatly enhanced by the existing modern and reliable transport network to the international markets. The Walvis Bay Corridor, with its efficient Walvis Bay port facilities and the Trans-Caprivi Highway linking it directly to Zambia and the DRC, through Katima Mulilo, Lusaka, Ndola on the Zambian Copperbelt, and Lubumbashi in the DRC, act as an effective catalyst for these ventures. The Walvis Bay port has been deepened to 12.8 metres and offers the shortest sailing route to Europe and the Americas with significant time savings of two to five weeks over other regional ports in southern Africa.

(Source: 'Ongopolo has big plans with Zambia, DRC', *The Namibia Economist*, 30 July 2004; www.economist.com.na)

Ongopolo's effort to boost community development in Tsumeb has started producing results. Neethling gave his company's support to Ondundu, a community development initiative, which enabled Tsumeb residents to grow vegetables on mine land. The Ondundu agricultural programme in Tsumeb testifies to the entrepreneurial spirit of many rural women in Namibia, and is one of the most successful agricultural projects embarked upon by rural women. During November 2003, four and half tons of carrots were harvested and sold weekly to a local caterer who supplies the Namibian army. The carrots were not only handpicked but also washed, top and tailed and put into bags of ten kilos each. In addition, seven hectares of potatoes, three hectares of squash, and half a hectare of sweet potatoes were harvested by January 2004, and a good price was received for these vegetables, which were much in demand.

(Source: www.ongopolo.com, and 'Life is good and green in Tsumeb thanks to Ondunda', *The Namibia Economist*, 23 November 2003; www.economist.com.na)

NamPower and NAMCOR, Namibian energy companies, have concluded a joint development agreement with South African energy companies Eskom and Energy Africa to develop a gas powered plant in Namibia, which will use gas from the proposed Kudu project, off Namibia's coast. A final investment decision on the Kudu gas and power plant projects was expected to be made by the end of 2005 and Namibian and South African officials are anticipating that electricity production will commence during the second half of 2009, should the projects go ahead. The project involves the offshore development of the Kudu gas field by Energy Africa and the local petroleum company, NAMCOR and the piping of gas to shore for treatment and delivery to an 800 MW power station to be developed at the diamond mining town of Oranjemund. The electricity produced will be sold to NamPower for resale into the Namibian market and the balance sold to Eskom. The Kudu gas project is expected to boost power generation in the Southern African Power Pool. The development of new energy sources is becoming more urgent as the region has of late been experiencing increased demand for electricity. Demand is growing at a fast rate and energy experts say by 2007 the region will face great difficulty in servicing peak demand for electricity. 'No one country can tackle this regional challenge single-handedly. The optimal solution can only be found through regional cooperation and joint planning effort,' says NamPower managing director Dr Leake Hangala. He says the Kudu project is the best option, offering the best solution to immediate electricity supply needs.

(Source: www.nampower.com.na, and 'Electricity production from Kudu seen around 2009', *The Namibia Economist*, 9 July 2004; www.economist.com.na)

The Leviev Group of Companies (LGC) has invested in a marine diamond company, Sakawe Mining Corporation (SAMICOR), Namibia's youngest role-player in the off-shore diamond industry, at a cost of N$300 million. The company is a smart-partnership between LL Mining Corporation, the Namibian government, a black empowerment group and the workers of the new factory. LL Mining is part of Israeli billionaire Lev Leviev's international group of companies. Namibia is now the third country after Angola and Russia where diamond tycoon Leviev has encroached on the business of De Beers, the South African company that has dominated diamond mining for more than a century. The Leviev Group, the second-largest diamond company in the world (behind De Beers), with annual revenue of some $2.5 billion, is a private company based in Ramat-Gan, Israel, and specialises in the cutting and polishing of rough diamonds.

SAMICOR will operate a fleet of four vessels and employ 300 people. SAMICOR holds a concession of about 14,000 square kilometres along the coast of Namibia with a minimum reserve estimate of 12 million carats. Kombadayedu Kapwanga, a director at SAMICOR, says SAMICOR would be in a position to provide enough diamonds to Lev Leviev's new diamond cutting and polishing factory which was opened in June 2004 at a cost of N$40 million. By July 2005, the Windhoek based factory was Africa's largest diamond cutting facility, employing 300 people (and with the potential to grow to 550 when it reaches full capacity), and processing between 25,000 and 30,000 carats per month.

(Source: 'Leviev factory to reach full production next year', *The Namibia Economist*, 27 August 2004; www.economist.com.na)

Traditionally, most diamonds have not been cut and polished in the countries from which they are mined. Although efforts to establish cutting facilities have been made in a number of diamond producing countries, to date many have not proved economical. Lev Leviev was a pioneer in opening Russia's vast diamond resources to local diamond manufacturing, and he apparently believes the same success can be achieved in southern Africa. Certainly, his company is making the investment in equipment and training that is critical to realising their goal. Such an investment has real merit for both parties. The Leviev Group gains by having even stronger ties to Namibia, as well as by developing a model that may have potential for other African countries. Namibia gains from the value added to its natural resources, the boost in employment, and the improvement in the quality of life.

(Source: William E Boyajian, 'Thoughts from the President: A Vision for Africa', www.gia.edu, 27 August 2004)

In November 2005, Leviev inaugurated a new hi-tech diamond polishing factory in Luanda, Angola. In his opinion it is completely possible to polish around 70 per cent of the local production of rough diamonds in Africa. He has also approached Botswana, the world's biggest diamond producer, with a proposal to develop its polishing sector with a view to tripling its current pool of polishers. He thinks it wrong to assume that African countries are not yet capable of polishing diamonds. In the US and Europe there is much talk about how to help poor African countries. Leviev believes the simplest solution is to help them help themselves and to invest in processing raw materials in Africa. Leviev's interests in the diamond industry range from mining, cutting and polishing right through to retail jewellery.

In 2005, Leviev's Africa-Israel company began operations in Namibia. It entered into a joint venture agreement with a local construction company owned by the government of Namibia. The partnership is working towards the construction of a government office building in the capital, Windhoek. This project will be carried out using the PFI (Private Finance Initiative) method, and will include the construction of the building by the partnership, rental to the government for a pre-determined period, to be followed by a transfer of ownership to the government at the end of the lease period.

(Source: www.africa-israel.com)

The Ramatex Textile & Garment Factory, a Malaysian company, was the first of its kind in Namibia. Ramatex operates in several Asian countries, and in Mauritius. The introduction of the African Growth and Opportunity Act (AGOA), providing for duty-free garment imports to the US from sub-Saharan Africa, prompted Ramatex to develop its African interests; the Ramatex project was officially launched in Windhoek in June 2001, and construction began in August 2001. As of 2004, Ramatex Namibia was Africa's highest-profile AGOA-related investment, having invested nearly US$100 million in its vertically integrated textile and garment manufacturing plant.

The Ramatex group has about 30 major buyers from international private label brands, discount stores and the majority of the established global brands. Ramatex Textile Factory Namibia exports branded clothes for large overseas shopping chains like Wal-Mart and Sears. The Ramatex products are mainly exported to markets in the USA (70 per cent) and EU (30 per cent), since the Malaysian investors qualify for the AGOA free duty, and free quota status. This project has significant bearing on the future course of Namibian economic growth in terms of employment creation, skills development and foreign exchange earnings. In 2004, Ramatex had about 9,000 workers and is expected to have a labour force of between 10,000 and 12,000 (mostly Namibians), once it is fully operational. Many of the job openings cater for the historically disadvantaged. The textile plant comprises three garment factories, one knitting mill, one spinning mill and one dyeing mill — with the capacity to produce about 12,000 tons of yarn, 10,000 tons of fabrics, and 24 million garments annually. However, this depends in part on the competitiveness of local supplies, which in turn depend on capabilities, and on the supporting domestic infrastructure, including packaging industries for the shipment of products, raw materials and the procurement of seeds, fertilizers and equipment.

The benefit of this project for a developing country like Namibia depends largely on its trade and investment policies. Namibia with an open trade regime continues to attract increased future competitive, outward-oriented foreign investment, which brings more efficient technology and skills' management, especially in the textile industry. There is no doubt that the Ramatex investment has various economic spin-offs, in terms of small business development, human resources development, and industrial linkages and increased tax revenue. It should generate further spillovers for the agricultural sector, especially in the cotton production sector. Another major benefit from the Ramatex development considering the current global economy is the increasing sophisticated communication and transport infrastructure development in the long-run. The transportation sector is crucial in this regard for the transportation of materials imported and the finished goods to be exported. Currently, the transport industry receives a monetary benefit for equipment handling and clearing of documents by NamPort, and for the transportation of containers by TransNamib Holdings, respectively. Also, during the construction phase, local natural resources and business opportunities have been utilized effectively for the procurement of sand, bricks, cement and paint from Namibia.

The success of the Ramatex project is a clear testimony of the City of Windhoek and Namibia's commitment to improve economic growth of Windhoek and Namibia in general, as it is through initiatives of this nature that the spending capacity of Namibians can be strengthened and the improvement in their living standard will eventually be accelerated. There is no doubt that various other businesses will spring from this venture which will create other vibrant economic activities. Since becoming AGOA-eligible, Namibia has benefited from high-profile foreign investment by Asian textile companies resulting in new factories, thousands of new jobs, and unprecedented levels of new apparel exports. Ramatex executive director Albert Lim's personal opinion is that Namibia has a lot of resources to offer to investors particularly in the agricultural sector, the northern and southern areas are fertile lands for cash crops and cotton growing.

Source: www.ramatex.com and www.windhoekcc.org.na

As editor of *The Namibian*, Gwen Lister's efforts to support the principle of press freedom in Namibia, both before and after independence, and her determination to defend the public's right to know have never wavered despite concerted efforts to silence her through harassment and intimidation. Lister was born in East London, South Africa. After graduating from the University of Cape Town with a bachelor's degree in 1975, she began her journalistic career with the *Windhoek Advertiser* in Windhoek, Namibia. Together with the former editor of the *Advertiser*, Hannes Smith, she started the *Windhoek Observer*, a weekly newspaper, in 1978. As political editor of the *Observer*, she incurred the wrath of the South African authorities with her critical reporting on South Africa's apartheid policies in Namibia. In August 1985, the first edition of her new independent paper, *The Namibian*, was published. From the beginning *The Namibian* was the only paper in Namibia to expose ongoing atrocities and human rights violations against Namibians at the hands of South African security forces. When Namibia finally became independent in 1990, *The Namibian* continued its watchdog role with the new government of the South West African People's Organisation. Lister's newspaper successfully made the transition from donor dependency to financial self-sufficiency shortly after independence from South African rule. Today, the paper continues its fiercely independent editorial stance as Namibia's largest selling daily.

Source: Kudlak, Michael. 2000. '50 Press Freedom Heroes', IPI Report Online (vol. 6, No. 2).

The Namibian was the first newspaper in Namibia to embrace new media technology. It now boasts having Namibia's biggest web site, which, among others, has become indispensable to Namibians living abroad. Lister thanks her many staff members, both past and present, as well as freelancers, who have contributed to making *The Namibian* what it is today. She says they have exciting plans in store as they endeavour to constantly improve on what they offer their readers as well as increase their involvement in communities in terms of social responsibility projects. She also thanks her readers, advertisers and supporters, in short the people of Namibia who have been with her, through bad times and good.

Since 1985, as a non-qualified journalist who learned the trade by baptism of fire, Gwen Lister has moved on to managing the entire publication, workforce, financial wellbeing and everything else that needs to be done. So it is in terms of many of her staff. It is a daunting task sometimes, she admits. Being modest in terms of size has also kept the staff in touch with their roots in the community, and this too, is undoubtedly a strong factor in their success. However, newspapers such as theirs, which have survived to a large extent due to their 'struggle credentials' and strong roots among their readership, Lister advises the staff cannot afford complacency. Times change and the struggle is no longer the same one. So they need to be innovative in bringing about change to give their readers more diversity and a fresher approach to content, and one of *The Namibian's* major projects is a weekly youth paper, which reaches out to youth in an educational and informative capacity, in a country where large scale unemployment and disillusionment about job prospects is a major problem for the next generation. *The Namibian's* growth in recent years has also been an interesting trend, when one compares with major newspapers the world over that are struggling to boost flagging readership. The answer to this, Lister believes, 'lies in connectivity to our communities and continued relevance to their aspirations and needs.'

(Source: www.namibian.com.na, and Gwen Lister. 2004. 'Managing Media in Times of Crisis.' Paper presented at Unesco Conference on 'Freedom of Expression and Conflict Management in Crisis Situations and Countries in Transition', Belgrade, 2-4 May 2004)

Botswana

There are more cattle than people in Botswana, with a 2004 human population of 1.8 million, the national herd of almost three million is enough for everyone to pick a cow and have sufficient reserve to start a new herd. Trade in beef makes the country stand out. It has benefited most from the lucrative trade in beef with the European Union. Where other developing countries have faced an uphill task in supplying quality beef to the superior standard European market, Botswana has prevailed. After independence in 1966, the Botswana government embarked on a deliberate program to improve the quality of Botswana's cattle. New breeds were introduced at subsidized prices to the farms. Artificial insemination has also played a leading role in improving on quality. Botswana has managed to turn subsistence cattle farming into organised beef ranching, which has a high demand in Europe and other countries. The quality has remained high because of highly trained personnel.

The formation of the Botswana Meat Commission (BMC) has ensured quality control. The BMC has been responsible for setting up cold storage facilities in Botswana, in Europe and in other markets. The craving for Botswana meat the world over was because the animals graze on chemically free vast ranch lands of more than 580,000 square kilometres. The BMC established by the government in 1996 coordinates the production of beef from a national herd of some two to three million. Facilities at the BMC headquarters in Lobatse have been designed and constructed as a complete and integrated complex of abattoir, canning, tanning and by-products plant to handle a throughput of 800 cattle and 500 small stock per day. Branch abattoirs are operated in the northwest of the country at Maun, with a capacity of 100 cattle per day, and in the northeast at Francistown, with a capacity of 400 cattle and 150 small stock per day. The BMC owns marketing subsidiaries in the United Kingdom, Germany and Holland, an insurance company in the Cayman Islands, cold storage facilities in the United Kingdom and South Africa, and transport companies in Botswana.

(Source: Patrick Luganda. 'Lessons from Botswana', Kampala: *New Vision*, 4 July 2002)

Botswana could benefit from the processing of its hides into fine leather, needed by manufacturing industries, but the BMC has no intention of further processing its leather beyond the wet blue hides stage. Motshudi Raborokgwe, BMC's executive chairman, says BMC has no intention of processing their leather to the crust and finished stage as this is not their core business. He adds that anybody is free to set up a tannery to process BMC wet blue hides into finished leather. BMC, Botswana's largest supplier of raw leather, only tans raw hides to the wet blue state, a process, which only removes the hair and fat deposits from the leather although the leather requires further processing into fine leather, which is needed by the manufacturing industries. As it is, Botswana is losing out due to the unfavourable balance of trade in importing leather goods and accessories. The processing of leather into finished leather could form the basis for the establishment of local leather manufacturing industries.

The BMC has previously attempted to privatize the BMC tannery and potential investors have expressed interest in buying it. BMC's gripe with the investors is that the latter are not prepared to buy the tannery at an acceptable price and they want the BMC to supply them with hides at below market prices. Raborokgwe adds that there are no new plans to add value to BMC's meat products and raw materials. The BMC already processes meat products by making corned beef, corned meat, stewed steak, stewed steak with vegetables, corned meat in chilli, ox-tongue, and pet food. Other than these, the BMC produces raw materials (beef, carcass meal) which entrepreneurs other than the BMC can process. BMC's value of export commodities for 2003 to the European Union markets and other African markets stood at P260 million. The United Kingdom commands 33.6 per cent; Norway 8.0 per cent, Germany 11.5 percent, Italy 7.7 per cent, and South Africa 15.2 per cent of the total export market of the BMC.

(Source: Donny Dithato. 'BMC has no Plans to process hides into leather', Gaborone: *Mmegi/The Reporter*, 30 July 2004)

In addition to the BMC, the Botswana Livestock Development Corporation (BLDC) was formed for the purpose of buying cattle not yet ready for slaughter — these are fattened after purchase and then sold to the BMC. The BLDC is designed to help cattle owners in more remote areas where prices for cattle are lower than in areas closer to the main abattoirs. Although most of Botswana's cattle are reared for beef production, there is also a dairy industry, still relatively in its infancy. Import controls have been instituted to encourage the production of milk and milk products. In addition the Botswana Department of Veterinary Services also helps in livestock production by providing livestock advisory services, operating a diagnostic laboratory for disease control and carrying out meat inspections.

(Source: Patrick Luganda. 'Lessons from Botswana'. Kampala: *New Vision*, 4 July 2002)

Owing to European import restrictions on meat, Botswana cattle must be kept inside fences to avoid disease. Environmentalists maintain that cattle raising, and the accompanying fences, have reduced the once plentiful wildlife of the country's plains and disrupted migratory patterns. Environmentalists are now fighting to preserve one of the continent's last great wild areas from cattle ranchers, whose fences are denying buffalo, zebra and wildebeest access to migration routes, and local Bushmen access to their traditional lands. Mark and Delia Owen, who wrote *Cry of the Kalahari*, protested vigorously against the fences across the wildebeest migration route and witnessed awful carnage — the destruction of almost all Botswana's wildebeest in just one season. They subsequently got thrown out of Botswana for their troubles. The Botswana government doesn't brook much opposition from foreign protestors. The fences affect all local people, not just Bushmen, and there have been cases of local communities breaking down fences. Cattle ranchers, however, argue that many areas of Botswana are still open and therefore the overall impact of enclosing some areas to migration is not overwhelming.

Another factor to meet EU requirements is the ability to trace cattle. A new company, AST Botswana, in partnership with the veterinary department is now tagging the entire national herd with a 'bolus.' They expect to tag five million cattle in five years. There are currently only about three million cattle tagged worldwide! This also gives an indication of the expected growth in the national herd.

(Source: www.bmc.bw)

Engine Component Enterprise (ECE) managing director Johan Sutherland says the manufacturing of light and heavy single trailers for the agriculture sector in Botswana has the potential to make a significant contribution to the gross domestic product (GDP). Sutherland, whose company specialises in building trailers for Botswana conditions, says Botswana's manufacturing industry has the capacity to generate revenue for the country through exports. Therefore, as the market expands, his company intends to venture into the manufacture of other products to satisfy the export market. Situated in Tlokweng, ECE, trading as Trail Quip, builds cattle, cargo and off-road trailers. Sutherland says that ECE employs 15 people trained on the job to do welding, auto-mechanics, sheet metal and steel work. Some women have undergone extensive training to become spray painters. They are looking at building cattle load bodies for trucks. With a skilful capacity to design and build trailers for Botswana conditions, ECE offers a one-year warranty on its goods. The company has been in Botswana since 1990, started building trailers 2002, and plans to explore the market to build agriculture trailers in 2005.

(Source: Martin Nyirenda. 'Entrepreneur Emphasises Importance of Machinery Manufacturer', Gaborone: *Mmegi/The Reporter*, 3 August 2004)

Tim Race, originally Zimbabwean, now lives permanently in Botswana with his wife Claire, a medical doctor. He hails from a long line of African safari operators and big game hunters and has family connections in most southern African countries. Tim runs his own company, Africa Insight, the only tourism company in Botswana to cater specifically for disabled clients. He has specially adapted vehicles for this purpose and offers wildlife and cultural tours and safaris throughout Botswana. 'We are not exclusively for disabled clients,' he says. 'We aim to be inclusive and as such you can now safari with your disabled family member — this is the only company in the whole sub-continent to offer this amazing opportunity.'

All the vehicles Tim uses for his tours and safaris are Land Rover-based and to counter the problem of getting spare parts he has also branched out into replacement parts distribution and is an agent for a large British company specialising in after-market parts. This has allowed him to widen his business interests rapidly and to supply other tour operators with Land Rover parts. Tim is also on the editorial staff of a leading monthly motoring magazine published in Britain, *Land Rover Enthusiast*. He provides regional reports, updates and anecdotes from his safaris to a worldwide readership. Tim's father is a partner in all his business interests, offering invaluable advice and direction.

Tim also offers location advice for filming and photography, as well as putting on a special Mma Ramotswe's Botswana Tour of the sites associated with *The No. 1 Ladies' Detective Agency* mystery novels by Alexander McCall Smith — probably one of the very few literary tours being offered in Africa — and he was the location manager for a film the BBC made about the background to McCall Smith's Botswana books. McCall Smith agrees that the unusual nature of Tim Race's activities is very different from the run-of-the-mill tourism outfit.

(Source: www.africainsight.com)

Gill Fonteyn runs an orphan-care centre, Dula Sentle, in the village of Otse (population 3,000). Seventy-five children come to the centre. Gill, an indefatigable Belgian, and his Batswana wife, Brenda, know who in Otse is sick and who is dying, so they know that in another year or two, they will be caring for about 300 orphans. When they began looking after the AIDS orphans, half the children were not going to school but now there is perfect attendance. 'It's the best orphan-care centre in Botswana,' says Dr Donald de Korte, whose African Comprehensive HIV/AIDS Partnerships (ACHAP) organisation provides some funding.

Otse village is a beautiful place with a big dam and is surrounded by hills and trees. There is much development. Work on a pool and camping area at Dula Sentle has been completed. The site of the Fairytales Furniture Showroom is officially opened and houses the showroom, a tea garden and tourist information centre. This will be linked to the proposed hiking path up to the top of Otse Mountain, at 1,491metres the highest point in Botswana!

In his September 2005 newsletter, Gill told the people and organisations who believe in Dula Sentle that he was already sure the September 2005 bookings for the campsite would, for the first time, secure staff salaries. In addition, the campsite was effectively providing weekend camp activities for Dula Sentle's own 106 children, and was providing skill training for some of the older children — and would eventually employment for some of the children when they grew up.

Gill reminded supporters that there was still a long way to go, but the indications were good, strong and sustainable. Their next step was to work hard to start self-generating enough funds to provide for programme expenses. The campsite and guesthouse, the furniture factory and showroom, the crafts and tea garden are all projects geared up to allow Dula Sentle to become more and more financially self-sustainable. He assured supporters: 'this allows us to ensure that your support is a 100 per cent direct support to our children. No cutting corners.'

People in Otse village support Dula Sentle, a place where beautiful children are taken care of and educated. Martin Fisher, creative at Marketing Communications PTY Ltd, Gaborone, is in partnership with Dula Sentle and Fairytales Furniture to help bring the furniture to market. Dula Sentle's long-term goal is to sell furniture in Gaborone.

Dula Sentle's music activities started in April 2002. From some simple songs the music developed into what it is today. It allows the children to write about their own feelings, emotions and experiences: the loss of beloved ones, grievance, coping with HIV/AIDS in the community — writing and singing about these issues has proved to be a powerful therapy tool. In June 2004, the children performed with Mary Wilson (former member of the Supremes). Gill and the children recorded some songs at the Mud Hut recording studio in Gaborone and a CD of the songs is available, along with a Dula Sentle documentary. On the cover of the CD, the children of Dula Sentle write: 'It has taken us a little bit longer than expected, but we feel that it was worthwhile waiting for. The story of our lives worked into a music CD. Eight songs that will tell you who we are, how we feel and who we want to be one day. We hope you enjoy listening to the music, as we enjoyed composing and singing the songs.' Dula Sentle's music therapy is one of the most powerful exercises to allow the children to become themselves again, and should be used all over to help children in Africa.

(Source: www.dulasentle.org.bw)

In May 2004, Academy Award-winning film director Anthony Minghella came to Otse and Dula Sentle. Botswana is thought to be a likely location for the shooting of a television series based on the bestselling *No.1 Ladies' Detective Agency* series by Alexander McCall Smith, which is set in the area. Minghella was given a short tour of the centre and hugely enjoyed the children and a performance of their songs, requesting encore after encore. Dula Sentle was visited in early June 2004 by BTV. Cameramen spent the day filming, and created a ten-minute documentary, broadcast nationwide, showing the children engaged in daily learning and craft activities. The documentary ended with the Dula Sentle children singing two of their songs.

Otse's Legodimo Trust Project offers vocational training and social support to 26 young adults aged from14 to 21, who have mental and physical disabilities. Legodimo also benefits the community by offering employment to local people and development assistance to other projects. Legodimo was founded in July 1996 by five Batswana residents. It is supported by the local authorities of Otse and is strongly affiliated with the Camphill Community Trust. The project is divided into a number of workshops and activities (all of which the young people are involved in) and the site also houses a mixed kindergarten for the village's younger children. Among these workshops and activities there is a shop which sells crafts from southern African and local projects, a tea garden serving snacks and drinks in a tranquil atmosphere and an orange orchard which donates up to 1,000 bags of oranges annually to other projects in Otse. The prize-winning gardens supply the project with its own fruit and vegetables and also provide another source of income, while the children learn to grow vegetables without use of pesticides.

In 1998, Mrs M Lesetedi became a teacher at Legodimo, having originally worked at Camphill School. She took over the Legodimo project from Gill Fonteyn in 2000. Her role is to oversee and market the project. Mrs Lesetedi describes Legodimo as a place where kids are trained to be independent and free — cooking and working on various projects for themselves. The skills that they acquire can then be used for the rest of their lives. Children come from all over Botswana and at present there are 26 children, with 22 living on the premises. She says that the best part of her job is working with the children. If she sees a student successful and happy then she is happy, and she is personally involved with the children's individual development. She describes the lows of the job as financial concerns. However, she reflects that projects such as the tea garden and conference room are good potential sources of income.

Mmegi, which was established as a weekly newspaper in 1984, is published by Dikgang Publishing Company (DPC). In October 2003, *Mmegi* went daily, becoming the only daily independent newspaper in Botswana at that time. Managing editor of Dikgang Publishing Company, Titus Mbuya, says the decision to go daily was a response to a need that existed in the market. The newspaper is read by a cross-section of the population including students, policy makers, intellectuals and the business community. Over the previous 10 years *Mmegi* had won the prestigious Institute of Bankers Newspaper of the year Award nine times. During 2000 the publishers of *Mmegi* added a new title to the stable — the *Mmegi Monitor*. With a circulation of about 16,000 copies a week the *Monitor*, which comes out on Mondays, is the fastest growing newspaper in Botswana. Both publications are printed at the DPC printing factory in Tlokweng, just outside Gaborone.

(Source: www.mmegi.bw)

Lesotho

In 1862 King Moshoeshoe allowed Father Gerard and his missionaries to settle in a vast amphitheatre, in an area known today as the Roma Valley. Here Father Gerard established the first Catholic mission in Lesotho. The valley is the most important educational centre in Lesotho, housing the National University of Lesotho whose humble beginnings as Pius XII College date back to 1945. Roma today is also home to three seminaries, St Joseph's hospital, two high schools and some junior schools. John Thomas Thorn established the Roma Trading Post in 1903, and lived there until his death in 1957.

The Trading Post is still owned by fourth generation Thorns: Ashley and Jennifer. Over the years the family used this base to pioneer their trade into the Blue Maluti Mountains and established other trading posts including one in Semonkong. Tribesmen still come from the surrounding mountains on horseback to buy supplies or to have their maize milled; the place had a very frontier feel to it as though nothing had changed over the years. The Trading Post Guest House, run by Ashley and Jennifer, is a lovely old sandstone building in a beautiful garden setting in the Roma Valley, alongside the original trading post that is still busy today. Today, the fifth generation of Thorns grows up in this scenic place deep in the Maluti Mountains with spectacular views across the Ramabanta valley. Andrea, daughter of Jennifer, spent a year travelling and working in the United States. She has taken a computer course, is a talented artist, and is currently working with the business in Roma. This is the ideal location for both the adventurer seeking the ultimate challenging off-road trails, and the traveller who wants the peace and tranquillity of trekking by horseback or hiking through the valley and mountains of Lesotho.

(Source: www.tradingpost.co.za)

Siiri Morley, a US Peace Corps volunteer working with the Elelloang Basali (Be Aware Women) Weavers in Lesotho spoke at the Third International Conference on Information Technology and Economic Development, held in Ghana in March 2004. She presented a paper (a finalist in the ICT Stories competition) titled 'AfricanCraft.com generating pride and publicity for Africa's artisans: A case study of mohair weavers in Lesotho', written by Morley and Manthabiseng Rammalane. The paper focused on the Elelloang Basali Weavers.

Elelloang Basali is 'a partnership of Basotho women who weave mohair rugs, tapestries, bags, table runners, tablemats, and knit mohair jackets. Their beautiful, high quality weavings, which have been washed, mothproofed, dyed, woven, and finished in their Lesotho studio, using local hand-spun mohair, add a unique touch to home or office and make wonderful gifts. Since 1997, they have been working to take control of their lives and improve the quality of life for their children. The proceeds from every purchase go back to them, all Basotho women, to help them pay school fees and medical bills. Any additional income goes to the development of the weaving partnership. Designs celebrate the Basotho cultural heritage through the revival of Basotho Litema patterns, originally drawn into the walls of traditional Basotho homes, depictions of the ancient Bushman rock paintings throughout the region and illustrate rural village life'

(Source:www.africancraft.com).

Morley's paper points out that 'Elelloang has had since its beginnings great difficulties with publicity, communication, and an inability to share their work with overseas customers. For several years, the weavers worked to build capacity in terms of product development, marketing, and exporting. With few overseas orders and limited local sales, they wanted to 'find the market,' but were unsure of how to specifically pursue and locate these abstract overseas clients. Without the use of the Internet, this was an enormous challenge. Thus, Elelloang pursued the connection with AfricanCraft.com in order to gain more visibility and to establish an online catalogue, which would allow the business and its projects to prosper and grow.'

Morley explains: 'In November 2002, AfricanCraft.com established a website for the weavers for free (as all artisan pages are) that includes a homepage with introductory information, a portfolio with over thirty weavings that customers can order, a photo gallery of images of the weavers at work, their price list, a map, and Elelloang's contact information. The site also includes a mailing list, which aims to document consumer interest in the product ... [Elelloang has] received high praise for the site and inquiries and orders have been sent from individuals and shops around the world, including Sweden, Lebanon, the United States, Canada, Japan, South Africa and the United Kingdom. AfricanCraft.com has also facilitated new orders with Elelloang's old customers in Namibia, Scotland, South Africa and the United States. Without the site, Elelloang would struggle for visibility; with it they are linked to a wider network of customers and African art enthusiasts ... Their business has strengthened and their many projects have led to women's economic empowerment, increased education, public health and HIV prevention initiatives, alternative building structures and solar energy, permaculture, improved nutrition, interest-free credit, the revival of indigenous Basotho designs, a strong women's support centre, and a powerful example of truly grassroots, self-initiated sustainable development.'

Morley writes: 'AfricanCraft.com, launched by Louise Meyer and John Nash in 1999, is an effort that aims to bridge the gap between the two worlds of artisans and western consumers. By recognising and giving publicity to the talent of African artisans, the site aspires to support efforts of fair trade, sustainable development, and women's empowerment; and additionally to instil pride and hope in disadvantaged craftspeople. This innovative and original website showcases the work of craftspeople, artists, and designers and additionally hosts retail catalogues, all with an African theme. It brings together [Africans] and Americans and proudly displays their work next to photos of the creators ... The site has helped numerous artisan groups, individual artists, and designers build their export clientele, obtain international recognition, and receive invitations to trade fairs and workshops. For some artisans, AfricanCraft.com is their only source of publicity. Perhaps the most important result of the site is one that is difficult to quantify, that of increased pride. Throughout Africa handicraft work is often seen as a low-status occupation, despite the fact it is sustaining families and takes great skill, for artisans to see their work presented with so much respect in an international forum is an extraordinary thing.'

(Source: Siiri Morley and Manthabiseng Rammalane. 'AfricanCraft.com generating pride and publicity for Africa's artisans: A case study of mohair weavers in Lesotho', presentation at 3rd International Conference on Information Technology and Economic Development in Ghana, March 2004)

Susan Hester, an accomplished marketing consultant and international trade specialist from Washington, who has extensive experience in marketing handicrafts from Africa, believes small Africa-based firms exporting handicrafts and textiles need to focus on specialty shops as an alternative to the large department- and chain-store markets in the USA, which are difficult to penetrate. She says it is appropriate to focus on smaller specialty entrepreneurs who demand smaller quantities and tend to be more open-minded and less rigid in their buying requirements. Hester notes that an alternative strategy that could be employed in order to penetrate the US market would be to target independently owned retail businesses such as furniture and home furnishing stores as well as clothing accessory shops.

Hester says one promising segment of the US market is businesses owned by or catering to African-Americans who number over 36 million and represent approximately 13 per cent of the American population. Hester says that 1.8 million affluent African American families spend more than US$32 billion on apparel and footwear as well as US$14 billion on household furnishings and equipment each year. She also observes that the USA has a staggering number of museums, art galleries and zoos, many of which have sophisticated retail shops designed to generate much needed revenue for the institutions. A key requirement is that an exporter must clearly define and understand its target consumers — and think about who will ultimately be using the products and where they will be sold. Hester notes that an honest objective assessment of the competition in the market, including market shares and strengths and weaknesses, is crucial if the exporter is to know how to out-perform its competitors.

(Source: Susan Hester, Speech at the Zambia Marketing seminar in Lusaka on 25 March 2004)

Lesotho is a world without fences. Breathtaking scenery abounds and every season has unique attractions. Malealea is a remote valley, set in the foothills of the spectacular Thaba-Putsoa range of mountains, in south-western Lesotho. Malealea Lodge and Pony-Trekking Centre is the ideal place for exploration. The Centre is tucked away in a remote rural area. Malealea dates back to 1905 when it was a trading post founded by Mervyn Bosworth-Smith, a charismatic colonial character educated at Oxford, who served in both the Anglo-Boer and First World wars, then fell in love with Basutoland and lived there for over 40 years. A small village subsequently developed round the trading store, which has changed hands several times since Mervyn's death in 1950.

In December 1986, Mick and Di Jones assumed management of the trading complex and in 1989 they bought the property and transformed Malealea into a fully functional self-catering lodge. Mick and Di had moved to Malealea to lease for three years, but when the shop burned down in February 1987, they were forced to make a decision — either to leave or rebuild and buy, which they did in April 1987. They bought the shop, knowing that it was running at a loss, but hoping they would get it going again. They liked the idea of starting a lodge for fun, not knowing at all whether or not it would take off, as the road at that time was a rocky track and a 4x4 was really needed to get to Malealea. The determined visitors managed to get there, bumping in their two wheel drives. They have now closed down the Trading Store and this is an opportunity for the local shopkeepers in the village to grow and improve their shops.

Mick and Di have made significant improvements to Malealea Lodge over the years to accommodate an increasing number of visitors, and made Malealea and Lesotho a cultural tourism destination. Mick and Di were both born in Lesotho and are credited with more local knowledge than anyone. They have made enormous contributions to Malealea, its people, and to Lesotho. They started an impressive model of ecotourism and community empowerment. In the evenings, around a campfire, guests are entertained by music and dance groups from the village, and payment is made directly to these entertainers, who are mostly students.

Mick and Di started the original lodge with five bedrooms, twelve beds and two shared bathrooms. Accommodations at Malealea Lodge now comprise 22 en suite rondavels, 17 en suite bedrooms in the farmhouse, as well as five Basotho huts with five outside communal bathrooms. Linen and towels are provided while catering is at an extra charge. Two communal kitchens are also provided. For budget travellers, there are nine forest huts with four outside communal bathrooms. Camping is also available. Electricity is supplied by a generator, which is turned off late at night, so it is recommended that guests bring a torch.

Mick and Di Jones specialise in horse trekking and can arrange one-hour to six-day treks. Villagers have been encouraged to form the Pony Owners' Association, and members take turns hiring their mounts to visitors. Accommodation on overnight treks is in basic Basotho huts, and this also provides an income to the owners. Young men from the village (who are able to speak some English) work as tour guides, for which they charge an hourly or daily fee. These treks explore spectacular mountain passes and provide opportunities for visitors to interact with local tribes.

Because of social involvement and environmental awareness, Malealea was the winner at the 2002 and 2003 Imvelo Responsible Tourism Awards. When the winners of the Africa 2004 SMME Awards were announced in October 2004, enterprises from all over the continent made their mark. Malealea was the winner of the award for the tourism sector.

(Source: www.malealea.com)

An important reciprocal relationship exists between Malealea Lodge and the surrounding community. The philosophy is one of interdependency. Mick and Di believe that tourism plays a constructive role in contributing towards the well being of the community who share their lives with tourists visiting the valley. The Malealea Development Trust was established to coordinate community development activities in the Malealea Valley. The two main (but not separate) areas of focus are development and education. Development activities engage members of the community in identifying and addressing their own needs in a way that can lead to an improved life. Education activities are integrally related to the development activities: people learn what they need to learn in order to carry out the development initiatives, which they have identified as appropriate. Development and education thus go hand in hand. Other Trust projects include the establishment of a small home for vulnerable children, a community library, a sports facility, a community hall, wetlands and soil reclamation projects, and a wind turbine which generates electricity for the local high school.

The Malealea community has identified income generation activities as a primary direction for development. They see these activities as a way to foster self-sufficiency and empowerment at both individual and community level. People engage collectively in meaningful work to generate income that will sustain their families and enable financial independence. This approach is more sustainable in the long-term, since it enables people to build their skills, as opposed to passively depending on the generosity of well intentioned tourists who give handouts on a short-term basis. Several income generation projects have been started. These include a handicraft project, a youth art project, and an agricultural project. These projects have been legally constituted into a multi-purpose cooperative, which is affiliated to the wider cooperative movement in Lesotho. Members of the cooperative sell their products to tourists as well as to other people in the community.

Every member of the cooperative has also participated in education and training activities, which have been identified as necessary for the growth and development of the cooperative. Education includes business skills training, management training, technical skills training, and training in basic English skills that will improve communication between members of the co-operative and tourists. Members of the cooperative have also participated in HIV-AIDS awareness workshops, a crucial aspect of any development initiative in rural communities.

Learning does not however take place only within the cooperative. Members of the cooperative have committed themselves to taking the development process forward through sharing their knowledge with others who live in more remote villages in the valley which tend to be cut off from the benefits of tourism. In this regard, village 'learning communities' have been established as 'engines' that promote learning and action in 14 villages scattered throughout the valley. A cadre of 25 cooperative members has received training in a participatory learning approach that supports the cooperative members to work more effectively with these village learning communities.

Training has been conducted by Gillian Attwood, a lecturer in Adult Education at the University of the Witwatersrand in Johannesburg. Each learning community meets twice a week for two hours, and the trained facilitators manage and monitor the learning and related action processes that take place during and after the meetings. Members of the village learning communities identify and take up development challenges relevant to their situation and context. In total, over 300 people have been involved in the 14 learning communities and their related education and development activities. Educational topics covered by members include health issues such as HIV-AIDS awareness, environmental issues such as soil and water conservation as well as reforestation, development issues, life skills and business skills, and gender issues. Appropriate literacy and numeracy skills have also been developed to enable members to address issues relevant to their everyday lives.

The facilitators of the learning circles in Malealea constitute a confident and capable cadre of community activists. In areas as poor as Malealea, apathy that grows out of poverty is often the biggest obstacle to development. However, the facilitators have become effective agents of change and have worked hard to establish a climate in which communities not only have a vision for their future, but a plan to make that vision happen. The ongoing challenge is to keep the learning circles alive. There is much work still to be done in Malealea, and communities are eager to take on this work. Some communities still need water and others want to improve their nutritional intake through establishing gardens. More trees need to be planted throughout the valley to address the very serious threat of desertification and of course communities want to take action to address the high HIV infection rate that is causing such devastation in their lives. Without these learning communities, community mobilisation is difficult and development in the area unlikely. People need to keep on learning and acting to address the almost overwhelming forces they face.

(Source: www.malealea.com/devprojects.html)

Swaziland

A number of the most successful groups of companies in Swaziland were founded by Nathan Kirsh, the Swaki Group being one of them, now equally owned by Kirsh and the Swaziland Industrial Development Company (SIDC). Kirsh, a multi-millionaire businessman, believed in the words of the 12th century philosopher Maimoinedes who wrote that the highest degree of charity is to aid a man in want, not by offering him a gift or a loan but by entering to partnership with him or by providing work for him so that he may be self-sufficient. Kirsh said this was his credo. He was not a man who believed in talk with no action. In March 1999, he backed up his belief by creating a one-million-dollar-plus fund, known as the 'Inhlanyelo Fund' to be used in small villages throughout Swaziland to give men and women with good ideas an opportunity to become self-sufficient. Kirsh was always accepted into the community right from his first day in Swaziland, and he said that if you're accepted by a community you give back to that community.

Kirsh, affectionately know as 'Natie', built an economic empire after coming to Swaziland in 1959 from South Africa. He began practicing his credo of partnership, moving from opening a maize milling business, to farm chemicals, then warehousing and many others. Thereafter he founded businesses in South Africa, the USA and in other countries. But he always kept his roots in Swaziland. In the manufacturing and commercial sectors, the most active investor in Swaziland has been the Kirsh Group. Kirsh with two other individuals helped to establish the Royal Swaziland Sugar Corporation and founded Swaki Ltd, working in cooperation with the SIDC. He went on to build shopping malls, and founded two textile companies. He invested in the banking sector and held franchises for Mercedes Benz, BMW and Nissan. However, he said he could only eat three meals a day, so he asked himself what he was going to do with his money.

Kirsh, a gregarious man with a million-dollar smile, had always been in the business of helping those around him. In the late 1960s he provided a home for the first orphanage in Swaziland, Enjabulweni, run by the Roman Catholic Church; donated money for construction at the University of Swaziland; and founded and developed the Computer Education Trust which, by 2006, will ensure that every high school graduate is computer literate. There is a long list of the civic organisations and boards he belonged to that were dedicated to the development of the people of Swaziland — amongst which was his 21-year stint as chairman of the Swaziland Electricity Board. The secret to his success, he said, was simple. When he looked at something, he was not just looking at what it was — he was looking at what direction it could go in. What he saw in Swaziland in 1959 made him put down business roots and he was right. The changes in Swaziland and the way it has progressed have been remarkable. In 1999, he wanted to speed up progress in the rural areas and to encourage entrepreneurship and show that to make money you had to decide what you wanted to do, and do it — but he appreciated that seed money was needed, hence the Inhlanyelo Fund (nhalnyelo means seed in Siswati). The background to the Inhlanyelo Fund was that a member of parliament came to Kirsh and asked for money to help people in his constituency start businesses. Kirsh agreed to help but insisted on giving the money directly to the borrower and asked the MP to bring him people with the right ideas. Three or four months later Kirsh had made unsecured loans to establish 28 businesses which, two years down the line, were almost 100 per cent successful. He was amazed. Again practicing his partnership credo, Kirsh twisted some arms. Two companies in which he had an interest, the Swaki Group and Standard Bank Swaziland Ltd, agreed to contribute to the fund.

The basic concept was that each of the 55 participating constituencies would be allotted approximately US$20,000, and a community panel within each constituency would determine whether an applicant should be considered. What the panel looked at was personal reputation and family, whether these people were the good players in the constituency. Management of the Inhlanyelo Fund would then evaluate and choose the most promising candidates and allocate the available cash as loans to those they thought had the drive to establish sustainable business projects. Loans of up to US$2,000 were thus made to individuals with good ideas and the will to work. Natie was seeking to promote a belief that it is possible to succeed in uplifting yourself, but he also recognised the importance of providing seed money. There was no requirement for people to repay if a business failed, but if it succeeded and did not repay then the constituency would put pressure to obtain repayment so as to recycle the money to the next person waiting for a loan. In this way peer pressure from the community ensured that those who succeeded would play the game so that money would flow back to the fund and be used again in the same constituency.

Although the Swaziland government had an enterprise fund to assist micro-enterprises, there were rules and regulations that required it to be used by communities rather than individuals. What Natie was trying to do was to promote a culture of entrepreneurship that the government's enterprise fund did not allow. By August 2005, 4,500 businesses had been started, creating over 10,000 jobs. Kirsh is confident, based on the cultural values and the sincerity of the Swazi people that he'd observed since 1959, that the fund will be a renewing spring of success, continuing to uplift the communities and the country as a whole. In 2004, with the first round of funding to all constituencies completed, Kirsh provided repeat funding for each constituency which, over the life of the new parliament, will be added to the money now being paid back and which will accelerate the number of new micro-entrepreneurs throughout the country. Historically the success rate is above 80 per cent, much higher than anyone expected, and 75 per cent of the loans have been to women. In Swaziland, Kirsh made a difference.

(Source: 2005 correspondence, and 'Swazi businessman gives back profits to rural poor', a special international report prepared by *The Washington Times* advertising department, published on 30 April 1999)

Amongst the mountains that encircle the tiny African Kingdom of Swaziland is one that resembles a basking crocodile. At its summit is the world's most ancient iron ore mine, dating back 43,000 years and at its foot is the remote village named Ngwenya (Siswati for crocodile). Here Sibusiso Mhlanga and a small group of Swazi craftspeople — with age-old artistry — breathe life into enchanting interpretations of the animals and birds of Africa, imbuing each with its own irresistible personality. As the master glassblower at Ngwenya Glass, Mhlanga creates works of art from molten 100 per cent recycled glass. The blower has only a few minutes in which to work his glass, between its initially being too soft and the moment when it hardens and becomes brittle. It is the measure of his skill to judge the few moments of its pliability to the best advantage.

Ngwenya Glass, set in large indigenous gardens, is considered one of Swaziland's major tourist attractions, where visitors can witness first-hand, the magical art of glassblowing from an overhead balcony and browse around the adjoining showroom which is well stocked with ornamental African animals, tall elegant drinking glasses, vases, jugs, shining glass jewellery and unique African tribal stem glasses. The factory was first started in 1979 by a Swedish company that employed Swazis and trained them in the ancient art of glassblowing. But in 1985 the factory closed down and went into liquidation. Two years later the Prettejohn family, who used to collect the glass craft made by the original business, took a leap of faith and re-opened the glassblowing factory. Although they knew absolutely nothing about glassmaking, through sheer determination, hard work and common sense the family brought the business successfully back into being. Now employing more than 60 workers, including the three original glass blowers first trained by the Swedes, Ngwenya Glass has proved in the 18 years since its re-birth in 1987, that it is here to stay.

(Source: 'Manzini market and craft shops hold Swazi treasures', a special international report prepared by *The Washington Times* advertising department, published on 30 April 1999; and www.ngwenyaglass.co.sw)

Situated within Ngwenya Glass gardens is a craft centre where local Swazi arts and crafts are made and sold. This incorporates Jody's Shoppe and Craft Market. Outside the door of the downstairs workshop is a sign headed 'The Toymaker' which reads, 'He is the hero of the village, because he works wonders for little boys and girls. He can make a single piece of wood come alive, and stir the imagination of any youngster. He is more than a toy maker, he is a dream maker.' Alan Taylor, an English immigrant carpenter/builder who was tired of the pressure of the construction industry, first established the Rocking Horse Company in 1995. This was the realisation of a childhood dream. In October 2003, Alan decided to retire to Dullstroom, South Africa, and Brian Roberts, a carpenter/joiner by trade, and Chas Prettejohn, the owner of Ngwenya Glass, acquired the business.

Each horse is created from local kiln dried hardwoods sourced from reputable timber merchants throughout southern Africa. The tack is handmade to fit each specific horse, which is sold with a certificate of authenticity. No two horses are the same; its creator endows each with its own irresistible personality. Horses can be personalised to meet the buyer's specifications, from choice of wood, colour of saddle and trimmings.

Since its rebirth in 1987, Ngwenya Glass has been more than an inspiring success story. It is an environmentalist's dream. Most of the glass used is from soft drink bottles, gathered from all over Swaziland. Not only are the people of Swaziland encouraged to collect the bottles, but Ngwenya Glass works with the local schools to instil in the children a sense of environmental awareness. In exchange for building materials and the sponsorship of the soccer team, the students must participate in roadside clean-up campaigns. Ngwenya Glass is proof that business success and commitment to the environment can, indeed, be a winning combination.

Ngwenya Glass products are found in homes worldwide, whilst custom-made light fittings and tableware are commissioned by the most prestigious hotels in southern Africa. In 1996, the company opened the first Ngwenya Glass Boutique in the hub of the exclusive V&A Waterfront in Cape Town. When the winners of the Africa 2004 SMME Awards were announced in October 2004, enterprises from all over the continent made their mark. Ngwenya Glass was the winner of the award for the arts and crafts sector.

(Source: www.ngwenyaglass.co.sz)

Swazi Candles bring the light of Africa to the world. Situated in the Malkerns Valley, Swazi Candles has been producing fine handmade candles since 1981. Their artists and craftsmen produce unique candle designs, which are renowned throughout the world. African trade beads, tiny colourful, intricately patterned pieces of art, were once the wealth of Africa, used as money for buying gold and ivory and other valuables centuries ago. Now expensive collector's items these beautiful beads are no longer in circulation. In the Kingdom of Swaziland creative remnants of the beads are being moulded out of wax. Swazi Candles, a company specialising in candle crafts in the form of African wildlife, birds and stunning balls and columns, is carrying on an African tradition in a unique form. The multi-layered technique of millefiore, or 'thousand flowers' is adapted from the ancient Egyptians in Alexandria who created glass beads.

The artistic team creates a new candle pattern every week. All designs are inspired by Africa. Jerry Mabuza, sitting at his worktable, his chest bare and dressed in animal skins and feathers, is proud of his African culture and craft. In his expert hands a block of warm, molten wax becomes an elegant elephant within minutes. Smiling at his own handiwork, Mabuza says that it is in his blood. Mabuza forms his elephants from a block of white wax, and then moulds a coloured, patterned hard wax veneer on top by folding the coloured wax squares around the original creation, melding it into one and cooling it off in a bucket of water. The result is a hard outer shell which hardly melts when the candle is lit and creates a mystical glow as the inner wax burns down leaving the outer layer intact. Tony Marshak, the founder of the innovative craft shop, says that although there are Chinese imitations of Swazi candles made more cheaply by machines, there is no substitute for the human touch. With pride, everything is handmade and hand finished. 'If you've got a good product, and you treat your staff well, you can't go wrong,' says Tony. Visitors can see the artisans at work at the Swazi Candles workshop and buy their creations in the storefront shop. There is also a tea garden where one can sit back, relax, have a light lunch and admire the African light sealed in wax.

(Source: 2005 correspondence; www.swazicandles.com; and 'Manzini market and craft shops hold Swazi treasures', a special international report prepared by *The Washington Times* advertising department, published on 30 April 1999)

In 1991, Jenny Thorne set up a small development company to realise the extraordinary potential of Swazi women making handcraft in the rural areas and to counteract the flood of handcraft coming into the country from other parts of Africa and being sold to tourists as 'Swazi handcrafts'. She called the company Gone Rural. The business has grown to the extent where there are now 772 women in 14 groups in the rural areas and 22 staff at the workshop in Malkerns. The lutindzi (mountain) grass is collected by the women and dyed into a range of rich colours at the workshop. The women create exquisite tableware, floor mats, baskets and clay pot candles which are supplied to over 525 retail customers in 32 different countries around the world (98.5 per cent of all Gone Rural's production is exported).

The products are of a high quality and many are works of art, bringing new designs and ideas to traditional craft. Since 2002, Gone Rural has won numerous Gold, Silver and Bronze Awards for Stand

Excellence at the bi-annual SARCDA Trade Show in Johannesburg. Gone Rural has become one of Swaziland's top three producers of handmade products. Most importantly, the rural women producers have an income which has vastly improved their quality of life and opportunities for their children.

Jenny Thorne was also highly practical, and by increasingly devolving responsibility to her business partner Zoë Dean-Smith and her design consultant Philippa Thorne, she ensured that the business would continue to evolve and provide employment for rural women. The new management structure comprises Zoë Dean-Smith as the managing director and Philippa Thorne as the creative director.

Gone Rural is committed to increasing its customer base to generate employment for more women and thus enhance local economies which are increasingly burdened with orphaned children.

The production and marketing are steered towards excellence and international success. In 2004, Gone Rural took a giant leap forward and shipped products to exhibit at the New York International Gift Fair in both January and August and at the California Gift Show in January 2005. They established some new business relationships with customers in the USA, Canada and South America. In 2005, Zoë was nominated as one of the candidates for Swaziland Business Woman of the Year 2005 and won a Pan-African Women Invent & Innovate Award 2005 in Ghana in September 2005, in the category of building capacity. Both of these events provided fabulous exposure for Gone Rural and a great opportunity for some useful networking.

In August 2004, Gone Rural was invited to take part in a joint project with Sebastian Conran (of Conran UK) and Woolworths in South Africa. In collaboration with 16 hand-picked southern African hand-craft producers (including Ngwenya Glass, also of Swaziland), Conran developed an exclusive range of products for the top 20 Woolworths flagship stores around South Africa. The range was called Conran-Africa and has been incredibly successful for Gone Rural, with Woolworths placing a number of top-up orders to keep up with an unexpectedly high consumer demand. A number of magazine and newspaper articles were published about the Conran-Africa range and Gone Rural received exceptionally favourable media coverage.

In 2005, Gone Rural supplied four of the Conran stores in London, Paris and Japan. Customers such as these continue to provide Gone Rural with the incentive and drive to continue to create fresh new designs that are consistently at the leading edge of the interior design world.

Gone Rural's work directly affects the lives of 772 families in the rural areas. When a woman joins a group, she is required to commit to a monthly meeting, attend workshops and complete the order that she has been given. Through rain, floods and hailstones, Gone Rural honours their monthly meeting with these women and relies on the women to do the same for them. That commitment has helped Gone Rural develop a solid, trusting partnership with this talented sector of the community, and Gone Rural makes the same pledge to their international consumers.

Gone Rural operates as a wholesale business and currently supplies about 525 retail outlets — mainly interior design and home living stores, game lodges, museum shops (in the USA), outdoor living shops and art galleries. The factory shop in Malkerns is supported by the local consumer market as well as tourists passing through the Malkerns valley.

In April 2005, Zoë was invited to attend a workshop at the IFC (International Finance Corporation) in Washington (Gone Rural has been working together with the IFC since late 2004). The workshop was attended by a number of international grassroots business organisations currently working with the IFC, and the objective was to take stock of progress and results, share lessons learned, brainstorm about key issues and discuss options for the future. The workshop was a practical and issues-oriented session with discussions focused around three operational themes: export marketing, scaling up, and monitoring and evaluation. Zoë was a key participant. She gave a presentation on Gone Rural's business operation and plans for the future with particular regard to the upliftment projects in the pipeline for the rural women; the current HIV/AIDS status in Swaziland, and export marketing. She also had discussions with James Wolfensohn, the outgoing director of the World Bank and met with several senior World Bank Group staff. The presentation was also attended by various other donor agencies.

One of the highlights of the workshop was that a number of the grassroots business organisations had recently noticed a very positive response from funding organisations and donors. It appears that profit-making 'businesses with a social mission' are finally being taken seriously and are being recognised for trying to be sustainable in their own right and 'looking for a hand-up, not a hand-out'. Gone Rural was a 2005 finalist for the Africa SMME Awards.

(Source: 2005 correspondence; and www.gonerural.co.sz)

Chapter 7: Madagascar, Mauritius, Seychelles, Comoros, Mozambique and Zimbabwe.

Madagascar

Mirado, a boutique in Antananarivo, Madagascar, is owned by businesswoman Mirana Abraham, who designs and sells high-end natural silk clothing accessories, raffia handbags, baskets and crafts. Mirana also employs a group of Malagasy women who manage the entire manufacturing process of lambas — traditional raw silk shawls worn by women and men in the highlands of Madagascar — from growing the silkworms, to spinning, weaving and dyeing the lambas. The texture and vast array of colours of lambas rival and surpass the beauty of the popular cashmere pashminas from India that have found a ready market in trendy boutiques and department stores in the West. Renowned for their high quality craftsmanship, most Malagasy women are poor and rely on income generating craft-related activities to support their families.

Mirana started the company in 1996. Since then she has expanded her business to represent other weavers and manufacturers of high quality shoes, bags and craft products, combining silk, raffia and crocodile in fashionable, creative combinations. In Madagascar, silk was the fabric of royalty, valued for its durability, luxury, and elegance. Mirana launched an integrated silk production, weaving, dyeing, and packaging facility, employing over 100 persons in all the production stages of her hand-loomed accessories. Her sense of design and colour has impressed buyers in both Europe and the US, and she has sold accessories to Yves St Laurent and Hermès. With the help of USAID, Mirana has participated in American trade shows, taking orders from specialty boutiques for hundreds of shawls.

The Wall Street Journal has observed that after decades of watching Asian countries use textile factories to galvanise their economies, Africa is finally getting a chance to stitch together its own success story. In June 2000, the US Congress passed the Africa Growth and Opportunity Act (AGOA), which gives 23 sub-Saharan countries the opportunity to ship a range of textile products to the US duty-free. This is good news to an industry always seeking the next low-wage country with good market access. As of January 2002, foreign investment has already risen sharply in Madagascar and the 11 other countries that have qualified for the trade benefits by setting up safeguards on customs and child labour.

Mathias Ismail, the director of Columbia Clothing Company, a local textile company, has made plans to manufacture Levi Strauss-Dockers Chinos, Liz Claiborne Bottoms or cotton camisoles for Victoria's Secret and boxer shorts for Gap. In his spinning room, as strands of cotton fly through the air, and the looms make such a din that workers are wearing earplugs, he proudly shows off his new looms in this room that he calls the AGOA room. This is his big chance. The biggest market in the world has opened for African textile entrepreneurs. He envisions planeloads of lingerie winging toward America.

Mathias is the son of a Gujrath family that emigrated from India to Madagascar a hundred years ago. His father, Salim Ismail, was born in 1939 and holds a textile engineering degree from ENSIT in Mulhouse and is a MBA graduate of the Institut d'Administration des Entreprises at the University of Paris (IAE). The family started out farming cotton, and then diversified to shrimp and fish farms. Salim joined his family group in 1964 entering La Cotonnière d'Antsirabé, 'Cotona'. He started his career in the spinning and weaving departments and was especially involved in the study which led to the realisation of an important extension programme which allowed Cotona to install 56,000 spindles, over 1,000 looms and complete lines of bleaching, dyeing and printing.

In 1967, Salim Ismail became director of the spinning section and was appointed technical director in 1969 and deputy director general in 1980. He took over as president director general in 1989 with responsibility for all textile activities of the group. Under his guidance, the group engaged in a broad development and diversification programme. In Madagascar this was by the upstream integration into Cotona of a cotton growing operation covering approximately 2,100 hectares. In Mauritius it was through the setting up of a weaving and finishing unit (Socota Textile Mills) equipped with the latest state-of-the-art technology, producing 10 million square metres of fabrics of high quality destined for the shirt market of well-known labels, in particular Marks & Spencer. This programme marked the first step towards the internationalisation of the Groupe Socota Industries, which has gradually become one of the principal industrial organisations of the Indian Ocean.

Mathias was born in Anstirabe in 1969. He grew up in Paris. He attended one of the top French Jesuit Schools and then graduated from Lyon Graduate School of Business and from University of Paris-La Sorbonne's Management programme. Mathias is also the representative of Madagascar at the International Federation of Aeronautics. He is married to an Anglo-French wife and is the father of two girls.

The Ismail Group has set up training classes for textile workers. Their flagship factory includes fire trucks that serve the surrounding suburbs. Perhaps most important for Madagascar's economic growth, they offer the chance for job mobility — mechanics hired to repair machines hope to use their experience to get into other industries.

The Ismails and other entrepreneurs are striving to reshape the way business development is done in Madagascar. Not content merely to sew together piecework, the group wants to have a hand in every step of textile production, every layer of value added to the clothing sent to America, from the cotton farmers grow out in the fields of Mahajanga up north, to the yarn spun on the new state-of-the-art spinning machines in Antsiarabe, and finally to the lingerie and trousers the group workers then sew. The Ismails and their joint venture partners are building the link between Madagascar's countryside and the American consumer.

The step towards Garment integration has been successfully made with the teaming of key strategic partners like Mast Industries' founder, Martin Trust, and the Sri Lankan-based partners of The Ltd, Phoenix Ventures (owned by the Omar family) and MAS Holding (owned by the Amalean family). US apparel industry giant Martin Trust is chairman of Brandot (USA), a holding company engaged in the production of apparel and textile products. Trust's global interests include the two garment factories in Madagascar known as Cottonline and Colombia Clothing Company (CCC). Both factories continue to expand their workforce and are adding equipment to broaden their product lines. Cottonline continues to focus its production on GAP, while CCC is working with Liz Claiborne, Abercrombie and Fitch, and Express. CCC recently received its first order from Sears. The investments in the Madagascar apparel sector by the joint ventures partners in both Columbia Clothing Company (woven bottoms) and Cottonline (knit products) are close to US$20 million. The investments are being financed by the partners and proposed to the leading international institutions like DEG (German Development Bank) and IFC (International Finance Corporation).

(Source: Helene Cooper, 'Madagascar's textile sector draws fresh life from US trade move', *The Wall Street Journal*, 2 January 2002)

By changing management practices, Madagascar farmers have been able to achieve some spectacular increases in rice yields — sometimes even higher than what has been considered as the biological potential of the rice plant. In Madagascar, where rice yields average two tons per hectare, farmers using methods known as le Systéme de Riziculture Intensive (SRI), have been able to average eight tons per hectare with some of the best yields reaching 20 tons per hectare. The impressive yields have been achieved without requiring new seeds or chemical fertilisers, and with reduced use of water.

The SRI methodology has only recently come to the attention of researchers and practitioners outside Madagascar where it was developed in the early 1980s by Père Henri de Laulanié, a French Jesuit priest. Fr de Laulanié came to Madagascar from France in 1961 and spent the next (and last) 34 years of his life working with Malagasy farmers to improve their agricultural systems, and particularly their rice production, since rice is the staple food in Madagascar. Rice provides more than half the daily calories consumed in

Madagascar, a sign of the cultural and historic significance of rice to Malagasies, but also an indication of their poverty. Fr de Laulanié established an agricultural school in Antsirabe in 1981 to help rural youths gain an education that was relevant to their vocations and family needs. Though SRI was 'discovered' in 1983, benefiting from some serendipity, it took some years to gain confidence that these methods could consistently raise production so substantially.

In 1990, Fr de Laulanié together with two Malagasy colleagues, self-taught agronomists, Sébastien Rafaralahy and Justin Léonard Rabenandrasana, established an indigenous NGO, Association Tefy Saina, to work with farmers, other NGOs, and agricultural professionals to improve production and livelihoods in Madagascar. The name 'Tefy Saina' means, in Malagasy, 'to improve the mind', indicating that this organisation is not concerned simply with rice, but also with helping people to change and enrich their thinking.

SRI has become a worldwide movement, yet the technique would have died with Père de Laulanié in Madagascar without the efforts of Rafaralahy and Rabenandrasana. Today, Tefy Saina is beginning to overcome the fear of change among Malagasy farmers. Rafaralahy and Rabenandrasana hope, in time, to help protect some of the planet's greatest biodiversity, their island's forests. In November 2003, Tefy Saina received the Slow Food Award for the Defence of Biodiversity in Naples, Italy.

In 1994, Tefy Saina began working with Dr Norman Uphoff, Director of the Cornell International Institute for Food, Agriculture and Development (CIIFAD) in the US, to help farmers living around Ranomafana National Park to find alternatives to their slash-and-burn agriculture. They would need to continue growing upland rice in this manner destructive to Madagascar's precious but endangered rain forest ecosystems if they could not significantly increase their yields from rice grown in the limited irrigated lowland area, about two tons per hectare. Farmers using SRI averaged over eight tons per hectare during the first five years that these methods were introduced around Ranomafana. A French project for improving small-scale irrigation systems on the high plateau during this same time period also found that farmers using SRI methods averaged over eight tons per hectare.

The SRI system optimises the potential of the plant and its root system. In effect, it achieves the 'edge effect' throughout the whole field. Transplanting of single plants is done early (8-12 days after emergence), with spacing that reduces nutrient competition between the plants and facilitates mechanical weeding. Tillering (the production of new stems) is optimised during the growing period, and then seed head formation and grains per head keep pace given root systems that take 5-6 times more force to pull up because they grow larger and deeper. Soils are kept well aerated for increased root growth for most of the period before flowering. With SRI methods the productivity of the land, water, capital and labour are all increased concurrently, and better results are usually obtained using organic than with inorganic fertilisers. Everywhere, there has been initial reluctance because the methods are counter-intuitive to the traditional belief that yield is maximised by close sowing and constant irrigation. Moreover, in Madagascar, the increased labour demand, at least in the first season or two of using SRI methods, has been found to conflict with need to be earning day-to-day off-farm income that is vital to the poor. It was not until 1999 that the yields obtained in Madagascar led to experiments in other countries of Africa and especially Asia. By July 2004, positive to spectacular results had been achieved in 22 countries. In June 2005, good results were reported in Senegal and Mozambique, as well as Vietnam and Pakistan (reported in 2004). In May 2005, the Government of India issued a press release that said it now advised farmers to use SRI methods. Much experimentation is now going on, both by scientists to understand the processes and by SRI farmers to adapt SRI ideas and practices to local conditions.

SRI has the potential for double yields (or more) without requiring chemical fertiliser or crop-protection agro–chemicals. In a several countries, it is seen that SRI methods can average about 8 tons per hectare, more than double the present world average. Adaptation of SRI ideas and practices to upland (rain fed) conditions in the Philippines has given average yield over 7 tons per hectare, so the principles and insights of SRI could have benefits beyond irrigated rice production. SRI requires only about half as much water per season as usual irrigated cultivation, and its seeding rate is only 10-20 per cent of that usually used. That fewer inputs can produce more outputs sounds too good to be true, but scientific evaluations are now confirming what has been seen for some years on farmers' fields.

(Source: Norman Uphoff, 'A review of the spread of and experience with the system of rice intensification (SRI) worldwide, with consideration of research issues', paper for National Workshop on SRI, organised by the China National Rice Research Institute, Hangzhou, 2-3 March 2003, http://ciifad.cornell.edu/sri/, and http://ciifad.cornell.edu/sri)

Mauritius

At different stages during the course of the history of Mauritius, people of diverse origins — Indian (Hindus and Muslims), African, European and Chinese — have settled on the island, bringing their cultures, languages, values and traditions. The country today is a recognised cultural melting pot and is often cited as a perfect example of the main religions of the world co-existing peacefully. Mauritius is also a good example of investor-friendly policies. Until 1982, Mauritius earned more than 90 per cent of its income from sugar exports. In 1982, a new government reversed the usual policy of inviting foreign investment in the worst areas of the country with the least infrastructure. The government instead invited investment in the areas with the best infrastructure: textile manufacturing and tourism. Four years later, manufactured textile goods replaced sugar as the leading export.

Tourism, the third pillar of the economy along with the manufacturing and agriculture sectors, has contributed significantly to economic growth and has been a key factor in the overall development of Mauritius, which is predominantly a holiday destination for beach-resort tourists with a wide range of natural and man-made attractions, a sub-tropical climate with clear warm sea waters, attractive beaches, tropical fauna and flora complemented by a multi-ethnic and cultural population that is friendly and welcoming. These tourism assets are Mauritius' main strength and are backed up by well-designed and well-run hotels, and reliable and operational services and infrastructures. The most prestigious beach side resort hotels are owned and/or operated by large groups such as New Mauritius Hotels' Beachcomber Group, and Sun Resorts.

An Integrated Resort Scheme (IRS) was announced by the minister of finance in the 2003/2004 budget, to further promote tourism. The concept aims at developing hotels, supported by golf courses for guests and villas which can be sold to foreigners for amounts in excess of US $500,000. In return, they would benefit from permanent residency. Mauritian investors groups have welcomed this scheme and presented to government a number of projects.

With the rising cost of living in Mauritius and world competition in the textile industry, Mauritius foresees a difficult and very competitive future. More than ten textile companies closed down in Mauritius in 2003/2004 to relocate overseas. Therefore, Mauritius has turned towards the information technology sector and has constructed a cyber city and business park and implemented new investor-friendly regulations concerning this industry in order to continue to attract the foreign investor. Mauritius' investor friendly regime has now turned to the more skilled, value-added sector of information technology (textile companies in Mauritius continue to produce but are smarter and more efficient, with methods being adopted to maintain their competitiveness — from using cheaper locations, to re-engineering the production line using new machinery, to refining its market and creating specialisations; and to ensuring that the industry is almost completely vertically integrated from the importation of the cotton to the finished product).

The financial sector has grown from strength to strength with reorganisation of the regulating bodies in 2002 and the complete updating and review of most laws governing the financial sector. Mauritius' financial sector now stands poised within the global business environment (formerly known as the offshore sector) to be a leader within the region. Many multinational companies have already set up regional headquarter operations in Mauritius to service their Africa operations: Coca Cola, Loita, HSBC, Barclays, Deutsche Bank, Jan de Nul, Mint Master Security and Hannah Instruments, to name a few.

The domestic corporations, in the meantime, remain strong, solid, stable and monopolised. If you cast a glance down the list of directors of almost any Mauritian company, you will see the same names cropping up again and again — Lagesse, Dalais, Espitalier-Noël, Harel, Leclèzio and Taylor. Between them, these six families control many of the top companies and most of its top hotels and sugar plantations.

Thanks to a complex web of inter-company shareholdings, the links between these families are very strong. The Espitalier-Noël and Taylor families together control the Rogers Group. The Dalais and Lagesse families share control of dozens of companies including Ireland Blyth, Sun Resorts and Consolidated Investments and Enterprises. In addition, each of these families has a representative on the board of the Mauritius Commercial Bank. Many of these families are going through a change in leadership as the old patriarchs hand over power to younger relatives. The most prominent members of the new generation are:
- Hector Espitalier-Noël, CEO of the Espitalier Noël Group and chairman of both New Mauritius Hotels and the Rogers Group;
- Arnaud Dalais (chairman of IBL and group chief executive CIEL Group);
- Christian Dalais (chairman of CIEL Investments, Deep River Beau Champ, and Sun Resorts;
- Antoine Harel (chairman of Harel Mallac);
- Thierry Lagesse (chairman of the FUEL Group, Mauritius' largest sugar provider and power generation provider, and also chairman and CEO of the Palmar Group); and
- Tim Taylor (CEO of the Rogers Group).

Having finally got their hands on the reins, these men are now looking around for new ways to grow their family businesses. They have all seen their wealth increase dramatically over the past 25 years thanks to the success of the island's textile and tourism industries. Now they have a fair bit of money to play around with and want to make their mark farther afield. The two big questions facing men like Dalais and Lagesse is how much money to commit to overseas expansion, and where to get it from. Most of these family businesses have opened their share capital and are now quoted on the Mauritian stock exchange, and have a very open-minded approach. Wanting to play in the global market, they have begun to bring in some outside equity partners. One example is the development of the Indian Ocean Fund, which has some major foreign equity shareholders. Moreover, there are other big companies doing very well in Mauritius and playing a predominant role in the economy. Mauritius Commercial Bank is a large public bank which does not belong to any particular group of families (its largest shareholder being Lloyd's Bank) and with no other shareholder owning more than 5 per cent of the bank. The Mauritius Commercial Bank is a very reputable bank with many shareholders and numerous clients.

Since independence and more precisely since the early 1980s, the economy has opened up to non-traditional players, as evidenced by the significant emergence of a generation of middle class of new economic operators from the non-traditional sector, who are particularly involved in commerce, manufacturing and tourism. Many of them have, through only one generation, reached the status of important economic players and have captured a fair share of the island's economic prosperity.

The Joint Economic Council was founded in 1970 and is the coordinating body of private sector business organisations. It must be pointed out that Mauritius has a long-standing tradition of government/private sector dialogue, which allows the private sector to voice its views on the development strategy of the country. The dialogue takes place in a structured manner as well as on an ad hoc basis. The Joint Economic Council consists of three core organisations: the Mauritius Chamber of Agriculture, the Mauritius Chamber of Commerce and Industry and the Mauritius Employers' Federation and five sector associations: the Mauritius Sugar Producers Association (MSPA), the Mauritius Bankers Association, the Mauritius Export Processing Zone Association (MEPZA), the Association des Hôteliers et des Restaurateurs de L'île Maurice (AHRIM) and the Insurers' Association.

The Food and Allied Group of Companies is a strong business performer and now rated tenth largest Mauritian business organization by virtue of turnover by the local business publication 'Top 100 Companies'. At a crucial time when the economy of Mauritius was shifting from a mix of sugar cane production and industrial products, including textiles, to an economy based on services, the Food and Allied Group of Companies has consolidated its position. In the mid-1960s the group launched into chicken production and became a pioneer of Mauritian industry. In 2004, under the leadership of Michel de Spéville (executive chairman of the the Food and Allied Group of Companies), it continued to demonstrate a significant commitment to the development of the local economy, while practicing good governance and maintaining the utmost respect for the country's heritage and the environment. Companies of the Food and Allied Group are actively engaged in various fields of production, manufacturing and services, including hotel development. Activities span integrated chicken production (which started in the mid 1960s), animal feed, Kentucky Fried Chicken franchising, flour milling, dairy processing, fruit and vegetable canning, food distribution and marketing.

In the early 1990s, seeing the growing demand for quality hotels in a safe destination, the Food and Allied Group of Companies diversified into the hospitality industry with the construction of the Labourdonnais Waterfront Hotel which, in just a few years, became a benchmark as a hotel for business people. Construction of a second 100-room three-star hotel in Port Louis, the Suffren Hotel and Marina, was completed in June 2004. The Group's third hotel, the Telfair Golf and Spa Resort, a 158-room high class resort, was officially opened by the prime minister of Mauritius in December 2004. Other service companies, within the Food and Allied Group of Companies, are involved in freight and transit, shipping, and advertising, including mobile billboard advertising. The Management and Development Company (MADCO) is the group's management core. It is involved in general management and strategic planning relating to the group's local concerns and to its expansion in the region. In 2002, the Food and Allied Group of Companies was the tenth largest group in Mauritius in terms of turnover, with a turnover of 4.6 billion Mauritian Rupees for the financial year 2003-2004. The Group employs around 2,200 people, and also operates in Madagascar and Mozambique.

The Espitalier-Noël family has been closely involved in the Mauritian sugar industry for nearly two centuries. In the late 1820s, Martial Noël started the Mon Désert sugar factory, which later merged with Alma Sugar Estate, to become Mon Désert Alma Co Ltd. The other family sugar estate, Savannah, dates back to 1882 and expanded, through a later merger, as part of the ongoing process of centralisation and streamlining in the Mauritian sugar industry. In 1944, a private company, Espitalier-Noël Ltd (ENL), was founded, in which the main components of the family business, in particular its shareholding in the two sugar estates mentioned above, were brought together. In the late 1950s, the company started to diversify into other sectors such as commerce, manufacturing and finance.

In 1969, with the setting up of its investment company, General Investment & Development Co Ltd, and of Espitalier-Noel Investment Trust (ENIT) at the end of the 1990s, ENL has developed a wide-ranging and dynamic investment strategy. As a result, it presently holds an attractive portfolio of shares in local 'blue chip' companies and a substantial stake in prominent business groups such as Rogers, New Mauritius Hotels, and the Food and Allied Group.

The New Mauritius Hotels are the leaders in hospitality in Mauritius and are wholly Mauritian owned. They own properties in Mauritius and in the Seychelles as well as companies in Europe and South Africa. The New Mauritius Hotels' Beachcomber Hotels Group currently operates eight premier resorts on the island of Mauritius, in the categories from five-star plus to quality accommodation. Situated along the most beautiful beaches of the island, the eight Beachcomber hotels reflect the group's philosophy of high quality, personal service and attention to detail. A strong emphasis is placed on the varying architectural nature of each property and the diversity of their management teams. The common thread of Beachcomber hospitality however, is evident in all hotels throughout the range.

Some of the main subsidiaries of ENL, namely Mon Désert Alma, Savannah Sugar Estate and GIDC were among the first companies to be listed on the stock exchange of Mauritius in 1989. ENL has remained at the forefront of the evolution in the economic, social, business and legal environment in Mauritius, in particular the diversification of the economy into non-sugar activities. The ENL Group consists of over 30 companies employing more than 5,000 people and covers the main business sectors of agriculture, manufacturing and services.

Compagnie Mauricienne de Textile (CMT)'s message for its eighteenth anniversary in November 2004 was clear and simple: Life is a journey. The company's path has proved it. From a small enterprise with 30 employees to third place in the top 100 company list of Mauritius, CMT is a success. But it has invested a lot and taken high risks, the latest being the opening of one of the most modern spinning plants in the world.

CMT has invested Rs 1.4 billion in its new spinning mill in La Tour Koenig and can now be proud to have the latest technology in the field: an entirely automatic spinning mill, one of the first in the world. The new factory is the biggest industrial building in Mauritius and employees will move around on roller skates. Its production capacity should be of 8,500 tons every year thus increasing the country's capacity to 18,500 tons (a third of the local needs). Moreover, the new factory should provide some 1,500 more jobs.

CMT has undoubtedly achieved many of its targets. Its success is largely due to the commitment of its employees and the family spirit that can be felt through the staff. 'CMT still has 53 among the 70 employees, which constituted its staff 18 years ago. They are the pioneers,' François Woo, managing director, told l'Express on the eve of the great celebration. In his speech, he added, addressing these same pioneers, 'You are the giants on whom we stood to build our vision.' François Woo is proud of and grateful to these employees, who helped him reach the top.

CMT reached the one billion Mauritius Rupees profit mark in 2004, but the company managers do not want to stop there. CMT intends to become the world leader of the textile industry. François Woo said, 'It will be naïve and irresponsible on my part to state that, with the opening of our new plant and having turned 18 years old, we have achieved our goal and objective and that it is the end of a chapter in our life cycle. As it is often said in the business world, the goal post is never reached. It keeps on being displaced further and further.'

The two other directors, Louis Lai Fat Fur and Marie Claire Woo, also paid tribute to their employees. They insisted that they started from a small enterprise to become the structured company they are today, with 5,500 employees. The solid achievements of the CMT testify to an unfailing team spirit within the company.

(Source: 'CMT and its ambitions come of age', www.lexpress.mu, 16 November 2004)

Currimjee Jeewanjee left his hometown in the state of Kutch, India, in 1884, and arrived in Mauritius at the age of 18. In 1890 he established Currimjee Jeewanjee & Company Ltd as a trading company dealing in the import of foodstuffs and commodities as well as the export of sugar. Over the next few decades, the company expanded into the bulk import and sale of primary consumption commodities.

Trading and commerce remained Currimjee Jeewanjee & Co's main activities until the mid-1980s. The company dealt in the sale of building materials. It initiated the direct selling of cookware and educational books through a network of door-to-door salespeople, and set up a unit for the bottling and distribution of liquefied petroleum gas. However, in the late 1980s, the company diversified into the services sectors: in travel, through its GSA office for Singapore International Airlines; in insurance, through Island Life and General Insurance; in Telecommunications and IT, through Emtel (a mobile cellular network operator), and its information technology division.

Following a decade of fast and innovative growth in new sectors in the 1980s, the 1990s saw a series of new ventures, which consolidated previous investments and maximised the synergies within different businesses. Satellite and direct-to-home pay TV and an internet communications management company, consumer finance and leasing, as well as a travel agency and a cargo company were all units which built on and strengthened the company's existing activities. Over the years, the company has also built up a sizeable property portfolio by investing in strategic properties.

From March 1998 to March 2000, Bashir Currimjee, Chairman and Managing Director of Currimjee Jeewanjee Ltd, was president of the Joint Economic Council (JEC). Founded in 1970, the JEC is the coordinating body of the main business organisations, the private sector of Mauritius. Mauritius has a long-standing tradition of government/private sector dialogue which allows the private sector to voice its views on the development strategy of the country. The dialogue takes place in a structured manner as well as on an *ad hoc* basis.

(Source: www.currimjee.com).

At the helm of Happy World Ltd, Antoine Seeyave Jr, says: 'We want to make Happy World a great business, as willed by the founders and everyone who is putting his trust in Happy World'. Born in 1908, his father, Antoine New Seng Seeyave, becomes in his thirties a bottler and distributor of rum. The son of a baker, he is on the way to being a self-made man. Antoine NS Seeyave sets up Happy World in 1952. The co-founders include Joseph Konfortion and Edward Leung Pin. Backed by 20 workers and Rs 50,000 of capital, the company produces ice cream. The name 'Happy World' sums up their vision to build success on the values of trust, value for money and innovation. Such a vision embraces the power and reach that is essential to the making of a great business. In the quest for sustainable growth, he favours policies that break new ground in tune with the evolution of Mauritius. This anchors the spirit and culture of the business in step with the dynamics of change that affect society at large.

In 1958 Antoine Seeyave decided to venture into frozen foods. The emerging market for frozen foods had made a huge impact on him in the course of a study trip to France and on his return, with newly acquired knowledge, he went into the storage and distribution of frozen foods. With the award of the Lyons Maid licence in 1966, Happy World was able to manufacture a famous brand of ice cream — testimony to its consistent compliance with exacting quality standards. Large-scale poultry farming was begun at 'Mauritius Farms Ltd' in 1973. Chicken products strengthen distribution operations as does the catch of the fishing vessel 'M.V. Stella Maru'. Following a merger with the food operations of Happy World, Mauritius Farms Ltd takes the name of Happy World Foods Ltd, and joins the Stock Exchange as a listed company in January 1996.

Meanwhile, Antoine Seeyave is implementing succession plans. The overriding principle is parity between his sons, René and Antoine Jr. They have the same and equal shareholding. On 23 December 1971, he appoints both of them as managers. When he retires in 1976, he entrusts Happy World jointly to René and Antoine Jr. on the basis of an equal shareholding and an equal say in the making of decisions. Further diversification takes the Group into the market for home appliances in 1977. Sony, Electrolux, and Casio put their trust in Happy World. Next, leading brands like HP and Ricoh entrust Happy World with IT and office equipment. More initiatives follow. Besides a chain of seven Pizza Hut outlets, Happy World sets up an agency service for Pacific Shipping Lines and stockbrokerage services. In the meantime, the headquarters moves into Happy World House — designed as a shopping-cum-office complex, Happy World House grows into a desirable address in the central business district of the capital city, Port Louis.

Meritocracy and governance take centre stage in 1992. Appointed chief executive, Antoine Seeyave Jr begins with reform at the top, the boardroom itself. Enriched with more talent, the new board fulfils a functional role in policy-making and strategy formulation besides the ongoing monitoring of performance. In the same stride, Antoine Seeyave Jr. drives a company-wide programme of reform with the aim of embedding the key drivers of excellence: meritocracy and empowerment. Superior results validate the reforms. In the period 1992-1996, Happy World is successful in lifting shareholders funds from Rs 144 Million to Rs 456 Million, a three-fold change. This is the outcome of rising satisfaction levels of customers and employees as borne out by the survey results. Set on the path to become a great business, Happy World suffers a setback in 1996 when a major disagreement at the top stops the train of reform in its tracks. In 2004, Antoine Seeyave Jr. obtains full control of the Group and relinquishes the food interests. As chairman, his committed goal is to make Happy World a great business as willed by the founders and everyone who puts his trust in Happy World.

The CIEL Group is an industry-based conglomerate whose growth and development have contributed to the general enhancement of the Mauritian economy. Through its textile and agro-industry activities, namely CIEL Textile and CIEL Agro-industry, the Group plays a leading role in textiles, sugar growing and milling. Its vision, and ambition to become a regional player, led to pioneering investments in both Madagascar and Tanzania. As of 2004, the group employed 12,500 Mauritians and 4,000 Tanzanians.

Operations in Madagascar were halted temporarily following political instability during the period 2001/2002, but were re-started in 2003. In addition to the above operations, the Group manages an investment holding company, CIEL Investment, through its internal corporate services company, CIEL Corporate Services.

The textile operations originated from the Floreal and Aquarelle groups of companies. The reshaping of those textile activities in 2001, under CIEL Textile Ltd, was considered necessary, in view of the current challenges facing export-oriented companies. Indeed, the pooling of resources allowed the creation of a stronger organisation more focused now after a split into six business units: knitwear, fine knits, shirts, spinning, dyeing and weaving for the textile activity. CIEL Textile is positioned as a world class multi-product textile and clothing group. With commercial offices in all major cities, it offers its international customers excellent quality products and services at competitive prices.

CIEL Agro-Industry encompasses all types of agro-industrial activities. It is based on sugar growing and milling at Deep River Beau Champ Ltd (DRBC), a sugar estate on the eastern part of the island. This sugar estate was the second private concern to provide electricity to the government-owned Central Electricity Board. Recently, DRBC extended its range of sugar interests. It became active internationally by acquiring, as part of a consortium, a majority stake in TPC Ltd, in the Kilimanjaro region of Tanzania. Over the years, diversification has led to energy production, fruit and vegetable growing and deer farming.

CIEL Investment is an investment holding company, with interests in a number of companies operating in various sectors of the Mauritian economy. CIEL Investment managed by CIEL Corporate Services acts as the development arm of the CIEL GROUP. Through careful selection and research, it seeks to strengthen its position in sound and well-managed companies. It also aims at active participation in the development of new economic sectors. The portfolio mix is balanced and allows CIEL Investment to engage in constant asset appreciation and, at the same time, distribute adequate returns to shareholders.

CIEL Corporate Services Ltd is a service company, which supports the three main operational clusters of the CIEL Group. It formulates the overall strategic planning of the group and also actively manages CIEL Investment's activities. Arnaud Dalais, group chief executive, points out that CIEL has become a leading investment company in Mauritius, with assets worth some Rs 2 billion in 2003. CIEL Investment has significant and focused interests in tourism, property and commercial activities. Its portfolio is further diversified in financial services, information technology, life sciences and construction. From March 2000 to March 2002, Arnaud Dalais was president of the Joint Economic Council.

Antoine Harel is chairman of Harel Mallac & Co Ltd, the flagship of a group of companies whose reputation for excellence has become a byword in Mauritius. Present in numerous areas of economic activity, Harel Mallac holds a prominent position on the island. Established in 1830, Harel Mallac has, during the past 175 years, increased services and diversified so as to adapt to a constantly changing market. Harel Mallac Group comprises 21 subsidiaries and 32 associated companies. They were listed on the stock exchange of Mauritius in 1991 and mainly operate in the commercial, industrial and services sectors. The group and their subsidiaries presently employ a workforce of around 740, including a great number of highly qualified experienced technicians, with the aim of offering the best service too their clients.

Patrice d'Hotman de Villiers is the chief executive of Ireland Blyth Ltd, which was incorporated in 1972 following the merger of Ireland Fraser & Co Ltd and Blyth Brothers & Co Ltd, two leading trading companies established in Mauritius since the beginning of the 19th century. The principal activities of the company and their numerous subsidiary and associated companies are in commerce, manufacturing, hotel and tourism, shipping, engineering, marketing and distribution, various services and projects. The group operates through a number of business units and is proud to be in the forefront of the diversification of the economy of Mauritius. The Group takes part in the development of Mauritius's industrial activities, of its free port operations, and of its international ambition, especially in the Indian Ocean and East African regions.

Sun Resorts is an associated company of Ireland Blyth and Mauritius' second largest hospitality concern. This international group owns five hotels in Mauritius, The One & Only Le Saint Géran Hotel Golf Club

& Casino, The One & Le Touessrok Hotel and Ile-aux-Cerfs Golf Club, the Sugar Beach, La Pirogue Hotel & Casino and the Coco Beach Hotel.

(Source: www.iblgroup.com)

From humble beginnings to one of the most successful companies in Mauritius, Rogers and Co celebrated its one hundredth anniversary in 1999. Starting in a small and modest way, Rogers was registered as a private company on 6 April 1899 by Walter Richard Rogers, its founder. In the early days, when business in Mauritius was almost entirely dependent on the sugar industry, Rogers' activities involved the importing of heavy machinery and equipment for use in sugar factories and the exporting of sugar. By 1920, after the death of Walter Rogers, his two nephews, Eddy and Eric, came into the firm as equal partners with Louis Goupille and René Maingard. In the 1920s and 1930s the activities of the company extended to shipping, initially as ships' agents and later as ship owners. In 1932, Rogers and Co formed the Colonial Steamships Company Ltd, a shipping company which, through its regular services to Rodrigues, played a major role in the development of the island.

Tim Taylor is chief executive of the Rogers Group, a Mauritian based company engaged in a number of economic sectors and, in terms of assets, one of the biggest groups in the country. They also operate in a number of other countries in Africa and Europe. Their business focuses on areas where they have a competitive advantage, and areas integral to the Group's broader business strategy. They are the leaders in cross border transportation, both freight and passengers. This business has been built around general sales agency agreements with a number of airlines including Air France and South African Airways and a special relationship with Air Mauritius, which they helped to found in 1967. On the sea transportation side, they represent a number of shipping lines calling at Mauritius, the major one being the Mediterranean Shipping Company, one of the world's global shipping lines. To support these activities, they have a number of freight forwarding, warehousing and transportation activities and new investments in small hotels.

In line with government's policy of promoting the financial sector as a fourth pillar of the economy, the Rogers Group has in recent years made important strides in financial services. Starting with a small insurance business in the 1970s, it is now a major player in insurance, leasing, consumer credit and offshore services, and recently took a major investment in the free port sector. In the field of commerce and industry, it has a wide variety of interests: the market leaders in the manufacture and/or sale of agro-chemicals, paint, steel reinforcing bars and rotomolded plastic products. It also holds substantial interests in marine engineering, air-conditioning, irrigation, environmental management and bulk petroleum transportation services. Other commercial interests include pharmaceuticals, food and consumer goods, and various retailing activities.

Deelchand Jeeha, former minister of information technology and telecommunications, was voted top African ICT achiever at the African ICT Achievers Awards 2004. In addition to being the overall individual winner, Jeeha won the Top Minister with an ICT Portfolio award for his key role in Mauritius' technology boom. During Jeeha's tenure, Mauritius has inter alia built a cyber city and ICT business park, provided computer literacy courses to citizens and created an incubation programme for ICT start-ups. In March 2005, e-government became a reality in the country, allowing Mauritians to interact with their government via the Internet. The cyber city, 15 kilometres outside Port Louis, has as its centrepiece the 12-storey Cyber Tower, an 'intelligent building' with advanced telecommunication facilities enabling ICT-related facilities including software and multimedia development; software and hardware design, development and support; hosting of Internet and application service providers; and ICT-enabled services. The cyber city includes a business zone hosting a number of office developments, a knowledge zone with several educational institutions, a residential village, a commercial centre and several government administrative headquarters.

Jeeha has also introduced laws aimed at growing the ICT sector. In 2001, a policy paper was drafted to liberalise the Internet service provider market, which in 2004 boasted several competitors. The liberalisation of the telecommunications sector led to the licensing of a second network operator. Internet telephony was introduced officially in 2003, followed by a new National Telecommunications Policy to prepare for the convergence of IT, media, telecommunications and consumer electronics.

(Source: Iain Scott, 'Mauritius makes its mark', *ITWeb*, 1 November 2004 www.itweb.co.za)

With the launch of third generation telephone technology in Mauritius in November 2004, the island nation's Emtel beat South Africa's Vodacom to become the first African country to launch 3G/UMTS. Jeeha, became the first person to make a third generation video call on the continent. Emtel, which has 154,000 subscribers, said the UMTS project bodes well for the government's objective to develop the ICT industry into a leading sector. 'It is with great pride that Emtel contributes to make Mauritius prime in the high tech sector with a 3G/UMTS as a first in Africa and along with the most developed countries in Europe, and ahead of most countries including South Africa, India and even the USA,' the group said in a statement. Jeeha, formerly a partner in Arthur Andersen, has now set up his own consultancy in finance and ICT, SC & A Ltd.

Moeletsi Mbeki, deputy chairman of the South African Institute of International Affairs, an independent think-tank based at the University of the Witwatersrand, asserts that South Africa and Mauritius are developing industrial economies that, if they are sustained over a significant period, could become important drivers for African development — not because of regional integration but because of their emerging role as foreign investors in the rest of Africa. As a matter of fact Mauritius is a good illustration of the relative unimportance of regional integration in the development process. At independence in the 1960s, Mauritius was a typical African country — small land mass, small population, single crop economy (sugar) which accounted for most of export earnings and formal employment, multi-ethnic society, low per capita incomes. Today Mauritius is, next to South Africa, the richest non-oil producing country in Africa. It boasts an economy that is almost as diversified as that of South Africa — Africa's economic giant — and per capita incomes that now surpass South Africa's. This phenomenal achievement was not driven by regional integration; it was driven largely by competitively priced, high quality clothing, and textile exports to world markets. Recently Mauritius has emerged, like South Africa, as an important foreign investor in other African countries.

(Source: Moeletsi Mbeki. Discussion paper presented at the United Nations Conference on Trade and Development, Germany, February 2004)

Seychelles

The Seychelles is the only granite island group in the world. North Island is about 42 kilometres northwest of the main island of Mahé, 15 minutes by helicopter. In June 2003, a fantastic luxury lodge opened on the old coconut plantation which Colin Bell, former managing director of Wilderness Safaris and a small consortium, had bought in 1998. Bell had the denuded ecological environment completely rebuilt to make an exclusive island retreat for top-paying tourists. North Island is one of the boldest initiatives that Wilderness Safaris has been involved in to date. This is an ongoing conservation plan that aims to turn back the Seychelles Island's ecological clock by 100 to 200 years through a rigorous rehabilitation programme, and reintroduce its critically endangered fauna and flora to the island. In 1998 Wilderness had introduced what Linda van Herck, North Island's environmental manager, calls the 'Noah's Ark concept' — a total ecological restoration to protect and restore North Island's native fauna and flora. In time, species like the Seychelles Magpie Robin and the Seychelles White-Eye will be introduced to the Island. The giant Aldabra tortoises, Seychelles Kestrels, Seychelles Swiftlet, Seychelles Sunbird, Seychelles Blue Pigeon and endemic Seychelles Fruit Bat have already been introduced.

'Haute Robinson Crusoe' is how South African architects, husband and wife, Silvio Rech and Lesley Carstens describe this new resort. What they and Wilderness wanted was to create something that represented the best of the Seychelles and at the same time celebrated nature. North Island's natural credentials are extraordinary. The nearly mile-long east beach is a ribbon of luminous, powdery white sand. It's here that the eleven villas sit, looking out to sea, an uncanny turquoise deepening to cobalt around the granite rocks at either end, and facing the sunrise. Architecture merges with its natural surroundings. It is this idea, conceived by Lesley and Silvio, which is behind the transformation of North Island into a gem for the more luxury-orientated island tourists. Besides the eleven villas, the resort has a spacious lounge, bar and restaurant deck, a spa and infinity pool hidden among jungle palms, a library, wine cellar, gym, and a world class diving centre.

The villas are constructed of sandstone, rock, and reclaimed takamaka wood. The bureaus, couches, and tables are of invasive woods like casuarina, some with butterfly ties; the beds from a chunky hardwood called banua. The decking is sandblasted pine, which has the look of bleached driftwood, and floors are teak with rosewood, weathered rather than shellacked. The style is casual rustic, with tactile finishes, including muslin-soft linens. Each villa's two bedrooms are larger than most presidential suites at other resorts, with a cavernous stone bathtub, indoor and outdoor rosehead showers, and a freshwater plunge pool.

The main lodge was designed to dramatise the Seychelles' ancient role as a crossroads of Asian, Indian and African cultures. Underlined with a hand-crafted ensemble of rich woods, intricate details and contrasting textures, the lodge's floors gleam with teak and sand-blasted pine, and thick, gnarled trunks of takamaka and casuarina trees support thatch roofs woven by Balinese artisans from imported ylang-ylang fronds. The rooms are open to every tropical breeze and sea sound. This resort's relationship with nature is carried through in all the important details, right down to the cuisine. The cuisine of North Island is based on the diversity and cultural influences which, in part, make up the Seychellois Creole flavour. Culinary aspects of Africa, France, southern India and Southeast Asia are combined with the tropical, organic resources of North Island and the abundance on offer from the Indian Ocean.

Readers of Hideaways magazine, which showcases the 'world's most beautiful hotels and destinations', honoured Wilderness Safaris' North Island as the recipient of the Hideaway of the Year 2005 award, which is testimony that North Island is achieving its goal of offering the highest standards of hospitality against a backdrop of sustainable, eco-friendly practice. Bruce Simpson, general manager of North Island expressed his appreciation by saying that it was an honour for North Island to receive the award, considering the calibre of the other nominees. 'It is fantastic to receive this award for North Island, knowing that Seychelles has also been recognised.'

(Source: www.north-island.com and Gunter Ned, 'The Magic of the Seychelles', Hideaways 2003, www.helicopterseychelles.com/hideaways+2003.html)

Comoros

Sarah Grainger, a BBC correspondent in Comoros, reported that not for nothing are the Comoros known as the Perfume Isles. They export around 80 per cent of the world's supply of ylang ylang essence, an essential oil that is the main ingredient of most expensive perfumes. Originally from the Philippines, the ylang ylang plant was introduced to the Comoros by the French in the late 19th century. Like vanilla and cloves, which are also grown in the Comoros, ylang ylang is a potentially lucrative crop that is subject to volatile markets. Even while still growing on the tree, the yellow flower has a strong, sweet fragrance which will eventually be used in perfumes, soaps and other toiletries. Walking through the fields with your eyes closed is like walking past a perfume counter in a big department store.

The flowers are picked three times a month, giving distilleries an income all year round. The flowers are placed in a vat and steamed; the steam rises into a pipe and is fed into a condensing chamber where it cools.

The perfume essence is then collected at the bottom of the chamber. It takes 100kg of flowers to produce three litres of essential oil and the distillation process alone goes on for 18 hours. In the treatment room, the oil is checked for impurities before it is put into barrels to be exported to France. The distillery does not only deal with its own crop of ylang ylang flowers but also buys quantities from small, independent farmers on all the islands of the Comoros, combining their lesser yields into a larger crop.

The exportation of essential oils and spices is a closed market and every exporter must be licensed for each crop, with separate permits for the export of ylang ylang, vanilla, cloves and pepper. Comore Vanille et Plantes (CVP) Biocom exports vanilla, ylang-ylang and spices. CVP Biocom stems from La Bambao SA, the first French company to be established in the country in 1907 and which traded in spices and ylang-ylang essential oil. In 1994, when La Bambao SA closed, Hassani Assoumani decided to establish the CVP Biocom distillery and export business in Mbeni on the main island of Grande Comore, in order to preserve the knowledge and experience acquired with the French. CVP Biocom supports the local economy with the production of qualitatively improved and environment-friendly products. Its department of agro-forestry has conducted several product quality controls, which resulted in a quantitative and qualitative improvement of vanilla, spices and ylang-ylang production.

Assoumani told Grainger that small-scale farmers do not have the money or expertise to distil the essence. 'Exporting essential oils is very different from distilling them. You have to have some know-how. You need expensive equipment to distil the oils and make sure that they are all to a very high standard.' A museum on the Comor Islands history and habitat, arts and local handicrafts is open to the public in Mbeni, at the CVP Biocom headquarters. The museum comprises a botanical garden with plants, rare animals and traditional sculptures. CVP Biocom regularly organises training courses for carpenters in order to transmit to new generations the necessary knowledge and skills for the realisation of traditional sculpture.

(Source: Sarah Grainger. 'Comoros seeks sweet smell of success', BBC NEWS, http://news.bbc.co.uk, 24 September 2004; and www.altromercato.com)

Mozambique

In October 2004, Mozambican President Joaquim Chissano, speaking at the eighth annual conference of the Mozambican private sector, declared that the dialogue between the government and Mozambican businesses had resulted in significant improvements to the environment for doing business in the country. He noted in particular the 2004 simplification of industrial and commercial licensing arrangements, the approval of terms of reference for revision of the country's labour legislation, and the government's commitment to a one-stop-shop for registering companies.

Chissano declared that the one-stop-shop reform proposed by the government should compress all procedures to within five days, anywhere in the country. The principle, as the name implies, is that businessmen will no longer have to go on a complicated paper chase from office to office, but should be able to deal with all the necessary authorisations in the same place. Chissano is pleased at the way relations between the government and the CTA (Confederation of Mozambican Business Associations) has developed. He says, 'It is now the sublime duty of all of us to consolidate and strengthen this partnership, looking for the best ways to improve it,' and points out that the Mozambican model of relations between public and private sectors has proved able to seek out solutions 'to the problems faced in our daily lives. Our model, though it needs adjusting, and it is we who demand the adjustments, has proved a source of admiration that has been studied elsewhere. When we know what we want, we should never vacillate when faced with difficulties. The important thing is clarity in our objectives. We need determination in order to put our country on the path of development and eradicating poverty.'

Sergio Chitara, executive director of the CTA stresses that the key goal for reducing red tape and improving the environment for business is to ensure that Mozambican companies can be competitive on the global market and that innovation and the adoption of new technologies are essential — a series of bureaucratic barriers continued to affect the competitiveness of the country and of the companies, and in 2004 Mozambique was still scoring poorly on several indicators used internationally to measure the business environment. Furthermore, the legal system was far too slow and ineffective. Chitara called for far reaching reform that would ensure a functioning legal system, which could enforce contracts and deal with business disputes. Among the controversial recommendations are that mechanisms should be found to ensure that land could be used as collateral when applying for bank loans. The CTA announced the creation of an annual 'entrepreneur of the year' award, and the first such award was granted to Chissano. The award is a statue of an ant, chosen because of this insect's reputation as a tireless worker.

The International Finance Corporation (IFC) of the World Bank Group works throughout Africa via specialised facilities:

- The Africa Project Development Facility (APDF) identifies African entrepreneurs and helps them organise, diversify and expand their businesses by assisting them throughout the project preparation cycle.
- The Enterprise Support Services for Africa (ESSA) assists small- and medium-sized businesses in developing their potential for achieving success, both locally and internationally, by helping businesspeople better to manage their enterprises.
- The African Management Services Company (AMSCO) supplies experienced managers and technical personnel to small- and medium-sized private companies. Customised training services to local managers and staff are offered to upgrade their skills and improve the performance and productivity of their companies. In 2004, AMSCO had in place around 151 managers under contract at 72 African companies and in 23 countries. More than 9,000 employees have been trained. Based in Johannesburg, AMSCO also had offices in Amsterdam, Nairobi and Accra. It plays a major role in job creation and in establishing long-term sustainable growth for its clients.

In November 2004, IFC appointed a Kenyan entrepreneur, Ayisi Makatiani, as chief executive officer and managing director of AMSCO. The appointment of Makatiani, known for his role in the founding of Kenya's premier ISP, Africa Online, was expected to bolster the focus and product offering, owing to his vast experience with private sector challenges. Makatiani will be based in Johannesburg. He says strategy for AMSCO is to become more sector focused and specialise in turnaround management as well as broaden training activities in order to develop and implement relevant solutions for the private sector. He says training and placement of managers should not be the end game; they must see clear developmental impact in businesses by way of turnarounds in profitability and product competitiveness. He sees a two-pronged role for AMSCO: turning around businesses and developing the next breed of African entrepreneurs.

In Mozambique, one private cotton company that has worked closely with newly empowered farmers, and that is regarded as a model for future investors, is Companhia Agro-Pecuária de Moçambique Lda (AGRIMO). Founded in 1995, AGRIMO provides seeds and know-how, and a guaranteed market at its cotton processing plant for the cotton produced by thousands of small farmers in Mozambique's Zambezia province. By doing so it helps to increase and diversify the incomes of the region's smallholder families, most of which were displaced during Mozambique's long and disastrous civil war. AGRIMO provides the farmers with pest control and micro-credit to help them start up. It buys all the cotton that the farmers produce, but the price is set by the government to ensure it is fair. The company's shareholders include Zamagri, a Portuguese company formerly half-owned by Mantero, an AMSCO shareholder.

In June 1995, AMSCO signed the first of three contracts with AGRIMO for the implementation of several training programmes and entered into a sub-contract with Mantero covering technical assistance and the seconding of an AMSCO-recruited manager. During the 2003 season, the company provided assistance to 16,000 small farmers seeding 8,000 hectares. Training is developed on a yearly basis, prior to each growing season, and carried out in different phases corresponding to the cycle of cotton production. Over the past several years, AGRIMO's permanent staff of 133 and its clients have received instruction in accounting, human resources management, transport and information technology.

An evaluation conducted in late 2000 found that participants in the programmes found them to have a strong and lasting impact. Average yields had grown dramatically since the start of the programme - from 300 kilograms to 1,000 kilograms per hectare — while cash was increasingly replacing barter in transactions in the region. Despite a decline in international prices for cotton fibre and catastrophic flooding in Zambezia province, AGRIMO continued to make progress in its mission to enhance the prospects of those involved in the local cotton industry. As AGRIMO prepared to graduate from its relationship with AMSCO, the company's AMSCO-seconded manager intensively trained his senior subordinates in anticipation of his departure and the buying out of Mantero by United States cotton merchant Dunavant Enterprises. In the future, AGRIMO could provide technical assistance to farmers in the production of maize, pigeon pea and sunflower, in addition to cotton.

The first Mozambican factory to produce teabags started production in June 2003, in Gurue district, in the heart of the tea-producing area of the central province of Zambezia. The factory belongs to the private tea giant, Chazeira de Mocambique, which is part of Momade Aki's local Gulamo Group. The teabag production line meets a growing demand; it produces 250 tons of teabags a year, which has allowed the company to diversify for the national and international markets. In 2002, Chazeira de Mocambique produced 12,000 tons of tea. In 2003, production was 15,000 tons, mostly for export. The teabags are sold under the brand name Five Stars, obviously to compete with the South African brand Five Roses, which has inundated Maputo shops. Mozambican tea production collapsed during the war of destabilisation, when many of the tea-processing factories in Zambezia were destroyed. Bit by bit, the industry is being rebuilt, with total production in 2003 reaching 30,000 tons. The tea units in Gurue and Ile districts have been rehabilitated.

Mozambique is forming close ties with South Africa, setting up economic development deals and opening up road, rail and harbour links for South African trade. Maputo Corridor projects have included a toll road from the industrial town of Witbank, east of Johannesburg, to Maputo, improvements to Maputo harbour and an aluminium smelter at Matola, outside the capital. Other development corridors are under way for the central area of the country, from the Zimbabwe border to the port of Beira, and in the north to the border with Malawi. On Mozambique's beautiful Indian Ocean coastline, local and South African entrepreneurs have built fishing and holiday lodges.

The Zambezi Valley, in the centre of Mozambique, could become one of the engines for the development of southern Africa. Its rich soils could help eliminate hunger in the region. The Valley covers 225,000 square kilometres of the provinces of Manica, Sofala, Tete and Zambezia. It has great potential for agriculture, livestock and forestry, and the sub-soil has proven reserves of coal, granite, titanium and other minerals. The Zambezi itself is a key resource for the generation of hydropower. There are plans to build a new 1,200-megawatt dam at Mepanda Ncua, some 70 kilometres downstream from the existing Cahora Bassa dam. The Zambezi Valley development programme is one of the typical projects of the New Partnership for Africa's Development (NEPAD), with impacts at local, national, regional, continental and international levels. Mozambique's ports and railways, and the development corridors located along the lines of rail are doubly important since Mozambique provides natural and privileged access to the hinterlands of Zimbabwe, Zambia and Malawi. The implementation of the SADC trade protocol is contributing towards a very promising emerging regional market.

In northern Mozambique, the major economic driver in the province of Cabo Delgado is cotton. Plexus Cotton Ltd, and its joint venture partner Caravel Developments, which operate a ginning factory in Montepuez and have revitalised cotton production in the province. In 2003, Plexus ginned 11,800 tons and had over 35,000 hectares planted and in 2004 this production rose to 17,500 tonnes. Plexus was the largest ginner in Mozambique.

Plexus supplies seed to the farmers and then buys the seed-cotton for use in its ginning factory, using its market expertise to ensure the best possible return to their growers, whilst at the same time ensuring the best possible quality and price to consumers worldwide.

Quilálea Private Island is the latest upmarket tourist development in the province of Cabo Delgado. Quilálea is an uninhabited island (a malaria-free retreat) of 34 hectares which rests in a marine sanctuary with Sencar Island, within the newly created Parque National das Quirimbas and lies alongside a deep 70-metre channel with direct access to the Indian Ocean. It is part of the Quirimbas Arquipelago, which stretches from Pemba to the Rovuma River, the natural frontier with Tanzania. Quilálea Private Island opened in November 2002 and guests can unwind in unexpected luxury in one of nine private villas that blend into the tranquillity of the East African coast, and enjoy five-star dining on the beach. Quilálea's professional multilingual staff ensure comfort, well being and relaxation. Activities include snorkelling and scuba diving, kayaking and dhow sailing, with bird- and whale-watching in season, deep sea sport fishing and diving instruction. Chris and Angelique Williams with Nathan Mhando, the executive chef, take care of the day-to-day running of the island and welcomes guests on arrival. All the Quilálea shareholders are resident in Cabo Delgado Province. John and Marjolaine Hewlett are Professional Association of Diving Instructors (PADI) dive masters. Pedro Cruz is a former Olympic swimmer. Peter Bechtel is an environmental consultant and technical adviser to the WWF. The design, concept, landscaping, and layout of construction on Quilálea were conceived by Marjolaine. Quilálea's buildings are of local rocks. Seawater was used in a traditional cement mix, so the fragile island ecology was preserved. Fresh water is produced by desalinisation. The island villas are roofed with traditional palm thatch (makuti), ideal for cool and unobtrusive comfort.

(Source: www.quilalea.com)

Indian Ocean Aquaculture (IOA)'s marine shrimp farming project in Pemba Bay advocates environmentally and socially responsible aquaculture. IOA's managing director Patrick Wood follows the stringent food safety standards that the Aquaculture Certification Council (ACC) developed to certify shrimp farms, processing plants, hatcheries and feed mills around the world. ACC, seeing the future of traceability, has built a network to make it work for the shrimp farming industry — and for all of aquaculture. Traceability seeks to trace and document the path a particular food — say, farmed shrimp — takes from hatchery to grocery. Traceability is the single biggest influence on the future of the world's food business.

(Source: www.indianoceanaquaculture.com)

The late Charles Norman, well-known angling writer, author of four books, and regular columnist for newspapers and magazines, reported in 2003 that one man has done more than any other to focus attention on northern Mozambique. This man is Sheikh Adel Aujan, a successful Saudi Arabian soft-drink producer and distributor, who first came to Africa on a hunting trip in the early 1980s and fell in love with it. Drawn to the Arab history of the east coast, he became especially smitten with Mozambique. He found Mozambique officialdom receptive to his long-term vision of tourism. Though Aujan stands to profit handsomely in the future, the millions of dollars he has injected into the local Mozambique economy are seen as an enormous act of faith. Aujan's first move in Mozambique was to buy the defunct Indigo Bay Lodge (formerly Sabal Bay) and completely rebuild it into the beautiful resort which was chosen in May 2003 by Conde Nast *Traveller* as one of the 80 'best new resorts in the world hot list'. This exquisite island resort is situated on the idyllic and pristine Bazaruto Island off the coast of Mozambique. It offers visitors the quintessential Indian Ocean island holiday, as well as a gateway to the unspoiled beauty of the Bazaruto Archipelago.

But the untouched coast and virtually uninhabited interior of northern Mozambique was where Aujan's true passion lay, in particular Pemba and the little-known 32 islands of the Quirimbas Archipelago that begin some 70 kilometres north of Pemba and continue right up to the Tanzanian border. The most visible manifestation of Aujan's influence has been the luxurious Pemba Beach Hotel which offers exclusivity and tranquillity in an idyllically beautiful and tropical setting on the unspoiled Mozambican coastline. Manicured lawns stretch down to the warm waters of the Indian Ocean. Coral reefs lie just off the coastline and their magnificent display of colourful coral species and tropical fish, as well as whales and dolphins, are waiting to be explored.

With the support of Governor Pacheco, Adel Aujan would like to see the entire Quirimbas Archipelago become a protected marine park, and it seems to be happening. Aujan's approach to this objective perhaps explains why he has succeeded with Mozambican officialdom. 'I discussed it with the governor,' says Aujan, 'and he agreed it would be a good idea, but said Mozambique didn't have the money for the boats that would be needed to patrol such a marine park. So I asked if I could contribute to such a fleet, and he graciously agreed that I could.' Aujan was genuinely grateful that the governor would allow him to spend his own money on Mozambique.

The Pemba Beach Hotel has kick-started all sorts of other developments in the area, starting with LAM Mozambique Airlines which now flies to Pemba several times a week, and the Makonde carvers creating their intricate ebony artworks under the shade of a tree are doing roaring business. Several cashew nut factories are working full-time to turn out the specialty of Mozambique. Aujan, who has a vision to uplift the local population, says he is just one of several like-minded people who want to develop the Mozambique coast for international tourism but at the same time protect it from destruction.

Opened in November 2004, Matemo Island Resort is an unspoilt, unexplored island paradise, with beautiful white beaches and thousands of palm trees swaying in the breeze. Matemo is eight kilometres in length and three kilometres wide — a magical destination with private beaches and countless coves to be discovered and blissful surroundings to be experienced. Situated in the magnificent Quirimbas Archipelago on the coast of northern Mozambique, Matemo Island Resort is one of two 2004 additions to the luxurious Rani Resorts portfolio. The Medjumbe Island Lodge was taken over by Aujan's tourism development company Rani Resorts and, after a complete rebuild, was reopened in December 2005. Medjumbe Island Resort offers guests a chance to experience Africa intimately. Seventeen and a half hectares of pristine tropical island, surrounded by bleached coral sand beaches, and kilometres of unexplored fringe reefs, offer snorkellers endless days of drifting over exquisite untouched coral formations teeming with exotic tropical marine species.

Rani Resorts specialises in exclusive resorts on the African continent. From the first inspiring vision right down to final completion, Rani maintains the highest standards to ensure that their properties provide an unforgettable holiday experience in a superb setting under the African stars. The Lugenda Wildlife Reserve (Luwire) was created to preserve and enhance the vast unique ecosystem found in northernmost Mozambique. One of the most pristine game reserves in Africa, Luwire includes part of the unspoiled Niassa Reserve in northern Mozambique and covers 7,200 square kilometres, which includes 300 kilometres of frontage on the Lugenda River. The reserve is rich in wildlife and hosts one of the largest undiscovered elephant populations in Africa as well as the rare and endangered Niassa wildebeest. In Zimbabwe, Rani's luxurious all-suite hotel, The Stanley and Livingstone Hotel at Victoria Falls, is situated near one of the world's natural wonders and the world heritage site of Victoria Falls, and caters for discerning guests seeking a tranquil and luxurious environment.

(Source: www.aujan.com.sa; www.sportfishafrica.co.za; www.raniresorts.com; and 'Under African Skies,' by Douglas Rogers, *Travel & Leisure*, October 2005, pages 244-56).

In 1996 five friends, all with a pioneering spirit and passion for Africa, embarked on a mission to build a new safari lodge in Mozambique, Nkwichi Lodge. Their dream was to provide guests with beautiful accommodation from which they could explore the surrounding wilderness and communities. One of the main goals was to ensure that the lodge helped to protect wildlife and provide social and economic benefits for local people. Nkwichi Lodge was set up as part of the Manda Wilderness Project, as a responsible tourism project. A separate UK charity, Manda Wilderness Community Trust (MWCT), was created specifically to carry out and develop the charitable activities, and works closely with Nkwichi Lodge to ensure that local communities also benefit from the growth of responsible tourism in the region.

With the commitment and active involvement of the local communities, an area of unspoiled wilderness

— brachystegia woodland and riverine forest, savannah, swamps and streams, mountains and miles of beaches with crystal clear fresh water — have been set aside to form the basis of Manda Wilderness Community Game Reserve, which was created to protect and manage a 100,000-hectare community reserve on the shores of Lake Niassa, owned by the 14 local villages, and managed by MWCT. Villagers vote for their priorities, be it a school roof, a clinic, a boat or a maize mill. The Nkwichi Lodge raises funds for materials — US$5 for every visitor night, coupled with donations from guests — while the locals supply the labour. There's an agriculture project aimed at improving nutrition and creating small-scale businesses, and a market in Cobue which opened as a result. Manda Wilderness emerged as the 2005 winner of the Africa SMME Tourism and Transport sector award and was also a third place finisher for the overall Africa SMME of the Year award.

(Source: www.mandawilderness.org)

Zimbabwe

Patterson Fungayi Timba is one the World Economic Forum's most distinguished Global Leaders for Tomorrow, 2003. Timba is the founder member and chief executive of ReNaissance Merchant Bank, successor to ReNaissance Advisory Services (RAS), a company specialising in financial advisory services. Prior to getting a merchant-banking licence in October 2001, ReNaissance had been offering merchant banking products in an advisory capacity through RAS. In the past RAS would come up with a number of new products and house them in other banks. This tended to delay their work, making RAS inefficient. ReNaissance is in a position to offer these services directly to clients as well as assume risk on their balance sheet. Timba says his team was forced to hunt for a merchant-banking licence in response to the dictates of the market and the desire to offer a total financial package. The package is anchored on a solid human resource base, state-of-the-art information technology, and a sound administration base. Timba says that although there were several banks operating in Zimbabwe, he was convinced of his capacity to offer innovative ideas and facilities.

ReNaissance is the first bank since 1980 to record a profit in its first year of operation. In 2002, ReNaissance posted an after tax profit of Z$1.2 billion (US$22.3 million), having kicked off with an initial capital of Z$200 million (US$3.72 million), a return of 600 per cent. ReNaissance declared a dividend of Z$500 million, giving back its shareholders 2.5 times their initial investment. The trend in Zimbabwe is that new banks make losses in their first year, break even in the second, and become profitable in the third year. Approximately eleven new banks have been licensed since 1992. In January 2003, the official exchange rate was Z$55 to US$1 with a parallel market rate of Z$1400 to US$1. The 2002 inflation rate closed the year at 198 per cent. Loans, interest rates and savings are based on the Z$, thus giving negative returns. Banks therefore have to work extremely hard to match and/or beat inflation, which is still feasible in a dislocated economy like Zimbabwe's. For example, to protect banks from any loss resulting from the depreciation of the Zimbabwe dollar, loan payments are often paid in the equivalent of US$, plus interest, plus a fee to partially cover exchange rate fluctuations.

Timba established RAS in November 1999 and assumed the role of managing director. Against stiff and established competition, the company won significant and high profile mandates and in most cases was appointed the lead financial advisor by both the public and private sector. By November 2001, the company was rated as one of the best financial advisors in Zimbabwe. Timba was formerly assistant general manager (corporate finance) at National Merchant Bank of Zimbabwe Ltd (now NMB Bank Ltd). He left NMB in October 1999 to spearhead the formation of Renaissance Advisory Services. He is a qualified Chartered Accountant with wide business experience. Prior to joining National Merchant Bank in March 1997, he was a senior manager (corporate finance) at Stanbic Bank of Zimbabwe. Timba had joined Stanbic from Standard Chartered Merchant Bank, where he was manager in the corporate finance department.

Timba says his selection as a Global Leader for Tomorrow was important in that it reflected international recognition for Zimbabwe's young businessmen. He believes that if international organisations can consider it fit to equate Zimbabwe's young businessmen with other world players it effectively vindicates his conviction that Zimbabwe has the capacity to develop businesses which can operate on a global scale. His selection as a Global Leader for Tomorrow was also important because he endeavoured to be a role model to other upcoming business people. Timba says the selection was a process and not an event, and put a responsibility on him in that one had to continuously strive to perform and maintain one's integrity, both from an individual and institutional perspective. He has taken this as a launching pad to be firstly an international businessman and use business linkages to develop Renaissance into an international business, bearing in mind that as the business develops it will always carry the Zimbabwe flag. He hopes that as he and his staff progress and develop the business into an international one, economic benefits will flow through into the country as well. He sees this as 'a challenge and a blessing from God'.

(Source: 'Timba joins world's 100 most-distinguished list', Zimbabwe Independent, 6 December 2002)

Since 2002, the ReNaissance brand has further grown with the creation of ReNaissance Financial Holdings Ltd (RFHL) in August 2003. RFHL is now the holding company of the bank, and in 2004 two other subsidiaries were added to the stable. The Group now offers asset and fund management through its licensed subsidiary, ReNaissance Asset Management; and securities trading through its other subsidiary, ReNaissance Securities, a member of the Zimbabwe Stock Exchange. Timba is now group chief executive with each subsidiary having its own executive management. In addition, RFHL was granted licences to offer financial advisory services, securities trading and asset and funds management by the Capital Markets Authority of Uganda. The Uganda operations operate ReNaissance Capital Uganda Ltd and opened their doors to the public in January 2005. This was achieved when Zimbabwe's banking sector had gone through a severe crisis with 11 of the 40 banking institutions collapsing.

When the winners of the Africa 2004 SMME Awards were announced in October 2004, enterprises from all over the continent made their mark. The ReNaissance Merchant Bank was the winner of the award for the banking and finance sector. Timba credits the success and growth of ReNaissance to the grace of God, as ReNaissance is anchored on strong Christian values. He says, 'The sky has never been the limit but a target; when we get there we pick another target.' ReNaissance Merchant Bank was also a 2005 Finalist for the Africa SMME Awards.

Internet and mobile phone usage is taking off in Africa. The numbers of dial-up Internet subscribers and cell phone activations are soaring. More mobile phones were turned on in five years than landline connections completed in an entire century. Internet access via corporate or shared networks is growing even faster than dial-up usage, and cybercafes and other public access centres have popped up rapidly in urban areas. Telecommunication entrepreneur Strive Masiyiwa believes information and communication technologies are a chance for Africa — not a magic formula to solve all the problems but powerful tools for economic growth and poverty eradication, which can facilitate the integration of African countries into the global economy.

Masiyiwa is the founder and group chief executive officer of South African based, diversified international telecommunications group Econet Wireless. Under his leadership and guidance, Econet Wireless has grown into a global telecommunications company operating in the core areas of mobile cellular telephony, fixed line networks, satellite services and Internet operations. The company is headquartered in South Africa and currently has operations and offices in Africa, Europe and the East Asia Pacific region.

A recognised entrepreneur, Masiyiwa has also been involved in the development of Africa's independent media. He is a well-known international business leader who has won numerous international recognition and awards for business excellence. In 1999, he was named by the Junior Chamber International (Jaycees) as one of the 'Ten Most Outstanding Young Persons of the World'. In 2003 he was chosen as one of the '15 Global Influentials of the Year' in a CNN/*TIME* Magazine poll. Over the years Masiyiwa has served on many international boards and foundations, and has also been involved in numerous initiatives to promote entrepreneurship and social development in Africa. He was on the board of the American government funded Southern Africa Enterprise Development Fund from 1995 to 2004 and is now a member of the advisory group of the Nelson Mandela Foundation. He joined the Rockefeller Foundation board of trustees in 2003.

Outside his business interests Masiyiwa is also active in promoting awareness on the impact of AIDS in Africa. A foundation, which he and his wife founded and fund, currently provides scholarships for more than 25,000 orphans. As one of the most respected African business leaders today, Strive Masiyiwa speaks regularly on African business at major international business gatherings, and has been regularly featured in leading international publications and television programs, among them *The Economist, Newsweek*, CNN, Barron's of New York, and *The Financial Times*.

Chapungu Sculpture Park of Harare has one of the largest permanent collections of Zimbabwean stone sculpture. It was established by its director, Roy Guthrie, as the Gallery Shona Sculpture in 1970 and moved to its present park location in 1985. Many of the works depict matters closest to the hearts of the artists — their own way of life, their culture and their daily living experiences — and are representative of eight universally human themes: custom and legend, family, nature and the environment, the role of elders, the role of women, social comment, spirit world, and village life. Chapungu is dedicated to acquiring and safeguarding as many of these works as possible as part of the sculptural heritage of Zimbabwe, hoping that viewers of the sculptures will be able to gain an insight into African culture.

Stone sculpture from Zimbabwe emerged during the 1960s, initially through the encouragement of Frank McEwen, first director of the National Gallery of Zimbabwe (then Rhodesia). McEwen argued that he was resuscitating in Africans the creative relationship with local stone which was evident in late stone age rock art and the building of the great and lesser Zimbabwes. The proliferation of stones suited to sculpture in Zimbabwe provides a surrounding for other developments in the history of the sculpture. For example, the discovery of serpentine in the Eastern Highlands encouraged Tom Blomefeld, a tobacco farmer of Tengenenge Farm, who saw stone sculpture as an alternative occupation for his farm workers when sanctions against Rhodesia decimated the tobacco industry, and a way of expressing their cultural background in sculpture. Through the efforts of supporters such as Frank McEwen and Tom Blomefield, an emergent western market for the stone sculpture led many people to turn to sculpture as a potentially lucrative profession and today thousands of rural and urban people earn their living through carving stones, making sculpture which is often serious, unpretentious, powerful, immediate and engaging.

Out of these beginnings have risen some of the most famous names in African art history such as Nicholas Mukomberanwa, Henry Munyaradzi, Joram Mariga and many more. With the second and third generations of artists we can see, more than ever, the great diversity of impressions and materials used. Dominic Benhura and Agnes Nyanhongo are representatives of the new generations. Dominic has developed a very easily recognisable contemporary sculpting style. His technical ability and emphasis on form and movement, rather than facial features, make his work timeless and universal. Agnes has mastered the ability to capture human emotions in stone, especially the bonds between husband and wife, child and parent, and the spiritual world and oneself

(Source: www.chapungusculpturepark.com).

In October 2005, Loveland, Colorado, USA, became home to a permanent collection of world-renowned Zimbabwean stone sculpture. Chapungu Sculpture Park is developing a 27-acre sculpture park in Loveland that will house an extensive outdoor collection of Chapungu's contemporary sculpture. The park and lifestyle centre will blend together — through trails, landscaping, and design features. Many areas of the lifestyle centre will overlook the sculpture park, including outdoor restaurant patios. Trails around the lakes, wetlands, and other natural features of the park site will connect with the lifestyle centre. Roy Guthrie, curator for Chapungu, opened a gallery in January 2006.

The sculpture park will enhance Loveland's art culture. Chapungu has future plans to build a cultural centre that would have activities such as workshops and artist visits. It is envisaged that this cultural centre, due to open in fall of 2007, will be key to cultural art and music exchanges between Zimbabwean artists and their American counterparts. It will also provide educational programmes to include schools and disadvantaged communities. These cultural exchanges and sculpting workshops have been key components in the exhibits Chapungu has held throughout the United States. Guthrie has made Loveland the international headquarters for his 'Chapungu: stories in stone — An African perspective of family' touring exhibit.

Roy Guthrie believes that the future holds much promise for the committed sculptors of Zimbabwe. In Africa today Guthrie points out that there is a great upsurge of artistic expression, some beholden to traditional means of art practice and creative expression, linked still to African ceremonial and ritual. Other art praxes follow and indeed initiate new developments in art in the North, a result of African artists travelling and representing their countries at Biennales and Art Fairs the world over. The stone sculpture of Zimbabwe remains conceptually representative of both the traditional and modern way of life in Zimbabwe. Other art forms in Africa may succumb to fashion and come and go. Others may become obsolete as traditions die out. The stone sculpture of Zimbabwe and its new and exciting developments Guthrie thinks may show that the best future of art for Africa comes from this troubled but highly spiritual continent.

Australian Celia Winter-Irving, a former gallery director in Sydney and a major writer on sculpture and art for serious art journals, was appointed curator at the National Gallery of Zimbabwe in January 2004, a position she still holds and is widely respected for, locally and internationally. She is in charge of organising all exhibitions, selection of work, documentation, writing, media and liaising with artists the world over. Celia came to Zimbabwe professionally in 1987. She pioneered the publication of books with substantive texts on Zimbabwe's stone sculpture. Many of these books have influenced international buyers of substance and repute as to the sculptors whose work they buy and exhibit. Celia has been jurist and national monitor for Zimbabwe's National Arts Council Merit Awards in the field of visual arts since 2000.

Celia is the author of *Stone Sculpture in Zimbabwe: Context, Content and Form* (1992), a standard reference work on the stone sculpture of Zimbabwe, locally and internationally. She writes that Zimbabwe's stone sculpture is unique, not only because of its individual form and content, which is highly valued and acclaimed in the art centres of the world, but because it springs from the indigenous talents that lay hidden until the 1960s. This is a classic work on the stone sculpture and still relevant to contemporary developments. Since 1992, ten more books on Zimbabwe's stone sculpture by Celia have been published. Her tenth book on Zimbabwe's stone sculpture, *Pieces of Time*, was launched at Dominic Benhura's Sculpture Studio in June 2005, and was well reviewed in Zimbabwe. Her latest book, *Merchers Chiwawa Sculptor, Following the Footsteps of Wisdom*, will be published by Shona-Art of Witten Germany in March 2006.

Ashoka is a global non-profit organisation that searches the world for social entrepreneurs, extraordinary individuals with unprecedented ideas for change in their communities. Ashoka identifies and invests in these social entrepreneurs. It does so through stipends and professional services that allow 'Ashoka Fellows' to focus full-time on their ideas for leading social change in education and youth development, health care, environment, human rights, access to technology and economic development. Ashoka has invested in more than 1,100 Ashoka Fellows in 41 countries, who have transformed the lives of millions of people in thousands of communities worldwide.

Ashoka launched its Africa programme in 1990 with the election of the first Ashoka Fellows in Zimbabwe. Nigeria and South Africa followed in 1991, West Africa and the Sahel region in 1992, and East Africa in 2001. By 2003, there were approximately 170 Ashoka Fellows in 15 African countries, and about 25 new Fellows elected each year in Africa. Across the continent, Ashoka Fellows are attacking persistent social problems with innovative solutions — from developing new ways to face the AIDS epidemic in west and southern Africa to promoting civic participation in Nigeria's burgeoning democracy. Ashoka Africa is strengthening efforts to build the Ashoka Fellowship, improve services to Fellows in the region, and build partnerships with the business sector.

Among the entrepreneurs Ashoka has backed is Esinet Mapondera, who was elected to the Ashoka Fellowship in 2000. Esinet founded the first micro-finance institution in Zimbabwe to pioneer group-lending methodology. Inspired by the Grameen Bank idea in Bangladesh and based on Esinet's belief that the poor can help themselves, she formed the Zimbabwe Women Finance Trust (ZWFT). As a result of her work, Esinet has played a leading role in a host of international endeavours addressing women's issues. Esinet had a dream that women could be more than housewives, domestic workers, teachers or nurses. She believed that if women could start their own businesses and make their own money through their own efforts, they would be empowered and independent. Influenced by her communal background, her lifetime of experience as a social worker, 28 years as a successful businesswoman in Zambia and her frustration at being refused venture capital in Zimbabwe to start a market garden business, Esinet created ZWFT in 1989.

This institution was the first to offer group lending to women in Zimbabwe and began as an affiliate of Women's World Banking. Created out of the discovery that women were poorly skilled to manage themselves financially, ZWFT offers technical training for members, strengthens linkages with other groups, encourages self sustainability and offers vocational skills training to women who want to start their own small scale industries. The organisation also aims to protect the environment and impact on HIV/AIDS through micro-lending. Since its inception in 1989, ZWFT has had more than 6,000 members and has provided project assistance valued over Z$25 million. ZWFT is well spread over Zimbabwe's rural, suburban and urban areas and has had an impact on over 30,000 beneficiaries.

ZWFT targets poor women who are involved in income generating activities. These women face enormous difficulties in accessing credit through the formal financial institutions, for not only do they face gender discrimination from the business sector but also deep rooted prejudices against micro-enterprise development, and a lack of depth in the Zimbabwean capital markets. When funds are made available for venture capital, the interest rates are too high for the sustainability of new enterprises. In most cases, these micro-enterprises are the only source of income to support families. High interest rates mean that there is virtually nothing left after servicing the loan.

The rapid growth of the organisation is attributed to the introduction of a group-based lending methodology. Initially the organisation used an individual-based approach to lending. This meant that women were assessed as individuals and even the repayments were made by the individual borrower without any commitment from the beneficiaries of the revolving loan funds. It led to high incidences of non-payment of loans.

The group lending method assesses the group and requires that the women form themselves into groups of seven to ten members where each member is a co-guarantor for the other. All members must be involved in micro-enterprise and must have been in operation for 12 months — an assessment of commitment to the venture. ZWFT encourages the women to save as well as obtain credit, and gives them business advice and training assistance once they qualify for loans. ZWFT has an excellent repayment record and the credit delivery method allows for constant contact with the women through regular visits by field officers.

Esinet Mapondera is a born leader and people person. She was influenced by her strong, hardworking family, especially her grandmother, who taught her to think for herself and not to blindly follow others. Throughout her life, she has challenged unfair systems and initiated reforms. After graduating from college, Esinet worked as an industrial social worker at the Chilanga Cement works in Zambia. While employed there from 1964-76, she established a community school for employees' children and the first cottage industry training centre for employees' wives. In addition to her employment as a social worker, Esinet developed her own independent enterprises, including a clothing shop and a vegetable shop. She left Chilanga in 1976 to become a full-time market gardener. She was the first Zambian woman to export vegetables to Europe. Upon moving to Zimbabwe in 1979, she wanted to continue gardening work but, as a black woman, could not get a loan. She managed, however, to create a successful trading business, and her experiences eventually led her to create the Zimbabwe Women's Finance Trust in 1989, to assist other women in establishing independent enterprises.

Throughout her career, Esinet has been recognised for her successful work and invited to advise and lead others. In 1980 to organise a women's NGO conference. After her report of the conference, in which she had recommended that the government create a women's affairs desk in one of the ministries, the government decided to establish the Ministry of Women's Affairs. In 1985, she set up Zimbabwe Women Business Promotions and, in 1989, the Zimbabwe Women Finance Trust (ZWFT), of which she is the chairperson. She served as vice president of the Zimbabwe Women's Bureau from 1982-84, its president from 1984-88 and its general secretary from 1988-90. She has served as a board member of the Inter University Consortium of International Development since 1990 to date. She was the first African representative at the Ecumenical Church Loan Fund in Geneva as a board and committee member from 1991-97. She travels often to present papers at international conferences. In 2001, Esinet was awarded the prestigious Desmond Tutu Footprints of Legends Leadership Award. The award is offered to 'persons who proceed from sunrise to sunset, promoting the ideals of social justice and equity while selflessly serving their vision and their dream of an Africa free from poverty and prejudice'.

(Source: www.ashoka.org)

The Africa Centre for Holistic Management operates as a sister organisation to Holistic Management International, a US-based NGO with headquarters in Albuquerque, New Mexico. Located close to the Victoria Falls, the Africa Centre owns Dimbangombe Ranch sitting between a large communal lands community and vast tracts of big game country. The Africa Centre is governed by a board of trustees, on which all the chiefs of this region of Zimbabwe are sitting members. It has established a college of wildlife, agriculture and conservation management to train people particularly from this region to better their lives through improving the environment, wildlife and agriculture.

Dimbangombe is a working ranch managed holistically as outlined in the book *Holistic Management: A New Framework for Decision Making* by Allan Savory and Jody Butterfield. In 2003, the work was recognised through the Australian Banksia Environmental Foundation's International Award. This award, previously given to achievers like Rachel Carson and Sir David Attenborough, is given to the person or organisation doing the most for the environment on a global scale.

The work of the Africa Centre incorporates a series of interrelated projects that together seek to resolve some of the world's most pressing problems. Objectives include:

- Establishing an international training facility and learning site that serves as a working example of holistic management in practice on the land and in local communities, and that brings governments, scientists and local communities together, working in collaboration at all levels.
- Empowering the people in the neighbouring Hwange communal lands to become self-sufficient and to achieve a long-term sustainable future of their own design, through community training in holistic management.
- Restoring desertifying land in Zimbabwe and developing a model programme that can be implemented anywhere in Africa.
- Enhancing the survival of threatened wildlife populations by working to restore damaged habitat, and to improve the quality of life for the people living among and around them.
- Researching and documenting the successful use of livestock and wild ungulates to recycle old vegetation, as an alternative to fire.
- Creating a successful micro lending 'village banking' programme to assist people in improving their personal quality of life and that of the community, and assisting the women of the banks to make sound social, environmental and economic decisions.

Although intended to benefit Africa mainly, people from as far afield as Indonesia, Argentina, Canada, Australia, New Zealand and the United States have requested holistic management training in Zimbabwe where the knowledge originated.

The Africa Centre is reversing desertification and restoring biodiversity. People and wildlife depend on the health of the land to survive. Land degradation through much of Africa and other seasonal rainfall regions of the world was initiated by the human-caused disruption of a vital relationship that once existed between herding ungulates, the plants and soils that nourished them, and the pack-hunting animals that preyed on them. This destruction has been exacerbated by human management, especially attempts to maintain grasslands through the frequent use of fire and, in the settled areas, through the manner in which livestock have grazed. Numerous fires are deliberately set throughout most of Africa's wild lands and national parks to remove excess old vegetation, and thus keep grasslands alive. In the past, massive herds of wild grazers cleared away the old growth, making way for the new. Modern managers have tried to simulate the role performed by using fire, but the repeated use of fire also produces many undesirable effects.

The Africa Centre is providing evidence that livestock can be used far more effectively to simulate the presence of the formerly massive wild herds. Managed holistically, livestock can be used to clear away the old growth on grass plants while at the same time helping to cover exposed soil, and to enhance the diversity of plant and animal life by creating the habitat for them. They also feed people.

In 2005 Holistic Management International was awarded a substantial grant by USAID to further its work in the Hwange community. This is taking the form of establishing two pilot projects in which the villagers are being trained to apply the techniques that have been so successfully demonstrated on Dimbangombe ranch. In addition the project has major components involving training in HIV/AIDS awareness and gender awareness. Many of the micro-credit banks are simultaneously being converted from money as currency to goats as currency due to the hyper-inflation in Zimbabwe.

None of the projects of the Africa Centre is for as little as three or five or ten years. Holistic Management International and its sister organisation are in it for the long term. Their relationship with their neighbours in the Hwange Communal Lands is for the long term; their training programmes have to continue from one generation to the next and must be for the long term; and their work in restoring the land and the habitat, for both people and wildlife, is for the long term because their vision of how it must be, and can be, is long-term.

(Source: www.holisticmanagement.org)

Chapter 8: South Africa: Mining, Agriculture, Construction, Transport and Tourism

South African President Thabo Mbeki is shifting his country to the nuts and bolts politics of sound economics and government performance. Backed by a 2004 mandate from nearly 70 per cent of voters, Mbeki has set his sights on an African renaissance that would strengthen the continent politically and economically and restore the dignity of Africans everywhere. South Africa, with a population of about 45 million, a stable democracy, and an economy that churned out more than 38 per cent of sub-Saharan Africa's gross domestic product in 2004, is the best-equipped nation on the continent to provide indigenous economic and political leadership. Mbeki has positioned South Africa for a leading role in the African Union and its economic platform, the New Partnership for Africa's Development (NEPAD).

At home, Mbeki is tackling one of his country's core problems, what he refers to as its 'two economies', amounting to two starkly disconnected populations. The first economy is an exporter of BMWs, a skilled purveyor of telecommunications and banking services, and a major producer of raw materials such as gold and platinum. The second economy is the sector of society that includes the unemployed, who account for as much as 42 per cent of the working-age population. These South Africans, many of them shoved by the apartheid government into rural areas where they did their best to live as subsistence farmers, are barely literate, and many have never held a formal job. They are virtually unemployable in the high-skill jobs market.

Mbeki plans different prescriptions for each sector. For the mainstream economy, he aims to attract investment by sticking with the government's macroeconomic discipline and by lowering the cost of doing business in South Africa. To lower the cost of doing business, Mbeki is cracking the whip on quasi state-owned companies such as Transnet, the transportation conglomerate that owns everything from the nation's ports and railroads to its flagship airline. Mbeki has pledged his government will open a major new shipping port by September 2005, and that it will expand rail capacity 30 per cent by 2009. He has also vowed to license a private competitor to the state-owned phone operator, whose prices are high relative to those in other countries.

For the abject second economy, Mbeki says South Africa will 'go the route of a New Deal', launching an expanded public-works programme designed to transfer skills — and provide temporary jobs — to more than a million South Africans by 2010. His government is also reinvigorating skills training and adult education programmes, and is turbo-charging its micro-credit system to help incubate small businesses. He promises every household will have running water by 2009, and electricity by 2012. Mbeki thinks about the broader political consequences of poverty, believing that social instability will sink all, black and white.

(Source: Mark Schoofs. 'Mbeki sets sights on details', *The Wall Street Journal*, 12 October 2004)

Patrice Motsepe is one of the most successful of the new generation of black South African mining entrepreneurs. Patrice began his business training in 1977 at the age of 15 when he would wake early to help his entrepreneurial father by selling liquor to mineworkers to supplement the income his father earned from owning a beer hall and bottle store. He went on to earn a BA from the University of Swaziland and an LLB from the University of the Witwatersrand, and become a partner at the law firm of Bowman Gilfillan, where he specialised in mining and business law. In 1994, he shifted to the mining industry. Nobody would give him a loan when he started and so for the first nine months he ran his business from his briefcase. He founded a contract mining operation called Future Mining, which provided various services to the then Vaal Reefs gold mine, now part of AngloGold. That put him in the right place at the right time to benefit from the restructuring of the South African gold mining industry.

Major South African gold groups like AngloGold were restructuring their operations to survive an extended downturn in the gold price. Part of the solution was to dispose of marginal shafts (which were high-cost or had a short life) to focus on the remaining low-cost, long-life shafts. Motsepe formed African Rainbow Minerals (ARM) in 1997 and acquired a number of marginal shafts at Vaal Reefs in January 1998 on favourable financial terms. He followed that with the purchase of other marginal shafts owned by AngloGold in the Free State. The purchase of the Free State shafts was a joint venture with Harmony Gold Mining. The challenge was then to turn them around through tighter cost control and better working efficiencies.

In just eight years after leaving Bowman Gilfillan, Patrice had established ARM as the fifth largest gold producer in South Africa. By 2002, ARM owned and operated 13 gold mining shafts, had become the eleventh largest gold producer in the world and employed approximately 9,000 in its Sandton offices and Orkney and Welkom mining operations. In May 2002, the company achieved a major milestone. ARM's gold assets were listed on the Johannesburg Stock Exchange as ARMgold, the first black empowerment mining company to list on the JSE and the first new gold mining company to list on the JSE in 15 years. Patrice had become a rand billionaire since various Motsepe family trusts owned a total of 55.8 per cent of ARMgold, which in 2002 had a market capitalisation of nearly R7 billion. The company began focusing on acquisition opportunities, primarily in South Africa and then in the rest of Africa.

Each of the separate units in ARMgold was given free reign to exhibit entrepreneurial spirit. As an innovator, Patrice had an employee pay scheme of a low basic salary supplemented by performance-rated bonuses. ARMgold intended to focus on its strengths to enhance shareholder value by increasing gold production and reserves through acquiring mines where its management style and operating principles could be applied. By improving operating performance and reducing costs, ARMgold management felt they could pursue increased profitability aggressively. ARMgold aimed to optimise its resources and improve its ore reserve management.

Still privately held and unlisted in 2002 was ARM's 50 per cent stake in the new Maandagshoek platinum mine being developed by Anglo American Platinum, a project likely to be worth far more than the R1.35 billion development cost. Asked about his plans for platinum, Motsepe said it took five to six years to get the gold company listed; however, he suggested that a million ounces of output from the platinum division would probably trigger another stock exchange listing. Motsepe added that, like ARMgold, platinum would become part of an internationally competitive company.

In September 2003, Harmony Gold Mining and ARMgold shareholders overwhelmingly approved the merger of the two companies. The merger created South Africa's largest gold producer. The ARMgold listing was terminated and the 'new' Harmony is now chaired by Patrice Motsepe. In October 2004, Harmony made an unsolicited takeover bid for South African rival, Gold Fields, a move that would create one of the world's largest gold producing companies. The deal faced major hurdles and set off heated bickering among executives on three continents. If the deal were to go through, it would consolidate Motsepe not only as one of South Africa's pre-eminent black entrepreneurs, but also as a major dealmaker.

Patrice's strong personality, innovation and determination, coupled with an unflinching desire to succeed, has enabled the development and implementation of a 'we do it better' management style, culminating in a set of management and operating principles focused on enhancing operations. He values strong corporate governance and believes in empowering employees at all levels, training them in basic business principles and the necessary skills and expertise to make appropriate decisions. He takes the approach that mining is about people and not rocks; it is important to Patrice that his employees participate meaningfully in any decisions relating to the company's operations. This strategy improves productivity and employee understanding of the business's objectives. Patrice says the most important elements in business are employee buy-in and applying innovative leadership to maintain a contented workforce. He regards developing a relationship of trust as the cornerstone of a happy working environment.

With Motsepe's business success has come broader corporate exposure and responsibility. Patrice participates in a number of global and local business organisations. He is a member of the World Economic Forum (WEF), where he has been elected a Global Leader of Tomorrow, and is also part of the WEF's annual global meetings where the world's most influential businessmen and country leaders evaluate and deliberate global affairs. Patrice is a past president and member of the executive committee of the Chamber of Mines. As of 2004, he was the president of the Black Business Council of South Africa. He was elected as the president of the National African Chamber of Commerce & Industry (NAFCOC) in 2002 and re-elected unopposed in 2004. Patrice points out that NAFCOC's vision for empowerment is to nurture and develop small black business in order to create a successful black middle class. While Patrice recognises the need for empowerment he says the time will come when race will no longer be a criterion. He says it is critical for black and white business to unite and that it is his dream in the long term to talk about business, not black or white business.

(Sources: 'Mining is about people, not about rocks', Johannesburg: *Business Day*, 10 October 2002; Brendan Ryan. 'In the right place at the right time', *Financial Mail* 27 September 2002; Hilton Shone. 'From zero to hero in just five years', Johannesburg: *Sunday Times*, 6 October 2002)

In September 2003, South Africa's four business chambers merged in a move that united the business community for the first time. The National African Chamber of Commerce and Industry (NAFCOC), the South African Chamber of Business (SACOB), the Foundation for African Business and Consumer Services (FABCOS) and the Afrikaanse Handelsinstituut (AHI) agreed to unite. A group of members from the four chambers, headed by Patrice Motsepe, oversaw the process. The move was a sign of how the business landscape — previously fragmented along racial lines and by in-fighting — had changed. Unification had become necessary so that government could interact with a strong business community on certain issues relating to the country's economy. Motsepe sees the unification as having spin-offs for both business and greater society. From an empowerment perspective it exposes young black entrepreneurs to those who have been in business longer. It is an exciting opportunity to work together. Unification also enables business to identify common issues and influence economic policies. Overseas players now know where to go if they want to meet the country's business community.

In October 2002, in recognition of his successful leadership of ARMgold, Patrice was named as South Africa's Best Entrepreneur for 2002 and runner-up in the global competition. He says that competitions such as this play a vital role in fostering a proudly South African entrepreneurial spirit by identifying local talent and putting it on a global stage. It gives business leaders an international platform to demonstrate their ability. Patrice was chosen from an impressive line-up of local finalists, which included Kananelo Makhetha of BTI Connex Travel, South Africa's largest black empowerment travel company; Zeth Malele of arivia.kom, global ICT company; Reg Lascaris of TBWA Hunt Lascaris advertising agency; Annette van der Laan of IT company CS Holdings; Fred Robertson of Brimstone Investment Corporation; and Capital Contracting Services' Wayne Stainforth.

Robert Emslie, managing executive of Absa Business Banking Services, co-sponsors of the award, says that Motsepe has created a world-class company. ARMgold competes on a global stage and truly reflects the spirit of South Africa — energy, determination, perseverance, ingenuity and an African philosophy and way of life called *ubuntu* (humanness).

Motsepe wants to be known not only for running successful companies but also for creating opportunities that empower many other people. He believes that those black entrepreneurs who are successful have a duty to plough back into the community and that they have to share their experiences with those who are still struggling to make it. Motsepe spent a year without an office when he started his business. He operated from a briefcase and it was difficult to raise capital from financial institutions. He wants to share that experience with others and help them see that they can make it too. He thinks big business — irrespective of colour — needs to play a leading role in uplifting emerging entrepreneurs and poor communities. There cannot be a business elite unperturbed by the concerns of small business, for that elite's survival depends on the wellbeing of its fellow citizens, he believes.

Motsepe is today one of the richest people in South Africa. Yet he is a down to earth person who finds it as easy to relate to ordinary people as to the rich and famous. Those close to him attribute this to the fact that, as a mining baron, he interacts with thousands of workers. Others say it has to do with his upbringing as the son of a businessman and hereditary chief. At the age of 15, Motsepe would travel to neighbouring villages selling liquor from his father's bottle store. It was from his father, Motsepe says, that he learnt about running a business. His father taught his children to be compassionate. If a student came to him looking for money to pay fees, Motsepe's father would give it to that student, even though he had not yet paid school fees for his own children. That taught Motsepe the importance of helping those in need.

His father's teachings have made the Motsepe family one of the most powerful in post-1994 South Africa. Motsepe's sister, Bridgette Radebe, is founder and executive chairperson of empowerment group Mmakau Mining. Patrice Motsepe's and Bridgette Radebe's passion for the mining industry began in their childhood when their father implored them to fight for royalties due to their tribe as part of an agreement with a mining house which mined vanadium on tribal land. It is his approach to business that has endeared him to many in the corporate world. At a time when it was fashionable for empowerment groups to form consortiums that had their fingers in every pie that came along, Motsepe cautiously invested in businesses of which he could have operational control. Many of his peers burned their fingers, but Motsepe remains one of the icons of true empowerment.

(Source: S'Thembiso Msomi. 'The man with the Midas touch', Johannesburg: *Sunday Times*, 6 October 2002)

Bridgette Radebe, founder and executive chairperson of Mmakau Mining and chair of the South African Mining Development Association (Junior Mining Chamber), is a highly respected global opinion-maker and mining strategist. She was the first black South African deep level hard rock mining entrepreneur in the late 1980s, and the first black woman in South Africa to engage in production and executive management in gold, platinum and diamond mining. She achieved this under circumstances that forbade her access to the industry on the grounds of her gender and race.

Radebe is not only a major player in South Africa's mining industry — she is also a woman with a mission. She has a lot of very important things to say concerning compassionate capitalism and economic activism, the new voice of African economic transformation. Radebe says, 'The total focus, discipline, and passion invested by our icons such as Nelson Mandela into achieving the goal of the political liberation of South Africa, needs to now be translated into a new breed of economic activists — pioneers pursuing the economic liberation of South Africa and the continent of Africa. In the same way that Mandela and his colleagues were prepared to die for the cause, we need economic activists that are dedicated to ensuring a balance between profits, bottom line and the creation of a sustainable economy.'

What she has to say is of crucial importance to anyone considering business or development in or with Africa. Make profits in business by all means, she says, but make sure that the process of doing so leaves a sustainable economy in place. Radebe says, 'It does not make sense for investors in Africa to pursue models of wealth creation in which the primary focus is shareholder value, bottom line and profits — in an economy that is characterised by poverty, unemployment and underdevelopment. Investors need to strike a balance between labour-intensive and capital-intensive practices and should not seek to mechanise operations at the expense of job creation in a rural mining environment.'

Radebe entered the mining industry with the objective of redressing the injustices she saw as a child in her home community. Her community owned the mineral rights to the land, but never received royalties from the mining company extracting the ore. She has received widespread acknowledgement for pioneering efforts on behalf of previously disadvantaged communities, particularly in the mining industry. She has been instrumental in creating highly successful joint-venture partnerships between Mmakau Mining and disadvantaged communities in the rural areas, whereby communities utilise dividends to fund community development projects. Her model for wealth creation through empowerment procurement practices, managed empowerment partnering and entrepreneur development is being implemented throughout the country.

As chairperson of the South African Mining Development Association (Junior Mining Chamber), representing companies with an asset base of R18 million to R1 billion, Radebe is playing a key role in the development of the junior and small-scale mining sector, an important sunrise industry in South Africa. She is also the founder and a member of the Board of Trustees, of the New Africa Mining Fund to aid junior mining companies, particularly the empowerment companies, with finance and skills. She says the mining industry in Africa needs to keep evolving. She sees a need to develop entrepreneurs, a new breed of players in the mining industry, pioneers of value creation rather than beneficiaries of value accumulation. She would like to see the science of mining and technological research being fast tracked and the universities in the rural areas concentrate on mining-based curricula because there is a need to localise skills in mining through degrees in these areas, since that is where the resources are.

Radebe would like to see owners, entrepreneurs, and shareholders who are operational, both under the ground and above, and that is why she pursued contract mining, to learn about all aspects — how to extract the mineral; do feasibility studies and geological surveys; engage in the construction of a min; how to sink a shaft; concentrate the ore and market it. She talks about the science of value creation and capacity building. A company profits on one deal and then reinvests the money into other projects, so creating growth, infrastructural development and rural renewal. She hopes to see an Africa where one can see how communities have used dividends, paid through partnerships with mining companies like Mmakau Mining, to build roads, clinics, schools and rural renewal projects.

'Success will not come knocking on your door, you must go out and find it,' is the firm belief of Robert Stodel, a man of humble beginnings who went on to found one of the Cape's most successful garden stores. Sally Hetherington of *Bizland News* reports that Robert arrived in South Africa from Holland at the age of 16, having to adjust to a new school, learning languages that he did not understand. He struggled for the next two years, failing at both, and realised that in order to succeed he must first become fluent in English and Afrikaans. He decided to leave school and follow his dream to become a farmer but, having no money or skills, ended up working as a labourer on a farm near Port Elizabeth, moving down to work on a Cape wine farm a short time later. The work was both physical and uninspiring, so in order to stimulate his mind, he studied horticulture in the evenings — good preparation for the future. Robert's interest in horticulture had begun at an early age, when he worked for flower bulb farms during his school holidays in Holland.

Robert used his contacts and horticultural knowledge and bought flower bulbs, selling them by mail order to garden services he had found in the telephone directory. He soon expanded on this by going door to door, something he found very rewarding, as he was well received by elderly people who would offer him coffee and biscuits in exchange for a little company. Robert also sold his bulbs twice a week as a hawker on Cape Town's Grand Parade. In those days, each sale was a major achievement and the foundation of greater things to come. He began a mail order flower bulb business, which burgeoned into the biggest bulb retailer in South Africa. He imported up to 20 million flower bulbs from Holland per year and posted nearly 600,000, 36-page full-colour catalogues annually. He was soon asked by the Consumer Council to team up with *Reader's Digest* to form a direct mail association, in order to regulate the industry. Robert soon extended his passion and fast-growing experience into expanding his business.

It is testimony to his skill as an entrepreneur that he saw and captured the market for gardening and accessories by opening the first one-stop retail garden centre. At this stage most nurseries were farm-like operations with muddy footpaths, so the introduction of the concept of a one-stop retail nursery revolutionised the gardening industry. In 1968, at age 23, he opened the first branch of Stodels Nursery in Kenilworth. He then began his programme of expansion. Two years later, an additional garden centre on a three-hectare property was opened along the national road in Bellville. Four more branches followed. The philosophy of selling the best available quality at the best possible prices, together with personal service, paid off.

It was at this point that Robert reached a crossroads in his career — to expand or not. He felt that he was not sufficiently trained to handle a much larger company at that stage, and he also enjoyed the hands-on approach of being with his staff and customers on the floor. In his mind, success was not shown by the amount of money you could throw around, but rather by the joy you get from your work — something he felt he would lose if he expanded too quickly. Instead he scaled the business down to three larger branches, in order to be able to work more closely with them and keep his systems in check, which in the long run he found to be more profitable. Robert firmly believes that bigger is not always better, and has since seen many similar companies come and go while trying to expand too quickly. He comments: 'It is crucial to regularly assess yourself, your company and your future objectives.'

Robert's emphasis on marketing started at the beginning when he sent bulbs to radio announcers in the hope of a mention. He also sponsored bulbs for city councils to beautify pavements and road islands, and soon started selling bulbs at cost to schools, churches and other organisations as part of their fund-raising efforts, using these opportunities to push his brand. Robert believes in looking for marketing opportunities, has organised for various dignitaries to plant his trees as part of environmental awareness, and has in fact seen the likes of Nelson Mandela, the Queen of England and Hilary Clinton planting trees on various occasions.

Robert Stodel was the first nursery to guarantee that each plant sold would be a success. Robert has four very simple philosophies when it comes to managing his business: customer service, respect for the individual, development of all staff, and the search for excellence. His staff members take a very personal approach with customers. In 2004, the company had 215 staff members, with 17 horticulturists and 10 managers, and Robert was in the process of handing over the business in its entirety to his son Nick, who is keen to expand in the future. Robert believes that he has been a success if he can hand over a well-managed business with complete closure. He plans to enjoy more time on his farm, and pursue other interests such as hiking, diving and travelling.

He offers the following advice to aspiring entrepreneurs: 'Success can come to anyone, but you must go out and look for it as it will not come knocking on the door. You cannot wait for opportunities. You must make them happen. The harder you work, the luckier you will become.' Robert Stodel continues to be inspired by the words of Cecil John Rhodes: 'Whoever plants a tree is creating a monument for himself and provides capital for his successors, while what they gain for posterity is incalculable.' This philosophy has certainly helped this humble man achieve his dreams.

(Source: Sally Hetherington. 'Planting the seeds of success - Robert Stodel of Stodels Nurseries', *Bizland News*, April 2003; www.bizland.co.za/newsletter/bizlandnews19may03.htm)

Jana Smit, journalist for the *Krugersdorp News*, reports that Jenneth Prinsloo from Plantwise, a Krugersdorp-based nursery, 'has green fingers and a heart of gold'. When the 2005 winners of the Regional Business Achiever Awards for the Johannesburg branch of the Businesswomen's Association were announced, this dynamic businesswoman won in the Entrepreneur category. People lie close to Prinsloo's heart and in between grabbing awards (she also walked away as the Woman Entrepreneur and Individual Entrepreneur in the medium business category at the 2005 Mogale Chamber of Commerce and Industry Awards); she is uplifting less privileged communities and involving disabled people in her business. 'Whenever I take on a project, I use people from within the community,' she says. Prinsloo says that even if a person has two fingers, those two fingers can plant a seed.

In 1989, Jenneth Prinsloo was offered the opportunity to start up a wholesale nursery with one of the area's best-known nurserymen. Without any knowledge of the industry, but with plenty of enthusiasm, she dedicated herself to the success of the project. Then, after a dispute about the partnership, for which there was no recognised legal contract, Prinsloo was left with nothing. Believing this to be a blessing in disguise, again with nothing but enthusiasm and the will to succeed, Prinsloo started Plantwise in 1991 'from scratch' as a professional plant brokers and growers company. The company specialises in consulting, sourcing and the transporting of plants, flowers and horticultural products from around the world.

Sheer guts and determination led to Plantwise entering the export business in 1998, doing what has never successfully been done in South Africa before — shipping fully-grown palms and trees to the Middle East.

Apart from a host of logistical challenges, they even had to develop a watering system to ensure that the plants arrived in good shape, Prinsloo reported. After they had grabbed the attention of buyers from the Emirates, China became the next big challenge and the next successful market. Plantwise has exported very large palms to China successfully since 2004. The United Kingdom is the next market Plantwise will be tackling.

Today, Plantwise's enormous success finds its roots in Prinsloo's passion, drive, and sheer determination to succeed. Prinsloo, one of the SA Flower Growers Association member exporters, and co-opted member of the SA Flower Export Council (SAFEC), was the 2004 winner of the Gauteng Exporter of the year award. She says that this award was a great honour, not only to have been nominated but also to walk away as a winner. Prinsloo is now studying for a masters' degree in horticulture from the University of South Africa. Plantwise was a 2005 finalist for the Africa SMME Awards.

(Source: Jana Smit. 'Businesswoman grabs up entrepreneurial award', *Krugersdorp News*, 15 July 2005, and August 2005 e-mail correspondence with Jenneth Prinsloo)

Near Graaf-Reinet, in the dry but beautiful Karoo, grows a blue-grey leafed plant, which farmers often call the American aloe, and which is a member of the Agave family. It is hard to imagine, looking at this plant, that it could be used to produce alcohol, but that is precisely what the owners of Agave Distillers are doing. The first Agave plants were introduced into the Graaf-Reinet district in the 1830s, as a feed for goats and sheep during drought periods. Although a different variety from that in Mexico, the final product is virtually indistinguishable and in some ways superior to Mexican tequila. Many centuries ago the indigenous peoples of Central America produced the first wine from the Agave plant, which they called Mescal. When distilled, Mescal was found to produce a potent drink. In the 1950s, the product was improved and formally branded as tequila.

In the late 1990s, a group of entrepreneurs established a factory to produce Tequila in Graaf-Reinet. The project was funded largely by venture capital, but over-capitalisation on inappropriate technology resulted in the project going insolvent before producing anything. Prior to bankruptcy the original producers also became aware of the fact that their product could not be marketed as 'Tequila', as this is a trademark of Mexico. One of the minor shareholders in the original distillery, the McLachlan Family Trust, decided at this point to diversify and invest further in taking the distillery to market. At this point the name was changed to Agave Distillers. Agave Distillers proceeded to add the necessary equipment for the distillery to come into full production, the intention being to produce character alcohol identical to the Tequila brand of Mexico.

Agave's distillery is situated just outside Graaf-Reinet and consists of state of the art plant and machinery. The high standards of technology, sterility and safety are impressive. The capacity of the plant is approximately 200,000 litres per month of Agave Spirit. It is estimated that, without replanting, the quantity of Blue Agave necessary to fulfil these production objectives is sufficient to last for ten years. In an area with high unemployment it is encouraging to see that where possible people have been employed instead of machines. The distillery has initiated a replanting programme utilising local government participation and the farming community.

Keith McLachlan brings to the new venture his wealth of entrepreneurial skills, while Roy McLachlan, as managing director of Agave Distillers, applies his expertise to the challenge of establishing a first for South Africa. In numerous blind tastings with Tequila experts, Agave Distillers' Blue Agave spirit has consistently achieved a superior rating to that of most of the Tequila brands. This superior taste is rapidly spring boarding Agave Distillers' product on to the local and international market. As of December 2004, the products being marketed are Agave Silver, Agave Gold, 100 per cent Blue Agave, Agave Sours, and Agave Cream Liqueur.

(Source: http://www.agaveblue.com; and Garth Cambray. 'Agave - Gems in the Karoo', Science in Africa, May 2002; http://www.scienceinafrica.co.za/2002/may/agave.htm)

From the vineyards of the fairest Cape, Cybercellar.com offers an eminently enjoyable range of specially selected South African wines for delivery around the globe. Fiona Phillips is the chief executive officer. Fiona has extensive business experience gained during 11 years as an equity derivatives trader in London and Johannesburg. She is a member of MENSA (UK) and has an MBA. from the University of Cape Town's Graduate School of Business. Fiona has completed several Cape Wine Academy courses, culminating in the Diploma II. Her passion for wine and her fascination for the limitless possibilities of the Internet motivated the start-up of Cybercellar in 1998.

Cybercellar.com was the first Internet site to specialise in marketing South African wines, and was the first Internet-focused wine retail company in South Africa. Cybercellar is an established wine marketing, distribution, consulting and web enablement company based in the Cape wine lands. Fully e-commerce enabled, Cybercellar.com currently retails over 1,000 specially selected South African wines from nearly 250 different producers to clients all over the world.

Cybercellar's core business over the first two years was one of business-to-consumer in the domestic market, and they have since additionally focused their efforts on the global market, particularly to the US and Europe, in addition to B2B diversification. Cybercellar hosts a number of wine industry websites including the very successful John Platter Online, and facilitates e-commerce for several wine producers and other non-wine e-commerce companies. Cybercellar is additionally involved in e-enabling the South African wine community by offering web design and web hosting to wine producers and other related organisations, creating an online community for the wine industry. Cybercellar aims to be the facilitator of Internet sales of South African wine to as many consumers on a global basis as humanly possible.

In 1937, Charles Back, an immigrant from Lithuania, bought Fairview Farms. The farm already had a reputation for its wines, which in those days were mostly fortified. Charles Back passed away in 1955 and the running of the farm was taken over by his son, Cyril, who replanted the whole farm. In the early days, Fairview vinified its grapes and delivered the wine to the large merchants and cooperatives that controlled the South African wine industry at that time. Cyril, a man ahead of the times, saw the need to break free from this restrictive grip and decided to go it alone. In order to circumvent the stranglehold held by the large merchants, Fairview decided to auction its first bottled wines in 1974. This was the first wine auction in South Africa, predating the now famous Nederburg auctions. Cyril also introduced milking goats in 1980, which led to the development of cheese production at the Fairview Wine and Cheese Estate.

In 1978, Cyril's son Charles joined Fairview after completing a winemaking degree and a practical spell at another wine cellar. Charles is responsible for the building of Fairview's famous goat tower, which was completed despite the initial reservations of his father. When Cyril passed away in 1995, Charles assumed full responsibility of Fairview. The policies and initiatives started by Cyril Back continue to be evolved by Charles, ensuring that Fairview is planted with suitable grape varieties such as Shiraz, Viognier and Pinotage. The best cheese styles from Europe, enhanced by Fairview's innovation, provide cheese lovers with a wonderful selection of distinctive cheeses. In 1998 Charles Back bought the farm Klein Amos Kuil, situated in Malmesbury. The farm is the home of the Spice Route Wine Company. Spice Route has had a stratospheric climb into the top echelons of the South African wine industry. The dry land vineyards on this prime site are enormously expressive, and have encouraged Fairview to seek and source fruit from a number of special vineyard sites throughout the Western Cape. The Fairview operation markets three tiers of wines — from lowest to highest priced, Goats Do Roam, Fairview and Spice Route.

In 1997, a group of black Fairview farm workers formed an association, and with a government grant formed their own Fair Valley farming community on eighteen hectares adjacent to Fairview donated by Charles Back. The group has been making wine since 1997 with help from Back, who sometimes offers advice and donates space in the winery. Fair Valley wines are made from grapes sourced elsewhere and then produced in the Fairview cellar. The intention is to build a Fair Valley dedicated cellar on the property. In 2004, Fair Valley began exporting wines to the United States. Income from the sale of Fair Valley wines is directed to a communal property association. Its revenue is augmented by income derived from cheese packing at Fairview Estate. In addition, cottages on Fairview are being converted to provide tourist accommodation and rentals charged will also go towards the property association. Back is cautiously optimistic about the chances for success of the more than a dozen empowerment projects underway in the South Africa wine industry.

(Source: Jerry Shriver. 'South African wines blend quality, playfulness', *USA Today*, 16 April 2004; May 2004 e-mail correspondence with Charles Back)

Fair Valley's elected cellar master Awie Adolph is a bright-eyed grandfather. He told journalist Tom Hiney in 2002 that he remembers his first day at Fairview as a labourer on the farm in 1982. He had never worked on a farm before, and says he was frightened, as there were many horror stories about farm life among the rural population. He says he began in the fields, before being moved into the main cellars in 1994, where he still works for Charles Back. Here, after hours, he turns his attention to new Fair Valley labels, often working late into the night on a Chenin Blanc and a Pinotage. At picking time, relatives come from other farms to help them out. Everyone has a job, and they cook a big communal meal in the afternoon. Everyone has shares in the income. After a storm, they are all out checking the plants at dawn. Their vines are doing very well. Things don't always run smoothly and he says he wants to learn more about the winemaking side of things. Awie Adolph says, 'I will get better. We never thought this would happen. We never even asked for the land. I would like to visit some other farms and see how they do things.' Do he and his fellow workers ever argue? He answers, 'Sometimes, good arguments.'

(Source: Tom Hiney. 'Grape of Good Hope', *The Observer*, 10 March 2002)

After 300 years of white supremacy in South Africa, other white farmers near Paarl, one of the earliest settler towns in the Western Cape, are also engaged in this bold experiment to give black workers a substantial stake in their vineyards and olive-growing estates. The amazing thing, reports Hiney, is that everybody wins. It's the brightest and the best Cape farmers who embrace affirmative action initiatives. For example, in pursuit of a childhood dream, Alan Nelson acquired wine lands in 1987 out of a bankrupt estate. Since then, the lands have been lovingly restored by the Nelson family and their team of dedicated workers. Nelson told his workers that if they helped him turn the estate's fortunes around he would give them some land. He conceived of the idea as one of many to inspire his farm workers to help him realise his dream of producing South Africa's best wine. All that he could offer in exchange when he bought the land on a shoestring was a promise to share in the fruits of any success that their dedication in the vineyard would bring. His workers took him up on this offer.

Between 1987 and 1994 approximately 50 hectares of old vines were replaced under the watchful eye of the best viticulture consultants in the Cape with noble cultivars, including Cabernet Sauvignon, Merlot, Shiraz, Pinotage, Sauvignon Blanc, Chardonnay and Semillon. Between 1993 and 1995, a state of the art wine cellar was constructed with the help of Elsenburg oenologist Eugene van Zyl. Wine production commenced in earnest in 1995. The very next year, the estate won an award for the best Chardonnay in South Africa and was in the same year crowned as the champion private wine producer in the Boland region. Since then, the estate has never looked back. The estate has become internationally known as Nelson's Creek, named after the Nelson family and the small stream, that winds its way through the estate. It inspired and is depicted on the unique two-part label.

In 1996, when Nelson's Creek won the trophy for South Africa's best Chardonnay and was adjudged the champion wine producer in this region, it was time for Nelson to deliver. He gave his farm workers 11 hectares of prime vineyard, access to his cellars, and told them they could start their own label alongside their work for him. Wine farming is very intensive and 11 hectares is a lot of vine. In 1998, New Beginnings produced the first wine ever to be made by people of colour from grapes grown on their own land. Currently they export wine to Europe, Asia and America. All revenue derived from the sale of their wine accrues to the workers.

In 2004, the Nelsons again achieved unparalleled success at the South African Veritas Awards by winning a total of five medals for each of the five wines that they entered at the show, including a double gold medal for their Shiraz and a gold medal for their Cabernet/Merlot blend. In recognition for their efforts the estate's labourers have now been given land upon which to construct their own homes.

Some of the world's finest olives are grown at the southern tip of Africa. Nestling in the fertile Western Cape, and protected by the Drakenstein Mountains on the east and the 'pearly' Paarl Mountains on the west, is Cape Olive. Here, 10,000 kilometres away from Spain, olives of a quality to rival the world's best are grown. Cape Olive is made up of six farms located at the foothills of the Drakenstein mountain range — an area ideally suited to olive farming as it has deep soil, low humidity and a warm climate. Owing to this location on the foothills, there is a dramatic difference in altitude between the various farms, which enables Cape Olive to grow many different cultivars of olives.

The olive tree was introduced commercially to South Africa by Ferdinando Costa (1884 - 1969), an Italian immigrant. From Genoa, Ferdinando had joined his brother in Cape Town in 1903, and started his own nursery there in 1904. He began experimenting with olives at his Rosebank and Plumstead premises, grafting his imported olive trees onto the native olienhout (Olea Africana) tree, which grows abundantly in many areas of South Africa. He propagated thousands of grafted olive trees at his nursery on the lower slopes of Table Mountain. But it was in Paarl that Ferdinando started his olive growing in earnest on a stony hill at Huguenot on the eastern side of the village. He purchased a farm in Paarl in 1925, which he named Nervi after his birthplace, a seaside resort near Genoa. When he started planting olive trees, the local farmers considered him touched. He pressed his first oil in 1936, and one branch of the family is still pressing oil. Ferdinando had two sons and a daughter. The oldest son Philip continued on the original Nervi farm until his death in May 2005, and the same farm is now being run by Philip's oldest son, Guido. Ferdinando's second son Nino meanwhile played a leading role in the local wine industry, while the olive trees that he planted on his farm La Valle (also in Paarl), were growing. In 1968, he left the wine industry to develop his own brand of table olives, Buffet Olives. His vision was to have tasty, quality olives on the market at affordable prices. The history of Cape Olive was a success story because of the hard work, brilliance and hands-on management approach of Nino Costa, who laid a solid foundation, which Buffet Olives' new ownership, the Cape Olive Trust, is continuing.

In 2002, journalist Tom Hiney visited Cape Olive Trust's 300-hectare Buffet Olives farm and processing plant. Since 1999, the 40 black workers, who live permanently with their families on the farm, have had an equity share in the farm. Since the farm produces 750 tons of olives a year, and processes and packs them on site with European machinery, that equity share is a motivator. The workers have received training in making investment and management decisions. For example, the workers' self-appointed committee has built its own trout hatchery by the farm dam and is obtaining land to build private housing. Meanwhile, the workers have continued to receive improvements to their current houses. Everyone is delighted and, according to the farm's books, sharing equity is proving profitable — as one worker put it, 'When the workers on a farm want that farm to succeed, things happen.' Another worker explains that owning shares in the company gave the workers an opportunity to become part of a business, to learn how decisions are being made and to get the right inside knowledge. The workers in general are proud of what they have achieved. They are very much involved in the company, but they say they are not working harder now, they are working 'smarter'.

(Source: Tom Hiney. 'Grape of Good Hope', *The Observer*, 10 March 2002)

The Costa family continues its interests in South Africa's olive industry. Guido Costa continues to run the original family olive business, F Costa & Son, in Paarl. It is one of the industry's biggest, and deals in table olives, olive oil and, importantly, olive trees for planting and propagation. Guido's brother Carlo is a senior agricultural scientist with the ARC Infruitec-Nietvoorbij research centre in Stellenbosch. He has extensive experience in olive growing and processing. With his excellent qualifications in horticultural science, Carlo has become a highly successful consultant, and has written a superb book titled *Olive Growing in South Africa*. Nino Costa's daughter Linda is the principal of Olives In Fact (Pty) Ltd, which provides table olive factory design, advice about table olive production, assessment of table olives, and olives and olive oil seminars for the industry.

Whilst the olive industry was previously dominated by the Costa family, there are a number of emerging growers and processors making their marks: Vesuvio, Willow Creek, El Olivar and Morgenster. In the Northern Cape there are very large areas planted since 1998 and there is a brand called Olives South Africa, which will be a very large producer in the future. This is indicative of a growing industry, but consumer demand is what makes it sustainable. EU subsidies are a major threat despite demand exceeding supply, but this needs to be handled with care if the markets are to be kept free. The olive industry also complements wine farming by providing additional employment for workers during the winter season.

A number of South African extra virgin olive oils have received international quality awards. Under the management of one of South Africa's most respected olive oil makers, Carlo Castiglione, Vesuvio Natural extra virgin olive oil won top international awards. The two farms which produced the brand are Sorrento near Paarl and Positano near Wellington, and they comprised some 450 hectares, 300 of which were planted with olive trees between one and 55 years old. Castiglione, who studied agricultural science in his home town of Naples before coming to South Africa to visit a friend in 1965, saw a radical change in the country's attitude towards olive oil, and 40 years later local demand for olive oil is so great that two million litres are imported every year and demand continues to grow. Castiglione worked at the farm, first when it was started in the 1950s by an Italian baron, and then in the 1970s when it was owned by a Cape Town engineering group.

In 1996, Castiglione returned to the farm when it was bought by his Neapolitan friends and present owners, Arturo Dotoli and his wife Elra. The Vesuvio brand was then created. In 2003, there was a two-phase extraction cycle system in place, and the farm was producing about 100,000 litres of olive oil a year, all of it sold in South Africa. Castiglione retired after handing over the running of the farms to a young, strong management team, Gert van Dyk (oil maker and general manager), Kobus van Niekerk and Waldo Kellerman (field operators) and Alinda van Dyk (finance and administration).

With the purchase of another farm, Amalfi, and the importation of the biggest oil extraction plant in the southern hemisphere — a state of the art machine made in Italy by Rapanelli — just in time for the 2004 pressing season, owners and managers started a new development programme that includes the planting of 50 000 extra olive trees. Vesuvio's three farms now comprise some 500 hectares, 350 of which are planted with olive trees. With the new ultra modern two-phase extraction cycle system in place, Vesuvio now produces about 150,000 litres of extra virgin olive oil a year, a quantity that will increase when all the existing young trees and those that will be planted in the near future will be in full production.

(Source: Gill Moodie. 'Celebrated olive farm for sale', Johannesburg: *Sunday Times*, 4 May 2003)

The Willow Creek Estate is situated in the picturesque Nuy Valley between Worcester and Robertson in the Western Cape, where the Rabie family has been farming since the late 1700s. Traditionally, wine and wheat were produced in the Nuy Valley and on Willow Creek the Rabie family expanded into table grapes and potatoes. Willow Creek has a typical Mediterranean climate, very low rainfall and the optimum soil conditions to produce healthy, robust olives. Together with the worldwide growing demand for olives and specifically good olive oil, the stage was set for Willow Creek Extra Virgin Olive Oil. In 1999, Andries and Louise Rabie planted their first olive trees and a new course was laid out for the estate.

Andries did extensive research on olive production and sourced information and guidance from leading figures in the field from Italy, Spain, Australia and Argentina to form the blueprint for the best planting and growing techniques specifically for the Nuy Valley. Cultivars were chosen with the production of top quality olive oil in mind and include Frantoio, Leccino, Coratina, Favoloza, I77 and Nocellara. By December 2005, 163 hectares of 130,000 trees planted in high density had been established, and time is the only limitation to further expansion, the aim being 600 hectares by 2008. The trees are cut and pruned to a mono cone to make them suitable for mechanical harvesting which is the only way to ensure that once in full production, the large quantities of olives could be harvested at their peak stage of ripeness for the production of consistently high quality olive oil. Open hydroponics is used to achieve the optimum in both growth potential and yield of robust olive harvests. A nursery with a hothouse was also established on the farm to supply most of the trees to be planted on Willow Creek, as well as to provide for other customers.

Frikkie and Danila Naude's farm El Olivar borders the Breede River in the Breede River Valley in the Robertson District. As the rainfall is less than 250 mm a year, they have to irrigate all their trees from the river. They have deep red soils and their trees grow vigorously. The trees are harvested from March to end of June. The trees are pruned and cut to a height of 2.2 meters during June and July, which ensures that they do not have to pick with ladders. They have Mission, Frantoia, Leccino and Manzanilla varieties planted. In 2004, they had 33 000 trees, all bearing olives. The first trees were planted in 1995; they are presently planting 3 000 trees per year and intend to stop at a total of 50 000 (a manageable quantity) in 2010. They were working with a Pieralisi press, which they replaced with the latest Pieralisi Panorama at the end of 2004. The oil is marketed as estate oil (all the fruit is from the estate) and the oil is sold under the Olyfberg ('olive mountain') trade mark. They also process mission olives under the same name. The character of the oil is soft, fruity and unfiltered. Frikkie and Danila have a passion for the olive tree because an olive tree is planted for generations, whereas grape vines have a maximum productive life of 25 years. Frikkie and Danila are also wine farmers in the Stellenbosch area, on the Yonder Hill farm, and feel that 'wines and olives form a gentleman's partnership'.

Historic Morgenster ('morning star' estate was originally part of Vergelegen, a picturesque farm nestled against the foothills of the Helderberg and Hottentot Holland mountains in the Western Cape. A retired Italian businessman from Piedmont, Giulio Bertrand, bought the Morgenster farm in 1992 and decided that he was still too active to be on retirement. He saw the beautiful slopes on the farm and imagined producing olive oil and wine. At that stage the farm's future olive oil maker Gerrie Duvenage, was busy with research on olives at Stellenbosch Research Institute and together they made some olive oil from the local Mission, Manzanilla, and other mainly table cultivars. After tasting these olive oils Giulio realised that it was not the style of olive oil he would ever get used to, and immediately decided to look for assistance in Italy and made contact with Professor Giuseppe Fontanazza, director of the Istituto di Ricerche sull'Olivicoltura in Perugia. This institute is well known for olive research and breeding of new cultivars. After seeing Morgenster, the professor decided that initially he would have to import 12 cultivars from Italy to see how they performed. The importation was not easy but they managed to get the first 3,000 trees through quarantine and planted in 1994, the year Gerrie had become the olive oil maker at Morgenster, After proper evaluation they found that the cultivars Frantoio, Leccino, Coratina, Peranzana, Nocellara Del Belice, I77 — and especially the patented FS17 and Kalamata on DA12I — were doing very well. They erected a nursery and propagated a further 25000 trees to plant 45 hectares over a five-year period on Morgenster. The nursery started to concentrate on these cultivars and now Morgenster supplies most of the new producers in South Africa with these excellent cultivars.

On Morgenster there is a wide range of soil types, from fertile loamy soil in the flat areas to poor rocky soil on the terraces. Management of these rocky areas is quite complicated and it is also the reason why certain blocks on the farm produce lower yields than others of the same age or even younger. The irrigation system is designed to be able to irrigate every day if needed. Harvesting is from mid-March to the end of June. Olives are harvested by hand on younger trees and by shaker on older trees. The shaker works very well on trees with a high production and the real advantage is that you can harvest and deliver to the press in a very short time (it is very important to get the olives to the press within 24 hours after harvesting if your aim is to produce the best extra virgin olive oil).

(Source: Gerrie Duvenage. 'Morgenster and the South African olive industry', unpublished presentation delivered at the Olive Expo, Napa Valley, California, Exposition Centre, February 28 2004)

In the centre of South Africa, lies the fertile and beautiful Vaalharts Valley formed millions of years ago by a giant glacier. Here, in the midst of the semi-dessert of the Northern Cape Province, lay the 43 000-hectacre Vaalharts Irrigation project, cradled between the Vaal and the Harts Rivers. Hartswater, the main centre of the project, is home to Olives South Africa. The first trees were planted in 1995 and at present Olives South Africa's Eden estate has 30 000 trees. There is also an experimental grove of more than 60 different varieties, which helps them to select those varieties best suited to the unique conditions. As of 2003, a total of more than 200 000 trees were planted in the area, most of which are already producing excellent crops.

Since Olives South Africa has the only olive processing plant in this area, almost all these olives are processed at its plant. At first, mostly Mission, Kalamata, Manzanilla and Uovo di Picione trees were planted, but since 1998 other varieties such as Frantoio, Leccino, Coratina, FS 17, I 77 and Nocellara del Belice were introduced. Of the table varieties, Uovo di Picione performs excellently, with high yields and fruit that is firm and full of rich olive tastes. Frantoio and Coratina are the only oil cultivars in production and have excellent yield both in crop and in oil. Through 2003, the oil came mainly from the cultivar Mission, but this changed in 2004 when the cultivars mentioned above came into production.

A new Pieralisi oil press was imported in January 2003, and a big factory was built to process the oil and the table olives. Special care is taken during all the production stages, from the loving care of the groves, to the bottling of the final products. High standards of hygiene and cleanliness are maintained throughout all the production stages. All olives are handpicked, and the olives used for oil are picked when half ripe. Olives are transported to the mill, and pressed within 12 to 24 hours of harvesting. The unique tastes and aromas in Olives South Africa's olive oil and table olives are due to the rich soils deposited by the glacier, to very hot summers and mild winters, with less than 400mm of rain (mainly during the summer months), and a water table no more than two meters deep. An additional benefit is the fact that the olive trees are protected from pests and diseases by natural enemies and the isolation of the area, limiting the use of pesticides.

Visser says that Olives South Africa is still expanding, and has new very big project in the pipeline, which will be one of the largest in the world, and will benefit previously disadvantaged communities, which will have the major shareholding. Visser is excited about the successes of the olive industry in his area and truly believes olives have the potential to help local people to climb out of the poverty net in which they have been caught up for so long. It would give them their pride back, and could certainly make a big difference in their lives.

Marula Natural Products Pty Ltd (MNP) is a company dedicated to community-based values that produces marula oil and fruit pulp. For centuries in southern Africa, local communities have relied on the marula tree and its fruit for numerous health and nutritional benefits. Today these traditional practices are the foundation of a growing community enterprise in the Limpopo Province. Following the principles of fair trade, MNP buys fruit from the surrounding communities at a fair, community-negotiated price. Communities are involved throughout the process, including pulp and kernel extraction as well as oil pressing.

Marula fruit pulp is a natural product of the organically grown and harvested marula fruit. The high-quality pulp contains up to four times the Vitamin C of orange juice and is being marketed as a delicious new natural base for beverages. Marula oil is rich in antioxidants and oleic acid, essential components for the maintenance of healthy skin. It is an ideal and innovative ingredient of modern cosmetics and carrier oil for aromatherapy. Both products, pulp and oil, are steeped in the marula legends of old, and carry with them a fascinating cultural history from ancient African traditions.

Originally begun under the wing of the Mineworkers Development Agency in 1995 as a rural development project for unemployed women, Marula Natural Products (MNP) now successfully brings its natural products to companies in South Africa and globally. Its administration offices are in Braamfontein, Johannesburg, while fruit collection and production (and sales and marketing) take place in Limpopo. Marula is the culmination of a vision of sourcing natural marula products for commercial use. What started as an empowerment initiative was converted to a commercial enterprise in 2003. In 2005, 42 communities were partners in the supply chain and over 4,000 people, mainly women, earned incomes by supplying MNP with fruit and kernels.

Kate Philip, chief executive officer of MDA during the development phase of the Marula programme, says that it has been thrilling to see Marula grow from its roots as a community development project. Winner of the Gauteng Premier's award for women achievers in the category for business and the economy, Kate Philip held the helm at MDA, since its inception in the National Union of Mineworkers, until October 2002. MDA has pioneered a number of ambitious programmes. The successful launch of MNP is one project of which Kate Philip is especially proud. She says they have been working to bridge the traditional gaps where commercialisation of new products generally falls down. By creating links between research and development, on one hand and the creation of markets on the other hand, MDA has been able to facilitate products into commercial production.

MDA's track record in creating jobs and income for southern African communities is remarkable. From stonework to marula products to fence making and skills building, they have had a big impact wherever they work. The key challenge for MDA as a development agency has been how to bridge the gap between the significant commercial opportunities identified for MNP and the communities that hold the resource and need the economic benefits. Kate explains that MDA has piloted the research and development, the marketing, the initial production, and the community facilitation processes required to deliver marula products to market-readiness. They have demonstrated that where market demand is created, they can provide the community interface required to deliver the raw and pre-processed products at the volumes required. She believes this intermediary implementation function has been a key gap in many attempts at the commercialisation of indigenous resources to date.

MNP is therefore the outcome of an extension of this intermediary implementation role. All of the marula products identified depend on supply of the marula resource through local marula collection strategies. This is the main way by which income opportunities are provided for local people. This is because the marula grows in the wild. It has never been commercially propagated on any significant scale. Unlike so many resources in South Africa, the marula resource has never been colonised. It remains in the hands of local communities, who control access to it on their homesteads and in the communal areas, and harvest and farm the trees. Of course this may change, so it is all the more important to develop a viable and vibrant strategy of commercialisation that ensures local communities lead the process and derive the maximum benefits.

In 2005, MNP was led by Girlie Njoni, who became CEO in 2003 from the parent company, MDA. Girlie develops develop appropriate business models and accelerates the establishment of market relationships which will create demand for innovative marula products.

(Source: Neil Pendock. 'Karoo sunrise drink', Johannesburg: *Sunday Times*, 21 October 2001; 2005 e-mail correspondence with Kate Philip and Girlie Njoni; and website www.marula.org.za)

Ultimate Sports Nutrition (USN) is a prime example of a company that correctly anticipated changes in consumer needs. USN has developed a range of nutritional supplements that draw on the world's leading scientific research to help consumers reach the ultimate in fitness levels and enjoy the benefits of a healthy lifestyle. USN founder Albé Geldenhuys correctly foresaw a surge in the need for sports drinks. The company he launched from his bedroom in 1999, Ultimate Sports Nutrition, had 260 products in its January 2006 range, including food supplements for professional sportspeople and sports drinks aimed at a wider mass-consumer market. These are exported across the world and used by world-class athletes such as swimmers Ryk Neethling and Roland Schoeman, South African cross-country champion Heidi Muller, and Jenna Warlock, who won the title The World's Fittest Woman in 2004.

USN has cornered an enviable percentage of market share in various countries in the face of fierce competition from rival products. It holds a 60 per cent share of the health supplement market in South Africa and turnover has grown from zero in December 1999 to R18 million a month in 2005. Annual growth has been between 60 per cent and 80 per cent. The product range has doubled since 2004 to meet the growing demand for sport supplements. In October 2005, USN was a close runner-up for the overall Africa SMME award for being the top small- to medium-sized business in Africa and was winner of the Food and Beverage Production category in the 2005 Africa SMME awards.

(Source: www.usn.co.za, www.acia.sun.ac.za, and Sasha Planting, 'Muscling in on the mass market', *Financial Mail*, 7 October 2005; www.fm.co.za)

Huge quantities of vegetables are produced annually by farmers in South Africa. The owners of Greenway Farms became acutely aware that the problem is not to find the vegetables; the problem is to find the desired quality. South African vegetables leave much to be desired when it comes to shelf life. Sophisticated refrigeration/retail packaging cold chain distribution is only available at wholesaler/processor level. No primary producers offer adequate forced cooling refrigeration facilities.

A general rule of thumb is that for every hour delayed between the harvesting of the crop and achieving a forced cooled core temperature of 2 degrees takes a day off the shelf life of the product — not to mention the effect it has on taste and vitamin content. Most suppliers deliver their produce within 24 hours. Even so called 'fresh on the national markets' is already 24 hours old. At best there is some rudimentary cool room at the farm pack-house that might achieve a core temperature of a degree or two below ambient temperature. Wholesalers, processors and pack-houses spent millions of rands on sophisticated refrigeration and other shelf life enhancing techniques. In many instances the battle has already been lost when they put inadequately cooled product through their process line. The days where we called 12 hour old vegetables as 'fresh' are long gone! The exporter/processor/wholesaler who accepts this reality and seeks quality at primary producer level is tomorrow's success story.

Greenway Farms guarantees that all their products are brought to a 2-degrees Celsius core temperature within 60 minutes of being harvested. This ensures that they pass on to their customers the benefit of the best shelf life that money can buy. They are primary producers focusing on carrots only. Customers will gain maximum benefit from the enhanced shelf life of their vegetables, which they call 'Africa's favourite carrots'. A hundred tons of carrots are produced every day.

Laser beam technology has been extensively used to grade lands and create optimal growing conditions This ensures that Greenway's yield and quality remain consistent through the year. Greenway Farms has access to 1,500 hectares of ground owned or rented in order to be sustainable. Crop harvesting has been mechanised, to reduce back-breaking manual labour and enhance the practical manageability of the business, since manual systems are flawed and unreliable. Another benefit of mechanisation is that working hours can be reduced, quality of life can be improved and wages can be increased. Computerised irrigation maximises water resource utilisation and crop growing conditions. Greenway partners Vincent Sequeira and Vito Rugani, are extremely grateful today that they had the foresight to embark on full-scale mechanisation in 1996 since the cost of mechanising today would be far in excess of the original cost, bearing in mind the lower rate of exchange.

Sequeira and Rugani have always practiced a philosophy of providing people with a career and not just a job. This philosophy has radically influenced staff structures on the farm today. Every single manager has been promoted from the ranks of the workers. Greenway has never brought in supervisors from outside sources. This was possible because of a sophisticated grading system that has been in place since 1988. The objective of the system is to build people by motivating them to improve themselves and then reward them in accordance with their achievements.

In 1999 this ethic came to a logical conclusion when the loyal core of the workforce became shareholders in the business. The Masibumbaneni Farm Workers Trust was formed in 1999 to serve as a vehicle to hold the shareholding interest of the workers in the business. This spearheads Greenway farms' staff development programme.

Vincent Sequeira started Greenway in 1988. He had come from a vegetable farming family and he himself is the third generation in the industry. Johannesburg born, bred and educated, his early twenties was spent working on American farms to gain experience. He ran a vegetable retail operation with his uncle and spent a number of years working as a farm manager. All this experience was of great value when he made the big decision to go on his own. Vincent's portfolio in the business is production, irrigation, chemigation, fertigation, workshop maintenance and construction. He is extremely competent, with a strong practical instinct on how to get the job done.

Vito Rugani is a fourth generation vegetable farmer, also born, bred and educated in Johannesburg, and has a BSc in agriculture. Having worked on the family farm during his twenties, he joined Vincent in 1992. Vito's portfolio in the business is administration, labour, finances, pack-house and marketing. Most of all, he enjoys working with people and grappling with the abstract and the unknown. The combination of Vito and Vincent is a typical example of 'opposites attract'. It is Sequeira's and Rugani's objective to give the customer the best quality that his money can buy. They do not desire to be the biggest but, rather, to be the best. They believe that 'farming smarter is better than farming harder'! The most valuable people, to them, are their staff.

(Source: www.greenwayfarms.co.za)

Fhatuwani Ramabulana has always loved chickens, particularly their eggs. She kept a few chickens to ensure that she always had fresh eggs, and in 1985 she decided to leave her teaching job to start a small poultry farm. By 2003, Fhatuwani's Khumbe Poultry Farm had an annual turnover of R4 million, and her 80,000 chickens produced eggs in the thousands every day. Wamondo village in Limpopo Province is a small, disadvantaged community of people who desperately needed a way to earn an income. Fhatuwani's farm has achieved this. She has created 55 jobs, and uses her teaching skills to train members of the community in good farming practice. She hasn't stopped there, either: Fhatuwani sponsors the local football team and provides holiday employment for the village's schoolchildren. The farm has also been instrumental in improving the nutritional health of the Wamondo people. With a cheap and readily available source of fresh eggs, they have all managed to up their protein quota. The benefits have even spread to prisoners in nearby jails, who also get to eat Fhatuwani's eggs. Fhatuwani's incredible achievements have not gone unnoticed. In 2002, she won the award in the business entrepreneurship category of the Shoprite Checkers/SABC Women of the Year competition, and was also nominated as the overall winner. Fhatuwani's story is an inspiration to all South Africans, giving them reason to believe in the future of the country and the difference that one individual can make.

(Source: The International Marketing Council of South Africa: 'Fhatuwani Ramabulana: The power of one'; www.imc.org.za/2003/fhatuwani.stm)

Since 1998, the residents of the idyllic Valley of the Huguenots have been striving to transform their town, Franschhoek, into a model development, which would link the town's economic growth to the upliftment of those who had been disadvantaged in the past. The town's main asset, the valuable 100ha municipal commonage on the slopes below the Franschhoek pass, is being developed commercially, with the proceeds used to provide affordable housing, grow the local economy through the creation of new business, and generate employment. Land has been bought for low-cost housing, with the 770-unit first phase completed and title to their new homes handed to proud squatters turned home-owners. A further 230 homes are envisaged for phase two. A thousand Franschhoek squatter families are to get fully-subsidised houses that would normally cost over R38,000 each in a deal supported by property developers and the local council.

Willem Steenkamp, a property development lawyer, was South Africa's first ambassador to 'black' Africa, accredited to six central African nations. Steenkamp is chief executive officer of Frandcevco a private sector development company, which was created to partner the municipality and the community in this public/private/community joint venture. Steenkamp says the three main components of the commonage project (a tourism orientated commercial node, an upmarket residential development and an agricultural estate) will benefit the entire community and help integrate marginalised groups into an expanding local economy. The commercial node will comprise a hotel, resort and spa complex; the proposed South Africa Food and Wine Museum and Training Centre; themed restaurants; an exhibition and convention hall; an art gallery and craft centre; the estate's winery and cellar; and an olive press and bottling plant. With the support of the Development Bank of Southern Africa, the Department of Trade and Industry and Wesgro, bulk infrastructure has been established and participants are being short-listed. The farming operation consists of vineyards and the harvesting of fynbos and other aromatic herbs and plants, and an endemic plant nursery. One of the largest wine estates in the valley, this venture will give the disadvantaged to the agricultural sector for the first time.

Community participation is through the Franschhoek Empowerment and Conservation Trust which is chaired by John Samuel, a Franschhoek resident who is also former head of the Nelson Mandela Foundation. It is intended that the Commonage developments provide the previously disadvantaged community with access to the agriculture and tourism sectors, from which high land prices have hitherto excluded them. Thus the hotel will be co-owned by investment vehicles benefiting the disadvantaged, and the wine farm will be operated by a company in which disadvantaged individuals will have a majority equity stake. Analysts have estimated that the Commonage projects will create 4,400 jobs in the construction phase, and 750 permanent employment positions.

Thanks to the ground-breaking Franschhoek empowerment and Development Initiative (FEDI) Franschhoek's land claimants, victims of the Group Areas Act, were fast-tracked by Government and have received payment of their state compensation. They have also received a prime development plot of two hectares, as well as R1.2 million from the Franschhoek community (resulting out of the Commonage development) as local contribution.

The Development Bank of Southern Africa awarded a R1 million planning grant to the Commonage project, and has provided more than fifty million rands in development funding to date.. The project was chosen by the Department of Trade and Industry (DTI) as one of only three to be showcased at the Earth Summit held in Johannesburg in September 2002, as models of sustainable development. Frandevco was invited to be part of the South Africa National Pavilion at the MIPIM International Property Exposition in Cannes in March 2003, and in 2005 the Franschhoek Hoek Estate Tourism Node was part of the national Tourism Investment Pavilion of the DTI at the Durban Tourism Indaba, promoted by the DTI and Wesgro as government's leading private-sector driven investment priority in the tourism sector.

The Commonage development received numerous accolades from the media for its commitment to conservation of the natural and cultural environment. On 1 January 2003, it was, for example, featured on the SABC-TV main evening news for its efforts in identifying and conserving a red data book endangered plant species, the serruria gracilis. The public participation and research underpinning Frandevco's applications for development rights in respect of the Commonage land was hailed by environmentalists as well as planning and conservation officials as a model for such applications. It elicited not a single public objection but instead received large numbers of written statements of support. The Commonage developments moved into the construction phase in 2003, and by mid-2005 the first residential phase has been serviced and transferred to purchasers, bulk infrastructure in respect of roads, electricity and water have been provided (substantially upgrading the facilities available to Franschhoek village) and the farm establishment is nearing completion.

(Sources: Dave Marrs. 'Franschhoek turns into a model of sorts', *Business Day*, 28 June 2002; Anna-Marie Smith. 'Flavour of the month', *Business Day*, 15 April 2005, and August 2005 e-mail correspondence from Dr Willem Steenkamp)

In 1999, Peter Harley had an idea to start a construction company. He wrote a business plan, applied for funding and, most importantly, thought through his ideas critically. Today, Peter Harley Construction (PHC) is a multi-million rand company having completed numerous government tenders. PHC specialises in construction and building projects, and is primarily involved in government projects. It is capable of a wide range of projects that include government projects such as schools, police stations, community halls, libraries, clinics, museums, electrical sub-stations and museums. PHC has also successfully completed private commercial and industrial projects. Peter himself has won numerous entrepreneurship awards. Peter Harley Construction was a recipient of the Western Cape Business Opportunity Forum (WECBOF) Business Person of the year 2001, Western Cape Sanlam/Vodacom/BMF Entrepreneur of the year 2002, and an Africa SMME Award for 2003.

In 1997, Sandra Africa left behind her role as a housewife and took on the men when she pulled on her gumboots and entered the construction industry. She has since registered Corporal Construction, a company that has been subcontracted by construction giants such as Group Five and Grinaker. Africa has put her hometown of Dysselsdorp near Oudtshoorn on the map as a major construction player in the area, and her company's involvement in building projects has brought employment and a better life to the majority of the town's 23,000 residents. Empowering the people around her, Africa has assisted community members in everything from achieving their drivers' licenses to opening their own businesses. Her building, civil and road construction company has landed a number of contracts in the Oudtshoorn area, and she often manages contracts worth several millions of rands. From her early days of buying one bag of cement at a time and owning a hammer and a screwdriver, Africa now plays a key role in the region's development. She was the winner of the Shoprite Checkers/SABC Woman of the Year award for business entrepreneurship in 2003.

(Source: International Marketing Council of South Africa; www.imc.org.za)

Moladi Construction System (MCS) is a unique construction method that has been developed in Africa, initially for Africa, to enable the construction of affordable housing without compromising on quality. This innovative technology will help many millions of South Africans in obtaining equity in their country. Hennie Botes is the founder and CEO of MCS Technologies, which is based in Port Elizabeth, and is the producer of Moladi, a patented, lightweight, reusable, plastic injection melded formwork system applied in the construction of houses, classrooms, clinics, and various other structures. Because of the holistic approach of the construction system focusing on the process and end result, the construction phase is streamlined, resulting in an economical building system. Botes believes Moladi to be the beginning of an exciting new era in the construction industry, creating job opportunities and facilitating the speedy delivery of much needed, low-cost quality houses, clinics and schools. Communities are trained and assisted to build their own houses more quickly and for less than conventional brick and mortar.

In 1986, with the intended purpose of 'housing the nation', Botes designed and patented the plastic injection moulded shutter system, Moladi, to construct durable structures of quality in the shortest possible time. In the years that followed Moladi has developed into a construction technology that addresses the three key challenges embodied in the low cost housing shortages facing developing countries: lack of funds, skills and time. While focusing on the aspects of the construction industry, it is intended through the technology to generate wealth and opportunities for the emerging black communities in South Africa by introducing and facilitating mutually beneficial projects between these communities and the established formal sector.

Botes sees the provision of housing as a human right and not a privilege. Health and welfare, the sense of dignity, security, motivation and empowerment that go hand in hand with owning one's own home is further extended by the employment opportunities afforded by the technology. The community not only actively participates in the upliftment of their environment, but also benefits economically. This is an important consideration with the current high unemployment rate in South Africa. Moladi construction technology can contribute to strengthening South Africa's new democratic dispensation. Unlike the conventional building method of brick and mortar, Moladi is not dependent on traditional skills associated with building. Moladi is a cost-effective and environmentally friendly formwork that can be recycled. It is simple to produce and overcomes the manifold problems of traditional steel and timber formwork, for example skilled artisans required for the manufacturing and erection, the high cost and weight disadvantage, slow assembly and susceptibility to damage.

The concept of the technology is plastic shutter panels used in conjunction with a South African Bureau of Standards-approved lightweight mortar, providing a fast-track construction method fulfilling all the requirements of the South African financial institutions. The panels measuring 300mm x 300mm are joined to form a wall configuration of any desired length or height, depending on the structure. These panels are linked together to form wall cavities of either 100 mm or 150 mm. Wall reinforcing, windows, doors and services are located *in situ* before these cavities are filled with a cement-like material consisting of local river sand, cement, water and a admixture. This produces a fast curing aerated mortar that is flowable, waterproof, and possesses good thermal, and sound insulating properties. The wall forms are removed in sections, not panel by panel, and can immediately be re-erected on an adjoining site, thus speeding up the entire construction process. Cast in one day, the structure is now ready to receive the roof and other finishes necessary to turn the building into a home. Once removed, the smooth-off shutter finish eliminates the need to plaster, allowing structures to be extended as needs and budget permit.

Millions of new homes are needed, not only in South Africa but throughout the world, and housing remains a primary sector of industry that can contribute towards the upliftment and empowerment of communities. Traditional building methods cannot possibly hope to meet the demand in time without forfeiting quality and standards, even if the necessary skills and materials were freely available. The Moladi construction technology can be used not only in South Africa but globally in the construction of houses, schools, clinics as well as agricultural and mining applications. Combining shelter and economic development, Moladi is set to change the tradition bound construction industry in order to allow for the participation of contractors and entrepreneurs to empower and develop communities on a global basis.

(Source: correspondence with Hennie Botes)

Tjeka Training Matters (Pty) Ltd is an organisation with a specific training and entrepreneurial development focus in the building and civil engineering construction industries. Tjeka, a South Sotho word meaning 'to dig in', was formed by a group of training facilitators with a total of 130 years of construction industry and training experience. Previously disadvantaged individuals have 80 per cent shareholding in the company and 80 per cent board of director representation. The company is in association with Tjeka Development Solutions and Tjeka Business Development, consultants in education, development and training, the development of workplace skills plans, undertaking needs analysis, compiling competency profiles, developing learning interventions and the writing of unit standards. Training is conducted through mobile units whereby accredited training is conducted on the project as well as accredited institutionalised training in both the building and civil construction industries.

Chief executive officer Frans Toua points out that Tjeka has been awarded the Construction Education and Training Authority (CETA) group skills development facilitator project for the Gauteng and Western Cape provinces. They are able to assist SMMEs (between 1 and 50 employees) to set up their training systems to the CETA requirements at no cost. This is an opportunity for small companies to get return on their investment and not only see the 1 per cent skills development levy as a tax that has to be paid. As a result of the company's contribution to the growth of the economy, job creation and transformation, Tjeka has been honoured as one of South Africa' top 300 empowerment companies during 2003 and once again in 2004. The company was also nominated as one of the finalists in the category education, training, and consulting services for the 2004 Africa SMME Awards.

South Africa's no-frills airline kulula.com has a good claim to having invented a new, easy way to fly. In the process, it may well have created a new mass market for air travel in South Africa. This commercial aviation revolution was achieved by adopting the easy model (*kulula* is Zulu for 'easy'). Flights are easy to afford, book and fly. Customers book direct via the kulula.com website, or telephone its call centre. Booking, confirmation and payment are simultaneous. Travel agents use the same channels. Kulula.com had made the whole online experience so simple that it became South Africa's largest revenue-generating website soon after launching. In 2003, the airline saw 65 per cent of its bookings made online. Ticketing is unnecessary;

passengers arrive with their personal identification document so that their names can be ticked off the passenger list. Seats are filled on a first-come, first-served basis and there is no business class. If a passenger does not arrive on time, the plane won't wait. It's a bus service on wings. Kulula.com intends to grow by keeping close to its public — the consumer, the call centre and travel agents. Fast, accurate and reliable data has to be on tap concerning flight schedules, inventory profiles, aircraft, and destinations, while managing data from call centre agents and the travel trade.

Kulula.com won the Best Domestic Airline award 2002 at the annual Airports Company South Africa (Acsa) Service Awards. The airline's executive director, Gidon Novick, was obviously delighted to receive the award.

Acsa contracted an independent company to conduct sample surveys of airport and airline users, capturing the extent and size of the domestic market. In 2004, kulula.com replaced its three 737s with four MD-82s, which also enabled the carrier to boost capacity by 20 per cent. Gidon reported that the acquisition of the four MD-82s cut existing operational costs by 30 per cent, savings that were passed through to travellers. Gidon also said that they got their new fleet at a time when the rand was particularly strong, which had enabled them to bring costs down and offer the lowest fares to the public. Gidon asserts that the airline is focused first and foremost on safety and reliability and, following that, offering the lowest possible price.

Journalist Chris Barron, writing for the *Sunday Times* of Johannesburg, reports that Gidon Novick is a 'Joburger', schooled at King David, Linksfield, and the University of the Witwatersrand, where he received B Com and B Acc degrees. He started his career with accounting articles at Fisher Hoffman. During articles, he successfully completed the board exam towards his chartered accountant qualification. After three years of articles, Gidon completed an MBA at Chicago's Kellogg Business School. During his time in the US, Gidon also spent three months at AT Kearney, a global management consulting company with headquarters in Chicago. What he took out of his time in the US was the importance of differentiation in business. Gidon says, 'You've got to be different. Understand the market and be bold enough to be different. Not just for the sake of being different, but find out what people really need, then be different around that need.'

Which is precisely what kulula.com is all about. Returning home in 1998, Gidon joined the management team at Comair, with which his father Dave Novick — now chairman — has been associated for 35 years. Gidon was involved in various roles, including strategy, marketing and operations.

In 2001, Comair noticed how successful airlines around the world with low-cost operating structures were proving to be. It saw the way the Internet was able to cut the costs of running a carrier and realised that Internet culture in South Africa had reached a sufficient level of maturity to make the same thing possible there. At the same time, it sensed that South African passengers were tired of exorbitant flying costs. There was a growing need for affordable air travel. Passengers were beginning to look more critically at the value of all those extras they had been in the happy habit of accepting as freebies.

The Comair board put all this together and arrived at kulula.com, the first retail airline in the country. Instead of selling its product to the customer via an expensive intermediary, it would do so directly and pass on the savings. Gidon Novick, young, flush with qualifications, passionate about flying (he has a pilot's licence), the airline industry and business, was clearly the right person to head the venture. The average age of his management team is somewhere in the late 20s, which is reflected in the hip-hop happening vibe which has become the kulula.com trademark, along with its prices, of course. Kulula.com has managed to achieve an average load-factor of 75 per cent. Between 75 per cent and 80 per cent is what its counterparts in the US (where South West is the model) and in Britain (where Easyjet is the favoured model) are targeting. Any less than 75 per cent and any more would not work for them, says Gidon. He's happy to keep it where it is, and this has made kulula.com profitable from day one.

Kulula.com has expanded its offering to include car hire though a partnership with Imperial's black economic empowerment partner, Khaya. It is also looking to offer accommodation. Gidon Novick says the key is that the booking process is extremely quick and extremely easy. He is driven by the competitive aspect of the business; he believes being a single player in an industry would be lovely financially but 'as boring as hell'. In the name of competition, kulula.com spends around R1million a month, or about 2 per cent of expenditure, on vastly colourful advertisements the public won't forget. What Gidon says is needed is 'top of mind awareness', so ads are very, very important. He doesn't intend increasing this amount much. What counts far more than advertising is customer service — holding on to the customers the ads encourage to 'try this zany outfit just once for kicks'.

(Source: Chris Barron. 'Kulula boss gives the airline game a new spin', Johannesburg: *Sunday Times*, 5 October 2003)

Craig and Jill Hunter first set eyes on the beautiful Pear Tree Farm in November 1979. While on a business trip to the Cape, they decided to visit Plettenberg Bay to look at a thatched farmhouse that friends had told them about. 'Just what Jill would love, and plenty of room for your family,' they had said. It was, in fact, love at first sight for Jill, who had been longing to leave city life and return to the country, especially to a thatched house. The day they saw it was November 10th, Jill's birthday. An option on the property was secured, and to cut a long story short, by April the following year, 1980, the Hunter family was installed at Pear Tree Farm. Their friends thought they had gone soft in the head and had been seduced by the charm of the thatch, the beauty of the countryside, mountains, sea and indigenous forest. Would this compensate for water pumped from the river down in the valley, using the ancient tractor that came with the deal, and the power supplied from an old diesel generating set, which had to be started by hand cranking every morning?

Over the first two years, alterations and additions were carried out to accommodate the family of five children in a greater degree of comfort, power was laid on and dams were built to ensure the water supply. As the children left home for school, university or work, they found themselves rumbling around in a very large home. It was suggested that since they had two empty cottages in the garden, they should accommodate paying guests in them. Reluctantly, they were persuaded to do so. They enjoyed meeting their guests. It was very stimulating, and this started the move towards a Country House Hotel. They had been used to entertaining and Jill was known for her dinner parties, her flair for decorating and her style, so it was just an easy step (so they thought) from this to the hotel situation. In the late 1970s there were very few country house hotels of any consequence, and they identified a need for this style of establishment.

They were told by many people, some of them in the hotel business, that they were mad. Thoughtfully and prayerfully they weighed it up, and decided that it was the way to go, and in faith stepped out. They built a home on the next door farm which they had purchased a few years before, and moved out of the Pear Tree Farm homestead that they had grown to love. Finance was arranged and eight new garden suites were added to the two existing cottages, plus further alterations and additions to the main building. Hunter's Country House, boasting 10 garden suites, opened its doors to guests on 8 November 1989, almost ten years to the day that they had first seen the property. The design of all the garden suites, alterations, and additions were done by Jill and Craig (as has been the case up to the present time) and the construction was carried out by their family construction company. All the decorating and furnishing by Jill and the furniture, pictures and paintings, ornaments and much of the crockery and cutlery were supplied by Jill's antique business. Advertising and marketing had been done simply by sending out letters and faxes, and by phoning selected local and overseas agents and operators. Many of those first contacts have grown into close friendships. They introduced themselves and told them what they were offering their guests. They were fortunate in being featured in a number of publications that were interested in this family initiative.

The first season 1989-90 was a great success, eldest daughter Jacqui having been brought back from her travelling in Europe to assist them in the management. Many friendships with guests were established, which have endured. It was hard work, running from morning till night: entertaining, cooking, transporting staff, maintaining and repairing — the list is endless. It was a tiring season, but they were on their way. Eldest son Rob had supervised the building operation, Ian, who was working in Cape Town, assisted with the setting up of systems and the marketing. Youngest son Cameron worked on the cutting of the forest trails, and so it was that they set it all up. A few years after they opened, daughter Mandy, having obtained her chef's qualification in Cape Town, joined them as assistant chef, later moving on to head chef. During these early years, the hotel was enlarged to 15 garden suites and later to 18 suites. It was at this stage that their son

Ian and his wife (another Jill) joined the establishment, Ian taking over the management from Jacqui who, having taken the hotel through the early years, decided to gain further experience elsewhere, Jill playing her part in function management and the flower arranging.

After their first year of operation they had been invited to join the association Leading Hotels of Southern Africa. In the following years they were fortunate to win numerous awards and accolades for service excellence. They were awarded a four-star rating, followed by a silver classification for exceptional service and quality, upgraded to a five-star silver classification a year later. In 1996 they were awarded South Africa's Hotel of the Year. The hotel was firmly established on the international map, and the need to satisfy the ever-increasing demand for excellence led to the construction of their forest suite, a suite to satisfy the most discerning traveller, complete with private pool. The main outdoor living area was remodelled to include a new swimming pool. A year or so later, two classic suites, were added, superb accommodation, each with private pool and timber pool deck. In addition, the chapel in the forest was built in mid-1997 for the use of guests, staff and family. People have fallen in love with the beautiful chapel and it is now used for christenings, weddings and study groups, in addition to worship. A conservatory has been added lately, which has been enthusiastically received by guests and visitors. Membership of the prestigious Relais and Chateau was invited in 1998, an invitation that they were delighted to accept.

The Hunter family is dedicated to the concept of service excellence. In addition to their guests, the Country House welcomes visitors for breakfast or lunch in the conservatory or in the shade of the vast, beautiful garden — Jill's creation over the past two decades. Fine dining is also available in the evening in one of three dining rooms.

However, the Hunter family is not content with what has been achieved and is reaching out with new and exciting ventures which will complement the Country House. The Gorah Elephant Camp is a Hunter Hotels premier game-lodge, set in the heart of the malaria free Addo Elephant National Park, home to the densest elephant population on earth. The original 'Gorah House' is restored to its 19th century colonial splendour. Following the opening of Gorah, was Tsala Treetop Lodge. Tsala is located on the edge of the indigenous Tsitsikamma forest overlooking the spectacular Piesang River. The Hunters lifted it into the tree tops to take advantage of the views over the valley. However it also fits into the 'legend' that they decided to create and around which is based the architecture, decor, food and music, as well as the dress of the staff. Very briefly, the legend tells of a people far to the north, who as a result of drought in their land decided to migrate south, bringing with them their culture, their builders, stone masons, blacksmiths and other skilled people. Finding themselves in this beautiful forest land next to river and sea, they decided to settle here and so a settlement was built. They used the natural materials, wood from the forest, and stone from the quarries at Robbeberg. They built their dwellings off the ground for security, and here they lived — for how long nobody knows but, like so many civilisations, they disappeared.

The Hunters decided that Tsala should be built using the same materials and employing similar skilled workmen. Every aspect of the lodge was designed to reflect the great diversity, colour and excitement of the African continent. Tsala, with its refreshingly different concept, has won wide acclaim. Since Hunter's Country House was accepted as a member of Relais and Chateaux in 1998, both Tsala Treetop Lodge and Gorah Elephant Camp have become members as well.

The Hunter family has been fortunate in having been able to establish their hotels, lodges, and camps in some of the most beautiful spots in the world. As a result of this they have become very conscious of the necessity for man to fit in with nature and not alter it to suit his ends. They can only be as successful as the cooperation of their staff allows them to be. In other words all need to buy into the vision. The Hunter family subscribe to the 'triple bottom line philosophy' (environmental, social, and financial responsibility). They have believed that it is essential for their industry to guard against greed and complacency. It is thus essential that there be the greatest degree of attention to detail in all the many aspects of the hospitality industry, plus a constant measuring of the quality of the service one is delivering, the need to provide the very best value for money (service excellence and great value). To enable the Hunters to retain good staff, it is necessary to provide opportunities for them to fulfil their aspirations. For this reason, it is the Hunter family's plan to steadily expand their business, in accordance with the demands of the market, while at the same time creating the opportunities for staff advancement and empowerment.

In November 2004, the Hunters signed a concession agreement giving them a 26-year concession over 23 000 hectares in Limpopo Province and the right to establish three game lodges. The concession area belonging to Marakele Park (Pty) Limited, adjoins the Marakele National Park in the south and the Welgevonden Game Reserve to the east. Marakele Park was established to assist South African National Parks in the expansion of the Marakele National Park. This awesome new area under the mighty Waterberg Mountains with the Matlabas River running through it, offers the visitor a 'big five', malaria-free experience. This latest project is called Marataba Safari Company, and the opening of the first lodge is scheduled for November 2005. The Hunters feel extremely privileged to have been given the opportunity of being part of this new wilderness and game project. It adds a further dimension to the African experience that Hunter Hotels is able to offer their guests. They will continue to add to this experience in the future, as opportunities are identified. They go forward confidently in the knowledge that South Africa, the land and the people offer their visitors unique unforgettable experiences.

(Source: www.hunterhotels.com)

James Fawcett Bailes originally acquired Castleton and Ravenscourt, two farms in the area between the Sabi and Sand Rivers, in 1925, as a private game reserve. The Sabi Sand region was a remote corner of the lowveld, three days' hard driving from the coast, teeming with game, a raw and beautiful landscape. In 1994, as South Africa was opening itself to the rest of the world, the Bailes family decided that the time had come to open Singita, their piece of Africa, to discerning visitors. Cape Town based businessman Luke Bailes founded South Africa's private and luxurious Singita private game reserve. Bailes' passion to create the ultimate African bush and wildlife experience for discerning guests has redefined the concept of luxury ecotourism. It is a magnificently exclusive 18,000-hectare wildlife sanctuary overlooking the Sand River adjacent to the internationally renowned Kruger National Park.

Singita offers 18 suites, nine each in the Ebony and Boulders lodges, and six rooms in Castleton camp. In the Ebony lodge one encounters the quiet opulence of African colonial style at its most refined. Set in the dappled shade of ebony trees on the banks of the Sand River, the suites at Ebony are completely private, cool and spacious, and each with its own plunge pool. Contemporary and airy, the lodge at Boulders is inspired by the rough natural geometry of the rocks among which it is built. Overlooking the expanse of the Sand River and the plains beyond, Boulders is furnished in simple luxury, using natural materials.

Africa's big five — elephant, lion, leopard, buffalo and rhinoceros — and spectacular birding are in easy view from all venues. Game safaris are available night and day in open Land Rovers and are accompanied by a personal ranger and tracker team. Guests enjoy traditional evenings in the boma and savour refined cuisine accompanied by vintage South African wines from the 12,000 bottle underground wine cellar.

(Source: www.singita.com)

Castleton camp, once the private home of the Bailes family, houses intimate small groups and families and is ideally situated for viewing large herds of wildlife. Surrounding the classic stone farmhouse with its wide veranda, the chalets at Castleton are luxuriously appointed in a comfortable colonial style, and enjoy beautiful views of a waterhole. At Castleton parties of guests are attended by their own personal tracker and game ranger. An open Land Rover is placed at their disposal.

The premier Singita private game reserve, South Africa's celebrated safari destination, was crowned 'Best in the world' at the Conde Nast Traveller (UK) magazine's seventh annual reader Travel Awards 2004 ceremony in London. This was the second major international travel poll to name Singita world number one in 2004, after the readers of *Travel & Leisure* in the USA gave this exclusive African property their vote. Singita propelled to the number one spot in the Conde Nast Traveller (UK) poll by attaining the highest score overall of 97.08 per cent and a flawless 100 per cent in three criteria: location, environmental friendliness and accommodation. Over the past three years, Singita has been named best in the world in no less than five leading international travel polls: Conde Nast Traveller (UK), Conde Nast *Traveller* (USA) (twice), *Travel and Leisure* Magazine (USA), Andrew Harper's *Hideaway Report* (three times), and *Tatler* Magazine (UK). 'We never made it a goal to win awards. Our goal was to make the experience at Singita faultless in every detail of the guest's stay. The fact that repeat guests have commented that they are amazed at how we get better with each successive stay, is testimony to our quest for constant improvement,' said an elated Mark Witney, Group General Manager of the Cape Town based Singita Group. Having garnered so many international awards, Singita has established itself firmly among the top resorts in the world.

In response to the Conde Nast honours, Singita owner, Luke Bailes, says 'It has been hugely rewarding for us as a South African-owned property with a team of South African staff to receive international recognition for our efforts. These achievements on the world stage emphasise that safari destinations rank high in the preference of travellers and that we are in good company with other southern African award winners and the many fine properties and products around the world.' Bailes has no doubt Singita will maintain its standard of excellence. He points out the competitive advantage of being in the midst of the world's most outstanding wildlife. He notes that the resort itself has managed to capture the beauty and tranquillity of its natural surroundings and has the ongoing benefit of a genuinely friendly staff, which feels responsible for each guest's pleasure. Bailes adds that the African spirit is strong at Singita and has proved itself to the many guests who return year after year.

In March 2003, the Bailes family's 78-year commitment to luxury ecotourism was extended to the opening of the Singita Lebombo Lodge on their newly acquired 15 000-hectare concession within the Kruger National Park on the Mozambique border. Voted Hotel of the Year in the prestigious UK *Tatler* Travel Awards 2004, Singita Lebombo offers guests a wilderness experience with spectacular scenery and an abundance of game. A major focus of the Singita Lebombo project was to minimise construction impact on the natural terrain. This two-lodge facility has 15 elevated, fully air-conditioned loft style luxury suites in one lodge and six in the other. Lebombo rests lightly on a pristine site among ancient boulders overlooking the confluence of the Nwanetsi and Sweni Rivers, the Lebombo Mountains and the savannah plains rich with indigenous vegetation such as aloes and euphorbias. Travelling along the single dust road into this remote wilderness, guests are overwhelmed by the scale and the silence. Rangers who have walked on foot through the area say it has the largest concentration of game they have seen in Kruger.

In February 2004, Singita Lebombo continued to set new boundaries in game lodge living with the opening of yet another design and architectural masterpiece, Sweni Lodge. The new Sweni Lodge is a collection of six intimate suites nestled in dappled shade on the banks of the Sweni River. Whilst similar in architecture and design as the 15 elevated loft style suites at Singita Lebombo, the Sweni interior has a more classic safari feel. Constructed almost entirely of glass, slatted wood and bleached, woven branches, the suites merge into the intimate vistas of the river and surrounding euphorbia trees. By staying at both Singita Private Game Reserve and Singita Lebombo/Sweni, a complete African experience can be had, as the two resorts differ vastly in tone and setting.

(Source: www.singita.com)

Mala Mala looks out over the Sand River, and covers 70 square miles of Mpumalanga province, sharing a border open for game with Kruger National Park. It supports a very broad selection of wildlife in its varied habitats, which include riverine forest, acacia bushveld and savannah. The owners, Michael and Norma Rattray, are personally involved in the environmental and hospitality management to ensure that the highest standards of game viewing and comfort are maintained. Mala Mala is one of Rattray Reserves' three destinations in southern Africa, all within a 60-minute flight of each other. Owned and managed by the Rattray family over three generations since 1964, the organisation strives for the perfection inherent only in family managed organisations. Each one of these destinations is markedly different and each one compliments the others thus guaranteeing a complete African safari. From the 'big five' experience of the award winning Mala Mala Game Reserve alongside Kruger National Park to Mashatu in Botswana to Mount Anderson in the eastern highlands of South Africa, the three game reserves provide consistent year-round African game viewing.

(Source: www.malamala.com)

Africa's largest and leading hotel group, Protea Hotels, now displays its special brand of hospitality in 11 African and Indian Ocean Island countries. Each Protea hotel is different in character and they range from small country hotels, seaside and lakeside resorts to mountain retreats, bustling city-centre hotels and the prestigious portfolio of Premier Protea Hotels. Protea Hotels roots go back to the Heerengracht hotel and to the then receptionist, Otto Stehlik. After hotel school in Vienna, Austria, Stehlik worked in Guernsey in the Channel Islands, where he met his wife, Suzan. The couple was lured to South Africa initially by the new Carlton Hotel in Johannesburg. The opening of the new Carlton Hotel was delayed, so Stehlik took a job at the new Heerengracht. By the time the Carlton was ready, Stehlik and Susan had settled in Cape Town and were reluctant to leave.

In 1973 Stehlik was appointed marketing director of the Heerengracht and in 1978, managing director. He intervened when the owner, Sanlam, was on the brink of selling the Heerengracht to Southern Sun Hotels, then controlled by Sol Kerzner. He went to see his boss, Sanlam's Fred du Plessis, and told him he was making a big mistake. Du Plessis listened when Stehlik said that the Heerengracht could be turned around. The upshot was that Kerzner was told the deal was off. Stehlik's timing was not brilliant. It was shortly after the 1976 Soweto riots and the hotel industry was bankrupt because its international market had disappeared. But then came what was popularly known as the Argentinean invasion, where thousands of people took charter flights from Argentina to visit South Africa. They were lured by a relationship between the US dollar, Argentine peso and South African rand that made South Africa cheap. Starting with the Heerengracht, Argentineans packed the hotels. Stehlik laid on three sittings for dinner in the Heerengracht's Van Donck restaurant. This comforted Du Plessis and soon Sanlam had expanded its hotel interests to include the Capetonian, Protea Gardens and San Lameer.

It was after these were running successfully that Du Plessis allowed Stehlik to reach the second landmark in Protea's history. Although Du Plessis had the option of either selling the hotels or embarking on slow expansion, he went with a third option suggested by Stehlik — rapid expansion through the route of the management contract. There had been a drain on expertise following the 1976 riots, and Stehlik believed that he could convert what had become a need into a business. He told Du Plessis that all he needed from Sanlam were the management contracts for the four Sanlam hotels. Du Plessis offered Stehlik 40 per cent of the new management company, Protea Hotels, which was formed on 1 July 1984, with an initial base of the four managed properties which were controlled by Stehlik and his partners: the Heerengracht and Capetonian Hotels in Cape Town, the Protea Gardens hotel in Johannesburg and the San Lameer resort on the Natal South Coast. Within a year, Protea grew from four to 20 hotels. Stehlik, together with Ron Stringfellow, was also instrumental in forming the Hotel Industry Liaison Group, which represents about 80 per cent of South Africa's international hotel rooms.

(Source: 'Why Protea hotels grew wings', Johannesburg: *Financial Mail*, 29 September 2000)

Protea Hotels continued to expand rapidly and is today the largest hotel group, in terms of numbers of hotels, in Africa, with the most extensive network. It has management and franchise agreements, as well as several joint ventures, with over 100 hotels. These are spread throughout South Africa, as well as Réunion, Mozambique, Swaziland, Zimbabwe, Tanzania, Malawi, Nigeria, Zambia, Namibia and Egypt, thus completing the Cape to Cairo tourism axis.

In 2000, Protea Hotels was also awarded a management agreement for Aventura Resorts, which is recognised as South Africa's foremost self-catering/serviced resort group with 17 resorts in the most scenic parts of the country. Six of their resorts are within or adjacent to provincial nature parks where guests can enjoy guided game drives, nature walks, cross country horse-riding and lectures on the local environment and culture. Two resorts are renowned for their hydro and mineral spa treatment facilities, while the balance offer a wide range of family fun and leisure activities. Aventura Resorts offer an unrivalled diversity of conference expertise in relaxing, natural settings, with modern caravan and camping facilities also available.

Negotiations are continually taking place regarding Protea's expansion into other African regions on both the east and west coasts of Africa — areas where Protea has a distinct trading advantage. For example, Protea Hotels now manages and markets three new hotels in Nigeria, the first hotels to be built in Nigeria since 1991. The three new hotels are the Protea Hotel Lagos, the Protea Hotel Oakwood Park and Protea Hotel Victoria Island. Protea also manages and markets two upgraded and renovated properties, Protea Hotels Apapa Apartments and Protea Hotel Nike Lake Resort. Whilst managed and marketed by Protea Hotels and carrying the Protea name, Protea Hotel Lagos is owned by the Honeywell Group. Headed by Chief Oba Otudeko, Honeywell is one of Nigeria's leading conglomerates, with interests in oil and gas, engineering, marine services, fishing and flour milling.

The partnership concept has worked well and has enabled Protea to help people grow through the organisation and to develop a dynamic corporate culture which, in turn, forms the platform of its future growth. Key to this growth will be Protea's ability to empower those around them. Many people have been marginalised through circumstances beyond their control. Protea is assisting in the creation of the kind of future that Africa's children will all be proud to live in.

Protea Hotels launched African Pride Hotels, their superior-deluxe brand, in 2001. It is through this brand that the Protea Hotel Group has been able to successfully break into the exclusive top-end market, an area, which they had previously not pursued. Stan Evans, who is known for his dynamic leadership in the tourism and hospitality industry, is at the helm, with the main purpose of developing and acquiring new properties for this new brand. Evans says that the last 10 years have seen the African continent firmly emerging onto the world tourism stage. He adds that with its unrivalled diversity of wild life, culture and scenic beauty, Africa has increasingly become the destination of choice for millions of seasoned tourists from all over the globe. He maintains that with this African renaissance come increasingly higher expectations of quality service levels, coupled with the demand for a superior physical tourism product. He proclaims that African Pride Hotels is exactly that — an exclusive African collection of luxury hotels and game lodges offering the highest standards of service, accommodation and facilities that meet and exceed these expectations and demands.

Lion Sands private game reserve was the first superior deluxe property to launch under Protea's new brand, African Pride Hotels. Lion Sands, with its superb setting and luxurious accommodation, gives guests the choice between River Lodge and South Camp, both situated on the banks of the Sabie River, ensuring breathtaking views and magnificent game viewing. With 10 kilometres of river frontage, this game reserve offers guests access to one of the most highly concentrated game viewing areas in South Africa. Launched in 2001, it has already gained wide spread recognition in this luxury market. This has been achieved by including a range of specialised activities that are available in addition to all standard packages and which include special interest lectures, bush breakfasts, river fishing, hippopotamus tours, survivor skills, wine tasting, bush cookery lessons, star gazing, full moon walks and bush sleep-outs.

Thula Thula, an exclusive private game reserve in Zululand has also joined African Pride Hotels, and expects to realise increased growth and market exposure. Known for its blend of cultural and wildlife heritage, this is the oldest and one of the most established private game reserves in KwaZulu-Natal. Thula Thula, which is soon to form part of the new Royal Zulu Umfolosi Reserve, is situated only 30 minutes from Richards Bay harbour and airport, and less than two hours' drive from Durban. Known for its exclusivity and superb wildlife, Thula Thula will fit effortlessly into the African Pride brand and Evans was delighted to welcome it into the group.

One of the reasons that have been cited for this brand's rapid growth is that is has taken advantage of Protea Hotels' marketing and management infrastructure and vast experience throughout the African continent. One of the most exciting additions to the African Pride brand is a new superior deluxe urban hotel, the Melrose Arch Hotel. This hotel is located within the multi-billion rand Melrose Arch development in Johannesburg. The development is a first of its kind in South Africa, incorporating living, working and recreational space into a single development, comprising 275,000m^2 of building, on a 16.5-hectare site. Melrose Arch includes features such as its own digital telephonic exchange, complemented by a fibre-optic intelligent spine. This development is not only pleasing to the eye, but is also very aware of the environment, taking into account issues such as waste and air management.

The five-star boutique hotel further establishes Protea Hotel's superior-deluxe brand, alongside its other top-end properties. This hotel incorporates 117 luxury bedrooms, modern and sophisticated. This property appeals to both the domestic business traveller, as well as the international market which is accustomed to, and expects, nothing less than the best. Melrose Arch includes suitable conference facilities as well as an exclusive auditorium. A theme restaurant, located within the hotel, serves guests as well as the public, complementing the numerous restaurants and eateries located in the Melrose Arch precinct. Evans says they are incredibly excited to be part of this fantastic hotel, which ensures that they will be leading the hospitality industry into a new era.

(Source: e-mail correspondence with Otto Stehlik and his personal assistant Debbie Mulliner.)

Hans Enderle left school at 15 to become a pastry chef and union activist. After five years of toil, he put himself through the tough hotel school in Lausanne, Switzerland. He immigrated to South Africa in 1966, taking up the less than fabulous post of receptionist at the Langham Hotel in Kerk Street, Johannesburg. Four years later he had been headhunted to run Holiday Inn's hotel at Jan Smuts Airport. By 1984 he was managing the whole company. As boss of Holiday Inn in South Africa, he saw profits draining from his coffers with every frill the hotel chain offered. He knew all about the expenses and he had an idea. What if his guests didn't feel like paying more for unwanted extras like lunches and dinners and porters and concierges and waiters? What if they would happily eat out in exchange for paying less for their hotel rooms? It made sense to Enderle and that is why, under his management, the first 'select services' City Lodge was about to open in Randburg, north of Johannesburg. 'Homely, friendly and modern,' is how he described the concept at the time. 'Nothing plastic, sexy or glittery.' Suddenly in 1985 the rising hotel giant Southern Sun swooped in to buy Holiday Inn. 'They offered to let me stay on as deputy, but I said I was a conductor, not first violin,' says Enderle, 'the wizard', as his people like to call him. 'I said if they'd let me buy the 123-room City Lodge in Randburg, then I'd depart.' Southern Sun let him have the half-built structure at cost, including the trademarks, concept and architectural plans. Needless to say, it may be a decision Southern Sun rues today.

The City Lodge Hotels Group has come a long way from its relatively humble beginnings. The City Lodge in Randburg opened on 1 August 1985 and became the catalyst for what today is South Africa's leading select service hotel chain. Year after year since then, on 1 August, the Swiss national day, a batch of new frills-free City Lodge hotels has opened their doors. There are now 37 in South Africa. From the start, emphasis was placed on quality accommodation, homely ambience and friendly service. These are still hallmarks of the group today. After pioneering the quality, select services hotel concept in South Africa, the group was incorporated in July 1986 and has since substantially grown and diversified its product offering to meet different travellers' needs. Enderle has never been tempted to diversify from his original concept of select services. Every five years he opens another version of the City Lodge brand. Top of the range is the Courtyard Hotels, dramatically less expensive than its full-service peers in the four-star category. Next, with three stars, is the original City Lodge concept. Then there is Town Lodge and down in economy class is the Road Lodge chain, aimed at the 'emerging market'.

In 1990, the second-tier Town Lodge concept was started and has proved highly popular. On 18 November 1992, the group successfully listed on the Johannesburg Stock Exchange. In 1995, the group acquired a 50 per cent interest in the companies associated with the upmarket Courtyard Hotel chain and also opened its first Road Lodge, a concept aimed mainly at budget conscious travellers. With six Courtyards, eleven City Lodges, seven Town Lodges, and thirteen Road Lodges, the City Lodge group has 4,049 rooms and suites and ranks amongst the 250 largest hotel chains in the world. Commitment to service and excellence from a highly motivated and dedicated staff is a common thread throughout the group's hotels, which have developed a loyal clientele of both business and leisure travellers over the past years.

City Lodge Hotels Group has created an extensive online database and search engine that will be able to tell prospective guests exactly what rooms are available on auction in their hotels at all times. The benefit of this site is that the bidders get instant confirmation whether they are successful or not concerning a room at any of the City Lodge group of hotel brands including the Courtyard, City Lodge, Town Lodge, and Road Lodge of their choice.

Hotels, say the economists, are a 'leading indicator' of a country's fortunes. Their room occupancy rates are a handy insight into both international tourism and domestic business travel trends, not to mention reflecting that woolly term 'consumer confidence'. Every City Lodge investment is made out of cash reserves. Unlike most hotel groups in the world, City Lodge owns most of its land and all its buildings. City Lodge is thriving. In 2000, the group invested almost R60 million in new hotels. Indeed the last 17 hotels it built have been financed through cash flow. The group is considering expanding in southern Africa and is looking at Namibia, Botswana, Zambia, Malawi and Mozambique.

Enderle, along with group chief executive Clifford Ross and his team, is doing his best by offering good, affordable accommodation, but his business sense extends into the very heart of the company. On 1 August 1995, on the occasion of the group's 10th anniversary, the City Lodge 10th Anniversary Employees Share Trust was launched which enabled all employees to become shareholders. All employees own shares and receive a dividend every year that reflects the company's financial performance. The bonus is drawn from R35 million of trust shares that include personal shares worth R6 million donated by Enderle.

The company has sponsored many black staff members to take part in a three-year International Hotel School course. Upon graduation they take their place in the City Lodge hierarchy. Cross cultural training and skills development programmes run year-round. The group has a pragmatic human resources policy that is, in most respects, well ahead of legislative requirements. Liaison for all aspects of pay and working conditions is conducted through elected employee bodies and a trade union. History, Enderle says, must look forward. He believes that evil concepts like apartheid have had their time and failed and that human rights have come to the fore. He says, 'There's no point in looking backward finding people to blame. We must move on.'

(Source: Jeremy Thomas. 'Overnight success: The man who introduced economy hotels to South Africa is now living a five-star life', Johannesburg: *Sunday Times*, 7 October 7 2001, and 2005 e-mail correspondence with Hans Enderle).

Stefan Knipe and Koos-Jérard Louw have created a company known as Superior Choices that offers a unique approach to marketing upscale hotels, lodges and restaurants and tailor-designing unique holidays and corporate getaways for international tourists and businesspersons to southern Africa and the Indian Ocean Islands. Superior Choices is a DMC (destination marketing company) with offices in Pretoria and a sales and marketing office in Boston, USA. A flexible, technologically advanced e-commerce solution enables Superior Choices to take real time confirmed reservations through the Internet.

Superior Choices represents 150 hand-picked hotels, resorts, game lodges and small boutique guesthouses, together with 120 restaurants selected individually for a Superior Choices Platinum membership. Memberships are offered based on a rigorous screening process whereby each property is reviewed in four qualifying categories: location, service, special features and architecture and decor.

Successful programmes managed by Superior Choices include the Standard Bank Platinum Concierge Restaurant and Travel programme, the MasterCard Platinum Hotel programme, the Standard Bank Lifestyle Choices Home Loans programme, the Rennies Bank Corporate Concierge programme, the Boe Private Clients Circle of Appreciation programme, the Absa Bank Superior Gold Stay programme and the Nedbank-MasterCard Golf Concierge programme.

Superior Choices implemented its Internet booking engine for a two-month banner promotion on the CNN web site, CNN.com, starting in July 2000. Stefan Knipe, managing director of Superior Choices and responsible for all marketing activities, says that the high profile exposure of the CNN campaign necessitated linking their website with a technologically advanced real time reservation system, enabling potential guests to book online and receive an instant confirmation. After the CNN campaign, the booking engine remains on the Superior Choices website, allowing the general internet public to make real time reservations at Superior Choices' discounted rates and benefit from the built-in advantages to guests such as room upgrades, complimentary breakfasts, free transfers and many more. In addition to providing internet connectivity, the system allows for a reduction in operating and administrative costs while capturing important reservation statistics and customer preferences. It also allows a hotel's preferred clients or travel agents to book directly at their negotiated rates, secured by a unique user ID and password.

Superior Choices enjoy the privileged formal endorsement by MasterCard International Globally, offering all member properties a direct website link to MasterCard International's website. Since inception, Superior Choices has aligned itself with top blue chip companies for marketing and distribution alliances such as Ferrari, Maserati, Möet & Chandon, Dom Perignon, LG Electronics, Budget Car rental, Nedbank, Standard Bank, Bridgestone, Abbot Laboratories, L'Oreal, BMW, ABSA Bank, BoE Private Bank and Rennies Bank.

(Source: e-mail correspondence with Koos-Jérard Louw)

Sally Hetherington of *Bizland News* reports that Allen Ambor, founder of Spur Corporation, is the personification of entrepreneurial success. Never given anything on a silver platter, Allen built from scratch, initially with a small team. Spur Steak Ranches is now one of the most successful brands in South Africa, with operations across South Africa's borders in Africa, as well as internationally — in Ireland, Australia and the United Kingdom. Yet Allen's beginnings were humble, a fact which pushes him forward, rather than holding him back. Allen matriculated in 1959 from Highlands North High School in Johannesburg. He went overseas shortly thereafter and was employed in London as a trainee in sales with a textile manufacturing group, which his father represented in South Africa. He returned to South Africa and accepted a job as a manufacture's representative in the agency business in Johannesburg. After working for two years he decided to further his education, and began the study of the History of Art, Economics and English, with the possibility of becoming a lawyer.

Allen put himself through university by working in a steakhouse in Johannesburg, where he developed an interest in the restaurant business, and a dream to eventually own his own restaurant. This was put on hold, however. After attaining a BA degree at the University of the Witwatersrand, Allen took up a position in the personnel department of a shoe company. It was on the last of many scouting expeditions to Cape Town, on the verge of taking up another position, that he met a builder who was building a shopping complex in Newlands. At age 23 with R2,000 in his pocket and no surety, he signed the lease to open a restaurant. The complex took some time to build, during which time he took on various *ad hoc* positions, including working part-time as a waiter and manager at sundry steakhouses, and as a high school and primary school teacher of commerce, arithmetic and soccer.

The doors of the first Spur Steak Ranch, the Golden Spur, as it was then named, officially opened in Newlands, Cape Town, in 1967. Allen's hard work and dedication had paid off, and from day one the Golden Spur was a success, due largely to Allen's high standards of customer service and quality food. Little did Allen realise at the time that this was the beginning of a multi-store franchise, so successful was the family orientated sit-down restaurant concept that Allen soon found himself opening several more stores in quick succession. By 1986, the franchise had grown to 43 Spur Steak Ranches, and since then that number has more than quadrupled, with approximately 15 new Spur Steak Ranches developed every year. Many outlets have been opened internationally, with plans for further expansion already under way.

In December 1990, the first Panarottis Pizza Pasta restaurant was opened in Tygervalley, Cape Town. Within a decade, over 50 further outlets were opened, and the Panarottis brand is now as instantly recognised as its big brother, Spur Steak Ranches. Following hot on the heels of the Panarottis success story, since December 1998 Spur has developed the Kelseys Grill & Fish restaurants, located in Cullinan Hotels in Cape Town and Johannesburg, as stylish, upmarket restaurants catering for the tastes of the more discerning diner. The Spur Group first listed on the JSE in 1986-87. In 1999, a major restructuring was undertaken, to provide management incentives and capital for growth. Spur Corporation is now forging ahead in taking Spur Steak Ranches and its associated brands to new heights.

In 2005, Spur acquired a controlling stake in a seven unit franchise trading in Natal called John Dory's Fish and Grill. Concentrating on fish and grilled chicken, this outfit trades in a niche very similar to Spur and to Panerottis Pizza Pasta in the sit-down family market. The originators are go-getters with a concept Spur admires. Together with Spur's Natal regional director, they head up this new initiative. When you walk into a John Dory's restaurant the cosy Mediterranean style is prominent. Boats, ropes brass bells and a host of nautical paraphernalia adorn the walls and ceilings. A huge stocked marine tank takes pride of place in all the stores. Spur management is excited about the prospects this new area of endeavour offers the company.

As chairman of the Spur Corporation, Allen is still extremely involved in franchising. Allen remains what he calls the 'brand custodian', in that he still maintains control of marketing and development of the corporation. Allen attributes his success to his sheer grit and persistence. He believes that one should always maintain one's caring and humility, and never become arrogant. Customer service is of the essence, as he believes: 'Your competition don't bankrupt you, your customers do'. He also stresses the importance of maintaining a good relationship with franchisees, allowing for an open flow of information. Allen says that he will always remain involved in the business. 'I am not an old person, and will never retire. Life is like surfing — you have to stay ahead of the wave or risk getting dumped'.

(Source: Sally Hetherington. 'Spurring ahead - Allen Ambor of the Spur Corporation', *Bizland News*, March 2002; www.bizland.co.za/newsletter/bizlandnews5march02.htm)

In 1993, successful Spur franchisee Duncan Paul opened his first Spur Steak Ranch, the Nevada Spur, at the Cascades Centre in Pietermaritzburg. After five years, armed with juicy results, he approached Business Partners, South Africa's leading small- and medium-enterprise investment company. Business Partners agreed to finance another Spur, this time the Kansas Spur at the Pavilion Centre in Westville. Soon a third Spur was added, the 280-seater Mustang Spur at Musgrave Centre. Duncan then decided to incentivise his operation by creating three different companies as small business units, with each manager having the opportunity to acquire a stake in the business. Trading results have subsequently soared. Another two outlets have been added to the portfolio of Spurs: the Boulder Creek Spur, a 277-seater in the Liberty Mall, Pietermaritzburg, and the Eldorado Spur in Hillcrest, Durban. Paul was a regional finalist for the 2003 Business Partners Entrepreneur of the Year Award.

In 2002, Five Flies, Cape Town's slick city restaurant, changed ownership after a management buyout, with Alex van Nes the vibrant general manager since 1999 firmly at the helm. At 34, Van Nes is the proud owner of this good-looking hotspot situated in a historic Cape Dutch landmark in the heart of Cape Town's legal and financial district. Van Nes has been the driving force behind the Five Flies success story from the outset. His vision, innovative flare and unbridled energy have made Five Flies one of the city's most successful establishments that appeals both to the local and international market. It was his winning formula of exceptional food, ambience, outstanding service and value for money that catapulted Five Flies onto the city's fine dining restaurant scene. As one of the first highly successful restaurants to operate in Cape Town's central business district, Five Flies has played a major part in the revitalisation of the city centre. Van Nes says that improved security, safe parking and cleaner streets have led to the establishment of a vibrant dining hub of restaurants and cafes that has seen life come back into the city. Van Nes does not intend making any changes to his winning formula.

Van Nes has a solid grounding in the hospitality industry. After studying hotel management in Switzerland, he tested England's culinary limits as part of the opening team of the trendy brasserie, Le Palais du Jardin, in Convent Garden. His global inspiration, evident in the cosmopolitan cuisine at Five Flies, can be attributed to his world travels, with memorable visits to Mexico, Venezuela and Italy. Totally in tune with what's happening at all times, Van Nes has just given the cigar lounge a facelift and is looking at redeveloping the third floor into a conference facility and boardroom. Five Flies epitomises energy and ultimate enthusiasm, which is what Van Nes is all about. High on life and terribly social, he loves drawing energy from the people around him. When Van Nes senses that a patron appreciates the better things in life and that he's happy, Van Nes is happy. From the moment you cross the threshold with its heavy stable doors, a feeling of continuity, of dining with history, pervades the interleading rooms. This presents an agreeable contrast to the contemporary buzz of diners.

(Source: E-mail correspondence with Alex Van Nes)

In 1996, Christine Cashmore started the annual Cape Gourmet Festival in Cape Town. The Festival is Africa's biggest, most comprehensive and diverse food festival. As a major player promoting tourism in the Western Cape, the Cape Gourmet Festival is one of only eight selected events that have been given the official Cape of Great Events endorsement by the Western Cape Tourism Board. The Festival has earned its rightful place as South Africa's premier gourmet event. Locals and tourists, who want to experience South Africa's cutting edge cuisine and culinary excellence firsthand, find that the Festival has a scrumptious menu of palate-pleasing activities. This internationally acclaimed, locally loved festival showcases South Africa's finest produce and wines. The anchor event is The Good Food and Wine Show, the largest four-day consumer food and wine exhibition in southern Africa, held at the Cape Town International Convention Centre in May, with a sister exhibition held at Gallagher Estate, Midrand, each September.

(Source: www.gourmetsa.com)

Cashmore is the author of nine books as well as former editor and publisher of a national magazine, *Food & Home*. She produced and presented a series of cooking programmes on television. Her community involvement has resulted in over R3 million being donated to various South African children's charities including the Red Cross Children's Hospital, the African Children's Feeding Scheme and Copes Clinic. Cashmore has also been directly involved in the self-help children's gardening scheme at the Valley Trust in Natal. In 2000, Cashmore launched the Table of Unity, a peace initiative to unite all South Africans regardless of colour, race or creed. This initiative was taken national in 2003 and also extended into local communities and homes, raising funds for the children's charities listed above.

(Source: E-mail correspondence with Christine Cashmore)

BTI Connex Travel is one of the country's leading travel businesses and South Africa's largest black empowerment travel management company, bringing international expertise and buying power to the business of providing its clients with consistently reliable, highly organised and cost-effective travel arrangements, both locally and globally. In 1996, Kananelo Makhetha was hired by Connex Travel to spearhead its restructuring and further development.

Connex Travel started as part of the process that saw SA Transport Services give way to Transnet. Connex Travel and Makhetha piloted the privatisation process and participated in negotiations that brought in Rennies Travel, Shumi Travel and Leisure as new shareholders, and awarded a 10 per cent stake in the company to employees. A measure of the company's success is that the bottom line profit grew by 350 per cent after its privatisation in 1999. Another is its blue chip client profile. BTI (Business Travel International) Connex Travel is widely recognised for its record of service excellence.

Makhetha has made a vital contribution to the development of the tourism and travel industry through his dynamic leadership of the Association of South African Travel Agents (ASATA) from 1998 to 2001 and as a member of numerous related associations. He is credited with being instrumental in changing the face of the South Africa tourism and travel sector. As the first black president of ASATA, Makhetha was one of the first senior industry executives to call for real transformation in the local travel industry. Along with placing transformation high on the agenda of ASATA, he took a public stance against window dressing. He has long been known as an outspoken proponent of constructive dialogue between travel agents and suppliers. Over the years he has built lasting relationships within the travel industry, both locally and around the globe.

As former chairman of the Tourism, Hospitality and Sport Education and Training Authority (THETA), Makhetha sees training and education as being key to the transformation of the South African travel and tourism industries. Under his leadership, BTI Connex Travel has reached new heights in an industry grappling with major commission cuts, the events of September 11 2001 and the subsequent demise of many airlines.

BTI Connex Travel has become a role model for real and successful black economic empowerment. In the past few years there have been many efforts to create companies in which black people are significant shareholders. Unfortunately, many have resulted in spectacular failures with little if any benefit for the black shareholders and employees. However, Makhetha and BTI Connex Travel have proved that empowerment can work in a fundamentally sound manner that adds real value to shareholders and customers alike. Makhetha and his management team have turned BTI Connex Travel into a dynamic, highly professional and people-focused organisation that is making travel and tourism a positive, enriching experience for clients, so that they will keep returning.

Since his appointment as MD in 1996, Makhetha has been the driving force behind the transformation and strategy that has propelled the company into the top 10 travel agencies in South Africa, competing favourably with large multinational agencies. In 2002, Makhetha received an award from South African Airways as the individual who has made the most outstanding contribution to the travel and tourism industry, and BTI Connex was a finalist in 2003 SA non listed company awards.

Calabash Tours has developed a sustainable model for township tourism. Bringing benefit to the community has been its imperative from the start. Using community projects and black-owned businesses as service providers has also generated financial benefits for township residents. They realised early on that placing well-resourced first-world tourists into third-world conditions creates a lot of opportunity for both parties, which led to their establishing the Calabash Trust, an independent entity that mobilises and manages tourist and other third party donations in support of social development projects in communities that host their tours.

By August 2005, the Calabash Trust had distributed more than R1 million into disadvantaged communities around Port Elizabeth. Calabash tours are helping to correct historical imbalances, particularly in terms of whose stories are told — and who benefits from tourism. Co-owner Paul Miedema says they were uncomfortable with the one-sided way that city tours in South Africa are typically conducted, focusing only on 'white' or 'black'. Their tours weave the story of their city into one story, embracing all aspects of their heritage.

Miedema is focusing strongly on 'pro poor responsible' tourism strategies. In August 2005, Miedema was in the process of selling 30 per cent of Calabash Tours to three staff members, both as a black empowerment process, and the completion of the vision Miedema had when he started Calabash in 1997. Briefly, Miedema sees the Calabash owners as social entrepreneurs, working for profit for sure, but with a 'win/win' business attitude. He says, 'Since the collapse of socialism in the 80s, the dominant ideology worldwide, and in developing Africa, is a capitalist model. However, we operate from the premise that this can be a humane, fair model, not intrinsically exploitative, and business can be an effective development tool for the poor. Tourism has massive potential in this regard, which we are effective at unleashing.' Miedema emphasises that, 'We work from a position of love for the poor, we see the poor of South Africa as our partners, not because we are do-gooders or bunny huggers, but because poverty is the largest threat to global sustainability.

South Africa is a country of potential, massive potential, but is threatened by instability which can arise out of poverty. Even HIV/AIDS thrives more readily among the undernourished than the well fed.'

In 2004, Calabash Tours was a worthy joint winner of the fiercely contested Responsible Tourism Awards, which attracted more than 700 entries. Calabash won the 'poverty reduction' section of the awards (based on tourism that directly helps to alleviate poverty). It was then selected by the judging panel as a co-winner of the most outstanding overall entry award. Harold Goodwin, director of the International Centre for Responsible Tourism, Greenwich University, UK, and chair of the judging panel, said: 'We have heard nothing but good things about Calabash. They are really pushing the right type of tourism in South Africa. What is so important is that Calabash is bringing into the mainstream a kind of tourism that benefits the black community.'

(Source: www.responsibletravel.com and August 2005 e-mail correspondence with Paul Miedema)

Chapter 9: South Africa: Business, Manufacturing, African Arts and Crafts, Health, Education and Media

The consensus of many at the Africa Economic Summit 2003 concerning the role of post-apartheid South Africa vis-à-vis the rest of the continent was that there is an extremely fine line between 'economic powerhouse' and 'big bully'. To be sure, South Africa enjoys a grossly lopsided trade imbalance with its neighbours. Yes, some South African businessmen seemed to ignore or disrespect local manners, customs, linguistics and traditions. And, true, there was growing foreign resentment of the brusque way certain brand name South African companies appeared to swoop in, crush their regional competitors and dominate the market through economies of scale. But some asked whether it was always such a terrible thing since it brought more competitive and transparent economic dynamics. And furthermore, noted moderator Antonio Matos, chairman of the Mozambican Austral Consulting Group, aren't these relatively minor discomforts compared with having a champion and leader in your corner?

'We need a strong leader,' said Alhaji Tukur, group chairman of Bhi Holdings, Nigeria. 'Sometimes there is only one country that holds the power and has the obligation to use it wisely.' A participant from Lesotho agreed, noting that there are times when a big brother is needed to help quell the differences between peoples and nations. A Zambian businessman pointed out, 'South Africa, whether we like it or not, is an African country. Where we used to report to London or America, now we report here. And that brings confidence that it is coming from within Africa.'

Gugu Moloi is the chief executive at Umgeni Water, a company producing bulk potable water and dealing with water sanitation management and consulting in all its aspects. Umgeni Water is the largest water authority in the KwaZulu Natal province. It sells over 300 million cubic metres of water annually to approximately 5 million people in KwaZulu-Natal; it manages and operates 12 storage dams, 13 waterworks ranging in capacity from 500 to 750,000 cubic metres a day, a number of wastewater works and an extensive network of well-maintained pipelines, inter-basin transfer systems, major pump stations and reservoirs.

Umgeni Water has an integrated and holistic approach to the planning and implementation of water and environmental management services. Recognising the need to control water quality from source to sea, Umgeni Water's highly rated water quality monitoring programme continues to deliver a high quality output. Umgeni Water leads the way in the empowerment of women, as it is the first water utility in Africa to boast a female chief executive officer.

Gugu Moloi heads an executive team of five members, of which three are women. Moloi obtained a degree in law from the University of Durban-Westville and a postgraduate degree in urban and regional planning from the University of Natal. She is a mentor for the Mandela Leadership Foundation and is passionate about bringing water and infrastructure to developing countries, especially to poor rural communities, and is very involved in a number of water infrastructure projects. She has extensive experience in development work, and a sound financial management background.

On her appointment in 2002, Gugu initiated an extensive restructuring process to enable Umgeni Water to reposition itself to become a competitive force in the South African and African water services market. The six corporate divisions were reworked into operational divisions and some of the divisional directors were replaced by a new breed of general manager committed to drive this water utility towards its vision of being number one in the developing world. The benefits of this restructuring process became evident in the financial year 2004/05.

Gugu envisions Umgeni Water moving under her stewardship towards a profitable future and having a positive impact in the water sector. Umgeni Water has put in place a province-wide programme for the delivery of water in the next five to ten years. This is a joint initiative between Umgeni Water, Umhlathuze Water and Uthukela Water. Although it has been conceptualised by Umgeni Water, other utilities as well as other government structures have come on board. This will need an investment of over R11 billion. Umgeni Water has committed to providing R500 million. The project will create in access of 78,000 jobs. There are currently discussions with various donors on the c-funding of this initiative.

Gugu also expects that more SMMEs will develop and that more broad-based empowerment will occur. She would like to see further good relationships developing between white and black business. In October 2004, Gugu was appointed to the Forum of Young Global Leaders of the World. She is a member of the Water Supply and Sanitation Collaborative Council Steering Committee in Switzerland and has been appointed on the Advisory Council of the Nelson Mandela Foundation in April 2005. She is also chairperson of the Forest Sector Charter Steering Committee, appointed by the Minister of Water Affairs and Forestry in June 2005.

Gugu is a staunch supporter of Africa and has recently started a motivational business, Iman' Africa (meaning 'rise, Africa'), where she talks to people in all sectors of society about what they need to do to make Africa the continent of the future. Although she finds the talks exhausting, she is driven by her strong belief that this initiative will encourage all Africans to view Africa as a continent of opportunities. Her dream is to ensure that all sectors of society become active participants in the economy within the context of the African Renaissance. Because she has been fortunate she feels it is her responsibility to help others so that she can leave a legacy of a youth able to lead the country to greater heights in the future.

(Source: www.umgeni.co.za)

Global recognition has the power to inspire and encourage young entrepreneurs to dream and succeed. In recognition of his leadership of international investment holding company Bidvest, executive chairman Brian Joffe was awarded the South African Chapter of the Ernst & Young World Entrepreneur Award 2003. The judges selected dealmaker Joffe for his ability to identify opportunities in stagnant industries and his record of acquiring and turning around under-performing businesses. Bidvest's decentralised and entrepreneurial business model has proved that solid operational performances are possible in volatile markets. Bidvest's June 2004 market capitalisation of R16.6 billion makes it one of the largest industrial companies listed on the JSE Securities Exchange. The group has operations in South Africa, the UK, Europe, Australia and New Zealand, and employs almost 80,000 people worldwide. The award identifies and rewards visionary entrepreneurs who increase the number of successful business ventures that add real value to the formal sector of the economy, create jobs and develop skills on a large scale. Joffe represented South Africa at the world award ceremony in Monaco in May 2004 and competed against finalists from 35 other countries.

According to its 2005 group annual report, Bidvest plans to invest about R2 billion in major capital expenditure programmes over the next five years. The conglomerate, which supplies office support services in South Africa, Europe and Australia, reports that its Bidfreight transport division alone would spend about a billion rands on new port-landside infrastructure. The investment dovetails with the South African government's plans to step up investment in port, rail and other infrastructure. 'The smart money is going into our infrastructure, not out of the country,' says Joffe.

(Source: www.bidvest.co.za)

Premier auctioneering group Aucor grew from humble beginnings in Johannesburg, where it was established in the late 1960s. Eddie Winterstein, the current Aucor Group chairman, founded Aucor and remains its prime entrepreneur. Subsequently, he was joined in business by his brothers, Clive and Brian, the company's financial director. The three brothers put Aucor on the auctioneering map in its formative years during the 1970s: in its early days it was a small outfit selling items such as coal stoves and radiograms (they even sold their office desk to an interested buyer and had to work off the kitchen table for the next few weeks). Recognising a gap in a remarkable industry, Aucor became more involved in the industrial and commercial fields and grew from strength to strength. A breakthrough came in 1983, when Aucor was awarded the tender to conduct an auction of excess equipment for Sasol. Winterstein reckons that the auction sale of some R8 million nearly two decades ago is probably the equivalent of a sale of R100 million today.

(Source: *Sunday Times*, 26 November 2000)

Clive Winterstein, a metallurgist, heads up Aucor's mining and earthmoving equipment divisions. He says auctions are an efficient and cost-effective method of asset disposal, eliminating the problem of holding costs which can add up to a considerable percentage of the stock value annually. Aucor director Chico da Silva, who is head of the group's industrial, plant and machinery division, notes that with emerging black-led companies tendering for and securing government contracts, there has been a major demand for fabrication equipment at auctions. Da Silva says South Africa buyers need to be educated about the advantages auctions offer. 'They are undoubtedly the quickest way to purchase assets at realistic prices. You can get pre-approved financing from a bank and a letter of credit qualifies you to buy at an auction. You don't need cash.' He says the division is increasing auction sales in other African countries.

(Source: *Sunday Times*, 26 November 2000; www.suntimes.co.za)

Aucor has been instrumental in introducing a code of ethics for use within the company. It also assisted the South African auctioneering industry to establish the South Africa Institute of Auctioneers, a voluntary body which acts as a watchdog for the profession. With more than 40 years in the business, group chairman Eddie Winterstein is one of the longest-serving auctioneers in South Africa. He believes there is a strong need for a statutory body in South Africa to regulate the industry and says it would serve to give auctioneering in South Africa true credibility. For example, in the United States auctioneers are required to put up a bond as security in order to obtain an auctioneering licence. 'Anyone can stand up on a box and start selling,' he says, 'but to know what the true value of an item is and to give a fair and honest deal requires a deep knowledge of the industry. This can only come from proper education and training — with proper recourse for the buyer in the event of comebacks. This is lacking in our industry.' Auctioneering expertise and experience is essential. The strength of Aucor's operation is the expertise of its executives who are able to make decisions individually and stick to those decisions. The philosophy of shared responsibility extends to Aucor's branches, each of which is 50 per cent group owned (the balance is owned by the local manager).

(Source: *Sunday Times*, 26 November 2000)

Brian Winterstein is the managing director of Aucor's online auction company AucorActive. After 32 years in the traditional world of auctioning, Winterstein found the transition into the world of digital business easy. 'I did not intend to allow an Internet start-up to hijack our market,' he says. His online initiative was seized by his son and nephew, who were both already involved in the business. Shannon Winterstein was given his first computer at 13 by his uncle, Brian, and computers have become part of his life. While studying at university in the United States he became adept at using computers to complete tasks at hand; from creating digital images for photography classes to history research online, and undertaking statistical work for various theses, computers were always part of his tool kit. Even in his first 'real' jobs, such as working for a US government-funded research institute, he used computers to model economic development. On his return to South Africa in 1996, he began working for a company which supported what are called GISs (Geographic Information Management Systems). His most important client required a huge database that was linked to its global user base via secure online access. He had been using the Internet since 1990, which put him in a perfect position to work on the project.

In 1998, in discussions at family gatherings, the family finally decided that it was time to implement all the ideas and research that they had all seemed to have done (without ever being asked) regarding online auctions. As Shannon was at this point working for himself as an independent consultant, he began to spend much of his time in the specification and design of AucorActive, the online website. By September 1999, Aucor's website was coming to life as planned. Fully e-commerce enabled, with integrated logistics, and a system of guarantees to online users, it was a world first. Despite the odd hiccup, the system flourished, and Aucor was in need of someone to take full-time responsibility for it. Having been involved from the beginning, and not being committed to any other part of the business, Shannon became the perfect candidate. He worked on the website for two years, watching the rise and fall of the 'dot comers' and always aware that AucorActive was essentially a brick and mortar company. The more Shannon worked on the website, the more he started to get excited by the 'real world' auction environment and he slowly started working for both the 'real world' and online areas. Most recently, Shannon has been brought into the entire group structure as a director, having a strategic role for the Internet offering, whilst at the same time becoming more focused on getting real world auction experience under his belt.

Shannon and his cousin, Dale Winterstein (Brian Winterstein's son) started out project-managing the site's development. Today they manage AucorActive's strategic alliances, and procure 200,000 articles a month for auction. These range from bulldozers to watches and from T-shirts to garden benches. From the first day of business, in October 1999, growth projections fell far short of reality. 'We thought it would take us a year to populate the site with 30,000 to 40,000 items. It took us three months to reach 200,000 items,' he says. The company was started with a marketing and development budget of five million rands, and today enjoys over 300,000 page impressions per month. Over 50 per cent of these are from people who would not ordinarily have put foot in a 'real world' auction. Much of the company's success is due to its role as a middleman. Unlike other auction sites, it guarantees the seller with payment and the buyer with the article as advertised.

(Source: Sasha Planting. 'AucorActive', Future Company, 7 July 2000)

Dale Winterstein is no longer directly involved with Aucor, but his brother Darren joined Aucor in 1994 and has progressed through the Aucor ranks from laying out a wide range of commodities (from catering equipment, engineering and trucking equipment) to his current directorship. Darren now heads up Aucor's furniture, office automation, appliances, and information technology divisions. He is also an experienced auctioneer.

Aucor is the only national auctioneering company in South Africa and South Africa's only online and offline auctioneers with branches in Johannesburg, Durban, Cape Town, Pretoria, Free State and Windhoek. Aucor also has affiliations with partners throughout southern Africa and the rest of the world. Its client base ranges from major corporations such as Goldfields, ABSA Bank, First National Bank, Sasol, Standard Bank, Nedcor, BOE., Investec and various governmental departments, to the man in the street. Aucor's success is the ability to relate to the needs of each of its clients.

Aucor has realised the need to establish a new trading mechanism that caters to the needs of the new digital economy in our exciting world, and AucorActive is the most progressive and dynamic on-line auction website in South Africa with a unique system of guarantees to buyers and sellers on conclusion of all deals. AucorActive is not merely online auction, but a virtual auction house tailored to the digital economy of the new millennium. Its nerve centre is the Aucor Group of Companies, which boasts over 30 years of growth and leadership in the auction industry and its base of executive expertise with a wealth of experience and impeccable reputation established it as the first fidelity bonded auction house in South Africa. Strategic partners, both national and international, have been added to the team to create a wealth of skills tailored to the new generation.

(Source: www.aucor.co.za)

The digital divide is a reality that developing countries like South Africa have been forced to accept, but through a commitment to uplifting poor local communities, FreeCom Group is making inroads into bridging this divide. 'Our pure focus is to provide affordable computer solutions for the first-time buyer end of the market,' says FreeCom Group managing director Rob Packham, a chartered accountant with extensive experience in financial and marketing management of distribution and retail companies. The company buys used computers in bulk from the United States and Europe, where the life of computers in a corporate environment is traditionally 18 months to two years. Its technicians peel open, professionally clean, and then run the machines through a thorough diagnostic system before rebuilding and preparing them for sale. The quality of their refurbishing has won status as an official IBM used broker, and they are now accredited as one of the only Microsoft approved refurbishers in the southern hemisphere. Packham says, 'What we're trying to do is build an appropriate, credible market of affordable computers, not just refurbished but new as well, and trying to offer the first time buyer or small business entrepreneur an alternative, but at the same time widening the base of people who are now able to access and afford a computer.'

The company was founded when Packham started doing research into the IT consumer market, looking for a gap into the market. 'What we found was that the inherent demand was there, but the market was very quick to say 'but we can't afford it'. With this information we looked around and saw that the hardware was there, with 18-month old, end of lease computers being discarded into dumps in the US and in Europe. We said, 'well there had to be an opportunity here and there had to be an appropriate channel to which we could distribute these computers into the middle market'.' The key was to create and deliver a credible and affordable distribution model. It was then that Packham met Swiss investor, Eric Meier-Ruegg, who had taken a liking to the idea of affordable computers as a way to bring development to poor communities. 'What we do is no different to that of the top-end operators in the used car market,' says Packham. 'The used car industry now is a highly credible and discerning option for customers to choose. We're trying to create the same level of confidence in used and refurbished computers. And because it's priced at an affordable level and sold with a full warranty, it gives people who otherwise think they were excluded from the market the opportunity to own a home computer.' Meier-Ruegg introduced the company to the Andromeda Fund, a private equity social investment firm based in London. Andromeda seized the chance to invest and support the venture.

However, Packham points to lingering opinions as the first real hurdle FreeCom Group had to face in setting itself up as a second-tier business in the ITC industry. New computer vendors initially saw the entry of refurbished computers into the market as competition that would take a bite out of an already competitive pie. 'In the beginning we were scorned by the new vendors, as being almost irritants in the market, whereas now we have a much healthier relationship with quite a few of them. They see that credible, quality, refurbished computers narrows the digital divide, but at the same time it gets their own brands out there into the market a second time around, to people who wouldn't see them or know them otherwise. And the next time they buy, they will have developed an affinity for whatever the product was, and it won't do the original equipment vendor any harm.'

FreeCom Group also runs a learnership programme, the FreeCom Digital Workshop, training IT graduates from previously disadvantaged communities. 'The learnership kind of evolved. We looked at our core business — and about 80 per cent of it is refurbished computers and we didn't have a logical route to market. So we started thinking that if we then had to open our own grid of distribution/retail centres, then inevitably they would need to be run and owned by individuals who understand what it is we're trying to do,' says Packham. 'And because our business is primarily a technical, labour-intensive activity, we decided that instead of hiring a lot of technicians into effectively dead-end positions, we would bring those individuals in on a twelve-month learnership basis.' The learnership, which is soon to be accredited by the Information Systems, Electronics and Telecommunications Technology Sector Education and Training Authority (ISETT SETA), focuses on hiring A+ graduates from the previously disadvantaged communities, and aims to give them experience in the IT world as well as general business skills, with three months' worth of commercial business and entrepreneurial training. 'After the course, and if they are the right kind of people, they will be able to work in one of the company-owned stores, or hopefully they have the courage to set out on their own and own and run their own FreeCom franchise. Our hope is that as many as possible would be able to go through the course, come out, and set up their own business, and create new opportunities and new jobs for others.'

Although small, FreeCom Group is quick to look towards partnerships in the future. FreeCom has been appointed a member of IBM international dealer/broker network, and identified by Microsoft as a business partner. It is accredited as one of the only Microsoft Approved Refurbishers in the southern hemisphere. Locally the group is partnered with Telkom, who see the introduction of affordable hardware as a necessary move in increasing the momentum of their rollout of home Internet access. FreeCom Group has also teamed up with E-Degree, with the partnership offering affordable computers to their students. The company is starting to develop ties with countries in Africa, with enquiries from Nigeria, Rwanda and Namibia about setting up FreeCom Group franchises in those countries. Explaining the company's success, Packham again draws on the used car example: 'You don't need a sports car to get to school or do your grocery shopping, as nice as it is. A two-year old Toyota Corolla — for a first time car owner, bought from a reputable dealer — is their new car. They don't have to buy a new one out of the box. They can buy a used one from a credible dealer.'

(Source: www.freecomgroup.com; and e-mail from Rob Packham, October 2004, updating Top Tech 100 story: http://196.4.91.173/toptech/story.asp?StoriesID=85&TimeLine=Arch)

Combining management and staff from three parastatals led to the creation, in January 2001, of Arivia.kom as a major black-managed global information communications technologies company. As chief executive officer, Zeth Malele leads the team at Arivia.kom. Malele chaired the consolidation management committee and the leadership burden rested squarely on his shoulders. Bringing together management and staff from three different state-owned entities was a challenge that Malele embraced as he built a management team from the most promising of those he inherited. Malele spared no effort in bringing all relevant stakeholders together, including unions, shareholders, customers and external business partners, to create a single, formidable team. From its inception, the company's vision has been to be a player of note, not just an also-ran, in the local, regional and global markets.

Ariva.kom's goal is to be a profitable, successful and global player in a sector of the economy most affected by globalisation and the challenges that accompany it: information communications technologies. Arivia.kom also has a division, Niche Market Solutions, which focuses on state of the art technology applications in the areas of smartcard and biometric technologies.

The company now has an impressive global reference of installed information and communications technology solutions and prospects in Africa, South America, the US, EU and the Middle East. The nature of its business is such that the solutions, methodologies and technologies it provides must be world class because the sector is dynamic and competitive. Customer needs change as businesses need to adapt to competitive pressures themselves. In order to be responsive to the needs of the market it is imperative that the company does not focus only on the technology solutions of yesterday. Arivia.kom looks ahead of trends in applications and technologies, so that innovative solutions, based on the most current and appropriate technologies, can be provided to customers on a proactive basis. This ensures that the company stays competitive.

Malele has achieved recognition in the market and has addressed international conferences such as the World Congress on Information Technology in Australia in 2002. He is a computer science graduate from the University of the North and has also studied business and management with Wits Business School. He won the Black ICT Personality Awards in 1999 and 2000, and the Computer Society of SA IT Personality of the Year in 2001. In 2002, he was the vice president of the Black Information Technology Forum and the Information Industry South Africa Organisations, and served as a member of the management committee of the Black Business Council and as non-executive chairman of the boards of Reed Exhibitions Company SA and Sybase SA. In addition, Zeth is non-executive director of the South African Electrotechnical Export Council and a member of the Presidential National Commission on Information Society Development.

(Source: www.arivia.co.za)

The dynamic and agile company Integr8 IT, founded in 2001, and focused on the design, deployment, support and maintenance of network infrastructure, has offices in Johannesburg, Cape Town, Durban and representation in Port Elizabeth, East London; across the southern African region, and internationally as well. Lance Fanaroff, managing director of Integr8 IT, says their model is quite different from that of other players in that they will never attempt to sell technology if it is not going to ease a process, streamline a procedure or do something that results in a more efficient activity. They first investigate how a company operates and then use the various technologies to provide the most viable solutions for each individual client's business needs and requirements. The company's service capabilities and lifecycle approach are structured to focus on the needs of a client's project or existing infrastructure at the appropriate point in the life cycle — whether it's design and consulting, integration, operations or maintenance services. Fanaroff believes that companies should view IT expenditure as a long-term investment — one that will not only help them remain competitive but, in the long run, save them money. Companies are tired of having technology products pushed onto them in order to solve business process requirements, and this is where the solutions model is key.

Having established a pattern of organic growth, the company has made a significant investment in the creation and retention of a solid skills base. Integr8 IT employs almost 200 highly skilled full-time specialists. Rob Sussman, joint managing director, says the company only recruits brilliant people who are attracted to working with the best. This approach is focused on transforming intellectual capital, the knowledge that is retained in employees' heads, and converting it into structural capital, which is knowledge retained within the organisation and that can be passed on to new employees. It doesn't go home at night. This is imperative for the accumulation of the organisations experience in its lifetime. They strive to improve their skills, nurture their relationships with customers and treat the accumulation of new experience, processes, systems and policies with the necessary respect, for the key component of any company is its people. In order to capitalise in this market and work towards a common goal, companies need a strong team of dedicated professionals — people who are willing to learn and who are motivated to come up with new ideas.

A key factor in Integr8 IT's success has been its strategic enterprise alliances and partnerships with Microsoft, Citrix, Computer Associates, Cisco, 3Com, Intel, Sun Microsystems and MTN Network Solutions. These partnerships have enabled the company to combine industry-leading products and technologies with their services, aiding them in implementing next generation solutions. Fanaroff believes there is a fortune of opportunity in South Africa and success lies in being driven and hungry enough to take advantage of it. He says there are many aspects of South Africa that are first world, and many that are still third world — and that business opportunities lie in bridging that gap. He thinks IT can play a leading role in this arena.

Integr8 IT has been growing at a phenomenal rate and the next challenge lies in controlling this growth. The IT market is no longer driven by large companies eating up the small but by the quick eating the slow. Fanarof believes that they have been ear-marked as the future giants within the industry.

Integr8 IT has been accredited as the Mid-Market Infrastructure Integrator of the Year for the last two consecutive years, and has been honoured with a position among South Africa's Technology Top 100 Companies. In 2004, Integr8 IT was named Microsoft's Global Small Business Partner of the Year and Security Partner of the Year for Europe, Middle East and Africa (EMEA) at Microsoft's Global Partner Award ceremony held in Toronto, Canada. Fanaroff says Microsoft's recognition of Integr8 IT as the number one international small business partner is an extraordinary feat, especially for a South African company that was born in 2001. He adds that it is a remarkable milestone for the company and a tremendous victory for the country and continent in terms of skills levels, expertise and capability within this increasingly competitive global arena. They are extremely pleased with these awards, which elevate South Africa's capability within the dynamic field of information and communications technology, and reflect very positively on the contribution Integr8 IT continues to make within these key market segments.

In September 2004, Integr8 IT added another coveted title to its growing list of achievements, clinching the prestigious Microsoft Gold Partner of the Year award. Mark Reynolds, group manager, Partner

Development and Marketing, Microsoft South Africa, noted that Integr8 IT has consistently proven itself to be an outstanding business partner providing significant value and consistently outstanding service to their mutual customers and that Microsoft was proud to be associated with Integr8 IT. In the November 2004 African ICT Achievers Awards, which honour and reward excellence in ICT from both a company and individual perspective, Integr8 IT was a finalist in three categories. 'We are delighted to have received this recognition. It is an honour to be nominated, no less as finalists for three categories. Our vision is to continue to be leaders in our field and the African Achiever Awards represents a huge boost forward,' commented Rob Sussman, who the African ICT Achievers Award Chief Information Officer of the Year 2005 for Africa (Private Sector), a very prestigious award. In 2005, Integr8 IT won the Microsoft Network Infrastructure Solutions Award, the Best Customer Experience Award.

Integr8 IT was selected in 2004 as the official information technology partner to a national ICT training and vocational guidance initiative known as the National Centre for Self Knowledge Academy (NCSK). Based in Johannesburg, the NCSK is targeted at historically disadvantaged individuals who want to enter the field of IT/ICT. It is positioned as a nation-building project, funded through government and corporate partnership and collaboration, to provide holistic professional skills development and training for employability and business development of SMMEs for job creation. The service level agreement with Integr8 IT will ensure NCSK has all the necessary IT infrastructure (software and hardware), services and support for its entire national operation — including setup, configuration and maintenance of all equipment and systems. In addition, the comprehensive ICT base will enable full connectivity with sponsors (government, social and corporate) as well as with current and prospective students and eventually form the network between digital villages that will be established in key regions throughout the country.

Fanaroff and Sussman believe the company has a specific role to play in helping to address key education-related issues of affordable, sustainable access to reliable technology, all-round training and skills development. 'We are pleased to be involved with this ongoing project and look forward to laying down the platform for reliable connectivity between digital villages, an exciting and very necessary vehicle for knowledge transfer and practical application of IT skills,' adds Sussman.

(Source: www.integr8it.com)

In pursuing its initial focus, creating geographic information systems, Intermap has reached the point where today the company is acknowledged as a market leader in the customised development of web-based project and programme management, software and support services. Managing director Ross Lewin practised as a consulting engineer prior to establishing Intermap in 1999 (the name 'Intermap' links the words 'Internet' and 'interpretive' with 'mapping'). Having recognised the need for Internet-based geographic information systems, Lewin set out to create an environment in which like-minded IT professionals could develop innovative Internet-based products that not only satisfied a need in the market but also created new opportunities. His vision was to 'break the paradigms' of IT.

Today, a significant aspect of Intermap's business is the eTrack platform, which accounts for over 60 per cent of its business activities. This tool was developed as a platform for business process management' and is based on established workflow principles. eTrack organises the business processes of Intermap's clients in order that optimum business information management systems may be developed and established. Also featuring dominantly is the eMap platform, which is designed to present meaningful displays of spatially located business information together with current information sourced directly from existing business systems, in a real-time environment. New on the market is the metadata management tool, which is used to administer and manage spatial data, providing system administrators and end users with the means to visualise spatial data though a web interface and then to request the use of it.

In addition, Intermap realised that many clients required a 'bundled service' and thus established Application Service Provider, a service run out of the Pietermaritzburg head office and which provides 24/7 technical support and maintenance at the end of a toll-free telephone line. Other products include eTime, a comprehensive time management solution, and Issue Manager, a SMS based event management system. Intermap is a certified Microsoft partner. It was a recipient of an Africa SMME Award for 2003 in the information and communications technology category. The business has grown from four to 30 staff members since 1999 and was acquired by MICROmega Holdings (MMG) in January 2004. Ross Lewin is still managing director. MMG is a listed company on the JSE.

(Source: www.intermap.co.za)

Fanus Nothnagel is the managing director of Massdiscounters, a subsidiary of Mark Lamberti's Massmart Holdings. As of January 2005, Massdiscounters operated 59 Game and 11 Dion stores. Nothnagel says Massdiscounters' strategic decision in 1999 to stay in the city centres while other retailers were abandoning inner city trading has been richly rewarded, with these shops currently showing greater turnover growth than many other stores in the group. The company initially did expect the decay of the central business districts to have a negative impact on performance — which indeed was the case. But the fact that other retailers fled the CBDs eventually counted in favour of the group's trading there. The three CBD Game stores (in Durban's West Street; on the corner of President and Joubert Streets in Johannesburg, and next to the Grand Parade in Cape Town) are now among the fastest growing in its network. The investment of about R500 million in the CBD stores is made up of lease commitments, salaries and wages, and start-up costs.

Nothnagel says it is certainly paying dividends. The CBD stores were essentially established to provide a service to city workers and fringe-of-town residents as well as commuter shoppers. Subsequent sales growth of the three stores has proved this to be the correct strategy. He says the new inner-city phenomenon, whereby office buildings are being converted into residential apartments, should add to the CBD stores' customer base. Game opened another store in September 2004 in Mitchells Plain, Cape Town, and in November 2004 in the Gateway shopping centre north of Durban. A further five stores are planned for South Africa in 2005. The group is also expanding its African operations, with a store opened in Kampala, Uganda, in June 2004; a store in Maputo, Mozambique, in December 2004; and one in Lagos, Nigeria, in November 2005. Game also has stores in Botswana, Namibia, Zambia and Mauritius with future stores planned for Tanzania, Angola and Ghana. Massdiscounters contributed about R6.2 billion to Massmart's annual sales for the fiscal year ended June 2004.

Logistically it is more complicated trading in other African countries. Game will spend US$135 million on operating and stocking its newly opened store in Kampala. Nothnagel says that the store employs up to 160 workers, only three of whom are not Ugandans. The initial investment was around US$15 million on land, buildings, capital costs, the initial stockholding and working capital. Game will spend, over the next ten years, some US$135 million on operating and stocking this store. Ugandan President Yoweri Museveni officially opened the Lugogo Mall, which houses the state-of-the-art new Game discount store set to revolutionise the retail market in Uganda (more than 10,000 customers came on its first day of business and Nothnagel thanked them for their patience and amiable behaviour). Uganda is the first country in which the South African firm has invested in land and buildings for a new store. Economic reforms (including reduced inflation levels), improved infrastructure and domestic security are some of the reasons that attracted Game to Uganda. Nothnagel congratulated President Museveni on having transformed Uganda into an investment-friendly country with investment legislation that is pragmatic, uncomplicated, and free of bureaucratic obstacles. He says additional turnover was among the benefits of expanding into other African countries and that the profitability of stores in other African countries is generally better than in South Africa because of limited competition in these countries, and adds that previously consumers in these countries have had limited general merchandise shopping options and no exposure to aggressively low pricing.

(Source: www.massmart.co.za)

Game Stores is not the only South African retailer seeking opportunities in African countries. In 2005, the Shoprite Group was firmly entrenched as the largest supermarket group on the African continent, with operations comprising 763 stores in 15 African countries with 61,500 employees. In August 2005, The Africa Centre for Investment Analysis presented Shoprite with an Africa Economic Developer Award on behalf of NEPAD. Shoprite invested over US$8 million to build the Lugogo Mall in Kampala, a shopping centre featuring 12,380 square metres of rentable space and 570 fenced-in secure parking bays. It houses the Shoprite supermarket, as well as the Massdiscounters Game store, and 1,700 square metres of line shops, accommodating Uganda's four biggest banks, cellular phone shops, a pharmacy, an optometrist, a coffee shop and a Ugandan craft store. Shoprite CEO Whitey Basson said at the opening of the shopping centre that he was proud to strengthen the group's investment in Uganda following the success of its first supermarket in Kampala. Shoprite's presence had given Ugandan consumers access to a wide range of local and imported products at the lowest prices.

Shoprite was also delighted to be able to create jobs and contribute in a tangible way to the economy of Uganda. The new store employs over 100 Ugandans, with a large percentage of products sold in the store locally sourced. The Shoprite Group procures goods from Uganda's biggest producer of soap powders and oils (Mukwano) to its smallest supplier of honey (Kusoro). To promote local fisheries, the new supermarket also features a fresh fish deli which stocks, amongst other species, Nile perch and Tilapia, sourced from Lake Victoria by local suppliers. A wide selection of alcoholic and non-alcoholic beverages is available in the store as well as a selection of locally produced coffees including Rwenzori Premium Ground Coffee. In 2005, Rwenzori Coffee, which plans to open branded coffee shops in South Africa and Uganda to boost its brand profile, opened its first coffee shop in the new centre. Also doing its bit for the environment, Uganda's Roko Construction Ltd, contracted by Shoprite to build the shopping mall, renovated surrounding areas on Lugogo bypass, on the main route to Uganda's border with Kenya.

The Shoprite group, today a flagship retail operation on the African continent and neighbouring islands, is a company that started as a mere eight-store chain operation with a turnover of about R13 million in the 1980s. From small beginnings the group grew aggressively in the 1990s, with an acquisition trail, and bought out three of the five major supermarket chains in South Africa. The first acquisition was Grand Bazaars, a Western Cape-based operation, followed by the acquisitions of the Checkers group in 1992 and the OK Bazaars group five years later in 1997. Despite doomsayers' gloomy forecasts, these takeovers proved to be enormously profitable, effectively earning the Shoprite Group the number one market share position in the South African retail arena. With the South African market nearing saturation the group ventured into the broader African market, starting to open supermarkets towards the latter part of the 1990s in various African countries. Basson points out that although the African countries are relatively small in GDP terms, they constitute a large untapped consumer market with little threat of competition apart from small-town operators. He explains that Shoprite's decision to enter the African market was based on the fact that the group is well equipped for the Africa continent, not only understanding the market but also being better positioned than most international companies to handle the difficulties of service and logistics specific to Africa.

(Source: Basson interview in *The Wall Street Transcript*, 28 May 2003)

Shoprite established its presence in Uganda by opening its first supermarket in Kampala in December 2000. Later, during the Lugogo Mall negotiations in Uganda with President Yoweri Museveni, Whitey Basson, and Andrew Rugasira (Rwenzori Coffee founder and chairman) attending, a niche market opportunity was recognised. Rugasira was confident of putting a value-added coffee product of international quality on supermarket shelves, and an offer of collaboration from Basson gave Rwenzori Coffee of Uganda access to the South African market. Rugasira points out that it requires a conscious effort with a high level of support from retailers to penetrate shelf space in any new market.

(Source: www.shoprite.co.za)

By 2004, Rugasira's dream of supplying Rwenzori Finest Coffee to South African consumers became a reality. South Africa was potentially a huge market for Rwenzori Coffee, and Basson and Rugasira believed that trade rather than aid was the best way to create economic growth. Rugasira wanted to move Uganda away from its 2004 position as the world's eighth largest exporter of raw coffee to being a major player in the market segment where value-added coffee is sold and traded. Rugasira was also deeply committed to promoting wealth creation for the small scale coffee growers that supply his company.

According to Rugasira, projects such as the export of Rwenzori Finest Coffee to South Africa form an integral part of Uganda's plans for economic diversification and commitment to regional markets. In identifying primary export markets in 2004, Rwenzori Coffee initially focused on South Africa because of the logistical benefits in terms of proximity and existing strategic relationships between Uganda and South Africa. Rugasira felt they could grow in that market and make a significant contribution to the character of coffee consumption. He believed that the time was right to launch a quality African national coffee, and the company looked forward to exploring other market opportunities such as China and Egypt.

Rwenzori Finest Coffee consists of a range of three core products of individually chosen Arabica coffees. According to Rugasira, there had been a considerable increase in the global consumption of ground roast coffee and a clear shift from away instant coffees. The industry had seen the emergence of specialty niche segments where consumers had become more conscious of quality and differentiation in terms of packaging, roasting and presentation. Rugasira believed that Rwenzori Finest Coffee offered a richly aromatic, full-bodied and well balanced blend that would be highly competitive in the existing South African market.

According to Rugasira, the agreement his company signed in 2004 with Shoprite was a tremendous opportunity for Uganda. Rugasira, a graduate of the London School of Economics, was confident that Rwenzori coffee would become a serious contender in the South African market by 2009. They were committed to providing a true value-for-money product and would not compromise on their high standards of quality. They were determined to live up to the opportunity they had been given. The Rwenzori Coffee Company's introduction of their range of premium ground coffees onto the South African market played a significant role in strengthening trade links between South Africa and Uganda.

In July 2005, Andrew Rugasira became the first African supplier to place his range of 'Good African Coffee' on the shelves of a major British supermarket chain; the prestigious Waitrose group, and announced his pioneering company commitment to 'trade not aid'. Rugasira has emphasised that his projects are based on empowerment through trade and are rooted in the African tradition of commitment to the community. Fifty per cent of company profits will be directed into self-sustaining social projects. Rugasira's goal is to address wealth creation rather than poverty reduction. He points out that for centuries Africans have been sharing their resources, and that commitment to their communities represents their unofficial welfare system. Rugasira believes if profit sharing leads to the empowerment of African growers, employees, and shareholders, then this is what needs to be done.

(Source: www.rwenzoricoffee.com)

Cobus Cronjé, a mechanical engineer from the Cape, and managing director of Viböl Marketing International (Pty) Ltd, has re-engineered the technology of exhaust emissions that reduce fuel bills, breakages and downtimes. This is another example of South African ingenuity with global reach, as major truck manufacturers around the world adopt this home-grown innovation.

Viböl Exhaust Vibration Balancer started as the family-owned Exhaust City in Cape Town, building and repairing exhaust systems for cars, 4 X 4s, trucks, and special off-road vehicles. Numerous requests were put by customers looking for a way to replace the standard flexible joint attaching their exhaust systems to their engines. There was nothing on the market, which could be fitted with confidence and dependability. With the demand as it was and the opportunity realised, Exhaust City was transformed to Viböl in 1995 with the patenting of the first ever successful exhaust vibration balancer. Since then Viböl and the exhaust vibration balancer have grown into a successful multinational corporation engineering solutions in Germany, England, Australia and South Africa.

Viböl International is more than the sum of its parts, more than its products. It represents the search for and implementation of quality filled mechanical products. With the refinement of ideas into workable, practical solutions, the company has been able to provide both companies and people with affordable, durable and environmentally friendly alternatives.

Viböl's core philosophy is that things can always improve; not simply the product but also the systems designed to complement and enhance it. Through long hours of research and development, Viböl has benefited from the problems faced and overcome. Talk to any truck owner about his main technical operation problems and most likely the ongoing difficulties encountered with flex joints in trucks between the engine and exhaust system will figure prominently. Flex technology, which dates back to the 1950s, is basically a stainless steel spiral and is known to often crack, leak and break. Sometimes it has to be replaced after only eight months of operation. Now there is a new breakthrough solution, the Viböl exhaust vibration balancer invented by Cronjé. Patented worldwide, the design is fairly simple and is proving to be an extremely cost effective alternative consisting of a male and female section, designed to ensure that a perfect seal is achieved. The taper on the ball (male) fits on a different taper into the female and allows for emission gas to form a second seal. The diesel gas emission is high in carbon, which under heat and pressure turns to graphite — which is the best anti-friction agent — thereby extending the life of the moving parts.

Viböl, the trademark, is derived from 'exhaust vibration balancer', which describes the motion that balances the vibration, torque and road shocks between the engine of the vehicle and the exhaust system. Cronjé points out that vibration caused by diesel engines, in particular, is the major contributing factor to metal fatigue and stress placed on pivotal joints on an exhaust system. When the vehicle is in motion uneven road surfaces and gear changes are further contributors to untimely breakages to the manifold, front pipes and exhaust system. The Viböl has the properties to swivel 17 degrees in any given direction, whereas the flex, spiral and slip joint arrangements presently being used are very limited in their intended application. Cronjé says that the new Viböl design has not only reduced fuel bills, breakage and downtime, but has also increased engine power and durability.

The company has spent in excess of R2.7 million in design and patenting costs alone to establish its product in the major trucking markets of the world. In Europe, MAN ERF has accepted the Viböl as original equipment. MAN South Africa has given the Viböl OE status and Daimler Chrysler (Stuttgart) is presently studying OE approval. Iveco and Nissan South Africa are testing Viböl prototypes for approval, which have been approved in Germany by TUV Automotive. Locally, fleet operators like Autonet, Engen, Tanker Services, Duens, Stellenbosch Farmers Winery and La Farge have given the product their stamp of approval. Cronjé says the aim is now to open up obvious markets like fishing vessels, agriculture, mining and industry even further. On the design boards are also plans for Vibölls for passenger vehicles. The Viböl exhaust vibration balancer won the SABS Design Institute Engineering Award for 2000 and South Africa's Top 300 Companies New Product Award for 2003.

(Source: www.vibol.co.za)

BreatheTex Corporation (Pty) Ltd, based in Port Elizabeth, was established in September 1999 as a result of the successful commercialisation of a lamination technology developed by the Council for Scientific and Industrial Research (CSIR). The company, a joint venture between several local entrepreneurs and a majority black empowerment consortium, includes the CSIR as its technology partner, and Brait Technology & Innovation Fund, Vantage Capital and the Industrial Development Corporation (through the European Investment Bank) as funding partners. Managing Director George Yerolemou says BreatheTex is the only company in Africa, and one of only four companies worldwide, that can deliver high performance laminated waterproof, breathable fabrics that meet the most stringent international specifications for high-tech fabrics.

BreatheTex has modified the latest screen print technology into a highly advanced process for laminating lightweight, breathable membranes to textiles in order to produce state-of-the-art products. These improvements to the technology allow them to laminate a variety of polytetrafluoroethylene (a versatile polymer like teflon) polyester and polyurethane membranes to any type of fabric, foam or other substrate, using various types of adhesives including reactive hot melts. The laminated fabrics are completely waterproof and windproof, resistant to wear and abrasion, and show a high degree of breathability. They allow perspiration in the form of moisture vapour to escape into the atmosphere, thus helping the wearer to remain cool, dry and comfortable. These fabrics are used for specific applications in the military, fire fighting, protective work-wear, sports and leisurewear and medical markets: raincoats, sleeping bags, surgical coats, gloves, trousers, operating theatre covers, curtains and mattress covers.

BreatheTex operates in a niche market where there are few competitors. The market is protected by the large corporations, which have had a monopoly for the past 20 years. BreatheTex has therefore focused on using innovative business strategies to successfully penetrate the market. Since 1999, BreatheTex has achieved: turnover growth from R9.5 million in 2000 to approximately R41 million in 2004; staff growth from nine employees in 2000 to 47 in 2004; winning key tenders in Europe and the Middle East against the three global giants in the industry; and national recognition through 16 awards for export, technology and business excellence. 2004 proved to be the turning point for BreatheTex in this niche market. BreatheTex managed to achieve growth in export sales of 86 per cent and was awarded the second largest contract in the history of the industry worldwide. This was as a result of clear proactive strategies through all areas of their business, including marketing, sales, product development, production and finance. The contract is valued at over R200 million for five years, and the prestige of having beaten the largest company in this industry has provided BreatheTex with instant credibility in Europe. In 2004, BreatheTex was awarded an exclusive licensing agreement from Donaldson Membranes to market their Tetratex (r) polytetrafluoroethylene membranes into the European, Middle Eastern and African market.

BreatheTex is committed to the development of South Africa and the success of the textile industry, providing the local market with access to cutting edge technology and customised world-class products. Yerolemou says that with a global vision of 'providing innovative solutions to our material world', BreatheTex proactively sets out to exploit all available opportunities. The successes of this newly established, progressive business are clearly evident from its export sales achievements, environment management systems and standards accreditations and the various awards the company has received in its first five years of operation.

When the winners of the Africa 2004 SMME Awards were announced in October 2004, enterprises from all over the continent made their mark. The three top enterprises were not only from different corners of the continent, but also from different industries. BreatheTex was the overall winner of the Africa SMME of the Year award, the winner of the regional award for Southern Africa, and the winner of the award for the manufacturing sector.

(Source: www.breathetex.com)

The Bumbo Baby Sitter Seat is an award-winning patented baby seat. While caring for his infant grandson, mechanical engineer Johan Buitendach noticed that babies reach a natural stage where they want to sit up and observe their surroundings, but they lack the physical coordination to do so. So he designed a seat that could comfortably hold and support an infant in any surroundings. He started with a block of polystyrene and an exacto blade. Eight years later Buitendach has a comfortable baby seat for the next crop of grandchildren and a product that is sold in more than 40 countries. The Bumbo provides comfortable support for baby's posture and allows for enhanced interaction between parent and child. This award winning infant chair is manufactured to the highest safety standards from low-density foam material, which makes it lightweight and portable. It is soft and comfortable for the baby, safe, hygienic and non-toxic. The integral outer skin of the material is durable and easy to clean. Bumbos are versatile and can be used safely and conveniently anywhere on any level surface. The Bumbo has been approved by standards bodies around the world.

Buitendach knew that taking an idea from concept to commercial reality is not a walk in the park but his experience of global trade fairs meant he was already familiar with the principles of design and manufacture, intellectual property protection and marketing. He owns and manages Jonibach Patterns & Toolmakers, which specialises in tool making for the motor industry. This established company was able to help fund the start-up — with some help from the department of trade and industry's export arm for international trade fairs. To find the correct formulation for the seat, Buitendach worked with AECI subsidiary Industrial Urethanes, a supplier to the automotive industry. Together they developed the ideal chemical composition for the seat, patenting the product locally and abroad. Agencies and distributors began to show an interest and he hired a colleague, Donald Pillai, to drive global sales.

Then began a global journey in which the company visited mother and baby trade fairs. Buitendach knew that to penetrate the US market he had to produce the seats in higher volumes at lower cost so he geared up his factory at Rosslyn in Pretoria to utilise the full extent of the premises, producing up to 300,000 units a month. In 2004, the Bumbo Baby Sitter Seat was the winner in the economic category for South Africa's T-Systems Age of Innovation & Sustainability Award, which celebrates innovation in the private sector. In 2005, Bumbo was assigned a Vendor from the Target Group USA, and Target had placed a test order for 600 of their stores. Buitendach has other inventions and possible products up his sleeve. However, his priority is to develop the Bumbo markets and the networks that support them. Bumbo was the 2005 winner of the Africa SMME Award for the manufacturing sector.

(Source: Sasha Planting. 'Recognising Brilliant Ideas', *Financial Mail*, 3 September 2004; and www.bumbobabysitter.com)

Like his father and grandfather before him, the late Cornelis Nouwens became a craftsman in carpet making in Tilburg, the wool textile hub of Holland at that time. In the early 1950s he moved to Harrismith, South Africa, in the foothills of the Drakensberg. It was there, in one of the town's old garages, that he established his own carpet factory in 1962. Under his guidance, Nouwens Carpets flourished. In the early years the factory made haircords, woven on an old converted blanket loom. Later, conventional Wilton wire-looms and Axminsters were used to produce carpets from home-spun yarns. Over time, Cornelis Nouwens saw his company develop into an innovative market leader, enjoying a sound reputation for quality and craftsmanship.

Cornelis Nouwens was a craftsman fired with enthusiasm and innovation. Over the years, these qualities have inspired Nouwens to invest in the most up to date equipment and technology, enabling the modern Nouwens craftsmen to produce exceptional products of quality and innovation. Cornelis favoured traditional Wilton looms to weave his pure new wool carpets. Old favourites like Ankara Twist and Kabir spring to mind. Being an open-minded craftsman, Cornelis identified the need to move with the times, introducing synthetics and tufting. However, these modern advances have been introduced without compromising the traditional craftsman's spirit. The love of the art of carpet making, and carpet making skills, allowed Cornelis to reinterpret the traditional beauty of carpets using today's technologies, fibres and systems.

Nouwens has always been a family business and over the years, Cornelis Nouwens had always enjoyed the support of his wife and children, two of whom, Luci and Pieter, have become carpet craftsmen in their own right. In 1990, Cornelis Nouwens handed over the reins to Luci and Pieter. They now jointly own Nouwens Carpets. In 1970, after matriculating, Luci Nouwens began working at Nouwens Carpets, starting from the bottom, under strict supervision of Cornelis. At first, she worked on the factory floor and was involved in basic administration functions. This ensured her a good grounding and thorough foundation of the workings of the company. Pieter Nouwens qualified as a mechanical engineer and started at Nouwens Carpets in March 1980. With an engineering background and exposure to production at all levels, Pieter has planned and managed the commissioning of various systems at the mill to enable Nouwens Carpets to produce leading edge carpet styles. In spite of large and financially strong competitors, the business grew with a strong commitment to quality products. There are also three young Nouwens sons exposed daily to the family tradition of carpet making.

Nouwens Carpets was the first company to develop a commercially viable product from Karakul wool and this was a major breakthrough for the industry. In its early years, only pure new wool products were made at this fully vertical mill, but the 1970s saw the introduction of synthetic fibres. The need for large ongoing capital investment and risk related to commissioning the right plant is a major challenge to a company of this size. If large parts of such projects had not been improvised and built in-house, Nouwens Carpet would not have been able to compete. Today the company houses a state-of-the-art yarn processing and tufting plant, complemented by one of the most modern Axminster systems in the world. It is with such constant updating and commissioning of the latest systems available worldwide that ensures that Nouwens Carpets hold their own internationally.

(Source: www.nouwens.co.za)

Sulzer Pumps launched its new Aya Duma-Duma oil-free air powered drill in 2004. Aya Duma-Duma (Zulu for 'many thunders') has been designed to be robust and durable, with minimal moving parts, and is constructed mainly of stainless steel. Weighing approximately 22 kilograms, it operates with air and uses only water for lubrication. With water lubrication the exhaust water cools the working environment and suppresses dust, leading to improved visibility and faster drilling rates, while the absence of oil eliminates oil vapour inhalation by the operator and contamination of the ore body. This heavy-duty rock mining drill took the honours in the most outstanding technological innovation category at the Technology Top 100 awards in November 2004.

Mike O'Connor, general manager of the hydro mining division at Sulzer Pumps, says the new product was set to be shipped to international markets after a prototype was developed in 2003. 'The water hydraulic drill is a breakthrough in drilling technology in that it significantly reduces the cost of drilling, protects workers and the environment, and out-performs normal drills — there is no oil in the drill, which is likely to make it a hit in developed markets.' O'Connor anticipates huge demand for the drills, which will probably replace existing air-powered and oil-lubricated machines, as well as those that use expensive biodegradable oil. 'We have taken our background and understanding of metals, plastics and engineering and combined this with new technology to produce these new drills. This is a good example of how South African technology can be applied anywhere in the world, and the drills carry an international patent,' he says.

O'Connor has been associated with Sulzer SA Ltd for nine years. Before that he held various senior positions with engineering groups in England and South Africa in the accountancy field. His principal activities ranged from assessing poor company performance and how it could be corrected quickly, to systems implementation from simple accounting systems to full blown manufacturing resource planning systems, and now he is developing and controlling a very successful rock drill business. His philosophy is, 'If you attempt to perform a task, do it to the best of your ability, no half measures. In the workplace, believe in promoting from within, and equipping people with the best tools to do the job.'

(Source: www.sulzer.com)

Jooste Cylinder & Pump Co has developed and manufactured a revolutionary borehole cylinder for wind pumps, hand pumps and power heads. It is revolutionary because of the materials used in its manufacture. Christie Jooste, the owner, who was a drilling contractor before he developed the borehole cylinder, explains that they use materials that last five times longer than traditional materials and as a result their product operates five times more smoothly than traditionally manufactured products.

Pumping water with a wind pump causes difficulties because of the excessive friction in the pumping cylinder caused by leather cup washers that tend to bite into the sides of the cylinder. It was impossible to determine exactly what the delivery of that particular wind pump would be and how much water could be expected under certain wind conditions. There was also breakage in windmill heads, rods and pipes. To eliminate this hazard, Jooste Cylinder and Pump spent considerable time and money on research and testing with an exciting end result — the introduction of the Jooste stainless steel borehole cylinder. By using modern materials like stainless steel, polyurathane and injection moulded polyethelene, a zero friction result has been attained with considerable less power to operate, making the windmill tops for economical water supply.

Christie Jooste developed the Jooste borehole cylinder over a long period of time; finally, in 1967, he started his company. At first he worked with five other directors, but he quickly bought them out. Jooste had to market his products very carefully. Financial restraints prevented mass manufacture. Finance came from any profit made selling the product. This has assisted Jooste in learning what he considered the biggest lesson in business. 'You have to know how to work with money if you are going to be in business.' Jooste always made very sure, for example, that when he purchased something for his business it was worth what he was paying for it. Today the product's success has led to the formulation of a computer program that can produce the correct requirements if the available details are entered. If the pumping depth, the surface lift and distances are noted, the program will tell you what wind pump you need, the size of the cylinder, how much water you can expect and the exact weight required to operate. Jooste's product is revolutionary and won him the Cullinan Design Award in 1993 for good engineering, and the Disa Award for South African design excellence.

Although much money was spent in development, the company has secured its financial position quite well and no further development on a large scale will be necessary. The product can now be marketed on a solid background. More products — check valves, water level control valves, air vessels, force heads, foot valves pipe protectors and rust retainers — have been developed and are more advanced than existing products on the market. In addition to increasing the efficiency of the wind pump as a pumping unit, Jooste Cylinder & Pump has developed affordable stainless steel riser pipes replacing corrodible galvanised steel piping. This can make the unit productive for many years.

Jooste Cylinder & Pump has also produced borehole cylinders for the Namibian market. They export to Botswana as well as Namibia. With the agricultural development of the sub-continent already under way, the demand for such equipment in a desert-encroaching sub-Saharan Africa will undoubtedly increase. South Africa could become a world leader in this field for there is not only the African hinterland and Indian Ocean islands, but also countries with similar physical geographic factors such as Australia, North and South America, China, India and Russia.

Floppy Sprinkler has grabbed the attention of technologists and farmers with its innovative agricultural sprinkler system. Floppy Sprinkler has developed, and patented in 34 countries, a new generation irrigation system called Floppy Sprinkler, a revolutionary new design that has dramatically challenged conventional irrigation systems used over the past 50 years, with water savings of 29 per cent and yield increases of up to 40 per cent. The system was independently tested by the South African Water Research Commission, confirming dramatic water and energy savings compared to conventional irrigation systems.

The Floppy Sprinkler is an original South African product. The sprinkler consists of a plastic nipple on which a silicone tube is mounted. When water passes through it the tube snakes to and fro while slowly rotating through 360 degrees, forming uniform droplets similar to rain drops without any mist formation. Each sprinkler is fitted with a flow controller. The flow controller regulates the flow of water regardless of pressure. The Floppy Sprinkler is installed as a solid set system with variations according to the irrigated crop's cultivation practices. It provides a combination of cost and performance efficiency benefits, not only offering lower water consumption, but it also rendering lower labour, installation and maintenance costs with a dramatic increase in yield, even on rocky or sandy soils.

Managing director Johann Hiemstra explains that the solid set Floppy system can save up to 75 per cent in labour costs — no pipes need to be moved around, making it easier to manage. The system has no moving and wearing parts and therefore requires little or no maintenance. Hiemstra says the Floppy solid set system makes it possible to irrigate more frequently, which eliminates stress conditions. The total root area is irrigated resulting in optimum root development and yields. The popularity of the Floppy Sprinkler irrigation system among farmers is increasing at a staggering rate because the system is such an effective, simple, easy to operate, low maintenance and economical system.

The Floppy Sprinkler system has been successfully installed across the globe and past projects include: Swaziland (Maguga host area, 185 hectares, sugar cane); Swaziland (Big Bend, 75 hectares, sugar cane); Swaziland (His Majesty King Siswati, 35 hectares, sugar cane; Zimbabwe (Tanganda Tea, 35 hectares, tea, coffee); Zimbabwe, (Marondera, 150 hectares, vegetables, flowers); Mozambique (Xinovane, 640 hectares, sugar cane); Mozambique (Frutas Libombos, 110 hectares, bananas); USA (Hawaii, 150 hectares, sugar cane); and Egypt (Armament Authority, 600 hectares, lucerne, corn, wheat). Hiemstra says the Floppy system is ideal for Egyptian conditions, which require an irrigation system that lends itself to extreme environmental conditions and temperatures, is easy to manage, adaptable, flexible and more water efficient than conventional irrigation methods.

Over the years the Floppy Sprinkler has become highly acclaimed and is currently the winner of ten international and national awards.

(Source: www.floppysprinkler.com)

Graham Mackay, chief executive of SABMiller was appointed in 1999. Born in 1949, Mackay was brought up in Swaziland, Natal and Zimbabwe. He graduated from the University of the Witwatersrand in 1972 with a BSc in engineering, and in 1977 he gained a B Com from the University of South Africa (Unisa). He joined South African Breweries, the group's wholly owned South African subsidiary, in 1978 as a systems manager. Mackay held a number of senior positions in SAB including chairman of SAB Ltd. in South Africa and SAB group managing director, before becoming chief executive in March 1999 on the group's relisting as South African Breweries plc on the London Stock Exchange (Johannesburg remains as its secondary listing).

Building on its strength in Asia and Africa, SAB splashed into the US beer market in 2002 by agreeing to acquire Miller Brewing Co. As of 9 July 2002, South African Breweries was renamed SABMiller. SAB agreed with Philip Morris Companies Inc (now known as Altria Group Inc) to acquire Miller for approximately US$5.6 billion in total, including the assumption of US$2 billion of debt, and Altria became a 36 per cent shareholder in SABMiller with 430 million shares of which 24.99 per cent were voting shares. At the time, the buyout made SABMiller, formerly the world's fourth largest brewer by volume, the second largest brewer in the world behind Anheuser-Busch. Miller widened SAB's geographic reach and offered the group a solid distribution network in the US, the opportunity to sell Miller products in growing Asian and eastern European markets, and substantial US dollar earnings.

Mackay says that this was a deal that reshaped the top tier of the global brewing industry. The Miller buyout was a big step in the group's strategy to become a top player in the consolidating beer business. In May 2003, SABMiller bought a majority stake in the family-owned Italian brewer Birra Peroni. The deal added some well-known Italian brands, such as Peroni Nastro Azzurro. Control of the 157-year old Peroni gave SABMiller the number two spot in the Italian beer market.

SABMiller's turnaround programme at Miller is beginning to deliver results, with particular momentum around Miller Lite. Elsewhere, SABMiller has brands that dominate Africa and is among the market leaders in Asia, much of central Europe, and in Central America. In Africa, the group has operations in 29 countries, including 17 through its strategic alliance with Castel, whilst through its joint venture company in China, China Resources Snow Breweries, the group is one of the country's and most profitable brewers. SABMiller has also made investments in India and is now India's second largest brewer. In Europe it has leading positions in Italy, the Czech Republic, Poland, Hungary and Romania, as well as major operations in Russia, Slovakia and the Canary Islands, and in Central America, the group is the largest brewing company in El Salvador and Honduras. The group's international brand portfolio includes Miller Genuine Draft, Nastro

Azzurro and Pilsner Urquell, and it has a strong regional portfolio, including major brands such as Miller Lite in the USA, Castle in southern Africa, Tyskie in Poland, Zolotaya Bochka in Russia, and Snowflake Beer in China.

Mackay's strategy for SABMiller's future development, now that the group is established in the top tier of international brewers, is based on growth over three time horizons. In the short-term the aim is to achieve sustainable growth in earnings by building on existing operations: in the medium-term growth with be achieved through the turnaround programmes at Miller and Peroni, and in the longer term growth will be through the strengthening of its position in China and India, as well as widening the reach of its international brands.

In November 2004, SABMiller confirmed that it would invest R5 billion in South Africa over the next five years, commencing in early 2005. Approximately half of this is in new expansion. The decision was taken as a direct result of SABMiller's confidence in the South African economy and its future prospects. The company has invested some R4 billion in South Africa over the past decade, including the construction of the Ibhayi brewery. SABMiller's share of the South African liquor market increased to just under 60 per cent in 2004, while in the last few years they have added three new beer brands to the market plus two flavoured alcoholic beverages.

This investment will create a number of opportunities for employees and suppliers of the company and, as importantly, will boost SABMiller's impact on the South African economy. While some specialised equipment will be sourced abroad because of proprietary supplier considerations, the company will be taking this opportunity to boost local suppliers and, particularly, seek new black economic empowerment opportunities in procurement. As far as local purchasing is concerned, the intention is to source all civil works, building expansion, brew house expansion, glazing, roofing, sheeting and pipe work locally. SABMiller spent over R700 million with 1,500 black economic empowerment suppliers in the 2004 financial year, a 21 per cent increase over the previous year. A similar percentage increase in black economic empowerment spend was envisaged for the 2005 financial year.

(Source: www.sabmiller.com)

Toyota South Africa started in 1961 when Dr Albert Wessels imported 10 Toyopet Stout pick-ups, and July 2005 marked a very important development in the 44-year history of Toyota South Africa. In July 2005 Toyota SA reached a milestone as a volume exporter of vehicles to Europe and Africa. Although Toyota SA had been the overall leader in terms of sales in the domestic vehicle market for the past 25 years, they had not been a major player in terms of vehicle exports to destinations outside Africa. However, since Toyota Motor Corporation increased its shareholding in Toyota South Africa from 28 per cent to a controlling 75 per cent in 2002, Toyota SA has become more and more an integral member of the Toyota global supply network.

In 2003, Toyota SA started to export outside the African continent for the first time, with regular shipments of Corollas to Australia. July 2005 marked the first shipment of new Hilux to Europe and Africa. Importantly, Toyota SA is the sole supplier to this market of a number of Hilux derivatives. This means Toyota SA has to ensure they meet all Toyota's requirements for global suppliers in terms of volume targets, quality standards and reliability of supply.

Fortunately, Toyota SA's experience with Corolla exports to Australia has proved a valuable training ground for their manufacturing team members, as well as the crucial development of a logistical infrastructure to handle production of a myriad of models. By 2006, Toyota SA will be producing more than 180 variations of Hilux single and double cab models and the sports utility vehicle derivative on one assembly line, so the demands to maintain standards will be immense. However, Johan Van Zyl, CEO and president of Toyota South Africa, has complete faith in his team at the plant in Prospecton to rise up to meet one of the biggest challenges Toyota SA has faced in its 44-year history.

Toyota South Africa will be responsible for the supply of Hilux models to more than 70 countries in

Africa, Europe (including Mediterranean countries), the Indian Ocean Islands and a number of Latin American and Caribbean countries. The initial annualised volume to these markets was 60,000 units. There are many benefits flowing from this export programme, with the local communities in KwaZulu-Natal being major beneficiaries. Importantly, this included job creation, with the attendant flow of money into the local economy. Toyota had created more than 1,100 new jobs in Durban between November 2004 and July 2005, all for production line and logistical support team members.

In addition, Toyota SA is encouraging some of their local suppliers to either relocate existing operations or set up new facilities in the Durban area, while also attracting international suppliers to set up new facilities near the Prospecton plant. For instance, Denso Corporation is involved with joint ventures with Smiths Industries, while Boshoku Corporation of Japan, is investing approximately R280-million in setting up a facility in Umbogintwini to produce seats and door trim panels. Boshoku intends employing 800 people when the plant is fully operational in 2007, with annual sales of R885-million. Van Zyl says, 'This type of development is exactly what is needed for our industry, our region and our country.'

Toyota South Africa, itself has made major investments of almost R3.5-billion from 2000 to 2005. This was kicked off with R1-billion for the launch of the current generation Corolla and RunX in 2002 and now a further R2.4-billion has been invested in the IMV programme. This is made up of R2-billion by Toyota SA itself to prepare for a production capacity of 120,000 IMVs a year by 2007 and R400-million for supplier tooling. In addition, construction of a new, state-of-the-art paint facility, costing a further R1-billion, was underway and scheduled for completion by mid-2006. This new facility will have the capacity for painting 200,000 units a year – 80,000 units a year more than the current facility. It will be a water-based plant, instead of the current solvent-based system, thereby contributing to a cleaner environment.

This whole IMV project has also required significant investments in training. Not only have there been many specialised training courses for large numbers of team members at Toyota SA's plant, but more than a hundred team members, team leaders, group leaders and managers went to the Hilux plant in Thailand for on-the-job experience.

Component exports are another important aspect of growing Toyota SA's business. Catalytic converters and maniverters make up the bulk of these exports, with more than 2.4 million units a year being dispatched to TMC facilities in Europe and South America. Foreign exchange earnings from this operation alone are in excess of R1.5-billion. This makes Toyota SA one of South Africa's biggest exporters of this type of component.

(Source: Address by Dr Johan van Zyl, CEO and president of Toyota South Africa at export ceremony, Durban Harbour, 25 July 2005, and www.toyota.co.za)

Cora's Costumes started in 1987 in Boksburg, with very little capital, a lot of enthusiasm, hard work, willpower and faith. A small opportunity is more than often the beginning of a large enterprise, and Cora's Costumes is no exception. The business has over the years rocketed into the South African and international mascots, fancy dress and walk-a-about character costumes market. Cora's Costumes was the first one-woman business of its kind in the country. Cora Simpson, the founder, had seen the gap in the market for a business that would design, manufacture, sell and rent out character and fancy dress costumes. Cora made it business policy not to reject any job that is too big or too small. She had no formal experience in this field except for helping to renovate old costumes for amateur dramatic societies doing fundraising musical shows for charity. As Cora did not have any business experience, she knew nothing about running a rental company or a business, but she believed in herself and her prayers.

Cora is also focused on the development of people, especially the underprivileged. She has realised how difficult it is to make it in the outside world with no financial backing, no skills and no knowledge. In 2002, she registered a promotional company, Phakamani, for mentoring and advising young entrepreneurs. It is also a character promotions and events company and arranges children's workshops and fantasy parades in shopping centres.

Cora's Costumes was very small at first, situated on the first floor of an old building. From a turnover of R28,000 in the first year, it grew to an annual turnover of more than R3.5 million in 2004. In 2004, Cora had four rental outlets in three cities in South Africa, stocking approximately 60,000 costumes, and was building and renovating some old buildings in Boksburg to start a complete new business. Individually created costumes have been shipped to Denmark, the US, Portugal, Canada, Australia, United Kingdom, Italy, Bahrain, Madagascar, Dubai, Spain, Israel, Kenya and central African countries.

Cora Simpson's sympathy for people less fortunate than herself keeps her involved with them in some way or another. Since 1984, Cora has been determined to develop people, and her commitment to playing a role in the country's social development has frequently been recognised. In 2002, Cora arranged for Radio 702, at her own expense, the hugely successful 'Christmas in July' parade at Gold Reef City, involving over 100 participants and characters, to collect food parcels, blankets and warm clothing for the poor. She initiated the upliftment of the Driefontein squatter camp and organised the cleaning-up projects in the camp. She was involved in the building of a new crèche, as the previous crèche was looted and stripped of all desks and books. Off-cuts of material were given to the women of the squatter camp, and those who were interested were taught to sew. Some of these women are already successful entrepreneurs. Since 1986, Cora's Costumes has been feeding an average of between 30 to 50 hungry and homeless people daily. Cora does not allow any of her staff to show away anyone who knocks on the door and is thirsty, cold or hungry. Cora believes that to be committed you must get involved in helping the local authorities in your city, organisations and people.

In 1986, Cora instituted a development programme for her staff members, who are mostly illiterate and unskilled when they start at Cora's Costumes, by means of opportunity and constant training which is given daily by Cora and her husband. Since 1996, a qualified adult educationist has been coming to Cora's Costumes premises twice a week to teach the entire illiterate staff the skills of reading and writing. Every year the staff have an awards day and are honoured in different categories for their achievements and progress. Every year one member becomes the Gold Star achiever. An example is David Mbewe, who started working for the company in 1988 as a cleaner, and has a standard two certificate. His potential for quality work, and a keen brain, inspired Cora's Costumes to offer him the opportunity to be trained as an artist mould-maker in characters (mascots). He now owns his own house two blocks from Cora's Costumes; for him and his family it is a big change from the squatter camp where they resided before. Other designers have left the services of Cora's Costumes, but still sub-contract to the company, from their private dress designing and dressmaking companies. The 2004 branch manageress, of The Costume Shoppe, near the East Rand Mall, Priscilla Msiza, was employed as an ironing girl when she started in 1987 and had only a standard seven certificate; she has run numerous branches of Cora's Costumes, and in 2004 was also the head liaison person between branches.

There is always communication between staff members and owners. Cora's Costumes does not have a closed door, closed book or closed anything else policy, as it is imperative to get the staff motivated. Cora believes that staff need to know what is going on in the company. Morale is high as everyone feels free to talk about their problems openly.

Cora has also won numerous business awards for the high productivity and high morale maintained in her company. In 1987 and 1990, she was a finalist for the Johannesburgse Afrikaanse Sakevroue entrepreneur of the year award. In 1996, Cora was awarded the entrepreneur of the year in the Eastern Gauteng Area, by the Transitional Local Council. In 2001, Cora was a finalist in the Lebone/SABC 2 women entrepreneur programme and received the South African Woman Role Model award. In 2002, Cora was nominated as one of the 20 finalists in the Shoprite Checkers/SABC 3 Woman of the Year competition and was second in the women entrepreneur category. In 2002, the § chose Cora as one of the three top women entrepreneurs in South Africa. She was one of the recipients of the first Proudly South African Homegrown Awards 2004 SME Winners — Category 'Bridging the Divide' award. The Homegrown Awards were created to showcase the achievements of Proudly South African members and the diverse spectrum of South African companies, large and small, whose dynamism and innovation display a positive contribution to local sustainable growth.

The very first ceremony, held in Johannesburg, was fittingly opened by President Thabo Mbeki whose moving speech focused on the power of the Proudly South African campaign in building a sense of national pride amongst businesses.

(Source: www.proudlysa.co.za)

The 'vuvu' sound, which South African soccer fans love to blow on their horns, has a new note. The Vuvuzela sounds better, is better and is creating jobs through its sale. The Vuvuzela is made by Masincedane Sport, a black-owned South African sports promotions company, an initiative of the South African Breweries Kick-Start Youth Entrepreneurship programme. Masincedane Sport wants to transform the local and international sporting culture by developing South African sports promotional items that will excite fans and contribute to the solidarity culture the way that only sport can. After winning the South African Breweries Kick Start Initiative in 2001 the company received an injection of funds with which to create proper infrastructure. Masincedane then developed a local version of the soccer plastic blow horn, which has been an overwhelming success on the stands.

Neil van Schalkwyk, the director and one of the founders of Masincendane Sport, is a qualified toolmaker by trade. He used his combination of skill in plastics to develop a better quality horn and ensured that Masincedane created a horn with a better sound too. Masincedane works together with vendors who market the vuvuzela at stadiums all over the country and receive a healthy profit on mark-up. Masincedane created the transport infrastructure and set up regional collection points for the vuvuzelas by the vendors. Co-owner and co-founder of the company, Beville Bachman says his company is committed to true empowerment and social upliftment. It is their dream that the vuvuzela becomes the icon of the Soccer World Cup 2010 and that each supporter has one (when England played South Africa in May 2003, some international supporters were buying more than five horns each). In the last three years, Van Schalkwyk says they have sold more than 30,000 vuvuzelas, most of them over the last year and especially since South Africa was awarded the 2010 World Cup. What next? It doesn't stop there. Masincedane's thethazela, a version of a megaphone, began production in 2004.

Set up in 1999 and affiliated to the 15 year old Siyazisiza Trust, the non-profit company KhumbulaZulu Craft was established to help revive traditional art forms and techniques, product development, fair pay and sustainable jobs. Mary Rose, executive director of both organisations, long ago recognised the potential for craft development in terms of job creation. KhumbuluZulu is the trading arm of the Siyazisiza Trust, which is involved with training, job creation and sustainable incomes in rural areas of KwaZulu-Natal and expanded to two other provinces in 2002. Both organisations are highly respected and supported by the business sector and government. They operate at a local level, with a head office of only six staff and a team of 15 highly experienced field staff. The communities are encouraged to self-sufficiency, and assisted, for example, in market gardening or finding retail outlets in the bigger cities for their craftwork. At any one time the trust gives support to some 5,500 people and 250 projects, always with the intention of moving on once the community has become self-reliant.

Khumbulani Craft, as it is now known, has a strategic alliance agreement with Tourvest Holdings, which has led to KhumbulaZulu Craft being made a shareholder in Tourvest's two shops in the international departure hall at the Johannesburg International Airport and a total of 14 shops in the Kruger, Addo and Tsitsikamma national parks. Funds received from dividends are earmarked for traditional craft development. Tiger's Eye, a subsidiary of Tourvest Holdings, buys much of the craft. As a result, Khumbulani Craft is expanding its activities in Mpumalanga and the Eastern Cape. Khumbulani Craft has established a number of other markets for craft workers. The Siyazisiza Trust's field staff is superb, dedicated to their work and great motivators.

Income generating activities include block-making, vegetable gardening, organic fruit production, bee-keeping, candle production, poultry production, net wire production, metal work (production of gutters, mealie meal and flour bins and so on), carpentry, furniture and coffins, mat making, knitting, crop production, hand embroidery and craft production. Training is included in record keeping (including income and expenditure), financial literacy, business training, opening and running bank accounts and savings clubs, bulk buying, committee work (including drawing up constitutions and the establishment of associations especially for the craft workers.

All these ventures have a market in the areas in which they occur and many community associations are now becoming commercial entities in their own right. For example, fresh vegetables are sold to the Ulundi Holiday Inn, to the Schools Nutrition Programme, to ten Boxer Stores in northern KwaZulu-Natal, to local stores in small Zululand towns like Nkandla and Nongoma, and also to some SPAR shops. Poultry is sold to the local communities as are all the products from other activities with the exception of craft work and hand embroidery. In 2002, an organic fruit project was funded from overseas and was aiming at eventual export. This venture, for which the trust held very successful trials, occurred in Maputaland.

Ceramic artists Barbara Jackson and Shirley Fintz, passionate collectors of African beadwork and art, have facilitated a revival of an ancient beading tradition in southern Africa. Together with Mathapelo Ngaka, they made their dream come true. A desire to create employment and empowerment for disadvantaged women in Cape Town has led to the creation of Monkeybiz. Monkeybiz supplies richly coloured glass beads to women in the townships of Cape Town. The 450 women involved in the project are currently producing exquisite hand beaded artworks, each a one-off creation. Each woman is paid for every doll produced and, since they work from home, can look after their families and avoid transport costs.

The beaded artwork is creating sensations wherever it appears, locally and abroad. Monkeybiz is captivating the international arts world with its vibrant, one-of-a-kind pieces. Recent sell-out exhibitions at Sotheby's in London; in the Conran design stores in New York, London, Paris and Tokyo; at The Nancy Hoffman Gallery in New York; and at The Flow Gallery in Notting Hill and Anglo American Plc (both in London), have placed Monkeybiz at the forefront of gaining accolades and recognition for South African craft.

Beadwork in South Africa is about a language: a language of ritual, courtship, oaths, gender, decor, wealth and posterity. Every tribe in South Africa has its own code of beadwork. The remarkable phenomenon of Monkeybiz is not only its commercial success, but also the already established handed down codes of traditional beadwork now being used in exhilarating contemporary styles. Historically, beadwork in a South African context has been the domain of women largely within the Xhosa, Zulu, Ndebele and Sotho Communities. The women are introduced to it directly through their mothers, grandmothers and other women in the community who have a natural aptitude for the craft. Monkeybiz has become a flourishing beading collective, which is now producing arguably the most remarkable, and comprehensive collection of beaded works since the days of Shaka. In November 2005, Monkeybiz received the DO UKCARES HERO AWARD in London, along with Nelson Mandela who received the International Hero Award. Monkeybiz received the award for working on the front-line in Africa and empowering people living with HIV in innovative ways.

(Source: www.monkeybiz.co.za).

Streetwires Artists Collective, a well-known wire art company and social enterprise, creates and markets the very best contemporary wire and beadcraft, blending first world resources with traditional third world craft skills to the benefit of everyone involved. Using the core tenets of upliftment, sustainability and innovation as their guide, they are seeking in Streetwires to create a microcosm of what they are striving for in South Africa — individuals, taking responsibility for their destiny, bringing their diverse skills together and working to build their future.

Started in 2000 with two artists and two marketing coordinators, Streetwires is a socially aware small business that is tackling the problems of unemployment and poverty head on. Focusing on the unique and dynamic genre of wire art, their Proudly South African project is providing the skills training, support and raw materials necessary to enable over 120 formerly unemployed men and women to channel their natural creative energies into this vibrant art form.

Street wire art is a living testimony to the industriousness and creative spirit of their people. Born in the shanty towns and dusty back roads and baptised on the streets, today this genre is a thriving, legitimate and innovative art form in its own right. Using wire, tin, beads and metal as their medium, talented wire artists are able to shape, mould and create. In January 2005, Streetwires was honoured for achievement in proactively embracing the challenges presented by the rainbow nation at the Proudly South African Homegrown Awards 2004, and an SME Winner of the Bridging the Divide Award. In August 2005, the city of Cape Town awarded R268,000 to Streetwires to set up Streetwires Training and Development. The aim of this initiative is to inspire job creation through the development and marketing of original and culturally significant works of art, based largely on the customs, traditions and beliefs of the Xhosa people. Through this investment the city of Cape Town hopes to contribute to economic growth and job creation by partnering with the private sector in skilling people and creating income generation opportunities. This initiative further demonstrates the significance of cultural heritage as a tourism resource.

A marketable range of wire and bead craft has been developed that has already led to employment opportunities for young South Africans. Project goals have been exceeded, with 15 jobs already created and a projection that this will grow to 30 by December 2005 as a direct result of the project, says Anton Ressel, Streetwires co-founder and marketing manager. There are various Xhosa narratives and subjects in the range such as the Nguni cow range and Xhosa Christmas range. The research and development phase has provided a value-added product, an exhibition that creates a rich backdrop for the products and the ranges.

(Source: www.streetwires.co.za)

Carrol Boyes is the internationally-known creator of what she calls 'functional art'. Her sleek pewter, spun aluminium, stainless steel, and cast aluminium shapes can be found in stylish homes from Canada to Norway and from Hong Kong to Australia. Her individual style has captured the hearts of people around the globe. Carrol graduated with a degree in fine arts, having majored in sculpture. She was a teacher for 11 years in Cape Town, after which she resigned in 1989 to pursue her lifelong passion as an artist and designer in silver. She loved the glow of the metal, but silver is very expensive and she wanted to work on a bigger scale. Pewter filled the bill. It's an alloy of copper, tin and antimony and has a usefully low melting point. It is easy to cast and doesn't require heavy industry to work it. Carrol also felt it was rather a neglected metal that needed to be given a new lease of life, instead of being used only for beer tankards.

Carrol explains that she had to be an artist, but soon realised she couldn't make it as a fine artist; her work had to be functional if she was to survive. She reasoned that it's easier for a buyer to justify buying a water pitcher rather than a freestanding sculpture. Her first break came when Peter Visser offered to display some of her pieces in his upmarket decor shop, and soon many buyers were admiring Carrol's functional art. Soon there was a bigger demand for her stuff than she could handle alone. Ex-South Africans living overseas wanted to sell it for her. Sales spread mainly by word of mouth.

Carrol Boyes Functional Art soon became known worldwide as a South African manufacturing company specialising in innovative, contemporary designs for the kitchen and home. With an emphasis on functional art, they produced a variety of distinctive and uniquely South African items that were both useful and beautiful to own. Carrol is the chief executive officer of the company, which designs and manufactures a range of more than 2,000 exclusive lifestyle products and is continually on the look-out to introduce further new and exciting products.

The head office is situated in the Bo-Kaap on the slopes of Signal Hill in Cape Town and commands a stunning view of the sea and of Table Mountain. It is in Cape Town that Carrol and her artistic team create the prototypes for the new designs. When Carrol is satisfied with the results most designs are sent to the company's own manufacturing facility, located near Tzaneen in Limpopo Province. Carrol's father, who is a doctor, had a farm near Tzaneen and when Carrol started producing her functional art he offered her an unused building in which to work. As things progressed, her father and her businessman brother became involved in the factory full time. It is here that the casting and stamping of the metals is done and larger items are assembled. Upon completion, all finished articles are returned to the Cape Town head office where a final quality control check is performed. Once the quality control process has been completed, the final product is packed and shipped to local and international markets.

Carrol employs a large multi-cultural staff which assists with the sales, administrative, accounting, quality control, packaging and dispatch functions in Cape Town, and all aspects of manufacturing in Limpopo Province. Carrol remains dedicated to encouraging local talent. Her passion for South Africa infuses her work and she has been saluted as a South African icon by leading national and international decor and lifestyle magazines. Carrol Boyes Functional Art has grown rapidly from its humble beginnings in 1989, with new customers being attracted globally to stylish and distinctive products.

(Source: www.carrolboyes.co.za and Dave Biggs. 'A functional artist', *Good Taste*, July/August 1999)

Stephen Saad is the group chief executive officer of Aspen Pharmacare Holdings Ltd, a major supplier of branded pharmaceutical and healthcare products, and the leading producer of affordable generic medicines in South Africa. Saad is a founding shareholder of Aspen Healthcare with more than ten years' experience in the pharmaceutical industry. Aspen Healthcare Holdings was formed to develop a pharmaceutical marketing organisation offering a comprehensive branded product range, backed by promotional support to stimulate consumer demand. In its relatively short history, Aspen has obtained a formidable range of products and, through strategic alliances and acquisitions, has secured the manufacturing and marketing of an extensive pipeline of future products.

The consolidated Aspen Pharmacare is headed by a team of entrepreneurs, intent on transforming the company into the largest and most dynamic pharmaceutical house in South Africa. Aspen has stayed firmly on the acquisition trail since listing on the Johannesburg Stock Exchange in 1999, concluding no fewer than seven other deals including the purchase of Columbia Pharmaceuticals and the rights to Apotex and Steifel Labs in South Africa. Aspen Pharmacare has tied strategic knots with global multinationals such as GlaxoSmithKline, Bristol-Myers Squibb, Lilly, and AstraZeneca in order to expand its presence beyond the world of generic medicines. Saad says that the alliances are a thumbs-up from the world's largest pharmaceutical groups, which could lead Aspen to benefit from other strategic alliances. In 2003, GlaxoSmithKline and Bristol-Myers Squibb granted voluntary licences to Aspen Pharmacare to produce generic versions of their ARV drugs in South Africa.

The biggest drawing card for Aspen in the Pharmacare business was the Lennon brand. Lennon products make up Pharmacare's generic division and have been a yardstick of market leadership in the South African pharmaceutical industry for decades. Aspen's management therefore had a great sense of the potential value in Pharmacare when the opportunity to acquire the company arose. The Lennon facility in Port Elizabeth forms part of the manufacturing division and is South Africa's biggest pharmaceutical site producing produces large quantities of generic products including liquids, solids and ointments. The East London facility is Aspen Pharmacare's second manufacturing site and produces penicillin, aerosols, solids, liquids, laxatives and oral contraceptives.

In October 2003, former US President Bill Clinton announced that his foundation had reached an agreement with South Africa's Aspen Pharmacare and three other leading multinational manufacturers on major price reductions for HIV/AIDS drugs in developing countries. The agreement, building on previous price reductions, promised to bring the 2003 annual best rate of US$255 per year (around 70 US cents per day) for antiretroviral therapy to as low as US$140 per year, or just over 38 US cents per person per day. Stephen Saad said that the agreement further endorsed Aspen's quality manufacturing, scientific and development capabilities, placing Aspen in a league with the leading international generic pharmaceutical manufacturers. Aspen has continually stated its commitment to contributing toward the fight against the HIV/AIDS pandemic.

In a dramatic shift in its AIDS policy in November 2004, the South African government said it would undertake the world's largest AIDS treatment programme by providing the expensive and complex AIDS drug regimens free of charge. Aspen has licences to produce almost all of the AIDS drugs South Africa plans to use. In 2004, an independent study found that 38 of 42 generic medicines sold in South Africa are on average cheaper than in Australia, Brazil, Canada, Germany, the Netherlands, the United Kingdom and the United States. Aspen is Africa's largest manufacturer of generic pharmaceutical products.

Stephen Saad was named as the SA winner of the Ernst & Young World Entrepreneur of the Year Awards for 2004/2005. Saad went on to represent South Africa at the global awards ceremony, held in Monte Carlo in May 2005. Previous winners of the South African leg of the World Entrepreneur of the Year Awards are Brian Joffe (Bidvest Group), Patrice Motsepe (ARMgold), Mark Lamberti (Massmart), Zitulele 'KK' Combi (Master Currency), Ivan Epstein (Softline), and Adrian Gore (Discovery Holdings).

(Source: www.aspenpharma.com)

In 1971, Hermann Röthig, a mechanical engineer who had emigrated from Germany to South Africa after World War II, founded a precision/production engineering firm, Table Bay Engineering, in Cape Town. Table Bay Engineering employed skilled German, Austrian, Swiss and British artisans and from the beginning established themselves as a leading manufacturer of precision made components, tools and machines, in areas as diverse as printing, packaging machinery and gearbox manufacture. Strong emphasis was also placed on the training of South African artisans and an in-house apprenticeship programme was established.

In 1985, members of the South African orthopaedic fraternity approached Table Bay Engineering with a view to manufacturing implants for the local market. The demand for these implants grew rapidly and this trend necessitated the establishment of a specialised production facility in 1989, Trauma Surgical Services CC. This family business was initially geared at supplying the South African market exclusively. The first exports ensued a few years later, initiated by Thomas Röthig, the eldest son of the company's founder. In 1992, Röth Medical Components was established in order professionally to manage this fast-growing sector of the business and in 2003, the company was exporting its extensive product range to some 40 countries around the world.

Röth Medical invests in the development and design of new products such as the innovative technological features of the new external fixation systems. Today, Röth Medical seeks to supply affordable orthopaedic implants, devices and instruments to a world market which is increasingly feeling the effects of budgetary constraints, without ever compromising the conviction of its founder and chairman, Herman Röthig, who believed in 'quality without compromise'.

In November 2002, , Röth Medical Components walked away with the Minister of Arts, Culture, Science and Technology's Award for Technology Excellence in a Small Enterprise, at the MTN/Business Day Technology Top 100 Awards, for their world-class design and production of medical devices and orthopaedic implants. Röth Medical Components was cited for its world class machining shop, which achieved international recognition for quality and its outstanding culture of innovation as well as a series of new products in the field of medical implants and external fixators. The company was also the adjudicators' choice as Best Small Enterprise in the Western Cape.

In October 2003, Röth Medical Components was declared the top small business in Africa at the first Africa SMME Awards function held in Johannesburg, South Africa. The aim of the awards is to promote and reward small businesses that strive for excellence in order to be competitive in regional, national and international markets. The businesses that enter are expected to be well established, in good financial shape and enjoy a reputation for quality, integrity and service. Furthermore, they should operate in a socially responsible manner, support community development efforts and create a work environment in which their employees can learn and grow.

According to the panel of judges, Röth Medical Components came out tops in the competition because of the high quality and reputation of its products produced for the medical industry, and because the business is built on solid business principles, and has established itself as a world-leader in orthopaedic niche products.

Röth Medical Components won two important Proudly South African Homegrown Awards in 2005 in the categories product of the year and innovator of the year. The award ceremony was held in Auckland Park, Johannesburg, during January 2005 and the guest of honour was South Africa's president, Thabo Mbeki.

(Source: www.rothmed.co.za; and www.acia.sun.ac.za)

During her July 2005 trip to Cape Town, American First Lady Laura Bush discovered that through a project called Mothers' Creations, women learn how to make arts and crafts to sell in the international market (the making of crafts, is a cultural and traditional practice in Africa). The mothers create beaded accessories — and Laura Bush got a few of them during her visit — such as cellphone holders, bookmarks, purses and belts. What does it mean to earn this money? Laura Bush discovered that 'earning money means self-confidence, as women realise that they have talents that are in demand. Earning money means independence, as women find a way to support themselves and their children. Earning money means security, as women discover that they don't have to remain in an abusive situation because they can be independent.'

(Source: Press Release, Office of the First Lady, 12 July 2005)

The Mothers' Programmes were founded in 2001 by an American doctor, Mitch Besser, a charismatic and energetic man, someone who lives his days to the fullest and is always willing to help or to solve a problem. With his motivation and interpersonal skills, he created the Mothers' Programmes, one of the most successful models for HIV/AIDS peer support in the world. The advocacy work of Mothers' Programmes is spreading. In August 2005, the group had over 80 programmes at 64 sites in five South African provinces, as well as four in Ethiopia and two in Botswana, with 190 mentors who work with as many as 5,000 women each month.

Mothers' Programmes use education and empowerment as tools to prevent mother to child transmission of HIV, support a mother's adherence to medical treatment and reduce the likelihood of AIDS orphans. Located in clinics that offer medical treatment to HIV-positive women, the programmes provide a secure, warm environment where these women can feel safe to share their fears and concerns: fears for the health of their children; fears of disclosure to their partners, friends and family; and the feelings of helplessness engendered by being alone, pregnant and infected with the AIDS virus. Mothers' Programmes is composed of four distinct projects, but they are rapidly evolving to meet the needs of even more people affected and infected by HIV and AIDS by including fathers and by partnering with different countries. Their current projects in South Africa include Mothers-2-Mothers-2-Be (M2M2B), Mothers-2-Mothers (M2M), Mothers-2-Community and Mothers' Creations.

Many of the mothers enrolled in the Mothers' Programmes are the primary financial providers for their extended families. Mothers' Creations was therefore developed to promote economic empowerment by providing mothers enrolled in M2M or M2M2B with a sustainable income. The women are trained by the site coordinator to produce high quality beadwork that is distributed to domestic and international markets. In October, 2004, Mothers' Creations secured work space at the Zenzele Training Centre in Khayelitsha, a township outside Cape Town. As with the other programmes, mothers at the beading centre typically engage in casual conversation over a nutritious meal, ensuring a relaxed and comfortable atmosphere.

When the project first began, Mothers' Creations consisted of a small number of beaders making a select few items. As of July 2005, Mothers' Creations was employing over 100 beaders producing more than 15 products ranging from decorative bra straps to stylish cellphone bags, bracelets, lanyards and condom carrying cases. Since the inception of the project in November 2002, participating beaders had collectively earned over R2 million. Many commercial craft cooperatives don't pay their workers until items are sold but workers for Mothers' Creations are paid in cash by the non-profit organisation as soon as they complete an item. The money has enabled 25 women to purchase homes with the money they have earned.

Christopher Cooper, Staff Reporter of *The Wall Street Journal*, reported in July 2005 that 'the next hot trend in US charity fashion may come from Mothers' Creations. Thanks in part to Robin Smalley, a former Los Angeles television producer who now heads the group's umbrella organisation, Mothers' Creations beads are being catapulted into the international fashion scene.' Smalley arrived in Cape Town from Los Angeles, with her husband and two daughters in August, 2004 and has brought structure and focus to the Mothers' Programmes while overseeing the organisation's rapid domestic and international development.

Mothers' Creations baubles have drawn the attention of a few stars. Sean 'P Diddy' Combs visited the workshop during a 2002 trip to South Africa, while Mothers' Creations website shows Beyonce Knowles rifling through a selection of the beaded accessories. Beyonce and Bono visited Mothers' Creations in 2003. Kenneth Cole discovered Mothers' Creations during a visit in May 2005. Intrigued by the materials, Cole sat on the floor and sketched out a few designs for beaded sandals, which the non-profit organisation says it is now in talks to produce. They had a substantial order to produce lanyards to be distributed to his staff and sold in his US stores during the 2005 Christmas holidays. The Cole contract and the money it will bring in are nice but what really thrills the women is the prospect of seeing their creations displayed on 5th Avenue.

While they previously were only sporadically available in the US, mostly at charity fund-raisers, Mothers' Creations beads now are being adopted by some big companies too. MTV's retail store in Times Square started carrying Mothers' Creations cellphone covers in 2003. Entertainment company Showtime purchased about 1,000 lanyards for a 2005 event, while Church & Dwight's Trojan condoms division commissioned 500 condom carrying cases featuring the brand logo in beads, for guests of the October 2004 SHINE awards. In August 2005, Smalley was in talks with Bono's AIDS awareness organisation.

(Source: Christopher Cooper. 'Beaded lanyards, cellphone cases are stars of charity chic', *The Wall Street Journal*, 15 July 2005)

Dr Besser says that even he couldn't have imagined how far-reaching the Mothers' programmes would become. He is careful, though, to point out that he is just one of many who are working to eliminate HIV in South Africa, and nowhere near the most important, citing Dr Fareed Abdullah, a local health official who set up the first HIV treatment programme there. Dr Abdullah, head of the Western Cape's AIDS programme, says 'the Mothers' Creations and the Mothers-2-Mothers-2-Be (M2M2B) Project harnesses the enormous wellness and economic potential of the poorest of poor women who have the added burden of living with HIV. The sheer humanity of these women who, under the weight of their own infection and the spectre of stigmatisation, find it in their hearts to voluntarily counsel other women, is an exhibition of the strength and moral courage of our species in the face of tragic events created by the AIDS pandemic.'

(Sources: E-mail correspondence with Robin Smalley, Dr Fareed Abdullah, and Dr Mitch Besser; Office of the First Lady 12 July 2005 press release; www.mothersprogrammes.org; Christopher Cooper. 'Beaded lanyards, cellphone cases are stars of charity chic', *The Wall Street Journal*, 15 July 2005; Bettijane Levine. 'By starting an ambitious program in South Africa for HIV-positive mothers, Dr Mitch Besser proves that one person can make a real difference', *Los Angeles Times*, 24 June 2005)

Dr Ernest Darkoh is one of the world's leading authorities on AIDS in Africa. Educated at Harvard and Oxford, Darkoh was born in the US and grew up in Kenya and Tanzania. He was previously a management consultant for McKinsey & Co in New York and South Africa. After launching one of Africa's most successful HIV/AIDS antiretroviral programmes in Botswana, Dr Darkoh turned his attention to South Africa, recruiting two partners (Jeff Butler, chief executive officer and Dr John Sargent, president and chief operating officer) and founding BroadReach Healthcare, a private company that is setting up HIV programmes. Through an innovative international joint venture with South Africa-based Aid for AIDS (AfA), BroadReach offers ARVCare — a comprehensive and turnkey treatment management solution for HIV/AIDS programmes. The venture combines BroadReach's and AfA's respective expertise in the development of public and private sector HIV/AIDS treatment initiatives.

Medscheme's Rodney Cowlin is the Managing Director of AfA and brings extensive experience in the founding, development and ongoing management of the largest HIV/AIDS disease management programme in the world. He has extensive leadership, operations and marketing experience in the sub-Saharan Africa healthcare market. Dr Leon Regensberg is one of the world's leading experts in HIVAIDS disease management. As the Medical Director for AfA, he was involved in creating and developing the programme, which has evolved into the largest treatment programme in Africa — with highly impressive clinical outcomes. He now oversees the quality of care for all enrolled in the programme and is extensively involved in training and assisting doctors with AfA patients.

ARVCare's Africa Remote Centre in Cape Town houses the ARVCare patient and doctor call centres, IT patient databases and electronic medical records, physician specialist panels for difficult case consults, educational material mailing facilities, financial claims office, and is the launching-off point for ARVCare's programme management consultants and social marketing staff. The ARVCare centre is staffed by over 50 expert HIV/AIDS specialist physicians, nurses, pharmacists, patient counsellors, biostatisticians, financial managers and operational consultants. Through the centre ARVCare provides treatment to over 30,000 patients in over 10 countries throughout Africa.

Together, BroadReach and AfA are setting an example for how organisations from across the globe can work together to win the battle against HIV/AIDS. As BroadReach's chairman, Dr Darkoh feels strongly that global health is everybody's business. In 2005, BroadReach was setting up additional HIV programmes in Ethiopia, Haiti and Vietnam, making liberal use of churches and existing AIDS advocacy groups to get treatment to the largest number of people possible. 'It's got scarily good potential,' says Darkoh.

(Source: www.broadreachhealthcare.com; and Jeffrey Kluger and Megin Lindow. 'Efficiency Expert, Ernest Darkoh', *TIME* Magazine, 7 November 2005)

Dr Anna Mokgokong, co-founder and executive chairperson of Community Investment Holdings, and a 2005 finalist for the South African Chapter of the Ernst & Young World Entrepreneur Award, says 'I have achieved success, having started from humble beginnings, but the life I lead is quite skewed towards work. I work long hours, sometimes seven days a week......which is quite an antisocial life!'

Dr Mokgokong was named South Africa's Businesswoman of the Year in 1999, and has been twice selected as one of the 50 Leading Women Entrepreneurs of the World by the Star Group of the United States, in 1998 and again in 2002. Anna is today one of the most confident female entrepreneurs in South Africa. She started from very humble beginnings, and has overcome significant obstacles to build a diversified investment holdings business worth in excess of R1 billion.

Anna was born in Soweto in 1957 and, from a tender age in primary school, traded sandwiches for cash. She acknowledges that she was fortunate in having parents who placed a premium on a good education; her parents moved the family to Swaziland to ensure the children got a better education than what was on offer in South Africa. All six Mokgokong children went on to get degrees. Anna completed her schooling in Manzini, Swaziland. In 1979, she obtained a BSc from the University of Botswana and went on to attend the Medical University of South Africa (Medunsa), where she completed a MB ChB degree in 1984 and won the Best Family Medicine Student Award, the first of the many awards that have marked her path through life. It was during this time that Anna's real entrepreneurial flair came into being.

In 1981, whilst studying medicine, Anna started a business selling handbags and belts to her fellow students and residents at Medunsa. Through a contact in Swaziland, she was given R40,000 worth of stock. The business became a huge success and diversified to include African clothing and curios. The lecturers at medical school did not like the fact that Anna was running a lucrative business whilst studying, and tried to persuade her to drop her business interest and focus on her studies even though she was one of the top performing students at Medunsa. Undeterred, Anna continued with her business and, by the time she completed her medical degree, was able to sell her business for R200,000, using the capital to establish the Hebron Medical Centre in the North West Province. Overcoming significant obstacles, she built the centre from zero into a primary healthcare and baby welfare clinic with over 40,000 patients.

With the advent of the new democracy in South Africa, Anna realised that there were real opportunities in the healthcare arena and she established Malesa Investment Holdings which later became Community Investment Holdings, a 100 per cent black owned investment holding company with investments within the four key areas of healthcare, transport and logistics, power and energy and telecommunications.

As a dynamic and energetic business entrepreneur, Anna is passionate about ensuring that previously disadvantaged South Africans have the opportunity to participate in the broader economy. She believes that while CI Holdings strives to maximise shareholder value, it is companies which promote the wider interests of their stakeholders and of society that have the strongest chance of long-term success.

Four of CI Holdings' divisions have a joint turnover of over R4 billion and this figure is increasing with their development under the CI Holdings umbrella. This development is currently driving participation in other sectors that will extend the focus of CI Holdings over time. With also JSE listed Jasco, a company over which CI Holdings has 51 per cent control, the group operates predominantly in South Africa and sub-Saharan Africa. Anna has played a key role in sculpting the new South Africa and enjoys the trust of both government and industry. Being a 2005 finalist for South Africa's Best Entrepreneur Award is a tribute to Anna's dedication to upliftment and empowerment, and to her stature in business circles both in South Africa and abroad. Anna is a phenomenal entrepreneur, who has contributed greatly to society, especially to the communities within which CI Holdings has a presence.

(Source: www.ey.com; and www.ciholdings.co.za)

The Technology Top 100 Awards Programme is one of the foremost business awards programmes in South Africa, addressing large, medium and small enterprises. For four successive years, the TT100 Awards have recognised adult education specialist Media Works for its innovative use of technology in developing a unique, interactive multimedia computer software programme that is highly complex yet can be operated by an illiterate adult who has received little or no formal education. The result is a more literate and numerate employee, who also has computer skills. Media Works Development Director Dennis Lamberti says the software programmes that they have developed have helped over 120,000 previously illiterate adults, around South Africa, to read and write and develop basic numeracy skills. To have this software recognised by the Technology Top 100 Awards Programme again in November 2005 was very exciting for Lamberti. The Technology Top 100 Awards Programme clearly recognises Media Works' efforts in continuously striving to improve the technology that it offers its clients. In October 2005, Media Works was also the Education, Training and Consulting sector winner of the 2005 Africa SMME Awards.

(Source:www.mediaworks.co.za)

ABC Ulwazi is a NGO dedicated to preserving culture and rebuilding civil society through the medium of community radio. Since 1994, it has been producing educational and developmental radio programmes and providing training for community radio station broadcasters in content and presentation skills as well as other aspects of broadcasting such as marketing and management. It has trained over 800 community radio broadcasters and has provided nearly R4 million in bursaries for the participants. In 2004, ABC Ulwazi produced over 3,000 hours of programming in all 11 official languages on all the most urgent issues of the day that affect civil society: HIV-AIDS, children's rights, women's rights, youth job creation, governance and poverty relief, and reclaimed lost areas of culture such as histories of the many traditional musics of South Africa. It is also dedicated to making the community radio sector sustainable through good management practice in order for it to be *'The Voice of the People'* as the title of the book it published in 2003 proclaims. Increasingly, ABC Ulwazi is fulfilling a consultancy role throughout southern and East Africa, especially in terms of identifying gaps in educational radio production capacity, and then providing remedial training programmes. It is also assisting several regional start-up radio stations with training in basic management and programming techniques. Staff numbers grew from eight in 2000 to 18 full-time members in 2005. ABC Ulwazi also uses part-time and freelance trainers to support the full-time staff. Managing director Professor John van Zyl is the editor of the 2003 handbook *Community Radio: The Voice of the People*. A new book, *A Sense of Belonging: Community Radio and Civil Society*, reflects his belief that community radio is the voice of civil society, developing dialogue within communities and between communities, and creating a public sphere between grassroots organisations and central government. A collaborative project between UNESCO and ABC Ulwazi resulted in a combined book and CD of exemplary educational radio scripts, *Innovative Radio*. ABC Ulwazi was the recipient of the Best African SMME Award in education, training and consulting for 2003.

(Source: www.abculwazi.org.za)

CIDA City Campus is the first virtually free university level institution in South Africa. It is a national solution to open access to higher education for all South Africans, so that a true social and economic democracy can be created. CIDA offers an accredited Bachelor of Business Administration degree. This is a foundation year plus 3-year business degree that also has a strong technology and lifeskills focus, covering over 40 subjects for all students. The degree prepares students for over 50 professions and careers including accountancy, banking, entrepreneurship and leadership. CIDA is one of only 13 private higher education institutions in South Africa offering a business degree. It is situated in central Johannesburg, and in 2005 had over 1,300 students who came from financially disadvantaged backgrounds. Some have achieved high grades and have proven to be leaders in their communities.

The Community and Individual Development Association (CIDA), founded in 1979 by Richard Peycke and others, was one of the first NGOs of its kind to begin work in South Africa's townships. CIDA hopes to help transform South African society and the economy by making education affordable to everyone. The organisation subscribes to the old adage that says if you teach a man to fish, you feed him for life. It was hard work getting the CIDA City Campus project up and running, but CIDA was very passionate about it and had help from corporations, and thought-leaders in the country. CIDA City Campus has been so successful that CIDA has received invitations from around the world to replicate what they've done in Johannesburg. A branch of the campus has already opened in Cape Town.

CIDA City Campus is part-managed by the students, allowing them to learn and get work experience simultaneously, while studying. Students do administrative work, computer maintenance, admissions, marketing, computer training — and are even involved in the canteen. Every one of the students has an important responsibility to help build their local or rural community; they play a practical bridging role between the first world economy and their community's world. There is an African saying that it takes a village to raise a child; CIDA believes it now takes a child to raise a village. Students come to CIDA not as individuals but rather as a representatives of their village. Nelson Mandela's Extranet programme ensures students return home to share the knowledge gained and in this way skills are raised throughout the country. It is wonderful to see how passionate and proud students are to contribute to their own communities and the social and economic development of the nation.

Students have trained 500 hawkers in Johannesburg's city centre in financial literacy and entrepreneurship through the Skills for the City initiative. The hawkers were from markets in the city and their training took place in languages including English, Sotho, Zulu, Xhosa, Shangaan and Tsonga. On completion of the hawkers' training, students managed and ran Entrepreneurs Anonymous meetings, creating a kind of support group where students responded to specific queries and entrepreneurs could share their experiences and support one another. The hawkers show strong entrepreneurial spirit.

CIDA City Campus was founded in 1999 by four extraordinary people, Dr Taddy Blecher, former actuary and management consultant; Thembinkosi Mhlongo; Richard Peycke, systems analyst, former IT manager of a national construction group, and teacher of self-development programs; and Mburu Gitonga, teacher and educationist. In the mid-1990s, these individuals ran projects in black township schools to upgrade levels of education. Pass rates increased dramatically which created the impetus for starting a tertiary education institution. High school students would pass their final year with a great effort, but had no prospects at all.

They were stuck in a poverty spiral with no money for further education and no way of finding work. The decision was taken to develop a model for mass higher education which would develop Africa's future leaders. CIDA and Monitor Company put together a think tank to conceptualise a workable model. CIDA City Campus is the result.

CIDA City Campus started with nothing — no government funding, no student fees and R40,000 worth of debt incurred while working in the townships. In no time it became a virtually free, accredited and registered degree-granting institution with 1,300 students all on tuition scholarships. Students were initially attracted to CIDA through letters sent to school principals across the country encouraging them to send their brightest and best students to a university that did not yet exist. In short, CIDA had nothing behind it but a dream, a purpose, a vision, a phenomenal sense of commitment and an unshakable belief that miracles can, and do, happen. Inspired and driven by a small group of dedicated individuals, CIDA City Campus was born.

Many of the students come from rural areas and townships, and several now also coming from other countries in Africa. By 2008 CIDA expects to have thousands of students at the campus in the centre of Johannesburg. It is believed that CIDA City Campus is a gold mine of an idea in the field of education and skills transfer, and is a pilot project that can be replicated. In 2002 and 2004, Blecher was honoured by the World Economic Forum for his efforts in creating CIDA City Campus and a better world.

American talk show host Oprah Winfrey has donated over one million US dollars to the campus to build a much-needed residence for its students. For two years the Oprah foundation followed CIDA's progress. There was frequent contact and they came out to visit CIDA every year. In December 2003, in a surprise visit to the Johannesburg campus, Oprah presented CIDA directors with the first instalment of R1 million to build an African style residence for the students, for whom accommodation had been a problem for some time as it was insufficient especially for students who came from far away and from financially disadvantaged families. Whilst their education is virtually free, students still need to pay for accommodation, food and transport. In extreme situations students resorted to sleeping on the streets and many have been unable to continue with their studies. Oprah commended students for their display of maturity as well as dignity and urged them to work hard on their studies.

In April 2006, CIDA City Campus was the recipient of a US$1,015,000 (approximately R6,3 million), three-year award from the Skoll Foundation to establish a replication centre which will strengthen the Johannesburg campus as a centralised hub for further expansion. It will also be used to develop a franchise model and build a master's degree programme for CIDA and other graduates to be trained for leadership, teaching and administration for future urban and rural campuses. Dr Taddy Blecher explained, 'We have always wanted to strengthen and expand our campus so it can meet the tremendous need for the social and economic development of the continent. The money will be used initially to create a stronger and more stable educational platform at the Johannesburg campus from where we can replicate. We will however continue working to reach our funding goals for the future sustainability of the campus.' Dr Blecher was presented with the award by Jeff Skoll, the co-founder of eBay and chairman of the Skoll Foundation.

(Source: www.cida.co.za)

At a time when government and the private sector are racing to bridge the digital divide, which threatens to leave millions of African children behind in the technology revolution, Futurekids South Africa is at the forefront of introducing ICT into schools and training teachers in South Africa. Futurekids provides computer skills training, IT integration and curricula to schools and professional educators, currently teaching over 100,000 students locally. The Futurekids approach is to teach the use of the computer as a tool, with the focus, not on the technology, but rather on the subject or learning area — and integrating computer skills into the school curriculum to make learning more exciting. Futurekids is an international franchise company, founded in 1983 by an ex-South African, Peter Markovitz, in the USA. As the world leader in school computer technology training, Futurekids is able to offer a unique product and service to schools at an affordable price. The Futurekids curriculum is taught in 60 countries around the world, and is licensed in 70 countries.

Futurekids International awarded the South African regional franchise to the current owners in June 1994. Futurekids SA also holds the Futurekids rights for Lesotho and Swaziland and has a 50 per cent stake in Futurekids Mauritius. Futurekids Inc twice named Futurekids SA as 'Star Performer', and in 2001 and 2002 Futurekids SA was selected as regional franchiser of the year.

SkillsPro is the development division of the group and the holding company of Futurekids SA. Its shareholders are Trustee Board Investments, Nedbank, management and staff, and BEE Partners. SkillsPro develops all the curricula, course material and assessments for the group.

By 2004, over 430 South African schools had selected Futurekids SA as their partner in developing a dynamic computer technology education and Internet strategy. Futurekids SA occupies the top position for dollar-based turnover in the international group, and has twice been selected as one of the top ICT companies in South Africa by the Corporate Research Foundation. Futurekids SA is involved in actively seeking innovative ways not only to empower people through computer skills training but also to stimulate economic growth in disadvantaged areas and create jobs and opportunities. Futurekids SA has been involved, as a member in two of the private sector consortia, in the Gauteng Online Pilot Project, a provincial government initiative to bring ICT to schools starting with Gauteng province, with the ultimate objective of rolling out to the remainder of the country in the future. Futurekids also promotes the use of its computer centres for adult literacy training and community training. The company sees the biggest challenges as lack of facilities and funding and believes Internet access to be the most critical aspect in helping African children to catch up.

(Source: www.futurekids.co.za)

The Dikhatole Digital Village community project is a unique public-private partnership between ORT (Organisation for Educational Resources and Technological Training), Hewlett-Packard and the South African company MacSteel. Established in 1936, ORT South Africa is a non-profit NGO that specialises in technology education and vocational training. ORT's goal is to assist the very poor community of Dikhatole to develop itself with the help of computer-based training and education. Since the project's inception in January 2002, hundreds have benefited from the project and additional donors, Microsoft and the city and state of Geneva, have since come on board.

Dikhatole, located near Johannesburg, is both a formal and informal settlement which has developed over a number of years. The community has mushroomed from a few hundred people a decade ago to a largely transient population of perhaps as many as 50,000, attracted by the area's proximity to the main industrial heartland of Gauteng. Dikhatole is an extremely poor and marginalised urban community, with very high levels of unemployment and very poor basic service provision. The community comprises many different ethnic and linguistic groups, including those speaking different African languages such as Xhosa, Zulu, and Sotho as well as so-called coloured people, whose first language is Afrikaans, and a small population of Indian South Africans who speak English as their first language. It is unusual in South Africa to find such a racial and linguistic mix of people in a relatively small community such as this. Accommodation in Dikhatole varies from brick houses to tin shacks, often both forms of housing growing up side by side. Shacks can also be seen nestling up against the boundaries of industrial complexes. Roads and service provision are very basic and mostly inadequate. Shacks are built with no roads between them, making access to police and service providers impossible. Young children can be seen playing in dirty water ditches which sometimes have live electricity cables running through them. As the area is industrial, strong smelling emissions from factories and other buildings make up part of the air that is breathed every day by Dikhatole residents. A single primary school in Dikhatole is attended by almost 1,400 children and there are likely to be over 15,000 other children below the age of 15 in the community currently receiving no formal education. There are no high schools nearby for Dikhatole residents; the most popular and cheapest schools are a 45 minute walk away from the township across open land and along a very busy road. One small clinic serves the entire area and is overstretched at the best of times. There are currently no doctors who visit the clinic, so the nurses replace these services as best they can. The ambulance service to the nearest hospital is erratic. Substance abuse, alcoholism and prostitution are considered a great problem in the community and the number of teenage pregnancies, STIs and HIV-AIDS is extremely high. Access to family planning, sexual health services and counselling services are vastly inadequate and in particularly urgent need.

Despite this backdrop of extreme poverty, this unique and diverse community of people has managed to demonstrate a resilience that allows them to get by from day to day. Young people in the community, as well as their parents and elders, show a strong desire to contribute and lead the development of Dikhatole. Community leaders have already emerged to lead initiatives to help youth, clean up the township, start football clubs, run small businesses and form women's groups. The potential for Dikhatole to develop itself is already present in the resourcefulness of its people and the largely untapped possibilities offered by representatives of different sectors to be found in and around Dikhatole. ORT has worked with the community since January 2002 towards increasing the level of employable people (especially young people); increasing the number of people (especially women) running small businesses; enabling more children and teachers to use computers in school to improve their lessons and learning; building the capacity of local government to use computers in the workplace; and building the capacity of the community to lead their own development process.

As of 2004, outputs included 366 young people placed in jobs; 20 young people enrolled in a youth programme, the President's Award; five young people who have set up a coal business as a result of training from Junior Achievers South Africa; four women trained and working on a road tarring project; two women running their own candle business; 80 metropolitan municipality council and social services workers trained in computers in the workplace; and a community management committee established with a terms of reference, wide range of members and partners representing different stakeholders, and a stronger capacity to organise and set up small projects.

Importantly, in trying to achieve these objectives and outputs, additional areas of a more community development nature have been strategically included along the way. For instance, employability skills for young people are strongly linked to more general youth development work that ORT now implements in Dikhatole; and women's training and entrepreneurial activities are linked to training on human rights, conflict resolution and leadership skills, traditional marriages and domestic violence. In addition, the creative partnerships that ORT has developed and maintained with local organisations, businesses, government departments and others has been key to the success of the project. These partnerships are either created directly between ORT and another organisation or by inviting organisations to sit on the CMC. For example, the CEO of the local chamber of commerce and industry is part of the Dikhatole CMC. Getting people into work or self-employed in Dikhatole is extremely challenging. However, so far this project has shown that the key aspects needed to achieve this are based on creative thinking and good partnerships (private, public and other), specific job-related training with extensive follow up and support; broader training which impacts on people's everyday living conditions; and significant efforts to build the capacity of the community to represent different interest groups and plan and implement activities.

(Source: Lucy Hillier. 'Dikhatole Digital Village community project'. E-mail from regional coordinator, World ORT International Cooperation, Southern Africa, 3 November 2004)

BigNews for Growing Business, a publication edited by Barrie Terblanche, was launched in 1996 by Terblanche and a group of young entrepreneurs who were previously involved in various anti-apartheid and adult education organisations during the 1980s and 1990s. They saw the need for an information source that would assist black small business owners to make full use of the opportunities that were becoming available as part of the democratisation of South Africa. The aim was to provide a voice to small business owners and to help them to grow their businesses and create jobs.

BigNews is independent from the large media groups and operates as a small business itself, since, as the launching members believed, you need to practise what you preach. The business proposition was that advertising would provide the revenue for publishing the paper and start-up funds would come from a bank loan. The launching members registered a limited liability company and secured the required start-up loan. The paper's ownership is 68 per cent black (in itself an example of black empowerment in South Africa) and 47 per cent female. The regional pilot, then known as *Big News for Small Business* and launched in the Western Cape, saw a steady growth of readership — the circulation increasing from the initial 20,000 to 30,000 copies monthly. Viability through advertising support was also proven with the Western Cape edition. So successful was the regional free sheet in reaching the black small business community in the Western Cape that by 2001 it had expanded into a regular national publication.

A monthly national edition of *BigNews* is provided for free collection by entrepreneurs at 1,400 distribution points in all nine provinces of South Africa. In Gauteng and the Western Cape provincial supplements provide the opportunity for regional specific editorial content and advertising. Of the 200,000 copies distributed nearly 95 per cent are validated by the Audit Bureau of Circulation certification, which stands at 190,835 (January to June 2002) and on average 4.65 people share each copy (Readership Survey 2001). *BigNews* is the largest business publication in South Africa that reaches more than 850,000 readers every month. In 2003, Barrie Terblanche was announced as the Africa SMME Journalist of the Year for his objective and informed style of writing. In October 2005, *BigNews* journalist Stephen was Africa SMME journalist of the year.

(Source: www.bignews.co.za)

In June 2002, Barrie Terblanche reported that the small business community in South Africa has rapidly expanded since 1995. Estimates of the number of business owners vary from 600,000 to about one million, or 4 per cent of South African adults. If one weighs up the forces working for and against small business development, the forces working for are stronger. A key positive influence has been the political emancipation of the majority in 1994 and the human potential it unlocked. When one asks black small business owners when they started their businesses, the answer is often 1995 or 1996.

Outsourcing by the government, parastatals and corporates is opening up unprecedented opportunities. Government spending is estimated at R120 billion a year. Coupled with this is affirmative procurement by the government. A preference policy exists for all levels of the government and parastatals, according to which previously disadvantaged businesspeople can receive up to 20 points advantage, with 80 points going to the lowest price tendered. Some estimates put the amount of government business that is going to black business as high as 30 per cent — or R40 billion a year. A further impetus is the perception among white employees that career paths are closing in the corporates and they should start their own businesses sooner rather than later. Relatively successful government programmes, including the Khula guarantee scheme and the Competitiveness Fund, have also contributed.

The small business myth and the lack of business management skills in South Africa are among the forces impeding small business development. Added to this is a strong labour movement and the misconception by organisations, including Parliament, that labour costs for small businesses are measured in monetary terms. In fact, they should be measured largely psychologically. The gatvol (had enough, fed up) factor pushes small business owners back into employment.

A further drawback is the enormous need in corporates and the government for black management. The country's most talented black entrepreneurs work for corporates and the state.

The department of trade and industry incentive schemes are poorly marketed. For example, Cape entrepreneur Cobus Cronje made millions with an invention for diesel exhaust systems, but was almost ruined by the cost of international patents. Only afterwards did he and his accountant discover that the government sponsors certain international patents by up to 75 per cent.

(Source: Barrie Terblanche. *Mail and Guardian Online*, 28 June 2002)

The founder and CEO of digital media company Three Blind Mice Communications, Pierre van der Hoven, epitomises the new breed of South African entrepreneurs. He says, 'The key lessons for entrepreneurs in the media industry — or any other industry — are the same. You must have an idea and absolutely believe in it. The key is passion, but don't expect everyone else to share your vision. Many people think entrepreneurship is glamorous. They think it's easy; it's not — 90 per cent of the time it's pure hard work, focus and perseverance.'

Van der Hoven thrives on making start-up enterprises successful. 'Start-ups fail for many reasons: if their strategy is wrong, they lack resources (and spend too much money) etc, but the most common reason is they give up too soon,' he says. A qualified chartered accountant with an MBA, he has extensive media experience. Van der Hoven started his media career at the SABC where he was exposed to virtually every aspect of broadcasting and it was there that he learnt how to think on a grand scale. 'I've been in media all my life, so it's what I do; it's what I know. I've been lucky to have been exposed to many different media disciplines. It's a passion — once you're in the media, it's very difficult to get out and I have no desire to do that,' says Van der Hoven.

After leaving the SABC in the early 1990s, he founded Mopani Media which went on to win a commercial radio licence (Yfm) and the only private free-to-air national TV licence (eTV). Today, Yfm has over 1.8 million listeners, making it the largest regional radio station in South Africa. Van der Hoven is still involved with the Yired group. 'Yfm is undoubtedly the most successful new radio station launched in the history of South African media with an extremely powerful brand that has captured the imagination of its audience. Here's another lesson you learn as an entrepreneur — you've got to believe in people. The right team of people is pivotal to success. We weren't experts in urban black music culture, so we found people who were, and since they weren't business experts we gave them the backing,' he explains.

Van der Hoven's entrepreneurial ventures at Yfm and eTV have been central in providing him with an understanding of South Africa's highly competitive media market. His unique skills, experience and qualifications made him the ideal person to head up Three Blind Mice Communications and it was the challenge of converging different technologies that first captured his imagination. The story of how the mix of technology, capital and business gave rise to this exciting entrepreneurial venture is an inspiring one. When the company launched in 1999 it broke new territory. 'The idea of satellite transmission of visual TV content to plasma screens in highly visible places evolved into a new media solution. The initial challenges were mainly technical and had to do with using satellite technology and having a return path to confirm that the content got there, but we had to do it cost effectively, so we broke the rules,' he recalls.

TBM started as a technology-driven company and then identified gaps in the electronic out-of-home media market. 'We have a fantastic broadcasting model and because of the technology that drives it we can tailor-make content for individual sites from a central location. This is what makes it incredibly powerful,' he explains. Today TBM sells cost effective advertising on more than 1,000 screens around South Africa, including the country's three largest airports. It also operates visual communication networks for corporate clients or government, which are used for business to consumer communication, staff training and communication, and education. Van der Hoven's leadership skills are part and parcel of how he runs businesses. 'It's all about teamwork, respecting other people's points of view, and working together towards a greater vision,' he notes.

Van der Hoven has spoken at various conferences including Adfocus, the African Telecommunications Summit and the Broadband and Convergence Summit, and has appeared on Summit TV's 'The Entrepreneurs' series. He addresses various MBA classes on the subject of entrepreneurship and was recently appointed to the Academic Advisory Board of the Da Vinci Institute for Technology Management. TBM also sponsors various awards including the Age of Innovation and Sustainability Awards, the Technology Top 100 Awards and the National Science and Technology Forum Awards. 'We try to put something back into promoting innovation and entrepreneurship,' he concludes.

In 2005, Van der Hoven was appointed an 'innovation ambassador' by South Africa's minister of public service and administration to champion the cause of sustainable innovation across the country's public and private sectors. The appointment was made at the launch of the call for entries for the Innovation and Sustainability Awards 2005. These awards celebrate the entrepreneurial and creative spirit of South African organisations as a means of adding sustainable value. Van der Hoven was the only individual from the private sector to be recognised as having made a significant contribution to the cause of innovation and he said, 'I am extremely honoured to have been one of the people acknowledged and singled out to act as a role model and to be an inspiration to South Africa's innovators.' Van der Hoven, who thrives on making start-up enterprises successful, truly represents the new breed of entrepreneurs. TBM Communications was a 2005 Finalist for the Africa SMME Awards.

(Source: 2005 press releases issued by TBM Communications: www.tbm.co.za, and August 2005 e-mail correspondence with Pierre van der Hoven)

Chapter 10: South Africa: Investors, Bankers and Exchanges

African markets offer immense investment opportunities and the continent's business landscape has great potential for lucrative returns, yet potential investments are often hindered by the risky nature of Africa's financial infrastructure, coupled with an unpredictable economic backdrop. Nonetheless, access to capital remains critical to fuelling the growth of African markets, both private and public. In this chapter, Jo' Schwenke (managing director of Business Partners Ltd); Ibrahima Diong (manager, SME Solutions Centres); Justin Chinyanta (one of the founders of Loita Capital Partners International); Alan Gordon Stokes (managing director of Equity Africa); (Ron den Besten (who heads up the Aureos Southern Africa Fund); and Cyrille Nkontchou (founder and managing director of LiquidAfrica) share their experiences in making investments and accessing capital in Southern Africa.

Business Partners is South Africa's leading specialised investment group for small and medium enterprises. It is a private equity company at the forefront of entrepreneurial development, with the stated mission of investing capital, skill and knowledge into viable small and medium enterprises. The company offers a wide range of investment, property, venture capital and equity products tailored for SMEs, as well as pre- and post-investment mentorship services. Its focus is on enterprises requiring between R250,000 and R15 million to finance a start-up phase, expansion or development. The financing, enablement and support of SMEs is one of the most significant challenges facing South Africa today and Business Partners is at the forefront of meeting this challenge.

The SME sector is a powerful business force worldwide, with SME entrepreneurs accounting for an international average of 90 per cent of all business owners. SMEs have a vital role to play in the growth and stability of South Africa's economy. Business Partners' focus is on enabling development in this sector and on opening up the opportunities of business to a broad base of entrepreneurs. Business Partners already has an impressive track record and aims to use a marketing-focused approach to build on that foundation.

For the fiscal year ended 31 March 2005, Business Partners invested R660.5 million in 538 entrepreneurial businesses across South Africa (2004: 513 investments to the value of R449 million; 2003: 496 investments to the value of R400 million), facilitating the creation of 7,550 new jobs (2004: 7,400 and 2003: 7,800). Since its inception in 1981, under the stewardship of Anton Rupert, Business Partners has invested R6.55 billion in private equity into emerging new businesses and has directly facilitated the creation of more than 500,000 jobs through its investment and business activities. The company's current investment portfolio stands at R1,066 million. Business Partners is one of the most significant driving forces of entrepreneurial growth in South Africa.

Business Partners operates under the non-executive chairmanship of Johann Rupert and is managed by Jo' Schwenke, managing director since 1996. The objective is to provide tailored investment, management and mentorship products to South Africa's entrepreneurs and to strengthen awareness of the brand across a broad spectrum of target markets and influencers.

Business Partners has a remarkable success rate; about 75 per cent to 80 per cent of the start-ups survive, and about 90 per cent for other deals. Net bad debts written off annually have been running at between 2 per cent and 3 per cent of the investment book. In May 2005, Jo' Schwenke announced an R850 million investment budget for the 2005/2006 financial year, up R250 million on the previous year. The main focus of the new budget is on black economic empowerment in the entrepreneurial sector and on providing better access to investment financing for all entrepreneurs.

'Black economic empowerment (BEE) remains one the highest priorities on the business agenda,' says Jo' Schwenke. 'Only through equitable economic participation can economic growth be assured and, as small and medium enterprises are the power-house of empowerment, job creation and economic growth, we feel BEE is a key focus for us at this time.' This is reflected by the fact that BEE receives the single largest allocation in the budget, with R357 million having been earmarked for investment in entrepreneurs from historically-disadvantaged communities.

'The 2004 SME Survey showed that small and medium enterprises still rate the impact of BEE initiatives on their sector as low,' says Schwenke, 'with only 28 per cent of the 2,919 respondents indicating that these had had any positive impact for them. Business Partners is determined to turn the tide on this trend and to make BEE a reality for independent businesses.' Business Partners invests in black entrepreneurs across all industries and sectors and in all types of businesses, including start-ups, expansions, franchises, management buy-ins, and management buy-outs. A specialist investment fund, the Business Partners Umsobomvu Franchising Fund, also affords young black entrepreneurs aged between 18 and 35 the opportunity of joining the lucrative franchise industry. Participation of black entrepreneurs in the industry more than doubled between 1995 and 2000 and, according to an Institute of Race Relations survey, more than 40 per cent of new franchise outlets opened during the 2001/2002 financial year were black-owned — a clear indication of the BEE potential afforded by the industry.

'It is vital for South Africa's future economic success that we create a new generation of entrepreneurs,' says Schwenke. 'Not only do small and medium enterprises account for 25 per cent of the country's GDP, but they are also one of its most important engines of job creation.' Year-on-year, Business Partners reports that an average of 15 new jobs are created every time the group makes an investment in a new or existing business and government figures show that approximately half of all the people in full-time employment in the country work in small or medium enterprises. By monitoring these trends and by establishing specialist investment funds, Business Partners is at the forefront of real economic empowerment for ordinary South Africans.

The Business Partners budget also aims to create and enable more female entrepreneurs, with R297.5 million budgeted for the 2005/2006 financial year for investment into businesses run and owned by women. The group's female client base is growing steadily and represents a low overall risk profile. Business Partners aims to increase the percentage of women in its client portfolio and to make it easier for women to enter business than ever before. Business Partners has a 'blue sky vision' of enabling more and more women to take up meaningful roles in the business community, to create wealth for themselves, facilitate the creation of new jobs, and contribute in a real way to the growth of the South African economy.

'Approximately 30 per cent of our client base comprises businesses owned and run by women,' says Schwenke, 'and these businesses are spread across all sectors.' Business Partners' female clients own and run construction companies and service stations, supermarkets and clothing factories, hotels and B&Bs, franchises and quantity surveying practices, travel agencies and tour operators, biotechnology labs and medical practices; one even owns a marine fishing fleet and processing plant. 'Our experience has shown that women can take on absolutely anything they set their minds to, are a better business risk than men and have a significantly lower rate of failure,' says Schwenke. 'Women in all business sectors prove themselves to be very good at setting goals and at pursuing them in a focused and innovative way.'

One example is Gail Behr, the proprietor of Crags Clothing in Plettenburg Bay. In 1989, Gail moved down to the coast from Johannesburg and, with the help of Business Partners, purchased a quaint Victorian schoolhouse in the Crags area. There she established a small business manufacturing hand-embroidered bed linen and hand-knitted sweaters. So successful was this enterprise that Gail soon recognised she could grow and develop it by opening a retail outlet. In 1990, she opened her first Homework store in Plettenburg Bay selling a beautiful range of resort-style garments not previously available in the popular holiday town. Homework sold out its summer range before the December season was over and another idea was born — to franchise the retail concept. There are now seven franchised Homework stores along the Cape coast and in Mpumalanga, and the company employs more than 50 people.

'Homework Romantic Resort Clothing' designed and manufactured by Gail Behr uses natural fabrics, imported and carefully selected, making up a mix and match range with coordinated outfits. A new range is prepared each year and each outlet makes its selection in May. The clothes are made up in the quantities ordered and are never repeated; the selection is therefore completely limited and exclusive. Gail's next plan is to enter into the export market with a range of stores called 'Africa's Son'. 'It is this ability to recognise the opportunities inherent in a business — and to seize and develop them — that makes women such successful entrepreneurs,' says Schwenke. 'It also makes them a relatively low investment risk.'

Another example of bold innovation — in a completely different sector — is Valmé Stewart of Swift Micro Laboratories. Swift is a company servicing the food, cosmetics, pharmaceutical and related industries with microbiological testing, hygiene audits, quality management system training and implementation. In September 2000, the Council for Scientific and Industrial Research (CSIR) was moving its focus back to its core objective, research. The microbiology services business area was identified as being in conflict with this objective (it offered a commercial service). A management buy-out by the now managing director, Valmé Stewart, was approved by the CSIR board. With the help of Business Partners and ABSA Bank, Valme Stewart's entrepreneurial success story was born. 'The core focus of our business is service,' says Valmé, 'and that has made all the difference.' Clients trust the quality service and the superior operating procedures at Swift, which is constantly seeking ways to improve its service offering through close personal contact and involvement with client companies.

'According to management guru Tom Peters, this kind of emotional intelligence is another reason women are so successful in the contemporary business environment,' says Schwenke, 'particularly as so many women entrepreneurs work in the services sector, where understanding of and empathy for the customer is paramount.' Business Partners operates in all the country's major sectors and women are strongly represented in all of them, not least in manufacturing.

Elke Herbst, for example, owns and, with her husband Shawn, runs a very successful plastic manufacturing concern in Durban called East Coast Flexibles. Elke had operated a successful plastic flexibles supplies business, and in 1997, with the support of her husband she purchased a plastic film extruder and went into production with plastic bags of various thicknesses and a range of film products. The business was so successful that Shawn joined it full-time and they soon expanded production with the purchase of another extruder. They estimated that, after expansion, capacity would be 45 tons per month. However, through astute marketing, tailored products and old-fashioned hard work, they are now averaging 60 tons per month. They also recognised another opportunity to develop their business and now supply state-of-the-art degradable plastic products using additives purchased under licence from UK-based Symphony Environmental. They obtained this licence in recognition of their dedication to quality, of both product and client service.

'Women entrepreneurs are changing the face of business in South Africa,' concludes Schwenke. 'Not only are they creating wealth for themselves, but they are generating valuable new jobs and fostering overall economic development.'

Business Partners invests in SMEs across all sectors and industries apart from agriculture, with a few accounting for the largest portion of investment exposure and activity. These are manufacturing, travel and tourism, franchising and retailing, leisure, professional services, and marine fishing. This is a definite indicator of the sectors in which visible economic growth is taking place. Schwenke says each sector requires a unique approach. The organisation is configured to meet the specific demands of each, with specialist advisors located in both the investment funds and the property management division. Business Partners knows that entrepreneurs need solutions that offer both investment and added-value services. These are provided through the product and services portfolios of the group's three operating divisions, Business Partners Investments, Business Partners Properties and Business Partners Mentors.

While Business Partners Investments provides a free business planning model for entrepreneurs, free initial consultations for entrepreneurs and extensive due diligence and counselling during the pre-investment phase, the other two divisions provide for the added-value needs of entrepreneurs post-investment. Business Partners Properties provides property broking and management services to meet the site needs of SMEs. In 2005, properties under management represented 670,000 m^2 of lease space and accommodated more than 3,470. Business Partners Mentors provides a range of professional counselling, management consulting, turn-around and sector-specific services for both start-ups and developing businesses. This is done through a base of mentors servicing sectors as diverse as retailing, mining, construction, IT and hospitality. In 2005, 430 professional mentors were available to provide mentorship and consulting services as well as skills transfer.

Business Partners' shareholding demonstrates how broad the base of influencers is and the strength of commitment to entrepreneurial development in South Africa. Shares are held variously by corporate bodies, banks, investment companies, government and individuals, with major shareholders including Firstrand Ltd, Standard Bank Investment Corporation, De Beers Holdings, Anglo South Africa, Billiton SA, ABSA Group, Sanlam, Nedcor, Old Mutual Nominees and Remgro. The Business Partners Employee Share Trust holds 10 per cent of the 178.8 million shares in issue, while government holds 20 per cent through Khula Enterprise Finance Ltd.

Established in 1989 the Business Partners Entrepreneur of the Year competition is open to any clients who have been in business for at least three years. The criteria include both qualitative and quantitative aspects, each accounting for 50 per cent. Qualitative criteria include entrepreneurial and marketing flair as well as realising the opportunity within a particular market segment, and growth in terms of turnover and profit. Owners' equity, employment opportunities and the development of employees' skills as well as community involvement account for the quantitative criteria. The winners clearly demonstrate the necessary inspiration, dedication and drive to deliver the best product and the discipline which leads to business success. Business Partners initiated the competition to give prominence and honour to the entrepreneur with the courage to independently own and operate a small- to medium-sized business. With small and medium enterprises being recognised for their contribution to job creation and economic activity, this competition fulfils that necessary role of identifying and rewarding their collective impact on the country's economic infrastructure.

Protea Service Station, Foodworld and Nika Clothing won the annual Business Partners Entrepreneur of the Year Award competition for 2001. Nika Clothing, manufacturers of a range of children's clothing, won the Blue Sky award and Protea Service Station and Foodworld shared the award for the Lifestyle category. Blue Sky recognises entrepreneurs whose businesses have unlimited potential to grow into the corporates of tomorrow. The Lifestyle category, on the other hand, recognises businesses, particularly franchises, that perform exceptionally well but will probably remain SMEs.

With 11 branches throughout the Western Cape, the Foodworld Group also has a cash and carry division (wholesale/bulk), with six branches trading under the Saveworld brand. The group has successfully differentiated itself through merging family values within a corporate culture. It has developed a niche market in providing basic foodstuffs to customers at the lowest possible price. The Foodworld Group was founded under the leadership of L A Parker, the CEO of the group, with Ilyas Parker and Iqbal Abdurahman. The entrepreneurs have a firm belief that everyone should benefit from Foodworld's success and this is evident in the treatment of their staff and the many social projects supported by the group, which is actively involved in uplifting the communities where their stores are situated.

When George and Maria Negota purchased Protea Service Station in Soweto it was under-performing but through the expert management, hard work and commitment of Maria it was turned into a profitable business. A qualified attorney, George, who has always recognised the advantage of caring for employees and delivering good customer service, is also a director on several company boards. Maria is a trained nurse and also completed a business and a financial management course at the Rand Afrikaans University in 1997 and 1998. She assisted George in managing his other filling station, where she gained experience. She now manages Protea Service Station. Twenty-one well-trained and motivated staff members, all from previously disadvantaged groups, provide assistance. George and Maria believe that customer service is the key to their success and they provide training on a regular basis to ensure service standards are maintained at the highest level. With two other filling stations, George is familiar with the petrol industry and derives much of his support from local motorists and the taxi industry.

Nika Clothing manufacturers a range of children's clothing and is owned by Nina and Donald Brown. In 1987, with a loan of R5,000 from Business Partners, she started Nina Brown Weavers in Stellenbosch, selling cotton carpets in street markets. This loan was used to purchase two weaving machines and the business was started in her garage with eight labourers. In 1989, she also started selling clothes and the Nika children's clothing range was born.

In 1993 she opened her first retail outlet in Somerset Mall and the business started to flourish. She opened her first franchise in Namibia. Nika clothing is now sold countrywide in South Africa in 13 franchised outlets and Nina is planning to add another two soon.

'Nika' was derived from the names Nina and Karin (her sister) and also means 'to give' in Xhosa. The clothing range is sold overseas by agents and is also exported to various countries on a large scale. A full time agent was employed to handle all exports from South Africa. In 1997 Brown obtained another loan from Business Partners to buy a factory in Stellenbosch and now employs about 60 people excluding agents and staff in retail outlets. In September 2000 Brown started a new range of clothing with the label 'Icing', targeted at teenagers. This range is imported from Europe and the East and marketed countrywide through magazines and to retail outlets in the Western Cape. Imports and exports as well as her drive to seek new ideas take Brown on overseas trips as often as every six to eight weeks. Brown believes that in order to stay ahead in the extremely competitive clothing industry, new ideas are a necessity.

The winner of Business Partners' prestigious Entrepreneur of the Year award for 2002 was the Western Cape finalist, Ruwekus Fishing (Pty) Ltd. Recognition was awarded to the fishing group for its entrepreneurship and contribution to the empowerment of the fishing community. Ruwekus Fishing is a partnership entered into by south coast rock lobster fishing rights holders and comprises four main companies, Arniston Fish Processors (Pty) Ltd, Bluefin Fishing Enterprises CC, Cisco Fishing (Pty) Ltd and Imbumba Fishing CC. On behalf of the company, Steve Dondolo, Sabelo Magwaca and Xola Makapela, Andrew Durrheim, Joy Grey and Brian Flanagan received the award. Having its own fully equipped vessel enabled Ruwekus to harvest south coast rock lobster, one of the highest quality coldwater lobsters in the world. The Rigel Brand, produced by the group, is highly sought after by the American market. The vessel has an on-board factory with packing and excellent freezing facilities, ensuring that the lobster is instantly processed and ready for export.

Jo' Schwenke says the story of Ruwekus Fishing, since its inception in 2000, is one which typifies what is good about the 'new' post apartheid South Africa. It contains the ingredients required to ensure success in business, in South Africa and the increasingly smaller globalised world in which South Africans now live. According to Schwenke, four very diverse groups — in terms of race, gender, social and business philosophy and culture — pooled their resources to purchase a fishing vessel so that they could harvest the south coast rock lobster for which they all had rights, since the fishing quotas of individual groups were not sufficient to justify the acquisition of a vessel by each of the groups. The individuals in each of the group set aside their differences, recruited professional management highly experienced in the harvesting, processing and marketing south coast rock lobster, and called in investors with industry-specific knowledge. As the industry specialist investors in small and medium businesses, Business Partners was able both to finance and to structure a deal for the four groups to jointly acquire an expensive fishing boat crewed by 30 people.

The fishing authority, the marine and coastal management branch of the Department of Environmental Affairs and Tourism, has recognised Ruwekus Fishing's status as a beacon of transformation and black economic empowerment in the fishing industry. Ruwekus Fishing applied for and was awarded a 20 per cent increase in its fishing rights when the medium term (four year) rights were issued in 2002. Ruwekus Fishing earns sought-after foreign currency for South Africa, since its product is primarily exported to the USA. Nazeem Martin, executive director and deputy managing director, comments the entrepreneurs associated with Ruwekus Fishing have built up a business worth millions in less than two years. This is a prime example of a business getting off the ground, growing steadily and contributing not only to economic growth but also to the lifestyle enrichment and financial security of the persons who own it.

Schwenke says Business Partners knows from experience that one of the most important factors in the success of small and medium enterprises is the drive and vision of the entrepreneur, and 2002 saw remarkable achievements displayed by all the finalists. The finalists were all exceptional entrepreneurs drawn from a variety of businesses across South Africa. Schwenke concludes that the winners clearly demonstrated

the necessary inspiration, dedication and drive to deliver the best product and the discipline, which leads to business success. The other finalists were:
- Dan Maluleke of Maluleke Supermarket (Pty) Ltd (a group of successful businesses, including four supermarkets and two filling stations);
- Heinz Fischer, CEO and founder of Heinz Fischer Engineering (Pty) Ltd trading as Fischer Profile S.A. (specialises in rollforming, pressings and assemblies for the automotive, building and shelving industries);
- Jan Kruger & Petrus Hoyer of Pusela Easy Meals (Pty) Ltd of Tzaneen (who produce soya-based foods); and
- Sturu Pasiya of SOS Security Services in the Eastern Cape.

Dan Maluleke took his first small steps as entrepreneur when he became a herder of his father's goats. When he was a boy his father gave him the responsibility of ensuring the accuracy of the numbers in the flock, as well as overall care of the goats. Dan says his father was not an easy man to please. From these humble beginnings, Dan Maluleke has established a group of successful businesses, including four supermarkets and two filling stations, and in 2002 he provided employment to 280 in the Gauteng area. Dan Maluleke was born in Wallmanstal north of Pretoria where his father owned a small general dealer business. After matriculating in Makhado (formerly Louis Trichardt), he joined the existing family business and later completed a B Com at the University of Limpopo (formerly University of the North) in 1980. Upon completion of his studies Dan had no intention of becoming a retailer and was looking for a profession that would give him the status which he felt was commensurate with his academic qualification.

Family persuasion and the words of the British author, Lord Macaulay: 'a people which takes no pride in the noble achievements of remote ancestors will never achieve anything to be remembered with pride by remote descendants,' were the turning point for Dan. He took over the full-time responsibility of managing the family business, Maluleke Savemor in Soshanguve. He became the managing director of Maluleke Supermarket Holdings (Pty) Ltd.

In 1983, Dan approached Business Partners for financing to open a Spar franchise. He also needed suitable premises for his business venture to replace the 60m² converted home then serving as the Maluleke family-owned store. During 1984 Dan converted Maluleke Savemor into Maluleke Spar. Loan finance was granted and Business Partners erected a 580m² custom-designed building to accommodate Dan's first Spar franchise in Soshanguve, which operated from the business premises leased from Business Partners. This property was later purchased from Business Partners. The store has been enlarged twice to accommodate the needs and growth of the business. It is now three times the size of the original store and includes a bakery, a butchery, new refrigeration and fresh produce areas. Turnover per square metre has increased dramatically. The successful operation of this business has led to various expansions, such as the opening of Mathambo Spar in Spruitview in 1993, Katlehong Spar in 1997 and Soshanguve Spar in 1999. The Spar group has recognised Maluleke's achievements. In 1996, he was named Retailer of the Year for the Spar Inland Division, and in 1997, he won the coveted national Spar Retailer of the Year award. He presently serves on various regional and national committees within the Spar group.

The business interests were later diversified when Maluleke expanded into the petroleum retail industry. In addition to this, Maluleke has interests in the food distribution company Guild Sibanye and is a director of Umphakati Investments, a property investment company in Katlehong. Management of the business interests displays strong family participation with Maluleke's wife, two sisters and nephew playing an active role in management. His elder brother George, a practising attorney, and younger brother Abel, are co-shareholders. Apart from his business achievements, Maluleke played an active role in various community organisations over the years.

Heinz Fischer Engineering (Pty) Ltd. trading as Fischer Profile S.A., specialises in rollforming, pressings and assemblies for the automotive, building and shelving industries. It is the policy of Fischer Profile S.A. to operate a documented quality management system that complies with the requirements of ISO / TS 16949:2002 (the International Organisation for Standardisation (IOS) Technical Specification (TS), which aligns existing American (QS-9000), German (VDA6.1), French (EAQF), and Italian (AVSQ) automotive quality systems standards within the global automotive industry, with the aim of eliminating the need for multiple certifications to satisfy customer requirements).

Established in Port Elizabeth in 1979, Fischer is regarded as the leading designer and manufacturer of automotive seat slide systems and special purpose machines in South Africa. The company also manufactures window guide- and drip rails, inner door frames, seat backrest hinge assemblies and steel bumper sections. The subcontracted surface treatments including phosphate, e-coating, zinc plating and powder coating comply with current environmental regulations.

CEO and founder Heinz Fischer says, 'Today, while we continually strive to adapt and improve our technology in order to remain at the forefront of manufacturing developments, we are firmly committed to the founding values that have made us a recognised player in the global automotive sourcing market.'

(Source: www.fischerprofile-sa.com).

Sturu Pasiya started his security company, SOS Security Services, in the Eastern Cape with just one guard, in 1997. In 2002, SOS had a staff of 1,200 of whom 90 per cent are trained security personnel. SOS has also set up a registered training company not only to train their own guards but to also provide training for other businesses to ensure higher service levels within the industry. Sturu, a qualified teacher left his teaching career to help his father's ailing cartage business which, at that time, operated with only two trucks. By the time Sturu decided to move on, the fleet consisted of 25 vehicles. His passion for sport led to his establishing his own football club. Today this club, BushBucks, is nationally recognised, with Sturu still at the helm. His knowledge of and contribution to this sport ensured his appointment as a board member of the Professional Soccer league, the South African soccer governing body. His enthusiasm for success however, did not stop there. He identified a business opportunity and, with a partner, opened a panel beating repair shop in Umtata, S&K Panel Beaters, one of the larger, independently owned outlets in the area. It was here that he identified another opportunity, the need for a viable and reliable security company.

SOS, a truly successful black owned and managed security firm has grown from a single control room in Umtata to a company with offices in Durban, Kokstad, Umtata, Lusikisiki, Butterworth, Queenstown, East London and Cape Town. Business Partners played a role in this growth, after Pasiya approached them for funding after landing a huge new contract and needing to acquire additional vehicles, weapons and uniforms. Business Partners invested in Pasiya's business and also helped him with cash flow management. Sturu has big plans and dreams to become the biggest, most successful business in the industry and go for public listing one day. SOS plans include the expansion of electronic security. With the demand for security continuing to grow, and, with the successful track record and peace of mind offered by SOS Security Services, the future for this company looks ever the more favourable.

UKD Marketing, the brainchild of Bengy and Shereen Premraj of Chatsworth, scooped the 2003 Business Partners' Entrepreneur of the Year Award. Bengy and Shereen Premraj embody everything that it means to be an entrepreneur. Bengy started Unique Kitchen Designs in 1980, trading from his brother's garage. With one machine, one employee and initial capital of R500 he started manufacturing custom-made kitchens units. From these early beginnings UKD has grown into a respected mass manufacturer of modular kitchen units and now distributes through furniture chains across southern Africa. Over the years the business has consistently won numerous awards from Ellerines, the furnishers, for best supplier, quality of workmanship, delivery and excellent customer service. The business is run according to Bengy's proven motto: 'Big challenges and hard work are the road to success.' Never daunted by a big challenge, Bengy and Shereen have grown a back-yard business into a thriving enterprise that now employs 130 staff in production and 30 administrative and distribution personnel.

The other finalists in the 2003 Business Partners Entrepreneur of the Year Award were Sally Marengo of KPL Aluminium Die Casting in Gauteng; Celeste Diest of Impala Fishing in Cape Town; Rick van Zijl of

Lalibela Game Reserve in the Eastern Cape; and Vernon and Robert Padayachee of Amarel Labs in Limpopo. Each business has an inspiring and interesting story to tell.

Sally Marengo of KPL Aluminium Die Casting has established a unique aluminium manufacturing and distribution business. It supplies everything from seat belt spindles for the local motor vehicle market, to ball and claw bases for baths in the export market, as well as components used in the armaments industry. From a housewife looking for a viable business opportunity, Marengo has built what started out as a small import business into a thriving manufacturing concern. Marengo started importing bathroom accessories from Italy and used her garage as her sales office. She soon had to face the cold hard world of business when her supplier shipped incomplete sets and she had to improvise by convincing a local toolmaker to manufacture the missing parts. After she discovered that the manufacturer was based in Taiwan, she decided to pay them a visit to understand the manufacturing process better. During her visit she realised that the technology and the manufacturing process could be duplicated in South Africa. Her first step was to convince her husband Giuseppe, a toolmaker by trade, to assist her with making the required moulds. With Sally's never-ending enthusiasm the company quickly grew into a successful business and she managed to obtain some lucrative contracts. Sally Marengo is the sole owner of KPL, a business consists of three adjacent factories measuring 1,500 square metres in total.

Celeste Diest of Impala Fishing has, on the other hand, built on the legacy of her father, a fisherman who founded the business over 50 years ago. Impala Fishing is a pioneer black empowerment company in the fishing industry. Celeste's father, the late Harry Cottle, started in the fishing industry over 50 years ago as a fisherman. Later, he purchased his first vessel and operated it by sub-contracting on behalf of other quota-holders. The company, Impala Fishing, was established in 1994 and has expanded at a phenomenal rate by growing from strength to strength as a result of good leadership and sound management.

Impala Fishing is a fully-fledged black empowerment company. The business has grown through many difficulties and persevered through many adverse business conditions, such as obtaining quotas and financial assistance. However, it has progressed in the fishing industry despite these difficulties. Celeste Diest has also on numerous occasions experienced doubts from many who doubted she was capable of running the company successfully. Impala Fishing now owns a small fishing fleet, operating successfully in both the local and export markets, and dealing mainly in pelagics (pilchards and anchovies), as well as long-line and trawl hake.

Another successful, but very different, enterprise is Lalibela Game Reserve, the pride and joy of founder and owner Rick van Zijl and his wife Sue. Entrepreneur, businessman and visionary are apt descriptions of Rick, who has been instrumental in providing an inflow of much needed foreign capital into the Eastern Cape, where the game reserve is regarded as one of the leading tourist attractions. Lalibela, which caters to photographic tourists, is located off the N2 highway between Port Elizabeth and Grahamstown, and stretches approximately 30km inland. The 7500-hectare reserve spans five ecosystems (valley bushveld, acacia woodland, grassland, fynbos and riverine forest), boasts an impressive diversity of flora and fauna and is one of the busiest in the region.

Lalibela has three luxurious game lodges catering to foreign tourists. The buildings are elevated above natural water pools, allowing game to roam freely nearby. Sundowners are enjoyed on spacious decks or open-air lapas.

Rick and Sue have introduced rhino, lion, buffalo and elephant in establishing a 'big five' game reserve. From a conservation point of view, the goal at Lalibela has been to re-introduce indigenous game that once roamed the Eastern Cape in profusion. Rick and Sue have also increased their staff to 75 and are concentrating on training local people to fill vacant positions. During 2005, Rick has been busy masterminding the expansion of the game reserve and the acquisition of more land, the design and construction of a cultural village and day centre and the building of Lalibela's fourth lodge, Idwala.

Rick came into the wildlife industry through his hunting operation, John X Safaris, which he and Sue founded in 1983, at Merriman in the Great Karoo. A professional hunter, he is also a member of the Professional Hunters Association of South Africa, the International Hunters Association and a life member of Safari Club International. He is an expert on hunting in Southern Africa and has since 1983 successfully guided both local and international sportsmen and women. He is well known overseas, especially in America, and regularly attends shows in the United States, Canada and Europe. John X Safaris caters exclusively for overseas trophy hunters and attracts approximately 260 hunters per season.

Today, Lalibela Game Reserve and John X Safaris are operated as two distinct and separate businesses. It is these kinds of businesses that are at the forefront of strengthening South Africa's international reputation as an eco-tourism destination. Rick is not one to sit around talking about possibilities. He says, 'You can't afford to when you are running one of the most successful game reserves and hunting operations along the 34th parallel of southern Africa.'

Amarel Labs is an excellent example of how to create a successful niche business. It was founded in December 1996 when father-and-son team, Vernon and Robert Padayachee, found that there was a growing need to provide hair care products at an affordable price to the Limpopo province's previously-disadvantaged communities. At its inception in 1997, the sole aim was to manufacture products for other companies, but by the end of 1997 Amarel Labs was approached by many professional ethnic salons to manufacture a product that was of a high quality and affordable. Alvin Padayachee, Amarel's chief marketer, decided to give their products to salons in Limpopo province on a consignment basis. Almost all the salons came back with a positive report and started purchasing. Amarel's range has now gained huge popularity in salons all over Limpopo. Amarel Labs was the Business Partners EOY monthly winner for August 2003 and has previously won the Technology Top 100 Award in 2000 and the Small Enterprise Award in 2002.

'I'm often asked what it is that makes a successful entrepreneur,' says Jo' Schwenke. 'Our experience has shown us that it is the entrepreneurs who have a combination of a unique vision, strong personal drive, a sound business plan and unlimited energy who succeed,' he says. 'Entrepreneurs are very different to the traditional "company man". It is their individualism and hands-on approach that makes the best of them so successful.'

When Dedreich Otto wanted to raise capital to grow his power generator company Megatron, he realised quickly that it would be a tough task as South African banks were nervous about funding small and medium enterprises. Megatron generates about R5 million a month. 'It's difficult, there's no denying that. There are so many opportunities that small businesses can take in South Africa, but the lack of support is a hindrance,' says Otto.

Starting out as a sheet metal company supplying a single client in 1994, Otto's business has since diversified into supplying diesel and petrol electricity generators for standby power, and servicing electrical substations for clients like Anglo American, Eskom, and Siemens. Another principal component of the business is supplying components for distribution boards and electrical panels for motor control centres, all of which the company sources and imports.

All aspirant entrepreneurs should take the lessons that Otto learned along the way to heart:

- Lesson one is that perseverance wins. 'Ultimately, you have to make your own way, and you can't rely on people and institutions,' says Otto.
- Having the appropriate skills is a major challenge: 'One cannot discount the importance of knowing the industry that you want to get into inside out,' says Otto. 'On-the-job training is crucial: academic qualifications mean nothing without experience.' Otto started out by learning the ropes of the engineering trade at GEC (now Alstom), working his way up the ladder.
- Funding is another stumbling block that needs to be overcome: 'When we intended to acquire Marqot (the Siemens metal workshop) in 1994, we approached all the major banks for financial assistance and were turned down. It was at this stage that our relationship with Business Partners commenced,' says Otto.

Today, nine of the Megatron Group's clients are blue-chip companies, and the company now distributes generators to Ghana, Guinea Conakry, Mali, Burkina Faso and Nigeria in West Africa, as well as all of the Southern African Development Community (SADC) states. The company distributes to these countries from Zimbabwe, and is currently setting up another distributorship in Angola.

For these reasons, Business Partners named Otto its entrepreneur of the year in 2004. Otto says that after obtaining funding, Megatron has expanded operations and focused the business. The group has been appointed as distributors of Brazilian MWM diesel engines. 'Business Partners is helping us with funding to import the sets,' says Otto.

The company has grown its staff complement from 20 to 100. Turnover has increased ten-fold from the company's beginnings to its current R5 million a month. Otto also attributes the business's success to family involvement. His accountant son Ryan is now the group's financial director and managing director of three of the group's companies, while Otto's sister Lyn van Staalduinen is an operations director. 'Our relationships are excellent, with all of us working towards a common goal. In fact, we see work as a way of spending time together.' Otto's long-time business associate, Carlos Fidalgo, started Megatron Engineering with him and is now an operations director on the engineering side.

(Source: Ana Monteiro, Ana. 'SME success secrets unveiled', Moneyweb, 18 October 2004)

In 1989, Johnny Parbhoo started his business Labora Shoes with little capital and a single machine, operating from premises shared with another tenant at Business Partners' Chatsworth Factories in Durban. Although highly skilled in the shoe industry, Johnny had no formal business training, and Business Partners encouraged him to enter a training programme for inexperienced entrepreneurs. Business Partners provided start-up premises at an affordable rent. The advice and training Johnny received during the programme stood him in good stead. He was able to dramatically expand his market, and started supplying shoes to large chain stores. Over the years, Labora Shoes has developed from an informal business, initially employing three people to a formal operation, employing well over 75 workers, and a member of the Durban Chamber of Commerce.

Johnny retains his competitive edge by regularly travelling overseas to study the latest shoe trends and styles. Currently, Labora Shoes manufactures up to 2,500 shoes per day. Business Partners' property manager maintains contact with Johnny, offering advice and solutions to problems ranging from his premises to his business operations. Johnny says that without Business Partners they would never have been able to achieve what they have. By providing value adding services, adopting a flexible approach in meeting his business accommodation requirements and displaying a genuine interest in his business, Business Partners' property investments division, has contributed to Labora Shoes' success in a highly competitive industry. Monica Frank, Johnny's daughter and Labora Shoes' financial manager, says that Business Partners offers people an opportunity to recognise their goals and gives them the means to reach them.

(Source: www.businesspartners.co.za)

In 1996, Cecil Shannon formed Cellulose Derivatives (Pty) Ltd to accommodate the management buy-out of Norilose CMC. CMC is the common abbreviation for sodium carboxymethylcellulose, a chemical with many and diverse uses. The technical grades of Norilose CMC are supplied primarily for use in detergent powders and in the recovery of platinum group minerals. Noristan Ltd had closed down the Norilose CMC manufacturing facility during 1995, and Cellulose Derivatives' purchase included the plant, machinery and the trade name. Because markets had been satisfied by imported products, and now had to be regained, limited production with only seven employees resumed intermittently on the Noristan site. Business Partners provided the necessary financial backing by way of a risk partner transaction. In terms of the agreement with Noristan, the factory building on the site had to be vacated by the end of 1997. A piece of land was purchased with Business Partners finance, and production in the new factory started in 1998, with a staff complement of 15. Despite initial problems, 65 per cent of rated output was achieved during the first month of production. Output has further increased by streamlining the process, and production is now higher than anticipated. The new factory has, however, been unable to meet the demand for Norilose CMC from both local and export markets, and plans to extend the factory are well advanced. The company supplies a high quality product and excellent service and was awarded the prestigious Supplier of the Year Award by Lever Ponds, the leading manufacturer of washing powders in South Africa.

(Source: www.businesspartners.co.za)

Vusi Mvelase had been employed in the motor trade for 17 years, dreamed of having his own motor dealership, but was unable to obtain the required funding. He shared his dream with a friend, Pat Magubane, who already had a supermarket in Hammarsdale, KwaZulu-Natal. Pat realised the potential of Vusi's idea and they decided to start the project together. Topcars is the first black-owned used car dealership in the Durban central business district. Obtaining finance from financial institutions proved to be extremely difficult as the risk element seemed to be too high. The motor trade has been experiencing numerous problems; stocks, which traditionally appreciated in value, have been depreciating in recent years, and there is also the problem of high theft levels. Vusi and Pat approached Business Partners for start-up funds and initial stock requirements in 1998. Business Partners wanted to help them realise their dream of establishing this business and rendered value adding services by convincing Petronet to upgrade the premises to suit the dealership, becoming involved in negotiations for a favourable lease and sourcing a reputable auditing firm with knowledge of the motor industry. Pat says that Business Partners demonstrated entrepreneurial spirit and brought them to where they are today. Topcars is one of the city's busiest dealerships, and Vusi and Pat are now considering opening branches in Empangeni, Umtata and Pinetown.

(Source: www.businesspartners.co.za)

Simon Boikanyo was born in 1954 in Oukasie just outside Brits in North West province, and is the sole owner of Boikanyo's Funeral Home. He took the plunge and started his business in 1988 after having worked in the undertaking industry for over ten years. He saw the need in the black business community for such a service and decided to start his own business, taking a loan of R50,000 from Business Partners to service the Letlhabile area near Brits. Simon was one of the chosen few asked to render service at the funerals of the late Oliver Tambo, bearing testimony to the esteem in which he is held. Simon says that when running a funeral home one must be honest and must have a heart as well. When he started his undertaking business, there was an old age home close by and whenever one of the occupants died, they were given a pauper's funeral. He couldn't let that go on, couldn't allow mothers and fathers to be buried in such an undignified fashion. He therefore volunteered his services free of charge. Luckily, he received payback he didn't expect. People in the community heard that he was providing this service and rewarded him by supporting his business.

It's amazing what the power of good service and word of mouth can do. The esteem in which the community held him grew and he established himself firmly in the area. But Simon is not just heart; he is also a very astute businessman who certainly knows a thing or two about marketing. He realised that he had to give people reason to choose his service above anyone else's and therefore decided to invest a little more to provide something special which would draw clients. That something was imported vehicles. He got the idea after visiting America to see how they conduct funerals, and he was impressed. He decided to try and achieve the same standards in South Africa, importing a number of vehicles over a period of time, and it worked. He believes people use his service because they feel special when they come to him. Simon now has a total of 90 vehicles, 40 of which are imports. To further market his business he maintains close ties with the community by often addressing groups of people on the merits of joint burial policies. Many form themselves into societies and join these schemes, which are mutually beneficial to both the community and his business. He repaid his first loan before the term expired and took a second loan. In 1992 he bought the premises from which he started operating and has now expanded his business by opening branch offices in other parts of North West province.

(Source: www.businesspartners.co.za)

When Malcolm Craig, founder of Robberg Seafoods, arrived with his suitcase and fishing rod in Plettenberg Bay in 1970 for a holiday, he never thought he would one day head up one of the leading fishing and fish processing companies in the region. First he started a small fish and chips shop in Plettenberg Bay, and caught fish himself to supply his shop. As many other fishermen from the community took over the supply side later, Malcolm saw the opportunity to harness their expertise to build a bigger fishing venture and to help community fishermen set up a market for their catches.

Robberg Seafoods was established in 1979 in Plettenberg Bay as a small retail fish operation. Since then it has expanded considerably into fishing, processing, retail and wholesale distribution as well as the export of squid and line caught hake. This has made a sizeable contribution to the local economy, as well as providing valuable foreign exchange to the country. The company began operations in 1979 with one ski boat and agreements with two private boats for the supply of squid and other fish species.

In 1980, recognizing the potential for squid, the company was involved in pioneering the fledgling export squid industry. A small loan from Viskor, a government department in the fishing industry (later incorporated with Business Partners) helped in the early eighties to set up a small fish processing factory. The processing plant grew from the outset and Blaine Dodds, a former navy man and then skipper on a fishing boat, joined the business as a partner in 1983.

In 1983 operations were relocated to larger industrial premises. This enabled the partners to pack and freeze squid for the export market, as well as carry on their normal wholesale and retail operations. Fishing capacity developed steadily with further acquisitions and upgrading of the fleet. Today their fleet comprises one sea freeze squid vessel and four 13-metre ice vessels licensed for line fish and squid, plus another nine privately owned ice vessels that supply them. They also have a large offloading vessel with a 3-ton carrying capacity, which they use to offload their catches on a daily basis to ensure the best quality for the export market. Their factory has been granted EC approval and is listed as establishment F4 on the EC list of approved factories.

The partners' philosophy has always been to endeavour to provide permanent jobs for the local community although owing to the seasonal nature of line fishing this has been difficult. Even so, they have enjoyed an exceptionally good record of labour relations, with no staff turnover for at least nine years. In fact many of their original staff are still with them today. This has been due to a good working relationship between management and staff in which ability and performance are the criteria for advancement. In house training has provided the partners with an excellent management team who have been promoted through the ranks. Their style of management is one of engendering team spirit in which all workers are valuable participants.

Craig and Dodds are proud to note that their minimum wage is on par with the big fishing companies. They work a 45 hour week, provide four weeks paid leave, a thirteenth check and a provident fund. This has been in place for the last five years thereby making Robberg a forerunner in complying with, and even exceeding, the minimum requirements of the new labour relations act. As far as the partners are aware, they are the only line fishing company that has managed to achieve this goal.

Due to the seasonal nature of squid fishing it was the partners' utilisation of hand line caught hake, between squid seasons, that enabled them to provide permanent employment for their factory staff and the fishermen manning their vessels. As records show, Robberg was the only fishing company in South Africa utilising and developing this particular fishery. Because they were traditionally losing money on hake catches and because of the abundance of cheaper trawled hake, they were forced to look into other markets for superior quality line-caught fish. According to the SABS, in 1991, Robberg Seafoods became the first company in South Africa to export fresh hake to the more lucrative European market, thereby initiating what has now become a major export industry.

Even then they realised the need for increased productivity, to make the line-caught hake fishery more viable, and the idea of long lining for hake was broached. This eventually led to many meetings with the Department of Sea Fisheries, and a two day workshop at Stellenbosch University, which evolved into the three year South African longline experiment. Robberg Seafoods was involved in the experiment from the beginning and was initially the only inshore component of the experiment to successfully catch its allocation. Thy not only initiated the line-caught hake export industry, but also caught and processed substantial quantities of squid before the squid industry was officially recognised. Robberg Seafoods has firmly established itself as an innovative and resourceful member of the South African fishing industry.

With no harbour in Plettenberg Bay, Robberg Seafoods contributed largely with innovative management to key scientific, logistic and socioeconomic information on fishing in the area that impacted favourably on the growth of the industry. Off-loading of catches is still done under difficult circumstances using smaller craft, but this does not prevent the town from building a strong reputation as a leading supplier of fresh hake to European markets. Robberg Seafoods exports to Spain, Portugal, France and the United Kingdom.

Robberg Seafoods started out as, and still is, a company that empowers its employees and community whenever possible. With assistance from Business Partners the company has established three independent fishing companies with four current and two former employees now the new business owners. In turn, these owners have also empowered their employees who work on board their respective vessels. In total, employees have a 51 per cent equity stake in the respective fishing companies.

Craig says that by transferring skills and knowledge, jobs are created and with empowerment of people from the industry in business, the growth of the fishing industry is ensured. The next step in their empowerment and transformation program, is the formation of Plettenberg Bay Fish Processors. This comprises a new purpose-built SABS registered factory where staff and transformed fishing companies will be the majority shareholders. Talks have started with Business Partners to finance this venture. Craig and Dodds are optimistic of future prospects in the industry. Fishermen are reputed to be survivors. The partners are confident that the industry and its people will manage the industry to benefit all.

(Source: www.businesspartners.co.za)

Rubber Rollers had its beginnings in Pinetown in 1971, starting off as a small company, recovering rollers for the printing industry. Since then the company has expanded through a merger with Capital Rollers in 1997 and, under the ownership and management of executive chairman Tony Hesp and managing director Harold Chouler, has grown into the largest roll coverer in Africa. The company has factories in four major centres in South Africa as well as Zimbabwe and Kenya. The company is structured into five manufacturing divisions, four of which are strategically located to service a broad client base, whilst the other is centralised in KwaZulu-Natal to supply manufactured rubber compounds, and to provide technical support and product development. The company's factories are ISO 9001 accredited and are designed to supply specialised and standard roll coverings to a number of industries. The major industries serviced are paper, steel, aluminium, print, textile, metal decorating and packaging.

The vision of the company is to become the preferred supplier of roll coverings in Africa and to provide customers with exceptional quality and service excellence, thus ensuring the future of the company. The company's commitment and meticulous attention to detail, tested by regular audits, ensures its ability to compete with the best. The experienced sales and customer service staff, supported by export agents, are able to service wide-ranging customers' needs.

In 1999 the shareholders took a strategic decision to own premises at their various factory sites, and approached Business Partners for financial assistance. A loan was approved by Business Partners to purchase the property from which the Cape Town division was operating and in the next year further finance was granted to purchase the properties from which the Pietermaritzburg and Wadeville divisions had been operating.

Rubber Rollers believes in giving its customers personalised service and attention, which has earned it an excellent reputation in the industry. Manufacturing methods are continuously reviewed to improve efficiency. Rubber Rollers continually focuses on marketing itself in an attempt to further increase its share of both the local and international markets. The portfolio manager of Business Partners, describes Rubber

Rollers as an excellent client which, through high levels of integrity, professionalism and commitment has emerged as industry leader.

(Source: www.businesspartners.co.za)

In July 1989, two young people took over the management of the Toyota dealership in Belfast, Mpumalanga province. Today, Plato Motors/Belfast Toyota is one of the top dealerships in South Africa, winning every conceivable award year after year, from the 'top customer service provider' to 'most vehicles sold'. If there was an award for personnel loyalty, they would probably have won that as well, as they boast what must be one of the lowest personnel turnover rates in the country. Liset Kotze and her husband Gerhard confirm that they and their staff remain committed to their dedication to excellence in customer service. To this end they expanded their operations in 2000 to include a larger, totally modernised forecourt and a 24-hour La Boutique. Business Partners Ltd. provided the funding for the project, which is already showing positive returns.

In 2001, Business Partners Ltd. and SANLAM chose Liset Kotze and her husband Gerhard as the entrepreneurs of the month from among many top contenders in Mpumalanga. Their total dedication to the business, successful participation management style and involvement in the community made them the obvious choice. Needless to say their commitment to excellence is clearly reflected in the profitability of the business. Business Partners Ltd and SANLAM were proud to honour successful entrepreneurs such as Liset and Gerhard Kotze for their achievements. In July 2002, Liset and Gerhard opened a new Landini and McCormick franchise in Belfast, selling and servicing tractors, and they are doing very well.

(Source: www.businesspartners.co.za)

Under ownership of Alex and Jabu Shazi, Umlazi Plaza Butchery is a household name synonymous with well priced best quality meat. In 1991, Alex and Jabu Shazi acquired Umlazi Plaza Butchery at V section in Umlazi. This was the beginning of their success story. From the profits of this butchery, Alex Shazi acquired a second in J section. Together these butcheries traded successfully and Shazi embarked on an expansion drive, acquiring butcheries in Isipingo, Alice Street (central Durban), Congella (King Edward Butchery), Isipingo Rail and Clairwood. The success of his butcheries comes from buying quality meat at best prices and then passing these discounts onto customers.

A proud yet humble Alex Shazi paid tribute to the woman behind his business empire, the soft spoken Jabu, co-owner of the Shazi group of butcheries. Being named Business Partners' Regional Entrepreneur of the Year 2004, made him a very happy man. 'All my life, I have struggled. I started off selling fruit and vegetables on the streets of Umlazi to pay for my schooling,' he recalled, 'but the words of my mother always inspired me. She used to say, "There are two ways. Find the other way."' It was this philosophy that inspired him to reach greater heights. Today, Shazi maintains that his greatest achievement is building two churches, one in Umlazi and the other in Kwa Vulindlela and he gives credit for his success to God. He also pointed out, however, that there were still too many obstacles facing emerging black entrepreneurs today, and he exhorted banks and large corporates to give small and medium enterprises a chance at proving themselves in business.

(Source: http://ushauncut.co.za and www.businesspartners.co.za)

Naseem and Ashraf and their father, Abdool Kathrada, who own and run Cool Ideas 24 (Pty) Ltd, the Levi's franchise in the Western Cape, were selected as finalists in the much sought-after award for the Business Partners Entrepreneur of the Year 2004. In 2001, Levi's sold off their retail stores to individuals, and the Kathrada family was the franchisee awarded rights in the Western Cape. Ashraf owned the Levi store in Canal Walk when the franchisee opportunity for the Western Cape arose. Subsequently, the family took over five Levi's stores and opened three new stores within two years, currently running seven stores: V&A Waterfront, Tygervalley, Canal Walk, Cavendish Square and shops in Kenilworth and Kuilsriver. The brothers are assisted by their wives and their father, who has 40 years retail experience. The Katharadas grew up in a family with a retail background, owning various clothing concerns, working on the shop floor, assisting with administration and purchasing decisions. Both brothers studied (Naseem has an MBA) and compliment each other well with experience and expertise.

Land Mobility Technologies (LMT) is a private South African-based company situated in the Persequor Techno Park, Pretoria. The company specialises in the design, development, simulation, testing and manufacturing of automotive and mechanical systems, sub-systems and components.

LMT offers automotive, mechanical, electrical and logistic engineering services and products in the commercial and military fields to local and international clients. Its team of highly qualified and experienced engineers provides independent and objective engineering services. These services and products include design and development (through LMT Consulting), manufacturing (through LMT Products) and logistic support (through LMT Logistics).

Business and turnover has doubled every year since LMT's inception in 1997. Exports to Europe and the Middle East amounted to more than 70 per cent of turnover in 2004. LMT is allied with major European suppliers as South African engineering partners for key army vehicle acquisition programmes. The South African army's future infantry combat vehicle will be supplied by a consortium involving Patria of Finland, Patria's part-owner, EADS (European Aeronautic, Defence and Space Company), Denel, BAE Systems OMC and Land Mobility Technologies (LMT). The vehicle the group will supply is Patria's 8x8 armoured modular vehicle (AMV), as redesigned for southern African conditions by LMT.

(Source: www.lmt.co.za and www.businesspartners.co.za)

Coastal Bricks is the brainchild of Jacque Bellingham who, in the early 1990s, saw the opportunity to supply high-quality, durable and affordable cement maxi blocks for low-cost housing developments in the Eastern Cape. So strong was the demand for his new product that, at one stage, his production line ran on a 24-hour cycle for a full year. After expanding to accommodate this demand, he later added cement pavers to his range and a contract to supply cement building products to the Coega Development Corporation consolidated his company's market position. In 2005, Coastal Bricks' range included custom-purpose cement blocks and pre-cast cement flooring and walling, all of which are SABS 1029 approved. Jacque Bellingham was Business Partners' Entrepreneur of the Year Award for 2005. As always, competition for the award was stiff, with companies from across the country vying for the title. The five finalists, apart from Coastal Bricks, included Kulucrete South Coast (Pty) Ltd, Dyer Island Cruises (Pty) Ltd, Long Run Labels cc, and M&M Hiring cc.

'I'm often asked what it is that makes a successful entrepreneur,' says Jo' Schwenke, 'Our experience as a company is that the successful entrepreneurs are those who have a combination of unique vision, personal drive, solid management capabilities and, of course, a good business plan. These are the qualities we look for in our award winners — and the qualities which we believe separate the leaders from the pack.'

(Source: Business Partners Media Release, 17 November 2005)

KuluCrete Concrete Products is a large-scale manufacturer of bricks, blocks, roof tiles, paving bricks, and Loffelstein retaining blocks, and is located on the Umzimkulu River near Port Shepstone. For decades, KuluCrete has harnessed the natural resources of the mighty Umzimkulu River Valley to the benefit of the region, which includes not only the sprawling south coast but also a significant segment of KwaZulu-Natal and the bordering regions of the Eastern Cape. Contributing to the company's success has been a core of dedicated employees who have distinguished themselves in the challenging task of turning sand, stone and cement into a large range of innovative building products.

KuluCrete's brick and block works is capable of manufacturing 100,000 bricks or 30,000 concrete blocks daily. Additionally, the separate tile works can turn out up to 9,000 roof tiles daily. These facilities enable the company to compete for the most demanding building materials tenders in the region. PMSA VB45 automatic brick and block making technology enhances KuluCrete quality in several ways; the computerised system guides the batching process to provide a consistent ingredient mix; the use of super cement and the compaction inherent in the PMSA system allows KuluCrete to produce a block which is 25 per cent to 30 per cent lighter than typical concrete blocks.

KuluCrete paving bricks are made to the size, shape and strength requirements of the South African Bureau of Standards. Quality ingredients and the PMSA system have been instrumental in earning SABS approval and in the production of paving bricks capable of a long service, giving strong and attractive underfoot support. KuluCrete interlocking pavers offer even greater load-bearing strength.

KuluCrete employs the vortex hydro concrete roof tile manufacturing system. This advanced technology is used to make SABS approved roof tiles competitively and in quantity. For the landscaping sector of the market, KuluCrete manufactures the distinguished Loffelstëin retaining blocks under licence to Infraset. Another factor in KuluCrete's success has been a large fleet of heavy-duty delivery trucks which is largely maintained in the factory's own workshops. KuluCrete uses only 100 per cent pure 'super cement', regularly collected from the Durban cement factory in the company's own sealed cement tanker truck.

Expansion is the keyword these days at KuluCrete. Managing director Gerrard Stott says that in recent years the company's products have played a major role in the construction of much needed low-cost housing in southern KwaZulu-Natal and the Eastern Cape. 'Supplying these housing projects has taken most of our production capacity and in order to do a better job of meeting the needs of local contractors we've built a new brick and block-making production line which will increase our output by more than 30 per cent,' says Mr Stott, who is also a civil engineer.

Interacting with newly developing communities has proven to be an interesting and sometimes challenging experience. 'In some cases we have supplied cement blocks to communities where the people, rather than contractors, are building their own homes. We have undertaken to provide our products to many emerging communities across a large geographical region and it has required a lot of dedication from our factory and supervisory staff.'

To keep pace, KuluCrete has purchased new equipment, added new trucks to its heavy-duty delivery fleet, beefed up security with a 16 camera CCTV system and expanded its office building. Factory manager Stephan Pretorius says, 'Our new production line gives us more than increased output capacity. With a more sophisticated input system, we can more easily innovate. We look forward to enhancing the features of our paving brick range and adding more design options.' The new production facility will result in employment for up to 30 local personnel.

(Source: http://www.kulucrete.co.za)

Dyer Island Cruises is a socially responsible company that contributes proceeds from its cruises to benefit conservation, education, marine research and local community development projects, so while guests are having a great time discovering the ecosystem they are also helping to protect it and improve the quality of life of people who live in it. The boat, Whale Whisperer, was the first boat in South Africa to be designed specifically for whale watching. It is extremely comfortable and spacious, with an onboard toilet, observation deck, PA system and even a hydrophone! Whale Whisperer is 11.5m long, can take up to 24 passengers and complies with all the safety regulations set out by the marine authorities. The trained marine guides are qualified biologists and conservationists and provide commentary about the marine life during the trip. Dyer Island Cruises has worked with many photographers and film crews. The boat has a raised photo deck where the view is incredible.

Dyer Island Cruises operates from Gansbaai, near Hermanus in the Western Cape. Businessman and skipper, Wilfred Chivell, grew up in the area and has been a spear fisherman and wreck diver since 1985. He took part in gruelling offshore boat races in the early 1990s. He has a long relationship with conservation and has worked with the South African Cultural History Museum, Maritime Museum and South African Museum in Cape Town and the Shipwreck Museum in Bredasdorp. Wilfred has a vast amount of knowledge and is very familiar with the Dyer Island area. He has worked with top marine wildlife photographers as well as scientists specialising in whales, dolphins, seals and seabirds and has visited the Prince Edward Islands as a member of the bird team, to do counts on penguin and albatross colonies. Yvonne Kamp is a qualified nature conservationist and marine guide, who has been guiding whale watching tours since 2001. Dyer Island Cruises works very closely with CapeNature, particularly with regard to Dyer Island, where Yvonne and Wilfred assisted an international team with the tagging of Cape fur seals.

All cruises depart from Kleinbaai harbour near Gansbaai. Dyer Island is located 8 km from shore and is completely protected for the conservation of its many resident bird species, including African penguins. Adjacent to Dyer Island is Geyser Rock, home to a 60,000-strong Cape fur seal colony. The channel of water between Dyer Island and Geyser Rock is the renowned Shark Alley. This channel is part of the Whale Whisperer's voyage. On their whale watching and Dyer Island trips guests also see great white sharks, Bryde's whales, humpback whales, southern giant petrels, Cape gannets, and dolphins.

(Source: www.WhaleWatchSouthAfrica.com)

M&M Hiring is the story of David Naidoo, the truck driver who became a function hire tycoon. M&M specialises in the hiring out all of the requirements for a memorable function. David began his working career as a truck driver for companies in the catering and hiring industry. In 1993, with capital of R15,000 he started his own hiring business from a one-bedroomed flat. By 2005, M&M had sufficient tents and marquees to cover 17 rugby fields, enough carpeting for 70 houses, over 9,000 chairs, and more than 15,000 crockery items. M&M's head office is situated in a warehouse in Johannesburg with access to all main highways and roads. Owing to the demand in the Pretoria area, Naidoo also established a branch in the heart of that city.

(Source www.mandmhiring.co.za).

David has wide experience in event logistics, marquees, and hiring — an area he has been associated with for some 15 years. David joined the board of directors at Effective Event Management (EEM) in early 2002. EEM's scope of operation under managing director Garth Kirkman is the production, planning and coordination of crowd control services together with the management of major events. EEM has built an enviable client base and reputation for its professionalism in the handling of most of the major cultural and sporting events hosted in South Africa.

(Source: www.eem.co.za)

David also bought into The Event Production Company (TEP) in 2002. Established by Karen Ashwin in 1993, TEP is regarded as a leader in corporate communications. With a reputation honed serving blue chip companies, TEP conceived and organised the opening ceremony of the World Summit 2002, the launch of the logo, mascot and banquets for the Cricket World Cup 2003, and Nelson Mandela's 85th birthday bash.

Those who work with Karen to create show-stopping events say they have never seen her lose her temper. Karen makes sure her attitude leads her all the way to the top. 'I'm ambitious. I'm driven. I love success. I love to be number one,' she says. Karen says a certain company 'gave me a break in life,' and brags how one of her lavish Christmas parties made it into the Guinness Book of Records for serving a three-course meal to 7,000 people. She explains that events are actually 'parties with a difference'. Companies strive to be the best in their field, but then blow their image by staging the same functions year after year.

(Source: 'Building a model company', www.suntimes.co.za, 5 October 2003)

TEC Multi-Media and TEC Video Production are owned by The Event Communication (TEC). Established as an affiliate to TEP in 2001, TEC Multi-Media came into being as the direct result of the need for a design house specialising in event packaging - from designing storyboards and mock-ups to producing posters, invitations, menus, programmes, audio-visual presentations and branded gifts. TEC Multi-Media co-directors, Karen's daughters, Leigh Glicksman and Candice Ashwin, offer clients a full range of branding and integrated marketing solutions from initial strategy through to implementation.

TEC Multi-Media expanded its range of services to include a video division in October 2003. The founding of TEC Video served to complete the group's vision of positioning itself as a below-the-line agency, offering clients an integrated service from strategy through to implementation, with the overall objective of building clients' brands. Candice, TEC Video's managing director, develops, directs and produces high impact corporate and commercial videos from concept and graphics to final edit, as well as branding the video through creative graphics and DVD compilations.

(Source: www.tecmultimedia.co.za).

In April 2003, a new investment fund aimed at enabling and empowering South Africa's young entrepreneurs, particularly those from previously disadvantaged communities, was launched in Johannesburg. The Business Partners Umsobomvu Franchise Fund is a private/public sector joint venture between Business Partners and the Umsobomvu Youth Fund, an initiative of the national government. With an initial investment allocation of R125 million, the fund's specific aim is to make all of the opportunities and benefits of franchising available to the country's new generation of entrepreneurs.

'Franchising is an accessible and powerful retail delivery model,' says Jo' Schwenke, 'providing access to the mainstream economy for youth of all groups.' Statistics from all over the world bear out this statement. In the USA, nearly 50 per cent of all retail business is conducted through franchises. 'As franchising currently only accounts for 7 per cent of retail sales in South Africa, we at Business Partners feel there is huge potential for growth in this sector, particularly in non-food franchising, and we hope to enable young entrepreneurs to realise this potential,' says Schwenke.

Since its stated objective is to provide investment financing for viable youth-owned franchises across all sectors, applicants will, first and foremost, need to have some knowledge of and experience in business. The composition of the business will also be a vital qualifying factor. Entrepreneurs will only qualify for financing from the fund if young black people between the ages of 18 and 35 have an equity holding of at least 30 per cent. Individual applications will be assessed on the viability of a sound business plan and on the drive, vision and competency of the individual entrepreneur or entrepreneurs.

Ultimately, the benefits of franchising extend way beyond access to an established brand, comprehensive training, operational support and integrated marketing. 'Franchising is not only a vehicle for the creation of personal wealth, but for skills development and job creation as well,' says Schwenke. 'In the USA, 8 million people are employed in franchising and the industry accounts for US$1 trillion in turnover annually. One in every twelve retail outlets in the States — approximately 320,000 independent enterprises in 75 different industries — is a franchise. 'There can be no doubt about it,' he concludes, 'with the business franchising model, everyone benefits, and we hope to see more emerging entrepreneurs having access to the rich opportunities it provides.'

During the 2005 financial year, R40.8 million was approved for investment through this R125 million fund, with new entrepreneurs receiving active mentorship and business skills transfer as part of each deal. One of the early success stories of the Business Partners Umsobomvu Franchise Fund is Kirshan Gounden, financed through Business Partners' East Fund in Durban. Gounden is a certified systems engineer who took on the challenge of entrepreneurial enterprise when his father passed away and he assumed management of the family business. In 2003, he saw the potential of expanding his business interests to include a service station that had excellent potential, but which had been neglected by its previous owner. Seizing the opportunity, he purchased the Engen franchise off the Phoenix Highway in Durban with investment financing from the new fund. Adopting a market-related focus, he improved the image of the business and concentrated on upgrading service delivery. Employing other young people to assist him in the management of the business, Gounden is demonstrating the vast potential for success that lies in South Africa's youth.

Another of the fund's early successes is Mtobeli Mlahleki of Motherwell in Port Elizabeth, financed through the Business Partners West Fund in the city. A business management graduate from the University of Transkei, Mlahleki took ownership of the Nobulali Spar in the area in November 2003, since which he has exceeded all projected targets. Nobulali is situated in one of the fastest-growing areas in the Port Elizabeth/Uitenhage area and is regarded by the franchise organisation as one of its best franchises. Mlahleki is a director of Masakhane Employment Consultants and a managing member of Six Bar Trading, a stationery distribution company. Mlahleki has been involved in various business development initiatives in the Nelson Mandela Metropolitan Municipality and the greater Eastern Cape Province. He is currently the General Secretary of the National African Federated Chamber of Commerce (NAFCOC) for Nelson Mandela Bay.

In the Western Cape, young black entrepreneurs are taking advantage of the opportunities offered by the new investment fund. Recently financed through the Business Partners South Fund in Cape Town, PK Phera is one of these. Phera is the co-owner and manager of the Ubuntu Service Station, an Engen and Quickshop franchise in Khayalitsha. After managing a service station for some years, he heard about the Umsobomvu Franchise Fund on the radio and decided to buy the franchise in partnership with another young entrepreneur, Lennox Gesha. Together, they are working towards taking the previously sluggish business to new heights.

The first two women to receive investment financing from the new fund are both from historically disadvantaged communities and are blazing a trail for other young women to follow. In 2004, Yoliswa Jaftha purchased a flourishing Spar franchise in Montpelier and Nilay Naidoo established a popular Barcelos franchise in Johannesburg's bustling Gandhi Square.

Yoliswa Jaftha opted for an established store with a loyal clientele in an excellent location. This decision enabled her to minimise her business risk, show a healthy profit right from the start and build on the infrastructure already in place. Yoliswa is both the owner and manager of the store and is focusing on expanding its product range to better meet the needs of its diverse clientele. 'Not only is this a perfect example of the kind of empowerment through franchising that we wish to invest in,' says Jo' Schwenke, 'it's also testimony to the important role that entrepreneurs have to play in job and wealth creation in the country.' Montpelier Spar employs 18 people, most of whom work in its grocery, hardware, butchery and bakery departments. The remainder work in stores and administration, making use of a computerised point-of-sale system that is directly linked to the Spar Distribution Centre. 'This is a well-structured and well-run business,' says Schwenke, 'and with an owner-manager fuelled by the passion of entrepreneurship, it can only go from strength to strength.'

Nilay Naidoo, on the other hand, chose to establish a new franchise from scratch. In the first four months after opening, the busy fast food franchise became a favourite with the business lunch-time trade. Bringing a taste of European flair to the square, the new Barcelos is not only filling a much-needed gap in the local market, but is making a real contribution to the developing fusion culture unique to South Africa's urban areas. 'Buying this franchise was quite a leap for me,' says Nilay, previously a stay-at-home mother to two young children. 'Despite the fact that I had to step out of my comfort zone, though, I'm enjoying every minute of it and am delighted to see that the business is becoming quite a landmark here on Gandhi Square.' In 2004, the Barcelos franchise group operated 75 sites in six African countries. Their original Portuguese home style flame grilled chicken is known for its quality and generous portions.

Like all entrepreneurs funded by the Business Partners Umsobomvu Franchise Fund, both Yoliswa Jaftha and Nilay Naidoo received mentorship and coaching through Business Partners Mentors as part of the deal. This arrangement ensures that young entrepreneurs have the skills required to get the business off the ground and the best chance of long-term success. 'Investing in entrepreneurs is about more than just providing investment financing. It's about investing in the people that run the business too, so that they can not only build a successful enterprise, but also grow it successfully,' says Jo' Schwenke.

In February 2006, the state-owned finance institution Khula Enterprise Finance and Business Partners launched a R150-million start-up fund for new entrepreneurs. Khula is the anchor investor of the fund and contributed R130-million. Business Partners contributed the rest of the money. Khula managing director Xola Sithole says the fund is aimed at black-owned and black-managed SMEs with preference being given to female entrepreneurs. This fund also targets entrepreneurs in provinces other than Gauteng, Western Cape and KwaZulu-Natal. Interest on the loans varies and is likely to be higher than prime. Although the fund was initially capitalised at R150-million, Sithole says Khula has intentions to raise the capitalisation to at least R300-million. Khula and Business Partners are providing technical help to entrepreneurs in starting, planning and running their businesses. Mentors are drawn from Khula's Thuso Programme and Business Partners' mentorship programme. An additional R15-million has been set aside for the technical assistance. Jo Schwenke says. 'Our philosophy is to stand by the entrepreneur. That is why it is important to get involved and understand the nature of their business.'

The International Finance Corporation (IFC), the private sector arm of the World Bank, promotes sustainable private sector investment in developing countries to help reduce poverty, and improve people's lives. IFC's strategy for poverty reduction in Africa consists of three main areas: enhanced support to SMEs, proactive project development and improved investment climate

The SME Solutions Centres (SSCs) are one of IFC's vehicles for enhancing SME support in Africa. These SSCs were established in response to the four major challenges for SMEs which include access to finance, relevant market information, capacity building services and inadequate Business Environment. The SSCs are one-stop shops that provide both technical assistance and financing solutions to SMEs, along with market information and services for business enabling environment. These one-stop shops seek to address the four SME challenges by establishing:
- Risk capital fund: providing equity and debt finance to SMEs and related technical assistance funding;
- Digital and text-based databases providing up to date sector and market information;
- Business development services, diagnostics, training and enterprise support services; and
- Advocacy and enhancement of investment climate.

IFC has entered into a joint venture with Business Partners to establish Business Partners International (BPI), a platform for rolling out Business Partners' unique financing model throughout sub-Saharan Africa. Three areas, Madagascar, Kenya and a SADC country or region yet to be named, are to be pilot sites for the initial phase of this initiative. An investment fund in the amount of between US$10 to US$15 million will be established in each area, as will a technical assistance facility with a budget of US$2 to US$3 million to provide mentorship to local entrepreneurs. Each fund will be managed by a team of local professionals based in the respective capital cities and will be supported by a dedicated international back-office team in South Africa. As of January 2006, two SSCs have been opened in Antananarivo and Nairobi, with expectations to expand beyond these cities as operations become established. 'If the pilot projects are successful they will become full blown in these countries, with possible extensions into other developing countries,' says IFC's Ibrahima Diong, SME Solutions Centres manager.

Jo' Schwenke and Mark Paper, BPI's chief operating officer, were both present on June 2004 at the Antananarivo opening where the guest of honour was Marc Ravalomanana, the president of Madagascar. The SSCs cater for all the needs of small and medium enterprises including access to information, capacity building, technical assistance, and generally mentoring existing and new SME entrepreneurs and, of course, BPI provides the financing window. Their normal products are made available to clients and they have good prospects in Madagascar. Mark Paper spent three months in Madagascar to oversee the successful recruitment of a local area manager and the professional deployment of Business Partners' first-ever office outside South Africa. He believes the quality of the people and the potential of the country is very promising. The opening of the SSC and their Business Partners window was very well received and BPI received press mentions in all Antananarivo's newspapers.

An article in 2001 in the *New York Times* pointed out that Africa is extremely dependent on unlocking the value of the emerging entrepreneur. Smaller businesses are particularly important in Africa because they are efficient at creating jobs. With many workers unemployed in Africa, the people who are willing to finance small businesses are an increasingly important element in Africa's economic development. Justin Chinyanta, a young Zambian banker, saw this opportunity in 1992.

Chinyanta and a few of his colleagues at Citibank founded their own financial services firm to help small- and medium-sized businesses get their start. Since then, the firm, Loita Capital Partners International, has grown into a unique pan-African group with a dedicated team of professionals from around the world. The group originates and completes transactions across Africa from a network of company and affiliated locations and relies on this local network to share and apply best practices, which take into account the reality and demands of their markets.

Chinyanta, chief executive officer and chairman of Loita Capital Partners, was presented with The Best Financial Consultancy of the year award at the inaugural Africa Investor Awards, which he collected on behalf of the Loita Group at a gala dinner in Dakar, Senegal, in November 2004. The award recognised Loita Capital Partners' support and development of capital markets, facilitating the availability of local currency funding, thus avoiding exchange risk for local companies. Loita's seven year bond issue in Kenya created long-term assets and liabilities critical for sustainable lending and growth.

Chinyanta is a specialist and an expert in the financial markets of eastern and southern Africa, with over 20 years of professional experience in commercial and investment banking in the region. He has had extensive experience in structured finance during his tenures with Citibank and HSBC/Equator Bank. In both, he was in charge of formulating the overall business strategy and action plan for countries in the southern African region. In addition, he was a senior transactor responsible for originating, structuring and managing financial solutions for clients in the region. Chinyanta maintains relationships at the highest levels of various donors, central and commercial banks, and ministries within the region.

What firms like Loita have to offer, Chinyanta says, are years of experience and contacts in first-world finance, coupled with an insider's knowledge of third-world business. The trick, he says, is to provide financing that will yield respectable returns while conforming to 'local market sensitivities'. In Malawi, for example, Loita helped two tobacco traders, Clive Douglas Le Patourel and Michael John Gange-Harris, start their own company after their previous employer, Intabex Holdings Worldwide, was bought out. With US$3 million in financing arranged by Loita, Le Patourel and Gange-Harris founded Africaleaf. Le Patourel says they did not secure or guarantee the loan because they weren't in a position to do so. The bet paid off. Africaleaf repaid the loan and now routinely arranges financing through Loita's office in Malawi.

Loita has since grown its financial network to include a pan-African leasing house that is listed on the Johannesburg Securities Exchange. According to Chinyanta, leasing is an extremely important financial option for the smaller business in that it offers longer-term financing on a much more tax efficient basis. In Zambia where Loita owns Industrial Credit Corporation, the market dominant leasing entity with a 74 per cent market share, the group writes leases from as little as US$50,000 to those running into several millions. The Zambian debt market by its nature is short term and therefore a company such as ICC offers an excellent leeway for borrowers to increase their tenors. In South Africa, ICC has found a niche in the newly emerging market for black entrepreneurs by offering leases to entrepreneurs in the transport sector who for the first time have now been able to own the vehicles they drive under contracts with blue chip companies.

The bank management operations have been part of Loita's portfolio of operational skills since the first technical management agreement was signed with an indigenous bank in Angola and the incorporation of a wholly owned subsidiary in Malawi. Since then, Loita has assisted with the restructuring and management of banks leading to the privatisation of the same; as well as the management of the largest indigenous bank in Zambia and technical management agreements in Côte d'Ivoire and Sudan. In 2005, Loita further expanded its banking network to include the acquisition of majority shares in a commercial bank in Kenya.

Loita and Business Partners say they are profitable, though the risks are great in a continent where entrepreneurs need business experience, bureaucracy can be stifling and corruption is common. Business

Partners' Jo' Schwenke thinks there's room in the market for more people to play, but it's not an easy playing field. He says that you've really got to know what you're doing. He points out that it is a specialised field, and that is why people cannot expect ordinary banks to fill the need. He says that banks are in the business of secured lending, small and medium enterprises generally don't have collateral, so there is risk and a specialist firm has to handle that.

(Source: Henri E Cauvin, 'Small-scale financing takes hold in Africa', *New York Times* 17 December 2001)

The Johannesburg *Sunday Times* of 1 April 2001 reported that the next time South Africans order a side portion of mushrooms at their favourite eatery, they could well be eating the produce of Tropical Mushrooms. This is a business founded by Peter Nyathi and nurtured with help from Equity Africa, a private equity fund manager with a difference. Equity Africa is a partnership between banking group Absa and Shanti Industries, a company, which encourages black entrepreneurs. Established in 1999, Equity Africa invests and manages the partners' Resource Initiative Trust Fund. It typically takes minority stakes of between R1million and R10million in entrepreneurial businesses, aiming to help them become financially independent in three to seven years.

Nyathi's story is familiar. Peter Nyathi was a top grower for one of South Africa's major mushroom companies and studied mushroom production in Holland. When expected career opportunities did not materialise, he decided to strike out on his own. He had a bright idea, a sound business plan and the skills to implement it. However, without any assets to secure a loan, his track record, technical knowledge and management experience counted for little in credit applications, and he struggled to secure finance for his dream of building an organic mushroom farm. And it was not as if he did not knock on enough doors. You could say that every time he approached a financial institution, he felt more like the little mushrooms he was growing — although, to his relief, the banks did not actually throw organic compost on top of him.

Then along came Equity Africa, whose core team members have years of experience in identifying, cultivating and promoting black entrepreneurs with a good reputation and a sustainable business idea. Nyathi says, 'It was like a breath of fresh air when I walked into Equity Africa's offices. It was exciting to be given a platform to speak, almost like finding water in the desert, when at last I saw the opportunity to realise my dream.' Equity Africa decided to make the investment based on Nyathi's sound business plan and his reputation as one of the top mushroom growers in the country. The investment was made in September 1999.

Since then Tropical Mushroom has created 50 full time jobs in an area (the Magaliesberg) that suffers from serious unemployment. It is now one of the premium production employers in the Magaliesberg sub-region, with a staff empowerment trust owning 18 per cent of the company. Tropical Mushrooms, one of the first black managed cultivated mushroom growers in South Africa, now produces an average of four tons per week of premium white button and brown mushrooms. And Peter Nyathi has become widely recognised for his technical abilities, his dedication, and outright determination in designing, commissioning and running a profitable mushroom production facility. Tropical Mushrooms was judged the Best Agriculture SMME in Africa for 2003.

Equity Africa MD Alan Gordon Stokes says private equity investment is not just about providing cash in exchange for an equity interest. It extends to hands-on support like facilitating training in financial monitoring and IT systems, continuous product development and even distribution alliances. Gordon Stokes highlights the very real commitment made by Absa which not only provided R100 million of seed capital for the fund, alongside significant funding from Shanti Industries, but also ensured that its top managers took an interest in Equity Africa's underlying investments.

Absa group executive director Bert Griesel sits on Equity Africa's board and Absa group chief executive Nallie Bosman, known within Absa for his ability to roll up his sleeves and talk directly to customers at the bank's call centre, has taken a close personal interest in Nyathi's business. Griesel says: 'Absa is proud to be associated with the Equity Africa joint venture and sees it as a tangible commitment towards furthering prosperity and growth for small, medium and micro enterprise development in South Africa.' There may only be a handful of private equity houses contesting Equity Africa's tightly defined empowerment segment, but few can lay claim to the sort of on-the-ground credentials of the Shanti Industries team, which has worked in the community for 12 years.

Equity Africa has other investments in the agricultural and consumer goods sectors, including export-focused essential oils producer Edmar; retail market vegetable grower Greenway Farms; and Isis ice-cream, a three-way venture between Isis Denmark, a black woman entrepreneur and Equity Africa. Recent investments include decorative foliage exporter Singoflora and household detergent manufacturer Colprochem. Gordon Stokes stresses Equity Africa is not fixated on particular sectors but just keeps an eye out for opportunities combining backable people, growth and empowerment.

(Source: Richard Stovin-Bradford. 'Business mushrooms with seed capital', Johannesburg: *Sunday Times*,1 April 2001)

Aureos Southern Africa Fund is a new entrant to the Private Equity Segment in the Southern Africa Region. This US$50 million fund targets small and medium sized businesses across southern Africa, up to a maximum investment of US$4 million. Aureos is owned by Actis and Norfund and the Aureos Southern Africa Fund is funded by Commonwealth Development Corporation, European Investment Bank, the International Finance Corporation, Norfund, and Nordic Development Fund. Aureos Southern Africa Fund is one of six emerging market funds operating under the Aureos banner around the world. It is an amalgam of several country-specific funds previously operating throughout the region. The fund's regional hub is in Johannesburg, with regional offices in Mauritius, Mozambique and Zambia.

'We've pooled the human resources and infrastructure of these various funds, but we still have people on the ground in the various countries, which is how we generate deal flow,' says Ron den Besten, who heads up the fund. Den Besten says sectors earmarked for investment include retailing, manufacturing, logistics, mining services, tourism, franchising and telecommunications. 'South African companies have been very successful in expanding into Africa. Originally it was the larger corporations that rolled out across the border; now we're seeing smaller companies doing it very successfully, and this is one area where we will be focusing our investments.'

Cyrille Nkontchou, a Harvard MBA graduate from Cameroon, started LiquidAfrica to make it easier for investors to buy stocks in Africa. In 2000, Nkontchou left his London job as a Merrill Lynch analyst to start Johannesburg-based LiquidAfrica. It was to be an online trading site that provided a one-stop shop for Africans and international investors to trade and invest in the African securities markets. 'It would have been like an E-Trade for Africa,' he says. 'It was a no-brainer.' In 2004, he concluded that it worked well; the only problem was that there weren't enough investors as the client pool had actually shrunk. So LiquidAfrica has been forced to evolve to survive. Investors can still use the website to trade shares and get price alerts, but Nkontchou's focus has shifted from the individual investor to institutions, and from trading to information. The LiquidAfrica website offers a broader menu of market news in English and French, corporate filings, country profiles, brokerage research and other business intelligence — some free, some for a fee.

Nkontchou started LiquidAfrica with US$250,000 of his own money and US$2.5 million from the Washington-based private equity fund Modern Africa Fund. The surge in emerging markets investing has largely passed Africa by, the lone exception being South Africa, by far the most dominant market in the region. There are roughly 500 listed companies in South Africa, and they account for nearly 80 per cent of the continent's market capitalisation. 'I've learned to be more patient,' says Nkontchou, who also has seen an opportunity to make money by matching buyers and sellers. The plan now is to charge fees for research on industry sectors such as tourism, energy, mining and telecoms. LiquidAfrica also wants to add commentary and research on government bonds and hopes to offer bond trading online.

Nkontchou wants to turn LiquidAfrica into more than an information provider and trading platform. He plans to set up a corporate finance advisory service for African companies looking to raise capital and is also considering setting up a stock index fund and a debt fund, both dedicated to African securities. 'I realise that would be a conflict of interest [in the USA]. But in Africa, the only way to get things going is to gain critical mass,' he says. Stephen Cashin, managing director of Modern Africa, says that LiquidAfrica provides terrific research to a fledgling equity market that may provide a global opportunity going forward. Among America's emerging class of black professionals there is a lot of interest in Africa at the cultural level and in cultural tourism, but when it comes to investing money in Africa, they just haven't. Nkontchou says, 'They are generally ignorant of African economic conditions, and their interest is still fairly superficial.' He dreams of the day there is a 'clear signal' to the world that it's time to invest in Africa.

(Source: James Cox. 'Invested in future of African markets', *USA TODAY*, 9 February 2004)

Africa's equity markets, a synopsis

As diverse and contrasting is the continent of Africa, so too are Africa's capital markets. With 53 countries, the African continent has over 20 active stock exchanges, including one of the only regional stock exchanges in the world, linking eight French-speaking countries in West Africa. With a market capitalisation of over US$ 180 billion in South Africa, Africa hosts one of the largest stock markets in the world. This is in stark contrast to the other African stock markets that have comparatively small market capitalisations.

With the exception of the South African market and to a limited extent the North African markets, African stock markets are described as 'frontier markets'. These markets are typically characterised by a relatively small capitalisation and liquidity levels. As a consequence, most of these markets are excluded from the main regional equity market indices and as a result attract little Global Emerging Markets (GEM) portfolio funds.

However, amid bearish performance of developed stock markets over the past two and a half years, several leading African markets such as Botswana have bucked the negative trend and recorded solid performance. Smaller African markets have proved relatively immune to global jitters hitting share values worldwide, due to their lack of correlation with developed markets. This distinct characteristic of African equity markets offers positive benefits in terms of risk diversification.

African stock exchanges face a number of challenges before they could enter a new phase of rapid growth. The most critical issue is to eliminate existing impediments to institutional development. These include a wider dissemination of information on these markets, the implementation of robust electronic trading systems and the adoption of central depository systems. A number of countries have already begun implementing necessary changes notably in the area of trading and settlement systems and regulatory regimes that will continue to improve.

The 1990s witnessed a deliberate shift by a number of African governments to free market policies driven by the desire to reduce the burden on government finances. This was achieved by implementing market-friendly reforms. A central component of this process was the privatisation of state-owned companies.

A number of these privatisations were effected by listing on the local exchanges. In order to further stimulate the development of a local capital market, many subsidiaries of large international companies were also encouraged to list their local operation. For entrepreneurs as well as emerging private companies, capital raising in African equity markets is vibrant despite the relative small size of issues.

Some African governments have taken advantage of the development of the local capital markets to issue stock exchange listed treasury debt instruments. Kenya and Ghana are a case in point, where these governments have been able to issue longer-term instruments thus better managing local debt. The spin-off of this has been improved transparency in pricing of local bank lending facilities and increased competition within local banking industries. We continue to witness rapid development in the debt segment of the African capital markets.

An increasingly encouraging trend is the development of the local pension fund industry. With the exception of South Africa and to some extent southern Africa, private and institutional cash flows have traditionally been invested mostly in real estate, term bank deposits and treasury bills. A number of African countries have introduced as part of wider financial sector reforms new laws enabling the emergence of a local fund management industry.

Looking ahead, African capital markets represent the final frontier of global capital.

Robert Bunyi, Robert. 'Africa's equity markets, a synopsis', *African Stock Markets Handbook -2003*, United Nations Development Programme (page 4). http://www.undp.org/dpa/publications/AfricanStockMarkets.pdf.
Reproduced by permission of the UNDP.

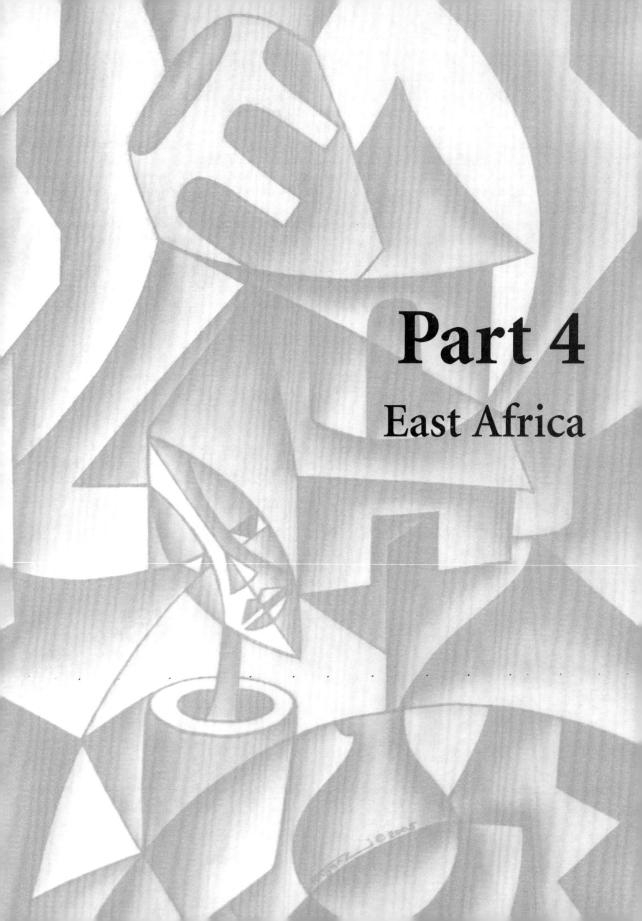

Part 4
East Africa

The eastern region of Africa is home to the great wildlife reserves of the Serengeti plains and the rich volcanic soils surrounding the Great Rift lake system, which stretches across the countries of Kenya, Uganda and Tanzania. Further north are the countries of the Horn of Africa. From its source in Uganda (the White Nile), and its source in the Ethiopian highlands (the Blue Nile), the Nile, the longest river in the world, flows northwards over 6,690 kilometres to end in the Mediterranean Sea. Ethiopia is a large inland country, while Somalia occupies the Indian Ocean coastline. On the coast of the Red Sea are the two independent republics of Djibouti and Eritrea. The East Africa region exhibits the strong influences of Arab traders and European colonisation.

In December 2004, the head of states for three East African countries — Uganda, Tanzania and Kenya — agreed on a full political federation to commence in January 2010. Presidents Mwai Kibaki of Kenya, Benjamin Mkapa of Tanzania and Yoweri Museveni of Uganda decided to fast track political integration and make the East African Community more meaningful to their people. The new federal state will have its own elected parliament, a cabinet, federal judiciary and a head of state. Tourism throughout the region is expected to receive a massive boost through such measures, as expatriates in the three sister states will also find that work and residence permits will be standardised, allowing them freedom of movement and the opportunity to visit without having to pay visa fees when crossing a border.

Chapter 11: Horn of Africa: Ethiopia, Eritrea, Djibouti and Somalia

Ethiopia

About 90 per cent of Ethiopia's people earn their living from the land, mainly as subsistence farmers. Agriculture is the backbone of the national economy and the principal exports from the sector are coffee, oil seeds, pulses (peas, beans, lentils and similar plants having pods), flowers, vegetables, sugar and foodstuffs for animals. Ethiopia produces less than 500 megawatts from a few hydropower dams, providing electricity to less than 10 per cent of the population. The Ministry of Water Resources estimates its rivers, chiefly the Blue Nile, have the potential to produce more than 15,000 megawatts of power and irrigate nearly nine million acres, if the country gets the cooperation and investment it needs. 'The international community has to understand this, rather than just give us food handouts,' said Shiferaw Jarso, the Minister of Water Resources, in 2003. 'This year, the United States gives us 500 million dollars in food aid and it's gone within one year. People get the food, but it never brings additional value for the country. If this money goes to a power project or irrigation, it can keep on helping every year.'

According to the region's new mathematics, what helps Ethiopia can also help Egypt. The countries are studying a plan for four hydropower dams on the Blue Nile which could produce enough energy not only to supply Ethiopia's domestic demand but also to feed into Egypt's extensive power grid for sale to users all the way to Europe. The dams would also serve as sediment traps for the topsoil that washes down from Ethiopia's denuded hillsides. Currently, the silt from the Blue Nile is building up in Egypt's Aswan Dam and a couple of smaller dams in Sudan. Over time, if the runoff isn't controlled, the silting could cripple the dams. Engineers from both countries agree that dams in the cool and moist Ethiopian highlands, storing water in deep natural gorges, would lose far less water to evaporation than the Aswan Dam in the hot, dry Egyptian desert. They calculate the savings on evaporation could compensate for the amount of water Ethiopia proposes to use for irrigation. 'There's enough water. It is a matter of managing it. To look at the Nile from a selfish point of view won't help anyone,' says Abdel Fattah Metawie, the chairman of the Nile water sector in Egypt's Ministry of Water resources and Irrigation.

(Source: Roger Thurow. 'Ravaged by famine, Ethiopia finally gets help from the Nile', *The Wall Street Journal*, 26 November 2003)

Ato Tadesse Haile, Ethiopia's Minister of Trade and Industry, remarked in August 2002 that there is a lack of innovative entrepreneurs who can stand up to the challenges of fostering entrepreneurial talent in Ethiopia. He believes that inadequate appropriate training is an impediment to the development of entrepreneurship. Ato Tadesse says that in almost every aspect, the concept of entrepreneurship is novel to Ethiopia, and only recently have the glaring problems facing the country been put into perspective. A concerted effort is needed. Ato Tadesse adds that efforts to promote entrepreneurial initiative should have been started earlier, and should now be gaining momentum.

Ato Tadesse says that Ethiopia is confronted with the problems of reconstructing the economy and laying the foundation for future rapid growth. Profound changes are taking place all over the world and globalisation is forcing developing nations to grapple with unprecedented burdens. In addition, the crushing burden of population growth is accompanied by threats of mounting poverty and unemployment. These and related factors require Ethiopians to concern themselves with efforts to effectively and efficiently tune their pace to emerging trends, since never has it been truer than today that nations cannot live in isolation. Tadesse believes that small- and medium-sized enterprises and innovative indigenous entrepreneurs have to play a significant role in the development of Ethiopia's economy. What Tadesse doesn't mention is that the policies of the Ethiopian government have forced many talented entrepreneurs out of the country or into bankruptcy. It is ironic that Tadesse laments the lack of business talent in Ethiopia. There appears to be a poor understanding in Ethiopia of the role of government behaviour in affecting the stock and rate of growth of indigenous businesses and entrepreneurs.

(Source: Michael Eskinder. 'Minister says more innovative entrepreneurs needed', Addis Ababa: *The Daily Monitor*, 29 August 2002)

M H Alli, United Nations Industrial Development Organization (UNIDO) representative and head of regional office, stresses that the state needs to ensure that there are favourable conditions for the development of entrepreneurship. He says that if a market economy is to be vibrant it will require a state that provides an enabling environment for business but which is able to maintain some autonomy and avoid capture by the business or entrepreneur class. The implications are relevant for policy makers, government officials, entrepreneurs, trade unions and members of international and regional organisations — and he thinks these are enough reasons for legislative bodies to revisit and revise regulation.

Ethiopia's Entrepreneurship Development Programme (EDP) was launched for the first time in 1994, and focuses on creating a new breed of Ethiopian entrepreneurs. The programme is sponsored by United Nations Industrial Organisation (UNIDO), United Nations Development Programme (UNDP), and Department for Development Support and Management Services (DDSMS). It organises forums, so that people can get together and discuss how to develop entrepreneurship according to Mulu Solomon, president of the EMPRETEC Ethiopia Business Society. The follow up programme is meant to help youth to start and sustain businesses. Musa believes that Ethiopians need to work hand in hand to create a vibrant private sector, for it is the corner stone of the economy. Presently, entrepreneurial workshops organised by the EMPRETEC Ethiopia Business Society in collaboration with UNIDO, UNDP, and the Ethiopian and Addis Ababa Chambers of Commerce are attended by businesspeople who receive training in credit schemes for the development of small and medium enterprises.

(Source: Michael Eskinder. 'Minister says more innovative entrepreneurs needed', Addis Ababa: *The Daily Monitor*, 29 August 2002)

The Ethiopian agriculture sector is in a troubled state. The interests of farmers and the private sector have become secondary to those of party-affiliated enterprises. Ethiopia's economy is heavily dependent on the development and growth of agriculture and so long as discriminatory practices in the Ethiopian agricultural sector are in place, Ethiopia will remain in poverty and looking for handouts from the world community. The manner in which the affairs of farmers are handled, people living from hand to mouth is disgraceful, as is its effect on the overall economy. The United Nations, the World Bank, and other international agencies should take note and work towards effecting change.

Agriculture is not a one way street. In order for the farmers of Ethiopia to produce, they need returns on their investment in time, land, and money. But without a growing private sector this will not be possible.

Agro-economists at Michigan State University have submitted that increased use of chemical fertilisers, more productive seed varieties, and improved crop husbandry practices will be preconditions to the bridging Ethiopia's wide food gap, at least in the immediate future. According to the *FAO Fertilizer Yearbook 1997* Ethiopian farmers use roughly 15 kilograms of fertiliser nutrient per hectare of cropped land, compared with 71, 93, and 65 kilograms per hectare in Latin America, Southeast Asia, and the Near East/ North Africa in 1996/97. Commercial fertilisers are more concentrated (contain more nutrient per unit) than organic wastes or manure, making them cheaper to transport and store. More importantly, there are simply not enough organic fertilisers to get the productivity increases needed. Farmers need to adopt improved cultural practices that combine available organic matter with chemical fertilisers. Increasing the adoption of improved agricultural technology should become an important part of the Ethiopia's strategy to increase agricultural productivity in both high and low potential areas.

Specific objectives should include strengthening public and private participation in seed research, extension, multiplication and distribution services; increasing the availability of fertilizers and pesticides, and improving their distribution through the private sector and service cooperatives; expanding rural credit and savings services; and improving the extension service, and strengthening links between extension agents, farmers and the research system.

The agro-economists at Michigan State University propose that the Ethiopian government should recognise the important role that agricultural markets play in motivating farmers to increase their agricultural production. Farmers will have little incentive to increase production if there is no marketing system through which they can sell their products, and buy agricultural inputs and consumption items at fair prices. The Ethiopian government should encourage and assist, not hinder, the private sector in playing a much larger role in agricultural development than previously: for example, in the provision of marketing and transportation services, investment in the seed industry and the development of agro-industry. The formation of farmer organisations should also be encouraged to facilitate farmer participation in the political and development process.

Thom S Jayne, professor of international development in the Department of Agricultural Economics at Michigan State University, points out that there are political impediments to helping improve poor peoples' fate (which are mainly the same impediments obstructing African private sector entrepreneurs). Many local politicians may perceive that it is in their interests to control power, to prevent people from being able to make money, because money allows entrepreneurs to develop a political support base that can be used to challenge incumbent politicians. As in many developed countries such as the United States, people in Africa become politically powerful from their ability to provide benefits to others, which allows them to mobilise a political support base. Incumbent politicians whose priority is to maintain power can often be threatened by an economic system that provides the means for competition in the political arena to arise, so it is not surprising that active support for an entrepreneurial class is not more forthcoming in many countries.

Jayne says it is not as simple as sending in ground agronomists to help African farmers grow food. He points out that Nobel laureate Norman Borlaug tried this in Ethiopia, Ghana, Mozambique and elsewhere, under the assumption that the technology was on the shelf, and all farmers needed was to be shown how to use it. Borlaug worked with Jimmy Carter and a Japanese billionaire, Sasakawa, to form the Sasakawa-Global 2000 programme which financed huge on-farm demonstration plots using hybrid maize seed, fertiliser and appropriate agronomic practices. The project delivered these inputs to the villages, and in-depth education and extension programmes showed farmers optimal row spacing, planting density and timing of input application. Participating farmers typically obtained three times greater maize yields! The programme looked like a dramatic success in each country until it withdrew, feeling that farmers now had the knowledge and ability to continue.

What they found out was the importance of markets: no one was there to provide the fertiliser; no-one provided credit; no-one distributed the hybrid seed to remote areas — so, very quickly, farmers' yields fell back to near their original low levels. The SG-2000 programme people have now fully accepted that developing sustainable markets for both inputs and commodities are crucial; it is not merely a technical issue of getting agronomists to show farmers how to cultivate their crops. Why haven't markets developed so far? Jayne points out that there are major political constraints. Agro-businessmen can certainly tell about those in Ethiopia.

Jayne is an economist who writes reports, advises government officials, and trains African analysts, and has lived and worked in three African countries for a total of eight years. What he does is to try to raise awareness of the importance of markets. He emphasises the importance of developing Africa's private sector entrepreneurs (not as an objective in its own right, but because this will be necessary to link African farmers and consumers with the technology and markets that they need to become productive and profitable in an increasingly globalised world). Jayne's research often runs counter to that of other academics that contend that markets fail and that private traders are exploitative. Based on his work with other African researchers, he has found that generally private agricultural entrepreneurs are providing valuable services that raise the living standards of farmers and consumers. However, they are often constrained from being allowed to invest further because this interferes with the politicians' moneymaking activities and often threatens them. Markets and private traders need a supportive government that provides key public investments that allow markets to function effectively. Alas, some government officials feel that they are in competition with the private sector, not in partnership. This needs to be exposed and brought out into the public eye much better.

Hawas Agri Business Plc was established in 1994. Ato Bulbula Tulle, a commercial farmer in Ethiopia's southern and western highlands and grain trader for all of Ethiopia — and a very experienced and influential figure — is the co-owner and managing director of the company. Hawas is primarily engaged in the grain wholesale trade, provision of combine harvesting and ploughing services, export of primary agricultural produce such as maize, wheat, chick peas and oil seeds, and in farming. Its assets include 1,600 hectares of land (100 hectares irrigated and 1,500 hectares rain fed), a commercial building, a 600 square metre warehouse, six combine harvesters, six farm tractors, seven commercial utility vehicles and 10,000 square metres of urban land which can be utilised for various kinds of projects. The company produces various cereal crops, including soy bean and maize, using mechanisation and modern farming methods.

Hawas has expanded its business to include large scale commercial farming, real estate development and import and export trade. In order to expand further, Hawas has charted out a five-year business plan that includes food processing, vehicle assembly and floriculture for which the necessary ground works are already completed. Hawas holds three international certificates of award for business excellence and quality service. The company has been awarded two certificates of excellence from the World Summit of Young Entrepreneurs based in Canada and an international gold category award from Business Initiatives Directions for excellence and business prestige. Hawas has also been awarded certificates for good performance from donor organisations: the World Food Programme, Euro Aid, the German Technical Cooperation Programme and the Disaster Prevention and Preparedness Commission of Ethiopia.

2001 was a hard time in Ethiopia for farmers of grain producing regions, which were hard hit by declining prices owing to surplus production while the country was depending on food aid for more than 15 per cent of its population. Little provision had been made to support Ethiopia's fledgling free market with storage facilities, transport and financing. When a bumper harvest came in 2001, the markets were overwhelmed. Prices collapsed, sapping the incentive for farmers to produce as much as they could. Bulbula Tulle knows that when he cuts the size of his farm, he is contributing to the food shortage. But at least he is not losing money. In 2001, he planted 1,200 hectares of corn, reaped one of his best yields ever and lost nearly US$200,000 because prices fell below his costs for labour, seed, fertiliser and fuel. The next year, to reduce his costs and his exposure to the market, he planted only about 250 hectares. The rest of his land has gone to grass and is feeding grazing cows rather than hungry people.

(Source: Roger Thurow. 'Road to hunger: Behind the famine in Ethiopia', *The Wall Street Journal*, 1 July 2003)

Bulbula Tulle comments that the price crisis should be seen as crisis of marketing management to handle properly what the farmer delivers to the local market. There are different factors aggravating the problem:
- Most of the deficit areas of the country were crowded with aid foods that were sold at lower prices in the local markets.
- The inefficiency of Ethiopia's food processing industry to convert grain to different food items contributed to the crisis. Ethiopian food industries are inefficient due to their weak financial and technical capacity. In many supermarkets, foreign-produced wheat flours are sold cheaply, but the local industries could not stand up to the challenge.
- The regulatory body, the Ethiopian Grain Trade Enterprise (EGTE), should play a leading role in the grain market, purchasing grains from the farmer to stabilise the falling market price. EGTE can get loans on overdraft from banks, but its role was minimal during the price crisis, which shocked the country.
- Various donor agencies, which were not able to implement their schedule of purchase of grain on time contributed to the crisis. Donor agencies pledged to buy about 1.1 million quintals of grain, the tender of which would be announced in March 2001. Because their programmes failed farmers were compelled to sell their yield more cheaply.
- Farmers have storage problems and there also is a problem of loan settlement. There is no way to settle

except by selling the grain that farmers have at hand at available prices
- Farmers are getting less income — not enough to pay the last year's fertiliser debt, let alone to buy fertiliser for the present year.
- EGTE has not fulfilled its role of stabilising seasonal grain price fluctuation without violating the operation of a free market system.
- Local grain traders like Hawas should be the main actors in the local purchasing stratagem, but because of inadequate logistics, finance, human resources and other factors they could not play their important role.

They also lack proper programmes for the purchasing of grain at the right time. The lack of perfect economic policies, liberalised bank loans and efficient grain market management are the main reasons for the crisis of the grain prices. Ato Bulbula asserts that this should be considered as a national crisis, instead of regarding the decreasing price as a sign of prosperity. Voices of the financial institutions, government bodies, the private sector and the farmers should be heard. He advises that there should be a change of discipline in production and marketing management and points out that Ethiopia has a production extension package for the agricultural sector and additionally needs a market extension package.

(Source: Melaku Demissie. 'Declining grain prices threaten further production', Addis Ababa: *Fortune: Ethiopia's Business Weekly*, 1-7 July 2001)

In 2004, Hawas Agri Business and Progressive AgCo, a progressive agriculture company based in the USA, established a joint venture company, Hapac Agri International, which is developing about 3,000 hectares in Ethiopia with full irrigation, aiming at cotton and horticulture. The project will create about 2,500 jobs, mostly for Ethiopians and a few expatriate professionals. In October 2004, Hawas Agri Business Plc won a World Quality Commitment (WQC) International Star Award for Excellence and Business Prestige Trophy: Platinum Category. The award was part of the 21st annual programme of Business Initiative Directions Awards, designed to recognise the prestige of the outstanding companies, organisations and businessmen in the business world. In 2004, the awards were handed out at the International Star Award Conference in Paris. The ceremony was attended by companies from 70 countries, together with leaders from different business fields, professionals from the worlds of economics, the arts and corporate image, quality experts and academic personalities and representatives from the diplomatic corps.

East African Agribusiness Plc (EAAB), a member of East African Holdings (EAH), was established to facilitate EAH's entry into the agricultural sector by establishing commercial farms to meet local demand for agricultural produce. EAAB also plans to set up commercial farms that will rely strictly on organic farming principles and methods in order to supply high quality agricultural produce to local and export markets. Managing director, Buzuayehu Tadele Bizenu, says this exemplifies EAH's concern for the environment and its emphasis on the need to respect and preserve ecological processes and principles.

EAAB's first venture and success story has been the establishment of Chewaka Tea Estate, a 3,435 hectare tea plantation situated in the scenic beauty of the south west highlands of Ethiopia. At an altitude of 6,000 feet with an average rainfall of 80 to 90 inches per year, it is a most favourable climatic environment for black tea production. Tea bushes are established on virgin soil, rich in organic nutrients, with very little supplementary fertiliser being required for optimal production. EAAB also owns the Chewaka Tea Packaging Factory, where the machinery is the latest technology in the tea industry. Transportation services for delivery of products mainly for the export market is accomplished by a sister company, East African Transport Plc.

EAH is a family-owned business started in 1891 by Bizenu Cheru, who passed it over to his son Tadele in 1920. He too left the company to his son, the current managing director, Buzuayehu Tadele. With the benefit of work experience from 1975 to 1992, and with a degree in business management from Cambridge College in England, Buzuayehu converted the age-old family business into a vibrant import-export operation, which has exploited the opportunities of economic liberalisation in Ethiopia, as well as the scarcity of products being offered in the 1993 Ethiopian market. Buzuayehu is an example of educated Ethiopians taking over their parents' traditional businesses and converting them into dynamic and vibrant conglomerates.

EAH now comprises seven subsidiary companies operating over a variety of sectors such as manufacturing, trading, distribution, transport, real estate development, and the production and processing of agricultural goods and commodities. It has become a major player in the industrial sector. The primary focuses of EAH industrial operations are the light and consumer goods industries such as the production of foodstuffs, cosmetics, soaps and detergents. EAH has also expanded into the transport, agriculture and real estate sectors and has witnessed phenomenal growth in terms of its capacity, specifically in human resources, production capacity, and technological upgrading of techniques, skills and machinery. As of January 2006, EAH employs over 4,000 workers throughout Ethiopia.

Besides East African Agribusiness, the EAH subsidiary companies include:

- East African Group, responsible for the management of five factories: East African soap and detergent factory; East African Flour and Pasta Factory; East African Food Processing and Packing Plant; East African Printing and Packing Plant; and a 60 per cent stake in Dire Dawa Cement Factory, of which the main export focus is Somalia.
- East African Industrial Park. Located within 35 kilometres from the capital at Dukem, the industrial park extends over 50 acres of land, large enough to accommodate over 20 different plants ranging from light to medium industries. Envisaged are plastic, engineering products, health care products, building materials and chemical plants. By January 2006, EAH owned 13 factories at the industrial park. The list includes Miki Biscuit, various detergent products, Anbessa Flour and Pasta, and Berchaco Cosmetics. EAH also sees the industrial park as a potential opportunity for cooperation with foreign and domestic investors.
- East African Trading House. Established to efficiently promote and distribute all the products under the EAH umbrella, it has played a pivotal role in the development of market share. It has a central distribution centre in the capital Addis Ababa from which it serves distributors. It is supported by a fleet of vehicles, nine branch offices and 50 agents spread across the country. It also imports and distributes various material and consumer goods to market, including generators, pipes and fittings, submersible pumps, tyres of different types, hand pumps, liquors, incense sticks and foodstuffs. In the interest of specialisation and coordination, the promotion, marketing and distribution of the whole product line and range of commodities produced by the EAH group is the responsibility of the East African Trading House.
- East African Transport. Established in the overall interest of EAH's diversification, expansion, and specialisation needs, it presently meets the transportation needs of the companies under the EAH umbrella. The fleet under EAT is comprised of liquid and dry cargo trucks with a load capacity of 40 tons each transporting raw materials, finished goods and commodities to sister companies. EAT has opened branches in Moyale (Kenya) and Djibouti. It also handles the transport needs of external customers, companies and institutions.
- East African Real Estate Development. This represents EAH's opening venture into the real estate marketing and development sector in Ethiopia. Its primary focus is the construction of residential housing, office complexes and warehouses. Recently it completed the construction of an important office complex in Addis Ababa.
- Berchaco Ethiopia. With 40 years' experience in the field of cosmetics products manufacturing this is a leading player, with a wide product range of perfumes, skin and hair creams and nail polish as well as health care products - all based on natural and environmentally friendly raw materials. Before being distributed, the cosmetics undergo stringent quality control and testing.

(Source: www.ethioexport.org/adv/eaab.htm)

Oxfam International claims that the world's largest coffee companies are destroying the lives of millions of impoverished third world farmers. It blames the big four roasting companies, Kraft, Procter & Gamble,

Sara Lee and Nestle, for driving subsistence farmers into even greater hardship. In a 2002 report, 'Mugged, poverty in your coffee cup', Oxfam claims that there is a crisis destroying the livelihoods of 25 million coffee producers around the world. 'Despite the stagnant consumer market, the coffee companies are laughing all the way to the bank,' the report says. 'With farmers getting a price that is below the cost of production, the companies' booming business is being paid for by some of the poorest people in the world.' The report, which was launched in Uganda and Ethiopia, adds, 'The coffee crisis is becoming a development disaster whose impact will be felt for a long time. The coffee market must be made to work for the poor as well as the rich.'

Ethiopia, the birthplace of coffee and Africa's leading exporter, has been crippled by the huge slump in prices making it more dependent on aid from rich nations. Coffee accounts for more than 60 per cent of exports generating vital income for its 65 million people, more than half of whom live on less than a dollar a day. Ethiopia's farmers are paid less than US$0.10 per kg for coffee, which will sell in western countries for around US$26. Five years ago they received more than six times that amount. Ethiopia's coffee income dropped by US$110million compared to the US$58million it was set to save in debt relief in 2002, hitting the one million families who are dependent on coffee for their income.

In September 2002, Ethiopia's prime minister Meles Zenawi made an impassioned plea to rich nations on behalf of millions of impoverished coffee farmers in Ethiopia. Speaking at the first ever coffee exhibition, which was hosted in Ethiopia, and launched by Oxfam International, Meles declared that companies selling coffee in western countries were reaping huge benefits while coffee farmers were being driven into the ground. He says this is a damning indictment of the global trading environment and startling proof of the totally unfair global trading environment. Meles told delegates that farmers faced a sharp increase in poverty and hunger as a direct result of a massive slump in prices.

The International Coffee Organisation says world coffee prices slumped to record lows in 2002, falling by more than 70 per cent since 1998. Oxfam, which argues that fair trade will help impoverished countries more than aid handout alone, is trying to introduce a 'rescue plan' for coffee. Oxfam criticises the World Bank and the International Monetary Fund for encouraging countries into export-led growth without warning them about the potential of catastrophic price falls. The coffee campaign is part of Oxfam's fair trade strategy designed to make consumers aware of the importance of trade and globalisation in the fight against poverty.

(Source: Oxfam. 'Coffee companies hurting third world farmers', Oxfam press release, 18 September 2002)

Sophia Bekele is the founder, president, and chief executive officer of CBS International. Sophia is well educated and a successful young woman doing business internationally. Always career oriented, Sophia left Addis Ababa after graduating from high school. Landing in San Francisco, she was soon studying computers at San Francisco State University and working as a professional model on the side. Recruited fresh out of college by Bank of America, with a bachelor of science degree in computer and information systems, Sophia became one of a handful of women working in information data security, a highly specialised field at the time.

An MBA in management information systems from Golden Gate University, San Francisco, led to managerial positions with Mitsubishi Bank of California and Coopers & Lybrand. Sophia maintained a successful career track record spanning over a decade of constant professional activity working for multinational consulting firms and large financial and banking companies in corporate America. From these corporate contacts, Sophia gained invaluable practical experience in diverse areas such as technology risk assessment of financial markets and instruments, financial engineering risk management, computer quality assurance, information systems security/auditing, systems controls, technology evaluation and project management.

In 1998, Sophia was lured back to Addis Ababa by her family and the opportunity at CBS, a company that had successfully pioneered the computer market in Ethiopia in the early 1990s, but was then foundering due to increased competition and poor management. Taking over at CBS, Sophia engineered a top-to-bottom restructuring that repositioned the company as the provider of total system solutions. The overhaul included new management and staff, an aggressive marketing campaign and, unheard of in the Ethiopian business community, strategic partnerships with her local competitors and with high tech firms in the West, also setting up a satellite office in California.

The first year was the hardest in her life. Sophia explains that Ethiopia has always been influenced by Middle Eastern culture, where women are mostly expected to be submissive and quiet. Sophia then rose to be a figure in the Ethiopian business community, known for her efforts to adapt western business methods. Sophia believes the Internet, satellite and wireless communications are going to be keys to economic development in Africa. She looks at how the Internet has transformed business in the United States and says Africa could skip a lot of the mistakes the West has made and take a quantum leap into the 21st century.

(Source: Kay Kaufman. 'I'm creating something from scratch', *Connections Magazine*, Fall 1999)

As an affiliate of CBS International, Sophia started up SbCommunications Networks (SbCnet), a company specialising in systems integration and dedicated to serving emerging economies from Addis Ababa. Sophia focused on international technology issues and third world technological development, using Ethiopia as a base model. She participated in several international meetings and technology workshops, including speaking at the UN General Assembly on ICT and the digital divide and a presentation to the 5th African Telecom Summit in Maputo, Mozambique in 2003 on cost-effective solutions to developing the ICT business in Africa.

In 2000, Sophia's company, CBS International, won its first multi-million international contract with UNOPS (United Nations Agency for Project Services), to deploy a sophisticated turnkey fibreoptic-based information technology infrastructure, for the African Union General Secretariat within Conflict Management and Prevention. Sophia put together the entire project, management strategy and structure for the AU, and was implemented on a turnkey basis. CBS International handled technological inputs and services procurement while SbCnet provided field management and strategic technology integration services. The project was successfully implemented.

During 2000, Sophia was elected to the Advisory Committee of the UNECA-sponsored African Information Society Initiative (AISI), an action framework to build Africa's information and communication infrastructure. In her tenure in AISI, Sophia has co-authored the blueprint for Africa's ICT challenge ('Common position for Africa's digital inclusion'), recommendations, which reflect Africa's position in the global arena on ICTs, to include the G8 Digital Opportunity Task Force, ECOSOC, United Nations Task Force and World Economic Forum.

In 2002, SbCnet was awarded yet another multi million dollar international contract for the implementation of an integrated data networking infrastructure project at the Ethiopian Parliament. SbCnet was the prime contractor, handling all front-line liaison and project services delivery and working closely with its foreign implementation partners.

While the project opportunities her company has been offered in ICTs in Ethiopia have been worthy, it has not been without lessons learned. Sophia has been patient in navigating the treacherous waters and the complicated politics between the various organisations. For example, the project opportunity for the Ethiopian parliament precipitated a big crisis in government and afforded an opportunity to directly confront and challenge government by holding it up against the higher ideals underlining justice, transparency, accountability, probity and issues of illegality. Sophia's continued lobbying for almost seven months finally resulted in the suspension and subsequent cancellation of the project that was started by the contractor and then reversed to SbCnet on grounds of irregularities of the tender evaluation process and the illegal contract award.

(Source: 'Auditor says parliament's IT project award improper', Addis Ababa: *Fortune: Ethiopia's Business Weekly*, 5-12 August 2001; 'Is justice served?' *Fortune: Ethiopia's Business Weekly*, 6 January 2002; 'Our government and parliament should be free of inefficiency', *The Reporter Weekly*, 9 May 2001; and 'Parliament's computerisation project delays', *Fortune: Ethiopia's Business Weekly*, 13-20 May)

Since February 2004, Sophia and her companies have focused on the international issue of corporate governance, and have been engaged in business consultancy to various US-based international public/private companies in areas including public/investor relations, corporate communication and governance, Sarbanes-Oxley implementation, business strategy and process re-engineering. Some of her company's clients in this area include Intel Corp, BDO Sieldman LLP, and NMMI/On-Screen Technologies, Inc.

In 2005 Sophia was appointed into a key leadership position to serve on the Internet Corporation for Assigned Names and Numbers (ICANN) board of advisors, a position responsible for balancing the needs and interests of the larger Internet community. Sophia was formerly appointed into the Advisory Interim Steering Committee of the African Regional Network, the second global regional network formed for ICT, under the sponsorship of the United Nations.

Sophia is a member of many technological alliances and professional associations. She is a certified information systems auditor, a professional designation for competent knowledge and proficiency in the field of information systems audit, control and security. In the United States, Sophia has served on the board of the International Information Systems Audit and Control Association, San Francisco Chapter, and the international 'Who's who in information technology' in 1998. In 2003, Sophia was nominated to serve on the board of governors of the Golden Gate niversity San Francisco International Alumni Association.

Sophia is also a published writer and contributes often to local and international publications on various topics including technology for development, risk management, good governance, public affairs issues, business and women's issues and sports. Her volunteer work includes helping students achieve educational excellence and pursue vocational training and a college education via personal assistance and recommendations, member and contributions to the Paul Harris fellow Rotary Club and a contribution to public affairs as one of board members in the North California-based World Affairs Council.

In June 2002, the Society of Ethiopians in Diaspora (SEED) honoured and awarded Ato Gebreyes Begna and his wife Weizero Yeweinshet Dessalegne in recognition of their contribution to their community both at home and abroad. Ato Gebreyes and his wife were honoured for providing opportunities to the less fortunate children, orphans, the disabled and the aged in the community, as well as for their inspiring entrepreneurial leadership and family values. The Begna family pioneered private enterprise in its modern form in Ethiopia. Ato Gebreyes founded Ethiopia Amalgamated Ltd, with a little or no capital but with a clear vision of the future and recognition that the private sector is the engine for accelerated economic and social growth. Ethiopia Amalgamated engaged in diversified economic and social development activities, including modern logistics and ships management; the transformation of the Addis Tyre Company (from antiquated facilities to modern technology), and the establishment of the Kotobe Metal Tools Factory, which is engaged in the production and distribution of essential agricultural tools.

Ethiopia Amalgamated played a pioneer role in the introduction and promotion of the widespread use of fertiliser in Ethiopia and linked the farmers to national and international markets where they can get equitable prices for their produce.

(Source: Society of Ethiopians in diaspora (SEED) press release)

Teshome Kebede, born into a farming family in Bale Province, graduated in accounting from the Commercial School of Addis Ababa (now Commercial College) in 1969. He pursued higher studies at Addis Ababa University and graduated with a BA in management in 1974. Since graduating he has worked in institutions as varied as a private bank and a vegetable oil milling factory, progressing from a junior clerk in the Addis Ababa Bank to becoming commercial manager of the United Oil Mills and Soap Factories (now Addis Modjo Food Complex). Kebede has been running his own business for 26 years, the last 12 at Genuine Leather Craft. His prominence in the national business circle of the country has earned him several official posts (vice-president of the Addis Ababa Chamber of Commerce, president of the Commercial Graduates Association, and currently acting president of the Ethiopian Private Industries Association). In operating his leather garment-producing firm, he uses the Internet and ultra-modern foreign trade methods.

Kebede writes that Ethiopia's livestock resources are one of the largest in the world — in fact the 10th in the world and the largest in Africa. It is not only the quantity of leather harvested that is significant but also the quality. Some of the varieties have become synonymous with sovereign standards in the international leather market which recognises, for example, 'Bati Genuine' as a type of goatskin that is extremely high class and high value, while anything close to it is referred to as 'Bati Type'. Similarly, sheepskins from Ethiopia's highland are known as 'Selallie Genuine' and the hides are also known for their uncommon dense fibre texture.

The establishment of Genuine Leather Craft, which specialises in high class leather garments, was inspired by the paradox that the country has not been known as a source of these raw materials. In the traditional foreign trade system, the company's finished consumer goods could not easily find their way onto the world market. A pair of fashion gloves made in Japan from one and a half square feet of Ethiopian sheepskin costs more than a jacket made from a 42-square foot sheepskin of the same quality made in Ethiopia. E-commerce has done a lot to change this.

Genuine Leather Craft was established in 1992. It attempted to enter the leather garment market in Europe through the conventional export channels, and participated in prestigious fashion fairs there at least twice a year. Each was preceded by visiting the known fashion centres for current trends, creating up-to-date collections and printing eye-catching catalogues for free distribution. The entire exercise was indeed very expensive.

E-commerce enables the producer and the consumer to meet in the information superhighway and transact at their will without any intermediary. The multiple benefits include that the chain between the consumer and the producers is reduced and GLC's outreach has increased to encompass the whole world. The garments pictured on their website are available to buyers around the world 24 hours a day, and GLC can promote its business to the entire community of virtual shoppers. E-commerce also links GLC to small importer-retailers who offer even better unit prices than big importer-wholesalers. Equally the small importer-retailer benefits by cutting out the margin otherwise payable to the middleman, importer-wholesaler.

Between 1997, when GLC's first few web pages were published, and March 2001, more than 100,000 browsers have visited their website, and learned something about GLC and Ethiopia. GLC's online sales grew by a yearly average of 25 per cent for 1998-2000, reaching 42 per cent of their total sales in 2000.

GLC's presence on the web has also helped their domestic sales substantially. The large international community in Ethiopia that buys a lot for relatives and friends abroad, and the huge number of Ethiopians in the diaspora, visit GLC's website and specify their preferences. As a result, GLC's market share assessment survey for 2000 showed that they had been able to control a significant portion of the domestic market in spite of larger companies with wider traditional market outlets. GLC believes domestic sales to foreign buyers have made a direct contribution to the foreign currency transfer into Ethiopia.

Even GLC's traditional export marketing has benefited from its online activity. GLC receives inquiries from places that they could never have been able to reach otherwise. Keeping track of trends has now become a click away for GLC. As many sources of fashion publish their creations on their websites, they are now able to follow seasonal developments and even foresee trends. Teshome Kebede concludes that Ethiopia can be an example of benefiting from the development of e-commerce. Ethiopia has been associated with supplying crude agricultural raw materials, mainly coffee and raw hides and skins. Ethiopia's emergence as a supplier of finished industrial consumer goods such as high fashion leather garments is a new development in the market, and its potential is only comprehended by a few.

(Source: www.genuineleathercraft.com and Teshome Kebede. 'The potential of electronic commerce', paper prepared for the 'Ethiopia in the Knowledge Age' Conference, 11 June 2001)

Menbere Alemayehu is a self-employed businesswoman engaged in fashion designs since 1984. She exports mainly pillows, table runners, wall hangings, shawls and scarves, made from elegant traditional, hand-woven Ethiopia fabrics. Menbere has acquired years of experience in the design and production of women's garments. She has been in the business from her childhood, following in the footsteps of her mother, who was a tailor who designed and made wedding dresses, casual dresses and uniforms.

Menbere has a degree in design from the University of Delaware, where she was honoured with a 'woman of promise certificate of distinction' in recognition of her dedication to academic excellence and determination in facing up to challenges. She owns a design studio, Menby's Design, in Addis Ababa, where she works as a head designer. She uses local weaving threads (Dirna-Mag) and imported Indian threads as a raw material. Through her products, Menbere introduces Ethiopian culture, tradition, and art to the world. After Menbere completes the design work on new products, she works with the weavers to turn her designs into new products. Sometimes the weavers fail to effect orders on time, and Menbere says they need to be made aware of the urgency of time.

She has now established a business partnership with Ellen Dorsch, an American committed to expanding markets for Ethiopian products in the United States. While Menbere facilitates the production in Ethiopia, Dorsch does the marketing and selling in the United States. Together, they plan patterns and colour to attract the American market, shopping in New York to observe popular colours and styles. They have participated in various international exhibitions such as at the Javitts Trade Centre in New York, the Smithsonian Museum in Washington, and at the San Fransisco Trade Fair.

In September 2005, Menbere was employing four women and working with 45 weavers. She wants to expand her business and needs the moral support of the government, and more space, for mass production.

(Source: www.creativewomen.net and Muluneh Gebre, 'Introducing local products with foreign tastes and preferences', *Addis Tribune*, 28 May 2004)

The Gamo people in the Gamo Goffa region of southern Ethiopia have a reputation for making the best traditional costumes. In Addis Ababa, there is a Gamo cooperative of spinners and weavers, producing not only materials for the traditional costume but also suiting and decorative fabrics. This cooperative is the capital's major supplier of traditional costumes. A member of the cooperative notes that they never fail to get a supply of raw cotton as they have good contacts with their region, where cotton is widely cultivated.

The process of spinning and weaving is carried out through a division of labour between the sexes. The women clean the cotton filament and spin the thread, which is then woven by men. The finest fabrics are woven by hand on looms. Warp threads are strung on a framework of stripped sapling poles and are moved as the weaver chooses, by means of foot-powered leather throngs. The woof threads are carried across in a pod-shaped wooden shuttle. This way transparent cloths and cloths with the heavy texture of drapery material are produced. They work from dawn to dusk six day a week, and rest on Mondays, says 30-year-old Mesfin Bashu, a member of the cooperative since its establishment some years ago.

On Sundays, people converge on Shero Meda to buy traditional clothes of various colours and designs ranging in price from 70 to 200 birr. In one year, the cooperative has made a substantial profit and with the money they want to expand their business so as to cope with the local and even foreign demand. Genet Belay is an Ethiopian businesswoman living in America who receives large orders for traditional costumes. She says that Ethiopians in the diaspora, especially women, want to wear the *kemis*, a long, full-sleeved cotton gown embroidered at the neck, cuffs and hem. Mesfin says business is good, and the cooperative is seriously considering its own cotton farms in the Gamo Goffa region in order to have its own supply of cotton on a regular basis.

Until recently, most members of the cooperative didn't really bother to send their children to school. Mesfin never went to school himself and yet he is better off than most people in the civil service. He teaches his children how to spin and weave, and this skill provides them with a safe livelihood. With a family of eight, he is now convinced of the necessity to educate his children. He has now realised the importance of education in becoming efficient entrepreneurs and worthy citizens, and proudly says that he has already enrolled his four children in a nearby school.

(Source: Yohannes Ruphael. 'Clinging to traditional costumes', Addis Ababa: *Addis Tribune*, 12 November 2004)

Daniel Mebrahtu has been a dynamic entrepreneur since 1974. After graduating from Bahir Dar Polytechnic in electrical technology, he wanted to establish his own business instead of seeking employment. However, there were many challenges, as he had no permanent place of his own or any start-up capital. Under these prohibitive circumstances he started a business virtually empty handed. The only asset he possessed at that time was some brushes and paint that he had bought for 15 Birr, but his heart was set, and he was ready to tackle whatever came along with determination. That was how he established Dan Technical Studio and started signboard writing in a garage of a private house. He learned new ideas from the books he bought out of his savings. Then he started his first manufacturing business, crafting traditional cotton clothes from locally-available materials. When that was not enough he added making gift articles, jewellery boxes, brief cases, decorated chairs and several items for office and home decoration — again from locally-available materials.

Mebrahtu went through many ups and downs. Some individuals who did not want to see him succeed were continually threatening him. As pressure was mounting, he had to leave Ethiopia and flee to Kenya in 1985, returning to his country in 1991. He was determined to transform his company from handicraft to technocraft, and so he travelled to America and to European and Asian countries to study the manufacture of steel office furniture. Today, his company, Dan Technocraft, is one of the finest and largest office furniture manufacturing companies in Ethiopia and compares well even in the regional markets. Since 1997, Mebrahtu has become the only manufacturer of elevators and traffic lights in the country. It gives Mebrahtu special satisfaction to see posters in front of new buildings promoting elevators supplied by his company.

Mebrahtu says that the mission and vision of his company is to be the hub of technology and to be engaged in technology transfer and contributing to the development of essential, appropriate and affordable technology in the country. In December 2001, he sponsored and organised a symposium under the theme 'Technology development, transfer and its future in Ethiopia' in which academics, government officials, industrialists, and important personalities participated. He has assisted in the development of Ethiopia's first private university, the American University of Ethiopia. In 2001 he also established the Industrial Technology Institute. Mebrahtu is an inspiration for many Ethiopians who strive to break out of the vicious circle of poverty. He says that if you are determined you will succeed.

Since his high school days Mesfin Teshome has been known as a shy and reserved person. But when it comes to business development and exploring potentials, Mesfin has magical powers. When Ethiopia fell under a military dictatorship over 30 years ago, Mesfin Teshome, then only a fresh graduate aspiring to a respectable occupation, went into exile in to East Africa. There he engaged in various businesses including tea blending and packing. He soon climbed the ladder of success to acquire enough experience and resources to take him back to Ethiopia, when the situation changed. His company, Almeta Impex, is very well known in East Africa and is now also identified with import-export and agro-industrial activities in Ethiopia.

Yirga Haile started by working with his older brother in the shoe business more than 30 years ago but left his brother to start the Kangaroo shoe factory. He has managed to live up to the highest standard of quality in the country, which has earned him well-deserved recognition. His children, all of who have received higher education (since he himself had little formal schooling), have returned from educational institutions equipped with skills and managerial competence and contributed to the growth of the company. Today, while Yirga oversees, as managing director, the Kangaroo Industrial Group (KAN) of companies is involved in various facets of manufacturing, from the traditional shoes to plastics, foam products and laundry soaps. KAN is living testimony to the fact that lack of formal education cannot limit the entrepreneurial potential of an individual.

Batu Tannery was built by the Kangaroo Industrial Group at a cost of about US$ 4.2 million, and started production in January 2001. According to Belachew Yirga, general manager and shareholder of the tannery, the construction of the factory took six years to complete. A US$2 million loan from the African Development Bank partially covered the investment, while the remainder came from contributions made by the three shareholders. Located on the outskirts of Addis, Batu Tannery has the capacity to process 3,500 units of hides and skins a day. The tannery plans to supply 85 per cent of the hides and 50 per cent of the skins it processes. The remaining products would be supplied to the local market, mainly to the Kangaroo Shoe Factory, which is part of the industrial group. Belachew sees good markets locally, but fears that the increasing price of hides and skins in the local market might pose challenges in competing with different kinds of products in the international market. Nonetheless, Belachew says the company plans initially to export seven kinds of leather products. The factory is equipped with up-to-date technology and Belachew hopes they can contribute to bringing foreign currency to Ethiopia.

Samuel Getachew is the managing director of Nile Shoe & Sole, a privately owned company established in 1994 to produce shoe components and accessories for local and foreign market consumption. It was established with an initial capital of US$112,360. The company supplies shoe soles and has many clients who are engaged in producing complete leather shoes as well as synthetic leather shoes as per the market demand. Nile also produces synthetic leather for shoe uppers, linings, upholstery, bags and covers. By 2004, it had grown to a big company capable of producing 6,500 shoe soles and plastic shoes a day. Nile Shoe is planning to diversify to sports shoes and various similarly-produced items such as U-PVC pipes and packing juice bottles. The company was run by only five personnel at the start. By 2004, it had an annual turnover of US$792,994 and 132 full time employees of whom 55 are permanent. By endeavouring to compete in the market, which is highly affected by cheap finished shoes imported from China, the company is contributing to the struggle for the survival of the African economy.

Getamesai Degefu is devoted to work and takes his duties seriously. At one time, employed as a junior staff member in an electronic appliances company, he learned the serial numbers of a whole spare-parts manual by heart to make sure his clients were given the response they wanted on the spot. Such commitment and hard work were sure to bear fruit sooner or later. Mesai started Omedad Plc with four friends some ten years ago, to import office machinery and equipment, and did extremely well. He continued to work hard with his partners to nurture and bring Omedad to what it is today, one of the biggest exclusive furniture and domestic appliances importers and retailers in Ethiopia. Besides that, he has recently acquired establishment manufacturing modern furniture. It is often said at Omedad that there is always an option to 'no'.

National Oil Ethiopia Plc, member of the MIDROC Group, introduced Chevron-Texaco products to the Ethiopian market under its own trademark in November 2004. National Oil was established in April 2004 by Sheik Mohammed Hussein Al-Amoudi, Abnet Gebremeskel, and former general manager of Shell Ethiopia, Tadesse Tilahun. In May 2004, National Oil reached an agreement with American Chevron-Texaco to package and then distribute Chevron-Texaco products in specially designed plastic and tin containers selected by National Oil. The same month, National Oil began the construction of ten filling stations in Addis Ababa, two in Adama (Nazareth), two in Bishoftu (Debre Zeit) and one each in Mekele, Gondar and Asayta. Chevron-Texaco sent its experts to train managers of National Oil in August and the constructions were completed and the filling stations became operational in November.

National Oil planned to increase its share of the market to 25 per cent during 2005 by constructing more filling stations. Invitations were extended to individuals and companies that had convenient spaces to join the company. Each filling station would have its own restaurant, supermarket, Internet cafe and car-wash facilities. Buildings of one-story and above were being constructed alongside each station, with parts of the buildings to be rented to other companies involved in areas such as insurance and banking. National Oil was building its head office in Addis Ababa and was awaiting a reply to its application for a plot in Dukem, 35km south, to construct a depot. Among the plans for 2005 was the distribution of liquid petroleum gas.

(Source: Dawit Taye. 'National Oil to launch lubricants under own brand', *Addis Fortune*, 17 October 2004)

A Glimmer of Hope has been called 'the most effective approach to private assistance in the world today' by Tibor Nagy Jr, the former United States ambassador to Ethiopia. In the May 2004 edition of the *Foreign Service Journal*, Ambassador Nagy suggested the US government should partner more with innovative emerging NGOs such as A Glimmer of Hope, a Texas-based family foundation focused on Ethiopia. Formed and funded by high-tech entrepreneur Philip Berber and his wife Donna, A Glimmer of Hope, has been operating with remarkable success in Ethiopia since it launched its national aid programme in 2001. By the end of 2005, the foundation will have completed more than 1,600 projects and directly affected approximately 1.5 million Ethiopians living in poverty in remote, rural villages.

By the end of 2004, the foundation had invested approximately US$8 million in water wells, schools, health posts, veterinary clinics and emergency famine relief. A Glimmer of Hope has helped by building schools and classrooms, providing desks and books, supplying medicines, restoring a hospital, and providing potable drinking water in rural villages. In 2005, the foundation is funding more than 1,150 projects throughout Ethiopia. Its goal is to help indigenous people in rural areas to help themselves. It gives to humanitarian causes, invests in development projects and lends to social enterprise. It deals directly with local organisations and uses an entrepreneurial and business-like approach to project selection and management.

In 2000, a windfall from the dot.com boom left the Berbers in a position to fulfil their dream of making a difference in the lives of less fortunate people around the world. Initially, they were drawn to Africa — specifically, Ethiopia. After researching existing channels of international giving, they decided that if their money was going to have any real impact they would do it themselves. Philip Berber notes that the more they learned about the international aid business, the more appalled they became at the inefficiency and misuse of funds. Donna Berber explains that they work with national governments, not through them, and deliver aid directly through local indigenous NGOs. She explains that in some cases, traditional aid organisations deliver as little as 15 cents on the donated dollar to the people it was intended for. Part of the Berbers' motivation is to make sure all the money gets to where it is needed and that it is used effectively.

Since all costs are covered by income arising from its endowment, A Glimmer of Hope is able to assure donors that 100 per cent of their donations will be forwarded to its Ethiopian partners for those in need. Donors are able to make non-specific donations but they are also able to select which type of project to help. For those able to fund an entire project, they will receive recognition at the project site as well as feedback on the impact of the project from the foundation. Philip Berber says A Glimmer of Hope's new model of international aid involves social entrepreneurs and social investors seeking long term, sustainable social impact. He believes the days of handing money to governments and bureaucratic aid organisations, and only a small part of that aid getting to the people, must be put behind us. New approaches drawn from the commercial, entrepreneurial, and technological fields can and are making a real difference. They are already seeing this at A Glimmer of Hope.

(Source: www.aglimmerofhope.org)

Eritrea

When Eritrea got its independence in 1991, the government brought commerce to the centre stage of its activity. Eritrea has certainly coped well. Trade is now valued more than aid. The government is promoting free trade agreements with regions as far apart as Latin America, Africa, and the Middle East. The search for capital, technology and markets has become an important component of Eritrean diplomacy, particularly over the last few years.

Ravinder Rena, professor of economics at the Eritrean Institute of Technology, believes that Eritrea should exploit its unique geographic inheritance. Eritreans are acutely conscious of their geostrategic location at the crossroads of Europe and the Middle East, the Persian Gulf and Asia. Eritrea therefore seeks to establish harmonious relations with neighbours and to adopt policies of economic modernisation.

Professor Rena underlines Eritrea's need:
- to focus on trade and investment partnerships;
- for imaginative economic strategy towards neighbours;
- to promote economic integration in the region;

- for incentives and facilities to promote border trade between Eritrea and its neighbours;
- for the reduction of tariffs for goods from the rest of Sub Saharan Africa; and
- for the removal of restrictions on investments from other countries.

Rena suggests that if Eritrea looks at the strategic significance, over the long term, of economic integration with neighbours, it should be more than eager to bilaterally force the pace of creating a single market in Africa and end the economic fragmentation of the continent. Unlike in the past, African countries are seeking to globalise their economies and are planning for a single currency. Rena states that all the countries are under compulsion to take full advantage of the natural imperatives for market integration with each other.

Rena points out that Libya, Pakistan, United Arab Emirates and Bahrain are seeking deeper links with Eritrea. Djibouti, Yemen and Sudan want duty free access for their goods to the Eritrean market. Qatar, France and Italy which have already agreed to cooperate in promoting Eritrea's economy, are seeking modernisation of this relationship and the removal of many distortions that have crept into the trading regime with Eritrea.

Rena concludes that the economic success of neighbouring countries is linked to the trade and fiscal policies of every country in the region. The question is no longer whether the region will integrate. The unanswered questions are about how effectively and quickly Eritrea will take advantage of this reality in the African continent.

(Source: Ravinder Rena. 'Eritrea and its trade linkages - some observations', from Shaebia.org, 31 October 2005)

Professor Rena believes that Eritreans in the diaspora have to invest substantially in their motherland to boost the Eritrean economy. The soundness of government policies and the performance of the economy will increasingly condition the preparedness of the diaspora to make savings available to the country and influence the sustainability of the public finances. Rena points out that Eritrea can set up economic zones exclusively for non-resident emigrants (NREs) to facilitate more investments. The economic zones with state-of-the-art infrastructure will have hotels, motels, higher educational institutions, and IT industry and research centres. The government can work out a package to attract NRE investment in tourism and education and facilitate transfer of technology and joint ventures with local Eritreans.

According to the available statistics, Rena points out that of the about a million Eritrean diaspora, at least 100,000 could invest substantial amount in the country projects. Both fiscal and external sustainability depend critically on the continued support of the diaspora. Rena says that some of the Eritrean people are very rich in the diaspora in the US, Europe, Saudi Arabia etc. Hence, the government has to create conditions to make NREs invest back in their country. In the meantime, the government has to be committed to protect the interests of NREs. In fact, it is for this purpose that a separate department can be established as a nodal point to address all issues related to the diaspora.

Rena explains that the Eritrean NREs or investors should be confident that their investments can create new job opportunities, improve the quality of life for all Eritreans, and improve the infrastructure of Eritrea. He emphasises that Eritrea's government has already taken some steps in this move, but he believes it has to expedite the process to make things comfortable for NREs, as Eritrea also belongs to them. Rena points out that other countries such as China, India and Israel have created conditions to facilitate their diasporas to invest back, and concludes that Eritreans in the diaspora can also join their hands in building the strong and multifaceted economy of Eritrea (for all of Africa, remittances from Africans working abroad in the period 2000-2003 averaged about US$17 billion per annum, overtaking Foreign Direct Investment flows which averaged about US$15 billion per annum during the same period).

(Source: Ravinder Rena. 'NRE investment - an impetus to boost Eritrea's economy', from Shaebia.org, 20 July 2005)

In late 2001, Giovanni Primo, an Eritrean investor, entrepreneur and businessman residing in Italy, with the ambition to see a developed Eritrea, started a new project comprising the renovation of a hotel in Asmara, expansion of another in Massawa, and establishment of a tourist village on an island off the coast of the Red Sea. Primo has invested more than 120 million Nfk in the project. He believes that with its great natural resources potential, Eritrea could make huge progress in the tourism industry. 'We have the sea, the sun. What more could we ask for?' he asks, adding that Eritrea would be an ideal place for foreigners who wish for a wonderful time. It's why he decided to buy hotels that could attract and comfortably accommodate tourists. One of these hotels is Albergo Italia.

Built in 1899, the Albergo Italia (previously known as Keren Hotel) is the oldest hotel in Asmara and contains perhaps the most elaborate stucco plasterwork in the country. Primo re-opened the hotel in the second half of 2005, after a thorough renovation to restore its original grandeur, fully complying with the standards of a five-star hotel. Visitors who come to Eritrea to explore the sea can stay in this hotel and directly proceed to Massawa or Dessey Island, where resort hotels are being built.

Primo also owns Dahlak Hotel in Massawa. In 2006, an expansion complex to the hotel will be completed next door, working in connection with its sister hotel in Asmara. As a third step, Primo has initiated a tourist village project in Dessey, one of the islands in the Dahlak Archipelago. The project comprises a resort hotel made up of a number of traditional huts but fully equipped with modern hotel appliances. The hotel will provide scuba diving equipment for those interested and will have jetties to harbour boats. There will also be some residential houses and the hotel's own swimming pools.

Primo expresses his sincere hopes that Massawa will be another Venice. With everything being restored and renovated, and with the free trade zone operational, Massawa will surely prosper. If Eritreans abroad came back and help in rebuilding their country, Primo can't see any reason why Eritrea couldn't become as rich and attractive as other developed nations.

(Source: 'Come and invest in Eritrea: Giovanni Primo', www.shaebia.org, 14 September 2003)

Negash-Bokre Saba, owner of Barocko Eritrea Ltd, was born in Asmara but left Eritrea in 1971, living in Switzerland and the United States, earning a bachelor's degree in marketing from UCLA. She worked as a fashion representative in Italy and the United States before returning to Eritrea in 1998. She saw an opportunity and with US$4 million of her own money and a loan from the government, she purchased the Barocko textile factory, which had opened in 1993. She named her company Barocko Eritrea, developed the slogan 'New fashion for a new nation' and had visions of manufacturing brightly-coloured mini-skirts and hot pants, but during the war with Ethiopia, Saba, a consummate businesswoman, saw a new opportunity. Her factory manufactured camouflage. She employed 850 workers, 80 per cent of whom were women, working as electricians, mechanics, spinners, seamstresses and floor supervisors, earning on average US$45 to US$65 a month, depending on the worker's skills and responsibilities. Saba talks of the future with optimism. She has purchased a plantation in western Eritrea so she has her own supply of raw cotton.

(Source: Cheryl Hatch. 'Wonder women of Eritrea', www.zreportage.com, March 2000)

Saba was among business executives drawn from over 70 different countries of the world who received the prestigious European Market Research Award for 2002. The award is presented by the European Market Research Centre (EMRC) to those entrepreneurs who are successful in penetrating regional and foreign markets, and for contributing to the development of economic cooperation within their regions and towards Europe. The EMRC appreciates the activities of such business leaders and urges producers and industrialists to bring their competitive products and services to the international marketplace.

In 1992, the National Insurance Corporation of Eritrea (NICE) was formed as an autonomous public enterprise transacting all classes of insurance business. NICE has fully-fledged insurance facilities and can provide all classes of insurance required by individuals and companies. In 2004, Eritreans around the world expressed an interest in buying NICE shares. About 750 Eritreans at home and more than 1,000 abroad have bought. Other shares are owned by the Martyrs' Trust Fund, with the remainder still retained by the Government. With the transfer of shares to the public, NICE is now looking for ways to establish an over the counter market for the trading of its shares.

Owing to its skilled and prudent financial as well as operational management, NICE has shown remarkable growth since its establishment in 1991. The corporation's gross profits have risen from a mere 4 million Nakfa in 1992 to 54.4 million Nakfa in 2004, and it is expected to yield even higher profit levels in the future in the hands of investors.

Zeru Woldemichael, general manager and chief executive of NICE since 1991, has extensive insurance knowledge having worked in the insurance industry since 1972. From 1972 to 1982 he held various positions within the Ethiopian Insurance Corporation, starting as a department head, subsequently promoted to branch manager and further promoted to operations manager before leaving the company. In 1983 he joined the Khartoum Insurance Company in the Sudan acting as technical manager. Woldemichael, born in 1951, holds a Bachelor's degree in business administration from the Haile Selassie University of Addis Ababa and is a chartered insurer by professional qualification.

Woldemichael is responsible for ensuring the smooth daily operations of all departments, the overall risk management of the corporation, business development and the sound financial standing of the corporation. He reports directly to the board of directors. Woldemichael is also the vice chairman of the board of Africa Re, a director of PTA Re (where he also acts as the chairman of the audit committee), and Eritrean Airlines and sits on the executive committee of the African Insurance Organisation, as well as being a member of the board of trustees of AIO Software Trust Fund.

(Source: www.nice-eritrea.com)

The Tesinma Share Company assembles a wide range of commercial vehicles such as buses, cargo trucks, tippers, skip loaders, hook loaders, garbage compactors, incinerators and weigh bridges, using imported chassis and drive trains. Tesinma shareholders are Tesfai Yehdego, an Eritrean engineer, and Delia Brox, his German wife, both qualified production engineers. They have invested significantly in Tesinma and have trained the firm's staff in modern production methods. Yehdego specialised in automotive engineering at the Technical University of Hamburg, worked in Germany for nine years, and made working visits to many African and Middle Eastern countries.

The Tesinma factory, with a capacity to build from 50 to 70 buses yearly, is located in Dekemhare, a town planned for industrial development, about 40 kilometres west of Asmara. Tesinma also produces laundry machines (for hotels and hospitals), solar collectors, agricultural equipment and prefabricated halls and hangers. It is also actively involved in developing human capacity, which is vital to technological advancement. Annually, about 50 students take courses in seven subjects; one-year courses are given in auto CAD design, painting, industrial and auto-electricity, welding, toolmaking and office management. The criteria for admission are completion of high school, exemption from national service and a pass in the entrance examination. Those who fulfil these criteria take the courses free of charge. 'We are putting much effort in developing the country's human capacity,' says Yehdego. The employees also take on-the-job training in modern production methods.

Engineer Jurgen Krafft, from Germany, said, 'I am surprised to find such a company in this small country. It has the same modern facilities and equipment as those in Germany.' Tesinma has about 150 Eritrean employees and eleven foreign experts (from Germany and India). Bereket Tesfai is one of the Tesinma employees who graduated in civil engineering from Asmara University. He is working as a structural and architectural designer of pre-fabricated steel houses. 'I have learned in class how to design using different software but here I could see what I have designed. Above all, I have acquired confidence,' he notes. Aster Elias has worked for Tesinma for four years since graduating from Pavoni Technical Institute. 'I have acquired much experience in general drawing and details about auto CAD designing,' says Aster.

Tesinma finished assembling seven BMC type buses made for Asmara Bus Company, at a cost of Nfk 980,000, in March 2004. The buses were tailor-made according to the customers' needs, at a price comparing favourably to the imported buses that fetch about one and half million Nfk. Girmay Haregot, the manager of the Asmara Bus Company, says, 'The buses we bought are designed according to our demands with Euro two–engine (anti-pollution), first of its kind in the country.' Girmay further noted that local products should be encouraged in order to save hard currency.

According to Yehdego, buses are built by taking into consideration vehicle weight, pay load and the roads of African countries which require special reinforced structure. The future plan of the company is to produce its own chassis and dies using computer aided machines. Yehdego has opened a head office in Asmara with its maintenance and spare parts section, and plans to export Tesinma products to neighbouring countries in Africa and the Middle East.

(Source: www.tesinma.com and Yorsalem Abraha. 'Tesinma: A promising vehicle assembling company', www.shaebia.org, 5 May 2004)

Like this young nation, founded only in 1993, Tesinma was created with great optimism. Yehdego returned home with his wife to help build something different in Africa — a country that would not only succeed, but also do so defiantly on its own. 'We can't just leave Africa, with all its resources, as a professional begging society. We can train people to have them develop themselves,' Yehdego insists.

(Source: Ian Fisher. 'War dims Eritrea's hopes, but clears its eyes', The New York Times, www.nytimes.com, 24 April 2001)

The Elabered Agro Industrial Estate is 'a unique place not only in Eritrea but in the whole Africa,' says general manager Morgan Hoff. You need only to travel about 68-km north-west of Asmara in order to reach Elabered Estate. When you come near the village of Elabered you pass along a narrow road bordered with flowers that stretches for 50 metres. On the right there is place where the Anseba River and the Balwa River flow. These streams are diverted in seven dams in order to satisfy the water requirements of the farm. When you arrive at the gate of the farm you see the signboard of Elabered Estate and when you get inside you are inspired by the beauty of the place with its huge duma tree, garage and well equipped guest house, and the natural vegetation.

On the outskirts of Elabered, the estate has a moderate climate and an elevation of about 1,400 to 1,500 metres above sea level. It is an integrated farming system producing fruits (oranges, lemons, mandarins, mangos and custard apples), vegetables (potatoes, green and sweet peppers, egg plant, zucchini, green beans, lollo Rosso, lollo Biando, endive, oak leaf, fennel, leeks, curled parsley, sweet melon, celery and radishes) processed milk, livestock and other products. There are 1,200 hectares within the Elabered Estate of which 300 hectares are arable; the rest is occupied by houses of workers, ponds and dams containing fish — and trees and grass during rainy season. Ato Selebe Kahesay, a researcher from University of Asmara, and administrator of Elabered Estate, has found that more than 100 different species of birds exist in the estate, which is not only a farm but also a tourist site.

In describing the place, Morgan Hoff says, 'When I came in 1996 to do a general study of sustainable farming, I came in touch with the beautiful farm in Elabered and I was very enthusiastic because I have never seen a place like this in my whole life as an agricultural consultant.' One of the amazing things about Elabered Estate is the underground pipeline which stretches for about 236 kilometres, and which was built when it was set up as a private sector establishment by an Italian entrepreneur.

The Elabered farm has upgraded its dairy factory by introducing new machinery from Norway. In explaining the reason for the crowd of people in the dairy shops, the estate's marketing manager, Ato Kidane Melles, says that in order to stabilise the market and to minimise exploitation by businessmen the organisation sells directly to the consumers.

Other livestock production is the outdoor swine (pig) area. The estate, which has about 1,300 pigs, delivers pork to hotels and restaurants. Elabered Estate is in a transition from a traditional to a modern system of irrigation and water management. It is introducing new technologies like the drip, micro, mini, and overhead sprinkler systems.

Many people say that the Elabered Estate is in ruins because the area along the road where the orange trees used to grow is now barren. But from what journalist Yorsalem Abraha observed, and from the words of the general manager, the farm is being revived through the replanting of new trees, some of which have already started to bear fruit. In 2003, vegetables were the main export item. The marketing manager says that the exported vegetables can compete with those from South America, California, Mexico, Europe, Australia, Egypt and Holland.

(Source: Yorsalem Abraha. 'Elabered Farm, Part I', www.shaebia.org, 15 December 2003)

The Energy Research and Training Centre (ERTC), within the Department of Energy in the Ministry of Energy and Mines, has designed a new and improved stove that is safer to use for the cooking of injera, a pancake-like bread that is served with most traditional Eritrean dishes. The improved stove has been carefully designed by ERTC Director, Debesai Ghebrehiwet Andegiorgish, renewable energy specialist, to ensure complete and efficient combustion of the fuel used in it. It has an enclosed fire-holder, with enhanced ventilation so that the fire burns more efficiently, and a chimney to take smoke out of the house. The stove also burns a wider range of fuels, working well with twigs and leaves and animal dung. Being raised above the floor and having an enclosed fire-holder, the stove is no longer a danger to children. ERTC is disseminating the use of this new stove to rural communities throughout Eritrea, teaching women how to build the stoves themselves, and also paying them to teach other women, who are, in turn, teaching others.

ERTC was presented with a first prize of £30,000 in the Food Security category of the Ashden Awards for Sustainable Energy in June 2003 for developing and introducing their energy-efficient smokeless and fuel-efficient clay stove for baking injera. The award funding was used to provide an additional 2,000 stoves and train over 400 artisans in stove production. As of November 2005, over 32,000 stoves had been installed, about 6,400 women were totally trained, and the users are delighted with the improved quality of life that the stove has brought them. The benefits are lower consumption, reduced or eliminated health problems and saved cooking time. Less wood is collected for fuel, and fewer trees are cut down. This stove has also been recently improved in its simplicity and implementation process. Debesai came up with a new idea and innovation and built a mould with which the users can build the hollowed brick for the firebox with insulation, and the chimney part of the stove. So the rate of implementation will be more than doubled.

In early 2005, Debasai also designed a multifunctional efficient portable setarit (solve any problem) stove that uses less fuel and has fewer carbon emissions. It was designed to prevent heat loss and increase the combustion rate. In testing, it was seen that this stove is very convenient for remote communities, especially for nomads who travel from one place to another, with many improved features. It burns wood and dung more efficiently (a considerable benefit in a region where forests are becoming increasingly difficult to sustain). Using only dung, small pieces of wood, or a small amount of charcoal, one can cook any type of bread, make coffee and sauce, or boil water in a very short time. The stove also offers innovative safety measures. It can be manufactured relatively easily, since it does not require complex and expensive tooling or high capital expenditure. Debasai believes his stove also has a promising future in neighbouring countries like Ethiopia and Sudan where the way of cooking resembles Eritrea's.

The ERTC was established in 1994 with the help of the Lower Saxony government in Germany through the coordination German branches of the World University Service (WUS). Since independence in 1993, ERTC has been responsible for introducing all energy saving and sustainable energy systems in Eritrea. ERTC has been active in various renewable energy activities for different applications, and conducts training and does research to transfer the know-how of the renewable energy technology in Eritrea actively and effectively.

Thirty-five health centres and more than 150 clinics have been powered by photovoltaic systems to run refrigerators, lighting, small operating systems and centrifuges in remote areas of the country. Eighty-five solar water pump systems have been installed around the country for community use, providing access to pure drinking water. Seventy-two schools are equipped with school lighting systems, helping the villagers to continue their education during evening classes, and supporting the students and teachers to study and to prepare lessons respectively.

ERTC is also responsible for repairing and maintenance of all the installed solar systems in the country. It has been doing wind and solar assessment projects in Eritrea for about six years at 25 meteorological stations around the country. Eritrea is presently in the stage of establishing wind parks in the high wind potential areas.

Phaesun Asmara is focused on the sustainable development of Eritrea, offering photovoltaic (solar electric) applications and solutions for the provision of electricity, potable water and water for irrigation. Phaesun Asmara is owned and managed by Francis Hillman and his wife Almaz Tecle. Hillman managed successful BP Solar operations in East and Southern Africa for ten years before moving to Eritrea to start up a new comprehensive service for the local and East African market. He has extensive experience in the engineering of water pumping and irrigation systems.

Hillman's main focus is on small-scale projects providing sufficient electricity for individual families or rural communities (solar energy solutions for rural infrastructure). He encourages Eritreans living abroad to purchase solar home systems for their relatives and friends living in rural Eritrea. He sells solar energy home packages to power lights, radio, black and white or colour TV, and offers battery backup systems. Phaesun Asmara is a shareholder in Phaesun GmbH in Memmingen, Germany.

Presently, Hillman is working on an integrated stove and fee for service solar home system programme in which small (12 watt peak/wp) two lights and radio solar home systems are supplied to individual houses in a group of villages. Each household pays a monthly service fee for the electricity provided. A local energy agent is appointed who is responsible for monthly fee collection, system maintenance and general liaison with Phaesun Asmara. The agent takes a small commission from each fee. In this way, 140 houses had been electrified in four villages as of November 2005.

Part of the income from the programme is being used to build improved Mogogo cooking stoves in collaboration with the Energy Research Centre. These stoves are eligible to earn carbon credits which are sold to earn hard currency for replacement batteries for the solar home programme as a sustainability mechanism since hard currency is not readily available in Eritrea.

(Source: www.phaesun.com/phaesun_asmara)

Seawater Farms Eritrea was one of the world's first commercial-scale integrated seawater farms. It is located on the west coast of the Red Sea on a vast stretch of barren desert just north of the Eritrean port of Massawa. It is here that the future of a new Eritrea is being built, a model that could provide a fruitful future for all the nations of the region. Carl Hodges, an atmospheric physicist at the University of Arizona, came up with an ingenious plan to overcome the freshwater shortages that many farmers face in arid countries. This plan came in the form of a seawater farm, which uses clean, untreated seawater instead of freshwater to raise its crops. An integrated seawater farm combines the growing of salt-loving edible plants and mangrove trees with the integrated breeding and raising of shrimp and fish. Integrated seawater farming has been engineered to address the problems of our time: hunger, environmental degradation, rising temperatures, drought and desertification, collapsing fisheries, shrinking cropland, disappearing forests, the loss of plant and animal species, poverty — and, indirectly, the growth of population.

They began its construction by cutting a huge channel from the Red Sea. This saltwater river, wide enough for small boats, runs onto the land, providing water to the land-based brick and concrete circles in which they raise their shrimp, filling the three salt lakes that hold the bulk of their fish, nurturing the thousands of mangroves that will shade its shores, irrigating their field crops, and draining, finally, into a sea garden park that is also accessible to boating. This park, forested by several varieties of mangroves, shelters innumerable species of flora and fauna, herons, flamingos, and other shorebirds, marine animals of many kinds, and provides controlled grazing for domestic animals, including goats and camels.

By eventually planting hundreds of thousands of hectares of field crops, they will be greening a substantial portion of coastal desert. By planting millions of new mangrove trees, they will be creating new mangrove forests. Both fields and forests will absorb immense amounts of atmospheric carbon, helping to lessen global warming. Newly green fields and forests will also create new micro-climates, making the surrounding area more liveable and more attractive to tourism. The sea garden provides a new and attractive habitat to numerous animal and plant species and an attractive and aesthetically pleasing amenity to visitors.

Nothing here is wasted. The bricks used to construct their shrimp circles are made on the farm. So is the food they give their shrimp. Their feed mill also makes feed for chickens, goats, cattle and camels, which is much needed in Eritrea. Wastes from the fish and shrimp help to fertilise their field crops. After the fish are filleted, their skins are tanned for leather and their bones and innards go into the shrimp food. One of their principal field crops, salicornia, provides a gourmet vegetable from its young shoots, and the mature plant provides seeds, which are used to produce a fine, edible oil and a high protein meal. There is also a large amount of biomass which can be used, along with other seawater-irrigated crops they grow, for animal fodder, particle board, and fire bricks. Combinations of salicornia straw and meal with fish and shrimp meal provide a complete feeding regimen for most domestic animals and a significant part of human feed.

They expect this first commercial-scale integrated seawater farm and its associated research facilities and industries to be a magnet for eco-tourism, for academic study, and for interested government and agribusiness officials from all over the world. Accordingly, they have a visitors' centre, a Seafalls Restaurant, and plan a luxury Sea Garden Hotel. Guided boat tours will traverse the entire expanse of the farm, and opportunities will be afforded for close observation of their technology and direct discussions with their agronomists and aqua-culturists.

Land has already been set aside for the establishment of a new seawater-based community providing homes and jobs for some of Eritrea's displaced people. Training will be provided to equip workers with the skills necessary to operate downstream industries creating the by-products of integrated seawater farming. New factories will make edible oil, particle board, fire bricks, lumber, fish leather goods, goat cheese, cereals, shrimp and fish specialties and numerous other products.

Seawater Farms Eritrea ships shrimp and fish to European markets as a way of earning much-needed hard currency. In the long run they envision duplicating this farm many times up and down the coast of the Red Sea, sharing this development with other nations in the region and providing a dependable source of food for all the people in the region and for their livestock as well. They see this as a giant step forward towards creating new wealth in the region, building stable new communities with new industries and rewarding employment. They see this as a major guarantor of future peace in the region and of self-sufficiency for its people. They see it as a way of greening the desert coastline, remaking the environment, creating comfortable new micro-climates, and encouraging tourism. Ultimately they believe this new technology will make the region one of the most productive shrimp and fish producers as well as one of its more productive agricultural areas using saltwater to irrigate new forests and to produce vegetables, oil, meal, and biomass for fuel, building materials, fodder and grazing.

In September 2005, war between Ethiopia and Eritrea still had not come to an end. The latest result is that Eritrea has expelled all USAID activity, and is in general making it difficult for NGOs to work in the country. Even with these problems, however, Carl Hodges continues to believe in the integrity and humanity of the people of Eritrea. He also continues to believe that Seawater Farms Eritrea will one day be revitalised and make significant contributions to improvement of the quality of life of the people of Eritrea, and that the seawater irrigation technology from Eritrea will spread to other countries such as Sudan and Egypt. In fact, if he were to have his greatest dream, there will be a seawater canal either on the southern border or to the north of Massawa, where the benefits would also be available to Ethiopia. Because of the situation, the Seawater Farms Eritrea project is on hold but Seaphire International has made a proposal to the government of Eritrea for the revitalisation of Seawater Farms Eritrea.

(Source:www.seawaterfoundation.org)

Djibouti

The Port of Djibouti is located at the crossroads of one of the busiest shipping routes in the world, linking Europe, the Far East, Africa and the Arabian Gulf. Djibouti, as a main maritime passage and a main trading route between East and West, stretches back 3,500 years, to the time of maritime explorations of the Red Sea. A strategic meeting point between two worlds (of Africa and Asia), the Red Sea was a place of contact and passage used by the Egyptians, the Phoenicians, the Ptolemaists, the Romans, the Greeks, the Byzantine, the Arabs, and then by the Europeans in search of the spices route. Its apogee came with the opening of the Suez Canal.

The Port of Djibouti evolved out of Ethiopia's search for a maritime outlet to its railway line, and Djibouti's coastline provided both easy access and sheltered anchorage. Work on the railway began in 1897, as did the initial construction of the port. Once the line was completed, in 1917, the port grew rapidly. Development at the port increased further between 1948 and 1957 with the construction of four deepwater quays and the dredging of the port access channels. On land, new warehouses and oil storage facilities were built, electricity and water supplies provided and railway lines laid.

Between 1960 and 1970, port activity was developed as part of an international maritime exchange network. The Red Sea had become one of the busiest shipping lanes in the world and Djibouti found itself acting as its service station. Bunkering traffic quadrupled in the ten years from 1954, reaching a peak of 1.8 million tons in 1965.

Djibouti's strategic location enabled the port authorities to rise successfully to the challenge of turning the port into a regional hub for the Red Sea and Indian Ocean, and in a wider context the three continents of Europe, Africa and Asia. Containerisation was the defining concept behind this new period of development and Djibouti's first modern container terminal began operations in February 1985.

In June 2000, the Port of Djibouti signed a management agreement with Dubai Ports World (DP World). Under the agreement, DP World will manage and develop the port over 20 years. DP World is a leading global port operator with a management portfolio of cargo and container operations at ports in Asia, Australia, Europe, Latin America, North America, Africa and the Middle East. Since 2000, Djibouti has become one of the most productive terminals in Africa and one of the fastest-growing container terminals in the Red Sea.

DP World has been engaged in an important programme of development of the port's facilities and equipment which will help in providing the high return performances made necessary by international and regional economic competition. Local and transit traffic has shown high levels of growth in line with the economic performance of Djibouti and Ethiopia. DP World has invested in new handling equipment to increase Djibouti's capacity to 350,000 TEU per annum. Four container cranes with 41 ton container load capacity with up to 50 ton heavy lift, and ten rubber-tyred gantry cranes are operating in the container terminal.

Effective systems are placed in the Container Terminal such as NAVIS system, which performs container terminal operations. This system has two main modules, EXPRESS and SPARCS, which provide complete terminal operations such as container movement's history, vessel and berth schedules, real-time planning, and control and information management, also a manifest management system based on an electronic manifest transmission process implemented in the commercial department. However, shipping lines and agents also use it to transmit cargo manifest details. This system is shared between port and customs. A bulk terminal is being constructed on berths 14 and 15.

MIDROC Ethiopia, owned by Sheik Mohammed Hussein Al-Amoudi, a Saudi businessman with Ethiopian blood and family connections, was granted the bulk terminal concession. In 2005, MIDROC commenced its project to build a bulk carrier terminal, designed to handle annually 1.2 million tons of bulk goods, such as fertiliser, wheat, and salt. The new bulk terminal is designed for Ethiopian fertiliser and grain transit traffic. Storage for bulk fertilisers and cereals will be created, with a capacity of 60,000 tons. The construction of the bulk terminal will enable the Port of Djibouti to compete with other large international ports. Large consignments will be unloaded, packed, and soon dispatched to their destinations. Packing, which used to take a month, will be completed within a minimum of two or three days following the construction of the terminal.

As of 2006, the Port of Djibouti was the most efficient and the shortest corridor to the potential Ethiopia market, being the only port in the region connected to the Ethiopian capital by rail. Since DP World commenced operational management, Djibouti Port's container productivity has doubled to 25 moves per hour, putting it amongst the highest in Africa. At the same time, local and transit traffic have shown high levels of growth in line with the economic performance of Djibouti and Ethiopia. Port and customs documentation are computerised and connected by EDI systems; storage, cargo clearance and transit procedures are efficient and reliable and most, if not all, donated food aid to Ethiopia is efficiently and promptly handled by private companies.

DP World is attracting and contributing new investments in Djibouti Port. Another tool has been put in place to complete the good working of the port — a dedicated health and safety department. It controls and monitors safety measures within the port area, especially waste disposal, and hazardous cargo and emissions. Shipping lines have gained confidence in the ability of Djibouti Port to serve their needs. DP World officials hold regular meetings with their Ethiopian clients and port users to discuss ways and share ideas on how the services rendered by the port can be more suitable.

As part of DP World's ability to provide a total logistics' solution to the government of Djibouti, DP World's sister organisation, Jafza International, manages Djibouti Free Zone, and as a result of the success of the port contract, DP World also took over management of Djibouti International Airport with effect from June 2002. In addition to improving the efficiency and financial performance of the airport, DP World is actively working with Dubai-based companies to establish air-sea services operating out of Djibouti's free zones, taking advantage of the synergies and common management of the airport. Djibouti lies on the main east-west aviation trade route with minimal deviation and provides a secure hub within the region for trans-shipment and relay business. In 2005, Dubai Customs signed a strategic agreement with Djibouti Customs to undertake the management of all regimes, measures and customs procedures of the Republic of Djibouti.

Djibouti has proven its ability to adapt at short notice to significant volume increases. When an explosion damaged the French super tanker 'Limburg' off the coast of Yemen on 6 October 2002, causing it to catch fire and leak oil into the Gulf of Aden and diverting shipping lines from Aden, a large portion of the business moved to Djibouti. Despite not being set-up as a trans-shipment hub, Djibouti terminal handled a 100 per cent increase in business, until the Aden situation normalised. This proved the attractiveness of Djibouti as a potential trans-shipment location and DP World has now invested in additional equipment to cater to this growing potential.

With the current demand levels, Djibouti will soon need additional capacity. And in this regard, a new and much larger port is being developed by DP World at Doraleh, about 10 kilometres east of the current facility. Djibouti will then become one of the major seaports of East Africa. The new port will have a huge impact on the local economy, generating jobs and driving other types of industry. The Djiboutian authorities hope, in particular, that tourism will be developed.

At a cost of around US$450 million, the port is being built in two phases. The first phase is the construction of the oil terminal, which became operational in August 2005, and will be completed in 2006 with a total capacity of 370,000 cubic meters. Phase two, the construction of the container terminal started in April 2006 and will be operational in 2008. The investment cost of the container terminal will be around US$300 million. The container terminal will have a quay length of 900 metres in the first phase, which will be expanded to 1200 metres in the second phase. The container terminal capacity will be over 1.7million TEUs. A twenty-foot equivalent unit (TEU) is a measure of containerised cargo equal to one standard 20 ft length x 8 ft width x 8.5 ft height container.

The port of Doraleh will allow Djibouti to expand and broaden its economic base by attracting new private investors, by encouraging new business ventures and by expanding international trade routes. The new port will encourage the business development of the country and will offer unlimited possibilities for the future well-being of Djibouti's citizens.

In February 2006, Sultan Ahmed bin Sulayem, DP World's chairman, officially opened the new US$100 million Doraleh Oil Terminal facility in which DP World itself had invested some US$30 million. The official reception heralding the opening of the terminal was held on the guided missile cruiser, U.S.S. Vicksburg. Bin Sulayem said the expansion was accelerated by the United States Navy, which had been a key driver of the project and a close partner with DP World and the Djibouti government, along with the oil companies. He added that DP World invests for the long term, working in partnership with its customers to meet their needs today and tomorrow, and is the largest contributor to Djibouti's economy, investing extensively outside the port, including in the free zone, the airport, and in roads, to facilitate the movement of fuel and goods. Dubai is also investing in other business in Djibouti, including the construction of a 400-room five-star hotel and resort by Nakheel Hotel and Resorts, recognising Djibouti's potential as a tourist destination. Bin Sulayem also told his listeners that security was essential to Djibouti officials, and a prime focus of DP World as well which worked closely with customers such as the US Navy, oil companies, and international shippers, all its precautions exceeding regulators' demands.

Besides the projects of the oil terminal and the container terminal to make Djibouti into a comprehensive logistic hub port for East Africa, another important element will follow: the Free Zone, which will be managed by Jebel Ali Free Zone (JAFZA). The present free zone with an area of 17 hectares serves about thirty companies and will accommodate more companies when fully operational. It is situated at two kilometres from the sea port and is managed by JAFZA International, which will also manage the Doraleh's Free Zone, and has made studies on the establishment and feasibility of the project which show that there are opportunities for the multinationals operating in Dubai, to be present in the expanding East African market especially in the Horn of Africa. JAFZA International, a regional leader with more than 4,000 multinational companies, wishes to make Djibouti an international logistics hub.

The free-trade zone will provide space for storage, manufacturing, assembly, conditioning and banking services on a 40-hectare area near the port, airport and railroad. Conceived on the model of Jebel Ali in Dubai, this space will benefit from synergies with the free zones of the port and the airport and will combine air, sea, and ground services.

(Source: www.dpworld.com and www.dpiterminals.com)

The government of Djibouti, in recognition of the owner of Groupe Boreh, Abdourahman Boreh, and his business acumen and entrepreneurial ability, has installed him as the chairman of the Djibouti Ports and Free Zones Authority. Boreh was the one who originally contacted DP World and invited them to negotiate with Djibouti authorities concerning managing Djibouti's port operations.

Boreh champions the creation of the free-trade zone that will enable Djibouti to become an effective eastern gateway to the rest of east and central Africa. Boreh would like to see Djibouti become the Dubai or the Singapore of Africa and says that Djibouti should attract companies needing to store goods before sending them into central Africa. Companies such as Sony, which presently operates from Dubai, would benefit from using Djibouti, which is nearer to these markets. Boreh believes Djibouti represents a fantastic opportunity for trade between the countries of the Red Sea, the Gulf of Oman and the Indian Ocean, and African countries like Congo-Kinshasa, Uganda, Rwanda and Burundi.

Groupe Boreh was founded in Djibouti in 1908, and has grown to comprise eight companies: Red Sea Central (tobacco, sole distributor of Benson & Hedges for all eastern Africa; Soprim Construction (which built the residential complex for the French military); Sodras (Air France supplier); Sodeca (duty free stores at Djibouti's airport); Sotram (maritime transport); Sotsom; Sompec (storage of petroleum products); and Boreh International (international trade). The origin and headquarters of the group are in Djibouti, but Groupe Boreh is active in Dubai, Somalia and Ethiopia. They intend to continue their growth internationally. Their success is without borders.

(Source: www.borehgroup.com)

Somalia

BBC News has reported that rising from the ruins of the Mogadishu skyline are signs of one of Somalia's few success stories in the anarchy of recent years. A host of mobile phone masts testifies to the telecommunications revolution which has taken place despite the absence of any functioning national government since 1991. Three phone companies are engaged in fierce competition for both mobile and landline customers, while new Internet cafes are being set up across the city and the entire country. It takes only three days for a landline to be installed, compared with waiting-lists of many years in neighbouring Kenya, and once installed, local calls are free for a monthly fee of just US$10. International calls cost 50 US cents a minute, while surfing the web is charged at 50 US cents an hour — possibly the cheapest rate in Africa, according to the manager of one Internet cafe. But how do you establish a phone company in a country where there is no government?

In some respects, it is actually easier, since there is no need to get a license and there is no state-run monopoly which prevents new competitors being established. And of course there is no-one to demand any taxes, which is one reason why prices are so low. 'The government post and telecoms company used to have a monopoly but after the regime was toppled we were free to set up our own business,' says Abdullahi Mohammed Hussein, products and services manager of Telcom Somalia, which was set up in 1994 when Mogadishu was still a war zone. 'We saw a huge gap in the market, as all previous services had been destroyed. There was a massive demand.' The main airport and port were destroyed in the fighting but businessmen have built small airstrips and use natural harbours, so the phone companies are still able to import their equipment. Despite the absence of law and order and a functional court system, bills are paid and contracts are enforced by relying on Somalia's traditional clan system, Abdullahi says.

In a country divided into hundreds of fiefdoms run by rival warlords, security is a major concern. While Telcom Somalia has some 25,000 mobile customers — and a similar number have land lines — you very rarely see anyone walking along the streets of Mogadishu chatting on their phone, in case this attracts the attention of a hungry gunman. The phone companies themselves say they are not targeted by the militiamen, even if thieves occasionally steal some of their wires. Mahdi Mohammed Elmi has been managing the Wireless African Broadband Telecoms Internet cafe in the heart of Mogadishu, surrounded by the bustling and chaotic Bakara market, for almost two years. 'I have never had a problem with security,' he says and points out that they have just a single security guard at the front door. Abdullahi says the warlords realise that if they cause trouble for the phone companies, the phones will stop working again, which nobody wants. 'We need good relations with all the faction leaders. We don't interfere with them and they don't interfere with us. They want political power and we leave them alone,' he says.

While the three phone companies, Telcom, Nationlink and Hormuud, are engaged in bitter competition for customers, they have cooperated to set up the Global Internet Company to provide the Internet infrastructure. Manager Abdulkadir Hassan Ahmed says that within 1.5 kilometres of central Mogadishu, customers — mostly Internet cafes — can enjoy service at 150Mb/second through a Long Reach Ethernet. Elsewhere, they can have a wireless connection at 11Mb/s. His company is able to work anywhere in Somalia, whichever faction is in charge locally. 'Even small, remote villages are connected to the Internet, as long as they have a phone line.'

The Internet sector in Somalia has two main advantages over many of its African neighbours. There is a huge diaspora around the world (between one and three million people, compared with an estimated seven million people in Somalia) who remain in contact with their friends and relatives back home. E-mail is the cheapest way of staying in touch.

'We are planning to introduce 3G technology, including live video calling and mobile Internet, next year,' says Abdullahi. But despite their success, the telecoms companies say that, like the population at large, they are desperate to have a government. 'We are very interested in paying taxes,' says Abdullahi — not a sentiment which often passes the lips of a high-flying businessman. And Abdulkadir at the Global Internet Company fully agrees. 'We badly need a government,' he says. 'Everything starts with security … all the infrastructure of the country has collapsed — education, health and roads. We need to send our staff abroad for any training.'

Another problem for companies engaged in the global telecoms business is paying their foreign partners. At present, they use Somalia's traditional Hawala money transfer companies to get money to Dubai, the Middle East's trading and financial hub. With a government would come a central bank, which would make such transactions far easier. Taxes would mean higher prices but Abdullahi says that Somalia's previous governments have kept taxes low and he hopes this will continue under the regime due to start work in the coming months. Somalia's telecoms companies are looking forward to an even brighter future with the support of a functioning government, as long as it does not impose punitive tax rates or state control in a sector which obviously needs very little help to thrive.

(Source: Joseph Winter. 'Telecoms thriving in lawless Somalia', *BBC News* 19 November 2004; http://news.bbc.co.uk/go/pr/fr/-/2/hi/africa/4020259.stm)

Telcom Somalia is the largest and leading communications network operator in Somalia and, in February 1994, the first major privately owned company to enter the fully deregulated marketplace. Since then, Telcom has have expanded to meet the demands of customers and set new benchmarks in service, technology development and performance in one of the most competitive telecom marketplaces in the world. The diversity of Telcom's business portfolio adds to its knowledge of the entire spectrum of telecom services. Telcom Somalia is Somalia's leading provider of mobile, Internet and landline services for voice/fax, video and data transmission. In addition, it owns a 25 per cent stake in the Global Internet Company. The expertise and funding brought by equity partners have allowed the company to focus on developing the company to international standards. Mohammed Hagi Abdullahi is the chairman and Abdullahi Mohammed Hussein is the products and services manager of Telcom Somalia.

(Source: www.telcom-somalia.com)

Somaliland

The late Michael van Notten in his important and highly original work *The Law of the Somali: A Stable Foundation for Economic Development in the Horn of Africa* (2005) outlined Somali customary law and pointed the way to a practical synthesis between the modern world economy and the traditional institutions of the Somali people. A practicing lawyer in the Netherlands, Michael van Notten married into, and lived, as one of the Samaron Clan during the last twelve years of his life. His libertarian cast of mind was an asset in understanding the culture and institutions of this people whom he adopted and who received him as a fellow clansman. It enabled him to gain a deep understanding of traditional African institutions.

His book might seem to straddle two horses, law and commerce, but each presupposes the other: economic development presupposes law, and the growth and development of the law proceeds largely from the hustle and bustle of economic activity. In a stateless setting, especially, these are two aspects of a single phenomenon and hence the author's emphasis on economic development, in which he envisions 'free ports' playing an important catalysing role. Economic development will have the capability of stimulating the growth of the customary law into a full body of common law capable of meeting the complex needs of a developed society. Such growth is essential if, as seems likely, Somalia is to continue towards an effective decentralised government.

The question as to whether significant economic development is even an option in a region lacking a legislative authority is squarely addressed in this book. The last chapter contains innovative thinking on how, in the absence of a central government, free ports might be designed to operate in the world economy while being fully compatible with traditional Somali institutions. Such tradition-friendly development could enable Somalis to assume a respected place in the world by leaving aside their colonial legacy and building on their indigenous institutions.

(Source: Michael van Notten and Spencer Heath MacCallum. *The Law of the Somali: A Stable Foundation for Economic Development in the Horn of Africa*, Red Sea Press, 2005)

In 1999, Van Notten and his business associate Jim Davidson began work on a detailed plan for an Awdal free port on the Gulf of Aden, south of Djibouti — a planned community project that Michael worked on until his death in June 2002. In January 2000, Van Notten and Davidson established the Awdal Roads Company to build a toll road designed to make possible the transportation of all goods from the harbour/free port to the 70 million in Ethiopia and the highlands of Awdal. Van Notten and Davidson identified many business opportunities in Awdal and were pursuing opportunities in port development, road construction, toll road operation, communications, fishing and import/export services.

Davidson has been continuing the business on his own, and Awdal Roads Company is the major shareholder in Awdal Roads Building Company, Somali Freeport Services and Awdal Utilities. Davidson's plan is to continue the endeavour and to identify and work as a facilitator for businesses involving mining, manufacturing and financial services. Business opportunities in mining would be pursued with Resource Commission Awdal. An initial phase of investment and opportunity would involve coastal power and water. There would be the possibility of several financial infrastructure companies.

A subsidiary, Somali Fishing, had been pursuing a set of business opportunities in fishing, shipping, import/export, warehousing and related services. The company expected to market fish in Awdal and in Djibouti, Kenya, Ethiopia, other parts of Somalia, Yemen, United Arab Emirates, Saudi Arabia, Egypt and in Europe. The company would forego the limitations of onshore seafood processing facilities, which are largely prevented by trade barriers. Instead the company has identified freezer trawlers with processing facilities. These would clean and gut fish to be frozen for trans-shipment without ever reaching shore. Fish waste would be sold locally for fertiliser.

Another significant business opportunity exists in operating an abattoir run according to Islamic traditions. Livestock raised locally would be slaughtered and frozen for export or later consumption. The major customers for livestock from Somalia are Islamic countries such as Yemen, Saudi Arabia and the Gulf States.

(Source: www.awdal.com)

MoMatrade is a young and dynamic company presently focusing its efforts within Somaliland. The core of its business is consultancy, with the objective of being the preferred link between the Horn of Africa region and companies around the world. MoMatrade is a partnership between M. Aden Hassan from Somaliland, M S van Muiswinkel from the Netherlands, and I Awil also from Somaliland. The company was founded because of the great affinity with Somaliland, and after a comprehensive research of the market the partners are confident of the opportunities. For example, MoMatrade's division, Nomadic Herbs and Incense, has built an international network and is a significant participant and leader in providing high quality frankincense and myrrh in solid form (resin gum).

There is a steady market for frankincense and myrrh from the Horn of Africa region, especially incense from Somaliland, the 'Land of Punt'. Frankincense and myrrh continue to be well regarded, and have been since well before the kings of the orient brought them, along with gold, to give to the 'newborn king'. MoMatrade has an undivided interest in land in Somaliland where myrrh and frankincense grow. The problem has always been distribution, especially to the West, and the lack of management. MoMatrade's strategy has been to build a sales/distribution team to realise its vision of rapidly growing from an established base to become a significant international participant and leader in the field.

The trading history of Somali frankincense dates back to the early Mediterranean civilisations, with the ancient Egyptians mounting expeditions to the Horn of Africa to purchase resins. The Arabian Peninsula has always dealt in gums. It is generally understood that Somalia's commercial history began with frankincense and that northern Somalia gained its importance from the incense trade. There is strong emerging evidence that the ancient Egyptians may have traded directly with Somali collectors and merchants.

Somalis chew *maydi* to help teeth, gums and breath. It burns evenly, like candlelight, so the low grades are used as fire to produce light at night in addition to being burned as incense. By comparison, Somalis have many uses for *beyo*. It produces a mass flame and smoke so is used like a fire lighter to start fires. It is used to fumigate, and purify homes and vessels. It perfumes garments, wedding guests and hair. *Beyo* is used for backaches, cough, and chest congestion. It is also used as incense in mosques.

(Source: www.momatrade.com)

Five telecommunications companies operate out of Somaliland, offering possibly the cheapest rate calls in the region because of intense competition between them. Independent telephone operators require only a satellite dish, a foreign carrier and a small office with booths for callers. Abdirazak Osman, a Somali expatriate from the USA, persuaded his American partners to finance telephone companies in collaboration with Somali businessmen, first in Hargeisa, then in Mogadishu. In 1998, he brought telephones and electricity to his hometown of Galkayo in Puntland. The telephone network is used not only by relatives, but also by businesses to strike livestock deals with Middle Eastern customers. Half of Somaliland's three million inhabitants are nomadic herders. These communication links have been vital to connect Somaliland with the diaspora. Remittances from abroad, once mainly used to enable families to survive, are now being directed towards businesses. Remittances from Europe, North America and the Middle East are estimated at between US$150 million and US$500 million a year, exceeding international aid. There is no private banking system in Somaliland, so clan-based networks channel remittances. The UNDP has established a programme to identify skilled Somali expatriates who might be willing to return to assist development.

(Source: 'A nomad's life is hard', *The Economist*, 7 August 1999; 'A failed state that is succeeding in parts', *The Economist*, 28 August 1999; and 'Peace and development in northern Somalia', Africa Policy Information Centre: *African News*, 12 September 1999)

In 1970, Mohamed Said Duale founded Dahabshiil Ltd in Burao in the former Somali Republic. Duale is the sole owner of the family business which has its head office in Hargeisa, Somaliland. Dahabshiil's principal business since 1988 has been money-transfer services, together with import/export trading and, more recently, the establishment of a postal system in Somaliland, a construction company and Somtel International, in which Dahabshiil is a major shareholder. Somtel International currently operates ten telecommunications stations in the country. Dahabshiil is the biggest private sector employer in Somalia and Somaliland, employing over 1,000 staff.

Dahabshiil is the oldest remittance company in the Horn of Africa, with the largest worldwide network. It provides money-transfer services throughout the Somali regions. Dahabshiil has the largest network of agents, is the leading company that transfers remittances and has established its reputation as a most trusted company. Since late 2001, Dahabshiil has more than doubled money-transfers to Somalia and Somaliland from its international offices in 34 countries worldwide, with 400 branches in total, including 50 branches in the United Kingdom and 25 in the United States of America. In 2004, Dahabshiil was the only Somali remittance company with fully licensed and bonded branches in ten states of the USA. Duale emphasises the importance of adhering strictly to guidelines on anti- money-laundering laws and regulations. He recognises the importance of new regulations and requires Dahabshiil agents and employees to fully comply with these laws. Dahabshiil has 36 branches in Somalia and Somaliland, 17 of them in Mogadishu. The services provided by Dahabshiil are highly competitive; the company competes with 20 smaller remittance companies.

As for the future, Dahabshiil is vigorously planning to become a fully-fledged commercial bank and will give clients the option, where correspondent banks exist, to deposit remittances with an international bank for direct transfer to and from the existing Dahabshiil branches in Mogadishu, Hargeisa, Bosaso and Burao and other branches. Dahabshiil's banking clients include United Nations organisations such as UNDP, UNOPS, UNHCR, UNICEF, WHO, UNCHS (Habitat), some international and local NGOs, the Somali diaspora, the BBC and those Somalis in Somalia and Somaliland who remit and receive funds.

In November 2004, the Dahabshiil Tower in Hargeisa was completed. It was designed by Daryeel Architects and built by Daryeel Construction. The six-storey hotel provides 36 rooms and is conveniently located along the heart highway (Waddada Halbawlaha). On the sixth storey, is the most luxurious restaurant in the capital city of Hargeisa.

Daryeel Construction and Contracting Ltd is locally owned, and Somaliland's largest and leading construction company, employing around 500 staff of professional builders and surveyors, and completing approximately 300 constructions annually. Daryeel is a well-established contracting company with over 25 years of experience in building almost every type of architecture and providing a complete range of construction and programme management services in all in the segments of the residential and business building market, from pre-construction services to construction management or general contracting services. Since its inception in 1982, Daryeel's homes have featured the best of the local craftsmen.

In recent years, Daryeel has renewed its focus on premium hotel construction, with the completion of several successful projects. Project sites have ranged from congested urban centres and suburban locations to extensive developments adjacent to major airports. Cost-effective construction, strict schedules and quality guest amenities characterise this work which includes the Ambassador Hotel Hargeisa, Dahabshiil Tower Hargeisa, and Indha-deero Burco Plaza.

Daryeel's founders believe that their strong commitment to the vision and value under which they operate are of paramount importance. Safety, quality, customer satisfaction and all the values associated with being an ethical, responsible and innovative company will guide their company in the 21st century. Daryeel's management is led by the managing director, Kayse Shukri Jama. The administrative personnel have diverse experience in their respective departments of finance, engineering, marketing, operations and various workshops. All work towards achieving the goals set by the management, which emphasises the introduction of new ideas in building, and new styles of homes to satisfy customers returning from abroad. Daryeel's management puts customer satisfaction first, knowing that it is the best way to maximise profits.

(Source: www.daryeel.com)

The Ambassador Hotel Hargeisa is a five-star international hotel in the heart of downtown Hargeisa which vividly represents the optimism of its stakeholders, especially founder, co-owner, and manager Khader Aden Hussein, a 1993 graduate of Sheffield Hallam University in England. The hotel towers on a hilltop with a panoramic view of the city. It has 45 spacious guestrooms, and eleven fully furnished villas; three ballrooms for special family celebrations, conventions and seminars; spacious indoor restaurants with stand-in bars, and rooftop restaurants with star gazing amenities. To every single guest and visitor, Ambassador Hotel Hargeisa strives to be known for its excellent customer service and authentic Somali hospitality. Guests enjoy the comfort of living in style. They experience the ambiance of home away from home, as well as satisfying their discriminating taste for delectable cuisine. Hussein endeavours to create a wholesome environment, conducive to international, national and local visitors and guests to unwind and bring new businesses. Hussein is also committed to making his hotel a wholesome workplace, one that breeds respect, trust, and loyalty. He is proud that the presence of the Ambassador Hotel Hargeisa has served to inspire Somalilanders, giving them a sense of pride, nationalism and hope that there is something to look forward to in their motherland.

(Source: www.ambassadorhotelhargeisa.com)

Chapter 12: Kenya

James Shikwati, director of the Inter Region Economic Network (IREN Kenya), and editor of online and hardcopy magazine: *The African Executive*, reports (2002) that Joseph Barrage Wanjui, former chairman of the Kenya Association of Manufacturers, believes that a flourishing private sector is critical to economic growth in developing countries. Wanjui enumerates the tremendous development opportunities that exist in developing African countries for entrepreneurs, assuming that these countries commit themselves to full free enterprise economies and permit free market principles to work. Wanjui emphasises that governments stand as the most serious impediment to new business creation and growth, in that they control funds instead of permitting them to flow directly between business enterprises or individuals. Since governments are not the most effective channels for development funds, Wanjui recommends that government's role should be to foster an environment which encourages individual freedom, risk taking and generation of profits. Wanjui adds that governments must recognise individual initiatives as the cornerstone of economic growth. Given a free market environment, the problems of financing growth will be resolved by the market forces. Wanjui maintains that the underlying problem to economic growth is a lack of freedom for individuals to engage in activities that would lead to prosperity.

Shikwati summarises:
- It is important that Africans pursue strategies to encourage growth in local businesses, entrepreneurial spirit and a vibrant private sector to spur economic development.
- It is in Africa's interest to address underdevelopment through appropriate trade, aid and investment policies.
- If Africa has to develop and compete in the present world driven by market economics then it ought to invest in entrepreneurship.
- It is entrepreneurs who seek out profitable opportunities, organise productive units, and compete fiercely, keep innovation high and make their country wealthy as well as enriching themselves.
- The debate on economic recovery for Africa ought to focus on how economic growth can be achieved.
- Give the private sector a chance to be the engine of growth.
- Simplify rules and regulations governing the establishment of small firms into medium to large sized business.
- Put in place tax reforms to promote investments and savings, enticement for foreign direct investment, privatization of state owned enterprises to enhance efficiency and help reduce the external obligations.
- It is prudent for government policy makers to focus on promoting intra African trade and providing an environment that can make local entrepreneurs thrive.

Shikwati concludes that if individuals are let free, then they will strive to better their lot through their talents. Enhanced rule of law will encourage both local and international businesspeople to engage in activities that generate income without fear of confiscation and insecurity. Economic freedom will lead to the society making use of man's fundamental desire to claim fruits of his labour. He emphasises that it is urgent therefore that African countries attain economic freedom in order to allow individual talent to thrive irrespective of tribe or race.

(Source: James Shikwati. 'The benefits of economic freedom to Kenya', Nairobi, Kenya: Inter-Region Economic Network, 7 February 2002; www.irenkenya.org)

In East Africa, the private sector must take a leading role in forging economic integration if the East African Community (EAC) organisation of Kenya, Uganda and Tanzania is to succeed. It must be committed to the establishment of the EAC Customs Union and eventually a free trade area. The common market will have a population of 81 million people and a US$25 billion economy. When fully integrated, it will be the third largest market in sub-Saharan Africa, dwarfed only by South Africa's (42 million people, US$133 billion) and Nigeria's (125 million people and US$38 billion) markets. Kenya entrepreneur Mohamed Jaffer, chief executive officer of Grain Bulk Handlers in Mombassa, says that the EAC would become a force to be reckoned with if the private sector in the three East African countries continued to invest in the region. As a matter of fact, Jaffer points out that East Africans are one people, despite the lines drawn up by some people in London to divide East Africa into three different countries.

When it was clear that major improvements had to be made at the port of Mombassa, with vision and tenacity Jaffer managed to convince his government and international financiers that not only was a new grain terminal essential, but that it was also a viable proposition. Grain Bulk Handlers invested US$35 million for the grain handling facility, the silos being located just outside the port, the grain being transferred using conveyor belts. The facility was officially opened in March 2000. The new terminal is designed to be environmentally friendly, with strict dust controls, and the spillage problems have been eliminated using enclosed offloading conveyors. The method of discharge is designed to reduce vessel turn around times by as much as 75 per cent. This ultimately results in lower ocean freight costs which, together with other increased efficiencies in the terminal, provide a reduction in commodity prices for the end user. There are storage facilities for 100,000 tons.

In addition to grain and fertilisers, the terminal is designed to handle other vital food supplies. It can be used as a strategic food storage facility for the region, serving landlocked countries. The storage area is divided and completely segregated into food and non-food areas, as are the warehouses for bagging. On reaching the handling complex, commodities can be loaded in bulk directly into rail cars or trucks or alternatively stored in a controlled environment ready to be bagged. Materials handling equipment from the dockside, conveyors and storage silos feed to the eight complete bagging lines. The bagging lines are designed to simultaneously handle up to 5,000 tons of grain and 5,000 tons of fertiliser per day. The design of the weighers and feed equipment allows delicate commodities such as long grain rice, beans and lentils to be handled with the minimum of breakage. Grain Bulk Handlers intends to set up a facility in Jinja, Uganda, for procurement of produce for the regional market.

(Source: www.grainbulk.com)

Vimal Shah is the CEO of Bidco Group, East Africa's enterprise success story. Through a combination of the right business practices, dedication to the customer and a clear and well communicated vision, Bidco has in a short time risen from an unknown company to become East Africa's most respected manufacturing company, according to the PriceWaterhouseCoopers and Nation Media Group CEO's survey carried out in 2004. Bidco was founded in 1970, and has maintained an impressive growth in east and central Africa to emerge as the market leader. The group has a combined edible oil refining capacity of over 1,700 metric tons per day. Bidco's success story is not confined to the East African region; the company has a clear vision of attaining number one status in Africa by 2030. Its success in Kenya, Uganda and Tanzania is only a demonstration of what the company seeks to attain in Africa. Bidco seeks to become the first African company to be a world benchmark.

Bidco started operating in Kenya in 1970 when the company chairman and founder Bhimji Depar Shah set up a garment manufacturing company in Nairobi. Following the liberalisation of the textile industry in 1980, which led to the near collapse of the industry, Bidco shifted from garment manufacturing to soap manufacturing.

In 1991 Bidco moved its operations to Thika with the opening of the Bidco Oil Refineries plant. This marked the turnaround for Bidco as it now concentrated on the core competencies of manufacturing and marketing edible oil, fats and hygienic products. Between 1994 and 1997 Bidco increased its manufacturing capacity by 500 per cent. This growth led to the acquisition of the Elianto oilseed crushing business from Unga Group Ltd in 1998. The year 2002 demonstrated Bidco's prowess when the company acquired leading brands in East Africa from Unilever. These are Kimbo, Cowboy and Veebol vegetable cooking fats.

At an early stage of its operation, Bidco recognised the importance of investing in technology for efficient management and decision making. In 1998 Bidco networked all its locations through VSAT, and by 1999 Bidco was the only company of its kind in the region with fully integrated BaaN Enterprise Resource Planning (ERP) and Intelligent Resource Planning (IRP) systems. A year later, Bidco was the first sub-Saharan edible oil processing company outside South Africa to be awarded the ISO 9002 certification by the Bureau Veritas Quality International of Geneva, Switzerland. Today, Bidco's operations in Kenya, Uganda and Tanzania are all on real-time online systems interlinked via VSAT and leased lines.

In July 2004, the Bidco Group realised part of its long-term vision of setting up an oil palm plantation on East African soil. With an investment of over US$130 million, Bidco and its partners have already commenced work on the largest oil palm plantation in Africa. Once fully operational, this plantation on Kalangala Island will cover over 40,000 hectares of oil palm plantation. In addition the project will create over 6,000 direct jobs and make Uganda self sufficient in palm oil requirements, leading to an annual foreign exchange saving of over US$90 million.

Bidco is implementing the oil palm project in partnership with Wilmar Group, Josovina and ADM. Wilmar Group of Malaysia is one of the largest operators of oil palm plantations in the world; Josovina, based in Singapore, is the primary exporter of crude oils to East Africa and ADM, based in the USA is the largest oil seeds processing entity in the world. Together, the sponsors represent an impressive group of global expertise and pedigree.

Bidco is also using the latest technology to set up Africa's finest edible oil complex in Jinja, Uganda. This plant, with a capacity of 400 metric tons per day, commenced commercial production in May 2005. This ensures Uganda reaps the maximum benefits of full value addition on oil palm products produced on Kalangala Island.

Bidco initially entered the Tanzanian market through direct exports from Kenya. However, in 2001 Bidco purchased an existing soap plant in Dar es Salaam to start its manufacturing and operations in Tanzania. Bidco has since expanded the soap plant operations and has successfully installed a 500 metric ton-per day edible oil refinery. Bidco's investment in Tanzania now stands at US$25 million and over 700 direct jobs have been created. Bidco plans to invest more in the field of oil palm and oilseed plantations once the processing of locally grown seeds becomes viable, and is already supporting local farmers in Kigoma in western Tanzania by purchasing all their oil palm produce.

The above major milestones represent one of Africa's well managed corporate organisations with a passion to identify new ways of doing business. Bidco believes in identifying consumer needs and providing solutions to satisfy customers. But, most importantly, Bidco will only rate itself successful if it leaves a positive impact on the community in which it operates. Bidco is therefore constantly seeking opportunities to partner with the community and assist the less fortunate members of society.

(Source: www.bidco-oil.com)

Craftskills Enterprises started working on wind power machines in 2001, and has so far been able to manufacture wind generators and their accessories, with over 30 units sold all over Kenya, Rwanda and Tanzania. The firm was started by a Nairobi resident, Simon Mwacharo Guyo. After realising the burgeoning demand for alternative sources of energy, especially renewable ones, the computer engineer started out to design affordable wind energy generators. Electricity is inaccessible to the majority of Kenyans, in both rural and urban areas. This in itself has allowed wind generators from Craftskills Enterprises to find a ready market in all parts of Kenya. Customers come knocking, and therefore Craftskills has not undertaken any major marketing campaign according to Philip Osula, the Craftskills sales and marketing executive responsible for marketing the *WindCruiser* wind power machines.

The majority of Kenyans relies almost exclusively on biomass-wood, charcoal, and organic waste for cooking and heating, given that over 75 per cent of the population has no access to grid electricity or other forms of modern commercial energy. Ironically, renewable energies such as wind and solar power remain under-utilised despite being abundant. Indeed, fuel wood supplies are fast dwindling in the country and poor families are compelled to spend more time and money to procure it. Indoor smoke pollution in rural Kenya contributes to a large extent to many respiratory infections and deaths which put a heavy financial load on the poor rural folk. On the other hand, the high cost of imported wind generators has hindered harnessing of wind energy in the country in the same way the cost of solar panels has prevented many households from utilising solar power. Thus, the Craftskills initiative to locally manufacture affordable wind generators filled a big void at an opportune time.

After experimenting on a range of technologies that could provide cheaper, durable and efficient wind turbines and accessories, the firm managed to devise *WindCruisers* of various specifications. The average *WindCruiser* ranges in weight from 10 to 70 kg, with 6 to 10 feet in propeller diameter, has tails that can furl when there is too much wind thrust and has a peak power output between 150-6000 watts. Unlike conventional wind turbines, which use gears and hence require strong winds to start generating and reach cut-in voltage, Craftskills machines operate on bearings. Hence they are direct drive, rugged, strong against windstorms and utilise the slightest breeze. Smaller or bigger *WindCruisers* can be made to suit the needs of individual customers. The bearings they run on take years to replace, and their spare parts are locally available. The machines also have charge controllers that enable them to regulate themselves during high winds. Craftskills Enterprises sources 90 per cent of the materials used to manufacture its machines locally. It uses recycled metals to make the machines, and the only imported components are magnets.

The demand for the *WindCruiser*, which unlike conventional wind machines automatically seeks wind in any direction and can also be used alongside solar panels, is phenomenal. Clients include schools, hospitals, urban and rural communities. Osula says that owing to the high demand for their wind power technology, they intend to venture into the neighbouring countries of Uganda and Tanzania. Craftskills is aiming to start small wind firms/standalone power stations to provide sustainable localised electricity grid to rural market places, hospitals, schools and homes. This will compensate the national electricity grid covering the major towns and highways (a skeleton of the country).

(Source: www.craftskills.biz; Justus Wanjala. 'Blowing life into rural Kenya', islam-online.net, 26 July 2004)

Peter Silvester started Royal African Safaris, a franchise operation that spans several countries. Today, Kenya is finally winning back its pre-eminence from the southern African nations. The Kenya Professional Safari Guides Association (KPSGA), established in 1996, has qualified more than 1,000 guides under its bronze award, and launched a gruelling silver examination in 2000. 'Guiding is at last being recognised as a proper profession,' says KPSGA founder Peter Silvester, 'and more bright young Kenyans are setting out to make it their career.' Peter was also the tourism director of Loisaba Wilderness, which was run by a team of young go-ahead white Kenyans with a keen vision for the future of safaris. Peter says, 'Being on safari is not about designer interiors, it is about the bush. We want to get people out there.'

Located on the edge of the Laikipia Plateau, 70 kilometres north of Mount Kenya, the Loisaba Wilderness 61,000-acre private wildlife conservancy is in the heart of the Ewaso eco-system. Incredibly rich in both biodiversity and topography, Loisaba is in the heartland of the Laikipiak Masai community. Loisaba offers a rare insight into cultures, traditions and a way of life that has stood the test of time. At 6,500 feet above sea level, Loisaba has a temperate climate making all activities pleasurable year-round. The same size as Tanzania's Ngorongoro Crater and larger than many of Kenya's national parks, the Loisaba wilderness is a haven for more than 250 species of birds and 50 species of wildlife. The area offers some excellent big cat and wild dog viewing opportunities.

Loisaba Lodge is built entirely of local materials and offers stunning views of Mount Kenya. The seven en-suite rooms each have a private deck built into the escarpment; all the furniture at the lodge is handmade. The lodge has a swimming pool and tennis court. Loisaba is part of an enterprise in which all profits generated from tourism are dedicated to the conservation of the 61,000-acre private wilderness area. In addition, Loisaba supports community health, education and enterprise programmes outside its boundaries with the neighbouring Samburu and Laikipiak Masai people.

Loisaba has long been a successful cattle ranch with a luxury lodge, but today the ranch is at the centre of a promising new partnership involving its tribal neighbours and an emerging mix of land uses, including cattle, wildlife tourism and local industry, operating and cooperating on the same land. Its latest tourist venture involves a series of 'Star Beds', luxury open-air sleeping platforms scattered across the open bush of Laikipia, which offer a unique new wilderness experience with transport by camels and evenings under the stars. After opening to wide acclaim on Loisaba itself, a fourth Star Bed is soon to start operations on neighbouring land owned by the Koija community. The community will run the Star Bed as their own enterprise. Together with several complementary spin-offs such as handicrafts and mat-making, the project will give the community a new incentive to conserve the big game on land where such animals have never been considered anything other than a costly danger.

Peter was involved in creating this project in northern Kenya but left the project in June 2001 and has returned to his core business of guiding safaris. He believes that there are a number of very exciting investment opportunities, especially in the area of privatised conservation. Peter believes that natural economics is about the symbiosis of a number of different industries that all directly or indirectly benefit from the resource on which they rely. Combining a number of different industries can therefore yield substantial returns to an investor.

Peter asks us to consider the fact that in Kenya there are over 50 game reserves and national parks although only six have a positive cash flow. Put into the equation the fact that Kenya has become more and more democratic since 1990. Consider the fact that democracy means the people have an input into government policy and spending, and the fact that if given a choice at the polls most Kenyans would chose more pressing socio-economic issues as a priority for public spending than wildlife. In an odd sort of way democracy and an understandable hunger for land may be the downfall of government sponsored conservation.

Peter asserts that profit driven privatisation of this resource may then be the only way that some areas can exist. If one was to take a private lease on a 500 square mile national park or game reserve, was able to raise the required investment capital and produce a natural economic model, a model that integrated tourism, community industries, and environmentally responsible agriculture, Peter believes one should be able to produce a sustained rate of return in the plus 15 per cent region. With large sections of the major funds looking for ethical investments, Africa and its many conservation investments are obvious choices.

Peter states that this is attractive stuff in a world, where land with elephants on it is becoming a rare and precious commodity. In addition of course the technological revolution has meant that it would be possible for one to live anywhere one chooses on the planet and remain in contact, a choice between living in downtown New York or out in the African bush. Peter concludes that perhaps he goes too far. However, he does believe that within a generation the world will see a massive exodus from cities, a vestige of the last, industrial, revolution to a more rural lifestyle.

Tanzania and Kenya were rated as the world's leading eco-tourism destinations through an August 2005 travel poll conducted by an online travel agency, responsibletravel.com. The success of Tanzania and Kenya was attributed to both becoming the first countries to understand the importance of tourism for wildlife conservation and poverty reduction strategies to their local communities, especially those abutting the wildlife parks.

(Source: www.royalafrican.com)

Peter points out that in Masai and Samburu land, the traditional tribal cultures clearly offer a rich source of horizon-broadening experiences for more earthy eco-tourists (ecotourism means encouraging local communities to conserve their wild surroundings, respecting and promoting their culture, educating visitors about the value and fragility of their land). In Shompole, south-west of Lake Magadi in the Great Rift Valley, 150,000 acres is currently at the centre of a brave new partnership between the Shompole Group Ranch and a company formed in 2001, The Art of Ventures. Art founder Anthony Russell and the Shompole Group Ranch community have together formed a third company, Maa O'Leng ('deeply of the Masai'), which they call a partnership in community, conservation and commerce. It promises to delve deep into the wellspring of cultural and historical attractions that remains untapped on most of Kenya's tribal lands.

A first-class lodge, straddling a panoramic spur beneath the Nguruman escarpment, has been built. Water from a local spring has been diverted through the open-plan suites, which feature their own outdoor bathrooms and rock wallows. Russell has a considerable reputation for eco-friendly lodge construction and innovative design, and everything was constructed from local materials. Sewage is treated through an eco-friendly tank system, 80 per cent of power is provided by solar panels, and all landscaping is designed around local plants. The lodge at Shompole comprises six rooms completed in January 2002. Latterly added are two magnificent suites at Little Shompole which share an exclusive mess and dedicated team of staff.

With the Kenyan wildlife experience still largely restricted to game drives and rushed wildlife encounters, the emphasis at Shompole is on a more sedate, unintrusive wilderness experience. Here, there are game and night drives, sundowners, mountain biking, canoe trips, massage and beauty therapy, camel rides, fossil exploration, a salt spa, and a mobile camp that has enabled the ranch to double its occupancy. Highly trained local guides conduct nature walks. A resource centre exhibiting historical artefacts and facets of modern Masai life is planned for the future. Besides employment and a steady stream of revenue, the development channels part of the profits into a trust fund that finances an array of local initiatives, from piped water, roads and clinics to projects planned for improved livestock practices, fast-growing tree nurseries, a fish farming industry and small-scale vegetable farming.

The aim is that the Masai will eventually buy a greater stake in the lodge, becoming majority shareholders. With a few years of solid training and on-the-job business practice, there seems no reason why the famously astute Masai will not be able to run such a venture. Russell is assisting them. He has translated his business plans into the language of the Masai — not on paper into Maa as most of the members of the group ranch cannot read. However, every effort has been made through numerous meetings to communicate Russel's intentions to the leaders who then ensure that their people know about the project. The point is to give back the responsibility to the people as soon as possible. 'You cannot change people's minds overnight,' concedes Russell. 'This kind of process has to be very slow and very diplomatic. But the fact that people are gradually warming to the idea offers great hope for those who want to save the last wild spaces of this beautiful country.' It can only be hoped that honourable projects like Anthony Russell's will be given the support they deserve, and that the fresh blood of new leaders will create greater room for the nationwide cooperation and planning strategies that are so desperately needed if Kenya is to reclaim its ecotourism crown.

(Source: www.shompole.com; Ralph Johnstone. 'Communing with Nature', *Ecotourism Observer*, July 2001, www.ecotourism.org; and Ralph Johnstone. 'Ecotourism: The greening (and greenwashing) of Kenya's tourism industry', *EcoForum* 'Short Rains' 1999 issue, www.elci.org)

Sandstorm (Africa) Ltd began life in Nairobi in the 1980s as a successful safari tentage business called Beach 'n Bush. Journalist Kate Patrick reports for *The Scotsman* that it was founded and managed by a second-generation Kenyan, Gary McIntyre, a designer and craftsman who decided to diversify to protect against volatility in the safari market.

In the late 1990s he began using robust, water-resistant, heavy-gauge cotton canvas to create some basic holdalls. Encouraged by the response from both the local market and tourists, he brought in Robert Topping, a leather specialist who had worked with bag designer Bill Amberg in London, and combined the canvas with pulled-up leather, which is finished to give it a worn, lived in appearance that improves with age. Soon he had come up with a whole raft of ingeniously designed safari accessories, all in earthy African tans and olive greens with solid brass fastenings. These included a champagne cooler, a wash bag based on a Victorian design and a fishing (or painting) stool.

But why stop at safari gear? thought McIntyre; and promptly came up with a canvas executive briefcase complete with phone and computer compartments, a natty collection of urban rucksacks and a separate pride of travel bags in camel and cowhide, the smallest of which would not look out of place in a first-class lounge or a style bar. Now all McIntyre needed was a partner, to bring Beach 'n Bush to the attention of the rest of the world and generate some foreign hard currency.

Enter Kenya-born entrepreneur Keith Steel, based in Edinburgh, who was on the lookout for a new venture, having successfully marketed both Glenmorangie Scotch Whisky and Nepalese pashminas to a variety of world markets. His lifetime passion for Kenya had led him to look at Kenyan artisanry — beads, woodwork, soapstone and other African tribal work — and it was while he was circling, two-and-a-half years ago, that he came across McIntyre's products. It was a serendipitous meeting. 'Quite simply, I fell for it and bought the company,' he says.

Steel's ambition for Sandstorm is to turn it into a global brand with a safari image. The bags, made in workshops in Nairobi, are hard-wearing but, as McIntyre had done, Steel saw the potential for them to look good beyond the Kenyan reserves or the European countryside: Louis Vuitton meets North Face, but with the unmistakable stamp of Africa. The authentic link with Kenya, however, would provide the degree of integrity increasingly sought by customers in Europe and America's luxury markets.

'I loved the products from the start,' says Steel, 'but what we brought to the party were some refinements necessary to the creation of a luxury brand. We changed the name to Sandstorm, adopted the gecko as our signature icon, which would be embossed on every piece, and incorporated elements such as hard bases, proper linings and better quality zips ... I've always loved the people of East Africa and the variety you find from one tribe to another, depending on whether they come from the coastal areas or the mountains. The Luo, from Lake Victoria, are particularly good with their hands, well-practised in making fishing nets. They are good at stitching and very particular in their work. They pay close attention to detail and finish. 90 per cent of our workforce at Sandstorm is drawn from the Luo.'

Needless to say, an important part of relaunching the business has been to improve the logistics of moving the product from Nairobi to distribution points in the UK and US. Back in Nairobi, Sandstorm Africa under Gary McIntyre remains true to its roots by continuing to produce tents as well as bags. Affluent travellers started to return in 2003, and in May 2004 safaris were ranked the hottest adventure travel activity in a survey of 6,000 worldwide travel specialists by Virtuoso, a network of upmarket travel agencies with annual sales of $US3 billion. So it's a good time to be in this market; but McIntyre and Steel know better than to sit still, and have also started to create canvas and leather seat covers for off-road vehicles — potentially launching Sandstorm into a whole new sector of the international markets.

Steel has committed one US dollar for every Sandstorm bag sold worldwide to the work of the Lewa Wildlife Conservancy, a wildlife and community development operation based on the Laikipia Plain in the north of Kenya, which works to protect the wildlife from poaching, and also to educate the Masai and Samburu to understand the value of conservation. 'I want this to be an international brand with a genuine future,' Steel says. 'Quality, craftsmanship, durability, style; these are all fundamental components. But so is our connection to Kenya and its ecosystems. Without that, and without a sense of Africa, we would be just another manufacturer of bags.'

Steel is aware of the challenges the company faces in progressing the manufacturing process in Kenya. They are already using more camel hide than they can source there, for example, and will have to look outside the country — to Sudan or Egypt — for future supplies. But he and McIntyre operate a strong, mutually supportive partnership. 'Faced with problems, we'll just go off together for a beer until we've worked out the solution. I feel very strongly that the way to help Africa get back on its feet is to invest in appropriate business and wildlife enterprises. Soft grant aid is not the answer. You have to keep the local people involved.'

(Source: Kate Patrick.' Out of Africa', *The Scotsman*, 27 November 2004)

Lewa Wildlife Conservancy started as a private cattle ranch, Lewa Downs, named after the Lewa Springs, which runs through its heart. The conservancy has been in the Craig family since 1924, when the Craig grandparents came from England and began raising cattle in Kenya. The late Alec Douglas took up land rights on Lewa Downs under the British government's post war 'Soldier Settler' scheme. He established a cattle ranch there and the property has remained in the family ever since. Alec Douglas was a pioneer in every sense. Unusually for those early days, he sought to manage his farm in harmony with the wildlife that he found there, a tradition that has passed down the generations. 'Always make room for the wildlife' has been the Craig ethic since the 1920s. His daughter, Delia, inherited the property on his death and, together with her husband David Craig, ran the farm for 26 years before handing over to their eldest son Ian.

Three generations of the Craig family continue to be involved in daily operations on Lewa. The Craigs managed Lewa as a cattle ranch for more than 50 years, but as commercial farming became unprofitable, the farm evolved first into a rhino sanctuary and then into today's conservancy. In 1985, David Craig started a rhino sanctuary on their property. David provided 5,000 acres for the start of the Ngare Sergoi Rhino Sanctuary. Owing to the success of the Rhino Sanctuary, this 5,000 acres soon became 10,000 acres. Since 1990, donated funds have been used to purchase a surveillance aeroplane, a large lorry (truck), patrol jeeps, fencing materials, and pay the salaries of the armed guards needed near every rhino to keep them safe from the *shifta* (poachers). Recognising the tremendous success of Lewa Downs, the Kenyan government allowed 15,000 acres of the Ndare Forest to be enclosed under the protection of Lewa Downs. In April 1993, the Ngare Sergoi Rhino Sanctuary, the Lewa Downs Ranch, and the Ndare Ngare Forest were opened up to the rhinos and became the 61,000 acre Lewa Wildlife Conservancy.

Lewa director Ian Craig has made one of the largest contributions to community wildlife conservation. Ian discovered early on that communities really needed security and transport, before healthcare, education, and clean water, which had been the traditional cornerstone issues. By developing close personal relationships with tribespeople to the north of Lewa, Ian has managed to build a radio network, literally with herdsmen carrying a handheld radio. This has enabled fast reports to reach the security services, whenever there is cattle rustling or poaching in the area. Conservation projects such as IL Ngwesi, Tassia and Sarara, are direct spin-offs of their approach.

Lewa is one of the biggest employers in Kenya's Eastern Province. In addition to LWC's 300 full-time staff and 50 part-time staff, an additional 150 people are employed in tourism enterprises and other local craft workshops within Lewa's boundaries. LWC's ambition is not only to conserve the environment, but also to act as a stimulus to development and economic growth in the wider area. On Lewa's southern and eastern boundaries there are arable farmers trying to make a living off small plots of land with unreliable rainfall, while to the north its neighbours are cattle and camel herders accustomed to living with wildlife.

Ian and his brother Will, who runs the private homestead operation called Wilderness Trails on the conservancy, have pioneered a new kind of ecotourism that involves the creation of 'group' ranches owned by whole villages or communities. The Lewa Wildlife Conservancy has been assisting the nearby Masai, Samburu and Rendille Group ranches to develop community-based tourism. The Craigs and their associates helped the tribespeople design and build up market tourist lodges, organised for them to go on catering courses, and helped provide the infrastructure necessary for looking after wealthy Europeans and Americans. By building several small, simple guest lodges, the local people have been able to promote their game-rich areas to tourists; generating a considerable income that benefits the tribes as a whole. Schools and medical clinics have been the main focus of this development.

(Source: www.lewa.org)

Well-known conservationist, Oria Douglas-Hamilton has launched Elephant Watch Safaris in Samburu Reserve, northern Kenya. This is a totally new concept in the world of safaris where visitors will be introduced to individual elephants, recognise them through their photo filing system and learn about elephant society. While on safari, Oria's guests will be able to stay in her beautiful upmarket tented camp, set on the western shores of the Ewaso Ngiro River inside the Reserve.

The rationale behind Elephant Watch Safaris is borrowed from whale watching: that there is more value in the live animal from people watching it than there is from killing it for its products of meat, skin and ivory. Oria is delighted to be able to offer her guests this wonderful experience. While venturing into the secret world of elephants, visitors will also see many of the unusual wild animals: the slim necked gerenuk, the reticulated giraffe, the Grevy zebras, and over 400 species of birds, as well as all the big cats, including the now famous 'miracle lioness', who has taken to adopting baby oryx.

Oria's exotic camp is perched on the sandbanks of the Ewaso Nyiro River, beneath big *kigelia* trees and *acacia elatiors*. The trees are filled with a multitude of birds and monkeys; at dawn a gentle chorus echoes overhead announcing the new day in the wild. It is home to some of the largest bulls in Samburu: Mungu, AB Lincoln, Martin Luther King and many others, who can often be seen resting under acacia trees or picking pods beside the tents.

The camp, which is eco-friendly, has been specially constructed for comfort and coolness. Using wood from dead trees pushed down by the elephants, every piece has been used and recycled, which gives the camp its unusual appearance. The camp can accommodate a maximum of ten guests in its wide and breezy desert-style tents, individually designed, draped with colourful cloth and unusual furniture. Bathrooms are built around trees, giving guests a novel washing experience, with hand-painted shower buckets and plenty of sun-heated water and sun-powered lights.

Everything about Elephant Watch Camp is a feast for the senses, starting with the central thatched area with its bright swathes of cotton fanning in the breeze, huge cushioned sofas, woven local mats and special Daliesque furniture made from twisted branches. Menus are a fusion of bush gourmet, flown in fresh from their farm, with tropical fruit and drinks and a selection of good wine. Books, films and information on elephants are provided for guests. At night, flame torches and lanterns light up the camp along the river. Baboons call out, as leopards stalk, while lions and elephants are always nearby. It is the only camp of its kind in Kenya.

Elephant Watching begins on arrival. Elephant Watch guides meet their guests at either of the two airfields and drive them gently through the Reserve spending time with many of the well known elephant matriarchs and their families as well as the big bulls. A special visit to the Save the Elephant Research Centre can also be organised. Each day opens with a new adventure. Early morning or evening bush walks along well travelled elephant paths are a must, where one can collect medicinal plants and honey, accompanied by Samburu warriors. At times one can witness the great river crossings of camels and cattle, learn the techniques of fire making, and participate in Samburu ceremonies.

Oria and her husband Iain have been privileged to work with elephants for more than 30 years. They wrote the books *Among the Elephants*, an account of their six years spent studying elephants in Lake Manyara and *Battle for the Elephants*, which documents their years undertaking an Africa wide elephant census to put an end to the slaughter of elephants for the ivory trade. Iain and Oria have recently installed log beehives in specific trees liable to destruction by the elephants, by using bees as the guardians of the trees, from observations in their studies showing that elephants have an inborn fear of bees.

Dr Iain Douglas-Hamilton is now the chairman of the registered charity, Save the Elephants. He was awarded an OBE for his conservation work in Africa and was also involved in the production of the Discovery Channel IMAX film, 'Africa's Elephant Kingdom'. Iain and his team from the Save the Elephants Research Centre are currently monitoring long-distance movements using high-tech GPS radio collars on some of the wild elephants roaming throughout Samburu in northern Kenya. He can down load their specific location via satellites and transmit to his computer in Nairobi.

(Source: www.elephantwatchsafaris.com)

In her comprehensive book, *Ecotourism and Sustainable Development: Who Owns Paradise?*, Martha Honey, American writer, analyst and executive director of the International Ecotourism Society and the Centre on Ecotourism and Sustainable Development (a joint project of the Institute for Policy Studies in Washington, and Stanford University in California), presents an overview of the ecotourism industry and a first-hand account of ecotourism projects around the world. Based on interviews and visits to eco-tourist hotspots in Latin America and Africa, the book offers a vivid description and analysis of projects that meet the goals and standards of ecotourism, as well as those that claim to be ecotourism, but in reality fall short. Honey presents in-depth case studies of seven destinations (Galapagos, Costa Rica, Cuba, Zanzibar, Tanzania, Kenya and South Africa) that illustrate the economic and cultural impacts of tourism development on indigenous populations and ecosystems.

Martha Honey argues that the responsibility of ecotourism operators stretches far beyond their physical impact on the land. She argues that real ecotourism must involve seven vital and interrelated characteristics: travel to nature destinations; minimising negative environmental impact; building environmental awareness; direct financial benefits for conservation; financial benefits and empowerment for local people; the respect of local culture; and the support of human rights and democracy. Her book is an excellent account of worldwide ecotourism. It is an important guide for students and researchers involved with international development, geography, or tourism, as well as for anyone interested in becoming a more environmentally sensitive traveller. She is currently working on a new edition of this popular book.

(Source: Martha Honey. *Ecotourism and Sustainable Development: Who Owns Paradise?* Washington: Island Press, 1999)

The beautiful Bay and Marine Park of Watamu just south of Malindi has always been a big favourite with all who love the Kenya coast. Its beach is second to none and the waters within the reef are broken up by huge coral outcrops. Watamu was visited by Dicky Evans in the 1970s and he was captivated and eventually bought land and built a holiday home there.

In the late 1980s one of the two established locally-owned hotels on the beach, Seafarers, came up for sale and a big corporation was in the final stages of negotiation for its purchase. Dicky knew nothing about hotels but the prospect of losing the Watamu he knew was sufficient spur for him to find out very quickly how they worked and secure the purchase of Seafarers in early 1988.

The old hotel was mostly knocked down and rebuilt and Hemingways, as had been advertised, opened on 1 November 1988. The main terrace overlooking the bay had been raised by 15 feet and now looked down across the beach and collected all available wind, which allowed comfortable dining even in the hot season. The bar and restaurant were high roofed and airy, and the place soon became a local favourite.

Dicky is an avid fisherman, and with Watamu also a very well-known base for the big game variety, Hemingways soon had a respected fishing fleet and started to host international events. The ethic of the hotel (together with the African Billfish Foundation) brought tag and release of game fish to those waters and, happily, this is now the norm with most who fish there.

During the years that followed, the south wing of the old hotel was demolished and a spacious and comfortable new wing went up in its place. With a large and loyal following, Hemingways is a place where faces are easily recognised from the last trip and friendships are easy to come by.

(Source: David Bird. 'Hemingways revisited' www.big-gamefishing.net/hemingways.htm, 2001)

Mahmud Jan Mohamed is the managing director of Tourism Promotion Services Ltd (TPS), a subsidiary of the Aga Khan Fund for Economic Development. TPS is the operating company behind Serena Hotels. Mohamed has been with Serena since 1970 and has climbed every rung of the corporate ladder, from resident manager of Kenya's Serena Beach Hotel to the top. As a result, he believes that pressure for change must come from the bottom up rather than from the top down and describes his management style as 'open, fair and consultative'. He was the prime mover behind Serena's expansion into Tanzania, where two ruined but historical Stone Town buildings were transformed into the splendours of the Zanzibar Serena Inn. Zanzibar Serena was opened in 1997, after skilfully restoring the two dilapidated near ruins and adding the amenities and back of house facilities, a top hotel requires today. It is one of the rare spots, where one can look over the Indian Ocean and see the sun set, as normally one sees the sun rising out of the sea in this part of the world. Dozens of dhow sailing boats with their typical triangular sails ply the waters around the island, offering picturesque sights across the water to the small islands, dotting the horizon towards the Tanzania mainland.

Asked about the future, Jan Mohamed says he wants to consolidate Serena as an East African organisation by establishing the group in Uganda and flinging wide the doors of Serena hospitality in the Great Lakes region. He doesn't believe in standing still; whereas ten years ago it was fine for Serena Hotels to measure themselves against the benchmark of local competition, now they must look towards Mauritius, the Maldives and other 'hot' destinations to see who's doing what, where and how.

Jan Mohamed is a formidable networker, the founding chairman of the Kenya Tourism Federation, an umbrella body that pulled together the many strands of the Kenyan travel industry to allow them to speak with one voice and lobby with joint resolve. During his two-year leadership, the federation established a tourism security nerve centre and fought some notable skirmishes in the long-running visa war. Jan Mohamed is also a member of the USA's Cornell University Hotel Society that meets tri-annually to update and exchange views on the state of the industry. In 2001, he was appointed to the board of the private sector governance body that is dedicated to promoting good governance and sound business practice throughout Kenya.

Under Jan Mohamed's leadership, Serena Hotels has re-invested, most especially in infrastructure, both front of house and behind the scenes. Good housekeeping apart, Serena Hotels has also made some shrewd property moves: Mountain Lodge on the slopes of Mount Kenya and Kilaguni Safari Lodge in Tsavo West, both of which received a radical revamp before adding their charms to Serena's all-star luxury line-up. The cast includes: in Kenya, the Nairobi Serena Hotel, the Mombassa Serena Beach Hotel and the Amboseli, Mara and Samburu Serena safari lodges and in Tanzania, the Ngorongoro, Serengeti and Lake Manyara Serena safari lodges plus the Kirawira Camp in western Serengeti and the Zanzibar Serena Inn.

Serena has not only invested in property. Serena Hotels' accolades include winning the Company of the Year Award for Human Resource Management Practices and overall second place in the same event. Jan Mohamed says they have also invested heavily in people; claiming that not only are human resources their greatest asset but also that they offer handsome dividends to any organisation willing to invest in them. That such an investment must include the provision of an enabling environment and the right tools for the job is repeated with mantra-like conviction by Serena's management. Serena Hotels puts much time and effort into the employer/employee relationship and is keen on training and the provision of health and recreational facilities, and meticulous in offering top quality uniforms and good staff accommodation. All the upper management echelons encourage information feedback from everyone, from doorman to front-desk manager.

Jan Mohamed is quick to point out that Serena should know how to deal with people as they're in the people business. As part of their commitment to keeping the purse strings of the world-tourism-spend elastic in their direction, Serena Hotels believe in keeping their fingers firmly on the global tourism pulse. They've introduced adventure sports such as mountain climbing, biking and canoeing. They've brought on board all manner of educational pursuits, cultural visits and discovery walks orchestrated by battalions of highly trained naturalists and educators. The reason, according to Jan Mohammed, is simple: it's no good standing still in a globally positioned market, especially one that is clamouring for cultural interaction, sport and eco-experience as well as reading, relaxing and roasting.

Serena Hotels have also blended skilfully with the greenness of the times and are right where they should be when it comes to the ecologically correct disposal of waste and effluent. They also work alongside local communities to promote cultural and financial exchange and pay their dues on time to organisations such as the Kenya Wildlife Service. In this way, they can help minimise human-wildlife conflicts, embrace bio-diversity, protect wildlife and promote those wonders that still remain of the natural paradise of Kenya. They won the 2000 American Society of Travel Agents Award for Achievements in Conservation and Preservation of the Planet for their Amboseli reforestation project. Drastic climatic changes had prompted Serena Group to start a reforestation project in Amboseli; more than 250,000 trees were planted by tourists and the Serena

Hotels management. The Amboseli initiative shows how a company can rejuvenate a devastated area and restore the eco-balance of the vegetation and wildlife. Serena's mission is to conserve rather than exploit nature.

All Serena Hotels' meals are prepared by East African chefs, many of whom have returned from sabbaticals in the kitchens of some of the highest-profile eateries in the world. The trademark African decor of the hotels draws heavily upon local art, textiles and sculpture. They have won the Gold Award for Excellence in Architecture from the Architectural Association of Kenya. The more exuberant tropical output of the East African horticultural industry blooms in their foyers. Serena Hotels are creating buildings of outstanding ethnic design.

(Source: Jane Barnsby. 'As Kenya Tourism goes belly-up, Serena Hotels are baking the perfect croissant', Nairobi: *The East African*, 2 December 2001; www.nationaudio.com)

In recognition of their achievements, in the annual business survey of the most respected businesses in East Africa, carried out by PriceWaterhouseCoopers and the Nation Media Group, Serena Hotels was voted one of the top 10 most respected companies in East Africa in 2002. Jan Mohamed, who has a very steady hand on the tiller, was voted one of the top 10 most respected chief executives in East Africa in 2002. In 2003, Serena Hotels was voted the most respected hotel group in East Africa, and once again one of the top ten most respected companies overall in the region. In November 2004, Serena Hotels was again awarded the Most Respected Company award in East Africa in the Hotels and Tourism category for 2004.

In February 2004, TPS signed a 30-year lease concession agreement with the government of Uganda and agreed to invest US$26.5 million for extensive refurbishment and upgrading of the former Nile Hotel and International Conference Centre, which would re-open in November 2005 as the five-star Serena Kampala Hotel. New facilities will include three restaurants, swimming pool, health, fitness and spa facilities, two bars, a new lobby and seminar rooms. The meeting rooms at the Nile conference centre will be renovated and new systems related to fire and safety will be installed. A leading landscape designer has been appointed to ensure the project takes full advantage of the seven hectares of land which will include retaining mature trees on site and adding water features. Prince Amyn Aga Khan, chairman of AKFED, announced that the Serena Kampala Hotel would help TPS expand the established Serena safari and leisure circuit in East Africa, and it would also enable TPS to advance tourism development throughout Uganda and act as a spur to other investors in this sector.

In Kenya, ongoing and new developments include the conference centre at Mombassa Serena Beach Hotel (opened September 2004), the ongoing rehabilitation of bedrooms at Kilaguni and Amboseli Serena lodges and the Serena Beach Hotel. Construction on the new state of the art conference facility at the Nairobi Serena Hotel commenced in November 2004 and was completed by April 2005.

(Source: www.serenahotels.com)

Uhuru Kenyatta and David Stogdale have done a fine job of building the Heritage Hotel chain. Kenyatta, former chairman of the Kenya Tourist Board, has been involved in the tourism industry since 1989 through his company, previously called Prestige Hotels and which he and Stogdale have re-launched as Heritage Hotels. The experienced pair has a younger and more dynamic outlook, well in tune with the new directions being adopted by the industry. Stogdale has worked in a number of hotels during a local career spanning some 30 years, and was responsible for overseeing Kenya's award-winning stand at the World Travel Market in 2000. The main point about Stogdale, which was true at Block Hotels, at Conservation Corporation Africa, and certainly at Heritage, is his drive to empower local Kenyans into senior management positions in the local hospitality business.

In October 2001, the Heritage Group took over the spectacular Siana Springs tented camp, becoming the biggest safari group in the world famous Masai Mara National Reserve, where it also runs Mara Intrepids and Mara Explorer luxury camps and Voyager Safari Lodge. Siana Springs offers incredible opportunities for getting up close and personal with the area's famous wildlife. Mara Intrepids is a luxurious tented camp along the Talek River. Mara Explorer is a five-star camp with secluded tents and the finest personal service. Voyager Safari Lodge is situated to the north east of the Masai Mara National Reserve, within the borders of the Koyaki/Lemek Wildlife Trust.

Voyager Safari Camp is situated in the shadow of the majestic Mount Kilimanjaro on the edge of Tsavo West National Park. A natural choice for a few days' break, Samburu Intrepids is a tented lodge in the Samburu National Reserve, complete with camels and bush walks for the intrepid traveller. Great Rift Valley Lodge and Golf resort is an unusual lodge and championship golf course overlooking the Great Rift Valley and beautiful Lake Naivasha. Kipugani Explorer is a romantic getaway situated two degrees south of the Equator on a deserted stretch of Lamu Island beach. Voyager Beach Resort is one of Kenya's leading coastal destinations. The resort overlooks the white sands of Nyali Beach, seven kilometres north of Mombassa.

For years, children have been accompanying their parents to Africa to witness the world's greatest creatures, marvel at its wildest landscapes, and partake of its oldest cultures, only to return home knowing very little about what they have actually seen. The Heritage Group offers the ultimate children's holiday, thanks to its uniquely educational and inspirational Adventurer's Club, a complementary kids' club that provides an interactive education about Africa's wilderness and its human and wild inhabitants. The club operates at six Heritage properties around Kenya. Accompanied by highly trained naturalists and cultural specialists, children are treated to an enlightening series of walks, talks, visits to neighbouring schools and villages, games and activities designed to help them better understand their wild surroundings.

In November 2002, Heritage launched an exciting new five-star eco-tourism portfolio, the Explorer Collection, which is making great headway in bringing more discerning eco-tourists to Kenya and Tanzania. The Explorer Collection brings together 20 of the finest, most responsible private eco-tourism retreats in Kenya, Tanzania and Zanzibar and offers visitors an exceptional eco-tourism experience in some of Africa's most exclusive and remote locations. Heritage's flagship camp in the heart of the Masai Mara and their enchanting desert island hideaway on Lamu Island offer the very best of both beach and bush. Heritage's private partners invite guests to visit some of Africa's most luxurious properties on wildlife reserves in Laikipia, Masailand and the Great Rift Valley.

(Source: www.heritage-eastafrica.com)

Wangari Maathai, Kenyan professor and environmental activist was the recipient of the Nobel Peace Prize in October 2004, for her work as leader of the Green Belt Movement, which has sought to empower women, improve the environment and fight corruption in Africa for almost 30 years. Maathai is Kenya's deputy minister for the environment and the first African woman to win the prize, first awarded in 1901. She has battled to stem deforestation across the African continent and to promote democracy and women's and children's rights. She gained recent acclaim for a campaign for planting 30 million trees to stave off deforestation. 'We believe that Maathai is a strong voice speaking for the best forces in Africa to promote peace and good living conditions on that continent. Peace on earth depends on our ability to secure our living environment. Maathai stands at the front of the fight to promote ecologically viable social, economic and cultural development in Kenya and in Africa,' the Nobel committee said in Maathai's citation.

Caroline Kihato, Kenyan citizen and policy analyst and editor in the Development Bank of Southern Africa, reports in *Earthyear* magazine that environmentalists around the world have hailed Wangari Maathai's conservation work. For rural women in Kenya, Maathai has been a liberator. Through her NGO, the Green Belt Movement, she has facilitated their economic and social empowerment where their own elected leaders have usually failed them. Maathai was the first woman in East and Central Africa to obtain a doctorate, and the first woman professor at the University of Nairobi. In 1977 she founded the Green Belt Movement, whose objectives centre on the restoration of Kenya's rapidly diminishing forests. The movement also seeks to promote the empowerment of rural women through environmental conservation.

Rural women's daily lives are intricately intertwined with their environment. They are responsible for fetching water and ensuring that there is enough firewood in the home for cooking and heating. As forests diminish because of the demands made on them to satisfy household needs, it is women who walk further and further in search of the increasingly scarce resources. By planting trees, the movement not only ensures greater environmental sustainability, it also alleviates the daily burdens faced by women by providing a close, sustainable source of fuel. The Green Belt Movement gets seedlings and distributes them free of charge to rural communities. A network of locally trained community members, often women, provides advice to women farmers about planting, maintenance and nurturing of the seed-lings. Farmers are paid for every tree that survives, thus providing women with an independent source of income. What began as a small nursery in Maathai's back yard has grown into about 3,000 nurseries giving job opportunities to 80,000 people, most of them rural women. About 20 million trees have been planted in Kenya, and nearly 80 per cent have survived. The movement has also grown beyond Kenya's borders and now has local chapters in Tanzania, Uganda, Malawi, Lesotho, Ethiopia and Zimbabwe.

In the 2002 historic elections in Kenya, Maathai stood for a parliamentary seat, this time with a united opposition under the National Rainbow Coalition banner, which succeeded in ousting Moi. Notwithstanding attempts by her political rivals to disrupt her rallies and hurl insults and abuse at her, Maathai won her parliamentary seat with an overwhelming majority.

She is now deputy minister for environment and continues her struggle for the protection of the environment. Maathai's ministry is involved in rooting out the corrupt practices of the previous government, which illegally sold state forests and gave illegal logging permits to individuals with connections to the Moi regime. The way the new government deals with this kind of corruption will allow Kenyans to determine whether real political transformation has occurred.

Wangari Maathai is a role model for young Kenyan women. She has opened cultural and political doors that have traditionally been strict male domains. To some extent she has made it easier for young Kenyan women since they have a precedent where she had none. A green, safe environment is not the only gift she will bequeath to posterity. Her inspiration, hope and fighting power will endure for generations to come.

(Source: Caroline Kihato. 'Kenya's green role model, Wangari Maathai', *Earthyear*, Volume 3, 2003; www.earthyear.co.za)

Professor Maathai spoke at the Africa Diaspora and Development Day in London on 2 July 2005 where thousands of Africans met to discuss their own future. 'One of the worst outcomes of injustices is poverty,' says Wangari. 'It robs human beings of their dignity. When people are poor and when they are reduced to beggars, they feel weak, humiliated, disrespected and undignified ... They hide alone in corners and dare not raise their voices. They are therefore, neither heard nor seen. They do not organise but often suffer in isolation and in desperation. Yet all human beings deserve respect and dignity. Indeed it should be unacceptable to push other human beings to such levels of indignity. Even before any other rights, perhaps it may be time to campaign for all human beings to have the right to a life of dignity: a life devoid of poverty in the midst of plenty because such poverty demonstrates gross inequalities. As long as millions of people live in poverty and indignity, humanity should feel diminished. A time such as this gives all of us, and especially those in leadership, the opportunity to reduce poverty. There is a lot of poverty in Africa. This is largely due to economic injustices, which must be addressed not only by the rich industrialised countries but also by leaders in Africa.'

The African Women Agribusiness Network - East Africa (AWAN-EA) is a business support organisation that promotes women's small and medium enterprise growth through facilitation or direct provision of need based services and through advocacy aimed at creating a better business environment for women within East Africa and the region. AWAN-EA builds the capacity of the women and their organisations; enhancing their competitiveness in the global market and thus fostering social development, gender equity, income generation, environmental sustainability and good governance. AWAN-EA members include Women's SMEs who have excelled in local markets and are seeking export markets and SMEs already involved in export trade and which are looking to expand their market base. The AWAN-EA is funded by the USAID/REDSO/ESA office.

Headquartered in Nairobi, with seven country chapters in East Africa and the region (Eritrea, Ethiopia, Rwanda, Tanzania, Uganda, Kenya and Southern Sudan), AWAN-EA facilitates access to a wide set of business development services to their members in the region.

The purpose of AWAN-EA is to enhance trade and market development; to facilitate access to risk management and financial services; to strengthen quality mechanisms and compliance through training and co-financing certification; lobbying and advocacy (promoting law reforms, regulations and other barriers to agri-business growth); and to strengthen institutional capacity and skills through training and facilitating access to technical assistance.

Women's small and medium sized enterprises are increasingly playing a strategic role in economic growth and development through their contribution in the creation of wealth, employment and income generation. In most developing economies they have taken the role of the primary vehicles for creation of employment and income generation through development of self-employment, becoming effective tools for poverty alleviation. Access to finance has been identified as a major constraint in the development of the sector with others being unfavourable business environment and lack of access to business development and advisory services. Finance, however, still ranks as the biggest handicap. AWAN-EA was a 2005 finalist for the Africa SMME Awards. Fresh Approach Ltd and Woni Vegetables and Fruit Exporters Ltd of Kenya are excellent AWAN-EA success stories.

(Source: www.awan-ea.net)

Fresh Approach Ltd deals in horticultural exports which include passion fruits, mangoes, French beans and avocados. Frida Muya is the managing director of this company and a member of AWAN-EA. The company's key markets include France, Sweden and Canada. Frida took advantage of a AWAN-EA trip to Dubai to establish business linkages with some of the buyers that had been identified there (this was the first time the company was exporting to Dubai). As of 2005, the company had made several shipments to Dubai. Results were: income increased by $364,614; increased out reach to rural farmers (12 new small-scale outgrowers to meet this increased demand); increased employment (the company has recruited five additional permanent staff members ranging from an extension officer to pack house supervisors and clerks); her intake of casuals has increased by approximately 30 per cent; business expansion (two new cold storage facilities installed); and certification (the first AWAN member to be certified for EUREGAP protocol).

Woni Vegetables and Fruit Exporters Ltd is a medium sized company that deals in horticultural and floricultural exports which include flowers, mangoes, avocados, passion fruit, French beans and snow peas. Managing Director Jane Mutiso's export markets include France, the United Kingdom, Holland and Dubai. The company has 55 employees — 25 permanent and 30 casuals. The company has sub-contracted 60 small scale farmers in rural Kenya for the production of French beans, sugar snaps and snow peas.

Jane Mutiso participated in the AWAN-EA regional workshop on implementation and audit technique for international standards. In a letter of appreciation to the AWAN-EA secretariat she said, '...The training served as an eye opener to me. The best part of the workshop was the organised reference material that was provided which was self-explanatory; now I know without doubt the specific standards and their requirements and I am able to supervise their implementation.'

As a result of this awareness, Jane Mutiso embarked on the implementation of the recommendations laid out by Eurepgap, which included the computerisation of traceability systems; the training of field technicians and farmers using the training manuals she has developed; the testing of water and soil samples (700 different samples are scheduled for testing); and the implementation of food hygiene processes at the warehouse.

Jane Mutiso states that Woni's audit for Eurepgap was pegged to the farmers' preparedness. She subcontracted 60 farmers who were organised into groups of five to work together in developing grading sheds together with other infrastructure necessary for accreditation. By 2005, 18 structures had been completed. Woni was audited and certified for Eurepgap in 2005. After conforming to the laid down standards, Woni was assured of a market for her products in the European Union market. This is going a long way in ensuring that Kenya does not lose the foreign exchange earnings generated by exports of fresh produce to this trading bloc.

Magana Flowers Kenya Ltd is 100 per cent owned by Magana Holdings Ltd. With 500 employees, it is one of Kenya's most successful exporters, growing a variety of roses for the European market. Kenya is considered a giant in the international floriculture industry occupying the top position as the leading supplier to the European Union, the country's leading trading block, with a 25 per cent market share in 2004. With an annual turnover of more than US$ 130 million and employing about 60,000 people, Kenya's flower industry has been a spectacular success.

Magana Flowers' farm is situated in the village of Kikuyu, about 18 kilometres from Nairobi's city centre, on the main highway between Nairobi and Nakuru, and 30 kilometres from the international airport. The farm is surrounded by eleven villages, one of which, Gichungo, is where the founder of Magana Flowers, Dr Magana Njoroge Mungai, was born.

The operation started in 1994 with two hectares. Now it covers 18 hectares and two more hectares are in development. All are under cover in greenhouses. The farm has moved away from growing on the soil. It uses pumice and cocopeat as media. Fertigation is done through drip irrigation; fertigation fluid is collected from the troughs where it flows to the collection tank. It is pumped to recirculation tanks, cleaned, pumped into irrigation tanks and some more fresh water and fertilisers are added. It is then pumped back into the greenhouses. This saves water, fertilisers and ensures that soil is not polluted by fertilisers. It also saves money.

Dr Mungai has introduced high agronomical standards on the farm which ensure high quality export products and thus help Kenya sustain its position as a quality horticultural producer. To achieve and maintain the high standards required, Magana Flowers is audited and inspected by organisations from the countries where it exports flowers: FLP, German Flower Label; FLO-Cert of Germany; Milieu Programma Sierteelt (MPS), Dutch Flower Labs; Max Havelaar, from Switzerland; Flower Plus, from United Kingdom; EUREPGAP, on behalf of European Union; KFC, Kenya Flower Council; and individual supermarkets.

Auditors and inspectors are sent every year and spend a lot of time on the farm, interviewing workers privately, looking at all aspects of farming to ensure that Magana Flowers is keeping and maintaining a code of practice and ethics to conform with good agricultural practices. In all cases, this village farm at Kikuyu has passed and has been certified by all of these organisations. Magana Flowers exports to various importers in Europe including the supermarkets Migros in Switzerland, Carrefour in France, Kaizer Tanglemann in Germany and Somerfield in the United Kingdom. Magana Flowers also exports to the Middle East.

Quality of product is important to the company, but more important to Dr Mungai and Magana Flowers are their employees and the environment. Magana Flowers states in its mission statement and values: 'Our most important assets are our employees, their families, health, housing and welfare in general. We are committed to continuously maintaining, protecting and improving our environment consistent with sustainable development for current and future generations.' The area in the farm that is not covered by greenhouses is covered by grass and indigenous trees. Trees are continuously being planted including around the blocks of greenhouses. This is aesthetically pleasant it conserves the soil from water and wind erosion. It has increased bird population and animals are now occasionally sighted.

Magana Flowers as a company is very aware of social and environmental corporate responsibility. At the farm all employees are provided with protective clothes — boots, masks (where necessary), gloves, overcoats, overalls and helmets for those in construction. Already under construction are changing rooms with hot showers (for women and men separately), a day care centre, and a dining hall where one can get a hot meal. Special attention is given to those who handle chemicals, like spray teams and care is taken that they are not over exposed to injuries. They undergo regular medical examinations and blood tests.

All employees, their spouses and children are provided with free medical care at the farm. Arrangements are made for their hospitalisation if needed. Expectant mothers are given three months leave with pay. After delivery and when they return to work they get one hour in the morning and one hour in the afternoon for breast feeding. The company keeps the CBA, the common bargaining agreement, as laid down between employees and labour unions. All aspects of wages and conditions are maintained.

In the farm and the whole company, management respects the rights of all employees, irrespective of age (they do not employ children), sex or religion. In fact the term that is gaining popularity in addressing workers is 'colleague'. The workers committee is composed of both men and women and management looks out for the rights of women in the farm to make sure there is no sexual harassment or exploitation. The company believes that a healthy, respected and happy worker produces more gains and profit for the whole community. This is in keeping with Magana Flowers' mission statement.

Dr Magana Njoroge Mungai was educated at Kikuyu Elementary and Primary School and Alliance High School, Kikuyu. He went to the University of Fort Hare in South Africa for a B Sc in 1950. He was admitted to the University of London Medical School in 1951 but changed his mind and instead went to Stanford University in California for a BA and MD. He did his residency in New York City, associated with Columbia University, and at McGill University for purposes of registration to practise medicine in Kenya. In 1963 he was on the team that negotiated for Kenya's independence from Britain, served in government in the cabinet as minister of health, housing, internal security, defence, foreign affairs and environment. Now retired from politics, Dr Mungai keeps active with his farming and private businesses.

When the winners of the Africa 2004 SMME Awards were announced in October 2004, enterprises from all over the continent made their mark. The three top enterprises were not only from different corners of the continent, but also from different industries. Magana Flowers, Kenya, was the winner of the second runner up award, the winner of the regional award for East Africa, and the winner of the award for the agricultural, food and beverage production sector.

(Source: www.maganaflowers.com).

Flamingo Holdings, a vertically integrated horticultural business involved in the growing, processing, packaging, marketing and distribution of cut flowers and fresh vegetables, has significant interests in Kenya through its wholly-owned subsidiary, Homegrown Ltd. 77 per cent of the shareholding of Flamingo Holdings is owned by the staff, with 14 per cent held by Actis in London, and the balance of 9 per cent by Barings representing OPIC, the overseas development arm of the US government.

Flamingo sells direct to supermarkets in the UK, where the demand for such premium products continues to grow. To help it service and develop this customer base, Flamingo has established processing, distribution and marketing operations in the UK. Flamingo Holdings' growth plans include the acquisition of other horticultural businesses in Africa and the UK to strengthen its supply chain and expand its capacity and product range.

Thanks to continuous innovation, high product quality, efficient distribution channels and value for money, Flamingo is now the leading supplier of flowers and premium vegetables to supermarkets in the UK including Marks & Spencer, Tesco, Sainsbury and Safeway.

Horticulture is the fastest-growing sector of Kenya's economy, bringing in an estimated US$450 million in 2003. Flamingo developed out of Homegrown Ltd, Africa's largest exporter of vegetables and flowers to the UK. In addition to Kenya, the group also sources products from Zimbabwe, South Africa, Guatemala, Thailand, Spain and the Netherlands and now has a worldwide annual turnover of US$350 million. Michael Turner, Actis's East African director, comments that Flamingo is exactly the type of business Actis is looking to invest in — an integrated business with control of the entire supply chain, managed by an excellent team of experienced and committed professionals with a successful track record. He adds that its position as an innovator and supplier of the highest quality products means that it has exciting growth prospects.

As well as having excellent commercial prospects, Flamingo meets world benchmarks in terms of its social, environmental and health and safety policies. Flamingo is an active participant in the Kenya Flowers Council, the industry body set up to encourage businesses to adopt acceptable social and environmental policies. When the battalions of giant plastic greenhouses on the flower farms attracted criticism from environmentalists for draining and polluting the beauty spot of Lake Naivasha, Homegrown responded by building a natural water filter. All storm water runoff from the greenhouses now winds through a custom-built waterway between its farm and the lake, planted with a variety of specially chosen local water plants that clean up the runoff, and by the time it reaches the lake it is full of fish, with kingfishers hovering overhead. The water re-entering the lake is cleaner than the water leaving it.

Other aspects of Homegrown's operations attest to their efforts to improve social and environmental performance. Homegrown's packing stations look like operating theatres, and employees scrub up with soap and alcohol spray before entering in hairnets and overalls.

Homegrown is also at the forefront of commercial Integrated Pest Management (IPM) a method of pest control using natural enemies of pests such as indigenous beneficial insects. The success of this research and development — undertaken by a Flamingo subsidiary called Dudutech — in the last six years has been instrumental in obviating the use of all toxic organophosphates on its commercial vegetable crops throughout Kenya. Dudutech employs over 185 scientists and production staff and the successful implementation of IPM on its vegetables has now been extended to its more than 200hectares of flower production where, for instance, the use of toxic acaricides for spider mite has been reduced by 90 per cent. Not only are the benefits clear for the crop and the consumer, but the key upside is the positive effect it brings whereby staff are never exposed to any toxic materials in the production stage, ensuring worker safety.

Flamingo Holdings employs more than 10,000 staff worldwide and over 9,000 of them are in Kenya. It has recently invested in South Africa acquiring a small chrysanthemum operation near Johannesburg. The challenges in South Africa are different to Kenya but the group hopes to emulate its Kenya success in South Africa.

Flamingo Holdings' Chief Executive, Dicky Evans, says Flamingo will continue to grow, creating a world-class business, coupling the resources that exist in Africa with the added-value technologies that exist globally. This will ensure Flamingo continues to develop its product range providing top quality products for major supermarket customers. In the meantime, Homegrown Ltd in a short time has risen to become East Africa's most respected agri-business according to the PriceWaterhouseCoopers and Nation Media Group CEO's survey carried out in 2004.

(Source: Duncan Green. 'Growing pains', CAFOD: www.cafod.org.uk, 23 November 2004)

Agriculture is the backbone of the Kenyan economy. In fact, exports of tea and coffee are Kenya's major foreign currency earners. Presently, tea is even more important than coffee, so it is no wonder that tea growing is very popular. Both large plantations and smallholder farmers grow tea and the sector contributes 20 per cent of Kenya's total export earnings. There are a couple of large plantations in western and central Kenya, but the smallholder farm group Kenya Tea Development Agency (KTDA) is the biggest producer. The KTDA was established in 1964 as a state corporation mandated to promote tea cultivation by Kenya's indigenous smallholder farmers. To this end, the authority advised small holders on the best method of tea growing. It also collected leaf from small-scale tea farmers, and processed and marketed the tea on their behalf. Spread across all tea growing districts, the KTDA became the biggest single tea producer and exporter in the world.

The elections of June 2000 saw the former Kenya Tea Development Authority change from a governmental parastatal to a public company limited by a guarantee now known as the Kenya Tea Development Agency. About 360,000 small-scale tea growers participated in the June 2000 elections drawn from five provinces. All 28 tea growing districts participated in the elections where 11,368 farmers were elected representatives to leaf collection centres, 255 directors to tea factory boards, 12 to the Kenya Tea Development Agency and 11 to the Tea Board of Kenya. Prior to 2002, the KTDA managed 45 tea factories on behalf of their growers but by the end of 2002, nine new factories had been completed, serving smallholder farmers, and a tenth was being built. Its completion increased the number of small-scale tea factories managed by KTDA to 55. The ten factories have an installed annual capacity to process 10 million kilograms of green tea each, providing a new capacity of 100 million kilograms of green tea leaf. This is a 15 per cent increase over KTDA factories' 2001 capacity (665 million kilograms of green leaf per year). Processed tea is transported to Mombassa and sold in auction for export, with Pakistan, the United Kingdom and Egypt being the biggest buyers.

The building of each factory at an average cost of Sh350 million was financed 35 per cent by local tea farmers and 65 per cent by a combination of local and international financiers. In 2001, Kenya's tea industry turnover reached Sh38 billion (US$475 million) of which Sh35 billion (US$437.5 million) was accrued from export earnings, with the balance being the value of domestic tea sales. Kenyan tea output was 280 million kilograms for 2001. Currently the small-scale tea sub-sector under KTDA produces over 60 per cent of all Kenyan tea from a planted area of 90,000 hectares. Kenya normally records an average production of 500 million kilograms of green leaf in the smallholder tea sub-sector and 300 million kilograms from the estate category. It is also estimated that in addition to the member growers, another two million Kenyans indirectly derive their livelihood from the agency.

Kenya has more than 110,000 hectares of land devoted to tea, which is grown in the highland areas with adequate rainfall and low temperatures. The main tea-growing area is in the Kenyan highlands, west of the Rift Valley, at altitudes between 5,000 and 9,000 feet. The bushes are harvested throughout the year, with the best quality being produced in January and February and again in July, during the drier periods of the year. The average tea growing area is 0.26 hectare/smallholder farmer. The KTDA represents 360,000 small-scale growers, mainly in western and central Kenya. Roads in growing areas are improved through a special levy on the crop, and the agency provides hundreds of tea collection vehicles. Delivery of tea is improving as the KTDA is moving more tea to factories. As the question of roads is continually dealt with, the farmers are happier.

Joseph Nganga Mwaura is a KTDA tea grower from Kagwe. His tea growing area is 1.2 hectares which he manages together with his family. By KTDA standards Joseph is a big farmer, as their members' average is 0.26 hectares. Tea is giving a stable income to small-hold farmers, as they can sell green leaves throughout the year. In addition to tea, Joseph is also eagerly growing cabbage. He can sell cabbage to bigger cities and gets a good price, too.

In his 1991 study, *African Successes: Four Public Managers of Kenyan Rural Development*, David Leonard focused on four public officials who had a great impact on rural development in Kenya. He especially mentioned the entrepreneurial and innovative capability displayed by Charles Karanja, who was general manager of the KTDA from 1970 to 1981. With a commitment to efficiency that characterised his career, Karanja steered the KTDA through its period of greatest growth from a fledgling institution into one of the world's top producers of quality tea. Under Karanja's guidance, the KTDA became one of the world's greatest success stories in rural development. With startling success, the KTDA took over from the multinationals the manufacturing, wholesale marketing and retailing of tea. Household incomes from Kenya tea rose to three times the national average by 1995. Eric Kimani was KTDA's managing director 2002-2004 while Lerionka Tiampati became KTDA's managing director in January 2005.

(Source: www.ktdateas.com and David K Leonard. *African Successes: Four Public Managers of Kenyan Rural Development*. Berkeley: University of California Press, 1991)

In 1991, social entrepreneurs Martin Fisher and Nick Moon co-founded a Nairobi based non-profit company called Appropriate Technologies for Enterprise Creation, or simply ApproTEC, now known as KickStart. They know full well about working within the market while having to continuously operate, and think 'outside the box'. Nick Moon grew up in India and South East Asia and learned woodworking and general building skills. He started a small enterprise in London that prospered from its work for big city firms. Uneasy in his role as a fully-fledged businessman, and not being sure about his place as 'joiner to the gentry', Moon sold his share of the company and left for Kenya in 1982 to work as a volunteer technical instructor. Later in Kenya he joined ActionAid and met Fisher. Martin Fisher received his PhD at Stanford in theoretical and applied mechanics, but it wasn't until he made friends from developing countries in graduate school, and spent a summer in Peru, that he actually considered how to apply his learning to help the developing world. He went to Kenya on a Fulbright scholarship in 1985. He never looked back.

KickStart seeks to develop a significant middle class in Africa by stimulating the growth of a thriving entrepreneurial sector. Beginning with Kenya and Tanzania, it seems well on its way to attaining that goal. KickStart creates new businesses and jobs by developing and promoting new low-cost technologies that are bought and used by local entrepreneurs to establish profitable small businesses. By identifying, developing and marketing technologies with a high benefit-cost ratio, KickStart enables poor but industrious individuals to play an effective role in the market economy, substantially increasing their incomes and creating jobs and a host of backward and forward linkages. As of December 2005, over 58,000 East African entrepreneurs had bought KickStart-designed machines and tools and used them to establish some 39,000 currently active profitable small-scale businesses, generating over US$42 million per year in new profits, and providing waged employment for over 36,000 others. Every month, 750 more entrepreneurs in East Africa buy KickStart technology. By 2006, the turnover at enterprises that use KickStart products is expected to be equivalent to one per cent of Kenya's GDP.

In the industrialised world, governments subsidise research and development to promote new technologies that the private sector leverages for economic growth. But in the developing world there is almost no expenditure on technological research and development, particularly if the technologies are aimed at the poorest whose purchasing power is minimal. Poor governments have other priorities, and private sector companies rarely develop new products and technologies for the poor. KickStart responds to this 'market failure' by subsidising, through grants and donations, the research and development needed to develop innovative appropriate machinery that is both affordable and directly increases the efficiency of small and medium enterprises in Kenya and Tanzania. It collects detailed case studies and statistical data on the impact of its technologies, and maintains an awareness and demand creation programme for as long as it takes to build the market to sustainable levels. KickStart's operating principle is 'the greatest good to the greatest number in the shortest time and at the least cost'.

Several technologies developed and promoted by KickStart have substantially improved agricultural production. For example, in 1998 Jane Mathendu, a single mother of two living on the eastern slopes of Mount Kenya, decided to save up all her money and buy a KickStart manually operated oilseed press. The press extracts oil from sunflower seeds and has a filter to produce cooking oil and a seedcake by-product for animal feed. Mathendu already worked as a local schoolteacher but she needed to make more money to pay for her children's higher education. She looked around and saw that there would be a big market for the sunflower cooking oil and the by-product seedcake, which is a nutritious animal feed. She rented a small shop in Chuka town to start the business, but initially couldn't buy enough sunflower seed to keep the press busy. She soon solved this problem by contracting some local farmers to grow the seeds and she quickly made back her initial investment (US$350) and much more. Today she has left her job as schoolteacher to manage her business full-time. She now contracts 20 local farmers to grow seeds and employs two full time workers, who press over 16 litres of oil a day. She sells oil in bulk to a local hospital and school and in labelled bottles to her other customers. The seedcake is very popular with local farmers and she is now planning to buy a second press to meet the growing demand. The new business makes Jane over US$10 profit a day - a lot in a country where the average person lives on much less than a dollar a day, and more than four times what she made as a teacher — and it has drastically changed her life. She has become a leader in local social groups and has managed to pay for her oldest daughter's university education — something she could only dream about before she bought her new KickStart press.

Another product, the KickStart SuperMoneyMaker, is a leg-operated two-piston water pump with two treadles that makes it look like a Stairmaster and was priced at US$76 in 2004. It uses a pressurised head so that water can be driven through a sprinkler or up a slope and into Kenya's hilly fields. It can irrigate up to two acres of land. Moses Chumo and his bride had a small plot of land and were using one-eighth of an acre to grow kales, which they watered with a bucket. The SuperMoneyMaker allowed them to irrigate an entire acre, and with the profits, buy seven acres of additional land. They now grow irrigated crops for local and export markets.

Journalist Lisa Margonelli, writing in *Wired Magazine* in April 2002, said that it's clear that low-tech tools, like the KickStart MoneyMaker treadle pumps, can help kick-start an economic transition in Kenya. She maintains that the pump helps the country's struggling farmers put food on the table, and it gives them a foothold in the country's fledgling market economy. She points out that more family farmers have goods to take to market, where they can earn the cash needed to expand their operations, hire workers, buy a cow and invest in new businesses by purchasing, say, a sewing machine. She suggests that in some areas the pumps are slowly and subtly shifting traditional social roles. Margonelli feels, after talking with other people in the pump field, worldwide, that one of KickStart's greatest strengths is its all-out culturally appropriate marketing campaign, which has given the pumps extraordinary visibility. Out of curiosity, she asked everyone she ran into casually in Kenya if they'd heard of the KickStart MoneyMaker treadle pumps, and nearly everyone had. This is a big deal in a country with little mass media, a lousy road system and poor distribution.

(Source: LisaMargonelli. 'The rainmaker: How a low-cost lightweight pump is changing the economy of a nation', *Wired Magazine*, April 2002, pp. 108-115)

Fisher and Moon say that KickStart's strategy is to identify profitable small-scale industries for which capital investments can be recovered in three to six months with the introduction of appropriate technology. Once identified, KickStart's research team works to design a product that meets tough criteria. It has to be affordable (US$50 to $1,000), manually operated, energy-efficient, easy to transport by bicycle or bus, durable, require minimum training to install and use, be easy to repair and be manufactured from locally available materials. KickStart designs the tooling for mass production of the equipment and trains local manufacturers to mass-produce the technologies. It buys the technologies from the manufacturers and mass markets them to poor entrepreneurs, using innovative marketing techniques and selling them through local retail shops. Is KickStart concerned about others imitating its products? Quite the contrary! Its goal is to subsidise the development and establishment of the new technologies until they become firmly rooted in the society. At that point, there is no longer the need for marketing. Other manufacturers will step in to copy the product and compete with KickStart.

Martin Fisher and Nick Moon were two of the twenty social entrepreneurs worldwide selected as 'Outstanding Social Entrepreneurs' for 2003 by the Schwab Foundation for Social Entrepreneurship in Geneva, Switzerland. The Schwab Foundation provides recognition for outstanding social entrepreneurs whose work has significantly improved people's lives. Every year, they look for candidates and receive hundreds of suggestions through their network of nominators. Nominees undergo an extensive due diligence process which includes research, interviews, expert evaluations and site visits. Social entrepreneurs identify practical solutions to social problems by combining innovation, resourcefulness and opportunity. Deeply committed to generating social value, these entrepreneurs identify new processes, services, products or unique ways of combining proven practice with innovation, driving through pattern-breaking approaches to seemingly intractable social issues. Most importantly, they act as social alchemists, converting under-utilised resources into productive assets by working with, and motivating, groups of people and communities.

Professor David Kelley the Founder and Chairman of IDEO in Palo Alto and Professor of Design at Stanford University says that he has been 'wildly impressed' by the work that KickStart has accomplished in Kenya and that their contribution is amazing. Martin has shown him that it is possible for a small group of people to make an amazing impact, even change the world. He says that the creative leap they have made shows that the way to contribute in East Africa was not to simply give aid, but to empower the inevitable existence of entrepreneurs within a culture. Kelley emphasises that this was impressive. He points out that giving people the hope, the ability and the tools to make their dreams come true has been incredibly successful, but not obvious until KickStart proved that these individuals would surface and rally to the cause. Kelley believes that KickStart's irrigation and other technologies are feats of engineering and design that deserve recognition on their own. He emphasises that the success experienced by Kenyan entrepreneurs using KickStart's approach is a testament to the potential for KickStart-like models in developing economies worldwide. He concludes that, 'there is no telling how huge an impact this work can have'.

More recently Fisher and Moon have been recognised by others too. In 2003 they won the UK's prestigious Beacon Prize for Creative Giving, 'for developing an entirely new form of income generation and creative and innovative approaches to solving problems that are capable of imitation and replication'. In the same year, the AGFUND International Prize for Pioneering Development Projects was given to them, for 'innovative initiatives in the field of poverty alleviation'. And in both 2005 and 2006 they won *Fast Company* magazine's 'Social Capitalist' award that cited social impact, aspiration and growth, entrepreneurship, innovation and sustainability as the qualities which distinguish KickStart.

Kenyans remember KickStart/ApproTEC as the social enterprise that makes and markets irrigation pumps to help end poverty in Africa. In 2005, KickStart announced a major grant that will help them lift 400,000 people out of poverty by 2008. This is a practical example of corporate America partnering with a social enterprise to tackle the issue of global poverty. On 8 June 2005, The John Deere Foundation said it plans to provide US$3 million over the next three years to KickStart, an innovative social enterprise that creates and markets tools to help end poverty in developing countries. KickStart's three-year plan is to enable some 80,000 African families - approximately 400,000 people — to raise their standard of living by introducing small, inexpensive irrigation pumps and other money making equipment. 'It is fitting for John Deere, with a long history of advancing agriculture, to align with KickStart in Africa, where access to water for farming is particularly challenging,' said Robert W Lane, chairman and chief executive officer at Deere & Company. 'Through this grant, the John Deere Foundation can help improve the lives of the small family farmer by partnering with a successful organisation that is already working to strengthen agricultural economies in Africa.'

As of December 2005, KickStart products had helped lift 39,000 families out of poverty. On average, farmers who buy KickStart's foot-operated irrigation pumps multiply their income ten-fold as they move from subsistence to first-level commercial farming by growing high value fruits and vegetables. 'By partnering with the John Deere Foundation, KickStart will be in a position to help thousands more families to properly feed and educate their children and afford good healthcare,' said Dr Martin J Fisher, co-founder and executive director of KickStart. 'For the first time, these families will be able to plan for their futures.' Fisher said that the John Deere Foundation grant provides a solid foundation for the organisation's three-year, US$16 million plan to expand to six new countries and help 80,000 more families create successful farm businesses.

(Source: www.kickstart.org)

Davis & Shirtliff Group (D&S) is East Africa's largest water supply equipment specialist, founded in 1946. The company's activities are concentrated in importation, distribution, servicing and installation of surface and borehole water pumps; and water treatment, swimming pools and solar equipment. The company also manufactures and assembles water treatment and swimming pool products, sourced from various world-leading manufacturers including Grundfos, Pedrollo, Davey, Ajax KSB, Koshin, Lister, Shell Solar, Certikin and Sundaya.

Company headquarters are situated in Nairobi's industrial area with subsidiaries in Uganda (Kampala), Tanzania (Dar es Salaam and Arusha), Zambia (Lusaka and Kitwe) and Rwanda (Kigali). The company also has branches in the following towns in Kenya: Mombassa, Eldoret, Kisumu and Nairobi's Westlands suburb.

In 1995, the pump centre concept was introduced whereby D&S distributes its products through established outlets dealing in similar or related products in many major towns countrywide.

The D&S branch network has grown tremendously since 1995. In 2005, the company had revenues of US$15 million. The company has doubled in size in the three years 2003-2005 with the 2006 number of employees standing at 170. D&S has a training school where regular courses in management, engineering and other related courses are carried out for staff and customers. In 2005, over 700 staff members and D&S customers were trained in various courses.

D&S also has a strong culture of quality and innovation. Developments have included ISO 9001 Certification and various product initiatives, some examples being the establishment of a solar products division and new water treatment products, including equipment for softening water and fluoride removal, and the successful introduction of the revolutionary Grundfos SQ Flex water pumps powered by the sun or wind launched in Kenya in 2002.

CEO Alec Davis says the pump has become quite common in remote areas because of its flexible alternatives over how to pump water up. The solar pump gets power through conversion of sunlight to electricity using solar panels which then runs a motor and the wind pump is turned by wind turbines which power the pumping of the water. Battery and AC generator power is also available to run the pump motor for standby operations. One benefit of using renewable technology in such systems is that there are no running costs. Davis adds that with the ever increasing requirements for economic and sustainable water supplies in remote areas, renewable energy pumping systems have become a logical solution. D&S also distributes KickStart pumps.

In 2005, Grundfos, D&S's most important business partner, marked its 60th Anniversary, and as part of the celebrations, Grundfos decided to make a substantial charitable donation to Africa. Working in conjunction with UNICEF, Kenya was selected as the beneficiary and an agreement was reached to supply twenty-five SQ Flex Solar water pumping systems to schools in deprived arid areas. D&S was commissioned to implement on the ground and the first three installations were completed in December 2005. All included a tower supporting the polycrystalline solar modules and a tank to provide a complete water supply installation. Other installations were to be completed in 2006. These facilities are transforming lives at the benefiting schools (www.dayliff.com and www.grundfos.com).

Farouk Jiwa and Honey Care Africa have revitalised Kenya's national honey industry. Jiwa is a Kenyan born in 1974 and the recipient of several degrees in environmental science from Queen's University and York University in Canada. In the late 1990s, he undertook research on possibilities to revive the Kenyan honey sector and came across Honey Care International, a start-up that aimed to promote Langstroth beehives in Kenya. However, the company was not progressing. In 2000, Jiwa convinced two Kenyan businessmen to take control, acting as his financiers while he re-launched the company. Though they initially toyed with the idea of commercial large-scale production, Jiwa convinced them to work with small-scale farmers in order to create a social benefit for a population with little economic opportunity.

Central to Jiwa's success is an innovation in production technology, the integration of honey production with marketing (a departure from previous standard practice) as well as the development of a tripartite model, a synergistic partnership between the development sector, the private sector and rural communities. Honey Care successfully introduced a more advanced bee-keeping technology, the Langstroth hive. As a result, bee-keeping has become less risky, more productive, and attracted more women bee-keepers. Additionally, Honey Care has created a new honey production and marketing model. Honey Care also offers extension services to farmers either directly or through a network of local NGOs. Honey Care purchases the honey from the farmers in its network at guaranteed Fair Trade prices, manages all collection logistics and then processes the honey at its small Nairobi plant. Honey Care has captured 27 per cent of the domestic honey market within four years and established a network of 2,750 bee-keepers who, as a result, are earning between US$200 and US$250 a year, doubling their previous incomes.

For Joel Akaki, a polio victim and father of four from rural western Kenya, Honey Care provided his family with a way out of grinding poverty. He had an apiary consisting of outdated log and pot hives. Then he attended three-day training in Nairobi that demonstrated the Honey Care system. In the year after, Joel added US$200 to the family income thanks to the new techniques and the sale of his honey to Honey Care, his yield increased from 10 kilograms to 56.6 kilograms of honey. The income enabled Joel to pay school fees for his children and to buy more food for his family.

Honey Care manufactures Langstroth hives and other bee-keeping equipment. It then sells the hives to farmers. In 2004, a hive cost US$57. Since most farmers cannot afford such a big up-front capital investment, Honey Care initially charges a deposit fee of 20 per cent of the sale price, and then deducts the outstanding balance over time from the accounts payable to farmers who sell their honey to Honey Care. Honey Care's 2004 network of 2,750 farmers is located in extremely poor, subsistence-based rural communities in western Kenya and elsewhere across the country. Working with Honey Care has allowed these farmers to surpass the poverty line and provide a better life for their families. Honey Care partners with NGOs to provide micro-finance and beekeeping training. Having supplied beekeepers with beehives and trained them in the new technology, Honey Care subsequently acts as purchaser from the communities. Farmers gladly sell their honey to Honey Care since the company's purchasing price is consistently above that of its commercial competitors. Honey Care then processes and packages the honey in its Nairobi plant. Honey Care has taken the strategic decision to focus initially on the domestic market before serving export markets, with marketing slogans on t-shirts such as 'Bee Kenyan, Buy Kenyan'. As a result of this, and the emphasis on quality, Honey Care products are very popular. Honey Care supplies major retail outlets, hotels and industries in Kenya with its pure, natural and organic honey and other related bee products. In June 2004, Honey Care launched Honey Care Africa Tanzania, as a joint venture with a Tanzanian partner, based on a model similar to that as in Kenya. Plans are also underway to expand its operations to other countries in the region.

In June 2004, Farouk Jiwa, as Director of Honey Care Africa, signed an agreement with James Wolfensohn, the president of the World Bank Group, in Washington. Under the terms of this agreement, Honey Care Africa receives grant funding and considerable direct investment in the form of patient capital through the recently established Grassroots Business Initiative (GBI) within the International Finance Corporation/World Bank (www.ifc.org/gbi). In addition, Honey Care Africa also receives technical assistance through the Africa Project Development Facility of the International Finance Corporation. This support helps Honey Care Africa strengthen its current operations in Kenya through the development of an integrated MIS system, undertake a country-wide assessment of its social, economic and environmental impact at the village level, increase the number of field staff to improve service delivery to small-scale beekeepers across the country, develop and implement a comprehensive marketing strategy, as well as renovate and expand its hive manufacturing and honey processing facility in Nairobi. In addition, the funding from the GBI of the World Bank and International Finance Corporation also assists Honey Care in replicating and establishing its successful model of community-based beekeeping in other countries in the East Africa region. Jiwa says the agreement underscored the World Bank's commitment to supporting innovative business models that are making a direct contribution to poverty reduction at the grassroots level. It was also an important achievement for Honey Care Africa and would help strengthen their business in Kenya and assist them in the expansion of their operations into neighbouring countries.

(Source: www.honeycareafrica.com)

Jiwa has received a number of prestigious international awards: the Equator Initiative Prize, at the World Summit on Sustainable Development, for his contribution to poverty reduction and biodiversity conservation; the International Development Marketplace Innovation Award, from the World Bank and George Soros Open Societies Institute; and the World Business Award, for his contribution to UN Millennium Development Goals. He was also recognised at the 2005 World Economic Forum in Davos as among the World's Most Outstanding Social Entrepreneurs (www.schwabfound.org). At the 2005 Africa SMME Awards, Honeycare Africa emerged as both winner of the renewable energy and environment category and also as the recipient of the overall Africa SMME of the Year award. Jiwa is now a senior manager at CARE Enterprise Partners, a division of CARE Canada that applies innovative, market-based approaches to poverty reduction in the developing world. Jiwa remains both director and shareholder in Honey Care and is actively involved in its strategic planning and overall direction.

Much has been said and written about the great variety of curing powers of the leaves, twigs, bark and roots of the neem tree and each year more is becoming known of its role in plant and animal health. The champion of neem tree commercialisation in Kenya is Kenyan-born entrepreneur Dorian Rocco, who has almost 50 years of experience in pest control and agribusiness. Dorian began the first commercial development of neem products. He is the founder of Saroneem Biopesticides, which made the leap from marketing imported synthetic pesticides to working almost exclusively on developing local pest control products. A key hurdle was getting these products registered with the Pest Control Products Board, a process that took nearly two years of tedious testing to complete.

Saroneem carried out a survey on the availability of neem seeds and developed methods of extrusion, dehydration and formulation for various parts of the neem tree. Each year at the onset of the long rains, Kenya's naturalised neem trees produce hundreds of tons of small yellow fruits similar in size to coffee berries. Saroneem established a network of neem seed buyers up and down the Kenya coast. Storing the seed at the coast turned out to be unworkable, due to the high temperatures and humidity, which quickly spoil the seed quality. The raw seeds contain up to 40 per cent oil. Yearly, around 50 tons of clean seed are brought to the Saroneem processing facility.

Using fairly basic equipment, Saroneem has found it economical to transform large quantities of raw seed into commercially viable products, which work successfully where others have failed. In 2006, Saroneem was producing a variety of herbal pest controllers and human remedies, which were being sold in Kenya:

- Neemroc: An emulsifiable concentrate, formulated by mixing neem oil with an alcoholic extract of neem cake. Both are good insect controllers, the oil acting on sucking insects and the cake on biting ones. In addition, the oil has properties which make plants grow more vigorously. By combining the oil and extract a wide spectrum of activity can be obtained from the formulated product.
- Neemros powder: This is a combination of neem seed cake and neem seed shells, mixed and ground together. This product is mainly utilised as a fertiliser as it acts as a phytotonic to plants and is useful in the fight against soil borne pests. Neemros can also be used against worms in domestic animals.
- Neemleaf powder: This product made of ground, dried neem leaves is utilised as a vermifuge in domestic animals and is excellent for the control of Newcastle disease in poultry.
- Neem fertiliser: A combination of extracted neem cake and neem shells, this is a powerful insect and disease controller as well as stimulating plant growth by its phytotonic action. Particularly recommended in passion fruit plantations for its control of root fungi.
- Neemsar O: Specially filtered neem oil that cures all forms of infections in animals, including the poultry disease, coccidiosis.

Saroneem's two newest neem products are: Neemroc+, a combination of neem seed cake, neem leaves, and the leaves of a tree called *Warburgia Ugandensis*, specifically to control nematodes; and emulsified neem oil against white flies and powdery mildew. Plants and animals that are treated with neem emerge disease-free and healthy, especially when compared with untreated specimens. Saroneem's small garden plot of several rows of vegetables demonstrates the hidden effects of regularly spraying with neem. Cabbage, kale, tomatoes and peppers regularly sprayed with Neemroc are all thriving on exceptionally poor soil. Meanwhile, new ways of using neem for pest control are still emerging.

(Source: A Varela and D M Rocco. 'The use of neem seed extract to control pests in horticulture', paper presented to the World Neem Conference, Vancouver, 1999; and 'Plant and animal health: Neem comes into its own', by Muthoni Wanyoike, Nairobi: *The East African*, 3 June 2002)

Apart from insect control, neem has many other benefits, particularly in the para-medical field. After spending two years developing pest control products, Dorian went on to manufacture a whole series of human health products, now being sold under the company Saroneem Herbals. Treating many of the forty diseases claimed by Kiswahili speakers, Saroneem manufactures soaps, shampoos, creams and lotions as well as producing tea and pure oil. These are used in combination with other local herbs to cure asthma, malaria, diabetes, non-cancerous prostrate problems, typhoid and many other local ills.

Dorian emphasises that one of the main uses of neem in the future is in the fight against desertification and supplying adequate timber, charcoals and firewood. Contrary to most forest trees which require rich soil and adequate rainfall, conditions also sought by most farmers, thus causing continuous battles between the forest departments and the agriculturalist, neem can grow on land that nobody wants. Except for a few goats and camels, there are millions of acres where the tree would grow well.

In a forgotten spot in Kenya, 170 miles north east of Garissa, lies a small village called Dadaab. In it reside 140,000 refugees from Somalia who have been there for as long as 14 years. However, it is not the refugees that make it important but the presence of 100,000 neem trees, planted by some settlers and by refugee aid organisations. Dorian points out that, aged up to 35 years, there are signs of self growth and a slow spread of the trees (this in land which at most holds a few scruffy acacias). The fact that it would be possible to plant them in a huge belt south of the Sahara makes this one of the most important crops to be established. It will naturally take money but the results could be spectacular.

Mombassa resident G L Antoni has entrepreneurial development ideas, which would benefit Uganda, Tanzania and his country of Kenya. One concerns poverty reduction by helping rural communities to have permanent sources of water. This would be achieved by using small, efficient, environmentally friendly dredging machines with adequate digging/suction capacity. The function of these dredging machines would be to service and maintain (for the first time since their existence) the numerous village dams. Eighty per cent of the population of Kenya gets its water from the village dam. Over the years the silt from deforestation has dramatically reduced the capacity of the dams. As a result many of them dry up at the first failure of the rainy season. This has critical consequences to the rural people. The machines Antoni envisages would be capable of de-silting a ten-acre dam in about 20 days of dredging. There are dozens of small- to medium-size dams in Kenya that would benefit from this service. Thinking even bigger, with two rainy seasons in a year, Lake Victoria and many rivers in East Africa, there is no reason why East Africans cannot hold/store the water and get it out all over East Africa to cater for extreme flooding to the driest periods.

Antoni is the former managing director of Divecon International Ltd, from which he retired after about 30 years. He absolutely cannot sit about 'watching the grass grow', so he has started a small consultancy company which caters to individuals, companies and NGOs. Antoni has an impressive amount of experience working on the east coast of Africa, from Sudan to Madagascar. He has undertaken many projects in many disciplines, from farming to salvage. He has an entrepreneurial instinct, which helps him to see opportunities clearly when they arise. For example, since 2001, several companies (usually with Asian capital) have established EPZ (export promotion zones) which are manufacturing textiles. However, manufacturing is not enough. Kenya must have its own raw material input. Cotton must be planted that will be sufficient in quantity, of the required quality, and cost effective. Antoni's answer is simple, an industrial agricultural venture. If an agro/industrial outfit were to start to grow cotton seriously, Antoni believes Kenya is looking at the employment of 5,000 Kenyans.

Antoni points out that in 1964 the Netherlands government made a present to the then emergent Kenya — a fully functional agro-industrial venture of 12,500 acres on the Tana River. This venture had pumps, irrigation canals, go-downs, factories, accommodation for workers, schools for workers children, hospital and infrastructure (vehicles, tractors, dozers, weld sets). The venture was designed to grow cotton. The going concern was handed over to the government. By 1984 it had completely collapsed. Most of the infrastructure is still there. The land is not utilised (without irrigation this land cannot be cultivated). The Tana River is an inexhaustible source of water that pours uselessly into the Indian Ocean, all the time. Thus irrigation is no problem. Using GM seeds and plenty of agricultural inputs, Antoni believes a very high per hectare production can be achieved. The cotton could be ginned and sent to the textile mills. Cottonseed could be exported or rendered to oil and cake, for local cattle feed.

Joanna Schouten is the African Trading Partner Liaison for PEOPLink. She informs us that around the world, an organisation known as PEOPLink is helping bridge the gap between traditional artisans and their ultimate consumers by training and equipping them to use digital cameras and the Internet to market their crafts and showcase their rich cultural heritage. Numerous African groups are using CatGen, PEOPLink's new communications system. Three groups with web catalogues made with CatGen are Crafts of Africa in Nairobi, the Patina self-help organisation in Kisii and the Undugu Society in Nairobi.

A few years ago Crafts of Africa had a web catalogue made by a company in Kenya which helped them find some loyal customers. With the new web catalogue they have total control over themselves and hope to reach more new buyers. Crafts of Africa was founded in 1988. As a self-help grassroots orientated development organisation, its major focus is to enable the self-help income generating handicraft producer groups to meet their basic needs of food, shelter, education and healthcare.

Crafts of Africa's vision is guided by the ideals of self reliance and nurturing of the participatory development process. The organisation's motivating principles are job creation, poverty alleviation and cultural heritage promotion through crafts, whilst creating a source of income for self-help artisans. Another priority task is to seek market networks both locally and overseas. The organisation is directly involved in promoting alternative trade ideals, in that it is committed to uplifting the socio-economic situation of the impoverished grassroots communities such as squatter dwellers, urban poor, small farmers, pastoralists, and the handicapped who are striving to become self reliant through their handicrafts.

Crafts of Africa long-term objective is that these groups may build a future for themselves and that the handicrafts industry may become a meaningful economic activity through which the nation's deepest cultural heritage and traditions, customs of folk and art can be passed on from one generation to the next. Crafts of Africa is a member of fair trade organisations like the International Federation for Alternative Trade (IFAT) and Fair Trade Federation (FTF-USA) among others. In 2000, the CEO of Crafts of Africa, Peter Wahome, presented a paper 'Home based enterprises: The case of Crafts of Africa'. In November 2001, Crafts of Africa was nationally awarded the first prize of *jua kali* (informal sector) organisations offering services category. This was in recognition of Crafts of Africa's contribution to the socio-economic and cultural development of the communities among other factors. Crafts of Africa has also been honoured internationally for addressing the social problems in Kenya.

Wahome has tentative plans to come up with a one-stop shop/gallery with a collection of craft products of intrinsic value from all over the African continent. The Craft of Africa Cultural Gallery will be an integral part of the People to People Tourism-Kenya project, which Wahome is already conducting. Elvis Kombe is the coordinator of the project, which won the 2003 Kenya Bureau of Standards first Kenya Quality Award in the service category. The KQA Award is designed and developed in the same way as the coveted Deming Awards of Japan, the European Quality Award for the EU, and the USA Malcolm Bridge National Quality awards, among others. The People to People Tourism idea, and related activities, have also won Peter the Ashoka Award fellowship, the first Ashoka fellow in Kenya.

(Source: www.peopletopeopletourism.com and www.ashoka.org or www.changemakers.net)

In Kisii, Kenya, mainly young people run the Patina self-help organisation. Only about a month after they uploaded the first products to the web catalogue, they received an order through the catalogue. Patina was formed in 1998 to bridge the gap between handcraft production and marketing by the Gusii (Kisii). The demand for professionalism in commercial crafts made it necessary to form Patina. Patina uses the natural eco-friendly materials found in western Kenya to produce marketable handcrafts.

The Undugu Society, in Nairobi, has reported reactions from new customers and an actual order three months after they uploaded the first products to their web catalogue. The philosophy of this organisation is based on the principles of 'respect, involvement and helping each other'. Undugu means 'solidarity' in Kiswahili and that is exactly what it is about. The society was established in 1973 to respond to the plight of Nairobi street children. For the last 30 years the society has expanded and diversified services in response to children in difficult circumstances and the urban poor. In the last eight years, it has embarked on activities which can facilitate its own fund raising through the export of handicrafts, articles which are made by individuals and groups, who have no external markets for their products, and in many cases are exploited by middlemen and women. There are other African groups (in Kenya, Uganda and Tanzania) working on their web catalogues and they will soon be ready for the Internet.

The Wikyo Akala Project educates, trains, and employs the residents of the Korogocho slums of Nairobi to make sandals and sell them over the Internet. The project educates, trains, and employs residents of the Korogocho slums in sandal making and computing. The sandals, made primarily from recycled tyres, are then sold around the world through the project's award winning e-commerce web site, Ecosandals.com. A network of global volunteer assistants helps the project to sell and distribute its footwear, enabling an extraordinary level of profits to go to the shantytown project. Started with less than US$3000, the project now provides 33 people with a living wage. The project has been featured in the global press, including on CNN. But the project's work can best be summarised by the inspiring stories of the sandal-makers and web artisans who provide sandals and online service to a growing international customer base. Agnes Andachila uses her share of the dot-com profits to feed, clothe and educate her five children. The money 21 year-old Joel Chege has made enabled him to launch a community recycling business. The project presents some hope and dignity in a place where globalisation rarely offers any. A young Korogocho woman today can creatively design a sandal style that within weeks could be worn by customers in Tokyo, Timbuktu or Tallahassee.

Mrs Elizabeth Mary Okelo has been a leading banker in Kenya, and now operates several family concerns, including being the co-founder and executive director of Makini Schools and Makini College in Nairobi. Okelo holds a degree from Makerere University of East Africa. After being the first woman manager at Barclays Bank in Kenya, and senior adviser to the president of the African Development Bank, Okelo started Makini School with her husband in 1978. It soon grew into a respected primary school, adding grades 9-12 in 1996 in response to parental demand. The IFC provided a US$545,000 six-year loan in 1996 to complete the new secondary school and add a second K-12 campus in Nairobi, increasing enrolment by 500. The IFC advised the sponsors to make the new K-12 school co-educational rather than boys only, as originally planned. Makini has an enrolment of 2,000 (kindergarten to 12th grade) and offers quality education at affordable fees. Of the students enrolled, 10 per cent receive free education. Some of these students are orphans and disadvantaged children.

Makini has been a top performer since 1985 when it first sat the Kenya certificate of primary education examination. Makini has consistently produced excellent results in national and international examinations. In the 2000, 2001 and 2002, it has been the best school in Nairobi province and in 2000 it performed the best in the country and also made history during the Nairobi City Council prizegiving awards by winning all the trophies in the private schools category in the Kenya certificate of primary education examination. Makini was the first in Kenya to introduce computer studies at primary level and now provides guidance and support to many schools on computer studies. Makini is also a training centre for teachers countrywide on information technology. Makini adheres to good cooperative governance in which all stakeholders, especially parents, are invited to play an active role in the affairs of the school. It was the first private school in the country to introduce a parent-teachers association. Makini is now consulted on the establishment and running of PTAs by other schools. The directors and managers of the Makini group of schools in Nairobi are hailed as a guiding light in the management of private schools in the region. In less than two decades, Makini has used original management styles to grow from a simple nursery school into several primary and secondary schools of international standard.

Okelo says she came into education more out of the love of children than anything else, although her decision was also partly based on necessity. When she worked at the bank, she was very busy. Her daughter was only three, and it was becoming very difficult to manage; while she maintained a very busy professional schedule, at the same time she had to make sure that her daughter was not neglected. So she started a school in her house, partly to be able to help her daughter and other children as well. One of Okelo's friends, who had a school, lent her some of her teachers as a start. They began with 15 children, but had to move out of the house when the numbers got bigger. The school now has three locations.

The school is called *Makini*, a Swahili word that more or less translates to 'work with diligence, keenness, and integrity'. It reflects one of Okelo's philosophies, which is to encourage her students to do their very best at whatever they choose to do. They focus on setting goals, and they do Okelo proud. One of her students became the first woman pilot at Kenya Airways, and because of her example, many others are now pursuing aviation. Another had the best score in the country in the 1997 Kenya certificate of primary education, and Okelo believes he will go far. He is focused, disciplined, and self-motivated. Africa certainly has its leadership problems, but Okelo is trying to build its leaders of tomorrow by reminding her students of what US President John Kennedy said: 'Ask not what your country can do for you, but what you can do for your country'. The school instils discipline and a profound sense of responsibility in each student so they can internalise it. Okelo tells her students that they can accomplish nothing without self-discipline, because their teachers will not follow them everywhere. The school also teaches them to be self-reliant because they can no longer rely on government, which has its own problems.

The curriculum is essentially the same as the public schools' but matched with better facilities and more motivated teachers (public schools in Kenya can have classes with up to 60 students per teacher). The school encourages and involves its students in many extracurricular activities such as athletics, drama and music. But in particular it emphasises social responsibility — for example working with HIV orphans, street children, the aged, people with cerebral palsy and the disadvantaged members of the society. An example of her emphasis on social responsibility is the fact that Okelo has set up a small rural school for poor children in her home area of Nyanza province, using old Makini materials. It's just a single-building school but before it existed the children who live there had had to walk four to six kilometres each way, which is hard for five-year-olds in the hot weather and means that many of them don't go to school at all. Okelo felt obliged to do something, because she knew they needed to be in school, otherwise they would grow up to be nothing but labourers like their parents. Makini provides assistance to, and has helped, many people who want to set up private schools, especially teachers including former Makini teachers, parents and entrepreneurs. This assistance has also been provided to schools in other African countries such as Uganda, Malawi and Ghana.

Aoko Midiwo-Odembo, a prominent businesswoman, is the owner and managing director of Legacy Books, Nairobi. She is the coordinator of the Kenya Enterprise Network and a member of the executive committee of East Africa Enterprise Network. Aoko is an experienced development consultant and entrepreneur and is very active in the informal sector as a manager and consultant. Aoko holds a master's degree in public administration from Atlanta University in the US, a BA in political science and history from the University of Nairobi and a postgraduate certificate in personnel management from the Royal Institute of Personnel Administration in London.

In 1996, having until then worked in NGOs, Aoko decided to become an entrepreneur and set up Legacy Books. This is a development bookshop, perhaps the only one of its kind in Africa. Since 1999, the bookshop has been located in an upmarket area a few kilometres north of Nairobi's central business district, at the in the Yaya Centre, which is the second largest shopping mall in Kenya. The bookshop also has an outlet in another Nairobi shopping mall. Aoko established an active online catalogue at www.legacybookshop.com. This has been in operation since 2000. Since 2003, the bookshop has diversified to include a restaurant and a cybercafe in its Yaya branch.

In addition, Aoko has recently introduced Legacy Books Press, a publishing wing focusing on development and books on culture. This is a logical growth area and Aoko intends to strengthen this as necessary. She says, 'A key opportunity exists to open an additional branch of the shop and the snack restaurant in the central business district of Nairobi. This would provide better access to existing and potential customers.' The business has an established management structure with 15 employees, some who have college and university education. The products and services offered within the product mix ensure that one component supports another. For instance the snack restaurant supports the bookshop and the cybercafe, and vice versa. With the development of suitable locations, Legacy Books envisions further growth.

At the beginning, Aoko's primary objective was to stock titles on women's issues. Since 1996, the bookshop has become the premier resource centre for books on community development and areas such as environment, micro-enterprise, disaster and conflict; business and administration; and African books on history, politics, culture, women and gender, children and youth and agriculture. The bookshop stocks topical and current global issues on international development, economics and current affairs and has distribution rights for some small presses and development publishers such as the World Bank, United Nations, Commonwealth Institute, Intermediate Technology Group, Oxfam, and Save the Children. Legacy Books intends to continue to focus on market needs not currently adequately catered for in Kenya. It is Aoko's sincere belief that the potential for growth is real and this been demonstrated by the sales records since inception.

It is Aoko's hope that in a liberalised and increasingly competitive market, Legacy Books will become a leading Kenyan bookshop with a publishing firm and successful franchises in other countries of East Africa. Legacy Books will be a Kenyan corporate success story in the same league as other companies that have weathered a difficult economic and uncertain political environment since 1996. Aoko has accumulated strong knowledge of the product and market and she has full confidence in Legacy Books' ability to continue to meet the reading requirements of planners, development workers, professionals and students.

Aoko is a member of an initiative that involves eight Kenyan business persons and institutions, collaborating with the University of Georgia (Office of International Public Service and Outreach) and the East Africa-America Business Council concerning AGOA US — Africa trade and finding markets for East African entrepreneurs. The AGOA project is meant to assist small- and medium-sized Kenyan enterprises to gain access to American markets. It targets dynamic entrepreneurs who want to expand their knowledge of American markets and build links with firms that desire to trade with East Africa. Aoko is also the coordinator for the advisory board (Kenya Women Entrepreneurship Board) for International Finance Corporation's SME Solutions Centre in Nairobi and she participates in an entrepreneurship development programme at the Moore School of Business in Columbia, South Carolina, USA.

Chapter 13: Tanzania

The Sumaria Group is a large East African business house with operations in Tanzania, DRC, Nigeria, Kenya, Mozambique and the United Kingdom. This chapter talks about the Sumaria Group, Tanzania, of which Jayesh Shah is the managing director. The group was founded in Tanzania by its chairman Gulabchand Shah in the late 1950s and has grown from a small trading enterprise into a giant industry. Known for its progressive outlook and professional approach, the group commands an enviable reputation in the Tanzanian business scene. In the 'most respected company' survey carried out by PriceWaterhouseCoopers and the respected weekly *The East African* in 2003, the company was ranked eighth most respected company in East Africa.

The group is a leading player in Tanzania in plastics, pharmaceuticals, soaps and detergents, beverages, agriculture and agro-processing. Jayesh came on the scene in 1982. His progressive outlook led him to introduce concepts such as human resource development, strategic planning and information technology — concepts hitherto untried in Tanzanian enterprise.

In the early years, the Sumaria Group started with general trading. At that time, there were few manufacturing operations and most of the products were imported. Understanding the Tanzanian economy, the group decided to move into manufacturing. Plastics were the first line of manufacturing and gradually the company diversified into pharmaceuticals, beverages, detergents and agriculture. Today this diverse portfolio helps the group in neutralising the cyclic nature of business.

Sumaria is one of the largest private sector groups in Tanzania, employing over 3,000 people. The companies in the group include Sumaria Holdings Ltd (the holding company); Shelys Pharmaceuticals Ltd (manufacture of pharmaceuticals); SDL Ltd (manufacture of soaps and detergents (Foma Brand)); Simba Plastics Company Ltd (manufacture of industrial plastics); Nyanza Bottling Company Ltd (Coca-Cola bottling); Royal Dairy (milk and dairy products); S&C Ginning Ltd (cotton ginning); Sumagro Ltd (agriculture); DPI Simba Ltd (pipes and water transport products); Henley Industries, Congo (distributers and general trading); G S Holdings Limitada, Mozambique (manufacture of edible oil); Socieda Sabao de Nacala Limitada, Mozambique (manufacture of soaps); Farinal, Mozambique (manufacture of wheat flour); IPAN, Mozambique (manufacture of biscuits).

Dar es Salaam-based-Shelys Pharmaceuticals is the largest pharmaceuticals company in Tanzania. It plans to build a US$9 million plant to manufacture drugs primarily for export to the neighbouring countries in east and central Africa. The company acquired a 15-acre plot and is constructing a modern plant that meets international good manufacturing standards. Shelys' mission is to double turnover every three years by launching and branding innovative quality healthcare products, widening its distribution network and maintaining a respectable presence in the export markets. In 2004, Shelys was not manufacturing anti-retrovirals, but if government policy opens up this category for the local manufacturers, the company is ready to develop affordable anti-Aids drugs. It exports drugs to Malawi, Congo, Zambia and Mozambique and exports are expected to rise with the installation of the new plant.

In October 2003, Aureos Capital and Sumaria Group were pleased to announce that the Aureos East Africa Fund had invested US$4 million in Shelys Pharmaceuticals to finance the acquisition of Beta Healthcare Kenya Ltd. With this acquisition Shelys becomes one of the largest pharmaceutical companies in east and central Africa. Shelys is the market leader in the Tanzanian pharmaceutical industry, in over-the-counter and ethical products. 'Coldril', 'Koflyn', 'Sheladol', 'Mucolyn', 'Malafin', 'Sulphadar' and 'Malathar' are just a few of the household names manufactured by Shelys. Beta is a market leader in Kenya in analgesics and manufacturers two of the strongest over-the-counter brands in Kenya, 'Action' and 'Mara Moja'. Like Shelys, Beta also produces a range of other products including anti-malarials, throat antiseptics and general pain relievers. Commenting on the deal, Jayesh Shah said, 'Sumaria Group continues to strive for growth and excellence. The acquisition of Beta is the perfect representation of what we believe is the right course for many of Sumaria's businesses to develop to the next stage in striving to become a regional/pan-African business group.'

The group company SDL Ltd, based in Tanga, a northern Tanzanian city, is the largest detergent manufacturer in the country. It produces detergents, laundry soap and scouring powder. Its brand 'Foma' is a household name across the country. The success of Foma in Tanzania is a classic example of a local African company making products as good, if not better, than imported products. Today, Foma is the market leader in its business.

Sister company Simba Plastics is another market leader in its own field. The company is the largest plastic converter in Tanzania. It has dedicated facilities for injection moulding, blow moulding and film extrusion. In 2001, the company spun off its pipes extrusion business to form a joint venture with a leading South African pipes company, DPI Plastics. The new company, DPI Simba Ltd, is geared up to cater to Tanzania's growing mining industry and infrastructure projects.

Situated on the shores of Lake Victoria, is the Nyanza Bottling Company, a Coco-Cola bottling franchise for the Lake Zone of Tanzania with the distinction of winning the Coca-Cola gold award for four years in a row. The newest Tanzania addition in the Sumaria family is Royal Dairy Products Ltd. This company was taken over by Sumaria Holdings in 2001. The largest milk processing company in Tanzania, the company makes pasteurised milk, yogurt, ice cream, ghee and cream.

Each of these group companies operates as an independent strategic business unit. All operational decisions are taken at the company level. Only decisions affecting group policies are taken by the corporate executive committee, which consists of the executive directors of all companies. All companies are self sufficient in all aspects of management. The various strategic business units of the group function in complete synergy as self-managed and multi-disciplined teams and promote a work culture that aims at mobilising, directing and sustaining individual efforts, and encouraging the active involvement of every member. Each of these companies also has direct access to the group's management resources available in the holding company.

After achieving market leadership in most of its businesses in Tanzania, the group is now looking beyond its immediate borders. The commitment to this thrust is reflected in the mission statement of the company. The group aims to be one of the largest and most successful business groups not only in Tanzania, but also in east and central Africa, and that good progress has been made is evident from the growth in exports in the last few years. Apart from exports, some of the group companies are in the process of setting up joint ventures in other African countries. The Sumaria Group has formed a joint venture in Mozambique and invested in four consumer products companies in the northern port town of Nacala. The Shah family owns a plastic-processing unit in Nairobi, Kenya. Their major customers include Unilever Kenya and Bidco and their main product line includes thin wall plastic containers for margarine and cooking fat. They are also one of the main producers of disposable ball pens in Kenya, sold under two brand names, Speedo and Aim. In October 2002, the group formed a joint venture company, Henley Industries, to market and distribute detergents and other sundry items in Mbuji Mayi, DRC, with the Roffe group.

Over the past few years the Sumaria Group has seen spectacular growth. A large part of the credit for this success goes to Jayesh Shah who transformed a small trading company to one of the largest industrial groups in the country. Shah's business acumen is well known. Peer CEOs acknowledged Shah's stature by rating him as the ninth most respected CEO in East Africa in a 2002 survey carried out by PriceWaterhouseCoopers and the respected weekly The East African. Jayesh Shah was recognised as an eminent leader, steering Tanzanian business. He is second vice chairman in the Confederation of Tanzania Industry; a member of the CEO Roundtable; a member of Investment Committee of Aureos East Africa; and a member of the board of directors of Alliance Insurance and Standard Chartered Bank (Tanzania) Ltd. Shah says, 'Things are looking up in Tanzania. I am very upbeat about Tanzania and the opportunity of the East African Community. Our Group looks forward to playing an effective role in the growth of the region.'

(Source: www.sumariagroup.com)

Mohammed Enterprises Tanzania Ltd (METL) has businesses in trading, agriculture and the manufacturing of a wide variety of products. METL is the leading company of the METL Group, which consists of a number of independent operational companies each registered as a separate unit. Gulam Dewji formed METL as a trading business in the early 1970s. It has traditionally dealt in imports of commodities – wheat, maize, rice, sugar, edible oil and a wide range of consumer goods. METL promptly established a nationwide structure for the local procurement of cereals, cotton, cashew nuts, lentils, timber, beeswax and oilseeds at the farm gate. These goods are marketed within Tanzania and exported to neighbouring African countries and elsewhere. In early 1998, METL entered into agriculture and marked its presence in manufacturing through the processing of sisal. Since then it has gone into edible oil refining, soap-making, grain milling to the tune of 1,000 metric tons per day, beverages such as juices and drinking water, composite textile mills and plastic products.

METL is emerging as a widely diversified business conglomerate with interests in agriculture, product distribution, export/import, trading, and manufacturing and with 27 branches spread all over Tanzania. This network places it in a unique position, and gives it competitive advantage in commodities procurement and product distribution. It also has branch offices in Uganda, Rwanda, Burundi, Mozambique and London. METL employs over 3,500 people in Tanzania spread over various group companies, and is one of the largest private sector sources of employment for Tanzanians. METL is committed to being a responsible corporate citizen sensitive to the communities and environments in which it works. METL is consolidating the gains it has made in core competencies and is making forays into new areas with a conscious desire to expand, diversify and succeed. The goal will be to continue identifying ideas and challenges and converting them into opportunities and success stories.

METL is a major player in the agricultural sector in Tanzania. Sisal, an endemic tropical crop whose leaves provide the world's most important hard natural fibre used in the production of twines, ropes, sacks and carpets, is the thrust area for METL, which owns ten sisal estates with a combined total area of 30,000 hectares. Combined production was 6,500 tons of sisal fibre in 2003. METL's sisal estates provide permanent employment to 800 workers and temporary employment to about 1,500 workers. Dairy farming, beef cattle ranching and inter-cropping of many annual crops with immature sisal are diversification activities in some estates. Extension of the cashew area from the current 300 hectares to 5,000 hectares over a six-year period in two estates is in progress. Forest plantations with eucalyptus, casuarina and teak are established in two of the estates. There are plans afoot for growing cotton, sunflower seeds and cassava on a commercial scale. METL is in the process of acquiring sisal-spinning mills and more sisal estates to effectively compete with synthetic and jute products and to expand the product line to include sisal twine and carpet buffing cloth. Sisal's botanical name is 'agave sisalana' and is therefore the same agave family from which Mexican agave is used for distilling alcohol, which is marketed as tequila. Tanzanian sisal can also serve as raw stock for producing alcohol, but METL has not yet invested in that option. As of April 2003, METL had developed an integrated agriculture sector development plan, and was in discussions with international funding agencies towards structuring a financial package.

There is forward integration with a METL Group Company, the Morogoro-based Tanzania Packages Manufacturers Ltd (TPM), which manufactures sisal bags. Tanzania has the capacity to produce about 16 million sisal bags annually. TPM has managed to attain standards conforming to the specifications of such associations as the Association of Chocolate, Biscuit and Confectionery, the International Jute Organisation and the International Organisation of Cocoa, Coffee and Confectionery. The firm produces sisal sacks emulsified in vegetable oils, instead of mineral oils in line with international health requirements for packing cocoa and coffee beans, shelled nuts and cloves for both export and local markets.

METL is the leading import house of Tanzania. Its main focus is on essential items of consumption for the Tanzanian population, the sourcing and the importing of varied items from rice to tyres and tubes, from salt to shoes and from fertilisers to crockery and enamelware. METL is the largest importer of maize and rice into Tanzania. It is also actively involved in transit trade for the neighbouring countries of Uganda, Zambia, Zimbabwe, Burundi and Malawi. METL also has a well-oiled distribution machinery and actual end-user retail mechanism set up in over 27 cities and towns of Tanzania.

METL is one of the largest procurer and exporter of commodities from Tanzania and one of the largest foreign currency earners of Tanzania through its export activities. It has been a major procurer and exporter of raw unprocessed cashew nuts for two decades and is also active in other major agricultural exports of Tanzania including pigeon peas, groundnuts, cocoa, green moong, bees wax, gum arabic, coffee and castor-seeds.

For coffee, in particular, the group company Tanzania Commodities Trading Company Ltd (TCTC) focuses on its procurement and storage. TCTC holds a Tanzania Coffee Board licence as a coffee buyer and exporter, and participates in coffee auctions. TCTC has branches in Zanzibar for exporting, and in Moshi, Mbeya and Songea, important coffee growing areas in Tanzania. TCTC also acts as a focal point for imports of various commodities by METL such as rice, sugar, maize, wheat flour and cooking oil.

A network of 27 branches represents the group in all the regions of the country. Each branch is equipped with warehouses, delivery vehicles and manpower. These branches act as crucial hubs for further secondary and tertiary distribution into the remote hinterland of the country. In Dar es Salaam, where more than 10 per cent of the population lives, over 40 trucks deliver the products six days a week to a network of wholesalers and retailers, an effort which is supported by an in-house fleet of over 400 vehicles of different carrying capacities. This distribution system handles a basket of over 600 different products, some manufactured by the group companies, and some imported for trading purposes. These branches also serve as hubs for the procurement of agricultural commodities at the farm gate.

METL's successes as the leading processor and distributor of essential commodities in Tanzania have bolstered its resolve to focus even more on the manufacturing and processing sector in the coming years. Major thrust areas for the manufacturing sector have been:

- Processing and packaging high quality consumer items at affordable prices throughout Tanzania;
- refining and packaging palm oil, soya oil, sunflower oil and cotton oil;
- manufacturing popular brands of laundry, bath and beauty soaps;
- manufacturing pet bottles, jars and containers used for bottling water, juices, cooking oil, rice and wheat flour;
- bottling two brand leaders, 'Masafi' pure drinking water and 'Pride' soft drinks;
- milling, packaging and marketing of wheat and maize flour, rice, and by-products; and
- fully integrated textile and garment manufacturing units.

The encouraging progress of METL's Afritex is a challenge to other textile factories in the country to develop the textile sector and create employment for more Tanzanians. According to Mohammed Dewji, the managing director of Mohammed Enterprises, which is the major shareholder in Afritex, the Tanga-based Afritex textile mill already exports cloth to the US under the African Growth and Opportunity Act, and by 2004 the factory will be exporting ready-made clothing. METL is evaluating a wide range of opportunities in agro-processing and service industry sectors.

The stated mission of achieving a dominant presence has led METL towards:

- Clear identification of core business areas;
- aiming at entire supply-chain management by going backwards into agriculture and agro-processing industries or going forward into more and more value-added products;
- aiming at manufacturing quality products at as low a cost as possible; and
- strategic presence in services infrastructure that reduces cost and adds value to core business areas.

METL has developed a mission statement that incorporates its ethos and helps in decision making: 'The group has carefully charted its course by mapping out development plans that underpin its resolve to achieve a dominant presence in its core business areas, in an ethical and socially responsible manner, by manufacturing and supplying quality products that give value-for-money to buyers and consumers-at-large.'

(Source: www.metl.net)

AFRICA: CONTINENT OF ECONOMIC OPPORTUNITIES

Ali A Mufuruki is one of Tanzania's pre-eminent business leaders. He founded Infotech Investment Group Ltd in 1989 and since then has served as chairman and chief executive officer. Headquartered in Dar es Salaam, his company employs 60 people and is composed of four operating divisions.

Infotech Computers Ltd is one of the leading IT companies in Tanzania and has been in operation since 1989. M & M Communications is a full service advertising agency incorporated in Tanzania since 1993. W-Stores Company (Tanzania) Ltd, the first ever Tanzanian Woolworths franchise, was incorporated in 1999 and started operations in Dar es Salaam in December of the same year. It is the first formal retail business in Tanzanian history. In 2002, W-Stores expanded to neighbouring Uganda. Tellus Africa Ltd is a Norwegian-Tanzanian technology joint venture specialising in the development and distribution of tourism information systems over the internet. It was established in December 2000.

Mufuruki speaks fluent German and holds a degree in mechanical engineering from the Fachhochschule Fuer Technologie und Wirtschaft in Reutlingen, Germany. Prior to founding Infotech, he was head of the mechanical engineering design department for National Engineering Company Ltd, a state-owned engineering company in Dar es Salaam. He also worked for Daimler-Benz (now Chrysler) in Germany from 1985 to1986, as an engineer in the planning department. Mufuruki sits on the boards of several businesses and research institutions in Tanzania and has been involved in policy formulating bodies both in Tanzania and overseas.

In 2001, Mufuruki was appointed a member of TechnoServe, a non-profit organisation 'on the ground' in Tanzania and other African countries, working to build businesses to fuel rural economic growth. Mufuruki says that organisations such as TechnoServe contribute by quickening the pace of wealth creation in poor societies. They share their considerable experience and help promote well-tested international best practices, be it in farming, trading, business methods, management skills or organisational skills. Organisations such as TechnoServe become goodwill ambassadors for poor economies in the raging debate on globalisation, by urging developed countries to adopt trade policies that are fair and supportive to developing nations. Mufuruki was asked by TechnoServe to describe the challenges Africa faces, as countries there strive to bolster economies, increase living standards and become bigger players in the global economy. He states that Africa has been in a leadership crisis for many centuries. The nature of the problems keeps changing, but the crisis has been the most constant of all occurrences on the continent. Africa's leadership crisis has affected the private/business sector. Private-sector growth requires a stable political environment coupled with sensible policies and, of course, good governance. Business people can help provide leadership in the field of economics. By creating wealth, not only for themselves, but also for others, African entrepreneurs are contributing to the creation of a society that is less prone to political bribery or bullying, and thus a society in which the quality of leadership will become an important social issue. Through this process and over time, the leadership crisis facing Africa will be brought to manageable levels if not overcome altogether. Mufuruki believes the private sector will ultimately take the driving seat, but it will take time.

Mufuruki points out that Tanzania has a CEO Roundtable made up of chief executive officers of some 20 leading companies based in Tanzania. They represent interests in mining, manufacturing, agriculture, telecommunications, energy, banking, information technology and retail trading. This CEO Roundtable, which is an informal group, holds meetings with the president and ministers. Another forum for this kind of dialogue is the Tanzania National Business Council (NBC). Mufuruki says the purpose of the NBC is to create a platform for genuine and binding deliberations between the government and the private sector, civil society, labour and academia — basically all stakeholders in Tanzania. It surely is a step in the right direction.

Mufuruki's role in the NBC is rather small but perhaps very significant in some ways. In early 1996, shortly after the current president came to office, he attended a meeting at the State House. During this meeting Mufuruki read a statement he had prepared on behalf of the private sector that emphasised the importance of a genuine dialogue between the government and the private sector in their effort to build a successful, private sector-led economy in Tanzania. This started a huge discussion on whether or not there was a private sector in Tanzania worth its name, and, if there was not, what needed to be done to create one. Mufuruki stepped back from active participation in the dialogue sometime in 1998 to focus on building his business, but he continues to be involved in the background, as a member of several boards of directors and through informal groups such as the CEO Roundtable.

(Source: www.infotech.co.tz)

In November 2001, for the second year running, Reginald Mengi was voted by his peers to be the second most respected CEO in East Africa in the annual survey conducted by PriceWaterhouseCoopers and the Nation Media Group's regional newspaper, *The East African*. Speaking at the ceremony, the Nation Media Group's CEO, Wilfred Kiboro, urged governments to create an enabling environment for business. He told companies to tap their strengths to turn around their countries' economies. The chief executive also advised companies to learn to adapt in the face of economic decline and global recession. 'Our competitors are hoping that we give up the fight so that they can come in and take over everything,' he told the CEOs. Kiboro said regional governments and companies were facing challenges in the face of global recession and increasing grip on resources by transnational conglomerates. He urged governments to stick to the core business of creating an enabling environment for social, political and economic development, and praised winning CEOs for setting clear objectives, providing effective leadership in their businesses and taking risks in decision-making. In 2003, Mengi was again picked second most respected CEO in the region, making it three times in past three years.

Mengi says that Africans as a whole are not very good at identifying their role models, talking about them, writing about them and following in their footsteps. Magazines, newspapers and books are full of great people around the world, especially in America and Europe, but you hardly read about Africans who have been able to perform. Young people in Africa read about these great achievers in America and Europe, but can't relate to them. Mengi does not say that he is a role model for East Africans, but he believes that any exercise to identify role models helps create future leaders in business. Mengi points out that human beings like to be recognised. It gives hope to others that they will be recognised too, and so it motivates them to perform and go down in history as achievers. Peer recognition also sends a message to the outside world that East Africans appreciate excellence. It enhances the image of East Africa as a region.

Mengi is the founder, owner and executive chairman of the IPP Group, one of the largest private sector companies in Tanzania. The history of IPP dates back to the mid 1980s, when Mengi started a small scale, hand operated ballpoint assembly at his Dar es Salaam residence. From this humble beginning, the company has mushroomed into diversified manufacturing business and service industries, which play a major role in the social and economic development of Tanzania.

IPP is a holding company of manufacturing, bottling (Coca Cola Kwanza) and media subsidiary companies (IPP Media Group: television and radio stations and newspaper publications such as *The Guardian*). Coca Cola Kwanza is a joint venture between IPP and SABCO. His direct employees number about 2,500. Of course, there is a multiplying factor when one takes into account distributors and other indirect employees (over 32,000). Mengi believes a businessman has a social responsibility and ensures that his factory's operations don't pollute the environment. Mengi does not make huge profits from the media. The money he invested in the media was made from Tanzanians, and the media was one way of delivering a social responsibility. Mengi is extending his TV and radio network to Uganda and Kenya.

Darhotwire.com is part of Mengi's IPPMedia group, providing a platform that allows the exchange of information, ideas and knowledge necessary to coordinate Africans' thoughts into defining, pursuing, realising and acknowledging the African dream, a vision many have lost sight of at collective and even individual levels. It is a long way, but DHW is determined to pursue it step by step from Dar es Salaam to Tanzania in total, from Tanzania to East Africa and beyond.

In 2003, Mengi announced that his company planned to go into large-scale mining of, among other minerals, platinum, tanzanite, diamonds, rubies and sapphires. The company has already started investing in the mining of tanzanite at Mererani in Simanjiro district, Arushta, in partnership with JS Magezi. Mengi also announced that he was going into partnership with one Alfred Peter to mine sapphires and rubies in

Korogwe, Tanga region. It is heartening that a home-grown Tanzanian entrepreneur is ready to invest in the country's mineral wealth. It is estimated that Tanzania has over a hundred types of metals, minerals and gemstones including iron, coal, uranium, silver, nickel, gold, silver, diamonds, garnets, emeralds and mica. Mengi's venture into large-scale mining promises many benefits for the local people. His track record bears him out. Tanzanians have high expectations that his venture will pave the way for the emergence of a local entrepreneurial base in mining and manufacturing.

A chartered accountant, Mengi was previously chairman and managing partner of Coopers and Lybrand Tanzania. He is vice president of ESABO and chairman of the National Board of Accountants and Auditors-Tanzania. He is also a member of the National Environment Management Council-Tanzania; the Poverty Alleviation and Environment Protection Committee-Tanzania; CPU, Tanzania Chapter; Tanzania ICC National Committee; and a patron of LEAD Tanzania and of several Tanzanian NGOs. Also, he funds the Kilimanjaro afforestation campaign, youth employment and disabled persons' projects. He was awarded the EAEN environmental leadership award, the Environmentalist of the Century Award 2000 in Kilimanjaro Region, and national awards of the Order of the United Republic of Tanzania and the Order of the Arusha Declaration of the First Class for exemplary contribution to Tanzania.

(Source: www.ipp.co.tz and Joseph Mwamunyange and James Mwajisyala. 'Businessmen care only about profits, not the environment', *The East African*, 26 February 2001)

Steve K Mworia of Dar es Salaam is chairman and chief executive officer of the Computer Corporation of Tanzania. He is a graduate of St Francis College, Pugu, the School of Aviation in Nairobi, and the Copenhagen School of Aviation in Denmark, having earned several degrees in air traffic control. He was awarded a doctorate in humanities from Kings College, Pennsylvania in 2002 in recognition of his efforts to help the poor and needy. He serves as the chairman of the board of several businesses and charitable organisations, including three companies he founded, as well as two organisations that provide scholarships for students and care for orphans and needy children.

In 1980, Mworia founded Computer Corporation of Tanzania Ltd (CCTL), a computer dealership. At that time, there were only three computers in Tanzania, all imported by special dispensation against an order prohibiting imports because of the belief that they would destroy jobs. Mworia successfully lobbied to have the prohibition lifted. For about three years, the business grew steadily because of the increasing demand for computers and the fact that there was virtually no competition. By the mid-1980s, several companies had entered the computer dealership business and CCTL faced severe competition. Mworia realised that he had to diversify his product line in order to stay in business and grow.

In 1987, Mworia decided to delegate the running of CCTL to an employed manager, so that he could concentrate on developing new ventures. The CCTL has now branched into four subsidiaries each handling a specialised activity. Mworia has, in recent years, established or acquired significant interests in a number of medium-sized companies dealing with insurance, a hotel and banking. He acknowledges that his strategy now is to start enterprises that he does not have to manage and that give him the time to move to the next one. He is a shareholder in Akiba Commercial Bank, Royal Insurance Company, and the Kilimanjaro View Hotel.

(Source: Donath Olomi, Jan-Erik Jaensson and Per Nilsson. 'Evolution of entrepreneurial motivation: The transition from economic necessity to entrepreneurship', paper presented at 2001 Babson College-Kauffman Foundation Entrepreneurship Research Conference.)

Students from Tanzania are growing roots in Sioux City, Iowa, USA, that will pay off when they return home. Briar Cliff College has become the college of choice for more than a half dozen students from Tanzania, the first of many who may study in the American Midwest says Mworia, whose daughter Helen is a good example. In 1997, Helen graduated from Briar Cliff College with a major in business administration. Two of her brothers followed her in studying at Briar Cliff. After Briar Cliff, Helen attended the University of South Dakota and obtained her master's degree in business administration and a law degree. She has returned home to Tanzania, has become an entrepreneur, and helps people set up their own businesses.

The Siouxland-Tanzania connection was made stronger when Helen's parents visited Sioux City. They stayed with Dr Steve Meyer, an orthopaedic surgeon who has travelled to Tanzania several times on mission trips. Dr Meyer has organised Siouxland-Tanzania Educational Medical Ministries (STEMM), whose goal is to raise money for high school scholarships, to support a girls' school and to finance medical missionary efforts in Arusha, near Mount Kilimanjaro (Mworia's company, Computer Corporation of Tanzania was headquartered in Arusha). Mworia has talked to Dr Meyer about broadening STEMM's outreach to cover other East African countries. Mworia has the business connections to involve other Africans in the project. Anna J Mkapa, the first lady of Tanzania, is the honorary Patron of STEMM and Mworia has served as its board chairman from its inception. Dr Meyer says he would like STEMM to help support a school for Masai girls in Monduli, situated on an old German coffee plantation, where the students help produce coffee to finance their education. The gourmet blend of coffee, Blue Mountain, is found only in two places in the world, Jamaica and Tanzania. Meyer bought 27 kilograms and sold the coffee in Sioux City to help support the school. He also bought five crates filled with Tanzanian and Masai art work, including oil paintings, intricate wood carvings and ebony nativity sets, and has set up a corporation in Sioux City to sell the artwork, with much of the proceeds going to STEMM.

Rashid Mbuguni and Richard Nyaulawa are the founders of Business Care Services (BCS). Their mission is to contribute to the socio-economic and political development of society through harnessing individual and group enterprise with the view to achieving the highest good to the greatest number. From its inception, BCS has been pursuing its mission through provision of management advisory and business development services to government and parastatals as well as private sector institutions and individuals. These services include:

- systems development and implementation
- operations review
- business planning and growth strategies
- market research
- project designing and implementation
- public relations
- web design, networking and hosting
- capacity building and mentoring.

BCS has also successfully initiated and managed its own economic projects that provide a range of products and services to the public, including newspaper and book publishing, printing, distribution, courier services and funds management. In 1988, a business weekly, the *Business Times*, began publication.

The management of BCS is headed by Richard Nyaulawa, the managing director and also the chief executive officer of the Business Care group of companies, assisted by a general manager and a core staff of 20 employees (13 consultants and seven support staff). In addition to the core staff, BCS has collaborative arrangements with a large network of local individual and institutional consultants as well as foreign firms. BCS has its head office in Dar es Salaam, and branch offices in Tanga (north-eastern zone), Mwanza (north-western zone) and Mbeya (southern zone), which are connected by telephone and email.

(Source: www.businesscareservices.com)

Anuj Shah is the CEO of A to Z Textile Mills Ltd, the largest privately held manufacturer of bed nets in Africa. A to Z employs approximately 2,500 workers and in 2005 was producing 6 million bed nets annually for distribution in Tanzania and other African countries. A to Z is also the lowest cost manufacturer in Africa, owing to an intense focus on innovation and productivity.

New technologies for malaria prevention and treatment, combined with an increase in available funding, and A to Z Textiles, the first factory in Africa to produce long-lasting insecticidal mosquito nets, are fuelling optimism in the fight against malaria. With the planning and start-up of their plant supported by the World Health Organisation, the Sumitomo Chemical Company and the Acumen Fund, A to Z Textile Mills is producing a long-lasting bed net made of knitted polyethylene supplied by ExxonMobil Chemical and infused with an insecticide manufactured by Sumitomo Chemical Company that will maintain effectiveness for five years.

Acumen Fund provides the business assistance to A to Z to create a sustainable enterprise that serves the poor of Africa. An old man living in a mud house, was sleeping without a net and covering his body with a sheet. Mosquitoes would bite him all night. Since using a bed net he has slept well, with no more mosquito noise or biting.

Traditional polyester bed nets require fresh insecticide treatment every six months (which in practice seldom occurs), and without it they lose effectiveness. In addition to saving lives, the plant is providing employment for some 2,500 people, mostly women, who are earning better wages than they ever have and in improved working conditions.

Environmental management is increasingly difficult, so the use of Long Lasting Insecticidal (LLIN) is seen as a practical solution. A to Z's reasoning in getting involved was twofold, says Binesh Haria, one of the company's directors. In humanitarian terms, A to Z realised that a large number of people could be protected from malaria by using ITNs and, in pure economic terms, there was a demand for them.

Anuj Shah says that A to Z will export 70 per cent of the nets produced to over 25 African countries, while 30 per cent will be sold locally in Tanzania. Shah expects plant production capacity to exceed 7 million bed nets a year by 2006, compared with an initial capacity of 400,000 a year when operations began in November 2004.

In the city of Dar es Salaam, there is a trading company with the fascinating name of Foot Loose Tanzania Ltd. An enterprising couple, Ndelle and Joyce Mbwette run this company. Foot Loose is an exporter of sisal fibre, raw cotton, graphite, ferromanganese, sulphur and other ores. Ndelle is a participant in Envconsult Ltd, Dar es Salaam. Ndelle and Joyce are also interested in the export of handcrafts that they source from organised groups of women. They create jobs for these people and teach them the quality and technology transfer needed to make markets happen. The lead NGO which Foot Loose works with in Tanzania is the Mothers' Empowerment Group (MEG), a cooperative of people who make handicrafts, grow fresh flowers, and mine and cut gemstones. Foot Loose cannot deal with all NGOs so MEG does it for them, coordinating production groups, doing training, controlling quality, and monitoring production trends for all groups. Joyce Mbwette is the chairperson and managing director of the Mothers' Empowerment Group. An American import company based in Florida helped Foot Loose to secure a market for their products in the United States by taking all of Foot Loose's initial orders, promoting them on television and distributing brochures. Foot Loose exported handcrafts to the importer which wholesaled or retailed to their customers in the USA thus helping to start the whole thing rolling.

In January 2003, Great Lakes Consortium for International Training and Development (GLC) sent eight people from Ohio to provide workshops and assistance to over 500 people in Tanzania. After these workshops, GLC focused on those who had the most chance to be successful, and who would be able to help the highest number of people. They invited Joyce and five other businesspeople from Tanzania to the United States for a three-week visit to see how handcrafts are sold, retail and wholesale, in the USA (the workshops and visits were funded by the US State Department Bureau of Educational and Cultural Affairs). GLC works with businesspeople, academics and non-profit organisations locally and around the world. Tanzania is one of those countries where they have strong community ties and through their Tanzania representative, Karl Gingrich, active participation and support. Foot Loose is just one of several GLC success stories in Tanzania. GLC is now helping Foot Loose to expand their business in the US. Thanks to AGOA policy and by working with American companies, Foot Loose has thus managed to source the basic products produced by talented poor people who have for a long time been exploited. Foot Loose is receiving orders for a variety of carvings, paintings, folklore items and batik textiles. It has created employment for 1,200 women and men in both rural and urban Tanzania. For a small company like Foot Loose, this was surely no mean achievement.

In December 2003, USAID sponsored Ndelle and Joyce's visit to Washington for the third AGOA Forum. They took a lot of samples from the group, putting a tag with a good story concerning the artisan on every item for sale. They managed to start a relationship with the Smithsonian Museum stores, which are now buying Foot Loose products. 'In the United States alone, the market for handcrafted articles is US$10 billion a year,' deputy assistant secretary of commerce for Africa, the Middle East, and South Asia, Molly Williamson, told the audience of African artisans, American importers, and US and African government officials attending the third AGOA Forum. Williamson said there is a strong desire to find unique and interesting products with a story. This consumer market, large and growing, is something that opens a very special market for African products through AGOA. Throughout the United States, specialty shops and big chains are looking for all manner of products and crafts that come from, among other places, Africa.

Angelina Dimitrova Mbaga is a flower seed exporter who buys seeds from small-scale suppliers. Angelina is a Bulgarian who married her Tanzanian college-sweetheart. She has developed a flower seed business, getting local small farmers to grow the flowers, for which she provides seed stock (in order to maintain quality), and has been doing this since 2000. In the first year she shipped 20 tons of flower seeds to Holland, Belgium and France (think about how many tiny flower seeds there are in 20 tons); in 2001, she shipped 40 tons; and in 2002, she hit 60 tons. That's growth! In May 2003, the Great Lakes Consortium (GLC) brought Angelina to the US and put her in front of seed dealers and companies. She told Karl Gingrich in January 2004 that she now has her first contract from the US. It won't surprise Gingrich if he finds out she has the same growth pattern in the US as she had in Europe.

Deo Kafwa is the general manager of Handcrafts Marketing Company Ltd (MIKONO) in Dar es Salaam. MIKONO, which means 'hands', deals with handcrafted giftware, alternative use giftware and original works of art of ethnic and cultural value such as chairs, weapons, figures, wood statues, baskets and mats, pottery, decorations, paintings and various musical instruments. MIKONO primarily seeks to promote income generation, sustainability and self-reliance among artisans. MIKONO avoids buying from middlepersons, instead making sure that they buy direct from the producers, which assures better pay to the producers. Other primary goals include preservation of indigenous crafts and arts traditions as well as development and promotion of unique artistic talents. In 1997, the company hired Kafwa, who had 15 years' experience in handcraft marketing.

As general manager, Deo Kafwa made changes. Company products either positioned as cultural items or given functional values. For example, African bowls previously sold as tourist collections were now being sold as salad bowls. The management engaged in market research and participated in exhibitions such as the Ambiente Fare in Frankfurt, Germany. The company also joined the International Federation for Alternative Trade (IFAT), which gives marketing information to members, and the Fair Trade Organisation of Holland (FTO) and the FTO in Culemborg, The Netherlands. The company also obtained support from the Board of External Trade (BET) to undertake a market survey. MIKONO also has received a grant from the municipality of Bolzano, Italy. This initiative was possible through CTM. The grant worth 60,000 euros aimed at improving the producers' workshops based at MIKONO premises.

The company agreed with craftsmen to produce items on company premises for sale to the company or directly to customers. The company also made direct contacts with other producers in the regions and in Dar es Salaam production centres. Since 1997, the company has purchased handcrafts from 400 groups and since each group has 20 or more artisans, the company has been able to provide employment for 20,000 artisans in addition to the number employed permanently by the company. To speed up communication with overseas centres, the company acquired a digital camera and developed a website, which made it possible to send pictures of products to customers who reviewed them and could send feedback within less that an hour. After this feedback the company can then send samples of preferred items, thus reducing costs and saving time. The company also started a systematic training scheme for staff on product adaptation, quality and customer care.

In 2001, the company opened the IPS Twiga Gallery in the city centre where various handcrafts are displayed. At the MIKONO Chang'ombe gallery are the workshops for tie and dye and sculpture. Company export sales grew from US $10,000 in 1997 to US $100,000 in 2000, exceeded US $150,000 in 2001, and $165,000 in 2005. According to Deo Kafwa the centre has been able to train more than 200 people in various skills before going to establish their own workshops. Each student pays about Tsh 50,000 (US$ 57.50) for a period of three months. MIKONO is connected to about 20,000 artists countrywide who send their products to MIKONO to fetch market value on their behalf. MIKONO participates in a number of local and international exhibitions.

Gulf Africa Petroleum Company (GAPCO) is a multinational petroleum marketing company with operations in the East African region. Although it is incorporated in Mauritius, it was started in Tanzania and is owned by two Tanzanian Indian brothers. Founded in 1980, GAPCO was incorporated to purchase the assets of oil majors exiting the region. GAPCO acquired the operations of Esso in Uganda and Tanzania, Caltex in Tanzania and Agip in Sudan, to become a dominant petroleum distributor in the region. In 2003, GAPCO had a network of 2,000 petrol stations across Uganda, Tanzania, Zambia, Malawi, Sudan, Mauritius, Kenya, Rwanda and Burundi. The GAPCO group companies, principally owned by Yogesh and Dhiran Kotak, have a range of business activities which cover the spectrum of petroleum retail and wholesale marketing, trading, storage, distribution, bunkering and inland road haulage.

GAPCO is on the lookout for more opportunities throughout the continent. Dhiran says that he is still very confident that the group is going to be even bigger. Over the past decade, the company has clocked up a remarkable increase in revenues. Clearly, the company has come a long way from the single petrol station opened by the brothers' grandfather in 1931. Dhiran puts this success down to strong management, tight control and a thorough understanding of the market. A key advantage is the fact that GAPCO is vertically integrated and owns its own trucks and oil tankers as well as storage and retail outlets. This extensive and complete downstream infrastructure is the real strength of the company, giving it a competitive edge in all its markets.

In Tanzania, the petrol market is intensely competitive and any price advantage is critical. GAPCO is the leader, with a 42 per cent market share. Its facilities are a real strength: a 5 million-gallon petrol oil tank in Dar es Salaam is the largest in East Africa. As the Tanzania road network improves and is extended, traffic will pick up with a resulting increased demand for petrol. Such factors make Tanzania the centrepiece of the company's regional strategy. This is where the lion's share of GAPCO's revenues comes from. But it is also strong in Kenya, Uganda and Sudan and is aggressively pursuing market share in these countries.

The advantages of a strong infrastructure are integral to GAPCO's ongoing success, as the company adapts to offer new services, such as the clean fuel LPG, which is widely anticipated to become increasingly important. Taken as a whole, from a regional rather than a country basis, the market is large, as there are 130 million people in the East African region. But a company needs to have that regional, if not a continental, vision to really grow, and for GAPCO, eyeing new opportunities throughout Africa, the market is looking ever more promising. In 2004, GAPCO acquired four prized lodges in Tanzania: Lake Manyara Hotel, Ngorongoro Wildlife Lodge, Seronera Wildlife Lodge and Lobo Lodge, which has a stunning setting on a huge kopje (hill) in the northern Serengeti. There were also reports that GAPCO was negotiating to take over a Kenyan hotel group.

(Source: 'Gasoline Alley', *Washington Post* www.washingtonpost.com, 3 October 2001)

Hotel Tilapia in Mwanza was founded in 1991 by Manjit Singh Sandhu and is known for its excellent service, hospitality and cuisine. The hotel offers forty air-conditioned rooms and suites, most of which have a panoramic view of the lake. Seven of the rooms are located on its houseboat, the 'African Queen', a boat straight out of the movie that featured Humphrey Bogart and Katherine Hepburn. Hotel Tilapia has an outdoor swimming pool and an air-conditioned business centre providing guests with modern facilities. The hotel accommodates six different restaurants to add to the ambience — such as the Japanese restaurant

Tepanyaki, built on a jetty in the lake surrounded by water. Dinner is also offered on the yacht MV Rubondo at sunset on Lake Victoria. The hotel offers pre-training facilities for students of the hotel management schools. This assists the students in first hand training before they start their careers as hotel staff. In 2005, the hotel opened Mbalageti, a five-star luxury tented safari lodge located in the western corridor of the Serengeti National Park, near the Mbalageti River. It will cater to environmental tours. The hotel also runs the Kijereshi tented camp, in the Kijereshi game reserve. The reserve also acts as a buffer to conserve nature and poaching in the Serengeti National Park. The camp can cater for up to 50 persons. It has a swimming pool and a bar and restaurant where continental cuisine is served. The staff interact with communities around the game reserve to educate them about tree planting, and supplies seedlings.

Boundary Hill Lodge is one of Tanzania's newest wildlife safari experiences for visitors to Tanzania, helping to attract new visitors to the country. The 16-bed upscale lodge is located high above the savannah, perched on the edge of Tarangire National Park. Built of natural materials, predominantly local stone, wood and burnt brick, the lodge offers outstanding views over the Silale and Gosuwa swamps. In an era where words such as community and ecotourism are increasingly used in attempts to differentiate supposedly new approaches to tourism activities, Boundary Hill Lodge sets high standards in community partnership and conservation. It is owned jointly by the local Lolkisale village, where 4,000 Masai reside. Their partner is the King family, an established tour operator with long ties to the community. The lodge helped to spur the creation of a 35,000-acre wildlife conservation area, and employs the local Lolkisale villagers, thereby benefiting the local people and the environment, and providing economic development options for the local economy.

(Source: www.hoteltilapia.com and www.mbalageti.com)

Mary Kalikawe, Managing Director of Kiroyera Tours in Bukoba, says their African Safari itineraries offer visitors a directory of scenic lands: Lake Victoria (the largest fresh water lake in Africa); water activities, beaches and islands; animals, culture, traditional music, religious pilgrimage, historical monuments and leisure; and a wide variety of holiday activities. She says the romance of Bukoba begins with its geography. Unlike the gradual rise of the Italian Riviera or the abrupt rising of the hills of Corfu in Greece, Bukoba, an inland lake port town, sits like a low lying soap dish on the edge of the vast Lake Victoria basin. It is set between the water's edge and a rugged backdrop of rock cliffs that are like a massive protective shield around the African town.

Colonists, missionaries, traders, explorers, international aid organisations, friends of people of Bukoba and refugees from other parts of Africa discovered Bukoba many years ago and have been blended into the rhythm of its present society. The history of Buhaya in Kagera region lies in eight kingdoms, which lasted for about five centuries ending in the early years of the independence of Tanzania. Kings lived in elaborate palaces. The demise of these kingdoms left ruins of which some can still be seen. Now, Mary is helping Bukoba to open up its gates to tourists for a treat to an African safari of a lifetime, where they get a chance to experience Bukoba's rich history, culture and natural beauty.

Mary Kalikawe is a pioneer tour operator and the founder of Kiroyera Tours Ltd, which has eight full-time employees. It opened in 2002. Prior to that, this very lovely area of Tanzania, which is among the lowest GDP regions in the country, was definitely not on the tourist map of Tanzania. Indeed, there was hardly any promotion of Lake Victoria as a viable tourist attraction in Tanzania. By 2005, tourism was finally generating income and creating jobs, thus confirming the name 'Kiroyera' that comes from the local language meaning 'turn the dark day bright'.

During the 2004/2005 Kiroyera Tours served tourists from Holland, Germany, the UK, the USA, Switzerland, South Africa, Uganda, Canada, Denmark and Japan. The tourists visited historical and cultural tourist attractions in Bukoba, Lake Victoria, Rubondo Island National Park, Serengeti National Park, Mount Kilimanjaro, Zanzibar — and the Ugandan gorillas. The company is opening up Kagera region, on the western side of Lake Victoria, to tourism, the fastest growing industry in the world.

Kiroyera Tours markets and advertises its business operations through several means including the company website, wide distribution of brochures, attending trade fairs and conferences within and outside the country. Word of mouth by tourists is also another way of making the company known in international circles. In addition to marketing, Kiroyera Tours is gaining international recognition through local and international awards and competitions. The most recent award is the trophy won by Mary Kalikawe in Accra, Ghana (September 2005) as one of the top ten Pan African Women Inventors and Innovators (PAWII) at the PAWII awards competition.

The company's public image is good, as it is a favourite of Tanzanian media houses, and client loyalty is ranked at 95 per cent, as the number of customers has been increasing year after year. Kiroyera Tours supports several community development projects including the Bukoba Disabled Assistance Project where disabled people are trained to make drums which are then sold locally and abroad. This project generates jobs and a decent income for disabled people of Bukoba Town. Kagera Museum, the first museum in Kagera region, was established and is operated by Kiroyera Tours. Kiroyera Tours has spearheaded the development and operations of the Kagera Tourism Development Association (KATODEA).

Kiroyera Tours employees have undergone in-house training sessions as tour guides and tourist services managers, and its employees are computer literate. The company also supports its employees to go on exposure visits to Tanzania's — and neighbouring countries' — tourist attractions. In 2005, Kiroyera Tours worked on a structured staff training programme lasting at least three months in recognised institutions within Tanzania or outside the country to Swaziland, South Africa and Kenya

(Source: www.kiroyeratours.com and December 2005 correspondence with Mary Kalikawe)

International trade in organic products is growing rapidly and providing an ideal opportunity for African exporters to find premium export markets. The Export Promotion of Organic Products from Africa (EPOPA) programme was therefore created by the Swedish International Development Agency (Sida) from 1994 and established in 1997, and is a valid instrument for African exporters to improve their business, and for thousands of farmers to improve their livelihood.

Since 1995, about 70,000 African farmers have been taking part in the EPOPA programme. The income of the participating farmers has increased considerably and viable export operations have been established. From April 2002, the programme, funded by Sida, has been implemented jointly by Agro Eco (The Netherlands) and Grolink (Sweden). The contract was for a three-year period and has a budget of around 5 million Euro. In 2004, Sida made an external evaluation of the programme which showed it had made a positive impact, and as a result Sida decided to extend it up to 2008 with a budget of seven million euro.

Contrary to common belief, organic agriculture is not only relevant for an ever increasing numbers of farmers in rich countries, but also for farmers in developing countries. Many of these farmers can't afford the costs of inputs, and in some areas they practice traditional forms of agriculture that easily can be converted to organic. The EPOPA programme combines these conditions for organic farming with marketing opportunities for exports. Increased income for farmers in developing countries is a key for development, and that is a main result of EPOPA.

In EPOPA projects, exporters work with groups of smallholders to organise the production for organic certification and to improve quality as well as implement organic techniques. The projects are supported mainly with technical assistance in areas of management, setting up internal control (to facilitate organic certification), quality assurance and marketing. Certification costs are supported initially. Substantial investments in organisation and crop-finance are to be made by the exporter, assuring that only serious and committed companies participate.

In 2005 in Tanzania, EPOPA was involved with the Kagera Cooperative Union in an organic Robusta and instant coffee project, which has been extended from the previous phase of EPOPA. This project works with close to 3,500 farmers and is targeted to export 500 tons of organic certified green coffee beans and 15 tons of instant coffee annually. EPOPA works in close cooperation with Fair Trade and part of the coffee is sold as Fair Trade. An Arabica coffee project involves 4,000 farmers and is expected to export 900 tons of organic coffee. In the coastal area, 600 farmers are involved in the production of 400 tons of organic hand-shelled cashew nuts. The programme is looking into increasing the number of projects and diversifying into other crops and products, for example, sugar, honey, condiments, spices, herb teas, fresh vegetables and oil. The cocoa project in Kyela Tanzania, completed in Phase I, continues on its own and involves about 16,000 farmers under the management of Biolands International (Tanzania), which buys and exports the organic cocoa. Since September 2002, Agro Eco had established a regional office in Dar es Salaam. In 2005, the programme activities in Tanzania were managed by Marg Leijdens.

Agro Eco has set up an office, Agro Eco Uganda, from which several small and large organic projects are run. In 2005, Alastair Taylor was serving as the country manager for the EPOPA activities in Uganda. Within projects his activities include management, technical support, financial management and capacity building. Kawacom is the exporter in one of the EPOPA projects in Uganda that covers both Arabica and Robusta coffees, and works with 13,000 small holder farmers in three different areas. On another project, EPOPA works with Olivea Kayondo, co-founder of Outspan Enterprises Ltd, an exporter of organic agricultural products, who has approximately 6,000 farmers producing sesame and cotton in the Apach and Kaberamaido districts in the northern part of Uganda. In 2003, Kayondo endeavoured to have sunflowers and peas grown by the same farmers certified as organic. The results confirm that there is a virtue in private sector led (organic) export development projects that benefit the rural poor. EPOPA has shown that it is possible to organise farmers around organic farming, to set up an internal control system and to kick off export businesses that are rewarding for all parties. However, all projects have to go through cycles of good and bad times. To develop sustainable agriculture more time is needed. Solid trade relations need to be developed.

In 2004, the EPOPA programme was extended to include Zambia in addition to Uganda and Tanzania. Zambia started with a pilot lemon grass project with the company AOFI, which deals in organic essential oils and wild tree nut oils. A positive evaluation from Sida decided to make the year 2005 an interception phase with focus on the extension of the running project, research study of the South African market, and support to the local organic Association. The EPOPA programme in Zambia will start operating fully in 2006.

In 2005, EPOPA benefited a number of selected exporters. Other exporters, not benefiting directly from EPOPA, share experiences through flanking activities such as training. EPOPA has also been working with flanking activities: setting up domestic certification bodies and to provide training to a wider public, so as to provide a solid basis for the organic sectors in the respective countries. The founding of two certification bodies during 2004, UgoCert in Uganda and TanCert in Tanzania, is a pleasant development that EPOPA is part of. There is potential for more EPOPA type projects in other countries. The consultants have been asked by Sida to expand EPOPA into additional African countries, especially those where Sida has offices.

Gunnar Rundgren, chief executive officer of Grolink, has a lot of respect for Agro Eco and its hands-on approach to organic agriculture and development. Bo van Elzakker, director of Agro Eco, says Grolink makes marketing in Scandinavia easier and he appreciates their experience in institutional development. Agro Eco has been the implementer of EPOPA since 1995. Both consultancies are key actors in the organic sector; Agro Eco in Bennekom, Netherlands is the older with a turnover of euro two million euro; Grolink has its office in Höje, Sweden and has a turnover of euro 2.9 million euro.

Rundgren says that there are people who wonder how organic production will feed the world. Today, he says, people are starving through to social and economic conditions, not because of inadequate food production. He emphasises that in the short-term the solution is found in political and economical change and not in agricultural methods. However, in the long-term, he believes no agriculture will be able to feed an ever increasing population. He asks whether we want to feed 12 billion people for 50 years at the cost of massive exploitation of natural resources, loss of bio-diversity and environmental degradation ending with collapsing fertility of the soils. Or do we want to feed a somewhat smaller population for a long time in a sustainable way. Organic agriculture, as Rundgren knows it today, is the most sustainable kind of agriculture. Nevertheless, he concedes that there are still many improvements to be made in organic agriculture.

(Source: www.epopa.info)

Zanzibar

Chumbe Island Coral Park and Eco-Lodge is the brainchild of Sibylle Riedmiller, a German former aid worker who first came to Tanzania in the early 1980s to manage school agriculture and environmental education projects for a German aid agency. While sailing around Zanzibar in 1991 in search for a suitable reef for a marine park, Sibylle came across uninhabited Chumbe Island, a diminutive 24-hectare rocky island, and was captivated by it: The fringing reef to the west was still relatively intact, the pristine coral rag forest was one of the last coastal forests remaining in the region; and the island had historic ruins that gave evidence of its past significance in the trade relations of the Indian Ocean.

Sibylle decided to campaign for a marine protected area in Zanzibar to counter the serious coral reef destruction from dynamite fishing, over-fishing and careless tourism. She chose Chumbe because, when studied, it was found to be host to an incredibly bio-diverse reef system; so much so that Professor J E N Veron, a leading coral expert from the Australian Institute of Marine Science, described the Chumbe reef as '...one of the most spectacular coral gardens to be found anywhere in the world'.

'I was lucky to find Chumbe,' Riedmiller recalls, 'as the island was uninhabited and fishing in its western waters was traditionally not allowed for strategic reasons. Therefore, no local people lost their fishing grounds and livelihoods when creating the marine park. This is normally one of the biggest challenges in marine conservation and park establishment around the world.'

Sibylle embarked on the ambitious plan of building a private, not-for-profit, eco-lodge using responsible, nature-based tourism. She lobbied the government, and based on her investment proposal, in 1994 the government of Zanzibar gazetted the island as a protected area, making Chumbe Island the first, and only, private Marine Protected Area (MPA) in the world. Chumbe Island Coral Park Ltd (CHICOP) is the management company responsible for managing the MPA.

Chumbe Island was uninhabited for many decades, but had historical buildings that were either left untouched or carefully restored by CHICOP. A historic lighthouse, built by the British in 1904, is kept functioning with the AGA gas system installed in 1926. The Chumbe Park Rangers now make sure that the lights are working for the traditional dhows that have no modern means of navigation. The lighthouse also facilitates monitoring of the reserve and provides spectacular views of the Chumbe Sanctuary and Zanzibar. A protected historic mosque on the island is left untouched and still used daily by the Chumbe staff on the island. This is one of the few mosques of Indian architecture in Zanzibar, built for the Indian lighthouse keepers by their community at the turn of the 20th century.

Sibylle was the investor in the baseline research, park management and the infrastructure of the entire project. Her investment was in the form of an interest free loan, with profit being put back into the project to run the non-commercial components (the park management, various research projects, the education programmes for local schoolchildren). Therefore, once established, the project relied on its own funds for the management of the MPA (unlike nearly all conservation initiatives in Africa, which rely on unsustainable and politically entangled aid and donor assistance).

The Chumbe revenue is generated through closely managed eco-tourism. While developing the park, Sibylle was helped by some small amount of donor funding and, above all, around 50 professional volunteers, marine biologists, ornithologists and educationists who spent between a month and a year on biological baseline surveys, training the park rangers, and producing a management plan. Unlike many other eco-tourist ventures, Chumbe is genuine, as visitors to the island must, by definition of a protected area, have zero impact on the environment. Therefore on Chumbe a unique visitor centre and eco-bungalows have been developed, all built with state of the art eco-architecture and eco-technology (solar water heating, solar photovoltaic electricity, rainwater catchment systems, grey water filtration and composting toilets).

These bungalows are so revolutionary in the field of eco-design that Chumbe was chosen to represent Tanzania at the EXPO2000 in Germany, where a bungalow was re-constructed, and has been finalist twice for the Aga Khan Award of Architecture. As there are only seven eco-bungalows, numbers of guests are limited which in itself ensures that impact on the island environment is avoided.

Chumbe's chefs serve up local produce and seafood in a variety of African, Indian and Middle Eastern dishes in the former lighthouse keeper's home, which has been remodelled into a giant-clam-shaped visitor centre. The authentically traditional cuisine allows the employment of local women as cooks and has became a real success story! None of the women had ever received any training as chefs, but they routinely produce culinary delights, with meals based on seafood, local spices and sweets, and indigenous vegetables and fruits. This also creates a market for local produce over imported foods, reduces environmental pollution with packaging materials, and raises pride for the local culture.

The visitor centre also contains a classroom for visiting schoolchildren and teacher training workshops. Most students who come to Chumbe Island have never seen a coral reef. Getting the conservation message out to this generation is one of Chumbe's most important goals. The children receive free snorkelling lessons, and learn about the importance of coral reefs and coastal forests and the threats they face. In the local Islamic culture, women do not learn how to swim. Therefore, as is done in Chumbe, teaching schoolgirls how to swim and snorkel in coral reefs provides environmental education. This also serves as an eye-opener necessary for developing feelings of ownership and more political support for marine conservation. In 2003 alone, 778 schoolchildren and 111 teachers from Zanzibar and mainland Tanzania took part in the Chumbe Education Programme. In 2005, they brought young fishermen to the island to teach them good fishing practices. Most sons of fishermen go on to become fishermen themselves.

In November 2005, Sibylle Riedmiller concluded that, 'Fifteen years of successful operations prove that coral reef conservation can work on the ground and be sustained by eco-tourism. The Chumbe experience suggests that private management of marine protected areas is technically feasible and efficient even, when state enforcement is not available or ineffective. This is probably the case for reefs that are not yet over-exploited by communities depending on them for their survival. Effectively managed, a private protected area such as Chumbe can provide important biodiversity conservation as well as community benefits.'

'With an overall investment of approximately US$1million over nine years, the cost of private management is considerably lower than would have been the case with a donor-funded project through government agencies. And, most importantly, there are better prospects for sustainability, as the incentives to struggle for commercial survival are much stronger for private operations than for donor-funded projects.'

'Chumbe Island combines sustainable tourism with sustainable conservation area management. While most protected areas around the world are dependent on financial support by governments or donor agencies, the revenue generated from tourism on Chumbe Island finances the conservation and education programs run in the park.'

(Source: www.chumbeisland.com; Darryl Leniuk. 'Coral meets candlelight on Chumbe', Toronto: *The Globe and Mail*, 15 January 2005; and November 2005 e-mail correspondence with Sibylle Riedmiller)

Zanzibar, the actual name of which is Unguja Island, is a partner in the United Republic of Tanzania, located in the Indian Ocean about 35 kilometres off the coast of mainland Tanzania. Zanzibar's Bluebay Beach Resort is situated on 300 meters of the finest wide, white, sandy beach on the island. Located on the east coast in an area known as Kiwengwa, the resort is only 35 minutes' drive from the town and the airport on a recently built tarmac road. Blue Bay Beach Resort opened in December 1999 and offers a wide range of facilities in addition to the magic Indian Ocean 'spice island' itself. The resort is spread out on the most beautiful 50-acre site with its bedroom cottages located on rising ground overlooking verdant gardens, the public areas, the pool, the more than 1,000 beautiful palm trees, the sparkling white beach, and the azure sea with its coral reef offering particularly warm and safe swimming. It is this beach which delights guests — the most, pristine clean white beaches with sand as soft as cotton wool and miles on each side of the hotel to walk uninhibited, with no beach vendors disturbing the enjoyment of nature, according to eco-tourism entrepreneur Wolfgang Thome. The Bluebay is owned by an old Kenya hand, Steve Smith of Alliance Hotel fame at the Kenya coast and the Naro Moru River Lodge on Mount Kenya. His son Andrew is the managing director of the company.

(Source: www.bluebayzanzibar.com)

Yvonne Adhiambo Owuor is the executive director of the Zanzibar International Film Festival (ZIFF), an NGO established in 1997 and a unique initiative for the sustained preservation and development of the region's rich cultural heritage and the work of contemporary artists. ZIFF's mission is to promote internationally and to develop film and other relevant cultural industries as tools for social and economic growth in the region, as exemplified in Zanzibar. ZIFF aims to make Zanzibar the focal point for promoting Dhow culture through films and other media. ZIFF's main activity is the organisation of the annual Festival of the Dhow Countries, one of East Africa's largest multi-media cultural events, which takes place around the first two weeks of July, in magnificent historical venues along the waterfront of Stone Town. The festival celebrates the unique cultural heritage of the dhow countries of the African continent and the Indian Ocean region and their global diaspora. The festival promotes an extensive programme of films, music and performing arts, exhibitions, and workshops for women, children, the film industry, the music industry and literature. The festival also includes events in selected villages of the Zanzibar islands, Unguja and Pemba.

The 2003 festival featured the Sidi Goma people from Gujarat, India. Sidis are African-Indians, whose various African origins go back centuries. They arrived in India as sailors, navigators, soldiers, merchants and slaves. The Sidi Goma performances are situated within their dedication to the Sufi saint, Bava Gor. These performances infused a sacred passion into non-sacred spaces. Their presence at the ZIFF Festival of the Dhow Countries marked the public debut of the Sidis on African soil. In 2004, a Certificate of Commendation was given to *'Gardiens de la Memoire'* (Keepers of Memory) by Eric Kabera (Rwanda), for its documentation of the painful memory of a people struggling to reconstruct its identity and chart ways to live positively beyond hate, demonstrating the inexhaustible human capacity and responsibility to rise from the debris. This film also received the Silver Dhow from the ZIFF jury and the Award of the People's Choice.

Under the theme Monsoons and Migrations ZIFF's Festival 2005 builds on the strategic foundations established and outlined in the ZIFF three year plan. To this aim ZIFF, utilising the festival as an aggressive tool to intervene in the regional arts and cultures, intends, for the next three years, to:
- Focus on excellence in the capacities, structures and systems leading to the various artistic interventions, including building the internal human resources necessary to the successful growth of the regional arts industry;
- build its technical production capacity to deliver on high, standard setting, production values;
- nurture connections that would enable the sustainability of festival units;
- develop the capacity of ZIFF to deliver on the expectations for the Festival of the Dhow Countries; and
- establish production oriented skills transfer processes whose outcomes are highlighted at the Festival of the Dhow Countries.

(Source: www.ziff.or.tz)

Yvonne Adhiambo Owuor was awarded the 2003 Caine Prize for African Writing, and US$15,000 prize money, for her short story 'Weight of Whispers', published in *Kwani*, a literary magazine that has been in operation as an online publication (www.kwani.org). The prize is awarded annually for African creative writing, for a short story by an African writer, published in English (whether in Africa or elsewhere), with an indicative length of 3,000 to 15,000 words. An 'African writer' is taken to mean a writer born anywhere on the African continent whose work reflects that cultural background. There were 120 entries in 2003, of which 70 fulfilled all the criteria for entry and were submitted for judging. The three African winners of the Nobel Prize for Literature, Wole Soyinka, Nadine Gordimer and Naguib Mahfouz, are patrons of the Caine Prize.

Yvonne reveals that she has always written. It is her way of expression. She writes. It is the way she unties the knots of things she does not understand. However, Yvonne does not consider herself a writer — more of a human being who happens to write as a way of making sense of things. After high school, Yvonne went to Kenyatta University for her first degree and then later on went to the University of Reading in the UK for an MA in Television/Video for Development. She reveals that her interests in writing were richly rewarded. She thinks that Africans need to do more than they are doing to increase Africa's works of art at the global market.

Chapter 14: Uganda

Although Walusimbi Mpanga died in 1987, he is the father of modern day Ugandan entrepreneurship. Walusimbi was the first indigenous Ugandan to put up a big commercial building, Mwebaza House in Mengo, in the early 1960s. He was the mayor of Kampala from 1971 to 1982. At a time when Kampala was experiencing shortages in nearly every sector, he would finance the city projects using his own money. Walusimbi did not go beyond primary school but in spite of that he was a most successful businessman. He had the Toyota dealership; he was into big time real estate development; he built the Bunamwaya Church and many others. He sent his children to good schools in Uganda and abroad. James Mulwana and Gordon Wavamunno give glowing accounts of their good friend and mentor. The story of Africa's success in entrepreneurship is incomplete without Walusimbi Mpanga.

Walusimbi's father was also a very successful businessman, trading in cattle. In the early 1950s he built a storied house in Mutundwe, a very significant achievement at that time. Walusimbi's son and heir, Sam Walusimbi, is the owner of Walusimbi's Garage, the Toyota distributor in Uganda, and is also the owner of the Hotel Catherine on Bombo Road in Wandegeya.

James Mulwana runs several businesses, the Nice House of Plastics Ltd being his flag ship company. Mulwana spearheaded the revival of the Uganda Manufacturers Association in 1988, serving as its chairman until 2000 and as chairman of its advisory council until his voluntary retirement in 2003. Born in 1936, Mulwana was an early bloomer who, by 1960, was already involved in the import-export business, selling goods on an indent basis. At one time, he ran a mail order business, exporting wooden combs to the UK.

Life would have probably followed much the same routine had it not been for the late William Kalema, a friend who saw manufacturing as the basis for the development of emerging economies such as Uganda's. Kalema introduced Mulwana to Chloride, a British company that was at the time looking for partners in Uganda. In 1967, in a joint venture, Chloride opened a motor battery manufacturing line in Kampala, with James Mulwana as managing director. That assignment took Mulwana to various exhibitions around the world where he identified niches he could exploit back home.

Mulwana's investments have always been user-focused, given the nature of African economies. In 1970, he set up Ship Tooth Brush Factory Ltd (renamed Nice House of Plastics Ltd), a company producing household plastic ware and ball point pens, and was also the first manufacturer of toothbrushes on the African continent. The Nice product line has now diversified into tableware, packaging products like jerry cans for oil packers, crates for Coca Cola and the beer industry, and knapsack sprayers. His other operations range from the manufacture of automotive batteries and dairy products to commercial property development.

Mulwana is the managing director of Jesa Farm Dairy Ltd, which was founded in 1988 as Jesa Mixed Farm with a seed herd of 82 Friesian cows and became a dairy processing plant in 1996. It has a processing capacity of 20,000 litres of milk per day with a herd of 600 cattle and produces milk, butter, cream and yoghurt. The farm includes a milking section, an animal spraying section, a manure harvesting unit, animal feed preparation machines and a milk processing plant. Altogether his businesses employ 450 people.

His other positions of responsibility include that of chairman, Standard Chartered Bank Uganda Ltd, chairman BATU Ltd, and chairman Private Sector Foundation Uganda Ltd, a body which represents private sector interests to government and the donor community and is funded by the World Bank, and Honorary Consul of the Royal Kingdom of Thailand to Uganda. Community and volunteer activities include holding the position of senator (African Continent) of the International Senate of the SOS General Assembly and vice chairperson SOS Children's Village Uganda.

Mulwana was judged by his East Africa peers as Uganda's 'Most Respected Chief Executive Officer' for three years in a row: 2000, 2001 and 2002. In 1998, the French government awarded Mulwana the prestigious

'Chevalier in the National Order of the Merit' in honour of his continued contribution in promoting the private sector. For all his success, Mulwana remains modest about his own achievements, preferring instead to give the credit to team effort. He believes that his success is the result of the contribution of many people. Regardless of their status, interacting with them has been an enriching experience for him. 'Treat people with respect because they have their own values. Listen to them carefully because their ideas will contribute to your success,' he says of the vision that was his guiding light as he navigated his way from a simple trader to a leading industrialist.

(Source: Gertrude Kamuze. 'Mulwana: Uganda's most respected CEO', *The East African*, 13 January 2003)

William Kalema is a prominent member of the Ugandan private sector, former chairman of the Uganda Manufacturers Association and current board chairman of the Uganda Investment Authority. He is chairman of the board of the DFCU group, one of the strongest financial institutions in Uganda dating back to 1964. DFCU group was incorporated in 1964 to boost the development of the Ugandan economy by providing financial services to Ugandans in the form of long-term lending followed by leasing in 1999 and banking in 2000. The parent company is DFCU Ltd with DFCU Leasing, DFCU Bank, Rwenzori Properties and Rwenzori Courts as subsidiary companies. Forty per cent of DFCU's shares are listed on the Uganda Securities Exchange (Uganda's brokerage firms have taken the marketing of DFCU shares to Nairobi and Dar es Salaam, treating the region as one market). According to Kalema, DFCU is the most diversified financial institution in the country with a strong position in some businesses such as leasing and long-term finance and fast growth in others, such as commercial banking and mortgage finance. DFCU is also the fastest growing financial services group in Uganda. 'DFCU will seek to grow shareholder value while playing a key role in transforming the economy of Uganda and enhancing the wellbeing of society. Through our dynamic and responsive teams, we will provide innovative financial solutions and maintain the highest levels of customer service and professional integrity,' says Kalema.

(Source: www.dfcugroup.com and A Mutumba-Lulu. 'Listing of DFCU Ltd to boost trading on Uganda Bourse', Nairobi: *The East African*, 23 August 2004)

Kalema also heads UMACIS Consulting, the firm that conducted investment climate assessment surveys in Uganda for the World Bank in 1994, 1998 and 2003. The 2003 survey of firms was part of the Bank's RPED programme and indicated that finance obstacles, high tax rates, electricity provision and corruption continue to be some of the major disincentives to private sector investment and growth in Uganda. The findings contained in an investment climate assessment report compiled by UMACIS Consulting shows that 60 per cent of firms surveyed reported that the cost of finance is a major or severe constraint and 45 per cent reported the same for access to finance. When the results are disaggregated by the size of the firm, it is obvious that the cost of finance is a constraint felt across all firms of different categories. The survey was done between 2002 and 2003, and 392 firms were sampled in the manufacturing, tourism and commercial agriculture and services sectors. The survey done in central, north east, and south western Uganda was funded by the World Bank. It said that some foreign firms forfeited almost 4 per cent of their earnings to informal payments. They also report more sensitivity to certain investment constraints.

Kalema received his bachelor's and master's degrees from Cambridge University and his doctorate in chemical engineering from the California Institute of Technology. He worked in several divisions of the Du Pont Company in the USA before returning to Uganda in 1992. He is a member of the UK Commission for Africa recently established by the British government to advise on strategies to empower Africa to achieve social and economic development and meet the millennium development goals.

(Source: www.dfcugroup.com and Sylvia Juuko. 'Finance obstacles bog down investment'.)

Gordon Wavamunno is the founder and chairman of the Spear group of companies. He has built a vast business empire in a wide range of fields including transport, manufacturing, tourism, motor vehicle distribution, trade, insurance and banking, commercial farming, electronic media, entertainment and property development.

In his biography (2000), Wavamunno writes that he has a very modest academic background. Although he passed his examinations very well and was admitted to Mbarara High School, he decided not to go further, but to join his father's business. After a year, he went to work as a cashier for a chain of businesses in Mbarara and was attached to the agricultural produce buying section. After gaining enough experience, he left in 1961 to venture into produce buying. Trading in agricultural produce did not require much working capital or specialised knowledge.

After saving enough money, Wavamunno bought a car and started a taxi hire business. Later, he bought two mini buses, financed from his agricultural produce and taxi operations, and partly by hire-to-purchase arrangements. In 1969 and 1970, he procured two buses with a guarantee from the Uganda Commercial Bank. Apart from trading in agricultural produce and passenger transport service, he also started a number of other businesses in Mbarara, including a dry cleaning business and a driving school. He also supplied food and beverages to Nganwa Hostel and, for two years, he managed the accommodation, bar and restaurant facilities at the hostel. He used to organise regular dances which attracted the social elite, not only in Mbarara but throughout Ankole. Under his management, Ngwanwa Hostel became the most popular social spot in Mbarara town.

Wavamunno later decided to expand his business to Kampala. He became partners with two friends who were jointly running a company known as Uganda People's Transport and Taxi Service, joining the company with a fleet of six vehicles, which were mostly hired by government officials and departments, and tourist companies. Later, he formed his own company, Spear Touring Safaris. He then borrowed money and used it as a deposit to buy a fleet of ten vehicles; six Mercedes Benz cars and four Volkswagen mini buses. In 1975, after prolonged negotiations, he acquired an exclusive franchise from Daimler Benz to import Mercedes Benz passenger cars, trucks, buses and corresponding spare parts, and to provide after sales service in Uganda. Owing to the political turmoil of the 1970s and early 1980s, Wavamunno had to rebuild his business empire twice, almost from scratch, in 1979 and 1985, but today, his Mercedes Benz franchise is one of the most popular motor vehicle dealerships in Uganda.

Wavamunno says he owes his success to 'flexible business diversification by putting my eggs in as many baskets as possible' — he has followed a flexible and varied approach to doing business. Wavamunno still owns a fleet of tankers and trailers that transport goods to and from Mombassa. Companies in which he has stakes include GM TUMPECO, Wava Holdings, Spear House, Wanno Engineering, Batunga Quarry, Radio Simba, WBS TV, Nile Bank, United Assurance Company, Nakwero Farm and Victoria Flowers Ltd located in Entebbe near the airport.

Wavamunno also has good managers, excellent at marketing, finance, public relations and human resources. Whenever Wavamunno comes up with a business, he engages consultants to find out who is doing what in Europe and America. His managers are expected to treat workers with respect, firmness, fairness and empathy. They honour entitlements — but they do not tolerate laziness, shoddy work, rudeness to customers or dishonesty.

Wavamunno should be commended for his far-sighted investment in the increasingly popular WBS Television, while improving on Uganda's professionalism in the broadcasting industry. WBS TV, which was opened in January 1999, operates on Channel UHF 25 and provides broadcasting services to viewers within a radius of 120 kilometres from Kampala, with repeater stations extending its services to Entebbe, Masaka, Jinja, Mukono and Mityana. WBS intends to keep number one position, and dreams of growing in Uganda and beyond Uganda. The station now uses a satellite, is going digital, and has built a new home on Naguru Hill with a state-of-the-art studio to seat 500 people.

In 1995, Rene Guy Bartoli and Gordon Wavamunno started Victoria Flowers Ltd with 2.5 hectares of roses. The farm is located in Busamba at the lakeside, ten minutes on a good road from Entebbe Airport. The farm has been through many fortunes and misfortunes, among which was growing the incorrect varieties advised by international consultants. Currently, the farm is growing more suitable varieties (Inka, Birdy, Red Calypso, Escimo, Bixa, Lambada and Sunbeam). There are 250 employees.

One of the high points of the farm project is that it has resulted in the development of the surrounding areas. There have been improvements to social amenities in the area, such as recreation facilities and electricity. The project is also doing in-house training and upgrading of the local employees. In order to promote Ugandan flowers further in a competitive environment on the international market, future plans are to expand the acreage, carry out suitable flower diversification, and find a partner to be associated with. Bartoli's advice to fellow growers is to carefully study the industry before investing in the business. He urges that the Uganda Flower Exporters Association (UFEA) continues to be vigilantly managed so as to avoid division among growers, and constantly make them understand that strength and survival is through union.

(Source: Gordon Wavamunno, *The Story of an African Entrepreneur*, Kampala: Wavah Books, 2000)

There is much potential for the flower industry in Uganda because of the favourable tropical climate, water from Lake Victoria and average production costs. The flower farms pay above minimum wages but labour is still much cheaper than for flower farms in Europe.

The flower industry in Uganda was found in 1992, and recorded its first exports in 1993. The UFEA was established in 1995, currently has 19 members, and is recognised nationally and internationally. The function of the Association is to:

- Represent the interests of all the flower exporters in Uganda;
- lobby to promote flower growing and the floricultural industry in Uganda and for an improved investment climate to attract new local and foreign investment;
- seek recognition, cooperation, and support of the government of Uganda, relevant government institutions and other bodies;
- seek recognition, cooperation, and support of other exporters' associations in Africa, and other international institutions connected with the floricultural industry worldwide;
- coordinate donor funded projects for training, capacity building and development of the flower industry in Uganda and manage allocated donor funds in a transparent and professional manner;
- encourage, assist and support members of the association to succeed in their business enterprises;
- ensure that proper standards and business ethics are maintained throughout the trade;
- discourage unfair competition;
- promote friendly relations and cooperation among the members of the association;
- provide machinery for consultation and negotiation between the association and other organisations, donors, government and institutions concerned with the development of the floriculture industry in Uganda; and
- advise the government about developments in the floriculture industry both locally and internationally.

The flower industry consists of cut flowers and cuttings. Roses are the major flower exports from Uganda. There are 39 different rose varieties of which sweetheart roses are commonly grown and yield better than the tea hybrids, due to adaptability to the climate. Production from sweetheart roses ranges between 250-350 stems per square metre, while tea hybrid roses yield 110-200 stems per square metre. Cuttings include chrysanthemums, kalanchoe and poinsettia. They grow well in the Ugandan climate. Most flower farms are located in the Mpigi district near Lake Victoria and on the way to Entebbe airport, although a few are located in the Mukono and Mpigi districts. New flower farms are now opening up in the west of Uganda to grow the larger roses and to diversify into other types of flowers, taking advantage of the cooler night temperatures at the higher altitudes. The flowers are transported from farms to the airport in refrigerated trucks to maintain quality through cold-chain maintenance. By the end of 2005, there were 210 hectares under production.

Uganda flower exports have increased from a meagre 313 tonnes in 1994 to 4,000 tonnes in 2002, 5,000 tonnes in 2003, 6,300 tonnes in 2004, and in excess of 7,200 tonnes in 2005. Exporters have worked at improving the quality requirements in order to meet the international standards of flowers set by the flower council. Good flower varieties are being grown according to market trends in the auctions. Uganda is now specialising in growing sweetheart roses.

The 2006 Chairman of UFEA, Jacques Schrier, the Managing Director of Royal Van Zanten Ltd, points out that Uganda exports to Europe increased over 80 per cent in the four years from 2002 to 2005. He attributes the success to the dedication of the growers in continuing to reinvest in further expansion of their farms and to a strong growers' association (UFEA) which has given the industry strength and direction by unifying the growers and developing a sound industry development strategy based on the collective views of the grower members. Ugandan growers have invested in their own dedicated handling and storage facility, Fresh Handling Ltd, which has been successful in keeping handling costs to a minimum. Uganda's flower exports already meet western market standards and all growers are registered under the MPS/EUREPGAP standard to comply with European market requirements for traceability, minimum chemical usage, worker welfare and health and safety requirements. Further growth in production is expected in the flower industry due to increase in cultivated hectares and higher yielding varieties. The flower industry provides employment to about 6,000 people, 60 per cent of them women.

In May 2002, visiting US Secretary of the Treasury, Paul O'Neill, and rock star Paul Hewson, popularly known as Bono of U2 fame, toured the UFEA Research Trial Centre at Nsimbe Estates, where research on 62 rose varieties from different breeders is carried out. The flower research centre was set up in 1995 with financial assistance from USAID as part of Uganda's Investment in Developing Export Agriculture (IDEA) Project. Other supporters are Africa Project Development Facility (APDF), a facility of the World Bank Group's Small and Medium Enterprise Department. The breeders are Kordes, Interplant, Tantau, Schreurs, Agriom, Terra Nigra, Brill, Meilland and De Ruiters.

This research facility was useful to Uganda's flower growers. They are able to determine which roses grow better in Uganda's climate and soil, and they are also able to monitor their productivity. In addition, the varieties are sold to the auction to test their marketability especially in the quality, the head size and length and how they compare to similar varieties from other countries. The growers include Aurum Roses Ltd, Expression flowers, Belflowers, Florema, Fiduga Uganda Ltd., Jambo Roses, Magic Flowers, Mairye Estates, Mellisa Flowers, M K Flora, Pearl Flowers, Uganda Horticulture/SCOUL, Ugarose Flowers, Royal Van Zanten, Venus Flowers, Rosebud, Victoria Flowers Ltd, Wagagai Roses, Wagagai Chrysanthemums and Oasis Nurseries.

Through UFEA there are many training programmes each year whereby supervisors and managers receive training in production techniques, quality management, human resource management and the marketing of flowers. During the training, they share experiences in flower management and together they come up with solutions to the problems. The training is always crowned with visits to Kenya and Holland in order to observe how growers in those countries manage their flowers and what the market requires of the Ugandan flower exports. Close by is the 40-hectare Fiduga Uganda Ltd chrysanthemum-exporting flower farm.

The Uganda Agribusiness Development Centre produces monthly bulletins of market information, giving the auction price trend of some major rose varieties grown in Uganda: the exported volumes, market share in comparison to other suppliers and volumes of the specific flower varieties. The market trend is analysed from the available information. The floriculture industry has emerged as one of the success stories in the government's campaign to promote non-traditional exports.

Approximately 60 per cent of Uganda's flower exports go to the auction and 40 per cent to direct sales. Most of the Ugandan roses go to Bloemen Veiling Holland (BVH) auction and the rest to Aalsmeer Auction. Roses for direct sales are sent to Taasal Koos Mink, Roto Flowers or Zurel. In fact, all the Ugandan flowers go to Holland and then are distributed to countries like the USA, Norway, Sweden, United Kingdom and Germany. The chrysanthemums are sold directly to their parent companies in Holland — Fides Holland, Deliflores and Van Zanten.

In January 2006, Keith Henderson, executive director UFEA, said that UFEA is beginning to also target the Far East through the Dubai hub, and America through Miami. Most of the UFEA markets have traditionally been Europe and Holland, but they are now looking for other additional markets they need to move the flowers to where the prices are high. Sometimes, the prices are very low in Holland because the market can become over supplied at times.

Statistics indicate that flower exports have kept on growing despite lack of new investors in the industry. Volumes have increased dramatically, purely through existing investors re-investing their money on their own farms. Henderson points out that the floriculture industry is playing a major role in poverty eradication and bringing in foreign exchange revenue — US$36 million in 2005. He believes that if UFEA could get new investors coming in, they could double the volumes, and encourages the government to attract more investors to the flower industry, and to find a way of making finance accessible and affordable to investors.

Fresh Handling Limited (FHL) handles the flower exports of all the UFEA members. It organises airfreight for the exporters by chartering planes, and books cargo space for the flowers. This has been very useful in preventing bottlenecks, especially in the peak exporting periods. Dairo Air Service (DAS) is the commonly used carrier because it flies direct to Amsterdam.

Dairo Air Services (Das Air), Uganda's private international airfreight company, was founded in 1983 and is owned by two of Uganda's most successful entrepreneurs, Captain Joe Roy and his wife Daisy. Das Air operates a fleet of ten aircraft, including five DC10s, with 40 flights a month into Entebbe airport. It also has aircraft maintenance facilities in the United Kingdom, and employs 400 people. Dairo has vast entrepreneurial experience in aviation. Roy's Das Air Cargo is a very successful airfreight company flying out of the UK to Africa and the Middle East. In December 2005, the Roys' passenger airline, Dairo Air, began a twice weekly service from Entebbe to Yei, Rumbek, and Juba in the southern Sudan. For early 2006, additional routes are being planned for Johannesburg, Dubai and Bombay, which would be a boost for Uganda tourism besides firmly restoring some Ugandan ventures in aviation.

Born in the Hoima district in the Bunyoro Kingdom of western Uganda, Daisy Roy was an air stewardess and Joe Roy was a pilot for East African Airlines. When the airline went out of business the couple moved to Nigeria where Joe Roy found work as a pilot. In 1980, Daisy Roy moved to London with their four children, started trading internationally, and then rented planes to transport freight. She earned an MA at the London School of Economics before the family returned to Uganda. Besides Das Air, the Roys have interests in ranching, horticulture, and represent a Japanese vehicle company. Daisy Roy is up-to-date on technology including the internet. 'It's a very competitive world out there,' she says. In 2001, Daisy Roy was Uganda's distinguished woman entrepreneur of the year.

(Source: Margaret Snyder. *Women in African Economies: from Burning Sun to Boardroom*, Kampala: Fountain Publishers, 2000)

Joe and Daisy Roy are also key pillars in wildlife conservation. They have leased 18,000 acres of their land at the Nakasongola based Ziwa Ranch, near Masindi, half way between Kampala and Murchisons Falls National Park, to the Rhino Fund Uganda, to establish a rhino sanctuary. The lease is for an initial 30 years. They have also contributed to the establishment of the rhino enclosure at the Uganda Wildlife Education Centre in Entebbe. They were the main sponsors of the DAS 2000 challenge, where several teams rowed across Lake Victoria from Mwanza, Tanzania to Munyonyo, Kampala — with most of the proceeds going again to the Rhino Fund. Professor Wolfgang Thome, president of the Uganda Tourism Association, is the current chairman of the board of trustees of the Rhino Fund Uganda and says that without Roy and Daisy's support to this project, rhinos would probably never return to Uganda in any meaningful numbers.

(Source: www.rhinofund.org)

Wolfgang is German born and moved to East Africa in the mid 1970s to start work in Nairobi and, after moving twice back and forth to Mombassa, eventually ended up in 1992 in Kampala. He has been married to his wife Esther for over 25 years. Esther is Ugandan, an accomplished artist in her own right and a pillar of strength in their companies under the name 'The Travel Group', which deal in representations, consulting and project developments. Wolfgang's other direct interest is in cargo aviation, where he co-owns a cargo airline under the name of Great Lakes Airways (Uganda) Ltd. Throughout his career in East Africa, Wolfgang has participated in trade association work. In 2000, he was elected president of the Uganda Tourism Association, Uganda's private sector apex body for the tourism industry.

In the financial year 2001, the tourism sector climbed to the top of Uganda's foreign exchange earners list with US$163 million earned by and through tourism. By the end of 2004, tourism earnings had risen to over US$350 million and arrivals to Uganda since 2000 had also risen by over 400 per cent to more than 512,000 visitors (January-June 2005 stands at over 301,000). Wolfgang is proud to preside over the tourism industry at a time when Ugandans are managing to achieve such a substantial turnaround as a result of hard and sustained efforts and work. Wolfgang represents Uganda at the East African Community in Arusha, Tanzania, where he serves on the East African Tourism Council, and as a member of the EAC Committee on Tourism and Wildlife.

Wolfgang's educational background is an MBA, followed in 2001 by a PhD in economics. He lectures at Ugandan universities and other tourism training institutions in East Africa and beyond

In July 2005, Wolfgang was appointed by the Ugandan government as chairman of the Uganda national Hotel and Tourism Training Institute at the Crested Crane Hotel in Jinja and is now tasked, together with his colleagues on the board, to oversee the construction of new facilities (groundbreaking took place in mid-July 2005) and the integration of the Institute into the newly formed public University of Eastern Uganda. Wolfgang also serves as chairman of the Rhino Fund Uganda, which reports that the fencing of its 18,000-acre sanctuary and the holding bomas for the new rhinos were completed in February 2005. The first four rhinos were introduced in July 2005 and the official opening of the sanctuary was expected by late 2005, after the relocated rhinos had settled down in their new home. The Disney Corporation of the United States will also shortly fly two of their rhinos to the sanctuary as part of their commitment to support re-introduction of the species to Uganda.

In September 2005, Wolfgang reported that Softpower Education, an NGO with roots in the UK and associated with Nile River Explorers, a leading rafting and river activities company in Jinja, has of late recorded more support from visitors coming to Jinja for kayaking and rafting. Many of them give small donations or send funds after their return home, having seen the impact of the school support programme of Softpower, which engages in the rehabilitation of school buildings and classrooms and adds water tanks and hygiene facilities. Softpower works closely with local communities in the rural areas, who then take charge of the maintenance of such projects. Visitors also come to Jinja to support building projects by working on site for the duration of their holiday. Near Bujagali Falls a full community centre, clinic, pottery and education centre is presently under construction by Softpower.

(Source: www.softpowereducation.com)

Nile River Explorers' proprietor John Dahl came to Uganda in 1995, scouted the Nile River, and obtained a commercial licence for river rafting. The source of the Nile is one of the most spectacular white-water rafting locations in the world. Dahl has invited experienced river guides and world-class safety kayakers from around the world to lead NRE's trips. From offering an unforgettable rafting day along a 30-kilometre route filled with wild, churning rapids, to organising expeditions down the Nile into Sudan and Egypt, NRE can customise trips to satisfy the various desires of white-water rafters and kayakers. NRE also offers a safari-styled tented camp, the Nile Porch, and a 50-seat a la carte restaurant, the Black Lantern, which are situated high up on the banks of the Nile at Bujagali (eight kilometres from Jinja), offering beautiful views of the river below.

In 2006, the management of SN Brussels Airlines in Uganda concluded a strategic deal with Nile River Explorers for kayaking enthusiasts, who come to the upper Nile valley for their annual winter training, taking advantage of warm weather and warm white water, rapids and falls. SN began flying kayakers, free of charge on their network, to Entebbe, subject to space. Within weeks the offer was taken up by dozens of kayakers spending a holiday in Jinja and measuring their strength and skills against the mighty River Nile. SN connects some 58 European destinations with 14 African capitals, making it one of the most intensive networks to Africa from Europe.

(Source: www.raftafrica.com)

In the newly refurbished lobby cafe and lounge of the Kampala Sheraton, connoisseurs now have a choice of either pure Uganda Arabica or Uganda Robusta coffee, a Kampala Sheraton House Blend or a mix of one's own blending. Uganda produces some of the finest coffee grades in the world and the pure or blended choices have made an instant hit with hotel guests as well as casual visitors. Wolfgang was treated to a sampling by the hotel's director of food and beverage, Kwashie Gbedemah, in January 2006, and had the opportunity to ascertain the rich flavours of coffee now available at the hotel, including such crowd favourites as espresso (also made of choice beans) and cappuccino. Wolfgang praises the Kampala Sheraton for demonstrating that Uganda is a country richly endowed with some of the best pure coffee in the world.

The Grand Imperial Hotel in Kampala, which is owned by Karim Hirji, chairman and managing director of the Dembe Group, is a shining showcase for the liberalisation and privatisation policies that germinated in the early 1990s. It was a dilapidated state-owned eyesore until Hirji bought and renovated it in the mid-1990s. Known originally as the Imperial, the first hotel in Kampala, Grand Imperial has been restored to her previous grandeur and offers a five-star world-class luxury setting amidst the nine-acre Independence Park Gardens, in the heart of the business district of Kampala. Karim Hirji is a pioneer in the hotel industry in Uganda. His Dembe Group of Companies purchased the Hotel Equatoria in 1991, the Grand Imperial Hotel in 1994, and the Botanical Beach Hotel in 1996. These three properties were extensively refurbished and remodelled to retain the traditional colonial style but with modern comforts added.

Karim Hirji, being a shrewd businessman, realised that the success of the Dembe Group's ventures required capable managers. The Grand Imperial Hotel is run by general manager Y D Sharma. The hotel has 103 attractive rooms and suites. All feature air-conditioning, long baths, work desks, video and satellite television, and hand-made classic wooden furniture. The hotel itself has three restaurants, two bars and a colonial ballroom complementing its conference and banqueting facilities. There is a swimming pool, as well as steam and spa baths, saunas and jacuzzis. There is also a business centre and it is possible to get access to the internet from every hotel room. The Hotel Equatoria has 130 fully equipped en-suite bedrooms, all with air-conditioning. There are four restaurants, six bars, a business centre, and a banqueting suite with a capacity of 350. The Botanical Beach Hotel is a fine hotel in Entebbe with facilities of a resort and conference centre sprawling on ten acres overlooking the beautiful Lake Victoria. Ideally located near the airport, it has 122 rooms finished to the finest taste.

In 2002, Karim bought the Resort Beach Hotel in Entebbe. After an ambitious re-development plan, in May 2004, 191 rooms and suites became available on one of the finest beaches of Lake Victoria. Long a favourite spot for Kampaleans on weekends, the private beach near Entebbe runs almost a mile along the lakeshore. The resort offers meeting and sports facilities, lake excursions and fishing trips, and is within easy reach of the Uganda Wildlife Education Centre and the Botanical Gardens, two 'must visit' attractions for visitors to the Pearl of Africa.

The Dembe Imperial Group of Hotels now has some of the best hotels in Kampala and Entebbe, catering to the needs of upscale tourists and corporate travellers and enhancing the image of the country worldwide. These hotels do not operate under any international chain but are professionally managed and maintain the highest level of standards and personalisation. The group commenced construction in 2005 on another hotel between the Nile Hotel and the Sheraton Kampala Hotel.

Olive Kigongo, president of the Uganda National Chamber of Commerce, is the first woman to hold the position. She is a prominent businesswoman and the managing director and owner of an apartment complex and of the Homes Ltd furniture and accessories store in Kampala. For a luxurious alternative to a traditional hotel, the influential Kigongo business family's MOSA Court Apartments are a popular choice. The complex consists of 90 apartments of various sizes, including modern air-conditioned executive suites. The hotel services include satellite television, direct-dial telephones, fully equipped kitchens, internet access, daily maid service, airport services and a tranquil garden setting. Olive Kigongo says the biggest asset is definitely the location and quality of the apartments, which are located right in the business hub of Kampala, next to the Kampala Sheraton hotel. MOSA Court Apartments also contain a restaurant, a kidney-shaped swimming pool with poolside bar, steam bath, sauna, health centre, a gym and a beauty parlour. In addition to international business people, clients include visitors from various NGOs, expatriates and visiting diplomats.

Crater Valley Kibale Beach Resort (CVK) was started by Pelusi Ruyooka and Professor David Ruyooka in 1994 in a rural area of Kabarole District, western Uganda. CVK Resort is an ecological and community business, situated on the shores of tranquil Crater Lake Nyabikere ('lake of frogs'), facing the Mountains of the Moon (Rwenzori), whose snows are visible on a clear day. CVK is mostly famous for its clean, picturesque lake, hills and the presence of 12 species of chimps, monkeys and baboons in the nearby Kibale tropical rain forest. There are also elephants and very many interesting birds. CVK is a family-run establishment with a friendly ambience, offering the best food one will find in the area. CVK offers fine accommodation in attractively grass-thatched, ecological cottages (bandas) and newly constructed self contained rooms. The terraced campsite, covered by a soft carpet of evergreen grass, overlooks the blue and tranquil lake. The bandas are spaced out among broad-leaved evergreen trees. CVK also offers a guest house, a bar, restaurant, conference hall, bird watching, guided nature walks, fishing, canoeing, swimming, handicraft development programmes using natural dyes and material for community women and youth, and CVK tree planting activities programmes for youth and women in the neighbourhood.

CVK has enjoyed good systematic development since 1994. It started as a mere campsite and now is a full rest camp with a lodge which can accommodate about 48 people. It has a good accounting and management system and is an exemplary eco-tourism business in Uganda, having promoted self-reliant economic development in a rural area. CVK is free from loans and grants. Revenues collected are put back for more developments. CVK Resort provides many benefits to the community: free tap running water to about 600 people; ICT (telephone connection); employment; market for community products (foodstuffs, milk and milk by-products), handicrafts; and the community enjoys free development awareness courses from CVK Resort development programmes.

CVK Resort and Ruyooka have achieved the following recognitions: National Enterprises Award by the Kampala Rotary Club 1998; Woman of Year Award by Kampala Rotary Club 1998; Arch of Europe Gold Medal Award by Business Initiative Development of Europe 2000; Investor of the Year Award, Small Scale Category, first runner-up by Uganda Investment Authority 2003; and certificate and an award for excelling in environment management by the Uganda Environment Management Authority, 2004. For networking purposes, CVK Resort and Ruyooka are registered members of the Uganda Community Tourism Association; Uganda Chamber of Commerce and Industry; Uganda Women Entrepreneurs; Uganda Investment Authority, Eco-Village of Europe; and Kabarole Tourism Association. Future plans for CVK Resort include: waste management project in order to conserve the environment around the Nyabikere Lake; internet cafe and e-mail for CVK Resort and Rwetera Village; stocking fish and lake management; purchasing vehicles for rental to tourists and other visitors; and gender awareness seminars on environmental conservation and management at the grassroots.

The Madhvani Group was started by Muljibhai Madhvani in the late 1920s, but as he died suddenly of a heart attack in 1957, Jayant, his eldest son, took the reigns of the group and expanded it after attaining academic degrees (a BSc and a law degree). Jayant took charge of the group, as all his six brothers and six sisters were still very young. After Jayant inherited the business from his father as a liability company, he turned the group around and expanded it internationally to Kenya, Tanzania, Lebanon, the United Kingdom, Canada and India. Jayant was the first man in sub-Saharan Africa to secure a loan from the IFC, a member of the World Bank Group, for sugar in 1970, and he managed to secure a sugar quota to the USA for Uganda. *Time* magazine ran a feature on him in 1967. When Jayant died suddenly of a heart attack in New Delhi in 1971, the group was worth US$800million worldwide. A year later, Idi Amin put Jayant's brother Manubhai in jail in Uganda and expelled all the Asians from Uganda.

In 1980, the Ugandan citizens were invited back to reclaim their properties. The Jayant Madhvani family, the only Ugandan citizens in the family, returned to take back ownership on behalf of the whole family under the leadership of Mrs Meena Madhvani the widow of the late Jayant Madhvani, with her son Nitin, as the sugar was a joint family asset. Members of the family had gone separate ways, but now decided to cement themselves back together and re-form the Madhvani Group under the leadership of Manubhai Madhvani, the next brother after Jayant. After him was Pratap, and then Surendra, represented by his son Rickin and daughter Priya. Mayur was the youngest of Muljibhai's sons.

Since coming back in 1982, the Madhvani Group has renewed its commitment to the development of Uganda and Africa, has expanded its interests to Kenya, Zanzibar, Angola, and Kenya, and is open to investing in other areas. Family members are all working to contribute to the growth of the company and adding to Uganda's economy. Roni Madhvani worked for the success of Nile Breweries and its sale to SABMiller. Roni also manages the Muljibhai Madhvani Foundation buildings established by the late Jayant Madhvani in the 1960s to raise funds through rent for scholarships for Ugandan students. This organisation had run down during the reign of Idi Amin and was revived in the early 1980s after repossession. Roni has successfully turned it around and has issued scholarships once again to some 70 students in one year. Roni's brother Nikesh runs the tea estate, as well as the steel plant, while Rickin runs the sweet factory. Amit works with the fencing. Hrishikesa recently graduated from Manchester and is working to expand the IT sector of the group. Jayant's eldest son Nitin initiated the energy sector with AES/Bujagali. However, it was suffocated by politicians who did not grasp the urgent need for this sector. In 2006, the World Bank was again assisting to mobilise funding for the Bujagali and Karuma dam projects in Uganda. The group's Kakira Sugar Works has begun to set up an alternate energy project which uses the residue of sugar cane production (bagasse) as a cheap source of primary boiler fuel. Nimisha represents Uganda at all international forums. Natasha works to look after the sugar factory with her father's training and Mayur and Kamlesh are managing the success of the sugar factories in Uganda and Rwanda.

The Madhvani Group now comprises some 52 industrial, commercial and agricultural enterprises operating throughout East Africa, with its head office in Jinja, Uganda. Activities include the manufacture of soap, confectionary, steel, tea, sugar, edible oil, insurance, floriculture, packaging and tourism. The group produces toilet and laundry soap (some 2,200 short tons per month), safety matches, steel and metal products, glassware, crown corks, and cardboard packaging. Its consumable products include corn flour and tea. Mayur, one of five family directors, says that the group started with sugar, and after that, cotton, and slowly developed from trading to industry. Mayur is a charming young family-minded man. In the spirit of his father and brothers, he not only rejuvenated the group's sugar activities, but embraced the whole family and embarked on re-establishing all the group's industries.

To give an idea of its magnitude, the Madhvani Group contributes around eight per cent of the total tax revenue collection in Uganda. It is one of the most prominent employers in the country and takes its social role seriously. Kakira Sugar Works is part of the Madhvani Group of companies which has a turnover in excess of US$ 120 million a year and provides a livelihood directly and indirectly for over 100,000 individuals in eastern Uganda. The plant produces over 87,000 tonnes of sugar and has a workforce of over 6,500. The estate consists of some 8,700 hectares of land, and in addition to this, over 4,000 outgrower farmers supply sugar cane to the factory. After expansion, this venture will produce 132,000 short tons of sugar, saving Uganda an estimated US$80 million a year at 2005 import parity prices. Kakira Sugar Works has an extensive social infrastructure including staff housing, electrical distribution systems, roads, its own 100-bed hospital, and free education facilities (12 schools) for all employees' children.

The Madhvani Group already has a number of international alliances. Mayur says that the group is always interested in partners, especially in steel and energy. He hears a lot about possible foreign investments in

Uganda, and he would like to see more of them. He believes that Uganda is one of the more lucrative countries to invest in. Besides the enormous untapped potential in agriculture, Mayur thinks that tourism could play a very important role in the development of the country.

Roni Madhvani is the director of Marasa Holdings, a subsidiary of the Madhvani Group of companies that looks after tourism. Marasa now owns two of the most luxurious lodges in East Africa, the five-star Safari destinations of Mweya Safari Lodge located on a peninsula within the heart of the spectacular Queen Elizabeth National Park, and the Paraa Safari Lodge located high above the Nile River in Murchinson Falls National Park. The two lodges provide a circuit for tourists who usually prefer to visit several locations in Uganda. Both lodges are headed by Mani Khan, the director of operations. The group also owns the Inter-Continental Hotel in Lusaka, Zambia, and has other properties in other countries including Zanzibar, which the group is currently looking to develop into five-star tourist facilities. They are also planning a stage development of the Chobe Safari Lodge as an excellent fishing resort in the Murchison Falls National Park, which is only a five hour drive from Kampala. In 2001, Mweya Safari Lodge won the Investor of the Year Gold Award.

In 2005, Nimisha Madhvani, daughter of Jayant Madhvani, and Mayur's niece, was the first secretary of Investment and Trade at the Uganda Embassy in Washington. Nimisha places special emphasis on encouraging foreign investment in Uganda in the agricultural industries, including sugar, ethanol, beef, edible oils, vanilla, silk, asparagus, strawberries, tea and cotton. She also recommends investments in soft drinks, soap, container glass and plastic manufacturing, power projects, tourism and textiles. With her colleagues, Nimisha also tries to implement Uganda economic policy by attracting investors to set up export orientated industries for processed goods to benefit under AGOA in the USA, which allows duty free/quota free exports to the USA from eligible AGOA countries (of which Uganda is one) to some 6,000 products, along with continuing to work with US agencies, the US Administration, the Chambers of Commerce and international organisations.

When Ugandan President Yoweri Museveni recruited Nimisha into the Ugandan Foreign Service, he envisioned the appointment of an Asian Ugandan woman as a step forward in setting the stage for a new global Uganda. Museveni's vision and Madhvani family support has given Nimisha strength in her efforts. She would like her experience to benefit other Asian women so that they do not have to be worried about dependency. She is a role model to encourage women in her family, along with other Asian women, that you can achieve and contribute in different ways to your family and not just depend on the men, especially in a big family. The credit for this goes to President Museveni, who had the vision to appoint her. In 2006, Nimisha is scheduled to be based in New Delhi, in Uganda's high commission to India.

In 1942, Narsi Bhai Thakrar left India and went to Africa to work as a labourer. By 1972 he was an established trader in salt and steel until Idi Amin, the despotic leader of Uganda, threw him out together with many other foreigners. Thakrar did not return to India. Instead, he went to England and re-established himself, this time in rice trading. The Thakrar family has developed businesses in the rice industry in 40 countries and is based in the United Kingdom and in India. Vipul Thakrar (Narsi Bhai's son) now manages the family's business.

In 1997, the Thakrar family was back in Uganda involved in the privatisation, rehabilitation and development of the Kibimba Rice Scheme, which had been established in 1973. About 550 hectares were developed for cultivation of rice paddies, but the scheme languished because of lack of investment, poor management and weak technical expertise. The Thakrar family bought the land and existing facilities from the government of Uganda in March 1997.

The project was situated about 90 kilometres northeast of Jinja near the Kenyan border (between Jinja and Tororo). The Kibimba estate incorporated an irrigation system and the key structures included a mill, storage areas workshops, housing and a school. 'On 6 March 1997, we formally took over,' says the enthusiastic manager Venugopal Pookat, 'and we have never looked back. Our production is expanding year by year and we aim to get 15 per cent of the market in Uganda and 5 per cent of Kenya's much bigger market. Do you know that Kenya imports 220,000 tons of rice a year?'

Since privatisation, Tilda has entirely refurbished and replanted 3500 hectares of the old scheme. A new rice processing plant has been built and Tilda employs more than 1,000 workers compared with the 120 who were trying to cope at the time of privatisation. 'We have a further 2000 hectares we could use, though not all of it is suitable for development. Most of our rice (about 95 per cent) is irrigated, but we are encouraging outgrowers to grow upland rice and sell it to us for milling, processing and branding,' says Venugopal.

'We have adopted a policy of continuous cropping, planting every week and fertilising after each crop to replace essential nutrients. We are already getting yields of about four tons per hectare', says Venugopal. To achieve these high yields Tilda has set up a modern laboratory, continually testing the soil and levels of fertilisation to ensure continuous cropping without upsetting the ecological balance. The whole project is run on modern scientific principles. Tilda already offers consultancy to other agricultural projects and programmes and does soil and tissue testing and land development surveys. Venugopal hopes eventually to get up to 30 per cent of the market share by increasing yields and relying on a growing number of successful outgrowers. 'We can expand our production quite considerably, despite high fertiliser costs,' he says.

Tilda will soon have three basic types of rice. Already on the market are the long grain Tilda Kibimba rice and a classic aromatic (usually known as Basmati rice). The company is now developing another brand of broken rice for the economy market, which will be called Tilda halves. It also grows a little maize and sorghum, which is currently used by the Nile brewery to make its Eagle brand beer. 'Uganda's future is in agriculture, and we are determined to play our full share. Nothing is more important than rice for this country,' says Venugopal. Tilda Kibimba rice is now advertised as the 'finest everyday rice for all the family, grown and fresh milled in Uganda'.

(Source: www.tilda.com; and 'A nice dish of rice', in Bhupendra Taylor (Ed), *2004 Investor's Guide to Uganda*, Imprint International)

The Alam Group ranks among Uganda's major industrial, construction, trading and financial corporations. The multiple business activities are arranged into specialised business houses. The diversified field of the Alam Group of companies ranges from aluminium, steel, glass, and uniports (round metal huts) (Casements Africa Ltd); hot- rolled high tensile reinforcement steel (Steel Rolling Mills Ltd); wire products and security systems (Roofclad Ltd); industrial and medical gases (Oxygas Ltd); construction (Alam Constructions Ltd); tourism (Inns of Uganda Ltd); business accommodation (Alam Properties Ltd); timber industry (Ama Ply Ltd); wooden prefabricated buildings and furniture (Ekono Homes Ltd); domestic and farm hand tools (Crocodile Tool Company Ltd); and agricultural implements tools (SAIMMCO Ltd).

The Alam Group has focused primarily on the manufacturing sector and has made major inroads into industrial production in Uganda. Today, they can be proud to have 1,200 Ugandans employed in their various organisations.

The Alam Group of companies was first founded in the building and construction fields by the present chairman of the Alam Group, Manzur Alam. In 1965, the first company, Uganda Steel Window Ltd, was established with an aim of manufacturing metal doors, windows, louvres, shop fronts, slotted angles, hacksaw blades, wire ropes, welding rods, fencing, steel trunks, BRC, all kinds of furniture and steel pipes. In 1967, Uganda Steel Window Company Ltd became Casements Africa Ltd, the flagship company of the Alam Group and the largest fabricator of steel and aluminium building products in Uganda.

Casements Africa fabricates aluminium and steel windows and doors and makes glass furniture with beautiful sand blasted artistic designs (all made in-house). The company will soon be making windscreens for vehicles. It also fabricates uniports for both residential and security purposes, and makes quality steel furniture complemented by Ekono Homes and Ama plywood materials. Branches in all regions supply their products through outlets in Arua, Kabale, Mbarara, Jinja and Kampala.

Steel Rolling Mills Ltd (SRM) manufactures round, square, deformed and twisted steel bars, T and Z window and door sections from high tensile rolled steel. SRM has the largest furnace in East Africa, with other small furnaces in operation. Roofclad Ltd, manufactures security and wire products such as barbed wire, chain link, gabion boxes, nails, roofing sheets, meshs, BRC wire mesh and farm fences. Oxygas Ltd manufactures industrial and medical gases like acetelyn, nitrogen, industrial oxygen, argon, medical oxygen, an exclusive agent for ESAB (Sweden) for all their welding machinery and accessories, and imports ammonia.

Saimmco Limited (Soroti Agricultural Implements Machinery Manufacturing Company) was acquired in 1999 together with Crocodile Tool Company (Uganda) Ltd (formerly Chillington Tool Company), manufacturing garden tools. Saimmco manufactures agricultural implements, most of which are oxen driven, such as the sungura plough, carts, dam scoops, harrowers and other machinery like the potato slicers, oil pressers and brick moulders. The company intends to start exporting regionally. Its products have already been successfully sold in Sudan, Rwanda and Burundi.

Abid Alam is the managing director of the group and the 2004 chairman of the Uganda Manufacturers Association (UMA). He says organisations in Uganda require skilled, energetic, progressive managers, who can work beyond normal working hours and have new ideas to help firms compete in a stiff market. Other Alam Group directors are Shahid Alam, managing director of Casements Africa Ltd, Khalid Alam and Zahid Alam, managing director of Ekono Homes Ltd and Inns of Uganda Ltd, pioneers in the safari industry in Uganda, operating two luxury lodges in Uganda.

(Source: www.alam-group.com)

Zahid Alam is a businessman and entrepreneur. In 1993, he travelled north from Kampala, to camp out in the wilderness. He approached from the south, driving through bush in an uninhabited area until he saw the River Nile and stopped at a spot about 12 miles downriver from Murchison Falls, an explosion of water where the Nile bursts through a 130-foot ravine on its long journey to the Mediterranean. Today, you can see why he did. Zahid acquired the rights to build a small resort on the banks of the Nile in the heart of the jungle. Rather than build something large that dominated the landscape, he decided to respect the environment, and aimed to integrate the design of the resort with the environment. The Nile Safari Camp, which Zahid established in 1994, is situated on the River Nile in Murchison Falls National Park. Its location has been described as one of the ten most beautiful sites in Africa. The lodge has a close-to-nature atmosphere with spectacular views of the river and the park beyond. The view of the river from the swimming pool is especially lovely.

Zahid's idea in building Nile Safari Camp was to provide a low-key, yet supremely comfortable place to enjoy the beauty of Uganda. Zahid also wants the camp to do something for the local people, who have a hard time finding jobs in the isolated and neglected region. Of the 30 permanent staff at the camp, 20 are from the surrounding area. They are being trained to advance in the company, which also has built a school in the neighbouring village and paid for a headmaster and a teacher. Scholarships are being established to allow two students a year to study at the university level, and a clinic is planned.

The success of Zahid's Nile Safari Camp venture has led to other successful eco-tourist projects in Uganda. Zahid's Jacana Safari Lodge in Queen Elizabeth National Park is the Inns of Uganda's newest and most exciting addition. Elevated amongst the trees, Jacana is surrounded by views of lakes, mountains and forest. Set on the edge of a crater lake, this tree house lodge grew out of the forest, at one with nature. The delicate use of local rock, gum poles, wood, rope, organic furniture, and rich textures blends with forest smells, a crackling fire conjuring a magical atmosphere to remember. Much effort and imagination went into the creation of Jacana Safari Lodge, which comes as no surprise when you consider its prime locality and the visionary mind of the man behind its creation. Queen Elizabeth National Park, Uganda's prime wildlife sanctuary, is rich with bird-life, boasting one of the highest numbers of endemic species in the world, and the delicate style and comfort of Jacana offers very eco-friendly accommodation for visitors to the park.

Following the signing of a concession agreement between Inns of Uganda and the National Forest Authority, work has now commenced in Mabira Forest to build an eco-tourism lodge in the deep of the forest. A canopy walk will be one of the key features and attractions of the new lodge, which was expected to open in late 2005 with initially eight cottages. Further expansion into other areas of tourist value is being assessed.

Uganda will soon be getting floating hotels on Lake Victoria, according to an agreement signed in July 2004 between the Uganda Investment Authority, the Ministry of Agriculture, Animal Industry and Fisheries officials, and the management of the African Development Incorporation (ADI) based in Cairo. ADI's chairman, Moustafa El Gendy (the financier who brought tourism to Egypt's Lake Nasser), runs a 120-room floating hotel on Lake Nasser in Egypt and he launched ADI in 2003, with an eye to doing the same on Lake Victoria. In Uganda, El Gendy has established a boat construction company at his shipyard in Jinja, west of Kampala, where the Nile begins its long journey northward. Cruises on the river, with its verdant islands and nature reserves, are but one aspect of El-Gendy's plan, which also includes upgrading the quality of local fishing vessels (responsible for a US$100 million annual haul of Nile tilapia and perch) and barges. El Gendy offers training sessions in Egypt for Ugandans, and Egyptian experts also come to Jinja to train Ugandans. He is already marketing his Nile project, code-named Nile A-Z. El-Gendy's hope is to create the beginnings of a lake- and road-supported trade corridor that will eventually connect all of eastern Africa. Given Egypt's position at the terminus of the Nile, its growing population and its dearth of arable land, it could benefit by a more active presence in the fertile lake region, but, in the words of El-Gendy, 'paradise isn't for everyone'.

President Yoweri Museveni has been a progressive leader, whose economic reforms have led to steady economic growth in Uganda, a remarkable performance that has made Uganda one of the fastest growing African countries. In May 2002, Museveni led a 50-person trade mission to the United States. The group was seeking US partnerships and investments, rated by the Ugandan president as the formula for Africa's integration into the 21st century global system. Museveni called on Ugandan entrepreneurs to invest their profits innovatively and create more skills, because Uganda is faced with heavy competition all over the world.

While launching the Enterprise Group Uganda in March 2002, chairman of the group Patrick Bitature said that the primary objective was to advance business and professional interests through advocacy, networking and project investment, as well as supporting other up and coming young entrepreneurs and professionals. With strong institutional capacity, Bitature hopes the group will have the ability to link up with other institutions in order to exploit synergies in pursuing its goals. The group consists of individuals with diverse business and professional interests ranging from the law, entertainment, public relations, information technology and business. As young people in business, they are the future of Uganda.

Patrick Bitature is the managing director of Simba Telecom, the biggest managed mobile phone dealer in East Africa, with over a hundred retail outlets dealing mainly in the distribution of airtime cards, service fee cards, starter packs, mobile phones and accessories. Simba Telecom is the main dealer for MTN in Uganda, Safaricom in Kenya and Vodacom in Tanzania. Bitature attributes the success of his company to hard work and sticking to the business code. As a college student, Bitature was forced to abandon his studies at Makerere University for political reasons; he then fled to the United Kingdom. When he returned to Uganda after the fall of Milton Obote in 1985, he started a business on Kampala's Luwum Street, which he soon abandoned in favour of starting a nightclub. He started importing vehicles from Dubai and Japan, but gave this up before he realised that importing reconditioned vehicles would become big business. When Uganda liberalised foreign exchange operations, he opened a foreign exchange bureau, Simba Forex, which he still operates. When he married in 1991, he left the nightclub business to open Simba Tours and Travel, and also went into the property business.

When MTN was given the second national operators' licence in 1998, Bitature was already working with Celtel. Under the deal with Celtel, he was being paid US$100 per connection. MTN then offered him a better deal. When he was approached by MTN he took a big gamble, selling all his property to raise funds to open up shops to sell MTN products. The gamble paid off. A new market soon opened up in Tanzania, and Simba Telecom became an agent of Vodacom, one of the mobile telephone operators in the country. The opening up of the market in Kenya provided another opportunity to become an agent of Safaricom. In each country, Bitature deals with one network and, in the three countries together, employs almost 500 people. Simba Telecom is also in Nigeria. Bitature's business empire ranges from agriculture on a small-scale, through commercial micro-finance, to foreign exchange operations through Simba Telecom, Simba Tours, Simba Property and Simba Distribution. He is also a director of Radio West.

AFRICA: CONTINENT OF ECONOMIC OPPORTUNITIES

For several weeks before the 28 October 1998 switching-on of its network in Uganda, MTN Uganda ran a series of intriguing advertisements. An ad that showed a forlorn row of wooden poles along a highway, without telephone cables, read 'We are going to disconnect the whole of Uganda'. Five years and 450,000 subscribers later, the company has largely succeeded in disconnecting Uganda from an archaic telephone system. In the words of Charles Mbiire, the only Ugandan shareholder in the South Africa-based multinational, the market has been kind but customers have also remained loyal because the company offers a quality product. 'We had an obligation to roll out 89,000 telephone lines over a five-year period. We are talking about nearly half a million subscribers today. We are rolling out our fibre-optic network on schedule and we have maintained our position as Uganda's number one brand in every sense of the word,' he said.

It seems that MTN Uganda has maintained its lead partly by mirroring the enigmatic personality of its Ugandan shareholder. Trained as an economist at the University of Essex, in the UK, Mbiire keeps an extremely low profile. 'Business is like warfare, and the more your enemy knows about you the easier it is for him to disorganise you. So I prefer to keep my armaments in the armoury and bring out a few pieces during anniversary parades — that is how I operate,' he says.

Focused on the long-term, MTN Uganda has stuck to its business plan and is the only operator still charging subscribers a monthly service fee, which has not stopped the company's growth. 'We have MTN International, which has a very good understanding of the African telecommunications landscape and then we have Telia Overseas AB, which is one of the biggest telecommunications companies in Sweden and which brings an international perspective to the business. Combine that with the local input that comes through my company, Invesco Uganda Limited, which has an intimate knowledge of the local landscape and the regional knowledge brought by Tristar of Rwanda, and you have a winning combination,' he says.

MTN Uganda recruits the best personnel, has remained apolitical, and has made it clear to employees that opportunities for individual growth are open to whoever keeps pace with the company's strict regime. 'We focus on the communications industry and avoid other areas that are not our core business. We learn our business and stick to it. I think we owe this to the global experience of our partners and quality leadership, but overall the policy environment has also been supportive. As owners, we don't interfere with day to day management of the company, although we keep a close eye,' says Mbiire.

At a time when many potential investors are still judging Africa through the prism of conflict and instability, MTN has placed its faith in Uganda. The initial plan to invest US$70 million in Uganda was revised upwards and US$120 million had been invested as of January 2004. The company rolled out Africa's first door-to-door fibre-optic cable network and more than 400 kilometres of cable have been laid in Kampala and its environs. A fibre-optic ring was laid all the way to Jinja, 80 kilometres east of Kampala, while another ring runs to Masaka, 136 kilometres away. MTN's thrust has been aided by a growing realisation in Uganda that however small a business might be, communication is always crucial.

In recognition of their achievements, in the 2003 business survey of the most respected businesses in East Africa, carried out by PriceWaterhouseCoopers and the Nation Media Group, MTN Uganda was voted the most respected in the telecommunications/ICT category and the third most respected company overall in the region. Mbiire says of the ranking, 'It is a valuable tool that positions us against the best. It is also a motivator towards excellence because once an independent survey puts you in a particular position, you can only want to get better. You don't want to slip. The ranking also enhances shareholder value company perception and shows that your efforts are appreciated, boosting morale.' On specific returns attributed to the survey, Mbiire says, 'It has motivated us. It boosts confidence in our customers, investors and bankers.'

(Source: Michael Wakabi, 'MTN: Reconnecting Uganda to itself', Nairobi: *The East African*, 1 December 2003)

In 2003, MTN Uganda began to extend widespread telecommunications access to rural villages across Uganda while also creating jobs in the region. MTN Village Phone is a joint venture between MTN Uganda and Grameen Foundation USA. The Village Phone concept is operated in partnership with micro-finance institutions, allowing potential village phone operators to take a micro-loan of as little as US$230, which is repaid over a period of up to 12 months, for the MTN Village Phone equipment. In addition to the antenna, the equipment package also includes a car battery or solar power panel, a wireless handset, a user manual and a fixed-line dedicated SIM card that can be loaded with the prepaid airtime and requires no service fees. The Village Phone project is a sustainable initiative that aims to alleviate poverty and empower rural Ugandans through the provision of communications services. These village phone operators resell cellular services to local residents. The project is instrumental in increasing local economic activity and business opportunities through the creation of entrepreneurs and small enterprises. The average villager used to travel up to five kilometres to make a call and was also charged a considerable rate per minute. Through this project, MTN Uganda provides its communications services where no such viable, affordable or accessible alternatives existed before. In 2004, the head of MTN Village Phone, Richard Mwami, said the goal of village phone is to provide 5,000 MTN Village Phone micro-enterprises by 2008, thus bringing affordable information and communications technologies to millions of rural villagers in Uganda.

With Uganda stable — save for the north — some Asians are now returning. Abhay Shah sold his home in Kent, England, in 1999 to live in Kampala. In 2004, he runs UltraTec, supplying power solutions to Uganda's telecom providers, professional applications, rural community and industry. He gets personal satisfaction doing something he likes and in an industry he likes, and seeing the difference supplying power solutions can bring. One strand of Shah's enterprise says everything about business in Uganda: mobile phone use is going through the roof in Africa. For farmers, the technology is vital because they can access up-to-the-minute world commodity prices on their handsets. Price information stops middlemen ripping them off. The trouble is that Ugandan energy provision was so poor in 2004 that few people could charge mobile phones and less than 3 per cent of the population had access to power (one of the lowest connection rates in Africa). Businesses take power blackouts as a fact of life. Shah devised a phone charger powered by a solar panel. It sells for US$75, but average wages are about US$300 a year, so his breakthrough is only available to farmers through some form of consumer finance facility.

(Source: Nick Mathiason. 'Back from Amin's abyss, Uganda is on the cusp of being an African success story'. *The Observer*, 13 June 2004)

Shah established UltraTec in 1999 to serve the needs of the growing energy and telecommunication sectors for appropriate products and services. The company represents reputable international manufacturers, which has ensured that the products and services offered are of the best performance and high quality standards. UltraTec renewable energy division provides power solutions and renewable energy including solar power for rural and professional applications. UltraTec represents Shell Solar, which is one of the world's leading PV systems companies. It supplies PV systems for a wide range of applications including water pumping, telecommunications and lighting. UltraTec also represents Free Energy Europe, a leader in high quality, stable and reliable amorphous solar modules. They also represent Solahart Industries of Australia, the makers of the world's most popular solar water heating system.

UltraTec also represents Sun Ovens International Inc of the United States, manufacturers of premium quality solar cookers designed to last a very long time. UltraTec is working with the Sun Ovens, TTT International's East Africa Programme and the Ministry of Energy to further the penetration of this product by manufacturing it in East Africa. This move is likely to raise the quality of life for the rural community as the numbers of lives lost in the collection and burning of wood fuel from accidents and fumes will be dramatically reduced. The government, hopefully, will react positively by removing most of the taxes from the importation of these solar devices. Then UltraTec has a chance to grip the market that is made up of the poorest of the poor, refugees and the rural folk who spend hours of the most productive time of their lives collecting increasingly scarce firewood. Many NGOs have reacted positively to working with UltraTec on this project.

UltraTec also represents Steca GMBH of Germany which produces very high professional quality balanced system accessories for PV systems, and OutBack Power Systems Inc from the USA, known for rugged inverter/chargers that produce ultra clean power. UltraTec's products fall into three categories:

lightning and power surge protection, telecommunications and lighting products. UltraTec's recent innovation is its agreement with German Development Cooperation (GTZ) in bringing energy efficiency to Uganda's industry and bringing innovative small lighting systems to rural people at an affordable price using the latest LED lighting technology. The trick here is to make a system that can be self-installed and requiring no, or low, maintenance to make it a low cost system to buy and own.

UltraTec provides the highest quality of installation, maintenance, design, and consultancy in the niche areas of its expertise building and installing major solar PV systems, major solar water heating systems, complete industry-wide surge and spike protection and the design of power conditioning/stabilisation and voltage transient protection systems for broadcasting, telecommunications and manufacturing sectors. Major industries now rely on UltraTec's power analysis/audit service to implement their energy usage and efficiency and protection systems. UltraTec provides wireless support including VSAT installations to major telecoms carriers in east and central Africa.

UltraTec's customers include major fixed line telecoms operators: UTL; major GSM operators (MTN, Celtel, Mango, and Safaricom); manufacturing industries (some of the biggest industries use their services and products); educational institutions; broadcasting companies (major radio and TV stations); banks and financial institutions; hospitals; schools; NGOs; hotels (Sheraton, Grand Imperial, Serena, Paraa and Sunset); consultants; government and ministries; major supermarkets (Shoprite, Uchumi, Metro and Capital Shoppers); major electrical outlets; and solar retailers, wholesalers and installers. Ultra Tec was a 2005 Finalist for the Africa SMME Awards.

In 2006, UltraTec was getting more involved in the Energy Efficiency Initiative of the German Development Cooperation (GTZ). The idea is to save Uganda's industry precious money by using energy efficiently, and to improve on the quality of the power. This is a major initiative as Uganda suffers from chronic power shortages and thus whatever UltraTec can do to reduce the power wastage and make it available for others will go a long way to improving the quality of life for other industries and domestic users. Using demand control, energy efficient lighting, power factor correction for industry, and improving furnace and steam system efficiency are some of the technicalities UltraTec gets into everyday.

Hans Verkoijen has been working as a technical assistant in development aid. He was sent out in 1990 as an internal controller for SNV, the Dutch development aid organisation, in a local micro-finance institution in Burkina Faso. This organisation served 10,000 clients from six regional offices. Administration was done manually but Verkoijen saw that some automation might do wonders, so he developed a plan, got funding, and started implementing things. A computer room was set up, some computers were bought, and a small network was installed. For accounting purposes, suitable software was readily available, but for micro-finance, there was no suitable software at the time (1990), especially not in French. Verkoijen started his first steps in developing suitable software for micro-finance. During the period of his contract, a membership registration and a savings module became operational.

In 1995, Verkoijen was sent, again by SNV, to Uganda to assist the Uganda Women Finance Trust (UWFT) in their automation efforts. This also was a micro-finance institution of about the same size. An automation plan was developed, some computers bought and again, now five years later, there was no suitable software on the market. So new efforts were made to develop something in-house, suitable to the way UWFT worked. By the time Verkoijen's contract ended, a client, savings and loans module were operational. Instead of going to a third organisation and repeating the same process, Verkoijen was looking for a more general solution. He first asked SNV whether they were interested in the production of micro-finance software that would suit more than just a single organisation, but this was not in SNV's line of work and the organisation was not interested. Next, Verkoijen negotiated with UWFT to take the source code with him, start a company in Uganda and continue working on the software to make it a more general product suitable for a wide variety of micro-finance organisations. UWFT asked for some compensation and an agreement was made.

In 1998, Crystal Clear Software Ltd was registered in Uganda with the purpose of developing suitable micro-finance software. Verkoijen registered a name for his product, Loan Performer, and created a website to stimulate sales. In the first year only a single licence was sold. It was not easy to promote software that was developed for a single organisation to a level where it was suitable for many. But after the first year, slowly the customer base of Loan Performer grew. In 2004, total sales of Loan Performer had reached 174 organisations of which about 125 were active clients. What is amazing is that these clients are located in a wide variety of countries. Loan Performer has been translated into French, Spanish and Russian, and is being used in about 40 different countries. The geographical spread is about 70 per cent in Africa, 15 per cent in the Caribbean and 15 per cent in Eastern Europe and Asia. In 2004, Crystal Clear Software also had installations in the UK, in the USA and in Latin American countries (Mexico, El Salvador and Peru). In July 2004, a branch of Crystal Clear Software was registered in Costa Rica to serve the Latin market.

In 2005, there were two developments: Loan Performer was also going to be available on a client-server platform so that bigger organisations can also use the software — and Crystal Clear Software Ltd was working with a team from the World Bank to develop a tool with which payments could be entered by the credit officers on a handheld device. These payments are transmitted via a mobile phone network to a central server which then updates the Loan Performer database. Once the payment is successfully processed, an acknowledgement is sent out and the handheld device prints a receipt. The World Bank will get access to the payment behaviour of micro-finance clients and expects to draw conclusions on poverty eradication by combining this information with other collected data. Crystal Clear Software was a 2005 winner in the information and communications sector for an Africa SMME Award.

Mango Tree Educational Enterprises produces high quality, durable, and inexpensive educational tools designed to meet the special needs of Ugandan teachers, parents, and anyone working to uplift the country's educational standard. Grain sacks, bottle tops, recycled slipper material, jerry cans, wire, wood off-cuts, and other locally available materials are the raw materials that Mango Tree uses to make its innovative line of educational products. In addition, they provide employment to local artisans, many of them members of marginalised groups like people with HIV/AIDS, the disabled and street children.

Mango Tree Educational Enterprises was founded by Craig Esbeck in Busolwe, a village in eastern Uganda. Craig, who has a bachelor's degree from the School for International Training in Brattleboro, Vermont, and a master's degree from Holy Names College in Oakland, California, was a teacher in Iowa and Minnesota before coming to Uganda in 1997 to work as a Peace Corps Volunteer. In Uganda, he worked as an outreach tutor for Mukuju Primary Teacher College for two years. When the Peace Corps abruptly suspended its Uganda programme in May 1999, Craig decided to stay on and start a business that would provide teachers, especially those in rural primary schools, with relevant and appropriate teaching tools. He called the business enterprise 'Mango Tree' because its focus was to serve rural schools, many of which are under mango trees.

Mango Tree Educational Enterprises' products reflect the realities of the village classroom. They are made from locally available materials and are designed especially for the Ugandan primary school curriculum. In addition, Mango Tree's teaching tools are designed to encourage teachers to use more participatory, child-centred teaching strategies. Empowering teachers to see that their environment is rich in potential learning tools is part of Mango Tree's mission to educate teachers.

In addition to producing teaching tools, Mango Tree understands that an equally important part of its mission is to provide training so that teachers use these tools effectively. Ugandan education is lecture-based, teacher-centred, and focused on rote learning and memorising. Mango Tree encourages teachers to try methods that encourage student participation, develop teamwork and focus on problem-solving skills.

Mango Tree has two of its own workshops. The original workshop in Busolwe employs ten artisans. In 2003 Mango Tree set up a graphic arts studio in Kampala which employs 14 graphic artists who design and draw most of Mango Tree's teaching tools. Mango Tree's employees pay taxes and contribute to the National Social Security Fund. Playing its small part in the development of Uganda's private sector is another facet of Mango Tree's mission. In addition, Mango Tree works with a wide range of other organisations, both public and private, which assist in the manufacture of their products. Partners include NGOs working with the disabled, street children, women with HIV and people with epilepsy. They also contract with other small- and medium-scale enterprises to assemble their products.

Mango Tree exists to serve teachers. In Uganda, the average primary school teacher faces many challenges. For example, the pupil to teacher ratio, especially in the early years, is often 100 to 1 or more. Even in upper primary a teacher often has 50 to 75 pupils in a class. Mango Tree listens to teachers and responds to their needs. In November 2002, Mango Tree hired a consultant to do a market research survey to improve its line of products. A Teacher Advisory Board has been created to test products in the classroom. Mango Tree also hires teachers to write lesson plans and other support materials for their products. Their future vision is to identify, reward, and bring together superior teachers who can be role models for the profession. Mango Tree was the first place winner in the business sector for Ashoka's 2005 Changemakers Innovation Award.

(Source: www.mangotreeuganda.org)

Uganda is among the ten biggest users of the Internet in Africa. The internet has been popularised by the mushrooming internet cafes and service providers, by the falling cost of the computer, and by the inherent advantages of the net. It is easy to use, cheap, and versatile and has useful information on virtually every topic. Edward Baliddawa is the founder and chairman of Uganda Home Pages Limited (UHPL), the firm credited with popularising the Internet in Uganda, and he is the founder and director of the Cyberworld Cafe in Kampala. In 1995, Baliddawa launched UHPL, the pioneering and first ever Internet website (www.uganda.co.ug) in Uganda. This was an endeavour he began while earning a Master of Business Administration degree at Abilene Christian University in the USA. After graduating in 1996, Baliddawa returned home to continue his work.

With over a decade of design experience, the creative professionals at UHPL have earned a reputation for excellence in website design. They offer professional design solutions plus proven marketing services and fast, reliable website hosting. The internet is communication at its finest and UHPL makes sure Ugandan entrepreneurs are heard loud and clear. UHPL provides good and valuable information about Uganda for investment and tourism opportunities. The site provides readers with up to date and comprehensive information about Uganda's recorded road to recovery, which has become a beacon of the renaissance in Africa. Baliddawa maintains that his driving motivation and passion is that the internet be in every home in Uganda.

In 2002, UHPL introduced a new concept, Easy Web, to enable small businesses to acquire exposure on websites. Baliddawa says that Easy Web is basically a web presence package for small businesses, NGOs, schools and individual entrepreneurs, to access websites at very low costs. Easy Web enables one to have a five-page site for 12 months at Shs 200,000 (US $115), to be paid before any work is done. Baliddawa says that if UHPL is to promote the small-scale industries, they have to offer them opportunities through affordable packages like easy web. He says the sites are simple and cheap, with basic facts about the company such as the logo, profiles, service range and local contacts. Baliddawa says an extra US$10 is charged each time the users want to update their sites.

The idea of information technology enhancing competitiveness has given rise to the prominence of such concepts as electronic commerce (trade on the internet), video conferencing, tele-health, long distance learning, cyber shopping malls, electronic banking and virtual tourism. With this in mind, UHPL designed the first e-commerce site in Uganda, which Baliddawa calls the Uganda Mall, where various made-in-Uganda items are sold. Inevitably, developments in digital technology will dramatically change Ugandan society. Baliddawa has been pleading the case of internet use by Ugandans with almost evangelical zest. He imagines the Makerere University Medical School, and all hospitals in Uganda, accessing information on the latest developments in medical science. The Buganda website (www.uganda.co.ug/buganda) that Baliddawa set up on the Internet was visited by over 50,000 Ugandans and other people abroad who wanted to learn about the royal wedding in Buganda.

The first-ever district website project aimed at providing affordable communication services to rural areas in Uganda was launched in July 2003 in Mbale. The Uganda Communications Commission (UCC) corporate affairs officer, Fred Otunu, says the Shs 140 million project subsidises operational costs of private Internet investors in 26 districts. Uganda Home Pages is executing the project. This was after it had won the bid to host and design the district websites also known as district information portals. The internet will change what Ugandans know, and the most influential person in Uganda in the early 21st century will be the one who spreads this phenomenon as widely as it is desperately required. This person so far is Baliddawa.

Julian Adyeri Omalla was named the Most Distinguished Woman Entrepreneur of 2004 at the Uganda Investment Authority's Investor of the Year Awards. One would never guess that at 40, Adyeri has achieved what more seasoned businessmen only dream about — being recognised as one of Uganda's most enterprising local investors. Adyeri owns five companies worth about Shs 6.3 billion, employing more than 400 workers. She has invested Shs 1.6 billion in poultry, fruit and mixed farms and Shs 4.6 billion in value addition to agro products.

Adyeri's most widely known business is Delight Uganda Limited (DUL) which produces a variety of soft drinks under the brand name 'Cheers'. Worth Shs 4.6 billion, DUL operates in a two-storied building that also houses Adyeri's Kampala home, a bakery (cakes, buns and doughnuts) and an engineering section. The soft drinks company, which started as a cottage industry with only one worker, now employs 180 and is competing favourably with other industries. DUL plans to expand its factory premises and open up sister companies in neighbouring countries — Rwanda, Burundi, Democratic Republic of Congo and Nigeria. Aderi says, 'It's a long process but we are determined to expand and introduce new products by making sure every single coin of the profit is put back to the business, even if it takes five years.'

Adyeri's other businesses include Kidera Demonstration Farm, located in West Budama, Tororo district, where Adyeri has a stock of 38,000 layer chickens producing 600 trays of eggs (30 eggs per tray) a day; Ndejje Bongole Farm, on a 12-acre piece of land on Entebbe Road, grows purple passion fruit, which, when ready, will be used by DUL to make fresh juice concentrate; Senge Farm covers 21 acres in Wakiso district and deals in mixed farming; Brigton Students, a six-storied hostel in Makerere Kikoni, has become an attraction for Makerere University students (it has 144 self-contained rooms, a library, conference hall, grocery, laundry and a large packing yard); and in addition to these, Adyeri owns a fleet of 21 vehicles, all used in her businesses.

The Most Distinguished Woman Entrepreneur award was started three years before by the Uganda Investment Authority to recognise successful businesswomen in a world where business and many other areas of life are male-dominated. Like Adyeri, all its previous winners — including Ms Mariam Luyombyo (2002), director of Taibah Schools, and Ms Fang Min (2001) of Fang Fang Hotel and Restaurant — are from the membership of Uganda Investment Authority Women Entrepreneurs Network (UIA-WEN), which gathers women managers and investors.

Adyeri is Catholic from the radical Charismatic Renewal faith, and prays at Christ the King Church every evening. In her office hangs a framed photo of herself, her husband and the Cardinal, His Eminence Emmanuel Wamala, who visited her in 2003. Also all lined up on the sideboard are many award plates she has won, her certificates from training courses with Uganda Revenue Authority, Uganda Manufacturers' Association, and others. Adyeri says she has learned to rely on her faith to solve all her problems. 'In the early 1990s I was trading in Busia when I was robbed of Shs 20million. I went back to scratch,' she says. Adyeri used the only Shs 500,000 she was left with, and the knowledge she had acquired doing a certificate course in food science and technology from Frutarom, Israel, in 1988, to start mixing fruit juices in Kikuubo. 'I was creative. I had one worker, and designed my own labels,' she says.

Adyeri says that apart from God, her involvement in associations like the Uganda National Chamber of Commerce and Industry, where she is chairperson for the central region, UIA, WEN, Enterprise Uganda, and others, have seen her through stiff competition. Her Cheers juices are a favourite for boarding students' school, including her own. Adyeri is a mother of three — two girls, and a boy, who often serves as a model to advertise her brands. Her husband, Felix Omalla, is a lawyer, who serves as legal advisor for DUL and reportedly supports her in everything she does. 'When it comes to following those who have cheated me, Felix never rests till they are netted,' says Adyeri.

(Source: Dorothy Nakaweesi. 'Cheers for calm entrepreneur', Kampala: *The Monitor*, 4 December 2004)

Fiona Kobusingye is a businesswoman and designer. A Hamite, she is a cattle raiser and farmer. She is currently spearheading a poverty eradication and entrepreneurial initiative in Uganda in which she has organised women — mostly school dropouts and single women, raising children. The project called 'The Kogere Bagg of Uganda', uses traditional mats, hand-woven by the women in her group, to make handbags. She has begun exporting the bags to the USA. The Smithsonian Museum is one of the clients she is currently developing to market her creations. As a designer, Fiona is a forward and creative thinker whose mission is to explore the commercial possibilities of her African cultural heritage and traditions in a post-modern, industrialised global environment and marketplace. Her immediate goal is to provide avenues through which women can earn money to support their families.

In September 2002, people in the book industry from Zambia, Ghana, Kenya, the United Kingdom and Uganda held a four-day seminar in Kampala with the aim of discussing books for development. The theme of the workshop was 'Bringing key stakeholders in the book chain together'. The participants included booksellers, publishers and librarians. James Tumusiime, the chairperson of the National Book Trust of Uganda, believes that perhaps nowhere in Africa have efforts to sensitise government and donors on the importance of books paid off as well as in Uganda. Words like democratisation, decentralisation, universal primary education and globalisation have for some time formed part of Uganda's vocabulary, but there was no book industry to back them up. As of 2002, there are 20 publishing houses, over 100 booksellers and a number of libraries are coming up in schools. A participant from Ghana, however, was not impressed with the stock. He visited Mukono Bookshop in Kampala and all he saw were books from Cambridge and Oxford. He looks forward to a time when he will walk into an African bookshop and find books from Ghana, Zambia or any other part of Africa.

(Source: Joan Mugenzi. 'African book publishers, sellers chart new ways', Kampala: *New Vision*, 20 September 2002)

James Tumusiime is the founder and managing director of Fountain Publishers Ltd. In a 1998 conversation with Katherine Salahi, coordinator of the Bellagio Publishing Network, Tumusiime traced his love of books back to the days when his older brothers and sisters used to bring books back from school. He liked them, and each time someone brought home a book he had to go through it. Sometimes he'd write in it too. His parents were farmers, 'newly-literate' converts to Christianity, and the only books at home were the Bible and occasional religious tracts.

Tumusiime trained as an agricultural economist and went to work for Idi Amin's government in the 1970s. At the same time he started writing for the local newspaper as a political satirist and he narrowly survived to tell the tale. He also drew cartoons; at one stage he was arrested for a particularly apposite one. When Amin was overthrown, there followed a brief period of press freedom. Tumusiime moved into newspapers and became publicity officer for one of the political movements of the time, the Uganda Patriotic Movement. Meanwhile the threat of civil war grew day by day. Tumusiime engineered time off from the Ministry of Livestock, where he still worked as an agricultural economist, to take a degree course in Nairobi. But the ministry soon discovered they were dealing with a rebel. They cut off his scholarship, leaving him stranded without money in Nairobi.

His newspaper experience stood him in good stead. He joined the *Nation* newspaper as a humour writer, moved to the *Nairobi Times* as economics correspondent, then joined mainstream journalism full-time and became the paper's business editor. The paper was bought by the *Kenya Times*, where he worked till 1985, moving to *The Standard* for a short time before joining a magazine publisher. Alongside his writing he continued as a political cartoonist. Indeed, he was so successful that the newspaper's sales went up when he started his cartoons in Kenya. Sometimes the whole letters page was devoted to his cartoon of the day. *The Standard* published books of his cartoons, which sold well in Kenya and beyond to Tanzania and as far as Swaziland, earning him more in royalties than all his writing put together (even today in Uganda cartoonists are some of the best paid people on the newspaper).

Then, in 1986, the government in Uganda changed. Immediately he went back. There were lots of Ugandans in Kenya just waiting to return. He started the *New Vision* newspaper, the largest English daily and its four sister local language papers. He was the group deputy editor-in-chief, a position he remained in for 11 years. He wasn't satisfied with the way things were going in the book industry and felt there was more to do in this virgin territory than in newspapers that had taken root. There were no books, nothing, no record covering the years of the war and Amin's time. As an editor, he really needed reference material, so with his wife and sister in law he started a small publishing house, Fountain Publishers, mainly to publish directories giving basic information about the country. He started in 1989 with a *Who's Who in Uganda*, with a print-run of 3,000 copies which sold out straight away. He became excited. He followed with a directory chronicling the failures and achievements of the National Reconciliation Movement's first five years of government. That quickly sold out, as did the *Uganda Districts Information Handbook*, which became a bestseller. By this time he was co-publishing with the British publisher James Currey, and selling abroad through the African Books Collective.

In 1991, Fountain Publishers launched a children's book series, stemming from Tumusiime's interest in culture and the need he felt to record tales from the past that were in danger of dying out. To get texts he set up a Ugandan folktale writing competition in the newspaper. DANIDA helped with a grant of US$3,000 towards the series. But the multinationals dominated the scene; when the World Bank funded textbook provision for Uganda, every single title was imported. Uganda publishers lost US$35million in World Bank funding of books, World Bank funding left no trace on the economy. So in 1992, in the run-up to a USAID textbook project, Tumusiime and a few other local publishers first formed a publishers' association with US$20,000 support from CODE, and then Tumusiime talked to the local USAID officials, who listened to him, he says, with some surprise. USAID informed the Ugandan government that the old selection method for books was no longer acceptable. This time, users must select the books. USAID called for a tripartite meeting with the Uganda publishers' association and the government, where it was agreed in principle that publishers would submit books. They would be evaluated to see if they met basic criteria. Then schools would select the titles they wanted. That was the beginning of their participation in the book purchasing projects.

Tumusiime worked with the more established Kenyan educational publisher Henry Chakava in order to meet the deadline. Their submission was included on the suppliers' list, and in the event Fountain Publishers sold a lot of copies — the only indigenous publisher to have books included on the final list. Things moved relatively smoothly, although the government people never appeared to be fully convinced, perhaps because they felt denied their authority: this way, publishers were dealing with schools directly.

The government is still doing the purchasing and distributing. Ugandan publishers would prefer that to happen through a bookshop network, which would stimulate growth, and would help for non-textbooks. They would also appreciate support in the form of guaranteed purchase of a number of finished copies, rather than upfront grants: That way, says Tumusiime, the publisher keeps the copyright and feels independent, while the distribution of copies stimulates readership. The Netherlands Embassy made a guaranteed purchase for a series of storybooks on the environment, for example, which were then distributed to district education authorities.

Fountain publishes a number of titles in local languages. James has been surprised at times by Fountain's success in some of the more widely-spoken languages, such as a reader in Kinyankole, which had to be reprinted three times in one year. Fountain publishes a small fiction list, which has sold well beyond Ugandan borders, and poetry. Tumusiime is no longer involved with newspapers.

Coming from that faster, more immediately dynamic world, does he miss the buzz of the newsroom? He says not. His main desire was always to communicate. He never trained as a journalist. Anyway, it was time for him to slow down. He likes having his own company, and products that will endure. A newspaper becomes boring after a while. He is an artist, closely involved in artwork and book design. His love for local music and culture propelled him to convince some friends to set up Radio West, a regional radio station that broadcasts mainly in Runyankole, of which he is board chairman and which is one of the most successful radio stations in the country.

He's also a good businessman. After what he calls his initial relative success he needed to expand his activities, which required developing editorial, accounting and marketing departments. Fountain's initial funding had come from his other activities. Now he added a bookshop to help finance the publishing, something he says most Ugandan publishers do. Five years later he bought the university bookshop at Makerere, which had been closed for over three years. Now the publishing house has four editors, four typesetters, modern pre-press equipment, and publishes around 40 titles a year.

How does Tumusiime's involvement with the African Publishers Network (APNET) (he was its vice-chair for five years) affect his publishing? It's inspiring for him to find there are many other people all over the continent who share his problems and his aspirations, and therefore he feels he is working with a community that understands. It revives his interest and determination. He has applied what he learned from APNET at home, by setting up the National Book Trust of Uganda (NABOTU), an umbrella organisation for all stakeholders in the book industry — authors, publishers, booksellers, printers, librarians and teachers. The trust is involved in campaigns to promote a reading culture in Uganda, and hosts an international book fair in Kampala every year. Now people talk about books and publishing, previously there was no one to talk to, so Uganda has benefited from his membership of APNET. He has made useful contacts with donors. It takes a lot of time, but it's time well spent.

And if money were no object, what would he do? He says he'd publish more and more books, of course, especially linked to art and crafts. He has a special interest in culture, and would like to start a heritage trust, conserving Uganda's history and culture, and developing cultural tourism. He confesses he's not much of a reader of fiction himself — there's no time. He is so interested in virtually everything! He writes children's books, not just for work but also for pleasure. They're often full of wisdom; and there's so much to read about publishing. He thinks he'll carry on publishing into a ripe old age, because he hasn't run out of ideas. He tries something out — sometimes it works, sometimes it doesn't — if it does, he is spurred on to try again.

The hardest problem in Ugandan publishing is getting skilled and interested personnel. Fountain competes with other possible employers, and it's difficult to pay the salaries needed to get the best staff. Tumusiime has another concern: publishing is a long-term industry, and his family doesn't have a publishing tradition, so it's hard to know who to bequeath it to. He'd like to hand it over to his children, but he can't know what his children will do His father wanted him to take up farming.

(Source: 'Talking books: James Tumusiime in conversation with Katherine Salahi'. *BPN Newsletter*, Issue No 24, December 1998)

Alexander Calder, the curator at The Art Room, San Francisco Fine Arts Center for East Africa, and David Kibuuka, Ugandan artist, write that during Uganda's early post-independence period, the early to mid-1960s, Ugandan artists such as Mugalula Mukiibi, Teresa Musoke, Elly Kyeyune, Norbert Kaggwa, David Wasswa Katongole, Francis Musango, Mwebwe, Mark Mutyaba, Wilson Lukenge and Henry Lumu demonstrated exceptional brilliance and originality. These artists, and others, rose to prominence in a thriving art scene centred on the Makerere University School of Fine Art, in Uganda's capital city of Kampala.

While many in Uganda's art community chose to remain in Uganda after this period, increasing political unrest during the 1970s forced others to emigrate to other parts of the world. Nairobi, the capital of neighbouring Kenya, became a focal point where much of this transplanted talent began to collaborate, exhibiting works through local galleries, and participating in group exhibitions at Kenya's National Museum. During this time, award-winning Ugandan artist the late Henry Lumu and his younger brother David Kibuuka worked among fellow Ugandan artists such as Dan Sekanwagi, Nuwa Nnyanzi, Joseph Mungaya, Jack Katarikawe, Emanuel Lubega, James Kitamirike, and others. They brought their unique and refined styles to Kenya's burgeoning art scene, exerting a broad influence upon other local artists. Helping to define the emerging East African Modern Art Movement, artists of the Ugandan School helped gain international recognition for styles, mediums and colours unique to this group. Since then, these artists and their work have continued to evolve and emigrate further, expanding their impact as they influence other artists throughout the world.

Born in Uganda, David Kibuuka was a blossoming prodigy who began selling his painting to international collectors through local galleries at the age of eleven. Protégé to his brilliant late mentor and older brother Henry Lutalo Lumu, the artist shared a passion for the work of European art masters. From Lumu, Kibuuka learned a deep respect for the achievements of representational painters such as Rembrandt, Leonardo, Raphael and Michelangelo. This early passion found Kibuuka creating works such as 'The Royal Guardian', featured on the cover of Kibuuka's 2000 Art Calendar. In this work, exquisite anatomical details capture the regal stature of a Masai warrior. Spending six years in Kenya, Kibuuka made this legendary tribe a favourite subject for his early work executed in high renaissance-styled tight realism. As Lumu exposed Kibuuka to modern western styles, Kibuuka's work evolved to include impressionism and surrealism, infusing his deep love of human anatomy and natural form with a vibrant new energy. One result of this evolution is 'Ceremonial Dance'. In this striking piece, a group of young Masai warriors dances proudly in precisely unified fragments of bold primary colours, continuing his use of new forms of semi-abstraction; in 'Baganda Dancers' figures blend effortlessly with brave splashes of colour animating each dancer with unforgettable visual vibrations. Composed of mixed media and created with Kibuuka's fragmentation technique, the dancers spring to life with radiant energy.

Although Kibuuka is equally fluent in oils, acrylics, watercolours, pencil and mixed media, a favourite medium has emerged. 'I love the versatility of acrylics. You can use them to create all kinds of interesting effects. At one end of the range, on paper, one can lightly apply a very thin layer to simulate watercolours. At the other end, as in 'Pure Innocence', I use the palette knife on canvas to create heavy layers of paint, imparting an oil-like impressionist flavour to a traditional African village scene.' Kibuuka hopes to provide inspiration for generations of emerging talent. 'There are a number of East African modernists who have emigrated to North America to develop their careers outside Africa,' he says. 'As we move into the 21st century, we are likely to see the expansion and maturation of the East African modern art movement in North America'.

(Source: www.kibuuka.com)

Nuwa Wamala-Nnyanzi is a celebrated, self-taught, Ugandan artist of international repute, and a visual arts practitioner and consultant. He was born in 1952. His father was a laboratory assistant and late mother a retired midwife and nurse. Nnyanzi attributes his talent and success to the grace of God. He has contributed much to Uganda society. He owns and runs the Nnyanzi Art Studio, a studio gallery in Kampala which employs three people on a permanent basis (during exhibitions the number increases to between 10 and 15). Nnyanzi offers industrial training to students to equip them with skills to practice as freelance artists. He offers free consultative services to practicing artists to improve on their marketing skills. A number of artists sell their work through the gallery, which promotes and markets artists' work in and outside Uganda. Since Nnyanzi returned to Uganda from Kenya he has influenced a change in attitude towards art. Today there are more artists depending on the sale of their art. As a result of Nnyanzi's sensitising programmes on art appreciation in the media, parents are sending their children to art institutions whereas previously art was not considered a noble profession.

Nnyanzi's works of art are in batik, pastel, acrylic, and oil and watercolours. They are earthy, vibrant and reflective of the strong and sweet African sun; the lines of his works of art flow and turn with the fluency of an African drum. Looking at his art, one feels the vibrant life in an African setting.

In 1996 Nnyanzi had the privilege and honour of hosting, among many other dignitaries, US President Bill Clinton's Commerce Secretary, Ron Brown, at his studio gallery. In 2001, Nnyanzi hosted the former president of the USA, Jimmy Carter and his wife. Mrs Carter actually bought one of his prints, 'The Awakening', which portrays the twelve apostles receiving the Holy Spirit. Outside Uganda, Nnyanzi's works of art are on permanent display at The Gems of Africa Art Gallery, Atlanta, Georgia, USA; The Art Odyssey Gallery, Pasadena, California, USA; The Museum fur Voelkerkunde, Frankfurt, Germany; The Monaco Fine Arts, Nairobi, Kenya.

Although Nnyanzi works in many other media, he specialises in batik painting. Through extensive research and experimentation he has managed to come up with a style where more than one dye can be applied to get tones and varied shades, as in his famous batik painting 'The Pearl of Africa'. After all the required dyes have been applied, the wax is removed by placing the batik between two absorbent pieces of paper and pressed with a very hot flat iron. The wax melts with the heat and is absorbed into the sheets of paper, leaving the batik crisp and clean. The rugged edges of the images are retouched using black dye in a fountain pen. A talented and articulate orator, Nnyanzi convincingly addresses the audience, eloquently and emotionally, through his art. In fact, his art has so touched people's hearts that some viewers have shed tears. His art has also been used in psycho-therapy whose beneficiaries include traumatised children, single parents and senior citizens.

Nnyanzi's knowledge of Ganda culture and traditions and also of the neighbouring people has its roots in the close association his family has had with the royal courts of Buganda, Bunyoro and Tooro for a number of generations. He is a descendant of Baganda chiefs, among whom was his great grandfather Paulo Nsubuga Bakunga, who participated in the making of the 1900 agreement which laid the foundation for the creation of modern-day Uganda. At the beginning of the 20th century, his paternal grandfather, Kesi Mukasa Bagandanswa, was among the first Ugandans to visit the United Kingdom as a reward for his swift grasp of the English language.

On top of international exhibits, Nnyanzi has also made several slide/talk presentations on Uganda's rich cultural heritage at universities, colleges, and select interest groups. Nnyanzi's art has inspired many scholars who have used it as a subject of reference when writing their theses and art books. Nnyanzi has appeared as guest speaker at fundraising functions and he has on several occasions donated his art in support of charity. Nnyanzi's batik painting, 'Homage to the first born', features in the UNICEF greeting card collection. Another of his works, a 1987 batik painting 'Desperately longing for shelter', was selected to be used in minting a medallion by the United Nations High Commission for Human Settlement (Habitat) to be presented to distinguished world leaders. In 1993, during the Pope's visit to Uganda, Nnyanzi's design, 'The Pentecost' was used in executing a wood sculpture, which was presented to Pope John Paul II. In 1995, Nnyanzi was commissioned by the University of Transkei in South Africa to paint a mural (depicting Xhosa life-style) in the administration block. The American Red Cross, in 1993, used Nnyanzi's design the 'Dialogue' on the cover of its book on AIDS. In 1997, Coca-Cola International commissioned Nnyanzi to make an eight-foot Coca-Cola bottle portraying Uganda's rich cultural heritage. The sculpture is part of the art collection of Atlanta-based company. In 1998, the head of the Roman Catholic Church in Uganda, who is also the chairman of the ecumenical movement in Uganda, commissioned Nnyanzi to produce portraits and a collage which were presented to the Archbishop of Canterbury when he visited Uganda. One of his batik paintings 'Working Woman' appears on the cover of the 1999 World Health Report by the World Health Organisation.

Len Folkes of Sabbokai Gallery in London writes that for the black diaspora settlers in Europe, Nnyanzi's work has been a spiritual key for identity seekers. In Britain's racially mixed inner cities for example, the demand for his work in schools and commercial outlets greatly increased in the mid-1980s. His images were used as teaching aids for the reclamation of the black child's identity. In a number of primary schools, his works in blue were compared with Picasso's Blue Period. Perhaps for the first time, Folkes writes, 'the African artist was taken outside of the particularistic confines of his culture and accorded universality'.

Nnyanzi has been involved in electronic commerce with the help of Uganda's information technology evangelist Edward Baliddawa, as he sees that in future money will also come from doing business on the internet. Photos of Nnyanzi's works are displayed on the Nnyanzi Art Studio website. For sale are high quality prints on acid-free paper in limited and open editions published from the original batik paintings, plus original batik paintings (dyes and wax on cotton fabric), inspired by Nnyanzi's concern for humanity. Selected original works are also available as limited Giclee editions, individually numbered high-resolution digital replicas of original art works, which are produced on canvas or watercolour paper. These limited reproductions allow collectors to own a work which Nnyanzi has compared favourably with his original. In order to expedite shipments, Nnyanzi keeps some artwork in a gallery in the United States, from which he can post to the customers the artwork that they have chosen. In July 2005, Nnyanzi received his MA degree in design from Middlesex University in the UK.

(Source: www.nnyanziart.com)

James Finlay Ltd, which was founded in 1750, is a wholly owned subsidiary of the John Swire and Sons business empire, a privately owned international trading company with diverse interests in Asia and the Americas. Now one of the largest independent tea growers in the world, Finlay has extensive plantations in Uganda, Kenya, Sri Lanka and Bangladesh. Established in early 1994, James Finlay (Uganda), formerly Rwenzori Highlands Tea Company Limited, has grown rapidly to become Uganda's largest single producer of black tea, accounting for over 25 per cent of the total production and country's tea exports. All five James Finlay, (Uganda) tea factories produce black Crush, Tear and Curl (CTC) teas. The factories have recently been rehabilitated. Four of the factories use screw fomenters and eucalyptus fired fluid bed driers. At Kiko Estate the tea is made using Williamson fermenting trolleys and a state-of-the-art Kilburn vibrating fluid bed drier.

Unlike many other East African tea companies, James Finlay (Uganda) is geographically spread with its six actively managed tea estates strung out along the Rwenzori range on Uganda's south-western border with the Congo, an area that offers ideal climatic and fertile soil conditions for tea production. James Finlay (Uganda) estates now comprise over 3,000 hectares of mature seedling tea, and an expanding area of high yielding clonal tea (clonal teas are processed from a single variety of genetic material which has not been propagated sexually). These teas usually offer a uniform and attractive appearance with well pronounced character). The tea estates are all situated around large areas of indigenous equatorial forest that provide habitats for a variety of species of flora and fauna. The preservation of the environment is crucial to the future of James Finlay (Uganda) and is therefore a core factor in its business strategy. Since 1995, James Finlay (Uganda) has planted Eucalyptus grandis (fast growing energy wood suitable for wet areas) at all the estates, which is used for fuel wood and the company is now virtually self-sufficient.

In 2002, James Finlay (Uganda) produced 8,200 tons of tea out of the 33,000 tons produced in the country. The company employs more than 5,000 people at six large estates in the Bushenyi, Kabarole, Kyenjojo, Kibaale and Hoima districts. The Kabarole district accounts for more than 70 per cent of the tea produced in Uganda. James Finlay (Uganda) production reached 9,500 tons in 2003.

If the economic environment continues to improve, the total output of tea in Uganda could hit 40,000 tons. With the revival of the East African Community, the future is bright. The EAC will play a bigger role in infrastructural development, especially regarding transport to the port of Mombasa. In 2002, it took ten days to transport tea to Mombassa whereas James Finlay (Uganda) chief executive Laurie Davies dreams of shipping from Uganda by rail to the port of Mombasa in one day.

There was an increase in the volume of cargo between the Malaba railway station in Kenya and Tororo in Uganda during 2003. Uganda Railways Corporation (URC) officials at Tororo and their Kenyan counterparts said they have given more time and energy to the clearance and delivery of the customers' cargo arriving at the border. Importers of cement and perishables said URC officials have eliminated congestion at both Malaba and Tororo, which used to delay wagons by up to three weeks. There has been a great improvement in the limited capacity utilisation. In 2003, an average of eight trains ran to Kampala every day.

President Yoweri Museveni has emphasised the need for Uganda to repair its railway network, and to develop and link it with Rwanda and the Democratic Republic of Congo as well as Burundi, Zambia and South Africa. Uganda's railway system needs to be extended to the DRC through Kisangani. With the restoration of peace in southern Sudan, as a way of improving railway transport, an extension of the Ugandan railway line from Pakwach, Uganda, to Juba via Yei in southern Sudan, would be an economically viable venture. Railways are costly to build but ideal for Uganda because they provide a better alternative to roads which are often washed away during rainy seasons.

In October 2005, Rift Valley consortium, a group led by South African company Sheltam Trade, won a 25-year contract to manage Kenya's and Uganda's railways, and took over Kenya Railways Corporation and Uganda Railways from 1 April 2006. Sheltam bid US$1 million for the passenger business. The Sheltam bid means the group will pay the countries Sh73 million (at current exchange rates) a year as concession fees. Sheltam will also remit 11.1 per cent of its gross revenues every year to be shared by the two countries.

The two railway systems expect to be upgraded over the 25-year initial concession period, and additional routes are expected to be opened up into the southern Sudanese city of Juba, generating more traffic for the networks. The Uganda business sector is hopeful that the joint rail network will be a stepping stone extending the railway to the potentially lucrative Democratic Republic of Congo and Sudan markets.

Sheltam Trade was incorporated in 1999 in South Africa. It is involved in management services, locomotive maintenance, mining and railway operations. It was contracted to supply locomotives and operating crew on the 650-kilometre Nacala Corridor and Beira-Mutare (300-kilometre) lines in Mozambique, and 400 kilometres of railway in Zimbabwe. It also operates 65 kilometres of mine tracks in South Africa.

St Mary's Lacor Hospital of Gulu, provincial capital of northwest Uganda, is a non-profit institution committed to providing health care and development to the most disadvantaged and deprived. Its mission is to provide high quality health care comparable to that in developed countries. Lacor is a fully developed referral hospital with 474 beds, a full range of diagnostic and curative services, well-established primary health care activities, several training and research programmes. Daily activity concerns on average 500 admitted patients, and another 500 patients are seen every day in the outpatient departments. Lacor is the only sizeable private economic institution in northern Uganda providing salaries and local expenditures in 2003 of over US$1,500,000 yearly and having over 520 permanent employees. Director Dr Bruno Corrado points out that Lacor contributes not only to human development through fighting diseases and educating a large number of young people, but also to economic development by injecting a sizeable amount of funds into the local economy.

The Comboni Missionaries and the Diocese of Gulu started Lacor as a dispensary in 1959. After the maternity ward was added in 1960 it was licensed as a hospital. In 1961, the Italian doctor Piero Corti persuaded his Canadian colleague Lucille Teasdale, one of Canada's first female surgeons, to spend her summer months helping him as a surgeon at the medical mission in Uganda. Overcome by her love for Piero and for her adopted country, Lucille decided to settle in Uganda to help Piero expand the missionary clinic. The dignity and humanity of the local patients struck a chord with Lucille, who devoted her life to improving their condition. Lucille and Piero were married, and their daughter Dominique is now a qualified physician in Italy and works for Lacor's fund raising foundation and the hospital's logistics and support group without any remuneration. Together, Lucille and Piero expanded Lacor amidst the chaos of civil war. Despite the human madness, they kept the doors open to care for the wounded and to give shelter to thousands of refugees. The Italians deserve credit for helping in capacity building, especially training the local African staff and making it possible for many of them to take over skilled jobs and high responsibility as doctors and nurses.

The as yet undiscovered AIDS virus soon changed the course of Lucille's life, but not her work and determination. Lucille's and Piero's story depicts how selfless dedication can triumph by leaving a legacy of hope for generations to come. Lucille succumbed in 1996 to professionally acquired HIV-infection. In over 30 years of activity, Dr Teasdale carried out more than 13,000 major operations and cared for four generations of patients in the wards and outpatient department. Dr Piero Corti continued to direct the hospital until his death in 2003.

Matthew Lukwiya was one of the first native Ugandan residents at Lacor. Just a couple of weeks after his arrival, Piero and Lucille admitted to each other that Matthew was a truly brilliant person and physician, and that if he remained at Lacor, his excellent leadership qualities would certainly assure the hospital's future. Dominique said that this was evident to everyone who had the chance of meeting Matthew for just a few minutes. 'He had a really amazing personality, very quiet man, always calm and smiling, always treating everyone in the same respectful way, and yet so incredibly medically brilliant and dedicated.' Piero told his wife on her deathbed: 'Matthew was sent by providence to keep this hospital running'.

In late September 2000, student nurses fell sick at Lacor. In the space of a few days, three students of the nurse training school and two nurses of the hospital had died of a mysterious disease. Matthew was in Kampala for study, and was summoned urgently back to Lacor. As soon as he arrived, he spent the night going through the medical charts and reports of patients. The very next morning, Matthew had already formulated the hypothesis of viral hemorrhagic fever, probably Ebola. He knew the consequences if they failed to stop the spread of the disease. Under his inspirational leadership, the hospital staff set about creating isolation conditions. They formed a team of nurses prepared to risk their lives and they went out into the towns and villages to try to bring the sick in before the illness spread. Inevitably the staff themselves fell ill, and towards the end of the epidemic, Matthew also succumbed to the virus.

In December 2000, as he lay dying from the most vicious virus known, Matthew Lukwiya, the doctor who alerted the world to Uganda's Ebola outbreak, asked to be buried beside the grave of his mentor, Lucille Teasdale-Corti. Matthew has set a shining example for all medical workers. The example is total devotion to the medical service, and not only because of his fight against Ebola. Matthew could have worked and lived in prosperity in Europe, America, or anywhere else in the world. He eschewed these alternatives, and even Uganda's capital of Kampala, instead choosing to go to the rather remote and less glamorous Gulu District, which is near the Kitgum District where Matthew was born in 1957. This sacrifice, together with that of Lucille who could have lived more comfortably in Italy, is a fine example of global humanity at its best, working together to alleviate human suffering, service above self.

At Lacor, where there is now a monument in memory of all the fallen health workers during the Ebola fight, the hospital is even better prepared. They have learnt from the Ebola experience and now have an infection control committee, so that standard practice is observed even without Ebola, to protect the staff. Everything seems to be done with extra care — even the blue and white nurses' uniforms seem to hold extra starch. Business is back to normal. The bed occupancy is at full capacity. The former isolation unit has been transformed into the children's ward after thorough cleaning, repainting and disinfecting. The hospital's name is now recognised internationally. The Italians have offered ten scholarships for young Ugandan doctors to pursue postgraduate studies. The Austrians have given the hospital an automated laundry to spare the staff from handling the soiled materials from the wards. They have also got an incinerator from other donors.

(Source: www.lhospital.org)

Dr Peter Mugyenyi of the Joint Clinical Research Centre in Uganda is renowned throughout sub-Saharan Africa as an infectious-disease expert, especially in the area of HIV/AIDS research, care and treatment. He is best known these days for his crusade, going back to 1992 when he introduced antiretroviral therapy (ART) in an organised programme in Uganda. He was one of the first African physicians to insist his patients were capable of taking the complicated daily regimen of medicines that was revolutionising treatment of HIV/AIDS in the United States. There was, then, widespread belief that AIDS treatment was just impossible in Africa. In fact no organisation was prepared to provide any funds for ART or support any programme providing the treatment. As early as 1992, Dr Mugyenyi formed a partnership between his patients who could pay for the drugs and started providing ART to them in Uganda thus saving them thousands of dollars for which they used to spend travelling abroad for the same service.

Then he launched a campaign for more affordable prices explaining that exorbitant prices for ART drugs, was the real constraint to the widespread use of ART in Africa. Although prices slowly started to fall, the vast majority of Ugandans could not afford the therapy. In 1998, Mugyenyi described watching helplessly as numerous patients died while the life enhancing drugs were available and yet out of reach simply because patients could neither afford them nor get any help from any other source. Since health insurance was practically nonexistent, and the government was hard-pressed to pay for the care, even a well-off Ugandan making US$600 a month couldn't buy drugs that were then priced at about US$12,000 a year. Patients were too poor to afford treatment and therefore paid with their lives. Dr Mugyenyi believes that African governments now have the opportunity to successfully plan an AIDS care and treatment programme that will greatly increase the number of Africans accessing ARV therapy.

(Source: Michael Waldholz. 'Ugandan doctor crusades for cheaper AIDS drugs', *The Wall Street Journal*, 13 June 2002)

Dr Mugyenyi, working with a team of African scientists, founded the Africa Dialogue on AIDS, an African led initiative to enhance focused AIDS research, coordinate HIV/AIDS related activities, including the promotion of best practices as a way forward for mass prevention, care and treatment of HIV/AIDS in Africa. He also provides technical and management expertise to the Ugandan Ministry of Health as AIDS task force chairman to plan for national scaling up of HIV. Dr Mugyenyi carried out an in-depth study, on the impact of HIV/AIDS in Africa defining the scope of the problem, country responses, trends, gaps and research priorities. In April 2002, he testified to the US Senate decrying the devastation of HIV in Africa, and put a strong case for international emergency support for Africa. In recognition of his international leadership in HIV/AIDS and treatment advocacy, Mugyenyi became the first non-American to be invited to sit in the US Congress Royal Box during the 2003 State of the Union address as the American president announced US$15 billion emergency funds to alleviate the AIDS crisis in Africa and the Caribbean.

Subsequent events have vindicated Dr Mugyenyi's position and foresight. In Africa in 2004, the cost of HIV/AIDS drugs for antiretroviral therapy (ART) had finally fallen to as low as US$140 per year, or just over 38 US cents per person per day. Although there is increased international funding for AIDS treatment, including Global AIDS Fund, World Bank and President Bush Emergency Fund for AIDS, Dr Mugyenyi insists that much more work and funds are still required to put a stop to the carnage of AIDS in Africa. He now leads one of the most successful ART scale-up programmes in Africa — Timetable for Regional Expansion of ART (TREAT), aiming at universal access to all Ugandans in need of AIDS treatment. Dr Mugyenyi has received a number of local and international awards including Lifetime Achievement Award (India), an international Award of Hero of Medicine 2003 (USA) and a Doctor of Science degree (Uganda), a special Uganda Parliamentary honour 2004, and was appointed Professor of Medicine, Mbarara University.

(Source: 'ART rollout: The Uganda experience', presentation by Dr Peter Mugyenyi, 30 March 2005, www.fshealth.gov.za)

Part 5
Central Africa

AFRICA: CONTINENT OF ECONOMIC OPPORTUNITIES

The Economic Community of Central African States (ECCAS) was created in October 1983 in Libreville, Republic of Gabon. The treaty became effective in December 1984 and the Secretariat was set up in 1985. The ECCAS comprises 11 countries covering nearly 6.7 million square kilometres of geographical space, and has a combined population of about 113 million.

The small landlocked central African countries of Rwanda and Burundi form part of this economic union of countries in the central African region. Rwanda's exports are mostly agricultural — primarily coffee and tea — and Burundi's are coffee, tea, cotton and hides.

Other members of ECCAS are: Cameroon (crude oil, petroleum products, lumber, cocoa beans, aluminium and coffee); Central African Republic (diamonds, timber, cotton, coffee and tobacco);

Chad (crude oil, cotton, cattle and textiles); Equatorial Guinea (petroleum, timber and cocoa);

Congo (Brazzaville) (crude oil, lumber, plywood, sugar, cocoa and coffee); Gabon (crude oil and timber) and the vast country of the Democratic Republic of Congo (diamonds, copper, coffee, cobalt and petroleum products).

Situated south and north of the DRC's access to the Atlantic Ocean are Angola and its oil-rich enclave of Cabinda (crude oil and diamonds). In the Gulf of Guinea off the coast of Gabon is the small island-state of Sao Tomé and Principé (cocoa).

Chapter 15: Republic of Congo, Gabon, Central African Republic, Cameroon, Chad, Equatorial Guinea, São Tomé and Principé

Republic of Congo

Mme Guili Tsoumou-Gavouka is the director of communication at the UN Development Programme (UNDP) in Congo's capital, Brazzaville. She reports that the traders and merchants of Brazzaville paid a heavy price during the successive waves of civil wars that gripped that country over the past decade, often losing all the tools of their trade to looters and destruction. Before the war in 1994, Lydie Mouyokakani started a small business, Farila, which produced a highly nutritional flour that mothers could use in food preparation during the weaning process (at the time, mothers were using imported cornstarch or a fermented paste that is widely available but nutritionally lacking). Business had been good and Farila was producing 3,000 sacks of flour every month. The war wiped out the business, and when the war ended Mouyokakani found herself with no capital to restart it. Through a grant from UNDP's Community Action Project, which was aimed at reviving and promoting small businesses, she was able to recruit three employees and buy the necessary equipment, including a roaster, a crusher and a drier, to get back into business. Farila now offers two additional varieties of flour. In addition to Farila Maize and Soya, there is Farizso (corn/rice) and Foufou Riche (containing cassava, manioc and soya). To market her flours, Mouyokakani demonstrates the nutritional benefits of the Farila products. She says mothers now use Farila, not only for their babies, but for baking cakes as well. Production is still at only half the pre-war level, or about 1,500 sacks per month, but Mouyokakani reports that 'you can find Farila in every district of Brazzaville'. Each sack costs 250 CFA francs (US$0.42) and, on average, she sells 900 sacks of flour a month. The total revenues from the flour amount to 220,000 CFA francs, all on an initial investment of 30,000 CFA francs.

Gabon

After American biologist J Michael Fay of the New York-based Wildlife Conservation Society completed his 2,000 mile hike across central Africa in 2000, he began an even harder task — lobbying to save the wildest places he had seen. Twenty months later in an August 2002 meeting with Gabon's government ministers, Fay described the extraordinary biological riches residing in the trackless forests, the remote mountains and the inland and coastal waters of Gabon. He explained the extraordinary opportunity — an economic as well as conservation opportunity, considering the potential earning from ecotourism — that might be seized by protecting those riches with a network of 13 national parks. Fay and others persuaded Omar Bongo, president of Gabon, to set aside 11,292 square miles, 11 per cent of Gabon, as protected national parkland, a remarkable gift to conservation. Since then, Gabon has received help from developed nations and from some non-governmental organisations like the Wildlife Conservation Society, Conservation International and the World Wildlife Fund. With continued help, Gabon is creating the training programmes, the infrastructural developments and the management and enforcement regimes necessary to make the park gambit a tangible success, both in economic terms (through ecotourism) and for conservation.

Having no existing park service before the announcement, and virtually no infrastructure in place, gives Gabon the unique opportunity to build something truly world-class from the onset. President Bongo hopes the new parks will make tourism a viable alternative to logging. For Gabon, he sees a future based on enjoying nature, not exploiting it. He says, 'By creating these national parks, we will develop a viable alternative to simple exploitation of natural resources that will promote the preservation of our environment. Already there is a broad consensus that Gabon has the potential to become a natural Mecca, attracting pilgrims from the four points of the compass in search of the last remaining natural wonders on earth.'

(Source: www.gabonnationalparks.com; and David Quammen. 'Saving Africa's Eden', *National Geographic*, September 2003)

The World Bank International Finance Corporation's privatisation advisory work specialises in providing advice to the governments of developing countries on the privatisation of state-owned infrastructure assets or the implementation of private-public partnerships. It covers existing businesses, as well as green field projects. The IFC has been at the forefront of advisory services in the water, power and telecommunications sectors. Prominent recent transactions include Cameroon's electricity utility (SONEL), Mauritania telecom (Mauritel), Uganda Telecom (UTL) and Gabon's water and electricity utility (SEEG).

Sophie Trémolet, senior consultant at Environmental Management Resources in London, reports that Veolia Water plays a leading role in Gabon, through Société d'Energie et d'Eau du Gabon (SEEG), which manages water and electricity services for the country's entire population of 1.1 million under a 20-year concession. Veolia Water, a subsidiary of Veolia Environment, is the leading global provider of water and wastewater services for municipal authorities, as well as industrial and service companies. It provides the entire range of outsourcing and design-build services, as well as equipment and systems. In 2002, Veolia Water was serving over 110 million people worldwide. With 77,600 employees, its revenues amounted to 13.3 billion euros. Veolia Water holds a 51 per cent interest in SEEG; the remaining shares were successfully sold to institutional investors (20 per cent), employees (5 per cent) and the general public (24 per cent), with a Golden Share reserved for the state. The Golden Share is one share held by the state, with special rights — two board members, without voting rights, but veto power on the sale of shares.

In Gabon, SEEG's targets for increasing coverage for water and electricity services have been met or exceeded. Since privatisation, Gabon's former money-losing utility has not only turned profitable, but has cut its water losses to 13 per cent and enabled public use of electricity to rise by more than 10 per cent and of water by more than 8 per cent. The now profitable company is regarded as a model for future privatisation in Africa. Hydroelectric stations account for 71 per cent of Gabon's electricity production. The primary sites are at Tchimbele (69 MW) and Kinguele (57.6 MW) on the M'Bei River and Poubara on the Ogooue River. There is an estimated total hydropower potential of 6 000 MW if all possible sites were to be developed.

In July 1997, SEEG signed a 20-year concession contract with the government of Gabon for operating both water and electricity services throughout the country. This was the first privatisation of a sub-Saharan water and electricity utility that entails full commitment for future investment by the private operator to upgrade and modernise the systems. The contract also introduced coverage targets for expanding service to previously unconnected rural areas. SEEG offers both water and electricity services, with the electricity business cross-subsidising the less developed water business and, in particular, electricity revenues from the two main towns, Libreville and Port-Gentil. Since 1997, the concessionaire has performed well in its existing service areas, often exceeding targets, but less progress has been made in more isolated areas.

During times of public ownership, SEEG grew out of private municipal companies that provided water and electricity services in the two main urban centres with half the population, Libreville (the capital) and Port-Gentil (the main port, serving the country's primary oil-producing region). Rapid expansion followed the nationalisation of SEEG in the early 1960s, so that by the time the company was privatised in 1997 it provided electricity to 39 centres and water to 32. Given Gabon's small population and dispersed rural communities (a population of just over 1 million people, with four people per square kilometre on average), some of these centres are tiny, with just over a thousand inhabitants.

Gabon can be seen as a relatively successful case of private sector participation, one in which strong government commitment has been key. Although the government was initially slow to pay its bills, undercutting the company's performance, it has been a good payer since signing a debt moratorium in 1999.

SEEG has consistently improved service quality and reduced tariffs substantially. It has already made 80 per cent of the contractually required investments, self-financing all of them. It has posted good profits since the start of its operations and paid its shareholders higher dividends every year (dividends rose from a contractually guaranteed 6.5 per cent of the share price in the first year of operations to 20 per cent in 2000). Finally, the company has managed to become truly independent in the face of potential political pressures, as demonstrated by the improved payment record of government customers.

SEEG is gradually fulfilling one of the main objectives of the contract, to expand services in small towns and rural areas. It has met or exceeded its targets for 2002 (and, in some cases, for 2015) in all regions except the centres that were previously not serviced. In centres where it missed the targets, the reason was often delays in government investments, either in roads (indispensable for reaching the villages) or in electricity transmission networks. Coverage targets have provided effective incentives for quickly increasing network density in newly served areas. The company has carried out active commercial campaigns in small villages to encourage people to connect, and has developed innovative technologies (such as pre-paid meters) to reduce the costs of providing services to these difficult to reach areas.

SEEG collaborates with small-scale informal providers, and uses them as 'service relays' in areas that are difficult to reach. This means that tolerance towards such providers may be a better business strategy than open confrontation. SEEG found that it was better to accept the laying of informal networks to extend their services rather than to try and suppress them — as long, of course, as the line eventually connects to a functioning meter. Collaboration with small-scale private operators is also required for innovative service solutions such as prepayment.

SEEG developed two types of prepayment meters for electricity. The system EDAN (Electricité des Années Nouvelles), used in urban areas (mainly Libreville and Port-Gentil), is more sophisticated and requires access to SEEG's computer network. With that system, each consumer is granted a 20-digit number corresponding to each payment — this number is specific to each meter and each particular customer. With such meters, the customer can have access to a lot of information that helps track consumption and manage demand. In rural areas, a much simpler system is used, requiring less technical input. Customers can purchase swipe cards from vendors — usually the village's shopkeeper. The swipe card is not meter-specific and the meter itself is less sophisticated, so they have access to less information. But, thanks to this system, people who previously might have had to walk for a day to go and pay their bill at the closest branch do not have to do so any more. Organising the distribution of such cards has proven challenging, but rewarding in commercial terms, as it reduces the need for regular visits by the utility's personnel. Pre-paid metering cuts the costs of customer management substantially for SEEG. Sophie Trémolet, however, believes the benefits of this system could be even greater if it were also used for water services.

Sophie Trémolet points out that in rural areas SEEG offers services far superior to those provided by the government outside SEEG's service area and at prices that remain affordable because of the high degree of cross-subsidisation. Although the government is nominally responsible for providing services in rural areas, lack of financial resources and poor technology choice has led to ineffectiveness. Overall, it appears that services provided by the government in rural areas are insufficient compared to need. In some areas, an extension of SEEG's perimeter could potentially offer a better alternative to government services, owing to the difficulties in organising maintenance services at village level. Although in theory SEEG's perimeter only includes villages with more than a thousand inhabitants, some villages with less than this are included. In fact, some villages have SEEG's electricity supplies and government's water supplies or (more rarely) vice-versa. Based on this observation, it appears that some rationalisation could be effected to open the possibility for SEEG, or other private sector operators, to offer private rural infrastructure where the Government has failed to do so.

(Source: Sophie Tremolet and Joanna Neale. 'Emerging lessons in private provision of infrastructure services in rural areas: Water and electricity in Gabon' report for World Bank PPIAF, Environmental Resources Management, September 2002)

Central African Republic

The Central African Regional Programme for the Environment (CARPE) is a 20-year regional initiative that was begun in September 1995 by USAID to address deforestation and biodiversity loss in the Congo Basin forest zone, in the middle of the African continent. One of the least developed regions of the world, the Congo Basin holds massive expanses of closed canopy tropical forest, second only to the Amazon Basin in area. Much of this forest remains relatively intact, yet unsustainable timber exploitation, shifting cultivation, urban expansion and other human themes are posing increasing threats to this globally-significant tropical forest resource. Loss of forest cover on this scale imposes serious risks of loss of biodiversity, and emission into the atmosphere of carbon dioxide previously locked up in forest biomass.

CARPE began in four countries, the Central African Republic, Equatorial Guinea, Gabon and Republic of Congo. Five other countries were later added: Burundi, Cameroon, Democratic Republic of Congo, Rwanda and São Tomé and Principé. In 2002, CARPE shifted its strategic focus and changed the location of its management functions. In its first phase, CARPE's partners focused on increasing their knowledge of central African forests and biodiversity, and on building institutional and human resources capacity. In the next phase, CARPE partners are applying and implementing sustainable natural resource management practices in the field with an added emphasis on the US contribution to the Congo Basin Forest Partnership (CBFP). CARPE is also improving environmental governance in the region, and strengthening natural resources' monitoring capacity.

In March 2004, when European timber companies, environmental groups, research organisations, and African forestry officials sat down to negotiate the future of logging in central Africa, the discussion took an unusual turn, reports Curtis Runyan, managing editor of WRI Features, an international news features service on environment and development issues.. After years of debating how to track logging practices in remote African rainforests, industry groups invited Global Forest Watch (GFW) to start keeping tabs on their logging operations. 'It's a big step; the logging companies are asking us to monitor them and their practices in Africa,' says Dr Ralph Ridder, deputy director of World Resources Institute's GFW. 'This is a breakthrough for improving the management of central Africa's forests.' WRI is an independent non-profit organisation with a staff of more than 100 scientists, economists, policy experts, business analysts, statistical analysts, mapmakers and communicators working to protect the Earth and improve people's lives.

The central African rainforest is threatened by poor governance and forest management. Illegal activities are commonplace, logging often extends beyond concession boundaries or into protected areas, and harvests often surpass the allowable timber cut. Widespread corruption in the region has been an obstacle to instituting better practices. Logging companies are under growing pressure from consumers in the European Union to ensure that the timber they sell is responsibly harvested. Some European countries are moving towards closing markets to all tropical timber lacking a certificate of legal origin. Consequently, industry is concerned that it may lose sales in European markets unless it develops a legitimate system to document forest management practices.

A number of more progressive logging companies approached GFW to serve as an independent monitor. GFW has partnered with the InterAfrican Forest Industries Association (IFIA), the World Conservation Union (IUCN), and the World Wildlife Fund to develop a monitoring system that can independently document the industry's logging practices in the region, and highlight the companies that are making the most significant strides toward sustainability. The higher prices for timber paid in European markets provides an incentive for companies to improve their practices to retain access to these markets. Ridder says, 'When the monitoring process is up and running, it could be a win-win for the forests and the companies. These companies expect that there will be a positive market reaction if they make these changes. They are convinced that the better-acting companies will rise to the top of the market.'

To ensure transparency and neutrality, the industry has agreed to allow its logging data to be reviewed by GFW. 'Ideally, forest monitoring would be conducted in a way that is open and transparent to all parties. The best way to ensure this is to have a neutral third party conduct the monitoring in collaboration with governments, industry and non-governmental organisations. It is a monumental task in the Congo Basin, given the challenges facing countries there,' says WRI researcher Jim Beck. Stephen Cox, GFW's executive director says, 'This move by industry alone will not create sustainable forestry in central Africa, but it is a positive new development that could lead to a vast improvement in the management of Africa's rainforests.'

(Source: Curtis Runyan. 'Timber companies agree to oversight in Africa', *WRI Features*, 15 March 2004; http://newsroom.wri.org)

Cameroon

African Investment Corporation (AIC) has made a firm commitment to sustaining Africa's economic growth. Founded by Joseph Tegue in 2000, AIC is an international business development enterprise that offers consultancy services in Cameroon and has corporation agreements and working relationships with major US export finance banks and multilateral financial institutions through which it packages, sources and procures finance facilities from the US to local companies. AIC has been particularly involved within the US Export Import Bank financing programmes and has successfully sourced US$40 million worth of financing to companies in Cameroon.

As a consulting firm, AIC also helps loan recipients adopt management strategies which will enable them to pay back; carries out due diligence on behalf of the lenders, and conducts market research to identify competitive US sources for their customers' products or machinery and develop related marketing or business plans and feasibility reports to support their applications. In 2002, an Ex-Im Bank Short Term Financing helped a company that imports fish regain financial stability and made it one of the biggest fish importers in Cameroon. Quality makes for expertise.

AIC has made a firm commitment to providing quality services consistently through innovative and scientific methods, working closely with accounting, legal and credit reporting firms to provide suppliers and lenders with accurate information and ratings on local businesses. AIC has also set up a quality management firm, Compatible Qse that prepares companies for certification to international norms.

In a bid to bring global perspectives and experience to the services they offer, AIC is also networking with such international organisations as the Corporate Council on Africa, the US department of Agriculture, Export Canada, (a governmental agency that provides financing for Canadian companies that export products), and is the Commonwealth Business Council's selected partner for Cameroon.

This experience, coupled with intra-African trade and regional economic development goals, has led AIC to business opportunities in Gabon, Niger, Nigeria, Senegal and Chad where they and Canadian partners working with the different governments, are realising a project for the construction of low-cost housing units worth about US$1 billion. AIC is also currently working with the Port Management Association of west and central Africa.

AIC also works closely with WESGRO, the official trade and investment promotion agency for the Western Cape Province in South Africa and is also a member of the Indo-African society for promotion of investment from India into Africa. AIC provides multilateral financial institutions and exporters with a platform for people-to-people contact and business-to-business interaction, between lenders, exporters and African buyers.

(Source: www.africaninvest.biz)

Heineken is the most international brewer in the world. The Heineken brand is sold in more than 170 countries and the company owns over 115 breweries in more than 65 countries. It has confidence in the future of Africa. Thomas de Man, Heineken's managing director responsible for sub-Saharan Africa, says his company believes that in the long term Africa will be a good continent for the beer business. But growth requires a professional approach in all aspects of the beer business — technologically, financially and commercially. To underline this, in 2003 Heineken's affiliated company, Nigerian Breweries, commissioned a 3.5 million hectolitre high tech brewery in Enugu at an investment of 250 million euro. Heineken creates its own professionalism through the training and development of employees and by recruiting and selecting young, promising Africans who aspire to a career in the brewing business. Heineken is a major employer in Africa, directly employing over 10,000 people (but, given that many in Africa with regular salaries salary support as many as ten others, over 100,000 people could actually be dependent on Heineken breweries). Moreover, Heineken indirectly gives work to suppliers of goods and services, transport providers, farmers and shopkeepers. The company also works hard to ensure that its brewing activities do not affect the environment and surrounding communities in harmful ways.

Each brewery has its own facility through which Heineken actively promotes employee schooling and training. Larger regional facilities are located in West Africa (Lagos, Nigeria), as well as in central Africa (Kinshasa, Congo). Courses run from one week to two years and cover the entire scope of the modern brewery business. Heineken must attract, develop and retain young African talent if it is to be successful. The company is always looking for the best African graduates from leading universities in Europe and North America who are interested in management traineeships in their home countries. Candidates must be flexible, dedicated, willing to learn and have a strong sense of integrity. Heineken needs results-oriented people with a strong work ethic who would enjoy being part of the Heineken culture in a continent full of contrasts. Potential Heineken managers must look beyond the borders of their nations and aspire to international job postings. As management trainees, they will learn the basics of the brewing business. Through training courses, actual experience, and with the advice of senior management mentors, they will be on their way to a promising career as an international manager.

The rates at which Heineken compensates its employees are among the highest in each African country. But Heineken's responsibility goes beyond that. In countries where public health care is not sufficient or inaccessible, it provides medical services and medicines (generally free of charge), to employees and their families. In practice, this means that there are medical departments on the premises of all Heineken's African breweries. More than 20 Heineken-run clinics are operating in Africa. In addition to prevention, Heineken has expanded its health care to include HIV/AIDS treatment. Owing to their complexity, the introduction of HIV/AIDS treatment services took place country by country. The programme was first rolled out in Burundi and Rwanda, and then in Congo Brazzaville and the Democratic Republic of Congo. The introduction was completed in 2003 in all locations with adequate infrastructure. Staff and their families who are within reach of a Heineken medical clinic now have access to full HIV/AIDS facilities, including the most advanced blood tests and latest disease-fighting drug cocktails.

(Source: www.heinekeninternational.com)

The Castel Group has beer, carbonated soft drink and mineral water interests, primarily in the francophone countries of west and central Africa. Its operations cover Angola, Benin, Burkina Faso, Cameroon, Central African Republic, Chad, Côte d'Ivoire, Democratic Republic of Congo, Ethiopia, Gabon, Mali, Tunisia, Morocco, Mozambique, Niger, Senegal and Togo. In the year ended 31 December 2000, the Castel Group had total beer production of 9.1 million hectolitres, its entire beer production comprising clear beer. It had total carbonated soft drink and mineral water production of 7.3 million hectolitres.

Veteran businessman Pierre Castel is keen to explore opportunities. The French entrepreneur, whose beverages group has an alliance with South African Breweries (now SABMiller, the second-largest brewer in the world), shuns publicity. Born in 1926 in Berson in south western France, the seventh of nine children, Castel left school at the age of 13 to work on the vineyards to help his family. He says this helped nurture the two values, unpretentiousness and perseverance, that have helped him build the Castel Group into France's biggest wine merchant. At the age of 23, Castel and his three brothers started a small wine trading company, the Castel Group, in 1949 in the Médoc cellars in Bordeaux. They grew the group internally during the 1950s and 1960s. Driven by a gut feeling that the African market might be receptive to his company's products, Castel set sail in 1950 for Senegal and Côte d'Ivoire. He was correct.

In 1990, he tightened his group's hold over francophone Africa's beer and carbonated soft-drinks market by buying brewer Brasseries et Glacières Internationales from Axa, the French financial services multinational. Back in France, Castel ventured into the bottled-water business in 1993. He quickly grew subsidiary Neptune into France's third largest by buying several water brands from Nestlé, the Swiss food and beverages multinational. 'Africa is a continent I know well and there are still a lot of opportunities,' says Castel who, despite his age, intends remaining actively involved in the running of the group. 'I have no intention of slowing down,' he says. Control of the Castel Group is likely to remain within the family, as Castel's nephews are also involved in running it.

In February 2001, South African Breweries and the Castel Group, Africa's two largest beverage companies, consolidated their positions in Africa through a pan-African beverage alliance. Pierre Castel says that the strategic alliance emphasises the commitment of both groups to the African continent. The respective operations are geographically complementary, and their alliance provides scope for further development across the continent. The ties between the two groups enable the pooling of their resources, which presents new opportunities for investment and enhances each company's prospects for growth. Pierre Castel is confident that the close relationship with SABMiller will result in faster growth for both groups in Africa in their chosen beverage markets.

(Source: Jabulane Sikhakane. 'Quiet clink to African deal', Johannesburg: *Financial Mail*, 30 March 2001)

Zogo Andela, who heads Andela Group, has seen his tea bag factories in Cameroon thrive since he began packaging tea in 1983. His initial aim was to develop the sector for exports and bring Cameroon's tea industry up to par with traditional rivals. 'Today we're in very diverse sectors. Besides the tea, we ventured into the fishing and lumber industries,' says Andela. A firm believer in African potential, Andela is convinced that, at the end of the day, only quality counts. 'We will continue to fight for the quality of our products,' he says. The Andela Group employs 1,200 people in Cameroon and company ranks could rise if there is breakthrough into target markets in the US and Europe. The fishing side of the business manages a fleet of 30 shrimp trawlers, one of Africa's largest. 'Cameroonian shrimp has a very good reputation abroad and because of this prices are going up,' says Andela. But the group's main export offensive involves wooden flooring systems. Andela came to the lumber industry out of a personal interest in woodcarving and he acts as something of a patron to local artists. The group is involved in the second and third transformation stages of wood in Cameroon, especially parquetry. Andela sees both technical and financial advantages in a partnership with American retailers. 'We will have to respect their norms, which will be a definite plus for our companies,' says Andela.

The Résidence Hôteliere La Falaise in Douala was started in 1985. It is part of an international chain of hotels owned by Michael Monkam. Résidence is a unique concept in Douala. The 133 air-conditioned apartments are small residences suited for business people and tourists. Monkam's daughter Jeannette, director of Résidence, says, 'We chose apartments rather than rooms as they are more spacious, allowing our guests to receive acquaintances or business relations without having to disturb the privacy of the bedroom.' Guests can cook in their own kitchen but there is always the option of relaxing or dining in the hotel bar-restaurant or taking advantage of room service. 'Foreigners coming here tend to be very surprised,' Monkam notes. 'They feel quite at home.' Résidence is near the Wouri River, five minutes from the airport, in the heart of the commercial and business centre of Douala, close to official buildings and the city's nightlife, and 80 per cent of Résidence guests are businesspeople. Asked about the future, Monkam replies, 'I want more international clients at our three-star hotel.'

Gisèle Yitamben from Cameroon founded the Association pour le Soutien et l'Appui a la Femme Entrepreneur (ASAFE) based on her belief that African women could develop into successful entrepreneurs if provided with business training and development services, alternative financing and access to e-commerce. ASAFE today supports thousands of women entrepreneurs in Cameroon, Guinea, Benin, Chad and the Democratic Republic of Congo. It has had to grow quickly to respond to the demand it has generated. But

Gisèle has found few second-stage financing mechanisms that will allow ASAFE to scale up as needed. Today, ASAFE is actively engaged with technology companies and business incubators to help African entrepreneurs overcome the digital divide.

After graduating from high school in Yaoundé in 1976, Yitamben studied economics in France, and got an MBA in the USA. On her return in 1982, she became a lecturer at the Pan-African Institute for Development in Douala. When she lost her teaching job, she decided to become a consultant, and through the projects that she dealt with she developed expertise in a wide range of women's business activities in Cameroon. She was impressed by the business savvy, vibrancy and capability for financial planning of the women. In 1986, Gisèle Yitamben completed a study for the African Development Bank, which found that women in Africa were systematically deprived of credit because their businesses were too small and they couldn't furnish collateral. Believing that many of these women could develop into successful entrepreneurs, she mobilised a group of professionals and businesswomen from Douala to support women's entrepreneurship. While fighting for legal permission to establish ASAFE, the group began providing business services to micro and small entrepreneurs in the region. In 1989, ASAFE was legally established.

In 1992, ASAFE launched the Femme Credit Epargne, a credit and savings service designed specifically for low-income women. ASAFE's teams of extension workers train women in management, pricing and marketing skills, always drawing on the women's knowledge of their socio-cultural environment. With 5,000 members, many of whom have built successful businesses, ASAFE is connecting its entrepreneurs to one another and to larger markets through technology. Working with the International Telecommunications Union and Chell.com, a business incubator, ASAFE has developed a leading e-commerce web portal for African businesswomen who are exporting products such as crafts and dried fruits to Europe, and translating documents for American educational institutions.

ASAFE takes in more than US$8,000 a month for translation work alone. ASAFE is also working with Cisco, the major US company, to provide networking training to members looking for new job opportunities in the very promising area of local and long distance computer networking, while seeking to expand well beyond its membership base to position itself as one of the leading Internet and e-commerce service providers in west Africa. 'Many African countries are still suspicious of information technology,' explains Gisèle Yitamben. 'They haven't understood the immense power of the internet. The solution to poverty among the womenfolk and their children is in information. There is no limit to our future.'

For 2002, the Schwab Foundation selected Gisèle Yitamben as one of the world's Outstanding Social Entrepreneurs. Upon accepting her award, Yitamben emphasised, 'We want to shift the focus from poverty reduction to wealth creation. The fight against poverty has existed for a long time, with the perverse effect of disempowering those it seeks to help. Shifting the focus enables us to prevent creating a mentality that reinforces the acceptance of poverty and enables us to recognise our capacity for change. Recognition of talent and ability is the foundation for creativity and the source of all wealth creation. As social entrepreneurs, we are investigating this explosion of creativity for all those we work for. Those who discover their gifts and their talents learn to confront obstacles through the creation of real outcomes'.

The category for non-profit organisations was introduced into the 2005 Africa SMME awards, and ASAFE won the category. Noting that ASAFE grew from an educational institution to one that offers entrepreneurs support services, including microfinance, Professor Nicholas Biekpe, head of the Africa Centre for Investment Analysis at the University of Stellenbosch Business School, and host of the Africa SMME Awards event held in Johannesburg in October 2005, believes that the development of best practices in the SMME sector could vastly alleviate poverty. 'Once a few key issues are in place, small businesses can thrive with relatively little effort. Yet we find that little is done to secure these enabling deliverables.' Among the factors that need to be addressed are excessive red tape when registering a business, as well as poor access to information and rule of law.

(Source: www.acia.sun.ac.za)

In 1999, Robert Jourdain, a well-known figure since 1954 in francophone Africa for his accomplishments in the poultry field, was officially given a merit award. In 1994-95, when Cameroon was going through a very difficult period, this bold entrepreneur took on a challenge considered unworkable by many. Against the advice of numerous experts and international financial organisations, he decided to re-open one of the three former state poultry complexes that had been forced to shut down. With the persistent support of Canadian Debt Initiative (CDI), he won the bet and succeeded in privatising and renovating the company. With two increases in capital since 1995, and annual production of more than two million chicks, the Mvog-Betsi poultry complex is an increasingly viable concern. The awarding of the Cameroon Knight of Merit on March 23 1999, by Hamadjoda Adjoudji, minister of breeding, fishing and animal industries, also honoured the efforts made by CDI to develop the poultry sector in Cameroon.

Ashundep Ettanki is building the base of remote rural economies in Africa by showing villagers how to pool their resources, learn ways around burdensome government regulations and utilise mass communications to coordinate their activities, for 69 per cent of Africans live in rural areas, of which perhaps as many as half live in areas best described as remote and isolated. To reinvigorate the economies of remote areas in Africa, Ashundep Ettanki is developing a model for promoting cooperative savings and production activities for farmers, incorporating credit formation, community re-investment and radio communications. Now piloting the model in his home region of Mamfe, Ashundep hopes, over the longer term, to see his approach to the development of remote rural areas applied throughout sub-Saharan Africa.

Ashundep hopes to reverse the feelings of isolation and, therefore, powerlessness, that characterise the more remote rural parts of Africa that have experienced deteriorating economic conditions. His approach involves stimulating savings and credit formation for investment by simplifying burdensome government regulations and the regular use of radio communication to spread the word about successful ventures. Since almost everyone listens to radio, Ashundep deploys it to create a virtual economic community among remote rural dwellers. Ashundep believes that with this regular broadcasting of collective endeavours, the pervading attitudes of hopelessness and fatalism will give way to a new self-image of action and achievement.

Much of rural sub-Saharan Africa, containing perhaps a third of the sub-continent's people, remains isolated by poor roads, the absence of other infrastructure including electricity and telephone and few, if any, government health services, education and security or commercial banks, brokers and transporters. Heavy seasonal rains render travel difficult at the best of times, making it sometimes impossible. In Ashundep's home region, for example, during the rainy season travel by road to the nearest town can take several days. In this context there are few opportunities for a local economy to grow. Farmers struggle to transport their produce to market. Very few goods are available for sale. There is little incentive to save, no savings or other banking institutions, and no tradition of saving to invest in the community. In those rare instances when an initiative to create a financial institution does take place, it is stymied by leaden and unresponsive government bureaucracy.

Ashundep introduces the practice of cooperative saving and investing by inviting villagers to pool their resources to buy a useful tool, such as a yam processing machine. Because the savings plan has a clear investment objective, it can overcome the initial distrust among villagers. The next step is to bring several villages together to scale up their purchases. And finally, he formalises the resulting organisation by helping it to register as a Common Initiative Group (CIG), a legal category that confers tax advantages and is a prerequisite for public or private sector credit. This involves yet another leap of faith by the villagers, this one prompted by their past success and Ashundep's patiently presented case for the benefits from moving to a formal status with the government and commercial institutions.

To register his projects as CIGs, Ashundep had to persuade government to modify the cumbersome registration procedures that had effectively blocked small rural farmers from accessing formal credit. Ashundep's projects were the first from the Mamfe area to be registered.

During his numerous visits to seats of government to convince officials to change regulations, Ashundep also took the opportunity to create a new programme for farmers with the regional radio station. The programme involves regular notices for upcoming meetings and activities of the CIGs as well as news about other events of interest to the small farmers (market opportunities and prices, government policies, and so on). The most popular element in the radio programme, however, has been a regular series of profiles of the activities and achievements of these new CIGs, in both English and French. These success stories have both affirmed the new CIGs and created widening interest in the region.

As a result of the success of the pilot project and the positive public attention it has received, Ashundep and his team have been asked to replicate this approach in other areas of Cameroon. His efforts have also caught the attention of institutions in neighbouring countries looking for ways to revitalise their rural economies as well. As part of his rural development strategy, Ashundep conducts workshops to train local residents to manage these cooperative associations so that he and his team are able to move from one area to another, forming new groups. As a way to ensure the sustainability of the projects that he helps to initiate, Ashundep is laying the groundwork for organising barter and trade relationships among the member groups and other national and international organisations to secure export markets for their products.

Ashundep is now meticulously documenting his methodology for publication. Based on the growing success of his pilot efforts, he is convinced that the formula of radio communication, appropriately attuned to remote rural farmers, followed by modest levels of direct support, will enable the approach to spread quickly across the continent.

Ashundep is one of only two from his village chosen to attend university since Cameroon's independence in 1961. He owes that opportunity to the intercession of his elder sister, who recognised that her brother had exceptional ability and succeeded in persuading the village elders to lead a village-wide effort to raise the funds to send him to university. Ashundep keenly feels the obligation that he has to his village to give back for what he received. But his commitment to village development runs deeper than reciprocal obligation. When Ashundep was a young man he saw faded photographs of his village that showed it as a centre of major yam cultivation. Further research revealed that the village had once been a large exporter of yams. His nascent determination to promote development could now grow in the soil of a better past.

While at university, he remained secretary of his village association and led an entirely local effort to build a school in the village and provide teachers and materials. Eventually the school was certified by the government, which had earlier rejected the village's request for assistance with the project. This success whetted Ashundep's appetite for initiating social change, and taught him a studied scepticism about what one could expect from government.

Ashundep asked to study economics at university but was prevented from doing so because he lacked sufficient mathematical training. Instead he took a degree in mass communications and worked for a year at a Yaoundé-based newspaper after he graduated from university in Nigeria.

The following year he returned to his village to help his elder sister and address the needs of the people in his area. He started a simple group savings plan in which each household contributed 100 CFA (20 US cents) per week. The project collapsed when the members demanded their money back, saying that they feared Ashundep might be using it for some other purpose.

Ashundep showed the members that the village chief, who was holding the money in trust for the villagers, had their savings. They insisted on having their money returned, and it was refunded in full. Through analysing this initial disappointment, Ashundep lit upon the idea of beginning by working with the village to identify a specific investment objective, and only then introducing a savings scheme.

Ashundep is now 34 years old, and has a wife and four young children. He continues to write articles for newspapers, but his passions are the community development projects he has undertaken.

(Source: www.ashoka.org)

Groupe des JAADIC (Jeunes Agronomes Actifs pour le Développement Intégré au Cameroun) was founded by Tsafack Djiague, an agricultural engineer, in 1999. All members at the initial stage were soldiers and volunteers. The objective was to give young Cameroonians self-employment. JAADIC is a company pioneered by young agricultural engineers which is initiating projects in agro-farming with the purpose of reducing unemployment, eradicating poverty, and contributing to sustainable development. JAADIC is active in many rural areas, favouring the integration of women and children providing the latter with education to enable them to be more easily rehabilitated in society. JAADIC aims its activities to satisfy foreign markets in order to grow its capacity to recruit a maximum number of graduates in the business. The opening of an office in the agro-ecological zone of Cameroon contributed to the halt of the intellectual exodus through the use of as many graduates as possible. Presently, JAADIC helps farmers in community development projects by identifying potential markets for agricultural produce, initiating projects for poultry, bees, pigs, cows, maize, cabbage and potatoes, and organising seminars and training sessions for farmers. Tsafack Djiague says future JAADIC projects will concern developing two major swamps for all-season production, helping communities on their projects to reach their potential, solving logistical difficulties and improving on the organisation of farmers into cooperatives for a better bargaining position in world markets. In 2004, the JAADIC received from the government 25 hectares of land for reforestation and they are looking for a financial partner or for a donor to implement the project.

In November 2004, JAADIC spun off the revenue generating part of the business, mostly agro-business and agro-consult into ABAC (Agriculture d'affaire et Consultations Agronomiques). They still have as their objective job creation for youth and women, but they also hope to halt the intellectual exodus. The objective of agro-business is to create farm enterprises to supply specific local and foreign markets, and to create their own stores. They are looking for partners in joint ventures to supply 100 per cent organic coffee to South Africa, the United States and Europe. Such coffee is controlled in the field by an agricultural engineer, for quality is the priority in foreign markets. They are also producing organic legumes, knowing that there is strong demand in the European and US markets. ABAC is looking for investors to provide better opportunities for farmers by helping build farm capacities. The potential markets for farmers are excellent since they have land which is capable of producing in all seasons. The coffee season starts at the beginning of January and ends at the end of June, and the total volume they can presently supply is 4,000 tons of 100 per cent organic coffee.

In agro-consulting, ABAC is aligned to the principles of High Performance Business (HPB). ABAC knows that companies are looking for dramatic performance improvement and that aggressive performance improvements present tough challenges. Restructuring creates uncertainty and a short-term outlook, and many of the traditional management approaches do not lead to sustained competitive advantage. HPB offers clients dramatic and quantifiable performance improvement; helps the client articulate and quantify performance improvement objectives and priorities; recognises that a primary source of performance improvement is though the re-design of the main business processes (BPR); and links process re-design to resources and organisation though a broad integrative framework.

Sustained performance improvement is achieved through multifaceted co-management programmes. ABAC offers four HPB products, or services, to clients: a diagnostic to identify key opportunities to improve business performance; business re-design to plan for business improvement; co-management to enable the implementation of a re-design of the main business processes plan; and change management to integrate the process of organisational change throughout the re-design effort. Each service is attractive to the market, despite intense competition.

As general director of ABAC, Tsafack Djiague says the company looks forward to representing South African, American and European companies in Cameroon in selling agricultural products such as organic coffee. ABAC can establish joint ventures. It has developed a good strategy to work effectively in agro-consulting in central Africa. There is a market and ABAC needs merely to reinforce the team and logistical equipment. ABAC will welcome investors from South Africa, America and Europe.

SURF has been providing marine support to the offshore drilling and production industry for nearly three decades. With a work force of over 400, and customers in France, Nigeria, Cameroon, Gabon, Congo and Angola, SURF operates a fleet of 109 workshops including straight supply vessels, anchor handling tug supply vessels and crew boats. The fleet includes 82 water jet powered crew boats, three conventional twin and triple screw crew boats and 24 larger vessels comprising eight anchor handling tug supply vessels, eight platform supply vessels, two multipurpose DP2 straight supply vessels, and six oil terminal tugs. A strong support structure covers all marine, personnel and engineering aspects of the business. Bases are located in Port-Harcourt (Nigeria), Douala (Cameroon), Port-Gentil (Gabon), Pointe-Noire (Congo) and Luanda (Angola).

SURF's benchmark services are based on efficient equipment, skilled personnel and high standards. In recent years, SURF has strengthened its operational performance in several key areas. Thanks to a strong shipbuilding programme, the fleet has been expanded, rejuvenated and upgraded. Special emphasis has been placed on meeting the unique demands of deepwater field development. The fleet now includes highly specialised vessels with deepwater capabilities ranging from platform supply and anchor handling to dynamic positioning and ROV (remote operated vessel) support. SURF has also gained market momentum by forming alliances with other leading offshore technology companies. A joint venture with the Angolan national oil company SONANGOL led to the creation of SONASURF for supporting deepwater offshore operations in Angola. Three vessels have already been deployed to support dynamically positioned rigs in the GIRASSOL field. SURF has also joined forces with INTEROIL Services Limited to provide crew boat and supply boat services to the Nigerian market. Continued development of this alliance strategy will enable SURF to undertake more complex projects and increase the scope of expertise offered to customers.

(Source: www.surf.fr)

Chad

The Chad Cameroon Petroleum Development and Pipeline Project, an ExxonMobil-led consortium, completed one of the largest private-sector investments, US$3.5 billion, in sub-Saharan Africa in 2003. The Miandoum I well started pumping from a one-billion-barrel oil reservoir in Chad. The crude flows 663 miles through a pipeline that slithers under hippo-filled rivers, parched savannahs, tropical rain forests and the hunting grounds of the Bakola pygmies, before emptying into storage tanks anchored in the Atlantic surf off the coast of Cameroon. The Chad-Cameroon project opens a vital new front in the battle against poverty. Chad's share of the oil money is to be spent on development projects such as schools, clinics and rural roads.

Chad's revenue is sent to an escrow account in a bank in London and 10 per cent of the revenue immediately goes into an international investment fund for future generations, to ensure that there is development money even after the expected 30-year life of the oil field. The remaining money moves to two commercial banks in N'Djamena, where an oversight committee of Chadian religious, political and community leaders apportions 80 per cent to pay for development projects in priority areas such as education, health, housing and rural infrastructure. The rest is divided up, according to a specific formula, for other needs. Dinanko Ngomibe, the budget director in Chad's Ministry of Finance in 2003, said that the revenue-management plan is a good thing. If it works, Chad will have drinkable water, hospitals and schools. Tom Erdimi, Chad's national coordinator of the petroleum project in 2003, said that Chad wants to be a pioneer in Africa.

At its 2003 annual meeting, ExxonMobil said that the two-year construction project had triggered a 10 per cent jump in Chad's gross domestic product. Exxon had improved more than 300 miles of roads and bridges, and had bought more than US$600 million in local goods and services from Chadian and Cameroonian companies. Esso Chad, EssonMobil's affiliate in Chad, has compensated land users for any effects and compensated villages that suffered a communal loss such as the destruction of fruit trees. Several villagers in Madjo received brick-making equipment. They now make and sell baked bricks for homes that can last 25 years, about three times longer than the traditional mud huts. So far, about 20 Madjo residents have replaced their old dwellings. In other villages, residents have started community gardens or bought sewing machines to make and sell clothes. In the production phase the project will require about a thousand employees and contractors, with over 65 per cent being nationals. During the construction phase of the project employment peaked at over 13,000 workers with over 80 per cent Chadian and Cameroonian nationals. The Chad-Cameroon project is part of Exxon's aggressive expansion plans in Africa. Exxon's 2002 net production base of about 350,000 barrels a day is expected to grow dramatically as a slate of exploration and production efforts in Angola, Nigeria, Equatorial Guinea, the Republic of Congo — as well as Chad and Cameroon — come online.

(Source: Roger Thurow. 'In war on poverty, pipeline in Chad plays unusual role', *The Wall Street Journal*, 24 June 2003)

Issa Doubgous, the general director of Diagnose Auto in N'Djaména, says he has funded a major expansion of his auto repair and rental business by gaining a contract with the project. In addition to car repairs, his business also rents cars, makes licence plates, and helps make arrangements for business and tourist travellers. The shop was created in 1982 and has grown to 32 employees and a rental fleet of 60 vehicles.

The company Climat Tchad installed and repaired air conditioners for the project, working in N'Djaména and in the oilfield area. Assistant manager Dimanche Ongtoin reports that the company has grown from five to 18 employees since starting work with the project. He says the extra business made it possible for him to buy a stock of air conditioners to keep in the warehouse, improving his chances for making sales. His firm also purchased power tools and other machines that make its work more efficient and profitable.

Manager Abdelkader Badaoui operates Alif, a furniture and decorating company in N'Djaména. Since founding the business six years ago, he says it has grown from its beginnings making traffic signs and billboards, and now makes furniture in wood and wrought iron, and has sold kitchen furniture and housing renovation services to the project. The company has been able to purchase two trucks to make deliveries.

In 2000, the International Finance Corporation (IFC), the private sector arm of the World Bank Group, provided US$200 million in A and B loans to the Chad-Cameroon Pipeline Project. Along with its largest ever single investment in Africa, IFC assumed responsibility for the Chad Small and Medium Enterprise Programme to accelerate development of the local private sector and ensure that the benefits from oil production accrue to the citizens of Chad. Hence, the SME Program was started in 2001/2002 to complements the work of the pipeline's sponsors, increase the participation of local enterprises in economic activity generated by the pipeline, and help better prepare local businesses for the new economy the project is creating. More concretely, the programme's assistance to small businesses includes supporting local entrepreneurship capacity building, facilitating financing opportunities in a country where financing is usually unavailable for periods of longer than a year, creating agri-businesses and promoting a more favourable business enabling environment in Chad.

Access to finance for micro and small businesses is an important component of the SME Programme. IFC continues to play a leading role in support of Finadev Tchad, the only accredited micro-finance institution in Chad, which was established in 2003 with technical assistance funding from IFC. As Finadev Tchad develops its institutional capacity, it is making an increasingly significant contribution to the availability of credit for micro-entrepreneurs, particularly in southern Chad. FINADEV serves three types of clientele: women micro-entrepreneurs (mainly traders); small enterprises; and low- and medium-income employees in the formal sector (who seek micro-credit for housing improvement or to establish a micro-enterprise). FINADEV serves over 2,300 clients, including about 1,300 women-owned enterprises.

In March 2005, the IFC inaugurated the Enterprise Centre in Chad, a partnership with the local Chamber of Commerce. The EC's first pillar rests on a massive local entrepreneur capacity building and development programme which is being delivered through the facilities of the EC in N'Djamena, with satellite centres located in Doba, Moundou and Sahr in the south. Local entrepreneur recruitment is entirely demand driven, with more incentives given to registration through targeted supplier development (linkages) with large companies, especially those active in the petroleum sector. A second pillar of the EC promotes the establishment of business linkages between producing entrepreneurs on the one hand, and buyers (primarily ESSO/Exxon-Mobil and its subcontractors) on the other hand. Hence, using a cadre of local training and support officers trained by the IFC, the EC contributes an integrated package of training and mentoring programmes for micro and small enterprises. In October 2005, the EC embarked on an innovative project to provide assistance to potential Exxon-Mobil bidders. Through the EC, potential suppliers are offered high speed internet access, and receive support and training throughout the electronic bidding process.

The focus of the IFC's strategy for Africa targets three areas: a much more active engagement with small businesses by increasing technical, managerial, and financial support to micro, small, and medium enterprises; improving investment climate issues that currently impede private sector growth by fostering improved dialogue between the public and the private sector; and promoting private investment in infrastructure and related services (including utilities, physical infrastructure, and telecommunications) to enhance the quality of services to businesses and the public. To underpin IFC's capacity to be a catalyst for sustainable private sector investment and growth in Africa, in July 2003, IFC launched a new technical assistance programme, the Private Enterprise Partnership for Africa (PEP Africa).

Equatorial Guinea

Equatorial Guinea has one of the fastest growing economies in Africa, with GDP growth in double digits. The economy is based on hydrocarbon production and forestry, which together account for around 97 per cent of total exports and have replaced reliance on the traditional production and export of cocoa and agricultural products. The economic expansion brought about by the establishment of petroleum production has permitted an acceleration of the infrastructure improvement programme and investment initiatives to diversify the economy. Malabo and Bata are the main sea ports and two other ports are used for timber exports and fishing. A new deep-water harbour and freeport is under development at Luba on Bioko Island.

(Source: www.equatorialoil.com)

Starting in 2007, Equatorial Guinea LNG Holdings Ltd (EGLNG) will produce 3.4 million tonnes per annum of liquefied natural gas (LNG) from the LNG liquefaction plant being developed by EGLNG on Bioko Island. Bechtel Engineering is overseeing the building of the US$1.5 billion liquefied natural gas project for EGNLG. The project is one of a string of plants Bechtel has built or is building to help meet surging demand for LNG, a highly compressed liquid form of natural gas that can be shipped economically in ocean tankers to distant markets. It will include everything needed to compress, cool and liquefy gas from a nearby field to minus 160 degrees Celsius, along with refrigerated tanks to store it and marine shipping facilities. When the project is completed, it will supply at least 3.4 million tonnes of energy to the market each year.

Construction began in 2004, and the plant is expected to be on-stream in October 2007. Steven Olerearnshaw, managing director of EGLNG, says that the venture employs 2,300 people, 850 of them locals, on the construction project. Feedstock gas for the project will be sourced primarily from the Marathon-operated offshore Alba Field. EGLNG is jointly owned by a subsidiary of Marathon Oil Corporation (60 per cent), the Sociedad de Gas de Guinea Ecuatorial (SONAGAS G.E) (25 per cent), Mitsui & Co., Ltd. (Mitsui) (8.5 per cent) and a subsidiary of Marubeni Corporation (Marubeni) (6.5 per cent). BG Gas Marketing Ltd (BGML), a wholly-owned subsidiary of BG Group plc, has signed a long-term agreement with EGLNG to purchase liquefied natural gas (LNG). The agreement provides for the supply of 3.4 million tonnes per annum of LNG for a period of 17 years, beginning in late 2007, from EGLNG's Bioko Island liquefaction plant.

The project promises an economic boost to Equatorial Guinea, which has a population of 1,014,000. It also could be a first step in creating a hub for gas and petroleum in the Gulf of Guinea, and could spur new energy production throughout West Africa, which in turn might be very good for companies like Bechtel.

(Source: www.bechtel.com)

Bata is Equatorial Guinea's second largest town and is also the capital of the continental territory. Bata alone is a macrocosm of what is happening all over Equatorial Guinea. The two parts of the country, the island of Bioko and the continental part, are a vast worksite. Previous visitors to Bata say the town has been radically transformed in the past few yeas. All the city's streets are now paved while the colonial buildings left by Spaniards in the 1960s, and abandoned, have been restored. The sea front is now a tourist's paradise with paved esplanades at the seafront. A new residential area is being constructed in the city's northern district of Asonga where a futuristic national assembly building, recently completed, dominates the skyline. Expensive houses are shooting out of the ground like mushrooms. Residents also say the banks are overflowing with liquid cash. Few participants can leave Bata with any doubt in their minds that Equatorial Guinea is set on becoming black Africa's Eldorado.

However, orphans and homeless children always need help everywhere in the world. In view of the misery of countless war orphans and homeless children after the Second World War, the Austrian Hermann Gmeiner initiated the construction of the world's first SOS Children's Village in the small Tyrolean town of Imst in 1949. SOS Children's Villages revolve around the effort to give children who have lost their parents, or who are no longer able to live with them, a permanent home and a stable environment.

In Equatorial Guinea, SOS Children's Village Bata is in the San Pedro de Lea district, about two kilometres from the centre of town. It was opened in January 2000, has a capacity of up to 100 children and consists of a total of ten family houses, plus a village director's house, an administration building and a house for the SOS aunts (SOS mothers-in-training who actively support the SOS mothers). It has a kindergarten and two schools, a primary and a secondary school. The SOS kindergarten can offer places to 30 children in six classrooms. It was opened in September 1996 and has a kitchen where warm meals are prepared for the children.

Up to 380 schoolchildren (boys and girls) can be taught at the SOS Hermann Gmeiner Primary School, which was opened in September 1998 and has ten classrooms, a library and office space. The Hermann Gmeiner Secondary School can offer 180 schoolchildren (boys and girls) a place. It opened in September 2002 and also has ten classrooms, a library and office space. The three schools are open to children from the SOS Children's Village, and to any child from the neighbourhood.

In 2001, an SOS medical centre was built to ensure efficient medical care for the people and to implement various preventive measures at a local level. The centre has a treatment room with beds, a consultation room, a laboratory, a dispensary and an operating theatre and delivery room. It also has a reception and administration area. Since it opened, up to 2,050 patients have been attended to each month.

SOS Children's Villages in southern and eastern Africa have geared their effort especially towards meeting the needs of families and young people affected by HIV/AIDS who are at a high risk of contracting HIV every day. Services offered include support to child- or grandparent-headed families, AIDS counselling and prevention, education and health services.

(Source: www.sos-childrensvillages.org)

São Tomé and Princípe

In April 2006, Chevron Oil was expected soon to disclose the results of an exploration well the company drilled off the West African coast, perhaps opening a new oil frontier and unleashing a gusher of revenue in the tiny island nation of São Tomé and Príncipe. A significant discovery would further underscore the growing importance of African oil supplies. It would be the first real test of a sweeping revenue-management law passed by São Tomé lawmakers hoping to avoid the so-called 'oil curse', whereby new oil wealth fails to improve living standards and instead leads to more poverty. São Tomé's measure, signed into law in 2004, requires transparent accounting of oil revenue and establishes an investment fund for a chunk of the money for the day when oil inevitably runs out. There was no guarantee Chevron would find oil, but industry experts agree that the acreage off São Tomé's coast holds huge potential. International development officials are banking on the former Portuguese colony as a model for how countries can avoid the corruption and mismanagement that newly discovered oil can often bring — especially in Africa, where petroleum riches have been squandered for decades. Even if Chevron does find oil, significant government revenue would not start pouring into São Tomé for several years.

(Source: Chip Cummins. 'Africa experiments with oil, *The Wall Street Journal*, 23 March 2006)

Entrepreneur Chris Hellinger is the proprietor of the Bom-Bom resort, an exclusive deep sea fishing, diving and eco-tourism tropical retreat on the island of Principé, a pristine island paradise. The island is lush, and the resort setting is beautiful, with bungalows set right onto the beach. The cost for the resort is all-inclusive, meaning that you only pay for excursions such as deep-sea fishing and scuba diving. There are 25 high quality fully air-conditioned and serviced chalets, a gymnasium/conference centre facility, resort shop, restaurant, fisherman's bar, licensed mini casino, fully-equipped fleet of deep sea fishing vessels and a marina and diving centre. All are serviced by a private power generation plant.

Chris Hellinger, businessman and wine connoisseur, is also the proprietor of much else on the sister-island of São Tomé. Hellinger's Island Oil Exploration Company was engaged in oil and gas exploration and development, as well as oil industry support activities. Hellinger also believes in the possibility of developing a deepwater support port facility in São Tomé and Island Oil Exploration has made such a proposal to the São Tomé government. Hellinger believes such a project would work on the island because it already has a runway and a drop-off zone on the north of the island where one can build a deep water port support centre within a free trade zone. This would be a viable development.

Chapter 16: Democratic Republic of Congo, Rwanda, and Burundi

Democratic Republic of Congo (DRC)

The DRC has the third-largest population and the second-largest land area in sub-Saharan Africa. It is rich in natural and human resources, including the second-largest rain forest in the world, fertile soils, ample rainfall and considerable and varied mineral resources. Agriculture and mining constitute the DRC's main economic activities.

Historically, mining of copper, cobalt, diamonds, gold and other base metals, zinc and petroleum extraction accounted for about 75 per cent of total export revenues, and about 25 per cent of the country's GDP (agriculture accounted for about 50 per cent of GDP).

Known primarily as a mineral producing economy, the DRC has such an ecological diversity that it is also rich in non-mineral resources. Approximately one-third of the total area is made up of the tropical rain forest. The whole area is dominated by the Congo River basin, and includes seven great and medium lakes, plus hundreds of rivers and small lakes. Africa has approximately 40 per cent of the world's hydroelectric potential, about half of it in the DRC, which has the potential to supply the entire African continent with hydroelectric power.

One location on the Congo River, the Inga Falls just north of Matadi, has a potential generating-capacity of over 40,000 megawatts. At a sharp bend in the river between Sikila Island and the mouth of the Bundi River (a Congo River tributary), the Congo falls 315 feet in nine miles (96 metres in 14 kilometres) and flows at a rate of about 1,500,000 cubic feet (42,480 cubic metres) per second. Part of this potential has already been harnessed through a small hydroelectric complex at Inga Falls which provides electricity to the DRC and some of its neighbours, including Zambia and Zimbabwe in southern Africa. In 2003, power was starting to be exported into the West African power pool region through Nigeria. South African president Thabo Mbeki proposed that the Inga Falls hydroelectric complex be expanded as part of a regional electric grid system, which would make energy more plentiful and cheaper across west, central and southern Africa. Furthermore, with twelve months of rainfall in much of the rainforest and plenty of rain in the two savannah zones on each side of the Equator, the Congo can also be a major food exporter to other African countries and the world.

(Source: Georges Nzongola-Ntalaja. 'The crisis in the Great Lakes region', speech presented at the African Renaissance conference held in Johannesburg, South Africa, 28-29 September 1998; www.africaaction.org/docs98/con9811a.htm)

Georges Nzongola-Ntalaja is a PhD in political science (University of Wisconsin-Madison), Director of the UNDP Oslo Governance Centre, and Professor Emeritus of African Studies at Howard University, in Washington. He was born in the former Belgian Congo and has written extensively on politics and nation building in Africa. His major work is *The Congo from Leopold to Kabila: A People's History* (2002).

Eskom of South Africa is driving the development of a major energy system for the continent, signalling its intention to implement five key projects falling under the New Partnership for Africa's Development (NEPAD) programme, located largely in sub-Saharan Africa. Together with several other parastatals, Eskom is the driving force behind several infrastructural development projects around the continent. In January 2004, Eskom's longstanding vision of harnessing the hydroelectric potential of the Congo River moved a step closer with the signing of an inter-governmental memorandum of understanding. Approval by the governments of the five southern African national utilities participating in the project will result in the building of the world's largest hydroelectric scheme which will have the capacity to supply the entire continent with electricity. Existing connections between Morocco and Spain, Jordan and the Middle East would facilitate the drive to supply excess power into European markets. Eskom and four other southern

African power utilities plan to build the 3,500-megawatt Inga III hydropower station in the DRC. About US$5 billion will be made available for the project. A joint venture company, Western Power Corridor (Westcor), owned by Eskom, Botswana Power Corporation, Nampower of Namibia, Empresa Nacional de Eletricidade of Angola and Société Nationale D'Électricité of the DRC will drive the Inga III project. All five stakeholders will have equal shareholdings in the firm. The venture is aimed at establishing a major power system across the five countries, incorporating power generation, transmission and telecommunications. The power utilities have been invited by the Congolese government to help in the rehabilitation of the Inga I and Inga II and two other power stations, and help the electrification programme in that country.

The University of KwaZulu-Natal and ESKOM established the High Voltage Direct Current (HVDC) Centre for capacity building and research in HVDC technology, which will be applied in the delivery of power over such long distances. The Centre has been conducting both basic and applied research for optimised design and operation of long distance transmission lines. The university's dean of engineering, Nelson Ijumba, said that harnessing the hydroelectric power on the Inga Dam would be developed in phases. Initially the Inga project would harness 3,000 to 5,000 megawatts, or 10 per cent of the total potential, and transmit the power over 3,000 kilometres to the member countries, at 800 kilovolts (kV). This will be the highest DC transmission voltage ever. Later phases would develop and grow the project towards the 40,000-megawatt potential. Ijumba says that the technical challenge will be to engineer a power system that employs large-scale run of river generation and the associated long-distance power transmission scheme incorporating the latest technology. He says the overall power system must be capable of integrating with existing and planned power systems in each of the five countries. The availability of power from the hydro sources will obviate the dependence on coal fired power stations which contribute to global warming. Also, power delivered cost effectively will ensure reduced energy cost, which will be attractive for large industrial developments.

(Source: Nicola Jenvey and Robyn Chalmers. 'Hydroelectric scheme in Congo could power Africa', Johannesburg: *Business Day*, 13 February 2003)

In July 1999, the Protestant University of Congo undertook a bold and visionary endeavour to begin a new entrepreneurship institute that should interest Americans in business. Dr. Jerôme Kinga Oveneke, a Congolese who had recently completed his doctorate in business administration from Liege, Belgium, joined UPC and announced his plan to lead the new institute. The University of Liege agreed to fund it. The new endeavour was envisioned to serve as a research centre for the creation of Congolese businesses, and it intended to seek funds for projects deemed worthy of assistance in the Congo, where loans to businesses are impossible to get. However, the endeavour was stymied by the war and was linked to the official resumption of cooperation (foreign aid) from Belgium to the Congo. In short, the Enterprise Institute at UPC was held hostage to politics, another victim of the tragic Congo war, and Dr Oveneke's plans were overturned by the unstable political, military and economic situation in the Congo. However, as a result of the 2002 peace negotiations in Sun City, South Africa, a Belgian delegation of businessmen headed for the Congo and contacted Dr Oveneke, resulting in renewed activity for the Entrepreneurship Centre at the Protestant University of Congo, and finally getting their promised financing from the Belgian government, via the University of Liege.

Priorities to encourage Congolese small and medium enterprises need to be defined. A tutoring authority should set up short-term programmes designed to encourage the entrepreneurial spirit or to help owners of existing businesses to improve their management. The country's chambers of commerce and industry have substantial experience in this field. Where chambers of commerce still remain operational, core operations are limited to establishing contact partners looking for business opportunities, and no initiative pretending to contribute to the reactivation of small and medium enterprises has come out from any chamber. However, there is hope that an effective reactivation of economic activities will take place. This time the economy should count on a solid structure of small and medium enterprises, which are the framework capable of reactivating the economy and creating employment.

The main objectives of the centre are to implement a training programme in entrepreneurship for young Congolese; to assist entrepreneurs in the design and the implementation of their projects; to ensure the follow-up of entrepreneurs' field projects in order better to contribute to the development of new enterprises; to contribute to the creation of micro credit institutions; and to implement a support programme. The objectives of the support programme are to promote the creation of enterprises in the technological/scientific, industrial and services sectors; to encourage new ideas that can contribute to the design of new products; and to ensure optimal growth conditions for the development of these new enterprises/products.

This support programme, promoting the creation of enterprises, will be managed by the Entrepreneurship Center of the Protestant University of Congo and will require investments in term of equipment and personnel. To finance the implementation of the programme and ensure its success, Dr Oveneke wrote financing proposals for UNDP and World Bank offices in Kinshasa. He hopes that the programme carried out by the Entrepreneurship Centre will indisputably contribute to the economic growth of the DRC through intensive support for the development of new small enterprises active in both industrial and services sectors. To ensure the success of the programme, one of the research teams of the centre is conducting a study with the objective of identifying the key explanatory factors of success and failure of enterprises in Democratic Republic of Congo. Finally, to make the programme known locally and internationally, Dr Oveneke plans to publish a working paper entitled 'Le Nouvel Entrepreneur Africain'.

Born in Kinshasa, Dikembe Mutombo is the seventh of ten children born to Samuel and the late Biamba Marie Mutombo. He arrived in the United States in 1987 on an academic scholarship to attend Georgetown University in Washington. As a pre-med major, his dream was to become a medical doctor and return to the Congo to practice medicine. In his second year at Georgetown, Coach John Thompson invited the extremely tall Mutombo to try out for the university's renowned basketball team. After joining the team, Mutombo re-directed his academic ambitions and graduated from Georgetown with dual degrees in linguistics and diplomacy. He is fluent in nine languages, including five African languages.

The Denver Nuggets basketball team drafted Mutombo after his graduation from Georgetown and in 1996 he signed a five-year free agent contract with the Atlanta Hawks. On 22 February 2001, Mutombo joined the Philadelphia 76ers NBA basketball team where the team advanced to the 2001 NBA Finals for the first time since 1983. Mutombo is a four-time NBA 'Defensive Player of the Year' and ranks first in NBA rebounds per game. In August 2002, he joined the New Jersey Nets and that team advanced to the finals in 2003. In late 2004, Mutombo joined the Houston Rockets.

In 1997, Mutombo created the Dikembe Mutombo Foundation to improve health, education and the quality of life for the people of his homeland. Because infections caused by poor sanitary conditions are a serious threat to both children and adults in the Congo, one of the Foundation's most important goals is to improve the present public health facilities that are currently lacking in both medical supplies and trained personnel. One major project of the Foundation is to build a new general hospital, Biamba Marie Mutombo Hospital, in the capital city of Kinshasa. The groundbreaking ceremony for the new hospital took place in Kinshasa on 15 September 2001. The US$29 million project is scheduled for completion in June 2006. The Biamba Marie Mutombo hospital will be the first new hospital in the Congo almost 40 years.

Mutombo believes that God has given him this opportunity to do great things for his country, especially in health care. This facility will create the most dramatic change in health care delivery, not only in the capital, but in the country and the whole region. Mutombo, who is full of the joy of life, is eager to share that spirit with a country desperately in need. He quotes a modern African proverb to explain why he has committed so much of his life and his wealth to the welfare of others. 'When you take the lift up to reach the top, please don't forget to send it back down, so that someone else can take it to the top,' saying that this is his way of sending the lift back down.

Mutombo also serves on the advisory board for the Fogarty International Centre at the National Institutes of Health and is a board member for the George Washington University's Africa Centre for Health and Security. In January 2005, Mutombo was nominated to be part of the Forum of Young Global Leaders, which works in close cooperation with the World Economic Forum. Other Mutombo honours and awards include the Wilt Chamberlain Award — Operation Smile; Honorary Degree, Doctor of Humane Letters — State University of NY/Cortland; NAACP Phoenix Award; the Henry Iba Citizen Athlete Award; the President's Service Award (2000) — presented by US president Bill Clinton; the J Walter Kennedy Citizenship Award — National Basketball Association; the Ernie Davis Humanitarian Award; the Samuel J Halsey Award — Georgetown University; and the Constituency for Africa's Trailblazer Award.

(Source: Dikembe Mutombo Foundation (www.dmf.org); and Jeff Chu. 'On the shoulders of a giant', *TIME* Europe, 20 April 2004)

In September 2004, the International Finance Corporation, the private sector arm of the World Bank Group, announced an agreement for a 15 per cent equity stake in the start-up of Pro Credit Bank, a microfinance bank in DRC. As well as credit facilities, the bank will also provide other financial services to micro and small businesses. IFC's US$0.45 million equity investment in Pro Credit Bank underscores the corporation's strategy of providing post-conflict support to DRC to boost private sector development. The bank will have a strong impact on the economy, helping bolster private sector wealth and job creation, accelerating the business growth of target enterprises and boosting confidence in the banking sector. Pro Credit Bank will also help strengthen microfinance banking in DRC by introducing commercially-oriented techniques — together with the equity investment, IFC is also providing a US$0.5 million technical assistance grant to the bank for institution and capacity building. Other foreign equity investors in Pro-Credit Bank include Stichting DOEN of the Netherlands, and Germany's Internationale Projekt Consult and Internationale Micro Investitionen, the latter in which IFC has an equity stake. Richard Ranken, IFC director for sub-Saharan Africa, says that IFC is committed to supporting and strengthening the financial sector in DRC to promote the development and growth of entrepreneurs in the micro and small business sectors, and adds that IFC is very pleased to support Pro Credit Bank Congo, which they hope will quickly become the country's leading provider of credit and banking services to micro and small businesses. Jyrki Koskelo, IFC director for Global Financial Markets, notes that the project is a good example of how a group of like-minded investors can support access to finance for low-income people in Africa and a significant development in the growth of the commercial microfinance sector in Africa.

The creation of the Forrest Group goes back to 1922. This was the year in which Malta Forrest created his company in the province of Katanga in the south of the Belgian Congo (the present DRC). From 1933 onwards, this transport company moved towards mining activities (copper, manganese, gold) and at the start of the 1950s, it developed its own activities in the fields of civil engineering and public works. In 1968, the company undertook the transformation to limited company status. After the death of the founder, Victor Eskenazi-Forrest and George A Forrest became the managing directors.

In 1986, George A Forrest took sole control of the company, and injected it with new vitality. He promoted the creation of the Forrest Group by diversifying activities and geographic locations. In 1989, the Forrest Group acquired the Belgian industrial assembly company New Baron & Leveque International (NBLI), as well as a Belgian machine construction company in the highly technological field of pyrotechnics, New Lachaussee. The Forrest group continued to develop with its 1992 acquisition of cement plants and coal mine in the DRC.

For more than 82 years, the Forrest Group has expanded, become stronger, and continued to develop, and it covers a wide range of activities as diverse as civil engineering, mining, metallurgy, high-precision mechanical technology for pyrotechnics, engineering, construction of power lines, assembly of industrial complexes, cement plants, flour-mills and trading. In this multi-technical mixing pot, the Forrest Group has built up global experience and a presence in Africa, Europe and the Middle East.

In recent years, the Forrest Group entered in several partnerships aimed at developing new projects in

DRC for reviving the mining and metallurgical industries.. Among others:
- The Forrest Group, OMG Group and Gecamines erected in 1999 a cobalt slag refining plant with a capacity of 5,000 tons of cobalt, 3,500 tons of copper and 15,000 tons of zinc per year.
- With Gecamines' partnership, the Compagnie Minière du Sud Katanga was created in 2004 for the production of copper and cobalt concentrates. The capacity is around 5,500 tons of cobalt and 12,000 tons of copper.
- With Copper Resources Corporation (CRC) and SODIMICO (a state owned company), the Forrest Group is developing a project for resuming operations in the mines of Kinsenda and Musoshi in south Katanga. Dewatering of the mines will start early in 2006, and a yearly production of 40,000 tons of copper and 500 tons of cobalt is expected within 18 months.
- The Forrest Group associated to Kinross within Kinross-Forrest Ltd has, with Gecamines, established a new company, the Kamato Copper Company, aimed at restarting mining operations in the Kamoto mine and the Dikuluwe, Mashamba and Musonoie open pits,; resuming concentration in the Komoto and DIMA concentrators; and restoring production of copper cathodes in the Luilu plant.

The project includes plants rehabilitation, development and restoration of infrastructure such as roads and electricity, and in the social sphere (housing, medical, schooling). Production is expected to reach 150,000 tons of copper and 4,500 tons of cobalt within six years.

The experience and professionalism of George Forrest's colleagues, enriched by the cultures of North and South, provide technical know-how, mastery of economic management and a good social sense, which are the foundations for success and a security for the future. Its president considers there is much work still to be done in the DRC, where it will continue to invest.

(Source: www.forrestgroup.com).

Mpakasa, the largest inland navigation group in the Congo River basin, is based in the DRC. It draws its name from the wild buffalo in the Lingala language. Since is foundation in 1926 with the name 'Mobali ya Tembe', the principal activities of Mpakasa have been agriculture, general trade, road transport and river transport. With a fleet of six pushers and 10 barges with a total power of 2,100 CV and a capacity of 3,500 tons, Mpakasa appropriately represents the force and the courage of the African buffalo. The fleet travels the Congo River on nearly 1,700 kilometres of inland waterway, carrying travellers, goods and containers to the localities between Kinshasa and Kisangani. Managing director Patrick Latour says that Mpakasa has the experience essential for the type of transport required on a gigantic river, which often crosses virgin country. Pusher *Mpakasa 1* is the most significant of the company's boats, with rooms that make it possible to live aboard comfortably while travelling on the river. *Mpakasa 1* takes with it two barges which are used as container ships, their holds filled with various products. Important international missions trust Mpakasa to transport passengers and freight between Kinshasa and Kisangani.

Mpakasa also has a fleet of six carrying trucks, 11 road tractor-trailers, 11 tow trucks and one tanker truck. All vehicles are especially well-adapted to the difficult roads of the DRC, with a total capacity of 360 tons — mainly all-terrain vehicles, which are robust and well-maintained. The tractor *Tatra* 148 8 x 8 is one of the principal types of vehicle, existing in various versions, such as buckets for civil engineering and platforms for general transport. Mpakasa also buys agricultural produce (corn, manioc, paddy, groundnuts, palm oil and coffee) inside the country and resells it in the capital. The company sells goods of first need (salt, soap, oil and second-hand clothes) in the main towns of Kikwit, Tshikapa and Idiofa. It is also active in the agricultural processing industry, with de-husking factories for the treatment of agricultural produce like paddy and groundnut in Idiofa, Bumba and in Kikwit; and in the handling industry, with a mobile 70 T mark Link Belt crane and a 7 T mark Tatra crane.

(Source: www.pageweb.cd/mpakasa/)

Bralima was founded in 1923 in Kinshasa and is one of Africa's oldest breweries. It now has production facilities in five other cities in the Democratic Republic of Congo, as well as one bottling plant of its own in the capital. Recently, an intensive programme of modernisation was begun at the plants at Kinshasa and Boma, which were re-equipped with new, state of the art machines. Other facilities will follow. Bralima produces a wide variety of beers and other beverages, including the African favourite Primus, alcohol-free Malta and many soft drinks. Economic activity in the DRC remained at a low level in 2003 and beer sales were adversely affected by declining purchasing power. Although Bralima's sales were down, restructuring enabled it to post an improved financial result. Bralima is owned by Heineken, one of the largest international breweries in the world.

The Jules Van Lancker Company, usually known as JVL, was established in 1927 in the Congo and neighbouring countries. JVL is an agro-industrial company working in livestock and agricultural productions, processing and marketing and has an office in Brussels consulting in agro-pastoral projects to international and government organisations and to the private sector. The success of JVL's African large-scale farming operations in integrating livestock and agricultural activities (such as its Kolo and Mushie ranches in the DRC), has contributed to its international fame. Developing these activities in remote areas has allowed the company to acquire good experience in rural socio-economic development, benefiting its employees and their families as well as surrounding populations. Its professional skills cover livestock production and related activities such as tropical agricultural practices, range land management, natural resources preservation and rural development.

In the DRC, its commercial operations include two ranches with 45,000 head of selected N'Dama cattle. These animals are raised mainly on natural savannahs; balances between grazing loads and fodder production are carefully maintained with pasture rotations and early fire schemes. These natural savannahs, exploited up to their maximum potential for the last 30 to 50 years, are preserved. Grazing schemes were studied and adapted to the very different soils, plants and rain patterns. Long trials on improved pastures and fodder production were carried out, screening most of the tropical fodder plants. Improved pastures are established and exploited over 1,000 hectares, allowing increased production and off-take rates. The animals are subject to continuous selection, and represent the world's only large reservoir of the pure improved N'Dama breed.

Commercial operations also include large-scale pig and poultry production units; animal feeds formulation and production; slaughtering and processing facilities for total animal production; design for the production of maize, beans, groundnuts and cassava; large-scale trials and screening in fruit (mainly bananas and pineapples) and vegetable production and on aromatic and medicinal plants; and long experience of palm tree plantations and full processing (refined palm oil, soaps, palm kernel oil and cake).

Accompanying these operations, inputs into rural development were necessary to allow normal socio-economic life in these remote areas. Extension work was provided. Around their ranches, villagers started cattle breeding, and over the years hundreds of herds have developed, totalling more than 30,000 head. The company, needing animal health protection, followed up these developments by providing veterinary services and surveys, husbandry advice and basic equipment. In the same vein, the company developed the concept of 'mutual guarantee herds', allowing farmers through cooperative membership to give a serious financial guarantee for the loans contracted when they bought veterinary products and breeding stock. These services developed into two cattle development projects funded by Belgian cooperation and the European Union.

Other inputs by the company allowed for the organisation of rural markets and exchange shops of agricultural products; transport and marketing circuits both through the company itself or through trader organisations; the organisation (and building) of schools, which provide education to more than 5,000 children, parents and employees and surrounding villagers; the building and equipping of the company's medical centres, providing care to its staff and surrounding populations, through its own medical staff and in collaboration with specialised agencies; the building of facilities to provide drinkable water; and the construction and maintenance of rural roads and tracks, with methods adapted to local resources.

(Source: www.jvl.be)

The Raga Group operates a cable TV subscription service, FM and television broadcasting station and a large ISP in Kinshasa which provides wireless data links for clients. Raga is the pioneer of the privately-run network media in the heart of Africa. It is radio and television, but also a network of cable television, and the first wireless internet network in the Democratic Republic of Congo. Raga FM is a popular commercial network, operating in several Congolese cities. The network re-broadcasts several BBC and Voice of America programmes.

Raga SPRL was incorporated in 1997 as a media company with a television and a radio channel. Starting with less than 10 people, Raga has grown to be a leader in media broadcasting, corporate internet solutions, and cable TV, which forms an average of 30 per cent of all the corporate business amongst all the ISPs and media houses in Congo combined. In 2006, Raga employed more than 200 people.

Raga is committed to providing services in those areas which will assist in the growth and development of enterprises in DRC, and providing progressive Africa with information, products, and services relevant to the 21st century. The company has strategically made the investment necessary for extending world-class IP networks and media broadcast to cover the DRC.

(Source: www.raga.net)

The 21st century's scramble for Africa is not happening out of the goodness of the hearts of aggressive investors such as retailers, banks and telecommunications companies. The opportunity of doing business in sub-Saharan Africa is clearly not one that South Africa's cellular operator Vodacom is going to miss out on. The market, if only because of sheer size, is potentially a very lucrative one. The risks involve committing vast capital expenditure to countries where even getting the equipment through irksome customs officials can be a mammoth task, and yet Vodacom is hungry for it. Getting the infrastructure into the country was one of Vodacom's biggest challenges when starting out in the DRC. Another was the erratic power supply, which meant the need for generators to keep its base stations operating.

The market in the DRC is estimated by Vodacom to be around six million subscribers over 10 years. But it is hoping for a 50 per cent market share, according to former Vodacom DRC chairman and deputy CEO of the Vodacom group, Andrew Mthembu. Vodacom's route into the DRC was not via winning a licence but, rather, through an acquire and merge strategy. Its joint venture partner Congo Wireless Networks (CWM) was awarded a GSM licence in the DRC in 2000. Since its inception, CWN has only been able to secure 12,000 customers but within three weeks of launching the joint venture Vodacom DRC multiplied this number by more than four, to 52,000 active subscribers. And so far, the customers are spending three to four times what its pre-paid subscribers in South Africa are spending, as measured by the average revenue per user: an estimated US$25 to US$30 in the DRC, against the equivalent of US$8 or US$9 in South Africa. In 2005, Vodacom had over a million subscribers in the DRC. The Vodacom roll-out is complete and even small towns like Uvira (next to Burundi and 2,000 kilometres from Kinshasa) were already covered by 2005.

Vodacom's cost of entry into the DRC was US$39 million for its 51 per cent stake in the joint venture. CWN needed a partner because it couldn't get support from institutions to continue funding its network. To fund the venture, Vodacom had a 24-month credit facility from its equipment partner Alcatel for phase one of the network, backed by an Absa facility. The second leg of the network roll-out was funded through a combination of project finance, arranged by Standard Bank, and through other potential funders with the appetite for this type of project.

To roll out the initial 88 base stations into the three major centres of Kinshasa, Lubumbashi and Mbuji-Mayi cost a further US$55 million. The second phase of the network cost US$45 million, which brings the total investment to around US$139 million.

Vodacom's further roll-out into the DRC hinterland depended on the market potential and the prospects for peace. Although the country was under a UN ceasefire in 2002, attempts by South Africa at encouraging peace between rebel groups warring for power was only partially successful. The main centres remained unconnected by workable roads and infrastructure, so the cost of rolling out the second portion of the network was greatly inflated. But that Vodacom went ahead in full knowledge of the political and other risks was instructive in terms of what kind of return it expects to generate in the DRC.

(Source: Belinda Anderson. 'Cellular operators vie for lucrative African market', Johannesburg: *Moneyweb*, 31 May 2002)

In 2003, Vodacom had GSM operations in South Africa, Lesotho, Tanzania, the DRC and Mozambique. In most African countries, the vast majority of the population is very poor but there is normally a wealthy segment prepared to pay for cellular services in US dollars, and large enough in size for investments to be very worthwhile. Vodacom offers the latest value-added services and products. Its GSM coverage usually includes all major cities and provincial capitals, as well as many smaller towns — plus major road coverage.

Mthembu is a formidable advocate for GSM in Africa. As former managing director of Vodacom International Holdings (Pty) Ltd, he led Vodacom's expansion into the rest of Africa. His reputation as a worldwide GSM industry heavyweight was cemented through his chairmanship of the GSM Association's Africa Interest Group. Mthembu believes that mature markets like Europe and the US need a better appreciation of the issues affecting the evolution of wireless services in less developed parts of the world. He says that Africa is potentially a massive market for mobile services. However, in the midst of all this talk about data, GPRS and third generation services the so-called developed nations need to realise that Africa requires basic telephony. With fixed-line infrastructure across much of Africa in disrepair, he believes that basic telephone services need to come in the form of GSM networks. The market's potential is clear from significant progress in 2000. At the end of 1999 there were almost six million subscribers in Africa and by the end of 2001 the figure had risen to just over 20 million. In addition, the number of GSM networks continues to increase: 56 live networks at the end of 2000, with a further 33 in 2001. This means that more than 90 per cent of African networks in 2001 deployed GSM technology, an astonishing statistic given the size and diversity of the region.

Mthembu says it is important, however, to consider these developments in context. Although Africa now has over 20 million GSM subscribers, this is only one in 40 of a total population of 770 million. In addition, more than 12 million of these subscribers are in one country, South Africa. Mthembu explains that the important point about this market is that only five operators had more than 100,000 subscribers in 2000. He says this has resulted in a shortage of investment and a roll-out strategy that tends to be piecemeal. Operators rollout in the most populated areas make a little money and this enables them to rollout a bit more.

This is clearly a far from ideal foundation for business growth, since the first priority for any operator in the early days of a network is to sell its services on the basis of its coverage. However, even when adopting such strategies, African operators invariably confront another problem — the shortage of disposable income amongst consumers. Mthembu says that the obvious answer is to introduce pre-paid services. The trouble is that pre-paid services require intelligent network platforms, which for most operators are prohibitively expensive in the context of the medium-term growth of their subscriber base.

There is no doubt that the GSM industry in Africa will only realise its considerable potential supported by foreign investment and strategic support from vendors. Mthembu believes advocates of GSM can make an important contribution to such developments: first, by lobbying governments to work together to create the foundations of a cohesive regulatory environment across Africa (which will be critical in the quest for foreign investment); and second, by persuading manufacturers to adopt a more long-term approach to financing infrastructure.

Finally, Mthembu believes that advocates of GSM must continue to encourage backward compatibility as a cornerstone of technology development. Mthembu says that the continuing evolution of GSM is one of its greatest strengths, but that there must be a strategy to bridge the gap between developed and developing countries. Backward compatibility must be at the heart of that strategy to ensure smooth migration for those regions that mature markets leave behind

(Source: 'Untapped potential: The work of GSM Africa',www.gsmworld.com)

In June 2004, Vodacom's decision to walk away from a contract to manage the second largest network in Nigeria, and eventually to buy a controlling stake in the business, led to the departure of Andrew Mthembu from his position as Vodacom's deputy CEO, in charge of Vodacom's African expansion.

In his book *Conversations in the Rainforest* (2000) Richard B Peterson emphasises that commercialised use, more than indigenous peoples' use of the forest, lies at the root of Africa's environmental problems. He says central African models of environmental management suggest that we would do better to try to control the market forces that lead to over-exploitation of the environment rather than unjustly restrict the subsistence practices of people who have lived in these forests much longer than ourselves. He points out that the environmental wisdom of central African forest peoples stems from the knowledge and belief that nature and humans are never separate entities but parts of one system. We are part of nature, not set apart from it. He stresses that nature and culture, humans and environment, social ethics and environmental ethics, ecology and justice go hand in hand. Peterson concludes that it is not humans or nature that are central; rather he stresses that it is life that is primary, and that includes the entire community of life, for all of life is important, all of life is bonded, all of life is sacred.

Peterson writes that in the early 1950s the Belgians set up an okapi capture station at Epulu for the capture, breeding and export of okapi to western zoos. He relates that in 1987 this work was taken up by the Gilman International Conservation (GIC), a private American conservation organisation funded by paper magnate Howard Gilman, who wanted to repay a dept of gratitude to nature, from which his family and company had prospered for over a hundred years, through three generations. White Oak's conservation programmes, both in situ and ex situ, improve the prospects for the survival of a part of the world's natural heritage.

(Source: Richard B Peterson. *Conversations in the Rainforest: Culture, Values, and the Environment in Central Africa*, Boulder, Colorado: Westview Press, 2000)

The authors of *The Okapi: Mysterious Animal of Congo-Zaire* describe a particularly creative form of aid involving local inhabitants, reserve guards, and personnel of GIC. Resident Bantu people and pygmies, traditionally hunters, of the Ituri forest where the okapis live, are employed by Gilman to capture temporary founder stock for the okapi centre at Epulu. For this, the local villages leave 'Zones de Capture' undisturbed and then receive food and medical care during capture operations in their zone. Each okapi captured brings its zone an incentive of its choice — anything from a school or medical facility to a sewing machine or bicycle. With the local people motivated to protect their okapi resource, the whole forest ecosystem benefits.

The last capture campaign took place in 1993. Because of the civil war over the past nine years in the region, the capture zones have gone through a lot of disturbance in the same sections where the zoning programme is underway. A thorough inspection of the reserve documenting human activities is the basis for a zoning programme demarking areas where certain types of human activity are allowed. Since the Okapi Wildlife Reserve was created in 1992, the capture zones where limited human activities are allowed are now known as green zones. Some of the areas converted to agriculture are being reclaimed through reforestation programmes. Presently, assistance to local communities is not compensation to maintain the capture zones but response to the needs of the population. Support to schools, health centres and distribution of seeds, plants, and road maintenance materials around the reserve do provide incentives for local communities to support protection of biodiversity and help to eliminate illegal mining and poaching activities in the Reserve.

(Source: www.giconline.org, and Susan Lyndaker Lindsey, Mary Neel Green, Cynthia L Bennett. *The Okapi: Mysterious Animal of Congo-Zaire*, Austin, Texas: University of Texas Press, 1999)

Since 1985, the New York Zoological Society, now called the Wildlife Conservation Society (WCS) has also been involved in a wide spectrum of ecological research and conservation initiatives in the Ituri. In 1992, the government of Zaire recognised the threat to its endemic okapi by creating the Reserve de Faune a Okapi

(Okapi Wildlife Reserve). Because post-independence regimes in DRC have had only limited funds for conservation work, the financial burden has fallen on international sources. WCS has established the Centre de Formation et Recherche en Conservation Forestiere (CEFRECOF) at Epulu with Terese Hart, John Hart, Robert Mwinyihali and Innocent Liengola as representatives of WCS. This is the Ituri tropical forest research and training centre set up to train Congolese students in field ecology and conservation management, and able to provide foreign researchers with research clearance. One purpose of the training is to familiarise future field leaders with survey methodology, protocols, data collection and analysis. The herbarium at CEFRECOF was developed as part of an active research and training centre. The plant collection is primarily from the Ituri Forest. There are approximately 3,500 fertile collections in the herbarium, and three staff botanists are employed by CEFRECOF. In 1998, Terese Hart of WCS and project senior staff members Robert Mwinyihali and Richard Tshombe completed meetings in the capital, Kinshasa, where they obtained authorisation for another five years of fieldwork at Epulu. Left unclear is the degree of commitment on the part of the new government to the reserve.

Bill Weber is a gorilla expert at the WCS in New York, and co-author with wife Amy Vedder of *In the Kingdom of the Gorillas: Fragile Species in a Dangerous Land* (2001). He says that what is needed now is a mix of protected areas, enforcement of protection for endangered species wherever they are located (inside and outside protected areas), and sound and sustainable natural resource management by local people outside reserves. This is the strategy that WCS has been promoting for the last 20 years in places like Rwanda. Most of the countries already have laws banning poaching, but there are insufficient staff and funding to enforce them. Some wildlife experts have been campaigning against poaching for bush meat for the last several years. Those most familiar with the issues on the ground recognise that hunting takes many forms, is conducted by different people for different reasons, and is done at very different intensities. Where endangered species are at risk, where national laws have been established to protect such species, and especially where the drivers for over-use are not local, Weber says that resources are needed for law enforcement. There were virtually no resources at all going into gorilla conservation when he first began work. He says groups should also work with the local communities to address their very real natural resource concerns.

Conservationists point out that Africans do not routinely eat gorillas. Humans and gorillas coexisted for thousands of years, but now, central Africa has growing human populations, shrinking forests and roads cutting into the heart of the forests. Bush meat satisfies a large and growing urban population that has retained a preference for the wild meat it grew up with. Gorillas were a traditional food source. Conservationists are not trying to turn everyone in the African forest into vegetarians but they would like to see gorillas and chimpanzees removed from the dining table. One way is to enforce existing laws. Weber says that '...blame also should not be put on the African governments for the lack of law enforcement, these governments have a lot of other priorities, and some continue to have very serious problems with security and outright warfare. Protecting wildlife is not at the top of their priority list, generating resources from our own deep bank accounts would help, we have to remember we're the ones with the resources and the interest in this right now.'

(Source: Bill Weber and Amy Vedder. *In the Kingdom of the Gorillas: Fragile Species in a Dangerous Land*, New York: Simon & Schuster, 2001)

The Ivugha hydro electric power station was the result of businesspeople from Butembo in northern Kivu in the Democratic Republic of Congo joining forces to build a hydroelectric power station. The energy for the Ivugha power station is drawn from a waterfall situated along the Mususa River near Butembo. The Mususa's waters were first diverted to a small turbine located 100 metres downstream. In its initial phase, the turbine produced one megawatt of power, enough to fuel the additional work that needed to be done at the site. In 2005, the completed dam was producing five megawatts. All work related to the power station, transmission line to town and the distribution prepayment system in Butembo is supervised, executed and managed by Clackson Power of South Africa. Certain streets, hospitals and schools in Butembo were the first to be electrified. Project coordinator Daniel Hangi needed to show people that the project was viable before he asked them to fork over their share of money to finish the project. This is the reason that his first act was to light public spaces, which would directly benefit the population. People were quick to notice how different it was from the days when they had to be afraid of being outside in the dark.

First proposed in 1996, the Ivugha project nearly didn't see the light of day. That year marked the beginning of the insurgency that saw deceased president Laurent Kabila overthrow Mobutu Sese Seko, leader of what was then Zaïre. When Kabila's Alliance of Democratic Forces for the Liberation of Congo laid siege to Butembo in 1997, the project was put on hold for three years. In 2000, another insurgency led by the Goma faction of the rebel Congolese Rally for Democracy isolated the region from the rest of the country. Nonetheless, the project's originators pressed ahead with their plans. They created the North Kivu Electrification Company (Société d'électrification du Nord-Kivu (SENOKI)) and enlisted the help of Clackson Power, which specialises in technology for rural electrification. Clackson put the cost of the project at US$3.7 million (various European companies put in bids at about US$9 million).

SENOKI raised 10 per cent of the total US$3.7 million capital. The 90 per cent balance was paid by Clackson Power which will, under contract, have sole control and administration of the project until the 90 per cent owed by SENOKI is paid to Clackson Power in full. Clackson Power uses monthly income of electricity sales to cover monthly expenses, and the balance is paid towards the outstanding capital. The 700,000 residents of Butembo supported the project. In addition to boosting development in the area, the hydro power station reduced their dependence on wood as the fuel of choice for household needs. Nonetheless, locals did not break down SENOKI's doors to buy power, largely as a result of widespread poverty. Most practised the subsistence farming of their forefathers but tea and coffee, two export crops that used to earn the region revenue, are mostly no longer in cultivation since an outbreak of coffee wilt disease decimated the 1993-1994 crop. 'We're satisfied just by the thought that electricity is now available in Butembo, even though we don't have enough money to buy it ourselves,' says Celine Maskika, a Butembo housewife. The electricity itself is very cheap (US$0.07 per kilowatt-hour), but what it expensive is the connection fee SENOKI imposes. Clackson Power is working to make connections to customers free of charge.

The project's backers are optimistic. According to the FEC, the precarious economic condition of people in the area was taken into account when the prices were set. Since they were born there and have experienced the same living conditions, they were aware of their people's economic situation, says Jean Muteti, a banker and member of the FEC. They talked about it a lot and tried to set prices while taking into account all the problems, so that the majority would have access to electricity. When the plant was finally finished, it produced more electricity and FEV was able to revise prices downwards. Previously, there were two types of electricity fee schedules for Butembo residents, depending on their financial status.

Prior to Ivugha's generation of electricity, non-governmental organisations had set up diesel generators to provide residents with power. Although the electricity produced by these generators was more expensive than that created by the hydro power station, the generators stayed in service and provided night-time illumination to certain neighbourhoods before they were finally linked to SENOKI. In 2004, Butembo residents did not yet need large amounts of electricity, says Joseph Malembe, executive secretary of COTEDER, a rural development NGO; essentially they merely needed to light up their houses and cook their food on a hot plate. In reality, the biggest beneficiaries of the electrification project are Butembo's entrepreneurs, who are starting up small- and medium-sized businesses, such as Maison Cafekit, which produces carbonated beverages. The manager of Maison Cafekit says he had worked with diesel generators for fifteen years, and they were very unpleasant; with the electricity produced by the power station, he definitely produces more at lower cost and has even been able to lower his prices.

(Source: Juakali Kambale. 'Power under uncertain circumstances', *Inter Press Service*, 14 July 2004)

In 2006, Clackson Power will be completing the Katende-I hydroelectric power station destined to supply the city of Kananga, capital of the diamond-rich western Kasai Province that counts a million inhabitants, and another hydroelectric power station in Kakobola, in western Bandundu Province. The power station in Katende, the first of the two to be completed, has a capacity of 18 megawatts, and Kakobola seven megawatts. These projects are valued at US$31 million. The Clackson Power Company was registered in 1992 in South Africa to specialise in designing and erecting small to medium power plants. Since its inception, the company has distinguished itself as the only hydro turbine manufacturer and independent power developer in Africa, specialising in turnkey hydro power schemes. This includes all civil works, earth moving, weirs and canals, turbines and generators, transmission and distribution and pre-payment systems.

(Source: www.clacksonpower.com)

In September 2002, Fiammetta Rocco was in the process of writing a book on the history of quinine. To complete her research, Fiammetta and her father Dorian Rocco visited Pharmakina in Bukavu, DRC, the biggest chincona plantation in the world today. Pharmakina had been established during World War II in the vicinity of Lake Kivu in order to supply chincona bark for antimalarial drugs, as most of the producing areas in Indonesia and Malaya were in the hands of the Japanese. The company remained in the hands of the Belgian Congo government until it was sold to Boehringer, the large German pharmaceutical company which had been engaged in the manufacture of quinine for half a century. Boehringer ran the estates and the factory for 30 years, through the revolutions and tribal wars, continuing production and employing up to 10,000 people. In the late 1990s, Boehringer was taken over by Hoffmann Laroche of Switzerland. The Swiss were not too keen to get involved in the DRC adventure so the general manager, Horst Gebbers, and his French partner, Etienne Erny, arranged a management buy-out and took over the company. Quinine had fallen on hard times as it was little used in the fight against malaria and, having been prescribed as remedy for some heart problems, had been superseded, so that sales were low.

By dint of active marketing and owing to the huge increase in malaria, sales have increased over the years and the factory is now being revamped and modernised. Dorian Rocco, as an entrepreneur who bemoans the difficulties of running a business in Nairobi, says that it is absolutely staggering to see the conditions in Bukavu. There is no bank, workshop or spares shop. All fuel must be brought by truck from Kenya, a distance of over 1,000 miles. Yet, in spite of this, a highly effective organisation run by the partners and their sons is flourishing.

All vehicles and machinery are repaired and maintained in-house. All requirements are air-freighted to Kigali from Europe. A local Indian businessman handles foreign exchange. He supplies their requirements in Congolese francs against US dollars or vice versa. Of course the local authorities have to be kept happy and it usually costs US$20,000 to obtain an export permit. Yet they have set up an extremely advanced laboratory for micropropagation of the trees, and run some 20 estates of 500 acres each which are kept separate as the trees are subject to a root fungus which can destroy the whole plantation — when that happens, the trees must be uprooted and a legume planted which must remain for seven years before the chincona can be returned.

(Source: www.pharmakina.de)

When Dorian and Fiammetta went to visit in 2002, they were rather perturbed that a series of armies and militias, Congolese, East Congolese, Rwandan, Ugandan, Interhamwe and various others were operating, some as close as 10 kilometres from Bukavu. Luckily, they were able to visit a plantation in Rwanda just a few miles over the border, where they were able to see the whole set-up. Dorian stayed at the Orchids Safari Club. Set above a flamboyant garden, the friendly, family-run Orchids' Safari Club waterside hotel has the most spectacular views over Lake Kivu — the setting for the famous Bogart/Hepburn film, 'The African Queen'. This is the starting point for a wonderful safari: rafting on the Luhoho River, visiting a tea plantation or pygmy families and trekking through the dense rain forest of Kahuzi-Biega in search of lowland gorillas who despite their formidable strength are gentle and rare patriarchs. The hotel has 25 rooms and three suites, and is run by Marc Moreau, who vaguely remembered hearing about Dorian's parents, who had made a one-year foot safari in the area in 1928. Dorian also worked with TMK (Transport et Messagerie du Kivu), owned by a Belgian, Hubert Esselen, and his three sons, transporting fertiliser to the Congo some 30 years ago.

(Source: www.ila-chateau.com/orchids)

Fiammetta Rocco's book, *The Miraculous Fever-Tree: Malaria and the Quest for a Cure That Changed the World* (2003) explores the history of the ravages of malaria, of the heroism and tragedy of those who have attempted to find cures, and the manner in which the discovery of quinine opened the door of the tropics to western imperial adventure.

(Source: Fiammetta Rocco. *The Miraculous Fever-Tree: Malaria and the Quest for a Cure That Changed the World*, London: HarperCollins, 2003)

Rwanda

Dorian Rocco was amazed, when he went to Rwanda in September 2002, to see what can happen when a country is properly managed. After the terrible events that occurred there in 1994, arriving in the Rwanda capital of Kigali, he noticed that the streets were clean and the buildings refurbished, and that there was a pleasant atmosphere when going through customs and immigration. In the countryside, the roads were perfectly maintained and the agriculture was very productive. In spite of working on tiny plots on steep hillsides, the farmers produced a surplus of maize in 2002, which was sold to the World Food programme for the starving Sudanese. He noted that money and investments were pouring in.

Georges Jaumain is an import/export entrepreneur in South Africa. His parents had agricultural interests in the Great Lakes region. Georges has heard of the progress of Rwanda and that it is the result of the very strict rule of law applied by an enlightened new regime. He believes that Africa needs new young leaders who want to develop instead of loot as their predecessors did. Once peace was achieved in the Great Lakes region, he saw that region once more becoming a real paradise on earth, one with arguably the most beautiful scenery on the planet.

Journalist Geoffrey Kamali reports that Kigali residents were bracing themselves for a different lifestyle as a number of new multi-million dollar facilities opened up in 2004. Overlooking the entire city is the new ten-storey Bank of Commerce, Development and Industry project, said to cost US$7 million. The rectangular building has ten pairs of panoramic oval offices, designed to be boardrooms, on either side, complete with curtain wall glazes to give occupants a scenic view of the entire city. This is the tallest building in the city and the country, says Franz Piller, the site manager. In the housing sector, Caisse Sociale (Rwanda's social security fund) has put up about 200 flats for civil servants. Elsewhere, Ugandan-based Roko Construction Company's construction workers built the exclusive resort facility the Kivu Sun. In the heart of the city is another new modern building, Karitas.

Other new facilities include two large supermarkets. One, a retail complex at Nyarutarama, a new exclusive residential area with palatial homes on the outskirts of Kigali, is operated by Tristar, a local company. The other large supermarket is in the city centre and is owned by a US-based Rwandan entrepreneur, Tribert Rujugiro. The US$6 million Rujugiro supermarket has five floors, one of which is used as a parking lot for over 200 vehicles. Rujugiro has also acquired a site at the Kigali Central Market to set up a seven-storey shopping mall. He also owns a large housing estate in Gikondo, a Kigali suburb stretching over two hills, with a recreation centre, a clinic and a school. Rwanda's high-roller also has interests in furniture, metal fabrication, banking, real estate, a brewery, and a cigarette manufacturing company, the Mastermind Tobacco Company, in east and southern Africa. In 2005, Rujugiro was the President of Chambre de Commerce et d'Industrie du Rwanda.

Other new facilities that will change the lifestyle in Kigali include a proposed Kigali city amusement park, to be set up by a group of individuals and several companies. The project, similar to Sandton City, Johannesburg, is the brainchild of another prominent Rwandan businessman, Eugene Nyagahene, whose other concerns include a franchise for the MNet pay-TV channel of South Africa; a major stake in Rwanda's first FM station, Radio 10 FM; and a partnership in MediaPost, a South African-based internet service provider. MediaPost, jointly owned with his brother, Patrick Ngabonziza, is carrying out a pilot wireless internet project, using technology similar to mobile telephony, around Kigali. The company also has licences to operate in a dozen African countries including Kenya, Uganda, Tanzania and Congo Brazzaville.

(Source: Geoffrey Kamali. 'Tycoons change Kigali', *Procurement News*, 26 April 26 2004; www.procnews.com)

Rwanda's private broadcaster, Radio 10 FM, kicked off programming in February 2004 and Rwandans really enjoy it. In 1994, a few months after the genocide, Radio 10's founder Nyagahene launched Tele 10, Rwanda's first private TV station, with the broadcasting of international TV channels using UHF and MMDS transmitters and satellite in Rwanda. Nyagahene says Radio 10 represents a new beginning for Rwandan radio, which had been controlled by the government for a decade. During the genocide, radio was used as a tool to foment violence. Between 1994 and 2004, the bulk of the news that Rwandans heard on national radio was news about the government. Nyagahene says that his station expands coverage to other social and cultural arenas. He says the US$125,000 he laid out to start Radio 10 was a small price to pay for the chance to give the microphone to the public.

The Rwandan government has granted six other broadcasting licences, three to commercial enterprises and three to community or religious broadcasters. All hit the airwaves in March 2004. These include Radio Contact, Radio Flash FM, Izuba Radio, National University of Rwanda-School of Journalism Radio, Radio Maria owned by the Catholic Church and another FM station owned by the Seventh Day Adventist Church. Contact Radio founder Albert Rudatsimburwa says that the new stations mean President Kagame truly intends to open the country to independent journalism. The government closely monitors the new stations, but Radio 10's Nyagahene claims that there are no limits to what radios can put on air except for appeals to ethnic hatred. His reporters cover all subjects, including political issues.

Radio 10 sits at the top of a red Kigali hill broadcasting in Rwanda's three official languages, English, French and Kinyarwanda, and targeting Rwanda's youth with a mixture of American hip-hop, African pop and Bob Marley-style reggae. The staff is young, hip, and articulate. They have broken all the rules of old-school Rwandan radio. Programmes include listener call-ins, chatty morning shows, modern pop music, and contests where winners get to talk on air. Broadcasts began in the capital city Kigali, and are gradually being expanded to the rest of the country. The majority of Rwanda's eight million citizens are not literate, and many rely exclusively on the radio for news and information. Besides Radio 10 and the other independent stations, Rwandans find an alternative to the state-run Radio Rwanda in the international BBC radio network and Voice of America, both of which broadcast in Rwanda. Nyagahene calls upon the Rwanda business community to support radio stations as part of boosting the economy through advertising. Nyagahene's next big project is the launch in 2006 of 'Kigali City Park' a recreational park which will include a theme park, movie theatre, cultural centre and botanical garden. Due to the required big investment of US$25 million, Nyagahene's company entered into a public-private partnership.

(Source: Mary Wiltenburg. 'After the genocide, redemption. Once filled with hate, radio now spins Kenny Rogers', *The Christian Science Monitor*, 7 April 2004)

When the winners of the Africa 2004 SMME Awards were announced in October 2004, enterprises from all over the continent made their mark. Tele 10 was the winner of the regional award for Central Africa. The Africa SMME Awards are an initiative of the Africa Centre for Investment Analysis (ACIA) at South Africa's University of Stellenbosch Business School.

Nyagahene applauds the Rwandan government for embarking on a very ambitious programme called VISION 2020, by which Rwanda's per capita annual revenue would grow 8 per cent to 9 per cent per year and would jump to US$950 a year in 2020 as against US$250 a year in 2004. All government and private investments will largely focus on ICT, tourism and agriculture. New companies in ICT are investing massively in Rwanda: Terracom, an American company, is laying fibre optics around the country; Mediapost (Nyagahene's company) is busy implementing a wireless network around the country; while the 2005 privatisation of Rwandatel is now done. TERRACOM won the tender, with ALLTEL (an American company) and ZTE (Chinese company). Before the end of 2005, they planned to launch a mobile telephone company based on GSM and 3G technology. Of course they are also busy setting up a fibreoptic network (1,000 km) around the country. The mobile phone company MTN-Rwanda had more than 175,000 subscribers in March 2005, and was expanding into the Kivu region, launching a GSM business called SuperCell. Many projects in ICT, like e-goverment platform, SIMTEL (the VISA card company in Rwanda), the post office network and Schoolnet, are under implementation, and were being launched in 2005.

Nyagahene points out that Rwanda's tourism industry is making more than US$30 million per year, the main attraction being the mountain gorillas. Many small businesses, in partnership with Kenyan operators, are active in the industry. New hotels, four- or five-stars, are opening in remote areas such as Gisenyi, Akagera and Kibuye. New golf courses are under construction. Coffee and tea are on top of the list of agriculture for export; vanilla bean plants, macadamia trees and geraniums are also being planted, and markets have been identified in Europe and North America. Businessmen are investing massively in speciality coffee and Rwanda expects to export about 10,000 tons a year to the USA within the next five years. Maraba Coffee was the pioneer in the coffee business, exporting about 1,000 tons in 2002. Several small microfinance businesses are mushrooming, with a positive impact on the purchasing power of people in rural areas.

In September 2005, a long-serving journalist in Rwanda, Mwiti Marete, won a first prize in the prestigious AISI Awards. Marete beat numerous other contestants from across Africa to bag the United Nations Economic Commission for Africa-sponsored AISI-IDRC Media Award on 'Reporting on Research and Innovation of Information and Communications'. Marete's entry, 'Internet users to surf in Kinyarwanda next month' (*The New Times*, 15-16 December 2004), was a front-page breaking news story about the invention of software that makes it possible for Kinyarwanda speakers to surf the Internet in their mother tongue. The story featured philanthropic American millionaire, software architect of Rwandan descent, Antoine Bigirimana. (Source: Joan Wangui. 'Journalist scoops media award', *The New Times*, 12 September 2005)

Antoine Bigirimana, an American business executive and ICT expert, released a Kinyarwanda language pack for Linux computing platform in 2005. This is significant for the 35 million Kinyarwanda speakers in the Great Lakes region. The great majority of Kinyarwanda speakers (90 per cent) speak only Kinyarwanda. A Linux system that speaks Kinyarwanda will allow this community to have access, in their own language, to Internet and other ICTs and this will significantly increase computer literacy in Rwanda. A number of literacy software applications are being developed for this platform, targeting the great mass of people who can't read or write. 'You can't develop a country with just about 10 per cent of the population who speak English and French. To achieve Vision 2020, you need the 90 per cent who speak and understand Kinyarwanda. And there is political will to do this,' says Bigirimana, an American of Rwandan origin. With Kinyarwanda as the national language spoken by almost everyone, the software is generating a lot of interest and development in Rwanda.

Together with others beyond the Rwandan borders, Kinyarwanda speakers make up one of the largest language blocks on the African continent. The choice of Kinyarwanda breaks the barrier faced by Kinyarwanda speakers who do not speak the mainstream computer languages. Citing cases of illiteracy in the rural areas, Bigirimana is emphatic that the project will greatly reduce illiteracy levels in Rwanda, as it will bring the mostly illiterate masses into the Internet and ICT world of unlimited access to information. He says that his organisation chose to embark on the project because Kinyarwanda is more widely spoken and understood in the country than English, French and other languages that are currently built into the commonly-used computer software.

(Source: Mwiti Marete. 'Internet users to surf in Kinyarwanda next month', *The New Times*, Issue No. 263, 15 December 15 2004)

Bigirimana is a prominent entrepreneur and philanthropist. Born in Rwanda, he now spends two of every three months there. He and Robert Fogler co-founded the Kigali Centre for Entrepreneurs, a non-profit organisation that provides resources to budding entrepreneurs to turn their ideas into formal written business plans. He is the chairman of E-ICT Integrated Training Centre, a non-profit training centre for IT workers in Kigali. He says E-ICT would like to work with any school, college, hospital — indeed any organisation in Rwanda — to enable them to gain affordable access to ICT and use it effectively in modernising their organisations. He is a central figure in Rwanda's ICT community, with access to entrepreneurs and businesses throughout its capital city. He has also invested personally in local businesses in Rwanda and is active in the country's efforts to facilitate regional trade and promote entrepreneurship. Bigirimana is also a proven entrepreneur himself, having founded and built the Electronic Tools Company, a successful software company in the San Francisco Bay area.

In 2005, Bigirimana and Fogler co-founded the Thousand Hills Venture Fund to demonstrate that US-based equity venture capital, carefully invested in new technologies and financial innovations in Rwanda, can support sustainable economic growth and generate high returns to its investors. Fogler is a lawyer in Denver, Colorado, who represents venture capital and other private equity investors and their portfolio companies. Through his involvement in the venture capital and Denver business communities, he brings a broad range of business resources to the Fund and its portfolio companies. He has also developed relationships with central figures in Rwanda's business community through meetings in Denver and Rwanda. Both Bigirimana and Fogler participated in Rwanda's Second International Investment Conference, held in its capital city, Kigali, in May 2004.

Bigirimana and Fogler want their Thousand Hills Venture Fund to be a world-class, added-value investor in small and medium enterprises, thereby facilitating wealth generation, job creation and economic development in Rwanda. Their mission is to fulfil their vision by investing capital, skill and knowledge into viable entrepreneurial enterprises in Rwanda. Their goal is to be one of the most internationally respected, successful and profitable investors in small and medium enterprises. Their values are business and personal integrity, superior client service, economic merit and entrepreneurship.

They founded and designed their venture capital fund in various innovative ways to address the significant challenges in providing equity funding (US$50k-500k) to true SMEs. They are looking for entrepreneurs who will strive for excellence in order to be competitive in regional, national and international markets, who will be socially responsible, will support community development efforts and will create a work environment in which their employees can learn and grow. Their fund will help these entrepreneurs establish and grow their enterprises and attain good financial shape while enjoying a reputation for quality, integrity and service.

Brasseries et Limonaderies du Rwanda (Bralirwa), Rwanda's internationally renowned brewer of quality beers and producer of soft drinks, was founded in 1957 with the construction of a brewery at Gisenyi located at Lake Kivu, followed by a soft drink plant at Kigali in 1974. Bralira is the producer of *Primus* and *Mutzig*, two of Africa's flagship brands. Bralirwa also supports local farmers to grow crops of sorghum, a main ingredient for the production of *Primus* beer. For this the farmers get seed, advice and the assistance of a specialised agronomist. Shareholders are Heineken (70 per cent) and the government of Rwanda (30 per cent). In 2001, Bralirwa, was judged the best-managed company among the Heineken group in central and west Africa. As the second-largest employer after the state, it plays an active and important role in Rwandan society. Its involvement with the Methane Gas project at Lake Kivu is one good example. The unusually deep (450 metres) lake holds 55bn m² of methane gas, an amount that could meet 60 per cent of the present energy demands of Rwanda for more than a thousand years. However, the reserves are continuously replenished and can last much longer and yield many times as much gas. The gas is found at the lower depths of the lake (below 270 metres), and much of it can be piped to the surface. A technical consultant from South Africa is behind a unique power station project in Rwanda, which will provide 60 per cent of Rwanda's electricity requirements. Philip Morkel, consultant to Murray & Roberts, has developed a process to extract methane gas from Lake Kivu. The gas will power a 30MW power station at Gisenyi, north of the lake. Gas will be piped to communities and cities in the area. The project, worth hundreds of millions of rands, is being led by Cogelgas, a joint venture between Rwandan Bralirwa and BCDI, a leading bank. Kivu's methane has also been tested on a vehicle as a substitute for petroleum fuel.

Building on its strategy to expand its footprint in Africa, Southern Sun Hotels of South Africa — the leading hotel operator in the southern hemisphere — has made its first appearance in central Africa with the opening of the InterContinental Kigali hotel in Rwanda. The InterContinental Kigali, which officially opened its doors to the public in January 2004, is situated in the commercial hub of Rwanda. It has an international convention centre, with conference facilities for 900 people and the capacity to host 600 people for a banquet; a translation centre, media rooms and state of the art audiovisual equipment. The hotel also contains a fully-equipped fitness centre, a business centre, shops and a swimming pool.

Gisenyi is a popular resort town on the famous Lake Kivu. In early 2004, the four-star Kivu Sun Hotel in Gisenyi opened, offering world class services and facilities for business and leisure.

Southern Sun's Managing Director, Helder Pereira says he is pleased to be expanding into central Africa and believes that there are definitely opportunities in both Rwanda and the DRC. Southern Sun has invested significantly in Africa in recent years, bringing to seven the number of African countries in which the group has a presence — Kenya, Zambia, Seychelles, Tanzania, Mozambique, Rwanda and South Africa. Southern Sun is focused on building its portfolio of successful global brands and continuing its expansion in sub-Saharan Africa.

(Source: www.southernsun.com)

The Tahal Consulting Engineering Group, an Israeli firm, pledged in October 2002 to help Rwanda improve its agricultural and energy sectors by introducing advanced technology in water supply and management, micro irrigation and sewerage treatment. The group agreed to set up a demonstration school in Rwanda, to improve Rwandan technology and farming techniques to achieve sustainable development. Tahal focuses on the training of personnel, on irrigation and livestock, and on the improvement of storage facilities in Rwanda. The Rwandan government set aside US$8 million for technological development and at least another $9 million for subsidising agricultural investors. It is important to develop projects for rural development, since 90 per cent of Rwanda is dependent on agriculture, which makes up for 40 per cent of the country's gross domestic product. The major cash crops are tea and coffee.

(Source: www.tahal.com)

Rwanda's tea is some of the best in the world and the current world market would support the expansion of good quality tea production, at both the factory and farm levels. The US government's Overseas Private Investment Corporation (OPIC) has had an investment guarantee in Rwanda since 1967. The major OPIC activity has been support for the American-owned Tea Importers' Société Rwandaise pour la production et la commercialization du Thé (Sorwathé). Cally Alles from Sri Lanka is director general of the entire project. Plantations and Sorwathé's tea factory, the largest in Rwanda and capable of producing 3,500 tons of black tea per year, are at Kinihira in Byumba Prefecture, which is located in the hills of northern Rwanda between Miyowe and Base. The view from the factory is one of the nicest in Rwanda — overlooking six volcanoes, some of which are in the DRC and one that is partly in Uganda and Rwanda. The factory premises and housing are picturesque, adorned with flower gardens maintained under the supervision of Cally's wife

Amithy. Sorwathé's Cyohoha tea factory produces fresh teas of Rwanda with a choice of two varieties of black tea grown in the swamp, two varieties of black tea grown on the mountains, a little green tea and Oolong tea. A special Cyohoha brand tea is sold in the US — bright yellow in colour and particularly pleasant when drunk with a teaspoon of milk.

Joseph H Wertheim, the majority shareholder of Sorwathé and president of Tea Importers Inc, a small business located in Westport, Connecticut, has credited OPIC with enabling his company to make investments in tea plantations in Rwanda and Ecuador. Wertheim says that OPIC has been a great help to Tea Importers and he can state unequivocally that without their assistance they would not have considered making the investments in the two tea plantations. With financing that included a loan from OPIC in 1975, Tea Importers established the only private tea factory in Rwanda. Tea Importers repaid the loan in 1990. Meanwhile, the company also purchased OPIC political risk insurance. Tea Importers do not own all of Sorwathé; US interests in Sorwathé are 65 per cent and Rwandan interests own 35 per cent.

During the 1990-1994 civil war in Rwanda, rebels shelled the company's Cyohoha tea processing factory and looted vehicles, office furniture and computers. OPIC political risk insurance was instrumental in rebuilding the tea factory after it had been damaged. OPIC's payment of four political violence claims for losses totalling US$200,000 encouraged Tea Importers to stay and rebuild. During the civil war both sides shelled the area and Sorwathé does not know which side caused the damage, but with or without OPIC Insurance the factory would have been rehabilitated when peace returned. Sorwathé was the first tea factory to resume production after the war. Wertheim sums up why Tea Importers has remained a driving force in Rwanda's tea business since 1975, despite a devastating five-year civil war, by saying they could not move 15 million tea bushes — that's where they were, so that's where they are.

In 1998, the Cyohoha tea factory in Rwanda produced approximately 6.6 million pounds of tea, which represented 20.3 per cent of the country's total production. The company was also the fourth largest taxpayer to the country that year and the only source of cash income to approximately 35,000 people in the area. The project supports 3,500 independent tea growers and employs 110 permanent staff, 450 permanent workers and 1,500 seasonal workers. Besides the economic benefits of the Tea Importers project for the company and for Rwanda, the local population now has proper housing and facilities. Schools have been built, health care is provided and, according to a World Bank study, the farmers in the area have a better income per acre of land than in other parts of the country.

OPIC has expressed interest in continuing its involvement in Rwanda. OPIC support for US private sector investments in emerging markets will continue to provide opportunities for US companies like Tea Importers. The long-term support and advocacy that OPIC can provide as a representative of the US government makes the agency a valuable resource for small businesses and other companies entering new markets.

Prior to the 1994 genocide and upheaval, Rwanda's chief export product was coffee. After 1994, many plantations went untended, their crops not gathered for export sale. With national and international help, the coffee industry is beginning a rebirth with a new gourmet blend of coffee beans bound for the international market. As with so many sectors of the Rwandan economy, women are playing a part in that rebirth. The story behind Bufcafe specialty coffee begins with Epiphanie Mukashyaka, who lost her husband in the genocide, but kept the family coffee farm going. 'I expected to spend the rest of my days begging for help from relatives and friends,' says Mukashyaka, who produces Bufcafe.

Needing to support her own seven children, plus many orphans from relatives who were also killed, Epiphanie used her husband's experience in the coffee trading business, secured a 54 million Rwandan franc (US$93,000) bank loan to build a washing station in Gikongoro, and began Bufcafe. She taught farmers — both genocide survivors and suspects — how to produce high quality coffee, and began buying cherries at higher prices. For the first time, local farmers were able to process their coffee cherries in a manner that meets specialty coffee standards, allowing them to receive better prices. The beans produced in Gikongoro have been highly rated as gourmet 'stand-alone' beans. The beans are grown at very high elevation, then milled by hand, with rigorous attention to detail. Bucafe has been judged by one of the world's top coffee tasters, Ken Davids, as one of the most exceptional among new coffee varieties. In the online edition of the Coffee Review, Ken Davids describes coffee from Bufcafe as: 'Superb aroma: sweet, balanced, and intense, with deep dimension and a grand range of nuance, ranging from floral top notes to mid-tones of papaya and perhaps pear.'

'Coffee helped me recover after the genocide and has restored my dignity,' says Mukashyaka, who now employs 54 workers. She says it has not only changed her life, but also the lives of villagers who used to live on a lot less than half a dollar a day and who are now paid at least 15,000 Rwandan francs (US$26) a month.

(Source: Rodrique Ngowi. 'Coffee will help farmers and gorillas', *Associated Press*, May 2004)

The 'Signature Coffees of Rwanda' programme offers a unique way for the world's importers, roasters or retailers to present some of the finest coffees of Africa. Rwanda's specialty coffee is second to none — citrussy bright and berry, but with floral notes that make tasters think of Ethiopia, it is 'distinctly African but uniquely Rwandan.' Everyone in Rwanda is focused on quality, and ten brand new washing stations support Signature Coffees of Rwanda's growing family of producers.

(Source: www.rwandacafe.com)

Parliamentarian Juliana Kantengwa says, 'The challenges on the ground necessitated the women to work extra hard. It's like we doubled the effort and shortened the time. Women emerged with new skills with new determination to move forward, it was no longer possible for them to go back.'

Katherine Blakeslee, director of USAID's Office of Women in Development, says, 'We are keenly aware of the effect of conflict on women...Yet today, women in Rwanda are building, governing and healing their country.' Women now hold 48 per cent of seats in Rwanda's lower house of parliament — the highest percentage in a parliament anywhere in the world. Women also constitute 90 per cent of the country's agricultural workforce.

(Source: 'Ladies first - Women rebuild Rwanda', PBS documentary; www.pbs.org)

Rwandan flori-culturist Beatrice Gakuba is one private entrepreneur who took a calculated risk with her business, Rwanda Flora, a now thriving flower farm and rose export business. Gakuba left a 20-year international development career to return to Rwanda, where she bought Rwanda Flora as it became liquidated in early 2004. It was a gamble that paid off. Gakuba says, 'My goal was to grow beautiful roses on the ashes of genocide.' Against enormous odds, her small farm grew, creating jobs for nearly 200 rural women. In 2005, Gakuba was exporting four tonnes of roses a week to Europe, and saying, 'Working with development taught me to integrate social services into my business.'

During his 2005 visit to Rwanda, World Bank President, Paul Wolfowitz met Gakuba and listened to her experiences as an entrepreneur in Rwanda. Wolfowitz lauded her resilience and entrepreneurship in an address to the United Nations General Assembly at the September 2005 World Summit in New York. He cited Gakuba's efforts in Rwanda, saying her hard work and determination symbolised the talents and dreams of millions of Africans. He asked that world leaders not forget the Beatrice Gakubas of the world, who stand poised to transform their countries, and noted that new and sound policies had enabled Rwanda to discard its horrendous past and register meaningful economic growth, coming a long way from its years of pain and conflict, and averaging more than six per cent annual growth.

(Source: www.worldbank.org)

In a November 2005 e-mail to the author, Gakuba wrote that her fight against poverty in Africa has been the focal point of her international development career for the last 20 years, mostly with UN organisations as a staff member or as a consultant. She still consults and has an international consultancy company headquartered in South Africa. Being in Rwanda, dealing with business in a post conflict/post genocide environment, has made her an entrepreneur with a human face. She will definitely put her experience to use benefiting other countries that are coming out of conflict, like her African neighbours Sudan, Liberia and Sierra Leone.

In late 2003, Liz Wald, founder and managing partner of Economic Development Imports (EDImports), a New York-based importer of handmade home goods, gifts and fashion accessories from Africa, came to Rwanda to investigate the export of handmade Rwandan goods to the United States. Shortly thereafter, a joint venture was formed between EDImports and Rwanda partners (and sisters), Joy Ndungutse and Janet Nkubana, the co-founders of Gahaya Links, and their first product, the Red Friendship Basket, was developed for export. One thousand of these baskets were sold in the first order and the team built on that early success. This venture shows how entrepreneurship at all levels — from grass roots village production to international marketing and sales — can combine to create a thriving business.

In 2004, more than 12,000 items were created for export, including the very popular 'peace fortune ornament' designed to commemorate the ten-year anniversary of Rwanda's genocide. Hand-woven by women of Gitarama, whose lives were shattered by the tragic events, the sisal ornaments are dyed in bright, holiday colours and feature authentic Rwandan proverbs inside such as *Agasozi kagufi kagushyikiriza akarekare* (climbing even a short hill will bring us to a higher point).

'The Rwandan peace fortune ornaments are significant on two levels,' says Wald. 'They spread the message of peace on a global scale, but also, when sold successfully in the US, directly benefit the women who craft them, creating a thriving and sustainable economy for a segment of the population that previously lived at the margin'.

(Source: www.edimports.com)

In 2005, Gahaya Links received interest from the large US department store Macy's, for its handcrafted 'peace baskets'. Macy's set-up a display of the baskets at one of the New York Macy stores from July to September 2005 at no cost to Gahaya Links. This display was used to test the market response to the 'peace baskets' and allow sufficient production lead-time for the Christmas season. It presented a great opportunity for Gahaya Links to make headway into the US market.

By September 2005, Janet Nkubana, the managing director of Gahaya Links, was sitting in her Rwanda showroom, recovering from a hectic day spent shipping 5,000 Christmas ornaments and baskets to Macy's in New York. It was the first of several shipments Gahaya Links would send to the department store. Amid displays of baskets, shawls and necklaces, Nkubana says reaching the US market is a big achievement for her and the 400 Rwandan women weavers whom she and her sister employ. 'I am proud our products are winning the USA market,' she says.

(Source: Gayle Tzemach. 'How to weave around the odds', *The Financial Times*, www.newtimes.co.rw, 13 September 13 2005)

In 2005, Colleen Taugher, senior associate at WSU's Centre to Bridge the Digital Divide, visited Rwanda Computer Network (RCN). During her visit she got the opportunity to see the major achievements of RCN, which was started by Immaculée Kalisa in 2003, with the aim of reducing the cost of computers in Rwanda and letting every Rwandan provide himself or herself with computer tools and ICT skills at an affordable price. Kalisa, the manager as well as founder of RCN, discovered that importing computers cost almost the same as importing component parts. By choosing to import parts, RCN could provide local jobs assembling the machines, and in maintenance and repairing services as well as in teaching. These component parts have a special advantage of producing a fantastic local product, which is now for sale in Rwanda and in the region. It is a PC marketed under the label 'Gorilla 1000' to convey the computer's power or strength and for Rwanda's fabled thousand hills.

In addition to the computer assembly, RCN also offers classes to people who want to learn new skills, mainly in computer advanced programmes like software applications, hardware and networking installation. Many of the students who attend the company's ICT Training Centre are victims of the war and confined to wheelchairs. Attending classes contributes somehow to their medical and psychological treatment since it gives them hope that they can still be helpful for themselves and others. Moreover, other learners are employees or students sent by their respective institutions and organisations. Others come on an individual basis. The opportunities that the company is providing under Kalisa's initiative are especially inspiring.

More particularly, since the inception of RCN Kalisa has been combating the belief that goods made in Rwanda are of less quality than those imported. 'Because we assemble computers here in Rwanda, people thought they weren't good,' she says. Kalisa fought to shed the image by letting people use some of her initial 50 computers for free. As a result of her struggle, the company is now receiving purchase orders from all corners of Rwanda.

In its strategy, Rwanda Computer Network offers a two-year guarantee to its customers on every delivered computer. It offers various computer services to public and private sector institutions as well as to individuals. As far as competitiveness is concerned, in 2005, Kalisa secured a contract with the government of Rwanda for 4,000 computers to be delivered to secondary schools through the ministry of education. By the end of November 2005, RCN had delivered 2,000 of the 4,000 contracted computers at the rate of 300 per month.

In order to achieve its goals, the company has arranged a minimum infrastructure comprising a well equipped workshop for computer assembly and configuration, a showroom, a conference hall and rooms for classes and administrative services. It plans to export its product in the context of regional cooperation and will soon open branches and representations where possible. RCN centres its programme on the national strategy of improving the living conditions of the population, reducing poverty, creating new employment and contributing to the promotion of computer literacy in the country. For these reasons, the RCN has developed collaboration with the Kigali Institute of Sciences and Technology, the National University of Rwanda, and other big institutions and companies at both national and international levels.

(Source: www.rcnrwanda.com)

During her visit, Colleen Taugher was very impressed with RCN's achievements. She was excited about working with Kalisa to get youth involved in getting the machines into the schools and to help embed an effective IT curriculum. Later in 2005, Colleen and WSU's Centre to Bridge the Digital Divide was awarded a grant from the US Department of State to continue building on the work that she started in Rwanda in February 2005. She began in February 2006 by bringing a delegation of Rwandese youth to Washington State for intensive technology training with 4-H youth there (4-H is a community of young people across America, learning leadership, citizenship and life skills). She also brought government representatives there to collaborate with the Washington State Workforce Training and Education Board. This team began work on drafting a strategic plan for growing an ICT-capable workforce in Rwanda. That experience was to be followed up with a group of 4-H youth travelling to Rwanda in June 2006 to deliver technology training to youth in Kigali. The Washington State Workforce Training and Education Board staff was to travel as well in order to complete the strategic plan and to learn more about the workforce development challenges in Rwanda.

Entrepreneurs are taking advantage of evolving market conditions, and sometimes becoming local heroes in the process. Two young film makers, a Briton and a Rwandan, teamed up to produce a very powerful film about the Rwandan genocide. Nick Hughes, the director, and Eric Kabera, the producer, depict in their moving film *100 Days* the horror which befell Rwanda in 1994. It was filmed in the southern province of Kibuye, a place of a stunning beauty. The actors, mainly Rwandans, are mostly amateurs, with the exception of a few non-Rwandan actors who play the UN and French soldiers, journalists and a western parish priest. The film was first launched in the Toronto Film Festival in September 2001 and later screened at the

Raindance Film Festival in the Metro Cinema in London's Leicester Square in October 2001. In early 2002, the film was released to the general public with the hope that the film would reach a wide western audience.

The producers of *100 Days* say the aim is to show the world what actually happened to the Rwandan people whose suffering sometimes is still remote to many people around the world. Alex Shoumatoff is the author of a forthcoming multi-generational saga of his Rwandan wife's family from the dawn of Rwandan history through the l994 genocide. He says that *100 Days* is a powerfully and chillingly authentic portrayal about the genocide of 1994 overtaking Kibuye, a beautiful, hitherto bucolically peaceful town on Lake Kivu in Rwanda. He believes it is a film not to be missed by anyone disturbed by the darkness and collective madness increasingly abroad in the world.

Eric Kabera has initiated the Rwanda Cinema Centre, the first film institution of Rwanda. This project trains and exposes Rwandan aspiring filmmakers to the industry and culture of cinematography through a training centre and an institution for foreign film producers who are seeking African film locations and talents. Eric created the structure to enable Rwanda to attract films that will carry the story and name of Rwanda. Eric Kabera is also the director and the producer of the gripping documentary *Keepers of Memory* (*Gardiens de la Memoire*), which commemorates the tenth anniversary of the genocide in Rwanda by telling the story of the extraordinary journey of a people's bravery. *Keepers of Memory* has been screened in Rwanda during the commemoration period (April 2004) and worldwide. Many film festivals screened this important film to the memory of the Rwandan genocide, and it is in this regard that the film obtained the Special Mention at the Vues d'Afrique, the main African film festival in Canada. The film became also the People's Choice, obtained the silver award of the East-African Production and the Signis Commendation at the Zanzibar International Film Festival (ZIFF). The film has also been screened in prestigious film festivals such as the Toronto International Film Festival, Milan African Film Festival and the Durban International Film Festival in South Africa.

Eric Kabera is now finishing his latest production *Through My Eyes*. The RCC is helping young men and women to become professional filmmakers. Three have been in North America for training. 'RCC will help sensitise policymakers on the importance of filmmaking and of their responsibility to support it,' says Kabera, a member of the East African Filmmakers Forum that seeks to boost the audiovisual profile of the eastern African region. The Forum brings together filmmakers from Kenya, Tanzania, Rwanda, Ethiopia, Somalia and Uganda.

Several other film companies have focused on the Rwandan genocide of 1994 when 800,000 Tutsis and politically moderate Hutus died in 100 days of ethnic slaughter. *Hotel Rwanda*, based on true events and starring Don Cheadle and Nick Nolte, tells the true-life story of Paul Rusesabagina (played by Cheadle), a Hutu who was the manager of a smart Rwandan hotel in Kigali. When the war broke out he thought of only saving his immediate family but as he saw what was happening he opened the hotel to Tutsi and Hutus seeking refuge from the killing. He used all the favours he had stored as manager of the hotel and saved over a thousand lives. In 2004, when the film was shown at the Toronto International Film Festival, there was a standing ovation. Rusesabagina was an adviser for the movie and he and his family attended the screening, at which he received a five minute standing ovation. He still can't believe they made a movie about him, since he is just an average person but he hopes people will see that even an average person can make a difference in someone else's life simply by opening their eyes and their heart.

(Source: Scott Bowles. 'Actor spreads word on Rwanda'. *USA Today*, 4 January 2005)

Another film, *Shake Hands with the Devil: The Journey of Romeo Dallaire* tracks the return to Rwanda of the Canadian general who led the undermanned UN force that failed to stop the killing. Assigned to the country only months before the madness erupted, UN commander General Romeo Dallaire found that, despite his best efforts, he was unable to curtail the mass slaughter. The film is based partially on Dallaire's book, *Shake Hands with the Devil: The Failure of Humanity* in Rwanda (2004), and tells the tragic and profoundly important story of this legendary general. Dallaire argues that Rwanda-like situations are fires that can be put out with a small force if caught early enough; however, the book and the film document in horrifying detail what happens when no serious effort is made. In Steven Silver's award-winning documentary, *The Last Just Man*, a haunted Dallaire relates his personal account of one of the 20th century's worst cases of genocide and explains how politics and timidity conspired to prevent the UN from keeping the peace. A feature film totally based on Dallaire's book is planned for release in late 2006.

Philip Gourevitch, author of *We Wish to Inform You That Tomorrow We Will be Killed with Our Families* (1998), writes that the civil war in Rwanda in 1994 produced few heroes. Gourevitch points out, however, that in the midst of the horror Paul Rusesabagina the quick-witted and courageous Hutu hotel manager of the Hotel des Mille Collines, managed to save more than a thousand people. Gourevitch says that although Rusesabagina may not have seen what he did as heroic, he saved many lives, something that almost everyone else was unable or unwilling to do. None of the people who took shelter at the hotel was killed during the genocide. In 2000, Rusesabagina was the recipient of the Immortal Chaplains Prize for Humanity and was running a small taxi company in Brussels, Belgium, and is still exceptionally modest about what he did.

(Source: Philip Gourevitch. *We Wish to Inform You That Tomorrow We Will be Killed with Our Families*, New York: Farrar Straus & Giroux, 1998)

In his autobiography, *My Life*, Bill Clinton wrote that the failure to try to stop Rwanda's tragedies was one of the greatest regrets of his presidency. In his second term, and after he left office, Clinton did what he could to help the Rwandans put their country and their lives back together. Today, at the invitation of President Paul Kagame, Rwanda is one of the countries in which the Clinton Foundation is working to stem the tide of AIDS.

The Hotel Chez Lando was built by university professor Landoald 'Lando' Ndasingwa and his French-Canadian wife Hélène in the mid-1980s. It was created with a vision to provide an environment where people of all social and economic backgrounds could meet to conduct business or simply mingle and have a good time. The quaint garden-style hotel was built on a stretch of grassy land along the main road to the only international airport in the country, long before the neighbourhood became the bustling Remera commercial center it is today. In 1991, Lando decided to join the pro-democracy movement and eventually he became the government's Minister of Labour and Social Affairs, the only Tutsi in the cabinet when the 1994 genocide started. He had been active in trying to facilitate the return of Tutsi refugees living in neighbouring Uganda and was always vocal on behalf of equal treatment for the country's minority groups. Thus, it was feared that he might be one of the presidential guards' primary targets. That fear was borne out. According to a witness, in the morning of 7 April 1994, about 20 members of the Presidential Guards came to Lando's house; after searching the house, they shot Lando, his wife, mother, and two children. Hotel Chez Lando was also partially destroyed, but the spirit of the founders prevailed, prompting Lando's siblings to take over, rebuild and expand.

(Source: Romeo Dallaire. *Shake Hands with the Devil: The Failure of Humanity in Rwanda*, New York: Carroll & Graf, 2004)

Hotel Chez Lando is managed today by Lando's sister, Anne-Marie Kantengwa. Daily and prolonged happy hours in the grill area have become a must for after-work relaxation for anyone living in, or visiting, Rwanda. Hotel Chez Lando offers two dining style choices. The Chez Lando barbecue grill offers a friendly and informal atmosphere while the La Fringale French restaurant offers more formal dining for couples or business groups needing privacy. Anne-Marie started to expand and revamp the hotel in mid-2004. Rwandan and Dutch architects worked together on a roomier barbecue area, with state of the art bar, ten additional old-style Rwandan hut bungalows with modern-amenities, a swimming pool, and a larger children's playing area. In 2005, Hotel Chez Lando has 32 quaint rooms with individual patios. Whether one stays in one of their bungalow-style villas or in the main building with views of the gardens or of the rolling hills of Kigali, one is surrounded by beauty.

The story of Anne-Marie Kantengwa illustrates the country's political awakening. During the genocide she hid in the roof of a neighbour's house for almost a month, having lost two children, three brothers, and four other family members. After the murders stopped, Anne-Marie emerged with a powerful will to rebuild her family's business. Still recovering from shock, she became a leader in Kigali's economic recovery; in 2005, she headed the Hotel, Tourism and Restaurant Association of Rwanda. Although apolitical before the genocide, she eventually took an active role in politics. In elections held in 2003, she was one of two dozen women elected to the lower house of parliament. Her sister believes Anne-Marie's efforts symbolise the sense of renewal and hope felt by many Rwandans.

(Source: Swanee Hunt. 'Rwandan women step forward', *Scripps Howard News Service*, 8 October 2003)

After the genocide, Odette Nyiramilimo and her husband ran a private maternity and paediatrics practice in Kigali, the Good Samaritan Clinic. She saw women who had never consulted a doctor or spoken about being raped. She says there was a sense of shame among the survivors. Those who were not in Rwanda during the genocide looked at those who were and asked 'How did you survive?' It was as though they had done something shameful to survive. Rwandan women had been subjected to sexual violence on a massive scale, perpetrated by members of the infamous Hutu militia groups known as the Interahamwe, by other civilians and by soldiers of the Rwandan armed forces (Forces Armées Rwandaises), including the presidential guard. Administrative, military and political leaders at the national and local levels, as well as heads of militia, directed or encouraged both the killings and sexual violence to further their political goal — the destruction of the Tutsi as a group.

By 2000, Odette had become Rwanda's Minister of State in charge of social affairs in the ministry of local government, information and social affairs. At a global conference in South Africa in October 2000, she proposed that the Rwanda government's main economic role was to create a helpful environment in which economic activity could take place effectively. Rwanda's thrust was to be towards a strong and competent state that provides a visionary leadership and management role. Odette said that a delicate balancing act needed to be created between market forces and the strong guiding and facilitative hand for the state. She proposed that the role of the state should include:

- Providing a stable macroeconomic environment;
- good governance and national reconciliation;
- enforcing a coherent legal and regulatory system which protects the property rights of all citizens, including the poor, and enabling entrepreneurs to operate in a business-friendly environment;
- maintaining quality infrastructure;
- promoting human resource development;
- protecting the environment; and
- intervening to correct market failures, promote equity and protect the vulnerable.

Odette said the government recognised that Rwanda's prosperity in the future would come from new insights, high quality human capital and attitudes and actions that embrace competitiveness and innovation. Rwanda needed to create a competitive edge out of its two natural advantages of human resources and bilingualism. Rwanda could transform its population into a highly skilled bilingual force through human resource development. The development of human resources could form a basis for a service economy based on skills in science, technology and management.

Odette completed medical school at the National University of Rwanda in 1981. She worked in various hospitals of Rwanda, and taught in nursing and medical assistant schools. While practising, she had training in medical pedagogy (Lome, Togo), and in gynaecology, laparoscopy and ultrasonography (Charleroi and Brussels, Belgium). From 1991 to 1994, she worked as a Peace Corps medical officer, and attended several continuing medical education workshops in various countries. At the same time, with her husband, she started their private clinic Le Bon Samaritain. From 1995 to February 2000, Odette worked at Le Bon

Samaritain as a gynaecologist, a counsellor for raped and/or widowed women and participated in various women's associations. From March 2000 to October 2003, Odette was Minister of State for Social Affairs and since then has been a senator in the parliament of Rwanda.

(Source: Odette Nyiramilimo. 'Poverty reduction strategy programme in Rwanda', speech presented at the ICSW International Conference on Social Welfare, Cape Town, South Africa, 23-27 October 2000; www.icsw.org/global-conferences/nyiramilimo.htm)

Odette sees VSAT technology as a unique fit for rural applications in Africa and around the world. Rwanda faced the enormous task of closing the technology gap of several generations, making time an essential element. Only VSAT technology allowed for the deployment of hundreds of sites, in difficult terrain, in a short period of time. In 2003, Artel Communications deployed, and now operates and maintains, a VSAT network for RwandaTel, Rwanda's national telecommunications company. The VSAT network provides consumers and businesses with telephony and high-speed internet service in the education, health care, financial services and government markets throughout Rwanda and central Africa.

Artel's former chief executive officer, Yves Godelet, says that Artel's mission is to use VSAT technology to bring the satellite-based telephony and Internet service to remote communities nationwide. Godelet adds that Rwanda's ambitious 'Vision 2020' plan calls for extensive use of information and communications technology over the next 20 years to support steady economic development. He says that Artel is proud to be participating in that plan through the implementation of VSAT technology. The VSAT network allows villages to communicate with law enforcement agencies, to support health care programmes and to assist international aid agencies. As in many African nations, reliable telecommunications in Rwanda was limited to urban areas. In fact, only about six per cent of the Rwandan population had access to telephone service. Now, satellite telephony and high-speed internet services are available to rural villages and are having a positive impact on the development of Rwanda.

A two-way satellite communications telephony network is now in use throughout Rwanda. The network is deployed evenly throughout the country, with each VSAT servicing two public phones using a pre-paid (scratch card) system and powered with solar energy. With its VSAT network Rwanda has one of the highest densities of public satellite telephone lines per square kilometre in the world (one public telephone per 30 square kilometres). Godelet says that the service provided is revolutionary for the African Great Lakes region and that it is truly gratifying to see that the 18 000 residents of a small, isolated island in the middle of Lake Kivu, on the Congo-Rwanda border, now have telephone communication and Internet access as a result of VSAT technology. In 2001, they were cut off from the world, but in 2003 they were enjoying the benefits of the Internet age. This is what is meant when one talks about bridging the digital divide.

The entire Great Lakes region is an emerging economy and thus presents enormous opportunities for investing in the service industry. In particular, Rwanda has designated the service industry as one of the pillars for the country's development agenda. Gerald Mpyisi wants to take the lead by providing quality ICT services in the region. Business Communication Solutions (BCS) is an ICT company established by Mpyisi and other Rwandans with the mission to be the number one ICT services provider in Rwanda and throughout the Great Lakes region and to help transform the Rwanda Economy into a knowledge-based economy. Currently BCS is headquartered in Rwanda and has branches in Burundi and the Eastern Congo. BCS services include SMS applications; internet services including VoIP; call centre; software development and resellers; business centre; computer equipment rental; foreign company representatives; taxi services; and community mobile pay phone. BCS is the biggest 'Tuvugane' community payphone service provider in Rwanda.

In March 2004, the MTN Group, Africa's second largest cellular network by subscribers, successfully introduced, in partnership with Business Communication Solutions, mobile communication to Rwandan communities through its 'Tuvugane' (KiRwanda for 'let us all talk') community payphone service. MTN Rwanda, whose subscriber base stood at 175,000 as of March 2005, has rolled out 1,600 payphones since 600 payphones were deployed at inception in March 2004. Subscribers in Rwanda were generating average revenue per user of US$50 a month. MTN claims the service offers the most affordable rates for mobile and global calls in Rwanda and is available where it has coverage, putting telecommunications within reach of 95 per cent of the rural population. MTN Rwanda is committed to the delivery of quality and innovative services while playing a leading role in the socio-economic development of the country.

The Tuvugane initiative is part of MTN's drive to increase tele-density in rural areas throughout its operations and put telecommunications within the reach even of those who cannot afford handsets. The project has also created many entrepreneurs — a move in line with the company's plan to empower the communities in which it operates. The Tuvugane public pay phone service is a partnership between BCS and MTN. All the operations are implemented by BCS (purchasing of the handsets, sales and marketing, repairs and maintenance, sending airtime and collection of airtime money). MTN provides the network and participates in promotional expositions.

(Source: www.bcs.co.rw, and www.mtn.co.rw)

There is a palpable atmosphere of blossoming domestic and foreign business activity in Rwanda. Multinationals, like BAT and Shell Uganda, are active in the country, and government agencies set up to encourage private-sector development are getting foreign support. The recent economic recovery has prompted a number of lesser-known multinationals actively to invest in agricultural and mineral processing industries, building materials, sugar manufacturing, telecommunications and other sectors.

(Source: Joel Stratte-McClure. 'Encouraging corporate activity', *International Herald Tribune*, www.iht.com, 5 February 2003)

James Shikwati, the Director of the Inter Region Economic Network and Coordinator of the Africa Resource Bank, reports that Rwanda and Uganda have superb roads that would turn Kenyan motorists green with envy. In December 2004, he reported that travelling by road from Nairobi to Kigali had been not only exhausting but exciting for him. The concept of cities changed as he moved through Uganda down to Rwanda — some of the cities shrank to what in Nairobi would be a mere suburb.

Touring the genocide memorial site in Rwanda left his group both angry and humbled. It illustrated the danger of a people surrendering their minds to their leaders. It depicts the extent to which politicians can go to attain their objectives. A student who accompanied Shikwati on his trip could not hold back her tears. But behind this heavy cloud of sorrow, Shikwati says a peaceful Rwanda is emerging; although it will certainly take years for the wounds to heal he adds that a new Rwanda with clean and safe cities has emerged from the ashes.

Shikwati reports that privatisation has taken centre stage in Rwanda. Private businesses, schools, universities and tour firms are competing with state-owned facilities. American Lawrence Reed told Shikwati that in making reservations for his gorilla safari via e-mail, he learned that all gorilla safaris are conducted by private, locally-owned and locally-run companies. In 2001, two Rwandan entrepreneurs started Primate Safaris, the firm with which Reed travelled in 2004. With six employees, they provided everything a gorilla safari enthusiast could hope for — a competent guide with a four-wheel drive, good meals and comfortable, though Spartan, accommodation. The lodge where Reed stayed at the base of one of the volcanoes is owned by a private Rwandan women's association now, but at the time they bought it in 2002, it was government property.

Shikwati says Rwanda, in the heart of Africa, is engaged in the continent's most ambitious privatisation campaign. It may be the most ambitious and systematic of any country's, anywhere. After experiencing the kind of stifling, socialist rule that consigned virtually all of Africa to grinding deprivation for ages, this is a country that is now embracing the private sector with deliberate policy and enormous enthusiasm. He points out that, since the privatisation drive started in 1996, assets sold by the Rwandan government include its hotels, its tea factories, a fruit juice factory, a printing firm and companies that produce insecticides, tobacco products, sugar, dairy products, processed fish and coffee. Electrogaz and Rwandatel have already been privatised and by the end of 2005 all the remaining state-owned companies, including banks, will be privatised. Shikwati foresees Rwanda remaining on this path until it creates a genuine free market economy complete with something else it has never had before — a stock exchange, to be launched in June 2005. Even the human resources for this project had already been recruited by January 2005. The Rwandan case illustrates the fact that, despite the past traumatic experience, individuals are rising up to change their economic circumstances for the better.

(Source: James Shikwati. 'Rwanda a privatisation revolution', *IREN Newsletter*, Issue No. 4, 22 December 2004)

Burundi

The success story in Burundi comes from the northern province of Ngozi, where Burundi's former prime minister, Pascal Ndimira, has organised the population in associations. Rural electrification was brought in for the first time in 1996. Then, in 1997, the first private scheme was initiated — thousands of people from all walks of life came together to raise US$1.5 million for a coffee processing plant, Sivca. Hutu and Tutsi alike bought 5 000 shares in the project and although some raised only tiny amounts, says Ndimira, they created a crucial and unprecedented sense of shared ownership, along modern business principles.

In 1999, Ngozi took the next step and raised US$2.5 million to establish Burundi's first private university, backed again by local people and the Catholic Church. It has fast become a popular alternative for the country's middle class, and its success has been replicated elsewhere. 'At first there was jealousy, and then replication,' says Ndimira. In May 2000, the town launched the Cofide micro-finance bank. It makes loans to small producers' associations, and has boosted coffee production through a tie-up with the state buying agency.

Locals speak of Ngozi's dedication. 'It is an integrated development programme for the whole town,' says Nicodeme Bugwabari, from the university's science faculty. 'This university makes war against war, by developing the region socially and economically. And we did it ourselves we couldn't do it otherwise.' New motels have been built, and many micro-finance projects have been developed. An abandoned former German aid-financed goat project is under private management. The town is filled with building sites, new micro-enterprises are being created, and infrastructural developments, such as a small hydro-power station, have been completed.

(Source: Mark Turner. 'Economic experiment thrives amid African conflict', *FT.com*, *Financial Times*, 23 October 2001)

In 2004, the province had its own university, a new bank, and a three-star hotel. Ngozi's main agricultural product is coffee. In 2004, all coffee planters had bank accounts and easy access to microfinance. Most of the population had a decent house and some were buying cars and electric goods such as TVs and radios. The revenue per capita in Ngozi is the highest in Burundi, about US$300 a year while the rest of the population earns US$150 a year. Mobile phone companies are also investing in Burundi, and in 2004, there were three of them: Telecel, Africell and Burcell, and three main internet service providers, CNI, USAN and SpeedNet, Eugene Nyagahene's company.

Prime Nyamoya, a well-known Burundian economist from the region, explains that it is not simply a coincidence - the benefits of free enterprise are unquestionable. Nyamoya sees a direct correlation between responsible business practices and political stability and security. He says Ngozi shows how private initiative, based on a common goal, can achieve peace.

(Source: Mark Turner. 'Economic experiment thrives amid African conflict', *FT.com*, *Financial Times*, 23 October 2001)

Nyamoya, formerly an economics professor, is now the Administrateur Directeur Général of the Banque de Crédit de Bujumbura with branches in Gihofi, Gitega, Kayanza, Muyinga, Ngozi, Rumonge and

Kirundo. The bank is specifically organised to offer a high-quality corporate service and personalised service to SME executives in financing foreign trade, including imports and exports. Prime Nyamoya is also president of the Burundi Enterprise Network (BEN), which has been successfully promoting entrepreneurship in Burundi since 1999. BEN members are successful entrepreneurs in various fields such as agro-industries, services and information technology and their companies have created numerous jobs in a very difficult economic and political environment. Prospects for the future are positive after the April 2005 elections.

Herménégilde Ndikumasabo is a prominent Burundian businessman with a coffee export business, a cattle ranch, a dairy plant in Bujumbura, and interests in the importation of wheat, fertilisers, sugar, pharmaceutical machinery, packaging material plants, polypropylene and jute bags. Ndikumasabo is the president of the Burundian National Chamber of Commerce and Industry. His vegetables and flowers export company produces high-quality cut roses for export by air to the European Union market on his 390-hectare farm located 12 kilometres from the Bujumbura airport. Three hectares have been developed to grow four varieties of roses in wood-framed plastic-covered greenhouses. In addition to creating rural employment and earning foreign exchange, Ndikumasabo's project demonstrates the viability of exporting non-traditional crops from land-locked Burundi by air to European markets, and is a powerful example of an alternative investment activity to traditional coffee and tea exports for local businessmen to follow.

Brasseries et limonaderies du Burundi (BRARUDI), Burundi's sole modern beer and soft drinks bottling company, has invested in new facilities in order to increase sales of its beers Primus and Amstel, sales of Coca-Cola, and sales of a carbonated water Vital O. These modern facilities cost some 10.0 million euro (10.0 billion Burundian francs). The creation of these facilities was the prelude to an investment plan of 40 million euro financed through equity capital. The new bottling line represents approximately 10 million euro of these 40 million, while the remaining 30 million represents new carbon dioxide (CO_2) reclamation plant, new cooling plant, new syrup plant, new water treatment plant, electrical distribution, waste water pre-treatment plant and civil work for the extension of finished products warehouse and loading area.

According to Marc Busain, Brarudi's managing director, this investment is useful in financing staff training and equipping the company with modern machinery intended for the creation of a new line of production manufactured by the German Krones Group.

Heineken, a 59.3 per cent shareholder of the Brarudi Brewery and the world's third-largest brewer, provides AIDS drugs to its 6,500 African workers in a programme started in 2001 in Rwanda and Burundi, where AIDS is the number one killer. Providing therapy and testing for HIV-positive workers at the Brarudi Brewery in Burundi increases the medical expense for the company by around 8 euros per employee but programme costs are almost completely recovered by savings in medical care. Burundi's HIV rate is almost 20 per cent in some urban areas. Heineken's work-based programmes are starting to overcome patients' hesitancy to seek treatment.

The Global Digital Solidarity Fund (DSF) provides financing for equipment, training and services in the field of information and communication technologies (radio, telephone, television, ICTs, internet). The objective is to complement national development programmes by responding to local development needs pertaining to the ICT sector. Therefore, the DSF supports community-based projects that are part of a national strategy. The DSF gives priority to South-South cooperation projects.

In November 2005, the DSF launched its first projects in three countries: Burundi, Burkina Faso and the Dominican Republic. These projects consist in providing a VSAT internet connection to structures committed in the fight against the AIDS, in order to allow certain applications like Télémedecine. These projects are run in collaboration with AIDS Empowerment and Treatment International. For Burundi, three stations VSAT were retained following redistributing the received connection with the other neighbouring structures by radio local loops: the head office of the SEP/CNLS in Bujumbura; the antenna ANSS for Gitega; and the antenna of the SWAA Burundi for Ngozi.

Jean Paul Nkurunziza believes the use of new information technologies opens promising prospects for those involved in the fight against HIV/AIDS. A connection internet with high bandwidth offers a better coordination between the communities, the public and deprived medical structures, the institutes of research, and NGOs. Thus, the communities far away from the urban centres, with few resources, will profit from a data base on the prevention, the assumption of responsibility and the treatment of patients.

Nkurunziza is one of the creators of the Burundi Youth Training Centre (BYTC), and is also its Secretary General. BYTC is a centre in Bujumbura that educates local youngsters in the use of computers and the internet. He is also the national coordinator for Burundi of a project named Independent Observatory of Internet Access in Africa (Observatoire indépendant des offres d'accès à Internet en Afrique) This project was launched in eight countries in Africa with the financial support of Fond Francophone des Inforoutes.

Nkurunziza's activities in the ICT area began in 1999 with the training of Burundian youth in Bujumbura, the capital city of Burundi. In 2003, he was nominated to be the head manager of the project, Internet Centre for Youth, which was launched with the financial support of the Intergovernmental French Speaking Agency. He has also been involved in the WSIS process as the national World Summit Award's expert (WSA) for Burundi. The WSA is an initiative led by the International Centre for New Media, which aims to promote best products and applications of ICTs for development.

(Sources: www.dsf-fsn.org, www.aidseti.org and www.bytc.bi)

In a bid to promote peace and stability in the region, foreign ministers from Burundi, Rwanda and the Democratic Republic of the Congo (DRC) met in July 2004 and decided to reinitiate economic cooperation by reactivating the Economic Community of Great Lakes Countries. The community, known by its French acronym CEPGL (Communauté Economique des Pays des Grands Lacs), was active in the 1980s before conflict in the 1990s put an end to free trade exchange in the region. In January 2005, Roger Nsibula of CEPGL pointed out that the eastern DRC, Rwanda and Burundi share common natural resources (rivers, lakes, natural gas), the same problems (ethnic conflicts, refugee movement, arms traffic, cross-border trade), and the same culture, and hence have to work together in order to find the best ways to address the socio-economic problems of their respective populations.

The CEPGL structures that are to be re-launched cover economic, energy, conservation and social domains. They will include the Development Bank of the Great Lakes States (Banque de Développement des Etats des Grands Lacs) based in the eastern Congolese town of Goma; the Great Lakes International Electricity Company (Societé Internationale d'Electricité des Grands Lacs) based in Bukavu in eastern DRC; the Great Lakes Energy Organisation (Organisation pour l'Energie des Grands Lacs) based in the Burundian capital, Bujumbura; and the Institute for Agronomical and Zoological Research (Institut de Recherche Agronomique et Zootechnique) based in the central Burundian province of Gitega. Social dialogue aimed at reinforcing the partnership among social partners and to implement conflict prevention mechanisms is to be revived.

The objective of the reactivation of the CEPGL is to consolidate peace and stability in the African Great Lakes Region, by acting as an element in the rebuilding of mutual trust. The CEPGL was created in 1976, with Gisenyi in Rwanda as its headquarters. The aim was to promote regional integration through the free circulation of goods and persons, the promotion of trade and cooperation in various fields including cultural, economic and scientific. President Domitien Ndayizeye of Burundi describes the organisation as being of 'extreme importance' for the populations of Burundi, Rwanda and the Democratic Republic of the Congo. The reactivation of regional economic structures will constitute a vital complement to the current peace and transitional phases in these countries.

Burundi and Rwanda were assured on 26 November 2004 that their long-desired admission to the East African Community (EAC) was a matter of time. President Mwai Kibaki of Kenya told the sixth Summit of the EA Heads of State that the two countries in central Africa should not consider themselves outsiders in the East African integration process. He said the two countries have not only applied to join EAC since the regional body was revived in the mid-1990s but have enjoyed observer status in all matters pertaining to regional integration under the Community. He attributed the delay to register them as members of the

Community to wars and instability in the two countries and the Great Lakes region as a whole. 'For the Burundi, I tell them agree at home first and decide where you want to go,' he said. In April 2005, Burundi held a general election under the Arusha Peace Process.

Burundi had been wracked by internal wars since 1993. President Ndayizeye told the summit that Burundi had applied to join the EAC as far back as 1999 and was still waiting to be admitted to the regional economic bloc. He said his country attached much importance to the EAC because of cross-border trade with Uganda, Tanzania and Kenya. He assured the Summit that peace would reign in his country after the April 2005 elections.

Rwanda's prime minister, Bernard Makuza, who represented President Paul Kagame, said his country was looking forward to joining the EAC, a move which would enable the East Africa region to benefit from Rwanda's fast-growing economy. Yoweri Museveni said African countries can build up their strengths through economic blocs and political federations like that now proposed for Kenya, Uganda and Tanzania. He reminded them of the Mbale Federation signed in Uganda in 1963 by East African leaders of that time, Mwalimu Julius Nyerere, Mzee Jomo Kenyatta and Dr Milton Obote, as being the brainchild of the EAC.

It's important for an investor to know that he can export easily in the whole region (EAC or CEPGL). It gives a better idea of what could be the market. Roger Nsibula (CEPGL) suggests that an ideal initiative would be to launch an organisation which would combine CEPGL and the EAC. The new organisation would be able to speed up economic integration from the Indian Ocean to the Atlantic Ocean. This unique economic space could easily implement transport and telecommunications programmes to physically form transcontinental systems.

The six countries are already members of the Transit Transport Coordination Authority of the Northern Corridor Transit Agreement (TTCA-NCTA), with its Secretariat based in Mombassa, Kenya. The northern corridor is the main artery of transport facilities and infrastructure linking landlocked countries in the Great Lakes region of east and central Africa — Burundi, eastern DRC, Rwanda and Uganda — to the seaport of Mombassa.

Nsibula reports that the transport system in the eastern Congo is in a bad situation compared to Uganda, Rwanda, Burundi, Tanzania and Kenya. He suggests that the eastern Congo region should launch a central corridor transit agreement involving the improvement of the transport network in eastern and central Africa. As a strategy to boost economic integration, the Kisangani Congo River port could be used as a regional port, which would allow access to the Indian Ocean from the Atlantic Ocean, plus a trans-African highway could be built from Lagos in Nigeria via Zongo/Bangui to Mombassa in Kenya.

Between Lagos and the border of the Central African Republic, you can drive. From the Central African Republic, through the Democratic Republic of Congo, up to the border of Uganda, about a thousand kilometres have not been built. Then through Uganda up to Mombassa, it's again free passage. The road involves about half a dozen countries. But because of the recent civil unrest in the Central African Republic and the Democratic Republic of Congo, the project has not been completed.

There is a TTCA member countries' proposal which supports the creation of a Central Corridor Transit Agreement. The idea is to set up a linkage between Dar es Salaam to east DRC (Kalemie and Uvira) and south DRC (Lubumbashi and Mbuji-mayi) via Bujumbura. This is to strengthen the integration with a proposed north corridor project from Mombassa to Kampala and thence to Kisangani (via Bunia or via Butembo), and Kampala to Kisangani (via Kigali or via Kigali-Bujumbura, or via Kigali-Goma-Bukavu, or via Kigali-Bujumbura-Uvira-Bukavu) (final routes have not yet been determined).

Nsibula suggests that many other things can be done to promote cooperation and integration in these six countries concerning energy, trade and industry. There is a great deficit in energy in east Africa. The Inga III hydropower station in west DRC could provide energy to Kenya, Uganda, Tanzania, Burundi and Rwanda via Zambia. The Great Lakes Initiative on Development of Infrastructure (energy, transport, communications, water and telecommunications) carried out by UNECA in 2000 has demonstrated that this interconnection could be possible. The greatest potential market for Kenyan, Ugandan and Tanzanian industries is the eastern region of the DRC.

Chapter 17: Angola, Zambia and Malawi

Angola

In February 2002, peace finally became a reality for Angola. Peace will allow the country's political process to mature and economic reforms to take root. Angola needs investment and assistance to recover from a quarter-century of fighting. US interest in the country has been predominantly due to the strong involvement in the Angolan oil patch, which presently accounts for about 7 per cent of US petroleum imports. The diamond deposits in north east Angola, where one of the largest kimberlites has recently been discovered, are among the richest in the world and also of significance to the US. There is a mutual attraction between the United States and that southern African nation, according to merchant banker Rodney Goodwin, executive director of HSBC Equator Bank plc and Chairman of the US-Angola Chamber of Commerce. Goodwin, whose bank has actively financed a wide range of projects in Angola, says that more American companies should take a look at what Angola has to offer. He points out that Angola has the resources to contribute to its post-war development, opening the way for attractive business opportunities. HSBC Equator was founded in 1975 as a merchant bank to pursue trade finance opportunities exclusively in sub-Saharan Africa. Because Africa has remained its only market, HSBC Equator has a unique understanding and perspective of how to do business on the continent. As its only market, Africa is critical to HSBC Equator's success.

Angola has extensive diamond reserves (estimated at 180 million carats), principally in the provinces of Lunda Norte and Lunda Sul in the central and north eastern parts of the country. The diamonds currently being exploited in Angola represent only the tip of the iceberg; although most are alluvial diamonds produced in the Lunda provinces, some 700 diamondiferous kimberlite pipes have been identified in the country, several of which could be mined profitably (kimberlite pipes are diamond-rich geological formations similar to those found at Kimberley in South Africa). Analysts predict that Angola's annual diamond production could eventually exceed eight million carats in the coming years as more kimberlite diamond mines are placed into commercial production. Although Lunda Norte has a healthy diamond sector, the real hub of gem extraction in north eastern Angola is the Catoca mine in Lunda Sul.

The Catoca Mine, which entered its initial phase of production in 1998, has one of the largest kimberlite pipes in the world and is the world's fourth-largest kimberlite mine. The kimberlite yields quality diamonds, of which 35 per cent are gem quality. According to Catoca's administrative director, Marcelo Gomes, the company has conducted geological studies to a depth of 600 metres, which reveal reserves of 130 million carats. Marcelo says that in 2002 Catoca was producing two million carats per year and through investments will have the capacity to produce four million carats per year in three years' time. This will represent between 3 per cent and 4 per cent of the world's rough diamond production. At four million carats per year it is estimated that known reserves will last between 35 and 40 years.

The Catoca mine employs 2,000 Angolans, most of who come from Lunda Sul. Although Catoca is forging ahead in terms of production, local power generation is a top priority. If investment were forthcoming, it would be possible to build a hydroelectric facility on the Chicapa River, which could provide energy to both Lunda Norte and Lunda Sul. This would not only improve living standards for the local population, but also make diamond mining more economically viable. Catoca has invested more than US$2 million in a two-year project to repair and restore the main hospital at Saurimo, not far from the Catoca Mine. Catoca supports the community with a soup kitchen that provides meals, water, milk and vegetables. It distributes cleaning utensils and soap and is also active in battling AIDS, and in efforts to help people affected by the civil war.

Capital outlays for the development of a kimberlite mining operation are extensive. Only foreign investment can provide such capital, and only under an agreement with Endiama, the state-owned diamond mining company. For example, Catoca is a joint venture between the Angolan government (with a 32.8 per cent stake), the Russian company Alrosa (also with 32.8 per cent), Brazil's Odebrecht Mining Services (16.4 per cent) and Lev Leviev's Daumonty (with 18 per cent). Angola is a country of opportunities, and the fact that large multinationals like De Beers, Lev Leviev of Israel, Souternera of South Africa and Oderbrecht of Brazil are coming to Angola is a good sign. There is also scope for developing small business in the diamond-cutting industry, and in the artisinal exploration for gemstones or industrial diamonds. Angola must, however, diversify from both petroleum and diamond mining in the medium to long terms in order to achieve sustainable development.

Etienne A Brechet has always considered Angola to be his home because he was born and raised there. He worked for Caterpillar in Africa, Europe and the Middle East, and returned in 1984 as its general manager in Angola. Having grown up in Angola, he understood the development that was expected to take place. In October 1989, he and his partner Claude Maeder decided to set up a business. These two young entrepreneurs created a company called Jembas in response to perceived customer needs in the key developmental areas of energy, communications, refrigeration and water systems. Their idea was to begin by developing power production through diesel and gas generators, and telecommunications services. At the time, whatever the needs of the country, they were going to assist in the supply of energy, water and telecommunications.

At that time, Angola had oil companies in the country — Chevron, Texaco and Elf — so there was some private enterprise. The rest of course was largely state-controlled, which meant the government was their main business partner. In fact, to this day the Jembas Group's main customer is still the government. The company provides cities, hospitals, the newspapers and other government facilities with power and telecommunications. Capitalising on its skilled personnel within the energy and communications and related sectors, the business has steadily expanded and diversified its activities into other related areas.

Jembas has installed, and services, equipment that provides the majority of the emergency diesel electrical power currently available in Luanda, as well as the prime electrical supply for Cabinda and Soyo. More than 2,000 generators of all sizes have been installed and are being serviced throughout Angola by Jembas experts and technical support staff. The sales, installation and service of generators and the development in wireless communications have represented much of Jembas' growth for over a decade.

Jembas' success is based on its technical reputation for knowing the quality products that it sells and services, and for the high calibre of its technicians and support staff. It has large stocks of equipment and spare parts and branch offices maintained throughout the country, offering a single source supplier from the initial application stage through to follow-up service and maintenance.

Brechet has not been surprised by the rapid growth of the company. Right from the beginning, instead of concentrating on import and export activities as everyone else does, Jembas concentrated on the service side. They knew that if they did not maintain their installations, they would become yet another import and export company. Brechet and Maeder began by investing their own small private funds that they had saved over the years working in Europe and Africa. Their strength was that they had already worked in the Angolan market and they knew where the needs were. They made a realistic assessment of their own personal abilities and skills as well as their professional capabilities. They were a small group of hands-on people with complementary skills who had a good feel for what they could achieve.

Electric power distribution and production activities account for the largest share of their turnover, followed very closely by wireless telecommunications. They are currently trying not to depend too much on other sectors of the economy for supplying their operational and logistic needs. They have their own catering and lodging facilities, they raise poultry and grow as many fruits, vegetables and other plants as they can. They keep substantial stocks of fuel, water and supplies and they stock large amounts of spare parts. This of course is contrary to all modern thinking, which prioritises outsourcing, but in Angola at the moment they must rely on themselves to satisfy their needs.

Brechet and Maeder started with three employees. Today, Jembas employs approximately 700 to 900 Angolans and 100 expatriates in its operations, depending on project requirements. They have sister companies and affiliates in different parts of the country. Their main customer continues to be the government. A government entity might be prepared to buy a complete turnkey project or it might be interested in a new power station for a town. If Jembas were to be involved only in power generation and telecommunications it might miss some opportunities. At this time in Angola's history, Jembas cannot depend on banking support or cheap and easily obtainable credit lines, so the company is concentrating most of its investment in power generation and telecommunications. It is also developing a third area of activity - construction.

Jembas avoids outsourcing as much as possible so when it gets an order for a power station it does the study, the application, the proposal, the supply, the installation and the contract services. It also builds the facility. This has led Jembas to do more building than necessary and the company has started supplying other projects with conventional and prefabricated building services. A sister company, Lon Top, has, in association with a Swedish company called Top Housing, installed several prefabricated office units on the Sonils base in Luanda. Jembas has erected numerous metallic structure buildings including warehouses and storage areas, and has built a variety of structures ranging from offices to housing complexes, storage tanks to communications towers, in numerous locations throughout Angola.

Luanda's electricity is generated by the Cambambe hydroelectric plant, which has a capability of up to 160 megawatts depending on the water level of the river. At times, the hydroelectric turbines are under repair or the power lines are in overhaul, which means that there is a need for emergency power stations. So, between 1994 and 1999 Jembas installed five turnkey projects which are totally government-funded. Together they have a generating capacity of approximately 77 megawatts in diesel emergency power. The Capanda Hydroelectric Dam is a 520-megawatt project providing power to the cities of Malange, Ndalatango and Luanda. However, electricity distribution to the whole country will not be a reality for many years. The Cazenga sub-station in Luanda is equipped with five turbines with approximately 132-megawatt capacity if all are operating. In Luanda, the problem of the poor distribution network will remain, which means that there will still be a lot of work to be done in the area of emergency power stations for the cities. For example, Luanda was built for 400,000 people whereas today's population is between three and four million. In colonial times, domestic electricity consumption was below today's needs because very few people had air conditioning and the quantity of household appliances and gadgets that exist today.

Jembas sees its line of business growing over the next five to ten years because of the availability of electricity from the Capanda Dam. The government has been making a good effort to develop the country's water and power distribution infrastructure. As the country becomes more peaceful, they will be increasing the funds available for road, bridge and rail reconstruction so there is going to be a need for a lot of power out there.

Jembas' investment comes from its own resources, step by step as the finance becomes available. Good partnerships with some of the big manufacturers such as Kohler of the USA or Neilsen of Germany make credit facilities available, thus relieving Jembas of immediate payments on equipment.

Today the government is encouraging private enterprise, so many companies have come into Jembas' market in the past five years and there are competitors in power generation and in telecommunications — which makes Jembas examine its quality, services and prices in order to stay ahead of competitors. In the area of power generation Jembas' competitors tend to be connected to manufacturers from India and Korea. They also have very well-known competitors such as Caterpillar and Barlows Equipment Company of South Africa.

New companies are using Asian products with unbeatable prices and a customer's tendency is to look first at the price of a product or service. However, customers are becoming aware that after-sales service is important, and that is where Jembas' strength lies. Jembas has an approximately 50 per cent market share in the category of generators greater than 200 kilowatts.

Angola is blessed with excellent opportunities for game fishing with special emphasis on sailfish and blue marlin. The beaches are magnificent, and with careful development Angola could become one of the best holiday hotspots on the continent. The Jemba group owns and runs a hotel and restaurant resort complex on the island of Mussulo off the coast of Luanda that caters to the needs of an upmarket clientele requiring international standards of lodging, cuisine and conference facilities. They began building the Pelicano-Onjango project with local materials and a more 'African' style in 1993, and inaugurated the hotel in 1996.

The Jembas Group is developing new areas and the markets that they already are in. Brechet says that the discovery of new petroleum fields along the Angolan coast will make possible the increased development of Angola in the next years. He affirms that the new discoveries open development chances in the region of the Lobito (Benguela) as well as in Luanda and areas of the interior. The Jembas Group is building a regional base for southern Angola in Lobito, and already has facilities in Namibe, Soyo and Cabinda as well as one in Luanda. The group has also invested heavily in its own telecommunications and computer facilities. All its offices in Luanda, from Mussulo Island to the city centre and to the base in Viana, are connected by a system that integrates their computer network. The challenges are going to take place as many more companies arrive in Angola with big investments, so Jembas' engineering and servicing capabilities must continue to improve, and Jembas must develop partnerships with outside groups. The company is acutely aware that it must be efficient, competitive, and responsive to the customers it serves in order to grow in the 21st century.

(Source: www.jembas.com; and 'Angola's tormented path to petrodiamond-led growth', *World INvestment News,*. www.winne.com, 18 February 2002)

In September 2002 in Luanda, Angola's President Eduardo dos Santos opened the interchange leading to the international airport. The US$5.5 million undertaking was concluded in six months by Dar Al Hundash, a contractor under the Portuguese building company Teixeira Duarte. The construction of the viaduct with four sloping access roads covering a total area of 18,000 square metres used 730 tons of steel and 450 cubic metres of concrete. The viaduct is part of a project meant to make road traffic easier in Luanda. It entails immediate and economic actions, through the construction of upper and lower routes and the rehabilitation of some streets. In 2002, Angola's programme of road restoration was already underway countrywide - for example, the stretch linking Ondjiva and Santa Clara townships in southern Cunene province had been concluded.

Teixeira Duarte's Engenharia e Construcoes SA's main activities are construction such as car parks, industrial buildings and warehouses, civil engineering and public works such as roads, airports, tunnels and bridges. The company is also active in property development, hotel management, vehicle sales, fuel distribution, refuge collection, distribution, food industry, investment management and other activities. Teixeira Duarte is owner of two of the bigger and more modern hotels in Angola, Hotel Tropico and Hotel Alvalade, which have the complete infrastructures of modern hotels, with around 300 rooms each and facilities such as private parking, conference rooms, internet and gyms. Teixeira Duarte has operations in Portugal, Mozambique, Venezuela and Angola.

Oil and gas infrastructure projects predict growing demand for telecommunications, energy and construction in the various regions of Angola. This is already happening in Luanda where tall cranes have become a part of the capital's skyline. The biggest investors are property developers and hotel chains from Portugal — in 2001 they accounted for over half the US$53million in foreign direct investment invested outside the oil sector. Jose Carlos Queiroz, the managing director of Habimat, explains that foreign construction companies in Angola import their own materials but despite this Habimat sales have grown by 50 per cent a year since they opened. Founded in 1998 by Portuguese-based investors, Habimat supplies local contractors with tiles, ceramics and bathroom equipment from Spain and Portugal. The construction boom points to a recovery in business confidence and is a strong indicator that local operators now believe in long-lasting peace.

Teleservice, Angola's largest security company, started with 120 men. With the surge in the demand for protection services in Angola, by 2002 they had employed over 3,000. They also have an important social role, providing work for ex-military personnel re-integrating into civil society, explains Henrique Morais, managing director of Teleservice. Morais, who counts multinational mining and oil companies and other corporate clients operating throughout the country amongst his clients, predicts his company will carry on growing as more companies start investing in Angola. He explains that the perception of insecurity in Angola overseas is exaggerated and does not reflect reality. The problem is lack of information and ignorance. He says that today there are ways to guarantee security in many areas where people from overseas think it is impossible.

Rui M Dos Santos is the founder, chairman and chief executive officer of Sistec in Angola. His training was as a chartered accountant. He was born in 1955 in the small village of Gabela, and lived there until he was 17. His first job was at the age of 14, as a photographer in the dark-room of a photo-shop. At 16, while still in school, he worked part-time at a grocery store where he was in charge of much of the office work, handling invoices and bills of exchange control. At 17 he moved to Luanda to train as a chartered accountant, and to pay for his studies he worked during the day as a salesman for Grollier and Angotur, while studying at night. In the last year of his chartered accountancy course he became an auditor for Price Waterhouse Angola, where he was part of the teams that audited and did the book keeping of approximately 60 companies. He was then invited to become controller for Abbott Laboratories, where he stayed until their New York office decided to close the branch after Angola's independence. He then became controller for Plessey Angola. After independence, and because there was a shortage of skilled personnel, Rui Santos and many other workers in Angola went beyond the specific specialisation of their jobs and worked in many fields inside the companies they worked for. Rui did things such as selling medical products, doing customs clearance, sales and marketing, planning and after-sales service and maintenance.

Because of the twelve-fold salary discrepancy between expatriates and locally-engaged staff, Rui Santos left Plessey and became a freelancer until he started Protecnica, with two other persons, in 1981. Protecnica was one of the first private companies created in Angola after independence (in those days Angola was under communist influence, and private enterprises were not very well received). However, Protecnica was an immediate success and held a position of leadership in almost all the markets it entered. It was the agent for Minolta copiers, Mitsubishi vehicles and Racal radios, and in 1982 it was the company which introduced microcomputers and COBOL business software to Angola. In 1989, the country started moving towards a free market economy. Protecnica's three partners had different views on how to manage the company in a free market environment. In 1991, the partners decided to divide Protecnica into three parts — Sistemas, Tecnologia e Industria and Sistec. Sistec was created out of one third of the capital, keeping the office equipment and computer divisions of Protecnica, and Rui Santos became Sistec's chairman and chief executive officer.

Sistec was officially launched in July 1991. Paid out capital was US$1.5 million and the company had 22 employees. At the time, Santos owned 100 per cent of the company, and he decided to open the capital to all its directors. He believed that the future of the company lay with computers and software. It was importing parts and assembling PC clones in Angola but their price was only a fraction cheaper than well-known branded PCs from abroad so he decided to stop that activity and become agents for Gateway 2000 and, later, IBM business partners. As soon as Sistec did that, sales increased threefold. In 1993/4, forecasting that the computers and entertainment markets would converge, they decided to open the home division of Sistec to sell TVs and other consumer electronics, becoming the agents of Philips in Angola. They also started to assemble their own TVs and radio sets with solar panel charging systems.

In 2003 and 2004, Sistec received approval for two major projects. The first was to build a full service network of 'Sismotels' in eight provincial capitals, with a total of 240 rooms, 98 mini shops, and 190 parking places; access to the internet, telecommunications, television, rental cars and a business centre. The second was to create Nexus, a new telecommunications company offering internet, VSAT and fixed phone services. In 2004, Sistec took a 31 per cent equity share in Mampeza Industrial, a company with a massive property of 36 million square metres close to the sea (which will become part of the Sismotel project later as a tourist resort), and 67,000 square metres in Benguela, which will be transformed into a condimonium project to be sold in a real estate programme.

In 2004, Sistec had nearly closed its industrial division through lack of competitive edge in the areas of work because big corporations are now arriving in Angola. Industrial areas are now being transformed into warehouses. Sistec continues its twin trends of investment in towns other than Luanda and of employing Angolan specialised personnel (only three foreign residents work for the company, and since its start in 1991 Sistec has never had more than five foreigners working in the company). In 2004, Sistec had 384 employees nationwide, with branches in eight towns of Angola. Sistec provided broadcasting equipment for the National Radio (RNA) and Angola TV (TPA) and much radio equipment to the national army. It provided over 5,000 Minolta copiers, 70,000 Gateway and IBM computers and over 1,000 data systems to over 3,000 clients.

In 2001, 2002 and 2003 Sistec received performance awards from IBM and other awards from other organisations. Sistec has several divisions based on work solutions for their clients and customers. There is the computer division, one of the market leaders and a business partner of IBM with its own business software recently re-named *Innovation* and installed for approximately 600 clients. There is the office division, a distributor of Minolta copiers, Riso duplicators and Rall furniture. There is the home division, a distributor of Phillips, Whirlpool and JVC. There is the systems division, where all sort of systems, such as broadcasting systems for radio and TV, fully integrated VSAT, computers and PABX systems for voice and data, special military software for data transmission, cipher and HF and VHF radio equipment for civilian and military use are installed. Sistec also represents Microsoft, Epson, Novell and Kenwood in Angola.

Sistec was one of the first Angolan organisations to be present on the Internet. In 1996, it applied for the licence to set up NetAngola, a web design company/ISP, and started training their personnel to work on LINUX. They hired one Angolan technician who was sent to university in Portugal; when he returned he started training the rest of the personnel. At the time, NetAngola predicted that web design, rather than internet access, was NetAngola's growth area. One of their competitors saw this with a different eye and concentrated on providing internet access — they were right and NetAngola was wrong. Nobody realised the potential of the Internet, so how could NetAngola sell anyone homepages?

But as of 1996, NetAngola also decided to concentrate on access. Sistec already had a very big name, while their competitors were unknown. They were also offering very competitive prices. In 2002, they had 3,000 subscribers and were adding 10 more every week and had a 40 per cent market share. They also had 38 clients serviced by a combination of a four-megabite wireless system and dedicated lines to large hotels, the government and the national media companies.

At present, NetAngola has local points of presence (POPs) in Cabinda, Sumbe, Lobito, Benguela, Lubango and Namibe and is the only Angolan ISP that has, without extra charge, POPs outside of Angola — in Portugal, Spain, Belgium, France, Germany, Italy, UK, USA, Canada, China and Japan. It also has an agreement with GRIC Communications and iPass Inc to 'roam at a fee a minute' in all other countries. NetAngola is the only ISP in Angola that can accept 'inbound' traffic from other ISPs such as AOL, Earthlink and all ISPs (over 10,000) which have agreements with GRIC and iPASS.

Sistec ISP activity ceased in May 2003 and all NetAngola activities were integrated into a new consortium named Nexus. Sistec realised that the market was too small to accommodate so many ISPs, and realised as well that new services needed to be added to its NetAngola business portfolio. The investment in skilled personal was too high so the company decided to take advantage of the de-regulation of the communications market that the government had decided to start. Sistec proposed to the other ISPs that they join forces and bid for one of the four full communications concessions that were going to be granted. Sistec also decided to suggest that they extend the offer to a VSAT company, Telesel SARL, in which they had a minority stake. Betting on the future, Sistec extended the offer to ENE and EDEL (national power companies) and BPC, the major local bank. Among the ISPs, Ebonet accepted the challenge and so did the power companies, BPC and Telesel.

The idea was to get infrastructures and clients (the ISPs and the VSAT hub) who were already prepared and get a foot into the future with optical fibre structures that the power companies were going to install nationwide. The idea was also to conclude a strategic agreement to start using the power lines to distribute Internet and communication services. The new company took the commercial name of Nexus ('connection' in Latin) and adopted the legal name of Telecomunicacoes e Servicos). The bid was submitted to Instituto Angolano das Comunicações (INACOM), the equivalent of the US's Federal Communications Commission (FCC) and they were in second position in the bidding process. Finally, after a long process of price negotiations, the concession was signed in November 2002, full operations beginning in July 2003. The integration of all the partners, the installation of all new equipment and the interconnection with Angola Telecom took up to August 2004 when the full services started being offered. The Internet part started in July 2003, the WASDL started in July 2004 and the public fixed phone service started in August 2004. In 2005, Nexus was sold to MSTelcom-Mercury as it was being very difficult for Nexus to maintain the investment pace necessary for sustainable growth.

Sistec has invested most of its profits in fixed assets because it forecast that rents would start rising sharply, and it would be very difficult for companies to survive in such conditions. The company is buying land and building new headquarters, which will also include its social club, between 10 and 20 business outlets and two cinemas. The cinemas and the internet promote each other. Sistec is tying to negotiate content with content providers, so hopes the cinemas will be a way to distribute quality films in Angola and, should the licence permit it, through the internet as well.

(Source: 'Angola's tormented path to petrodiamond-led growth', *World INvestment NEws Ltd*, www.winne.com, 18 February 2002)

PAcomm Lda is a private Angolan company and an Internet service provider that began to operate in July 1996. PAcomm started with the design, implementation and launching of EBONet, one of the first public commercial ISPs in Angola, and the primary resource in Angola for full internet access in October 1996. During 1997, PAcomm supplied, configured and set up the Internet POPs of Angola Telecom in the provinces of Cabinda and Benguela and to the backbone system of Angola Telecom in Luanda, which allowed, starting from October 1997, the entrance in the market of other local commercial ISPs. There are four POPs in Luanda to deal with the inter-exchange saturation in the city, and one each in Cabinda and Benguela.

PAcomm is the result of an association between two local firms — SInform (computer and training company) and Alma Services, a small company founded by the system administrators from the earlier dialup-based hosts, AngoNet and the SDNP node. AngoNet is closely working with EboNet and continues to support the NGO internet communications need. A proposal to sponsor connectivity for Universidade Agostinho Neto's Faculty of Law is being developed, the first phase of public university UniNet-Angola (Angolan University Network) is already in place interconnecting five faculties.

EboNet web portal has established a daily news service, which employs two journalists. The service, which is one of the seven local information sources for the World Bank on Africa, is EboNet's contribution to a project the company has launched called Conheca Angola (knowing Angola) which is seeking sponsorship from other companies. The aim of the project is to build a comprehensive web server hosting information about Angola's culture, population, history, political and economic situations and so on, including a forum for discussions (a large mailing list of local and international subscribers).

The technical quality of the staff and the know-how that PAcomm acquired and expanded allowed it in 1998 to create EboNetCorp, a division of services driven to the planning, monitoring and evaluation of the market and corporations, specialising in intranet/extranet solutions and the implementation of metropolitan networks, exploring new technologies and telecommunications systems based on wireless solutions. In 1999, EboNetMedia was launched, a new specialised area in web design and programming, multimedia and electronic publishing, with the objective of study, analysis, development, consulting and implementation of web applications.

One of the strategic objectives of PAcomm is to promote the use of the new communication technologies. Dr Haymée Pérez Cogle, *direcção de vendas* (director of marketing) and founder of PAcomm/EboNet, says that her company, in association with Empresa de Correios e Telegrafos (the National Post Office Company), created a new company Correios Business Centre, Lda. This new enterprise is opening telecentres, using national post office premises in the capital and in the provinces — public places which offer traditional post services (faxes and telegrams) plus electronic mail and the internet, among other services and communication products. The typical telecentre has a wireless local area network of eight PCs, plus three internet kiosks connected to Internet via wireless link at 128kbs. They offer internet, desktop publishing (printing, binding, digitalising), office/multimedia, telegram and fax services. The idea is the convergence of traditional post services with new information technologies. The first telecentre, Mondu, was opened in November 2001.

EboNet's constituency has quickly grown from the original handful of former FidoNet/AngoNet project users to more than 5,000 Angolan individuals and companies using the service, and also to more than 200 small and medium sized LANs connecting via dialup. In addition, users include more than 70 corporate leased line and wireless users, plus researchers and employees of the US Embassy, the US Information Agency (USIA), the United Nations and various international NGOs. The EboNet staff, which is very motivated, has developed a help desk service to learn more about how to support their growing user population.

PAcomm considers that the use of new information technologies introduced by the Internet constitutes a powerful tool against underdevelopment. PAcomm tries by all possible means to facilitate access to the Internet for public sector education and health services, maintaining free access in some schools and offering discounts for teachers, students and professionals in the health sector, as well special conditions of access for national NGOs, through the partnership with AngoNet, the non-governmental Angolan Network. Adhering to the slogan 'Internet for all', PAcomm promotes the school-networking, public points of access to Internet (Internet cafe), and KidLink projects.

PAcomm is the authorised reseller of Cisco Systems, RAD Data Communications and Nortel Networks in Angola and maintains partnerships with other companies in the field of telecommunications such as the Interpacket Network, ITCommserv and Interwave. PAcomm is a member of the Internet Corporation for Assigned Names and Numbers (ICANN).

On 2003, EboNet accepted a major challenge and decided to join the Nexus consortium, its main competitor, and others, in establishing a full communications operator. This meant that the main operations of EboNet ceased and the brand, equipment and staff were fully integrated into the new company Telesel (Telecomunicações e SERviços), the new company resulting from the merger of Telesel's Hub/VSAT operations together with Sistec's ISP activities, EboNet and other partners. Telesel's complete activities started in May 2003, and include all kinds of communications of data and voice (mobile cellular is the only service not covered by the concession signed with the Angolan regulator INACOM (Angolan Institute of Communications).

The year was 1996, the war was raging, the political situation had gone from fuzzy to opaque, and the country's economic indicators were virtually flattened. Not a propitious moment to be launching Angola's first private banking venture. But a select group of Angolan and foreign shareholders saw things differently and put their money down to prove it by endowing the Banco Africano de Investimentos (BAI) with start-up capitalisation that exceeded the government-set requirements by a factor of eight.

That spirit of confident dynamism has kept BAI at the forefront of the small but intensely committed core of Angola's private bank sector. Talent certainly helped (a former governor of Portugal's central bank is on the board of directors) as did the fact that many of the foreign partners were companies that had been operating in Angola for some time previously and had an insider's idea of the potential that was buried under discouraging official statistics.

The original partners were Portuguese, South African and French. But to hear the bank's president of the administrative council, Mário APM Palhares, tell it, the fact that over half the owners are Angolan is what makes the big difference. 'Our headquarters are here and our decisions are taken here. In my view, managers who are based abroad are not ideally situated to take or approve investment decisions.'

During an initial period of building up and consolidating its operations in Angola, BAI took on more commercial and trade-related services such as opening letters of credit and brokering foreign currencies for importers. 'Given the current state of the economy, this is what is needed. It also puts us in touch with future clients of our investment banking services, which is what we should be doing and want to be doing.' Palhares is convinced that a bank with those characteristics has to position itself regionally, and accordingly has got involved in syndicated operations such as financing breweries in Mozambique and Guinea, and part-funding a copper exploration survey in Zambia.

'People see there is an aggressive bank open for business in Angola and the profits we make outside can be repatriated and reinvested at home,' says Palhares, pointing to the US$12 million loan that has been put into the fishing industry, and funding for an air charter company to acquire a couple of Boeings, a submarine cable for Angola telecom, Coca-Cola, 'and any other project with a major focus on Angola's development. We feel that our natural scope would be to the countries of the region wherever there is a chance of bringing profits to the bank, so that we are in a better position to mobilise investments for Angola.'

(Source: 'Angolan private bank is key regional player', Summit Reports, 28 December 2001; www.summitreports.com/angola2/index.htm)

'According to the 2004 figures published by BNA, we have a 27 per cent share in deposits and a 20 per cent share in loans,' says Palhares, president of the administrative council. The bank has 22 branches, operating with 453 staff, which already give it one of the best banking networks in the country, and it hoped to extend these to 27 by May 2005. Total balance sheet value was US$657 million. Internationally, BAI opened a subsidiary in Lisbon and is planning to open branches in Cape Verde, Sao Tome and Principe, Brazil and South Africa.

With its leadership in the banking market solidly established, BAI is looking to re-launch in the investment market, with particular focus on the oil and mining sectors. 'We want to start providing specialised services to the higher end of the market,' says Palhares. 'We are consolidating our position by adopting more effective operating mechanisms and creating a culture of excellence in the provision of customer services.' To this end, the bank is training staff to the highest technical standards.

However, in addition to providing a modern and efficient banking infrastructure for investors, private banks want to take their services to ordinary citizens. BAI's commitment to new technology has led it to introduce many useful systems such as ATMs, cashing points, credit and debit cards, and electronic banking services. These encourage people to deposit their savings in banks, which in turn allows the banks to build up their resources and offer more loans. Micro-credits also are an excellent way of encouraging growth. BAI remains committed to encouraging small and medium-sized business to flourish in Angola.

(Source: 'Angolan private bank is key regional player', Summit Communications, 28 December 2001: www.summitreports.com/angola2/index.htm; and 'Banks creating favourable environment for business', Summit Communications, 26 December 2004: www.summitreports.com/angola2004/index.htm)

Mário Pizarro is the former managing director of the Banco Comercial Angolano/Angolan Commercial Bank (BCA). BCA is a fully-fledged commercial bank founded in March 1999 by a team of finance professionals to provide efficient banking services to multinational and local corporations as well as non-governmental organisations. Pizarro points out that the Angolan banking sector was dormant for years. He explains that until recently, owing to excessive controls and regulations, the banking sector was limited to serving as a *bureau de change* for Angolan businesses, with no effective role in financing their development. However, the promulgation of a new legal framework in 1999 resulted in the introduction of a floating exchange rate, freedom to open accounts in foreign currency, the introduction of the kwanza as the national currency, and the introduction of freely negotiable interest rates between banks and clients. Pizarro adds that, thanks to recent economic reforms, new opportunities have been created in financial intermediation, structured finance and consumer credit.

Despite current improvements, most potential investors see Angola as a high-risk country, explains Pizarro, who in 2001 convinced a Portuguese bank to add 30 per cent to BCA's capital. Pizarro believes numerous British, American and South African companies will be moving to Angola over the next few years.

Pizarro points out that over 80 per cent of the financial flows from the oil sector currently transit outside Angola's banking system. Government finally changed foreign exchange regulations for the oil sector; therefore it should be expected that in the near future, billions of dollars will start to transit through the Angolan banking system.

(Source: 'Angola's tormented path to petrodiamond-led growth', *World INvestment NEws Ltd.* www.winne.com, 18 February 2002)

Pizarro welcomes detailed descriptions of the experiences of Angolan entrepreneurs, as they constitute valuable information for potential foreign investors. He has pointed out, however, that there are important aspects of Angola's private sector that are worth mentioning because these aspects may have considerable impact in the future, and that the constraints are as worthy of mention as are facts and opportunities. In a recent article written for a foreign newspaper, and e-mailed to the author, he expresses his opinion on the subject. The article gives some insight on the present situation in Angola. He thoughtfully reveals that these constraints include lack of transparency, corruption, an unstable legal environment, inadequate basic services and the fact that the state is the main customer.

Pizarro can understand that Angola does not have adequate and reliable basic services, or even that there is still an unstable legal environment. He takes into consideration that the country had more than 30 years of a destructive civil war, and had no strong parliamentary opposition in recent years. But he considers that the lack of transparency and the fact that the state is still the main customer constitute the most important obstacles to market development. As has been reported widely, the Angolan government has still a long way to go towards better governance and more transparency. Since 2000, Angolans have seen reports produced by Global Witness concerning 'the President's men', the scandal involving arms exports to Angola (locally known as 'Angola-gate') and, more recently, the IMF report relating to hundreds of millions of dollars missing from government finances.

Since Angola's independence there has been a complete change in company ownership. In fact the private sector has almost disappeared. Decades of war and inadequate economic policies have further worsened the situation of the few private companies. The economic and political liberalisation which occurred prior to the 1992 elections created opportunities for the private sector but, in the absence of clear policies favouring the establishment of genuine Angolan companies, what happened was that foreign companies had much more success. The few Angolan companies with success are owned directly or indirectly by persons linked to the regime and, worse, is the fact that with the state being the biggest customer, no private entrepreneur is able to speak out against government. In other words, the Angolan private sector does not have the critical mass to be a player in Angolan development. It cannot influence government policies. In Mário Pizarro's opinion, the biggest challenge facing not only Angolan entrepreneurs but also the Angolan political class is to break this vicious circle of dependence.

Zambia

In January 2005, the Export Board of Zambia (EBZ) in conjunction with the International Trade Centre (ITC) of Geneva, Switzerland, published a handbook entitled *Trade Secrets, the Export Answer Book for Small and Medium-sized Exporters*. The handbook, which provides answers to the most commonly-asked international trade questions, is customised to suit the needs of exporting enterprises in Zambia. It covers export-related issues such as market research, marketing export products, market entry methods, agents and distribution, trade shows, foreign trade regulations, quality standards, export financing, pricing, transportation, packaging and labelling, trade agreements and export regulations. It offers overviews of WTO trade agreements, and contact information on trade support organisations, and it also includes a list of useful addresses of organisations dealing with export issues, and selected internet resources relevant to small- and medium-sized enterprises.

This 230-page handbook, which is the result of interaction with a large number of small entrepreneurs, export houses, libraries, trade support organisations and trade-related organisations, is a result-oriented guide to exporting. It is a user-friendly, affordable reference for existing and prospective exporters that should help them better understand the terms, processes and resources involved in exporting, as it addresses over 100 questions most frequently asked by exporters, and answers then in clear, plain language. The handbook provides a comprehensive overview of the export transactions in a logical step-by-step approach using a question and answer format.

(Source: Export Board of Zambia in conjunction with the International Trade Centre of Geneva, Switzerland. *Trade Secrets, the Export Answer Book for Small and Medium-sized Exporters*, 2005)

Catherine Mwanamwambwa, a Nigerian-born entrepreneur based in Zambia, is the managing director of Bimzi Limited (Zambia). She is an American-trained entrepreneur with diverse interests which include Zambia's largest rose export farm, which exports 13 million stems a year to the Dutch auction floor, and a multi-million dollar oleoresin factory which processes paprika into a high-quality oil used in the food industry both within the region and globally. She founded Bimzi Limited, a leather manufacturing business, in 1980. She has represented Zambia on the African Business Roundtable and the Eastern and Southern Africa Business Organisation. In 1995, she founded her agricultural marketing firm Agribim Limited, which has become a leading provider of credit to small-scale farmers engaged in out-grower schemes in Zambia.

One of the structural weaknesses of the Zambian economy is its over-dependence on the export of primary commodities. Among the common commodities that are exported in their raw and unprocessed forms are the various agricultural products grown in Zambia. By perpetuating this practice, Zambian businesses deprive themselves of the immense and profitable opportunities arising from the processing of agricultural products. All estimates show that agro-processing adds tremendous value over and above the price of the original products in what is often a simple operation using relatively cheap machinery and equipment. The opportunities that abound in agro-processing are offered by the many products grown in Zambia such as citrus fruits, edible oils, seeds, coffee, tobacco, paprika and many more. The domestic, regional and international markets have a vast appetite for various products which might include fruit juices, potato powders, tomato paste, paprika foods, colorants and castor oils. The sugar industry can manufacture, apart from sugar, immense quantities of by-products such as alcohol, spirits and molasses, while other avenues are provided in the area of meat and fish processing. An important consideration is that agro-processing and agriculture are mutually reinforcing. The absence of domestic industries and factories that draw on inputs from the agricultural sector has discouraged the growth of certain crops in Zambia. An emerging agro-processing sector would alter this and give a boost to agriculture while simultaneously providing good profits to those investors involved in the business of adding value. The agro-processing industry offers one of the best investment opportunities both for the small investor operating simple hand tools to the big investor with high technological and elaborate equipment. It is a sector with a place for every one. Mwanamwambwa strongly recommends the opportunities offered in Zambia to any prospective investor and she invites investors to put their money in agro-processing for the returns it promises.

(Source: Zambia Investment Centre website www.zic.org.zm , March 1998)

Mwanamwambwa, is one of the farmers who have taken up the challenge, and is now growing high value crops. She is the vice president of the Zambia Association for High Value Added Crops (ZAHVAC). According to Mwanamwambwa, the prices offered on food crops such as maize are low and do not allow a farmer to earn much profit. She believes it is time peasant farmers switched to growing cash crops, because there is a ready market for them. In 1997, Mwanamwambwa exported 400 tons of paprika and in 1998 planted about 2,000 hectares of the crop.

To change the farming trend in Zambia, ZAHVAC has introduced outgrower schemes for paprika, especially amongst small-scale farmers. Under this scheme, up to 6,000 small-scale farmers have been placed under big farmers, who supply them with inputs and help them manage their paprika fields. 'We have ensured that each small farmer plants two to four hectares of the crop, which will be marketed for them when it is harvested,' explains Mwanamwambwa. In 1998, a kilo of paprika fetched between US$1 and US$1.25.

Mwanamwambwa is confident that these small-scale farmers will finally mature into large-scale paprika growers. She says that in the long run this will require the establishment of more processing plants, which will add value to the crop before it is exported. Mwanamwambwa is already the founder of Enviro Oil and Colourants, a local paprika processing plant currently undergoing renovations. This modern US$3 million oleoresin plant became operational when her paprika farms and ZAHVAC's paprika out-growers schemes were able to generate sufficient produce in the middle of 2002.

(Source: Zambia Investment Centre website www.zic.org.zm , March 1998)

A World Conservation Society (WCS) project in eastern Zambia's game-rich Luangwa valley is helping to transform poachers into farmers and entrepreneurs. The key is the use of food aid to persuade poachers to turn in their guns and join conservation farmer/wildlife producer training centres, established by WCS to teach sustainable farming methods. WCS is linked to the Bronx Zoo in New York. 'I used to kill an average of seven elephants in a week,' says Royd Kachali of Manga Village in the Luangwa Valley. Now he is one of 98 previously notorious poachers in the area who have taken up farming.

Rainfall in the Luangwa Valley is erratic, and poverty has forced people into poaching, a high-risk occupation that required keeping one step ahead of armed patrols sent out by Zambia's National Parks and Wildlife Service. Through a 'food-for-better-farming' initiative, run since 2001, WCS uses World Food Programme (WFP) relief aid with Food and Agricultural Organisation tools and seeds to improve output and raise farmers' profits. Farmer groups in the Luangwa valley, representing over 30,000 people, have been formed and registered with CTCs, which provide agricultural training, as well as basic marketing, accounting and business management skills.

Conservation farming aims to meet the challenge of declining soil fertility and recurrent drought in semi-arid regions by using an array of soil and water conserving technologies. 'Since the commencement of the programme we have seen some excellent results. Conservation farming methods are paying off, production has increased, locally-based trading centres have been created, farmer groups are consolidating farm production into single production units with the aim of saving on transportation costs and attracting higher-end trading partners,' says WFP information officer Jo Woods. 'By passing on the increased profit to the farmer directly, farmers have become more committed to better farming practices, and are becoming increasingly self-reliant,' she adds.

Masautso Banda, the district administrative officer in Lundazi, on Zambia's eastern border with Malawi, praised the initiative. 'The WCS poacher transformation programme is the greatest thing that has ever happened in Lundazi and the valley communities. It is not easy to convert a poacher into a farmer,' he says. WCS-established trade centres have provided new markets for the farmers' produce and, says Banda, Lundazi was ready to reap the more sustainable rewards of its wildlife through eco-tourism.

(Source: 'Zambia: Turning poachers into cultivators', 2004. *UN Integrated Regional Information Networks*, 18 October 2004)

The Elephant Pepper Development Trust (EPDT) discovered a natural elephant deterrent while working with rural farmers in the Zambezi Valley. The farmers surround their crops with rows of chilli peppers, which are unpalatable to crop-raiding elephants, and make various concoctions using hot chilli to keep elephants at bay. Chillies are not only used in different ways to deter elephants from crops, but also serve as a lucrative cash crop for the farmers. EPDT trains rural farmers in the techniques developed to use chilli as an elephant deterrent and to promote chilli pepper production by the communal farming community in areas of Southern Africa where conflict exists between wildlife and farmers.

The chilli repellent methods are simple, affordable and accessible to rural farmers. The techniques include the use of a chilli grease — ground chillies mixed with old engine grease — which is then smeared on simple string fences surrounding the food crop. The chemicals in the chilli that makes them hot repels the elephants, as their olfactory senses are more acute than humans'. On the string fence are also hung pieces of cloth, seeped in the same mixture, and cow bells, to alarm the farmers should the elephants dare to touch the fence. Traditionally, farmers light fires around their fields to deter the crop-raiding animals. Chilli briquettes add a new dimension to the fire; by mixing dried chillies with animal dung, the farmers make chilli dung briquettes which they burn on the fires. These briquettes smoulder, creating an extremely noxious smoke which again keeps the elephants away.

EPDT advises farmers and wildlife managers on natural resource conservation and sustainable utilisation of such resources in relation to the management of conflict with wildlife. They also facilitate livelihood improvement of the communal farmers by the development of chilli pepper as a cash crop, by providing technical advice.

Via Elephant Pepper (Pvt) Ltd (South Africa), EPDT also assists the farmers with marketing the crop through the Elephant Pepper range of products. The products contribute to the survival of the elephants and the livelihoods of the rural farmers. Support for the projects comes partly from sales in markets and online sales at www.elephantpepper.com. The range consists of Zambezi Red (hot pepper sauce), Chilli Relish, Chilli Jam and a new addition of Baobab Gold — a product that also combines the use of natural products. Baobab Gold was developed with assistance from Phytotrade Africa — a natural product trade association. The fruit of the baobab tree is used to give this sauce its unique flavour.

Because of the deteriorating political and economic environment in Zimbabwe, EPDT was forced to look over the borders to Zambia. This has been a very positive move for the Trust, as it has now expanded its work into the 'four corners region', Botswana, Namibia, Zambia and Zimbabwe.

EPDT discovered that chillies are attractive to poor families suffering from crop predation because animals find chilli unpalatable which means it can be planted as a protection buffer for other crops. It is more intensive and requires less land than other cash crops for the same return; it has relatively low input costs, does not exhaust soil nutrients as cotton does, for example, and exhibits drought resistant qualities. The farmer can obtain higher yields per hectare and much higher per unit prices than for other cash crops.

Participative research with farmers in the Zambezi Valley showed that farmers were impressed with the deterrent properties of chilli peppers and were equally pleased with the high prices they received.

In 2002 elephant expert Dr Loki Osborn, the founder and project director for the EPDT, partnered with a commercial chilli trading company. He realised the importance in identifying a market for the cash crop being grown in the projects. The surplus chillies from problem animal control had a high value and as such needed a market. The Chilli Pepper Company (CPC) committed to buy the chillies produced at market prices.

Nina Gibson, EPDT Zambia project coordinator, has forged a similar partnership with African Spices (Pvt) Ltd in Zambia, which has committed to buy the chillies at fair trade prices, based on the world market rates. Nina explains that EPDT Zambia provides training, education and capacity building of farmers within the areas of wildlife conservation, biodiversity in agricultural practices, environmentally sound farming, HIV/AIDS awareness programmes and monitoring of African Spices, as a partner in ethical trade. Nina points out that the programme has developed slowly, but consistently. African Spices gains market access on behalf of the farmers and EPDT Zambia. The future for EPDT and African Spices is based around continued promotion of chillies as the ideal crop for rural Africa and a strong belief that what Africa needs is 'trade not aid'.

The Miller family has been operating a mixed farming enterprise on a 5,000-acre (2,000-hectare) spread of land, only 20 minutes' drive from Lusaka, since the early part of the last century. Their Lilayi Lodge provides the ideal setting for a relaxed stay. This 36-bed luxury safari lodge is situated in the 1,500-acre (600-hectare) game ranch section of the farm. Lilayi offers deluxe accommodation and high-class cuisine, as well as game viewing of over 25 species of mammals and 300 species of birds in the unspoiled countryside. There are modern conference facilities for company presentations and workshops, and for weddings and private parties. The lodge, which contains 12 thatched chalets (six deluxe and six standard), is set in rolling gardens and overlooks the wild forests of the reserve.

Most of the fresh produce served in the restaurant is grown organically in the Millers' highly-productive farm, where 875 acres (350 hectares) each of soybeans and maize are grown in the summer rains, whilst 750 acres (300 hectares) of wheat are grown in the winter under irrigation. Throughout the year, cabbages, broccoli and cauliflower are produced. Lilayi Farm is one of the largest producers of these vegetables in the country and supplies them throughout Zambia. Baby corn is also grown and is exported to Tesco's in the UK. Lilayi Farm is a leading breeder of pedigree Boran and Angoni cattle, both indigenous African cattle that thrive in Zambian conditions for both small- and large-scale farmers. All the above is grown using conservation farming techniques, where no ploughing is undertaken, therefore reducing fuel demand and cost. A more recent development is the establishment of a wholly organic plot, which is proving popular with Lusaka residents. The result of this farming activity is the employment of over 450 staff. The provision of a year-round supply of vegetables to urban dwellers at steady prices is a significant contribution to household food security. In the same vein Lilayi Farm's wheat crop is almost one day's total requirement for the city of Lusaka.

The Miller family business also includes the management of a public company, Farmers House Plc, which is listed on the Lusaka stock exchange. Despite its name and the family's involvement in farming, this is actually a property investment company, which owns prime property in Lusaka, principally its flagship Central Park on Cairo Road, Lusaka's premier business park which provides an address for the stock exchange itself and other prime tenants such as Barclays Bank and Standard Chartered Bank. Farmers House has also formed strategic partnerships with some of the key players in southern Africa's property development industry.

The Board of Farmers House has ambitious plans to transform it into Zambia's leading property development and investment company, with plans for other developments in Lusaka and proposals for developments on the Copperbelt and in Livingstone. Farmers House has formed a separate property management company, Minerva Property Management Company Ltd, which, in addition to managing the Farmers House properties, has secured contracts to manage properties owned by third parties. The establishment of a professionally operated property management company in Zambia is long overdue, and a welcome addition to the property industry.

Most recently, City Investments Ltd has formed a partnership called Lilayi Development Holdings Ltd which will be developing a 250-hectare part of Lilayi Farm into a new housing estate for almost 5,000 homes. The estate will be fully serviced, including electricity, water and sewerage supplies, and will have retail and commercial areas set aside for schools, health facilities and churches. As part of this project the company has structured a financing facility to allow low- to medium-income Zambians to access a mortgage over 15 years. This will be the first private sector development of its kind in Zambia for many decades, and will be the first opportunity that allows this sector of the market access to mortgage financing.

(Source: www.lilayi.com)

Sylvia Chabala Banda started her catering business in 1986 with a two-plate stove, a handful of vegetables, a few plates borrowed from her domestic collection, one chicken and a piece of meat liberated from the family refrigerator, and one worker — herself. In 2004, 18 years and a lot of tribulations later, her company, Sylva Professional Catering Services, employs 130 workers in the 12 cafeterias she runs all over the capital. These include canteens at the Zambia State Insurance, Amanita, Cabinet Office, Lusaka Water and Sewerage, National Council for Scientific Research and Unilever. She also runs a guesthouse, a catering college at the University of Zambia and is just about to start exporting dried indigenous vegetables.

Sylva Professional Catering Services is an accomplished food provider with a wide selection of nutritious menus. They also offer outside catering and on-site catering at a number of canteens. Their catering college offers one-year certificate courses in hotel management, food and beverage operations and food production. Students who enrol for either the certificate in hotel management or the certificate in food and beverage operations are sent on industrial attachment to a four- or five-star hotel. At the end of the course the student is awarded with a certificate which is approved and accredited by the examinations council of Zambia.

In 2004, the company was given the certificate to run a hotel management diploma course for two years. It also runs short courses in food production, food and beverage operations, house-keeping, front office management, cake-making and decoration and catering technician (where students are taught not only to cook but also to repair electrical appliances). These courses range between two weeks and six months. There is also a boarding house for foreign and local students. So far, students have come from Tanzania, Malawi, South Africa, Angola, DRC, Swaziland and Botswana, and graduates are working in different countries, including in some of the biggest hotels in England and South Africa.

Sylva Food Solutions is where food processing and packaging of local foodstuffs takes place, and the preservation of foodstuffs for out-of-season consumption by both local and export markets. The company has 14 food outlets in Lusaka, providing food to companies, government institutions and higher learning institutions such as universities. In addition to all this, Banda also manufactures natural jam and offers catering consultancy services. Banda's mission is to provide quality services to local and international clients.

Sylva Professional Catering attended the Japan Expo 2005, exhibited all the traditional foods available in Zambia and prepared Zambian traditional food during the 'Zambia week', also using the exhibition to promote Zambian traditional foods to other countries. Banda said her company used new packaging for dry vegetables and traditional fruits. The company is now receiving orders for dry traditional vegetables from Europe.

In 2002, Sylvia's husband, Hector Banda, an accounting and management consultant and lecturer, resigned his job at the Zambia Institute of Management to join her and help her run the business — and that, she says, was a long time coming. All these years, she'd been running things single-handedly and the pressure of work was getting too much for her. Frankly, she needed a hand because the outlets had increased and she couldn't be everywhere at the same time. So she started putting pressure on Hector to join her but his letter of resignation was rejected several times because they wanted him to stay.

And how has he settled in? 'Quite well, actually,' says Hector Banda. Through the nature of his work as a trainer and consultant, he has been able to help his wife with the administrative side of her business. He also brings his expertise to the training side of things, teaching the students management, communication excellence and entrepreneurship, in line with technical education, vocational and entrepreneurship training requirements. Hector, who spent 14 years at ZAMIM as lecturer and principal, says the move from academia to the world of private business has been fulfilling.

Sylvia Banda's goal is to consolidate her different businesses in one location and eventually to expand and open a five-star hotel in Lusaka. Her firm has the capacity to run a five-star hotel but what it doesn't have is sufficient funding, so she is looking for a fundraiser. There are also plans for a Zambian recipe book, if the money can be raised.

Banda's efforts to help develop Zambia include being the chairperson until 2004 of the Lusaka Province Small Business Association (LPSBA). The association was founded in 1996 and joined hands with CARE Zambia in 1997. In collaboration with CARE Zambia, LPSBA has the capacity to fund small-scale, Lusaka-based business projects. LPSBA assists its members by providing developmental types of loans to micro and small-scale entrepreneurs. Many donors allocate funds to the small-scale business sector through CARE Zambia. Banda says her association currently has sufficient funds awaiting appropriate micro and small-scale entrepreneurs to apply for them.

Banda says all micro and small-scale businessmen and women who are registered and running businesses in Lusaka are eligible for loan assistance. To qualify for a loan one needs to be a member of LPSBA. The loans, which are given in stages, range from a minimum of K250,000 to K100 million and sometimes slightly above, depending on how big one's project is. The first loan given is the working capital and the second or third is the capital investment. LPSBA members can begin servicing their loans after a year, though even two years are sometimes given, depending on the type of business. LPSBA currently has more than 700 members and is administered by 10 elected officials. Banda also urges women entrepreneurs to apply for land titles as this further enables them to secure other funds for the setting-up of businesses.

Banda also leads a finance sub-committee for Habitat for Humanity Zambia (HFHZ). HFHZ was formed in 1985 and is building houses of cement blocks, stone foundations and cement-tile roofs. It is part of a world-wide non-profit, ecumenical Christian housing ministry whose goal is to eliminate poverty by providing simple, decent houses for families in need and to make shelter a matter of conscience and action. HFHZ invites people from all walks of life regardless of faith, race or gender to work together in partnership to help build houses. HFHZ has already built over 910 houses in Zambia.

(Source: Edem Djokotoe. ' She started business with one chicken', Lusaka: *The Post*, 15 August 2004, and 2005 correspondence)

Sun Solar Systems proprietor Henry Mwape, an entrepreneur dealing in the installation of solar energy, says the government should set up a fund for rural solar power. He has appealed to the ministry of energy and water development to create a credit fund to assist local firms to take solar power to rural areas. He says there is a lot of potential for solar energy in Zambia, especially among rural farmers, because of the large amount of sunshine, and it is merely a question of sourcing the equipment for installing the solar panels, batteries and lighting. Being a small entrepreneur, he was unable to stock the required equipment because of lack of capital and he has minimal access to the necessary micro-financing facilities. Mwape's company, like the other indigenous solar installing firms, is disadvantaged because of lack of support from the government. The government should create a fund, which could be a revolving service, so that small entrepreneurs would be borrowing from the facility when they have orders, and paying off their loans as they receive payment for their completed work.

With the government making agriculture the cornerstone of the economy, Mwape boasts that he has a wealth of experience in solar power installation, having worked as a solar engineer for the landmark BP Zambia Solar Project that installed over 200 panels in rural health centres across the country. Sun Solar Systems was contracted by World Vision Zambia to undertake projects in Solwezi and Choma, which they successfully executed. Mwape charges that the Government and the Micro-Project Unit and the Zambia Social Investment Fund have been contracting foreign companies to install solar power in various parts of the country, leaving out Zambian entrepreneurs. He says they tend to favour foreign companies when awarding tenders, but when opportunities are given to foreigners there are no back-up facilities, so they fall back on local contractors for maintenance.

(Source: 'State should set up fund for rural solar power', Ndola: *Times of Zambia*, 20 December 2004)

Natural Valley is the producer of Zambia's leading brand of bottled water, popularly known as *Manzi*. The water is extracted and bottled at Natural Valley's new factory, designed and equipped to meet international standards. It is bottled at source from a geologically approved and protected underground source. Independent analysis of the water quality is done by the University of Zambia's Environmental Laboratory. Stewart Simpson and his father, Robert Simpson, initially produced *Manzi* water at Ngwerere Farm, situated 25 kilometres north of the Lusaka city centre, where the production of Sun Blest fresh fruit juices was one of their main activities. One of the pre-requisites for juice production was a supply of good clean water, which was available at the farm. Robert Simpson was the driving force behind the project, but he died in July 2002, and Stewart's wife Nkechinyerem took his place (she had been part of the team since the start). The processing and bottling of water started with supplying the now defunct national airline, Zambia Airways, as one of the main customers. Although Zambia Airways folded by 1994, the business of water supply to the open market grew. Intending to expand water bottling and supply, the promoters started Natural Valley in 2000 and relocated to new premises in the Waterfalls area of Chongwe District, 20 kilometres east of Lusaka.

Since 2001, Natural Valley has continuously expanded and modernised in order to improve efficiency, meet increased demand and stay ahead of the increasing competition. NORSAD, a joint Nordic/SADC developmental initiative, which started operations in 1991, has availed two loans to the company in 2001 and in 2004 of EUR 183 000 and EUR 150 000 respectively. NORSAD contributes to the development of the private sector through financing of small and medium sized enterprises in order for them to start up and/or expand. It uses the NORSAD fund, which has been provided by the four Nordic countries of Denmark, Finland, Norway and Sweden.

The first NORSAD loan was used to purchase machinery for the new factory, to increase and improve the standard of production and to manufacture in-house the polyethylene terephthalate bottles required for bottling mineral water. Producing the bottles in-house lowered packaging costs and enabled the company to have more control over supply, quality and hygiene standards. The equipment for bottling and labelling is fully automated whereas previously, filling of bottles and labelling were done manually. This loan enabled Natural Valley to modernise its production line and reduce shortages of bottles for packaging, as the company was now able to supply 25 per cent of its bottle requirements in-house whereas previously, bottles were 100 per cent controlled by an external supplier.

In 2003 the company purchased two injection machines using their own funds, for cap production and an additional polyethylene terephthalate blowing machine, and increased capacity to 50per cent of bottle requirements. It further purchased two additional completely new filling lines and two additional polyethylene terephthalate blow-melding machines under a Japanese non-grant aid loan facility given through the Zambian government. The 2004 NORSAD loan consolidated the company's activities by increasing production further (including two additional injection machines), and improving efficiency. A major requirement in the manufacturing of polyethylene terephthalate bottles is a pre-form, and the NORSAD loan enabled the company to stop importing pre-forms and make them in-house. It has also improved the distribution by replacing the fleet of ageing vehicles. Natural Valley's filling lines include equipment for filling water in plastic sachets in an attempt to reach the low-income group with affordable clean water. In 2004, the company completed the construction of its modern factory building and was able to meet the requirements of the Zambia Bureau of Standards. South African Bureau of Standards (SABS) standards were used as a guide in constructing the building.

Manzi water is distributed nationwide to some 1,300 outlets and is sold in various sizes ranging from 500 ml to 4-litre and 20-litre jars. The company has a distribution fleet of 13 vehicles ranging from three- to 25-ton capacity. It also offers dispensers for rent or outright sale, where *Manzi* is sold in 20-litre jars to bulk buyers — mostly offices, clinics and hospitals. The company is the only mineral water company in Zambia with a dedicated disinfecting and filling line for dispenser jars and its own dispenser servicing division. In 2004, the factory was completed with the addition of a clean room for water bottling, a filtration and treatment room for water, a shower block for staff and a laundry room. Apart from increasing its production capacity, in 2004 Natural Valley instituted a new sales routing programme to improve efficiency, and purchased four new computers to help with administrative work. In an attempt to protect the surrounding environment, Natural Valley acquired five hectares of land on three sides of the factory premises and embarked on a tree planting project. About 2,000 trees have already been planted. This will not only protect the water source from contamination by other developers but will also add to the beauty of the surroundings. Environmental protection is a major priority and all attempts are being made to ensure that the factory will eventually blend into its environment. Maximum efficiency and production is forecast to be achieved December 2006. Natural Water (*Manzi*) was a 2005 Finalist for the Africa SMME Awards.

(Source: www.norsad.org)

It was Brebner Changala's father-in-law who spotted the opportunity to make blackboard chalk for Zambia's schools. Brebner Changala, who had retired with a handsome cheque after 12 years in banking, realised it was an idea that could not go wrong. He says, 'I looked at the number of schools countrywide and

I saw gold. When I put in $100,000, I didn't see the risk. I saw a new turn in teaching-aid materials for our poor country.'

He approached the Japanese International Cooperation Agency for help and they were equally impressed. This would be the first chalk factory in central Africa. It would save Zambia foreign exchange, create jobs in a rural area and provide an educational tool from local resources. The Japanese agreed to provide the machinery, and the factory opened in August 2000.

Brebner School Chalk Ltd now makes 200,000 boxes a year, each containing 100 chalks. This is about a tenth of the chalk which Zambian schools use, saving Zambia $350,000 in foreign currency a year and providing 96 badly needed jobs. It plans to buy more machines and supply a fifth of the market by the end of 2004. It also plans to sell to other countries.

Blackboard chalk is made of calcium sulphate (gypsum), dug out the ground at Monze, 120 miles southwest of Lusaka. This is in a national park but is the only source of gypsum in Zambia. Brebner Changala says that the mining, in an area without good roads, was the biggest challenge. 'This area is tough, to say the least. We had to clear the land manually. At Monze, gypsum granules are found in clay soil, to a depth of one metre. Forty workers do the mining with pick and shovel, because park rules prevent the use of noisy machinery. This is only local employment apart from cattle. The clay is washed off the gypsum and then used to refill the open pits and restore the ground. 'This project is 100 per cent environment-friendly,' says Brebner Changala. 'You can't go wrong.'

A lorry and pick-up, also bought with Japanese aid, take the gypsum to Lusaka where it is first baked then crushed to powder in a hammer mill. The powder is mixed with a similar volume of water to make a paste which is formed into chalks in a moulding machine. The chalks dry in the sun. Women, to whom Lusaka offers few job opportunities, do most of the work.

Brebner has contracts with the ministry of education but still has to persuade schools to take its chalk, rather than that imported from China, India or South Africa. He believes that this imported chalk is subsidised in the countries of origin, while his chalk is unsubsidised and carries 17.5 per cent value added tax. The four-wheel-drive pick-up, however, enables Brebner to sell in the countryside, while imports sell mainly to schools near the line of rail from Lusaka to the Copperbelt. Brebner has a nationwide distribution network. It sells a fifth of its crushed gypsum as plaster of Paris to Zambia's hospitals and clinics. It gives chalk to community schools and churches.

Within two years it plans to start making pencils as well. It aims for a listing on the Lusaka stock exchange and will sell shares to workers and the public. Workers have their own union, which works with the management for their welfare. Brebner Chalk provides medical insurance, lunch, transport and recreation.

In January 2004, Brebner School Chalk Ltd received the UK Trade and Investment Award for Small Businesses. This award is given to a company with not more than 150 employees, for commercial activity that has contributed to viable economic development in a community in a developing country. The judges said that Brebner School Chalk Ltd provides an excellent example of a rural initiative. A great deal of thought has gone into how the enterprise is strategically diversifying into both the community and the business. The judges were impressed with the sustainability of the project, the plans to expand, the commitment to being 100 per cent environmentally friendly, and the significant saving it has provided the Zambian government. 'Brebner School Chalk realised that education and employment are important areas of development and took the initiative to produce a vital teaching aid resource, chalk,' said Baroness Amos in presenting the award.

(Source: www.worldaware.org.uk/awards/awards2004/brebner.html)

Zambia's fish and fisheries sector has been singled out as one with great potential for the economic development of the country, given the considerable water resources in form of rivers, lakes and swamps, and the different varieties of edible fish.

Tim and Nicola Fuller have a fish farm on the Zambezi River and started the whole thing from scratch in 1997. Tim Fuller funded it by trading in fish in Lusaka during the week and building the fish farm over the weekends. Tim and Nicola camped for the first few years, lived in a hut for a number of years and now have a more or less proper home with bedrooms. They cleared the road by hand, and the land almost entirely by hand. They planted bananas and grew fish and now have a thriving operation. Water from fish tanks goes onto bananas to save both water and power. Twenty staff houses (made entirely from farm bricks), fish tanks, and fish ponds have been built. Their Chirundu Bream Farm has been highlighted as a success story by NORSAD, which has loaned EUR 442,000 to the project.

(Source: www.norsad.org)

Robin and Jo Pope have worked to promote responsible tourism in South Luanga National Park, especially to support the local community in Kawaza village. The Robin Pope Safaris name is becoming synonymous with the South Luangwa in the safari industry. Robin is an 'old school' safari guide having lived and worked in Luangwa since 1975 and started his own safari operations with the opening of Nsefu in 1982, and the opening of Tena Tena in 1985. In 1990, Robin started his mobile walking safaris, a respectable upgrade on the walking trails that the late legendary guide Norman Carr initiated in the 1960s. Over the years, Robin has handpicked and trained a select team of knowledgeable and experienced safari guides to ensure the high guiding standards and personalisation at each camp. Robin himself is the Zambian member of the eight independent professional safari guides who make up the Safari Guide Company.

Robin and his wife Jo now operate three small, highly personal and authentic bush camps — Nkwali, Tena Tena and Nsefu — offering a professional but relaxed atmosphere. The food is excellent but the views are even better as each camp is set in the shade of giant ebony trees directly overlooking the meandering Luangwa River. Each camp has just five or six rooms (or large and airy tents in the case of Tena Tena) with huge beds, thatched roofs, and your own private but open air shower. Most guests spend a couple of nights in each camp and it is often possible to watch elephants, or a leopard walking along on the far bank, from the private veranda of each room.

The 2005 Responsible Tourism Best Personal Contribution award was given to Jo Pope for working tirelessly to promote responsible tourism in South Luangwa National Park in Zambia, in particular to support the local community and Kawaza village. Jo has also helped the community develop their own tourism facility — the Kawaza Tourism Village. This is now providing an income to a good number of villagers and also ensures a sense of involvement with the tourists by the community.

(Source: www.robinpopesafaris.net and www.icrtourism.org)

Dunavant Zambia Ltd promotes both public health and economic growth in Zambia. The company's HIV/AIDS workplace and outreach programme has contributed to Zambia's fight against HIV/AIDS, while its expansion of cotton production has improved the quality of life for thousands of Zambians. Dunavant operates in four provinces and has contacts with small-scale farmers in the rural areas where its ginneries are located. Dunavant Ginneries now contract approximately 200,000 cotton out-growers — up from 42,000 that were contracted under Lonhro's Cotton Company of Zambia in 2000.

Dunavant Zambia's HIV/AIDS workplace and outreach programme reaches over 150,000 people, including the company's own employees, cotton growers and members of their families and communities. The programme generates awareness on how to prevent the spread of HIV and how to care for those infected by the virus. The comprehensive programme includes training for 3,500 community educators, 1,500 caregivers, and 200 civic leaders as part of a multi-faceted effort to roll back HIV/AIDS. Dunavant Zambia has facilitated voluntary counselling and testing for thousands of Zambians and helped hundreds to access antiretroviral therapy. Dunavant's commitment to fighting HIV/AIDS in Zambia demonstrates its enlightened understanding that the best way to do well is to do good.

Dunavant Zambia Ltd is a subsidiary of privately owned Dunavant Enterprises Inc, which has its headquarters in Memphis, Tennessee, USA, and is one of the largest cotton merchandisers in the world, handling in excess of four million bales of American and foreign cotton a year. The company has ginning and warehousing operations in Australia, Uganda, Mozambique, Zambia, Argentina and Paraguay, as well as a commodities trading company, cotton farming operations and a truck brokerage that serves as agent for approximately 5,000 trucks used to haul cotton. William B Dunavant, chairman and CEO of Dunavant Enterprises, which his father founded in 1929, firmly believes that 'Entrepreneurism is the key to the survival of free enterprise and capitalism, and ... changing ahead of the times, not with the times.'

In the Chongwe farming block, 1,870 farmers grow cotton for Dunavant on plots of land averaging just over 3 acres each. In total, some 58,000 acres of cotton are grown for Dunavant in the Lusaka Province. Lusaka, however, is by no means the biggest producer of cotton in Zambia. More than 530,000 acres of the crop are cultivated in the eastern and central provinces, of which 350,000 are grown with credit inputs from Dunavant.

Maureen and her husband Grimsdale Chiyokoma are leaders in the Chongwe farming block. They look after the interests of 92 farmers. They say that although Dunavant had brought some financial relief in the area, the earnings are so meagre that it is almost a hand-to-mouth existence for the farmers. 'Cotton farming is labour intensive. We put all our energies in the crop, but at the end of the day we can barely manage to sustain ourselves,' she says.

Dunavant Zambia's Managing director Tony Isherwood notes that '... these farmers also grow maize and sunflower and, whilst [Maureen] is right, the current low world lint prices are not the real cause of their problems, which would be better attributed to the small acreages farmed, the low yields achieved and the high cost of living in Zambia.'

Isherwood says, 'Work done by Michigan State University in comparing on-farm prices received by smallholder farmers in Africa indicates that Zambian farmers receive a higher percentage of the value of lint than do farmers in other African countries, except in some instances like [west Africa], where there is state intervention and subsidy.'

Isherwood is not totally familiar with the situation in West Africa but he believes that it is the state controlled cotton industries that are being privatised because the subsidies were bankrupting their governments. He says that Dunavant Zambia is putting considerable effort into trying to raise the yields of all their crops, and as far as cotton is concerned the input financing which Dunavant Zambia provides on credit to the farmers allows the better farmers to achieve yields three to four times higher than the national average. Isherwood, concludes that 'world cotton prices are low because of world-over supply, which has only partially been caused by cotton subsidies in the EU and USA.'

Isherwood says that cotton farmers in Zambia are given a guaranteed minimum purchase price before planting the crop, which the company buys from its outgrowers. He believes that this guaranteed pre-plant price, plus Dunavant Zambia's willingness and ability to provide the full spectrum of necessary crop inputs on credit to farmers at farm gate, followed by the provision of free picking and packaging material, and purchasing their crop at farm gate, have been the main contributing factors to the substantial growth in cotton plantings in Zambia in the last five years. Cotton farmers know beforehand the ruling prices for the crop from the pre-planting announced minimum rates.

The challenge for Dunavant Zambia is to increase yields, which is the real potential, as opposed to the increase in hectarage. The company is working at finding improved cotton growing practices in collaboration with other institutions. The company is also promoting modern methods with the introduction of the Micron Ulva, which is a controlled droplet applicator for more economic and effective spraying than the conventional knapsack sprayer.

(Source: Gerald Mwale. 'Zambia qualifies for $3.9 billion debt relief under HIPC: but is it good news for cotton farmers?' Lusaka, 14 April 2005, www.millenniumcampaign.org; 'US government recognises Dunavant Zambia Limited for good business practices', US Embassy, Lusaka, Press Release, 12 January 2005; and 'We announce cotton prices before planting', *Times of Zambia*, 11 July 2005)

Malawi

In 2004, Mathias A (Matthews) Chikaonda, chief executive of the largest conglomerate in Malawi, the investment firm Press Corporation Limited (PCL), announced plans to list PCL on Botswana's and South Africa's stock exchanges. PCL has stakes in leading players in the Malawian economy such as BP Malawi, People's Trading Centre Group, Carlsberg-Southern Bottlers, National Bank of Malawi, Maldeco Fisheries, Malawi Distilleries, Ethanol Company, Tambala Food Products, Limbe Leaf Tobacco Company and H&P Steel. It led the consortium that was chosen to buy a stake in fixed-line phone operator Malawi Telecommunications. Chikaonda says if PCL is listed on the Johannesburg Stock Exchange, it will have more access regionally to capital markets and become more international. Chikaonda is an American-trained economics professor (University of Pennsylvania, MBA, 1983), former governor of the Reserve Bank of Malawi, (1995-2000) and former minister of finance and economic planning of Malawi (2000-2002).

PCL has embarked on a fish-farming venture on the shores of Lake Malawi with the support of NORSAD. Fishing is not a new ball-game to PCL. The company has been in the fishing industry for several decades through one of its many subsidiary companies, Maldeco Fishing. Largely, it has been fishing *chambo*, a species of the tilapia fish family unique to Malawi. Since 1993, however, the fish stocks in the lake have rapidly been dwindling — a report by the Malawi department of fisheries reveals that average fish landings declined from about 65,000 metric tons in the 1970s and 1980s to 50,000 metric tons in the late 1990s and this trend has continued. The depletion of the fish stocks is attributed to several factors, including over-fishing and usage of inappropriate fishing methods. The implications are serious and of concern not only to Maldeco Fishing — whose income is solely dependent on fishing — but to the nation as a whole, because the fishing industry has traditionally played an important role as one of the sources of food security, income and employment to the majority of the less privileged in Malawi. The situation becomes more worrisome with the assertion that fish constitutes over 50 per cent of the animal protein consumed by the country's population.

When most of the people could only see dark clouds over the fish industry, PCL through its newly formed subsidiary company, Maldeco Aquaculture, saw a business opportunity which drove them to embark on a multi-million euro project to produce its own *chambo* using the cage culture. Three thousand tons of whole raw *chambo* per year will be produced, processed and sold throughout the country. When the venture takes off, it will contribute to the improvement in the per capita fish consumption and thus animal protein intake, a nutrient vital to health but lacking in the diet of the majority. The development is the first of its kind in Malawi. Maldeco will therefore be a catalyst for aquaculture development through the transfer of technology and the provision of fingerling stock to small-scale fishermen on an outreach programme. This development will also contribute to the reduction of the fishing pressure on the lake, thereby making it possible to restore the *chambo* fishery as planned by government in the 10-year strategic plan. Moreover, more permanent jobs will be created in an economy where the majority is not in formal employment. NORSAD, through a term loan of EUR 2,000,000 to Maldeco Aquaculture, is supporting the initiative. PCL has set aside over EUR 2.8 million to complete the development.

(Source: www.norsad.org).

Ask any visitor to Malawi about the country and the answer may be that while Malawi is indeed the warm heart of Africa, much needs to be done about hotel accommodation. It is not easy to find reasonably priced decent accommodation. Obviously, this does not work well for tourism although lately the number of international visitors has been increasing according to the ministry of tourism, parks and wildlife. Given the country's vast but untapped potential for tourism, the numbers achieved are still far from satisfactory. As a way of contributing to the alleviation of accommodation problems and the development of the tourism industry, Eclipse Limited, with the support of NORSAD, has embarked on a lodge development that will offer accommodation meeting international standards and at affordable rates, as Eclipse's intention is to contribute to the creation of a competitive environment, which will eventually bring down rack rates to levels that will promote tourism in the country. The development, consisting of a 39-double room lodge facility and a food court, will be situated in the heart of Blantyre's business district. The site offers superb scenic views typical of Africa and, capitalising on this, the lodge has been planned on a safari theme within the city environment overlooking a valley and a mountain. In 2004, the city of Blantyre did not have a single food court where consumers could enjoy a variety of cuisines under one roof. Seeing a business opportunity, Eclipse Limited made representations to Innscor Africa for franchising of their Steers, Pizza Inn and Chicken Inn fast-food outlets. The food court will operate independently from the lodge. This development will undoubtedly bring a new lease of life in the business district of the city of Blantyre.

(Source: www.norsad.org)

Through its subsidiary company, Edulis Food Processors Malawi, Edulis Holdings Malawi has established a factory for processing a type of wild mushroom called boletus edulis found in pine and oak plantations. The wild mushrooms grow naturally in the spring, summer and early autumn, from October to April, and depend on the seasonal cycle of pine and oak forests, of which there are significant cultivated plantations in Malawi. To start with, the company has secured from the government exclusive rights for a minimum of 1,000,000 hectares of prime Malawi forests for the next 30 years. Wild mushroom species such as boletus edulis are in high demand in western culinary markets because of their unique flavour, and they command a premium price. It is projected that the Edulis Food Processors plant will produce a total of 350 tons of processed wild mushrooms.

The know-how in the processing, harvesting, and distribution of wild mushroom is coming from a South African company called Edulis Mushrooms, the principal shareholder in Edulis Holdings Malawi. Edulis Mushrooms, which boasts of being in the business for nearly three decades, was founded in 1974 when the Casaletti family saw the opportunity to develop commercially the wild mushrooms that grow in the pine forests of South Africa's eastern highveld. Over the years the company has acquired considerable know-how and has extended its operations beyond South African borders into Zimbabwe and Swaziland, with Malawi being the latest extension.

As a partner in development with investors in the private sector, NORSAD could not resist supporting such a venture, which has significant development potential. It is an export-oriented venture that will generate foreign currency at a time when the country is grappling with the idea of diversifying its export base. Over 60 per cent of the country's foreign exchange earnings come from tobacco exports. The market prices of most agricultural commodities, however, are unstable and have lately fallen, contributing to the destabilisation of the foreign exchange market. Job creation by Edulis Food Processors Malawi is estimated at 8,000 and will mostly be seasonal jobs, given the seasonal nature of wild mushroom processing operations.

(Source: www.norsad.org)

In 2004, Aleke Banda was not only the president of the People's Progressive Movement, (whose mission is to clear up the economic mess created by poor leadership and a lack of vision), but also an enterprising entrepreneur. A shining example of his business empire is Nation Publications Limited, which publishes and prints *The Nation* and *The Weekend Nation* and other publications. Although his media company is only a decade old, it is successfully competing against Malawi's oldest publications. While many people expected Aleke to be interfering with the editorial content of *The Nation* and *The Weekend Nation*, this has not been the case. The two papers are known for their unquestionable independence and balanced stories. By letting the two papers operate independently, Aleke also demonstrates his respect for media freedom. By publishing stories, which sometimes irk Malawi's leadership, Aleke and his daughter Mbumba Achutan demonstrate that they do not use their political influence to determine the type of articles that find space in the two publications. On several occasions, Aleke has even come under fire because of the articles that have been branded anti-government.

Combine Cargo (Malawi) Limited is a Malawian owned and operated freight services company that is represented both regionally and internationally. CEO and founder, Eddie Kaluwa, says their mission is to 'lead the freight industry with the commitment to deliver the most comprehensive, cost effective and time saving freight management service in the SADC region and beyond.'

Combine Cargo was established in 1994 with the intention of providing a professional and cost effective alternative for the shipping of domestic and international consignments. Combine Cargo serves some of the largest organisations in the country. What sets them apart from their competitors is their commitment to the quality service that their customers have grown accustomed to. They have dedicated their operations to providing the highest quality service at the most competitive cost. Combine Cargo is one of the fastest growing freight services providers in Malawi.

For Malawi, air cargo is by far the fastest mode of transportation from continent to continent. Sea cargo is the only practical means of surface transportation over long distances and for bulky goods. Combine Cargo has international partners worldwide that make the first choice for sea transportation globally. As a landlocked country, Malawi's best opportunity for imports and exports is in trucking. Combine works with a network of transport brokers to ensure that their clients' goods are moved into Malawi on time and under budget.

Combine Cargo delivers a comprehensive service using an advanced and sophisticated information system. They emphasise process simplification that reduces the overall transportation costs. Their performance has earned them the reputation as the best company of choice for freight services in Malawi, and their expanding client base is proof.

Combine Cargo has a regional network that spans eight African countries and includes Botswana, Mozambique, Swaziland, Zimbabwe, South Africa, Zambia and Tanzania. Combine Cargo is linked to market leader SRP shipping' this collaboration offers unparalleled benefits for regional trade. Combine Cargo maintains sound relationships with international freight forwarders

CEO and founder, Eddie Kaluwa stresses that 'at Combine Cargo we are committed to providing a quality freight service. In this regard we have made numerous advances that have set us apart from the rest of the pack. Even though we are committed to finding new ways of meeting our client's needs. Combine Cargo has ongoing feasibility studies to determine the best possible transportation options for your cargo.' Combine Cargo was a 2005 Finalist for the Africa SMME Awards.

(Source: www.combinecargo.mw)

In Malawi, as elsewhere in Africa, one of the most distinctive features of the landscape is the imposing presence of the baobab tree. Growing up to 40 metres high, the baobab stands out in a region suffering one of the highest rates of deforestation in Africa. The high water content of the baobab renders it useless for charcoal or fuel unless it is left to dry for over two years. However, it has many other uses: its fibres are used to make sturdy ropes, cloths, mats and fishing nets; its leaves are cooked as a vegetable relish; and its seeds roasted for snack-food. It is also used in a range of traditional medicines. But in the village of Kamimwamba it is the fruit that is highly prized. The towering heights of the tree have to be scaled to harvest the yellow-green, oval fruits and once collected they are taken to a small roadside processing centre and the pulp extracted to make into juice. The drink lasts up to six months and is rich in energy, vitamin C, calcium, iron and other minerals, so is ideal for children, pregnant women and is also recommended as a cure for hangovers. The villagers now make more from the baobab drink than they did previously from selling charcoal or firewood. In addition, the communities have taken a vested interest in protecting existing baobab trees, as well as planting more for use by future generations.

Malawi Entrepreneurs Development Institute (MEDI) has embarked on a project seeking to commercialise plant-based products, referred to as green pharmaceuticals, to take advantage of a growing multi-billion dollar world market. MEDI chief executive, Charles Kazembe, says Malawi is endowed with a favourable climate for a wide range of herbal plants, some of which have been used by communities to treat ailments for over a century. MEDI aims to empower local people to move from traditional to commercial use of herbal medicines because of the growing market in Europe and the United States. With proper knowledge and enabling structures, MEDI and its helpers believe people could benefit financially from exporting herbal products. According to Siodharha Sanka Dash, an entrepreneur development expert attached to MEDI, plant-based products have been a foreign exchange earner for some countries. He says that the market has seen a wave of herbal cosmetics, perfumes, condiments and confectioneries, adding that herbal medicines were used in developing countries for primary health care because of easier cultural acceptability and fewer side effects. Malawi has a rich bio-diversity and wealth of indigenous knowledge on plant life, and therefore has the potential to emerge as one of the producers of herbal products. Experts say the government and stakeholders should consolidate the traditional knowledge base, to start developing new herbal preparations and make these products available to the international community. The project is a complement to recent efforts by the Traditional Healers Association of Malawi (THAM) to conserve natural medicinal plants. THAM has several botanical gardens around the country, the largest of which is in Mwanza district in southern Malawi, where herbalists are trained on sustaining indigenous plants that have medicinal value.

The Mtwara Development Corridor Initiative has been launched by Zambia, Malawi, Mozambique and Tanzania to promote economic development and integrate their transport networks. The initiative aims at exploiting existing investment opportunities along an 850 kilometre stretch linking Zambia, Malawi, Mozambique and Tanzania. The corridor runs from the south eastern Tanzanian port of Mtwara through the country's southern highlands to Lake Malawi, into northern Mozambique and then to eastern Zambia. Under the initiative, the development of roads, electricity, postal services, telecommunications, agriculture, mining, fishery and tourism will be tackled in the four countries. An agreement signed between the leaders of the four countries will also ensure the implementation of an institutional framework to enable smooth operation of the corridor.

Support for corridors of development has been underscored in the SADC regional indicative strategic development plan. The initiative will cover three of Zambia's provinces: eastern, northern and Luapula, which share borders with Mozambique, Malawi and Tanzania. In Malawi, the project will target all the districts of the central and northern regions and Mangochi district in the southern region, while in Mozambique the northern Niassa and Cabo Delgabo provinces will have access to the corridor. A conference of investors and donors was to be convened in 2005 to highlight the projects identified for development in the four countries. A feasibility study for a railway line linking Chipata, capital of Zambia's Eastern Province, with Mchinji in Malawi's Central Province, a vital aspect of the Mtwara corridor, has already been concluded.

(Source: 'Development corridor linking four countries launched', *UN Integrated Regional Information Networks (IRIN)*, 21 December 2004)

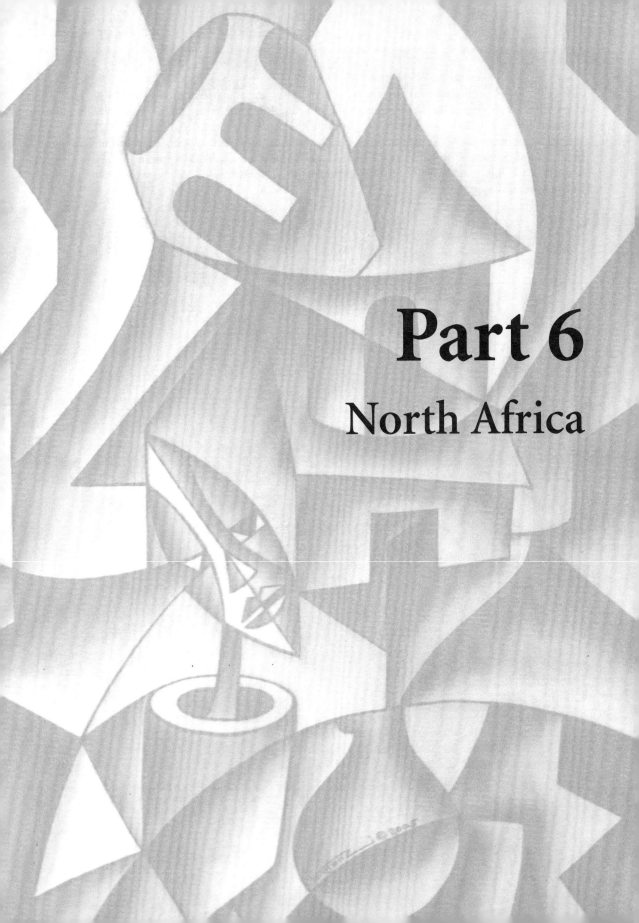

Part 6
North Africa

AFRICA: CONTINENT OF ECONOMIC OPPORTUNITIES

The countries of North Africa are heavily influenced by the ancient civilisations of the Middle East, Africa and Europe, as well as the more recent expansion of Islam. Bordered by the shores of the Mediterranean to the north and the Sahara to the south are the Muslim countries of Morocco, Algeria, Tunisia, Libya and Egypt. Egypt occupies the northeast corner of Africa and has an extension across the Gulf of Suez into the Sinai Peninsula, through which runs the Suez Canal, connecting the Mediterranean to the Indian Ocean. Two other Muslim countries are often included as part of North Africa, Mauritania on the Atlantic coast and Sudan south of Egypt.

Chapter 18: Egypt and Sudan

Egypt

A vast cultural complex rising on the shore of the Mediterranean, a stone's throw away from the location of the ancient Library of Alexandria, is an Egyptian enterprise of international scope and ambition, a worthy successor to the ancient Library of Alexandria. That great library, undeniably the greatest chapter in the history of Alexandria, was a unique ecumenical effort of the human intellect and imagination and remains engraved in the memories of scientists and intellectuals to this day. It is the setting for the new Library of Alexandria, a library for up to eight million books, three museums, five research institutes, several exhibition galleries, a planetarium and a conference centre that can accommodate some 3,000 seats. The beautiful new building, with its distinctive granite wall covered by the letters of the world's alphabets, is today a recognisable landmark of the new Alexandria.

The library forms partnerships with many eminent institutions of learning around the world, either ongoing or around specific events such as seminars, conferences and exhibitions. Equally important is the link to civil society in Egypt and the world, as it is linked up electronically with the rest of the world by a complex web of agreements that bring the digital age to Egypt and the region. And the library brings the fruits of Egyptian creativity and scholarship to the new digital world of instant communication and electronic publishing.

Journalist Paul Schemm reports that in 1996 American internet entrepreneur Brewster Kahle realised that the World Wide Web was going to become the premier information resource of the future. But he also realised that it was constantly changing, with old pages expiring and new pages being born every minute. He began taking full snapshots of the web every two months and archiving them. The result is the internet archive with 10 billion pages of information dating from 1996 to 2001. All this, together with 2,000 hours of Egyptian and US television, 1,000 hours of archival film footage and a book-scanning facility, was donated to the Library of Alexandria — a donation valued at US$5 million and a total of 100 terabytes of information. With a single book about a megabyte in size, this means that the library's collection has swelled with the equivalent of 100 million volumes, four times bigger than the US Library of Congress's collection of 25 million physical volumes.

The archive is an integral part of the library's mission. The web archive is made available to the world either at the library itself or through its website (www.bibalex.org). The idea of collecting all the knowledge of all the people in the world is within the grasp of this first truly digital library for the 21st century. Schemm explains that Kahle formed a partnership with the library because of its commitment to the ideal of the original library of antiquity to be a universal depository of knowledge. Other elements of the partnership have included sending trainees from Egypt to California and a project in cooperation with the Carnegie Mellon University to scan a million books. As far as possible, works are being digitised so that they are available to scholars and general readers all over the world.

Kahle revealed to Schemm that the idea of total access to information has been behind libraries from the beginning. He envisions a time when people in the remotest parts of Africa will be able to walk for a day and have access to the latest medical texts. The physical structure of the library itself serves as a locus for the human interaction of experts and researchers, who can meet and debate in person or online. The Library of Alexandria aspires to recapture the spirit of the ancient library but one way in which the library is different from its predecessor is that it is open to ordinary people. The original library was a scholars-only affair and the notion of public libraries only became widespread in the 19th century. Aside from priceless manuscripts and rare books, the majority of the collection of the Library of Alexandria (especially the digital material) is accessible to everyone).

(Source: www.bibalex.org, and Paul Schemm. 'Wired - with a new internet archive, the Alexandria Library keeps seeking to carve itself a niche'. *Cairo Times*. Volume 6, Issue 8, 25 April-1 May 2002)

AFRICA: CONTINENT OF ECONOMIC OPPORTUNITIES

Freelance journalist Hazel Heyer reports that Egypt is miles ahead of Arab and developing nations with respect to the private sector share in IT and telecommunications, and second only to the Gulf States in e-commerce. It has allocated massive investments from private coffers to develop and expand networks. There are 30 free internet providers competing for customers. LinkdotNet is at the top of Egypt's ISP ladder, the 'big five' comprising Nile Online, Yalla Online, MenaNet and the state-owned TE Data. LinkdotNet was founded by its president Khaled Bicharaand and 11 of his fellow graduates of the American University in Cairo. It is 64 per cent owned by Orascom Telecom, which is in turn owned by the billionaire Egyptian family of Onsi Sawiris and his sons. LinkdotNet has been managing Microsoft's Middle East web sites since 1997. By the middle of 2002, users of MSN Arabia were able to get access to the web wirelessly with Orascom's mobile telephones using wireless application protocol, a precursor of third-generation telephony. LinkdotNet has expanded its internet access services beyond Egypt, launching the first subsidiary, in Jordan, in January 2002.

Heyer reports that despite criticisms that Egypt cannot narrow the digital divide because of a floppy economy and poverty which hampers the entire population of 68 million from going cyber, the telecommunications minister Ahmed Nazif remains committed to the delivery of his five-year development programme. The programme includes the development of projects to achieve US$500 million worth of software exports, human resources, the training of 200,000 persons a year, modernisation of the telecommunications structure, and information and international telecommunications developments.

In Giza, Nazif opened the first giant electronic village, Pyramids Smart Village, an IT complex built at a cost £E100 million. The village brings together high-tech companies, notably specialised IT firms Microsoft, Oracle, Compaq, Cisco and Qualcom, to one location. A hotbed of creativity offering a set of advantages for local and international investors, it boasts a modern infrastructure for delivery of a high-speed communications network connected to satellites for data and TV transmission plus a state of the art stabilised electricity network. Ten per cent of the site is assigned to office buildings consisting of:
- A multi-purpose state of the art conference centre with seating for 2,400 and a fully-equipped press room;
- An exhibition hall for trade fairs and events, several hotels and hotel apartments, restaurants and commercial units, trade centres, recreation facilities, public libraries (print and electronic), international press centre, printing/publishing/translation business centres and health and first aid clinics.

Modern fresh water and irrigation drainage systems with greenery cover 90 per cent of the entire area. IT mega-projects, of the same dimension and function, are planned for Alexandria, Mansoura and Asiut.

(Source: 2003 correspondence with Hazel Heyer)

MenaNet Communications, founded in 1999, has grown rapidly to become the second largest ISP in Egypt with offices in Cairo, Alexandria and Sharm el-Sheikh in the South Sinai. With 60 employees, the company has an expansive service network that extends to Cairo, Alexandria, Suez, 6th of October City, Hurghada, Assiut and Sinai and is Egypt's number one provider both of corporate connectivity and dial-up access via Freenet. Built and headed by a senior management team of CEO Gamal Marwan and CFO Fred Murunga, MenaNet is positioned to offer home users and corporate clients across the Middle East and North Africa (MENA) region with quality Internet access, leased line and broadband access services. Gamal (grandson of former president Gamal Nasser) founded MenaNet Communications in 1999. Prior to founding MenaNet, he was Chairman and CEO of GAM Communication Services, one of Egypt's largest system integrators. Gamal holds a BSc degree in International Relations from the University of South Florida.

Since its inception, MenaNet has quickly established itself as a regional leader in Internet connectivity and has superior technical infrastructure for high speed Internet access and extensive value-added services that include Web Mail, e-calender, Global Roaming, ISDN and XDSL services. Gamal has forged numerous partnerships with a number of local and international companies. In addition, MenaNet has developed a free web-based mail service branded separately as FreeNet, which offers a range of value-added services, including a short message service. FreeNet is a toll-based internet access service operated on a revenue sharing basis with Telecom Egypt. The company also has a substantial stake in Global Data Broadcasting Systems, an Egyptian joint stock company trading under the name MenaSat, which provides high-speed broadband access to the internet via NileSat satellite downlinks. MenaSat's footprint covers most of the Middle East and North Africa and services are offered across the region.

In March 2001, Africa Online extended its operations into North Africa by acquiring MenaNet Communications. The US$8.7 million deal gave Africa Online a foothold in North Africa and the Middle East, and added Egypt, one of the most important markets in Africa, to a network that already covered eight countries: Kenya, Uganda, Tanzania, Zimbabwe, Namibia, Swaziland, Ghana and Côte d'Ivoire. Under the terms of the agreement, MenaNet Communications became a fully-owned subsidiary of Africa Online. Africa Online's services to the Middle East and North Africa will be offered under the MenaNet brand name, while maintaining the Africa Online brand for services to sub-Saharan countries. Gamal says that MenaNet's goal has always been to make it possible for anyone, anywhere, to enjoy the benefits of the internet. He believes that joining with Africa Online will help make that goal a reality. He is very excited about the opportunity to integrate MenaNet's state of the art technology and services into the Africa Online network.

Africa Online is part of the London-based African Lakes Corporation — a trans-African enterprise focused on the provision of internet access, online content, e-business services and solutions, as well as IT distribution. African Lakes' vision is 'Connecting Africa'. The company believes that transforming itself from a conglomerate to a focused technology group is the right way forward and will yield fruitful results, and it intends to continue to build upon group expertise and synergies to bring greater value to customers and shareholders. In November 2002, African Lakes appointed Fred Murunga as the new director of Africa Online Kenya. His appointment is expected to strengthen the important tie between the group's North African and sub-Saharan African ISP businesses, the two businesses being at the core of the group's strategy

(Source: www.menanet.net, and www.africaonline.co.ke)

Basel Dalloul, a successful businessman and recognised authority in IT, established Noor Advanced Technologies, a Washington and Cairo-based technology group, in response to the Egyptian government's decision to make Egypt the hub of the IT industry in the Middle East. Noor is leading one of the largest investments in data communications and infrastructure yet undertaken in the Middle East. The idea is to offer consumers and businesses regionally access to a data communications network comparable to any around the world. With a total investment estimated at US$170 million, Noor intends to be a single source for everything internet-related for consumers and businesses.

Basel Dalloul, chairman and CEO of the enterprise, explains that they want to transform the face of digital communications in the region, bringing the Arab world up to speed so that it can fully participate in the prosperity once the digital economy, the so-called 'new economy', takes off. He says that the digital economy is about much more than online trading. It's really about facilitating the rapid flow of information throughout business, as well as in government and education. The first step is designing and building the technological capacity to support such dissemination of information.

At the heart of it, then, Noor is an infrastructural project. Through an innovative agreement with Telecom Egypt (TE), Noor's infrastructure is based on locating its advanced data communications technology inside TE's exchanges. Using data-communications equipment, Noor has built a hardware infrastructure for fast, secure and reliable data communication services and internet access. Noor's most visible initial impact has been on the consumer service side with the company's introduction of the concept of free internet in Egypt. Noor connects consumers to the internet for the cost of a local phone call and shares revenues generated by phone usage with TE. Along with its free dial-up service, Noor will provide leased lines, global hosting services ASP services and enterprise solutions.

AFRICA: CONTINENT OF ECONOMIC OPPORTUNITIES

Enterprise solutions is a rapidly growing concept in the US, Europe and the Far East among establishments that require more complex and integrated IT services. Dalloul points out that many companies worry about who is going to manage their powerful new technology. He explains that Noor is bringing managed networks services to these companies. They will develop enterprise-wide solutions for their customers and then manage those solutions. If something goes wrong, Noor is responsible, end-to-end, because it controls the infrastructure end-to-end. This, more than anything else, is what makes Noor different.

(Source: www.noorgroup.net, and 'Bringing IT to the mountain'. *Egypt Investment Report* 2002; Arab Communication Consult Ltdhttp://www.arabcomconsult.com/egyptr/bringing.htm)

The Al Ahram publishing group, established in Cairo in 1875, has long been Egypt's generator of accurate and up-to-date news. Hazel Heyer reports that the chairman of the board, Ibrahim Nafie, holds the media group together through a strategy linking it to international changes, while developing it and the staff. Nafie got into the media business through working for Egyptian Radio in 1956, before joining Reuters News Agency. In 1959, he became economic reporter for the *Al Gomhoria* newspaper, and then moved to the US for further studies at a Californian university. On his return he worked between 1962 and 1971 as the economic news editor for the *Al Ahram* newspaper. His ambition was to be Egypt's top media executive, and to this end he worked in all media-related fields — radio, news agencies and newspapers. He was also able to deepen his knowledge of economics during a term at the World Bank.

The crux of the media challenge, according to Nafie, is to reach out to the audiences while maintaining a high level of credibility, and to adapt to the reader. This is achieved through accurate knowledge of public appetite, as well as the issues and atmosphere that surround us. Reaching out to audiences is possible in theory but difficult in practice as it is hard to satisfy all styles, trends and readers' tastes and to maintain credibility and use interesting methods to attract attention.

Consistent hard work and the exposure of reality are critical to success. The difficulty in the region is its long-standing political instability, poor economic conditions, and insufficient human resources. Nafie says that interconnected interests in the region are obstacles in the face of democracy that generate a negative impact. The ambitions of society are far higher than what is actually possible, and people are frustrated by their circumstances. Nafie stresses that his most important mission is to elevate the living standard of his people, and to see them attain a high level of progress.

In the regional context he pursues the development of Arab nations in general while hoping to contribute towards solving the problems and obstacles blocking Arab peace treaties. He vows to support the Al Ahram establishment in its target of expressing fairly all viewpoints in the region and of being a champion of freedom of opinion — an indispensable right in these times. He told Hazel Heyer that '…at the syndicate, I work to enhance professional levels of Arab and foreign press. I took the initiative to build a new, modern building for the syndicate to suit the spirit of the era. On the level of the Union of Arab Journalists, I try to unify the syndicate's movement, give it the opportunity to express a regional voice, increase media participation to achieve individual country aims. Inside me is a burning desire to step up cooperation between the Arab journalistic establishments to offer better service to Arab patrons.'

On the right to speech, he believes countries that prohibit press freedom will be marginalised. 'They will soon belong to the past. The Arab world is an effective region; freedom of the press must prevail. In Egypt, this right has become reality no longer ignored. It lays the foundation for a democratic system. As the economic society has an infrastructure so has the political sphere…it is imperative to prevent setbacks such as suffered by other governments.'

The internet has become a vital media tool that augments the communication processes and has proved that the age of information technology is reinforced by the entry of new media. Nafie says that radio did not defeat the press; TV did not defeat the press and radio. But the internet stretches communication channels and increases the ability of the established print media. He says, 'Print media are like the feet of a human being — indispensable despite the existence of cars, planes and rockets.'

Al Ahram's media 'pharaoh' sees himself and the group competing in the international arena, participating in the development of Egypt and building on links with Arab neighbours and the outside world through entering the world of television in addition to radio and newspapers delivered in English and French.

(Source: www.ahram.org.eg, and 2003 correspondence with Hazel Heyer)

In 1980, Mohamed Taymour started a financial service company, the Egyptian Financial Group (EFG), the first investment banking firm in Egypt. It offered its clients a variety of services and was involved in a large number of privatisation studies for the Egyptian government. EFG moved into brokerage in 1993, and asset management in 1994. It established the first equity index in Egypt. In 1994, Hermes Financial was established as a leading financial services company based on the international experience gained by its founders in the USA and on a young energetic team. Hermes showed great success in securities brokerage and fund management. When the local market had reached a point where large financial institutions were needed with real financial muscles and a wide network of local and international clients, the two firms decided to merge. In 1996, EFG-Hermes was born out of the highly publicised merger between the Egyptian Financial Group (EFG) and Hermes Financial. Hermes had a smaller company than EFG, but the right attributes and attitude, so the two companies were merged and became EFG-Hermes. That turned out to be a very important step in the expansion of EFG.

The EFG-Hermes group now employs over 300 people. It has centralised operation at its headquarters in Cairo and has developed its branch network to include offices in Alexandria coupled with an expanding presence regionally. It has offices of representation in Dubai, Saudi Arabia and Algeria. The asset management division has established an office in the United Kingdom to assist in managing its Middle East and emerging Africa fund and further developing its activities regionally. EFG has an excellent track record as a leading Egyptian investment bank involved in securities brokerage and investment banking, as well as corporate finance, advisory services, equity and debt offerings and asset management. EFG is the leading broker on the Cairo and Alexandria stock exchange.

Taymour, who earned a doctorate from Dartmouth College in the United States and a BSc in industrial engineering from Cairo University, envisions the future of Egypt and plans accordingly. His goal is for Egypt to become an international financial centre. It may not be able to compete with the New York stock exchange but, he says, it can certainly be the number one financial centre in the region, and EFG-Hermes is already beginning to expand outside Egypt — it has worked in Jordan and Algeria, and has visited Syria, Iran and Sudan.

In 2001, a year of stagnant business and limited returns, the most important news in Egypt's financial sector came from the two largest investment firms in the country, EFG-Hermes and its biggest competitor, Commercial International Investment Company (CIIC). In a move designed to create a financial institution large enough to serve the Middle East region as a whole, EFG-Hermes and CIIC announced that they were forming a strategic alliance. The end result of the process was two distinct identities with differing specialisations. EFG-Hermes would continue as a brand name in the market, but would focus on investment banking, while CIIC would focus on proprietary investments. Financial analysts, who had already rated EFG-Hermes highly, welcomed the strategic alliance. They pointed out that EFG-Hermes, being Egypt's largest financial services company outside the banks, stood a better chance of expanding its services abroad, especially to the Middle East, with the alliance. Taymour said the expansion would help the allied companies to penetrate the Arab world and to become greater regional players, rather than international ones. Thanks to strong management and networking they could outpace global players in the region'

(Source: www.efg-hermes.com)

Osman Ahmed Osman, founder of one of the largest indigenous civil engineering and construction firms in the Middle East and Africa, Arab Contractors (Osman Ahmed Osman and Company), died in 1998 at the age of 82 and was buried in Ismailia, his home town. Osman was construction minister for two years under former president Anwar Sadat. He played a key role in promoting Sadat's *'infitah'*, or 'open-door', economic policies in the 1970s and was a close adviser to the president. He was married and had five children; one of his sons married a daughter of the former head of state. Osman established Arab Contractors in 1949. It grew into one of the biggest construction firms in Egypt and the Middle East and is associated with all the new historical landmarks that have made Egypt famous on the world stage. Some of the history-making projects of Arab Contractors are the Aswan High Dam, bridges, tunnels, highways across the lands in Sinai, Luxor and Aswan, the underground rail system in Cairo, the indoor stadium that hosted the African Games and the land reclamation of the vast deserts.

Arab Contractors has been one of the few contractors successfully to blend the Middle Eastern classics with modern techniques of construction. Arab Contractors did not restrict itself to the borders of Egypt. With its management vision, it contributed substantially to the social and economic development of many nations in Africa and Middle East. Over the course of more than half a century, Arab Contractors has mastered every kind of engineering, construction, environmental, industrial, mining, operations and maintenance, power, transportation, management, development and financing challenge. Arab Contractors is a major worldwide engineering and construction firm with experience encompassing over 1,500 projects in 29 countries and employing a professional and technical staff of over 53,000, with projects underway on three continents.

Since the late 1970s, Arab Contractors has diversified its activities to include banking, insurance, agriculture, manufacturing of foodstuffs, industry, hotel services, health care and engineering services. It has 38 construction subsidiaries in the Middle East, Africa, Asia and Europe. It has participated in establishing 17 new companies, in which the Arab Contractors' percentage of ownership varies between 40 per cent and 100 per cent. Domestically, the conglomerate has 65 local companies, comprising joint ventures in which the Arab Contractors' ownership ranges between 5 per cent and 90 per cent. Since 1986, Arab Contractors has worked with the British, Germans, French and Japanese to build the Ahmed Hamdi Tunnel (underneath the Suez Canal), Cairo's underground metro, sewage systems, water purification plants, the Ferdan Bridge over the Suez Canal and the Alexandria Library. Arab Contractors was successful because it offered a cheaper model, and has the ability to utilise labour in a way the multinationals do not.

Ismail Osman, Osman Ahmed Osman's nephew and chairman until 2001, says the company has played an important part in the continuing development strategies of Egypt and other African and neighbouring nations by participating in the execution of projects of vital importance to the welfare and advancement of these countries. He says the main objectives of the company, set by Osman Ahmed Osman, have remained its striving for excellence, its leadership in its field and its maintenance of a sense of family atmosphere within the company. Throughout its history, Arab Contractors has proven its abilities as a leading construction company. Former and current clients, such as the government of Egypt and various African and Arab countries, can attest to this.

Ismail Osman took over as CEO in 1993. Designated by his uncle to work at Arab Contractors, he left an academic career in the 1960s to join the company and specialise in construction management. He worked on the High Dam and the Suez Canal, and at offices throughout the region, such as Libya, focusing on developing the company. In 1999, Osman obtained a Ph D from Loughborough University in England in performance assessment for large construction companies. During Osman's eight-year tenure as chairman, the Arab Contractors' turnover increased from £E1.5 billion annually to almost £E6 billion, as he steered the company along the fine line between minimising risk and trying to achieve the break-even point.

(Source: Aziza Sami. 'Enjoying bad news', Cairo: *Al-Ahram Weekly Online*, 13-19 December 2001)

In 2001, Ismail Osman's first deputy, engineer Ibrahim Mahlab, succeeded him as chief executive of the board of Arab Contractors. The move ended the tenure of one of the country's most popular CEOs and, with it, the pervasive influence the Osman family has wielded over Arab Contractors since it was founded in 1940. In Africa in particular the company has joined hands with local companies in numerous countries.

In 2004, Arab Contractors entered the Kenyan market. Engineer Medhat Askar, Arab Contractors' director for Africa, says the group is in partnership with a Nairobi firm, MG Consult, in a subsidiary called Arab Contractors Kenya Ltd. Arab Contractors had found a niche for their business in Kenya. The company's operations had already been established in 14 African countries, Kenya being the 15th. Askar says that the company is purely African, and he urges Kenyans to seize the opportunity to create African unity in working relations rather than rely on foreigners. He adds that the initiative will create jobs and develop nation-building. Askar says it had always been the group's wish to expand its operations to Kenya. The group would work closely with the government and the private sector in the construction and provision of affordable housing. The Kenyan government is keen on more investors to participate in key sectors, including construction and building.

(Source: www.arabcont.com)

Enviro-Civec is one of the leading engineering consulting firms in Cairo. It was established in 1984, as a private partnership between Diaa El-Monayeri and Khaled Souelim. Enviro-Civec has been growing ever since through its contribution to various vital projects in both private and public sectors. The main objective of the firm is to provide the highest possible quality of services within acceptable cost margins by calibrating new technology and science with the maturity of experience and professionals, while still remaining competitive. Enviro-Civec offers a wide range of engineering and project management expertise. The services rendered by the firm cover almost the full range of professional engineering services such as project identification, feasibility studies, property and site appraisals, selection of new sites for projects, design, detailed engineering of projects, geotechnical, construction management, procurement, environmental studies, construction supervision, inspection services, quality control and training of personnel.

Enviro-Civec's working team consists of a group of highly-skilled engineers who form the core of the various specialised departments, occupying the top and middle management positions. In 2004, there were ten PhD-holders trained in the US, Canada and Egypt. Departments include environmental (public utilities infrastructure, water treatment plants, water distribution networks, sewerage systems, industrial waste treatment, waste water treatment plants, fire fighting systems, irrigation networks, environmental impact assessment studies, flash flood protection studies and management, and storm water collection systems); civil and architecture (structure design and analysis, architectural and urban planning and design, and construction supervision); geotechnical (soil investigation, dewatering system, and geo-environmental); transportation (highway system planning and design, transportation planning and traffic impact studies, and bridges and tunnels planning and design); electro-mechanical (pump stations, treatment plants, and power generators); quality control (field supervision, construction management, surveying, and testing laboratories); and accounting and administration. A competent team is formed when various departments unite to work on the assigned project, headed by a project manager responsible for directing all the activities and organising the jobs required for the project.

By 2003 Enviro-Civec had become a consultant engineering experts office. To ensure proper application of its standards and quality of work, the firm has created its own built-in laboratories with experienced, professional staff supported by advanced equipment solutions which provide reliable and accurate test results and reports in the fields of soil, water investigations and environmental tests.

When the winners of the Africa 2004 SMME Awards were announced, enterprises from all over the continent made their mark. The three top enterprises were not only from different corners of the continent, but also from different industries. Enviro-Civec was the winner of the runner-up award, the winner of the regional award for northern Africa, and the winner of the award for the environmental and renewable energy sector. The Africa SMME Awards are an initiative of the Africa Centre for Investment Analysis at the University of Stellenbosch Business School in Cape Town.

(Source: www.envirocivec.com)

There are several systems for solid waste management — disposal by incineration, landfill and biological. Incineration can be a safe method if the generated gasses are dealt with properly. Dr Hisham Sherif does not prefer this method in Egypt because of the high investments required. There are two types of landfills — secure and non-secure. Sherif says secure landfills are acceptable in Egypt for governorates close to the desert; he points out, however, that this system is not good for Greater Cairo or the Delta governorates, where emitted gasses will pollute the air and leacheate (contaminated liquid which can seep from a landfill site) will pollute the ground water. Biological systems are either aerobic or anaerobic, but aerobic processes are most common.

Sherif says the Egyptian national economy cannot afford expensive incinerators, so solid wastes tend to be recycled, while organic matter is used for composting. Sorting units can be used to separate biodegradable from non-biodegradable wastes which will be sorted at the site, reducing the cost by at least 50 per cent. In 1995 and 1996, Egypt started 10 projects in 10 governorates. Then the number rose to 52 plants all over Egyptian governorates. They helped to reduce investment costs and consumed energy, and created job opportunities.

Sherif is the chief executive of Engineering Tasks Group (ENTAG), an Egyptian firm established in 1992 specialising in the design and supply of solid waste treatment systems. Sherif was a teacher of biochemical engineering at El Miniah University in the 1980s. Spending two years as a doctoral student in Scotland, he returned to Egypt to work as a consultant specialising in the conversion of solid wastes to compost (sorting, composting and recycling). He started his career at ENTAG, and later two sister companies for ENTAG were established — the Egyptian Company for Agricultural Residue Utilisation (ECARU) and Chemonics Libya.

ECARU was established in 1997 in the industrial zone in New Menya. Its operations include production of compost from recycling agricultural residues. It has facilities in Menya City and manages five facilities inside and outside Egypt with a staff of 400 highly skilled and professional staff (workers, technicians and administration). ECARU owns and manages the El Menya Composting Facility for agricultural residues treatment and manages four others: two 15 May facilities for municipal solid waste treatment with capacities 960 tons per day and 640 tons per day; the Obour Facility for market waste treatment; and the Tripoli Composting Facility, which is located in Libya for municipal solid waste treatment.

ECARU produces Nile compost, used widely in fertilising horticultural crops, fruit trees and ornamental plants; Nile compost is characterised by high organic content as a result of variety of wastes and being free from seeds of weeds; Obour Organic Compost, characterised by high content of organic material as a result of variety of wastes in the market (for example vegetables and fruit residue or banana tree leaves); pellets, characterised by flexibility in terms of modifying chemical specifications; humic acid; and *qattameya* compost, characterised by high level of purity compared to the local and international compost produced from municipal solid waste treatment.

ECARU facilities produce 50,000 tons per year of compost, and the company has a large customer base, keen to use composts free from chemicals. The research and development section was established in ECARU and staffed with specialist consultants to achieve the company objectives. In 2004, ECARU was awarded a contract with Cairo's cleaning and beautification authority for a new project in the southern zone of the city. This project includes the upgrade and operation of the authority's 15 May facilities which were designed and supervised by its sister company ENTAG, and the construction and operation of a sanitary landfill for at least 15 years. ECARU provides training for staff in the facilities.

ENTAG is an independent engineering firm established by a group of Egyptian professionals in 1992. The firm has nearly 50 full-time staff members consisting of engineers, chemists, urban planners, management specialists, financial analysts, and computer experts who understand the environmental business and bring years of both domestic and international expertise to every project they implement.

ENTAG has agreements with both local and foreign partners and cooperates with the largest manufacturing companies in Egypt to manufacture local supplies according to design and shop drawing from ENTAG and under its supervision.

The third sister company to ECARU and ENTAG is Chemonics Libya (a branch of Chemonics Egypt which was founded in 1992 in Egypt), founded in 2004 as an independent Egyptian consulting firm and also established by a group of Egyptian professionals committed to providing quality environmental services. Chemonics Libya has nearly 180 full-time staff members. It is able to draw on the resources of affiliate Chemonics International, a leading US international development assistance consultant firm, active in environmental projects on all continents.

(Source: www.ecaru.net)

Dr Ibrahim Kamel, one of Egypt's most successful business leaders, is the principal shareholder, chairman of the board and chief executive officer of Kato Investment, a diversified holding with primarily industrial interests, although it is also widely involved in construction, tourism and property development. With its scope of operations and its international sales, Kato represents one of the largest privately owned corporations in Egypt. Kamel himself is a deeply respected figure in Egypt, renowned not merely for his achievements in building a successful business, but also for the way he conducts it. Kamel would not feel he had succeeded if he had not contributed to the development of Egypt, for working only for money is the least of his incentives. His main business philosophy is to set a good example. It is this ethos that Kamel brings to his most ambitious venture, Sirocco Aerospace International.

With Kato Investment as the principal shareholder, Sirocco's first product is the Tu 204-120, a medium-range passenger jet capable of carrying over 200 passengers or 27 tons of cargo. Kamel says that the Tu 204-120 is a milestone in the industry, the result of the most technologically advanced and efficient commercial passenger jets available. The Tu 204-120 was designed by the Russian aerospace agency Tupolev and manufactured by Russia's Aviastar, Ulyanovsk. Sirocco, which is a minority owner of both firms and saw the potential in combining the aircraft's technologically advanced airframe with the highly efficient and reliable Rolls-Royce engine and state of the art avionics and interiors. The flight deck incorporates a level of technology seen only in new generation aircraft, including fly-by-wire flight control systems and a full electronic flight information system.

The plane, which is certified by the Russian Civil Aviation Authority (ARMAK) and the Egyptian CAA, and is undergoing European (EASA) certification, is comparable to the Airbus A321 and the Boeing 757, both of which have similar range and capacity. The advantage of the Tu 204-120, however, is that it is more cost-effective, not because of cheaper materials, cheaper manufacturing costs or lower quality, but because of the peculiar state of the Russian aviation industry. The development of the Tu 204 took place in the 1980s, which means that the huge cost involved in developing the aircraft was undertaken by the former Soviet Union. Sirocco, therefore, can sell each aircraft without having to amortise development costs.

But convincing an airline to buy aircraft from a newly-established company is not easy. Airlines need to know that the company from which it purchases will survive for decades to come and that the product will be widely used by other airlines or customers to ensure product support continuation and a good residual value of the aircraft. Sirocco's second major investment, therefore, is involved in developing round the clock product support including spare parts, training, technical assistance on maintenance, and engineering and operations wherever needed. Sirocco has so far invested over US$200 million but management is confident concerning their potential returns.

(Source: www.siroccoaerospace.com)

There are two other Kato projects inside Egypt. In Sahl Hasheesh ('grass coast'), the Kato Group is developing a tourist destination on the Red Sea on a scale not yet seen in the Middle East, a complete city where people will live, with schools and hospitals — a real community. The project is based on 3,200 square hectares, 20 kilometres south of Hurghada International Airport. It incorporates time-share villages and hotels, two 18-hole golf courses, a marina and marina housing, additional residential areas adjacent to the golf courses, a commercial and recreational centre and permanent employee housing. The Egyptian Resorts Company (ERC), which Kamel chairs, will act as the direct municipal operator of the community and coordinate the construction, which takes place in three phases. In 2002, 50 per cent of the first phase was sold to developers, while ERC is setting up the city infrastructure.

In a similar vein, but in a different location, is Kato's project at Ghazala Bay. Situated on the north coast of Egypt, the project is a fully-integrated resort development that coincides with Kato's construction of the nearby El-Alamein International Airport under a BOT scheme. This is a contribution to the Egyptian economy, for one of the objectives in building this resort is to set a model for other people to follow. The managers of the travel agency Thomas Cook believe that the north coast of Egypt could become one of the most popular places in the world for international tourism. Kamel says that God gave Egypt the most beautiful beaches in the world but Egyptians are not capitalising on them; he had not originally wanted to be involved but someone had to do something and now he is sure others will copy Kato and will try to create something even better.

Charm Life Grand Resort and Thalassotherapy — El Alamein opened the first luxury five-star resort and spa at Ghazala Bay in July 2004, a pioneering move on the north coast of Egypt. Behind the venture stands Ghazala Tourist Development Company, a subsidiary of the Kato Group, which had just completed the construction of the El Alamein International Airport in time for the opening of the resort and spa. The airport is a convenient 19 kilometre drive from the resort, allowing guests easy access. The new hotel will be at the core of a resort spanning 120,000 square metres of land, only 38,000 square metres of which will be developed. Eventually the resort will incorporate five hotels, a golf course, a shopping mall, a sports complex and a wide range of villas.

(Source: www.katoinvestment.com; and 'Setting the pace'. *Egypt Investment Report 2002*. Arab Communication Consult Ltd; http://www.arabcomconsult.com/egyptr/kato.htm)

Hussein Salem, another of Egypt's most prominent businessmen, leads one of the most successful showcases of the Egyptian tourist sector, the Hussein Salem Group, which is also involved in many other areas, including energy. A pioneer in the hotel and resort industry on the Red Sea and Luxor, the Hussein Salem Group helped put Sharm el-Sheikh on the map thanks to the Jolie Ville Mövenpick Resort and Casino in Naama Bay. The group's second hotel in Sharm el-Sheikh, the Jolie Ville Mövenpick Golf and Resort, was established in line with the new strategy of catering to a more luxurious form of tourism, offering the same five-star hotel service with the added advantage of attracting golfing enthusiasts. The hotel boasts an 18-hole championship golf course hosting international competitions. Ideally situated over a cliff, Jolie Ville Mövenpick Golf and Resort has 290 rooms, two presidential suites, 16 suites and six waterfront villas overlooking rich coral reefs, as well as nine restaurants and bars and a water theme park on 30,000 square metres.

The final link in the chain is the Group's Mövenpick Luxor. Located on a lush island in the Nile four kilometres south of Luxor, the hotel has 332 rooms within a low-rise development over 160,000 square meters, four restaurants, two bars, an enormous range of recreational facilities and banquet and conference services. The unique island environment has allowed the hotel to attract more than the cultural tourist interested in Luxor's archaeological heritage. Environmental tourists, such as bird and animal watchers, are an increasing source of business. Showcases such as this are proof that Egypt is definitely a serious competitor to the Mediterranean countries catering to leisure tourism.

(Source: www.hks-group.com, and 'Diversifying'. *Egypt Investment Report 2002*. Arab Communication Consult Ltd; http://www.arabcomconsult.com/egyptr/diversifying.htm)

Lobna Sabry, correspondent for Reuters, writes about a 'Spartan Egypt oasis inn that beckons city-weary visitors'. She portrays a remote corner of western Egypt, where the last of a string of oases borders the vast Saharan desert, and where one can stay in a room with no electricity. But the guests aren't complaining. They like to think of Adrère Amellal, the high-end eco-lodge situated on 75 acres of palm and olive groves, as 'tourism with taste' that attracts culturally and environmentally sensitive travellers. This exclusive hideaway addresses the concern that the pristine oasis of Siwa, with its unique Berber culture and language, is on the verge of losing its identity as the outside world encroaches upon it.

Mounir Neamatalla, creator of the eco-lodge, explained to Lobna that the main aim of this project is not merely profit, but its role in the sustainable development of the oasis and preservation of its natural environment and cultural heritage. He stresses that Siwa is an attraction for travellers, not tourists. Guests come from all over the world to the foot of the stunning rock called Adrère Amellal ('white mountain' in the Berber dialect) to experience the solace and beauty of the location. The lodge, which began operating in 2001, was built in keeping with the Siwan traditional architectural style using *kershef*, a mixture of salt rock and clay that not only sparkles but also insulates from both heat and cold. During the day, blocks of semi-transparent salt, which form the walls of the main restaurant, allow for a luminous sunlight to shine through. At night, candlelight turns the salty walls into gold. The walls of the 37 rooms are adorned with Siwan tapestries, local crafts and coin-like stones gathered from the desert. A stone-built basin is fed by one of the 230 natural springs of the oasis.

For the past 25 years, Neamatalla has headed Environmental Quality International (EQI), a Cairo-based company that consults on environmental management and social development projects throughout Egypt, North Africa and the Middle East. EQI began privately investing in the oasis in 1998, working with the local community to promote the sustainable development of Siwa. Adrère Amellal, the first of these investments, is the place where Neamatalla is committed to proving that economic sense and natural preservation are not mutually exclusive concepts.

In addition to bringing back the dying tradition of *kershef*, the project generated income opportunities for the Siwan community, working with local craftsmen and builders, cleaning the area, and reintroducing it to indigenous trees and plants. The land was assembled from 72 families, who worked with Neamatalla to build the lodge in old Siwan style with roofs made from palm-tree stems and furniture from olive-tree wood, the two principal crops cultivated in the oasis. Hag Abou El-Qassem is the oldest palm tree cutter in town and one of Siwa's tribal notables. He helped revive the dying skill by passing it on to the youngsters brought from a nearby village to work. Abou El-Qassem says the profession almost died some 25 years ago as Siwa became more accessible to the people of the Nile Valley and the north coast of Egypt, who in turn introduced modern concrete houses to the oasis. Neamatalla likes to think that visitors will contribute to the lives of the local community. Adrère Amellal does not have any marketing or advertising system. Nor does it rely on brochures or websites. It depends mainly on the word of mouth of its guests.

(Source: www.eqi.com.eg)

Since prehistoric times, the Nile River valley has provided one of the routes from the Mediterranean world to sub-Saharan Africa, with Nubia as the point of contact between the two worlds. For Pharaonic, Greek, Roman, Byzantine and Arab civilisations, Nubia served as a corridor to Africa, a highway for diverse cultures and political powers during thousands of years. In the 20th century, this region witnessed two of the greatest engineering feats in modern history. The first was the construction of the Aswan High Dam with the consequent creation of Lake Nasser. The second was the UNESCO project which saved the historical sites of Nubia threatened with permanent submersion beneath the waters of the lake.

The total volume of the dam itself has been calculated at 17 times that of the Great Pyramid, and to build it 30,000 men worked around the clock for 10 years. The resulting reservoir extends 500 kilometres, some 380 of which lie in Egypt, with an average width of 10 kilometres. No wonder then that Lake Nasser has been referred to as the Nubian Sea. Its coasts are uninhabited but it is the dream of the founders of the cruise ship Eugénie that someday this wealth of fresh water and land will create a verdant living space. When the decision was made in 1954 to build the dam, it was apparent that, in addition to the evacuation of the Nubian community, urgent attention was required to safeguard the Nubian monuments.

UNESCO responded to the appeal for assistance in the latter project by launching the resources of some 54 nations over a 20-year period. The degree of ingenuity required to save the temple represented a comparable task and fighting tribute to creative genius that accomplished their original construction. It was the first time in history that so many diverse countries, individuals and disciplines had united in an undertaking dedicated to the idea of a common cultural heritage and the universality of art. Since 1993, the immense lake and the temples on its banks have been accessible to travellers with a passion for a discovery and a taste for comfort — aboard the cruise ship Eugénie.

Hazel Heyer has written about her momentous cruise on Lake Nasser aboard the Eugénie, the 'gentle lady of the Nubian Sea', a ship dedicated to French Empress Eugénie Marie de Montijo de Guzman, countess of Tera. The ship in her majesty's honour was built by the family El Gendy, owner of the Bell Époque travel agency. The first boat to cruise the Nubian Sea, Eugénie was actually constructed in the desert since there was no way to haul it over or through the High Dam; its parts had to be brought from Cairo and assembled on the banks of the lake. Moustafa El Gendy, who initiated the idea to open up Lake Nasser to tourism, recalls that everyone except his brother Tarek (his partner in the business) thought he was out of his mind to build a boat in the middle of the desert above the High Dam but when the construction was completed, the boat became the newest, hottest and only sensation in the vast expanse, flooded with the reservoir water, but dotted with Pharaonic temples and monuments. Resembling an old paddle wheeler, the 74-metre 1000-ton ship boasts elegant interior decoration by Amr Khalil. This elegantly appointed vessel is arguably the most appealing and thoroughly comfortable cruise boat in Egypt.

(Source: www.eugenie.com.eg)

Sekem, an organisation that takes its name from an ancient Egyptian hieroglyph meaning 'vitality from the sun', has been practising and promoting biodynamic agriculture since 1977, and developing an increasing variety of projects and programmes in education, medical care and research. Dr Ibrahim Abouleish, the initiative's founder, returned to Egypt following his studies and many years of work as a pharmacologist in Austria. In 1977, he established a farm on 125 acres of desert, 40 miles north east of Cairo, at the edge of the Nile Delta. At one time, the Sekem farm was merely a barren desert like the surrounding environment, but now the desert sands have been converted into fertile soil, and green, flowering landscapes supporting livestock and bees. Trees were planted to serve as a new habitat for animals and to protect the farm from desert storms. Composting and cultivation of nitrogen-binding plants served to build up soil structure. Deep wells were dug for irrigation, pumping out precious water from a depth of more than a hundred metres.

In 1991, cotton (one of Egypt's most important agricultural products) was cultivated using biodynamic methods for the first time in history. This success led the ministry for agriculture to reduce pesticide applications and to stop application of pesticides by aeroplane. Within a few years, under the guidance of the German agronomist G Merckens, a wide variety of biodynamic crops and medicinal plants were introduced onto the local market and then exported to the United States and Europe. Working in close cooperation with Sekem, a countrywide network of farming based on biodynamic agriculture has spread through Egypt from these beginnings. Through consultation and training opportunities provided by the Egyptian Biodynamic Association, the number of new farms converting to biodynamic agriculture is constantly growing. Now, more than 800 farms are cultivating all kinds of crops covering 22,000 acres, under the guidance of Sekem.

The farms process and package fresh fruit and vegetables, make different varieties of teas and manufacture organic cotton textiles. Sekem founded companies that process agricultural raw materials into high-quality products, including natural cures (phyto pharmaceuticals), organic foodstuffs and textiles. Today Sekem is a group of firms consisting of six independent enterprises and in 2001 these were linked together under the umbrella of the Sekem holding company that oversees administration of all companies in the Sekem Group. Dr Abouleish's son, Helmy Abouleish, is the managing director of the Sekem Group.

Expanding Sekem's initiative into economic, social and cultural activities, the NGO Egyptian Society for Cultural Development (SCD) was founded in 1984 to carry out projects and programmes in education, medical care and research. There is the Sekem kindergarten and Sekem school for primary and secondary education. The children are educated through arts, crafts, and music. There is also an adult training centre and a vocational training centre. Gradually the project developed and diversified. The SCD cooperates with the German Association for the Promotion of Cultural Development in Egypt, founded at the same time as the SCD, and has made an important contribution to setting up social and cultural services, giving local people an opportunity to develop much-needed skills and perspectives.

Since 1999, the Sekem Academy for Applied Art and Science in Cairo has been the centrepiece of such activities. Through an international network of universities and institutions of higher learning, scientists and artists affiliated with the Sekem Academy investigate and develop practicable means for developing all areas of human life, particularly addressing the needs of contemporary society.

Sekem integrates the economic, social and cultural spheres of life in all aspects of its work. Employees are empowered to realise their full potential as responsible and capable members of society. At present about 2,000 people are employed by Sekem in its different companies. Every morning at a specific time, employees meet in a circle, where each person very briefly reports about his previous day's activities, as well as his work plans for the present day; this allows each employee to experience a sense of dignity as a member of the Sekem community. Each company has an administrator responsible for the interests of the workers, and the quality of their work environment. He organises their training and career development as well as their health care programmes.

Dr Abouleish highly values his friends and supporters from around the world for their support and cooperation. He always looks forward to an exchange of ideas concerning potential areas for future projects and development. In August 2003, the Schwab Foundation, World Economic Forum selected Dr Abouleish as one of the world's Outstanding Social Entrepreneurs, and in December 2003, Sekem was awarded the Right Livelihood Award in Stockholm — a prize for outstanding vision often thought of as the 'Alternative Nobel prize'.

(Source: www.sekem.com)

Sudan

The 2002 *World INvestment News* (WINNE) special country report on Sudan points out that, historically, the Sudanese economy is still very much run by family businesses, names such as Haggar, Aboulela, El Roubi, Hago, Abouda and Elnefeidi. For example, Gamal Elnefeidi is the managing director of Elnourus Transport of Khartoum. Elnourus Transport is part of the Elnefeidi Group, the leading transportation group of companies in Sudan, and the most diversified. It is said to be the largest logistic and transportation company in. Its main focus is the transportation of crude oil from some production areas to others not connected because there is no pipeline. The company transported the pipe from Port Sudan to the bending plants and then to the pipeline route, a distance of about 1,500 kilometres, obtaining cranes and earth moving equipment such as bulldozers, loaders and excavators. Nearly 200 trucks were imported to support Elnourus's own. When the project was completed, Elnourus decided to continue working in the area and, in 2000, established a company in Djibouti, the biggest port for landlocked Ethiopia. Working mainly with the UN and the World Food Programme, Elnourus transferred relief food from Djibouti to Ethiopia, and then from the main Ethiopian warehouses to small villages in Ethiopia.

A similar project, also related to oil and the pipeline, existed in Chad, and so an office was established there. According to Gamal, Egypt is a more difficult prospect because even though there are seven Elnefeidi brothers, none of them could go there and stay for a long period, and 'in the transport business you have to be very close to it, you have to follow it very close not like other projects like agriculture, construction...in anything like that you can depend on others but in [the] transport business you have to be there...'

Elnourus Transport represents more than 50 per cent of the group's turnover. The group's other transport companies in Ethiopia and Djibouti operate under different names but 'once they complete their projects they will be back and will join Elnourus. So Elnourus is growing this way'.

(Source: Interview with Gamal Elnefeidi at www.winne.com/sudan/vp03.html)

As shareholders with the government, the group developed a new bus terminal in Khartoum. The idea simply emerged after the group had started a new bus company, Gandala, and thought it had to do something different from other bus transport companies, so decided to create a more professional terminal. It is, according to Gamal, the kind of initiative that would make Sudan more competitive and provide a better service to the people while encouraging them to use the bus. Right now, he says, Sudanese hate to take buses even though they are more on time than the airlines, because the idea of stopping in some checkpoints and taking all the luggage up and down is too much hassle. People prefer to wait two or three hours at an airport rather than to go and check their luggage every 200 kilometres. 'For example, if you are going to Port Sudan, they check your luggage three times in different cities,' he says.

(Source: www.elnefeidigroup.com, and 'Sudan: Beyond perceptions'. *WorldINvestmentNews*, August 2002)

Arab Communication Consult of Beirut, Lebanon, reports that to anyone familiar with the business environment in North Africa and the Middle East, it is immediately obvious that it is the family unit that dominates. In Sudan, nearly all the private sector is comprised of family businesses. Indeed, the biggest private companies in Sudan — from transport, trade and industry — are family concerns. That is why one of the most important business developments in Sudan recently has been the establishment of one of the country's largest private businesses along distinctly corporate lines. The El Nilein Holding Company, established in 1999, represents the unification of more than 35 independent businesses with an enormous diversity of products and services.

The man behind the new company is Sudanese businessman and Chairman of El Nilein, Salah Idris. Idris was born in Shendi, Sudan, now spends much of his time in Jeddah, Saudi Arabia, and is a citizen of both countries. A former senior officer of Saudi Arabia's largest commercial bank, Idris has been an active investor in Africa, the Middle East and the United States. He has an office in London and a home in Cairo.

Idris became widely known internationally when the United States destroyed his pharmaceutical factory with cruise missiles in 1998. The attack, now widely viewed by the international community as a mistake, destroyed a factory that was responsible for 50 per cent of Sudan's pharmaceutical needs. Despite this international attention, in Sudan Idris is better known for his business activities, a part of his life he says he approaches from a dual perspective. 'Like any normal businessman, I want this to be a successful commercial enterprise. But at the same time, I was born in Sudan and in that way I'm indebted to the country, so I want this enterprise to be beneficial to the country and the people as well.'

In that sense, Idris wants El Nilein to be a successful combination of Sudanese and non-Sudanese business values. 'I'm against the family style of business; it cannot last for long, so we have to learn how business is done from the outside.' The company had its genesis in the economic difficulties Sudan experienced in the late 1980s and early to mid-1990s. Very high inflation and economic recession dragged many of the country's private businesses into financial difficulties, creating what Idris calls a buyers' market.

'In my opinion,' he says, 'we were in an environment in which the local businessmen, although very successful in their own right, were not experts in the foreign exchange side; they were more traditional traders, importers and exporters. They never thought to manage the foreign exchange risk and they were dependent on the fixed rate from the government. The dollar rate was almost fixed and the valuation was a political decision. So when the currency deteriorated, that had an enormous impact on their solvency and that's where the problems began. They were caught with Sudanese dinars in their hand while having financial commitments on the dollar side, so they could never catch up.'

Idris was able to generate a portfolio of businesses that span almost the entire spectrum of the economy. Many of these businesses were established names in the Sudanese market. For example, one of the holding's biggest companies is the Bittar Group, a conglomerate that covers multiple sectors of the economy and is one of Sudan's oldest private firms. With 10 independent subsidiaries, it specialises in heavy engineering, trade, industry, commodities and distribution.

(Source: 'El Nilein Holding Company marks the creation of one of Sudan's first multinational corporations'. *Sudan Investment Report 2001*. Arab Communication Consult Ltd. http://www.arabcomconsult.com/sudan/nilein.htm)

Investment is the most crucial aspect for the industrial sector, given that tariff barriers and the cost of energy are dropping. One of the most important of these investments is Saria Industrial Complex, one of the country's largest industrial initiatives, which is set to take advantage of recent improvements in Sudan's industrial sector. Saria is a group of seven factories located in southern Khartoum. Although it only began production in 1997, it already represents one of Sudan's largest industrial initiatives. Initially a public corporation, the complex was sold to the private sector in 1998 and is now fully owned by El Nilein and is its most significant holding. El Nilein produces a range of essential products for the local market and intends to become a major exporter to the region, particularly with the Common Market for Eastern and Southern Africa (COMESA) initiative set to free up regional trade. The holding's other industrial interests include flour milling, printing, plastics and textiles.

Saria began production by focusing on crucially needed consumer goods for the local market. The first factory specialises in producing car and truck batteries and the second focuses on manufacturing prefabricated packaging such as cardboard cartons. Factory three produces plastics such as PVC pipes and covers for the company's other products, including televisions, telephones and car batteries. The fourth factory is involved in manufacturing ready-made clothing such as uniforms for government institutions, while the fifth plant produces over 3,000 shoes and boots per day. The final two factories focus on electronics assembly and producing electrical fittings and household electrical appliances.

Under a joint venture with LG, the Korean electronics manufacturer, Saria is importing television components and assembling them for the local market. In total, Saria produces more than 60 different types of products. According to Saria's General Manager, Ahmed Alsamani Afaki, 'Sudan is a virgin country that is underdeveloped. But in the next 10 years, I believe Sudan will be the main developing country in the African region and Saria is going to be there to take advantage of this.' The majority of Saria's production is based on assembling imported components. The strategy of the company is to gradually increase its technical expertise till it manufactures most of the production. 'Our aim,' says Mr Afaki, 'is to move from assembly to genuine manufacturing once our experience increases over the next few years. For example, all electronic components are imported and we only produce the plastic covers, but with the technical assistance of LG, we want to turn that situation around.'

The success of this strategy depends on accessing the regional market. Saria is currently working at around 50 per cent of its capacity in supplying the demand of the domestic market. Afaki believes its spare capacity will be absorbed by its COMESA neighbours. A crucial addition to this strategy is further agreements and joint ventures with other international firms. 'While we have all the raw materials we need in Sudan, we lack technical know-how and have high capital costs. So we need more joint ventures.'

(Source: www.sariacomplex.com, and 'Saria Industrial Complex, one of the country's largest industrial initiatives, is set to take advantage of recent improvements in Sudan's industrial sector', *Sudan Investment Report 2001*, Arab Communication Consult Ltd; http://www.arabcomconsult.com/sudan/saria.htm

Another of El Nilein's interests is transportation, a key sector in a country the size of Sudan. Sabehat Transport, owned by El Nilein, is one of the country's largest private transportation firms specialising in car and truck rental and road freight. The holding also purchased a cargo airline, TransArabian.

However, the area that Salah Idris believes holds the most promise for the company is agriculture, particularly animal resources, one of Sudan's largest exports. El Nilein's interests in the sector include Ghanawa Meat Trading Company, which encompasses a US$10 million abattoir in Khartoum producing and processing meat for local consumption and export. It also owns Al Oswa Crop and Investment Company, which is involved in exporting some of Sudan's major agricultural products including sesame and peanuts, as well as Al Arab International Trading Company, which is active in the international commodity business and imports crops such as wheat, flour, sugar and rice.

The holding also has shareholdings in other very promising areas. In Sudan's growing oil and gas sector, El Nilein has a 75 per cent stake in Gulf Petroleum, which is active in both Sudan and Qatar. In telecommunications, the holding has a minority shareholding in Sudatel, Sudan's highly successful telecom company created from the privatisation of the state telecommunications utility. In banking, El Nilein has also taken a 30 per cent interest in Animal Resources Bank, which initially specialised in offering credit to the agricultural sector but is now expanding its services across the economy. On the international front, the company has businesses in Egypt, Syria, the United Kingdom, Sierra Leone and Saudi Arabia. In addition, Idris recently established another company in London to manage El Nileins' overseas businesses. Overseas activities include real estate, shopping mall construction and management, telecommunications, industry and nursing homes.

The key reason Idris decided to establish El Nilein was to give some focus to the diverse activities of the group. 'Eventually I see ourselves taking whatever we have under the holding company and going public,' he says. For this, he needs a company with a single identity that the Sudanese can recognise. 'We want to encourage the Sudanese to change their spending habits, to make them save by using the value of the markets and getting a higher yield than a regular savings account. So given that the stock market is properly set up and the right companies are included, that is something I believe we can achieve with El Nilein.'

For these goals to be realised, however, Idris reckons that Sudan must find peace and stability. 'We have been dealing with Sudan very professionally and commercially to the benefit of the people of the country and our business. We are confident about the potential of the country and we believe the economy will definitely take off given two conditions: peace and stability. I would love investors to come to Sudan for their benefit and the benefit of the country. We are open to working with investors'

(Source: 'El Nilein holding company marks the creation of one of Sudan's first multinational corporations', *Sudan Investment Report 2001.* Arab Communication Consult Ltd. http://www.arabcomconsult.com/sudan/nilein.htm)

Africa continues to be the fastest growing cell phone market in the world. In 2005, Africa accounted for 102 million GSM subscribers. Mobile subscriber numbers have increased on the continent by over 2,000 per cent between 1998 and 2005. However, penetration levels remain low with less than 13 per cent cellular penetration against the world average of nearly 30 per cent, and the market remains both fragmented and challenging. In sub-Saharan Africa, where Celtel operates, penetration levels are estimated to be even lower, averaging 6 per cent. The preference of Africans for mobile telephones is highest in the world (nearly 70 per cent of their total telephone connections are mobile). Most of the companies offer prepaid card services. Such a market growth was made possible because of liberalisation of the telecommunications sector. The leading companies are Celtel (whose registered office is in Netherlands), the South African companies Vodacom and MTN, and Econet and Orascom from Egypt. Factors like increased privatisation, more competition and the planned introduction of low-cost handsets are expected to propel the Africa's subscriber base to 248 million by 2010.

(Source: www.telecoms.com)

Mohamed Ibrahim is chairman of Celtel, which has GSM operations in 14 countries comprising over one-third of the population of Africa. Ibrahim is one of the most successful entrepreneurs in the mobile communications industry. He has a wide knowledge of the international scene. His original holding company, MSI Cellular Investments, changed its name to Celtel International in January 2004. From 1998 to 2004, Celtel invested more than US $800 million, which was raised from shareholders such as Citicorp, IFC, CDC, WorldTel, AIG and Old Mutual. Ibrahim chaired a prestigious board whose members included Lord Prior, Sir Alan Rudge, Marten Pieters (Celtel International's chief executive officer), and Felda Hardymon (professor of venture capital at Harvard). Ibrahim is an acknowledged global expert in mobile communications, with a distinguished academic and business career.

Ibrahim is an African by birth, a Nubian (Nubia was one of the earliest civilisations in Africa and now straddles the borders between Egypt and Sudan). He was born in 1946 in Sudan, grew up there and first worked for an African Public Telephone and Telegraph in Sudan. In an address delivered in Dar es Salaam in February 2001, Ibrahim spoke of suffering many of the frustrations shared by telecommunications engineers across the continent, and dreaming that one day he could make a difference and help his fellow Africans communicate better with each other and with the outside world. He believed his people deserved better.

His long journey took him first to England as an academic (he holds a BSc in electrical engineering from the University of Alexandria, Egypt; an MSc in electronics and electrical engineering from the University of Bradford, England; and a PhD in mobile communications from the University of Birmingham) and then as a radio engineer with the first cellular network in the UK. After six years as the technical director for Cellnet of British Telecom, he left to become an entrepreneur and founded MSI in 1989. To make the money necessary to develop Africa, he built the business into a leading cellular software and consulting company. Much was achieved very quickly. MSI built more GSM networks around the world than anyone else. Very soon, MSI established itself as the pre-eminent independent operation in the world. MSI also developed software, used to build and optimise cellular networks, which is probably used by a hundred operations around the world.

As MSI developed operations worldwide it was persuaded to take equity in cellular operations. MSI ended up with some equity in Hong Kong, in India and in Uganda. Very quickly, MSI realised that there was a conflict since it was providing cellular operators world wide with software and with consultants to build networks, but also competing with them to build networks, so it took the decision to separate its cellular operation from its services and software. That was a drastic decision for the group and it took a lot of soul searching.

In 1998, in Amsterdam, MSI Cellular was born as a different company, and in 2000 the original MSI was sold to Marconi. Ibrahim chose to go into the cellular operation and became the chief executive and the chairman of MSI Cellular. Ibrahim decided that MSI Cellular was going to focus on Africa. He invested the proceeds of the sale of MSI in Africa because he believes Africa needs investments, not charity.

Ibrahim made presentations to his board and shareholders indicating why he wanted to go back to Africa and build the continent. Tele-density in Africa was below one per cent. He had been to umpteen conferences worldwide. All the do-gooders would stand up and speak fine words. He had attended conferences in Johannesburg and listened, and thought the problem was solved, but nothing had happened. Ibrahim's plea to his board was that they had a historical opportunity to build a proper telecommunications company in Africa. With shareholders like theirs, with a board like theirs and with their technical expertise, they could do virtually anything. As of 30 June 2004, the number of employees in managed mobile operations was 3,341 in some 13 African countries: Burkina Faso, Chad, the Democratic Republic of Congo, the Republic of Congo, Gabon, Kenya, Malawi, Niger, Sierra Leone, Sudan, Tanzania, Uganda and Zambia. They had built large and small networks — from complex networks in cities like London, Munich, Berlin, Moscow or Singapore to rural networks in Zambia or Malawi. They had been to all sorts of markets, and knew what it took to build networks. In December 2005, Celtel expanded its reach across the continent, acquiring a majority stake in Madagascan GSM mobile operator Madacom, spreading its African operations across 14 countries and more than 8.5 million subscribers.

The strength of the management team that Celtel has assembled, the depth of its experience in the cellular market and the reputation that it can bring to deliver on projects in Africa lend it a lot of credence. The company has a track record of having worked and succeeded in some very difficult markets. Celtel's level of commitment in the training and development of its staff is encouraging.

In 2003, Celtel won the Netherlands inaugural SMO award for Foreign Direct Investment. The award, presented by the SMO Foundation for Business and Society, the Dutch industrial association, recognised Celtel as the best Dutch foreign investment company for 2003. It was a reflection of the high standards of corporate governance and healthy work ethic that Celtel maintains. Celtel has helped improve health and education by refurbishing schools and health centres, providing scholarships, supporting programmes for athletes and people with handicaps, and sponsoring the Africa Education Journalism Award. The company has embraced HIV/AIDS as a business and community issue and has worked with a specialised NGO, Pharmaccess, to deploy a comprehensive HIV/AIDS programme for employees and their families across all its operations. Celtel has also started a community phone initiative, installed solar panels for the recharging of phone handsets, and helped protect endangered species. In 2004, the IFC awarded its first annual Client Leadership Award to Celtel, recognising Celtel as a highly successful corporate client that, in line with IFC's mission, had made a significant contribution to sustainable development in Africa.

One of the problems that developing countries face is lack of equity financing. Telecommunications is a capital-intensive industry: it requires a lot of financing, equity, and debt. Celtel has built some of the best GSM networks in Africa. Ibrahim asserts that there is money willing to go to Africa, as long as it is backed by credible people. He warns that African telecommunications is no place for opportunists or amateurs, and that survival requires a very experienced management team, a successful record and the ability to attract finance. Celtel has transparency, institutional shareholdings and the backing of some of the best in the industry. Investors and bankers worldwide will continue that support as Celtel bids for new business throughout Africa. Ibrahim believes in the African century — for him not a slogan but about transforming the African continent from an under-developed continent into one that can export knowledge, technology and refined products. He believes in the creation of an African telecommunications network based on the philosophy of Africa's being the continent of opportunity in the 21st century. He asserts that the world's most marginalised continent offers one of the best business opportunities.

In March 2005, the board of Celtel International announced it had agreed to a cash offer for the company from Mobile Telecommunications Company (MTC) in Kuwait. Celtel will remain as a separate entity within the MTC group and retain its existing head office and management structures both in Amsterdam and in each of the 13 African countries of operation. Celtel will also continue to operate under its market-leading brand name. Post acquisition, a new Celtel board will include Dr Mohamed Ibrahim, the founder of Celtel, who said, 'In the past Celtel deployed European and American funds to assist the development of telecommunications infrastructure in Africa. Today we are engaging the Middle East in this process. This transaction represents a key step in bringing these sources of wealth to support the development of Africa.' Celtel's CEO, Marten Pieters, said, 'I look forward to working with my management team backed by the additional resources available from MTC. I am confident that, with our new partners, we have an exciting opportunity for our employees and customers to benefit from the full development of a vital service for emerging economies.' In recognition of the importance of the MTC/Celtel transaction for Africa, Celtel was awarded the Africa Investor award for the Infrastructure Deal of the Year 2005.

(Source: www.celtel.com)

Helping to meet the rising demand for housing in Sudan is the Danfodio Commercial and Contracting Company. Created in 1981, Danfodio has had a hand in almost every aspect of the national economy. It is now the largest integrated construction and engineering firm in the country and has built residential complexes, new offices, hotels, hospitals, government and industrial sites, infrastructural projects, the Khartoum International Airport, the national mint, roads, irrigation schemes and religious buildings. With the onset of oil production, Danfodio has been involved in work on Sudan's first oil and gas development to turn the country into an exporter of crude. Danfodio was responsible for completing pumping stations on the 1 600-kilometre pipeline from the oilfields in central Sudan to the oil export terminal on the Red Sea coast.

In addition to its construction activities, the firm runs functionally independent engineering, road transport, trading, agricultural and equipment rental divisions. The Danfodio Group has more than 20 companies, from subsidiaries to associate firms. Activities include vehicle imports, transport, engineering, grain stores and travel. Danfodio ventures into industry include cement and industrial oxygen production, and it is currently exploring the potential of petroleum by-products and power generation. Danfodio is a major consumer of ornamental stones, imported mainly from the European Union and China. The group also has ventured into dimension stones with the intention of carrying out several projects exploiting a number of quarries in Sudan.

With a presence in Dubai, Jeddah, Beijing and Seoul, Danfodio is also looking to expand its range of partners and joint venture agreements. Danfodio is now working in Chad with an Italian partner, building a bridge, and in Ethiopia it is working on oil transport and building a road through Ethiopia to divert most of the country's imports through Port Sudan. When this road is complete, the west and north of Ethiopia will be nearer to Port Sudan than Djibouti or Masawa. More recently, the company signed a joint venture with a Malaysian firm to build a new headquarters for the Bank of Sudan. Danfodio has also started a trading enterprise in Malaysia. The company plays an important social role in Sudan.

Management and its 800 employees believes the company can double its US$150 million turnover. They think it is feasible given the current economic situation. They are trying to serve their country by growing Danfodio since profits made by the company are shared with charities, such as hospitals and schools and for relief work both inside and outside Sudan. The company is diversifying projects to work in all fields in order to maximise profits. Many Sudanese are returning to the country as conditions improve. There are universities in Sudan but they teach mostly theory. They need foreign experience by getting companies to come to Sudan through joint ventures. There is a lot of work and it is apparent that investors are now starting to come to Sudan.

Hazel Heyer reports that the Sudan can no longer be oblivious to the several million dollars Hayat Abdoun's booming tannery business makes. As down-to-earth as she is, she would rather keep busy at work inside her little nook in her factory at the Omdurman Industrial Area than flaunt the rich harvest she reaps. Sudan's only woman in the tannery field (probably the only one in Arabia), is cultivating unprecedented success. But she hardly spoke about it until recently. 'It's a tough world out there. There's no way to loosen the grip. This business is perhaps the most difficult for women to engage in. Extremely demanding. It frightens them away. No wonder I am the only one doing it,' said Hayat Magzoub Abdoun, proprietor of the Sudan's Suliman Tannery.

Surprisingly, Hayat Abdoun is a newcomer in an industry she would have not known had her husband Suliman Hussein not died. She stumbled upon the activity by accident; more so of necessity as she was left to fend for herself and her four children alone. 'I was an ordinary housewife, a home-maker. I only looked after the kids. My husband ran the business of exporting hide until he passed away in 1994,' she narrated. Misfortune clearly thrust her into re-engineering her life chart. She and her offspring were caught in a financial vice. In desperation, Hayat decided to pick up the broken pieces and run the business herself, with the little technical background she had.

Even though, she had only basic education she pursued the impossible. 'Prior to my husband's death, I dabbled on the side in trading in raw leather, as back-up for Suliman. I was briefly exposed to salting raw hide in 1993 after watching my late husband conduct his operations. Most of the time, I preferred to stay home. One day, Suliman was gone. I was completely at a loss. Somebody had to take over what he'd left behind. Nobody was in charge; it just had to be me. Otherwise, I would have thrown away all that Suliman had worked for, for years, and let the family go hungry. I could not see my kids not have a good future,' she recalled.

'So I rolled up my sleeves and got to down to serious work.' The tragedy was not yet over. Her trials and tribulations were just about to begin. The government had banned the export of raw or undressed hide. In the face of numerous new learning curves in life, and a new law to contend with, Hayat did not buckle but confronted the issues head on. To conform to the authority's mandate, she set up the tannery from scratch. She bought the chemicals, barrels, tanning machines, packaging equipment, and tools whose names and purposes she did not know.

In due time, Hayat started rolling out the tannery's excellent main products such as pickled and wet-blue sheep and goatskins. Her factory was outputting a production capacity of 3,000 sheepskins and 2,000 goatskins daily. Barely a year after Suliman's demise and the threat of the company's closure, she was raking in US$3 to $5 million in annual sales. Her secret? 'I only applied a housewife's common sense to running a business, keeping costs down and questioning every expense. What saved me most was that I knew how to balance the books,' she quipped.

The other secret is serious, non-stop hard work. 'Tanning was, and still is, a very difficult line,' she confessed. Beyond faith and inspiration, Hayat has infinite capacity to take pains. It hurt, not seeing her children for days on end when she had to spend most of the time at work — 25 hours a day, eight days a week. But it was the only formula for success. There was no alternative — until a second pair of hands arrived. She said, 'My eldest son Mohamed has helped me a lot in the factory. He co-manages the tannery. He will most likely inherit from me. He has been of great help, ever since his father died when he was only eleven.'

Abdoun's Omdurman-based tannery is exported-orientated, with its main markets in Italy, Spain, Turkey, India and Pakistan. Weekly shipment is an estimated 70 to 90 tons per container. To Spain alone, Hayat exports four containers of leather to agents in Madrid and Barcelona; five to six containers are directed to Italy per week. Spain generates US$2 million sales per year. On leather quality control, Hayat said, 'I monitor closely every activity in the tannery. I inspect the quality of the hide supplied to us by the local farms. I only deliver superior-quality finished goods to my clients worldwide. As mine is the biggest private tannery in Sudan, competing with the government-owned Nile and Khartoum Tanneries, I am bent on keeping my position as the market leader. The government factories deal with reject hides, whereas mine only process first- and second-class skins. I would really not compromise on quality for volume. I will only risk losing my valued customers if I treat my 'raw' below standard.'

Recently, Hayat showed interest in participating in a pact with the Common Market for Southern and Eastern Africa (COMESA) in order to expand her export territory. 'Soon, I will open up markets in Egypt with the aid of this robust economic union. I am also looking into supplying my stuff locally to Sudan buyers with a view to extending a 50 per cent discount — the same percentage I would allocate to Egyptian clients. Egypt is very close to my heart; both it and my country drink from one Nile, so why should we not be very good neighbours?' said the 52-year-old entrepreneur, who owns a huge residential building at the heart of Cairo. Hayat's late father was the Sudan's foremost Supreme Court judge.

According to the old adage by William Feather, 'Success seems to be largely a matter of hanging on after others have let go'. Hayat Abdoun's story is not just an inspirational lesson in business administration. It reads like a tale of a loving mother, an excellent provider and an exemplary Sudanese. How many of them do you meet these days? You can count them on the fingers of one hand. The writer Hazel Heyer brushed tears from her eyes when she spoke to this woman, who had braved such a storm.

(Source: Author's correspondence with broadcast journalist Hazel Heyer, 2003)

Southern Sudan

Southern Sudan has bountiful natural resources and the potential to be a major producer of a wide range of agricultural commodities. Largely untapped livestock, fishery and forestry resources, adequate rainfall, fertile land, and water availability all point to the agricultural potential of southern Sudan. Constraints to agricultural production and marketing include poor infrastructure, lack of access to capital and low-level agricultural technical efficiency and skills in production, marketing and business management.

Southern Sudan has depended on manufactured goods and services from northern Sudan or the neighbouring countries of Kenya, Ethiopia, Uganda, the Democratic Republic of Congo and the Central African Republic. These are mostly consumer goods and include textiles, soap, salt, cooking oil, tea leaves, coffee, cigarettes and sugar. This is despite the fact that the raw materials for these goods are, or could be, produced locally. Soap, cooking oil, the fruit processing industry, the production of agricultural tools and processing equipment are not only feasible, but could be developed to meet some of the local demands. Other small or light industries, which are feasible and do not require very advanced technology, include leather processing, shoe manufacture, clothing or garment production, timber and furniture production, and the production of bricks and tiles. To promote these activities, appropriate institutions have to be developed to provide the needed skills, financial services, market information and appropriate technology. All these have to be made readily available to the general population through formal or informal training and media.

(Source: 'Peace through development in the Sudan', 1998. *SPLM Vision, Programme and Constitution*)

Sudan Mirror, the first national newspaper aiming to develop a culture of peace and justice in war-torn Sudan, was launched in October 2003. About 25,000 copies of the bi-monthly English-language newspaper are printed in the Ugandan capital, Kampala, and either bought in bulk by NGOs and flown into Sudan for distribution, or sold in shops and refugee camps in Kenya, Uganda and England for the diaspora. 'It's an informational and educational paper, written by Sudanese, for Sudanese, about Sudanese,' says newspaper director Dan Eiffe. 'We would like it be used as a tool, encouraging literacy, but also so people can become engaged in the peace process.' All the articles — which particularly target Sudan's literate youth — are geared towards development and peace, covering a wide range of issues from the environment, the economy, democratisation, gender issues, refugees and displaced people, reconciliation, education, human rights, the peace process and health and HIV/AIDS. Joseph Garang Deng, a renowned illustrator and fine artist, is currently the main illustrator for the *Sudan Mirror*. Many of his illustrations are published in the books for the new education curriculum for south Sudan. The English-language paper aims to encourage reconciliation and peace-building and offers a platform for the Sudanese people to contribute to the sustainability of peace in their country. The *Sudan Mirror* seeks to facilitate dialogue and understanding, and the initial public reaction has been fantastic. In March 2006, the editorial staff was in Kampala and the paper was printed there at the New Vision press. They are planning on moving into Yei and Juba in 2006.

(Source: 'Sudan media managers workshop opens in Nbo', *Sudan Mirror*, Vol 1, Issue 1, 6-18 October . www.sudanmirror.com)

ACROSS works in Southern Sudan, providing school and church literature, education for children and adults and training in agriculture, health and gender development. It has five bases in southern Sudan (Boma, Mayendiit, Dhiaukei, Yei and Yambio), and the work it does revolves around training. If it conducts a health programme it will not merely treat people, but will train them. In an agricultural programme it does not cultivate food and tell people 'Okay, the food is ready now, go and harvest.' No. It teaches skills so that they can grow vegetables or drought-resistant crops.

SLC was established in 1988 as a department of ACROSS, following requests from Sudanese individuals and church leaders for literature. The two major goals of the SLC are to assist the Sudanese Protestant churches in their evangelism and growth through the production and supply of Christian literature, and to assist the Sudanese educational authorities to improve the quality of education in southern Sudan through the provision of literature. Since 1988, the SLC has distributed over a million articles of Sudanese literature to individuals, schools, churches, health workers and adult literacy learners. The literature includes hymn books in different Sudanese languages, catechisms, a series of Sunday school books, theological books, tracts and other books published by Sudanese writers in English. SLC has also produced English books for adult learners and an AIDS awareness book in different Sudanese languages.

Since computers are the 'pen and ink' of modern book publishing, especially when working in 24 Sudanese languages including Arabic, in-house staff training is vital. SLC staff and other language consultants have been trained in the use of modern software programmes to improve the quality of the books produced. The centre has also been training Sudanese to sharpen their skills in translation, editing and reviewing. The trained personnel are then used by the centre in the production of more titles through short contracts. The centre's marketing strategy is done through the establishment of book distribution points (mostly other ACROSS bases) and through appointment of volunteer book agents (mostly from churches in the Sudan). Currently, there is a great demand for SLC books. One title in demand is an AIDS awareness book in different Sudanese languages, which aims at enlightening more Sudanese people about this epidemic and giving information on how to prevent it and how to live with it once infected.

Sudan Radio Service (SRS) started shortwave transmissions in August 2003, providing Sudanese living in Sudan and in the east Africa region with news and information. SRS head Jeremy Groce explains that programming strives to promote peace and development, especially in areas of civic education, health, agriculture and education. The service has multilingual programming in ten languages (Dinka, Bari, Nuer, Muro, Zande, Shilluk, Toposa, Arabic, Juba-Arabic and English) and is increasing its reach. Non-governmental organisations working in Sudan are able to use this radio service to provide information and training to the disparate population. SRS takes a strictly journalistic approach to its programming and does not broadcast any editorial commentaries. In its news reporting, SRS adheres to global ethical standards by balancing stories and seeking independent confirmation of information before airing it. Because of unstable conditions in Sudan, SRS first established its office in Kenya. The SRS will be transferred to Sudanese ownership once sufficient capacity is built and local conditions are favourable. SRS has a team of nearly 20 experienced Sudanese radio producers supplemented by stringers who operate throughout Sudan and the region, plus a correspondent in Washington. SRS programmes and top news stories are available daily on the internet at www.sudanradio.org.

Business in the southern Sudan at the time of war had been affected by the multiple currencies in use in various parts of the region — the US dollar, the Ugandan shilling, the Kenyan shilling, the Ethiopian birr and the South African rand. The main currency used was the old Sudanese pound, which is not a legal tender any more. Some areas also use the Sudanese dinar. With the signing of peace, this problem is being overcome. The wealth sharing agreement between the SPLA and the government of the Sudan highlighted the 2004 opening of a window of the Bank of Sudan in southern Sudan to regulate the issuance of currency in the southern Sudan. The Sudan People's Liberation Army (SPLA) has taken steps to print the new Sudan pound.

The Nile Commercial Bank Ltd (NCB) was established in Yambio in early 2003 by southern Sudanese working with various NGOs in southern Sudan. It has a proposed capital base of one million US dollars, with shares being offered to individuals, families and institutions. It is the first financial institution that allows small-scale entrepreneurs to start investing in the country. NCB extended operations to the southern towns of Rumbek and Yei in 2004, and Juba in February 2006. It provides varied services ranging from current accounts, saving accounts, foreign exchange, microfinance and commercial loans. NCB reduces the region's dependence on Ugandan and Kenyan financial institutions and thereby enhances economic activities. It facilitates business transactions in a region which previously had no formal banking system.

Yambio was chosen owing to its immense agricultural potential, links with important trade routes in the Central African Republic, the Democratic Republic of Congo and Uganda. Yambio has another advantage — internet access. Together with Rumbek, which lies in central Bahr el Ghazal, it was the only town in southern Sudan in 2003 with reliable, full-time internet, which has become an important communication tool in a region cut off from the rest of the world by war and lack of telecommunication and transport infrastructure. NCB is run by Nile Credit Management Ltd, a private company registered in Kenya, which has Kenyan and Sudanese directors. It is housed in premises previously occupied by a defunct former government bank, the Unity Bank in Yambio. The Sudanese diaspora and a number of local Sudanese and foreign NGOs are shareholders. NCB first concentrated on Yambio to stand on its own before embarking on other branches.

(Source: Matthias Muindi. 'SPLA to establish commercial bank'. *AfricaNews-Sudan*, 1-15 June

Established in June 2003 and opened for business in September of the same year, the Sudan Microfinance Institution (SUMI) provides working capital to micro-entrepreneurs in south Sudan. Potential clients are advised to form themselves into groups of five or more persons with a chairman, secretary and treasurer, so that they are able to solicit for the loan. Sanyangi Wangi, the branch manager, says that after an assessment they are able to determine whether or not the group is qualified for the loan. If the group qualifies for registration, then a savings account is opened for them. Among other qualifications, potential clients should be above 18 years of age and residents of Yei County and should own a small business. An individual should be prepared to work in a small group of at least five people through which the credit will be administered. The members must be known and trusted by all the members of the group. The first two members of a group to receive funds receive the loan after six weeks, followed by two others after nine weeks, and the last persons are given loans when the others have began repayment; the reason for such a staggered arrangement is to allow the first beneficiaries to begin repaying their loans. SUMI also introduced a grace period of two weeks for all new loans, to give their clients ample time for travelling to neighbouring DRC or Uganda in search of business products. The repayment frequency for the first and second loans is weekly, but fortnightly from the third loans onwards. This is the time SUMI builds confidence in the client. The approach has allowed SUMI to maintain a 100 per cent repayment rate. Sanyangi says, SUMI's mission is to offer financial services on a sustaining and efficient basis to micro-entrepreneurs and other business clients in south Sudan with a special emphasis on reaching the enterprising poor in the agriculture sector especially women, reintegrated refugees and internally displaced persons.

(Source: SilvanosYokoju. 'Micro-finance firm releases loan funds'. *Sudan Mirror*, Vol 1, Issue 5, 1-14 December 2003; www.sudanmirror.com)

Sanyangi Wangi points out that a woman named Cici joined SUMI when her own capital was USh150,000 (US$75). She progressed in a short time, managed to buy a piece of land, constructed some grass thatched tukuls and is now an independent woman. She has bought a pickup to run transport services between Koboko (Uganda) and Juba. Cici plans to use the pickup to transport her fish, the tiny type of dried fish locally known as *keje*, from Uganda (big smoked fish cannot be stocked in large quantities because of poor preservation facilities). Thanks to SUMI's support, Cici is diversifying her business and is currently rehabilitating a structure to be used for a restaurant in the near future. Cici's children are attending school. The older child is in standard three, one is in standard one and the youngest, who is four, is in nursery school. The responsibility of children and herself was the main motivator to work hard.

(Source: Correspondence with Sanyangi Wangi, February 2006)

Isaac Sadik, a used clothes dealer and tailor, started his business in 2001 with $40 he had raised by selling a bicycle. He joined SUMI in November 2003 with a loan of Ush200,000. His stock increased to Ush350,000. In 2005, his stall in Yei was too small so he looked for space to construct another.

Because Rose Anite, one of SUMI's first borrowers, is Sudanese and lives in Sudan, no one would lend her money in Uganda, but she uses the money from SUMI to expand fish sales (when she goes to Uganda on buying trips she can buy more fish). She wants to open another business in Yei selling used clothes.

Building on its experience in Yei, SUMI opened two more branches in 2004 in the towns of Yambio and Maridi, also in southern Sudan. Two additional branches were opened in 2005 in Rumbek and Tonj/Thiet in the Bahr el Ghazal region.

Sunday Bismark runs a general store in Yambio. He is one of SUMI's hard working clients, proving day in and day out the benefits of microfinance services for poor merchants. Having successfully repaid two loans from SUMI, in 2005 he was utilising a third loan to increase his stock and enable him to expand his business, adding soap to his inventory. He feels that the financial service SUMI is providing to micro-entrepreneurs has raised the standard of living of local businesspeople in Yambio County.

AFRICA: CONTINENT OF ECONOMIC OPPORTUNITIES

Yodita William owned a teahouse/restaurant when she heard about SUMI services. Thanks to two loans from SUMI, she is a partner with her brother Abdaraham and sells mixed goods in addition to running a thriving restaurant. According to Yodita, the SUMI programme has helped her to diversify into other income generating activities after only two loans.

(Source: USAID Sudan Agricultural Enterprise Finance Programme (AEFP), Quarterly Report No 10, 1 January - 31 March 2005)

Catholic Relief Services (CRS), Sudan's grant-making and capacity-building programme, supports community groups and local institutions in the implementation of economic rehabilitation projects through training, a start-up grant and business loans. The community based projects range from business enterprises such as grinding mills, wholesale shops, farmers associations and transportation, to professional and skills training institutes. After being reviewed and receiving final approval, these projects are implemented by the community and supervised by county development committees (CDCs). CDCs are facilitated by CRS to support county level development initiatives. Grant-making and community building projects were initiated to promote economic rehabilitation through small enterprise projects in southern Sudan. In 2001, the programme supported 30 projects approved in previous years, and 32 new projects approved in the year 2001. Existing groups such as the New Sudan Honey Producers' Association gained international recognition through exhibits in Kenya and South Africa, while newly-established groups such as the Lakes Transport Service are serving the needs of their community.

Lakes Transport Service, founded in 2001, was the first community-owned and managed transport service in Rumbek county, Lakes region Bahr el Ghazal. Sixteen community members; eight men and eight women, manage the trucking service. The group is excited to be serving the needs of their community while gaining business skills and improving the lives of their families. One member, Alam Daniel, says his life is the life of the community. Lakes Transport Service is changing the landscape of business in Rumbek — small-scale business activities create change because previously no one had their own business. Ramadhon Chadar, Lakes Transport Service Secretary, says they can see the impact of these activities on the market. Traders rely on Lakes Transport Service to transport their goods, and transporters rely on traders for business. People say they have hope for this project and want to see it succeed so that other community members will develop ideas for their own projects. Since becoming operational in December 2001, Lakes has transported goods for local traders and international humanitarian organisations, and has made many trips within Sudan and to Uganda. Chadar says that in previous years, traders walked with cattle to northern Uganda to purchase goods for the Rumbek market. This 780-kilometre trek was time-consuming and ultimately affected their businesses. The truck is helping the community, and now many traders and non-governmental organisations are interested in hiring the service as well.

Equatoria Foods Maridi (EFM) works with traditional beekeepers in southern Sudan to develop the beekeeping potential in western Equatoria province. The initiative is supported by USAID as a means of alleviating poverty using local resources in a sustainable manner. In 2004, EFM exported 60 tons of honey from Maridi to regional markets in Kenya and Uganda. EFM was established in 2000 with the aid of the CRS, to promote small-scale income generating activities in western Equatoria. An association called New Sudan Honey Producers Association (NSHPA), which covers Maridi and Tore in Yei County, was subsequently formed. The process of mobilisation of the local population for the purchase and production of honey was achieved after a series of workshops conducted among local processors on how to improve the quality of honey. Traditionally, local communities kept bees in fixed combs on hives and would normally supplement their honey production by hunting for wild bees in the forest. The trend has, however, changed as the whole business has been commercialised. The honey was traditionally consumed locally for food and local beer brews such as Duumo, Takayaa and Sikoo.

EFM has brought the market closer to home, says Ben Beda, the secretary of the NSHPA. Beda sold the association 292 kilograms of honey at 500 Ugandan shillings per kilogram, and has managed to buy himself a new bicycle. The Association has purchased 32 bicycles for some of the members operating as mobilisation agents, to ensure a constant supply of honey from the villages. Richard Wako, one of the honey suppliers for Equatoria Foods, is a married man with nine children to support. During the March–May 2004 honey season, he harvested a total of 1,154 kilograms of grade one honey from his 140 traditional bark hives. This honey earned Richard over US$500 — the equivalent of a year's wages in southern Sudan. With the money, Richard intended to start a business by buying a sewing machine. Honey is the only cash crop which can give Richard such a good return. Richard and other honey producers in Maridi are very happy that they now have a market for their honey, for until recently local markets could not absorb all the honey produced.

The EFM plant employs five female workers in Maridi County and this will increase as production and exports increase. The honey is processed through many stages and is tested for quality and grade before purchase from the traditional beekeepers. It is tested by a refrectometer to assess the humidity level. EFM will sensitise the traditional honey producers in the counties of Mundri, Yambio, Tambura and Wulu in Bahr el Ghazal region as it expands. The company may expand to Upper Nile although this will require the establishment of a sub location processing plant in Upper Nile. EFM has many tasks ahead to achieve its commercial objectives. EFM, an economic enterprise supported by USAID, is expected to make a profit, which is to be re-invested in its development. In 2006, Equatoria Foods was re-organising its business in Southern Sudan.

(Source: Tom Carroll, 2006, www.apiconsult.com and Silvanos Yokoju. 'Maridi to export honey', *Sudan Mirror*, Vol 1, Issue 8, 19 January - 1 February 2004; www.sudanmirror.com)

CRS conducted its first seed fairs in several locations in southern Sudan in the Lakes region of Bahr el Ghazal, eastern Equatoria and Bor County. Funded in part by the United Nations Food and Agriculture Organisation, seed fairs were implemented in partnership with Sudanese indigenous NGOs, the Sudanese Relief and Rehabilitation Association, the relief wing of the Sudanese People's Liberation Movement, and local community leaders and chiefs. In April 2001, seed fairs were sponsored by CRS in Rumbek County in the Lakes region of Bahr el Ghazal. The fairs were held in three different locations. Beneficiaries and sellers praised the seed fair approach, as both vulnerable households and the local host community benefited. Nineteen-year old Peter Magai, seed fair beneficiary, says, 'I came to Rumbek County to pursue an education. Formerly I was a child soldier. Through the seed fair I was able to purchase groundnuts and green grams which I cultivate to alleviate hunger.' Chol Tong Mayay, chairman of the Rumbek Grain Traders Association and seed fair seller says, 'The way of the seed fair is the best way — it is an idea to be encouraged. Through the seed fair, I was able to interact with people and enlighten them about different seed varieties. We also gained exposure to the community, we attracted new buyers. Seed fairs promote local farmers and strengthen food security in the county.' Seed fairs work in the following manner:
- Vulnerable households in need of seed are provided with vouchers worth a specific cash value to purchase surplus seed from sellers in the community.
- On a specified day and location, voucher holders and seed sellers gather for the voucher and seed and tool exchange. Farming households are able to choose which seeds and tools best meet their needs.
- At the conclusion of the seed fair, seed sellers redeem their vouchers to CRS for money.

This system draws upon locally-available resources, supports local farmer seed production, and actively involves civil authorities, traditional leaders, and Sudanese indigenous non-governmental organisations in the planning and implementation of the fair. In March 2002, in partnership with the International Crops Research Institute for the Semi-Arid Tropics, CRS trained over 50 Sudanese indigenous NGOs, international NGOs, and civil authority representatives on the seed voucher and fair methodology. Seed fairs have a number of benefits, including developing and strengthening local markets; providing a more equitable distribution of resources between displaced and resident communities; and empowering people to choose appropriate seeds and tools to meet their needs. Through the seed fair approach, CRS is now facilitating the purchase of seeds and tools locally.

AFRICA: CONTINENT OF ECONOMIC OPPORTUNITIES

Constance Nako is the chairwoman of the Yambio Women's Association (YWA), a network of 13 rural women's associations with an estimated 2 500 members from different ethnic and religious groups in Yambio county, western Equatoria, southern Sudan. YWA supports the development of income-generating activities that help women meet the basic needs of their families. The Association also advocates for women's issues and rights at the county administration level. Both the YWA Cooperative Shop and the Resource Centre, which are being strengthened through Oxfam Canada's support, create employment for women and generate profits that are then re-invested in the services provided to rural women by the Association. Skills and literacy training are some of the key services offered to the women and children served by this network. Oxfam Canada has been impressed by the spirit of self-reliance that guides the decisions of YWA's leadership, as the network works to expand in a manageable way and continues to provide relevant services to the women of Yambio County. The YWA is a good example of how small amounts of financial support can make a big difference to people's lives and livelihoods at the community level.

Crossroads Missions (Canada) has been involved in the rehabilitation and reintegration efforts of the people of south Sudan. Crossroads is building farms under the authority of Savannah Farmers Cooperative (SFC). Each farm has a manager. All the Sudanese involved in these farms have both experience and education in agriculture. For instance, Dr Samson Kwaje has a BSc in agriculture, an MSc in plant pathology/plant breeding and a doctorate in agriculture from West Virginia University, USA. Others have degrees in animal breeding. The co-chairman of the board, Steven Wondu, has degrees in commerce, philosophy, economic development and trade, an MA in accountancy and is a certified public accountant (Kenya). Cal Bombay is co-chairman of the SFC together with Steven Wondu.

These farms are being established with three major goals in mind:
- To mass produce food for consumption by the very hungry population
- To overcome and defeat the dependency syndrome, which has overtaken the population of southern Sudan through many years of manipulated famine caused by war and deliberate destruction by attacks on local farms and villages (it should be noted that for many years the United Nations through Life Line Sudan has been delivering food by air into starving areas).
- To develop farms which can be models for replication throughout southern Sudan to eventually make southern Sudan's food security dependable and long-range.

Cal Bombay, former vice president of Missions, now president of Cal Bombay Ministries Inc (CBM), has been asked by Crossroads to be their representative to southern Sudan and to administer the funds being given to the SFC for the operation and development of the SFC farms. Some of these farms are coming close to self-sufficiency. Bombay has given his assurance to Crossroads that his interest and commitment will continue in Sudan for years to come.

The areas around Kajo Keji and Yei are very fertile, and are now free from war and the conflict, which has been their horror for years. They want to help themselves. They want to get back their dignity and prosperity. They have the people with the drive and ability to accomplish their dreams. It is simply a matter of putting the basic tools and equipment into their hands under good management.

Seventeen tractors were put in place by Crossroads when Bombay was vice president of missions, at four locations (SFC farms are established at Morobo, Logobero, Romogi and Moje). The need still exists for operational funds as well as vehicles to deliver the produce to those in need. CBM has sent an additional seven tractors with implements to the SFC. Two more SFC farms are being established in Kagwada and Yambio in the immediate future, supported by CBM.

Appropriate systems are being set in place to market the product to NGOs, which will buy it from the SFC and give it to the hungry. The savings to the international community will be vast; the food will be fresh and of a kind which is staple to the diet of the southern Sudanese. These sales, will assure the ongoing operation of the farms as they develop enough acreage to become self-sufficient.

(Source: www.crossroads.ca/missions/sudan.htm), and www.calbombayministries.org)

In December 2005, Eagle Aviation, hitherto a predominantly domestic Ugandan carrier, commenced coach services from Entebbe to Juba twice a week, using their workhorse LET 410 equipment. Up to 19 passengers can travel on the aircraft and a limited amount of loose cargo can be taken onboard. This is the first Ugandan carrier on what is considered one of the most lucrative routes in coming years across east Africa. In January 2006, Eagle added Yei to their network, which is now served through an en-route stopover for passengers wishing to embark or disembark at that southern Sudanese town. Eagle's managing director Captain Tony Rubombora has firmly committed himself to developing routes into the southern Sudan and providing air links capable of allowing easy connections on to other international flights out of Entebbe for the south Sudan travelling public.

In 2004, the newly established Nile Air, with its headquarters in Rumbek, started flights within southern Sudan and into Kenya. The towns of Yei, Rumbek, Panyagor and Yambio were again connected by telephone in 2004 by Com-Carrier Satellite Services. The renewal of telephone services arose from the need to end expensive and inconvenient trips to neighbouring countries which citizens undertake to be able to communicate with their relatives living abroad. Many southern Sudanese travelled almost everyday to Kenya and Uganda for that purpose. These journeys cost money. The establishment of the Nile Commercial Bank, Nile Air, and telephone services makes it easier for people of southern Sudan to communicate and conduct business with each other once again. The South African-based Mobile Telecommunications Network (MTN) is reportedly set to extend its coverage to southern Sudan.

In order for the southern Sudanese to enjoy the benefits of peace, there is a great need to come up with a comprehensive plan that outlines priority areas to be given immediate attention. There are basic governmental structures in place, in the form of the various commissions and secretariats of the SPLA, to assist in this. Additionally, there are many Sudanese in the diaspora waiting to participate in the reconstruction effort. Before a self-rule government in southern Sudan takes shape, a minimum infrastructure in the form of roads, railway systems and telecommunications network is needed. The road and transport network should be at the top of the priority list. There should be plans to tarmac the roads between major towns and the roads leading to other countries, paving the way for the easy flow of goods and people. Power should be sourced from the River Nile, and the Fulla Falls would be a possible site for the construction of a hydro-electric power plant. A reliable and cheap source of electric energy will spur economic growth in southern Sudan. Appropriate connections by road, rail, and pipeline should be considered, and port authorities in Mombassa, Kenya, have started factoring this possibility into their development plans. Inevitably, infrastructural connections into southern Sudan portend much economic development for Kenya and southern Sudan.

In 2004, plans were underway for the construction of a railway line to link Sudan and Kenya. The German railway builder Thormählen Schweißtechnik AG is tackling the reconstruction of the old route, which is to be extended to southern Sudan. The estimated cost of that project amounts to 2.3 billion euros including support structures such as tunnels and bridges. The estimated line is to cover 4,100 kilometres and will stretch from Juba in southern Sudan via Lokichoggio to Nakuru in Kenya. Two additional lines are planned to connect southern Sudan with the towns of Gulu and Arua in Uganda. The financing is secured by the immense mineral resources of the country. The conflict parties agreed to sign the final peace agreement by the end of 2004, and the project is scheduled to start in spring 2006. Thormählen is a leading German railway constructor specialising in rail welding and the production of jointless rail. The firm has developed a mobile flash butt welding machine which can undertake mobile railway building anywhere in the world. The Sudanese pioneer project will be by far its most ambitious international construction to date.

Steffen Ralfs, a representative of Thormählen, says the building of the railway, from the swamps of southern Sudan across the plains of northern Kenya through a vast territory of undeveloped land, could provide much-needed infrastructure to a remote region. The planned railway line could become southern Sudan's lifeline and will constitute a first-ever stable transport link. The rail is meant to give southern Sudan access to the port of Mombasa, to be able to export oil from its vast oil fields on its own account. Thus far, all oil from southern Sudan is exported through a pipeline via Port Sudan under the authority of the government in Khartoum (the oil resources in southern Sudan were one of the reasons for civil war and at the peace negotiations both sides agreed to share equally any future oil revenue). Thus far, oil pipelines from the south lead only to the north. The company wants to employ many local labourers. Ralfs says that Thormählen wants to retrain former fighters into track layers and give them a new start — but the specialists would have to be brought in from Europe, as well as the machines and a large part of the construction materials. The Kenyan part of the route will be the easiest by far. The former British, single-track route will be replaced by a standard European one. Material and workers can be transported on the old route during the construction process.

(Source: www.thormaehlen-schweisstechnik.de; 'German Company builds railway line in Sudan', German Arab Chamber of Industry and Commerce, 2004; www.ahkmena.com)

On 31 December 2004, representatives of the Sudanese government and the rebel Sudan People's Liberation Movement/Army (SPLM/A) met their own 2004 deadline to reach an agreement by signing the two final protocols of a comprehensive peace deal, which established a permanent ceasefire and implemented all of their agreements on the ground, thus ending a 21-year civil war in southern Sudan that had claimed the lives of two million people and displaced up to four million others. The signing of the final two protocols joined earlier agreements signed by Khartoum and the SPLM/A on issues such as power-sharing and the distribution of economic resources, including oil. A formal signing ceremony was held in Nairobi on 9 January 2005, thus ending a war that drained the resources of Sudan for over two decades and inflicted unbearable suffering on its people. The agreement did not cover the separate conflict between Khartoum and other rebel groups that engulfed the Darfur region in Sudan's west. It is hoped that the peace agreement for southern Sudan will serve as a blueprint for resolving the Darfur crisis.

Chapter 19: Arab Maghreb Union: Mauritania, Morocco, Algeria, Tunisia, and Libya

Mauritania

Mohamed Abdellahi Ould Lahah is the founder and managing director of Groupement National de Nutrition, an enterprise incorporated in July 2002. He is a Mauritanian design engineer with more than ten years' experience in the mining, banking, IT and general commercial sectors. In 2003, he established a factory employing 72 people to produce a jam, a honey, and a 'compote' based on dates, groundnuts, acacia fruit, sorrel juice, rice and other locally produced ingredients. The factory has a capacity of 760 metric tons per year and turnover estimated at around 1.5 million euro per year. The products are sold in glass jars imported from Spain. A patent has been obtained and the products have been exhibited at national and regional trade fairs. The three products are merchandised in health food and baby food markets as well as emergency feeding programmes. They were initially sold in domestic and regional markets but Lahah is now establishing outlets with specialised food product traders and international agency feeding programmes such as the EU's ECHO (European Commission Humanitarian Aid Department).

Lahah's partner organisation is a firm in the food sector, which helped finance part of the equipment and start-up costs. He also received cooperation in technical experience, marketing and distribution and equipment leasing. Initially the three products attracted publicity in Mauritania and won first prize at the ministry of industry and mines trade fair in 2002. They were also exhibited at the African Intellectual Property Organisation's international fair at Libreville, Gabon. In October 2003, Groupement National de Nutrition won the prize as the Best SMME in West Africa at the Africa SMME Awards in Johannesburg.

The Mauritanian industrialist Mohamed Ould Bouamatou is the founder and director general of Générale de Banque de Mauritanie pour l'Investissement et le Commerce (GBM), Nouakchott, Mauritania. GBM was the first new private commercial bank to have been established in Mauritania since the restructuring of the country's banking sector began in 1988. It provides a full range of modern commercial banking services with a strong focus on project and trade finance. Headquartered in Nouakchott, with a branch in Nouadibou, Mauritania's second largest city, the bank uses state-of-the-art technology to provide services to large parts of the population which previously had no access to banking. Banque Belgolaise, a Belgian commercial bank, has a 30 per cent stake, and provides technical assistance to the Mauritanian management team. Générale de Banque de Mauritanie is presently one of the country's leading financial institutions. It is a member of the Belgolaise network and of the Fortis Group. It is active in financing international trade and supports European-Mauritanian partnerships.

In 2006, BSA Ciment SA, a company incorporated and owned by Mohamed Bouamatou, began a project involving the construction and operation of a greenfield cement grinding facility with a rated capacity of 480,000 tons per annum and a ready-mixed concrete plant with a capacity of 216,000 cubic metres per year at a total cost of 26 million euro. The plant will be located near the port on the western side of Nouakchott. The proposed site is 1.5 km from Nouakchott port and 15 km from the city centre.

Bouamatou is an executive vice president of the African Business Round Table (ABR), the membership of which consists of chief executive officers of leading companies from throughout Africa. The members are involved in a wide range of sectors, from petrochemicals, food processing, mining, banking, construction and aviation to tourism, agriculture and transportation. Most of the companies are multinational. The ABR has three principal objectives: to strengthen Africa's private sector, to promote intra-African trade and investment and to attract foreign investment to Africa.

The ABR was founded on the principle that free and competitive markets and a thriving private sector offer the best means of achieving sustainable development in Africa. In addition, the development of a dynamic private sector offers the only means by which Africa can hope to compete in global markets and beat the increasingly stiff competition for foreign investment resources. The ABR believes that Africa possesses a wealth of entrepreneurial talent that, if harnessed, can help the continent move from dependency to partnership, and it further believes that the quest for democracy and economic freedom is an inseparable one since greater accountability, transparency, initiative and popular participation in public decision-making are essential both to efficient and competitive markets and to democratic governance.

Abderrahmane Sissako is a Mauritanian-born film director. In 2003, his film *'Heremakono'* (*'Waiting for Happiness'*) won the most prestigious award, for best movie, at Africa's biggest and leading film festival, Le Festival Panafricain du Cinéma et de la Télévision de Ouagadougou (FESPACO). The coveted Stallion of Yennenga trophy, and prize money of more than US$11,000, was presented at a spectacular closing ceremony of FESPACO 2003 at the Municipal stadium in Ouagadougou, Burkina Faso. 'I am so proud as an African film-maker to win this great distinction,' said Sissako, who is also director of the acclaimed millennium film *'Life on Earth'*, presented at Cannes (Directors' Fortnight), Toronto, Sundance and New York.

'Waiting for Happiness' was also a standout of the 2002 Cannes and New York Film Festivals. It is quiet and haunting, one of the few films that grapples honestly with Africa's desperation, without itself falling prey to despair. It is a lyrical, meditative portrait of a young man who visits his mother in a small Mauritanian village before emigrating to Europe. It looks at issues of home, identity, longing for other lands, cultural up-rooting and exile. In the film we get to know the members of a small fishing community on the shores of Nouadhibou. Looking out to sea, the villagers dream of a hypothetical world far away. The interweaving stories of people in the community are told with the lightest touch.

Sissako is one of the most respected African film directors and his reputation can only grow after winning FESPACO 2003. In his shorts, documentaries and feature-length fiction films, he has often explored the exile experience and the relationship between African and western societies. Sissako has been following his destiny with both a sense of freedom and feelings of suffering.

Sissako feels like a citizen of the African continent first and then like a citizen of the world. He has followed quite a strange path. He is a child of exile, having lived outside his native country for many years; he was born in 1961 in Mauritania but, to his deep regret, does not speak the Hassania language. He spent his childhood in Mali and returned to Mauritania before leaving for Moscow where he studied cinema for six years at the VGIK film institute. He stayed in Russia for 12 years and then he went to France where he has been living since 1992. He doesn't know yet whether he is going to stay in France or go back to his homeland, but Africa is always at the heart of his films.

(Source: Robin Gatto. 'Abderrahmane Sissako sheds hope on exile', Cannes Interview, www.filmfestivals.com, May 2002)

Morocco

Transport is often a key cost-input in the competition to deliver physical goods or tourism services. The countries of the African Maghreb are extremely well-positioned to service Europe, so much so that they can consider major investments in pipelines, and even tunnels under the Straits of Gibraltar, confident that these will enable them to compete even more efficiently.

Rehab Saad, correspondent for *Al-Ahram* Weekly Newspaper (Cairo), writes that when tourism first took off in North Africa, and visitors began to arrive in large numbers, hotels and tourist villages were built and the number of restaurants doubled. As time passed, and the numbers increased, the importance of creating a balance between tourist development, and protecting the environment, was realised. In 1983, Morocco set a good example concerning the impact of tourism on the environment, on the role of local people in tourist development and on indigenous populations. The Moroccan ministry of tourism launched a project in the Atlas Mountains; according to ministry representative Jawad Ziyat, this area was chosen for eco-tourism projects because it included all the elements required — picturesque scenery, abundant wildlife and, above all, a local population with traditions and a unique way of life. He pointed out to Saad that the village houses in the area are all made of rosy mud brick to merge with the surrounding environment. Ziyat emphasised that the government was anxious to involve the local inhabitants in every aspect of development. The ministry encouraged villagers to rent rooms to foreign visitors and even to enlarge their houses to accommodate greater numbers. The ministry is strict in preserving the architectural style of the houses and the people are obliged to abide by its rules. They use young local people as guides for trips to the mountains, using mules as a means of transportation, and this has created one of the villagers' most important tourist activities. Visitors can wander around, which gives them a chance to communicate with the villagers. Ziyat told Saad that the number of travellers is increasing year by year and that the number of tourist rooms had increased from 30 in 1990 to 90 in 1998. When villagers get involved in these projects they earn money and are able to improve their standard of living, buying things (such as gas instead of wood) which they could not previously afford.

(Source: Rehab Saad, Rehab. 'Tourists take the green route', *Al-Ahram*, 10–16 December 1998)

Brothers Mike and Chris McHugo, founders and owners of Discover Ltd have been running field trips and educational tours for 25 years, offering students and teachers wonderful opportunities in spectacular settings. Their 'tour Morocco' trips visit their High Atlas Mountain Centre, the Kasbah du Toubkal, in the Toubkal National Park. Kasbah du Toubkal is a magnificent mountain retreat spectacularly situated in the heart of the High Atlas. Near the foot of Jbel Toubkal, the highest mountain in north Africa, it's only 40 miles from Marrakech but the peace and quiet and seclusion are so complete the city seems a million miles away.

Day visits, seminars, residential stays or as a base for more active pursuits — whatever you choose, the Berber people who staff the Kasbah will give you a warm welcome and a fascinating insight into their culture. Guests can explore the village, nearby hamlets and the surrounding mountain landscape, on foot or by mule, or just put their feet up and relax on the terrace or in the *hammam* (steam bath). The Kasbah is particularly suitable for groups and families. The meeting room, with digital projector and surround sound hifi, greatly extends the activities that can be carried out at the Kasbah. The upgrading of the *hammam* complex has been finished with a plunge pool and the construction of a spacious bedroom above this development, with exceptional views to the south and north.

With 11 en suite bedrooms and three Berber style salons the Kasbah has now become a near perfect location for family reunions, corporate off-sites and individual travellers. But the most important aspect is the friendly Berber atmosphere at the heart of the operation.

The Kasbah has become a most important facility for tourists and educational groups visiting Imlil and the surrounding valleys. The Imlil valleys are an area of truly outstanding natural beauty, with a rich cultural heritage among the traditional Berber communities. What is particular impressive about the Kasbah, is the way that the owners, Discover Ltd, have worked tirelessly with the local communities to develop the resources and improve the living standards of local people in an entirely sustainable manner.

Local people have been fully incorporated into crucial decision-making processes to plan the various development initiatives in the area, such that its rich environmental and cultural resources are managed sensitively so that they can be experienced by future generations. This coming together of an educational organisation with the local communities is a significant model of sustainable development planning which other similar bodies could well emulate. It is vital that the valleys of Imlil are conserved for future generations.

The Kasbah was converted into a Tibetan monastery by Martin Scorsese, for his film *'Kundun'* on the early life of the Dalai Lama. The Kasbah is now used as a 'corporate retreat centre' by some major international corporations, both for its unique position, and as a location where corporate values are evident. Kasbah du Toubkal was the first Moroccan operation to win a British Airways Tourism for Tomorrow Award in 2002, and the 2004 Responsible Tourism Mountain Award Winner, Best in a Mountain Environment.

(Source: www.cntraveller.com; www.responsibletravel.com; and www.kasbahdutoubkal.com)

Amyn Alami was the dynamic chief executive officer of the Casablanca Finance Group (CFG). Born in 1962, and an acknowledged financial expert, Alami is of the new breed of technocrats introducing Morocco to modern business methods. The CFG, which he co-founded in 1992, leads the way in the area of enterprise finance and venture capital. Currently, with a staff of 125, the CFG is the country's main player in capital markets. Alami's expertise received wider recognition in 1995, when he was elected the first president of the Casablanca Stock Exchange for its inaugural term. His message is clear: he wants the bourse to play an increasing role in the Moroccan economy. The long-term strategy is to attract more and more enterprises to be listed on the bourse because he believes that the stock exchange should reflect a wider picture of Morocco's active economic sectors.

Alami developed his financial skills early on at Banque Privée Edmond de Rothschild in Paris. Listening to him talk about his vision for his country, it is not difficult to figure out which age group is calling the shots in 21st century Morocco. He symbolises the new breed of designer-clad, mobile phone-toting Moroccans intent on turning Casablanca into the New York of North Africa and the country into a Mecca for entrepreneurs — and he was by far the oldest in his company of 60 employees, the average age of which is 27. When conducting visitors around his gleaming, state-of-the-art offices in Casablanca, he was able to point out that half of the people were women, and 90 per cent were executives.

Alami says the Morocco hotel industry's expansion is part of the overall modernisation of the country and an excellent source of jobs. One of the government's main aims is to attract international operators to Morocco to support and restructure tourism. The tourism industry is currently fragmented, and the underlying aim is to show that Morocco is a serious emerging economy with serious objectives. If this approach succeeds, it may be duplicated in other sectors.

In November 2000, Alami was entrusted with the chairmanship of the General Confederation of Moroccan Enterprises, a body representing the country's industry. Adil Douiri became the CEO of the Casablanca Finance Group. According to Douiri, you have to determine your core businesses and increase very sharply your exports in those industries. In Douiri's view, the Moroccan government should focus on the following core businesses:

- Tourism: Morocco needs some real professionals in the tourism sector, which has huge potential. Moroccan attributes that draw tourists are 12 centuries of written history, the sea, desert, mountains and snow.
- Phosphate: Phosphate products including fertilisers and chemical products derived from the phosphate industry.
- Food industry: Morocco has fish, a big rural population, much good soil and some irrigated areas — which means that the food industry can easily produce exports for Europe. Fishing, because of Morocco's large shoreline (approximately 3,000 kilometres of shoreline on the west coast and 800 kilometres on the Mediterranean), is important.
- Textiles: Moroccan textiles reflect a rich cultural history.
- The automotive component industry: The auto industry employs skilled workers to make components like seats, steering wheels, air bags, electric cables, tyres and shock absorbers.
- Electronic components: The mobile phone industry is a good example of a business that needs a slightly more skilled workforce, which is available at a low cost.
- Teleservices: Back office services performed out of Morocco through communication lines and directories.
- Engineering in general: Morocco's education system is strong in mathematics, which is excellent for the work force, and as a result of which there are many engineers and computer engineers.

Douiri attributes many of Morocco's economic woes to its arcane monetary laws, saying that Morocco's monetary policy is a little too strict, and too 'Teutonic', for a third world country like Morocco. A fixed peg against a strong currency basket is very tough for a third world country, rather like — in Douiri's analogy — chemotherapy, because it destroys all types of companies, the good with the bad. He thinks the dirham,

Morocco's currency, would do better if it were more flexible, which means focusing on the real economy and inflation risks, and being more flexible with interest rates; to do that, Douiri points out, you have to have a floating currency able to reflect what you're doing, whereas, under a fixed peg, you would lose all discipline. So, for the time being, what Morocco is doing is consistent, but tough on the economy according to Douiri. In 2005, Douiri was Morocco's minister of tourism.

(Source: Barbara Ferguson. 'No pain, no gain: cutting away at bureaucracy - making room for new investment', *The Washington Times*, 27 November 2000)

Othman Benjelloun, nationally-recognised business executive, particularly in banking and finance, has been the chairman and chief executive officer of the Banque Marocaine du Commerce Extérieur (BMCE Bank, www.bmcebank.ma) since its privatisation in 1995, and is the chairman of Finance.com, an operational holding involved in four sectors: banking and parabanking, with BMCE Bank at its heart; insurance, including RMA Watanya insurance company; telecommunications, media and technologies; and industry. Benjelloun is a member of several boards of directors, chairs the Moroccan Banking Association and is counsellor at the Centre for Strategic International Studies in Washington.

From 1998 to 2003 he acted as chancellor of Al Akhawayn University in Ifrane, aiming to position the university as an elite international academic institution founded on excellence and merit. In the field of corporate social responsibility, Benjelloun is the founder of the BMCE Bank Foundation, to which he assigned two main priorities: education (particularly the fight against illiteracy in rural areas) and environmental protection. He has been nominated Officier de L'Ordre du Trône of the Kingdom of Morocco and Commandeur de l'Etoile Polaire of the Kingdom of Sweden and awarded La Médaille de Commandeur dans l'Ordre National du Lion of the Republic of Senegal.

Othman Benjelloun has outlined his business philosophies:

'Beyond commercial and financial value-added, as the chairman of the bank and main shareholder, I wanted the bank to contribute to growth in social capital. Indeed, 'corporate social responsibility' has become anchored in our strategic decision-making. BMCE Bank is proud to be the first non-European corporation in the region to have solicited a social rating by the independent European social rating agency Vigeo, in the areas of human rights and community involvement. Moreover, through our Foundation, we aim at sustainable development by focusing on education, more specifically primary education in rural areas, as a means to reduce poverty and inequalities (whether socio-economic, cultural, gender, or technology related) and environmental protection. We have built a school network throughout the Kingdom called Medersat.com[1], based on three principles: opening to the outside world, tolerance and modernity.'

(*Washington Times*, July 2003)

Dounia Taarji of Morocco, a career banker, was selected in December 2002 to be one of the World Economic Forum's Global Leaders for Tomorrow 2003 in the category finance and consulting. After obtaining a master's degree from the Ecole Supérieure de Commerce de Paris (1987) and a degree in civil law from the Université de Paris II (Assas) (1988), Taarji began her career in 1987 as *chargé d'affaires* in project finance at Crédit Lyonnais. In 1990, she became adviser in mergers and acquisitions at Clinvest (the investment bank division of Crédit Lyonnais). In 1995, returning to her native country, she founded the stock exchange branch CDMC and later the asset management branch of an established commercial bank, Crédit du Maroc. She is also a co-founder and member of the executive committee of the Casablanca stock exchange. In 1998, she joined as a partner a young Moroccan investment bank, Casablanca Finance Group, where she is in charge of corporate finance activity. In 2001, Dounia Taarji was appointed as the new head of the Conseil Déontologique des Valeurs Mobilières (CDVM), the Moroccan Securities Exchange Commission. In her position, she is in charge of the regulation of the financial market, and of controlling the operators. An important part of her role is to enhance the values of modernity, transparency, and equal access to information. Dounia Taarji believes in building trust progressively among operators and investors, in order for the financial markets to gain credibility and efficiency.

The Association Al Amana pour la Promotion des Microentreprises is a leader in the Moroccan microfinance market; it has the largest loan portfolio in the market and takes a 45 per cent market share. The organisation's purpose is micro-enterprise promotion among Morocco's poor and underemployed and it is an active member of the Micro Finance Federation of Morocco (FNAM). When Al Amana was first created in February 1997, its goals were modest and it aimed at extending a total of 17,000 loans over a seven-year period through a 14-branch operational structure, but since the start of its activities it has undergone a significant expansion in the quantity and quality of its services, and the number of its active clients increased from 8,335 in 1998 to 37,195 in 2000, 78,114 in 2002 and 200,000 in May 2005. Al Amana had 27 branches in 1998, 49 branches by 2000, 80 branches by 2001 and 285 branches by April 2005 with an outstanding loan balance of over US$53 million and a staff of 759. The organisation is sustainable and self-sufficient and, as of April 2005, had extended a total of 777,000 loans since February 1997. In 2005, Al Amana was covering more than 120 per cent of its real operating costs and more than 100 per cent of its financial costs. Loan portfolio quality was excellent, with less than 0.3 per cent of loans being a day or more late at the end of any week. Al Amana's principle challenges included satisfying its clients, strategic planning, adapting its products to the needs of its clients, and mobilising funds (it was seeking an additional 50 million euros in financing according to the strategic plan for 2004 to 2007).

The target group consists of micro-entrepreneurs unable to access more formal sources of credit. This Grameen Bank-type system has been adapted to local customer preference, and works exclusively in urban areas. Three types of solidarity loans are granted to groups of four or five micro-entrepreneurs committed to investing money in short-term profitable investments and to be jointly and severally liable for the reimbursement of their loans. No other guarantee is requested from the borrowers. The duration of these loans ranges from three to nine months and their amounts from 1 000 to 10 000 Moroccan dirhams — approximately US$100 to US$1,000. Individual loans are intended for clients having had a successful experience with their loans in the solidarity system and who wish to invest in their company's equipment. Their tenor varies from six to 24 months and the amount from 2,000 to 20,000 Moroccan dirhams (approximately US$200 to US$2,000). They are tailor-made to the peculiarities of the businesses requiring finance, and are backed by guarantees adapted to clients' realities. Both solidarity and individual loans are repayable by fixed instalments, either weekly or fortnightly.

Al Amana's clients are poor men and women working in the old inner cities or in the outlying slums of Morocco. The organisation targets no particular sector of activity and places its services at the disposal of micro-enterprise promoters. Its clients belong to more than 160 types of activity: 48 per cent in commerce, 39 per cent in handicrafts and 13 per cent in services; customers are characterised by a parity between men (40 per cent) and women (60 per cent), and are generally able, honest, hard working and committed micro-entrepreneurs. Retail trade is by far the most common activity for male clients with sewing and embroidery the largest categories for women, many of whom work at home.

Halima Igamane has a hairdressing shop that she started in 2001 with her own money. Added to her own savings, a US$200 loan from Al Amana allowed her to buy a used hairdryer for her shop. Her second business is organising weddings and so she also bought an embroidered kaftan to rent to brides. She is very happy being in business, not only because she likes being independent, but because it enables her to support her family. She has several other business ideas, and plans to explore them after she pays off her first loan.

Fatima El Borj from Rabat is the mother of seven children. She owns the house sheltering the small shop where she works. With her loan of US$200, she increased her stock from 20 to 40 domestic gas bottles. Before contracting this loan, she ran the risk of losing some of her customers because she could not meet the demand for domestic gas. Now she is reassured. Her customers will not supply themselves elsewhere any more.

Since he bought a sewing machine with a loan granted by Al Amana, a tailor from Fès no longer has to worry about the quality and the punctuality of his services. Previously, Rachida, also from Fès, worked at home for an intermediary retailer, who provided her with the raw material and paid her by the kilo of wool transformed into carpet. Al Amana granted her a loan, thanks to which she could constitute her own working capital. Today she sells her beautiful carpets directly to her customers, her creativity from now on is developed and the quality of her work is better remunerated. Rachida intends to renew her loan to purchase an additional weaving loom and to urge another weaver to help her to increase her production.

(Source: www.alamana.org)

Fouad Abdelmoumni is the co-founder and executive director of Al Amana. He contributed to the creation of the organisation from 1996 to 1997 and has managed it ever since. Before working for Al Amana, Abdelmoumni managed MADI (Maghreb Développement Investissement), a social venture capital fund that is a member of the SIDI network, Société d'Investissement et de Développement International based in France. He has a degree in development economics from the University Mohammed V in Rabat and a MBA equivalent from ISCAE (Institut Supérieur de Commerce et d'Administration des Entreprises) in Casablanca. From 2001 to 2003, Abdelmoumni served as a member of the Consultative Group to Assist the Poor (CGAP) advisory board, CGAP being the coordinating body of the main international and bilateral donors. He also serves as chairman of the board of Sanabel, the Microfinance Network of the Arab countries.

Abdelmoumni is a former left-wing militant who 'disappeared' for six months and was sentenced to three years' prison at the beginning of the 1980s, but is now a respected civil society activist (vice president of the Moroccan Association for Human Rights, member of the Espace Associatif for the promotion of civil society). In 2000, Abdelmoumni pointed out that the population of the towns of Morocco, which absorb about 450,000 new arrivals from the country every year, and more in drought years, had quadrupled since the 1960s. In 2000, more than 55 per cent of the population lived in towns and almost 65 per cent lived below the poverty line. People in shantytowns were cut off from the elite. Before independence it was said that the French sucked Morocco dry for their own benefit. In 2000, the poor said the same about the middle classes and the rich. A gulf had opened between them. Since 1997, Abdelmoumni and Al Amana have endeavoured to help the poor close that gulf by becoming successful entrepreneurs achieving their dreams. Obviously, it is in the interests of Morocco to allow more social mobility, to give a chance to young graduates from underprivileged backgrounds, and to let new actors like Abdelmoumni and Al Amana come onto the scene.

(Source: Ignacio Ramonet. 'Morocco: the point of change', *Le Monde Diplomatique*, July 2000)

When the winners of the Africa 2004 SMME Awards were announced in October 2004, enterprises from all over the continent made their mark. Association Al Amana pour la Promotion des Microentreprises was the winner of the award for the non-profit organisations (NGOs) sector. The Africa SMME Awards are an initiative of the Africa Centre for Investment Analysis (ACIA) at South Africa's University of Stellenbosch Business School. The aim of the Awards is to inspire the entrepreneurial spirit of Africa.

Algeria

Cevital and Fertalge are two strong examples of how successful private industries can be in Algeria. Although the companies are different in size and conception, both have made a mark in a very short period of time. Cevital is a new industrial enterprise in Algeria's agro-foods sector. Strategically located on industrial land adjoining the Port of Bejaia, 250 km east of Algiers, Cevital is a US$200 million plus investment for the production of vegetable oils, oil derivatives and refined sugar. Group President Issad Rebrab initially suggested a partnership with the state-owned Enterprise Nationale de Corps Gras (ENCG), the erstwhile monopoly for vegetable oil production, through the purchase of an obsolete production unit, which Cevital would then reorganise and upgrade. When ENCG declined the offer, Cevital drew up a feasibility study and went out on its own, with impressive results. Its vegetable oil plant produces 1,800 tons a day, is the biggest such facility in Africa, and exceeds Europe's largest oil plants. The company currently has an approximate 50 per cent share of the local market and is now producing margarine, effectively eliminating the country's need to import the product. Cevital went public on the London Stock Exchange in 2002. It is also Algeria's largest sugar producer and doubled its production of white sugar to 900,000 tons in 2004 compared with 2003, cutting the north African country's import needs sharply. Foods, home and personal care giant Unilever, known for top brands like Dove, Lipton tea, Brayers ice cream, Ragu soup, and an impressive list of other brands, markets its products in Algeria through a partnership with Cevital.

(Source: www.cevital.com)

On a smaller scale, but equally impressive, is Fertalge Industries. In its short existence (Fertalge was established in 1997) this 100 per cent privately owned company became Algeria's eighth-largest exporter in its second year of production, overtaking the country's moribund state industries in a single bound. Aptly named, Fertalge produces UAN 32 per cent (Urea Ammonium Nitrate), a liquid agricultural fertiliser. UAN 32 per cent, a petroleum derivative, is said to be the future of agricultural fertiliser. It can be mixed with herbicide, and improves crop yields. It is used in the cultivation of cereal, vegetable gardens, and fruit trees. Fertalge is Africa's largest producer of UAN 32 per cent, and is an aggressive international competitor, selling to Europe and beyond. France is its biggest market, followed by Belgium, Germany, and Spain. By the end of 2004, Fertalge had the capacity to produce 800,000 tons annually. The company's CEO, Mohamed Amieur, asserts that Fertalge has managed to exploit the inherent advantages of Algeria: its cheap input costs such as energy and manpower and its proximity to one of the world's biggest single markets. 'There is a lot of money to be made in Algeria if you have a product of international standard,' says Amieur.

(Source: www.fertalge.com and 'Algeria: Investment Outlook 2000', 'Industry: Private Dynamos', *Arab Communication Consult Limited*, www.arabcomconsult.com)

World INvestment News reports that the private sector in Algeria is organised and managed in a very flexible way while having a great capacity for innovation, and there are many examples confirming this view. For instance, Fruital and ABC doubled their turnover thanks to lucrative contracts with Coca-Cola and Pepsi respectively. US Coca-Cola recently invested US$50 million to expand production capacity in Algeria. Moncef Othmani, chief executive officer of Fruital, a soft drink joint venture with Coca-Cola, says the US$50 million investment covered the setting up of new plants in the eastern city of Annaba and in Oran in western Algeria. The two units help Fruital to keep up with increasing demand and bring their products closer to consumers. Coca-Cola had previously invested US$70 million in building a plant in the Rouiba area, 18 miles east of Algiers. Coca-Cola employs approximately 1,500 workers in Algeria.

The clear evolution of Algeria's agro-business sector is well illustrated by the El Bousten Group, the biggest tomato canning industry in Algeria with 35 per cent of the market share. Beyond its economic success, the particular characteristic of the company is its direct commitment to agriculture by the introduction of new techniques such as chemical fertilisers. This is a way to teach farmers — who are often limited to basic agriculture — a new economic notion of the business. Abdelhamid Boudiaf, president of the El Bousten Group, says that before the creation of the company in 1992 Algerian tomato imports were about 25,000 to 30,000 tons per year, but now the company produces in excess of domestic needs, allowing 20,000 tons for export. The El Bousten Group has launched a company, AGRITEC, in partnership with AGIR, an international Canadian group. They have two factories producing liquid and solid fertilisers. Boudiaf also hopes to reinstate the cultivation of sunflowers in Algeria, amongst other projects.

Other private companies have emerged in different sectors, among them Union Bank in the financial sector. Union Bank, belonging to Chairman Brahim Hadjas, is one of the most prominent merchant banks in Algeria. Created in 1995, and considered the premier Algerian private bank, Union Bank increased its profits by 105 per cent in 1997, before its foreign trade licence was suddenly revoked. Three years later, however, Union Bank was able to get its licence back. After the liberalisation of the Algerian economy there remained no real legal framework behind the implementation of financing instruments, apart from classical banking instruments. After having fought to set up Union Bank, Hadjas is fully determined to develop the potential of Algeria's financial sector so as to provide the country with the necessary financing for its economic development. He says the country has to create its own businesses, and this requires a vehicle to allow foreign investment, so Union Bank is taking a leading role in offering investment services and funds.

(Source: www.ubgroup.com.dz)

Djamel Mehri is president of the Mehri Group, which has a diverse portfolio of activities, ranging from tourism to real estate and services, but agro-business figures prominently. Mehri's hometown is the southern desert oasis of El Oued where, for the past three decades, his family has run a 500-hectare agricultural scheme, including date palms, olive groves and glasshouse cultivation. Two processing plants are planned: one to turn dates into alcohol for export, as well as alcohol vinegar and livestock feed, and the other to process and package dates. Since 1995, the Mehri Group has been developing a larger agricultural scheme in Ouargla, where the traditional crops of dates and olives are supplemented with cereals, potatoes and cattle raising, notably dairy cows. They have a plant producing long-life milk.

The Mehri Group, which reflects the dynamic spirit of Algeria's private sector, also holds a franchise for the distribution of Pepsi-Cola all over the Algerian territory. Djamel Mehri is well acquainted with the Algerian market, and gladly shares his experience by saying, 'Algeria is what Egypt used to be in the 80s', a reference to the economic boom in progress in the country. Besides the partnership agreement with Pepsi-Cola, the company is partnered with Stella Artois for the production of the beer Tango, and with Savola for oil manufacturing. The group is also extending its activities to the hotel business. In 2004, Accor, a French hotel chain, formed a joint venture with the Mehri Group, with the aim of opening 36 two-star and three-star hotels across Algeria in three batches of 12. In 2005, the partners started work on eight hotels. The first two properties, one of them a 160-room Novotel, are being built in the north-eastern city of Constantine.

(Source: WINNE. 2001. 'Algeria: The time is now, the place is Algeria'. *World INvestment News*, www.winne.com, 12 November 2001; 'Algeria, la nouvelle generation'. *World INvestment News*, www.winne.com, 28 November 2002; and 'Towards the sustainable development of Algeria'. *World INvestment News*, www.winne.com, 23 May 2003)

Arab Communication Consult's experienced team of communications specialists and information analysts, (Beirut, Lebanon) reports that the 100 per cent Algerian-owned SIH is the firm behind Algeria's newest and largest five-star hotel, the Sheraton Club des Pins Resort and Towers. The hotel is located at the beautiful Club des Pins Beach in an absolutely secure area west of the city of Algiers. Equipped with one of the best conference centres in Algeria, it offers state of the art equipment and technology. The OAU African Summit was held there in 1999, and 57 heads of state were accommodated. The hotel is currently Algeria's only five-star hotel of international standard and represents the first in a chain of investments SIH is implementing. The next steps, in partnership with the Libyan firm LAFICO are a 331-room Sheraton in Oran, Algeria's western capital; a four-star hotel situated next to Club des Pins in Algiers; and another Sheraton in Hassi Messaoud, Algeria's biggest and longest-running oil field.

SIH's chairman, Hamid Melzi, has 30 years of experience in the tourism industry and is helping develop the country's coastline. He argues that the hotel sector will grow rapidly in the next five years, given certain requirements: he believes SIH can create 10,000 beds in that time and he sees the potential and the interest from investors, especially from the Middle East — but he warns that the Algerian infrastructure has to be developed and that hotel owners must invest more in employee training. SIH is creating a special school for hotel staff, to give guests the proper level of service. Interestingly, this flurry of activity is taking place without any significant competition. Melzi laughs that he is alone, 'People don't believe me. Good for me.'

(Source: 'Algeria: Investment Report 2002, Virgin Markets'. *Arab Communication Consult Limited*, www.arabcomconsult.com)

Tunisia

The Amen Group, which has been in business for generations, is one of the most active in Tunisia. The Group was established early in the 20th century by Brahim Ben Yedder, the founder of 'Cafés Ben Yedder', the first company of the group, which has expanded further under the aegis of his two sons, Béchir and Rachid Ben Yedder. At present, the Ben Yedder family controls the Group through a parent company, PGI Holding. Consisting of some twenty companies, the Group is strengthening its position in several branches of activity: finance, insurance, agro-business, trade in capital goods, IT, tourism, health and real estate.

The Amen Group has 3,000 employees and the overall turnover of its 26 members exceeds 400 million dinars. Well-known for its high moral standards, the Group relies on modern management techniques and youthful teams which constantly receive further training and are kept motivated and open to the international environment. Its deep roots in Tunisia's business community, its ethics and its creditworthiness have established it as a sound, high-performing and reliable business partner. Group members include farming (El Khir, Kawaris); olive oil (Huilerie Ben Yedder); coffee roasting (Cafés Ben Yedder, Cafés Bondin); tea packaging (Akyes); confectionery (Grande Fabrique De Confiserie Orientale); general trade (La Generale Alimentaire); trade in capital goods (Parenin-Caterpillar, John Deere, Atlas Copco); tourism (Majestic Hôtel, Hotel Dar Said); restaurants (Dar Zarrouk); real estate (Elimrane); health (Clinique El Amen); information technology (Tunisys, Amen Systems); insurance (Comar, Hayett); and finance (Amen Bank, Amen Lease, Amen Invest).

Amen Bank is Tunisia's first private bank, with origins dating back to 1906. It covers all areas of the banking business, boasting the most extensive multi-channel network in Tunisia. Amen Bank has created several financial subsidiaries and was the first Tunisian bank to receive ISO certification. Listed on the Tunis stock exchange, and acknowledged both nationally and internationally, Amen Bank manages several credit and financing lines for prestigious institutions such as the World Bank, the African Development Bank, and the European Investment Bank. Amen Bank employs 940 people and serves the whole country via its network of 79 branches and 62 automatic teller machines (ATMs). In 2003-2004 Amen Bank gradually implemented a new integrated multi-channel banking system enabling the bank to migrate to an information system combining customer services and products, in an open IT architecture. Amen Bank thus became the first north African bank able to coordinate its different remote services (Internet, ATM, interactive voice services, SMS, call centre, self-service terminals) via a single system used in all its branches. This allows real-time follow-up of all banking operations. In March 2001, Amen Group CEO Rachid Ben Yedder was named Manager of the Year by a panel of business personalities assembled by the financial magazine, *L'Economiste Maghrébin*.

The Poulina Group was founded in 1967 in Tunisia when five families decided to get into a partnership in order to achieve a common ambition, namely setting up a modern company, a company that would be a model for management in Tunisia. Started with capital of US$20,000 under the leadership of its chairman and CEO, Abdelwaheb Ben Ayed, Poulina has now become a group of 50 companies employing 7,000 people. Around its basic activity, poultry-farming, Poulina is active in various fields of industry (wood, ceramics, steel and printing), agriculture, agro-food (ice-creams, margarine, juice, yogurt, pastry, delicatessen, chips and snacks) and services (computers, hotels, timeshare, fast food restaurants) and thematic tourism.

Poulina's success comes from its innovating and pioneering strategy. Already a pioneer in the poultry industry, Abdelwaheb Ben Ayed was the first to believe in the potential of turkey consumption, at a time when turkey was not at all on the daily menus of Tunisian families. Poulina was also the first to believe in the future of thematic tourism. Médina Méditerranea is a reproduction of the medieval city of Arab-Muslim architecture relating the history of Tunisia, visited by more than three million people every year.

Abdelwaheb Ben Ayed willingly recognises that his success is due mainly to the people working with him, his staff who remain strongly attached to Poulina. The powerful company culture which characterises this group emanates essentially from innovating management systems, which combine strategy, remuneration, performance and local culture. This system, in continual development, based on meritocracy, has allowed Poulina to find its own style of management.

(Source:www.poulina.com.tn)

The Oxford Business Group has published *Emerging Tunisia 2003*, a review of events and trends in Tunisia's major economic sectors, including banking, capital markets (produced in association with Tunisie Valeurs), insurance, IT and telecommunications, industry, real estate and construction, tourism and agriculture. Tunisie Valeurs is one of the largest brokerage houses in Tunisia. Since December 1997, the Tunisie Valeurs research department has been publishing research reports at the end of each quarter, casting light on the most important events in Tunisia's financial market. Tunisie Valeurs was awarded the 'Best broker in Tunisia' award four years in a row by the *EuroMoney* magazine. Tunisie Valeurs offers a wide range of financial services:
- To individual clients: Brokerage and management of wealth.
- To corporate clients: Advisory services in the fields of mergers and acquisitions and fund-raising.
- To institutional investors: Research, advisory, placements in listed securities and government bonds.

Even though Tunisie Valeurs is totally independent in its research and management, it is closely related to a non-banking group, and benefits from the synergies of the companies, which operate in different sectors:
- Leasing with Tunisie Leasing, the sector's pioneer and leader in Tunisia;
- factoring with Tunisie Factoring, the first factoring company specialised in this sector of activity, and a joint venture with EUROFACTORS; and
- private equity management with Tuninvest Finance Group (TFG) a specialised company created in association with Siparex, with US$50 million funds under management.

The chairman of Tunisie Leasing Group, Ahmed Abdelkefi, started his career as a civil servant as the head of the Foreign Investment Department at the Tunisian Ministry of Planning and Finance. From 1973 to 1978, he was founder, chairman and CEO of Société d'Etudes et de Développement de Sousse Nord, a company established with the assistance of the IFC and various local and Arab investors. They developed the first integrated tourist resort in Tunisia, Port El Kantaoui, which today is one of the most attractive resorts in the tourist town of Sousse. From 1978 to 1984, Abdelkefi worked as advisor to the general manager of the Abu Dhabi Fund for Arab Economic Development where he was in charge of equity investment in several countries including the United Arab Emirates, Egypt, Tunisia, Morocco and Turkey. He set up for the federal government of Abu Dhabi the Abu Dhabi National Hotel Company, one of the blue chips listed on the Abu Dhabi Stock Exchange. On his return to Tunisia in the mid-1980s, Abdelkefi started the first leasing company in Tunisia. Tunisie Leasing has, over time, become a financial services group consisting of Tunisie Valeurs(the brokerage arm founded in 1991), Tuninvest Sicaf, Tunisie Factoring (founded in 1997) and Tunis Call Centre (founded in 1996). Abdelkefi is chairman of Tuninvest Finance Group founded in 1995 and which has a stake in Tunisie Factoring and Tunis Call Centre.

A number of international financial institutions have been investing regularly with the Tunisie Leasing group since the early 1990s, among them the IFC, the French development agency PROPARCO, the European Investment Bank, the Dutch capital development agency FMO, the French Natexis Banque Populaire group and other Tunisian banks and financial institutions. The group has also been involved as adviser to large takeover transactions such as the detergent SPCD takeover by the Unilever group with JP Morgan in 1999. Then, with BNP Paribas, the group advised the Tunisian government on the merger of the three largest investment banks in Tunisia, STB, BDET and BNDT. With Compagnie Financière Edmond de Rothschild, the group advised the Tunisian government on the sale in 1998 of the two largest cement plants in Tunisia to the Portuguese Cimpor and the Spanish Uniland. These are but a few of the local and international deals which have given the group a respectable track record. With the Tunisie Leasing Group,

Abdelkefi has always been innovative in Tunisia. He launched the first bond issue, the first initial public offering on the Tunis Stock Exchange and the first Tunisian call centre platform, which recently extended its telemarketing activities to France by selling French products from its Tunisian platform. In 1992, Tunisie Valeurs launched the first mutual fund, Tunisie Sicav. In 2005, the group established a leasing company in Algeria called in Maghreb Leasing Algeria, in association with FMO, Proparco, Maghreb Fund and CFAO, a branch of the French PPR Group.

(Source: www.tuninvest.com)

Taoufik Chaibi is chairman of UTIC (Ulysse Trading and Industrial Companies). The group is strong in distribution, packaging, electromechanics, food industry, tourism, and services fields. To meet their objectives, UTIC's winning strategy has always been the same: with an entrepreneurial spirit, aim for leadership, create new partnerships, anticipate future needs, and increase returns, while maintaining transparency and autonomy.

UTIC's partnership with Unilever, entering in its third decade, has been significantly reorganised through the signing of an exclusive distribution agreement for Unilever brands both in Tunisia (through its new company UTIC Distribution) and in Libya. In April 2001, Ulysse Hyper Distribution (UHD), UTIC's partnership venture with the Carrefour Group, opened the first hypermarket, which has been the biggest success in Tunisian retail distribution history. The consumer response reflected the level of effort invested by the UHD team, with the backing of UTIC and the assistance of Carrefour. UTIC continues to invest heavily in its packaging and food-making plants as well as in its carton mill. Its electro-mechanics companies continue to grow even stronger in the Tunisian market, thanks to the quality of their services and partners. This division is well positioned to take advantage of favourable market evolution. With the collaboration of the Marionnaud Group, UTIC entered the perfume and cosmetics retail distribution through its newly-created company, Point M. Finally, its tourism activity has been reinforced through an agreement signed with Mövenpick for the management of their five-star hotel, Ulysse Palace. UTIC's Ulysse Palace, Athenee Palace, Ithaque Palace, sea-line resorts on Djerba Island, are considered to be three of the jewels of Tunisian hotels.

(Source: www.utic.com.tn)

The Tunisian airline carrier Nouvelair was founded in October 1989 under the name Air Libetré Tunisie. Nouvelair is a subsidiary company of the TTS (Tunisian Travel Service) Group, one of the leading companies of the Tunisian tourism industry. Aziz Miled, chairman of TTS and Nouvelair, and his dynamic staff, have been able to develop Nouvelair's activities throughout Europe with its charter fleet of European Airbus A-320s departing from 90 European airports. In addition to its charter activities, Nouvelair has developed and expanded scheduled flights so as to respond to increasing demand. Nouvelair's aim was better to know the requirements of the more than one million passengers transported, and to anticipate their needs. Therefore, in 2003, Aziz Miled announced the birth of Nouvelair International, a new airline company directed towards serving the Middle East and other areas of the world. Years of assiduous work have produced solid operational and technical structures, while a healthy financial standing and remarkable human resources enable Nouvelair to challenge the development opportunities for Tunisian tourism to and from the Middle East and the Gulf Arab countries and to fill the vacuum of service to and from sub-Saharan Africa.

(Source: www.tts.com.tn)

Tunisia shatters all expectations and preconceived ideas regarding the place and the role of women in a Muslim country, for the situation of women in Tunisia has become a model in the African and Arab-Muslim worlds. The current status of Tunisian women is the result of a progressive policy started by President Habib Bourguiba at the outset of independence. In 1956, Bourguiba ushered in a new social era with the Code of Personal Status elevating the status of women in Tunisia. With better access to education, women are entering the workforce in record numbers, and are now present in all sectors of activity.

In 2003, 10,000 women headed business enterprises (compared to 68,000 men). The Chambre Nationale des Femmes Chefs d'Entreprises (CNFCE) (the Tunisian Chamber of Women Business Owners, founded in 1991), had over 5,000 women entrepreneur members. CNFCE members are active in all sectors of the economy, once the domain of men – from textiles to maintenance, to commerce, tourism and hotels, chemical industries, mechanical industries, food processing industries and the pharmaceutical industries. The objectives of the chamber are to:

- Promote women's entrepreneurship;
- defend the rights and interests of women entrepreneurs before policy makers;
- assure entrepreneurial skills training and the dissemination of information;
- assist in market access; and
- organise events that promote networking, partnership and business contacts, nationally, regionally and internationally.

ExpoFemina, a biennial exposition-forum, is an initiative of CNFCE aimed at promoting the 'made in Tunisia by women entrepreneurs' label. Tunisia has leadership skills in furthering the cause of women, and ExpoFemina has now become an international affair — in February 2004, women from more than 20 countries, participating from Europe, Africa, and the Middle East, displayed their products and services at the ExpoFemina Fair in Tunis.

Leyla Khaïat has been the president of the CNFCE since 1995. As president and general manager (CEO) of Plastiss, a group of manufacturing companies in the industrial textile sector employing 125 persons in Tunisia, Khaïat knows the ins and outs of business. After her husband died suddenly in 1985, she inherited the Plastiss group. Left to run five companies and to raise three children on her own, she was suddenly faced with a daunting task. In order to continue the family business, Khaïat learned to read and write Arabic during the day and studied business at night. There was no other option for the young widow, who by profession was a French professor. Her task was all the more difficult given that, though women in Tunisia had gained equal rights in 1956, in the 1980s women CEOs were pioneers in a business environment that was not accepting of their leadership. However, after mustering her strength, and proving her capabilities, she has managed to consolidate the companies from five to two and has dramatically improved the revenues. Today the group, consolidated to its core activities, consists of Plastiss, and Socotex, leading names in the manufacture of imitation leather fabrics. Khaïat's daughter Mounia and her son Sofiane both help run the Plastiss group. In 1999 Khaïat was the recipient of the Artemis international award of the Euro-American Women's Council for outstanding women entrepreneurs, and in 2000 Plastiss was awarded ISO 9002 certification.

As a female business-owner and president of CNFCE, Khaïat has been very active in promoting women's entrepreneurship at the local, regional and international levels. In 1998, she was elected World President of FCEM (Les Femmes Chefs d'Entreprises Mondiales), the world association of women entrepreneurs, a non-profit NGO association founded in France in 1945. FCEM is an international network of close to 60 countries from the five continents, and with an estimated half a million individual women business-owner members. Khaïat is the organisation's fifth president and the first from outside Europe.

Since taking over the helm of FCEM in 1998, Khaiat has focused on the needs of women entrepreneurs in countries in development and in transition, lobbying the United Nations, governments, and other international and regional institutions for programmes and policies that promote women's entrepreneurship as the means of poverty reduction, and for peace. Her international efforts have not gone unnoticed; the Together for Peace Foundation awarded her the 'Highest Acknowledgement Award' and she was decorated by President Wade of Senegal with the 'Chevalier de l'Ordre National de Lion' for her work for the women of Africa.

Khaïat's hopes for the future are that other Arab countries will call on the strengths and ingenuity of their own populations, creating sustainable development and economic growth increasingly based on non-oil exports. She believes that Arab countries must engage the complimentary potential of Arab women entrepreneurs. Khaïat sees women's active participation in socio-economic development as a means of assuring political and social stability, dynamism and development.

In Tunisia, the path for women wishing to create a business has been pioneered and little, if any, distinction remains between men and women business-owners, who all face the same challenges — competitiveness and innovation. A good example of the achievements of the newer generation of women entrepreneurs in Tunisia is Maille Fil, a cotton-spinning company owned and managed by the three Bouchamaoui sisters, and part of the Bouchamaoui Group. With a strategy anchored on three fronts — quality, equipment and training programmes for the labour force - the sisters have been able to carve a niche for their business. High-end designers, such as the children's clothes manufacturer Petit Bateau of France, are now using their cotton. Amel, one of the owners, was educated in the United States. She remembers that her classmates were always surprised to hear that women in Tunisia have been getting the same wages as men for equal work for the past 40 years. She equates the status of women in her country to that of women in the most developed countries. Protective policies are in place: women get 30-day maternity leave; they cannot work in the mill during the night shift and opportunities for women are the same as for men. Always forward-looking, Tunisia is now trying to stamp out the stereotypical view of women participating in the labour pool as hairdressers and stylists, and they are assuming a diversity of activities and positions in each sector of the economy

(Source: 'Equal pay for equal work for Tunisian women since 1957', *The Washington Times* (July 10-14, 2000); and Hazel Heyer. 'Tunisia's Leyla Khaïat leads world's women entrepreneurs', *Egyptian Millionaire* (May-June 2002)

Banque Tunisienne de Solidarité (BTS), was created in 1997 to help the state, in its job creation programme, to allow individual entrepreneurs with no collateral to benefit from small loans, and to encourage entrepreneurship. The BTS has also helped many women to own their businesses. Karima Ouertani went to the BTS to get a loan to start her own sewing business and she now makes traditional Tunisian wedding dresses encrusted in golden thread and beads that cost up to US$2 700. Hidri Najet needed a small loan to buy the kiln to open her own decorated ceramics factory. Although she did not have any collateral, the BTS granted her a small loan and now she re-sells her decorated ceramics to wholesalers throughout the greater Tunis area.

(Source: 'Creating the entrepreneurial spirit'. *The Washington Times*, 10-14 July 2000)

Essma Ben Hamida is the 1990 co-founder of ENDA Inter-Arabe in Tunisia, a non-profit organisation providing small business loans, or 'micro credits', generally the equivalent of a few hundred dollars, to small-businesspeople trapped in urban poverty. The micro-loans help Tunisian women in poor suburbs improve their lives and the lives of their families and communities by allowing them to support themselves with dignity and escape social dependency through their own entrepreneurial efforts.

ENDA Inter-Arabe, part of the ENDA Third World family founded in 1972 and now active in 21 countries worldwide, launched an urban development programme at Hay Ettadhamen in 1993. In the 13 years since ENDA first observed the women's situation at Hay Ettadhamen, a revolution has taken place. Women have invaded the public space: the markets, the streets and public transport. Today, women are fruit and vegetable vendors, run second-hand clothes shops, are hairdressers and photographers — and there is even a female butcher and at least one taxi-driver. Lamia produces elaborately embroidered wedding dresses, providing an excellent example of business skill development through improved management and networking. Souad, after losing her job in a factory, purchased a second-hand sewing machine with an ENDA loan. In 2004, six years later, she was employing 20 women producing textile goods for international clients.

In 2003, the ENDA programme was concentrating on support for micro-entrepreneurs. This included credit and business development services such as training in simple accounting and management; regular trade fairs where women sell their goods for cash (usually it is on credit); regular information sessions (health, legal matters, marriage and divorce, taxation, banking services, municipal services); and encouragement of networking between the clients, with ENDA staff as facilitators.

It is Essma Ben Hamida's experience that the micro-enterprise does provide a path to empowerment for many women. But that path is steep and has many pitfalls, for while micro-entrepreneurship can and does succeed in promoting viable businesses and households, it rarely acts in isolation as a mechanism for female empowerment. The economic and regulatory environment, family conditions and much else also exert a strong influence.

Starting in 1993 with a capital fund of only US$20,000, the programme, in 2004, had a portfolio of some US$3.6 million, has provided 65,000 loans to 24,000 micro-entrepreneurs for a total value of US$21 million, and has 15,000 active clients, with plans to reach 100,000 by 2008. 'Encouraging micro-enterprise through credit is a very efficient way to empower women: they become self-confident, break free from male domination, 'gain a say' in family affairs, and are generally more respected in their communities,' says Essma Ben Hamida.

In October 2003, co-directors Essma Ben Hamida and Michael Cracknell were proud to inform their supporters that ENDA Inter-Arabe had received two awards for its micro-credit programme from the University of Stellenbosch Business School. The best small, medium and micro enterprises (SMMEs) from all corners of the continent showed their mettle and ENDA Inter-Arabe received awards for Best Africa SMME in the Open Category and as the Best SMME in North Africa.

(Source: www.endarabe.org.tn)

Tunisia proposed in 1998 that the nations of the world should hold a summit on the information society with the sole aim of agreeing on strategies of bridging the digital divide. Tunisia had become a showcase of what an African country can achieve through political commitment. Every school and university in Tunisia had access to the internet. This was an example of a country bridging the digital divide within its own borders. Tunisia was economically and technically equipped to host a summit of such magnitude, with its civil society attempting to identify and exploit real opportunities offered by ICT for sustainable development. The World Summit on the Information Society (WSIS) was held in two phases. The first phase of WSIS took place in Geneva, hosted by the government of Switzerland, from 10 to 12 December 2003.

Phase two of WSIS was hosted by Tunisia, on 16-18 November 2005, with more than 16,000 delegates from 176 countries meeting in Tunis to focus on forging strategies to improve the accessibility and affordability of information and communication technologies. Development themes were a key focus in this phase. It was felt that what the South needed most were public/private partnerships to meet universal access goals. Development agencies showed a range of 'appropriate' technologies to bridge the digital divide. The highlight was a wind-up laptop retailing at US$100.

World leaders were asked to put information and communication technologies (ICTs) at the heart of their national economic and social development policies. Secretary-General of the International Telecommunication Union (ITU), Yoshio Utsumi, spoke passionately about the unprecedented opportunities offered by new technologies, and warned of the threat of increasing global inequality if access to these powerful tools for economic growth remained predominantly in the hands of the world's richest nations. 'We have within our grasp the opportunity to build a more just and equitable society, an information society in which developing countries, even with their lack of industrialisation, geographical challenges or troubled past, have — perhaps for the first time in human history — a very real chance to catch up with their more affluent neighbours,' said Utsumi.

The first edition of the Tunisian guidebook for new information and communications technologies came out in December 2004. The French-language 260-page *'Guidebook for professionals'* published by Symboles Media, provides detailed information about Tunisia's IT sector. It also presents the opportunities that the country offers for foreign investment as an 'emerging destination' in the fast developing sector of new technologies. The new reference resource (book and CD-Rom) provides data about specialised firms, web development companies, internet service providers, e-commerce outlets, call centres, and public agencies. According to the private publisher of the *Annuaire Professionnel des nouvelles technologies de l'Information et de la Communication en Tunisie*, the new guidebook came out at a time when the country was actively preparing for the second phase of the World Summit on the Information Society.

Tunisia is geographically diverse. The country has a Mediterranean coastline, a fertile mountain region and a region of Sahara desert. Many of the country's almost 10 million people live in rural areas, so training Tunisian professionals through distance learning is a major focus. Indeed, Tunisia has a national mandate to get 20 per cent of its university curriculum online by 2006. To oversee this process, Cat Holmes, a science writer with the University of Georgia College of Agricultural and Environmental Sciences, reports that Tunisia has created a virtual university. 'The focus isn't simply the technology of putting curriculum online but the pedagogy of online learning,' says Houcine Chebli, president of the Virtual University of Tunisia. Another focus — and an ambitious plan — is to create ten technology parks by the year 2010. In 2004, Tunisia had four such parks, which incorporate university research and technology and business technology and sales. Director of the Sfax Research Park, AbdelFettah Ghorbel, says that the technology parks are regarded as essential components in the development of the Tunisian economy. The parks are modern, low-density facilities catering to high-tech industries, and provide a range of shared, on-site resources. The main objectives of the parks are to:

- Promote the creation of start-ups;
- create job opportunities for university graduates;
- support the innovative project-holders by housing them in the science parks incubators;
- transfer the research and development results to industry; and
- encourage foreign enterprises to install principal activity or subsidiaries in the science parks.

A total of seven SPs (science parks) were to be in operation by 2006, specialising in technology of information and communication (SP of El Ghazala); food processing (SP of Bizerte); health applications of biotechnology (SP of Sidi Thabet); renewable energy (SP of Borj Cedria); textiles (SP of Monastir); informatics, microelectronics, and mechanics (SP of Sousse); informatics and multimedia (SP of Sfax).

(Source: Cat Holmes. 'Tunisian educators use UGA college as model'; http://georgiafaces.caes.uga.edu, 10 July 2003)

In November 2000, Madan Mohan Rao, editor of *INOMY* based in India, reported from the E-Commerce Summit in Tunisia that Tunisia has a diverse market-oriented economy with significant agricultural, industrial and tourism sectors. In 1991, it became the first Arab and African country to connect to the internet. Countries like Tunisia can take advantage of global trends in outsourcing infotech work via the internet. Tunisia has embarked on an ambitious strategy to develop its national Internet sector and be a regional player as well. One of the more notable projects has been TradeNet Tunisia, a one-stop online documentation and financial service for importers, exporters and freight organisations. Karim Gharbi, director of TradeNet Tunisia, says that this secure and convenient service cuts down on process delays in international shipping, and helps grow other business-to-business market spaces. Another successful initiative launched in October 1998 was PubliNet (public internet centres), which increases internet access options via community centres; there are over 200 such public access centres in Tunisia.

Dozens of companies have launched e-commerce services covering a wide range of Tunisian products including crafts, foodstuffs (dates, olive oil, desserts), textiles, tourist services, stamps and hotel reservations. Rapid Post (the Tunisian carrier for express postage) has reduced the transport tariffs for products sold through the Internet in order to promote this type of service, according to Lamia Chaffai Sghaier, e-commerce manager at the Tunisian Internet Agency (ATI). Many of these projects are grouped under the Tunisia Shopping Gallery site. Targeted countries for sales include the US, Germany, France, Switzerland, Lebanon, Hong Kong and Holland.

Internet Caravans were started in Tunisia in 1999 to take mobile workshops about the internet around the country. In November each year, an Internet Week series of events is held, featuring seminars, trade shows and training sessions; the highlight is a Web Oscars awards ceremony broadcast on national TV, honouring the best Tunisian websites of the year. There are also Open Internet Days in November when PubliNets offer free internet access to all users. By 2003, all universities and schools were online. Internet access is available via a local call across the whole country.

ATI has an SSL-based secure payment server called E-Tijara for users of Mastercard and Visa credit cards. E-Tijara is operated by ATI in cooperation with major Tunisian banks. Raken.com, an e-commerce site for Mediterranean, Arab and African art and decoration, is one of many vendors in Tunisia using ATI's E-Tijara payment server. ATI assisted the Tunisian postal agency with the smart card project called e-Dinar. These cards are available at most post offices in denominations of 20 to 50 dinars, are re-chargeable, and can be used for consumer e-commerce, says Abdelkrim Bouzid, chief technology officer at La Poste Tunisienne.

Tunisian ministries have an active presence on the web, as well as on the national broadcast TV and radio media. Other notable Tunisian sites include Yellow Pages Tunisia, ad agency Belmakett, Amen Bank, hotel reservation site Orangers.com, and portal TunisiaOnline. In addition to two private ISPs for commercial and consumer accounts, there are seven other ISPs in Tunisia providing access to government agencies, research centres, universities, schools, health institutes, agricultural organisations, and telecom affiliates. Entrepreneur Jamel Sghaier, who runs operations for RedHat Linux in Morocco, Algeria and Tunisia, says that Tunisian companies are also actively harnessing freeware and shareware operating systems and servers based on Linux.

PlaNet Tunisie, a private — and the leading — Internet Service Provider in Tunisia, was founded in 1997. PlaNet provides internet access by telephone lines (RTC), analogue, and digital leased lines, X-25 lines, and lines RNIS. The business focus of PlaNet is internet access for private subscribers. Mohamed Garbouj, general deputy manager for PlaNet, points out that their user base is rapidly growing. As of 2003, and with six years on the market, PlaNet had gained an overwhelming market share with 60 per cent in the home users' market and 70 per cent in the corporate market. As the leading ISP in Tunisia, PlaNet has kept up with technological standards and ensured manageable growth. To hold its market position the objective has been to create new services and differentiate from the competition through the quality of its services.

(Source: Madan Mohan Rau. 'E-Dinars, E-Tijara: Tunisia embarks on ambitious internet plan'. *INOMY*, 5 December 2000)

Libya

Libya is promoting itself as a changed nation desiring to join the world family of nations and aggressively courting foreign investors and, in particular, the travel industry. Sandy Dhuyvetter, executive producer of *Travel Talk Radio*, reported in March 2004 that Libya wishes to join the global community of peaceful nations and throw open its doors to international trade and commerce. Attracting foreign investors, resort developers and new industries is the logical step for developing Libya into a leading provider of leisure travel products. After all, the country is the size of Germany, France and Holland combined and has over 2,000 kilometres of undeveloped beachfront property on the Mediterranean sea. There is no doubt in Dhuyvetter's mind that Libya is ready to step up to the plate and compete with some of the finest destinations in the world. She advises that we need to learn about Libya's new role and aspirations in the world, its people and its natural resources, including some of the most incredible beaches on earth. With a population of only about five million people in a country nearly the size of Alaska, Libya offers a fantastic opportunity for outside investment and development.

(Source: Sandy Dhuyvetter. 'Libya: An about-face'. *Travel Talk Radio* interview with Ammar Mabrouk Eltayef, Libya's Minister of Tourism, 17 March 2004)

Libyan leader, Colonel Muammar Gadafy, has been sponsoring projects throughout the African continent. Gadafy says Libya is both an African and an Arab country. He asserts that Libya should export to satisfy sub-Saharan Africa's needs in agricultural production — such as farm equipment and machinery, fertiliser and chemicals, irrigation and horticulture and infrastructural development. These exports could in turn be exchanged for sub-Saharan Africa's agriculture exports to Libya, particularly of beef, coffee, tea, cotton, sugar, tobacco, soya beans and other horticultural products.

Libya is catching up with the times says Seif al-Islam Gadafy, son and rumoured heir-apparent to Col Gadafy. The younger Gadafy was 31 years old in 2004 and studying for his PhD in global governance at the London School of Economics. He had no official role, but he had become the public face of a westernising Libya. He said that the Libyan people hoped to establish a good relationship with America; to see Libyan students at American colleges; to import medicine, wheat and technology from America; to encourage American investment in the gas and oil sector; and to participate in a bilateral strategic programme for developing Africa.

These were the goals that Seif al-Islam believed could be achieved through mutual cooperation. Libya was ready for a dialogue based on mutual respect with Britain and America, to solve all their outstanding problems. The atmosphere was favourable, he thought, for taking positive steps.

In February 2004, Carla Anne Robbins, journalist for *The Wall Street Journal*, reported that the younger Gadafy's rising expectations were echoed with similar fervour by many others in Libya. A new foreign-educated, technocratic leadership had embraced private enterprise, globalisation and membership in the World Trade Organisation as Libya's newest creed. Another big player in Libya's future seemed to be Shukri Ghanem, who was called back from Europe in late 2001 to help repair the country's failing economy. An economist with a PhD from Tufts University's Fletcher School, and a mastery of American slang, Ghanem preached capitalism. Upon becoming prime minister in 2003, Ghanem had ambitious plans to privatise 360 of Libya's state-owned companies — including cement, shoe and soft-drink factories, banks and possibly part of the oil industry — by 2008. He wanted to attract billions of dollars of foreign investment to develop Libya's oil fields, tourism and other new industries.
(
Source: Carla Anne Robbins. 'In giving up arms, Libya hopes to gain new economic life', *The Wall Street Journal*, 12 February 2004)

Tourism is a labour-intensive sector, which would supply private sector jobs and draw hard currency from abroad while helping to re-integrate Libya into the world community. The US$135 million five-star Corinthia Bab Africa Hotel built by Malta-based luxury-hotel chain Corinthia Group illustrates the promise that awaits investors. New ownership and investment rules have enabled the Corinthia — a 300-room edifice on Tripoli's Mediterranean beachfront — to offer luxury accommodation for a new breed of visitor. There is good reason to expect the investment to pay off: in addition to myriad ruins, Libya has 1 200 miles of shoreline, friendly people and stunning geography to draw tourists. Tourism is a good way to diversify Libya's economy and reduce its dependence on oil. The economic potential of future tourism in Libya could prove to be the most important after oil. If well managed, it will be a sustainable resource and, unlike oil, it is undepletable.

(Source: Susan Rivers. 'Tourism spurs Libya evolution', *The Wall Street Journal*, 27 February 2004)

The Corinthia Bab Africa Hotel is located at the heart of Tripoli's central business district and opened to customers in 2003. This luxury hotel was built to attract the expected flow of foreign businessman looking for future opportunities in Tripoli. Corinthia was also planning to open more hotels in Libya by 2008. Alfred Pisani, Corinthia's chairman and chief executive officer, stated that the Tripoli hotel project emphasised his company's long-standing commitment to Libya. In those instances where Maltese contractors proved to be competitive on the international market, they had also been able to generate economic activity in Malta, their home base. The Tripoli hotel was one of the most ambitious undertakings so far by Corinthia.

The Corinthia Bab Africa Hotel features two imposing towers dominating the waterfront's skyline. The towers rise to 14 and 28 floors respectively, forming the central core of the hotel, as well as an adjacent commercial centre to be leased as offices to third parties. The hotel offers 300 bedrooms, a conference and banqueting centre, a spa and a shopping gallery. Since its inception in 1962, the Group has flourished and in 2005 it owned and operated 30 hotels in the Czech Republic, Hungary, Malta, Portugal, Russia, Belgium, The Gambia, Turkey, Tunisia and Libya — all under the banner of Corinthia Hotels International. Corinthia also operates a number of theme restaurants and other catering-related services. Alfred Pisani has been personally involved in the Corinthia's expansion, dedicating a considerable amount of time to identify new locations, new concepts, new designs, new facilities and new marketing strategies for each venture.

(Source: www.corinthia.com)

The Winzrik Tourism Services Group, Libya's longest established tour operator, aims to develop sites across the country, including a resort near Sabratha and a hotel in the desert town of Ghadames. 'There is no intention in Libya to create mass tourism like in neighbouring countries with nightclubs and alcohol,' says chairman and managing director Abdurrazag Gherwash. 'We don't want mass tourism, but quality tourism.' The main business of the Winzrik group is ground operator, travel agent, tourist village and hotel operator, and tourist transportation. They also handle land arrangements for cruise ships including full- or half-day programmes.

Abdurrazag studied in the UK as a mechanical engineer but became Libya's pioneer in the tourism industry, having started organising the first ever groups to Libya in the early 1990s. Today his company, Winzrik Tourism Services is seen as a leader in destination management. In 2001, the Winzrik Group celebrated its 10th anniversary and in the same year the Winzrik Hotel was opened. There is also the Ghadames Winzrik Motel, the Tasili Hotel in Ghat and the Al-Jazeera Tourist Village in Misurata, plus restaurants in Ghadames and Nalut, and an additional restaurant in old Tripoli 'Dar Winzrik,' decorated in traditional old Tripoli style serving a variety of dishes plus traditional meals.

Abdurrazag met Ivan Mifsud (managing director of Mifsud Brothers Ltd of Malta) in 1997 at the World Travel Market in London. Ivan wanted to expand his cruise business outside Malta and found he had so much in common with Abdurrazag that they formed an alliance in order to put together a professional team that would offer quality excursions in Libya. The alliance is Libya Cruise Services (LCS).

Ivan studied earth sciences at Oxford University but on his return to Malta found himself attracted to the tourism industry and gradually took over the family's tourism and shipping business (established in 1860). Ivan grew in this environment from his childhood following both his fathers and grandfather's footsteps. Today he is enjoying using these skills in developing the cruise services business in Libya together with partner and great friend, Abdu.

In July 2000, four members from Mifsud Brothers Ltd, who are established port agents and shore excursion operators in Malta for various prestigious cruise lines, paid a visit to Libya. After substantial groundwork, which included holding meetings with several destination management companies, a local agency was finally selected — one with which to develop and operate quality shore excursions for cruise lines. LCS launched its services in 2001 at Miami Seatrade and made its first breakthrough there.

Maria Mifsud is a director of Mifsud Brothers and is responsible for the shipping department, the cruise general sales agency and Libya shore excursions. Together with Abdu, she has handled every call in Libya.

Much groundwork has gone into designing, testing and marketing LCS shore excursions until LCS finally operated their first call in 2002. Since 2002, they have expanded their services in Libya and are now in a position to offer port agency services and shore excursions from the ports of Tripoli, Al Khoms, Benghazi, Derna and Tobruk. From 2002 until June 2005, shore excursions for over 30 cruise calls, as well as several site inspections, were organised, thus making LCS the most experienced ground operator in Libya. Maria, who is very knowledgeable about itinerary planning, coordinated these calls. She flies to Libya before every call and is the point of contact for the ship's shorex manager. In 2005, using the most modern air-conditioned coaches, and with guides selected according to their area of expertise and language fluency, LCS was the leading shore excursion provider in Libya.

(Source: Libya Part Two, 'Privatisation leads the way to take-off', Summit Communications, 10 July 2005; www.summitreports.com/libya2/index.htm and www.libyacruiseservices.com)

New companies are springing up to serve visitors to Libya. Among the most successful is Libtra Tours, part of the HB Group. After being in operation for just over a year in June 2005, the company had served almost 4,000 visitors. 'We mostly provide a full-package service,' explains General Manager Yousri Benyala. 'We organise the visas, the transportation, the accommodation, tour guides and the planning of all the sites that a tourist group or individual wants to visit.' Most go for a cultural tour. 'Throughout history, Libya has been a melting pot of cultures,' says Benyala. 'Some of the greatest civilisations that have existed have left their marks in Libya. We even have painting and engravings in caves from the pre-historic era. We have virgin coastlines, fascinating lakes in the desert, and even inactive volcanic sites.' Benyala believes tourism could become a main source of income for Libya in a relatively short period of time once the proper infrastructure is provided. Husni Ibrahim Husni Bey, CEO of the HB Group, says there are plans for Libtra to establish its own hotels and tour buses. Taking tours in Libya has proved to be a popular activity, but the hotel infrastructure is still very poor. Libtra is negotiating a plan to build a type of hotel with mini-flats.

(Source: Libya Part Two, 'Privatisation leads the way to take-off', Summit Communications, 10 July 2005, www.summitreports.com/libya2/index.htm and www.libtratours.com)

Esterlab Shipping Agency, also part of the HB Group, is one of the major privately owned shipping agents in the Libyan local market, with its head office in Tripoli and branches at Benghazi, Misurata and Khoms. Esterlab's human resources are its most valuable asset; dedicated staff can offer customers expertise and shipping knowledge. Esterlab specialises in moving products between Libyan ports and offering shipping services to destinations worldwide, including Europe, the Mediterranean, North Africa, Pacific Islands, North America and Asia. They also offer all types of containers for clients to use in the transport of their goods. Naser Alkshaik, Esterlab's general manager, believes that Libya offers huge potential for growth, and says that expansion is one of Esterlab's top priorities.

(Source: www.esterlab-ly.com)

Carla Anne Robbins concluded that the biggest complaint in Libya, especially among the young, was feeling trapped by a stagnant economy. College students could study, but there were not enough jobs in Libya when they finished, and it was hard to get a visa to go abroad. It was felt that Europe and America had everything, and they wanted their part. By the standards of its neighbours, Libya was well-to-do. In 2003, its oil export revenue was US$13 billion. With a population of just five million, the government had been able to buy off dissent with food subsidies, free medicine and free education. Streets were mostly clean and the people well dressed. In the capital there were few signs of extreme wealth or poverty. However, Robbins pointed out that Libya had a long way to go. The country had no trained civil service corps, no reliable legal system, and no guaranteed protections for foreign investors. Prime Minister Ghanem might talk about selling shares in privatised companies, but Libya had no financial markets, and the real political battles over selling off companies controlled by members of Gadafy's inner circle had yet to be joined.

(Source: Carla Anne Robbins. 'In giving up arms, Libya hopes to gain new economic life', *The Wall Street Journal* (12 February 2004)

In October 2004, Libya began pumping natural gas to Italy as part of a 7 billion euro project between Italy's Eni Spa and Libya's National Oil Co (NOC). The Western Libya Gas Project is the most important integrated project in the oil sector ever carried out in the Mediterranean and enhances the value of the Libyan natural gas through export and trading in Europe, writing a new page in the history of energy and cooperation between Italy and Libya. The gas produced from the Wafa field in the desert and Bahr Essalam, offshore, is sent to Mellitah and then transported to Italy through the Greenstream, the longest sub-sea pipeline in the Mediterranean. Eni's partner in the project is NOC, the Libyan state company. The project was launched in 1999 and was completed on schedule for an investment of around 7 billion euro (Eni share 3.7 billion) and a work force of nearly 20,000 people. The Greenstream connects Mellitah, on the Libyan coast, to Gela in Sicily, is 520 kilometers long, has a diameter of 32 inches (approximately 81 centimetres), and was laid at depths which reach 1,127 metres. The depth and dip of the seabed where the pipeline was laid, the numerous cable crossings, the careful attention paid to the environment and the time constraints made Greenstream a high technology challenge.

In March 2004, Voice of America's correspondent Roger Wilkison reported that American business executives, especially from the oil industry, were rushing to the oil-rich North African state of Libya, and Libyans were hoping that American tourists would discover their country as well. Libyan entrepreneur Sami Sadek, who owns a computer engineering firm, a furniture factory and one of Tripoli's most popular restaurants, says Americans have the best technology, and are willing to share their know-how with others. Young Libyans are surprisingly in touch with the outside world. Satellite TV dishes sprout from even the humblest apartment blocks. Teenagers listen to American pop music. Walid, who works at a travel agency, changes his name to Wally when he chats on the internet with Americans. He hopes Americans will visit his country, see its attractions and spend money there.

Wilkison points out that foremost among Libya's tourist sites is Leptis Magna, the ruins of a Roman city which, during the late second and early third centuries AD, rivalled Rome itself in splendour, architecture and wealth. Foreign visitors are stunned as they walk through what archaeologists say is the most splendid display of Roman civilisation that exists outside Italy. But Libya offers more than Roman ruins and a pristine Mediterranean coastline. Hussam Hussein Zagar is a tour operator who wants to entice Americans to visit Libya's vast desert. He says there is no animosity toward the United States despite decades of hostility between the American and Libyan governments. He says Libyans have welcomed large numbers of Italians, whose country was once the unpopular colonial ruler of Libya, and the Italian market is his country's main market because of the mutual historical background. Libyans welcome all nations. But before Libya can attract mass tourism, Wilkison asserts that the country needs to train its workers and build infrastructure such as hotels, restaurants, roads and airports like those of its neighbours Tunisia and Egypt. Only then will Libya be able to exploit tourism, its greatest untapped natural resource.

(Source: Roger Wilkison. 'Libyans hope opening to West will bring in money from US tourists', *Voice of America*, March 2004)

[1] Medersat.com, the name chosen by the BMCE Bank Foundation for its network of rural community schools, is rich in associations. The term medersatkoum means 'your school' in Arabic. Medersat.com also evokes the medersa, the place of learning in traditional Arab society; the Mediterranean locale; connection to satellites and new communications technologies, hence the dot.com; and the assets shared by the village community.

Part 7

Africa's Future

My first book, *Entrepreneurship in Africa: A Study of Successes* (2002) was meant to present entrepreneurial ideas, existing development projects and the entrepreneurs who are successful in Africa. The first book did not offer much of my own analysis; it was supposed to encourage readers to think for themselves and share their knowledge with others. It was also meant to be a story of all Africans, including those whose forefathers had been immigrants to their new African homes. It was supposed to impart the idea that the rule of law, and not the rule of one individual, are important for a country's development, and that the rights of minorities are to be protected. It was also meant to tell about cooperative efforts that are successful. It voiced an appeal for investment capital. Although African entrepreneurs are knowledgeable, they often lack the finances with which to translate their ideas into marketable activities.

The final chapter of this, my second book, *Africa: Continent of Economic Opportunities* (2006), contains commentary concerning how best to create economic environments and opportunities for skilled, innovative, and passionate entrepreneurs in Africa to successfully implement their ideas, achieve their dreams, and bring benefits to their communities. Africa is a continent rich in natural resources, cultures and the creativity of its people. It is by relying on this tremendous richness that Africans will build a 'new' Africa that is independent, self-reliant and prosperous. Unwavering faith will guide Africans in this quest.

Chapter 20: Commentary and Conclusions

A fiercely competitive world

Brian Paxton, managing director of MBendi Information Services in Cape Town, South Africa (2004), reports that one of the long-standing myths of the Internet is that people can merely put their websites in cyberspace and the whole world will come marching to their doors. As Africans watch Africa's political and business leaders in action, they sometimes get the uncomfortable feeling that a similar myth persists about joining the global community — once you're part of it, everyone will want to buy your products and services, and the future will be rosy.

The reality Paxton points out is that it's a fiercely competitive world out there and if Africa wants to survive, let alone thrive, Africans need continuously to size up their competition. In theory, African countries, with their low wage structures, should be able to compete with similar companies in the developed world. However, the competition for Africa on the wages front comes not from first world economies but from Asia, particularly China for manufacturing and India for software and services. African countries and companies need to monitor this closely and understand exactly where they are — and are not — competitive.

Traditionally, Africa has been an exporter of commodities — minerals, oil and agricultural produce — in competition with both first and third world countries. The challenges are, on the one hand, to be able to take up the slack quickly in the market when a rival is unable to deliver or, on the other hand, to be cost competitive when the price of a commodity falls, or an exchange rate firms, so that it is the operations in competing countries that are closed down by multinationals.

Transport is often a key cost input when competing to deliver physical goods, or tourism services. The countries of the African Maghreb are extremely well-positioned to service Europe, so much so that they can consider major investments in pipelines and even tunnels under the straits of Gibraltar, confident that these will enable them to compete even more efficiently.

Elsewhere on the continent, governments need to ensure that the costs of land transport and harbours are as low as possible so that they can compete in delivering goods to long-haul destinations.

Skilled manpower is an essential ingredient for any successful economy. Africans worry that African education systems are directed in giving a sub-average education to the masses rather than also providing a superb education to the gifted few. To make matters worse, the gifted few are often nabbed by greedy first world economies. Many of Africa's diaspora, to say nothing of potential immigrants, would love to be able to ply their professional trades back on their home continent, where the sun shines, but African countries often make no effort to provide an enticing environment. Africa's diaspora includes doctors, dentists, lawyers, economists and business executives. Harnessing their technical skills for the development of the African continent could play a decisive role in both short- and long-term measures to accelerate Africa's development.

After touching on these factors that Africa's leaders need to consider, Paxton concludes that it's a pity so many African leaders came through the military or career political route. He believes a couple of years spent as a trader in one of the bustling markets one finds across Africa would soon have taught them how to set up systems to monitor and benchmark the competition. African governments have the critical responsibility of providing enabling macroeconomic environments, in which small-, medium-, and large-scale businesses can prosper, create new jobs and spawn satellite businesses.

Trade liberalisation

Trade liberalisation alone will not boost growth and poverty reduction in Africa. That was the key message of the Economic Report on Africa 2004 (ERA 2004), published by the UN's Economic Commission for

Africa and entitled *'Unlocking Africa's trade potential'*. ERA 2004 argued that trade policies in many African countries have been applied haphazardly with too little relevance to overall development objectives. Data from African countries that have liberalised their economies showed that dynamic trade policies, together with gradual and targeted liberalisation, are more effective than liberalisation per se. The flagship report used a competitiveness index developed by ECA that combines the economic and political environment, availability of direct inputs to production and state of infrastructure, to provide insights into why development in Africa has fallen behind, compared to other regions. Mauritius, South Africa, Namibia and Tunisia are cited as Africa's most competitive nations.

ERA 2004 analysed the collapse of the Doha talks and argued for a comprehensive approach to development that prioritised poverty alleviation. It suggested that successful integration of Africa into the world economy would require better-educated and healthier workforces, improved economic and political governance and better-quality infrastructure. Reporting on the continent's overall economic performance, ERA stated that in 2003 Africa advanced to real GDP growth of 3.8 per cent, compared to 3.2 per cent in 2002. This encouraging increase reflected Africa's progress in a number of critical areas:
- the continent has continued to exhibit good macroeconomic fundamentals;
- fiscal deficits have been kept under control;
- inflation has largely stabilised;
- and the region's current account deficit fell.

The challenge lay in translating these achievements into faster growth. In 2003, only five countries (Angola, Burkina Faso, Chad, Equatorial Guinea and Mozambique) achieved the 7 per cent growth necessary to reach the millennium development goal of halving poverty by 2015. According to the ERA 2004, the regional outlook for 2004 was positive with growth projected at 4.4 per cent. However, there were several downside risks. The recovery of the global economy was marred by significant international imbalances because of the United States' large current account deficit, and the matching surplus concentrated in a few countries. According to the report, adjustment through sharp depreciation in the US dollar could interrupt the recovery.

The report also warned against protectionist sentiment, particularly in the form of cotton subsidies in the US and other industrial countries. These have damaged prospects for cotton-producing West African countries and further protectionist measures could seriously harm Africa in the medium-term, the report said (Unlocking 2004).

How can the developed world help Africa?

Jeffrey Sachs is the director of the Earth Institute at Columbia University. He believes Africa needs both trade and aid — trade to promote private investment, and aid to fight disease, provide clean water, and ensure universal education. All are necessary for growth. He believes a compassionate country like the United States, which leads the world in a war for freedom, must also be ready to offer billions more in help for Africa, a continent struggling for its very survival, and do it in a way that really supports economic development. Ann M Veneman, US Secretary of Agriculture, believes that in order to grow and prosper, developing countries must have markets for their products. Trade can and must play a critical role in addressing the world's food security needs. An open food trading system should be a world goal.

In May 2003, US President George Bush proclaimed that the spread of free markets, free trade and free societies was being threatened by plague, starvation and poverty. The advance of freedom and hope was being challenged by the spread of AIDS. Yet, this shadow, he believed, could be lifted. AIDS could be prevented, and AIDS could be treated. Lives could be saved, and others extended by many years. The long-term problem of hunger in Africa could be greatly reduced by applying the latest developments of science. By widening the use of new high-yield bio-crops and unleashing the power of markets, Africa could dramatically increase agricultural productivity and feed more people across the continent. Farmers in Africa must be given a fair chance to compete in world markets. When wealthy nations subsidise their agricultural exports it prevents poor countries from developing their own agricultural sectors. All developed nations should immediately eliminate subsidies on agricultural exports to developing countries so that Africa could produce more food to export and more food to feed Africa's people.

President Bush pointed out that half the human population lives on less than US$2 a day. Billions of men and women can scarcely imagine the benefits of modern life because they have never experienced them. For decades, many governments around the world have made sincere and generous efforts to support global development. Far too often, these funds have only enriched corrupt rulers and made little or no difference in the lives of the poor. He said it was time for governments of developed nations to stop asking the simplistic question 'How much money are we transferring from nations that are rich?' The only question that really mattered was 'How much good is being done to help people who are poor?'

President Bush concluded that the only standard worth setting and meeting was the standard of results. The lesson of our time is clear: when nations embrace free markets, the rule of law and open trade, they prosper, and millions of lives are lifted out of poverty and despair. So he proposed an entirely new approach to development aid. Money would go to developing nations whose governments are committed to three broad standards: they must rule justly; they must invest in the health and education of their people; and they must have policies that encourage economic freedom. These goals — advancing against disease, hunger and poverty — would bring greater security to the world and it would be by these efforts that a lasting, democratic peace would be built for all humanity (Bush 2003).

In June 2002, James Wolfensohn, the World Bank president, confirmed in a speech delivered at the InterAction Forum in Washington that, world-wide, agricultural subsidies in developed countries to the tune of US$350 billion a year are seven times what countries spend on development assistance, and roughly equivalent to the entire GDP of sub-Saharan Africa. Those subsidies are crippling Africa's chance of exporting its way out of poverty. Rich countries must dramatically reduce these subsidies. Rich countries' escalating tariffs, which peak with processed agricultural products, are stopping Africa's manufacturing in its tracks. Rich countries must work to dramatically reduce these escalating tariffs, which are huge barriers to processed products from Africa — confining Ghana and Côte d'Ivoire to export raw unprocessed cocoa beans; confining Uganda and Kenya to export raw coffee beans; and confining Mali and Burkina Faso to export raw cotton. Rich country subsidies to cotton farmers are increasing supply artificially on international markets and depressing export prices for African producers. Removal of US subsidies on this one crop alone would increase revenues from cotton by about US$250 million in west and central Africa.

In addition to efforts to improve market access and reduce trade-distorting subsidies in agriculture, rich countries should take immediate action on a number of fronts, which would substantially improve the potential of African farmers:
- Unilateral adoption of liberal rules of origin under preference schemes such as the African Growth and Opportunity Act (AGOA) especially for clothing and textiles; in the medium-term this would benefit African exports to the tune of about US$500 million.
- Rich countries should also give greater support to African countries and especially to small and medium enterprises to meet OECD product standards. Total gains to Africa with a truly international system of standards in place, followed by the rich and developed with a voice from the poor, would be more than US$1.2 billion in nuts, cereals, fruit and beef alone.
- And actions should be taken to increase competition on maritime and air transport routes to and from Africa. Collusive practices among shipping lines push up freight rates by up to 25 per cent on selected routes. A striking example is Benin, where shipping costs represent 22.7 per cent of trade. One step that can be taken by OECD countries is to eliminate antitrust exemptions for export cartels among transportation firms.

Wolfensohn says that no one who has travelled to Africa can doubt the potential of this great continent — the richness of its resources, the dignity of its diverse cultures or the limitless potential that beats in the heart of each African. There is no doubt that the future of Africa lies firmly in the hands of its people. They want only a chance to determine their own futures, to take advantage of what the world can offer in partnership, and to become full and equal members of the global family. Give Africans market access, give Africans a level playing field for their products and goods, and give Africans a trade partnership that is more than just in name. African countries need to follow through on the NEPAD agenda and work to break down internal barriers to trade and investment that limit the ability of farmers to market their goods (Wolfensohn 2002).

Judy M O'Connor, the World Bank's country director for Tanzania and Uganda, believes the key is to help African countries create an environment conducive to private sector development. A strong private sector-led growth would in turn help African economies effectively to combat pervasive poverty. It is therefore vital to deal with the constraints to private sector development and access to markets, through a combination of measures aimed at addressing the questions of distorting subsidies, excessive transportation costs, and gaps in the access to knowledge and capital by small entrepreneurs. The World Bank, through its policy dialogue and assistance programmes in its client countries in Africa and elsewhere, seeks to support and encourage private sector development and promote reforms to create a stable macroeconomic environment, conducive to investment and long-term planning. Indeed, they are actively working with their partners (governments, other donors, the private sector and civil society) to find lasting solutions.

The World Food Summit: Five Years Later

The World Food Summit: Five Years Later (WFS:fyl) took place in June 2002 at the headquarters of the United Nations Food and Agriculture Organisation (FAO) in Rome. At the Summit, UN Secretary-General Kofi Annan emphasised that progress in fighting hunger had been much slower than would be required to meet the 1996 World Food Summit target of halving the number of the undernourished by 2015. He believed that wider access to food and agricultural and rural development should be addressed at the same time. He said that farmers should be given greater access to land, credit, technology and knowledge, which would help them grow more resistant crops, as well as ensuring plant and animal safety. He also emphasised the key role of women, 'who are involved in every stage of food production, working far longer hours than men'. He also called upon developed countries to open their markets further and to remove the barriers to food imports from developing countries. He noted that the tariffs imposed on processed food, like chocolate, make it impossible for processing industries in developing countries to compete.

The President of Ghana, John Kufuor, said at the summit that there would be a sustainable solution to the problem of hunger when Africa's farmers are helped to modernise their farming methods. And there will be a sustainable solution when their produce does not have to compete unfairly with produce from the rich nations, who still protect their markets and whose farmers tend to be heavily subsidised.

In his speech at the summit, the FAO Director-General, Dr Jacques Diouf, said that fairer global agricultural markets and more investment are needed. He said that the global market for agricultural commodities has continued to defy any notion of fairness. For example, he too pointed out that the OECD countries transfer more than US$300 billion to their agricultural sectors, which means that they directly support each farmer to the tune of US$12 000 per year. He contrasted this to the same countries providing the developing countries with an estimated US$8 billion per year. This works out at US$6 for each farmer. He too declared that access to developed country markets is constrained by customs tariffs that average roughly 60 per cent for primary agricultural products, as compared to about 4 per cent for industrial products.

The Deputy Director-General of the World Trade Organisation, Miguel Rodríguez Mendoza, also said that reducing or eliminating trade-distorting subsidies and improving market access opportunities, particularly on the part of developed countries, would help boost domestic production. Thus it would also help boost farmers' income where food can be produced most efficiently, including in many developing countries, where problems of food security are endemic and where production was currently suppressed due to subsidised import competition. He also said that developing countries cannot compete with the fiscal profligacy of the industrialised nations which together, according to the OECD, currently pay out US$ one billion a day to their farmers in agricultural subsidies, which is more than six times all development assistance going to poor nations.

Producing food for the market

At the summit, the president of Uganda Yoweri Museveni, pointed out that more than 75 per cent of the poor in sub-Saharan Africa are rural people, obtaining livelihoods from agricultural activities or from non-farm activities that depend mostly on agriculture. There are only two ways in which food can be produced. Either one produces food for subsistence or one produces food for the market. The prime minister of Ethiopia, Ato Meles Zenawi, agreed with Museveni that transforming subsistence agriculture into small-scale commercialised farming is a key element of Africa's strategy. Improvements in rural infrastructure and marketing networks, including improved access to export markets, are critical to the success of Africa's economic development programmes.

Museveni points out that in Uganda, for the last 9,000 years, people have been producing crops for subsistence, which does not provide enough money to care for health, clothing, and housing. That is why youth gravitate from the rural areas to the towns, or even migrate to the countries of the north and the west, to Europe and America. Therefore, in the modern context the only sustainable way of producing food is to produce food for the market and then use the earnings to finance all other needs. Where is that market to be found? Unless significant and fundamental changes occur in African countries, disparities in income levels and economic growth rates are likely to continue and to lead to social unrest. However, there are considerable opportunities to accelerate the income growth rates in the slow-growing countries, especially those of sub-Saharan Africa, and to raise per capita incomes.

Museveni pointed out that Uganda is one of the nine African countries that are food-sufficient. Ugandans not only produce enough food for themselves; they also have plenty for export. Uganda produces 1.1 million metric tons of maize per annum, and although they do not eat much of that maize, Ugandans eat other foods of which they have plenty. Each year, Ugandans sell approximately 33,000 metric tons of maize to the World Food Programme, for distribution as relief in other parts of Africa. They are selling about 61,000 metric tons of maize in the region. They have surplus milk, a lot of bananas, sugar and many other types of food. Food shortages in Africa are not due to lack of technology. Many countries, including Uganda, have the technology to produce high yielding seeds for many crops and improved breeding stock for many varieties of livestock. Ugandans can also get what they do not have from other countries such as India and South Africa.

Museveni maintains that the main causes of food shortages in the world are really three: wars; protectionism in agricultural products in Europe, the United States of America, China, India and Japan; and protectionism in value-added products on the part of these same countries. The impact of war on agricultural and other forms of production do not need elaboration. It is the other two causes that need a little explanation. The structure of many countries in Africa is such that the majority of people live in the rural areas. Only a minority lives in the towns. In Uganda, 85 per cent of the people live in the rural areas and 15 per cent in the urban areas. The 85 per cent in the rural areas cannot buy from each other because they produce the same products. The 15 per cent who live in the towns are not enough to absorb the products of the countryside.

For instance, Museveni points out that Uganda produces 800 million litres of milk per annum. However, only 22 million litres a year are consumed in the towns, at a rate of 34 litres per year per person. The regional market is not well organised because of wars, lingering tariff barriers, and poor infrastructure. The only well organised and big markets are those in Europe, the USA, Japan, India and China — and they have been closed to African products, agricultural or value-added. Museveni says it is good that the USA promulgated the African Growth Opportunity Act (AGOA). The European Union has also adopted the Everything but Arms (EBA) policy vis-à-vis black Africa. China has also allowed Uganda's value-added coffee into their market for the first time.

By blocking value-added products, Museveni believes that Africa's partners in the world kill the following opportunities:
- The ability to earn more foreign currency;
- Employment, enhancing the purchasing power of the population;
- Expanding the tax base for the governments of Africa; and
- The chance to transform African societies from the backward, pre-industrial states which they are now, to modern ones, by building a middle class and a skilled working class.

Therefore, the most fundamental problems, Museveni asserts, are not the weather, are not the lack of improved seeds, are not the lack of education, and are not the lack of infrastructure. The fundamental problems are three: wars; protectionism against agricultural products; and protectionism against value-added products. All the others are problems but they are not as subversive of global development as are the above three.

There is, for instance, the problem that Museveni noticed in some of the African countries, the problem of interfering in the marketing of crops. This is, indeed, a problem in the short run for those countries. However, in the end, this cannot be the most basic problem. Even if those countries removed all the bottlenecks and production picked up, as it has done in Uganda, they would then face the real problem: where do they sell what they produce?

Museveni concluded by stating that Africa needs to get rid of wars. Africa needs to get rid of the intra-regional trade barriers. Nevertheless, as of 2004, this would not maximise trade for Africa because the total purchasing power of Africa is only US$550 billion while that of the USA is US$11 trillion. Even the enlightened self-interest of these countries dictates that enhanced purchasing power of the whole population of the world, six billion people, would be better for business all round. The empowered poor would buy more from advanced countries of the world. It would be a win-win situation. The new globalisation the world should talk about, Museveni emphasises, should be mutually beneficial globalisation (Museveni 2002).

Subsidies Create Cotton Glut

In June 2002, Roger Thurow and Scott Kilman, staff reporters on *The Wall Street Journal*, reported that lower world prices for cotton, along with higher fertiliser and pesticide costs, possibly meant eventual ruin for African farmers. However, half a world away in the US, there was no obvious sign that world cotton prices were at rock bottom. US cotton farmers were continuing to buy parcels of land. Subsidies were the biggest reason for US farmers' upbeat outlook and were also the biggest reason for African farmers' despair. American farmers get them in abundance. African tillers do not. In past years, farm subsidies have been criticised for widening the gap between rich and poor countries. Fearing that misery in the developing world may make it a breeding ground for instability and terrorism, the US government aims to promote development aid and open trade. But this strategy is undermined by subsidies to US farmers, which help depress global prices of some vital cash crops that developing countries count on. In Mali, the US spends US$40 million a year on education, health and other programmes. That investment is blunted by sagging prices for cotton, Mali's main cash crop.

A new US farm bill rich with subsidies meant that many US cotton growers received half of their income from the government in 2002. In June 2002, this contradiction was spotlighted when the leaders of the Group of Eight industrialised nations met in Canada with plans to launch a new effort to help develop Africa's economies. Back home, many of those same leaders were raising or maintaining subsidies and tariffs on a range of products that would further marginalise African trade. It goes to show that when push comes to shove, domestic policies trump foreign policies every time.

Subsidies protect growers in America and several other countries from falling world prices. However, they generally further depress prices by encouraging continued production and thus cripple growers in less subsidised countries. In few places are these skewed economics more evident than in the gap between the US cotton growers and west African cotton growers.

Armed with roughly US$3.4 billion in subsidy cheques, American farmers in 2001 harvested a record crop of 9.74 billion pounds of cotton, aggravating the US glut and pushing prices far below the break-even price of most growers around the world. In 2002, American cotton farmers pocketed even more, thanks to the US$118 billion, six-year farm bill signed by President Bush in May 2002. The government programme ensured that US farmers reaped about 70 cents a pound of cotton by making up for any shortfall in the market with federal cheque. Unlike several past farm bills, the latest one didn't require farmers to leave some of their land idle in order to qualify for the aid. In contrast, Mali's government is hard-pressed to provide even the most basic health care and education to a nation that is one of the ten least developed in the world and can't keep up with subsidies of its own.

The World Bank reports that cotton could be a key engine of poverty reduction for West African states. In west and central Africa, cotton cultivation employs more than two million rural households. African cotton, much of which is hand picked, is just as good as American cotton. The removal of US cotton subsidies — which account for much of the US$5 billion a year in subsidies world-wide — would produce a drop in US production that would lead to a short-term rise in the world price of cotton. In turn, that would increase revenue to west and central African countries by about US$250 million. That is a princely sum in a region where vast numbers of people live on less than one dollar a day. Instead, the opposite is happening. The 2002 US farm bill increased the amount of money a cotton farmer made in 2002 by at least 16 per cent. At the same time, in Mali, where cotton makes up nearly half the nation's export revenue, the government told cotton farmers they will be getting about 10 per cent less this year from the state cotton company. In the US there is little sympathy for such problems. American farmers don't want the added competition of Africa's farmers. With the US textile industry shrinking, American farmers must sell more and more of their crops to overseas buyers. In 2002, about half of the US cotton crop was sold into the world market, where it competed against cotton grown by lower-cost growers in China, Pakistan and Africa.

American farmers haven't always been so dependent on subsidies. In 1996, the booming Asian economy had boosted demand for US commodities so much that US farmers decided they didn't want the planting restrictions and red tape that came with government aid. Even cotton farmers, among the most dependent on aid, went along with other farm groups to successfully back a plan by Republicans in Congress that called for the elimination of subsidies by 2002. That would have marked an end to the more than US$500 billion in farm subsidies issued since such aid started, during the Great Depression of the 1930s. But US farmers lost their nerve shortly afterwards, when the Asian economic crisis punctured the export boom. Washington rushed in with record levels of aid. The new farm bill officially returned the country to the long-term policy of aggressively subsidising agriculture and with far fewer planting restrictions on growers than in the past. The upshot is that heavily subsidised crop production is likely to keep commodity prices depressed even as the world economy picks up.

In 2001, Malian farmers received about 13 cents per pound of cotton, after expenses. In 2002, they got about 11 cents. At the same time, the price of fertiliser went up about two cents a pound. In Mali, every cent counts, because cotton must pay for everything from school and food to malaria tablets. Money is also tight at Cie Malienne pour le Developpment des Textiles (CMDT), Mali's state cotton company, which runs the nation's entire industry, from providing the seeds to ginning the cotton. It is responsible for the livelihoods of the three million of Mali's eleven million residents who live off cotton.

In 2001, Malian farmers grew more than half a billion pounds of cotton on nearly 1.3 million acres. This was a record crop, but it only led to a bigger loss for the CMDT, where the total cost of each pound of ginned cotton exceeds the world price. This deficit restricts CMDT spending on other programmes, such as building roads and other infrastructural improvements in the cotton regions. It also puts pressure on the meagre budget of the Malian government, which owns 60 per cent of CMDT. The CMDT is restructuring itself and will rely more on the private sector, in order to pass more money on to the farmers. However, Malians wonder whether this will do much good without changes in cotton subsidy policies elsewhere in the world. They see US farmers as their competition, but the problem is that the competition isn't fair. African farmers want all of their children to have better lives. Beyond cotton, it is the one thing they have in common with other cotton farmers throughout the world (Thurow and Kilman 2002).

Improved market access

Patrick Asea, chief economist of the United Nations Economic Commission for Africa (UNECA), reports that improved market access offers African countries the best chance of increasing incomes. He points out that what the New Partnership for Africa's Development (NEPAD) wants above all from industrial countries is improved market access, in addition to more aid. But of the two it is trade that stands the better chance of improving African incomes. In 2002, the World Trade Organisation (WTO) calculated that the abolition of agricultural subsidies by the Organisation for Economic Cooperation and Development (OECD) countries would give developing countries three times what they receive in development assistance. UNECA said that gains from eliminating trade barriers between developing and industrial countries could be the equivalent of more than twice Africa's gross domestic product. The commission also estimated that the economic growth generated from lower protection could reduce poverty levels 13 per cent by 2015.

In 2002, the US gave a commitment to reduce all agricultural subsidies, and the EU spoke of the need to move away from its present agricultural policy towards a system that gives other forms of support to rural incomes. A reason the EU would abolish its form of subsidies was that the accession of new member countries from east and central Europe would place a considerable fiscal burden on the richer members. There are also commitments to liberalise trade in services, cut the peaks in tariffs (which hurt industrial exports), and reduce non-tariff barriers. The industrial countries are under increasing pressure to show that there are definite gains from globalisation. As the expansion of exports under the US's Africa Growth and Opportunity Act demonstrated, greater market access can be a rapid way of bringing about these gains.

Asea points out that NEPAD could provide a useful lever for African countries to ensure that many of the commitments made actually happen. Asea says African countries should actively lobby in Europe and the US for market access. As trade liberalisation offers substantial benefits to consumers, he says, African governments wanting to increase access for subsidised commodities such as sugar or cotton should join forces with consumer associations. Asea would like to see concrete action to improve on existing initiatives, such as AGOA and the EU's EBA, for greater market access. Apart from commitments to eliminate export rules and market distortions that impede trade, Asea would also like to see greater technical assistance for African countries to deal with trade issues.

Asea concludes that once granted expanded access, African countries will have to ensure they make the most of the opportunities. For this to happen, Asea believes there has to be an improvement in the investment climate, including macroeconomic stability and sound governance. Poor countries will also have to be sure to integrate trade into development and poverty reduction strategies. Asea stresses that the autonomy of African countries must be preserved, while respecting the legitimate objectives of importers to maintain high labour, social and environmental standards (Katzenellenbogen 2002).

Africa's economic potential

In November 2002, in his inaugural address in the Ambassador Andrew Young Lecture Series to the Africa Society of the National Summit on Africa, Ambassador Andrew Young focused on Africa's potential and what it meant for the United States. Young said that America's future was inextricably bound in Africa's rising. Too often is Africa viewed with a paternalistic attitude without recognition of its economic potential. He pointed out that with long-range planning, Africa could have a Marshall Plan that would pay for itself. He explained that the continent and its offshore waters hold vast supplies of oil reserves, but that Africa is not just oil – Africa is a market. Young said that Africa was soon to be a billion people with unlimited potential for consuming manufactured goods and needed everything that anyone could produce. He added that one unique thing that Africa had was the potential for wildlife tourism. With a little cooperation, he speculated, a wildlife preserve could be extended across the continent from Namibia to Mozambique that could attract billions of tourist dollars. Young said the continent could also benefit from a returning of its sons and daughters. He pointed out that there were millions of people of African descent in Europe and America and the Caribbean. All of those who came in the 20th century had migrated on their own, bringing or gaining skills and education. Many ran successful businesses. If they were to return to their homelands regularly, he suggested that they could create, and relate to, an African market. They could begin to share some of their skills and provide growth opportunities for the companies for which they worked.

The underlying mission of Ambassador Young's lecture series was really to focus the spotlight of attention on Africa in the United States. Julius Coles, president of Africare, a private aid organisation, said the lecture series was important in the sense that Americans, in general, are not very informed about Africa. He predicted that the exchanges would help in educating Americans about the political, economic and humanitarian aspects of Africa, its problems and its prospects.

An Ethiopian entrepreneur believes many opportunities in Africa are either foregone or delayed because many Africans, without whose direct involvement the development of the continent does not come, wait until everything has been smoothed out to allow them do what they want. When this fails to be so they either lose interest in their projects or they simply migrate to the developed west and try life there. The initiative to try to make a difference in the face of challenging situations in Africa, while at the same time working for the improvement of that challenging environment, is rarely seen. This may be taken as the sacrifice Africans need to make to bring about development to their continent. Africans must confront challenges at home rather than trying to contain them from remote positions in the diaspora, for it is only then that the problems ravaging the peoples of the continent will be felt at first hand by its educated citizens. These are the resources of the continent that can make the difference, and something has to be done to encourage them to come back home.

Regional markets in Africa

Many Africans note that ambitious market integration along the lines of the European Union cannot be imposed from above. Many initiatives in the past and in the present have largely confined their operations to inter-governmental institutions, leaving out non-governmental institutions, civil society and the indigenous private sector, some of which are key actors in national economies. They must be included this time. Integration should start at the regional level, as planned by ECOWAS in west Africa, for instance. Other regions like southern Africa can do the same thing. Then, gradually, the idea can spread throughout Africa.

William A Amponsah, associate professor of international trade and development, and director of the North Carolina A&T State University International Trade Center, says that as of 2002, regional economic arrangements in Africa still exhibit narrow patterns of trade, depend on primary products and involve low levels of intra-regional trade. In order to allow trade to flow regionally, he believes investment in physical infrastructure, roads, railways, pipelines, power lines, air services and telecommunications is necessary. Ultimately, the benefits of creating regional markets in Africa are many. Amponsah notes that integration would enhance industrial efficiency as larger markets allow exploitation of economies of scale. He envisions mobility across borders and harmonised policies spurring faster economic growth and providing greater opportunities to attract investors. He says that regional trade agreements can help countries build on their comparative advantages, sharpen their industrial efficiency, and act as a springboard to integrate into the world economy. He adds that a more open continent will build credibility for Africa's best reformers in the eyes of the world and, hopefully, reward them with greater access to markets (Mutume 2002).

An African living in London says that it is appropriate that regional groupings should be formed outside geographical boundaries and should sustain some level of stability and loads of cooperation amongst African regions. He believes the way forward is the revitalisation of African pride, the pride that is based on community aspects of life, protection of the people, their life and property and their rights. He sees a need for African leaders to develop a feel for the people as a whole rather than clinging to tribal and individualistic tendencies.

Africans inside and outside the continent believe that Africa can succeed with economic regional integration. In the past in Africa, or at least in large regions within Africa, there was a high degree of economic integration. Africa's present economic problems have been, at least partially, created by the artificial division of the continent into states. Accept as necessary the formation of continent-wide bodies aimed at producing greater economic synthesis. Imagine 54 nations coming together with all the natural resources that the continent holds, a day when Africa has her own flag that can be recognised all over the world. The African continent would be a powerful force. It is now time to stop blaming each other and start rebuilding the continent.

Facilitating investments in sub-Saharan Africa

There is a pathetic US$2 billion of intra-regional trade in Africa, yet there is a US$50 billion domestic demand for food crops, which is predicted to double by 2015. Professor Samuel Wangwe of Tanzania believes actual trade relations of sub-Saharan Africa can be classified as a hub-and-spoke arrangement, with Europe, North America and Asia as the hub and African countries as the spokes. The key feature of this arrangement is that trade between the hub and any spoke is easier than trade among the spokes, which in 2004, was probably only eight cent of total trade for sub-Saharan Africa. The hub-and-spoke trade arrangements exert a marginalising effect on the African economies. Although the cost of production in sub-Saharan African countries may be lower due to lower labour costs, higher trade costs (due to small markets as compared to those in the hub countries) are likely to more than offset the lower production costs. Trade liberalisation between the hub and the spokes favours location of investments in the hub, especially if intra-sub-Saharan African trade is not also liberalised. Hub-and-spoke trade liberalisation artificially deters investment in the spoke countries. Reduction of intra-sub-Saharan African trade costs would increase the chances that the lower production costs will outweigh these trade costs, and so would facilitate investments in sub-Saharan Africa (Wangwe 1995).

How can African governments help entrepreneurs?

Peter Evans, chairman of the department of sociology at the University of California, Berkeley, sees a basic connection between competent, coherent state bureaucracies and economic growth. He believes competent and adequately-compensated bureaucracies can help individual entrepreneurs overcome coordination problems that may be especially crucial in instigating new activities. He points out that they can also turn informational resources into public goods in ways that increase the likelihood and effectiveness of investment. For example, when entrepreneurs in small countries are trying to upgrade into world markets, he points out that collective action to gather data on external markets and enforce standards among local producers may confer important advantages. He suggests that respected bureaucracies could act as 'honest brokers' in overcoming collective action problems among exporters. A stronger version Evans says would see the bureaucracy itself as gathering information and providing advice and incentives that help local firms better to thread their way through the labyrinth of rapidly changing world markets.

Creating a conducive and enabling environment

A businesswoman from Ghana believes that creating a conducive and enabling environment does not depend on handouts. She explains that Africa needs investment in agricultural production, processing and packaging, and investors in telecommunication and the wireless Internet in urban and rural areas. She believes that if the atmosphere and the leadership are right, African people will develop Africa by themselves. She points out that there are trans-African highways, and railways, in very poor condition, linking almost all

Africa countries. Some countries have privatised these services. African countries are ready for investors in these infrastructural areas of toll roads and railways. Ato Gebreyes Begna, an entrepreneur from the Horn of Africa region, agrees that the lady from Ghana seems to have put her finger on the core issue.

Begna believes that new initiatives such as NEPAD are attempting to grapple with Africa's problems. He says NEPAD has started by articulating Africa's strategy for economic transformation and integration so that Africa will not remain a poor region out of step with the rest of the world, but would be integrated into the global economy. Ato Gebreyes points out that there is a tendency to view the development of a nation as the responsibility of the government or the educated elite in that nation. However, he sees it as a collaborative effort, a shared commitment between the public sector, represented by the government, and the private sector. This reality must sink in and the two sectors must learn to trust each other rather than engage in mutual hostility or suspicion. Having established the fact that the two sectors are the paramount stakeholders in national development endeavours, the next step is to define their respective roles.

Ato Gebreyes emphasises that there should be a mutual recognition of the notion that the role of the government is to create a conducive and enabling environment (or rules of engagement) for the private sector involvement. There should be a mobilisation of the intellectual resources of the country in achieving a national consensus as to what the rules should be, and the method of policing them. Equally, there should be recognition of the role of the private sector as the engine of growth and development and the need for it to actively participate in the policy formulation process. It is conceivable that both players may not have what it takes to fulfil their roles effectively. Nevertheless, recognising this constraint is in itself half the solution. They can find the other half by seeking the benefit of external advice. Once the nurturing of partnership and trust between the public and private sector takes hold on a national level, this can be extended to a regional or continent-wide level. All it requires is for like-minded leaders to get together and chart out the course for the continent's development. There is no shortage of models.

Ato Gebreyes believes that a sudden surge in patriotism, a call for making sacrifices for the motherland or the continent, and the revitalisation of African pride, have their places in nation- and continent-building. They are, however, no substitute for a macroeconomic environment that permits the unleashing of the energies of citizens. The solution must come primarily from rediscovering a sense of direction that provides context for embracing various models of economic development, including economic integration, with a renewed sense of urgency and purpose to unlock the region's vast potential by strengthening its production base and regrouping its fragmented markets.

The last and the inevitable question Ato Gebreyes asks is why certain African countries fail in their attempt at development, and find their economies in disarray. He answers that it is because some governments in Africa are not voted into office - they take office by force. They are not accountable to anyone but themselves. Because there are competing interests at work, collaboration is regarded as the surrendering of power, hence the lack of trust, the half-measures and the derailment of the development agenda. He asks whether it is true that nations deserve their lawmakers. Given the vastness of its untapped resources, he says that Africa could indeed qualify to be called a 'continent of opportunities', but what good are natural resources, he asks, if they stay buried in Africa's bowels when its children are falling like flies for lack of food to eat? His remedy is the rule of law, good governance and accountability.

Africa needs entrepreneurs of noble intent

2002 was a most remarkable and successful year for leading South Africa retailer Massmart and all those privileged to lead it, especially its founder and CEO Mark Lamberti. It was also an extraordinary personal honour for Lamberti to represent his country as South Africa's Best Entrepreneur of the Year for 2001. In October 2002, Lamberti thanked Ernst & Young and Absa for creating the forum for his recognition, and said that entrepreneurs are normally evaluated on the criteria of entrepreneurial spirit, financial performance, strategic direction, global impact, innovation and personal integrity and influence. He then gave his views on entrepreneurship, with emphasis on the particular entrepreneurial obligations in South Africa.

Lamberti pointed out that in recent times the world has been surprised and disgusted by the behaviour of too many entrepreneurs and business leaders. For too many, entrepreneurial drive turned into unbridled greed. Shareholders and employees of the companies involved were damaged, as well as all people in business. The credibility of business leaders was not what it should be. He quoted Winston Churchill, who had said, 'We make a living from what we get. We make a life from what we give.' Today throughout the world, Lamberti says society is telling us that too many entrepreneurs and business leaders got too much and gave too little. He suggests that South African society should evaluate its entrepreneurs on a number of additional criteria based on South Africa's unique history and situation.

Lamberti maintains it is a fact of history that most South Africans were denied almost every reasonable right and with it almost every reasonable opportunity. This has resulted in underdevelopment, high unemployment, and desperate poverty. Within this context, he asks, 'by what additional criteria should South African entrepreneurs be judged?' and quoted from a remarkable commentary on the new economy entitled 'The corrosion of character', in which Richard Sennett wrote that '...short term capitalism threatens to corrode character, particularly those qualities of character which bind human beings to one another and furnish each with a sense of sustainable self'. Lamberti suggests that much of the activity of the 90s had little to do with creative entrepreneurship and more to do with short-term opportunistic greed.

Lamberti emphasises that there is no such thing as short-term entrepreneurship, but that there are short-term opportunists. Sadly he enumerates three specific types of uniquely South African greed driven, short-term opportunists who sully the reputation of all entrepreneurs. The first group includes those who believe (or rationalise) that South Africa is doomed and that they should rip it off while they can. The second group includes those who believe (or rationalise) that their previous disadvantage entitles them to instant redress. The third group includes those who in the past legitimately flaunted apartheid laws in order to make progress in business, but now continue to do so with no legitimacy whatever. Lamberti says South Africans must distance themselves from these opportunists. Demonstrated commitment to the long-term he believes is therefore the first additional criterion on which South African entrepreneurs should be judged.

Lamberti believes a strong guide for the behaviour of entrepreneurs should be ubuntu, the cultural heart of South African society. 'Ubuntu,' says Lamberti, 'is best summarised as 'I am only a man through other men'.' He suggests this sense of unity with broader society means that commitment solely to shareholders is simply not a sustainable basis for business success in South Africa. The South African economy is too fragile for the abuse of customers. The talent and labour pool is too sensitive for the abuse of employees. South African markets are too small for the abuse of suppliers. South African social services are too essential to evade tax. South Africa's underprivileged communities are too many to be ignored. Given this, a demonstrated sensitivity to all stakeholders is therefore Lamberti's second additional criterion for South African entrepreneurs.

Lamberti's third, and perhaps the most important, additional criterion for South Africa's entrepreneurs, is humility. Sadly competence, confidence and humility are strange bedfellows. Flattering words are used to describe the characteristics of the entrepreneur: tenacious, focused, resilient, highly creative, single minded and driven. All of these are laudable personal assets when kept in check. But they translate into dangerous personal liabilities when unchecked, made worse by the negative consequences of success: over-confidence, arrogance, selfishness, greed, excess and abuse of power. Abraham Lincoln once said, 'Nearly all men can stand adversity, but if you want to test a man's character give him power.' Lamberti emphasises that the essence of character is humility.

Finally, in seeking to evaluate South African entrepreneurs, Lamberti says that South Africans should look for individuals who can debunk the myths of entrepreneurship. The first of these myths, he believes, is that entrepreneurship is about taking high risk. That is not his experience. The best entrepreneurs he knows are fanatical about the downside, and extraordinarily balanced in their assessment of risk. The second myth, he believes, is that entrepreneurship is about fast money. The most successful entrepreneurs he knows have accumulated wealth by delivering a service to society over many, many years. He concludes that South Africa desperately needs small entrepreneurs whose initial objective is simply to sustain their families. But South

Africa equally needs entrepreneurs of noble intent who build large organisations: organisations of integrity, which render honest added value to many customers, create sustainable jobs, and serve society indirectly through taxation and directly in their interface with the community.

The challenges that face Africa

Mark Shuttleworth, South African businessman and the first African in space, in an interview with Akwe Amosu of allAfrica.com regarding Africa's potential, advocated that there is a need for more and better teaching of maths and science in schools. He said there is an urgent need to push for an expansion of Africa's economic capacity, and that he was committed to developing African business and trade. He feels inspired, having been in space, to work towards the re-balancing of the world's distribution of wealth and opportunity. He has felt for a long time that Africa had tremendous potential and that the time was ripe for Africa's potential to be harnessed and, more and more, he feels that this is true. He now has the privilege of being invited to visit many African countries, of being able to go out and learn about those countries and see where the potential is, and of trying to find ways to promote what he does in an international setting.

Shuttleworth has lived in South Africa all his life. He recently moved to London. There, he has been exposed to a very rich melting pot of African expatriates. He found it a nice community to tap into because it contains representatives from all over the continent. He has received invitations to many African countries and hopes that over the years he will be able to take up some of these invitations and visit them, primarily to talk about education. And to try, if there's interest on their side, to get some of the excitement, enthusiasm and momentum that's been created around the continent channelled in a meaningful direction towards building up education, particularly science and mathematics. But who knows what else may come of it? That will be his focus in going, but he is interested in the process of learning more about Africa.

At the World Economic Forum in Durban in 2002 there was a tremendous opportunity for him to see people from different countries in action, and his overriding impression was one of increasing competence, increasing responsibility, increasing commitment from both government and business to principles of good governance, sound economic management and clean business. Those were all very different to the stereotypes and the prejudices that he thinks exist elsewhere about Africa and he thinks that if they are an indicator of real trends on the ground then he is very excited to get out there and learn.

Shuttleworth thinks that the challenges that face Africa will play a major role in uniting the continent, in getting Africans to focus their energies on specific issues, perhaps putting in place policies and procedures that could stave off future problems. One of the issues Africans face is the tremendous fragmentation on a continent with 54 different countries that will potentially make it a lot easier for Africans to move towards a pan-African view. It is his sense that Africans will be able to move towards a continent-wide view more readily than they would move towards a small, regional view.

Shuttleworth believes that new technologies are part of the African economic puzzle. He sees technology playing all sorts of roles. On the one hand, it's been demonstrated that one can create wealth through technology by investment and creating success in the technology marketplace. Africans can do this in Africa. He believes that Africans certainly have the talent and the expertise. If they can concentrate that effort in a few centres of excellence, they can create wealth in Africa because they have much lower costs in Africa than other regions of the international market. There's a natural arbitrage of opportunity.

One opportunity technology presents is wealth creation. Shuttleworth has benefited, personally, from being able to do this in Africa. He built a company that sold services and ultimately created tremendous wealth. He thinks many others will follow the same route.

The other option technology presents is to create infrastructure that reaches out to many more people far faster and for a much lower cost than has been possible in the past. Africa is already seeing how cell-phone communication, for example, is connecting people at a much higher rate than Africa has been able to for the last 60 years with traditional land-line telecommunication.

In 2002, the number of cell-phone subscribers in some African countries has equalled the number of fixed line subscribers. In South Africa that took five years, but there is still an incredible opportunity, especially when one thinks about the penetration rate, which is about 40 per cent of the adult population in South Africa.

Shuttleworth sees a need to unlock corporate value and untie the hands of the private sector. He also says that new technologies are often easier to deploy and sell than old technologies. To deploy fixed line infrastructure can take months. It is an enormous and slow process because every point needs a line and every line needs to be maintained, and so on, whereas wireless infrastructure is far less expensive and is far lighter and easier to deploy.

In the past, Shuttleworth has made investments in private equity. He has now found that often there are two independent needs, so he has allocated a certain amount of capital to technology investments in Africa and a certain amount of capital to promoting technology and education and so on. That leaves him free to learn more. At this stage he is not working personally every day towards the establishment of a new situation. He has made his investments, he has made his plays and the enterprises he founded must now carry that torch. Shuttleworth say his job now is to learn more about Africa, to understand what is happening on the continent, where it's going and based, on that, to see what opportunities he can find that will stimulate a new round of projects and investments (Amosu 2002).

In September 2000, Mark Shuttleworth founded HBD, which explores new territory by discovering innovative South African companies and people. The company has developed into two separate units, HBD Venture Capital and HBD Asset Management. HBD Venture Capital invests in innovative South African companies that have global potential. They also develop new internal business ideas from scratch, trying to capitalise on local skills and taking advantage of global trends and technologies. Many of the HBD team came from Mark' previous company, Thawte Consulting, which was sold to US company VeriSign in February 2000. These team members have all been involved in the early stage of entrepreneurship and have learned some tough lessons about the global technology marketplace through their experience. Together with new team members, HBD brings these skills to South African entrepreneurs.

In 2003, HBD Venture Capital started Upstarts, an incubator for entrepreneurs with innovative ideas that need funding and resources, and an environment to help them prove that their ideas are viable and accelerate their commercialisation. Upstarts is based in Durbanville, Cape Town. Philip Marais, the manager of Upstarts, says that they started operating at the beginning of 2003, and by 2004 they already have five businesses in the incubator. Their first business that they funded and helped is looking at developing a new type of electronic voting system, which will be marketed in South Africa, Africa and globally. What is unique about their incubator system, Marais believes, is that Upstarts does the funding, whereas with incubators in general a business has to look for its own funding. Another unique aspect of the project is that it offers a virtual incubation model. This means that a participating business does not have to be based in Cape Town, but can be situated somewhere else in the country, as long as it maintains a close relationship with Upstarts and an effective way of communication with the project. The idea is to support a number of small businesses which will benefit from low infrastructure costs and regular access to consultants and mentors who will help them to grow. If a project needs further funding in the form of venture capital, Upstarts will source this for the business immediately through HBD Venture Capital. All an entrepreneur needs is an idea. A business's stay in the incubator will be for one year, during which time a company will be formed, with Upstarts taking up to 40 per cent shareholding (Ismail 2003).

Mark also funds The Shuttleworth Foundation (TSF), a non-profit organisation dedicated to improving the quality of education in Africa. TSF supports innovation in education in Africa and seeks to fund projects that demonstrate a significantly better approach to some aspect of the education system and hopes to improve both the quality and the reach of education in Africa. Mark believes that developing countries need to find their own voices in the digital era. To this end, he also funds and serves on the board of bridges.org - an international non-profit organisation that seeks to address digital divide issues both through grassroots work and high-level policy dialogue. In December 2002, Mark was chosen as one of the World Economic Forum's Global Leaders for Tomorrow, 2003.

Mark is optimistic about opportunities in Africa because, he believes, people in many African countries are starting to demand better government, stability and democracy, and he predicts that Africans will see a trend toward the democratic helping hand of assistance over the demanding fist of power. Mark points out that the stability and predictability that Africans are beginning to demand of their governments are the same qualities which most foreign investors are also looking for. However, he believes it is a mistake for Africans to think that their continent will be best served by waiting for foreign investors to do the heavy economic lifting. He maintains that the reality is that success is always driven domestically. In terms of global opportunities for African entrepreneurs, Mark believes the natural target should be Europe, given the historical ties between the two continents, and because Africans understand European thinking, even if they differ from it.

The African Business Round Table

In 2002, an Africa-wide private sector organisation came up with a key initiative to provide an electronic database of economic activities by countries and sectors in Africa. According to Alhaji Bamanga Tukur, president and executive chairman of the African Business Round Table (ABR), an important factor of the African Renaissance will be the full embrace by African entrepreneurs of this initiative. It is hoped that this African Business Executive Program (ABEX) initiative will help catapult Africa from an agrarian society to an industrialised one, with the free flow of information playing the role of the catalyst. Ideally, entrepreneurs well armed with information available through the Internet will turn around the fortunes of Africa. The objective will be to promote trade, create consulting opportunities for private entrepreneurs and encourage local and foreign investment in Africa. The ABEX initiative aims to solve the critical lack of economic and business information about Africa, serving as an informational pool for business leaders, policy makers, the media and academics (Kanu 2002).

Many potential ICT entrepreneurs in Africa are limited by a lack of information about opportunities, potential partners, institutional contacts and resources. On the other hand, preliminary research demonstrates that many Africans in North America, and many others who feel committed to the development of Africa, have important skills and access to a wealth of human and material resources but perceive few avenues to apply them to benefit sub-Saharan Africa.

Brought together with the growing number of organisations, corporations, foundations, and academics promoting the application of ICT to assist Africa's development, members of the African diaspora would provide a rich source of ideas, skills and support for promoting digital opportunities in Africa. The Digital Diaspora Network reaches out to this scattered community in North America and Europe to facilitate the exchange of ideas and information in order to help ICT entrepreneurs create opportunities and find the partners and resources they need to make use of them.

AfriShare is an innovative initiative of the Digital Diaspora Network committed to unleashing the enormous potential of today's information and Internet technology to build a bridge to carry the resources and knowledge of the African diaspora back to Africa. Their mission is to:

- Develop a means for expatriate Africans in North America and Europe, and Friends-of-Africa, to contribute talent and resources directly to those in need;
- Develop a web platform that is accessible worldwide, where social investors and entrepreneurs can be matched, and where ideas and talent can be exchanged, and Africa-focused projects supported; and
- Deliver social and financial returns that will generate solid returns to investors.

AfriShare's objective is to mobilise and organise a cluster of stakeholders with a direct interest in Africa's sustainable development. African and US business leaders, government and intergovernmental agencies, foundations, NGOs and academics will combine efforts into a 'brains trust' that will help identify innovative projects on the ground in Africa and pinpoint ways that information technology can be used to trigger market-based solutions to the region's poverty. John Sarpong, chairman of Digital Partners for Africa (DAPA) says that there is a major opportunity to transform the historical brain drain problem in Africa into a new African brains trust that will uplift the continent socio-economically. The challenge for African expatriates wanting to change Africa's prospects through ICT is how to work with the energy and momentum created by recent policy initiatives in ways that will open new prospects for Africa's have-nots.

Social peace and economic dynamism

How did minorities achieve the economic success they now enjoy throughout Africa? It did not start yesterday. We have seen that many South Asians and mid-Easterners are third and fourth generation descendants of itinerant peddlers who in several generations went from rags to riches. We have read the fascinating stories of the economic success of these minorities. These successful minority entrepreneurs have not evaded the envy of others who blame their own relative lack of economic advancement on the groups that succeed. Distinguished international economist, Gerald P O'Driscoll Jr, points out that ethnic conflict has always existed and unfortunately continues to exist in many African countries. In the developing countries of Africa, the rule of law needs to protect minorities against the majority's backlash. It keeps the social peace and allows economic dynamism to go on unmolested. If only Africans would realise that the poor in Africa would advance absolutely when African economies grow and that the average income of the poor would keep up if the growth is widespread. Africans must distinguish between democracy's majority rule and a system that also enshrines the rule of law and constitutionally protected rights. O'Driscoll maintains that this distinction is surely central to the success of minorities, and to their protection. In a system of majority rule with no protected rights, he says that, 'democracy is just two wolves and a sheep deciding what is for lunch' (O'Driscoll 2002).

Africans, wherever they are, should get back home with their diversified experience and expertise to help out their motherland. Africans outside Africa can play a very important role in Africa's empowerment and improvement. African unity must be broadened to include the African diaspora. The ultimate goal of economic integration must be to benefit and improve the lives of Africans by creating new avenues of trade and creating an African bloc in terms of economic negotiations on the world markets. The United States and the European Union are driven by economic reasons upon which no individual African country can make a significant impact – but an African Union can make enough impact to cause the citizens of the US and EU to take Africa seriously. A successful AU will empower all of Africa, not merely the strong countries. Africa's abundant resources would then benefit the health, education and wellbeing of all Africans.

References

Amosu, Akwe. 2002. Mark Shuttleworth interview: Afronaut Shuttleworth sets sights on transforming Africa. Durban: allAfrica.com (12 June 2002).

Bush, George. 2003. Speech by US President Bush commenting on Aids, famine assistance in Africa in commencement address to United States Coast Guard Academy, New London, Connecticut, 21 May 2003.

Ismail, Moegsien. 2003. Shuttleworth starts incubator. Cape Town: *BigNews* (19 December).

Kanu, Okechukwu. 2002. ABR's new project to spread information. Lagos: *ThisDay* (17 October).

Katzenellenbogen, Jonathan. 2002. For NEPAD, trade would eclipse aid. Johannesburg: *Business Day* (18 October).

Museveni, Yoweri K. 2002. Speech delivered at the World Food Summit in Rome (10 June).

Mutume, Gumisai. 2002. How to boost trade within Africa: Lower barriers and diversify production. *Africa Recovery*, United Nations, Vol.16 #2-3 (September), p 20.

O'Driscoll, Gerald. 2002. Some succeed, others resent their success. *Wall Street Journal* (26 December).

Paxton, Brian. 2004. Africa competing in the world of 2004. Cape Town: *MBendi Information Services Newsletter* (30 January) www.mbendi.com.

Thurow, Roger and Scott Kilman. 2002. US subsidies create cotton glut that hurts foreign cotton farms. *Wall Street Journal*, 26 June, ppA1, A4.

Unlocking Africa's trade potential. *Economic Report on Africa 2004* (ERA 2004), published by the UN's Economic Commission for Africa.

Wangwe, Samuel M (ed). 1995. *Exporting Africa: Technology, Trade and Industrialization in Sub-Saharan Africa*. London and New York: Routledge.

Wolfensohn, James. 2002. Speech delivered at the InterAction Forum in Washington DC (4 June).

Other titles from STE Publishers

Cultural history
The world that made Mandela by Luli Callinicos
Johannesburg — One City Colliding Worlds by Professor Lindsay Bremner

Photographic
In the Company of God by Joao Silva
Jo'burg by Guy Tillim

Film
Come Back Africa by Lionel Rogosin

Biography / Autobiography
Makeba — the Miriam Makeba Story by Miriam Makeba in Conversation with Nomsa Mwamuka
Timol — A Quest for Justice by Imtiaz Cajee
All My Life and All My Strength by Ray Alexander Simons
Now Listen Here — the Life and Times of Bill Jardine by Chris van Wyk
Comrade Jack — The Political Lectures and Diary of Jack Simons, Novo Catengue Edited by Marion Sparg, Jenny Schreiner and Gwen Ansell
No Cold Kitchen — a Biography of Nadine Gordimer by Ronald Suresh Roberts
The Troublemaker: Michael Scott and His Lonely Struggle Against Injustice by Anne Yates and Lewis Chester

Reference
The South Africa Yearbook 2004/05 by the GCIS
Pocket Guide to South Africa by the GCIS

Art
Images of Defiance — South African Resistance Posters of the 1980s by the Poster Book Collective of the South African History Archive

Education
Turning Points in History series by Various
Turning Points in History cd-rom by Various

Literary Criticism
Indias Abroad by Rajendra Chetty and Pier Paolo Piciucco

Fiction
The Lotus People by Aziz Hassim
Bite of the Banshee by Muff Andersson

Law
Telecommunications Law in South Africa edited by Lisa Thornton, Yasmin Carrim, Patric Mtshaulana and Pippa Reyburn

Journalism
Radio Journalism Toolkit by Franz Kruger

Esoteric
Afternoon Tea in Heaven — Conversations with the Spirit World By Nanette Adams

Self Help
My Life Your Life — Steps to Heal the Heart By Michelle Friedman

To order contact: www.ste.co.za OR angela@ste.co.za